Index to Women of the World
of the World

from ancient to modern times:

A SUPPLEMENT

by

Norma Olin Ireland

The Scarecrow Press, Inc.

British Library Cataloguing-in-Publication data available

Library of Congress Cataloging-in-Publication Data

Ireland, Norma Olin, 1907-
    Index to women of the world from ancient to modern
times : a supplement / by Norma Olin Ireland.
        p.   cm.
    ISBN 0-8108-2092-7
    1. Women--Biography--Indexes.   2. Women--Portraits--
Indexes.   I. Title.
Z7963.B6I73   Suppl.
[HQ1123]
016.92072--dc19   87-35934

A TRIPLE DEDICATION TO "FRIENDS OF FORTITUDE"

To <u>Arlie and Harvey Lind</u> of Spring Valley, California (formerly of Ohio), who have been faithful friends for over 25 years. They have always been there when I needed someone, for every birthday and holiday, ready to help in all the crises of my life, and visiting me often although some miles away. Harvey passed on in 1986, but he saw this dedication in the manuscript and was very pleased. Arlie has had many hurdles since widowhood but has surmounted them all, with cheerful fortitude.

To <u>Mary and Dexter Woodford</u> of Akron, Ohio, friends of great personal courage and caring. Mary, totally blind since young motherhood, has kept on with church work, telephoning, etc., as well as swimming. Dexter, partially disabled, has given great love to his wife and son and carried on with his work and hobbies. He is a champion swimmer and was recently elected to a Swimmers' Hall of Fame. Whenever my husband and I came to Akron, the Woodfords met us and saw us off--with special friendship and consideration. Mary and Dexter are a couple of unbelievable fortitude.

To <u>Madge Liebole Curley</u> of Akron, Ohio, also struck down as a young mother. She has raised three children, been widowed, and still goes on with her art and other hobbies, as well as the housework she can manage. We were always welcomed in her home, and greatly value her friendship. Madge was one of the most beautiful women in our university; she has become one of the bravest women, in her later years, that I have ever known, carrying on with great fortitude.

CONTENTS

PREFACE

This volume is a supplement to our previous Index to Women of the World from Ancient to Modern Times: Biographies and Portraits (Faxon, 1970, now handled by Scarecrow Press). Although as a supplement it is of course much smaller, it includes many new biographies, as well as new sources for older ones, in books published since 1970. It also has a few earlier titles not indexed in the previous volume.

Scope

We have analyzed 380 collective biographies including a few magazine issues of special value. Once again we have emphasized "popular" works, rather than scholarly tomes, as our Index is intended primarily for large and small public libraries, schools, colleges, and universities, and some special libraries. We have included books for younger readers and have endeavored to find the latest editions and most volumes in some series (when available). We have necessarily omitted many "who's whos," indexing only those whose coverage is not found elsewhere.

Some may question the importance of certain women included. We tried to cover many fields, hitherto not found in biographical sources, and some may question whether they are "celebrities." Yes, they are or have been "celebrities" in their occupations or accomplishments they represent. For instance, Carnegie medal winners certainly deserve the honor. If some names are not familiar--remember today's celebrities' names may not be known or recognized tomorrow. A Civil War belle was known in her day-- just as a movie star is known today.

As in the previous volume, all periods of history are covered (from Biblical times) and even a few "mythological" women who have figured in history. After our first Index to Women was published, we received letters asking that certain names be included in any future supplement. Our book is an index to women as found in collective biographies, and if not in the ones we indexed, they are not included. Even some very famous women's biographies were only found in magazines or individual biographies. In a few cases we included "Women of the Year" in certain magazines.

Arrangement and Symbols, Dates

Arrangement of names is alphabetical by letter, as is usually found in biographical dictionaries. Dates of life (when available), nationality, and occupation are given for each woman, followed by symbols for analyzed references.

Symbols, to refer to list in the front, are simple in order that they can easily be used and remembered. In some cases, other than the first word of title follows the author.

Dates have been our biggest "bugaboo." Unfortunately, there are discrepancies in women's birth dates, due to their own "reporting." We have indicated "c." or "/" in such cases.

In some books, dates are not given, and we have used "fl." (for flourished), although it was used only after considerable search. At least it will give readers the time, a period in which the woman lived. Our assistants spent countless hours in libraries, which too often lacked the specialized "who's whos" needed.

Names

We have tried to index under the most commonly found names with cross-references to variations. Sometimes we have used pseudonyms, as users of the book would look for them first. In the case of "de," "van," "von," etc., we discovered that many books varied; therefore, we cross-referenced to the most used form. We followed ALA form, and also checked such standard sources as Webster's Biographical Dictionary, Brewer's Biography Almanac, and Wilson's Biography Index when making our decision.

In our previous volume we did not emphasize this cross-referencing, and sometimes were led astray by the forms used in different books. We trust that such discrepancies will not occur here.

Full names are given, as complete as possible, because of the incidence of first and last names of several women. Dates also distinguish and sometimes we have used (1), (2), (3) to separate individuals.

Percentage of Titles According to Date

Users of the book will also be interested to know the percentage of books indexed according to date of publication. Biographical books are seldom outdated, and certainly a book of biographies published 15 years ago may be just as valuable as a later one.

1980's	19.68%
1970's	73.13
1960's	4.25
1950's & earlier	2.94

We regret that several excellent recent books could not be included due to our publicity schedule. One, especially, we would like to recommend: <u>Women Remembered: A Guide to Landmarks of Women's History in the United States</u>, by Marian Tinling (Greenwood Press, 1986).

Length of References

Our best judgment was used in indexing each book, especially when uneven and scattered throughout the book. We have tried to evaluate material on the basis of its importance and length. Sometimes the references were so many, and scattered throughout the book, that we stated number of the index page. We checked into the indexes first, however, as some indexes had mistakes in them.

If sometimes the reference seems small, it was included because of its special information or summary data. Sometimes a student may wish to write of a person in depth and is searching for unusual information.

Inclusive paging is given; portraits are mentioned, but page numbers not given--for lack of space.

Occupations

In listing occupations, we have endeavored to be specific rather than general, e.g. painter, sculptor, etc., instead of just artist; novelist, historian, poet, etc., instead of just author. When women achieved in many fields, we did not spare space because we thought they deserved it!

There has been some overlapping, of course, such as feminist and suffragette, social reformer and humanitarian. We have not indicated special classes or ethnic groups, expect in the case of blind, deaf, etc. Inclusion in this volume is based on accomplishment alone.

Below is a chart showing number of books indexed according to occupations represented. "General" includes books covering many fields--and of course they are the highest count.

Occupations Represented

General	137
History and politics	69
Literature	34
Theater (including entertainment, movies, dance, etc.)	29
Art	22
Ethnic groups (some duplication in other categories)	15
Music	14
Science	13
Social workers, reformers	12
Religion	8
Sports	8
Business	8
Education	4
Society	4
Folklore	3
	380

Acknowledgments

Once again we wish to thank the Fallbrook Library, which in spite of an arson fire that destroyed the main building, still helped us in their small downtown quarters. Although interlibrary loans were difficult to get (over 50 titles not received), we still thank the San Diego County Library for trying to help us--and Rosa Castrow, the local librarian. We bought many books, not available elsewhere, which were absolutely essential to our work. We appreciated the books from the Carlsbad, Vista, and Oceanside libraries and the assistance of their reference librarians. And thanks to Helen Green who did last-minute work in those libraries--checking books and problems.

We acknowledge and thank most of all Mrs. Sally Meisenholder, our secretary, typist, and general "helper" for her assistance (four years), without whom this book could not have been compiled and completed.

LIST OF ABBREVIATIONS

Abyss.	Abyssinian	cont.	continued
A.D.	Anno Domini	Croat.	Croatian
Afr.	African	Cub.	Cuban
Alb.	Albanian	Czech.	Czechoslovakian
Alex.	Alexandrian		
Alger.	Algerian		
Alsat.	Alsatian	d.	died
Amer.	American	Dan.	Danish
Anglo.	Anglican	Dom.R.	Dominican Republic
Arab.	Arabian		
Argent.	Argentinian		
Armen.	Armenian	E.	East
Assyr.	Assyrian	E.Ind.	East Indian
Aust.	Austrian	Ecuad.	Ecuadorian
Austral.	Australian	Egypt.	Egyptian
		Eng.	English
		Est.	Estonian
b.	born	Ethiop.	Ethiopian
Babyl.	Babylonian		
Batav.	Batavian		
B.C.	Before Christ	Fin.	Finnish
Belg.	Belgian	fl.	flourished
Bohem.	Bohemian	Flem.	Flemish
Bol.	Bolivian	Fr.	French
Brazil.	Brazilian	front.	frontispiece
Brit.	British		
Bulg.	Bulgarian		
Byzant.	Byzantine	Galic.	Galician
		Ger.	German
		gr.	graduated
c.	circa (about)	Gr.	Greek
Camb.	Cambodian		
Can.	Canadian		
Carth.	Carthaginian	Hait.	Haitian
cent.	century	Haw. Isl.	Hawaiian Islander
Chile.	Chilean	Hung.	Hungarian
Chin.	Chinese		
Co.	Company		
col.	column	Ice.	Icelandic
Colom.	Colombian	Ind.	Indian

isl.	island	Pomer.	Pomeranian
It.	Italian	por.	portrait
		Port.	Portuguese
		pseud.	pseudonym
Jam.	Jamaican	Puert.Ric.	Puerto Rican
Japan.	Japanese		
Jav.	Javanese		
Jord.	Jordanian	Rev.	Revolutionary
		Rom.	Roman
		Rum.	Rumanian
Kor.	Korean	Russ.	Russian

Lat.	Latvian	S.	South
Lib.	Liberian	S.Afr.	South African
Liech.	Liechtensteiner	Salv.	Salvadorian
Lith.	Lithuanian	Sardin.	Sardinian
Lombard.	Lombardian	Scan.	Scandinavian
Ltd.	Limited	Scot.	Scottish
Luxem.	Luxemburgian	Serb.	Serbian
		Siam.	Siamese
		Sic.	Sicilian
m.	married	Siles.	Silesian
Madag.	Madagascarian	Slov.	Slovenian
Mesop.	Mesopotamian	Sp.	Spanish
Mex.	Mexican	supp.	supplement
Mon.	Monacan	Swed.	Swedish
Monte.	Montenegrin		
Moroc.	Moroccan		
Morav.	Moravian	Tas.	Tasmanian
		Thail.	Thailander
		Transyl.	Transylvanian
N.	North	Trin.	Trinidadian
N.Afric.	North African	Turk.	Turkish
n.d.	no date	TV	television
Nether.	Netherlander		
New Z.	New Zealander		
Newfound.	Newfoundlander	U.N.	United Nations
Nor.	Norwegian	unp.	unpaged
		Urug.	Uruguayan
p.	page		
pa.	paper	Venez.	Venezuelan
Pak.	Pakistani	Virgin Isl.	Virgin Islander
Palest.	Palestinian		
Palm.	Palmyrene		
Pan.	Panamanian	W.	West
Pers.	Persian	W.Ind.	West Indian
Peru.	Peruvian		
Phil.	Philippine		
Pol.	Polish	Yugoslav.	Yugoslavian

LIST OF COLLECTIONS ANALYZED AND
KEY TO SYMBOLS USED

ABDUL--FAMOUS
    Abdul, Raoul. Famous black entertainers of today. New York:
    Dodd, Mead & Co., 1974. 159p

ADAMS--GREAT (3RD)
    Adams, Russel L. Great negroes past and present. 3rd ed.
    Chicago: Afro-Am., 1969. 212p

ADAMS--WOMEN
    Adams, Jane. Women on top. Success patterns and personal
    growth. New York: Hawthorn, 1979. 227p

AMER.--MOTHERS
    American Mothers Committee, Inc. Mothers of achievement in
    American history, 1776-1976. (Bicentennial project 1974--
    1976). Rutland, Vt.: Tuttle, 1976. 636p

ANDERSON--PEOPLE
    Anderson, Christopher P. The book of people. Photographs,
    capsule biographies, and vital statistics of over 500 celebri-
    ties. New York: Perigree Books/Putnam's, 1981. 425p paper

ANTICAGLIA--12
    Anticaglia, Elizabeth. Twelve American women. Chicago:
    Nelson-Hall, 1975. 256p

ARCHER--FAMOUS
    Archer, Jules. Famous young rebels. New York: Messner,
    1973. 191p

ASIMOV--BIOG.
    Asimov, Isaac. Asimov's biographical encyclopedia of science
    and technology. new rev. ed. New York: Avon, 1972.
    805p paper

ASSOC. PRESS--PURSUIT
    The Associated Press and Grolier. Pursuit of excellence: The
    Olympic story. Danbury, Conn.: 1979. 384p

AVENEL--COMP. (1) (2)
  The Avenel companion to English & American literature. 2 vol-
    umes in 1. New York: Avenel, 1981. Vol. 1--575p, Vol. 2--
    280p

BACHTOLD--GIFTED
  Bachtold, Louise M. Gifted women in politics and the arts and
    sciences. Saratoga, Calif.: Century Twenty One, 1981.
    126p

BAGLEY--MILL
  Bagley, Bernice. The mill girls. New York: Antheneum, 1983.
    191p

BAINTON--FRANCE
  Bainton, Roland H. Women of the reformation in France and
    England. Minneapolis, Minn.: Augsburg Publishing House,
    1973. 287p

BAINTON--GERMANY
  Bainton, Roland H. Women of the reformation in Germany and
    Italy. Boston: Beacon Press, c1971, 1974 paper

BAINTON--SPAIN
  Bainton, Roland H. Women of the reformation, from Spain to
    Scandinavia. Minneapolis, Minn.: Augsburg Publishing
    House, c1977. 240p

BAKER--WOMEN
  Baker, Denys Val. Women writing: An anthology. New York:
    St. Martin's Press, c1978, 1979. 212p

BALLIETT--AMER.
  Balliett, Whitney. American singers. New York: Oxford Uni-
    versity Press, 1979. 178p

BANNER--WOMEN
  Banner, Lois W. Women in modern America. A brief history.
    New York: Harcourt Brace Jovanovich, c1974. 276 p paper

BASCH--RELATIVE
  Basch, François. Relative creatures: Victorian women in
    society and the novel. New York: Schocken Books, 1974.
    360p paper

BAUM--JEWISH
  Baum, Charlotte, Paula Hyman, and Sonya Michel. The Jewish
    woman in America. New York: Dial Press, c1975, 1976.
    290p

BEACH--DAUGHTERS
  Beach, Seth Curtis. Daughters of the Puritans: A group of

brief biographies. Essay Index reprint set. Freeport, N.Y.:
Arno, 1905, Books for Libraries Press, 1967. 286p

BEAL--20TH
Beal, George. 20th century timeline. New York: Crescent
Books, 1985. 237p

BEASLEY--FIRST
Beasley, Maurine Hoffman. First women Washington correspon-
dents. G.W. Washington Studies #4, n.d.

BENET--NEW
Benét, Laura. Famous New England authors. New York: Dodd,
Mead & Co., c1970. 150p

BERKIN--WOMEN
Berkin, Carol Ruth, and Mary Beth Norton. Women of America:
A history. Boston: Houghton Mifflin Co., 1979. 442p

BERNIKOW--WORLD
Bernikow, Louise, ed. The world split open: Four centuries of
women poets in England and America, 1552-1950. New York:
Random House (Vintage Books), c1974. 349p

BETTS--WRITERS
Betts, Glynne Robinson. Writers in residence. New York:
Viking, c1981. 159p

BIRD--ENTERPRISING
Bird, Caroline. Enterprising women. New York: W.W. Norton
& Co., 1976. 256p

BIRMINGHAM--GRANDES
Birmingham, Stephen. The grandes dames. New York: Simon
& Schuster, c1982. 299p

BLOOM--RELIGION
Bloom, Naomi. Contributions of women: Religion. Minneapolis,
Minn.: Dillon Press, c1978. 126p

BOASE--SKY'S
Boase, Wendy. The sky's the limit. Women pioneers in aviation.
New York: Macmillan Publishing Co., c1979. 223p

BOGIN--WOMEN
Bogin, Meg. The women troubadours. Scarborough, England:
Addington Press, 1976. 190p

BOLTON--SUCCESS
Bolton, Sarah K. Successful women. Boston: Lothrop Publishing Co., 1888. 233p

BOOK--LISTS (1)
The book of lists, by David Wallechinsky, Irving Wallace, and
Amy Wallace. New York: Bantam Books, 1977. 519p paper

BOOKS--LISTS (2)
The book of lists #2, by Irving Wallace, David Wallechinsky,
Amy Wallace, and Sylvia Wallace. New York: Bantam, 1980.
529p paper

BOORSTIN--AMERICANS
Boorstin, Daniel J. Portraits from the Americans: The democratic experience. An exhibition at the National Portrait
Gallery based on Daniel J. Boorstin's Pulitzer prize-winning
book. New York: Random House, 1975. 160p

BOOTH--WOMEN
Booth, Sally Smith. The women of '76. New York: Hastings
House, c1973. 329p

BOWMAN--ART
Bowman, Kathleen. New women in art and dance. Chicago:
Creative Education, Children's Press, c1976. 47p

BOWMAN--ENTERTAIN
Bowman, Kathleen. New women in entertainment. Chicago:
Creative Education, Children's Press, c1976. 47p

BOWMAN--MEDICINE
Bowman, Kathleen. New women in medicine. Chicago: Creative
Education, Children's Press, 1976. 47p

BOWMAN--POLITICS
Bowman, Kathleen. New women in politics. Chicago: Creative
Education, Children's Press, 1976. 47p

BOWMAN--SOCIAL
Bowman, Kathleen. New women in social sciences. Chicago:
Creative Education, Children's Press, 1976. 47p

BOYD--THREE
Boyd, Nancy. Three Victorian women who changed their world.
Josephine Butler, Octavia Hill, Florence Nightingale. New
York: Oxford University Press, 1982. 276p

BRANDON--DOLLAR
Brandon, Ruth. The dollar princesses: Sagas of upward nobil-
ity, 1870-1914. New York: Alfred A. Knopf, 1980. 214p

BRECHER--LIVES
Brecher, Bob, comp. Lives that shaped your life. London:
Proteus/Lippincott, 1980. 413p

BREE--WOMEN
Bree, Germaine. Women writers in France: Variations on a theme. New Brunswick, N.J.: Rutgers University Press, 1973. 90p

BRIN--SOCIAL
Brin, Ruth F. Contributions of women: Social reform. Minneapolis, Minn.: Dillon Press, Inc., c1977. 160p

BRINK--FEMALE
Brink, J.R., ed. Female scholars: A tradition of learned women before 1800. Montreal: Eden Press Women's Publications, 1980. 185p

BRINNIN--MODERN
Brinnin, John Malcolm, and Bill Reid. The Modern poets: An American-British anthology. New York: McGraw-Hill Book Co., c1963. 427p paper

BURGESS--EDUCATION
Burgess, Mary W. Contributions of women: Education. Minneapolis, Minn.: Dillon Press, c1975. 143p

BURT--BLACK
Burt, Olive Wooley. Black women of valor. New York: Julian Messner, 1974. 96p

CAHILL--WOMEN
Cahill, Susan, ed. Women and fiction: Short stories by and about women. New York: New American Library, 1975. 379p paper

CALLEN--WOMEN
Callen, Anthea. Women artists of the arts and crafts movement, 1870-1914. New York: Pantheon Books, 1979. 232p

CANNING--100
Canning, John, ed. 100 Great kings, queens, and rulers of the world. New York: Bonanza Books, 1967. 671p

CAVANAH--WE
Cavanah, Frances, ed. We wanted to be free: The refugees' own stories. Philadelphia: Macrae Smith Co., c1971. 207p

CHAMBERLIN--MIN.
Chamberlin, Hope. A minority of members: Women in the U.S. Congress. New York: Praeger Publishers, c1973, 1974. 374p

CHESTER--RISING
Chester, Laura, and Sharon Barba, eds. Rising tides: 20th

century American women poets. New York: Washington
Square Press/Pocket Books, 1973. 410p

CHINOY--WOMEN
Chinoy, Helen Krich, and Linda Walsh Jenkins. Women in
American theatre: Careers, images, movements. New York:
Crown Publishing, c1981. 370p

CHITTENDEN--PROF.
Chittenden, Elizabeth F. Profiles in black and white. New
York: Charles Scribner's Sons, 1973. 182p

CLAGHORN--BIOG.
Claghorn, Charles Eugene. Biographical dictionary of American
music. West Nyack, N.Y.: Parker Publishing Co., c1973.
491p

CLAGHORN--JAZZ.
Claghorn, Charles Eugene. Biographical dictionary of jazz.
Englewood Cliffs, N.J.: Prentice-Hall, c1982. 377p

CLARK--LEAD.
Clark, Electra. Leading ladies: An affectionate look at American
women of the twentieth century. New York: Stein and Day,
1972. 252p

CLYNE--PATRIOTS
Clyne, Patricia Edwards. Patriots in petticoats. New York:
Dodd, Mead & Co., 1976. 144p

COFFIN--FEMALE
Coffin, Tristram Potter. The female hero in folklore and legend.
New York: Seabury Press, 1975. 223p

COFFIN--PARADE
Coffin, Tristram Potter, and Hennig Cohen. The parade of
heroes: Legendary figures in American lore. Garden City,
N.Y.: Anchor Press/Doubleday, c1978. 630p

COHEN--MEET
Cohen, Scott. Meet the makers: The people behind the product.
New York: St. Martin's Press, 1979. 221p

COLBY--SINGULAR
Colby, Vineta. The singular anomaly: Women novelists of the
nineteenth century. New York: N.Y. University Press,
c1970. 313p paper

COLES--WOMEN
Coles, Robert, and Jane Hallowell Coles. Women of crisis.
Radcliffe Biography Series. New York: Delacorte/Seymour
Lawrence, 1978. 291p

COMFORT--GOOD
Comfort, Alex. A good age. New York: Crown, 1976. 224p

CONTEMP. BRIT.
Contemporary British artists, with photographs by Saranjcet
Walia. Edited by Charlotte Parry-Crooke. New York: St.
Martin's Press, n.d. unp

CRANE--MS.
Crane, Louise. Ms. Africa: Profiles of modern African women.
Philadelphia: Lippincott, c1973. 159p

CRAWFORD--FOUR
Crawford, Deborah. Four women in a violent time. New York:
Crown, c1970. 191p

CROSLAND--BEYOND
Crosland, Margaret. Beyond the lighthouse: English women
novelists in the twentieth century. New York: Taplinger,
c1981. 260p

CROSLAND--WOMEN
Crosland, Margaret. Women of iron and velvet: French women
writers after George Sand. New York: Taplinger, 1976.
255p

CROVITZ--COURAGE
Crovitz, Elaine and Elizabeth Buford. Courage knows no sex.
North Quincy, Mass.: Christopher, c1978. 186p

CUR. BIOG. '69
Current Biography Yearbook, 1969. Edited by Charles Moritz.
New York: Wilson, c1969, 1970. 508p

CUR. BIOG. '70
Current Biography Yearbook, 1970. Edited by Charles Moritz.
New York: Wilson, c1970, 1971. 509p

CUR. BIOG. '71
Current Biography Yearbook, 1971. Edited by Charles Moritz.
New York: Wilson, c1971, 1972. 483p

CUR. BIOG. '72
Current Biography Yearbook, 1972. Edited by Charles Moritz.
New York: Wilson, c1972, 1973. 488p

CUR. BIOG. '73
Current Biography Yearbook, 1973. Edited by Charles Moritz.
New York: Wilson, c1973, 1974. 480p

CUR. BIOG. '74
  Current Biography Yearbook, 1974. Edited by Charles Moritz.
  New York: Wilson, c1974, 1975. 491 p

CUR. BIOG. '75
  Current Biography Yearbook, 1975. Edited by Charles Moritz.
  New York: Wilson, c1975, 1976. 497p

CUR. BIOG. '76
  Current Biography Yearbook, 1976. Edited by Charles Moritz.
  New York: Wilson, c1976, 1977. 504p

CUR. BIOG. '77
  Current Biography Yearbook, 1977. Edited by Charles Moritz.
  New York: Wilson, c1977, 1978. 502p

CUR. BIOG. '78
  Current Biography Yearbook, 1978. Edited by Charles Moritz.
  New York: Wilson, 1978. 504p

CUR. BIOG. '79
  Current Biography Yearbook, 1979. Edited by Charles Moritz.
  New York: Wilson, 1979. 504p

CUR. BIOG. '80
  Current Biography Yearbook, 1980. Edited by Charles Moritz.
  New York: Wilson, 1980. 501p

CUR. BIOG. '81
  Current Biography Yearbook, 1981. Edited by Charles Moritz.
  New York: Wilson, 1981. 487p

CUR. BIOG. '82
  Current Biography Yearbook, 1982. Edited by Charles Moritz.
  New York: Wilson, c1982, 1983. 483p

CUR. BIOG. '83
  Current Biography Yearbook, 1983. Edited by Charles Moritz.
  New York: Wilson, c1983, 1984. 488p

CUR. BIOG. '84
  Current Biography Yearbook, 1984. Edited by Charles Moritz.
  New York: Wilson, 1984. 497p

CUR. BIOG. '85
  Current Biography Yearbook, 1985. Edited by Charles Moritz.
  New York: Wilson, 1985. 494p

DANIELS--WASH.
  Daniels, Jonathan. Washington quadrille: The dance beside
  the documents. Garden City, N.Y.: Doubleday, 1968. 370p

DAVIS--WOMEN
Davis, Mary L. Women who changed history: Five famous
queens of Europe. Minneapolis, Minn.: Lerner, c1975.
103p

DELDERFIELD--KINGS
Delderfield, Eric R. Kings and queens of England. Rev. ed.
New York: Weathervane, c1961, 1978. 160p

DE LEON--BELLES
DeLeon, T.C. Belles, beaux, and brains of the 60's. New
York: Dillingham, c1907, 1909. (Reprint: Ayer, 1974.)
464p

DEMETER--PRIMER
Demeter, Richard L. Primer, presses, and composing sticks:
Women printers of the Colonial Period. Hicksville, N.Y.:
Exposition, 1979. 155p

DePAUW--FOUND.
DePauw, Linda Grant. Founding mothers: Women in America
in the Revolutionary era. Boston: Houghton Mifflin, c1975.
228p

DePAUW--REM.
DePauw, Linda Grant, and Conover Hunt. Remember the ladies:
Women in America, 1750-1815. New York: Viking, 1976.
168p

DEW--WOMEN
Dew, Joan. The women of country music: Singer & Sweethearts.
Garden City, N.Y.: Doubleday (Dolphin), 1977. 149p

DIAGRAM--MOTHERS
Diagram Group. Mothers: 100 mothers of the famous and the
infamous. New York: Paddington Press, 1976. 267p

DIAMONSTEIN--OPEN
Diamonstein, Barbaralee. Open secrets: Ninety-four women in
touch with our time. New York: Viking, c1970, 1972. 474p

DONALDSON--HOW
Donaldson, Norman and Betty. How did they die? New York:
St. Martin's Press, 1980. 398p

DUNLAP--CALIF.
Dunlap, Carol. California people. Salt Lake City, Utah:
Gibbs M. Smith, 1982. 234p

EARLE--TWO CENT. (1) (2)
Earle, Alice Morse. Two centuries of costume in America,

1620-1820. Rutland, Vt.: Tuttle, 1971. V. 1, 1-388p
V. 2, 389-824p

EARNEST--AMERICAN
   Earnest, Ernest. The American Eve in fact and fiction, 1775-
   1914. Chicago: University of Chicago Press, 1974. 280p

EDELSON--KIDS
   Edelson, Edward. Great kids of the movies. Garden City, N.Y.:
   Doubleday, c1979. 121p

EHRLICH--OXFORD
   Ehrlich, Eugene, and Gorton Carruth. The Oxford illustrated
   literary guide to the United States. New York: Oxford
   University Press, 1982. 464p

EILLS--HERE
   Eills, Nancy, and Parker Hayden. Here lies America. New
   York: Hawthorn, 1978. 179p

EMBERLIN--CONT.
   Emberlin, Diane. Contributions of women: Science. Minneapolis, Minn.: Dillon, 1977. 160p

ENGLE--WOMEN
   Engle, Paul. Women in the American Revolution. Chicago:
   Follett, c1976. 299p

ENGSTEAD--STAR
   Engstead, John. Star shots: Fifty years of pictures and
   stories.... New York: Dutton, 1978. 250p

ENTERTAINERS
   The Entertainers. Foreword by Sir John Gielgud. New York:
   St. Martin's/Harrow House, c1980. 320p

EPSTEIN--INDIV.
   Epstein, Perle. Individuals all. New York: Crowell-Collier,
   c1972. 175p

EVANS--WEATHER.
   Evans, Elizabeth. Weathering the storm. New York: Charles
   Scribner's Sons, 1975. 372p

FABER--PRESIDENTS'
   Faber, Doris. The Presidents' mothers. New York: St. Martin's Press, 1978. 316p

FABIAN--ON
   Fabian, Monroe H. On stage: 200 years of great theatrical
   personalities. New York: Mayflower Books, 1980. 224p

FALLACI--EGO.
Fallaci, Oriana. The egotists: Sixteen surprising interviews.
Chicago: Henry Regnery, 1963. 256p

FAX--BLACK
Fax, Elton C. Black artists of the new generation. New York:
Dodd, Mead, c1977. 370p

FELTON--FAMOUS
Felton, Bruce, and Mark Fowler. Felton & Fowler's Famous
Americans you never knew existed. New York: Stein and
Day, 1979. 293p

FINDLATER--PLAYER
Findlater, Richard. The player queens. New York: Taplinger,
1977. 250p

FINE--WOMEN
Fine, Elsa Honig. Women and art: A history of women painters
and sculptors from the Renaissance to the 20th century.
Montclair, N.J.: Allanheld & Schram/Prior, 1978. 242p

FINES-WHO'S
Fines, (Dr.) John. Who's who in the Middle Ages. New York:
Stein and Day, c1970, 1980. 218p paper

FINK--GREAT
Fink, Greta. Great Jewish women: Profiles of courageous
women from the Maccabean period to the present. New York:
Menora, and Block, 1979. 97p

FIREMAN--TV
Fireman, Judy. TV book: The ultimate television book. New
York: Workman Publishing, c1977. 402p

FIRESTONE--SUCCESS
Firestone, Ross. The success trip: How they made it, how
they feel about it. Chicago: Playboy, c1976. 298p

FISCHER--LET
Fischer, Christiane, ed. Let them speak for themselves: Women
in the American West, 1849-1900. Hamden: Archon, 1977.
346p

FISHER--THIRD
Fisher, Dexter, ed. The third woman: Minority women writers
of the United States. Boston: Houghton Mifflin, 1980. 594p

FLEXNER--FACE
Flexner, James Thomas, and Linda Bantel Samter. The face of
liberty: Founders of the United States. Fort Worth, Tex.:
Amon Carter Museum of Western Art, c1975. 310p paper

FORBES--400 ('84)
   Forbes (Magazine). The 400 richest people in the world.
   Special issue, 1984 ed.

FORMA--THEY
   Forma, Warren. They were ragtime. New York: Grosset &
   Dunlap, c1976. 245p

FOWLER--ART
   Fowler, Carol. Contributions of women: Art. Minneapolis,
   Minn.: Dillon, c1976. 152p

FOX-SHEINWOLD--GONE
   Fox-Sheinwold, Patricia. Gone but not forgotten. New York:
   Bell, 1981. 224p

FRASER--HEROINES
   Fraser, Antonia. Heroes & heroines. New York: A. & W.,
   c1980. 263p

FRIEDMAN--OUR
   Friedman, Jean E., and Wm. G. Shade. Our American sisters:
   Women in American life and thought. Boston: Allyn &
   Bacon, 1973. 354p

FRY--1000
   Fry, Plantagenet Somerset. 1000 Great lives. New York:
   Exeter Books, c1975. 336p

FRYER--FACES
   Fryer, Judith. The faces of Eve. New York: Oxford University Press, 1976. 294p

FUNT--ARE
   Funt, Marilyn. Are you anybody? Conversations with wives of
   celebrities. New York: Dial, c1979. 339p

GAMMOND-ILLUS.
   Gammond, Peter. The illustrated encyclopedia of recorded opera.
   New York: Harmony/Crown, 1979. 256p

GELFMAN--WOMEN
   Gelfman, Judith S. Women in Television news. New York:
   Columbia University Press, 1976. 186p

GENETT--AVIATION
   Genett, Ann. Contributions of women: Aviation. Minneapolis,
   Minn.: Dillon, c1975. 113p

GIES--WOMEN
   Gies, Frances, and Joseph Gies. Women in the Middle Ages.
   New York: Crowell, 1978. 264p

GILBERT--PART.
   Gilbert, Lynn, and Gaylon Moore. Particular passions: Talks
   with women who have shaped our times. New York: Clarkson
   N. Potter, 1981. 340p

GILFOND--HEROINES
   Gilfond, Henry. Heroines of America. New York: Fleet, c1970.
   136p

GLASSMAN--YEAR '79
   Glassman, Judith. The year in music, 1979. New York:
   Columbia House, c1979. 184p

GOLD--UNTIL
   Gold, Don. Until the singing stops: A celebration of life and
   old age in America. New York: Holt, Rinehart and Winston,
   1979. 338p

GOLSON--PLAYBOY
   Golson, G. Barry. The Playboy interview. New York: Playboy,
   c1981. 721p

GRAY--WOMEN
   Gray, Dorothy. Women of the West. Millbrae, Calif.: Les
   Femmes, 1976. 179p paper

GREEN--SAINTS
   Green, Victor J. Saints for all seasons. New York: Avenel,
   c1982, 1983. 138p

GREENEBAUM--POLITICS
   Greenebaum, Louise G. Contributions of women: Politics and
   government. Minneapolis, Minn.: Dillon, c1977. 144p

GRIDLEY--AMER.
   Gridley, Marion E. American Indian women. New York: Hawthorn, 1974. 178p

GURKO--LADIES
   Gurko, Miriam. The ladies of Seneca Falls: The birth of the
   Woman's Rights Movement. New York: Schocken, c1974,
   1976. 328p

GURTMAN--MORE
   Gurtman, Bill. More modern women superstars. New York:
   Dodd, Mead, c1979. unp.

HAFTMANN--PAINT.
   Haftmann, Werner. Painting in the twentieth century, Vol. 1:
   An analysis of the artists and their work. New York:
   Praeger, c1965. 443p

HAHNER--WOMEN
   Hahner, June E. Women in Latin American history: Their lives
   and views. Los Angeles: UCLA Latin American Center, University of California, 1976. 181p paper

HALCOMB--WOMEN
   Halcomb, Ruth. Women making it: Patterns and profiles of success. New York: Ballantine, 1975. 290p paper

HAMALIAN--LADIES
   Hamalian, Leo, ed. Ladies on the loose: Women travellers of
   the 18th and 19th centuries. New York: Dodd, Mead, c1981.
   256p

HAMBLIN--THAT
   Hamblin, Dora Jane. That was the life. New York: Norton,
   1977. 320p

HARRIS--WOMEN
   Harris, Ann Sutherland, and Linda Nochlin. Women artists,
   1550-1950. Los Angeles: County Museum of Art. New
   York: Knopf, 1977. 368p paper

HAZEN--INTERV.
   Hazen, David W. Interviewing sinners and saints. Portland,
   Ore.: Binfords & Mort, 1942. 1st ed. 431p

HELLSTEDT--WOMEN
   Hellstedt, Leone McGregor. Women physicians of the world:
   Autobiographies of medical pioneers. New York: McGraw-
   Hill, 1978. 420p

HENDERSON--TEN
   Henderson, James D., and Linda Roddy Henderson. Ten notable
   women of Latin America. Chicago: Nelson-Hall, 1978. 257p

HENKES--EIGHT
   Henkes, Robert. Eight American women painters. New York:
   Gordon, 1977. 59p

HENRY--WRITTEN
   Henry, Sondra, and Emily Tartz. Written out of history: A
   hidden legacy of Jewish women revealed through their writ-
   ings and letters. New York: Bloch, c1978. 293p

HERRMANN--GER.
   Herrmann, Elizabeth Riitschi, and Edna Huttenmaier Spitz.
   German women writers of the twentieth century. New York:
   Pergamon, c1978. 148p

HERSHEY--BETWEEN
Hershey, Lenore. Between the covers: The lady's own journal.
New York: Coward-McCann, c1983. 242p

HIGHAM--CELEB.
Higham, Charles. Celebrity circus. New York: Delacorte,
c1979. 322p

HIRSCHHORN--RATING
Hirschhorn, Joel. Rating the movie stars for home video--TV--
cable. By the editors of Consumer Guide. New York:
Beekman House, c1983. 384p paper

HOLLANDER--100
Hollander, Phyllis. 100 greatest women in sports. New York:
Grosset & Dunlap, 1976. 142p

HOLME--JOURNAL
Holme, Bryan, with editors of the Viking Press and the Ladies'
Home Journal. The Journal of the century. New York:
Viking, 1976. 352p

HOOPLE--AS
Hoople, Cheryl G. As I saw it: Women who lived the American
adventure. New York: Dial, c1978. 187p

HORAN--DESPERATE
Horan, James D. The desperate years: A pictorial history of
the thirties. New York: Bonanza Books, 1972. 288p

HORNER--ENGLISH
Horner, Joyce M. The English women novelists and their con-
nection with the feminist movement. Northampton, Mass.:
Folcroft Library Editions, 1973. 152p

HOWARD--SEVEN
Howard, Maureen. Seven American women writers of the twentieth century: An Introduction. Minneapolis, Minn.: University of Minnesota Press, c1963, 1977. 380p

HUFSTADER--SISTERS
Hufstader, Alice Anderson. Sisters of the quill. New York:
Dodd, Mead, 1978. 329p

HURD-MEAD. See MEAD--HISTORY

HYMOWITZ--HISTORY
Hymowitz, Carol, and Michaele Weissman. A history of women in
America. Anti-Defamation League of B'nai B'rith. New York:
Bantam, 1978. 400p paper

INGRAHAM--ALBUM
Ingraham, Claire R., and Leonard W. Ingraham. An album of
women in American history. New York: Franklin Watts,
1972. 88p

INNIS--PROFILES
Innis, Doris Funnye, and Juliana Wee. Profiles in black: Bio-
graphical sketches of 100 living black unsung heroes.
Congress of Racial Equality, Core, 1976. 240p

JABLONSKI--ENCY.
Jablonski, Edward. The encyclopedia of American music.
Garden City, N.Y.: Doubleday, 1981. 629p

JACOBS--MODERN
Jacobs, Helen Hall. Famous modern American women athletes.
New York: Dodd, Mead, c1975. 136p

JAMES--NOTABLE (1)
James, Edward T., ed., and Janet Wilson James and Paul S.
Boyer. Notable American women, 1607-1950: A biographical
dictionary. Vol. 1. Cambridge, Mass.: Belknap Press of
Harvard University Press, c1971, 1974. 687p paper

JAMES--NOTABLE (2)
James, Edward T., ed., and Janet Wilson James and Paul S.
Boyer. Notable American women, 1607-1950: A biographical
dictionary. Vol. 2. Cambridge, Mass.: Belknap Press of
Harvard University Press, c1971, 1974. 659p paper

JAMES--NOTABLE (3)
James, Edward T., ed., and Janet Wilson James and Paul S.
Boyer. Notable American women, 1607-1950: A biographical
dictonary. Vol. 3. Cambridge, Mass.: Belknap Press of
Harvard University Press, c1971, 1974. 729p paper

JOHNS--DAMES
Johns, Eric. Dames of the theatre. New Rochelle, N.Y.:
Arlington House, 1974. 179p

JONES--RUTLEDGE
Jones, Barry, and M.V. Dixon. The Rutledge dictionary of
people. New York: Rutledge Press, 1981. 854p

JONES--WOMEN (1)
Jones, H. Wendy. Women who braved the far North: 200 years
of Alaskan women. Vol. 1. San Diego, Calif.: Grossmont
Press, 1976. 206p paper

JORDAN--BROKEN
Jordan, Pat. Broken patterns. New York: Dodd, Mead, c1974,
1977. 213p

KAHN--HILL.
Kahn, Kathy. Hillbilly women. Garden City, N.Y.: Doubleday,
1973. 230p

KAPLAN--SALT
Kaplan, Cora. Salt and bitter and good: Three centuries of
English and American poets. New York: Paddington Press,
1975. 304p

KEENAN--WOMEN
Keenan, Brigid. The women we wanted to look like. New York:
St. Martin's Press, 1978. 224p

KEIL--THOSE
Keil, Sally Van Wagenen. Those wonderful women in their flying
machines: The unknown heroines of World War II. New York:
Rawson, Wade, 1979. 334p

KELEN--FIFTY
Kelen, Emery. Fifty voices of the twentieth century. New
York: Lothrop & Shepherd, 1970. 192p

KELLEY-COURAGE
Kelley, Joseph J., Jr., and Sol Feinstone. Courage and candle-
light: The feminine spirit of '76. Harrisburg, Pa.: Stack-
pole Books, 1974. 240p

KEYLIN--HOLLYWOOD
Keylin, Arleen, and Suri Fleischer, eds. Hollywood album:
Lives and deaths of Hollywood stars from the pages of the
New York Times. New York: Arno Press, 1977. 312p

KIRK--CIRCUS
Kirk, Rhina. Circus heroes and heroines. Maplewood, N.J.:
Hammond, 1972. 93p

KLEVER--WOMEN
Klever, Anita. Women in television. Philadelphia: Westminster
Press, c1975. 142p

KOOIMAN--CAMEOS
Kooiman, Helen W. Cameos: Women fashioned by God.
Wheaton, Ill.: Tyndale House, 1968. 163p

KOOIMAN--SILHOUETTES
Kooiman, Helen W. Silhouettes: Women behind great men.
Waco, Tex.: Word Books, c1972. 170p

KOSTMAN--20TH
Kostman, Samuel. Twentieth century women of achievement.
New York: Richard Rosen Press, 1976. 178p

KRONENBERGER--ATLAN.
Kronenberger, Louis, ed. Atlantic brief lives. Boston: Little, Brown, c1965, 1971. 900p

KUFRIN--UNCOM.
Kufrin, Joan. Uncommon women. Piscataway, N.J.: New Century, c1981. 173p

KULKIN--HER
Kulkin, Mary-Ellen. Her way: Biographies of women for young people. Chicago: ALA, c1976. 449p

KUPFERBERG--FIRST
Kupferberg, Tuli and Sylvia Topp. First glance: Childhood creations of the famous. Maplewood, N.J.: Hammond, c1978. 192p

LAGEMANN--GEN.
Lagemann, Ellen Condliffe. A generation of women: Education in the lives of progressive reformers. Cambridge, Mass.: Harvard University Press, c1979. 207p

LAMPARSKI--WHAT. (2)
Lamparski, Richard. Whatever became of...? Second series. New York: Crown, 1968. 207p

LAMPARSKI--WHAT. (3)
Lamparski, Richard. Whatever became of...? Third series. New York: Crown, 1970. 207p

LAMPARSKI--WHAT. (4)
Lamparski, Richard. Whatever became of...? Fourth series. New York: Crown, 1973. 207p

LAMPARSKI--WHAT. ANNUAL (4, 5)
Lamparski, Richard. (Lamparski's) Whatever became of...? Giant 1st annual (includes some from Series 4, 5). New York: Bantam, 1976. 409p paper

LAMPARSKI--WHAT. (5)
Lamparski, Richard. Whatever became of...? Fifth series. New York: Crown, c1974. 207p

LAMPARSKI--WHAT. (8)
Lamparski, Richard. Whatever became of...? Eighth series. New York: Crown, c1982. 303p

LAMSON--IN
Lamson, Peggy. In the vanguard: Six American women in public life. Boston: Houghton Mifflin, 1979. 233p

LAND--NEW
Land, Barbara. The new explorers: Women in Antarctica.
New York: Dodd, Mead, c1981. 224p

LEARY--GOLDEN
Leary, Francis. The golden longing. New York: Charles
Scribner's Sons, 1959. 358p

LEONARD--DEAR
Leonard, Eugenie Andruss. The dear-bought heritage. Philadelphia: University of Pennsylvania Press, 1965. 658p

LePAGE--WOMEN
LePage, Jane Weiner. Women composers, conductors, and musi-
cians of the twentieth century. Metuchen, N.J.: Scarecrow
Press, 1980. 293p

LEVENSON--WOMEN
Levenson, Dorothy. Women of the West. New York: Franklin
Watts, 1973. 88p

LEWIS--PRIME
Lewis, Marlo, and Mina Bess Lewis. Prime time. Los Angeles:
Tarcher. New York: St. Martin's, c1979. 256p

LICHTENSTEIN--MACH.
Lichtenstein, Grace. Machisma: Women and daring. Garden
City, N.Y.: Doubleday, 1981. 369p

LINDBORG--FIVE
Lindborg, Kristina, and Carlos J. Ovando. Five Mexican-
American women in transition: A case study of migrants in
the Midwest. San Francisco: R. & E. Research, 1977. 111p

LONGFORD--EMINENT
Longford, Elizabeth. Eminent Victorian women. New York:
Knopf, 1981. 255p

LONGSTREET--QUEEN
Longstreet, Stephen. The Queen bees: The women who shaped
America. Indianapolis, Ind.: Bobbs-Merrill, 1979. 210p

LUTZ--CRUSADE
Lutz, Alma. Crusade for freedom: Women of the antislavery
movement. Boston: Beacon Press, c1968. 338p

McCULLOUGH--PEOPLE
McCullough, David W. People, books, and book people. New
York: Harmony Books, c1980, 1981. 182p paper

McFARLAND--INCRED.
McFarland, Kevin. Incredible people. New York: Hart, c1975.
192p paper

McHENRY--LIBERTY'S
McHenry, Robert. Liberty's women. Springfield, Mass.:
Merriam, 1980. 482p

MACKSEY--BOOK
Macksey, Joan, and Kenneth Macksey. The book of women's
achievements. New York: Stein and Day, 1975. 287p

McWHIRTER--GUINNESS
McWhirter, Norris, Steve Morgenstern, Roz Morgenstern, and
Stan Greenberg. Guinness book of women's sports records.
New York: Sterling, 1979. 192p

MAGILL--CYCL.
Magill, Frank N. Cyclopedia of world authors. New York:
Harper & Row, 1958. 1198p

MANCHEL--WOMEN
Manchel, Frank. Women on the Hollywood scene. New York:
Franklin Watts, 1977. 122p

MANDEL--SOVIET
Mandel, William M. Soviet women. Garden City, N.Y.: Anchor/
Doubleday, 1975. 350p paper

MARKS--WOMEN
Marks, Geoffrey, and William K. Beatty. Women in white. New
York: Scribner's, c1972. 239p

MARLOWE--GREAT
Marlow, Joan. The great women. New York: A. & W., 1979.
383p

MARZOLF--UP
Marzolf, Marion. Up from the footnote: A history of women
journalists. New York: Hastings House, 1977. 310p

MAY--DIFFERENT
May, Antoinette. Different drummers: They did what they
wanted. Millbrae, Calif.: Les Femmes, 1976. 156p paper

MEAD--HIST.
Mead, Kate Campbell Hurd-. A history of women in medicine:
From the earliest times to the beginning of the nineteenth
century. Haddam, Conn.: Haddam Press, 1938. 569p

MELICK--WIVES
Melick, Arden Davis. Wives of the presidents. Maplewood, N.J.:
Hamond, c1972. 93p

MEYER--PETTICOAT
Meyer, Edith Patterson. Petticoat patriots of the Revolution.
New York: Vanguard Press, 1976. 253p

MEYER--WHO'S
Meyer, Mary Keysor, and P. William Filby. Who's who in geneal-
ogy & heraldry. Vol. 1. Detroit, Mich.: Gale Research,
c1981. 232p

MIGEL--BALLERINAS
Migel, Parmenia. The Ballerinas, from the Court of Louis XIV
to Pavlona. New York: Da Capo Press, c1972. 304p paper

MILLER--FISHBAIT
Miller, Wm. "Fishbait" as told to Francis Spatz Leighton.
Fishbait: The memoirs of a Congressional doorkeeper.
Englewood Cliffs, N.J.: Prentice-Hall, 1977. 389p

MILLER--LIVES
Miller, Lynn F., and Sally S. Swenson. Lives and works:
Talks with women artists. Metuchen, N.J.: Scarecrow,
c1981. 244p

MILLER--WOMEN
Miller, Judi. Women who changed America. New York: Manor
Books, 1976. 254p

MILLSTEIN--WE
Millstein, Beth, and Jeanne Bodin. We, the American women:
A documentary history. New York: S.R.A., 1977. 331p

M.I.T.--WOMEN
M.I.T. Symposium on American women in science and engineering,
1964. Women and the scientific professions. Edited by
Jacqueline A. Mattfeld and Carol G. Van Aken. Cambridge,
Mass.: M.I.T. Press, 1965. 250p paper

MITCHELL--RECOL.
Mitchell, Margaretta K. Recollections: Ten women of photography. New York: Viking, 1979. 208p

MITCHELL--YESSIR
Mitchell, George. Yessir, I've been here a long time: The
faces and words of Americans who have lived a century.
New York: Dutton, 1975. 124p

MOERS--LITERARY
    Moers, Ellen. Literary women. Garden City, N.Y.: Doubleday,
    1976. 336p

MOFFAT--REVEL.
    Moffat, Mary Jane, and Charlotte Painter, eds. Revelations:
    Diaries of women. New York: Random House, c1974. 411p

MORDDEN--MOVIE
    Mordden, Ethan. Movie star: A look at the women who made
    Hollywood. New York: St. Martin's Press, c1983. 296p

MORLEY--LITERARY
    Morley, Frank. Literary Britain: A reader's guide to its
    writers and landmarks. New York: Dorset Press, c1980.
    510p

MUNRO--ORIGINALS
    Munro, Eleanor. Originals: American women artists. New
    York: Simon & Schuster, 1979. 528p

MUNSTERBERG--HIST.
    Munsterberg, Hugo. A history of women artists. New York:
    Clarkson N. Potter (Crown), 1975. 150p

NASH--INNOV.
    Nash, Jay Robert. The innovators: 16 portraits of the famous
    and the infamous. Regnery Gateway, 1982. 240p

NEIDLE--AMERICA'S
    Neidle, Cecyle S. America's immigrant women. Boston: Hall
    (Twayne), 1975. 312p

NEMSER--CONVERS.
    Nemser, Cindy. Conversations with 12 women artists. New
    York: Scribner's, c1975. 367p

NEULS-BATES--WOMEN
    Neuls-Bates, Carol, ed. Women in music: An anthology of
    source readings from the Middle Ages to the present. New
    York: Harper & Row, c1982. 351p paper

NEW YORK TIMES--GREAT
    New York Times. Great lives of the century, as reported by
    the "New York Times." Edited by Arleen Keylin. New
    York: Times Press (Arno), 1977. 305p

NEWLON--MEXICAN
    Newlon, Clarke. Famous Mexican-Americans. Foreword by Dr.
    Uvaldo H. Palomares. New York: Dodd, Mead, 1972. 187p

NIES--SEVEN
Nies, Judith. Seven women: Portraits from the American radical tradition. New York: Viking Press, 1977. 236p

OBERG--SPACE
Oberg, Alcestis R. Spacefarers of the 80's and 90's: The next thousand people in space. New York: Columbia University Press, 1985. 238p

O'CONNOR--SALLY
O'Connor, Karen. Sally Ride and the new astronauts. New York: Franklin Watts, 1983. 188p

OLDS--WOMEN
Olds, Elizabeth Fagg. Women of the four winds. Boston: Houghton Mifflin, c1985. 318p

100--GREATEST (1)
100 Greatest women. No. 1. Edit. Director, Roseann C. Hirsch. New York: Lexington Library, 1976. 114p paper

O'NEILL--WOMEN'S
O'Neill, Lois Decker, ed. The women's book of world records and achievements. Garden City, N.Y.: Anchor Books/ Doubleday, 1979. 798p

OPFELL--LADY
Opfell, Olga S. The lady laureates: Women who have won the Nobel Prize. Metuchen, N.J.: Scarecrow, 1978. 267p

OSEN--WOMEN
Osen, Lynn M. Women in mathematics. Cambridge, Mass.: M.I.T. Press, 1974. 185p

PACHTER--CHAMP.
Pachter, Marc, with Amy Henderson, Jeannette Hussey, and Margaret C.S. Christman. Champions of American sport. New York: Harry N. Abrams, 1981. 288p

PALMER--WHO'S
Palmer, Alan. Who's who in modern history, 1860-1980. New York: Holt, Rinehart, & Winston, 1980. 332p

PAPACHRISTOU--WOMEN
Papachristou, Judith. Women together. New York: Knopf, 1976. 273p

PARKER--OLD
Parker, Rozsika, and Griselda Pollock. Old mistresses: Women, art, and ideology. New York: Pantheon Books, c1981. 184p paper

PARKER--UNEASY
Parker, Jeri. Uneasy survivors: Five women writers. Santa
Barbara, Calif.: Peregrine Smith, 1975. 219p paper

PARTINGTON--WHO's
Partington, Paul G. Who's who on the postage stamps of Eastern
Europe. Metuchen, N.J.: Scarecrow, 1979. 498p

PEACOCK--FAMOUS
Peacock, Virginia Tatnall. Famous American belles of the nineteenth century. Philadelphia: Lippincott, c1900, 1901. 297p

PEARSON--WHO
Pearson, Carol, and Katherine Pope. Who am I this time? Fe-
male portraits in British and American literature. New York:
McGraw-Hill, 1976. 305p

PEDERSON--LEADERS
Pederson, Kern. Leaders of America: Capsule biographies of
over 260 famous personalities. Waukesha, Wis.: Country
Beautiful, c1976. 256p paper

PEOPLE--BEST
People's Weekly, ed. The best of People Weekly: The first
decade. New York: Fawcett Columbine, c1984. 255p paper

PEOPLE'S ALMANAC (1)
The People's Almanac, by David Wallechinsky and Irving Wallace.
Garden City, N.Y.: Doubleday, 1975. 1478p paper

PEOPLE'S ALMANAC (2)
The People's Almanac #2 by David Wallechinsky and Irving Wallace. New York: Bantam Books, 1978. 1416p paper

PEOPLE'S ALMANAC (3)
The People's Almanac #3 by David Wallechinsky and Irving Wallace. New York: Bantam Books, 1981. 722p paper

PERCIVAL--MODERN
Percival, John. Modern ballet. New York: Harmony Books,
c1970. 144p paper

PETERSEN--WOMEN
Petersen, Karen, and J.J. Wilson. Women artists: Recognition
and reappraisal from the early Middle Ages to the twentieth
century. New York: New York University Press, 1976.
212p

PLANTE--DIFFICULT
Plante, David. Difficult women: A memoir of three. New York:
Atheneum, c1979, 1983. 173p

POLLOCK--IN
   Pollock, Bruce. In their own words. New York: Macmillan,
   c1975. 231p

POMEROY--GODD.
   Pomeroy, Sarah B. Goddesses, whores, wives, and slaves.
   Women in classical antiquity. New York: Schocken, c1975.
   265p

PRAUSE--SCHOOL
   Prause, Gerhard. School days of the famous. Tr. and adapted
   by Susan Hecker Ray. New York: Springer, c1978. 216p

PRICE--GOD
   Price, Eugenia. God speaks to women today. Grand Rapids,
   Mich.: Zondervan, c1964, 1969. 192p paper

PRIESTLEY--PART.
   Priestley, J.B. Particular pleasures. Being a personal record
   of some varied arts and many different artists. New York:
   Stein and Day, 1975. 192p

PROCTOR--WOMEN
   Proctor, Priscilla, and William Proctor. Women in the pulpit.
   New York: Doubleday, 1976. 176p

P.W.--AUTHOR
   Publishers Weekly, editors and contributors. The author speaks.
   New York: R.R. Bowker, 1977. 540p

READER'S--STORY
   Reader's Digest Assoc., Inc. The story of America. New York:
   Pleasantville, Reader's Digest Assoc., 1975. 527p

REIFERT--WOMEN
   Reifert, Gail, and Eugene M. Dermody. Women who fought: An
   American history. Norwalk, Calif.: The authors, Cerritos
   College, 1978. 227p

RICH-McCOY--MILL.
   Rich-McCoy, Lois. Millionairess. Self-made women of America.
   New York: Harper & Row, 1978. 237p

RICHARDSON--GREAT
   Richardson, Ben, and William A. Fahey. Great black Americans
   2d rev. ed. Formerly titled Great American Negroes. New
   York: Crowell, c1956, 1976. 344p

RICHEY--EMINENT
   Richey, Elinor. Eminent women of the West. Berkeley, Calif.:
   Howell-North, 1975. 276p

RIVERA--SPECIAL
  Rivera, Geraldo. A special kind of courage: Profiles of young
  Americans. New York: Simon & Schuster, c1976. 319p

ROGERS--LADIES
  Rogers, W.G. Ladies bountiful. New York: Harcourt, Brace,
  & World, c1968. 236p

ROSS--YOUNG
  Ross, Pat, comp. Young and female: Turning points in the
  lives of eight American women--Personal accounts with intro-
  ductory notes. New York: Random House, 1972. 109p

RUDDICK--WORKING
  Ruddick, Sara, and Pamela Daniels. Working it out: 23 women
  writers, artists, scientists, and scholars talk about their
  lives and work. New York: Pantheon Books, 1977. 210p

RYAN--SPORTS
  Ryan, Joan. Contributions of women: Sports. Minneapolis,
  Minn.: Dillon, c1975, 1977. 133p

SABIN--WOMEN
  Sabin, Francene. Women who win. New York: Random House,
  1975. 171p

SAT. EVE. POST--MOVIE
  The Saturday Evening Post movie book. Indianapolis, Ind.:
  Curtis Publishing, 1977. 152p

SCHEUER--TEL.
  Scheuer, Steven H., ed. Who's who in television and cable.
  New York: Facts on File, c1983. 579p

SCHOENEBAUM--PROF.
  Schoenebaum, Eleanora W. Profiles of an era: The Nixon/Ford
  years. New York: Harcourt Brace Jovanovich, 1979. 787p

SCIENCE DIGEST--100
  Science Digest. America's 100 brightest scientists under 40.
  New York: Hearst, December 1984. 108p

SCOTT--SOUTHERN
  Scott, Anne F. Southern lady: From pedestal to politics,
  1830-1930. Chicago: University of Chicago Press, 1970.
  247p

SEED--SATURDAY'S
  Seed, Suzanne. Saturday's child: 36 women talk about their
  jobs. Chicago: J. Philip O'Hara, 1973. 159p

SEIFER--NOBODY
Seifer, Nancy. Nobody speaks for me: Self-portraits of American working class women. New York: Simon & Schuster,
1976. 477p

SEYMOUR-SMITH--NOVELS
Seymour-Smith, Martin. Novels and novelists: A guide to the
world of fiction. New York: St. Martin's, 1980. 288p

SEYMOUR-SMITH--WHO'S
Seymour-Smith, Martin. Who's who in twentieth century literature. New York: Holt, Rinehart, and Winston, 1976. 414p

SHERR--AMERICAN
Sherr, Lynn, and Jurate Kazickas. The American women's gaze-
teer. New York: Bantam Books, 1976. 271p

SHIPMAN--GOLD.
Shipman, David. The great movie stars: The golden years.
New rev. ed. New York: Hill & Wang/Farrar, Straus &
Giroux, c1970, 1979. 592p

SHIPMAN--INTERNATL.
Shipman, David. The great movie stars: The international
years. New rev. ed. New York: Hill & Wang/Farrar,
Straus & Giroux, c1972, 1980. 646p

SHOWALTER--LIT.
Showalter, Elaine. A literature of their own: British women
novelists from Brontë to Lessing. Princeton, N.J.:
Princeton University press, 1977. 378p

SHOWALTER--THESE
Showalter, Elaine, ed. These modern women: Autobiographical
essays from the twenties. Old Westbury, N.Y.: Feminist
Press, 1978. 147p

SICHERMAN--NOTABLE
Sicherman, Barbara, and Carol Hurd Green ..., eds. Notable
American women. A biographical dictionary. Cambridge,
Mass.: Belknap Press/Harvard University Press, 1980. 773p

SIGNIF.--AMER.
Significant American women. Chicago: Children's Press,
c1975. 78p

SIMON--BEST
Simon, George T., and friends. The best of the music makers.
Garden City, N.Y.: Doubleday, 1979. 635p

SIMON--BIG
  Simon, George T., comp. The big bands songbook. New
  York: Barnes & Noble (Harper & Row), c1975. 371p

SLIDE--EARLY
  Slide, Anthony. Early women directors. New York: A.S.
  Barnes, 1977. 119p

SMARIDGE--FAMOUS
  Smaridge, Norah. Famous author-illustrators for young people.
  New York: Dodd, Mead, c1973. 159p

SMITH--BREAK.
  Smith, Betsy Covington. Breakthough: Women in religion.
  New York: Walker, 1978. 139p

SMITH--DAUGHTERS
  Smith, Page. Daughters of the promised land: Women in
  American history. Boston: Little, Brown, 1970. 392p

SMITH--MOVIES
  Smith, Sharon. Women who make movies. New York: Hopkinson & Blake, c1975. 307p

SMITH--WOMEN
  Smith, George Barnett. Women of renown: Nineteenth century
  studies. Essay Index Reprint Series. Reprint of the 1893
  ed. Freeport, N.Y.: Books for Libraries Press, 1972. 478p

SNYDER--DAUNTLESS
  Snyder, Agnes. Dauntless women in childhood education.
  Washington, D.C.: Association for Childhood Education
  International, 1972. 405p

SOCHEN--HERSTORY
  Sochen, June. Herstory: A woman's view of American history.
  New York: Alfred, 1974. 448p

SOCHEN--MOVERS
  Sochen, June. Movers and shakers: American women thinkers
  and activists, 1900-1970. New York: Quadrangle/The New
  York Times Book Co., 1973. 320p

SOFTLY--QUEENS
  Softly, Barbara. The queens of England. New York: Bell,
  c1976, 1979. 128p

SOMERVILLE--WOMEN
  Somerville, Mollie, comp. Women and the American Revolution.
  Washington, D.C.: N.S.D.A.R., 1974. 67p paper

SORELL--THREE
Sorell, Walter. Three women: Lives of sex and genius.
Indianapolis, Ind.: Bobbs-Merrill, 1975. 234p

SPACKS--CONTEMP.
Spacks, Patricia Meyer. Contemporary women novelists: A
collection of critical essays. Englewood Cliffs, N.J.:
Prentice-Hall, 1977. 183p paper

SPARROW--WOMEN
Sparrow, Walter Shaw. Women painters of the world, from the
time of Caterina Vigri, 1413-1463, to Rosa Bonheur and the
present day. New York: Hacker Art Books, 1976 (reprint
from original London ed., 1905). 332p

SPRINGER--THEY
Springer, John, and Jack Hamilton. They had faces then:
Super stars, stars, and starlets of the 1930's. Secaucus,
N.J.: Citadel Press, c1974. 342p

STAMBLER--WOMEN
Stambler, Irwin. Women in sports. Garden City, N.Y.:
Doubleday, 1975. 155p

STARR--AMER.
Starr, Kevin. Americans and the California dream. Santa
Barbara, Calif.: Peregrine Smith, c1973, 1981. 494p paper

STEIN--FRAGMENTS
Stein, Leon, ed. Fragments of autobiography. (Women in
America, from colonial times to the 20th century.) New
York: Arno Press, 1974. (irregular pagination)

STEIN--LIVES
Stein, Leon, ed. Lives to remember. (Women in America,
from colonial times to the 20th century.) New York: Arno
Press, 1974. (irregular pagination)

STOBAUGH--WOMEN
Stobaugh, Beverly Parker. Women and Parliament, 1918-1970.
Hicksville, N.Y.: Exposition Press, 1978. 152p

STODDARD--FAMOUS
Stoddard, Hope. Famous American women. New York: Crowell,
1970. 461p

SULLIVAN--QUEENS
Sullivan, George. Queens of the court. New York: Dodd,
Mead, 1974. 96p

SWIGER--WOMEN
   Swiger, Elinor Porter. Women lawyers at work. New York:
   Messner, 1978. 224p

TALMEY--VOGUE
   Talmey, Allene, ed. Vogue: People are talking about ... people
   and things in   . Englewood Cliffs, N.J.: Prentice-
   Hall, 1969(?) 247p

TAYLOR--GENER.
   Taylor, Kethryn. Generations of denial: 75 short biographies
   of women in history. San Rafael, Calif.: Times Change Press,
   1971. 63p

TEITZ--WHAT'S
   Teitz, Joyce. What's a nice girl like you doing in a place like
   this? New York: Coward, McCann & Geoghegan, c1972.
   285p

THOMSON--AMER.
   Thomson, Virgil. American music since 1910: Twentieth-century
   composers. New York: Holt, Rinehart, and Winston, c1970,
   1971. 204p

TIME--WOMEN
   Time-Life Books, ed., and Joan Swallow Reiter. The Women.
   (Old West series.) Alexandria, Va.: Time-Life Books, 1978.
   240p

TOPPIN--BIOG.
   Toppin, Edgar A. A biographical history of blacks in America
   since 1528. New York: David McKay, c1969, 1971. 499p

TREASE--SEVEN
   Trease, Geoffrey. Seven sovereign queens. New York: Vanguard Press, c1968, 1971. 178p

TRUMAN--WOMEN
   Truman, Margaret. Women of courage. New York: Bantam
   Books, 1977. 210p paper

TUFTS--OUR
   Tufts, Eleanor. Our hidden heritage: Five centuries of women
   artists. New York: Paddington Press (Two Continents),
   1974. 256p

TUGGLE--GOLDEN
   Tuggle, Robert. The golden age of opera. With photographs
   of Herman Mishkin. New York: Holt, Rinehart, & Winston,
   1983. 246p

U.S.--WOMEN (89TH)
    U.S. Women's Bureau. Women of the 89th Congress. Washing-
    ton, D.C.: U.S. Government Printing Office (pamphlet).
    27p paper

U.S.--WOMEN (90TH)
    U.S. Women's Bureau. Women of the 90th Congress. Washing-
    ton, D.C.: U.S. Government Printing Office (pamphlet).
    27p paper

VALLANCE--WOMEN
    Vallance, E. Women in the House: A study of women members
    of Parliament. London: Athlone Press, 1979. 212p

VANCE--SIX
    Vance, Marguerite. Six queens: The wives of Henry VIII.
    New York: Dutton, 1967. 190p

WALKER--WOMEN
    Walker, Greta. Women today: Ten profiles. New York:
    Hawthorn Books, 1975. 174p

WARE--BEYOND
    Ware, Susan. Beyond suffrage: Women in the New Deal.
    Cambridge, Mass.: Harvard University Press, c1981. 204p

WARE--MEET
    Ware, Robert R. Meet the ladies: Personalities in Huntington
    portraits. San Marino, Calif.: Huntington Library, 1972.
    81p paper

WARREN--PICTORIAL
    Warren, Ruth. A pictorial history of women in America. New
    York: Crown, 1975. 228p

WASHINGTON--BLACK
    Washington, Mary Helen. Black-eyed susans: Classic stories
    by and about black women. Garden City, N.Y.: Anchor
    Press/Doubleday, 1975. 163p paper

WEBBER--WOMAN
    Webber, Jeannette L., and Joan Grumman. Woman as writer.
    Boston: Houghton Mifflin, 1978. 451p paper

WEBSTER'S--AMER.
    Webster's American biographies. Ed. by Charles VanDoren and
    Robert McHenry. Springfield, Mass.: Merriam, c1974.
    1233p

WELTER--DIMITY
    Welter, Barbara. Dimity convictions: The American woman in

the nineteenth century. Athens, Ohio: Ohio University
Press, 1976. 230p

WHEDON--ALWAYS
Whedon, Peggy. Always on Sunday: 1,000 Sundays with "Issues
and Answers." New York: Norton, c1980. 272p

WHITMAN--COME
Whitman, Alden. Come to judgment. New York: Viking Press,
1980. 373p

WHITNEY--COL.
Whitney, David C. The Colonial spirit of '76: The people of
the Revolution. Chicago: Ferguson, 1974. 440p

WHO DID WHAT
Who did what. The lives and achievements of the 5,000 men and
women--leaders of nations, saints and sinners, artists and
scientists--who shaped our world. New York: Crown, 1974.
384p

WILEY--CONFED.
Wiley, Bill Irvin. Confederate women. Westport, Conn.:
Greenwood Press, 1975. 204p

WILLIAMS--DEMETER'S
Williams, Selma R. Demeter's daughters: The women who
founded America, 1587-1787. New York: Atheneum, 1976.
359p

WILLIAMS--LEGEND.
Williams, Brad. Legendary women of the West. New York:
McKay, 1978. 142p

WILSON--HOLLY.
Wilson, Ivy Crane, ed. Hollywood in the 1940's. New York:
Ungar, c1980. 111p

WINTLE--MAKERS
Wintle, Justin, ed. Makers of modern culture. New York:
Facts on File, c1981. 605p

WOMAN'S ALMANAC
Woman's Almanac (Good Housekeeping). Edited by Barbara
McDowell and Hana Umlauf. New York: Newspaper Enter-
prise Assoc., 1977. 576p

WOMEN--RADIO
Women in radio. Illustrated by biographical sketches. Washing-
ton, D.C.: Department of Labor, Women's Bureau, Bulletin
No. 222, May 1947. 30p

WOMEN'S--FEMALE
Women's female artists, past and present. Berkeley, Calif.:
Women's History Research Center, 1974. 158p plus 5 pages
(supp.)

WORLD--WHO
World Almanac of Who. By the staff of the World Almanac.
Hana Umlauf Lane, ed. New York: World Almanac, 1980.
360p

YOUNG--REVOL.
Young, Philip. Revolutionary ladies. New York: Knopf, 1977.
225p

ZINSERLING--WOMEN
Zinserling, Verena. Women in Greece and Rome. New York:
Schram, 1972. 112p

INDEX TO WOMEN

A

AARON, BETSY (fl. 1960's-1980's)
Amer. TV newscaster
Gelfman--Women p67,142,160,
174-175
Scheuer--Tel. p1

AARON, CHLOE (1938-)
Amer. TV producer, executive
Scheuer--Tel. p1

ABAKANONICZ, MAGDALENA
(1930-)
Polish weaver, teacher
O'Neill--Women's p606

ABAYAH, JOSEPHINE (fl. 1970's)
Papuan & New Guinean MP
Macksey--Book p40

ABBAM, KATE (1934-)
Ghanaian publisher
O'Neill--Women's p480

ABBE, ELIZABETH (1950-)
Amer. geneaological
researcher, writer
Meyer--Who's p19

ABBOT, MARGARET (fl. 1900's)
Amer. golfer
Macksey--Book p256
O'Neill--Women's p561,572

ABBOT, SARAH (fl. 1820's-1830's)
Amer. educator, philanthro-
pist
Sherr--American p97

ABBOTT, BERENICE (1898-)
Amer. photographer
Bachtold--Gifted p36-37
Mitchell--Recol. p12-29, 199,
por.

Munsterberg--Hist. p135-137
O'Neill--Women's p613
Woman's Almanac p224
Women's--Female p62
World--Who p57

ABBOTT, DAISY RHEA (1891-)
Amer. politician, noted
Arkansas mother
Amer.--Mothers p47-48, por.

ABBOTT, EDITH (1876-1957)
Amer. social worker, educator,
philanthropist
Sherr--American p139
Sicherman--Notable p1-3

ABBOTT, ELEANOR HALLOWELL
(1872-1958)
Amer. children's book author
Ehrlich--Oxford p37

ABBOTT, ELIZABETH M. GRIFFIN
(1845-1941)
Amer. noted Nebraska mother,
civic leader, feminist
Amer.--Mothers p333-334, por.

ABBOTT, EMMA (1849/1850-1891)
Amer. opera singer
Claghorn--Biog. p13
James--Notable (1) p1-2
Sherr--American p64,242

ABBOTT, GRACE (1878-1939)
Amer. social worker, govern-
ment official
James--Notable (1) p2-4
McHenry--Liberty's p1
Macksey--Book p118
O'Neill--Women's p329
Sherr--American p139
Sochen--Movers p71,74,87-89,90,
272
Ware--Beyond p143-144, see also
index p197

1

Webster's--Amer. p4
World--Who p185

ABBOTT, MARY N. (fl. 1970's)
Amer. Air Force commander
O'Neill--Women's p550

ABBOTT, SARAH (fl. 1970's)
Amer. business woman
O'Neill--Women's p140

ABDY, IYA, LADY (fl. 1920's-
1930's)
Russian-French fashion
leader
Keenan--Women p56-58, por.

ABECASSIS, SNU (c1940-1980)
Portuguese book publisher
O'Neill--Women's p487

ABEL, ANNIE HELOISE (1873-1947)
Amer. historian
James--Notable (1) p4-6
McHenry--Liberty's p1-2

ABEL, HAZEL HEMPEL (c1888-1966)
Amer. Senator, noted Nebraska mother, Amer. business
executive, civic leader, educator, philanthropist
Amer.--Mothers p338, por.
Chamberlin--Min. p244-247

ABEL-HENDERSON, ANNIE HELOISE
See ABEL, ANNIE HELOISE

ABELLA (fl. 13th cent.)
Italian teacher, medical
woman, writer
Mead--Hist. p225,308

ABELN, MAURA J. (fl. 1970's)
Amer. Rhodes Scholar
O'Neill--Women's p434

ABERLE, SOPHIA D. (fl. 1920's-
1950's)
Amer. scientist, anthropologist
O'Neill--Women's p146

ABIERTAS, JOSEFA (-1922)
Filipino activist, WCTU
president
O'Neill--Women's p719

ABIGAIL
Biblical
Price--God p93-97

ABISH, CECILE (fl. 1970's)
Amer. sculptor
Women's--Female p84

ABOTT, BESSIE PICKENS (1878-
1919)
Amer. opera singer
Claghorn--Biog. p13

ABRABANEL, BENVENIDA (-1560)
Spanish business woman,
philanthropist
Henry--Written p138,140-141

ABRAHAM, SUSAN (fl. 1970's)
Amer. model, beauty
Keenan--Women p146-147,149, por.

ABRAHAMSEN, HANNA CHRISTIE
(1907-)
Norwegian woodworker
O'Neill--Women's p273-274

ABRAMOWITZ, BESSIE (1888-)
Russian-Amer. labor leader
Hymowitz--Hist. p248-249,
252-253

ABRAMSON, LYN (1940-)
Amer. psychologist
Science--Digest p70

ABREU, LUCILLE (fl. 1970's)
Hawaiian detective
O'Neill--Women's p374

ABSALON, ANNA PEDERSDOTTER
(-1590)
Norwegian accused witch
Bainton--Spain p128-133

ABUZA, SOPHIA
See TUCKER, SOPHIE KALISH

ABZUG, BELLA SAVITSKY (1920-)
Amer. Congresswoman,
feminist, lawyer
Bachtold--Gifted p103-104
Chamberlin--Min. p334-338
Clark--Leading p238
Cur. Biog. '71 p1-3, por.
Diamonstein--Open p3-6, por.

Gilbert--Part. p183-189, por.
Greenbaum--Politics p135-136
Hershey--Between p103-104,107
Lichtenstein--Mach. see index
    p357
Longstreet--Queen p193
McHenry--Liberty's p2
Miller--Fishbait p79-82,89-90,
    202
100--Greatest (1) p56, por.
O'Neill--Women's p44,71,448
Papachristou--Women p5,251,
    por.
Schoenebaum--Prof. p7-8
Sochen--Herstory p404-405, por.
Woman's Almanac p468-469, por.
World--Who p134

ACE, JANE SHERWOOD (1905-1974)
    Amer. radio actress, writer
    Curr. Biog. '75 p459
    Women--Radio p21

ACHER, VIRGINIA
    Amer. army flier
    Keill--Those p144-146,169,174,
    293

ACHEY, MARY ELIZABETH (1832-
    1885)
    Amer. artist
    Time--Women p114-115

ACHURCH, JANET (1864-1916)
    English actress
    Findlater--Player p165-167, por.

ACKERMAN, BERNICE (fl. 1970's)
    Amer. meteorologist
    O'Neill--Women's p172-173

ACKERMAN, MARGARET (fl. 1970's)
    Amer. art research worker
    Women's--Female p124

ACKERMAN(N), ROSEMARIE (fl.
    1970's)
    East German track and field
    athlete
    McWhirter--Guinness p177, por.
    O'Neill--Women's p577-578

ACKLAND, HARRIET CHRISTINA,
    HENRIETTA, LADY (1750-
    1815)
    Amer., wife of Major Ackland,

Parliamentary Member
Booth--Women p140-141, por.
Earle--Two Cent. (2) pxxi,
    p712-714, por.

ACKLEY, MARY E. (fl. 1850's)
    Amer. western pioneer, writer
    Fischer--Let p229-236

ACKROYD, MARGARET F. O'CONNOR
    (fl. 1920's-1940's)
    Amer. government worker,
    noted R. I. mother
    Amer.--Mothers p484-485, por.

ACLAND, CHRISTIAN HARRIET
    See ACKLAND, HARRIET
    CHRISTINA, HENRIETTA,
    LADY

ACOSTA, OFELIA URIBE (fl. 1960's)
    Colombian feminist
    Hahner--Women p117-122

ACTON, PENELOPE LEE (1764-1819)
    English socialite
    Ware--Meet p73

ACTON, SUSANNAH LEE (c1763-
    1789)
    English socialite
    Ware--Meet p73

ADAIR, BETHENIA ANGELINA OWENS
    (1840-1926)
    Amer. physician
    Gray--Women p128-134
    Hoople--As p143-150
    James--Notable (2) p657-659
    Millstein--We p64-65
    Sherr--American p194,196-197
    Time--Women p148-151,153, por.

ADAIR, THELMA DAVIDSON (fl.
    1940's-1970's)
    Amer. church moderator,
    teacher
    O'Neill--Women's p393

ADAM, JULIETTE LAMBER (1836-
    1936)
    French writer, editor, poet,
    salonist
    Crosland--Women p37-38

ADAM, MARIANNE (fl. 1970's)
    East German track and

field athlete
Hollander--100 p124-125

ADAM, SHARON (fl. 1960's)
Amer. sailor
Macksey--Book p246

ADAMCHICK, DONNA JO (fl. 1960's)
Amer. heroine, Carnegie
medal winner
O'Neill--Women's p734

ADAMOVA, EUGENIA MIKHAILOVNA
(1913-)
Russian painter
Women's--Female p3-supp.

ADAMS, ABIGAIL SMITH (1744-
1818)
Amer. first lady, letter-
writer, noted Massachusetts
mother
Amer.--Mothers p260-261, por.
Bird--Enterprising p29,32
Booth--Women, see index p323
DePauw--Found. p142-143,178,
202-205,208-211,219
DePauw--Rem. p146-147,149,
por.
Earle--Two Cent. (2) p570,
733,738-739
Earnest--American, see index
p271
Ehrlich--Oxford p64
Engle--Women p256-274, por.
Evans--Weather p1,5-6,19-20,
22,29-30
Faber--Presidents' p181-195,
por.
Fine--Women p90-91,94
Flexner--Face p110, por.
Hoople--As p32-37, por.
Hymowitz--Hist. p11,28,34-37,
69, por.
Ingraham--Album p13
James--Notable (1) p6-9
Kelley--Courage p15-57,232-233
Kulkin--Her p3-4
Levenson--Women p5
McHenry--Liberty's p2-3
Melick--Wives p12-16, por.
Meyer--Petticoat, see index
p245, por.
Millstein--We p30-32,38-40,por.
Moers--Literary p272
Neidle--America's p26-27
People's Almanac (1) p261

Sherr--American p108,110, por.
Sochen--Herstory, p73,75-76,84,
por.
Taylor--Gener. p8
Warren--Pictorial p53-54,56-57,
59,62-63
Webster's--American. p6
Whitney--Col. p90-91, por.
Williams--Demeter's, see index
p347
Woman's Almanac p486-541
World--Who p294

ADAMS, ALICE PETTEE (fl. 1890's)
Amer. social worker
Sherr--American p147

ADAMS, ANNETTE ABBOTT (1877-
1956)
Amer. lawyer, judge
Sicherman--Notable p3-5

ADAMS, BETTY (fl. 1960's)
Amer. WAC officer
O'Neill--Women's p542

ADAMS, EDITH (EDIE) (1927/1929-)
Amer. singer, actress
Scheuer--Tel. p3
World--Who p224

ADAMS, ELIZABETH (fl. 17th cent.)
Amer. founder of town
Sherr--American p151

ADAMS, EMMA HILDRETH (fl. 1880's)
Amer. western traveller,
newspaper correspondent
Fisher--Let p326-332

ADAMS, ENID ELEANOR (1909-)
Amer. genealogical researcher,
author, editor
Meyer--Who's p19

ADAMS, EVANGELINE SMITH (1865/
1872-1932)
Amer. astrologer
Felton--Famous p212-213

ADAMS, FAE MARGARET (fl. 1950's)
Amer. WAC physician
O'Neill--Women's p210

ADAMS, HANNAH (1755-1831)
Amer. scholar, historian,
essayist

DePauw--Found p206
DePauw--Rem. p98-99, por.
Fine--Women p92
James--Notable (1) p9-11
McHenry--Liberty's p3
Sherr--American p98,102
Stein--Fragments p1-110, por.
Williams--Demeter's p257

ADAMS, HARRIET (1893-1982)
Amer. children's book author
O'Neill--Women's p748

ADAMS, HARRIET CHALMERS
(1875-1937)
Amer. explorer, writer,
lecturer
James--Notable (1) p11-12
Sherr--American p22

ADAMS, JACQUELINE (fl. 1960's-1980's)
Amer. TV news correspon-
dent
Scheuer--Tel. p3

ADAMS, KATHERINE (1862-)
British bookbinder
Callen--Women p190,194-195,
198,222

ADAMS, LEONIE (1899-)
Amer. poet
Ehrlich--Oxford p151

ADAMS, LOUISA CATHERINE
JOHNSON (1775-1852)
Amer. first lady
James--Notable (1) p12-15
Kulkin--Her p4-5
Melick--Wives p26-27, por.
Woman's Almanac p487

ADAMS, MARIAN HOOPER
(c1843-1885)
Amer. photographer, hostess
Daniels--Wash. p11-21, por.
James--Notable (1) p15-16
Sherr--American p42

ADAMS, MARILYN L. (1931-)
Amer. genealogical research-
er, author, indexer, editor
Meyer--Who's p19-20

ADAMS, MAUDE (1872-1953)
Amer. actress
Clark--Leading p37-38

Fabian--On p108-109, por.
Gilfond--Heroines p110
Hazen--Interv. p88-90
Ingraham--Album p62
McHenry--Liberty's p3
O'Neill--Women's p654-655
People's Almanac (1) p862-863
Sicherman--Notable p5-7
Webster's--Amer. p10-11
World--Who p224

ADAMS, SARAH FLOWER (1805-1848)
English poet and hymn writer
Showalter--Lit. p322

ADAMS, SHARON (c1930-)
Amer. sailor
McFarland--Incred. p27

ADAMS, SUSANNA BOYLSTON
(1709-1797)
Amer. mother of John Adams
Amer.--Mothers p259
Faber--Presidents' p271-274

ADAMS, SUZANNE (1872-1953)
Amer. opera singer
Claghorn--Biog. p15

ADAMSON, JOY (FRIEDERIKE
VICTORIA) (1910-1980)
Austrian-Kenyan author,
animal expert
Cur. Biog. '72 p1-3, por.
Cur. Biog. '80 p449
Woman's Almanac p360, por.

ADATO, PERRY MILLER
Amer. producer and director
of documentaries
O'Neill--Women's p496
Scheuer--Tel. p3-4, por.
Smith--Movies p146,223

ADDAMS, JANE (1860-1935)
Amer. social worker, humani-
tarian
Anticaglia--12 p115-136, por.
Banner--Women see index p263,
por.
Bird--Enterprising p180-181
Brin--Social p55-75, por.
Callen--Women p222
Chinoy--Women p197-203, por.
Clark--Leading p31-34
Crovitz--Courage p125-151
Earnest--American p214-215,

222-223,234
Gilfond--Heroines p10-16, por.
Hymowitz--Hist. p223-233,273,
275
Ingraham--Album p43, por.
James--Notable (1) p16-22
Jones--Rutledge p5
Kulkin--Her p5-7
Longstreet--Queen p77-80, por.
McHenry--Liberty's p3-4
Macksey--Book p117-118,126,
por.
Marks--Women p188-196, por.
Marlowe--Great p172-177, por.
Millstein--We p148-149,159-161,
por.
Moers--Literary p272
O'Neill--Women's p699
Opfell--Lady p18-33, por.
Palmer--Who's p19-20
Papachristou--Women p152-153,
por.
Pederson--Leaders p175, por.
People's Almanac (2) p572,1044
Reifert--Women p184-187
Sherr--American p59-60
Signif.--Amer. p27, por.
Sochen--Herstory p207,214-215,
217,234,239,264, por.
Sochen--Movers p8-10
Stoddard--Famous p1-11, por.
Warren--Pictorial p148-149,167-
168, por.
Webster's--Amer. p13
Woman's Almanac p379-380, por.
World--Who p185-186

ADELAIDE OF SAXE--MEININGEN
(1792-1849)
English Queen
Jones--Rutledge p5
Softly--Queens p110-113

ADELBERGER, BERTHA (fl.
c750's-770's)
Italian physician
Mead--Hist. p103

ADELE OF ASSISI (fl. 13th cent.)
Italian bibliophile
Mead--Hist. p224

ADELICIA OF LOUVAIN (c1102-
1151)
English Queen
Softly--Queens p14-16

ADELMOTA, PRINCESS OF CARRARA
(fl. 1300's)
Italian obstetrician
Mead--Hist. p278

ADINY, ADA (1855-1924)
French opera singer
Claghorn--Biog. p16

ADIVAR, HALIDE EDIB (1883-1964)
Turkish educator, professor,
author, feminist
Macksey--Book p77,90

ADKINS, BERTHA SHEPPARD (1906-
1983)
Amer. government official
Cur. Biog. '83 p459

ADKINS, WILMA (1941-)
Amer. genealogical researcher,
author, indexer
Meyer--Who's p20

ADLER, POLLY (1900-1962)
Polish-Amer. "Madam"
People's Almanac (2) p933, por.
Sicherman--Notable p7-8

ADLER, RENATA (1938-)
Amer. reviewers, essayist,
short story writer, novelist
Cur. Biog. '84 p3-6
McCullough--People p1-2

ADLER, SARA LEVITZKA (1858-
1953)
Russian-Amer. actress
McHenry--Liberty's p4

ADLER, STELLA (1902-)
Amer. actress, director,
producer, teacher
Curr. Biog. '85 p6-10, por.
Diamonstein--Open p7-12, por.

ADOREE, RENEE (1898-1933)
French-Amer. circus performer
Keylin--Hollywood p2, por.

ADRI (fl. 1970's)
Amer. fashion designer
O'Neill--Women's p246

ADRIAN, IRIS (1912-)
Amer. actress
Lamparski--What. (8) p2-3, por.

ADRIANCE, JANE STERLING
    See STERLING, JAN

AELFLED
    See ELFLED

AELFLEDA, ABBESS
    English physician & surgeon
    Mead--Hist. p102

AEMILIA HILARIA MARTERTERA
    (fl. 4th cent.)
    Roman medical woman
    Mead--Hist. p83-84

AEMILIA, TERTIA (c169-c210 B.C.)
    Roman, Cornelia's mother,
    wife of Scipio Africanus
    Pomeroy--Godd. p162-163,177,
    181,192

AETHELFLAED (AETHELFLEDA)
    See ELFLED

AETHERIA
    See ETHERIA

AFFELBECK, MRS.
    See BAILEY, MARIE LOUIS

AGADJANOVA-SHUTKO, NINA
    (1889-)
    Russian magazine editor,
    political leader
    Mandel--Soviet p147

AGAR, SHIRLEY TEMPLE
    See BLACK, SHIRLEY TEMPLE

AGARISTE OF SICYON (c600-
    570 B.C.)
    Greek, daughter of
    Cleisthenes
    Pomeroy--Godd. p34-35,81

AGASSIZ, ELIZABETH CABOT
    CARY (1822-1907)
    Amer. educator, college
    president, scientific writer
    James--Notable (1) p22-25
    McHenry--Liberty's p4-5
    Neidle--America's p50-51
    Sherr--American p100

AGATHA, SAINT (-251/253)
    Sicilian medical woman, martyr
    Mead--Hist. p392

AGATHOCLIA (fl. 200's B.C.)
    Egyptian courtesan
    Pomeroy--Godd. p141

AGGER, CAROLYN (fl. 1970's)
    Amer. lawyer
    O'Neill--Women's p353

AGNES (fl. c1099)
    Jerusalem physician
    Macksey--Book p141

AGNES, ABBESS OF QUEDLINBERG
    (fl. c1200)
    German miniature painter
    Macksey--Book p194

AGNES, SAINT (291-304)
    Sicilian Christian martyr
    Kulkin--Her p7

AGNES OF BOHEMIA, BLESSED
    (-1280/1282)
    Bohemian queen-saint
    Mead--Hist. p220

AGNES OF MEISSEN, SAINT (fl.
    13th cent.)
    German tapestry weaver
    Munsterberg--Hist. p16

AGNESI, MARIA GAETANA (1718-
    1799)
    Italian mathematician, writer
    Macksey--Book p144
    Osen--Women p39-48, por.

AGNODICE OF GREECE (fl. c300
    B.C.)
    Greek physician, male imper-
    sonator
    Marks--Women p42, por.
    Mead--Hist. p45, 306

AGOULT, MARIE CATHERINE
    SOPHIE FLAVIGNY DE (1805-
    1876)
    French novelist, essayist
    Crosland--Women p31-32, por.
    Jones--Rutledge p7
    Moers--Literary p314

AGRANOFF, SHIRLEY HAFT (fl.
    1930's-1940's)
    Russian-Amer. pianist, hotel
    hostess, noted Washington
    state mother
    Amer.--Mothers p567-568, por.

AGREBI, SAIDA (1945-)
Tunisian labor organization
leader
O'Neill--Women's p709

AGRESS, ELLEN SHAW (fl. 1970's-
1980's)
Amer. TV executive
Scheuer--Tel. p4

AGRESTA, KIRSTEN
Amer. musician, child
celebrity
Woman's Almanac p52-53

AGRIPPINA I, THE ELDER (fl.
c13 B.C.-33 A.D.)
Roman empress, daughter
of Julia and Agrippa, wife
of Germanicus
Jones--Rutledge p8

AGRIPPINA, THE YOUNGER
(c15/16-59 A.D.)
Roman empress, mother of
Nero, wife of Claudius
Book--Lists (1) p284
Diagram--Mothers p182-183, por.
Fry--1000 p47-48

AGUILAR, GRACE (1816-1847)
English author, feminist,
poet
Henry--Written p226,235-246
Showalter--Lit. p325

AHBEZ, EDEN (1908-)
Amer. composer
Claghorn--Biog. p17

AHERN, MARY EILEEN (1860/
1865-1938)
Amer. librarian, editor,
teacher
James--Notable (1) p25-26

AHLMANN, LIS (1894-)
Danish weaver
O'Neill--Women's p270

AH LUN, MRS. (-1883)
Amer. Western pioneer
Sherr--American p9

AHRWEILLER, HELENE (1916-)
French Sorbonne president
O'Neill--Women's p408

AHUMADA, TERESA DE CEPEDA Y
(1515-1583)
Spanish, originator of Car-
melite Reform
Macksey--Book p106

AKYOKA (fl. 1820's)
Amer. Indian linguist
Sherr--American p192

AI (PELORHANKHE OGANA) (1947-)
Amer.-Japanese, Indian writer,
poet
Fisher--Third p543

AICHINGER, ILSE (1921-)
Austrian author, novelist,
radio playwright
Herrmann--Ger. p6,67-68

AIKEN, LORETTA MARY
See MABLEY, JACKIE ("MOMS")

AIMEE, ANOUK (1932-)
French actress
Shipman--Internatl. p2-5, por.
World--Who p254

AIMEE, SISTER
See McPHERSON, AIMEE SEMPLE

AIRPLANE, JEFFERSON
See SLICK, GRACE WING

AITCHISON, BEATRICE (1908-)
Amer. Federal Woman's Award
winner, P.O. Department
O'Neill--Women's p88

AITKEN, BARBARA B. (1938-)
Amer. genealogical researcher,
author, indexer
Meyer--Who's p20-21

AITKEN, JANE (1764-1832)
Amer. printer, bookseller,
bookbinder
James--Notable (1) p26-27

AITKEN, JANET (1886-)
British physician
Hellstedt--Women p23-25, por.

AKELEY, DELIA J. (1875-1970)
Amer., African explorer,
(wife of Carl Akeley)
Olds--Women p71-153, por.

AKELEY, MARY LEE JOBE (1878-
1966)
Amer. explorer, photographer,
educator, botanist, author
Sicherman--Notable p8-10

AKERMAN, LUCY EVELINA MET-
CALF (1816-1874)
Amer. hymnist
Claghorn--Biog. p17

AKERS, ELIZABETH CHASE
See ALLEN, ELIZABETH ANNE
CHASE AKERS

AKHMADULINA, BELLA A. (1937-)
Russian poet
O'Neill--Women's p684
Seymour-Smith--Who's p12

AKHVLEDIANI, ELENA
DMITRIEVNA (1901-)
Russian painter, graphic
artist
Women's--Female p2, Supp.

AKINS, ZOE (1886-1958)
Amer. screenwriter, poet,
playwright
Ehrlich--Oxford, see index p449
World--Who p9

AKIYOSHI, TOSHIKO (1929-)
Manchurian jazz pianist,
composer
Claghorn--Jazz p17

AKYOL, AFET
Turkish physician
O'Neill--Women's p552

ALAIS
French troubadour
Bogin--Women p145,178-179

ALAMANDA (fl. c1150-1190)
French troubadour
Bogin--Women p103,170

ALARDINE GASQUIERE, SISTER
(fl. 1450's)
French nun, nurse
Mead--Hist. p321

ALASDAIR, MAIRI NIGHEAN
See MacLEOD, MARY (2)

ALBA, MARIA DEL PILAR ROSARIO
CAYENTA FITZ-JAMES STUART
y SILVA, 18th DUCHESS
(1762-1802)
Spanish duchess, mistress of
Goya
Fallaci--Ego p175-186
O'Neill--Women's p745

ALBACH-RETTY, ROSEMARIE
See SCHNEIDER, ROMY

ALBANESE, LICIA (1913-1934)
Italian-Amer. opera singer
World--Who p69

ALBANI, EMMA (1847-1930)
Canadian singer, organist
Claghorn--Biog. p18

ALBEE, P.F.E. (fl. 1880's)
Amer. salesperson, 1st Avon
representative
O'Neill--Women's p519

ALBERG, MILDRED FREED (fl. 1950's)
Amer. TV producer
Marzolf--Up p162-163

ALBERGHETTI, ANNA MARIA
(1936/1937-)
Italian-Amer. singer, actress
World--Who p264

ALBERS, ANNI (1899-)
German-Amer. weaver,
tapestry artist
Fine--Women p198-200
O'Neill--Women p268

ALBERTINA, SISTER
See ROGERS, ELIZABETH ANN

ALBRAND, MARTHA (1911-1912-)
Amer. novelist
Seymour-Smith--Novels p89

ALBRECHT, GRETE (1893-)
West German physician
Hellstedt--Women p109-112, por.

ALBRECHT, SUSANNE (c1950-)
German terrorist
Lichstenstein--Mach. p165-166

ALBRET, JEANNE D' (1528-1572)
French poet, daughter of

Marguerite, religious re-
former
Bainton--France p43-73, por.

ALBRIGHT, LOLA (1924-)
Amer. actress
Lamparski--What. (8) p8-9, por.
World--Who p225

ALBRIGHT, TENLEY EMMA
(1935-)
Amer. skater
Assoc. Press--Pursuit p188,
208-209, por.
Hollander--100 p7,26-27,29,31,
por.
Pachter--Champ. p184-185, por.
Woman's Almanac p433-434
World--Who p209

ALCAYAGA, LUCILA GODOY Y
See MISTRAL, GABRIELA

ALCIBIADES
See HIPPARETE

ALCOCK, SARAH (-1665)
Amer. medical woman
Mead--Hist. p411, 487

ALCOTT, ABIGAIL (ABBA) MAY
(1800-1877/1878)
Amer., mother of Louisa
May Alcott
Diagram--Mothers p10-12, por.

ALCOTT, AMY (1956-)
Amer. gold player
Woman's Almanac p418-419

ALCOTT, LOUISA MAY (1932-1888)
Amer. children's book author
Avenel--Comp. (2) p16
Beach--Daughters p251-286, por.
Benét--New p84-91, por.
Betts--Writers p12-17, por.
Bird--Enterprising p97-98
Donaldson--How p7
Earnest--American p66-67
Ehrlich--Oxford, see index p499,
por.
Eills--Here p16-17
Fine--Women p93
Fry--1000 p240
Ingraham--Album p58, por.
James--Notable (1) p27-31
Jones--Rutledge p11

Kronenberger--Atlan. p11-12
Kulkin--Her p8-9
McHenry--Liberty's p5
Macksey--Book p188
Magill--Cycl. p17-19
Millstein--We p79-81
Moers--Literary p85-89,223,272,
por.
Moffat--Revel. p28-33
Seymour-Smith--Novels p89
Sherr--American p98, 102-103
Signif.--Amer. p15, por.
Stoddard--Famous p12-23, por.
Taylor--Gener. p51-52, por.
Warren--Pictorial p128-129, por.
Webster's--Amer. p19
Woman's Almanac p235-236,244-
245, por.
World--Who p9

ALDA, FRANCES (1883/1885-1952)
New Zealand opera singer
Neidle--America's p222
Tuggle--Golden p116-118

ALDAN, DAISY
Amer. poet
Chester--Rising p113-116, por.

ALDEN, CYNTHIA MAY WESTOVER
(1862-1931)
Amer. linguist, inventor,
humanitarian, journalist
McHenry--Liberty's p5-6

ALDEN, ELIZABETH ALDEN (1623-
c1717)
Amer. 1st white girl born in
New England
Sherr--American p206

ALDEN, ISABELLA MacDONALD
("PANSY") (1841/1842-1930)
Amer. author
Bolton--Success. p72-89, por.
Ehrlich--Oxford, see index p449
James--Notable (1) p31-33
McHenry--Liberty's p6

ALDEN, PRISCILLA MULLINS (1604-
1680)
Amer. Pilgrim
Ingraham--Album p6
James--Notable (1) p33-34
McHenry--Liberty's p6
Sherr--American p104,109
Woman's Almanac p75
World--Who p299

ALDERSON, NANNIE TIFFANY
(1860-1946)
Amer. Western pioneer,
noted Montana mother
Amer.--Mothers p321-322
Hymowitz--Hist. p179-180

ALDRICH, BESS GENEVRA
STREETER (1881-1954)
Amer. novelist, short story
writer, noted Nebraska
mother
Amer.--Mothers p337, por.
Ehrlich--Oxford, see index
p449
McHenry--Liberty's p7-8
Sherr--American p69,138-140,
por.

ALDRICH, DARRAGH (fl. 1940's)
Amer. novelist, radio pro-
gram director
Women--Radio p10-11

ALDRICH, MARISKA (1881-)
Amer. opera singer
Claghorn--Biog. p18-19

ALDRICH, MARY JANE (fl. 1970's)
Amer. TV director
Klever--Women p46-47,84-85,
93,103

ALEKSANDROVNA, TAMARA,
MAJOR
Russian aviator, war bomber
pilot
Macksey--Book p59

ALESSANDRA GILIANI
See GILIANI, ALESSANDRA

ALEXANDER, FRANCESCA (1837-
1917)
Amer. artist, author,
philanthropist
James--Notable (1) p34-35
McHenry--Liberty's p7

ALEXANDER, HATTIE (1901-1968)
Amer. physician, microbiolo-
gist, pediatrician
O'Neill--Women's p219
Sicherman--Notable p10-11

ALEXANDER, JANE (1939-)
Amer. actress

Anderson--People p6
Cur. Biog. '77 p13-17, por.
Hirschhorn--Rating p13, por.
World--Who p225

ALEXANDER, KATHERINE (1901-)
Amer. actress
Springer--They p10,269, por.

ALEXANDER, LUCIE (fl. 1970's)
Amer. activist, organization
co-founder
O'Neill--Women's p711

ALEXANDER, MARGARET ("DAISY")
(-1939)
British heiress
People's Almanac (3) p614

ALEXANDER, MARY (POLLY)
PRATT PROVOOST (1693/
1694-1760)
Amer. colonial businesswoman,
social leader
James--Notable (1) p35-36
Millstein--We p22

"ALEXANDER, MRS."
See HECTOR, ANNIE FRENCH

ALEXANDER, SHANA AGER (1925-)
Amer. magazine editor, jour-
nalist, columnist, radio and
TV commentator
O'Neill--Women's p477
World--Who p50

ALEXANDRA OF DENMARK (1844-
1925)
British queen, daughter of
Christian IX of Denmark
Jones--Rutledge p15
Softly--Queens p116-119, por.

ALEXANDRA, FEODOROVNA (1872-
1918)
Russian empress, Princess of
Hess-Darmstadt, wife of
Nicholas II of Russia
Jones--Rutledge p15
Macksey--Book p34-35

ALEXANDRA, SALOME, QUEEN (fl.
c104 B.C.)
Queen of Pharisees
Fink--Great p1-9

ALEXANDRIA, LOUISIANA
See STEWART, ELLEN

ALF, MARTHA (fl. 1970's)
Amer. painter
Women's--Female p32

ALI, VERONICA (1955-)
Amer. wife of Muhammed Ali
Funt--Are p3-25, por.

ALI KHAN, BEGUM LIAQUAT
Pakistani ambassador, gov-
ernor, feminist, professor
Macksey--Book p40
O'Neill--Women's p61

ALIA, QUEEN (c1949-1977)
Jordan queen, wife of
King Hussein
O'Neill--Women's p751

ALIQUIPPA (fl. 1750's)
Amer. Indian queen
Sherr--American p198,201

ALIX, MAY (1904-)
Amer. jazz singer
Claghorn--Jazz p18

ALIYEVA, SAKINA
Russian government official
O'Neill--Women's p59

AL-JOUA'N, KAWTHAR
Kwait lawyer, government
official
O'Neill--Women's p364

AL-KHANSA (fl. c645 A.D.)
Arab poet
Macksey--Book p179

"ALLA" (fl. 1970's)
Russian model
Keenan--Women p116,121, por.

ALLAN, ELIZABETH (1908/1910-.)
English actress
Springer--They p10,269, por.

ALLAN-SHETTER, ELIZABETH
Amer. water-skier, jumper
O'Neill--Women's p587

ALLARD, MARIE (1742-1802)
French ballet dancer

Miguel--Ballerinas p50-58,
por.

ALLEN, BARBARA
Amer. navy aviator
O'Neill--Women's p545

ALLEN, BARBARA JO
Amer. radio actress
Lamparski--What. (5) p204-205,
por.

ALLEN, BETSY (fl. 1830's)
Amer. Indian feminist
Sherr--American p128

ALLEN, BETTY (1930-)
Amer. singer
Claghorn--Biog. p20

ALLEN, DEBBIE (c1952-)
Amer. actress
Scheuer--Tel. p5-6

ALLEN, DEDE (1923-)
Amer. film editor
Gilbert--Part. p291, por.
Smith--Movies p74-76, por.

ALLEN, DONNA (fl. 1970's)
Amer. economist, feminist,
newsletter editor, publisher
Marzolf--Up p239-239
O'Neill--Women's p484,706

ALLEN, ELIZABETH ANNE CHASE
AKERS (1832-1911)
Amer. poet
Ehrlich--Oxford, see index p449
James--Notable (1) p36-38
McHenry--Liberty's p7

ALLEN, FLORENCE ELLINWOOD
(1884-1966)
Amer. judge, suffragist
McHenry--Liberty's p7-8
Sherr--American p188
Sicherman--Notable p11-13
Woman's Almanac p522

ALLEN, GRACE ("GRACIE") ETHEL
CECILE ROSALIE (1905-1964)
Amer. radio, TV actress,
comedienne
Fireman--TV p149-153
Mordden--Movie p137-139,284
Sicherman--Notable p13-14

Springer--They p10,269, por.
Woman's Almanac p316
World--Who p274

ALLEN, IDA BAILEY (fl. 1920's-1930's)
Amer. radio broadcaster
Marzolf--Up p122

ALLEN, INDRA
Amer. feminist, music maga-
zine editor
O'Neill--Women's p706

ALLEN, JAY PRESSON (fl. 1970's)
Amer. screenwriter
Smith--Movies p71

ALLEN, JUDITH (1913-)
Amer. singer, actress
Springer--They p10,269, por.

ALLEN, MARTHA FRANCES (1906-)
Amer. feminist, editor, or-
ganization official
O'Neill--Women's p706

ALLEN, MARY STAFFORD
Amer. P.E.O. founder
O'Neill--Women's p394,427, por.

ALLEN, MARYON (1926-)
Amer. senator
O'Neill--Women's p45

ALLEN, NATALIE PANNES (fl.
1970's)
Amer. National Labor Relations Board officer
O'Neill--Women's p333

ALLEN, PAULA GUNN (1939-)
Amer. Indian poet
Fisher--Third piv,126

ALLEN, ROSALIE (1924-)
Amer. singer, guitarist,
radio personality
Claghorn--Biog. p21

ALLEN, SAMANTHA
See HOLLEY, MARIETTA

ALLEN, SANDY
Amer., tallest living woman
Macksey--Book p12, por.

ALLEN, VIOLA EMILY (1867-1948)
Amer. actress

James--Notable (1) p38-39
McHenry--Liberty's p8

ALLENTUCK, MARCIA (fl. 1970's)
Amer. art history professor
Women's--Female p114

ALLERTON, MARY NORRIS (fl.
1600's)
Amer. Pilgrim
Williams--Demeter's p23

ALLILUYEV, NADYA
Russian, wife of Joseph Stalin
People's Almanac (2) p862-863

ALLILUYEVA, SVETLANA STALINA
(1926-)
Russian author, daughter of
Joseph Stalin
Book--Lists (2) p260
P.W.--Author p265-267,481

ALLIN, ROSE
English martyr
Bainton--France p220

ALLINGHAM, HELEN PATERSON
(1848-)
English artist
Sparrow--Women p69,109,137

ALLINGHAM, MARGERY (1904-1966)
English author
Seymour-Smith--Novels p89-90,
por.
World--Who p45

ALLISON, CYNTHIA (fl. 1970's-1980's)
Amer. news co-anchor
Scheuer--Tel. p6

ALLISON, FRANCES (FRAN) (1924-)
Amer. actress, radio performer
Fireman--TV p108-199
World--Who p225

ALLISON, MARGARET (fl. 1940's)
Amer. journalist
Marzolf--Up p75

ALLIX, MARTINE (fl. 1970's)
French yacht-racer
McWhirter--Guinness p188

ALLMAN, RUTH WICKERSHAM
Alaskan hostess
Jones--Women (1) p158-159

ALLSTON, ADELE
    Amer. Confederate rice
    plantation owner
    Wiley--Confed. p148

ALLWYN, ASTRID
    Amer. actress
    Springer--They p10,269, por.

ALLYN, MRS.
    Amer. army surgeon
    Mead--Hist. p487

ALLYSON, JUNE (1917-   )
    Amer. actress, singer
    Claghorn--Biog. p21
    Hirschhorn--Rating p15, por.
    Shipman--Internatl. p7-8, por.
    World--Who p225

ALMA-TADEMA, LAURA THERESE,
    LADY (fl. 1870's-1900's)
    English artist
    Sparrow-Women p70,156, por.

ALMIROTY, MARIA MARTINEZ DE
    PEREZ (1889-   )
    Puerto Rican mother, teacher,
    civic worker, politician
    Amer.--Mothers p471-472, por.

ALMUCS DE CASTELNAU (c1140-   )
    French troubadour
    Bogin--Women p93,165-166

ALMY, MARY GOULD (1735-1808)
    Amer. Revolution diarist
    Evans--Weather. p245-270

ALMY, SUSAN
    Amer. anthropologist
    O'Neill--Women's p36

"A.L.O.E.," PSEUD.
    See TUCKER, CHARLOTTE
       MARIA

ALONI, SHULAMIT
    Israeli lawyer, writer,
    radio editor, government
    worker
    O'Neill--Women's p364

ALONSO, ALICIA (c1921-   )
    Cuban ballet dancer
    Cur. Biog. '77 p17-20, por.
    O'Neill--Women's p643
    World--Who p73

ALPERN, ANITA F. (fl. 1970's)
    Amer. government official
    O'Neill--Women's p83,90

ALPERT, MIRIAM (-1976)
    Amer. officer, B'nai B'rith
    O'Neill--Women's p114

ALPHONSA, MARY (MOTHER)
    See LATHROP, ROSE HAW-
       THORNE (MOTHER MARY
       ALPHONSA)

ALSOP, FRANCES (JORDAN)
    (-1821)
    English-Amer. singer, composer
    Claghorn--Biog. p22

ALSOP, OLIVE "INEZ" (1905-   )
    Amer. jazz pianist
    Claghorn--Jazz p20

ALSTON, THEODOSIA BURR
    See BURR, THEODOSIA PREVOST

ALSTYNE, NANCY VAN
    See VAN ALSTYNE, NANCY

ALTHER, LISA (1944-   )
    Amer. novelist
    Seymour-Smith--Novels p90

ALVAREZ, ANNE MAINO
    Amer. plant pathologist
    O'Neill--Women's p28

ALVAREZ, CATALINE
    Amer., co-founder, Association
    of Family Women (AFW)
    O'Neill--Women's p108

ALVERIO, ROSA DOLORES
    See MORENO, RITA

ALVERSON, LEE RUTH
    Amer. naval aviator
    O'Neill--Women's p544

ALVING, BARBARA
    Amer. war correspondent
    Marzolf--Up p274

AMALASUNTHA (AMALASVENTA)
    (c498-c535)
    Italian Regent
    Macksey--Book p21

"AMALIA"
See HENTSCHEL-GUERNTH,
CHRISTINE DOROTHEA

AMAYA, CARMEN (c1913-1963)
Spanish Gypsy dancer
O'Neill--Women's p646

AMBLER, MARY (fl. 1850's)
Amer. Quaker heroine
Sherr--American p198

AMBROSINO, LILLIAN
Amer., co-founder of
Action for Children's Tele-
vision (ACT)
O'Neill--Women's p729

AMERICAN, SADIE (1862-1944)
Amer., organizing head,
National Council of Jewish
Women, feminist
Baum--Jewish p49,51,165-169,
171-174,176, por.

AMES, ADRIENNE (1907-1947)
Amer. actress, radio com-
mentator
Springer--They p10,12,269-270,
por.

AMES, AGNES H. (1916-)
Amer. genealogical research-
er, author
Meyer--Who's p21

AMES, BLANCHE AMES (1878-1969)
Amer. suffragist, botanical
illustrator, feminist
Sicherman--Notable p15-16

AMES, FANNY BAKER (1840-1931)
Amer., charity organizer,
industrial reformer
James--Notable (1) p39-40

AMES, JESSIE DANIEL (fl. 1930's)
Amer. social reformer,
suffragist
Berkin--Women see index p429,
por.
Scott--Southern p196,198
Sicherman--Notable p16-18

AMES, MARY E. CLEMMER (1831-
1884)
Amer. Washington correspondent, author

Beasley--First p10-12,23-24, por.
James--Notable (1) p40-42
Marzolf--Up p17

AMICO, ANN (fl. 1970's)
Amer. TV engineer
Klever--Women p51-52,66-67,105

AMIR, AZIZA (fl. 1920's-1950's)
Egyptian filmmaker
Smith--Movies p92

AMMERICH, JOANN
See EMMERICH, JOZIE

AMMERS-KÜLLER, JOHANNA VAN
(1884-)
Netherlands novelist
Magill--Cycl. p28-29

AMMUNDSEN, ESTHER (fl. 1960's)
Danish physician, Director,
Danish National Health Ser-
vice
O'Neill--Women's p228

AMRA (fl. c670's)
Arabian novelist
Macksey--Book p179

AMSTER, LINDA (fl. 1980's)
Amer. TV sales executive
Scheuer--Tel. p7

AMYTE (ANICIA) (fl. c300 B.C.)
Greek physician, poet, writer
Mead--Hist. p34

ANASTASIA (1901-)
Russian grand duchess,
daughter of Tsar Nicholas II
Jones--Rutledge p20

ANAXANDRA (fl. c228 B.C.)
Greek artist
Sparrow--Women p21

ANCAR, MURLENE B.
Amer. aviator, air force
instructor
O'Neill--Women's p546

ANCASTER, MARY, DUCHESS
(-1793)
English duchess, socialite
Ware--Meet p73

ANCKER-JOHNSON, BETSY
Amer. research physicist
O'Neill--Women's p141-142,190

ANDERSEN, ANNE MARIE (1767-
1833/1834)
Danish, mother of Hans
Christian Andersen
Diagram--Mothers p16-17

ANDERSEN, DOROTHY HANSINE
(1901-1963)
Amer. pathologist, pediatrician
Sicherman--Notable p18-20

ANDERSEN, YVONNE (fl. 1960's-1970's)
Amer. filmmaker
Smith--Movies p146-147,224,
por.

ANDERSON, ALLOA C. (1900-)
Amer. genealogical researcher,
author
Meyer--Who's p21-22

ANDERSON, ALTA (fl. 1970's)
Amer. singer
Glassman--Year '79 p92, por.

ANDERSON, ALYCE E.
Amer. mountain-climber,
educator, noted Alaskan
mother
Amer.--Mothers p16

ANDERSON, BETTE B. (c1929-)
Amer. government official
O'Neill--Women p82-83, por.

ANDERSON, BETTY HARVIE
British Parliament member
Vallance--Women see index p207

ANDERSON, BIBI (1935-)
Swedish actress
Cur. Biog. '78 p12-15, por.
Entertainers p283
World--Who p254

ANDERSON, BONNIE MARIE
(1955-)
Cuban-Amer. TV news
correspondent
Scheuer--Tel. p8

ANDERSON, CAROL (c1946-)
Amer. clergyman
Proctor--Women p1-21

ANDERSON, CAROL A. (fl. 1970's)
Amer. soil conservationist,
geneticist
O'Neill--Women's p26

ANDERSON, DOROTHY MAE
STEVENS (-1974)
Amer. freezing survival victim
Felton--Famous p204

ANDERSON, ELDA EMMA (1899-1961)
Amer. health physicist
Sicherman--Notable p20-21

ANDERSON, ELIZABETH GARRETT
(1836-1917)
English physician
Fry--1000 p263
Jones--Rutledge p20-21
Macksey--Book p150
Marks--Women p95-106, por.
O'Neill--Women p202
Palmer--Who's p29
Showalter--Lit. p333
Who Did What p14

ANDERSON, ELIZABETH JANE
(1930-)
Amer. singer
Claghorn--Biog. p23

ANDERSON, ELIZABETH MILBANK
(1850-1921)
Amer. philanthropist
James--Notable (1) p42-43

ANDERSON, EMILY (c1805-)
English, subject of portrait
Ware--Meet p73

ANDERSON, ERICA KELLNER
COLLIER (1914-1976)
Austrian-Amer. filmmaker,
photographer
Curr. Biog. '76 p463

ANDERSON, ERNESTINE IRENE
(1928-)
Amer. singer
Claghorn--Biog. p23
Claghorn--Jazz p22

ANDERSON, EVA
Amer. orchestral conductor
Neuls-Bates--Women p248

ANDERSON, FRANCES MARGARET
See ANDERSON, JUDITH, DAME

ANDERSON, (HELEN) EUGENIE
MOORE (1909-)
Amer. diplomat
McHenry--Liberty's p8-9
O'Neill--Women's p90

ANDERSON, IB (1954-)
Amer. ballet dancer
Cur. Biog. '84 p9-12

ANDERSON, IVY (IVIE) (1904/
1905-1949)
Amer. singer
Claghorn--Biog. p24
Claghorn--Jazz p22

ANDERSON, JANET H. (1920-)
Amer. genealogical research-
er, writer
Meyer--Who's p22

ANDERSON, JENNY (fl. 1970's)
Amer. softball player
Jordan--Broken p131-132,137

ANDERSON, JUDITH, DAME
(1898-)
Australian actress
Entertainers p203
Hirschhorn--Rating p16
Johns--Dames p117-122, por.
O'Neill--Women's p656
World--Who p254

ANDERSON, JULIA TAYLOR
(-1842)
Amer. philanthropist
Sherr--American p117

ANDERSON, JUNITA (1890-)
Amer. Alaskan mountain
climber, noted Alaskan
mother
Amer.--Mothers p18-19, por.

ANDERSON, KATHRYN
See FORBES, KATHRYN, pseud.

ANDERSON, LAURIE (1947-)
Amer. poet, composer,

sculptor
Cur. Biog. '83 p5-9, por.

ANDERSON, LOIS
Amer. heroine, Carnegie Medal
winner
O'Neill--Women's p732

ANDERSON, LYNN RENE (1947-)
Amer. singer
Claghorn--Biog. p24

ANDERSON, MABEL (1886-)
Amer., mother of Congress-
man John Anderson
Kooiman--Silhouettes p49-57, por.

ANDERSON, MADELINE (fl. 1960's-
1970's)
Amer. filmmaker
Smith--Movies p147,224

ANDERSON, MARGARET CAROLINE
(1890/1893-1973)
Amer. magazine editor, pub-
lisher, art patron
McHenry--Liberty's p8-9
O'Neill--Women's p472,613
Rogers--Ladies p29,33,147-153,
por.
Sicherman--Notable p21-23
Warren--Pictorial p184
Webster's--Amer. p28

ANDERSON, MARIAN (1902-)
Amer. opera singer
Adams--Great (3rd) p188, por.
Claghorn--Biog. p24
Clark--Leading p156-157
Gilfond--Heroines p114-118, por.
Ingraham--Album p65, por.
Jones--Rutledge p21
Kelen--Fifty p11-12
Kostman--20th p138-154, por.
Kulkin--Her p10-11
Longstreet--Queen p192
McHenry--Liberty's p9
Neuls-Bates--Women p273-277,
por.
O'Neill--Women's p620
Richardson--Great p31-39, por.
Signif.--Amer. p56, por.
Stoddard--Famous p24-35, por.
Toppin--Biog. p248
Truman--Women p130-143,200-201,
por.
Webster's--Amer. p28

Woman's Almanac p286, por.
World--Who p69

ANDERSON, MARY (1) (1859-1940)
Amer. actress
James--Notable (1) p43-45
McHenry--Liberty's p9-10

ANDERSON, MARY (2)
Amer. weaver
O'Neill--Women's p122

ANDERSON, MARY (3) (1872-1964)
Amer. labor leader, writer,
government official
Clark--Leading p68-70
Hymowitz--Hist. p262,305
Neidle--America's p126,130-132,
138,147-153, por.
O'Neill--Women's p285,289,329,
330
Sicherman--Notable p23-25
Sochen--Herstory p234,270,294
Sochen--Movers p67-71,74,87-88,
272
Ware--Beyond p144, see also
index p197
Warren--Pictorial p177-179

ANDERSON, MARY CHRISTOFFER-
SON (-1928)
Amer. writer
Sherr--American p58

ANDERSON, MARY REID MacARTHUR
(1880-1921)
Scottish labor leader, social
worker
O'Neill--Women's p286,292

ANDERSON, NANCY
Amer. Revolutionary patriot
Meyer--Petticoat p199-200

ANDERSON, NANCY (-1968)
Amer. heroine, practical
nurse, Carnegie Medal
winner
O'Neill--Women's p734

ANDERSON, ROBERTA JOAN
See MITCHELL, JONI

ANDERSON, STELLA BENSON
(1892-1933)
British novelist
Showalter--Lit. p347

ANDERSON, SUSAN
Amer. TV reporter
Klever--Women p34-35, 74-76,
106, por.

ANDERSON, THEODORA D.
Amer. radio director, research
Women--Radio p19

ANDERTON, CAROL
Amer. bowler
Hollander--100 p18-19

ANDRASSY, STELLA (COUNTESS)
Swedish-Amer. solar inventor
O'Neill--Women's p750

ANDRE, LONA (1915-)
Amer. actress
Springer--They p12,270

ANDREADIS, CHRISTINA ONASSIS
See ONASSIS, CHRISTINA

ANDREAS-SALOME, LOU (c1861-1937)
Russian-German philosopher,
psychoanalyist
Sorell--Three p131-214, por.

ANDREIANOVA, ELENA (c1821-c1855)
Russian ballet dancer
Migel--Ballerinas p253-255, por.

ANDREINI, ISABELLA (1562-1604)
Italian actress
Macksey--Book p223

ANDRESS, URSULA (1936-)
Swiss actress
World--Who p254

ANDREWS, CICILY ISABEL
See WEST, REBECCA, DAME,
pseud.

ANDREWS, ELIZA FRANCES (1840-
1932)
Amer. Civil War diarist,
editor, author, teacher,
botanist
Earnest--American p161-162
James--Notable (1) p45-46
Scott--Southern p119,132
Sherr--American p51

ANDREWS, ELIZABETH B. (c1911-)
Amer. Congresswoman
Chamberlin--Min. p343-345

ANDREWS, FANNIE FERN
PHILLIPS (1867-1950)
Canadian pacifist, author
James--Notable (1) p46-48
McHenry--Liberty's p10
Smith--Daughters p268-270

ANDREWS, JANE (1833-1887)
Amer. story-writer, edu-
cator, children's book author
James--Notable (1) p48-49

ANDREWS, JULIE (1935-)
English actress, singer
Anderson--People p13-14
Claghorn--Biog. p25
Higham--Celeb. p52-57, por.
Hirschhorn--Rating p17-18, por.
Manchel--Women p2,94, por.
Mordden--Movie p245,249-250,
269-270, por.
Shipman--Internatl. p11-14,
por.
Simon--Best p11-12, por.
World--Who p264

ANDREWS, LA VERNE (1915-1967)
Amer. singer
Claghorn--Biog. p25
Lamparski--What (3) p16-17,
por.

ANDREWS, LUCILLA
English novelist
Seymour-Smith--Novels p91

ANDREWS, MARY RAYMOND
SHIPMAN (1860/1884-1936)
Amer. novelist, short-story
writer
Ehrlich--Oxford p198,266-267
James--Notable (1) p49-50

ANDREWS, MAXINE (1918-)
Amer. singer
Claghorn--Biog. p25
Lamparski--What. (3) p16-17,
por.

ANDREWS, PATTI (1920-)
Amer. singer
Claghorn--Biog. p25
Lamparski--What. (3) p16-17,
por.

ANDREWS SISTERS
Amer. singers
Simon--Best p13-14, por.

Simon--Big p82-83, por.
Woman's Almanac p286-287, por.
World--Who p264

ANDREZEL, PIERRE, pseud.
See DINESEN, ISAK, pseud.
(BARONESS BLIXEN-FINEKE)

ANDRIAMANJATO, RAHANTAVOLO
African engineer
Crane--Ms. p112-122, por.

ANDROMACHE
Roman, wife of Hector
Pomeroy--Godd. p21-23,29-30,110
Zinserling--Women p16

ANDROMACHE OF EGYPT
Egyptian physician
Mead--Hist. p92

ANDRUS, ETHEL PERCY (1884-1967)
Amer. founder of Retired
Persons Association
O'Neill--Women's p721
Sickerman--Notable p25-27

ANER, KERSTIN
British Parliament member
Vallance--Women p148,163,169-171

ANGEL, HEATHER (1909-)
English actress
Lamparski--What. (5) p184-185,
por.
Springer--They p12,270 por.

ANGELA MERICI, SAINT (1474-1540)
Italian educator, nun, nurse,
founder of religious order
Macksey--Book p64
Mead--Hist. p431
World--Who p85

ANGELA, MOTHER
See GILLESPIE, ELIZA MARIA
(MOTHER ANGELA)

ANGELES, MARIA DE LOS
Spanish bull-fighter
Macksey--Book p261

ANGELES, VICTORIA DE LOS (1923/
1924-)
Spanish opera singer
Gammond--Illus. p236, por.

ANGELI, PIER (1932/1933-)
Italian actress
Shipman--Internatl. p14-15

ANGELINE (-1896)
Indian princess
Sherr--American p241, por.

ANGELIQUE LIELLE, SISTER
(1720-1742)
Amer. hospital manager
Mead--Hist. p490

ANGELITA, SISTER
See MYERSCOUGH, ANGELITA,
SISTER

ANGELL, MRS.
See COLEMAN, HELEN
CORDELIA

ANGELO, BONNIE
Amer. White House corres-
pondent
O'Neill--Women's p483, por.

ANGELOU, MAYA (1928/1929-)
Amer. author, actress,
dancer, playwright, song-
writer, script-writer
Curr. Biog. '74 p12-15, por.
Fisher--Third pvi,287
Hymowitz--Hist. p338
Kulkin--Her p11-12
Moers--Literary p272
O'Neill--Women's p671-672
Webber--Woman p118-122

ANGIOLINA OF PADUA
Italian obstetrician
Marks--Women p119

ANGLIN, MARGARET MARY
(1876-1958)
Canadian actress
Hazen--Interv. p101

ANGLOIS, ESTHER
See KELLO, (H)ESTER
ENGLISH

ANGLUND, JOAN WALSH (1926-)
Amer. children's book author,
illustrator
O'Neill--Women's p693
Smaridge--Famous p130-137, por.
Women's--Female p23

ANGOULEME, MARIE THERESE
CHARLOTTE (1778-1851)
French, daughter of King
Louis XVI and Queen Marie
Antoinette
Kulkin--Her p12-13

ANGST-HORRIDGE, ANITA (1897-)
Swiss physician
Hellstedt--Women p150-155, por.

ANGUIANO, LUPE (1929-)
Mexican-Amer. educator
Newlon--Mexican p153-163, por.

ANGUISSOLA, SOFONISBA (1532/
1535-1625)
Italian painter, musician,
scholar
Fine--Women p9-11
Harris--Women p13,21,23-31,34,
41-42,44,106-111,116,340-341,
por.
Macksey--Book p195-196, por.
Munsterberg--Hist. p19-21,23
Parker--Old, see index p177,
por.
Petersen--Women p25-26, por.
Sparrow--Women p24-28,36,39,
por.
Tufts--Our p20-29, por.
Woman's Almanac p220
Women's--Female p5

ANGUS, ANNE DENNY
See DENNY, ANNE

ANGUS, MARION (1866-1946)
Scottish poet
Avenel--Comp. ( ) p21

ANHALT, EDNA
Amer. film writer
Smith--Movies p41-42

ANICIA
See AMYTE

ANJOU, MARGUERITE D' (1429-1482)
French noblewoman
Leary--Golden, see index p353

ANKE, HANNELORE
East German swimmer
O'Neill--Women's p587

ANN, JUDITH
    Amer. insurance rater
    Hymowitz--Hist. p317

ANN-MARGRET (1941-)
    Swedish-Amer. actress
    Anderson--People p15-16, por.
    Cur. Biog. '75 p13-16, por.
    Hirschhorn--Rating p18-19,
        por.
    100--Greatest (1) p16, por.
    Woman's Almanac p331-332
    World--Who p225

ANN MEDICA
    English hospital officer
    Mead--Hist. p322-323

ANN, MOTHER
    See LEE, ANN (MOTHER)

ANNA COMNENA (1083-1148)
    Byzantine physician,
        founder Medical School
    Mead--Hist. p113,116,167-168,
        176

ANNA IVANOVNA (IOANNOVNA)
    (1693-1740)
    Russian Empress
    Jones--Rutledge p22

ANNA SOPHIA, OF HESSE
    German botanist, writer
    Mead--Hist. p424

ANNA SOPHIA, PRINCESS OF
    DENMARK
    Danish botanist, medical
        woman
    Mead--Hist. p360

ANNA, THE HEBREW (fl. 1500's)
    Jewish cosmetics dealer
    Henry--Written p147-149

ANNABELLA (1909/1912-)
    French actress
    Springer--They p13-14,270,
        por.

ANNE (1665-1714)
    British Queen
    Delderfield--Kings p97-99, por.
    Donaldson--How p13-15
    Jones--Rutledge p22-23
    Kulkin--Her p13-14

Macksey--Book p27
Softly--Queens p97-99, por.
Who Did What p14

ANNE BOLEYN
    See BOLEYN, ANNE

ANNE NEVILLE (1456-1485)
    English Queen
    Softly--Queens p52-53

ANNE OF AUSTRIA (1600/1601-1666)
    French queen, mother of
        Louis XIV, wife of Louis XIII
    Book--Lists (2) p266
    Jones--Rutledge p23

ANNE OF BOHEMIA (1366-1394)
    Bohemian queen, founder of
        nunnery & hospital, medical
        woman
    Mead--Hist. p220
    Softly--Queens p38-40

ANNE OF BRITTANY (1476/1477-
    1514)
    French queen
    Macksey--Book p23-24
    Mead--Hist. p302

ANNE OF CLEVES (1515-1557)
    English queen
    Jones--Rutledge p23
    Softly--Queens p66-69
    Vance--Six p95-101
    Who Did What p150, por.

ANNE OF DENMARK (1574-1619)
    English queen
    Softly--Queens p80-84, por.

ANNE OF FRANCE (1460/1461-1522)
    French regent
    Macksey--Book p23-24

ANNE OF SAVOY (1320-1360)
    Byzantine empress
    Partington--Who's p10

ANNE, PRINCESS OF BOHEMIA
    Bohemian founder of nunnery
        & hospital, medical woman
    Mead--Hist. p220

ANNE, PRINCESS OF GREAT
    BRITAIN (1950-)
    English princess

Cur. Biog. '73 p9-12, por.
Hollander--100 p61-62, por.

ANNEKE, MATHILDE FRANZISKA
    GIESLER (1817-1884)
    German-Amer. feminist,
    author, publisher, educator
    James--Notable (1) p50-51
    Marzolf--Up p12
    Neidle--America's p41-43
    Sherr--American p250

"ANNIE LAURIE"
    See BLACK, WINIFRED SWEET

ANNING, MARY (1799-1847)
    English fossil collector
    Kulkin--Her p14-15

ANNO, KIMIKO
    Japanese scientist
    O'Neill--Women's p7

ANSELMI, TINA
    Italian cabinet member
    O'Neill--Women's p44,55

ANSOLABEHERE, MARY JEAN
    ("DOLLY")
    Amer. Basque rancher
    O'Neill--Women's p18

ANSPACH, SUSAN (1944-   )
    Amer. actress
    Manchel--Women p16,19

ANSPACHER, CAROLYN (-1979)
    Amer. newspaper writer
    O'Neill--Women's p470

ANTHONY, C.L., pseud. (1896-   )
    British playwright, novelist
    Jones--Rutledge p723

ANTHONY, EVELYN, pseud.
    (1928-   )
    Seymour-Smith--Novels p91
    World--Who p23

ANTHONY, KATHARINE SUSAN
    (1877-1965)
    Amer. biographer
    Ehrlich--Oxford p284

ANTHONY, SUSAN BROWNELL
    (1820-1906)
    Amer. feminist, social

reformer, suffragist, humani-
    tarian
    Anticaglia--12 p73-94, por.
    Bachtold--Gifted p87-89
    Banner--Women see index p263,
        por.
    Clark--Leading p49-52
    Earnest--American see index p271
    Fine--Women p92,94-95
    Gilfond--Heroines p24, por.
    Gurko--Ladies see index p321,
        por.
    Hymowitz--Hist. p88,112-121,149-
        150,159-160,267-271, see also
        index p392, por.
    Ingraham--Album p26,33-34,37,
        71, por.
    James--Notable (1) p51-57
    Kulkin--Her p15-17
    Longstreet--Queen p33-38, por.
    Lutz--Crusade, see index p333
    McHenry--Liberty's p10-11
    Macksey--Book p86
    Marlowe--Great p74-79, por.
    Marzolf--Up see index p298
    Millstein--We p173-176, 184-185,
        por.
    Neidle--America's p30,41,45
    O'Neill--Women's p483,634,696
    Palmer--Who's p30
    Papachristou--Women see index
        pi, por.
    Pederson--Leaders p108, por.
    People's Almanac (2) p1203,1196,
        por.
    Reader's--Story p432
    Sherr--American p38,97,159,173-
        174, por.
    Signif.--Amer. p15, por.
    Smith--Daughters see index p370
    Sochen--Herstory p85,131,134-
        135,170,174-175,181,232, por.
    Stoddard--Famous p36-47, por.
    Truman--Women p10,115-130,198-
        199, por.
    Warren--Pictorial p67,99-100,
        113-130,159,170-172, por.
    Webster's--Amer. p33
    Woman's Almanac p544,546, por.
    World--Who p186

ANTILA, EVA (1894-   )
    Finnish textile designer
    O'Neill--Women's p274

ANTIN, ELEANOR (1935-   )
    Amer. sculptor

Munro--Originals p417-430, por.
Nemser--Convers. p267-301,365-
366, por.
Women's--Female p84

ANTIN, MARY (1881-1949)
Russian-Amer. author
Cavanah--We p14-19
Hoople--As p183-185
James--Notable (1) p57-59
McHenry--Liberty's p11
Neidle--America's p251,256-259,
265
Webster's--Amer. p33

ANTOINE, JOSEPHINE L. (1908-
1971)
Amer. opera singer
Claghorn--Biog. p26

ANTOINE, LORE (1895-)
Austrian physician
Hellstedt--Women p128-136, por.

ANTONIA DANIELLO (fl. 1386-
1408)
Italian medical woman
Mead--Hist. p276

ANYTE OF TEGEA (fl. c300 B.C.)
Greek poet
Macksey--Book p178-179

APGAR, B. JEAN (1936-)
Amer. research chemist
O'Neill--Women's p31-32,89

APGAR, VIRGINIA (1909-1974)
Amer. physician, medical
researcher, anesthesiologist
Curr. Biog. '74 p453
Diamonstein--Open p13-16, por.
McHenry--Liberty's p11-12
Macksey--Book p157, por.
O'Neill--Women's p209,469
Sicherman--Notable p27-28
Woman's Almanac p360

APHRODITE
Greek goddess
Pomeroy--Godd. p3,5-8,15-17,
141, por.

APPLEBEE, CONSTANCE (c1874-
1981)
British physical educator,
hockey coach

Hollander--100 p20-21, por.
Macksey--Book p258
McWhirter--Guinness p61

APPLEGATE, MELINDA MILLER
(c1812-c1887)
Amer. pioneer, noted Oregon
mother
Amer.--Mothers p444, por.

APPLEGATE, ROBERTA (fl. 1950's-
1960's)
Amer. political reporter
Marzolf--Up p251,257

APSLEY, LUCY
See HUTCHINSON, LUCY APSLEY

AQUINAS, M. THOMAS, MOTHER
See CARROLL, ELIZABETH,
SISTER

AQUINO, IVA IKUKO TOGURI D'
("TOKYO ROSE") (1916-)
Japanese spy
Dunlap--Calif. p205, por.
Lamparski--What. (3) p10-11,
por.
People's Almanac (1) p239
Woman's Almanac p450, por.
World--Who p301

ARAGON, YOLANDE OF
French mother-in-law of
"King of Bourges"
Leary--Golden p14,24,32

ARAGONA, TULIA D'
See D'ARAGONA, TULLIA

ARBELLA (ARABELLA)
See JOHNSON, ARABELLA, LADY

ARBER, AGNES (1879-1960)
British plant morphologist
Macksey--Book p167

ARBUS, DIANE NEMEROV (1923-
1971)
Amer. photographer
Marlowe--Great p357-362, por.
Moers--Literary p109,272
Munsterberg--Hist. p141-143
O'Neill--Women's p613-614
Sickerman--Notable p28-30
Woman's Almanac p225-226
Women's--Female p5
World--Who p57

ARBUS, LOREEN
Amer. executive producer
Adams--Women p145-146,184

ARBUTHNOT, MAY HILL (1884-
1969)
Amer. educator, children's
literature specialist
Sicherman--Notable p30-31

ARBUZOVA, ALLA
Russian feminist, professor
Mandel--Soviet p54

ARC, JOAN OF
See JOAN OF ARC

ARCHER, CORLISS
See WALDO, JANET

ARCHER, GEORGINA
British lecturer, Lyceum
founder
Macksey--Book p72

ARCHER, PATRICIA
British medical artist
Macksey--Book p209

ARCHIBALD, LIL(L)IANA
British lecturer, insurance
executive, history specialist
Macksey--Book p170
O'Neill--Women's p529

ARCHIPPE (fl. 2d cent. B.C.)
Greek goddess
Pomeroy--Godd. p125

ARCONVILLE, GENEVIEVE
CHARLOTTE D' (1720-1805)
French translator, medical
writer, chemist, anatomist
Macksey--Book p143-144
Mead--Hist. p491-492

ARDEN, ELIZABETH (1884-1966)
Canadian cosmetician, busi-
ness executive
Lichtenstein--Mach. p242-243
McHenry--Liberty's p12
Macksey--Book p172,271
Neidle--America's p269,280-281
O'Neill--Women's p512
Sicherman--Notable p32-33
Sochen--Herstory p291-292
Webster's--Amer. p34

Whitman--Come p14-20
Woman's Almanac p131
World--Who p192

ARDEN, EVE (1912-)
Amer. comedienne, radio-TV
actress
Fireman--TV p167-168
Hirschhorn--Rating p19-20, por.
Mordden--Movie p123,138-139,284,
por.
Scheuer--Tel. p10, por.
Shipman--Internatl. p16-18, por.
Springer--They p13,270, por.
World--Who p225

ARDEN, SHERRY W.
Amer. publicity director
O'Neill--Women's p490

ARENDSEE, MARTHA (1885-1953)
German politician
Partington--Who's p13-14

ARENDT, HANNAH (1906-1975)
German-Amer. writer, political
scientist
Avenel--Comp. (2) p20
Current Biog. '76 p463
McHenry--Liberty's p12
Marlowe--Great p328-332, por.
O'Neill--Women's p415
Sicherman--Notable p33-37
Webster's--Amer. p35-36
Wintle--Makers p13-15
World--Who p92

ARETE
Greek queen, mother of
Nausicaa, wife of Alcinous
Pomeroy--Godd. p22-23,28-29,31
Zinserling--Women p18

ARETHUSA OF ANTIOCH (fl. 4th
cent.)
Greek head of hospitals,
monasteries
Mead--Hist. p80

ARGENTINITA (1905-1945)
Spanish dancer
O'Neill--Women's p645

ARGETSINGER, LOUISE H. (1904-)
Amer. clubwoman, church
worker, noted Alaska mother
Amer.--Mothers p22

ARGUAS, MARGARITA (fl. 1920's-
1960's)
Argentinian lawyer, judge,
teacher
Macksey--Book p126
O'Neill--Women's p369

ARGUELLO, CONCHA MARIA DE
CONCEPCION (1791-1857)
Amer. nun
Sherr--American p12

ARIAS, MARGOT FONTEYN, DAME
See FONTEYN, MARGOT (DAME)

ARISTARETE
Greek painter, daughter of
Nearchos
Munsterberg--Hist. p10
Sparrow--Women p21

ARISTODAMA (fl. 218 B.C.)
Turkish poet
Pomeroy--Godd. p126

ARKHIPOVA, IRINA (1925-)
Russian opera singer
Gammond--Illus. p236, por.

ARLETTY (1898-)
French actress
Entertainers p203, por.
Shipman--Internatl. p20-25,
por.

ARLINGTON, JOSIE (1864-1914)
Amer. "madam"
People's Almanac (2) p930

ARMAND, INNA A.
French-Russian political
leader, friend of Lenin
Mandel--Soviet p42,59-61, por.

ARMATRADING, JOAN (1950-)
West Indies jazz singer,
guitarist, composer, songwriter
Claghorn--Jazz p22-23

ARMEL, PAULA (1949-)
Amer. TV director
Scheuer--Tel. p11

ARMER, LAURA ADAMS (1874-1963)
Amer. author, illustrator
O'Neill--Women's p691

ARMER, MARGARET McEVEY REID
(-1933)
Amer. goat herder
Sherr--American p156

ARMINE, MARY, LADY (-1675/
1676)
English scholar, philanthropist
Earle--Two Cent. (1) p60,69,243,
505, por.

ARMOISES, JEANNE DES (fl. c1439)
French imposter of Joan d'Arc
Leary--Golden p335-337

ARMOR, MARY HARRIS (1863-1950)
Amer. social reformer, noted
Georgia mother
Amer.--Mothers p129-130, por.

ARMOUR, JEAN
Scottish, wife of Robert Burns
Coffin--Female p67-68, por.
Morley--Literary p437-439,441-
444,450-451

ARMSTRONG, ANNE LEGENDRE
(1927-)
Amer. diplomat, government
official
Current Biog. '76 p6-9, por.
O'Neill--Women's p44,95
Schoenebaum--Prof. p26
Woman's Almanac p469

ARMSTRONG, BARBARA (1934-1969)
Amer. lawyer, professor
O'Neill--Women's p362

ARMSTRONG, CHARLOTTE (1905/
1906-1969)
Amer. author
Current Biog. '69 p463
Seymour-Smith--Novels p92

ARMSTRONG, JOAN (c1942-)
Amer. judge
O'Neill--Women's p371-372

ARMSTRONG, LIL HARDIN (1898/
1902-1971)
Amer. jazz pianist, singer,
composer
Claghorn--Jazz p131
O'Neill--Women's p631

ARMSTRONG, MARY ANN (c1800's-
c1928)
Amer., mother of Louis
Armstrong
Diagram--Mothers p18-19, por.

ARNAUD, MARIE-HELENE
French model
Keenan--Women p123-124, por.

ARNAUD, YVONNE (GERMAINE)
(c1892-1958)
French actress
Jones--Rutledge p30

ARNAZ, LUCIE (1951-)
Amer. actress
World--Who p225

ARNETT, HANNAH WHITE (1733-
1824)
Amer. Revolutionary War
patriot
Clyne--Patriots p127-128,134
Sherr--American p150
Somerville--Women p36-39

ARNIM, BETINA
See RUSSELL, ELIZABETH
MARY ANNETTE BEAU-
CHAMP, COUNTESS VON
ARNIM

ARNOLD, ANNE (fl. 1970's)
Amer. sculptor
Women's--Female p84

ARNOLD, EVE (fl. 1970's)
Amer. photographer, film-
maker
Smith--Movies p147-148,224

ARNOLD, HANNAH
Amer., mother of Benedict
Arnold
Books--Lists (1) p284

ARNOLD, JULIA SORRELL (fl.
1850's)
Tasmanian, mother of Mrs.
Humphrey Ward
Colby--Singular p127-128,173

ARNOLD, MARGARET ("PEGGY")
SHIPPEN (1760-1804)
Amer. Revolutionary patriot,
wife of Benedict Arnold

Booth--Women p167-168,224-225,
227-232,297-298, por.
DePauw--Found. p139-140
Engle--Women p153-162, por.
Kelley--Courage p141-167,234
Kulkin--Her p17-18
Meyer--Petticoat p142,144
Young--Revol. p44-49,53,80,143,
158,187-188,193,202-203

ARNOLD, MARY AUGUSTA
See WARD, MRS. HUMPHREY

ARNOW, HARRIETTE LOUISE SIMP-
SON (1908-)
Amer. novelist
O'Neill--Women's p685

ARNSTEIN, MARGARET GENE
(1904-1972)
Amer. public service worker
O'Neill--Women's p233
Sicherman--Notable p37-38

AROLDINGEN, KARIN VON (1941-)
German ballet dancer
Current Biog. '83 p19-21, por.

AROUET, MARIE MARGUERITE
DAMARD
French, mother of Voltaire
Diagram--Mother p248-249

ARP, LESLIE (fl. 1970's)
Amer. chef
Macksey--Book p176

ARP, SOPHIE TAEUBER
See TAEÜBER-ARP, SOPHIE

ARRIA (-42 A.D.)
Roman, wife of A. Caecina
Paetus
Pomeroy--Godd. p161
Zinserling--Women p64-65

ARRINGTON, MARIE DEAN
Amer. accused criminal
Woman's Almanac p508,510

ARROYO, MARTINA (1936-1940-)
Amer. opera singer
Abdul--Famous p29-35, por.
Claghorn--Biog. p28
Current Biog. '71 p11-14, por.
Diamonstein--Open p17-22, por.
World--Who p69

ARSAN, EMMANUELLE (fl. 1970's)
French-Eurasian writer
Crosland--Women p233

ARSINOE (1) (c316-271 B.C.)
Greek-Macedonian monarch,
daughter of Ptolemy I
Macksey--Book p19

ARTEL, LILI (fl. 1970's)
Amer. sculptor
Women's Female p84

ARTEMIS
Roman goddess
Pomeroy--Godd. p5-6,8-9,84

ARTEMISIA (1) (fl. 5th cent.
B.C.)
Greek queen, Halicarnassus
and Cos
Jones--Rutledge p33
Pomeroy--Godd. p100

ARTEMISIA (2) (352-350 B.C.)
Greek (Caria) queen, wife of
King Mausolus, botanist
Jones--Rutledge p32
Mead--Hist. p9,40
Zinserling--Women p37

ARTHUR, BEATRICE (1923/1926-)
Amer. actress
Anderson--People p17-18, por.
Cur. Biog. '73 p17-20, por.
O'Neill--Women's p662-663
Scheuer--Tel. p12
World--Who p225

"ARTHUR, DOLLY" (1919-1975)
Amer. Alaskan "gold rush
belle"
Jones--Women (1) p106-107

ARTHUR, ELLEN LEWIS HERNDON
(1837-1880)
Amer. first-lady
James--Notable (1) p59-60
Melick--Wives p49, por.
People's Almanac (1) p271
Woman's Almanac p489

ARTHUR, JEAN (1905/1908-)
Amer. actress
Hirschhorn--Rating p21-22, por.
Manchel--Women p60-61,63, por.
Proctor--Women p63-64,74-76,

89,114-115
Shipman--Gold. p20-22, por.
Springer--They p13-14,270, por.
Woman's Almanac p332
World--Who p225

ARTHUR, JULIA (1869-1950)
Canadian-Amer. actress
James--Notable (1) p60-61

ARTHUR, LEE (fl. 1970's)
Amer. TV sportscaster
Klever--Women p35-36,76-77,97-
99,105-106, por.

ARTHUR, MALVINA (1802-1869)
Amer., mother of Chester
Arthur
Faber--Presidents' p229-230

ARUNDELL, ISABEL (c1831-)
French, wife of Sir Richard
Burton
People's Almanac (2) p858-859,
por.

ARUSMONT, FRANCES ("FANNY")
WRIGHT D'
See WRIGHT, FRANCES ("FAN-
NY") D'ARUSMONT

ARWYLLER, FROMMET (fl. 1400's)
Jewish scribe
Henry--Written p115-117

ARZNER, DOROTHY (1900-1979)
Amer. film director
Marlowe--Great p309-315, por.
O'Neill--Women's p667
Slide--Early p92-101, por.
Smith--Movies p19-24, por.

ASAWA, RUTH (fl. 1970's)
Amer. sculptor
Women's--Female p84

ASCARELLI, DEVORA (fl. 1600's)
Jewish poet
Henry--Written p129-132

ASCHEIM, ELIZABETH FLEISCHMAN
(1859-1905)
Amer. X-ray technician
Book--Lists (2) p239

ASCUE, ANNE
See ASKEW, ANNE BYRD

ASH, MARY KAY (fl. 1960's-
1980's)
Amer. cosmetics executive
O'Neill--Women's p515

ASH, MARION (fl. 1960's)
Amer. publisher
Marzolf--Up p240

ASHBEE, AGNES (fl. 1870's)
British bookbinder
Callen--Women p222

ASHBY, DOROTHY JEANNE
(1932-)
Amer. singer, harpist,
pianist
Claghorn--Biog. p28
Claghorn--Jazz p24

ASHBY, VERA
See "SUMURUN"

ASHCROFT, PEGGY, DAME
(1906/1907-)
English actress
Entertainers p229, por.
Findlater--Player p209-227, por.
Johns--Dames p89-103, por.
Jones--Rutledge p33
Priestley--Part. p105-106, por.

ASHER, ELISE (fl. 1970's)
Amer. artist
Munro--Originals p312

ASHFORD, DAISY (1881-1972)
British child author
Avenel--Comp. (1) p25
Books--Lists (2) p224, por.
Jones--Rutledge p33

ASHKENAZI OF CRACOW (fl. 1593)
Jewish writer on morals
Henry--Written p90

ASHLEY, ELIZABETH (1939/1941-)
Amer. actress
Cur. Biog. '78 p19-22, por.
Firestone--Success see index
p297
Lichtenstein--Mach. p262-263
People--Best p166, por.
World--Who p225

ASHLEY, MARY ELLIOTT (1798-)
Amer. religious and social

patron, noted Arkansas
mother
Amer.--Mothers p40

ASHLEY, MERRILL (1950-)
Amer. ballet dancer
Current Biog. '81 p4-7, por.

ASHTON, SHARRON STANDIFER
(1940-)
Amer. genealogical researcher,
author
Meyer--Who's p23-24

ASHTON, WINIFRED
See DANE, CLEMENCE, pseud.

ASHTON-WARNER, SYLVIA (1908-
1978)
New Zealand novelist
Avenel--Comp. (1) p25
Crosland--Beyond p136-137
Moers--Literary p272
Moffat--Revel. p206-207
Seymour-Smith--Novels p92

ASHWELL, LENA SIMSON, LADY
(1872/1873-1957)
British actress
Jones--Rutledge p35

ASKEW, ANNE BYRD (1521-1546)
English, Protestant religious
martyr
Bainton--France p213-216

ASKEW, SARAH BYRD (1863/1877-
1942)
Amer. librarian
James--Notable (1) p61-62

ASKIN, ROSEMARY (c1949-)
New Zealand paleontologist
Land--New p89-102, por.

ASLAKSON, MARIAN (fl. 1910's)
Amer., Girl Scout, early
O'Neill--Women's p113

ASPASIA (1) (OF MILETUS) (470-
410 B.C.)
Greek scholar, adventuress,
consort of Pericles
People's Almanac (1) p859-862
Pomeroy--Godd. p89-91
Zinserling--Women p38-39

ASPASIA (2)
Roman physician
Mead--Hist. p63-66,73
O'Neill--Women's p197

ASPINWALL, NAN JANE (fl. 1910's)
Amer. equestrian
McWhirter--Guinness p57

ASQUITH, CYNTHIA MARY EVELYN
(CHARTERIS), LADY
English patron of arts
Rogers--Ladies p96-97,100-101,
105

ASTAIRE, ADELE (1898-1981)
Amer. dancer
Entertainers p209-210, por.
O'Neill--Women's p648
World--Who p262

ASTAIRE, MRS. FRED
See SMITH, ROBYN CAROLINE

ASTELL, MARY (1666/1668-1731)
English author, educator
Horner--English p24-25
Moers--Literary p272

ASTIN, ANNA MARIE
See DUKE, PATTY (ANNA
MARIE)

ASTIN, HELEN
Amer. education researcher
O'Neill--women's p423

ASTMAN, BARBARA (fl. 1970's)
Canadian photographer
Women's--Female p62

ASTOR, AVA WILLING
Amer. socialite
Forma--They p41,52,185-186

ASTOR, CAROLINE WEBSTER
SCHERMERHORN (MRS. Wm.)
(1830-1908)
Amer. socialite
Birmingham--Grandes, see
index p287
James--Notable (1) p62-64
Longstreet--Queen p21-31, por.
McHenry--Liberty's p12-13
People's Almanac (3) p149-150
Woman's Almanac p211

ASTOR, MADELAINE TALMADGE
FORCE
Amer. socialite
Forma--They p183,187-188, por.

ASTOR, MARY (1906-1987)
Amer. actress
Book--Lists (2) p188
Hirschhorn--Rating p24-25, por.
Lamparski--What. (4) p58-59,
por.
People's Almanac (2) p758-760
Shipman--Gold. p27-31, por.
Springer--They p14,270, por.
World--Who p225

ASTOR, NANCY WHITCHER LANG-
HORNE, LADY (1879-1964)
English Parliament member
Brandon--Dollar p112-113,149-150,
152-155,161-172
Brecher--Lives p310
Holme--Journal p180, por.
Jones--Rutledge p35
Longstreet--Queen p42-43, por.
Macksey--Book p38,103
Sherr--American p232-233
Vallance--Women, see index p207
Who Did What p20, por.
World--Who p154

ASTOR, SARAH TODD (1762-1832)
German-Amer. socialite
Bird--Enterprising p41-43

ASUNSOLO, DOLORES
See DEL RIO, DOLORES

ATALANTA
Greek Amazon huntress (god-
dess), wife of Hippomenes
Pomeroy--Godd. p5,19

ATANASSOVA, MARIA (fl. 1950's)
Russian aviator
O'Neill--Women's p742

ATHANASIA
See ANASTASIA

ATHENA (ATHENE)
Greek goddess
Pomeroy--Godd. p2-6,8-9

ATHERTON, GERTRUDE FRANKLIN
HORN (1857-1948)

Amer. novelist, biographer,
historian
Avenel--Comp. (2) p21
Clark--Leading p105-106
Dunlap--Calif. p5-6, por.
Ehrlich--Oxford p291,400,422
Hazen--Interv. p25
James--Notable (1) p64-65
McHenry--Liberty's p13
Richey--Eminent p97-123, por.
Seymour-Smith--Novels p92
Starr--Amer. p260-261,291,
345-364,443, por.

ATIENZAR, MARIBEL (c1959-)
Spanish matador
McWhirter--Guiness p45
O'Neill--Women's p744

ATKENSON, MARY MEEK (1884-)
Amer. author, lecturer
Sherr--American p244

ATKINS, EMILY (c1859-1889)
Amer. physician
Sherr--American p227

ATKINS, MARY (1819-1882)
Amer. educator, publicist
James--Notable (1) p65-66
Millstein--We p52,59
Sherr--American p12

ATKINSON, ELEANOR (1863-1942)
Amer. novelist
Ehrlich--Oxford p313

ATKINSON, TI-GRACE (1939-)
Amer. feminist
Sochen--Movers p257,273

ATUNEZ, FERNANDA
Spanish dancer
O'Neill--Women's p645

ATWATER, HELEN WOODARD
(1876-1947)
Amer. home economist,
magazine editor
James--Notable (1) p66-67
O'Neill--Women's p473

ATWOOD, ANGELA (1948-)
Amer. revolutionary
Woman's Almanac p507-508

ATWOOD, DONNA (c1923-)
Amer. skater

Lamparski--What (4) p64-65,
por.

ATWOOD, ERNESTINE F. (fl. 1900's)
Amer. heroine, Carnegie Medal
winner
O'Neill--Women's p732

ATWOOD, MARGARET ELEANOR
KILLIAN (1939-)
Canadian novelist, story-
writer, poet, professor
Cur. Biog. '84 p17-20, por.
McCullough--People p8-10
Seymour-Smith--Novels p93
Webber--Woman p177-187

ATZBERGER, CHRISTINA MARIE
(1947-)
Amer. genealogical researcher
Meyer--Who's p24

AUBIGNE, FRANÇOISE D'
See MAINTENON, FRANÇOISE
D'AUBIGNE MARQUISE

AUDERT, AUBERTINE
French socialist, suffragist
Macksey--Book p88-89

AUDIN, MARGARET (1926-)
English genealogical research-
er, writer
Meyer, Who's p24

AUDLEY, LADY
See CHURCHILL, SARAH, LADY
AUDLEY

AUDOUX, MARGUERITE (1863/1880-
1937)
French novelist
Crosland--Women p88-91,112

AUDREY, JACQUELINE (c1908-)
French film director
Smith--Movies p118-119

AUERBACH, BEATRICE FOX (1887-
1968)
Amer. business executive,
philanthropist
Sicherman--Notable p38-40

AUGSPURG, ANITA (1857-1943)
German suffragist
Macksey--Book p88

AUGUST, REBECCA (1883-   )
Latvian co-founder, Hebrew-
Trade Council
O'Neill--Women's p295

AULAIRE, INGRI D'MORTENSON
(1904-   )
Amer. children's book author
O'Neill--Women's p692

AULL, ELIZABETH (fl. 1860's)
Amer. educator, philanthro-
pist
Sherr--American p131

AUNE, REGINA C.
Amer. air force aviator
O'Neill--Women's p546-547

"AUNT FANNY"
See GAGE, FRANCES DANA
BARKER

AURA
See LEE, AURA

AURELIA PHILEMATIUM
Roman child bride
Pomeroy--Godd. p194

AURIOL, JACQUELINE DOUET
(1917-   )
French aviator
Kulkin--Her p18-19
O'Neill--Women's p40-41

AUSTEN, ALICE (1866-1952)
Amer. photographer
Sherr American p172

AUSTEN, ANNA, LADY (c1782-   )
English, friend of Cowper
Morley--Literary p297-298

AUSTEN, CASSANDRA (c1729-
c1827)
English, mother of Jane
Austen
Diagram--Mothers p20-21, por.

AUSTEN, JANE (1775-1817)
English novelist
Avenel--Comp. (1) p27-29
Brecher--Lives p195
Donaldson--How p18
Fine--Women p65
Fry--1000 p200

Horner--English p78-79
Jones--Rutledge p39
Kronenberger--Atlan. p23-25
Kulkin--Her p19-20
Kupferberg--First p6-7, por.
Macksey--Book p183-184, por.
Magill--Cycl. p57-60
Moers--Literary p273-274, see
also index p1321
Morley--Literary, see index p482
People's Almanac (2) p409
Seymour-Smith--Novels p93, por.
Who Did What p21
Woman's Almanac p245-246, por.
World Who p23

AUSTERLITZ, ADELE
See ASTAIRE, ADELE

AUSTIN, ANN(E) (-1655/1656)
Amer. colonial missionary
Neidle--America's p59
Williams--Demeter's p124

AUSTIN, BELINDA (fl. 1879-1880)
Amer. teacher, missionary
Jones--Women (1) p71-72, por.

AUSTIN, INEZ
Amer. designer
O'Neill--Women's p516

AUSTIN, MARY HUNTER (1868-1934)
Amer. novelist
Dunlap--Calif. p6-7, por.
Ehrlich--Oxford, see index p449
James--Notable (1) p67-69
McHenry--Liberty's p13-14
Sherr--American p156-157
Showalter--These p78-86
Starr--Amer., see index p481,
por.
Time--Women p111
Webster's--Amer. p46

AUSTIN, MILDRED MARIE LUCAS
(1874-c1972)
Amer. Girl Scout worker,
community worker, noted
Vermont mother
Amer.--Mothers p541-542

AUSTIN, PAULINE M.
Amer. meteorologist, director
of weather radar research
O'Neill--Women's p173

AUSTIN, SADIE (fl. 1900's)
Amer. cowboy
Time--Women p190-191, por.

AUSTIN, TRACY (1962-)
Amer. tennis player
Anderson--People p21-22
Cur. Biog. '81 p7-10, por.
Gurtman--More p47-62, por.
McWhirter--Guinness p152, por.
O'Neill--Women's p583
Woman's Almanac p413-414

AUZOU, PAULINE (1775-1835)
French artist
Harris--Women p46,48-49,198,
211-212,349

AVARINA, TATYANA (fl. 1970's)
Russian skater
McWhirter--Guinness p102, por.
O'Neill--Women's p563-564

AVARY, MYRTA LOCKETT (fl.
1900's)
Amer. author, sociologist,
editor, politician
Scott--Southern p97-98

AVENER, JUDI (fl. 1970's)
Amer. gymnastic coach
Jordan--Broken p68-70

AVERY, ALICE O'NEILL (c1917-)
Amer. millionaire
Forbes--400 ('84) p133

AVERY, BEVERLY
Amer., world record for
number divorces
Macksey--Book p129

AVERY, MARTHA GALLISON
MOORE (1851-1929)
Amer. socialist, Catholic
lay apostle
James--Notable (1) p69-71

AVERY, MARY ELLEN (1927-)
Amer. physician, Head,
children's hospital
O'Neill--Women's p230

AVERY, RACHEL G. FOSTER
(1858-1919)
Amer. feminist
James--Notable (1) p71-72

AVISA OF GLOUCESTER (1176-)
English queen
Softly--Queens p23-24

AVISON, MARGARET (c1918-)
Canadian poet
Seymour-Smith--Who's p24

AVIV, NURITH (fl. 1970's)
Israeli camerawoman
Smith--Movies p126

AVRAM, HENRIETTE D. (fl. 1970's)
Amer. computer systems
analyst, librarian
O'Neill--Women's p90,179

AW SIAN, SALLY (1931-)
Burmese editor, Head Inter-
national Press Institute
O'Neill--Women's p465

AXEMAN, LOIS (fl. 1970's)
Amer. illustrator
Seed--Saturday's p48-50, por.

"AXIS SALLY"
See SISK, MILDRED GILLARS

AXTELL, REBECCA, LADY (fl.
1700's)
Amer. colonial planter
Williams--Demeter's p188-189

AYCOCK, ALICE (1946-)
Amer. artist
Munro--Originals p394-395

AYER, HARRIET HUBBARD (1849-
1903)
Amer. cosmetician, business
executive
Bird--Enterprising p127-130
James--Notable (1) p72-74
O'Neill--Women's p510,512
Woman's Almanac p131-132
World--Who p193

AYHENS, OLIVE MADORA (fl.
1970's)
Amer. painter
Women's--Female p32

AYLONG, HELENE (fl. 1970's)
Amer. painter
Women's--Female p32

AYLWARD, GLADYS (1903-1970)
English missionary, heroine
Fraser--Heroines p233-237, por.
Macksey--Book p121
Who Did What p21

AYRES, ANNE (1816-1896)
English-Amer. religious sister
James--Notable (1) p74-75
McHenry--Liberty's p14

AYRES, GILLIAN (1930-)
English artist
Contemp. Brit. unp, por.

AYRES, RUBY MILDRED (1883-
1955)
English novelist
Jones--Rutledge p40

AYRES, MRS. WILLIAM (fl. 1600's)
Amer. accused witch
Williams--Demeter's p137

AYRTON, HERTHA MARKS (1854-
1923)
English physicist
Macksey--Book p152

AYSCOUGH, ANNE
See ASKEW, ANNE

AZALAIS DE PORCAIRAGES
(c1140-)
French troubadour
Bogin--Women p95,166-167

AZARA, NANCY
Amer. sculptor
Women's--Female p85

"AZA-YA-MAN-KA-WIN" (1788-
1873)
Amer. Indian, frontier
woman
Amer.--Mothers p285, por.

AZEVEDO, HELEN (1945-)
Amer. TV producer
Scheuer--Tel. p15

AZUMA, TOKUHO (c1910-)
Japanese theater co-founder
O'Neill--Women's p650

B

BABASHOFF, SHIRLEY (1957-)
Amer. swimmer
Hollander--100 p86-89, por.
Jacobs--Modern p85-98, por.
McWhirter--Guinness p131,136,
por.
O'Neill--Women's p586
Woman's Almanac p429

BABB, BELLE AURELIA
See MANSFIELD, ARABELLA
BABB ("BELLE")

BABBIN, JACQUELINE (fl. 1970's)
Amer. TV producer
Marzolf--Up p183
Scheuer--Tel. p17

BABCOCK, BARBARA ELLEN
Amer. lawyer, government
official
O'Neill--Women's p367

BABCOCK, BERNIE (1868-)
Amer. writer, museum founder
Amer.--Mothers p44, por.

BABCOCK, MARTHA CROSS (1814-
1873)
Amer., noted Rhode Island
mother, educator, Civil War
worker
Amer.--Mothers p478-479, por.

BABCOCK, MAUDE (fl. 1890's)
Amer. professor, feminist
Sherr--American p227

BABER, ALICE (fl. 1970's)
Amer. painter
Women's--Female p32

BABOTTA, CATHERINE COLORIA
See BALLARD, KAYE

BABS, ALICE (1924-)
Swedish jazz singer
Claghorn--Jazz p26

"BABY SANDY" (1938-)
Amer. child actress
Lamparski--What. (5) p156-157,
por.
Lamparski--What. (8) p22-23,
por.

BACALL, LAUREN (1924-   )
    Amer. actress
    Anderson--People p23-24, por.
    Current Biog. '70 p21-24, por.
    Engstead--Star p83-91
    Hirschhorn--Rating p28-29, por.
    Manchel--Women p77, por.
    Shipman--Internatl. p28-30, por.
    Woman's Almanac p328,332, por.
    World--Who p225-226

BACH, CATHERINE (c1954-   )
    Amer. actress
    Scheuer--Tel. p17

BACH, ELISABETH LAEMMERHIRT
        (1644-1694)
    German, mother of Johann
    Sebastian Bach
    Diagram--Mothers p22

BACHARACH, EVA (HAVA) (1580-
        1651)
    Jewish scholar
    Henry--Written p90-91

BACHAUER, GINA (1913-1976)
    Greek pianist
    Current Biog. '77 p459

BACHE, SARAH FRANKLIN (1743-
        1808)
    Amer. patriot, philanthro-
    pist, daughter of Benjamin
    Franklin
    Booth--Women p265-266
    DePauw--Found. p171-172
    DePauw--Rem. p86,93
    Engle--Women p236-243, por.
    James--Notable (1) p75-76
    Meyer--Petticoat p134-135
    Sherr--American p203
    Somerville--Women p48-51
    Warren--Pictorial p49-50
    Williams--Demeter's p257-259

BACH-LIIMAND, AINO GUSTAVOVNA
        (1901-   )
    Russian artist, book illus-
    trator
    Women's--Female p3--supp.

BACHMAN, MARIA
    See MARTIN, MARIA (MARIE)

BACHMANN, INGEBORG (1926-1973)
    Austrian poet, novelist,

radio playwright
Herrmann--Ger. p6,77

BACHNER, ANNETTE (fl. 1940's-
        1970's)
    Amer. filmmaker
    Smith--Movies p148,225

BACHRACH, DORO (fl. 1970's)
    Amer. filmmaker
    Smith--Movies p83-86,225

BACHVAROVA, RADKA (fl. 1960's)
    Bulgarian film director
    Smith--Movies p94

BAČKSTRÖM, MONICA
    Swedish glass-maker
    O'Neill--Women's p272

BACLANOVA, OLGA (1899-1974)
    Russian actress
    Springer--They p22,270, por.

BACON, ALBION FELLOWS (1865-
        1933)
    Amer. social reformer
    James--Notable (1) p78-79
    McHenry--Liberty's p15
    Millstein--We p151

BACON, ALICE MABEL (1858-1918)
    Amer. teacher, author
    James--Notable (1) p78-79

BACON, ANNE COOKE, LADY
        (c1528-1610)
    English, travel writer, religious
    worker
    Bainton--Spain p110-112

BACON, DELIA (1811-1859)
    Amer. author, lecturer,
    Shakespearean critic
    Felton--Famous p183-184
    James--Notable (1) p79-81
    McHenry--Liberty's p15
    People's Almanac (1) p85-87
    Sherr--American p32

BACON, DOROTHY
    Amer. magazine writer, news
    correspondent
    Hamblin--That p22-23,27-28,93,
        188

BACON, ELIZABETH (1842-1933)
Amer. author
Ehrlich--Oxford p333

BACON, ELIZABETH DUKE (fl.
1650's-1670's)
English, wife of Nathaniel
Bacon
Williams--Demeter's p162

BACON, GERTRUDE (fl. 1900's)
British aviatrix
Boase--Sky's p9-10

BACON, GEORGEANNA MUIRSON
See WOOLSEY, ABBY HOWLAND

BACON, KATHERINE (1896-)
English concert pianist
Claghorn--Biog. p34

BACON, MARY (c1950-)
Amer. jockey
Hollander--100 p66-68, por.

BACON, PEGGY (1895-)
Amer. illustrator, painter,
mystery writer
O'Neill--Women's p599

BADARZEWSKA, THEKLA (1834-
1861)
Polish composer
Macksey--Book p214

BADDELEY, HERMIONE (1906-)
English actress
World--Who p254

BADDELEY, MARY O'CALLAGHAN
(fl. 1760's-1770's)
Irish Tory
Booth--Women p188-190,273,
284-285

BADEN-POWELL, OLAVE ST.
CLAIRE, LADY (1889-1977)
English, organizer of Girl
Scouts
O'Neill--Women's p39,113

BAER, JO (fl. 1970's)
Amer. painter
Women's--Female p32

BAERWALD, SUSAN (1944-)
Amer. TV director
Scheuer--Tel. p18

BAETA, HENRIETTA LOUISE
(c1881-)
African, Ghana teacher
Crane--Ms. p15-20

BAEZ, JOAN (1941-)
Amer. singer, political activist
Anderson--People p25, por.
Claghorn--Biog. p34
Clark--Leading p210-212
Dunlap--Calif. p7, por.
Fabian--On p216-217, por.
Longstreet--Queen p169-171
McHenry--Liberty's p15-16
100--Greatest (1) p82, por.
O'Neill--Women's p710-711
Simon--Best p33-34, por.
Warren--Pictorial p205, por.
Webster's--Amer. p52
Woman's Almanac p287, por.
World--Who p264

BAEZ, MIMI (1945-)
Amer. singer
Claghorn--Biog. p34

BAGLEY, SARAH G. (1806-)
Amer. labor leader, telegraph
operator, social reformer
Bagley--Mill p117-180, por.
Hymowitz--Hist. p133,135
James--Notable (1) p81-82
McHenry--Liberty's p16
Macksey--Book p164
Millstein--We p89-90
Neidle--America's p114
Reader's--Story p436
Sherr--American p97,106
Warren--Pictorial p94-95
Woman's Almanac p177

BAGNOLD, ENID ALGERINE (1889-
1981)
English playwright, novelist
Current Biog. '81 p457
Jones--Rutledge p46
Seymour-Smith--Novels p94
Showalter--Lit. p349
World--Who p23

BAGSHAW, ELIZABETH CATHERINE
(c1881-1982)
Canadian physician
Hellstedt--Women p8-9, por.

BAI, A.R. KASTURI (1925-)
East Indian zoologist
O'Neill--Women's p6

BAILAR, BARBARA A.
    Amer. mathematician, govern-
    ment official
    O'Neill--Women's p179

BAILEY, ANN ("MAD ANN")
    (1742-1825)
    Amer. Indian, Revolutionary
    War patriot
    Clyne--Patriots p1-7
    McHenry--Liberty's p16
    Sherr--American p232,245

BAILEY, ANNA WARNER ("MOTHER
    BAILEY") (1758-1850/1851)
    Amer. Revolutionary War
    patriot
    McHenry--Liberty's p16-17
    Meyer--Petticoat p154
    Sherr--American p31

BAILEY, CATHERINE H. (fl.
    1960's-1970's)
    Amer. agriculturist, fruit
    breeder
    O'Neill--Women's p34

BAILEY, ETHEL (c1890-)
    Amer., curator of hortorium,
    zoologist, botanist
    O'Neill--Women's p34, por.

BAILEY, FLORENCE AUGUSTA
    MERRIAM (1863-1948)
    Amer. ornithologist, nature
    writer
    James--Notable (1) p82-83
    McHenry--Liberty's p17
    O'Neill--Women's p155-156

BAILEY, HANNAH CLARK
    JOHNSTON (1839-1923)
    Amer. philanthropist, social
    reformer, pacifist
    James--Notable (1) p83-85
    Sherr--American p90

BAILEY, HENRIETTA (fl. 1900's)
    Amer. potter
    Callen--Women p89

BAILEY, LILLIE (fl. 1860's)
    Amer. Southern belle
    DeLeon--Belles p149

BAILEY, LYDIA R. (-1869)
    Amer. printer
    Sherr--American p203

BAILEY, MARGARET JEWETT (fl.
    1850's)
    Amer. writer
    Sherr--American p197

BAILEY, MARIE LOUIS (1876-)
    Amer. pianist, composer
    Claghorn--Biog. p34

BAILEY, MARY WESTENRA, LADY
    (1890-1960)
    Irish aviatrix
    Boase--Sky's p45-62 (see also
    index p218), por.
    Macksey--Book p248

BAILEY, MILDRED RINKER (1903/
    1907-1951)
    Amer. singer
    Claghorn--Biog. p34-35
    Claghorn--Jazz p27
    Simon--Best p35-36, por.

BAILEY, MOLLIE (1841-1918)
    Amer. circus owner
    Kirk--Circus p30-33, por.
    Woman's Almanac p322-323

BAILEY, PEARL MAE (1918-)
    Amer. singer, actress, noted
    California mother
    Amer.--Mothers p57-58
    Claghorn--Biog. p35
    Claghorn--Jazz p27
    Clark--Leading p233-234
    Current Biog. '69 p23-25, por.
    Entertainers p249
    Ingraham--Album p62, por.
    Kulkin--Her p20-21
    100--Greatest (1) p48-49, por.
    O'Neill--Women's p137,628-629
    Simon--Best p37-38, por.
    World--Who p264

BAILEY, ROSALIE FELLOWS (1908-)
    Amer. genealogical researcher
    Meyer--Who's p27

BAILLIE, GRIZEL (GRISELL) HUME,
    LADY (1665-1746).
    Scottish song-writer, poet
    Avenel--Comp. p32

BAILLIE, JOANNE (JOANNA) (1762-
    1851)
    Scottish playwright, poet,
    actress
    Avenel--Comp. (1) p32

Moers--Literary p91,274
Morley--Literary p453-454

BAIN, BARBARA (1932/1934-)
    Amer. actress
    World--Who p226

BAINBRIDGE, BERYL (1934-)
    English novelist, actress,
    painter
    Crosland--Beyond, see index
    p253
    McCullough--People p10-12
    P.W.--Author p10-12,482
    Seymour-Smith--Novels p94

BAINTER, FAY OKELL (1891/
    1894-1968)
    Amer. actress
    Fabian--On p158-159, por.
    Keylin--Hollywood p11, por.
    Springer--They p22,270, por.
    World--Who p226

BAIRD, ELIZABETH (fl. 1840's-
    1880's)
    Amer. pioneer, writer
    Sherr--American p247

BAIRD, JACQUELINE DAVIS
    (1931-)
    British-Amer. manufacturer
    Rich-McCoy--Mill. p23-48, por.

BAITMAN, RASMAR (fl. 1970's)
    Russian dress designer
    O'Neill--Women's p246

BAJOR, GIZI (1894-1951)
    Hungarian actress
    Entertainers p195

BAKARICH, ALEXANDRA C. (fl.
    1960's-1970's)
    Amer. veterinarian, Air
    Force Reserve
    O'Neill--Women's p542

BAKER, ARCADIA BANDINI
    STEARNS DE (c1825-1912)
    Amer. rancher
    Dunlap--Calif. p7-8, por.

BAKER, BETSEY METCALF (fl.
    1790's-1800's)
    Amer. inventor, (1st straw
    hat)
    Sherr--American p114

BAKER, BETTY L.
    Amer. Air Force flier
    O'Neill--Women's p547

BAKER, BONNIE ("WEE") (1917/
    1918-)
    Amer. singer
    Lamparski--What. (4) p186-187,
    por.
    Simon--Big p239-240, por.

BAKER, CARROLL (1931/1935-)
    Amer. dancer, actress
    World--Who p226

BAKER, DOROTHY DODDS (1907-
    1968)
    Amer. novelist
    Avenel--Comp. p23
    Seymour-Smith--Novels p94
    Seymour-Smith--Who's p27

BAKER, ELIZABETH (fl. 1970's)
    Amer. magazine editor
    Women's--Female p121

BAKER, ELIZABETH PHOEBE
    Amer. pioneer
    Sherr--American p62

BAKER, FLORENCE (c1836-1916)
    Hungarian traveller
    Macksey--Book p238

BAKER, GLADYS L. (fl. 1930's-
    1970's)
    Amer. agricultural historian
    O'Neill--Women's p29

BAKER, IRENE B.
    Amer. congresswoman
    Chamberlin--Min. p307-309

BAKER, JANET, DAME (1933-)
    English opera singer
    Current Biog. '71 p19-22, por.
    Gammond--Illus. p237, por.
    Jones--Rutledge p47

BAKER, JOSEPHINE (1906-1975)
    Amer. dancer, singer
    Claghorn--Biog. p35
    Comfort--Good p130, por.
    Current Biog. '75 p460
    Entertainers p227, por.
    Jones--Rutledge p47
    Keenan--Women p173-174, por.
    Longstreet--Queen p187-188

McHenry--Liberty's p17
O'Neill--Women's p623,625, por.
People's Almanac (1) p899-900
Sicherman--Notable p40-41
Simon--Best p39-40, por.
Webster's--Amer. p56
Woman's Almanac p307, por.
World--Who p263

BAKER, KATHARINE LEE (1859-
    1929)
    Amer. educator, author
    Webster's--Amer. p74

BAKER, LINDA D. (c1956-)
    Amer. heroine, Carnegie
    Medal winner
    O'Neill--Women's p734

BAKER, MARGERY CLAIRE (1948-)
    Amer. TV news producer
    Scheuer--Tel. p19

BAKER, MARY (c1800-)
    English impostor
    Book--Lists (1) p482

BAKER, NORMA JEAN
    See MONROE, MARILYN

BAKER, SARA JOSEPHINE
    (1873-1945)
    Amer. pediatrician, public
    health worker, child health
    pioneer
    James--Notable (1) p85-86
    McHenry--Liberty's p17-18
    Millstein--We p151
    O'Neill--Women's p226-227
    Woman's Almanac p361

BAKER, TERRY (fl. 1970's)
    Amer. WAC M.P.
    O'Neill--Women's p545

BALAAM, ELLEN (1891-)
    Australian physician
    Hellstedt--Women p76-78, por.

BALAS, IOLANDA (1936-)
    Rumanian track and field
    athlete
    McWhirter--Guinness p166
    O'Neill--Women's p578

BALCH, EMILY GREENE (1867-
    1961)
    Amer. economist,

social reformer
    McHenry--Liberty's p18
    Macksey--Book p118
    O'Neill--Women's p700
    Opfell--Lady p34-49, por.
    Palmer--Who's p38
    Sicherman--Notable p41-45
    Warren--Pictorial p167,194-195
    Webster's--Amer. p57
    Woman's Almanac p381-382, por.
    World--Who p186

BALDAO Y CASTILLO, MARIA
    MARGUERITE
    See "MARGO"

BALDINE-KOSLOFF, ALEXANDRA
    (MME.)
    Russian ballet dancer
    People's Almanac (3) p525

BALDWIN, FAITH CUTHRELL (1893-
    1978)
    Amer. novelist
    Ehrlich--Oxford p117
    McHenry--Liberty's p18-19
    World--Who p9

BALDWIN, MARIA LOUISE (1856-
    1922)
    Amer. teacher
    James--Notable (1) p86-88
    McHenry--Liberty's p19
    Sherr--American p100

BALDWIN, MARY (fl. 1840's)
    Amer. educator
    Sherr--American p238

BALDWIN, RUTH ANN (fl. 1910's)
    Amer. director, screen writer
    Slide--Early p59

BALE-COX, PATRICIA (PATSI)
    (fl. 1970's)
    Amer. magazine publisher,
    feminist
    O'Neill--Women's p138

BALINE, LEAH
    Russian, mother of Irving
    Berlin
    Diagram--Mothers p28-29, por.

BALL, FLORRIE (fl. 1970's)
    English motorcyclist
    Comfort--Good p151, por.
    People's Almanac (3) p522-523

BALL, LUCILLE (1911-)
    Amer. comedienne, actress,
    TV personality
Anderson--People p26
Book--Lists (2) p260
Cur. Biog. '78 p31-35, por.
Engstead--Star p103-106
Fireman--TV p159-161
Higham--Celeb. p75-82, por.
Hirschhorn--Rating p29-31, por.
Kulkin--Her p21-22
Lewis--Prime p57,222-223, por.
McHenry--Liberty's p19
Mordden--Movie p135-139, por.
100--Greatest (1) p96, por.
O'Neill--Women's p660-661
Scheuer--Tel. p20-21
Shipman--Gold. p34-36, por.
Springer--They p22,270, por.
Webster's--Amer. p59
Woman's Almanac p332-333, por.
World--Who p226

BALLARD, ERNESTA DRINKER
    (1920-)
    Amer. horticulturist
Gilbert--Part. p283-289, por.

BALLARD, FLORENCE (1943/1944-
    1976)
    Amer. singer
Woman's Almanac p304-305, por.

BALLARD, KAYE (1926-)
    Amer. actress, singer,
    comedienne
Cur. Biog. '69 p25-28, por.
Scheuer--Tel. p21, por.

BALLINGER, THELMA (fl. 1970's)
    Amer. agricultural executive
O'Neill--Women's p15

BALLOU, MARY (fl. 1850's)
    Amer. Western pioneer
Fischer--Let p42-47

BALSAN, CONSUELO VANDERBILT
    (1877-1964)
    Amer. philanthropist, hostess
Brandon--Dollar, see index p213,
    por.
Forma--They p49,51-52, por.

BALUKAS, JEAN (1959-)
    Amer. pocket billiard
    player
McWhirter--Guinness p40

Woman's Almanac p437
World--Who p209

BAM, BRIGALIA (1933-)
    South African churchwoman
Crane--Ms. p129-140, por.

BAMBACE, ANGELA (1898-1975)
    Brazilian-Amer. labor union
    leader
O'Neill--Women's p300
Sicherman--Notable p45-46

BAMBARA, TONI CADE (fl. 1950's)
    Amer. writer, settlement
    house director
Fisher--Third pvi,196
Washington--Black p76-77

BAMPTON, ROSE ELIZABETH
    (1909-)
    Amer. opera singer
Claghorn--Biog. p37

BANCROFT, ANNE (1931-)
    Italian-Amer. singer, actress
Anderson--People p27, por.
Entertainers p278
Hirschhorn--Rating p31-32, por.
Shipman--Internatl. p30-33, por.
World--Who p226

BANCROFT, BETTINA (1941-)
    Amer. millionaire
Forbes--400 ('84) p150

BANCROFT, JANE MARIE
    See ROBINSON, JANE MARIE
    BANCROFT

BANCROFT, JESSIE HUBBELL
    (1867-1952)
    Amer. physical educator
Sicherman--Notable p46-47

BANCROFT, MARIE EFFIE WILTON,
    LADY (1839-1921)
    English actress
Findlater--Player p128-129

BANDARANAIKE, CHANDRIKA
    East Indian plantation manager
O'Neill--Women's p46

BANDARANAIKE, SIRIMAVO (1916-)
    Ceylonese prime minster
Jones--Rutledge p50-51
Macksey--Book p43

O'Neill--Women's p46
Palmer--Who's p40-41
Woman's Almanac p463-464, por.

BANDINI, ARCADIA
See BAKER, ARCADIA BANDINI
STEARNS DE

BANE, MARY E.
Amer. Marine Corps com-
mander
O'Neill--Women's p539-540

BANG, DUCK-HEUNG (1908-)
Korean physician
Hellstedt--Women p361-363, por.

BANG, MAIA (1877-1940)
Norwegian violinist, teacher,
author
Claghorn--Biog. p37

BANG, NINA HENRIETTE
WENDELINE (1866-1928)
Danish Cabinet Member
Macksey--Book p38
O'Neill--Women's p57

BANISTER, MARION GLASS
(1875-1951)
Amer. government official
Ware--Beyond p144, see also
index p197

BANISTER, ZILPAH POLLY
GRANT
See GRANT, ZILPAH POLLY

BANK, MIRRA (fl. 1970's)
Amer. artist, photographer,
film editor
Smith--Movies p148,225

BANKHEAD, TALLULAH BROCK-
MAN (1903-1968)
Amer. actress
Clark--Leading p179-182
Cur. Biog. '69 p463
Donaldson--How p22
Eills--Here p138-139
Entertainers p221, por.
Fabian--On p184-185, por.
Hazen--Interv. p82
Hirschhorn--Rating p32-33, por.
Jones--Rutledge p51
Keylin--Hollywood p14-15, por.
McHenry--Liberty's p20

New York Times--Great p4-5, por.
O'Neill--Women's p658
Shipman--Gold. p36-38,363, por.
Sicherman--Notable p47-49
Springer--They p22,24,270-271,
por.
Webster's--Amer. p61
Woman's Almanac p333
World--Who p226

BANKS, MRS. E.A.
See PICKETT, ELTLA

BANKS, ELIZA S. (fl. 1870's-1880's)
British pottery designer
Callen--Women p62-63,65,222, por.

BANKS, ELIZABETH L. (1870-1938)
Amer. author, journalist
Marzolf--Up p35-36

BANKS, ISABELLA VARLEY
LINNAEUS (1821-1897)
English poet, novelist
Showalter--Lit. p139,327

BANKS, LYNNE REID (1929-)
English novelist, playwright
Seymour-Smith--Novels p95

BANKS, MARY ROSS (fl. 1870's)
Amer. farmer
Scott--Southern p109

BANKY, VILMA (1898/1903-)
Hungarian-Amer. actress
Springer--They p24,271, por.

BANNERMAN, HELEN (1863-1946)
Scottish illustrator, author
Showalter--Lit. p342

BANNING, MARGARET CULKIN
(1891-1982)
Amer. novelist, short-story
writer
Cur. Biog. '82 p459-460
Ehrlich--Oxford p341

BANTA, GLORIA (fl. 1970's-1980's)
Amer. TV executive
Scheuer--Tel. p22

BANU, ARJUMAND
See MUMTAZ-MAHAL (MUMTAZ-
ZEMANI)

BANŪ, VĀLIDE, NŪR, SULTANA
(-1583)
Venetian, mother of Ottoman
emperor Murad III
Book--Lists (2) p252-253

BAÑUELOS, ANTONIA DE (fl.
1870's-1880's)
Spanish painter
Sparrow--Women p289,320-321

BANUELOS, ROMANA ACOSTA
(1925-)
Amer. government official
Signif.--Amer. p56, por.

BANVILLE, ANNE
Amer. co-founder of Organi-
zation for Women
O'Neill--Women's p516

BARA, THEDA (1890-1955)
Amer. actress
Banner--Women p164-165, por.
Engstead--Star p149,151-152
Hazen--Interv. p410
Keenan--Women p76-77, por.
Keylin--Hollywood p12-13, por.
McHenry--Liberty's p20
Manchel--Women p4,30-31, por.
Mordden--Movie, see index
p291
Shipman--Gold. p38-40, por.
Sicherman--Notable p49-50
Webster's--Amer. p62
Woman's Almanac p333-334, por.
World--Who p226

BARANOF, ANNA, PRINCESS (fl.
1790's-1818)
Russian, wife of 1st governor
of Alaska
Jones--Women (1) p15-21

BARAT, MADELEINE, SAINT
(1779-1865)
French founder, religious
order
Macksey--Book p67

BARBA, SHARON (1943-)
Amer. poet
Chester--Rising p352-357, por.

BARBAULD, ANNA LAETITIA
(1743-1825)
English poet, educator
Avenel--Comp. (1) p33

BARBE, VICTORIA (fl. 1970's)
Russian film manager
Mandel--Soviet p148

BARBER, ALICE
See STEPHENS, ALICE BARBER

BARBER, MARGARET FAIRLESS
(1869-1901)
English poet, essayist
Showlater--Lit. p344

BARBER, MOLLY (fl. 1700's)
Amer. pioneer
Sherr--American p34

BARBIER, ELISABETH
French writer
Crosland--Women p222-223

BARBOUR, PEGGY LEE
See LEE, PEGGY

BARCA, FANNY CALDERON DE LA
(1804-)
Scottish-Spanish, wife of
diplomat
Hahner--Women p35-42

BARCELO, GERTRUDIS (-1851/
1869)
Amer. Western gambling casino
operator
Sherr--American p156
Williams--Legend. p15-23, por.

BARCHUS, ELIZA (fl. 1880's)
Amer. painter
Time--Women p112,118-119

BARCLAY, DOROTHY (1921-)
French-Amer. editor, journalist
O'Neill--Women's p722

BARCLAY, FLORENCE LOUISA
CHARLESWORTH (1862-1921)
British novelist
O'Neill--Women's p693

BARCLAY, GRACE (fl. 1776)
Amer. letter writer
Williams--Demeter's p267-268

BARCLAY, POLLY
Amer. accused criminal
Sherr--American p51

BARD, ANNE ELIZABETH
See MacDONALD, BETTY

BARDINA, SOPHIA (fl. 1870's)
Russian feminist
Mandel--Soviet p23

BARDOT, BRIGITTE (1934-)
French actress
Anderson--People p28, por.
Hirschhorn--Rating p33, por.
Jones--Rutledge p52
Keenan--Women p186,204-205,
por.
People's--Best p204-205, por.
Shipman--Internatl. p33-38, por.
Who Did What p25
Woman's Almanac p334, por.
World--Who p254

BAREKMAN, JUNE BEVERLY
TERRY (1915-)
Amer. genealogical research-
er, author
Meyer--Who's p27-28

BARI, LYNN (1913/1917-)
Amer. actress
Lamparski--What. (4) p76-77,
por.
Lamparski--What. (8) p24-25,
por.
Springer--They p24,271, por.

BARILLI-PAVLOVIC, MILENA
(1909-1945)
Yugoslavian painter
Partington--Who's p20, por.

BARISH, SHERLEE (1926-)
Amer. executive, broadcast,
personnel, aging
Scheuer--Tel. p22

BARKER, A.L. (1918-)
English novelist, short-
story writer
Baker--Women p8-9
Seymour-Smith--Novels p96

BARKER, ARIZONA CLARK ("MA")
(1871/1872-1935)
Amer. criminal, gang leader
People's Almanac (3) p337-339,
por.

BARKER, FRANCINE
See "PEACHES"

BARKER, JANE (fl. 1715-1720)
English novelist
Horner--English p29-31,102-105

BARKER, KATE ("MA") (1872-1935)
Amer. accused criminal
Woman's Almanac p501-502, por.
World--Who, p294

BARKER, MARY CORNELIA (1879-
1963)
Amer. educator, labor leader
Sicherman--Notable p50-52

BARKER, PENELOPE PAGETT (fl.
1770's)
Amer. Revolutionary War
patriot
Clyne--Patriots p8-12
Meyer--Petticoat p27-28
Sherr--American p179
Somerville--Women p18-23
Williams--Demeter's p230

BARKLEY, DEANNE (fl. 1970's-
1980's)
Amer. TV official
Adams--Women p88,103,108,132-
135,162-163,204
Scheuer--Tel. p23

BARKLEY, JANE HADLEY (c1912-
1964)
Amer., wife of Vice President
Barkley
Miller--Fishbait p320

BARLOW, ALMIRA
Amer., Brook farm subscriber
Epstein--Indiv. p85,87,94,96

BARLOW, FLORENCE E. (c1873-1909)
British pottery decorator, de-
signer
Callen--Women p61-62,67,222, por.

BARLOW, HANNAH BOLTON (c1870-
1930)
British ceramicist, sculptor
Callen--Women p222, see also
index p230, por.

BARLOW, MOLLIE (1910-)
South African physician
Hellstedt--Women p393-397, por.

BARLOW, PHYLLIDA (1944-)
British artist
Contemp. Brit. unp., por.

BARNABY, RUTH (-1765)
Amer. colonial midwife
Mead--Hist. p411

BARNARD, A.M.
See ALCOTT, LOUISA MAY

BARNARD, ANNE LINDSAY,
LADY (1750-1825)
Scottish poet, ballad writer
Avenel--Comp. (1) p35
Pearson--Who p125

BARNARD, CHARLOTTE ALLING-
TON (1830-1869)
British ballad writer
Showalter--Lit. p330

BARNARD, HANNAH JENKINS
(c1754-1825)
Amer. clergyman
James--Notable (1) p88-90

BARNARD, KATE (1875-1930)
Amer. political, social re-
former, philanthropist
James--Notable (1) p90-92
McHenry--Liberty's p20-21
O'Neill--Women's p78
Sherr--American p191
Stein--Lives p587-593, por.
Truman--Women p10,147-161,178,
198,200, por.

BARNATO, DIANA (fl. 1940's)
Amer. aviatrix
Boase--Sky's p186,189,195, por.

BARNES, BINNIE (GERTRUDE
MAUDE) (1905/1906-)
English actress
Lamparski--What. (2) p140-141,
por.
Lamparski--What. (8) p26-27,
por.
Springer--They p24,26,271,por.

BARNES, DJUNA (1892-1982)
Amer. novelist, playwright,
poet, journalist, artist
Avenel--Comp. (2) p25
Ehrlich--Oxford p106,121
Moers--Literary p108,274

Seymour-Smith--Novels p96
Seymour-Smith--Who's p29-30

BARNES, ERNESTA
Amer. banker, executive
Adams--Women p140

BARNES, FLORENCE LOW ("PANCHO")
(c1902-1975)
Amer. aviatrix, resort owner
Boase--Sky's p117,126

BARNES, JANE (fl. 1810's)
Amer. Western pioneer
Millstein--We p52-53
Sherr--American p194

BARNES, LINDA
Amer. agricultural organizer
O'Neill--Women's p8-9

BARNES, MARGARET AYER (1886-
1967)
Amer. author, critic, play-
wright
Clark--Leading p124-125
Ehrlich--Oxford p7,37,318

BARNES, MARY DOWNING SHELDON
(1850-1898)
Amer. educator
James--Notable (1) p92-93

BARNES, MAYME LEE (fl. 1960's)
Amer. hero, Carnegie Medal
Winner
O'Neill--Women's p734

BARNETT, ALICE (1886-)
Amer. composer, song-writer
Claghorn--Biog. p39

BARNETT, IDA BELL WELLS
See WELLS-BARNETT, IDA BELL

BARNETT, JOAN (fl. 1960's-1980's)
Amer. TV executive
Scheuer--Tel. p24

BARNETT, MARILYN
Amer. tennis road manager
People--Best p62, por.

BARNETT, SUSANNAH (fl. 1770's)
Amer. Revolutionary War pa-
triot
Meyer--Petticoat p178-179

BARNETTE, ANNA LATHAM
(-1948)
Amer., noted West Virginia
mother, sculptor
Amer.--Mothers p577, por.

BARNEY, NATALIE CLIFFORD
(1876-1972)
Amer.-French writer, art
patron
Brandon--Dollar p173-178,180,
por.
Crosland--Women p74-86
Rogers--Ladies, see index
p226, por.
Sicherman--Notable p52-53

BARNEY, NORA STANTON BLATCH
(1983-1971)
English-Amer. civil engineer,
architect, suffragist
Sicherman--Notable p53-55

BARNSDALL, ALICE (-1946)
Amer. theater manager,
philanthropist
Sherr--American p15

BARNSDALL, LOUISE ALINE
(1882-1946)
Amer. heiress, philanthropist
Dunlap--Calif. p10-11, por.

BARNUM, GERTRUDE (1866-1948)
Amer. social worker, labor
reformer
James--Notable (1) p93-94

BARONE, JOAN S. (fl. 1970's-
1980's)
Amer. TV news producer
Scheuer--Tel. p24

BAROT, MADELEINE
Amer. ecumenical executive
O'Neill--Women's p394

BARR, AMELIA EDITH HUDDLES-
TON (1831-1919)
Amer. novelist
James--Notable (1) p94-96

BARR, JEANNETTE
See DERBY, JANE

BARR, MARY (fl. 1940's-1970's)
Amer. Forestry Service pilot
O'Neill--Women's p26

BARRENO, MARIA ISABEL
Portuguese writer
O'Neill--Women's p727

BARRERA, OLIVA SABUCO
See SABUCO, OLIVA BARRERA

BARRETT, ELIZABETH
See BROWNING, ELIZABETH
BARRETT

BARRETT, EMMA (c1905-)
Amer. singer, pianist
Claghorn--Biog. p40
Claghorn--Jazz p31

BARRETT, JANIE PORTER (1865-
1948)
Amer. social welfare leader,
educator
James--Notable (1) p96-97
McHenry--Liberty's p21
Millstein--We p149

BARRETT, KATE WALLER (1857-
1925)
Amer., noted Georgia, Dis-
trict of Columbia mother,
philanthropist, social worker,
lecturer, feminist
Amer.--Mothers p101-102,127-128,
por.
James--Notable (1) p97-99
McHenry--Liberty's p21-22
Sherr--American p46
Woman's Almanac p379

BARRETT, MELISCENT (fl. 1770's)
Amer. patriot, Revolutionary
heroine
Meyer--Petticoat p32

BARRETT, RONA (1934-)
Amer. columnist
Anderson--People p28-29, por.
Hershey--Between p150-152
Woman's Almanac p276-277

BARRETT, SARAH
See MOULTON, SARAH BARRETT
("PINKIE")

BARRIE, WENDY (1912/1913-1978)
English actress
Lamparski--What. Annual (4,5)
p210-215, por.
Springer--They p26,271, por.

BARRIENTOS, MARIA (1883-1946)
Spanish opera singer
Tuggle--Golden p135-137

BARRINGER, EMILY DUNNING
(1876-1961)
Amer. ambulance surgeon,
gynecologist
Kulkin--Her p22-23
Marks--Women p129-140, por.
O'Neill--Women's p212

BARRON, JENNIE LOITMAN (1891-
1969)
Amer., noted Massachusetts
mother, feminist, judge,
suffragist
Amer.--Mothers p264-265, por.
Sicherman--Notable p55-56

BARROWS, ANITA (1947-)
Amer. poet
Chester--Rising p389-393, por.

BARROWS, BELLA
See BARROWS, KATHARINE
ISABEL HAYES CHAPIN

BARROWS, KATHARINE ISABEL
HAYES CHAPIN (1845-1913)
Amer. ophthalmologist, sten-
ographer, editor, reformer
James--Notable (1) p99-101

BARRY, COMTESSE DE
See DuBARRY, MARIE JEANNE
BECU, COMTESSE

BARRY, ELEANOR
Amer., book, magazine,
newspaper "collector"
Felton--Famous p166

BARRY, ELIZABETH (1658-1713)
English actress
Entertainers p78
Findlater--Player p33-39, por.
Macksey--Book p224

BARRY, TRIS SYLVIA CRUMP
(1895-1969)
Amer. artist, museum direc-
tor, film critic
Macksey--Book p209
O'Neill--Women's p670
Sicherman--Notable p56-58

BARRY, JAMES (MIRANDA) ("DR.")
(c1793-1865)
Scottish army surgeon, male
impersonator
Book--Lists (1) p339
Longford--Eminent p227-248, por.
Macksey--Book p145-146, por.
Marks--Women p73-75
Marlowe--Great p45-51, por.
Woman's Almanac p447

BARRY, JOAN (1901-)
English actress
People's Almanac (2) p760-761

BARRY, LEONORA MARIE KEARNEY
(1849-1930)
Irish-Amer. labor leader,
social reformer
Hymowitz--Hist. p244
James--Notable (1) p101-102
McHenry--Liberty's p22
O'Neill--Women's p287
Webster's--Amer. p68-69
Woman's Almanac p162,177

BARRY-LAKE, MRS.
See BARRY, LEONORA MARIE
KEARNEY

BARRYMORE, ETHEL BLYTHE
(1879-1959)
Amer. actress
Clark--Leading p15-16
Donaldson--How p23-24
Entertainers p268
Fabian--On p127-129, por.
Gilfond--Heroines p110, por.
Hazen--Interv. p85
Hirschhorn--Rating p34-35, por.
Holme--Journal p30-31, por.
Ingraham--Album p62, por.
Keylin--Hollywood p17-19, por.
Kulkin--Her p23-24
McHenry--Liberty's p24-25
Pederson--Leaders p199, por.
Sicherman--Notable p58-60
Springer--They p26,270, por.
Stoddard--Famous p48-58, por.
Warren--Pictorial p157,159
Webster's--Amer. p69
World--Who p226

BARRYMORE, GEORGIANA EMMA
DREW (1854-1893)
Amer. actress, (mother of

Ethel, Lionel, John)
James--Notable (1) p102-103
McHenry--Liberty's p23
Warren--Pictorial p157
Webster's--Amer. p69,293

BARRYMORE, THOMAS
See STRANGE, MICHAEL

BARSKAYA, M. (fl. 1930's)
Russian film producer
Mandel--Soviet p146

BARTEL, JEAN (fl. 1940's)
Amer. beauty
Lamparski--What. (5) p22, por.
Woman's Almanac p139-140

BARTELME, MARY MARGARET
(1866-1954)
Amer. judge
Sicherman--Notable p60-61

BARTHOLOMEW, SHIRLEY (fl.
1950's-1970's)
Amer. TV news director
Marzolf--Up p155

BARTIMUS, TAD (fl. 1970's)
Amer., Head Assoc. Press,
Alaska
O'Neill--Women's p470, por.

BARTLETT, ANNA WARNER (1827-
1915)
Amer. author
James--Notable (3) p543-545
McHenry--Liberty's p430-431

BARTLETT, CAROLINE JULIA
See CRANE, CAROLINE JULIA
BARTLETT

BARTLETT, FREUDE (fl. 1970's)
Amer. photography researcher
Women's--Female p125

BARTLETT, JENNIFER (1941-)
Amer. artist, painter, deco-
rator, teacher
Cur. Biog. '85 p20-23, por.
Munro--Originals p396-408, por.
Women's--Female p33

BARTO, AGNIA (1906-1981)
Russian children's writer
Mandel--Soviet p192

BARTON, CLARA HARLOWE (1821-
1912)
Amer., founder of Amer. Red
Cross, nurse
Bird--Enterprising p98-100
Bolton--Success p198-222, por.
Earnest--American p170-173
Gilfond--Heroines p32-40, por.
Hoople--As p106-107
Ingraham--Album p26, por.
James--Notable (1) p103-108
Jones--Rutledge p57
Kulkin--Her p24-26
McHenry--Liberty's p25
Macksey--Book p113,123-124, por.
Millstein--We p121, por.
O'Neill--Women's p231
Pederson--Leaders p109, por.
People's Almanac (2) p1056, por.
Reifert--Women p80
Sherr--American p46,65,91,95-96,
108-109,150,159,233-234
Signif.--Amer. p17, por.
Stoddard--Famous p59-70, por.
Warren--Pictorial p108-109, por.
Webster's--Amer. p71
Woman's Almanac p453-454, por.
World--Who p186

BARTON, ELIZABETH (c1506-1534)
English visionary
Jones--Rutledge p57

BARTON, IVY
Amer. Marine
O'Neill--Women's p533

BARTON, LUCY
English, wife of Edward
Fitzgerald
Morley--Literary p79-80

BARTON, MRS. THOMAS PENNANT
See LIVINGSTON, CORA

BARTZ, JENNY (1955-)
Amer. swimmer
Sabin--Women p63-66

BAS-COHAIN, RACHEL (fl. 1970's)
Amer. sculptor
Women's--Female p85

BASCOM, FLORENCE (1862-1945)
Amer. geologist
James--Notable (1) p108-110
McHenry--Liberty's p23-24

O'Neill--Women's p171
Sherr--American p93

BASE, IRENE
British scientific artist
Macksey--Book p209

BASHKIRTSEFF, MARIE CONSTAN-
TINOVNA, MADEMOISELLE
(1859/1861-1884)
Russian painter, diarist
Crosland--Women p34-35
Harris--Women p53,56,221,255-
257,353
Jones--Rutledge p57
Macksey--Book p205
Moffat--Revel. p46-55
Parker--Old p106-110, por.
Sparrow--Women p182,289,293,
315,por.

BASILIO, ENRIQUETA
Mexican Olympic torch
carrier
McWhirter--Guinness p106

BASKETTE, LENA
See BASQUETTE, LINA

BASKIN, LISA UNGER
Amer. artist
Women's--Female p23

BASKINS, ADA (fl. 1970's)
Russian journalist, feminist
Mandel--Soviet p213-215,218,220

BASQUETTE, LINA (1907-)
Amer. ballet dancer, actress
Lamparski--What. (4) p178-179,
por.

BASS, CHARLOTTE SPEARS
(c1880-1969)
Amer. V.P. candidate, edi-
tor, social reformer
Millstein--We p257
People's Almanac (1) p127
Sicherman--Notable p61-63

BASS, MA (fl. 1970's)
Amer. wrestler
Jordan--Broken p29-31

BASS, MARY (fl. 1770's)
Amer. colonial midwife
Mead--Hist. p486

BASS, MARY ELIZABETH (1876-1956)
Amer. physician
Sicherman--Notable p63-65

BASSE, MARIE-THERESE
Senegalese food technologist
O'Neill--Women's p40

BASSETT, FLORENCE SCHUST
KNOLL
See KNOLL-BASSET, FLORENCE
SCHUST

BASSETT, KAROLYN WELLS (1892-
1931)
Amer. composer, pianist
Claghorn--Biog. p41

BASSETT, MISS
British bookbinder
Callen--Women p192-193, por.

BASSEY, SHIRLEY (1937-)
Welsh singer
World--Who p264

BASSI, (LAURA) MARIA CATERINA
(1711-1778)
Italian physician, anatomist,
physicist, philosopher, scholar
Marks--Women p118
Mead--Hist. p508

BASSIANO, PRINCESS DI
See CAETANI, MARGUERITE,
PRINCESS

BASTIE, MARYSE (fl. 1930's)
French aviatrix
Boase--Sky's p122-123,125, see
also index p218, por.

BAT HALEVI (fl. 12th cent.)
Jewish beauty, scholar
Henry--Written p9,86-87

BAT SHEBA (VERONA) (fl. c1594)
Italian-Jewish printer
Henry--Written p118

BATCHEFF, DENISE
See TUAL, DENISE PIAZZA

BATCHELOR, JULIA (fl. 1970's)
British canoeist
McWhirter--Guinness p48

BATEHAM, JOSEPHINE ABIAH
PENFIELD CUSHMAN (1829-
1901)
Amer. temperance, Sabbata-
rian reformer
James--Notable (1) p110-111

BATEMAN, ELLEN
Amer. actress
Webster's--Amer. p73-74

BATEMAN, KATE JOSEPHINE
(1842-1917)
Amer. actress
James--Notable (1) p111-113
Jones--Rutledge p58
Webster's--Amer. p74

BATEMAN, VIRGINIA (1853-1940)
Amer., wife of Edward
Compton, mother of Sir
Compton Mackenzie & Fay
Compton
Jones--Rutledge p58

BATES, ABIGAIL (fl. 1810's)
Amer. patriot
Clyne--Patriots p112-118
Sherr--American p111

BATES, ANN (fl. 1770's)
Amer. Revolutionary British
spy
Booth--Women p243-244
DePauw--Found. p138-139

BATES, BLANCHE LYON (1873-
1941)
Amer. actress, singer
Hazen--Interv. p100
James--Notable (1) p113-114
McHenry--Liberty's p24

BATES, MRS. D.B. (fl. 1850's)
Amer. Western pioneer,
diarist, traveller
Fischer--Let p301-312
Hoople--As p65-75

BATES, DAISY LEE (1919/1922-)
Amer. civil rights worker
Kulkin--Her p27
Signif.--Amer. p57, por.

BATES, KATHERINE LEE (1859-
1929)
Amer. poet, lyricist,

hymnist, educator
Claghorn--Biog. p42
James--Notable (1) p114-115
Kulkin--Her p28
McHenry--Liberty's p24-25
Sherr--American p25,105

BATES, MERCEDES A.
Amer. food industry executive
O'Neill--Women's p524

BATES, REBECCA (fl. 1810's)
Amer. patriot
Clyne--Patriots p112-118
Sherr--American p111

BATESON, MARGARET
See MEAD, MARGARET

BATESON, MARY (1865-1906)
English historian
Macksey--Book p189

BATHERICK, MOTHER (fl. 1800's)
Amer. patriot, heroine
Williams--Demeter's p248

MATHIA(T), (ARLETTE) LEONIE
See ARLETTY

BATHORY, ELIZABETH (ERSZEBET)
(1560-1614)
Hungarian princess, accused
criminal
Macksey--Book p132
People's Almanac (1) p1338

BATHSHEBA (1040-1015 B.C.)
Biblical, wife of King David,
mother of Solomon, Israeli
queen
Jones--Rutledge p58

BATSON, FLORA BERGEN (1870-
1906)
Amer. singer
Claghorn--Biog. p42

BATSON, NANCY (fl. 1940's)
Amer. aviatrix
Keil--Those, see index p320, por.

BATTCOCK, MARJORIE
English poet
Bernikow--World p183

BATTEN, JEAN (1910-)
New Zealander aviatrix

Boase--Sky's p157-176, see also
index p218-219, por.

BATTISTELLA, ANNABEL
See FOXE, FANNE

BATTLE, KATHLEEN (1948-)
Amer. opera singer
Cur. Biog. '84 p23-26, por.

BAUCHENS, ANNE (c1881-1967)
Amer. film editor
Sicherman--Notable p65-66
Smith--Movies p18,28,41,74

BAUCK, JEANNA (1840-)
Swedish painter
Sparrow--Women p287,300-301

BAUDIER, JACQUELINE (fl. 1960's)
French TV news director
Marzolf--Up p285

BAUER, CATHERINE KROUSE
(1905-1964)
Amer. housing expert, writer
O'Neill--Women's p610
Sicherman--Notable p66-68

BAUER, CHARITA (-1985)
Amer. actress
Scheuer--Tel. p28, por.

BAUER, CLARA (-1912)
German-Amer. educator,
founder & director of
musical conservatory
Claghorn--Biog. p42

BAUER, MARION EUGENIE (1887-
1955)
Amer. composer, musicologist,
editor, critic
Claghorn--Biog. p42
Jablonski--Ency. p202-203
Sicherman--Notable p68-69

BAUERMEISTER, MARY (fl. 1970's)
Amer. sculptor
Women's--Female p85

BAUGH, LAURA (c1955-)
Amer. golfer
Hollander-100 p51-52, por.
Kulkin--Her p28-29

BAUM, VICKI (1896-1960)
Austrian-Amer. novelist

Jones--Rutledge p59
Magill--Cycl. p78-79
Neidle--America's p259-262
Seymour-Smith--Novels p97
World--Who p9

BAUMANN, FRIEDA (1887-)
Amer. physician
Hellstedt--Women p26-29, por.

BAUMANN, LOUISE BLOOM (1922-)
Amer. genealogical researcher,
writer
Meyer--Who's p29

BAUMFREE, ISABELLA
See TRUTH, SOJOURNER

BAUMGARTNER, ANN
Amer. Army aviator
Keil--Those p258-261

BAUMGARTNER, LEONA (1902-)
Amer. physician, government
official
O'Neill--Women's p227-228

BAUSCH, PINA (1940-)
German ballet dancer, director
Percival--Modern p124,126, por.

BAWDEN, NINA (1925-)
English novelist, children's
writer
Seymour-Smith--Novels p97

BAXTER, ANNE (1923-1985)
Amer. actress
Cur. Biog. '72 p25-27, por.
Hirschhorn--Rating p37-38, por.
Shipman--Internatl. p40-42, por.
World--Who p226

BAXTER, ANNETTE K.
Amer. professor
O'Neill--Women's p426

BAXTER, ANNIE WHITE (fl. 1880's-
1890's)
Amer. politician, clerk of court
Sherr--American p129

BAXTER, ELLEN (fl. 1970's-1980's)
Amer. TV director
Scheuer--Tel. p29

BAXTER, LUCY E. BARNES (1835/
1837-1902)
English art writer
Showalter--Lit. p333

BAXTER, LYDIA (1809-1874)
Amer. hymnist
Claghorn--Biog. p43

BAXTER-BIRNEY, MEREDITH (fl.
1970's-1980's)
Amer. actress
Scheuer--Tel. p29

BAY, JOSEPHINE HOLT PERFECT
(1900-1962)
Amer. financier, philanthro-
pist
McHenry--Liberty's p25
World--Who p193

BAYARD, TRYPHENA CADY (fl.
1830's)
Amer. feminist
Gurko--Ladies p65-66,149,203

BAYER, ADELE PARMENTIER
(1814-1892/1893)
Belgian-Amer. Catholic wel-
fare worker
James--Notable (1) p115-116
Neidle--America's p75-76

BAYERLE, SHIRLEY B. (fl. 1970's)
Amer. teacher, heroine,
Carnegie Medal winner
O'Neill--Women's p734

BAYES, JESSIE (1890-1934)
British woodcarver, painter,
calligrapher, illuminator,
interior decorator, gesso
worker, gilder
Callen--Women p186-187,222

BAYES, NORA (c1880-1928)
Amer. singer, actress
Claghorn--Biog. p42
James--Notable (1) p116-117
McHenry--Liberty's p25
Webster's--Amer. p75-76

BAYLIS, LILIAN MARY, DAME
(1874-1937)
English theatrical manager,
philanthropist, heroine, composer, singer
Entertainers p164

Jones--Rutledge p59-60
Macksey--Book p229-230
Who Did What p28

BAYLY, ADA ELLEN (1857-1903)
English novelist, feminist,
politican
Showalter--Lit. p340

BAYNE, BEVERLY (1895-)
Amer. actress
Lamparski--What. (2) p184-185,
por.

BAZAN, EMILIA PARDO
See PARDO-BAZAN, EMILIA

BAZELLI, MADAME
See TETRAZZINI, LUISA (MADAM
BAZELLI)

BEACH, AMY MARCY CHENEY
(1867-1944)
Amer. composer-pianist
Claghorn--Biog. p42
Jablonski--Ency. p107-108
James--Notable (1) p117-119
McHenry--Liberty's p25-26
Macksey--Book p215
Neuls-Bates--Women p223-225,245
O'Neill--Women's p635-636
Sherr--American p148

BEACH, ELIZABETH (fl. 1630's)
Amer. landowner
Williams--Demeter's p32

BEACH, ELIZABETH JANE (fl.
1860's)
Amer. Civil War witness
Millstein--We p134-135

BEACH, MRS. H.H.A.
See BEACH, AMY MARCY CHENEY

BEACH, HULDAH (fl. 1770's)
Amer. colonial midwife
Mead--Hist. p414,487

BEACH, SYLVIA WOODBRIDGE
(1887-1962)
Amer. bookseller, publisher,
art patron
Avenel--Comp. (2) p27
McHenry--Liberty's p26
Rogers--Ladies, see index p226,
por.

Sicherman--Notable p69-71
Warren--Pictorial p184

BEACHBOARD, MOLLY
See BEE, MOLLY

BEALE, BETTY (c1912-)
Amer. columnist
Woman's Almanac p277

BEALE, DOROTHEA (1831-1906)
English educator
Jones--Rutledge p60
Macksey--Book p70-71

BEALE, JO A. (fl. 1970's)
Amer. Air Force officer
O'Neill--Women's p547

BEALE, MARY (1632-1697)
English portrait painter
Fine--Women p68-69, por.
Macksey--Book p198
Petersen--Women p34-35
Sparrow--Women p57-58,81

BEAN, MAURA
Amer. research food
technologist
O'Neill--Women's p32

BEAN, MRS. WILLIAM (fl. 1770's)
Indian captive
Booth--Women p80-81

BEAR, GRACE THARPE (1868-
1959)
Amer., noted New Mexico
mother, clubwoman
Amer.--Mothers p378, por.

BEARD, DITA DAVIS (1918-)
Amer. government official
Schoenebaum--Prof. p39-41

BEARD, MARY RITTER (1876-1958)
Amer. author, historian,
feminist
Sicherman--Notable p71-73

BEARDSLEY, CAROLINE LATTIN
(1860-1944)
Amer. organist
Claghorn--Biog. p43

BEASLEY, TERESA E.
Amer. heroine, Carnegie

Medal winner
O'Neill--Women's p732

BEATRICE, SISTER
See ROGERS, ELIZABETH ANN

BEATRICE OF SAVOY (fl. c1280's)
French physician
Mead--Hist. p217-218

BEATRIX (1938-)
Netherlands queen
Current Biog. '81 p13-16, por.
O'Neill--Women's p49

BEATTIE, ANN (1947-)
Amer. novelist, lecturer
Cur. Biog. '85 p23-26, por.

BEATY, SHIRLEY
See MacLAINE, SHIRLEY

BEAUCHAMP, HERTFORD
See HERTFORD, ISABELLA,
MARCHIONESS OF

BEAUCHAMP, KATHLEEN MANS-
FIELD
See MANSFIELD, KATHERINE,
pseud.

BEAUCHAMP, MARY
See RUSSELL, ELIZABETH MARY
ANNETTE BEAUCHAMP,
COUNTESS VON ARNIM

BEAUCHAMP-PROCTOR, MARY,
LADY (-1847)
English socialite
Ware--Meet p73-74

BEAUCHARNAIS, JOSEPHINE DE
See JOSEPHINE DE BEAUCHAR-
NAIS

BEAUCLERK, DIANA, LADY (1734-
1808)
English amateur painter
Sparrow--Women p58,82

BEAUFORT, MARGARET (1443-1509)
English educator, patron,
printer
Jones--Rutledge p61
Macksey--Book p64, por.
Mead--Hist. p307,320

BEAUFOY, MRS. HENRY (c1754-
c1824)
English socialite
Ware--Meet p74

BEAUREGARD, MRS. G.T.
See VILLERE, LAURE

BEAUVAL, MME. (c1648-1720)
French actress
Entertainers p75

BEAUVOIR, SIMONE LUCIE
ERNESTINE MARIA BER-
TRAND DE (1908-1986)
French novelist, philosopher,
essayist, memoir writer
Bree--Women p53-58
Crosland--Women, see index
p249 (under Beauvoir), por.
Cur. Biog. '73 p33-36, por.
Jones--Rutledge p62
Moers--Literary p274
O'Neill--Women's p485,703,727
Prause--School p121-123
Seymour-Smith--Novels p97,
por.
Seymour-Smith--Who's p32
Who Did What p28-29
Wintle--Makers p36-37
World--Who p32

BEAUX, CECILIA (1855-1942)
Amer. portrait painter
Fine--Women p114-118
Harris--Women p56,92,251-254,
352-353
James--Notable (1) p119-121
McHenry--Liberty's p26
Macksey--Book p207
O'Neill--Women's p596-597
Sherr--American p205
Sparrow--Women p76-78,121,162
Women's--Female p5

BEAVERS, LOUISE (1902/1904-
1962)
Amer. actress
Springer--They p26-27,271, por.

BECK, HELEN
See RAND, SALLY

BECK, JOAN (fl. 1960's-1970's)
Amer. newspaperwoman,
author
O'Neill--Women's p469

BECK, MARGIT (fl. 1970's)
Amer. painter
Women's--Female p33

BECK, ROSEMARIE (1923-)
Amer. painter
Women's--Female p33

BECKE, SHIRLEY
British policewoman
Macksey--Book p138

BECKER, HELEN
See TAMIRIS, HELEN

BECKER, LYDIA (1827-1890)
English women's rights leader
Showalter--Lit. p329

BECKER, MARIA (1920-)
German actress
Entertainers p250

BECKER, MARION ROMBAUER
Amer. cookbook co-author
O'Neill--Women's p132

BECKER, PAULA MODERSOHN
See MODERSOHN-BECKER, PAULA

BECKFORD FAMILY (1780's-1800's)
English socialites
Ware--Meet p63-64,74

BECKFORD, MARGARET (1784-1819)
English, subject of portrait
Ware--Meet p63-64,74

BECKFORD, SUSAN (1786-1859)
English, subject of portrait
Ware--Meet p63-64,74

BECKLEY, ZOË (fl. 1910's)
Amer. political reporter, inter-
viewer, columnist
Marzolf--Up p43-44,48

BECU, MARIE
See DuBARRY, MARIE JEANNE
BECU, COMTESSE

BEDELIA, BONNIE (1948-)
Amer. actress
World--Who p226

BEDELL, HARRIET, DEACONESS
(fl. 1910's)

Amer., noted Florida mother,
missionary to Indians
Amer.--Mothers p116-117, por.

BEDELL, SALLY (1948-)
Amer. newspaper reporter
Scheuer--Tel. p31

BEDFORD, ANNE, DUCHESS OF
(1402-1430)
French, daughter of John
the Fearless, wife of John
Duke of Bedford
Leary--Golden p13,71

BEDFORD, DUCHESS OF (c1866-
1937)
English aviatrix
Boase--Sky's p27-44, (see also
index p219), por.

BEDFORD, SYBILLE (1911-)
German-English novelist,
essayist, biographer
Moers--Library p274
P.W.--Author p224-226,483
Seymour-Smith--Novels p98

BEDOTT, "WIDOW"
See WHITCHER, FRANCES
MIRIAM BERRY

BEE, MOLLY (1939-)
Amer. singer, actress
Claghorn--Biog. p44

BEEBE, MRS. WILLIAM
See THANE, ELSWYTH

BEECH, OLIVE ANN MELLOR
(1903-)
Amer. aircraft company
executive, industrialist
Bird--Enterprising p197-199
Macksey--Book p172
O'Neill--Women's p508,513
Woman's Almanac p181
World--Who p193

BEECHER, CATHARINE ESTHER
(1800-1878)
Amer. educator, author,
school founder
Berkin--Women p145-146
Bird--Enterprising p67-72
Boorstin--Americans p61-62,
por.

Burgess--Education p135
Ehrlich--Oxford p78,154
Hymowitz--Hist. p82,129
James--Notable (1) p121-124
Lutz--Crusade p108,246-247
McHenry--Liberty's p26-27
Macksey--Book p15,68
Sherr--American p160,249
Signif.--Amer. p10, por.
Smith--Daughters, see index p370
Sochen--Herstory p141
Time--Women p91
Warren--Pictorial p71
Webster's--Amer. p80-81
Woman's Almanac p155-156
World--Who p99

BEECHER, HARRIET
See STOWE, HARRIET BEECHER

BEECHER, JANET (1884-1955)
Amer. actress
Springer--They p27,271, por.

BEEK, ALICE D. ENGLEY (1876-)
Amer. painter, author, lec-
turer
Sherr--American p243

BEEK, ANNA
South African Salvation Army
educator
O'Neill--Women p395

BEEKMAN, CORNELIA VAN CORT-
LANDT (c1752-1847)
Amer. Revolutionary War pa-
triot, social leader
Meyer--Petticoat p96-97,144-145
Whitney--Col. p120-121, por.

BEECKMAN, MAGDALEN (-1730)
Amer. colonial, (wife of
Gerardus Beekman)
Earle--Two Cent. (1) pxvi,104,
por.

BEERS, ETHELINDA (ETHEL LYNN)
ELIOT (1827-1879)
Amer. poet, lyricist
Claghorn--Biog. p44
McHenry--Liberty's p27

BEERS, EVELYNE CHRISTINE SAUER
ANDRESSEN (1925-)
Amer. singer
Claghorn--Biog. p45

BEERS, FANNIE A. (fl. 1860's)
    Amer. Southern belle
    DeLeon--Belles p382-383, por.

BESSE, NELLI (fl. 1910's)
    German aviatrix
    Boase--Sky's p21

BEESON, CONI (fl. 1970's)
    Amer. filmmaker
    Smith--Movies p148-150,227,
    por.

BEETHOVEN, MARIA MAGDALENA
    VAN (1746-1787)
    German, mother of Ludwig
    van Beethoven
    Diagram--Mothers p23

BEETON, ISABELLA MARY MAY-
    SON (1836-1865)
    English cookery authority,
    author
    Jones--Rutledge p65
    Macksey--Book p14-15, por.
    Showalter--Lit. p332-333

BEEVERS, JANE E. (1927-   )
    English genealogical re-
    searcher, writer
    Meyer--Who's p30

BEGIN, MONIQUE (fl. 1930's-
    1970's)
    Canadian minister
    O'Neill--Women's p51

BEGTRUP, BODIL ANDREASEN
    (1903-   )
    Danish ambassador, feminist,
    U.N. delegate
    O'Neill--Women's p62

BEHN, MRS. APHRA (OR AFRA)
    (1640-1689)
    English novelist, poet,
    playwright
    Avenel--Comp. p41
    Bernikow--World p68
    Entertainers p72, por.
    Horner--English p1-8,93-98
    Jones--Rutledge p65
    Kaplan--Salt p49-50
    Kronenberger--Atlan. p45-46
    Macksey--Book p181,227
    Magill--Cycl. p89-90
    Moers--Literary p144,274

Pearson--Who p67
Seymour-Smith--Novels p98
Taylor--Gener. p49, por.
World--Who p24

BEHRENS, EDNA (fl. 1940's-1970's)
    Amer. nurse, labor leader
    O'Neill--Women's p299

BEHRENS, HILDEGARD (1937-   )
    German-Amer. opera singer
    Cur. Biog. '85 p26-29, por.

BEHRINS, HARRIET FRANCES
    (c1830-   )
    Amer. Western pioneer, writer
    Fischer--Let p27-41

BEILENSON, EDNA (1909-1981)
    Amer. printer, publisher,
    editor, designer
    O'Neill--Women's p486

BEINHORM, ELLY (fl. 1930's)
    German aviatrix
    Boase--Sky's p123, por.

BEIS, MARILYN (fl. 1970's)
    Amer. carpenter
    Seed--Saturday's p94-97, por.

BEJART, ARMANDE GRESINDE
    CLAIRE ELIZABETH (1642-
    1700)
    French actress
    Entertainers p73
    Jones--Rutledge p66
    Macksey--Book p224

BEJART, MADELEINE (1618-1672)
    French actress
    Entertainers p63
    Jones--Rutledge p66
    Macksey--Book p224

BEKHTEREVA, NATALIE (fl. 1970's)
    Russian physician
    Mandel--Soviet p100-101

BELASHOVA, ALLA (fl. 1970's)
    Russian engineer
    Mandel--Soviet p101

BELASHOVA, CATHERINE (EKAT-
    ERINA) (fl. 1960's)
    Russian sculptor

Mandel--Soviet p132-133
Women's--Female p3 supp.

BELCHER, ELIZABETH (fl. 1770's)
English-Amer. Tory
Booth--Women p67-68

BELCHER, MARJORIE CELESTE
See CHAMPION, MARGE
CELESTE

BELFER, NANCY (fl. 1970's)
Amer. textile designer
Women's--Female p19

BEL GEDDES, BARBARA (1922-)
Amer. actress
Hirschhorn--Rating p40, por.
Scheuer--Tel. p31
Shipman--Internatl. p45-46,
por.
World--Who p226

BELKIN, SOPHIA (fl. 1960's)
Russian engineer
Mandel--Soviet p192

BELKNAP, MARTHA (1895-)
Amer. community worker
Gold--Until p191-203, por.

BELL, ACTON, pseud.
See BRONTË, ANNE

BELL, BARBARA (fl. 1970's)
Amer. art teacher
Women's--Female p114

BELL, BEULAH FRAZIER (1886-)
Amer. poet, social reformer,
noted Illinois mother
Amer.--Mothers p167, por.

BELL, CAROL WILLSEY (1939-)
Amer. genealogical research-
er, author
Meyer--Who's p30

BELL, CAROLINE (fl. 1940's)
English writer
Cavanah--We p70-79

BELL, CURRER, pseud.
See BRONTË, CHARLOTTE

BELL, ELIZA GRACE SYMONDS
(1809-1897)

British, mother of Alexander
Graham Bell
Diagram--Mothers p24-27, por.

BELL, ELLIS, pseud.
See BRONTË, EMILY JANE

BELL, GERTRUDE MARGARET
LOWTHIAN (1868-1926)
English traveller, archaeolo-
gist, government official,
author, scholar, naturalist
Avenel--Comp. (1) p42
Jones--Rutledge p67
Kulkin--Her p30

BELL, HANNAH TURPIN (-1939)
Amer. tanner
Sherr--American p183

BELL, MABEL GARDNER HUBBARD
(MRS. ALEXANDER GRAHAM
BELL) (1857-)
Amer. aviation patron, noted
District of Columbia mother,
deaf
Amer.--Mothers p99, por.

BELL, MARIE (1900-)
French actress
Entertainers p213, por.

BELL, REBECCA
Amer. TV newscaster
Gelfman--Women p20-21,45,48-49,
63-65,68,71-72,94,145, por.

BELL, VANESSA (1879-1961)
English painter
Harris--Women p60-61,63,283-285,
356
Petersen--Women p106
Women's--Female p5

BELLA, BEATRICE
See "SHOPP, BE BE"

BELLAMY, CAROL (1942-)
Amer. politician
Adams--Women p103-104,111,125-
126,177

BELLAMY, MADGE (1900-)
Amer. actress
Springer--They p27,271, por.

BELLAMY, MARY GODOT
    Amer. state legislator
    Sherr--American p256

BELLANCA, DOROTHY JACOBS
    (1894-1946)
    Latvian-Amer. union or-
        ganizer
    James--Notable (1) p124-126
    McHenry--Liberty's p27-28
    Neidle--America's p161,165-166
    O'Neill--Women's p296

BELLE, JENNIE JORDAN (fl.
    1860's)
    Amer. teacher
    Sherr--American p7

BELLINA, MADONNA (fl. 16th
    cent.)
    Jewish entertainer
    Henry--Written p128

BELLON, YANNICK (fl. 1940's-
    1950's)
    French editor, director
    Smith--Movies p118

BELLOWS, CAROLE KAMIN (fl.
    1950's-1970's)
    Amer. lawyer, rights advo-
        cate
    Swiger--Women p15-31

BELMONT, ALVA SMITH
    See VANDERBILT, ALVA
        ERTSKU SMITH BELMONT
        HAZARD

BELMONT, CAROLINE SLIDELL
    PERRY (fl. 1840's-1850's)
    Amer. socialite, daughter
        of Commodore Perry
    Birmingham--Grandes p225-226

BELMONT, ELEANOR ELISE
    ROBSON (1879-1979)
    English-Amer. actress,
        philanthropist, socialite,
        author, nurse
    Birmingham--Grandes, see
        index p288, por.
    Cur. Biog. '80 p450

BELLWOOD, BESSIE (1860-1896)
    English singer
    Entertainers p147

BELOFF, LEAH NORAH (fl. 1940's)
    English journalist
    Macksey--Book p190

BELOTE, MELISSA (1956-)
    Amer. swimmer
    Hollander--100 p87-89, por.
    Ryan--Sports p106-127, por.
    Stambler--Women p84-94, por.

BELOVA, ELENA
    Russian fencer
    O'Neill--Women's p560

BEMBO, ANTONIA (c1670-)
    Italian singer, composer
    Macksey--Book p211

BEMIS, LALU LATHOY (c1853-1933)
    Amer.-Chinese dancer, Western
        pioneer
    Sherr--American p56-57, por.

BENARIO-PRESTES, OLGA (1908-
    1942)
    German, Nazi victim
    Partington--Who's p28

BENAYAHU, MIRIAM (fl. 14th cent.)
    Jewish scribe
    Henry--Written p115

BENDEN, ALICE (fl. 1500's)
    English religious martyr
    Bainton--France p219

BENDER, KATIE (fl. 1870's)
    Amer. accused criminal
    Time--Women p179

BENDL, GERTA
    Amer., noted Kentucky
        mother, community worker,
        politician
    Amer.--Mothers p219-220, por.

BENEDICT, CRYSTAL EASTMAN
    See EASTMAN, CRYSTAL

BENEDICT, RUTH FULTON (1887-
    1948)
    Amer. anthropologist, edu-
        cator, author
    Ingraham--Album p67
    James--Notable (1) p128-131
    McHenry--Liberty's p28-29
    Macksey--Book p154

Moers--Literary p208,274
Moffat--Revel. p148-162
O'Neill--Women's p145
Signif.--Amer. p57, por.
Webster's--Amer. p87
Who Did What p32
Woman's Almanac p361
World--Who p93

BENEDICTA, MOTHER
See RIEPP, BENEDICTA,
MOTHER

BENEDUM, CAROLINE SOUTH-
WORTH (1869-1900)
Amer. pioneer, noted West
Virginia mother
Amer.--Mothers p574

BENERITO, RUTH R.
Amer. cotton chemist
O'Neill--Women's p31,89,165

BENGIS, INGRID (fl. 1970's)
Amer. novelist
Moers--Literary p274

BENGLIS, LYNDA (fl. 1970's)
Amer. sculptor
Women's--Female p85

BENGTSON, HERTHA (1917-)
Swedish industrial chemist
O'Neill--Women p273

BENGTSSON, ANNY (1918-)
Danish labor union leader
O'Neill--Women p320-321

BENHAM, EDITH
See HELM, EDITH BENHAM

BENHAM, GERTRUDE (fl. 1900's)
British walker
Macksey--Book p241, por.

BENINCASA, CATERINA (1347-
1380)
Italian Patron Saint
Macksey--Book p106

BENITEZ, HELENA Z. (fl. 1930's-
1960's)
Filipino home economist,
educator
O'Neill--Women's p105

BENJAMIN, ANNA (-1902)
Amer. war reporter
Marzolf--Up p27-28

BEN JOSEPH, ROJY (HANANEL)
(fl. 1960's)
Bulgarian-Israeli dress
designer
O'Neill--Women's p246

BENNANI, RABEA
Moroccan dress designer, TV
performer
O'Neill--Women's p252

BENNEDSEN, DORTE (fl. 1950's-
1960's)
Danish clergyman, chaplain
O'Neill--Women's p57

BENNETT, ALICE (1851-1925)
Amer. physician, hospital
superintendent
James--Notable (1) p131-132
O'Neill--Women's p203

BENNETT, BELLE HARRIS (1852-
1922)
Amer. missionary, church
worker
James--Notable (1) p132-134
McHenry--Liberty's p29
Sherr--American p80

BENNETT, BETTY (fl. 1950's)
Amer. youngest solo pilot
Macksey--Book p252

BENNETT, CONSTANCE (c1904-1965)
Amer. actress
Keylin--Hollywood p32, por.
Mordden--Movie, see index p291,
por.
Shipman--Gold. p55-58, por.
Springer--They p27-29,271, por.
World--Who p227

BENNETT, ERNA (1925-)
Irish wheat researcher,
genetic conservationist
O'Neill--Women's p39

BENNETT, JOAN (1910-)
Amer. actress
Hirschhorn--Rating p43-44, por.
Shipman--Gold. p58-60, por.

Springer--They p30,271, por.
Wilson--Holly. p116-119, por.
World--Who p227

BENNETT, JOYCE (fl. 1970's)
English priest
O'Neill--Women's p381

BENNETT, KATE (c1818-1855)
Amer. beauty
Sherr--American p133

BENNETT, KAY (fl. 1920's)
Amer. Indian writer
Fisher--Third piv,45-48

BENNETT, LEILA (fl. 1920's-
1930's)
Amer. actress
Springer--They p31,272, por.

BENNETT, MARY KATHARINE
JONES (1864-1950)
Amer. church, mission
leader
James--Notable (1) p134

BENNETT, SANDY (c1940-)
Amer., wife of Tony Bennett
Funt--Are p27-37, por.

BENNICH, AGATHE (fl. 1970's)
painter
Women's--Female p33

BENNY, MRS. JACK
See LIVINGSTONE, MARY

BENOIST, MARIE GUILLEMINE
(1768-1826)
French painter
Fine--Women p54-55
Harris--Women p48-50,209-210,
349
Munsterberg--Hist. p48-49
Petersen--Women p60-61

BENOIT, JEHANE (fl. 1950's-
1970's)
Canadian cookbook author,
TV, radio performer
O'Neill--Women's p133

BENSON, HELEN
See GARRISON, HELEN ELIZA
BENSON

BENSON, IVY
British band leader, manager
Macksey--Book p219-220, por.

BENSON, LUCY WILSON (1927-)
Amer. government official
O'Neill--Women's p96

BENSON, MARGARET (1)
Amer. 4-H scholarship winner
O'Neill--Women's p21

BENSON, MARGARET (2) (fl. 1970's)
Amer. chemist, professor,
feminist, writer
Sochen--Movers p22,262

BENSON, SALLY (SARA) SMITH
(1900-1972)
Amer. novelist, short-story
writer
Cur. Biog. '72 p459
Ehrlich--Oxford p358
World--Who p10

BENSON, STELLA (1892-1933)
English novelist
Avenel-Comp. (1) p44-45
Seymour-Smith--Novels p100
Seymour-Smith--Who's p39

BENTHAM-EDWARDS, MATILDA
(1836-1919)
English novelist
Showalter--Lit. p333

BENTLEY, ELIZABETH PETTY
(1945-)
Amer. genealogical researcher,
author, indexer
Meyer--Who's p31

BENTLEY, HELEN DELICH (1923-)
Amer. government official,
newspaperwoman
Cur. Biog. '71 p35-37, por.
Macksey--Book p131
O'Neill--Women's p461-462, por.

BENTLEY, PHYLLIS ELEANOR
(1894-)
English novelist
Avenel--Comp. (1) p45-46
Crosland--Beyond p108,123-124,
127-128
Showalter--Lit. p348

BENTON, BONNIE
    Amer. bowler
    McWhirter--Guinness p43

BENTON, LOANZA GOULDING
    Amer. missionary
    Smith--Daughters p196-198

BENTON, SUZANNE (fl. 1970's)
    Amer. sculptor
    Women's--Female p85

BENZELL, MIMI (1923-1970)
    Amer. opera singer
    Claghorn--Biog. p47

BEN-ZVI, MINA
    Russian-Israeli agricultural
    training director
    O'Neill--Women's p7

BERCKMAN, EVELYN (1900-   )
    Amer. pianist, composer,
    writer
    Claghorn--Biog. p47

BERCOVITZ, HELEN
    Amer. home bakery owner
    O'Neill--Women's p139

BERENGARIA, QUEEN (fl. 1200's)
    English queen, wife of Al-
    fonso IX of Leon, Spanish
    physician
    Mead--Hist. p176,219
    Softly--Queens p22-23

BERENSON, MARISA (1946-   )
    Amer. model, actress
    Anderson--People p44-45

BERENSON, SENDA (1868-1954)
    Lithuanian-Amer. sports-
    woman
    McHenry--Liberty's p29

BERETTA, CATERINA
    Italian ballet dancer, teacher
    Migel--Ballerinas p263

BEREZOVSKAYA, S.
    Russian feminist
    Mandel--Soviet p68-69

BERG, EDITH (fl. 1900's)
    Amer., early plane passenger
    Keil--Those p68-69

BERG, EVA
    Norwegian NATO nurse
    O'Neill--Women's p552-553

BERG, GERTRUDE (1899-1966)
    Amer. actress, radio & screen
    writer, producer
    Lewis--Prime p217-218
    McHenry--Liberty's p29-30
    Sicherman--Notable p73-74
    World--Who p227
    Women--Radio p5

BERG, MRS. HART O.
    Amer., early airplane passen-
    ger
    Woman's Almanac p369

BERG, ILENE AMY (fl. 1970's-
    1980's)
    Amer. executive producer,
    TV films
    Scheuer--Tel. p35

BERG, KARIN WESTMAN (1914-   )
    Swedish feminist
    O'Neill--Women's p426

BERG, PATRICIA JANE (PATTY)
    (1918-   )
    Amer. golfer
    Hollander--100 p40,42-43,48, por.
    McHenry--Liberty's p30
    McWhirter--Guinness p69-70, por.
    Pachter--Champ. p142-143, por.
    People's Almanac (1) p1182-1183
    Woman's Almanac p419
    World--Who p210

BERG, SIGRUN (1901-   )
    Norwegian textile artist
    O'Neill--Women's p273

BERGANZA, TERESA (1935-   )
    Spanish singer
    Cur. Biog. '79 p28-30, por.
    Gammond--Illus. p237, por.

BERGE, CAROL (1928-   )
    Amer. poet
    Avenel--Comp. (2) p32

BERGEN, CANDICE (1946-   )
    Amer. actress
    Anderson--People p45-46, por.
    Current Biog. '76 p26-29, por.
    Hirschhorn--Rating p45-46, por.
    World--Who p227

BERGEN, POLLY (1930-   )
    Amer. singer, actress,
    cosmetician
    100--Greatest (1) p70, por.
    World--Who p227

BERGER, MARILYN
    Amer. TV news correspondent
    Scheuer--Tel. p35

BERGER, VIVIAN
    Amer. lawyer
    O'Neill--Women's p363

BERGERE, OUIDA (-1974)
    Amer. actress, film writer
    Smith--Movies p17

BERGERY, BETTINA JONES (fl.
    1930's)
    Amer. fashion designer
    Keenan--Women p70,72, por.

BERGMAN, INGRID (1915-1982)
    Swedish actress
    Anderson--People p47-48, por.
    Book--Lists (2) p255
    Cur. Biog. '82 p460
    Fallaci--Ego. p51-62
    Hirschhorn--Rating p46-47, por.
    Jones--Rutledge p73
    Manchel--Women p64,69, por.
    Mordden--Movie, see index p291
    O'Neill--Women's p653-654,659
    People's Almanac (2) p761-762,
       por.
    Sat. Eve. Post--Movie p17-18,
       por.
    Shipman--Gold. p62-67, por.
    Springer--They p31,272, por.
    Wilson--Holly. p126-130, por.
    Woman's Almanac p334-335, por.
    World--Who p227

BERGMAN, STEPHANIE (1944-   )
    English abstract artist (fab-
    ric)
    Parker--Old p78-79, fig. 46

BERGMANN, AVA (fl. 1970's)
    Amer. socialite, designer
    O'Neill--Women's p250-252

BERGNER, ELISABETH (1898/
    1900-   )
    Austrian actress
    Entertainers p213

Shipman--Gold. p67-68, por.
Springer--They p32,272, por.

BERIOSOVA, SVETLANA (1932-   )
    Russian-English ballet dancer
    World--Who p74

BERK, ANN (fl. 1970's)
    Amer. TV advertising manager,
    writer
    Kelver--Women p47-48,58-60,92-
    93, por.
    O'Neill--Women's p506
    Scheuer--Tel. p37

BERKELEY, ELLEN PERRY
    Amer. architectural writer
    O'Neill--Women's p610

BERKELEY, FRANCES, LADY (fl.
    1630's-1690's)
    English-Amer., wife of colonial
    governor
    James--Notable (1) p135-136

BERKOWITZ, JOAN B.
    Amer. research & physical
    chemist
    O'Neill--Women's p170

BERLE, RUTH (fl. 1980's)
    Amer., wife of Milton Berle
    Funt--Are p39-49, por.

BERLIAWSKY, LOUISE
    See NEVELSON, LOUISE

BERLIN, KATHY (fl. 1970's)
    Amer. publicist
    Adams--Women p54,102,106,137-138
    Hershey--Between p131-132

BERLING, NATHANELLA SODERGREN
    (1885-   )
    Swedish-Amer., noted Texas
    mother, church worker
    Amer.--Mothers p514, por.

BERMAN, ARIANE R. (fl. 1970's)
    Amer. painter & plastic artist
    Women's--Female p33

BERMAN, AVIS
    Amer. writer, editor
    O'Neill--Women's p436-438

BERMAN, SARA MAE (fl. 1970's)
Amer. track and field athlete
Hollander--100 p139-140

BERMUDEZ, MARION
Amer. boxer
O'Neill--Women's p559

BERNADETTE OF LOURDES, SAINT
(1844-1879)
French saint, visionary
Donaldson--How p33
Fry--1000 p234
Green--Saints p45-47
Jones--Rutledge p75
Kulkin--Her p30-31
Palmer--Who's p47
Who Did What p33
World--Who p85-86

BERNARD, CAROLINE RICHINGS
(1827-1882)
English-Amer. singer,
teacher, composer
Claghorn--Biog. p48-49

BERNARD, JACQUELINE (1921-)
French-Amer., club founder,
journalist
O'Neill--Women's p722-723

BERNARD, JESSIE (1903-)
Amer. writer, editor, pro-
fessor
M.I.T.--Women p163-182
O'Neill--Women's p417

BERNARD, ROSINE
See BERNHARDT, SARAH

BERNARDINA, MOTHER
See MATHEWS, ANN TERESA

BERNASCONI, IRENE (fl. 1960's)
Argentinian hydrographic
(Antarctica) research
scientist
Land--New p21

BERNHARD, RUTH (1905-)
German-Amer. photographer
Mitchell--Recol. p30-47,199-200,
por.

BERNHARDT, SARAH (1844-1923)
French actress
Book--Lists (2) p213-214,273

Brecher--Lifes p337
Coffin--Female p177-190, por.
Donaldson--How p33-35, por.
Entertainers p133
Fry--1000 p268, por.
Holme--Journal p64-65, por.
Jones--Rutledge p76-77
Kulkin--Her p32
Macksey--Book p227-228, por.
Manchel--Women p24-26, por.
May--Different p119-152, por.
New York Times--Great p14-15,
por.
O'Neill--Women's p655
People's Almanac (1) p863, por.
People's Almanac (2) p425,1147,
por.
Taylor--Gener. p56, por.
Who Did What p34
World--Who p254

BERNHEIM, NICOLE (fl. 1970's)
French economic writer,
journalist
Marzolf--Up p281-282

BERNSTEIN, ALINE FRANKAU
(1880/1882-1955)
Amer. theatrical designer,
author
McHenry--Liberty's p30-31
Sicherman--Notable p74-76

BERNSTEIN, BERNICE LOTWIN
Amer. government official
O'Neill--Women's p86,89

BERNSTEIN, INA
Amer. TV executive
Scheuer--Tel. p39

BERNSTEIN, JANICE (1931-)
Amer. activist
Seifer--Nobody p88-134, por.

BERNSTEIN, JODY
Amer. lawyer, government
official
Adams--Women p142-144,164

BERRY, ETHEL BUSH (fl. 1890's)
Alaskan "gold rush belle"
Jones--Women (1) p101-105

BERRY, HARRIET MOREHEAD
(1877-1940)
Amer. civic worker, economic

resources expert
James--Notable (1) p136-137
Scott--Southern p117-118
Sherr--American p178,180-181,
por.

BERRY, LOIS M. (1911-)
Amer. genealogical research-
er, writer
Meyer--Who's p31

BERRY, MARTHA McCHESNEY
(1866-1942)
Amer. educator, foundress,
philanthropist
Burgess--Education p47-69, por.
James--Notable (1) p137-138
Kulkin--Her p33-34
McHenry--Liberty's p31
Sherr--American p49-50

BERRY, MARY (1763-1852)
English author, letter writer
Moers--Literary p125,274

BERRY, MARY FRANCES (1938-)
Amer. government, education
official (HEW)
O'Neill--Women's p410

BERRY, RACHEL B. ALLEN
(1859-)
Amer. state legislator,
noted Arizona mother
Amer.--Mothers p28-29, por.

BERRY, SUZANNE
Amer. labor leader
O'Neill--Women's p315

BERSSENBRUGGE, MEI-MEI
(1947-)
Chinese-Amer. writer
Fisher--Third p ix,560

BERTEAUT, SIMONE (1923-)
French biographer
P.W.--Author p227-229,484

BERTELS, THOMAS MORE,
SISTER
Amer. religious agriculturist
O'Neill--Women's p391

BERTHA, QUEEN (fl. c1126)
Turkish builder of hospital,
school
Mead--Hist. p168,176

BERTHAGYTA (-616)
English Abbess, physician
Mead--Hist. p100

BERTHILDIS, ABBESS (-680)
French, wife of Clovis II
Mead--Hist. p99

BERTHOLLE, LOUISETTE (COMTESSE
DE NALECHE)
French cookbook writer
O'Neill--Women's p133

BERTIN, ROSE (MARIE-JEANNE)
(1744-1813)
French fashion expert
Earle--Two Cent. (2) p559,745
Macksey--Book p265
O'Neill--Women's p234-235

BERTINELLI, VALERIE (1960-)
Amer. actress
Scheuer--Tel. p40

BERTOLACCINI, SILVIA (fl. 1970's)
Amer. golfer
McWhirter--Guinness p76

BERTOZZI, PATRICIA (fl. 1970's)
Amer. filmmaker, feminist
Smith--Movies p227, por.

BERTSCH, MARGUERITE (fl. 1910's)
Amer. film director
Slide--Early p103-105

BERURIAH (fl. 1210's-1280's)
German intellectual, feminist
Fink--Great p10-17
Henry--Written p9-10,44-47,54-58

BERVOETS, MARGUERITE (1914-
1944)
Belgian professor, spy
Macksey--Book p59

BESANT, ANNIE WOOD (1847-1933)
English theosophist, Indian
political leader
Jones--Rutledge p79
Longford--Eminent p129-150, por.
Macksey--Book p39,116,155
Palmer--Who's p48-49
Showalter--Lit. p337
World--Who p86

BESANZONI, GABRIELLA (1888-1962)
Italian opera singer

Tuggle--Golden p155-156, por.

BESHAR, CHRISTINE
Amer. Wall Street executive
O'Neill--Women's p357

BESPALOVA-MIKHALEVA, TAMARA
NIKOLAEVNA (fl. 1970's)
Russian ceramicist
Women's--Female p5, supp.

BESS, MINA
Amer. TV entertainer
Lewis--Prime p46-51,56-57, por.

BESSARABOVA, NATALIA NANOVNA
(1895-)
Russian ceramicist
Women's--Female p2, supp.

BESSERER, EUGENIE (fl. 1920's)
Amer. actress
Macksey--Book p234

BEST, EDNA (1900-1974)
English-Amer. actress
Cur. Biog. '74 p454
Springer--They p32,272, por.

BETANCOURT, ANA (fl. 1850's)
Cuban feminist, patriot
O'Neill--Women's p643
                    ι
BETHELL, MARY URSULA (1874-
1945)
New Zealander poet
Avenel--Comp. (1) p47-48
Seymour-Smith--Who's p43

BETHUNE, CYNTHIA (fl. 1970's)
Amer. TV graphic artist
Klever--Women p56,70-72,95,
108, por.

BETHUNE, JOAN (fl. 1840's)
British, college founder
Macksey--Book p72

BETHUNE, JOANNA GRAHAM
(1770-1860)
Amer. charity, Sunday
School leader
James--Notable (1) p138-140
Woman's Almanac p390

BETHUNE, LOUISE BLANCHARD
(1856-1913)
Amer. architect
James--Notable (1) p140-141
McHenry--Liberty's p31
Macksey--Book p166
O'Neill--Women's p608
Reader's--Story p436

BETHUNE, MARY McLEOD (1875-
1955)
Amer. college founder, educa-
tor, government official, noted
Florida mother
Adams--Great (3rd) p120, por.
Amer.--Mothers p104-105,113-114,
por.
Burgess--Education p111-134,
por.
Gilfond--Heroines p53-56, por.
Kostman--20th p21-33
Kulkin--Her p34-35
Longstreet--Queen p191
McHenry--Liberty's p31-32
Millstein--We p232
O'Neill--Women's p405
Pederson--Leaders p197, por.
Richardson--Great p184-194, por.
Sherr--American p39,43,212
Sicherman--Notable p76-80
Signif.--Amer. p38, por.
Stoddard--Famous p71-80, por.
Taylor--Gener. p44-45, por.
Toppin--Biog. p255-256
Warren--Pictorial p201-202, por.
Webster's--Amer. p97
Woman's Almanac p156-157, por.
World--Who p99

"BETSY THE BLACKSMITH"
See PRATT, ELIZABETH ("HAN-
DY BETSY")

BETT, MUM (fl. 1810's)
Amer. colonial painter
Petersen--Women p64-65

BETTERTON, MARY SAUNDERSON
(c1637-1710/1712)
English actress
Findlater--Player p20-22

"BETTINA," pseud. (fl. 1950's)
French model
Keenan--Women p108-109,121-122,
por.

BETTINGEN, BURTON GREEN
Amer. millionaire
Forbes-400 ('84) p124

BETTIS, VALERIE ELIZABETH
(1919-1982)
Amer. ballet dancer,
choreographer
Current Biog. '82 p460

BEVERIDGE, HORTENSE (fl.
1950's-1970's)
Amer. artist, writer, filmmaker
Smith--Movies p150-151,227

BEVERLY, PAT (fl. 1940's)
Amer. aviatrix
Boase--Sky's p186, por.

BEVERLY, TREVIA WOOSTER
(1931-)
Amer. genealogical researcher, writer, indexer
Meyer--Who's p31-32

BEVIER, ISABEL (1860-1942)
Amer. home economics
educator
James--Notable (1) p141-142
McHenry--Liberty's p32

BEYER, CLARA MORTENSON
(1892-)
Amer. government official
O'Neill--Women's p332
Ware--Beyond p145, see also
index p197

BHATIA, SHARJU PANDIT (1907-)
East Indian physician
Hellstedt--Women p348-353, por.

BIANCO, MARGERY WILLIAMS
(1881-1944)
Amer. children's book author
James--Notable (1) p142-144

BIANCOLELLI, CATERINA
(c1665-1716)
Italian actress
Entertainers p78

"BIBA"
See HULANICKI, BARBARA

BIBESCO, MARIE, PRINCESS
Roumanian-French author
Crosland--Women p110-112

BICE, AMY HAMADA (fl. 1970's)
Amer. sculptor
Women's--Female p85

BICKERDYKE, MARY ANN BALL,
("MOTHER") (1817-1901)
Amer. noted Illinois mother,
Civil War nurse, social reformer
Amer.--Mothers p161, por.
Bird--Enterprising p92-93
Hymowitz--Hist. p142
James--Notable (1) p144-146
Kulkin--Her p36-37
McHenry--Liberty's p32-33
Macksey--Book p149, por.
Millstein--We p121
Reifert--Women p80
Sherr--American p62
Sochen--Herstory p163-164, por.
Warren--Pictorial p108-109, por.
Woman's Almanac p453

BIDDLE, ADELE
Amer. diarist
Earnest--American p68-71

BIDDLE, ELLEN McGOWAN (fl.
1900's)
Amer. Western pioneer, author
Fischer--Let p124-136

BIDDLE, KATHERINE GRAHAM
CHAPIN (1890-1978)
Amer. poet
Cur. Biog. '84 p468

BIDDLE, REBECCA (fl. 1770's)
Amer. Revolutionary War
patriot
Ingraham--Album p14

BIEIRIS DE ROMANS (fl. 13th cent.)
French troubadour
Bogin--Women p133,176-177

BIESELE, ANNA EMMA JOHN (1888-)
Amer., noted Texas mother,
church, civic worker
Amer.--Mothers p515, por.

"BIG SISTER"
See MATTHEWS, GRACE

BIGART, ALICE WEEL (fl. 1940's)
Amer. radio & TV writer,
producer
Marzolf--Up p157

BIGGS, CAROLINE ASHURST
(1840-1889)
English women's rights
activist, journalist
Showalter--Lit. p335

BIGLER-ENGGENBERGER,
MARGRIT (fl. 1970's)
Swiss federal judge
Macksey--Book p129

BIGLEY, ELIZABETH
See CHADWICK, CASSIE I.

BIGOTTINI, EMILIE (1784-1858)
Italian ballet dancer
Migel--Ballerinas p93-111, por.

BIHERON, MLLE. (1730-)
French anatomist, medical
sculptor
Mead--Hist. p492

BILDERS, MARIE PHILIPPINE
VAN BOSSE, MADAME
(1837-1900)
Netherlands painter
Sparrow--Women p262,267,269,
272

BILLINGS, GRACE BEDELL
Amer., Lincoln "correspon-
dent" who suggested beard
Sherr--American p74
Woman's Almanac p52

BILLINGSLEY, BARBARA
Amer. TV actress
Lamparski--What. (3) p28-29,
por.

BILLINGTON, DORA (fl. 1900's)
British potter, ceramicist
Callen--Women p70

BINGAY, ROBERTA GIBB (c1942-)
Amer. track & field athlete
Hollander--100 p139, por.

BINGER, VIRGINIA McKNIGHT
Amer. millionaire
Forbes-400 ('84) p149

BINGHAM, AMELIA (1869-1927)
Amer. actress
McHenry--Liberty's p33

BINGHAM, ANN(E) WILLING
(1764-1801)
Amer. hostess, social leader
Earnest--American p38-44
James--Notable (1) p146-147
McHenry--Liberty's p33-34
Sherr--American p202-203

BINGHAM, EULA (fl. 1950's-1970's)
Amer. government official
O'Neill--Women's p340

BINGHAM, MARIA (c1784-)
Amer. member of "Republican
Court"
Earnest--American p41,43

BINGHAM, MILLICENT TODD (1880-
1968)
Amer. geographer, author,
conservationist, educator
Cur. Biog. '69 p464

BINGHAM, ROSE (fl. 1930's)
English socialite
Keenan--Women p44, por.

BINH, NGUVEN THI (1927-)
Vietnamese government official
O'Neill--Women's p60-61

BIRD, ADA (1859-)
Amer. musician
Sherr--American p252

BIRD, ALICE
Amer. P.E.O. co-founder
O'Neill--Women's p427, por.

BIRD, CAROLINE MAHONEY (1915-)
Amer. historian, lecturer, equal
rights activist
Cur. Biog. '76 p39-42, por.
Hymowitz--Hist. p315,372
O'Neill--Women's p417-418

BIRD, ISABELLA LUCY
See BISHOP, ISABELLA LUCY
BIRD

BIRD, NANCY (fl. 1930's)
Australian aviatrix
Boase--Sky's p131,134-136, por.

BIRD, ROSE ELIZABETH (1936-)
Amer. judge, state chief justice

Cur. Biog. '84 p26-29, por.
Dunlap--Calif. p17, por.
Lamson--In p185-218, por.
O'Neill--Women's p372
Woman's Almanac p523
World--Who p135

"BIRD WOMAN"
See SACAJAWEA

BIRDSEYE, CLARISSA STEIN
(1834-)
Amer., noted Oregon mother,
pioneer
Amer.--Mothers p445-447, por.

BIRGE, PRISCILLA
Amer. artist
Women's--Female p23

BIRGITTA
See BRIDGET, SAINT, OF
SCANDINAVIA

BIRJANDI, PARVIN (fl. 1950's)
Iranian, University Dean of
Women
Macksey--Book p77

BIRKENRUTH, MISS
British bookbinder
Callen--Women p196

BIRNEY, ALICE McLELLAN (1858-
1907)
Amer., noted Georgia mother,
organization founder, child
welfare worker
Amer.--Mothers p128-129, por.
James--Notable (1) p147-148
O'Neill--Women's p110
Sherr--American p49

BIRSTEIN, ANN (fl. 1970's)
Amer. novelist, story-writer
Moers--Literary p274

BISCOT, JEANNE, (ARRAS)
(1601-1664)
French nurse
Mead--Hist. p418

BISHOP, ANNA RIVIERE (1810-
1884)
English singer
Claghorn--Biog. p51
James--Notable (1) p148-150

BISHOP, BERNICE PAUAHI (1831-
1884)
Amer. Hawaiian high chieftess,
philanthropist, school founder
James--Notable (1) p150
Sherr--American p54

BISHOP, BRIDGET (-1692)
Amer. tavern keeper, accused
witch
Sherr--American p54
Taylor--Gener. p27
Williams--Demeter's p140

BISHOP, ELIZABETH (1911-1979)
Amer. poet
Avenel--Comp. (2) p34
Brinnin--Modern p35-41, por.
Cur. Biog. '77 p60-63, por.
Cur. Biog. '79 p458
Ehrlich--Oxford p31
McCullough--People p20-22
McHenry--Liberty's p34
Moers--Literary p274
O'Neill--Women's p615,680,688
Wintle--Makers p50,52-53

BISHOP, EVELYN (c1840-1926)
Amer. settlement school
leader
O'Neill--Women's p123

BISHOP, GWENDOLYN
British jewelry designer
Callen--Women p162

BISHOP, HARRIET E. (1817-1883)
Amer. teacher
James--Notable (1) p151-152
Sherr--American p122

BISHOP, HAZEL GLADYS (1906-)
Amer. industrial chemist,
manufacturer
McHenry--Liberty's p34
World--Who p193

BISHOP, ISABEL (1902-)
Amer. artist
Cur. Biog. '77 p63-66, por.
Fine--Women p205-208
Harris--Women p64,325-326,360-
361
Henkes--Eight p26-29,55-56
McCullough--People p22-24
Munro--Originals p145-153, por.
Women's--Female p33

BISHOP, ISABELLA LUCY BIRD
(1831/1832-1904)
English explorer, travel
writer, hospital founder
Hamalian--Ladies p169-184
Hoople--As p77-79
Macksey--Book p238
O'Neill--Women's p471
Sherr--American p28,52
Showalter--Lit. p331

BISHOP, MRS. SAMUEL (fl. 1770's)
Amer. Revolutionary War
patriot
Earle--Two Cent. (2) p xv,
por.

BISMARCK, LOUISE WILHELMINE
MENCKEN VON (1790-)
Prussian, mother of Otto
Von Bismarck
Diagram--Mothers p30-32, por.

BISSELL, ANNA (-1934)
Amer. executive
O'Neill--Women's p510

BISSELL, EMILY PERKINS (1861-
1948)
Amer. social welfare worker,
antisuffragist, (TB stamp
initiator)
James--Notable (1) p152-153
Sherr--American p37
World--Who p186

BISSET, JACQUELINE (1944/
1946-)
English actress
Anderson--People p49, por.
Current Biog. '77 p66-68, por.
Hirschhorn--Rating p48-49, por.
World--Who p227

BITAR, SALAH EDDIN (1912-1980)
Syrian foreign minister,
prime minister
Current Biog. '80 p450

BITKER, MARJORIE (1901-)
Amer. newspaper writer,
editor
Gold--Until p147-166, por.

BITTENBENDER, ADA MATILDA
COLE (1848-1925)
Amer. lawyer, suffragist,

temperance leader
James--Notable (1) p153-154
Sherr--American p141

BITTER, ADRIANA SCALAMANDRE
(1934-)
Amer. textile designer
O'Neill--Women's p276-277

BITTERMAN, KATHLEEN STUDDAR
(1916-)
Amer. economist, statistician,
government official
O'Neill--Women's p24

BITTERS, JEAN RAY LAURY
(1928-)
Amer. embroidery crafts-
woman, author
O'Neill--Women's p130

BIXBY-SMITH, SARAH (fl. 1870's-
1900's)
Amer. writer
Fischer--Let p247-259

BIZALION, ANNE CATHERINE,
SISTER
French-Amer. Dominican mis-
sionary
O'Neill--Women's p392

BIZE-LEROY, LALOU, MADAME
(c1934-)
French vineyard head
O'Neill--Women's p6

BJERREGAARD, MRS. RITT (fl.
1970's)
Danish education minister,
textbook writer
O'Neill--Women's p57

BJORQUIST, KARIN (1927-)
Swedish ceramicist
O'Neill--Women's p273

BLACHE, ALICE GUY (1873/1875-
1968)
French-Amer. film director
O'Neill--Women's p666
Slide--Early p13-32, por.
Smith--Movies p2-10, por.

BLACHE, SIMONE (fl. 1970's)
Amer. film writer
Smith--Movies p3-7

BLACK, CLARA BELLE (fl. 1900's)
Amer. Western casino operator
Sherr--American p183, por.

BLACK, JEANNETTE (1878-1952)
Amer., wife of Frank Norris
Starr--Amer. p198,262-264, por.

BLACK, JINNY (fl. 1970's)
Amer. painter
Women's--Female p33

BLACK, JOYCE M. (fl. 1940's-
1970's)
Amer., president of "Big
Brothers, Inc."
O'Neill--Women's p120

BLACK, KAREN BLANCHE ZIEGLER
(1942-)
Amer. actress
Anderson--People p50
Cur. Biog. '76 p42-45, por.
Hirschhorn--Rating p49-50, por.
People's Almanac (2) p1156
World--Who p227

BLACK, MAXENE
Amer. TV correspondent
Scheuer--Tel. p44

BLACK, NELLIE PETERS (1851-
1919)
Amer., noted Georgia mother,
agriculturalist, church, civic
leader, Southern kindergarten organizer
Amer.--Mothers p126, por.
Scott--Southern p158

BLACK, SHIRLEY TEMPLE (1928-)
Amer. child actress, noted
California mother, Ambassa-
dor, politician
Amer.--Mothers p58-59
Anderson--People p50-51
Banner--Women p162-163
Claghorn--Biog. p433
Current Biog. '70 p36-39, por.
Dunlap--Calif. p201, por.
Edelson--Kids p2,10-16,20,53,
por.
Hazen--Interv. p419-420
Hirschhorn--Rating p360-361,
por.
McHenry--Liberty's p407-408
Mordden--Movie p6,62,130,195-

196,205
100--Greatest (1) p110, por.
O'Neill--Women's p40,94-95
Sat. Eve. Post--Movie p140, por.
Shipman--Gold. p530-533, por.
Signif.--Amer. p76, por.
Springer--They p238,333, por.
Webster's--Amer. p1026
Wilson--Holly. p46-48, por.
Woman's Almanac p53, por.
Women's--Female p34
World--Who p250

BLACK, WINIFRED SWEET (1863-
1936)
Amer. journalist
Dunlap--Calif. p117, por.
James--Notable (1) p154-156
McHenry--Liberty's p34-35
Marzolf--Up p33-34
O'Neill--Women's p439-440
Sherr--American p19
Woman's Almanac p265-266

"BLACK SWAN"
See GREENFIELD, ELIZABETH
TAYLOR

BLACKADDER, ELIZABETH (1931-)
British artist
Contemp. Brit. unp., por.

BLACKBURN, HELEN (1842-1903)
Irish feminist, editor, writer
Macksey--Book p84

"BLACKFOOT INDIAN" WIFE (fl.
1835)
Amer. Indian
Hoople--As p49-51

BLACKFORD, MARY BERKELEY
MINOR
Amer., Southern slavery re-
former
Scott--Southern p51-52

BLACKMAN, WINIFRED (-1950)
British anthropologist
Macksey--Book p240-241

BLACKSHEAR, SUE (fl. 1970's)
Amer. portrait painter
Women's--Female p34

BLACKTON, PAULA (fl. 1910's)
Amer. director
Slide--Early p107-108

BLAGOEVA, VELA (1858-1921)
Hungarian revolutionary
Partington--Who's p37

BLAI(C)KLEY, CATHERINE
(c1695-1771)
Amer. colonial midwife
DePauw--Found. p41
Williams--Demeter's p172

BLAINE, ANITA EUGENE McCOR-
MICK (1866-1954)
Amer. philanthropist
Sicherman--Notable p80-83

BLAINE, CATHERINE (fl. 1850's)
Amer. teacher, Western
pioneer
Sherr--American p240-241
Time--Women p52

BLAINE, NELL (1922-)
Amer. painter
Munro--Originals p261-271, por.
Women's--Female p34

BLAIR, ARLENE (fl. 1970's)
Amer. textile artist
Women's--Female p98

BLAIR, MRS. EMILY NEWELL
(c1877-1951)
Amer. magazine associate
editor, feminist, politician,
government official
Hazen--Interv. p295
Sochen--Movers p146-147
Ware--Beyond p145, see also
index p198
Woman's Almanac p552-553

BLAIR, HANNAH MILLIKAN
Amer. Quaker, Revolutionary
War patriot
Sherr--American p180

BLAIR, JANET (1921-)
Amer. singer, actress
Claghorn--Biog. p53

BLAIR, KATHLEEN
Amer. musical composer
Sherr--American p82

BLAIR, MRS. L.C.
Amer. Southern prison re-
former
Scott--Southern p148

BLAIR, LINDA (1959-)
Amer. actress
Anderson--People p51-52
World--Who p227

BLAIR, MINNIE NICHOLS (1886-)
Amer., noted Nevada mother,
turkey rancher, restaurant
operator
Amer.--Mothers p351, por.
Sherr--American p143

BLAIS, MARIE CLAIRE
Canadian novelist
Moers--Literary p274

BLAKE, AMANDA (1931-)
Amer. actress
World--Who p227

BLAKE, KATHY (fl. 1960's)
Amer. tennis player
McWhirter--Guinness p163

BLAKE, LILLIE DEVEREUX (1833/
1835-1913)
Amer. feminist, author, social
reformer
James--Notable (1) p167-169
McHenry--Liberty's p37

BLAKE, MARIE (fl. 1920's-1930's)
Amer. actress
Springer--They p32-33,272, por.

BLAKE, MARY JANE SAFFORD
See SAFFORD, MARY JANE
(JOANNA)

BLAKE-ALVERSON, MARGARET
(1836-1923)
Amer. singer
Neuls-Bates--Women p131-134

BLAKE-BROWN, CHARLOTTE
AMANDA
See BROWN, CHARLOTTE
AMANDA BLAKE-

BLAKER, ELIZA ANN COOPER
(1854-1926)
Amer. kindergarten educator
James--Notable (1) p169-170

BLAKLEY, RONEE (c1946-)
Amer. actress, singer
People--Best p56-57, por.

BLALOCK, JANE (1945-   )
Amer. golfer
Woman's Almanac p419
World--Who p210

BLALOCK, MALINDA (SAM) (fl.
1860's)
Amer. soldier, male impersonator
Warren--Pictorial p109

BLAMAUER, KAROLINE
See LENYA, LOTTE

BLANC, SOPHIE, MADAME (fl.
1890's)
French pioneer aeronaut
Macksey--Book p246, por.
Smith--Daughters p207,224,260-
261,266-267

BLANCHAN, NELTJE
See DOUBLEDAY, NELTJE
BLANCHAN DE GRAFF

BLANCHARD, MADAME (-1819)
French balloonist, pioneer
aeronaut
Macksey--Book p246, por.

BLANCHARD, MARIA (1881-1932)
French painter
Women's Female p5

BLANCHARD, PHYLLIS (1895-   )
Amer. child psychologist
Showalter--These p105-109

BLANCHARD, THERESA WELD
See WELD, THERESA

BLANCHE OF CASTILE (1187/1188-
1252)
French queen, founder of
hospital, mother of Louis IX
Giles--Women p97-119, por.
Mead--Hist. p176,217,230,232,
270

BLANCHFIELD, FLORENCE ABY
(1884-1971)
Amer. U.S. Army nurse,
officer
Cur. Biog. '71 p460
McHenry--Liberty's p37
Sicherman--Notable p83-85

BLAND, DORIS ELLEN (1934-   )
Amer. genealogical researcher,
author
Meyer--Who's p33

BLAND, EDITH NESBIT
See NESBIT, EDITH

BLAND, MARTHA DANGERFIELD
(fl. 1770's)
Amer. Revolutionary patriot
Booth--Women p273-274

BLANDICK, CLARA (1880-   )
Amer. actress
Springer--They p33,272, por.

BLANDING, SARAH GIBSON (1898-
1985)
Amer. educator, social scien-
tist, college president
Cur. Biog. '85 p461
Webster's--Amer. p110

BLANE, SALLY (1910-   )
Amer. actress
Lamparski--What. (3) p186-187,
por.
Lamparski--What. (8) p30-31,
por.
Springer--They p33,272, por.

BLANK, BLANCHE
Amer., college vice-president
Adams--Women p119, 140-142

BLANKENBURG, LUCRETIA M.
LONGSHORE (1845-1937)
Amer. suffragist, club leader,
civic reformer
James--Notable (1) p170-171

BLANKENSHIP, BETTY
Amer. policewoman
O'Neill--Women's p373

BLANKERS-KOEN, FRANCINA
("FANNY") (1918-   )
Netherlands track & field
athlete
Assoc. Press--Pursuit p169-171,
por.
Hollander--100 p7,120-121, por.
McWhirter--Guinness p173, por.
O'Neill--Women's p573,575
People's Almanac (1) p1192
Woman's Almanac p425-426
World--Who p210

BLANKS, LILY FAULKNER (1856-
c1942)
Amer., noted Louisiana
mother, community worker
Amer--Mothers p229

BLATCH, HARRIOT EATON STAN-
TON (1856-1940)
Amer. feminist, lecturer
Clark--Leading p55-56
Hymowitz--Hist. p275,278
James--Notable (1) p172-174
McHenry--Liberty's p37-38
Millstein--We p177-178,211-212
Warren--Pictorial p160-161,163

BLATCHFORD, ELLEN C. (1900-)
Canadian physician
Hellstedt--Women p223-225, por.

BLATT, JOSEPHINE (1869-1923)
Amer. athlete, weight-lifter
Felton--Famous p273
Macksey--Book p258
McWhirter--Guinness p185

BLAU, GERDA (fl. 1900's)
Austrian-British agricultural
commodity expert
O'Neill--Women's p39

BLAU-LANG, TINA (1845/1847-
1916)
Austrian painter
Sparrow--Women p288,306,308

BLAUVERT, LILLIAN EVANS (1873-
1947)
Amer. singer
Claghorn--Biog. p54

BLAVATSKY, HELENA HAHN
PETROVNA (1831-1891)
Russian co-founder of
Theosophical Society, editor
Book--Lists (2) p290
Fry--1000 p243
James--Notable (1) p174-177
Jones--Rutledge p86
McHenry--Liberty's p38-39
Macksey--Book p116
May--Different p81-104, por.
Neidle--America's p67-70
People's Almanac (1) p16
Who Did What p37-38
World--Who p86

BLAZEJEWSKI, CAROL ("BLAZE")
(1956-)
Amer. basketball player
Gurtman--More p102-121, por.

BLEECKER, ANN(A) ELIZA (1752-
1783)
Amer. colonial poet, novelist
Booth--Women p130-131
Ehrlich--Oxford p170
James--Notable (1) p177-178

BLEGEN, JUDITH (1941-)
Amer. singer
Cur. Biog. '77 p69-72, por.

BLEIBTREY, ETHELA (fl. 1920's)
Amer. swimmer
Assoc. Press--Pursuit p81,83,
101, por.

BLENCOWE, AGNES
British embroiderer
Callen--Women p103-104

BLESSINGTON, MARGUERITE
POWER, COUNTESS (1789-
1849)
Irish author, salonist
Jones--Rutledge p86
Moers--Literary p176,275
Smith--Women p43-81

BLETTER, DIANA (c1958-)
Amer. letter-writer
Baum--Jewish p258-260

BLEVINS, RUBYE
See MONTANA, PATSY

BLEWETT, M. HILDRED (fl. 1950's-
1960's)
Canadian physicist
O'Neill--Women's p184

BLEY, CARLA BORG (1938-)
Amer. pianist, composer
Claghorn--Biog. p54-55

BLIND, MATHILDE COHEN (1841-
1896)
English-German poet
Kaplan--Salt p159-161, por.
Showalter--Lit. p335

BLISS, ANNA ELVIRA (1843-1925)
Amer. educator in South Africa
James--Notable (1) p607-610

BLISS, LIZZIE PLUMMER (1864-
1931)
Amer. art collector, philan-
thropist, museum co-founder
James--Notable (1) p178-179
Sherr--American p170

BLITCH, IRIS FAIRCLOTH (1912-)
Amer. congresswoman
Chamberlin--Min. p249-251
Miller--Fishbait p68

BLIVEN, KAREN, BARONESS
See DINESEN, ISAK, pseud.

BLOCH, SUZANNE (1907-)
Swiss musician
Neidle--America's p241-242,
245-248, por.
O'Neill--Women's p634

BLOCK, JOANNA (1650-1715)
Netherlands painter, glass-
engraver
Macksey--Book p198-199

BLODGET, REBECCA (fl. 1790's)
Amer. socialite
Earle--Two Cent. (2) p xxi,
por.

BLODGETT, FERN (fl. 1940's)
Canadian, ship wireless
operator
O'Neill--Women's p551

BLODGETT, KATHARINE BURR
(1898-1979)
Amer. research physicist,
chemist
Current Biog. '80 p450
O'Neill--Women's p180

BLONDELL, JOAN (1909-1979)
Amer. actress
Higham--Celeb. p58-63, por.
Mordden--Movie, see index
p291, por.
Shipman--Gold. p68-71, por.
World--Who p227

"BLONDIE"
See HARRY, DEBBIE (DEBORAH)

"BLOOD COUNTESS"
See BATHORY, ELIZABETH
(ERSZEBUT)

"BLOODY MARY"
See MARY I

BLOOM, CLAIRE (1931-)
English actress
Jones--Rutledge p87
Shipman--Internatl. p53-56, por.
World--Who p255

BLOOM, HELENE C. (fl. 1970's)
Amer. organization executive
director
O'Neill--Women's p517

BLOOM, SARA (1900-)
Amer. octogenarian
Gold--Until p219-229, por.

BLOOM, URSULA (c1898-)
English novelist
Macksey--Book p291, por.
People's Almanac (3) p545
Seymour-Smith--Novels p102

BLOOMER, AMELIA JENKS (1818-
1894)
Amer. feminist, social reform-
er, noted Iowa mother
Amer.--Mothers p185, por.
Hymowitz--Hist. p103, por.
Ingraham--Album p34, por.
James--Notable (1) p179-181
Jones--Rutledge p87
Levenson--Women p41, 44
Longstreet--Queen p57, por.
McHenry--Liberty's p39
Macksey--Book p266
Marzolf--Up p221-224
Millstein--We p73
O'Neill--Women's p236
Papachristou--Women p20,41,43-
46, por.
People's Almanac (1) p87-88, por.
Reiffert--Women p148-150
Sherr--American p70,140,175
Signif.--Amer. p17, por.
Smith--Daughters p125,127-128,
224
Sochen--Herstory p83,114,360
Stein--Lives p359-374, por.
Warren--Pictorial p135
Webster's--Amer. p113
Who Did What p38
Woman's Almanac p132
World--Who p186

BLOOMFIELD-MOORE, CLARA
SOPHIA JESSUP
See MOORE, CLARA SOPHIA
JESSUP

BLOOMFIELD-ZEISLER, FANNY
(1863-1955)
Silesian-Amer. pianist
Claghorn--Biog. p56
James--Notable (3) p705-707
McHenry--Liberty's p461

BLOOR, ELLA REEVE (1862-1951)
Amer. political radical, suf-
fragist, journalist, labor
organizer
McHenry--Liberty's p39-40
Sicherman--Notable p85-87

"BLOSSOM DEARIE" (fl. 1950's-
1970's)
Amer. singer
Balliet--Amer. p118-129

BLOUNT, BARBARA (fl. 1800's)
Amer., first coed
Sherr--American p217-218

BLOW, SANDRA (1926-   )
English artist
Contemp. Brit. unp., por.

BLOW, SUSAN ELIZABETH (1843-
1916)
Amer. educator, founder of
first public school kinder-
garten
Burgess--Education p136
James--Notable (1) p181-183
McHenry--Liberty's p40
Sherr--American p133
Snyder--Dauntless p57-85, por.

BLUE, MIRIAM
Amer. columnist
Woman's Almanac p279

BLUE, VIRGINIA NEAL (1910-   )
Amer., noted Colorado
mother, realtor, state official
Amer.--Mothers p71-72, por.

BLUM, ARLENE (fl. 1970's)
Amer. mountain climber
Lichtenstein--Mach. p14-26,
30-32

BLUM, BARBARA DAVIS (fl. 1970's)
Amer. government official,
social worker, environmentalist
O'Neill--Women's p87

BLUM, JUNE (fl. 1970's)
Amer. painter
Women's--Female p34

BLUM, MARIE ELIZABETH (1743-
1817)
Moravian widow
DePauw--Rem. p76, por.

BLUME, CLAIRE
See BLOOM, CLAIRE

BLUME, JUDY SUSSMAN (1938-   )
Amer. novelist
Current Biog. '80 p17-20, por.
World--Who p10

BLUMENAU, LILI (1912-1976)
German-Amer. textile artist
O'Neill--Women's p269

BLUME-SILVERSTEIN, ELIZABETH
(1892-   )
Amer. lawyer
O'Neill--Women's p352

BLUMHAGEN, HELEN M. (1922-   )
Amer. genealogical researcher,
writer
Meyer--Who's p34

BLUNSCHY-STEINER, ELIZABETH
(1922-   )
Swiss government official
O'Neill--Women's p50

BLUNT, ANN, LADY (1840-1922)
English writer, traveller
Hamalian--Ladies p134-145

BLUNT, KATHARINE (1876-1954)
Amer. chemist, college administrator, educator nutritionist
Sicherman--Notable p87-88

BLY, NELLIE, pseud. (1867-1892)
Amer. journalist
Banner--Women p36-37, por.
Boorstin--Americans p52, por.
Ehrlich--Oxford p211-212

James--Notable (3) p253-255
Kulkin--Her p39-40
Longstreet--Queen p87-91, por.
McHenry--Liberty's p374-375
Macksey--Book p190
Marzolf--Up p23-24
Millstein--We p169-170
O'Neill--Women's p x,439, por.
People's Almanac (1) p88-89,200,
  por.
People's Almanac (2) p379
Reifert--Women p180-183
Sherr--American p199
Webster's--Amer. p929
Woman's Almanac p264,273-274,
  por.
World--Who p294

BLYTH, ANN(E) (1928-)
  Amer. actress, singer
  Shipman--Internatl. p56-58, por.
  Wilson--Holly. p68-70, por.
  World--Who p227

BLYTH, MYRNA (fl. 1980's)
  Amer. magazine editor
  Hershey--Between p185,231

BLYTHE, BETTY (1903-1972)
  Amer. actress
  Lamparski--What. (3) p182-183,
    por.
  Mordden--Movie p5

BLYTON, ENID MARY (1897-1968)
  English children's writer
  Macksey--Book p192
  O'Neill--Women's p748
  People's Almanac (3) p545

BOADICEA (-62 A.D.)
  British Queen of Iceni,
  heroine
  Canning--100 p140-145
  Fraser--Heroines p97-102, por.
  Fry--1000 p46-47
  Jones--Rutledge p88
  Macksey--Book p49-50, por.
  Taylor--Gener. p18-19
  Trease--Seven p30-45
  Who Did What p39
  Woman's Almanac p445

BOARDMAN, ELEANOR (1898-)
  Amer. actress
  Springer--They p34,272, por.

BOARDMAN, MABEL THORP (1860-
  1946)
  Amer. Red Cross executive,
  nurse
  James--Notable (1) p183-186
  McHenry--Liberty's p40-41
  O'Neill--Women's p737
  Sherr--American p42

BOARDMAN, SARAH HALL
  See JUDSON, SARAH HALL
    BOARDMAN

BOATMAN, JANET
  Amer. archer
  O'Neill--Women's p558

BOCCHI, DOROTHEA (-1436)
  Italian, professor of medicine,
  moral philosophy
  Macksey--Book p63
  Marks--Women p51

BOCHKARYOVA (fl. 1910's)
  Russian soldier
  Mandel--Soviet p41,45

BOCKER, DOROTHY (fl. 1920's)
  Amer. physician, feminist
  Hymowitz--Hist. p296-297

BOCZON, MARY ANN (1941-)
  Amer. genealogical researcher,
  writer
  Meyer--Who's p34

BODARD, MAG (fl. 1960's-1970's)
  French film producer
  Smith--Movies p123

BODE, BARBARA
  Amer. Children's Foundation
  president
  O'Neill--Women's p37

BODE, MARION (fl. 1970's)
  Amer. craftswoman
  Women's--Female p19

BODENHEIM, NELLY
  Netherlands artist
  Sparrow--Women p12,72,262,292,
  332

BODICEA
  See BOADICEA

BODICHON, BARBARA LEIGH-
SMITH (1827-1891)
English artist, educator,
editor, feminist, college
founder, philanthropist
Basch--Relative, see index p347
Fine--Women p80-81
Macksey--Book p71-72,83
Showalter--Lit. p329
Smith--Movies p203,274

BODLEY, RACHEL LITTLER (fl.
1870's)
Amer. chemist, toxicologist,
botanist
Bolton--Success p149-174, por.
James--Notable (1) p186-187

BODLEY, ELIZABETH CLARK (fl.
1770's-1780's)
Amer. Quaker, town founder
Sherr--American p153

BODZIONY, GILL TODD (1953-)
Amer. genealogical researcher,
author
Meyer--Who's p34-35

BOE, SISSEL CATHERINE FINSETH
(1874-)
Amer. musical, religious
worker, noted South Dakota
mother
Amer.--Mothers p497-498, por.

BOELTE, MARIA
See KRAUS-BOELTE, MARIA

BOGAERT, SARAH RAPELJE
BERBER (1625/1685-1700)
Amer. pioneer
Williams--Demeter's p51

BOGAN, LOUISE (1897-1970)
Amer. poet
Avenel--Comp. (2) p36
Brinnin--Modern p42-45, por.
Chester--Rising p34-37, por.
Kaplan--Salt p273-274
McHenry--Liberty's p41
Moers--Literary p167,275
Sicherman--Notable p88-90

BOGARDUS, ANNETJE JANS
(1638-1661/1663)
Netherlands-Amer. midwife,
businesswoman

Mead--Hist. p415
Neidle--America's p9

BOGART, JENNEY
Amer., wife of Elliott Gould
Book--Lists (2) p252

BOGGS, CORINNE ("LINDY")
(1916-)
Amer. congresswoman
Keil--Those p310-315, por.
Miller--Fishbait p220
O'Neill--Women's p75
Woman's Almanac p469-470
World--Who p135

BOGGS, JEAN SUTHERLAND (1922-)
Canadian museum director
O'Neill--Women's p614-615
Women's--Female p117

BOGGS, LETTIE VAUGHN (1885-
1971)
Amer. community worker,
noted Delaware mother
Amer.--Mothers p87, por.

BOGLE, SARAH COMLY NORRIS
(1870-1932)
Amer. pioneer librarian
James--Notable (1) p187-188

BOHANNON, GRETE M.
Austrian-Amer. WAF, surveyor
O'Neill--Women's p542

BOHEN, HALCYONE H.
Amer. university dean
O'Neill--Women's p406

BOHLE, GEORGIA (1916-)
Amer. genealogical researcher,
writer
Meyer--Who's p35

BOHN, CAROLE
Amer. Catholic religious leader
Proctor--Women p158-160

BOHNER, BLYTH
Amer. artist
Women's--Female p101

BOHRER, FLORENCE FIFER (1877-
1960)
Amer. state senator, noted
Illinois mother

Amer.--Mothers p165,
por.

BOIKOVA, ANNA
Russian mayor
Mandel--Soviet p292-293

BOILLET, COLETTE (1381-1447)
French nun
Macksey--Book p106

BOISDECHINES, JOSEPHINE
(1831-)
Swiss circus freak
Entertainers p127

BOISSEVAIN, EDNA
See MILLAY, EDNA ST.
VINCENT

BOISSEVAIN, INEZ MILHOLLAND
(1886-1916)
Amer. lawyer, feminist,
journalist
Banner--Women p113-114,116-
117, por.
Clark--Leading p57-58
Hymowitz--Hist. p280
James--Notable (1) p188-190
Sherr--American p40,164,173

BOIT, ELIZABETH EATON (1849-
1932)
Amer. textile manufacturer
James--Notable (1) p190-191
O'Neill--Women's p509

BOIVIN, (MARIE) ANNE VICTOIRE
GILLAIN, MADAME (1773-
1841)
French midwife, obstetrician,
translator, medical writer
Marks--Women p68-69
Mead--Hist. p497,500-501

BOJOXHILL, AGNES GONXHA
See TERESA, MOTHER (1)

BOK, MARY LOUISE CURTIS
See ZIMBALIST, MARY LOUISE
CURTIS BOK

BOKYO, ELIZABETH
Austrian-Israelite agricultural
researcher
Macksey--Book p167

BOLAND, MARY (1880-1965)
Amer. actress
Hazen--Interv. p409
Springer--They p34,36,272-273,
por.

BOLAND, VERONICA B. (c1899-)
Amer. congresswoman
Chamberlin--Min. p159

BOLDAO Y CASTILLA, MARIA
MARGUERITE GUADELUPE
See "MARGO"

BOLDEN, DOROTHY (1920-)
Amer. domestic, activist
O'Neill--Women's p304
Seifer--Nobody p136-177, por.

BOLEN (BOLIN), LIN
Amer. TV newscaster
Gelfman--Women p160
Scheuer--Tel. p49

BOLEYN, ANNE (1507-1536)
English queen, mother of
Queen Elizabeth
Diagram--Mothers p74-75, por.
Donaldson--How p38-39
Jones--Rutledge p23
Pearson--Who p63
People's Almanac (3) p601-602
Softly--Queens p60-63, por.
Vance--Six p38-76
Who Did What p149-150, por.
World--Who p155

BOLIN, JANE MATILDA (1908-)
Amer. judge
Signif.--Amer. p58, por.

BOLING, YVETTE GUILLOT (1938-)
Amer. genealogical researcher,
indexer, writer
Meyer--Who's p35

BOLIVAR, MARIA CONCEPCION
PLACIOS Y VIANCO (1759-
1792)
Venezuelan, mother of Simón
Bolívar
Diagram--Mothers p33

BOLLAND, ADRIENNE (fl. 1910's)
French airplane pilot
Macksey--Book p247

BOLLING, MARY TABB (fl. 1860's)
  Amer. Southern belle
  DeLeon--Belles p436, por.

BOLLING, SUSANNA
  Amer. Revolutionary War
  heroine
  Sherr--American p235

BOLTON, DUCHESS OF
  See FENTON, LAVINIA,
  DUCHESS OF BOLTON

BOLTON, FRANCES PAYNE
  BINGHAM (c1885-1977)
  Amer. congresswoman
  Chamberlin--Min. p128-137, por.
  Cur. Biog. '77, p459
  Miller--Fishbait p65-67,348
  O'Neill--Women's p69
  U.S.--Women (89th) p5, por.
  U.S.--Women (90th) p3, por.
  Woman's Almanac p470

BOLTON, ISABEL, pseud.
  See MILLER, MARY BRITTON

BOLTON, SARAH (1814-1893)
  Amer., noted Indiana mother,
  state librarian, poet, social
  reformer
  Amer.--Mothers p175, por.
  James--Notable (1) p191-192
  Sherr--American p65-66,68, por.

BOLTZ, MAUDE (fl. 1970's)
  Amer. sculptor
  Women's--Female p86

BOMBECK, ERMA (1927-)
  Amer. columnist, author
  Anderson--People p54
  Cur. Biog. '79 p39-42, por.
  McHenry--Liberty's p41-42
  O'Neill--Women's p456, por.
  Scheuer--Tel. p49-50, por.
  World--Who p50

BONA DEA
  Roman goddess
  Pomeroy--Godd. p210

BONAPARTE, ELIZABETH (MRS.
  JEROME)
  See PATTERSON, ELIZABETH
  (BONAPARTE)

BONAPARTE, JOSEPHINE (1763-
  1814)
  French empress, wife of
  Napoleon I
  Kulkin--Her p42

BONAPARTE, (MARIA) LETIZIA
  RAMOLINO (1750-1836)
  French, mother of Napoleon
  Bonaparte
  Diagram--Mothers p174-179, por.
  People's Almanac (3) p492-494,
  por.

BONAPARTE, MARIE (1882-1962)
  French psychoanalyst
  O'Neill--Women's p413

BONAVITA, ROSE (ROSINA) (1921-)
  Amer. actress
  Lamparski--What. Annual (4,5)
  p268-272, por.

BOND, ANNA
  Amer. TV newscaster
  Gelfman--Women p159-160

BOND, CARRIE JACOBS (1862-1946)
  Amer. song-writer, composer,
  author, publisher, noted
  Wisconsin mother
  Amer.--Mothers p583, por.
  Claghorn--Biog. p58
  Jablonski--Ency. p112
  James--Notable (1) p194-196
  McHenry--Liberty's p42
  Macksey--Book p215
  People's Almanac (1) p898-899
  People's Almanac (2) p807
  Sherr--American p18,248

BOND, LILIAN (1910-)
  English actress
  Springer--They p36,273, por.

BOND, VICTORIA (1949-)
  Amer. conductor, composer
  LePage--Women p1-12, por.

BONDFIELD, MARGARET GRACE
  (1873-1953)
  British cabinet member, labor
  leader
  Fry--1000 p299
  Jones--Rutledge p92
  Macksey--Book p38

O'Neill--Women's p284,319,343
Vallance--Women, see index p207
Who Did What p41

BONDI, BEULAH (1892-1981)
Amer. actress
Lamparski--What. (4) p98-99,
por.
Lamparski--What. (8) p32-33,
por.
Springer--They p36-38,273, por.

BONDS, MARGARET (1913-1972)
Amer. pianist, composer
Claghorn--Biog. p58

BONDURANT, MRS.
Amer. Civil War patriot
Sherr--American p86

BONDY, BEULAH
See BONDI, BEULAH

BONFANTI, MARIE (1847-1921)
Italian ballet dancer
James--Notable (1) p196-197

BONFILS, WINIFRED SWEET BLACK
See BLACK, WINIFRED SWEET

BONGARTZ, EMMA (c1889-)
Swedish-Amer. teacher
Gold--Until p335

BONHAM-CARTER, VIOLET,
BARONESS ASQUITH OF
YARNBURY (1887-1969)
British politican
Jones--Rutledge p92

BONHEUR, ROSA (1822-1899)
French painter
Fine--Women p57-60, por.
Harris--Women p53,57-58,87,
223-225,249,349-350
Kulkin--Her p43
Macksey--Book p204-205
Munsterberg--Hist. p49-53
Parker--Old p35,37, fig. 24
Petersen--Women p74-78, por.
Sparrow--Women p180-181,195,
205,209-210,214-215
Taylor--Gener. p60-61, por.
Tufts--Our p146, por.
Woman's Almanac p220, por.
Women's--Female p5

BONNAY, MARCHIONESS DU (fl.
18th cent.)
French botanist, writer
Mead--Hist. p494

BONNER, KATHERINE (1849-)
Amer. writer
Sherr--American p126

BONNER, SHERWOOD, pseud.
See McDOWELL, KATHARINE
SHERWOOD BONNER

BONNEY, ANNE (1700-1720)
Irish pirate
Macksey--Book p133-134, por.
Woman's Almanac p498-499

BONNEY, MARY
See RAMBAUT, MARY LUCINDA

BONNEY, THERESE (1894/1895-
1978)
Amer. photographer, author,
journalist
McHenry--Liberty's p43
O'Neill--Women's p442-443

"BONNIE BLUE BUTLER"
See KING, CAMMIE

BONNIN, GERTRUDE SIMMONS
(c1875-c1936)
Amer. Indian, reformer,
teacher, author
Gridley--Amer. p81-87, por.
Hoople--As p163-166
James--Notable (1) p198-200
Stein--Fragments unp.

BONNY, ANNE
See BONNEY, ANNE

BONO, CHER
See "CHER"

BONOW, RAYSA R. (fl. 1970's)
Amer. TV producer
Klever--Women p20-21,62,103,105
Marzolf--Up p177

BONSIGNORI, MILI (fl. 1950's-1970's)
Amer. film editor
O'Neill--Women's p496

BONSTELLE, JESSIE (1871-1932)
Amer. actress, theatrical

producer
Chinoy--Women p4,106, por.
James--Notable (1) p200-202
McHenry--Liberty's p43-44
Macksey--Book p227

BONTECOU, LEE (1931-)
Amer. sculptor
Munro--Originals p377-387, por.
Munsterberg--Hist. p97,101-103
O'Neill--Women's p605
Women's--Female p86

BOODSON, ALISON (1925-)
English poet
Bernikow--World p176

BOOKER, LILLIE (-1891)
Amer. Southern belle
DeLeon--Belles p214-215, por.

BOOKER, SUE (fl. 1960's-1970's)
Amer. film director
Smith--Movies p151-152,228,
por.

BOOLE, ELLA ALEXANDER (1858-
1952)
Amer. social reformer
Sicherman--Notable p91-92

BOONE, CHERRY (fl. 1980's)
Amer., daughter of Pat
Boone
People--Best p238, por.

BOONE, DEBBIE (1956-)
Amer. singer
Anderson--People p54-55, por.

BOONE, JEMIMA (c1762-?)
Amer. pioneer, Indian cap-
tive, (daughter of Daniel
Boone)
Sherr--American p78

BOONE, MAGGIE AUGUSTA
(1867-?)
Amer., noted Maryland mother,
clubwoman
Amer.--Mothers p252

BOONE, REBECCA B. (1739-1813)
Amer. frontierswoman, wife
of Daniel Boone
Coffin--Parade p247
Kulkin--Her p45

BOOT, MRS. JOE
See HART, PEARL

BOOTH, AGNES (1841-1910)
Australian-Amer. actress
James--Notable (1) p202-203

BOOTH, ALICE LYNN (fl. 1960's-
1970's)
Amer. newspaperwoman
O'Neill--Women's p45

BOOTH, MRS. BALLINGTON
Amer. co-general of Volun-
teers of America
Hazen--Interv. p72

BOOTH, CATHERINE MUMFORD
(1829-1890)
English clergyman, "Mother"
of Salvation Army
Macksey--Book p113
O'Neill--Women's p395

BOOTH, ELLEN WARREN SCRIPPS
(1863-1943)
Amer. philanthropist
James--Notable (1) p203-204

BOOTH, EVANGELINE CORY (1865-
1950)
English-Amer. Salvation Army
executive, orator, musician,
poet
James--Notable (1) p204-207
Kulkin--Her p46
McHenry--Liberty's p44-46
Macksey--Book p113
Neidle--America's p76,79-84, por.
O'Neill--Women's p395
People's Almanac (1) p1276-1277
Warren--Pictorial p166
World--Who p186-187

BOOTH, HEATHER
Amer. feminist, co-founder
women's caucus, activist
O'Neill--Women's p704

BOOTH, JOYCE
British Parliament member
Vallance--Women p62,69,74,81,
108,178

BOOTH, MARGARET (fl. 1920's-
1970's)
Amer. film editor

O'Neill--Women's p666
Slide--Early p10
Smith--Movies p18-19,25,75

BOOTH, MARY ANN HOLMES
    Amer., mother of John Wilkes
    Booth
    Book--Lists (1) p284

BOOTH, MARY LOUISE (fl. 1860's)
    Amer. magazine editor,
    journalist, translator
    Bolton--Success p34-50, por.
    James--Notable (1) p207-208
    McHenry--Liberty's p45
    Macksey--Book p265

BOOTH, MAUD BALLINGTON
    (1865-1948)
    English-Amer. evangelist,
    social reformer, Salvation
    Army leader, co-founder of
    Volunteers of America
    James--Notable (1) p208-210
    McHenry--Liberty's p45

BOOTH, SHEILA (1928-)
    Amer. filmmaker
    Smith--Movies p152-153,228

BOOTH, SHIRLEY (1907-)
    Amer. actress
    O'Neill--Women's p653
    Shipman--Internatl. p62-63,
    por.
    World--Who p227

BOOTHE, CLARE
    See LUCE, CLARE BOOTHE

BOOTHROYD, BETTY
    British Parliament member
    Vallance--Women p65,70,91,104

BOOTH-TUCKER, EMMA
    See BOOTH, EVANGELINE CORY

BORA, KATHERINA VON (1499-
    1550)
    German, Christian wife of
    Martin Luther
    Bainton--Germany p23-44

BORACH, FANNIE
    See BRICE, FANNY BORACH

BORBONI, PAOLA (1900-)
    Italian actress

Entertainers p213-214,
    por.

BORCHARDT, SELMA MUNTER
    (1895-1968)
    Amer. educator, lawyer,
    labor leader, lobbyist
    Sicherman--Notable p92-94

BORDEN, LIZZIE ANDREW (1860-
    1927)
    Amer. (accused) criminal
    Eills--Here p82-83
    James--Notable (1) p210-212
    Jones--Rutledge p94
    McHenry--Liberty's p45-46
    People's Almanac (1) p576-578
    People's Almanac (2) p499-500,
    por.
    Sherr--American p104
    Webster's--Amer. p120
    Woman's Almanac p502-503, por.
    World--Who p294-295

BORDEN, MARGARET ANN
    See RICHARDS, ANN

BORDEN, MRS. (fl. 1770's)
    Amer. Revolutionary War
    patriot
    Meyer--Petticoat p74

BORDEN, OLIVE (1906/1907-1947)
    Amer. actress
    Springer--They p38,273, por.

BORDEREAU, RENEE (fl. 1790's)
    French Revolutionary heroine,
    male impersonator
    McFarland--Incred. p70-71

BOREN, LOUISA (fl. 1850's)
    Amer. Western pioneer
    Sherr--American p240

BORENTZ, HELENA MODRZEJEWSKA
    CHLAPOWSKI, COUNTESS
    See MODJESKA, HELENA

BORG, IRIS Y.
    Amer. geologist
    O'Neill--Women's p174, por.

BORG, VEDA ANN (1915-1973)
    Amer. actress
    Springer--They p38,273, por.

BORGESE, ELISABETH MANN
(1918-)
Amer. author
Smith--Daughters p236,287-288,
307

BORGIA, FRANCIS, SISTER
Amer. religious leader
O'Neill--Women's p392

BORGIA, LUCREZIA, DUCHESS
OF FERRARA (1480-1519)
Italian noblewoman
Fry--1000 p117
Jones--Rutledge p95
Macksey--Book p94
Mead--Hist. p350
Who Did What p42
World--Who p161

BORI, LUCREZIA (1888-1960)
Spanish opera singer
Claghorn--Biog. p60
Neidle--America's p222
Tuggle--Golden p107-109,218-
220, por.

BORSARELLI, FERNANDA (1904-)
Italian physician
Hellstedt--Women p261-266, por.

BORSTELL, GENERALIN VON,
FRAU OF COBLENZ
German botanist
Mead--Hist. p502

BOSOMWORTH, MARY MUSGROVE
MATTHEWS (1700-1760)
Amer. Indian leader, colonial
land negotiator
Gridley--Amer. p33-38
Sherr--American p50

BOSONE, REVA BECK (1895-)
Amer., noted Utah mother,
congresswoman, lawyer
Amer.--Mothers p531, por.
Bachtold--Gifted p106
Chamberlin--Min. p207-209

BOSSON, BARBARA
Amer. actress
Scheuer--Tel. p51, por.

BOSTAN, ELIZABETH (fl. 1960's)
Romanian filmmaker
Smith--Movies p143

BOSTWICK, CAROLINE (c1843-1852)
Amer. slave girl
Sherr--American p3

BOSWELL, CONNEE (CONNIE)
(1907-1976)
Amer. singer
Claghorn--Biog. p60
Claghorn--Jazz p45
Simon--Best p81-82, por.

BOSWELL SISTERS (fl. 1940's)
Amer. singers
Lamparski--What. (8) p36-37,
por.
Springer--They p38,275

BOTKIN, GORDELIA (1854-1910)
Amer. accused criminal
Woman's Almanac p502

BOTSCHAROVA, NINA (fl. 1950's)
Russian gymnast
O'Neill--Women's p572

BOTTA, ANNE CHARLOTTE LYNCH
(1815-1891)
Amer. author, teacher,
foundress, literary hostess
James--Notable (1) p212-214

BOTTOME, MARGARET McDONALD
(1827-1906)
Amer. author, religious organizer
McHenry--Liberty's p46

BOTTOME, PHYLLIS (1884-1963)
English novelist
Avenel--Comp. (1) p58

BOTTS, VIRGINIA M. (1904-)
Amer. genealogical researcher,
writer
Meyer--Who's p35

BOTYO, IVANKA PETROVA (c1830-
1910)
Bulgarian, mother of Khristo
Botev
Partington--Who's p45

BOUCHER, CONSTANCE
Amer. manufacturer
Rich-McCoy--Mill. p73-95, por.

BOUCHERETT, (EMILIA) JESSIE
(1825-1905)

English feminist, editor
Showalter--Lit. p328

BOUCICAULT, AGNES ROBERTSON
(1833-1916)
Scottish-Amer. actress,
singer
James--Notable (3) p175-177

BOUDIC(C)A
See BOADICEA

BOUDINOT, MRS. ELIAS
Amer., wife of President of
Continental Congress
Earle--Two Cent. (2) p xv, por.

BOUGUEREAU, ELIZABETH JANE
(1851-1922)
Amer. painter
Sparrow--Women p234,238

BOULANGER, LILI (JULIETTE
MARIE OLGA) (1893-1918)
French composer, conductor,
pianist, music teacher
Neuls-Bates--Women p242
O'Neill--Women's p636

BOULANGER, LOUISE
French couturière
Holme--Journal p154, por.

BOULANGER, NADIA JULIETTE
(1887-1979)
French pianist, conductor,
composer, teacher
Comfort--Good p84, por.
Cur. Biog. '80 p450
Jablonski--Ency. p211
Macksey--Book p217
Marlowe--Great p266-270, por.
Neuls-Bates--Women p239-246,
por.
O'Neill--Women's p634-637
Thomson--Amer., see index
p194
Who Did What p44
Woman's Almanac p287-288, por.
World--Who p74

BOULIAR, MARIE GENEVIEVE
(1762-1825)
French artist
Harris--Women p84,188,202-204,
348

BOURBON, CATHERINE DE (1559-
1604)
French governor, daughter
of Jeanne d'Albret, sister of
Henry of Navarre
Bainton--France p75-81, por.

BOURBON, CHARLOTTE DE (1546/
1574-1582)
French, wife of William the
Silent
Bainton--France p89-111

BOURBON, INFANTA DOÑA PAZ DE
Spanish painter
Sparrow--Women p289,318,320

BOURDEJJE, SARAH
See PHILLIPS, SARAH BOWMAN

BOURGEOIS, JEANNE
See MISTINGUETT

BOURGEOIS, LOUISE (1911-)
French sculptor
Cur. Biog. '83 p31-35
Miller--Lives p2-14, por.
Munro--Originals p154-169, por.
O'Neill--Women's p604
Women's--Female p86

BOURGEOIS, LOUYSE (1563-1636)
French midwife
Marks--Women p58-61, por.
Mead--Hist., see index p531,
por.

BOURGEOYS, MARGUERITE (1)
(1620-1700)
Amer. Saint nominee
People's Almanac (1) p1299-1300

BOURGEOYS, MARGUERITE (2)
(fl. 1850's)
Canadian educator
Macksey--Book p72

BOURKE-WHITE, MARGARET (1905/
1906-1971)
Amer. photo-journalist
Clark--Leading p147-149
Cur. Biog. '71 p460
Gilfond--Heroines p121-123, por.
Hamblin--That p48-50,55,60-61,
64-65, por.
Ingraham--Album p72

Kulkin--Her p47-48
Longstreet--Queen p191
McHenry--Liberty's p46-47
Marzolf--Up p66-67
Munsterberg--Hist. p139-141
New York Times--Great p18-19
O'Neill--Women's p447
Ross--Young p91-104, por.
Sicherman--Notable p94-95
Signif.--Amer. p55, por.
Webster's--Amer. p122
Woman's Almanac p266
Women's--Female p5
World--Who p50

BOURSIER, MADAME
See BOURGEOIS, LOUYSE

BOUSQUET, HATTIE
See BRIGGS, HATTIE

BOUSTANY, MYRNA
Lebanese construction
company manager
Macksey--Book p173

BOUVIER, CAROLINE LEE
See RADZIWILL, LEE BOUVIER,
PRINCESS

BOW, CLARA GORDON (1905-1965)
Amer. actress
Books--Lists (2) p188
Clark--Leading p90
Engstead--Star p8-10,12-13,122
Keenan--Women p74-77, por.
Keylin--Hollywood p43, por.
McHenry--Liberty's p47
Manchel--Women p4,42, por.
Mordden--Movie, see index
p291, por.
Shipman--Gold. p77-80, por.
Sicherman--Notable p95-97
Springer--They p38,275, por.
Warren--Pictorial p177-178, por.
Webster's--Amer. p123
Woman's Almanac p326,335-336,
por.
World--Who p227

BOWDEN, DORRIS (1915-   )
Amer. actress
Springer--They p39,275, por.

BOWDEN, MARGUERITE
Amer. Presbyterian elder
O'Neill--Women's p394

BOWDEN, MARIAN E. (fl. 1960's)
Amer. heroine, Carnegie
Medal winner
O'Neill--Women's p733

BOWDOIN, AUGUSTA (LADY
TEMPLE)
(painted by Copley)
Earle--Two Cent. (2) p xiii,290-
291,491-492, por.

BOWDOIN, ELIZABETH ERVING
(1731-1803)
Amer., wife of James Bowdoin
II
Flexner--Face p78, por.

BOWDOIN, SARAH (1761-1826)
Amer., wife of James
Bowdoin III
Flexner--Face p226, por.

BOWEN, CATHERINE (SHOBER)
DRINKER (1897-1973)
Amer., noted Pennsylvania
mother, historian, biographer,
essayist, lecturer
Amer.--Mothers p460-461, por.
Clark--Leading p234-235
Cur. Biog. '73 p450
Ehrlich--Oxford p196,199,221
Sicherman--Notable p97-99

BOWEN, ELIZA
See JUMEL, ELIZABETH (ELIZA)
BOWEN

BOWEN, ELIZABETH DOROTHEA
COLE (1899-1973)
Irish novelist
Avenel--Comp. (1) p60
Crosland--Beyond p59-69,71,76,
132,169,222
Jones--Rutledge p100
Magill--Cycl. p123-124
Moers--Literary p275
O'Neill--Women's p677-678
Seymour-Smith--Novels p104
Seymour-Smith--Who's p50
Showalter--Lit. p349
Who Did What p44
World--Who p24

BOWEN, LOUISE HADDOCK DeKOVEN
(1859-1953)
Amer. philanthropist, social
welfare leader

Sicherman--Notable p99-
101

BOWER, HOLLY
Amer. film photographer
O'Neill--Women's p317, por.

BOWERMAN, MYRELINE ELIZABETH
(1921-)
Amer. genealogical researcher,
author
Meyer--Who's p36

BOWERS, ADELE
Amer. book-club overseer
O'Neill--Women's p488

BOWERS, DORIS RONEY (1928-)
Amer. genealogical researcher,
author, editor
Meyer--Who's p35-36

BOWERS, EILLY ORRUM (fl.
1850's-1860's)
Scottish-Amer. Western
boarding-house owner,
pioneer
Sherr--American p145, por.
Williams--Legend. p35-39, por.

BOWERS, MARY
Amer. community leader
Innis--Profiles p106-107, por.

BOWERSOX, JERRY SUE GRAY-
(1944-)
Amer. genealogical researcher
Meyer--Who's p36

BOWES, ELIZABETH
Scottish religious worker
Bainton--Spain p84-88

BOWES, MARGIE (1941-)
Amer. singer, guitarist
Claghorn--Biog. p61

BOWES, MARJORY
Scottish, wife of John Knox
Bainton--Spain p83-88

BOWLES, MRS. A. LINCOLN
See HANK, HELEN

BOWLES, CAROLINE (1786-1854)
English poet
Moers--Literary p275

BOWLES, CATHERINE (fl. 1720's)
English surgeon, writer
Mead--Hist. p477

BOWLES, EVA DEL VAKIA (1875-
1943)
Amer. Y.W.C.A. leader
James--Notable (1) p214-215

BOWLES, HELOISE (c1919-1977)
Amer. columnist, author
O'Neill--Women's p456

BOWLES, JANE SYDNEY (1917/1918-
1973)
Amer. novelist, story writer,
playwright
Avenel--Comp. (2) p38
Seymour-Smith--Novels p104
Seymour-Smith--Who's p50

BOWMAN, MYRELINE ELIZABETH
(1921-)
Amer. genealogical researcher,
author
Meyer--Who's p36

BOWMAN, SARAH A. (1812-1866)
Amer. Western cook, hotel-
keeper, frontierswoman
Sherr--American p20,221

BOWN, PATRICIA ANNE (PATTI)
(1931-)
Amer. jazz pianist
Claghorn--Jazz p46

BOWNE, ELIZA SOUTHGATE (1783-
1808/1809)
Amer. diarist
Earle--Two Cent. (2) p xxiii,
524,579,756-757, por.

BOWRING, EVA (c1873-)
Amer. Senator
Chamberlin--Min. p240-244
O'Neill--Women's p66

BOX, MURIEL (fl. 1940's-1960's)
English director, producer
Smith--Movies p109-110

BOYADGIEVA, LADA (fl. 1940's-
1970's)
Bulgarian film director
Smith--Movies p94

BOYARS, MARION (fl. 1960's-1970's)
English publisher
O'Neill--Women's p487

BOYARSKA, RIVKA (fl. 1960's)
Russian composer, writer
Mandel--Soviet p192

BOYARSKIKH, KLAUDIA (fl. 1960's)
Russian skier
McWhirter--Guinness p121-122,
por.
O'Neill--Women's p574

BOYCE, NEITH (-1951)
Amer. feminist, writer
Sochen--Movers p75,77-79,83,
272

BOYD, BELLE (1844-1900)
Amer. Confederate spy,
actress, lecturer, Civil War
heroine
James--Notable (1) p215-217
Kulkin--Her p48-49
McHenry--Liberty's p47
People's Almanac (1) p647
Sherr--American p235,245,252
Warren--Pictorial p110-111, por.
Woman's Almanac p454

BOYD, JANE (fl. 1970's)
Amer. TV director
Klever--Women p19-20,61-62,
100,108

BOYD, LOUISE ARNER (1887-1972)
Amer. explorer, geographer
Cur. Biog. '72 p459
Dunlap--Calif. p21, por.
Olds--Women p231-296, por.
O'Neill--Women's p742

BOYD, MAMIE ALEXANDER
(1876-1973)
Amer., noted Iowa mother,
journalist, community worker
Amer.--Mothers p208-209, por.

BOYD, NANCY, pseud.
See MILLAY, EDNA ST. VIN-
CENT

BOYD, MRS. ORSEMUS BRONSON
(fl. 1860's-1890's)
Amer. Western pioneer,
author

Fischer--Let p111-123

BOYD, PATTIE (fl. 1900's)
Amer. journalist
Marzolf--Up p24

BOYE, KARIN (1900-1941)
Swedish poet, editor, novelist
Seymour-Smith--Who's p51

BOYER, LILLIAN (fl. 1920's)
Amer. aviatrix, (stunt flier)
Boase--Sky's p22, por.

BOYLAN, ESTELLE
See TAYLOR, IDA ESTELLE

BOYLE, CHARLOTTE (fl. 1910's)
Amer. swimmer
Macksey--Book p259

BOYLE, KAY (1902/1903-)
Amer. novelist, story writer,
poet, professor, foreign cor-
respondent, translator
Avenel--Comp. (2) p39
Cahill--Women p85,375-376
Chester--Rising p47-50, por.
Diamonstein--Open p23-27, por.
Ehrlich--Oxford, see index p450
McHenry--Liberty's p47-48
Seymour-Smith--Novels p104
Seymour-Smith--Who's p51-52

BOYLE, NINA (c1863-1943)
British policewoman, suffragist
Macksey--Book p137-138

BOYLSTON, HELEN DORE (1895-
1984)
Amer. author, novelist
Cur. Biog. '84 p468

BOZARTH, ELIZABETH (EXPERI-
ENCE) (fl. 1770's)
Amer. pioneer, heroine
Booth--Women p193-194
Sherr--American p244

BOZNANSKA, OLGA DE (fl. 1860's)
Russian portrait painter
Sparrow--Women p289,316

BOZZACCHI, GIUSEPPINA (fl. 1870's)
Italian ballet dancer
Miguel--Ballerinas p240-242,
251

BOZZIDINI, BETTISIA (fl. c1239-
1249)
Italian lawyer
Macksey--Book p122

BRACEGIRDLE, ANNE (1663/1674-
1748)
English actress
Entertainers p82
Findlater--Player p39-43
Jones--Rutledge p101
Macksey--Book p224
Who Did What p45

BRACEY, JOAN (1640-1685)
English, accused criminal,
male impersonator
Macksey--Book p133

BRACKETT, ANNA CALLENDER
(1836-1911)
Amer. educator
James--Notable (1) p217-218

BRACKETT, LEIGH (1915-1978)
Amer. novelist
Seymour-Smith--Novels p104

BRADDOCK, ELIZABETH (BESSIE)
MARGARET BAMBER (1899-
1970)
British Parliament member
Cur. Biog. '71 p461
Vallance--Women, see index p207

BRADDON, MARY ELIZABETH
MAXWELL (1837-1915)
English author, novelist
Jones--Rutledge p101
Showalter--Lit. p333

BRADFORD, CLEA ANNAH ETHELL
(1936-   )
Amer. singer
Claghorn--Biog. p62

BRADFORD, CORNELIA FOSTER
(1847-1935)
Amer. social worker
James--Notable (1) p218-219

BRADFORD, CORNELIA SMITH
(-1755)
Amer. colonial newspaper
publisher, printer
Demeter--Primer p46-57

James--Notable (1) p219-220
Stein--Lives, unp.

BRADFORD, DOROTHY (-1620)
Amer. Pilgrim
Warren--Pictorial p12

BRADFORD, MARY D. (-1943)
Amer. pioneer teacher
Sherr--American p248

BRADFORD, SUSAN (c1846-)
Amer. Civil War heroine
Hymowitz--Hist. p145

BRADLEY, AMY MORRIS (1823-
1904)
Amer. educator, Civil War
nurse, teacher
James--Notable (1) p220-222

BRADLEY, GERTRUDE M.
British illustrator
Callen--Women p204

BRADLEY, GRACE (fl. 1940's-1950's)
Amer. actress
Springer--They p39,275, por.

BRADLEY, KATHARINE HARRIS
See FIELD, MICHAEL, pseud.

BRADLEY, LYDIA MOSS (1816-1908)
Amer. philanthropist, college
founder
McHenry--Liberty's p48
Sherr--American p64

BRADLEY, PAT (fl. 1970's-1980's)
Amer. golfer
McWhirter--Guinness p77

BRADNA, OLYMPE (1920-)
French actress
Springer--They p39,275, por.

BRADSHAW, DALLAS (fl. 1970's)
Canadian radio officer
Macksey--Book p245

BRADSHAW, LILLIAN MOORE (1915-)
Amer. organization official
Cur. Biog. '70 p46-48, por.

BRADSTREET, ANNE DUDLEY
(c1612-1672)

Amer. colonial poet
Avenel--Comp. (2) p40-41
Bernikow--World p187
Ehrlich--Oxford p49,54-55,58
Fine--Women p92
Ingraham--Album p10
James--Notable (1) p222-223
Jones--Rutledge p102
Kaplan--Salt p27-28, por.
Kulkin--Her p49-50
McHenry--Liberty's p48
Macksey--Book p181
Millstein--We p13-14
Moers--Literary p275-276, see
  also index p322
Neidle--America's p7-8, 14-16
Pearson--Who p123
Reifert--Women p19
Sherr--American p107-108
Warren--Pictorial p24-25
Webster's--Amer. p129
Who Did What p45
Williams--Demeter's, see index
  p348, por.
Woman's Almanac p144
World--Who p10

BRADWELL, MYRA COLBY (1831-
  1894)
  Amer., noted Vermont mother,
  lawyer, publisher
  Amer.--Mothers p540-541
  Bird--Enterprising p107-110
  James--Notable (1) p223-225
  McHenry--Liberty's p48-49
  Macksey--Book p125
  Papachristou--Women p105-106,
    por.
  Reifert--Women p81-82
  Sochen--Herstory p103-104
  Warren--Pictorial p79
  Woman's Almanac p521-522, por.

BRADY, ALICE (1892-1939)
  Amer. actress
  James--Notable (1) p225-226
  McHenry--Liberty's p49
  Springer--They p39,275, por.
  Webster's--Amer. p129

BRADY, ELIZABETH PATTON (fl.
  1880's-1900's)
  Amer., Alaskan governor's
  wife, missionary
  Jones--Women (1) p75-80, por.

BRADY, MARY QUIGLEY
  Amer. Revolutionary War

martyr
Williams--Demeter's p274-275

BRADY, MILDRED EDIE (1906-1965)
  Amer. consumer advocate,
  editor, journalist
  Sicherman--Notable p101-102

BRADY, PAMELA
  Amer. director information
  services
  Scheuer--Tel. p53

BRAESTRUP, AGNETE MEINERT
  (1909-)
  Danish physician
  Hellstedt--Women p374-378, por.

BRAGG, MRS. BRAXTON (fl. 1860's)
  Amer. Confederate patriot,
  letter writer
  Wiley--Confed. p172-173

BRAGINA, LYUDMILA (fl. 1970's)
  Russian track and field athlete
  McWhirter--Guinness p169, por.
  O'Neill--Women's p573,575,577

BRAINARD, BERTHA (fl. 1920's)
  Amer. radio station manager
  Marzolf--Up p123-125

BRAITHWAITE, LILIAN, DAME
  (1873-1948)
  English actress
  Johns--Dames p66-74, por.

BRANCH, ANNA HEMPSTEAD (1875-
  1937)
  Amer. poet
  Bernikow--World p241
  Ehrlich--Oxford p11
  James--Notable (1) p226-228
  Sherr--American p33

BRAND, CHRISTIANNA (1907-)
  English novelist
  Seymour-Smith--Novels p105

BRANDEGEE, MARY KATHARINE
  LAYNE CURRAN (1844-1920)
  Amer. botanist
  James--Notable (1) p228-229

BRANDON, LIANE (fl. 1970's)
  Amer. filmmaker, university
  instructor
  Smith--Movies p153-154,229, por.

BRANDT, ASA
    Swedish craftswoman, (glass)
    O'Neill--Women's p273

BRANDT, YANNA KROYT (1933-)
    German-Amer. director, pro-
    ducer, writer
    Scheuer--Tel. p53-54

BRANICKA, ROSA, COUNTESS
    Amer. "self"-surgeon
    McFarland--Incred. p181

BRANN, MARTHA COBB (1882-
    1961)
    Amer., noted Maine mother,
    governor's wife
    Amer.--Mothers p243-244, por.

BRANSCOMBE, GENA (1881-1977)
    Canadian-Amer. composer,
    author, conductor
    Claghorn--Biog. p63
    Jablonski--Ency. p113

BRANT, ALICE (fl. 1893-1895)
    Brazilian diarist
    Hahner--Women p48-59

BRANT, MARY ("MOLLY")
    (c1736-1796)
    Amer. Indian leader
    DePauw--Found. p122-123
    James--Notable (1) p229-230
    McHenry--Liberty's p49-50
    Millstein--We p36
    Sherr--American p164
    Stein--Lives p95-108

BRANZELL, KARIN MARIA (1891-
    1974)
    Swedish-Amer. opera singer
    Cur. Biog. '75 p460-461
    Tuggle--Golden p192-194, por.

BRASLAU, SOPHIE (1888/1892-
    1935)
    Amer. opera singer
    Claghorn--Biog. p63
    James--Notable (1) p230-231

BRASSEY, ANNA (1839-1887)
    English travel writer
    Showalter--Lit. p334

BRATHCHER, TWILA
    Amer. scuba diver, shell
    author

O'Neill--Women's
    p157

BRATHWAITE, YVONNE
    See BURKE, YVONNE BRATH-
    WAITE

BRATTON, MARTHA (-1816)
    Amer., noted South Carolina
    mother, patriot, Revolutionary
    War heroine
    Amer.--Mothers p491
    Meyer--Petticoat p179-180

BRAUN, EMMA LUCY (1889-1971)
    Amer. botanist, conservation-
    ist
    Sicherman--Notable p102-103

BRAUN, EVA (1912-1945)
    German model, Hitler's wife
    Horan--Desperate p145-149, por.
    Jones--Rutledge p105
    World--Who p295

BRAUNWALD, NINA STARR (1928-)
    Amer. surgeon
    Diamonstein--Open p33-37, por.
    O'Neill--Women's p214-215

BRAUT, BESSIE (fl. 1910's)
    Amer. anarchist, labor union
    organizer
    Baum--Jewish p155-156

BRAVER, RITA
    Amer. TV news reporter
    Scheuer--Tel. p54

BRAWNE, FANNY (fl. 1800's)
    English, friend of Keats
    Morley--Literary p150-151,254

BRAYTON, MARIAN (1939-)
    Amer. TV executive
    Scheuer--Tel. p54, por.

BRAZIEL, MAUREEN (fl. 1970's)
    Amer. judo athlete
    O'Neill--Women's p564

BRAZIL, ANGELA (1868-1947)
    English children's author
    Jones--Rutledge p105

BRAZILLER, KAREN (fl. 1970's)
    Amer. co-founder publishing
    house

O'Neill--Women's
p491

BRECK, CARRIE ELLIS (1855-1934)
Amer. hymnist, author,
song-writer
Claghorn--Biog. p64

BRECKENRIDGE, MARY MARVIN
(fl. 1930's-1940's)
Amer. radio news reporter,
photo-journalist
Marzolf--Up p139-140

BRECKINRIDGE, AIDA DE ACOSTA
(1884-1962)
Cuban-Amer. aviatrix, or-
ganization official
Macksey--Book p246
O'Neill--Women's p115

BRECKINRIDGE, MADELINE
McDOWELL (1872-1920)
Amer. social reformer
James--Notable (1) p231-233
McHenry--Liberty's p50
Sherr--American p79-80

BRECKINRIDGE, MARY (1877/1881-
1965)
Amer. nurse, midwife
Kulkin--Her p50-51
Sherr--American p79
Sicherman--Notable p103-105

BRECKINRIDGE, SOPHONISBA
PRESTON (1866-1948)
Amer. social worker, educa-
tor, suffragist
James--Notable (1) p233-236
McHenry--Liberty's p50-51
World--Who p187

BREDIN, OCTAVIA MARY DU
PONT (c1913-)
Amer. millionaire
Forbes-400 ('84) p149

BREE, GERMAINE (c1907-)
French professor, literary
critic
Diamonstein--Open p38-42, por.
O'Neill--Women's p415-416

BREEDLOVE, LEE (fl. 1960's)
Amer. jet-car racer
Macksey--Book p254

BREEDLOVE, SARAH
See WALKER, SARAH BREED-
LOVE ("MADAME" C.J.)

BREEN, MARGARET (fl. 1840's)
Amer. Donner Party heroine
Sherr--American p22

BREENER, DORIS
Amer. country tour leader
O'Neill--Women's p17

BREENER, PAM (fl. 1970's)
Amer. country tour leader
O'Neill--Women's p17

BREESE, ZONA GALE
See GALE, ZONA

BREESKIN, ADELYN D. (c1896-)
Amer. museum director
O'Neill--Women's p595,614-615,
por.

BREHM, MANE CAROLINE (fl.
1920's)
Amer. Vice Presidential
candidate
People's Almanac (1) p127

BREMER, EDITH TERRY (1885-1964)
Amer. organization founder,
social worker
Sicherman--Notable p105-107

BREMER, FREDERIKA (1801-1865)
Swedish traveller, novelist,
feminist
Hamalian--Ladies p115-133
Macksey--Book p81,184
Moers--Literary p15,276
Sherr--American p203
Smith--Women p1-41

BREMER, LUCILLE (1923-)
Amer. dancer, actress
Lamparski--What. Annual (4,5)
p304-309, por.

BRENK, IRENE (1902-)
Swiss physician
Hellstedt--Women p240-243, por.

BRENNAN, EILEEN (1937-)
Amer. actress
Hirschhorn--Rating p58, por.
World--Who p228

BRENNAN, MAEVE (1917-)
Irish-Amer. writer
Cahill--Women p172,377

BRENNER, ELEANOR
Amer. fashion designer
O'Neill--Women's p246

BRENNER, SUMMER (1945-)
Amer. poet
Chester--Rising p348-351, por.

BRENNER, SUSAN
Amer. painter
Women's--Female p35

BRENT, ANNE (fl. 1600's)
Amer. farmer
Warren--Pictorial p32

BRENT, EVELYN (1899-)
Amer. actress
Lamparski--What. (3) p206-207,
por.
Springer--They p40,275, por.

BRENT, LINDA, pseud.
Amer., former slave, writer
Hymowitz--Hist. p53

BRENT, MARGARET (1600-1671)
Amer., noted Maryland
mother, plantation manager,
feminist
Amer.--Mothers p249
Friedman--Our p50-53
Gurko--Ladies p23-24
Hymowitz--Hist. p6
James--Notable (1) p236-237
McHenry--Liberty's p51
Macksey--Book p122-123
Neidle--America's p7-8
Reifert--Women p14-15
Sherr--American p96
Smith--Daughters p54-55
Taylor--Gener. p29
Warren--Pictorial p32-33
Webster's--Amer. p135
Williams--Demeter's p32,131-133
Woman's Almanac p520,540
World--Who p187

BRENT, MARY
Amer. farmer
Warren--Pictorial p32

BRES, MADELEINE (fl. 1870's)
French physician, surgeon

Macksey--Book
p150

BRESEGNA, ISABELLA (1510-1567)
Italian Reformation worker
Bainton--Germany p219-233

BRESHKOVSKAYA, CATHERINE
KONSTANTINOVA (1844-1934)
Russian feminist, political
leader
Mandel--Soviet p29-30,42,45-48
Marlowe--Great p134-141, por.
Taylor--Gener. p34

BRESLAU, (MARIE) LOUISA CATH-
ERINE, MADAME (1856-1927)
Swiss painter
Sparrow--Women p289,304,314

BRESOLES, JUDITH DE (-1673)
French nun, nurse
Mead--Hist. p417

BRESSE, MADAME DE LA (-c1876)
French, wealthy woman
McFarland--Incred. p103

BRESSLER-GIANOLI, CLOTILDE
(1874-1912)
Swiss opera singer
Tuggle--Golden p41-42, por.

BRETEUIL, EMILIE DE, MARQUISE
DU CHATELET (1706-1749)
French mathematician
Osen--Women p52-69, por.

BRETT, ARABELLA (-1803)
English singer, actress
Claghorn--Biog. p64

BRETT, CATHERINA, MADAME
(-1764)
Amer. landowner, pioneer
Sherr--American p158

BRETTESVILLE, SHEILA (fl. 1960's-
1970's)
Amer. artist
Munro--Originals p312-313

BREUER, LORE (fl. 1970's)
German magazine editor,
feminist
Marzolf--Up p296

BREWER, MARGARET A.
    Amer. Marine, brigadier
    general
    O'Neill--Women's p549-550,553

BREWER, THERESA (1931-)
    Amer. singer
    Claghorn--Biog. p65
    Claghorn--Jazz p48
    World--Who p265

BREWSTER, LUCRETIA (-1679)
    Amer. colonial medical woman
    Mead--Hist. p415

BREWSTER, MARY
    Amer. nurse
    Warren--Pictorial p148

BRIAN, MARY (1908-)
    Amer. actress
    Lamparski--What. (4) p174-175,
        por.
    Lamparski--What (8) p38-39,
        por.
    Springer--They p40-42,275,
        por.

BRIANZA, CARLOTTA (c1867-)
    Italian ballet dancer
    Miguel--Ballerinas p166-167

BRICE, FANNY BORACH (1891-
        1951)
    Amer. actress, singer,
        comedienne
    Claghorn--Biog. p65
    Clark--Leading p116
    Entertainers p188, por.
    Keylin--Hollywood p47-48, por.
    McHenry--Liberty's p51-52
    Sicherman--Notable p107-108
    Simon--Best p85-86
    Springer--They p42,275, por.
    Webster's--Amer. p136
    Woman's Almanac p316-317, por.
    World--Who p275

BRICKDALE, ELEANOR FORTESCUE
    See FORTESCUE-BRICKDALE,
        (MARY) ELEANOR

BRICO, ANTONIA (1902-)
    Dutch-Amer. musical conduc-
        tor, pianist, teacher
    LePage--Women p13-26, por.
    McHenry--Liberty's p52

Neuls-Bates--Women p252-259,271
O'Neill--Women's p637-638
Woman's Almanac p106
World--Who p69

BRIDGE, ELIZABETH SYRLING
    See STIRLING, ELIZABETH

BRIDGES, DOROTHY (fl. 1970's-
        1980's)
    Amer., wife of Lloyd Bridges,
        author
    Funt--Are p51-63, por.

BRIDGES, FIDELIA (1834-1923)
    Amer. painter
    James--Notable (1) p237-239

BRIDGET (BRIGID or BRIDE),
    SAINT (1) (453-525)
    Irish Saint, midwife, medical
        woman
    Jones--Rutledge p108
    Marks--Women p43
    Mead--Hist. p91

BRIDGET, SAINT OF SCANDINAVIA
    (2) (1302/1304-1373)
    Swedish Saint
    Marks--Women p52
    Mead--Hist. p279-280

BRIDGEWATER, DENISE (DEE DEE)
    (1950-)
    Amer. jazz singer
    Claghorn--Jazz p48

BRIDGMAN, ELIZA JANE GILLET
    (1805-1871)
    Amer. missionary educator
        (in China)
    James--Notable (1) p239-240

BRIDGMAN, LAURA DEWEY (1829-
        1889)
    Amer. blind, deaf mute
    James--Notable (1) p240-242
    Kulkin--Her p51-52
    McHenry--Liberty's p52
    Sherr--American p89,113
    Webster's--Amer. p137

BRIEL, MARIE (1896-)
    Amer. organist, teacher
    Claghorn--Biog. p65

BRIER, JULIET
    Amer. desert pioneer

Gray--Women p41-45
Sherr--American p13

BRIGGS, EMILY POMONA EDSON
(1830-1910)
Amer. war correspondent
Beasley--First p12-14,23, por.
James--Notable (1) p242-243
McHenry--Liberty's p52-53
Marzolf--Up p17

BRIGGS, HATTIE
Amer. P.E.O. co-founder
O'Neill--Women's p427, por.

BRIGGS, HELEN VIRGINIA
See BRUCE, VIRGINIA

BRIGGS, RUTH ELLA (1911-)
Amer. genealogical researcher,
writer
Meyer--Who's p37

BRIGHAM, BESMILR (1923-)
Amer. poet
Chester--Rising p117-121, por.

"BRIGHT EYES"
See TIBBLES, SUSETTE LA
FLESCHE

BRIGHT, MARY LEE
Amer. teacher, mother of
Bill Bright
Kooiman--Silhouettes p30-36,
por.

BRIGHT, VONETTE
Amer. religious worker
Kooiman--Cameos p148-160, por.

BRIGHTWEN, ELIZA (1830-1906)
Scottish naturalist
Showalter--Lit. p330-331

BRIGNONE, LILLA (1913-)
Italian actress
Entertainers p240

BRIN, RUTH
Amer. author
Brin--Social p160, por.

BRINDLEY, ARABELLA OWENS
(1892-)
Amer., noted Texas mother,
community worker
Amer--Mothers p517, por.

BRINGLE, CYNTHIA
Amer. potter, craftswoman
O'Neill--Women's p127,129

BRINK, CAROL RYRIE (1895-1981)
Amer. children's book author
Ehrlich--Oxford p336

BRINKLEY, CHRISTIE (c1954-)
Amer. model
People--Best p101, por.

BRINKMAN, MARIA (fl. 1920's)
German weaving-school founder
O'Neill--Women's p267

BRINVILLIERS, MARGUERITE MARIE
D'AUBRAY, MARQUISE DE
(c1630-1676)
French accused criminal
Jones--Rutledge p109
Macksey--Book p133

BRISEIS
Roman slave of Achilles
Pomeroy--Godd. p19,27,29

BRISTOW, GWEN (1903-1980)
Amer. novelist, journalist
Cur. Biog. '84 p469

BRISTOW, SUSANNAH
Amer. Western pioneer
Time--Women p32-33, por.

BRITAIN, RADIE (1903/1904-)
Amer. composer
Claghorn--Biog. p65-66
Jablonski--Ency. p341
LePage--Women p27-42, por.

BRITTAIN, VERA MARY (1893/
1896-1970)
English novelist
Avenel--Comp. (1) p64
Showalter--Lit. p348

BRITTON, ELIZABETH GERTRUDE
KNIGHT (1858-1934)
Amer. botanist, bryologist
Emberlin--Cont. p149-150
James--Notable (1) p243-244
McHenry--Liberty's p53
Sherr--American p166

BRITTON, NAN
Amer., friend of President
Harding

Felton--Harris
p128-130

BRITTON, SHERRY (EDITH)
Amer. burlesque star
Lamparski--What. (4) p42-43,
por.

BRLIC-MAZURANIC, IVANA (1874-
1938)
Croatian writer
Partington--Who's p51

BROADFOOT, ELEANORA
See CISNEROS, ELEANORA
BROADFOOT DE

BROADNAX, LYDIA
Amer., friend of George
Wythe
Kelley--Courage p227-228

BROADWELL, MARY (c1630-1730)
Amer. colonial midwife
Mead--Hist. p415

BROADWICK, GEORGIA ("TINY")
(c1893-1978)
Amer. parachutist
O'Neill--Women's p742

BROCKINGTON, JACKIE
Amer. TV weather reporter
Scheuer--Tel. p56

BRODELL, JOAN AGNES THERESA
SADIE
See LESLIE, JOAN

BRODERICK, GERTRUDE G.
(fl. 1940's)
Amer. radio education
specialist
Women--Radio p25-26

BRODERICK, HELEN (1891-1959)
Amer. actress
Springer--They p43,276, por.
World--Who p228

BRODSKY, JUDITH (1923-)
Amer. printmaker
Miller--Lives p15-36, por.

BRODSKY, LINDA G.
Amer. public relations
communications executive
Scheuer Tel. p57

BRODT, HELEN (-1908)
Amer. mountain climber
Sherr--American p15
Time--Women p116

BRODY, CATHARINE (fl. 1920's-
1930's)
Amer. journalist
Marzolf--Up p50

BRODY, SHERRY (fl. 1970's)
Amer. sculptor
Women's--Female p86

BROGLIATTI, BARBARA SPENCER
(1946-)
Amer. executive, embassy
communications
Scheuer--Tel. p57-58

BROKAW. ANN CLARKE (1925-1944)
Amer., daughter of Clare
Boothe Luce
Miller--Fishbait p69-70

BROKAW, JOANNE (1939-)
Amer. TV executive
Scheuer--Tel. p58

BROMLEY, SHEILA (1911-)
Amer. actress
Springer--They p43,276, por.

BRONNER, AUGUSTA FOX (1881-
1966)
Amer. psychologist
Sicherman--Notable p108-110

BRONSON, BETTY (ELIZABETH
ADA) (1906/1907-)
Amer. actress
Lamparski--What. (3) p194-195,
por.
Mordden--Movie, see index p291
Springer--They p43,276, por.

BRONSTEIN, YETTE (fl. 1960's)
Amer. Presidential candidate
People's Almanac (1) p128

BRONTË, ANNE (1820-1849)
English novelist
Avenel--Comp. (1) p64
Basch--Relative, see index p348
Donaldson--How p45
Jones--Rutledge p111
Longford--Eminent p29-60, por.
Macksey--Book p185-186

Sochen--Herstory p373-374, por.
Toppin--Biog. p258-259
Warren--Pictorial p220, por.
Washington--Black p49-50
Webber--Woman p71-78
Webster's--Amer. p140
Woman's Almanac p246-247, por.
World--Who p10

BROOKS, LOUISE (1906-1985)
Amer. dancer, actress, radio
performer
Cur. Biog. '84 p44-47, por.
Cur. Biog. '85 p462
Lamparski--What. (3) p178-179,
por.
Shipman--Gold. p84-86, por.
Springer--They p44,276, por.

BROOKS, MARIA GOWEN (c1794-
1845)
Amer. poet
James--Notable (1) p244-246
McHenry--Liberty's p54
Stein--Lives p413-424, por.

BROOKS, MARY T. (fl. 1960's-
1970's)
Amer., noted Idaho mother,
government official, ranch
manager
Amer.--Mothers p157-158, por.

BROOKS, MATILDA MOLDENHAUER
Amer. biologist, physiologist
O'Neill--Women's p218

BROOKS, PHYLLIS (1914-)
Amer. actress
Lamparski--What. Annual (4,5)
p134-138, por.
Springer--They p44,276, por.

BROOKS, ROMAINE (1874-1970)
Amer. artist, painter,
portraitist
Fine--Women p189-191, por.
Harris--Women p268-270,354-355
O'Neill--Women's p596,598
Petersen--Women p100-101
Sicherman--Notable p110-111
Woman's Almanac p223
Women's--Female p6

BROOMALL, ANNA ELIZABETH
(1847-1931)
Amer. physician, surgeon,

obstetrician, medical educator
James--Notable (1) p246-247
O'Neill--Women's p211-212

BROOME, CLAIRE (c1946-)
Amer. epidermiologist
Science--Digest ('84) p47

BROPHY, BRIGID (1929-)
Irish novelist, critic, journal-
ist
Seymour-Smith--Novels p106
Seymour-Smith--Who's p58-59
Showalter--Lit. p350

BROTHERS, JOYCE (1927/1928-)
Amer. psychologist, columnist,
TV & radio personality
Anderson--People p64-65, por.
Bowman--Social p4-11, por.
Cur. Biog. '71 p66-68, por.
Marzolf--Up p147,162
100--Greatest (1) p103, por.

BROTHERSON, SHIRLEY (fl. 1900's)
Alaskan lighthouse keeper
Jones--Women (1) p161-170, por.

BROUGHTON, RHODA (1840-1920)
English novelist
Moers--Literary p278
Showalter--Lit. p335

BROULON, ANGELIQUE (1772-1859)
French infantry officer
Macksey--Book p54

BROWER, TOCTOO (fl. 1960's-1970's)
Alaskan, wife of "King of the
Arctic"
Jones--Women (1) p114-121

BROWN, ABBIE FARWELL (1871-1927)
Amer. poet, children's books
author
James--Notable (1) p247-249

BROWN, ADA (1889-1950)
Amer. jazz singer
Claghorn--Jazz p49

BROWN, ALICE (1856-1948)
Amer. author
James--Notable (1) p249-250
McHenry--Liberty's p54

BROWN, ALICE VAN VECHTEN
(1862-1949)
Amer. art educator
James--Notable (1) p250-251

BROWN, ANGELINE
See DICKINSON, ANGIE

BROWN, ANTOINETTE
See BLACKWELL, ANTOINETTE
BROWN

BROWN, BARBARA J. (1921-)
Amer. genealogical research-
er, writer
Meyer--Who's p39

BROWN, BONNIE GEAN (1938-)
Amer. singer
Claghorn--Biog. p67

BROWN, CARO (fl. 1950's)
Amer. journalist
O'Neill--Women's p452

BROWN, CATHERINE (-1823)
Amer. teacher of Indian girls
Sherr--American p2

BROWN, MRS. CHARLES S. (fl.
1890's)
Amer. golfer
McWhirter--Guinness p67

BROWN, CHARLOTTE (fl. 1970's)
Amer. artist
Women's--Female p101

BROWN, CHARLOTTE AMANDA
BLAKE- (1846-1904)
Amer. physician, surgeon,
noted California mother,
hospital co-founder
Amer.--Mothers p52
James--Notable (1) p251-253
O'Neill--Women's p203
Sherr--American p19

BROWN, CHARLOTTE EMERSON
(1838-1895)
Amer. clubwoman
McHenry--Liberty's p54-55

BROWN, CHARLOTTE EUGENIA
HAWKINS (c1883-1961)
Amer. educator, school
founder
Sicherman--Notable p111-113

BROWN, CLARA ("AUNT") (fl.
1850's-1870's)
Amer. slave, religious worker
Sherr--American p24
Time--Women p131, por.

BROWN, DENISE SCOTT (1931-)
Zambian-Amer. architect, ur-
ban pioneer, teacher, writer
Gilbert--Part. p311-323, por.
O'Neill--Women's p610

BROWN, DOROTHY LAVINIA (fl.
1940's-1970's)
Amer. surgeon, medical educational director
Innis--Profiles p14-15, por.

BROWN, EARLENE
Amer. track and field athlete
Hollander--100 p124-125, por.

BROWN, EDITH P. (fl. 1970's)
Amer. physician
O'Neill--Women's p211

BROWN, ELAINE (fl. 1960's-1970's)
Amer. activist, head Black
Panthers
O'Neill--Women's p716

BROWN, ELEANOR McMILLEN
STACKSTROM (fl. 1920's-
1950's)
Amer. interior decorator,
business executive
O'Neill--Women's p280

BROWN, "GRANDMOTHER" MARIA
See BROWN, MARIA

BROWN, HALLIE QUINN (1849/1850-
1949)
Amer. educator, elocutionist,
women's rights leader
James--Notable (1) p253-254
McHenry--Liberty's p55
Sherr--American p187-188

BROWN, HANNAH (fl. 1770's)
Amer. patriot (Revolutionary
War), innkeeper
Meyer--Petticoat p70-71

BROWN, HARRIET CONNOR
Amer. writer
Sherr--American p71

BROWN, HELEN GURLEY (1922-   )
Amer. author, magazine
editor, feminist
Cur. Biog. '69 p56-59, por.
Diamonstein--Open p48-51, por.
Golson--Playboy p24-36
McHenry--Liberty's p55-56
100--Greatest (1) p39, por.
O'Neill--Women's p475-476, por.
Woman's Almanac p48,266,284,
por.
World--Who p51

BROWN, HELEN HAYES
See HAYES, HELEN

BROWN, HILARY
Canadian TV news corres-
pondent
Scheuer--Tel. p60

BROWN, J. MARGARETHE (fl.
1970's)
Amer. executive, religious
worker
O'Neill--Women's p385-386

BROWN, JEWEL HAZEL (1937-   )
Amer. singer
Claghorn--Biog. p68
Claghorn--Jazz p50

BROWN, JOAN (fl. 1970's)
Amer. painter
Women's--Female p35,155

BROWN, JUNE (fl. 1970's)
Amer. columnist
O'Neill--Women's p459-460

BROWN, KATHRYN
Amer. agriculturist
O'Neill--Women's p28

BROWN, KAY
Amer. graphic artist
Fax--Black p165-180, por.
Women's--Female p75

BROWN, LADY JOHNSON
See BRANT, MARY (MOLLY)

BROWN, LINDA
Amer. child celebrity
Woman's Almanac p52

BROWN, LOUISE (1978-   )
English, world's 1st test

tube baby
Anderson--People p66

BROWN, LUCY (1913-1971)
Amer. concert pianist, teacher
Claghorn--Biog. p68

BROWN, MARCIA (1918-   )
Amer. author, illustrator
Smaridge--Famous p118-123, por.

BROWN, MARGARET WISE (1910-
1952)
Amer. children's author
Sicherman--Notable p113-114

BROWN, MARGERY (fl. 1920's)
Amer. writer, aviatrix
Boase--Sky's p114

BROWN, MARIA ("GRANDMOTHER")
Amer. pioneer
Sherr--American p71

BROWN, MARION DOURAS
See DAVIS, MARION

BROWN, MARTHA ("MATTIE")
McCLELLAN (1838-1916)
Amer., noted Ohio mother,
social reformer, temperance
leader, lecturer
Amer.--Mothers p427-428
James--Notable (1) p254-257
McHenry--Liberty's p56

BROWN, MARY RICHARDSON (fl.
1970's)
Amer. TV advertising producer
Innis--Profiles p116-117, por.

BROWN, MARY WILLCOX
See GLENN, MARY (WILLCOX)
BROWN

BROWN, MAXINE (1932-   )
Amer. singer
Claghorn--Biog. p69

BROWN, MOLLY
Amer. Titanic heroine
Sherr--American p26-27,130

BROWN, MOURA
See FERRARS, ELIZABETH X.,
pseud.

BROWN, NANCY (1869/1870-1948)
Amer. journalist
James--Notable p390-391

BROWN, NORMA E. (fl. 1950's-
1970's)
Amer. aviator, Security
Wing Commander, brigadier
general
O'Neill--Women's p545

BROWN, OLIVE (1922-)
Amer. jazz singer
Claghorn--Jazz p51

BROWN, OLYMPIA (1835-1926)
Amer. clergyman, social
reformer, feminist
James--Notable (1) p256-258
McHenry--Liberty's p56
Papachristou--Women p52-53,
60-61, por.
Sherr--American p251
Webster's--Amer. p143-144

BROWN, PATRIKA
See DWYER, KAREN

BROWN, PHOEBE HINSDALE
(1783-1861)
Amer. poet, hymnist
Claghorn--Biog. p69

BROWN, PHYLLIS
Amer., college friend of
Gerald Ford
People's Almanac (1) p334

BROWN, PHYLLIS GEORGE
(c1949-)
Amer. TV co-host
Scheuer--Tel. p60-61

BROWN, RITA MAE
Amer. director, screen-
writer, playwright
O'Neill--Women's p670

BROWN, ROSEMARY (fl. 1970's)
English musician
People's Almanac (2) p1261-
1263, por.

BROWN, ROWINE HAYES
Amer. physician, lawyer,
hospital chief
O'Neill--Women's p229-230

BROWN, RUTH (1928-)
Amer. jazz singer
Claghorn--Jazz p51

BROWN, TABITHA MOFFAT (1780-)
Amer. Western pioneer, noted
Oregon mother
Amer.--Mothers p445
Sherr--American p195
Time--Women p101-104

BROWN, THERESA
Amer. TV newscaster
Gelfman--Women p89,95,99,118-
199,145-146

BROWN, VIRGINIA MAE (1923-)
Amer. lawyer, U.S. govern-
ment official
Cur. Biog. '70 p50-53

BROWN, VIVIAN (fl. 1970's)
Amer. artist
Women's--Female p101

BROWN, WINIFRED (fl. 1920's-1930's)
English aviatrix
Boase--Sky's p113,117-120, por.

BROWNE, BETSY
See ROGERS, MRS. ROBERT

BROWNE, FRANCES (1816-1879)
Irish Children's book author
Showalter--Lit. p325

BROWNE, IRENE (1893/1896-1965)
English actress
Springer--They p45,276, por.

BROWNE, L. VIRGINIA
Amer. TV writer
Scheuer--Tel. p61

BROWNE, MARY BURNET (fl. 1700's)
Amer., wife of William Browne,
daughter of Governor Burnet
Earle--Two Cent. (2) p xi,465-
466, por.

BROWNE, ROSE BUTLER
Amer., noted Rhode Island
mother, educator, (community
religious worker)
Amer.--Mothers p485-486, por.

BROWNING, ANDREA
    Amer. architect
    O'Neill--Women's p612

BROWNING, ELIZABETH BARRETT
    (1806-1861)
    English poet
    Avenel--Comp. p69-70
    Basch--Relative, see index p348
    Bernikow--World p104
    Book--Lists (2) p261,449
    Donaldson--How p48-49
    Ehrlich--Oxford p375
    Jones--Rutledge p113
    Kaplan--Salt p105-107, por.
    Kronenberger--Atlan. p96-97
    Kulkin--Her p53-54
    Magill--Cycl. p138-139
    Moers--Literary p278-280, see
      index under Barrett;
      Browning, por.
    Morley--Literary p207,288,360
    Pearson--Who p207
    People's Almanac (3) p603-604
    Showalter--Lit. p323
    Who Did What p50
    Woman's Almanac p247
    World--Who p24

BROWNING, LADY
    See DuMAURIER, DAPHNE,
      LADY BROWNING

BROWNMILLER, SUSAN (1935-)
    Amer. author, feminist,
      social reformer
    Cur. Biog. '78 p50-52, por.
    Hymowitz--Hist. p182, por.
    100--Greatest (1) p41
    Woman's Almanac p385-386, por.
    World--Who p187

BROWNSCOMBE, JENNIE AUGUSTA
    (1850-1936)
    Amer. painter
    James--Notable (1) p258-259

BROWNSON, JOSEPHINE VAN
    DYKE (1880-1942)
    Amer. social worker, educa-
      tor, catechist
    James--Notable (1) p260-261

BROYDE, RUTH (fl. 1970's)
    Israeli filmmaker
    Smith--Movies p125-126

BRUBAKER, JOAN BAKE (1931-)
    Amer. genealogical researcher,
      author
    Meyer--Who's p40

BRUCE, AILSA MELLON (1901-1969)
    Amer. philanthropist
    World--Who p295

BRUCE, BLANCHE KELSO (1841-
    1898)
    Amer. senator
    Toppin--Biog. p259-260
    Webster's--Amer. p145

BRUCE, CATHERINE WOLFE (1816-
    1900)
    Amer. philanthropist, astron-
      omy patron
    James--Notable (1) p261-262

BRUCE, GEORGIANA
    English-Amer. Brook Farm
      subscriber
    Epstein--Indiv. p88,93,97-98

BRUCE, MARY, LADY
    British microscopical researcher
    O'Neill--Women's p219

BRUCE, MRS. VICTOR (fl. 1930's)
    English aviatrix, sportswoman
    Boase--Sky's p125-126, por.
    Macksey--Book p254

BRUCE, VIRGINIA (1910-1982)
    Amer. actress
    Lamparski--What. (2) p202-203,
      por.
    Springer--They p46,276, por.
    World--Who p228

BRUCE-CLARK, EFFIE
    British lace-maker
    Callen--Women p142

BRUCH, BARBARA (fl. 1960's)
    Amer. heroine, Carnegie
      Medal winner
    O'Neill--Women's p732

BRUERE, MINA M. (fl. 1920's)
    Amer. banker, organization
      co-founder
    O'Neill--Women's p527

BRUMBERG, VALENTINA (fl. 1960's)
    Amer., (cartoon) film

director
Smith--Movies p137

BRUMBERG, ZENAJEDA (fl.
1960's)
Amer. (cartoon) film
director
Smith--Movies p137

BRUMELL, STELLA
British machinery manufac-
turer
Macksey--Book p173

BRUMER, MIRIAM (fl. 1970's)
Amer. painter
Women's--Female p35

BRUMMER, EVA (1901-)
Finnish designer, painter,
rug artist
O'Neill--Women's p274

BRUNAUER, ESTHER DELIA
CAUKIN (1901-1959)
Amer. government official
Sicherman--Notable p114-116

BRUNDTLAND, GRO HARLEM
(1939-)
Norwegian Prime Minister,
physician
Cur. Biog. '81 p42-45, por.
O'Neill--Women's p57-58

BUNHILDA (BRUNHILDE, BRUNE-
HAUT, BRUNHILD) (-613)
Austrasian queen, Visigoth
princess, wife of Sigbert I
Jones--Rutledge p116
Macksey--Book p21

BRUNSON, DOROTHY EDWARDS
(fl. 1970's)
Amer. radio station manager
Innis--Profiles p72-73, por.

BRUNSWICK, RUTH JANE MACK
(1897-1946)
Amer. psychoanalyst
James--Notable (1) p262-263
McHenry--Liberty's p56-57

BRUNTON, ANN
See MERRY, ANN BRUNTON

BRUNTON, MARY (1778-1818)
Scottish novelist

Moers--Literary p44,138,
280

BRURIA (fl. 1970's)
Amer. sculptor
Women's--Female p86

BRUSSELMANS, ANNE
British war heroine
Macksey--Book p60

BRUSTIN, MICHELE
Amer. TV executive
Scheuer--Tel. p61-62

BRYAN, ANNA E. (1858-1901)
Amer. kindergarten educator
James--Notable (1) p263-264

BRYAN, JANE (1918-)
Amer. actress
Lamparski--What. (5) p68-69,
por.
Lamparski--What. (8) p44-45,
por.
Springer--They p46,276, por.

BRYAN, MARY EDWARDS (1838/
1844-1913)
Amer. journalist, author,
editor, club leader
James--Notable (1) p264-265

BRYAN, MARY ELIZABETH BAIRD
(1861-1930)
Amer., noted Nebraska
mother, wife of William Jennings Bryan, lawyer
Amer.--Mothers p335-336, por.

BRYAN, PATRICIA J. (1946-)
Amer. genealogical researcher
Meyer--Who's p41

BRYAN, REBECCA
See BOONE, REBECCA B.

BRYANT, ALICE GERTRUDE (fl.
1890's-1900's)
Amer. physician
O'Neill--Women p213

BRYANT, ANITA JANE (1940-)
Amer. singer, TV performer,
social reformer
Anderson--People p67-68, por.
Claghorn--Biog. p71
Cur. Biog. '75 p56-59, por.

Golson--Playboy p550-577
People--Best p202, por.
World--Who p265

BRYANT, FELICE (fl. 1960's)
Amer. song writer
Pollock--In p135-146, por.

BRYANT, LANE
See MALSIN, LANE BRYANT

BRYANT, LOUISE (1890-1936)
Amer. actress
Ehrlich--Oxford p56,106

BRYANT, ROSALYN (fl. 1970's)
Amer. track and field
athlete
O'Neill--Women's p578

BRYANT, RUTH FLOWERS (1917-)
Amer., noted Kentucky moth-
er, community worker
Amer.--Mothers p221-222, por.

"BRYHER" (BRYER), pseud.
(1894-)
English novelist
Crosland--Beyond p37,160-162,
168
Rogers--Ladies, see index p227,
por.
Seymour-Smith--Novels p107
Showalter--Lit. p348

BRYK, RUT (1916-)
Arabian ceramic artist
O'Neill--Women's p275

BUBB, ELLA L. (1907-)
English genealogical research-
er, editor, writer
Meyer--Who's p40-41

BUCHANAN, ANNABEL MORRIS
(1888/1889-)
Amer. editor, teacher,
author, composer, lecturer
Claghorn--Biog. p71-72

BUCHANAN, ELIZABETH SPEER
(1767-1833)
Amer., mother of President
Buchanan
Faber--Presidents' p243-246

BUCHANAN, MARY MADALINE
(1908-)

Amer., noted Delaware mother, club worker
Amer.--Mothers p91-92, por.

BUCHANAN, SALLY RIDLEY (1750-)
Amer., noted Tennessee mother,
heroine
Amer.--Mothers p507-508

BUCHANAN, VERA D. (c1902-1955)
Amer. Congresswoman
Chamberlin--Min. p226-228, por.

BUCHER, HEIDI (fl. 1970's)
Amer. sculptor
Women's--Female p86

BUCHWALD, ANN (c1921-)
Amer. literary agent, wife of
Art Buchwald
People--Best p59, por.

BUCK, BERTHA ANN STANLEY
(1913-)
Amer., noted New Jersey
mother, community worker
Amer.--Mothers p372, por.

BUCK, LILLIE WEST BROWN
See LESLIE, AMY

BUCK, PEARL SYDENSTRICKER
(1892-1973)
Amer. author, noted Pennsyl-
vania mother
Amer. Mothers p459-460, por.
Avenel--Comp. (2) p45
Clark--Leading p122-124
Cur. Biog. '73 p451
Ehrlich--Oxford, see index p450
Gilfond--Heroines p104-106, por.
Hazen--Interv. p28
Ingraham--Album p58, por.
Kostman--20th p56-77, por.
Kulkin--Her p54-56
McHenry--Liberty's p57
Macksey--Book p191
Magill--Cycl. p147-149
Moers--Literary p92,280
New York Times--Great p28-29,
por.
O'Neill--Women's p678,693
Opfell--Lady p107-121, por.
Reader's--Story p425
Seymour-Smith--Novels p107, por.
Sherr--American p230,244-245
Sicherman--Notable p116-119
Signif.--Amer. p38, por.

Sochen--Herstory p323,340-343,
347, por.
Sochen--Movers p9-10,25-26,
177-183
Webster's--Amer. p148-149
Who Did What p52
Woman's Almanac p247-248
World--Who p10

BUCKEL, CLOE ANNETTE (1833-
1912)
Amer. physician, Civil War
nurse
James--Notable (1) p265-267

BUCKINGHAM, DUCHESS OF (fl.
1620's)
English socialite
Earle--Two Cent. (1) p xvi,
126,278, por.

BUCKINGHAM, KATE STURGES
(fl. 1920's)
Amer. philanthropist
Sherr--American p61

BUCKLES, MARY L. (fl. 1960's)
Amer. heroine, Carnegie
Medal winner
O'Neill--Women's p733

BUCKLES, TANJA (fl. 1960's)
Amer. heroine, Carnegie
Medal winner
O'Neill--Women's p733

BUCKLEY, HELEN DALLAM
(1899-)
Amer. singer, composer,
teacher, writer
Claghorn--Biog. p72

BUCKMASTER, HENRIETTA (1909-
1983)
Amer. author, editor
Cur. Biog. '83 p461

BUDANOVA, KATYA
Russian military flier
O'Neill--Women's p550

BUDBERG, MARIE (1892-1974)
Russian salonist
Macksey--Book p104

BUDD, ANNE DALLAS (1935-)
Amer. genealogical researcher,

editor, writer
Meyer--Who's p41

BUDD, CAROLINE MARY
Amer. early college student
Sherr--American p187, por.

BUDENBACH, MARY H. (fl. 1960's)
Amer. cryptologist
O'Neill--Women's p89,176

BUDEVSKA, ADRIANA KUNCHEVA,
pseud. (1878-1955)
Bulgarian actress
Partington--Who's p53

BUDWIN, FLORENA
Amer. nurse, Civil War soldier
Sherr--American p211

BUELL, HARRIETT EUGENIA (PECK)
(1834-1910)
Amer. hymnist
Claghorn--Biog. p72

BUENO, MARIA ESTER AUDION
(1940-)
Brazilian tennis player
McWhirter--Guinness p153-154,
156, por.
Woman's Almanac p414
World--Who p211

BUERK, MINERVA SMITH (1909-)
Amer. physician
Hellstedt--Women p369-373, por.

BUGBEE, EMMA (c1888-1981)
Amer. reporter, feminist,
journalist, suffragist
Marzolf--Up p44,49-50

BÜHLER, CHARLOTTE BERTHA
(1893-1974)
German-Amer. psychologist
Sicherman--Notable p119-121

BUHSE, SHEILA, SISTER (fl. 1970's)
Amer. nun
Proctor--Women p149,155

BUIC, JAGODA (1930-)
Yugoslavian weaver
O'Neill--Women's p607

BUJOLD, GENEVIEVE (1942-)
French-Canadian actress

Book--Lists (2) p274
Hirschhorn--Rating p64-65, por.
World--Who p255

BULETTE, JULIA (1832-1867)
Amer. Western pioneer
"Madame," philanthropist
Reifert--Women p137-138
Sherr--American p145
Williams--Legend. p25-34, por.

BULKELEY, CHRISTY (fl. 1970's)
Amer. editor, publisher
Marzolf--Up p110,113-114

BULL, MARY (fl. 1770's)
Amer. Revolutionary War
patriot
Meyer--Petticoat p83-84

BULLER, MARY (fl. 1910's)
English aviatrix
Boase--Sky's p21

BULLITT, DOROTHY STIMSON
Amer. millionaire
Forbes--400 ('84) p119

BULLOCH, KAREN (c1945-)
Amer. neuroimmunologist
Science--Digest ('84) p47

BULLOCK, ANNIE MAE
See TURNER, TINA (ANNIE
MAE) BULLOCK

BULLOCK, EDITH R.
Alaskan "tugboat queen"
Jones--Women (1) p145-150, por.

BULLOCK, REBECCA BURGESS
(1886-)
Amer., noted District of
Colbumia mother, religious
civic leader
Amer.--Mothers p107, por.

BULOW, KAREN (1929-)
Danish-Canadian fabric
designer, weaver
O'Neill--Women's p269

BULWER-LYTTON, ROSINA, LADY
See LYTTON, ROSINA DOYLE
BULWER-, LADY

BUMBRY, GRACE MELZIA (1937-)
Amer. opera singer

Gammond--Illus. p238, por.
World--Who p69

BUMPUS, BETTIE McSHANE (1935-)
Amer. genealogical researcher,
teacher, writer
Meyer--Who's p41

BUMPUS, (MERCY) LAVINIA WARREN
See STRATTON, (MERCY) LAVINIA
WARREN BUMPUS, COUNTESS
MAGRI

BUMSTEAD, "COOKIE"
See MUTCHIE, MARJORIE ANN

BUNCE, ELIZABETH T. (fl. 1940's-
1970's)
Amer. oceanographer
O'Neill--Women's p172

BUNDY, MAY SUTTON
See SUTTON, MAY

BUNFORD, JANE (1895-1922)
British, tallest woman
Macksey--Book p12

BUNIM, MARY-ELLIS (1946-)
Amer. TV executive producer
Scheuer--Tel. p63

BUNKE BIDER, HAYDEE TAMARA
(1937-1967)
German-Argentinean, Cuban
communist guerilla
Henderson--Ten p213-240, por.

BUNNELL, GOODWIFE (fl. 1650's)
Amer. colonial
Williams--Demeter's p88

BUNTING, MARY INGRAHAM (1910-)
Amer. microbiologist, editor,
college president
M.I.T.--Women p20-24
O'Neill--Women's p157
Warren--Pictorial p207

BUNYAN, MAUREEN
Amer. TV newscaster
Gelfman--Women p21,48,70,118,
132

BURBIDGE, ELEANOR MARGARET
English astronomer, director,
observatory
O'Neill--Women's p153-154

BURCE, SUZANNE
See POWELL, JANE

BURCH, LINDA
Amer. WAC, military science professor
O'Neill--Women's p541

BURCHENAL, ELIZABETH (c1876-1959)
Amer. folk dance narrator, folklorist
Sicherman--Notable p121-122

BURDEN, ELIZABETH (fl. 1870's)
British embroiderer
Callen--Women p94-95,101,104, 222

BURDETTE, BARBARA L. (fl. 1960's)
Amer. heroine, Carnegie Medal winner
O'Neill--Women's p733

BURDETTE-COUTTS, ANGELA GEORGINA, BARONESS (1814-1906)
English philanthropist
Macksey--Book p113
Marlowe--Great p58-63, por.

BURE, IDELETTE DE (fl. c1530's)
French, wife of Calvin
Bainton--France p87-88

BURFORD, ELEANOR
See PLAIDY, JEAN

BURGE, MARIANNE (fl. 1970's)
Amer. accounting executive
O'Neill--Women's p529

BURGESS, ABBIE (1839-1892)
Amer. lighthouse keeper
Kulkin--Her p56-57

BURGESS, DOROTHY (1907-1961)
Amer. actress
Springer--They p46,276

BURGESS, WILMA (1939-)
Amer. singer
Claghorn--Biog. p73

BURGHLEY, MILDRED COOKE, LADY
English religious worker,

daughter of Anthony Cooke
Bainton--Spain p113-116

BURGOS, JULIA DE (1914/1916-1953)
Puerto Rican-Amer. poet, journalist
Moers--Literary p280
Sicherman--Notable p122-123
Signif.--Amer. p39, por.

BURGOYNE, CHARLOTTE STANLEY, LADY (fl. 1770's)
British, wife of General Burgoyne
Booth--Women p125-127

BURGUNDY, ISABELLA, DUCHESS OF
See YORKE, MARGARET OF

BURKA, ILONA (fl. 1970's)
Hungarian MP in House
Macksey--Book p39

BURKE, BILLIE MARY (1885-1970)
Amer. singer, actress
Claghorn--Biog. p73-44
Hazen--Interv. p105
Keylin--Hollywood p50-51, por.
Shipman--Gold. p87-91, por.
Springer--They p46,48,276-277, por.
World--Who p228

BURKE, CATHERINE LYNN
Amer. Rhodes Scholar
O'Neill--Women's p434

BURKE, DENISE W. (1947-)
Amer. TV director
Scheuer--Tel. p54

BURKE, KATHLEEN (1)
Scottish, Secretary, Women's Hospital for Foreign Service
· Hazen--Interv. p311-312

BURKE, KATHLEEN (2) (1913-1980)
Amer. actress
Springer--They p49,277, por.

BURKE, KATHY (fl. 1960's-1970's)
Amer. undercover detective
O'Neill--Women's p373

BURKE, MARTHA JANE CANARY
See "CALAMITY JANE"

BURKE, MAUDE ALICE
See CUNARD, MAUD ALICE
BURKE, LADY

BURKE, MILDRED (fl. 1930's)
Amer. wrestler
People's Almanac (2) p1087-
1088

BURKE, (MRS.) F. (fl. 1940's)
Australian golfer
McWhirter--Guinness p79

BURKE, YVONNE BRATHWAITE
(1932-)
Amer. Congresswoman
Book--Lists (2) p261
Bowman--Politics p34-37, por.
Chamberlin--Min. p352
Cur. Biog. '75 p59-62, por.
Diamonstein--Open p28-32, por.
Miller--Fishbait p205-206,267
O'Neill--Women's p73
Warren--Pictorial p200-201
Woman's Almanac p470, por.

BURKHART, ANNA K. MILLER
(1868-)
Amer., noted North Dakota
mother, midwife, church
worker
Amer.--Mothers p415-416

BURLEND, REBECCA (fl. 1900's)
English-Amer. farmer
Neidle--America's p96-98

BURLIN, NATALIE CURTIS
See CURTIS, NATALIE

BURNE-JONES, GEORGIANA (fl.
1860's)
British engraver, embroiderer
Callen--Women p10,15,181, por.

BURNELL, JOCELYN BELL (fl.
1960's)
Amer. radio astronomer
O'Neill--Women's p154

BURNETT, CAROL (1933-)
Amer. comedienne, actress,
singer
Anderson--People p69-70, por.
Claghorn--Biog. p74
Hershey--Between p20
Hirschhorn--Rating p65, por.

Holme--Journal p324, por.
100--Greatest (1) p106-107, por.
Scheuer--Tel. p64-65
Woman's Almanac p317, por.
World--Who p275

BURNETT, FRANCES ELIZA HODG-
SON (1849-1924)
English-Amer. novelist, chil-
dren's writer
Avenel--Comp. (1) p77
Avenel--Comp. (2) p46
Ehrlich--Oxford p164,167,288
James--Notable (1) p269-270
Jones--Rutledge p124
Kulkin--Her p57-58
McHenry--Liberty's p58
Macksey--Book p188
Moers--Literary p246,263,280
Morley--Literary p137-138,369-370
O'Neill--Women's p690-691
Showalter--Lit. p338
Warren--Pictorial p129
World--Who p10

BURNEY, FANNY (1752-1840)
English novelist, diarist
Avenel--Comp. (1) p78
Fine--Women p65
Horner--English p50-51,59-67,
134-141
Hufstader--Sisters p273-309, see
also index p320, por.
Jones--Rutledge p124-125
Kronenberger--Atlan. p111-112
Macksey--Book p97,183,272
Magill--Cycl. p158-159
Moers--Literary p280-281, see
also index p323, por.
Morley--Literary, see index p483
World--Who p24

BURNINGHAM, CHARLENE
Amer. weaver
Bowman--Art p30-35, por.

BURNS, AGNES BROUN (1732-1820)
Scottish, mother of Robert
Burns
Diagram--Mothers p38-39

BURNS, ANNE
British glider pilot, aviatrix,
aeronautical engineer
Macksey--Book p252
O'Neill--Women's p591

BURNS, ELLEN B.
Amer. judge
O'Neill--Women's p372

BURNS, LORETTA ELLIOTT
(1928-)
Amer. genealogical researcher,
author, indexer
Meyer--Who's p42

BURNS, LUCY (1879-1966)
Amer. suffragist, feminist
Hymowitz--Hist. p279,281-282
Millstein--We p175,179,182,193-
194
Papachristou--Women p172-174,
176,182-183
Sicherman--Notable p124-125
Warren--Pictorial p160,162

BURNS, MARCIA
See VAN NESS, MARCIA BURNS

BURNS, MRS. ROBERT
See ARMOUR, JEAN

BURNS, SHEILA
See BLOOM, URSULA

BURNSTEIN, RONA
See BARRETT, RONA

BURR, EUNICE DENNIE (1729-1805)
Amer. Revolutionary War
patriot
Meyer--Petticoat p149-150

BURR, THEODOSIA PREVOST
(1783-1813)
Amer. scholar, society belle,
daughter of Aaron Burr
DePauw--Rem. p98-99, por.
James--Notable (1) p270-272
Peacock--Famous p18-38, por.
Warren--Pictorial p74

BURRAS, ANNE (fl. c1608)
Amer., first female servant
in Virginia
Williams--Demeter's p19

BURRILL, CHRIS (fl. 1970's)
Amer. cinematographer,
director, editor
Smith--Movies p154,230

BURROS, MARIAN (fl. 1970's)
Amer. journalist, food editor

O'Neill--Womens p467-
468

BURROUGHS, MARGARET (1917-)
Amer. writer, artist, curator,
lecturer
Innis--Profiles p110-111, por.

BURROUGHS, NANNIE HELEN (1878/
1883-1961)
Amer. educator, school founder, bookkeeper, club leader
Sicherman--Notable p125-127

BURROWES, M., MISS
British lace-maker
Callen--Women p143

BURROWS, ANNE
Amer. colonial servant
Ingraham--Album p5

BURSON, JOSEPHINE WAINMAN (fl.
1940's-1970's)
Amer., noted Tennessee
mother, humanitarian
Amer.--Mothers p509

BURSTYN, ELLEN (1932-)
Amer. actress
Anderson--People p70-71, por.
Cur. Biog. '75 p62-65, por.
Hirschhorn--Rating p67, por.
Manchel--Women p18-19,103,116-
117, por.
100--Greatest (1) p20, por.
Shipman--Internatl. p80-82, por.
Smith--Movies p68-69
World--Who p228

BURT, BERYL (fl. 1970's)
Amer. agriculturalist
O'Neill--Women's p28

BURT, KATHARINE NEWLIN (1882-)
Amer. novelist
Ehrlich--Oxford p381

BURT, OLIVE WOOLEY (1894-)
Amer., noted Utah mother,
teacher, newspaper woman,
world traveller, author
Amer.--Mothers p530, por.

BURTNETT, FLORISSA (1936-)
Amer. wheat insurance agency
owner
O'Neill--Women's p16

BURTON, BERYL (fl. 1950's-1960's)
British cyclist
McWhirter--Guinness p52-53,
por.

BURTON, ELAINE
British runner
Macksey--Book p258

BURTON, MRS. FRANCIS (fl.
1780's)
English socialite
Ware--Meet p74

BURTON, MARIE
Amer. painter, muralist
Bowman--New p36-39, por.
Women's--Female p35

BURTON, SYBIL
British, former wife of
Richard Burton
Hershey--Between p124-126

BURTON, TERRY
Amer. Coast Guard officer
O'Neill--Women's p549

BURTON, VIRGINIA LEE (1909-
1968)
Amer. author, illustrator
McHenry--Liberty's p58-59

BURWELL, LUCY RANDOLPH (fl.
c1770)
Amer. musician
DePauw--Rem. p113

BUSCH, MAE (1895-1946)
Australian actress
Springer--They p49,277, por.

BUSEY, KATE BAKER (1855-)
Amer., noted Illinois mother,
feminist, patriot
Amer.--Mothers p164, por.

"BUSH ANGEL"
See MILSTEAD, VIOLET

BUSH, DOROTHY VREDENBURGH
(fl. 1950's)
Amer. Democratic National
Committee secretary
O'Neill--Women's p74-75

BUSHFIELD, VERA C. (1889-)
Amer. senator

Chamberlin--Min. p196-
199

BUSHMAN, KATHERINE GENTRY
(1919-)
Amer. genealogical researcher,
author, editor
Meyer--Who's p42

BUSS, FRANCES (fl. 1940's)
Amer. TV director
Marzolf--Up p158
Women--Radio p29

BUSS, FRANCES MARY (1827-1894)
English educator, social re-
former, school founder
Jones--Rutledge p126
Macksey--Book p70-71

BUTCHER, GRACE (1934-)
Amer. poet
Chester--Rising p228-232, por.

BUTE, MARY ELLEN (fl. 1930's)
Amer. film producer, writer,
director
Smith--Movies p33-34, por.

BUTLER, ELIZABETH SOUTHERDEN
THOMPSON, LADY (1850-1933)
English painter
Fine--Women p83-84
Harris--Women p91,53-54,58,249-
250,352
Sparrow--Women p9,154

BUTLER, ELOISE (-1933)
Amer. botanist, founder of
Sanctuary
Sherr--American p120

BUTLER, MRS. GEORGE H.
See CHESTNEY, JOSEPHINE

BUTLER, GWENDOLINE (1922-)
English novelist
Seymour-Smith--Novels p108

BUTLER, JOSEPHINE ELIZABETH
(1828-1906)
English social reformer, social-
ist
Basch--Relative p105-106,121,195,
203,209
Boyd--Three p23-92
Jones--Rutledge p127
Longford--Eminent p109-128, por.

Macksey--Book p115, por.
Showalter--Lit. p330
Who Did What p54

BUTLER, MARGARET
    Amer. mathematician
    O'Neill--Women's p178,316

BUTLER, MARIE JOSEPH, (MOTHER)
    (1860-1940)
    Irish-Amer. nun, college
    founder
    James--Notable (1) p272-273
    McHenry--Liberty's p59

BUTLER, SALLY, (SISTER) (fl.
    1970's)
    Amer. Dominican nun
    Proctor--Women p148-149,164

BUTLER, SELENA SLOAN (c1872-
    1964)
    Amer. community leader,
    organization founder
    Sicherman--Notable p127-129

BUTT, CLARA, DAME (1873-1936)
    English singer
    Macksey--Book p215

BUTTELINI, MARCHESA
    Italian physician
    Mead--Hist. p508

BUTTERFIELD, JANE (fl. 1770's)
    English accused criminal
    Earle--Two Cent. (2) p676, por.

BUTTERS, DOROTHY GILMAN
    See GILMAN, DOROTHY, pseud.

BUTTERWORTH, MARY PECK
    (1686-1775)
    Amer. accused counterfeiter
    James--Notable (1) p273-274
    Macksey--Book p134
    Williams--Demeter's p186
    Woman's Almanac p499

BUTTONS, ALICIA (fl. 1970's-
    1980's)
    Amer., wife of Red Buttons
    Funt--Are p65-80, por.

BUZZI, RUTH (1936-)
    Amer. comedienne
    World--Who p275

BYARD, CAROLE (1970's)
    Amer. artist
    Fax--Black p61-78, por.

BYARS, BETSY (1928-)
    Amer. children's author
    O'Neill--Women's p691

BYATT, A.S. (Antonia Susan)
    (1936-)
    English, critic, novelist
    Seymour-Smith--Novels p109
    Showalter--Lit. p350

BYERLY, KATHLEEN
    Amer. training Commander,
    Pacific Fleet
    O'Neill--Women's p547

BYERS, ELIZABETH MINERVA SUM-
    NER (fl. 1850's-1860's)
    Amer. pioneer newspaper
    woman
    Sherr--American p27

BYERS, NINA
    Amer. physicist
    O'Neill--Women's p185

BYINGTON, ELLA GOOD (1858-)
    Amer. newspaper editor
    Scott--Southern p120

BYINGTON, SPRING (1893-1971)
    Amer. actress, radio, TV
    performer
    Cur. Biog. '71 p461
    Lamparski--What. (3) p78-79,
    por.
    Springer--They p49-50,277, por.
    World--Who p228

BYNOE, HILDA (fl. 1960's)
    Grenadan governor
    Macksey--Book p39

BYRD, ELIZABETH (BETTY) CARTER
    (1732-1760)
    Amer., wife of William Byrd
    Earle--Two Cent. (2) p xii,466-
    467, por.

BYRD, EVELYN
    Amer., daughter of William
    Byrd
    Earle--Two Cent. (2) p xi,464,
    498-499, por.

BYRD, MARY (fl. 1700's)
Amer. apothecary
Hymowitz--Hist. p8

BYRD, MARY WILLING (fl. 18th
cent.)
Amer. colonial plantation
manager
DePauw--Found. p27-28

BYRNE, ETHEL
Amer. social reformer
Hymowitz--Hist. p296
Sherr--American p167

BYRNE, JANE MARGARET BURKE
(1934-)
Amer. mayor
Cur. Biog. '80 p32-35, por.
McHenry--Liberty's p59

BYRNE, MARY
Amer. TV association presi-
dent
Scheuer--Tel. p68

BYRON, CATHERINE GORDON
Scottish, mother of George
Gordon, Lord Byron
Diagram--Mothers p40-41, por.

BYRON, KATHARINE EDGAR
(c1902-1976)
Amer. Congresswoman
Chamberlin--Min. p156-159

BYRON, MARION ("PEANUTS")
(1910-)
Amer. actress
Springer--They p50,277, por.

C

CABALLE, MONTSERRAT (1933-)
Spanish opera singer
Gammond--Illus. p238-239, por.
Neidle--America's p222
O'Neill--Women's p622,638

CABELL, MRS. CASKIE
See ENDERS, NANNIE

CABELL, LIZZIE (fl. 1860's)
Amer. Southern belle
DeLeon--Belles p146-147, por.
Peacock--Famous p230, por.

CABELL, MARY WASHINGTON (fl.
1860's)
Amer. Southern belle
DeLeon--Belles p207-208, por.

CABEZA DE BACA, FABIOLA (1896-)
Amer. writer
Fisher--Third p vii,321

CABRINI, FRANCES XAVIER, SAINT
(1850-1917)
Italian-Amer. orphanage
founder, Saint
Bloom--Pilgrim p123
Ingraham--Album p71
James--Notable (1) p274-276
Jones--Rutledge p130
Longstreet--Queen p192
McHenry--Liberty's p60
Marlowe--Great p147-151, por.
Neidle--America's p72-74
O'Neill--Women's p388
People's Almanac (2) p1196
Signif.--Amer. p27, por.
Stoddard--Famous p81-89, por.
Webster's--Amer. p165
Woman's Almanac p401, por.
World--Who p81

CACCINI, FRANCESCA (LA CECCHINA)
(1581/1587-c1640)
Italian singer, composer, poet
Neuls-Bates--Women p xiv,55-61

CADE, RUTH ANN (1917-)
Amer. mechanical engineer,
professor
O'Neill--Women's p195

CADILLA DE MARTINEZ, MARIA
See MARTINEZ, MARIA CADILLA
DE

CADWALADER, FRANCES, LADY
ERSKINE (1781-1843)
daughter of John Cadwalader,
wife of David Montague
Flexner--Face p218, por.

CADY, MARGARET LIVINGSTON
Amer., mother of Elizabeth
Cady Stanton
Hymowitz--Hist. p88

CAFFI, MARGHERITA (fl. 1662-1700)
Italian artist
Harris--Women p151-152,344

CAHIER, MARIE (1870/1874-1933)
Amer. singer, actress
Claghorn--Biog. p79
James--Notable (1) p276-277

CAHIER, SARAH JANE LAYTON-
WALKER (1875-1951)
Amer. opera singer
Claghorn--Biog. p79

CAHOON, MARY ODILE, SISTER
(fl. 1970's)
Amer. biologist, Antarctica
Land--New p21,63-67,109,137,
221, por.
O'Neill--Women's p163

CAIN, ELIZABETH (fl. c1755)
Amer. craftswoman
Williams--Demeter's p177

CAIN, JACQUELINE RUTH (JACKIE)
(1928-)
Amer. singer
Claghorn--Biog. p80
Claghorn--Jazz p60

CAINE, LYNN (fl. 1970's)
Amer. publicity manager,
writer
P.W.--Author p273-275,486

CAIRD, (ALICE) MONA (c1855-
1932)
British novelist, poet,
feminist, theoretician
Showalter--Lit. p339

CALAHAN, MARY A. (-1906)
Amer. educator
Sherr--American p1

"CALAMITY JANE" (c1852-1903)
Amer. Western frontier
character
Eills--Here p78-79
James--Notable (1) p267-268
Levenson--Women p69, por.
McHenry--Liberty's p57-58
People's Almanac (1) p99
Reifert--Women p144-146
Sherr--American p132,134-
135,214,256, por.
Time--Women p158-159, por.
Warren--Pictorial p96
Webster's--Amer. p153
Who Did What p57

Woman's Almanac p500, por.
World--Who p295

CALDERINI, NOVELLA (fl. c1349)
Italian lawyer
Macksey--Book p122

CALDERONE, MARY STEICHEN
(1904-)
Amer. physician, public health
educator
Bowman--Medicine p4-9, por.
Gilbert--Part. p255-263, por.
Gold--Until p312-328, por.
McHenry--Liberty's p60
O'Neill--Women's p228

CALDICOTT, HELEN (1938-)
Australian physician, social
activist
Cur. Biog. '83 p41-45, por.

CALDWELL, ANNE (1867-1936)
Amer. songwriter, librettist,
singer
Jablonski--Ency. p213

CALDWELL, HANNAH OGDEN (1737-
1780)
Amer., noted New Jersey
mother, Revolutionary War
martyr, patriot
Amer.--Mothers p369
Meyer--Petticoat p74-75,77,173-
174
Sherr--American p154

CALDWELL, JANET TAYLOR
See CALDWELL, TAYLOR

CALDWELL, MARGARET HOOD
(1940's-1970's)
Amer., noted North Carolina
mother, agriculturist
Amer.--Mothers p408-409, por.

CALDWELL, MARY GWENDOLIN,
MARQUISE OF MONTRIERS-
MERINVILLE (1863-1909)
Amer. philanthropist, socialite
James--Notable (1) p277-278
McHenry--Liberty's p60-61

CALDWELL, MARY LETITIA (1890-
1972)
Amer. chemist, professor
O'Neill--Women's p165

CALDWELL, RACHEL (c1739-1825)
Amer. Revolutionary War
patriot
Meyer--Petticoat p180-181

CALDWELL, SARAH (1928-)
Amer. opera director, con-
ductor
Cur. Biog. '73 p72-74, por.
Gilbert--Part. p239-249, por.
Kufrin--Uncom. p92-111, por.
McHenry--Liberty's p61
100--Greatest (1) p80
O'Neill--Women's p638
People--Best p134
Woman's Almanac p288-289, por.
World--Who p69

CALDWELL, SHIRLEY
Amer. labor union leader
O'Neill--Women's p315

CALDWELL, TAYLOR (1900-1985)
English-Amer. novelist
Cur. Biog. '85 p462-463
Ehrlich--Oxford p101,107
McHenry--Liberty's p61-62
People's Almanac (2) p1221-1222
Seymour-Smith--Novels p110
Signif.--Amer. p59, por.
World--Who p11

CALDWELL, ZOE (1933-)
Australian actress
Cur. Biog. '70 p64-66, por.
World--Who p255

CALHOUN, FLORIDE CALHOUN
(1792-1866)
Amer., wife of John Calhoun,
hostess, musician, furniture
designer
Sherr--American p210,213, por.

CALIFA, AMAZON QUEEN
Columbian jungle queen
People's Almanac (1) p738

CALIGIURI, NADINE
Amer. founder of "Handi-
capables"
O'Neill--Women's p117

CALISCH, MARIA, BARONESS VON
(1779-)
Hungarian physician
Mead--Hist. p507

CALISHER, HORTENSE (1911-)
Amer. novelist
Avenel--Comp. (2) p51
Cahill--Women p106,376
Cur. Biog. '73 p74-77, por.
Ehrlich--Oxford, see index p451,
por.
Moers--Literary p281
P.W.--Author p24-26,486-487
Seymour-Smith--Novels p110

CALKINS, MARY WHITON (1863-
1930)
Amer. philosopher, psycholo-
gist, author
James--Notable (1) p278-280
McHenry--Liberty's p62
O'Neill--Women's p412

CALL, MISS (fl. 1900's)
Amer. wrestler, sister of Joe
Call
Coffin--Parade p57

CALLAHAN, JEAN (fl. 1960's-
1970's)
Amer. free-lance writer
O'Neill--Women's p695

CALLAHAN, NANCY ("GRANNY
DOLLAR") (c1826-1931)
Amer. Cherokee pioneer
Sherr--American p1

CALLARD, CAROLE CRAWFORD
(1941-)
Amer. genealogical researcher,
indexer, writer
Meyer--Who's p45

CALLAS, MARIA MENEGHINI (1923-
1977)
Amer. opera singer
Brecher--Lives p229-230, por.
Claghorn--Biog. p80
Cur. Biog. '77 p460
Fabian--On p206-207, por.
Fry--1000 p323-324, por.
Gammond--Illus. p62,63,239, por.
Jones--Rutledge p134
Lewis--Prime p160-161
McHenry--Liberty's p62-63
O'Neill--Women's p621
Webster's--Amer. p168-169
Who Did What p56
Woman's Almanac p289-290
World--Who p69

CALLAWAY, MARY (fl. 1776)
Amer., Indian captive
Sherr--Amer. p78

CALLAWAY, VIRGINIA HAND
(1900-)
Amer., noted Georgia
mother, environmentalist
Amer.--Mothers p132-133, por.

CALLCOTT, MARIA, LADY
See GRAHAM, MARIA

CALLIRHOË
See KORA

CALLOT SISTERS
French fashion designers
Macksey--Book p266

CALLOWAY, BLANCHE (1902-1978)
Amer. jazz singer, composer,
orchestra leader
Claghorn--Jazz p61

CALLUM, AGNES KANE (1925-)
Amer. genealogical researcher,
author
Meyer--Who's p45

CALOGEROPOULOS, CECILIA
SOPHIA ANNA MARIA
See CALLAS, MARIA MENEGHINI

CALVE, EMMA (ROSA) (1858-1952)
French opera singer
Claghorn--Biog. p80
Jones--Rutledge p135
Tuggle--Golden p180-181, por.

CALVET, CORINNE (1925-)
French-Amer. actress
Lamparski--What. (3) p138-139,
por.

CALYPSO
Greek painter
Macksey--Book p194

CAMACHO, MATHILDE "DITA"
Amer. magazine reporter
Hamblin--That p110-114, por.

CAMARGO, MARIE ANNE DE
CUPIS DE (1710-1770)
Belgian-French ballet dancer
Jones--Rutledge p136

Macksey--Book p225, por.
Migel--Ballerinas p31-38, por.

CAMBRIDGE, ADA (1844-1926)
English novelist
Showalter--Lit. p336

CAMDEN, FRANCES, MARCHIONESS
(c1760-1829)
English, subject of portrait
Ware--Meet p27,75

CAMERINO, DUCHESS OF
See CIBO, CATERINA, DUCHESS
OF CAMERINO

CAMERON, DONALDINA MACKENZIE
(1869-1968)
Scottish-Amer. missionary,
crusader
Dunlap--Calif. p32, por.
Gray--Women p67-74, por.
O'Neill--Women's p399
Sherr--American p20
Sicherman--Notable p130-132

CAMERON, ELIZABETH SHERMAN
(fl. 1870's)
Amer., friend of Henry Adams,
wife of James Cameron
Daniels--Wash. p13-14,20

CAMERON, EVELYN JEPHSON,
"LADY" (fl. 1910's)
English photographer
Sherr--American p137, por.
Time--Women p107-109

CAMERON, JULIA (1815-1879)
British portrait photographer
Macksey--Book p203
Munsterberg--Hist. p121-123
Woman's Almanac p220
Women's--Female p6

CAMERON, MARGARET
English painter
Sparrow--Women p69,131,155

CAMERON, SHIRLEY (1944-)
English artist
Contemp. Brit. unp., por.

CAMP, MRS. ROBERT
See FISHER, ANNE

CAMPAGNOLA, IONA (fl. 1970's)
Canadian minister
O'Neill--Women's p51

CAMPAN, (JEANNE LOUISE)
HENRIETTE GENET (1753-
1822)
French educator, school
founder
Macksey--Book p66, por.

CAMPANINI, BARBARA (1721-1799)
Italian ballet dancer
Miguel--Ballerinas p39-45, por.

CAMPBELL, ADA
See IRWIN, MAY

CAMPBELL, ALLA BOZARTH (fl.
1970's)
Amer. Episcopalian priest
O'Neill--Women's p382,384

CAMPBELL, BEATRICE STELLA
TANNER (1885-1940)
English actress
Entertainers p152
Findlater--Player p167-171, por.
Jones--Rutledge p138
Springer--They p54,277, por.
World--Who p255

CAMPBELL, CAROLEE (fl. 1970's)
Amer, actress, white-water
river runner
Lichtenstein--Mach. p43-46

CAMPBELL, ELLA GRANT (fl.
1880's)
Amer. florist
Bolton--Success p127-148, por.

CAMPBELL, HELEN STUART (1839-
1918)
Amer. author, social reformer, home economist
James--Notable (1) p280-281

CAMPBELL, JANE CANNON (1743-
1836)
Amer. Revolutionary War
patriot
Meyer--Petticoat p116

CAMPBELL, JANET (1947-)
Amer. Indian writer
Fisher--Third p iv,54,106

CAMPBELL, JOYCE B. (fl. 1960's-
1980's)
Amer. TV executive, station
manager
Scheuer--Tel. p71

CAMPBELL, MARGARET W. (fl.
1880's)
Amer. suffragist
Papachristou--Women p108-110

CAMPBELL, MARY (1) (fl. 1759)
Amer., Indian captive, 1759
Sherr--American p184

CAMPBELL, MARY (2) (OF
AUCHAMORE) (-1786)
Scottish, inspiration of Robert
Burns
Coffin--Female p63-72
Morley--Literary p437,439,445-
446,456

CAMPBELL, MAUDE (fl. 1920's)
Amer., first Western passen-
ger on commercial airplane
Woman's Almanac p369

CAMPBELL, PERSIA CRAWFORD
(1898-1974)
Australian-Amer. economist,
consumer advocate
Sicherman--Notable p132-133

CAMPBELL, TIMOTHEA
Amer. painter
Women's--Female p35

CAMPBELL-PURDIE, WENDY
New Zealander tree expert
Macksey--Book p167-168

CAMPREDON, WAVA T. (fl. 1970's)
Amer. heroine, Carnegie
Medal winner
O'Neill--Women's p734

CANARY (CANARRY), MARTHA
JANE
See "CALAMITY JANE"

CANAVEZES, MARCO
See MIRANDA, CARMEN

CANAVIER, ELENA
Amer. craftswoman
O'Neill--Women's p129

CANCINO, ESMERELDA ARBOLEDA
DE CUEVAS
See CUEVAS CANCINO, ESMER-
ELDA ARBOLEDA DE

CANDEILLE, JULIE (1767-1836)
French singer, composer
Neuls-Bates--Women p88

CANDELARIA, ANDREA (fl. 1830's)
Amer. heroine
Sherr--American p223

CANDELARIA, MARIA (fl. 17th
cent.)
Central American Indian
"Jeanne d'Arc"
Henderson--Ten p xv

CANFIELD, DOROTHY
See FISHER, DOROTHY CAN-
FIELD

CANNING, ELIZABETH (1734-1773)
Amer. malefactor
DePauw--Rem. p69

CANNON, ANNIE JUMP (1863-1941)
Amer. astronomer
Emberlin--Cont. p7-27, por.
James--Notable (1) p281-283
McHenry--Liberty's p63
Macksey--Book p154
O'Neill--Women's p149-150, por.
Sherr--American p36, por.
Webster's--Amer. p173
World--Who p103

CANNON, DYAN (1939-)
Amer. actress, singer
Hirschhorn--Rating p73, por.
World--Who p228

CANNON, HARRIET STARR (1823-
1896)
Amer. Episcopalian Mother
Superior
James--Notable (1) p283-284
McHenry--Liberty's p63

CANNON, IDA MAUD (1877-1960)
Amer. nurse, social worker,
author
Sicherman--Notable p133-135

CANNON, ISABELLA W. (c1902-)
Amer. politician
Felton--Famous p130

CANNON, LOUISE E. (fl. 1960's)
Canadian heroine, Carnegie
Medal winner
O'Neill--Women's p733

CANNON, LUCRETIA ("PATTY")
(-1829)
Canadian outlaw, accused
murderer
Sherr--American p37

CANNON, MARTHA ("MATTIE")
HUGHES
Amer. feminist, school founder,
Mormon, nurse
Sherr--American p227

CANNON, SARAH OPHELIA COLLEY
See PEARL, MINNIE

CANOVA, JUDY (1916-)
Amer. singer, radio, TV
comedienne
Claghorn--Biog. p82
Mordden--Movie p138

CANSINO, MARGARET CARMEN
CANSING
See HAYWORTH, RITA

CAPERS, VALERIE (fl. 1970's)
Amer. jazz pianist, composer,
conductor
Claghorn--Jazz p61-62

CAPET, GABRIELLE (1761-1817)
French artist
Harris--Women p40,186,195-196,
348

CAPETILLO, LUISA (1880-1922)
Puerto Rican feminist, maga-
zine founder
O'Neill--Women's p698-699

CAPO, MARY ANN (fl. 1950's)
Amer. nuclear physicist
O'Neill--Women's p195

CAPONE, TERESA (c1867-1952)
Italian, mother of Al Capone
Book--Lists (1) p285
Diagram--Mothers p42-43, por.

"CAPTAIN MOLLY"
See CORBIN, MARGARET COCH-
RAN

CARAHER-MANNING, DOREEN
(1929-   )
Amer. genealogical researcher, author
Meyer--Who's p45-46

CARAWAY, HATTIE OPHELIA
WYATT (1878-1950)
Amer. Senator, noted
Arkansas mother
Amer.--Mothers p46, por.
Chamberlin--Min. p86-95, por.
Hazen--Interv. p207
James--Notable (1) p284-286
McHenry--Liberty's p63-64
Miller--Fishbait p63-64
O'Neill--Women's p66,68
Sherr--American p11,216
Signif.--Amer. p39, por.
Warren--Pictorial p179
World--Who p137

CARBINE, PATRICIA (fl. 1970's)
Amer. magazine publisher,
editor
Marzolf--Up p244
O'Neill--Women's p479-480,484

CARBONE, PAULA (fl. 1960's)
Amer. fashion designer
O'Neill--Women's p257-258

CARCOMO, MARIA TERESA (fl.
1940's-1970's)
Portuguese cabinet official
O'Neill--Women's p61

CARDEN, MAREN L. (fl. 1960's-
1970's)
Amer. feminist
Marzolf--Up p237

CARDENAS, TERESA TORRES
(fl. 1970's)
Amer. Chicano, wife of
labor unionist
Coles--Women p127-177

CARDEW, GLORIA
British illustrator
Callen--Women p194

CARENZA
French troubadour
Bogin--Women p145,178-179

CAREY, ELIZABETH TANFIELD,
LADY (c1585-1639)
English poet
Pearson--Who p117

CAREY, ERNESTINE MOLLER
GILBRETH (1908-   )
Amer. author, retail executive
World--Who p11

CAREY, JOSEPHINE
Amer. social reformer
Hymowitz--Hist. p242

CAREY, ROSA NOUCHETTE (1840-
1909)
English novelist
Showalter--Lit. p335

CARGILL, MARGARET (fl. 1980's)
Amer. millionaire
Forbes--400 ('84) p117

CARI, TERESA (fl. 1890's)
Brazilian seamstress, labor
worker, feminist
Hahner--Women p114-116

CARIA, MARIA ADELA (fl. 1960's-
1970's)
Argentinean, Antarctica
hydrographic research scientist
Land--New p21

CARITA, MARIA (c1918-1978)
Spanish-French wigmaker,
hairdresser
O'Neill--Women's p238

CARITA, ROSITA
Spanish-French wigmaker
O'Neill--Women's p238

CARL, ANN BAUMGARTNER (fl.
1940's)
Amer. aviator, (jet pilot)
O'Neill--Women's p742

CARL, MARY SISTER (fl. 1970's-
1980's)
Amer. nun, captain, U.S. Air
Force
People's Almanac (3) p61

CARLETON, MRS. THOMAS (fl.
1970's)
Amer. patriot

Young--Revol. p30-38,52-56,181,
187-188,201-202

CARLILE, JOAN (1600-1679)
English portrait artist
Fine--Women p67-68

CARLISLE, HELEN GRACE (1898-)
Amer. author
Hershey--Between p24-26

CARLISLE, KITTY
See HART, KITTY CARLISLE

CARLISLE, MARY (1912-)
Amer. actress, beauty salon
manager
Lamparski--What. (3) p202-203,
por.

CARLISLE, UNA MAE (1918-1956)
Amer. jazz pianist, singer,
composer
Claghorn--Jazz p62

CARLOS, WENDY (1939-)
Amer. musician, transsexual
Book--Lists (2) p327

CARLSON, CAROLYN
Amer. ballet dancer
Percival--Modern p83,86

CARLSON, CYNTHIA (1942-)
Amer. painter
Women's--Female p35

CARLSON, GRACE (fl. 1940's)
Amer. Vice Presidential
candidate
People's Almanac (1) p127

CARLSON, LYNNE (fl. 1970's)
Amer. veterinarian
Seed--Saturday's p52-56, por.

CARLSON, NATALIE SAVAGE
(1906-)
Amer. children's book author
Ehrlich--Oxford p237

CARLSSON, BRITT (fl. 1960's-
1970's)
Swedish labor leader
O'Neill--Women's p344

CARLYLE, JANE BAILLIE WELSH
(1801-1866)
Scottish-English letter writer,
author, wife of Thomas Carlyle
Moers--Literary p66,177,281
Morley--Literary p79,160-161,451

CARLYLE, MARY (1912-)
Amer. actress
Springer--They p55,277, por.

CARMACK, KATIE (fl. 1890's)
Canadian Indian "gold rush
belle"
Jones--Women (1) p91-93

CARMAN, MARIE ELENORE MAILLE
DE (fl. 1730's)
French, mother of Marquis de
Sade
Book--Lists (1) p285

CARMARVON, OTTILIE ETHEL,
COUNTESS OF
See LOSCH, TILLY, COUNTESS
OF CARMARVON

CARMEN SYLVA, pseud.
See ELIZABETH (PAULINE ELIZA-
BETH OTTILIE LOUISE)

CARMENCITA
Spanish dancer
Fabian--On p106-107, por.

CARNE, JUDY (1939-)
British actress, entertainer
World--Who p255

CARNEGIE, E. HATTIE (1889-1956)
Austrian-Amer. fashion designer
Neidle--America's p274-276
O'Neill--Women's p240-242,244,247
Sicherman--Notable p135-136

CARNEGIE, LOUISE (1857-1946)
Amer. philanthropist
James--Notable (1) p286-288

CARNER, JOANNE GUNDERSON
(1939-)
Amer. golfer
Woman's Almanac p419-420
World--Who p211

CARNEY, JULIA ABIGAIL (FLETCHER)
(1823-1908)

Amer. hymnist
Claghorn--Biog. p83

CARNO, MARIA DE
See MIRANDA, CARMEN

CAROL, SUE (1908-)
Amer. actress, (Mrs. Alan
Ladd)
Lamparski--What. (5) p54-55,
por.
Lamparski--What. (8) p52-53,
por.
Springer--They p55,277, por.

CAROLINE OF ANSPACH (WILHEL-
MINA CAROLINA) (1683-1737)
English queen, consort of
George II
Jones--Rutledge p147
Softly--Queens p100-104, por.

CAROLINE OF BRUNSWICK (AMELIA
ELIZABETH CAROLINE (1768-
1821)
English queen, wife of
George IV
Jones--Rutledge p146
People's Almanac (1) p1329
Softly--Queens p107-110

CAROLINE OF MONACO (CAROLINE
LOUISE MARGUERITE)
(1957-)
Monaco Princess
Anderson--People p79, por.

CARON, LESLIE (1931-)
French actress, ballet dancer
Hirschhorn--Rating p74-75, por.
Shipman--Internatl. p90-92, por.
World--Who p255

CAROOMPAS, CAROLE (fl. 1970's)
Amer. painter
Women's--Female p35-36

CAROUSSO, DOROTHEE HUGHES
(1909-)
Amer. genealogical researcher,
author
Myer--Who's p46

CARPEGNA, COUNTESS OF ROME
Italian philosopher, physician
Mead--Hist. p431

CARPENTER, HARLEAN
See HARLOW, JEAN

CARPENTER, KAREN ANNE (1950-
1983)
Amer. singer
Anderson--People p80-81, por.
People--Best p247, por.
Simon--Best p101-102, por.
Woman's Almanac p290
World--Who p265

CARPENTER, KATE (fl. 1750's)
Amer. pioneer
Sherr--American p246

CARPENTER, LIZ (c1920-)
Amer. press secretary,
journalist
O'Neill--Women's p446

CARPENTER, MARGARET SARAH
GEDDES (1793-1872)
English portrait painter
Fine--Women p79-80
Sparrow--Women p60,96,100, por.

CARPENTER, MARY (1807-1877)
English educator, philanthro-
pist, editor
Macksey--Book p69-70, por.
Smith--Women p271-319

CARPENTER, MRS. (HON)
British inlaid-wood craftswoman
Callen--Women p168

CARPENTIER, HARLEAN
See HARLOW, JEAN

CARPER, ELSIE (fl. 1970's)
Amer. editor
Marzolf--Up p101-102,215

CARPER, JEAN (fl. 1980's)
Amer. TV Cable reporter
Scheuer--Tel. p74

CARR, MRS. DABNEY J.
See DEANE, ANNA MEAD

CARR, DOLORES J.
Amer. heroine, Carnegie
Medal winner
O'Neill--Women's p732

CARR, EMILY (1871-1945)
Canadian painter, diarist
Moffat--Revel. p372-391

CARR, EMMA PERRY (1880-1972)
Amer. chemist
O'Neill--Women's p163-164
Sicherman--Notable p136-138

CARR, PHILIPPA
See PLAIDY, JEAN

CARR, SHIRLEY
Canadian labor union leader
O'Neill--Women's p319, por.

CARR, VIKKI (1941/1942-)
Mexican-Amer. singer
Newlon--Mexican p108-115, por.
Woman's Almanac p289, por.
World--Who p265

CARRASCO, MARIA (fl. 1970's)
Italian water skier
McWhirter--Guinness p183, por.

CARRE, MATHILDE (1910-)
French spy
People's Almanac (1) p649

CARREÑO, TERESA (1853-1917)
Venezuelan pianist, composer,
singer
Claghorn--Biog. p84
James--Notable (1) p288-289
Neuls-Bates--Women p226-227
O'Neill--Women's p630

CARRIERA, ROSALBA (1675-1757)
Italian painter (ivory minia-
tures, pastels)
Fine--Women p20-21, por.
Harris--Women p17,30,36,38-39,
40,42,44,161-164,345
Macksey--Book p200
Munsterberg--Hist. p35-37
Parker--Old p28-29,32,93,
fig. 18, 52, por.
Petersen--Women p47-48, por.
Sparrow--Women p20,24,37,48,
51, por.
Tufts--Our p106-115, por.
Woman's Almanac p220
Women's--Female p6

CARRILLO, GRACIELA (fl. 1970's)
Amer. graphic artist
Women's--Female p75

CARRINGTON, ELAINE STERNE
(1892-1958)
Amer. radio soap opera writer
Women--Radio p21

CARRINGTON, KARIN (fl. 1970's)
Amer. psychologist, mountaineer
Lichtenstein--Mach. p17-20,31-32

CARRINGTON, LEONORA (1917-)
English painter
Fine--Women p178-180, por.
Women's--Female p36

CARROLL, AGNES
See HEUSSENSTAMM, AGNES
CARROLL, COUNTESS

CARROLL, ANNA ELLA (1815-1893)
Amer. political pamphleteer,
military strategist, genius,
Civil War heroine
Hymowitz--Hist. p143-144
James--Notable (1) p289-292
McHenry--Liberty's p64
Macksey--Book p55
Millstein--We p123
People's Almanac (2) p560-562
Sherr--American p94
Taylor--Gener. p24, por.

CARROLL, BARBARA (1925-)
Amer. jazz pianist
Claghorn--Jazz p63-64

CARROLL, DELIA DIXON (-1934)
Amer. physician
Sherr--American p181

CARROLL, DIAHANNE (1935-)
Amer. singer, actress
Anderson--People p83
Claghorn--Biog. p84
Manchel--Women p108, por.
Toppin--Biog. p265
World--Who p265

CARROLL, ELIZABETH, SISTER
Amer. nun, social reformer
O'Neill--Women's p389

CARROLL, GEORGIA LILLIAN
(1914-)
Amer. singer, songwriter
Claghorn--Biog. p84

CARROLL, GLADYS HASTY (1904-)
Amer. novelist

Ehrlich--Oxford p17,46,
343

CARROLL, MADELEINE (1906-)
English actress
Hirschhorn--Rating p78-79, por.
Lamparski--What. (2) p74-75,
por.
Shipman--Gold. p98-100, por.
Springer--They p55-56,277,
por.
World--Who p255

CARROLL, MOLLY DARNALL
(1747/1749-1782)
Amer., noted Maryland
mother, (wife of member of
Continental Congress), patriot
Amer.--Mothers p250

CARROLL, NANCY (1904/1906-1965)
Amer. actress
Springer--They p56-57,277-278,
por.
World--Who p229

CARROLL, PATRICIA ("PAT")
ANN ANGELA BRIDGIT
(1927-)
Amer. actress
Cur. Bio. '80 p35-38, por.

CARROLL, SALLIE
See ESTERHAZY, CAROLINE,
COUNTESS

CARROLL, VINNETTE (1922-)
Amer. theatre director,
actress, comedienne
Cur. Biog. '83 p54-58, por.

CARSE, MATILDA BRADLEY
(1835-1917)
Irish-Amer. temperance
leader, financier, social
reformer, philanthropist
James--Notable (1) p292-294
Neidle--America's p45

CARSEY, MARCIA (1944-)
Amer. TV producer
Halcomb--Women p187-199
Scheuer--Tel. p75

CARSLEY, JOSEPHINE DONNA
SMITH
See COOLBRITH, INA DONNA

CARSON, JOANNA (c1940-)
Amer. (ex-wife of Johnny
Carson)
Funt--Are p83-97, por.

CARSON, KAREN (fl. 1970's)
Amer. artist
Women's--Female p101

CARSON, MARTHA (1921-)
Amer. singer, guitarist,
songwriter
Claghorn--Biog. p85

CARSON, RACHEL LOUISE (1907-
1964)
Amer. marine biologist,
author, social reformer
Anticaglia--12 p208-224, por.
Bachtold--Gifted p17-19
Clark--Leading p216-220
Emberlin--Cont. p81-105, por.
Gilfond--Heroines p106-109, por.
Ingraham--Album p72
Kulkin--Her p58-59
Longstreet--Queen p192
McHenry--Liberty's p64-65
Marlowe--Great p333-337, por.
New York Times--Great p34-35
O'Neill--Women's p156-157
Pederson--Leaders p245, por.
Sicherman--Notable p138-141
Signif.--Amer. p39, por.
Warren--Pictorial p204
Webster's--Amer. p180-181
Woman's Almanac p385, por.

CARSON, SALLY (BONNIE LOU)
(1926-)
Amer. singer, yodeler, guitarist
Claghorn--Biog. p85

CARSWELL, CATHERINE MacFARLANE
ROXBURGH (1879-1946)
Scottish novelist
Avenel--Comp. (1) p92
Crosland--Beyond p130-131
Morley--Literary, see index p484

CARTER, ANGELA (1940-)
English novelist
Seymour-Smith--Novels p112

CARTER, ANITA INA (1934-)
Amer. singer
Claghorn--Biog. p85

CARTER, BETTY (1) (1929/1930-)
Amer. composer
Claghorn--Biog. p85
Claghorn--Jazz p64
Cur. Biog. '82 p65-68, por.

CARTER, BETTY (2)
Amer. builder, executive
Macksey--Book p166

CARTER, CAROLINE LOUISE DUD-
LEY (1862-1937)
Amer. actress
James--Notable (1) p294-295
McHenry--Liberty's p65
World--Who p229

CARTER, CLAIRE (fl. 1980's)
Amer. TV news co-anchor
Scheuer--Tel. p76

CARTER, ELIZABETH (1717-1806)
English linguist, poet,
scholar, translator
Macksey--Book p182,272

CARTER, ERNESTINE
Amer. editor, museum
curator
Diamonstein--Open p52-55, por.

CARTER, EUNICE HUNTON (1899-
1970)
Amer. lawyer, community
leader
Sicherman--Notable p141-142

CARTER, JUNE (1929-)
Amer. singer, autoharpist,
songwriter
Claghorn--Biog. p85
Dew--Women p62-91, por.
O'Neill--Women's p629
World--Who p265

CARTER, (BESSIE) LILLIAN
(1898-1983)
Amer. nurse, mother of
President Carter
Anderson--People p87-88
Book--Lists (2) p255
Cur. Biog. '78 p66-69, por.
Cur. Biog. '84 p469
Faber--Presidents' p3-18, por.
O'Neill--Women's p18-19,40
Woman's Almanac p93

CARTER, LYNDA (1951-)
Amer. actress, TV producer
Scheuer--Tel. p76
World--Who p229

CARTER, MARY E. (fl. 1970's)
Amer. chemist, government
official, writer
O'Neill--Women's p24

CARTER, MAYBELLE ADDINGTON
"MOTHER" (1909-1978)
Amer. singer, autoharpist,
songwriter
Claghorn--Biog. p85-86
O'Neill--Women's p629
Woman's Almanac p290

CARTER, NELL
Amer. singer, actress
Scheuer--Tel. p77, por.

CARTER, ROSALYNN SMITH (1927-)
Amer. first lady
Anderson--People p88-89
Book--Lists (2) p261
Cur. Biog. '78 p69-72, por.
Lichtenstein--Mach. p303-304
O'Neill--Women's p129,299-300,594
People--Best p35, por.
Woman's Almanac p494, por.
Whedon--Always p152-154, por.
Wilcox--Amer. p324-346
World--Who p295

CARTER, SARAH (1898-1979)
Amer. singer
Claghorn--Biog. p86

CARTER, SUSAN SHIRLEY (fl.
1960's-1970's)
Amer. diplomatic courier
O'Neill--Women's p94

CARTER, VIRGINIA L. (1936-)
Canadian-Amer. nuclear physicist, TV executive
Adams--Women p24,90-94,97,99,
101,108,110-111,157,163,189,
200
Scheuer--Tel. p77

CARTHAN, HATTIE (1900-)
Amer. environmentalist
Woman's Almanac p108

CARTLAND, BARBARA HAMILTON
    (1901-)
    English novelist
Crosland--Beyond p217-218
Cur. Biog. '79 p64-66, por.
People--Best p150-151, por.
People's Almanac (3) p546
Seymour-Smith--Novels p81,112
World--Who p24

CARTWRIGHT, MARGUERITE (fl.
    1950's)
    Amer. journalist
Marzolf--Up p90

CARVILL, MAUD (-1944)
    Amer. physician, ophthal-
    mologist
O'Neill--Women's p205

CARY, ALICE (1820-1871)
    Amer. hymnist, poet
Claghorn--Biog. p86
Ehrlich--Oxford p69,135,297,
    por.
James--Notable (1) p295-297
McHenry--Liberty's p65-66
Macksey--Book p273
Sherr--American p170,184
Webster's--Amer. p182-183

CARY, ANNA (ANNIE) LOUISE
    (1841/1842-1921)
    Amer. singer
Claghorn--Biog. p86
James--Notable (1) p297-298
McHenry--Liberty's p66

CARY, CONSTANCE
    See HARRISON, CONSTANCE
    CARY

CARY, ELISABETH LUTHER
    (1867-1936)
    Amer. author, art critic
James--Notable (1) p298-300
McHenry--Liberty's p66-67
O'Neill--Women's p440-441

CARY, ELIZABETH (fl. 1600's)
    Amer. accused witch
Williams--Demeter's p141

CARY, HETTY (fl. 1860's)
    Amer. Southern belle
DeLeon--Belles p168-169, por.

CARY, MARY ANN SHADD (1823-
    1893)
    Amer.-Canadian pioneer,
    teacher, journalist, lawyer
James--Notable (1) p300-301
Sherr--American p37
Warren--Pictorial p85-86

CARY, PHOEBE (1824-1871)
    Amer. poet, hymnist
Avenel--Comp. (2) p53
Claghorn--Biog. p86
Ehrlich--Oxford p69,135,297
McHenry--Liberty's p65-66
Sherr--American p170,184

CARY SISTERS
    Amer. authors, poets
Sherr--American p170

CASA, LISA DELLA
    See DELLA CASA, LISA

CASALS, ROSEMARY (1948-)
    Amer. tennis player
Cur. Biog. '74 p66-68, por.
Kulkin--Her p60
McWhirter--Guinness p160, por.
Sullivan--Queens p84-91, por.
Woman's Almanac p414

CASANOVA, AURA CELINA (fl.
    1960's)
    Venezuelan cabinet minister,
    1969
Macksey--Book p43
O'Neill--Women's p61

CASARES, MARIA (1922-)
    Spanish-French actress
Entertainers p254, por.

CASAS, MARTHA (fl. 1970's)
    Amer. textile artist, fashion
    designer
Women's--Female p98

CASATI, MARGUESA (fl. 1970's)
    Italian jewelry designer
Keenan--Women p55-56, por.

CASCINI, FRANCESCA
    Italian singer, composer
Macksey--Book p211

CASE, ADELAIDE TEAGUE (1887-
    1948)

Amer. Episcopalian educator
James--Notable (1) p301-302

CASE, ANNA (1889-1984)
Amer. opera singer
Claghorn--Biog. p87
Tuggle--Golden p115-116, por.

CASE, LISA (fl. 1970's)
Amer. sculptor
Women's--Female p98

CASE, VALERIE PERCY (-1966)
Amer., daughter of Senator
Percy
People's Almanac (3) p309-310

CASEBEER, KAREN
Amer. machinist
O'Neill--Women's p316-317

CASERIO, MARJORIE C. (fl. 1970's)
British-Amer. chemist, writer
O'Neill--Women's p165,169

CASH, JUNE CARTER
See CARTER, JUNE

CASHIN, BONNIE (1915-)
Amer. fashion designer
Cur. Biog. '70 p69-71, por.
O'Neill--Women's p245,247,249

CASHMAN, KATHERINE (fl. 1970's)
New Zealander geochemist
(Antarctic) 1978
Land--New p11,201-213,por.

CASHMAN, NELLIE (1851-1925)
Amer. Western hotel owner,
prospector
Sherr--American p9
Time--Women p166-170,183, por.

CASILLAS, FLORENCIA BISENTA
DE
See CARR, VIKKI

CASLAVSKA-OKLOZIL, VERA
(1942-)
Czechoslovakian gymnast
Assoc. Press--Pursuit p262,
291-292, por.
O'Neill--Women's p562
Woman's Almanac p423
World--Who p211

CASO, PATRICIA (fl. 1970's-1980's)
Amer. TV producer
Scheuer--Tel. p78

CASPARY, ANITA, SISTER
Amer. nun, founder lay
community
O'Neill--Women's p388

CASPARY, VERA (1904-1987)
Amer. novelist, playwright
Seymour-Smith--Novels p112

CASS, E. ELIZABETH (1905-)
Canadian physician
Hellstedt--Women p306-312, por.

CASS, MELNEA
Amer. NAACP leader
O'Neill--Women's p702

CASSAB, JUDY (fl. 1960's)
Australian artist
Macksey--Book p209

CASSATT, MARY STEVENSON (1844-
1926)
Amer. painter
Bachtold--Gifted p29-31
Boorstin--Americans p146-147,
por.
Fine--Women p129-136, see also
index p232
Fowler--Art p7-29, por.
Harris--Women p57-58,66,90,197,
233,237-243,282,351-352
Henkes--Eight p1-7,48-49
Ingraham--Album p61
James--Notable (1) p303-305
Jones--Rutledge p151
Kronenberger--Atlan. p136
Kulkin--Her p61-62
Longstreet--Queen p117-119
McHenry--Liberty's p67
Macksey--Book p206
Munro--Originals p59-74, por.
Munsterberg--Hist. p56-59,109-110
O'Neill--Women's p596
Parker--Old p38-41, fig. 26
Pederson--Leaders p149, por.
Petersen--Women p87-90
Sherr--American p205
Signif.--Amer. p28, por.
Sparrow--Women p76-77,157,327
Stoddard--Famous p90-100, por.
Taylor--Gener. p61

Warren--Pictorial p154,156, por.
Webster's--Amer. p183-184
Woman's Almanac p221-222
Women's--Female p6
World--Who p57-58

CASSEL, FLORA HAMILTON (fl.
1890's)
Amer. temperance worker,
musician
Sherr--American p139

CASSELL, ROSALIE (fl. 1970's)
Amer. art teacher
Women's--Female p114

CASSION, EDITH GIOVANNA
See PIAF, EDITH

CASTAING, MADELEINE
French antiquarian, designer
O'Neill--Women's p280-281

CASTANIS, MURIEL (fl. 1970's)
Amer. sculptor
Women's--Female p86-87

CASTELLANE, ANNA GOULD,
MARQUISE DE
See TALLEYRAND-PERIGORD,
ANNA GOULD, DUCHESSE DE

CASTELLOZA (fl. c1200's)
French troubadour
Bogin--Women p119,175
Neuls-Bates--Women p22-23,26-27

CASTILLA, MARIA MARGUERITE
GUADELUPE BOLDAO Y
See "MARGO"

CASTILLO, ANA (fl. 1970's)
Amer. poet
Fisher--Third p vii-viii,386

CASTLE, BARBARA ANN BETTS
(1911-)
English labor leader, Parlia-
ment member
O'Neill--Women's p344
Jones--Rutledge p151
Vallance--Women, see index p208

CASTLE, IRENE FOOTE (1894-1969)
Amer. dancer
Claghorn--Biog. p88
Clark--Leading p85

Eills--Here p158-159
Jablonski--Ency. p118
Longstreet--Queen p192
O'Neill--Women's p238
Sicherman--Notable p142-143
Webster's--Amer. p184
Woman's Almanac p307-308
World--Who p263

CASTLEMAINE, COUNTESS OF
See VILLIERS, BARBARA,
COUNTESS OF CASTLEMAINE,
DUCHESS OF CLEVELAND

CASTORO, ROSEMARIE (fl. 1970's)
Amer. painter
Women's--Female p36

CASTRA, ANNE DE (fl. 1629)
Spanish philosopher, writer
Mead--Hist. p431

CASTRO, ARGEZ LINA GONZALES
(-1963)
Cuban, mother of Fidel Castro
Diagram--Mothers p44-45

CASTRO, INES (INEZ, AGNES) DE
(fl. c1360's)
Spanish, embalmed wife of
King Pedro of Castile
Book--Lists (1) p448

CASTRO, ROSALIE DE (1837-1885)
Spanish poet, novelist
Macksey--Book p188

CASTRO DE BARISH, EMILA (fl.
1970's)
Costa Rican, United Nations
Security Council member
O'Neill--Women's p65

CASTRO E SILVA DE VINVENZI,
MARIA DE LOURDES (fl. 1970's)
Brazilian ambassador
O'Neill--Women's p62

CATANEI, GIOVANNOZZA DEI
(1442-1518)
Italian, mother of Lucrezia
Borgia, businesswoman
Diagram--Mothers p34-35, por.

CATCHINGS, ROSE (1925-)
Amer. Methodist Mission sec-
retary
O'Neill--Women's p396

CATEECHEE
Amer. Indian patriot
Sherr--American p213

CATELA, JOAN SEGAL (fl. 1970's)
Amer. dairy farmer in Portu-
gal
O'Neill--Women's p7

CATHCART, LINDA (fl. 1970's)
Amer. museum curator
O'Neill--Women's p616

CATHCART, MARJORIE
Amer. painter
Women's--Female p36

CATHER, WILLA SIBERT (1873-
1947)
Amer. novelist, short story
writer, poet, journalist
Avenel--Comp. (2) p53-54
Betts--Writers p124-129, por.
Cahill--Women p27-28,373-374
Clark--Leading p77-79
Ehrlich--Oxford, see index p491
Gray--Women p147-158, por.
Howard--Seven p79-121
Ingraham--Album p58, por.
James--Notable (1) p305-308
Jones--Rutledge p152
Kronenberger--Atlan. p137
Kulkin--Her p62-63
McHenry--Liberty's p67
Macksey--Book p189
Magill--Cycl. p191-195
Moers--Literary p281-283, see
also index p323, por.
O'Neill--Women's p472,485,674
Parker--Uneasy p93-96
People's Almanac (3) p614-615
Seymour-Smith--Novels p112
Seymour-Smith--Who's p73-74
Sherr--American p140-142,147,
235, por.
Signif.--Amer. p40, por.
Stoddard--Famous p101-110, por.
Warren--Pictorial p179-180, por.
Webster's--Amer. p184
Who Did What p62
Woman's Almanac p248
World--Who p11

CATHERINE I (1684-1727)
Russian empress
Macksey--Book p28

CATHERINE II (CATHERINE THE
GREAT) (1729-1796)
Russian empress
Booth--Women p122,217-223,290-
291, por.
Canning--100 p509-515
Davis--Women p81-99, por.
Diagram--Mothers p200-203, por.
Donaldson--How p62-63
Fry--1000 p193, por.
Jones--Rutledge p152
Kulkin--Her p64-65
Macksey--Book p28-30,66, por.
Mandel--Soviet p14-17
Mead--Hist. p492,512
Trease--Seven p149-178, por.
Woman's Almanac p463
Who Did What p62
World--Who p162

CATHERINE DE MEDICIS (1519-1589)
French queen
Canning--100 p400-405
Diagram--Mothers p88-92, por.
Fine--Women p6
Fry--1000 p135, por.
Jones--Rutledge p152-153
Macksey--Book p12,95,224-225
Mead--Hist. p347
Who Did What p222
World--Who p158

CATHERINE HOWARD
See HOWARD, CATHERINE, LADY

CATHERINE OF ALEXANDRIA, SAINT
(-c307)
Egyptian Saint
Green--Saints p118-121

CATHERINE OF ARAGON
(1485-1536)
English queen
Bainton--France p139-152, por.
Donaldson--How p61-62
Kulkin--Her p63-64
Softly--Queens p56-60, por.
Vance--Six p17-58,102-118
Who Did What p149, por.
World--Who p162

CATHERINE OF BOLOGNA
See VIGRI, CATERINA DA

CATHERINE OF BRAGANZA (1413-
1705)
English queen, (wife of Charles II)

CAUSIRE, ANNE CHARLOTTE
(fl. 1760's)
French midwife
Mead--Hist. p491

CAVALIERI, LINA (1874-1944)
Italian opera singer
Tuggle--Golden, p118-129, por.

CAVANAGH, KIT (1607-1739)
English soldier (male
impersonator)
Macksey--Book p52

CAVANAUGH, KAREN BYERS
(1946-)
Amer. genealogical researcher,
writer, editor
Meyer--Who's p46

CAVANI, LILIANA
Italian filmmaker
Smith--Movies p126,128

CAVE, JESSIE KING (1897-)
Amer. dietician, noted Ohio
mother
Amer.--Mothers p432, por.

CAVE, MRS. WALTER
British furniture decorator
Callen--Women p169

CAVELL, EDITH LOUISA (1865-
1915)
English governess, nurse,
martyr
Brecher--Lives p157-158
Donaldson--How p63-64
Fraser--Heroines p214-219, por.
Fry--1000 p262
Jones--Rutledge p155
Kulkin--Her p65-66
Macksey--Book p57
People's Almanac (2) p447
People's Alamanc (3) p604-605
Taylor--Gener. p26, por.
Who Did What p62
Woman's Almanac p448

CAVENDISH, LADY
See MORRELL, OTTOLINE
VIOLET ANNE, LADY
CAVENDISH

CAVENDISH, MARGARET LUCAS,
DUCHESS OF NEWCASTLE

See NEWCASTLE, MARGARET
CAVENDISH, DUCHESS OF

CAWLEY, MRS. ROGER
See GOOLAGONG, EVONNE

CAYETANA, DUCHESS OF ALBA
(-1802)
Spanish, Goya's model
Book--Lists (1) p192

CAYVAN, GEORGIA EVA (1857-1906)
Amer. actress
James--Notable (1) p314-315

CAZALET, GILLIAN
Amer. aviatrix, (commercial
airline captain)
Boase--Sky's p215

CAZALET-KEIR, THELMA
British Parliament member
Vallance--Women p126-127,129,139

CAZALLA, MARIA (fl. 1525-1534)
Spanish religious leader
Bainton--Spain p33-39

CAZIN, MARIE, MME.
French artist
Sparrow--Women p182,227,239

CAZNEAU, JANE MARIA ELIZA
McMANUS STORMS (1807-1878)
Amer. journalist, publicist
James--Notable (1) p315-317

CECELIA, SISTER
Czechoslovakian nun, refugee
Cavanah--We p137-150

CELLA, PHYLLIS A.
Amer. executive
O'Neill--Women's p522

CELLIER, ELIZABETH (fl. 1642)
English obstetrician
Marks--Women p63-65
Mead--Hist. p395-396,398

CENCI, BEATRICE (1577-1599)
Italian noblewoman, daughter
of Francesco Cenci
Jones--Rutledge p157

CENTLIVRE, SUSANNAH (1667/
1680-1723)

English playwright, actress
Entertainers p78-79
Horner--English p10 (also note)

CERES
Roman goddess
Pomeroy--Godd. p154,184,214-217

CERRITO, FANNY (1817-1909)
Italian ballet dancer
Migel--Ballerinas p208-222, por.

CERVANTES, LORNA DEE (1934-)
Amer. poet, editor, publisher
Fisher--Third p viii,378

CESLIK, CAROLYN (1942-)
Amer. TV director
Scheuer--Tel. p80

CHACE, ELIZABETH BUFFUM
(1806-1899)
Amer., noted Rhode Island
mother, feminist, abolitionist
Amer.--Mothers p478, por.
James--Notable (1) p317-319
Sherr--American p206

CHACE, MARIAN (1896-1970)
Amer. dance therapist
Sicherman--Notable p143-145

CHADWELL, PATRICIA ANN
(1943-)
Amer. genealogical researcher,
writer
Meyer--Who's p46

CHADWICK, CASSIE I. (1857-1907)
Canadian impostor (swindler)
Book--Lists (1) p483
Felton--Famous p38-40

CHADWICK, FLORENCE MAY
(1918-)
Amer. swimmer
Dunlap--Calif. p35, por.
Hollander--100 p90-91, por.
Lamparski--What. (5) p98-99,
por.
McWhirter--Guinness p145
Woman's Almanac p429
World--Who p211

CHADWICK, NANCY GAILLARD
(1924-)
Amer. genealogical researcher,

indexer, editor
Meyer--Who's p46-47

CHAFFEE, SUZY (1947-)
Amer. skier
Hollander--100 p77-78, por.
Lichtenstein--Mach., see index
p359
100--Greatest (1) p34, por.

CHAIT, DONNA
Amer. basketball player
Hollander--100 p9, por.

CHALFEN, JUDITH
Amer. TV reformer
O'Neill--Women's p729

CHALL, JEANNE S. (fl. 1970's)
Amer. educator
O'Neill--Women's p422-423

CHALLANS (CHALLENS), MARY
See RENAULT, MARY, pseud.

CHALMERS, JOAN (1928-)
Canadian crafts leader
O'Neill--Women's p127

CHALUPEK, APPOLONIA
See NEGRI, POLA

CHAMBERLAIN, HOPE SUMMERELL
Amer. Southern feminist
Scott--Southern p72,215-216

CHAMBERS, ANNE COX (fl. 1970's)
Amer. ambassador
O'Neill--Women's p96

CHAMBERS, MARJORIE BELL
(1923-)
Amer. political activist,
AAUW president
O'Neill--Women's p433

CHAMPCOMMUNAL, ELSPETH
French couturière
Holme--Journal p153-154

CHAMPE, ELIZABETH (fl. 1780's)
Amer. Revolutionary patriot
Clyne--Patriots p82-88

CHAMPION, DEBORAH (1753-)
Amer. Revolutionary heroine,
military messenger

Booth--Women p55-57
Hymowitz--Hist. p33-34
Meyer--Petticoat p207-209
Millstein--We p46-48
Williams--Demeter's p245-246

CHAMPION, MARGE CELESTE
(MARJORIE CELESTE
BELCHER) (1923/1925-)
Amer. dancer, actress
World--Who p263

CHAMPLIN, JANE
Amer. army flier
Keil--Those p159-160,211-212

CHAMPLIN, "PEGGY"
Amer. belle, patriot
Earle--Two Cent. (2) p xiv,
710, por.

CHAMPMESLE, MARIE DES MARES
(1642-1698)
French actress
Entertainers p73-74
Macksey--Book p224

CHAMYNE
Greek Priestess of Demeter
Zinserling--Women p30

CHANDLER, ALICE JANE
See WEBSTER, JEAN

CHANDLER, ANNA PAINE (1738-
1811)
Amer. colonial patriot, wife
of Winthrop Chandler
Flexner--Face p119, por.

CHANDLER, ARTIE (1970's)
Amer. mountain woman
Kahn--Hill. p85-89,105-109,
110-112, por.

CHANDLER, DOROTHY BUFFUM
(1901-)
Amer. journalist
Diamonstein--Open p56-59, por.
Longstreet--Queen p175-176

CHANDLER, ELIZABETH
MARGARET (1807-1834)
Amer. poet, abolitionist
James--Notable (1) p319-320
Lutz--Crusade p3-4,6,8-20,
por.

CHANDLER, HELEN (1906-1965)
Amer. actress
Springer--They p57-59,278, por.

CHANDLER, JENNIFER (JENNY)
(fl. 1970's)
Amer. diver
McWhirter--Guinness p137, por.
O'Neill--Women's p584

CHANDLER, MARIE WILSON (fl.
1970's)
Amer. mountain woman
Kahn--Hill. p85-89,100-105,110-
112, por.

CHANDLER, MARJORIE
See COLLINS, DOROTHY

CHANDLER, NAOMI
Amer. agriculturist, textbook
critic
O'Neill--Women's p9

CHANDY, ANNA (1905-)
East Indian judge
Macksey--Book p128

CHANEL, GABRIELLE BONHEUR
("COCO") (1883-1971)
French fashion designer
Comfort--Good p163, por.
Cur. Biog. '71 p461
Holme--Journal p153, por.
Keenan--Women, see index p222,
por.
Macksey--Book p267, por.
New York Times--Great p42-43,
por.
O'Neill--Women's p240,263, por.
Wintle--Makers p101-102, #90
Woman's Almanac p132-133, por.
World--Who p295

CHANG CH'ING (c1913-)
Chinese political leader
Cur. Biog. '75 p77-80, por.

CHANG, DIANA (fl. 1950's-1960's)
Chinese-Amer. writer, (in-
cluding poetry)
Fisher--Third p ix,453,501,525

CHANG, MARGUERITE SHUE-WEN
(fl. 1970's)
Chinese-Amer. research
chemist, inventor

O'Neill--Women's p89,
167

CHANG, MOON GYUNG (1904-)
Korean physician
Hellstedt--Women p267-269,
por.

CHANNING, CAROL (1921-)
Amer. actress, singer
Anderson--People p94
Claghorn--Biog. p90
McHenry--Liberty's p68
O'Neill--Women's p677
100--Greatest (1) p52, por.
World--Who p265

CHANNING, STOCKARD (1944-)
Amer. actress
Shipman--Internatl. p97-98,
por.

CHANTAL, JEANNE FRANÇOIS
FREMIOT, BARONNE DE
(1574-1641)
French obstetrician, charity
worker
Mead--Hist. p357

CHAPELLE, GEORGETTE ("DICK-
EY") MEYER (1920-1965)
Amer. war correspondent,
photographer
Marzolf--Up p86
O'Neill--Women's p459

CHAPIN, AUGUSTA JANE (1836-
1905)
Amer. clergyman
James--Notable (1) p320-321

CHAPIN, EMILY
Amer. aviatrix, WASP
Keil--Those, see index p321,
por.

CHAPIN, LAUREN (1945-)
Amer. child actress
Lamparski--What. Annual (4,5)
p366-370, por.

CHAPIN, SARAH FLOURNOY
MOORE (c1830-1896)
Amer. temperance reformer
James--Notable (1) p321-322

CHAPLIN, MRS. CHARLES HILL

(-late 1920's)
British singer, mother of
Charles Chaplin
Diagram--Mothers p46-49, por.

CHAPLIN, GERALDINE (1944-)
Amer. actress
Cur. Biog. '79 p70-72, por.
Fallaci--Ego. p81-97
World--Who p229

CHAPLIN, LITA GREY (1908-)
Amer. wife of Charlie Chaplin
Lamparski--What. (5) p44-45, por.
Lamparski--What. (8) p56-57, por.

CHAPLINE, CLAUDIA (fl. 1970's)
Amer. sculptor
Women's--Female p87

CHAPMAN, CAROLINE (c1818-1876)
Amer. actress, Western pioneer
James--Notable (1) p322-324

CHAPMAN, JANE ROBERTS (fl.
1970's)
Amer. organization founder
O'Neill--Women's p707

CHAPMAN, MARIA WESTON (1806-
1885)
Amer. abolitionist, feminist,
philanthropist
James--Notable (1) p324-325
Lutz--Crusade, see index p334,
por.
McHenry--Liberty's p68-69
Millstein--We p92-93

CHAPMAN, MARION (fl. 1930's)
British mother
Macksey--Book p12

CHAPMAN, MARY F. (1838-1884)
Irish novelist
Showalter--Lit. p333

CHAPMAN, MAUDE (c1869-)
Amer. centenarian
Mitchell--Yessir p106-107, por.

CHAPONE, HESTER MULSO (1727-
1801)
English poet, essayist, story-
writer, feminist
Moers--Literary p283

CHAPPLE, WENDY WOOD (fl.
1970's)
Amer. film writer, director,
photographer, editor
Smith--Movies p154-157,231, por.

CHARAG-ZUNTZ, HANNA (1915-)
German craftswoman, potter
O'Neill--Women's p126

CHARISSE, CYD (1921/1923-)
Amer. dancer
Hirschhorn--Rating p82-83, por.
Shipman--Internatl. p98-100, por.
Woman's Almanac p308
World--Who p263

CHARLES, BULA WARD (1887-1974)
Amer., noted New Mexico
mother, author, executive,
community worker
Amer.--Mothers p382-383, por.

CHARLES, ELIZABETH RUNDLE
(1828-1896)
English novelist, poet
Showalter--Lit. p330

CHARLES, ETHEL (1871-1962)
British architect
Macksey--Book p166

CHARLESWORTH, FLORENCE
LOUISA
See BARCLAY, FLORENCE
LOUISA CHARLESWORTH

CHARLESWORTH, MARIA LOUISA
(1819-1880)
English children's book writer
Showalter--Lit. p326

"CHARLOTTE"
See RIDDELL, CHARLOTTE
ELIZA LAWSON COWAN

CHARLOTTE, GRAND DUCHESS
OF LUXEMBOURG (1896-1985)
Luxembourg monarch
Cur. Biog. '85 p463

CHARLOTTE AUGUSTA (1796-1817)
British princess, wife of
King Leopold I of Belgium

Jones--Rutledge p168

CHARLOTTE (SOPHIA) OF MECKLEN-
BERG (1744-1818)
English queen
Softly--Queens p105-107, por.
Young--Revol. p7,19,45,106,110-
111,120

CHARNAUD, STELLA
See ISAACS, STELLA CHARNAUD
(BARONESS SWANSBOROUGH)

CHARPENTIER, CONSTANCE MARIE
BLONDELU (1767-1849)
French sculptor
Fine--Women p53-54
Harris--Women p207-208,348
Munsterberg--Hist. p46,48
Petersen--Women p61-62
Women's--Female p6

CHARREN, PEGGY (1928-)
Amer. children's TV reformer,
executive
O'Neill--Women's p729
Scheuer--Tel. p84, por.
Schoenebaum--Prof. p121-122

CHASE, ALICE (-1974)
Amer. health food author
Felton--Famous p70

CHASE, ANYA
See SETON, ANYA CHASE

CHASE, CARRIE MATILDA MURRAY
(1876-)
Amer., noted Maine mother,
mother of Margaret Chase-
Smith
Amer.--Mothers p242-243, por.

CHASE, DORIS (1923-)
Amer. painter, sculptor,
filmmaker
Smith--Movies p231, por.

CHASE, EDNA WOOLMAN (1877-
1957)
Amer. (fashion) editor
Sicherman--Notable p145-146

CHASE, ELIZABETH
See ALLEN, ELIZABETH ANNE
CHASE AKERS

CHASE, ILKA (1903/1905-1978)
Amer. actress, author
Cur. Biog. '78, p466
Springer--They p59,278, por.

CHASE, KATE (1840-1899)
Amer. political hostess
James--Notable (3) p339-340
Peacock--Famous p206-229, por.

CHASE, LUCIA (1907-)
Amer. ballet dancer, director
Cur. Biog. '75 p71-74, por.
Fabian--On p192-193, por.
O'Neill--Women's p641-642

CHASE, MARY AGNES (1869-1963)
Amer. botanist, suffragist
Sicherman--Notable p146-148

CHASE, MARY COYLE (c1907-1981)
Amer. playwright, reporter
Chinoy--Women p163-170
Cur. Biog. '82 p461
Ehrlich--Oxford p384
World--Who p11

CHASE, MARY ELLEN (1887-1973)
Amer. novelist, educator
Cur. Biog. '73 p452
Ehrlich--Oxford p2,54
Hazen--Interv. p222
McHenry--Liberty's p69
Seymour-Smith--Novels p114

CHASE, REBECCA
Amer. TV news correspondent
Scheuer--Tel. p85

CHASE, SYLVIA (1938-)
Amer. TV newscaster
Gelfman--Women p17,59-60,82,
99-100,160, por.
Marzolf--Up p184-186
Scheuer--Tel. p85

CHASE-RIBOUD, BARBARA (1939-)
Amer. artist
Munro--Originals p370-376, por.

CHASSAIGNE, ANNE-MARIE DE
See POUGY, LIANE DE

CHASSEN, BELLA HURWITZ (fl.
1600's)
Jewish historian
Henry--Written p118

CHASTON, GLORIA DUNCAN (1920-)
Amer. genealogical researcher,
writer, editor
Meyer--Who's p47

CHÂTELET, GABRIELLE EMILIE LE
TONNELEVE (1706-1749)
French linguist, mathematician,
physicist, writer
Macksey--Book p143, por.
Mead--Hist. p494

CHATHAM, LOIS ALBRO (fl. 1970's)
Amer. government official
O'Neill--Women's p89

CHATTERTON, GEORGIANA, LADY
(1806-1876)
English novelist
Showalter--Lit. p322

CHATTERTON, RUTH (1893-1961)
Amer. actress
Hazen--Interv. p104
Manchel--Women p43, por.
Mordden--Movie p94-95,98,100,
109,139
Shipman--Gold. p109-113, por.
Springer--They p59,278,por.
World--Who p229

CHATTOPADHYAY, KAMALADEVI
(1903-)
East Indian union activist
O'Neill--Women's p695,738, por.

CHAUCER, ALICE
See SUFFOLK, ALICE, DUCHESS
OF

CHAUCHOIN, LILY CLAUDETTE
See COLBERT, CLAUDETTE

CHAUDET, JEANNE-ELISABETH
(1767-1831)
French artist
Fine--Women p60

CHAUDHURY, DEVIKA RANI
East Indian actress
Macksey--Book p235

CHAVARRI, EMPERATRIZ
See SUMAC, YMA

CHAYES, ANTONIA HANDLER
(1929-)

Amer. government official,
lawyer
Keill--Those p312-316

CHEATHAM, CATHARINE ("KITTY")
SMILEY (1864-1946)
Amer. singer
Claghorn--Biog. p91

CHEATHAM, MARIE
Amer. actress
Scheuer--Tel. p86, por.

CHEEK, ALISON M., REVEREND
(c1928-)
Amer. clergyman
O'Neill--Women's p377,382,384

CHEER, MARGARET (fl. 1760's)
Amer. colonial actress
Williams--Demeter's p222

CHEESMAN, EVELYN (1881-1969)
British entomologist,
explorer
Macksey--Book p240, por.

CH'EN SHU (1660-1736)
Chinese painter
Petersen--Women p156,160

CHENAI-MINUZZO, GIULIANA (fl.
1950's-1960's)
Italian skier
Assoc. Press--Pursuit p185,
204,206,230

CHENEY, AMY MARCY
See BEACH, AMY MARCY
CHENEY

CHENEY, EDNAH DOW LITTLEHALE
(1824-1904)
Amer. author, social reformer, philanthropist, lecturer
James--Notable (1) p325-327

CHENEY, JULIA
See ARTHUR, JULIA

CHENG, CHI
See CHI CHENG

CHENNEVIX, MARY (fl. 1730's-
1840's)
British toymaker
Callen--Women p152

CHENOWETH, ALICE DREW (1903-)
Amer. physician
Hellstedt--Women p244-248, por.

"CHER" (1946-)
Amer. singer, TV personality
Anderson--People p97-98, por.
Claghorn--Biog. p59
Cur. Biog. '74 p71-73, por.
Glassman--Year '79 p47,92, por.
Kulkin--Her p44
100--Greatest (1) p99, por.
People--Best p49,112-113, por.
Woman's Almanac p290-291
World--Who p265

CHERKASOVA, ANYA
See MOORE, BARBARA

CHERNIKOVSKY, MOLLY (fl. 1920's)
Russian-Amer. factory worker,
grocery-store owner
Baum--Jewish p92-98

CHERON, (ELIZABETH) SOPHIE
(1648-1711)
French painter, poet
Fine--Women p44, por.
Macksey--Book p197
Petersen--Women p34, por.
Sparrow--Women p173-174

CHERRILL, VIRGINIA (1908-)
Amer. actress
Lamparski--What. (8) p58-59, por.
Springer--They p60,278, por.

CHERRY SISTERS (ELIZABETH,
EFFIE, JESSIE AND ADDIE)
(fl. 1880's-1940's)
Amer. vaudeville performers
Book--Lists (2) p161
Felton--Famous p188-189
McFarland--Incred. p22-24
Sherr--American p69, por.

CHESHIRE, MAXINE (c1930-)
Amer. columnist
Diamonstein--Open p60-65, por.
Woman's Almanac p277

CHESLER, PHYLLIS
Amer. psychologist, lecturer,
feminist, writer
100--Greatest (1) p87, por.

CHESNUT, MARY BOYKIN MILLER
(1823-1886)

Amer. diarist
Earnest--American p59,164-165
Ehrlich--Oxford p248,251
Hymowitz--Hist. p61,147
James--Notable (1) p327-330
McHenry--Liberty's p69
Moffat--Revel. p270-287
Scott--Southern p29,46,48,50-55,
57,77
Sherr--American p209-210
Warren--Pictorial p112-113
Wiley--Confed. p3-38, por.

CHESSMAN, ANDREA
Amer. feminist, writer
O'Neill--Women's p484-485

CHESTER, LAURA (1949-)
Amer. poet
Chester--Rising p394-401, por.

CHESTER, PHYLLIS
Amer. psychologist, film
critic, author
Manchel--Women p19-20

CHESTNEY, JOSEPHINE (fl.
1860's)
Amer. Southern belle
DeLeon--Belles p413-414, por.

CHEVALIER, MARIE-CLAIRE (fl.
1970's)
French abortion reformer
O'Neill--Women's p727-728

CHEVALIER, MICHELE (1934-)
French abortion reformer
O'Neill--Women's p727-728

CHEVALIER, SALLY
Amer. belle
Peacock--Famous p118-119, por.

CHEVES, SOPHIA LANGDON (fl.
1860's)
Amer. Southern belle
DeLeon--Belles p162, por.

CHI CHENG (c1944-)
Taiwan track and field
athlete
Hollander--100 p133-134, por.
McWhirter--Guinness p166, por.
O'Neill--Women's p575-576
Woman's Almanac p426, por.

CHIANG CHING (1913/1914-)
Chinese, wife of President
Mao Tse-Tung, actress
Macksey--Book p38
O'Neill--Women's p421,713-714
Palmer--Who's p80-81
Woman's Almanac p389-390, por.

CHIANG, FAY (1952-)
Chinese-Amer. poet
Fisher--Third p ix,550

CHIANG KAI-SHEK, MAYLING
SOONG, MADAME (1898-)
Chinese political leader
Miller--Fishbait p354-355

CHIARA, MARIA (1939-)
Italian opera singer
Gammond--Illus. p239, por.

CHIBA, AYANO (fl. 1930's)
Japanese craftswoman (weaver-
dyer)
O'Neill--Women's p100,129

CHICAGO, JUDY (1939-)
Amer. painter, feminist,
writer
Cur. Biog. '81 p62-65, por.
Fowler--Art p149
O'Neill--Women's p605
Parker--Old p127,130, fig. 81
Petersen--Women p136-138
Women's--Female p36-37

CHIESMAN, LYDIA (fl. 1670's)
Amer. politician
Williams--Demeter's p162

CHILD, ABIGAIL (fl. 1970's)
Amer. photographer, filmmaker
Smith--Movies p156-157,231

CHILD, JULIA McWILLIAMS (1912-)
Amer. home economist, TV
personality
Anderson--People p100
Gilbert--Part. p219-225, por.
McHenry--Liberty's p69-70
O'Neill--Women's p133
Scheuer--Tel. p87, por.
100--Greatest (1) p64, por.
Woman's Almanac p267, por.
World--Who p296

CHILD, LYDIA MARIA FRANCES
(1802-1880)
Amer. author, abolitionist,
social reformer, editor
Beach--Daughters p79-119, por.
Ehrlich--Oxford p63,119
Fine--Women p93
James--Notable (1) p330-333
Kulkin--Her p66-67
Lutz--Crusade, see index p334,
por.
McHenry--Liberty's p70
Macksey--Book p184
Marzolf--Up p10
Millstein--We p95-96
Moers--Literary p176,283
Sherr--American p113-114
Webster's--Amer. p197

CHILDS, LUCINDA (1940-)
Amer. choreographer,
dancer, actress
Cur. Biog. '84 p75-7i, por.

CHILDS, MARLETA MARIE (1946-)
Amer. genealogical researcher,
editor, writer
Meyer--Who's p48

CHILTON, MARY
See WINSLOW, MARY CHILTON

CHILTON, RUTH (fl. 1920's-1940's)
Amer. radio, program direc-
tor
Marzolf--Up p122,142

CHILTOSKY, CHARLOTTE HORN-
BUCKLE (1868-c1936)
Amer. Indian, noted North
Carolina mother
Amer.--Mothers p404, por.

CHIMAY, JEANNE MARIE IONACE
THERESE DE CABARRUS,
PRINCESS OF (TALLIEN,
MADAME) (1773-1835)
French patriot, medico-
scientist, writer
Mead--Hist. p493

"CHINA MARY"
See AH LUN, MRS.

"CHINA POLLY"
See BEMIS, LALU LATHOY

CHINCHON, COUNTESS OF (fl.
1600's)
Spanish discoverer of "Peruvian bark," "Chinchon bark"
Mead--Hist. p432

CHINLUND, PHYLLIS JOHNSON (fl.
1970's)
Amer. filmmaker
Smith--Movies p157-158,232, por.

CHINN, MAY E. (c1896-1980)
Amer. physician
O'Neill--Women's p207

CHINNATAMBY, SIVA (fl. 1950's-
1960's)
East Indian physician, gynecologist, obstetrician
O'Neill--Women's p215

"CHIPETA" (1842/1843-1880)
Amer. Indian, noted Colorado
mother, queen, peace-maker,
heroine
Amer.--Mothers p63, por.
Sherr--American p29

CHISHOLM, DONNA GAGNIER
(1942-)
Amer. genealogical researcher
Meyer--Who's p48-49

CHISHOLM, SHIRLEY (1924/1925-)
Amer. Congresswoman
Bachtold--Gifted p104-106
Chamberlin--Min. p322-331, por.
Clark--Leading p238
Cur. Biog. '69 p92-95, por.
Diamonstein--Open p66-69, por.
Gilfond--Heroines p95-97, por.
Ingraham--Album p72, por.
Kulkin--Her p67-69
Longstreet--Queen p193
McHenry--Liberty's p70-71
Macksey--Book p42, por.
Miller--Fishbait p77-79, por.
Millstein--We p284-285, por.
100--Greatest (1) p57, por.
O'Neill--Women's p70-71
Ross--Young p15-24, por.
Schoenebaum--Prof. p123
Signif.--Amer. p59, por.
Sochen--Herstory p404-405, por.
Toppin--Biog. p270-271
Warren--Pictorial p197-198,204,
por.

Woman's Almanac p471, por.
World--Who p137

CH'IU SHIH (fl. c1550)
Chinese painter
Petersen--Women p155-156

CHIZHOVA, NADYEZHDA
Russian track and field
athlete
Hollander--100 p124-125

CHLAPOWSKI, HELENA MODREZE-
JEWSKA, COUNTESS
BORENTZ
See MODJESKA, HELENA

CHOLMONDELEY, MARY (1859-
1925)
British novelist
Showalter--Lit. p340

CHOPIN, KATE O'FLAHERTY
(1851-1904)
Amer. novelist, story writer
Avenel--Comp. (2) p57-58
Cahill--Women p1-2,373
Earnest--American p260-263,266
Ehrlich--Oxford p276,279,358
Fryer--Faces p207-208,243
James--Notable (1) p333-335
McHenry--Liberty's p71
Moers--Literary p283, see also
index p323, por.
Seymour-Smith--Novels p115
Sherr--American p82
Sochen--Herstory p199,223-224
Stein--Lives p487-494
Webster's--Amer. p199
Woman's Almanac p248
World--Who p11

CHOPRA, JOYCE (fl. 1970's)
Amer. filmmaker
Smith--Movies p158,232, por.

CHORPENNING, CHARLOTTE
(1873-)
Amer. children's playwright
Chinoy--Women p204-207

CHOUTEAU, BERNICE MENARD
(1801-1888)
Amer., noted Missouri
mother, Catholic worker,
friend of Indians
Amer--Mothers p310-311

CHOYNOWSKA-LISKIEWICZ,
KRYSTYNA (fl. 1970's)
Polish yachtsman
McWhirter--Guinness p188

CHRISTENSEN, ETHYN
Amer. labor leader
O'Neill--Women's p324

CHRISTENSEN, FERN BREAKEN-
RIDGE (1923-)
Amer. genealogical researcher,
editor
Meyer--Who's p49

CHRISTIAN, ANGELA
Ghana food, agriculture
specialist
O'Neill--Women's p39

CHRISTIAN, ANNIE (c1871-)
Amer. centenarian
Mitchell--Yessir p119-124, por.

CHRISTIAN, LINDA (1923/1924-)
Mexican-Amer. actress
Lamparski--What. (3) p122-123,
por.

CHRISTIANS, MADY (1900-1951)
Austrian actress
Springer--They p60,278, por.

CHRISTIANSON, PEGGY
Amer. TV executive
Scheuer--Tel. p88, por.

CHRISTIE, AGATHA (MARY CLARIS-
SA) MILLER, DAME (1890/
1891-1976)
English novelist, playwright
Avenel--Comp. (1) p101-102
Book--Lists (2) p435
Brecher--Lives p123-124, por.
Cur. Biog. '76 p465
Entertainers p189
Fry--1000 p320
Jones--Rutledge p174
Macksey--Book p191, por.
New York Times--Great p60-61,
por.
O'Neill--Women's p675-676,748,
por.
People's Almanac (1) p903
Seymour-Smith--Novels p76-77,
115
Showalter--Lit. p347

Woman's Almanac p248-249, por.
World--Who p45

CHRISTIE, JULIE (1941-   )
British actress
Anderson--People p101-102, por.
Hirschhorn--Rating p83-84, por.
Manchel--Women p96,105, por.
Shipman--Internatl. p100-102,
por.
Woman's Almanac p336, por.
World--Who p229

CHRISTINA (1626-1689)
Swedish queen, astronomer,
geologist, chemist, linguist,
scholar, medical woman
Fry--1000 p152
Jones--Rutledge p175
Macksey--Book p26-27, por.
Mead--Hist. p432
People's Almanac (2) p346-350,
por.
Prause--School p151-154, por.
Taylor--Gener. p23-24, por.
Trease--Seven p97-124, por.

CHRISTINA (1943-   )
Swedish princess
Miller--Fishbait p353

CHRISTINA OF HESSE (1758-1658)
German mathematician
Macksey--Book p143

CHRISTINA OF MARKYATE
(c1097-c1156)
English religious woman
Fines- Who's p58-61

CHRISTINE DE PISAN (1363/1364-
1431)
French poet, feminist,
scholar
Bree--Women p16-22
Mead--Hist. p256-259, por.

CHRISTMAN, ELIZABETH (1881-
1975)
Amer. labor leader, govern-
ment official
O'Neill--Women's p295,332
Sicherman--Notable p148-150

CHRISTOPHER, JEANNETTE MAY
(1920-   )
Amer. genealogical researcher,

editor
Meyer--Who's p49

CHRISTY, JUNE (1925-   )
Amer. singer
Claghorn--Biog. p93
Claghorn--Jazz p70

CHRISTY, MARY ROSE, SISTER
Amer. nun, political activist
O'Neill--Women's p389

CHRYSSA (VARDEA) (1933-   )
Greek-Amer. artist
Cur. Biog. '78 p72-75, por.
Women's--Female p101

CHUBBUCK, EMILY
See JUDSON, EMILY CHUBBUCK

CHU CHING-CHIEN (fl. 265-420)
Chinese calligrapher
Petersen--Women p149

CHUDLEIGH, NORMA LANE (1938-   )
Amer. genealogical researcher,
writer
Meyer--Who's p49

CHUKOVSKAYA, LYDIA (fl. 1930's)
Russian novelist
Moers--Literary p283

CHUMAKOVA, NADEZHDA (HOPE)
(fl. 1970's)
Russian mayor
Mandel--Soviet p293-294

CHUNG, CONNIE (1946-   )
Amer. TV anchor-newscaster,
journalist
Gelfman--Women p94,125
Marzolf--Up p177,190-192
O'Neill--Women's p500-501
Scheuer--Tel. p89

CHUPAK, LYDIA (fl. 1970's)
Russian labor leader
Mandel--Soviet p294-295

CHURCH, ANGELICA SCHUYLER
(1877-1954)
Amer. sculptor
Kelley--Courage p61-63,71,76-80,
89,92-93,223-224

CHURCH, CAROL R. (1934-   )

Amer. genealogical researcher,
editor
Meyer--Who's p49

CHURCH, ELLEN (c1905-   )
Amer. airline hostess,
"flying" nurse
Felton--Famous p100-101, por.
Macksey--Book p248
Woman's Almanac p172

CHURCH, MARGUERITE STITT
(1892-   )
Amer. Congresswoman
Chamberlin--Min. p220-222

CHURCHILL, ARABELLA (1648-1730)
English, sister of Duke of
Marlborough, mistress of
James, Duke of York
Jones--Rutledge p175

CHURCHILL, CAROLINE N.
(1833-   )
Canadian teacher, pioneer,
writer, journalist, feminist
Fischer--Let p166-176
Time--Women p220, por.

CHURCHILL, CARYL (1938-   )
English playwright
Cur. Biog. '85 p59-63, por.

CHURCHILL, CLEMENTINE OGILVY
HOZIER SPENCER, LADY
(1895-1977)
English, wife of Sir Winston
Churchill
Cur. Biog. '78 p477

CHURCHILL, ELEANOR FRANZEN
(fl. 1900's-1940's)
Amer. weaver, designer,
company founder
O'Neill--Women's p123

CHURCHILL, FRANCES, DUCHESS
OF MARLBOROUGH (-1899)
English, mother-in-law of
Jennie Churchill
Book--Lists (2) p253

CHURCHILL, JEANNETTE
(JENNIE) JEROME, LADY
RANDOLPH CHURCHILL
(1854-1921)
Amer.-English socialite,

mother of Winston Churchill
Brandon--Dollar p56,58-59,64-65,
127-128
Diagram--Mothers p50-56, por.
Earnest--American p179,196,199,
203-205
Forma--They p42-43, por.
James--Notable (1) p335-336
McHenry--Liberty's p71
Peacock--Famous p239-256, por.
Woman's Almanac p92-93, por.

CHURCHILL, MARGUERITE (1909-   )
Amer. actress
Springer--They p60,278, por.

CHURCHILL, ODETTE MARY CELINE
BRAILLY SANSOM (1912-   )
English war worker, spy
Fraser--Heroines p242-243, por.

CHURCHILL, SARAH, LADY AUDLEY
(1914-1982)
English actress, daughter of
Winston Churchill
Cur. Biog. '83 p462
People's Almanac (2) p1103

CHURCHILL, SAVANNAH (1919-   )
Amer. singer
Claghorn--Biog. p93
Claghorn--Jazz p70

CHYTILOVA, VERA (1929-   )
Czechoslovakian film director
O'Neill--Women's p668-669
Smith--Movies p100-101

CIBBER, CHARLOTTE (1713-1760)
English actress
Entertainers p91

CIBBER, SUSANNAH MARIA (1714/
1715-1766)
English actress
Findlater--Player p70-76, por.

CIBO, CATERINA, DUCHESS OF
CAMERINO (1501-1557)
Italian Reformation worker
Bainton--Germany p187-198

CILENTO, PHYLLIS, LADY (1894-   )
Australian physician
Hellstedt--Women p113-119, por.

CILLEY, ELSIE
Amer., noted New Hampshire

mother, Revolutionary patriot
Amér.--Mothers p359

CINCOTTA, GALE (c1930-)
Amer. political action re-
former
Woman's Almanac p391

CINTRON, CONCHITA (1922-)
Chilean bullfighter
Macksey--Book p260-261
McWhirter--Guinness p45
O'Neill--Women's p744

CIOBOTARU, GILLIAN WISE
(1936-)
English artist
Contemp. Brit. unp., por.

CISNEROS, ELEANOR BROAD-
FOOT, DE (1878-1934)
Amer. singer
Claghorn--Biog. p120
James--Notable (1) p450-451

CISSE, JEANNE MARTIN (1926-)
Guinean, President of U.N.
Security Council
O'Neill--Women's p65

CIXOUS, HELENE (fl. 1880's-1890's)
French professor, novelist
Crosland--Women p225,240

CLAFLIN, ROXANNA (ROXIE)
Amer. feminist, religious
worker, mother of Victoria
and Tennessee Claflin
Hymowitz--Hist. p165,171

CLAFLIN, TENNESSEE (1846-1923)
Amer. editor, publisher,
feminist, broker
Earnest--American p130-131,197,
250
Gurko--Ladies p243-244
Hymowitz--Hist. p164,166-167,
169,172-173
James--Notable (3) p652-655
Longstreet--Queen p63-65,68
Macksey--Book p166,169, por.
Marzolf--Up p20
Sherr--American p168
Smith--Daughters, see index p372
Woman's Almanac p548

CLAFLIN, VICTORIA
See WOODHULL, VICTORIA CLAF-
LIN

CLAIRE, BERNICE (1907-)
Amer. actress
Springer--They p60-61,278,280,
por.

CLAIRE, INA FAGAN (1892-1985)
Amer. actress
Cur. Biog. '85 p463
Lamparski--What. (2) p176-177,
por.
Springer--They p61-62,280, por.
World--Who p229

CLAIRMONT, CLAIRE (1798-1879)
English, step-daughter of
William Godwin, governess,
friend of Shelley and Lord
Byron
Book--Lists (1) p239

CLAIRON, CLAIRE, MADEMOISELLE
(1723-1803)
French actress
Entertainers p94
Macksey--Book p226

CLANTON, REITA (fl. 1970's)
Amer. athlete
O'Neill--Women's p569

CLAPP, CORNELIA MARIA (1849-
1934)
Amer. zoologist, teacher
James--Notable (1) p336-338
McHenry--Liberty's p71-72

CLAPP, HANNAH (fl. 1860's-1870's)
Amer. pioneer teacher, build-
ing contractor
Sherr--American p143

CLAPP, MARGARET ANTOINETTE
(1910-1974)
Amer. educator, government
official, historian
Cur. Biog. '74 p457
Sicherman--Notable p150-151

CLAPPE (CLAPP), LOUISE AMELIA
KNAPP SMITH (1819/1820-1906)
Amer. author, teacher
Gray--Women p46-59,63,121-122
Hoople--As p127-134
James--Notable (1) p338-339

CLAPPER, OLIVE EWING (1896-
1968)
Amer. author, lecturer,
government official
Cur. Biog. '69 p464

CLARA (CLARE) OF ASSISI
(1193/1194-1253)
Italian Saint, nun, nurse,
founder of order
Macksey--Book p106
Mead--Hist. p220,278,354
Who Did What p72

CLARA D'ANDUZA (fl. 13th cent.)
French troubadour
Bogin--Women p131,176

CLARE, ADA, pseud. (1836-1874)
Amer. novelist, poet,
actress, bohemian
Avenel--Comp. (2) p58
Ehrlich--Oxford p250
James--Notable (1) p339-340
McHenry--Liberty's p72

CLARE JOSEPH, MOTHER
See MATHEWS, ANN TERESA

CLARENBACK, KATHRYN (c1920-)
Amer. feminist, NOW chairman
O'Neill--Women's p416-417

"CLARIBEL," pseud.
See BARNARD, CHARLOTTE
ALLINGTON

CLARISSE OF ROTOMAGO (OR
ROUEN) (fl. 1300's)
French medical woman
Mead--Hist. p271

CLARK, ADELAIDE
Amer. house designer
Sherr--American p243

CLARK, ARIZONA DONNE
See BARKER, KATE ("MA")

CLARK, CARMEN ERCELL (1914-)
Amer. genealogical researcher,
writer
Meyer--Who's p49-50

CLARK, CATHERINE T. (1906-)
Amer. business corporation
head

O'Neill--Women's p135-136
Rich-McCoy--Mill. p49-72, por.

CLARK, DEENA (DEENER) (fl.
1960's)
Amer. radio, TV personality
Marzolf--Up p147

CLARK, ELEANOR (1913-)
Amer. writer
Cur. Biog. '78 p79-82, por.
Ehrlich--Oxford p411
McCullough--People p39-42

CLARK, ELOISE E. (1931-)
Amer. biologist
O'Neill--Women's p86

CLARK, EUGENIE (1922-)
Amer. ichthyologist, oceanog-
rapher, marine biologist
Emberlin--Cont. p125-148, por.
Kulkin--Her p69-70
O'Neill--Women's p162, por.

CLARK, FRANCES ELIOT (1860-
1958)
Amer. record producer,
music educator
Macksey--Book p215

CLARK, GEORGIA NEESE (1900-)
Amer. government official
McHenry--Liberty's p72

CLARK, JOAN (fl. 1940's-1970's)
Amer. government official
O'Neill--Women's p93

CLARK, JULIA (-1912)
Amer. pioneer airplane pilot
Macksey--Book p247
Woman's Almanac p369

CLARK, KARI (c1943-)
Amer., wife of Dick Clark
Funt--Are p99-112, por.

CLARK, KATE FREEMAN (-1957)
Amer. artist
Sherr--American p126

CLARK, KATHERINE (1602-1671)
Amer. colonial business
woman
Earle--Two Cent. (1) p57,70-71,
539,xv, por.

CLARK, KATHRYN HAUGH (fl.
1970's)
Amer. craftswoman, print-
maker, teacher
Women's--Female p155

CLARK, MAMIE PHIPPS (1917-   )
Amer. mental health worker,
clinic co-founder
Talmey--Vogue p229, por.

CLARK, MARGUERITE (1883/1887-
1940)
Amer. actress
James--Notable (1) p340-341
McHenry--Liberty's p72-73

CLARK, MARIE TAYLOR (1933-   )
Amer. genealogical researcher,
author, indexer
Meyer--Who's p50

CLARK, MICHELE (1943-1972)
Amer. TV executive
Marzolf--Up p106,189

CLARK, PETULA (1932/1934-   )
English singer, actress
Anderson--People p103
Claghorn--Biog. p94
Cur. Biog. '70 p83-85, por.
World--Who p265

CLARK, SEPTIMA POINSETTE
(1898-   )
Amer. educator
Burt--Black p71-88, por.

CLARK, SUSAN
Amer. TV reporter
Scheuer--Tel. p91

CLARK, YVONNE (1929-   )
Amer. mechanical engineer
O'Neill--Women's p194-195

CLARKE, AGNES MARY (1842-
1907)
Irish scientific worker
Showalter--Lit. p335

CLARKE, AMY
Amer. Confederate soldier,
male impersonator
Warren--Pictorial p109

CLARKE, CATHERINE (1890's)

Amer. hotel proprietor
Time--Women p132-133

CLARKE, EDITH (1883-1959)
Amer. electrical engineer
Sicherman--Notable p151-153

CLARKE, GRACE GIDDINGS JULIAN
(1865-1938)
Amer. clubwoman, suffragist
James--Notable (1) p341-342

CLARKE, HELEN
Amer. Indian "reformer"
Time--Women p210-211, por.

CLARKE, HELEN ARCHIBALD (1860-
1926)
Amer. magazine co-founder,
author, editor
James--Notable (3) p83-85
McHenry--Liberty's p73-74
O'Neill--Women's p471

CLARKE, HELEN J. (fl. 1890's)
Amer. music writer
Neuls-Bates--Women p211-213

CLARKE, MAE (1910-   )
Amer. actress
Lamparski--What. (4) p106-107,
por.
Lamparski--What. (8) p60-61, por.
Springer--They p62,280, por.

CLARKE, MARIAN WILLIAMS (1880-
1953)
Amer. congresswoman
Chamberlin--Min. p103

CLARKE, MARY
Amer. WAC director, engineer
O'Neill--Women's p552

CLARKE, MARY ANNE THOMPSON
(1776-1852)
British salonniere, courtesan
Macksey--Book p102

CLARKE, MARY BAYARD DEVEREUX
(1827-1886)
Amer. poet, editor
James--Notable (1) p342-344
Sherr--American p180, por.

CLARKE, MARY COWDEN
See COWDEN-CLARKE, MARY
VICTORIA

CLARKE, MARY FRANCES,
MOTHER (1803-1887)
Irish-Amer. foundress
McHenry--Liberty's p74

CLARKE, NANCY TALBOT (1825-
1901)
Amer. physician
Marks--Women p81-82

CLARKE, REBECCA SOPHIA
See MAY, SOPHIE, pseud.

CLARKE, SARA JANE
See GREENWOOD, GRACE,
pseud.

CLARKE, SHIRLEY (1927-)
Amer. film director, dancer
O'Neill--Women's p669
Smith--Movies p42-48, por.

CLAUDIA, MOTHER SUPERIOR
Amer. nun, religious worker
O'Neill--Women's p391

CLAUDIA PROCULA
Biblical, Pilate's wife
Price--God p161-164

CLAUDIA QUINTA (fl. 204 B.C.)
Roman patrician
Pomeroy--Godd. p179

CLAUSEN, FRANCISKA (1899-)
Danish painter
Harris--Women p321-322,360
O'Neill--Women's p596

CLAUSS, CARIN ANN (fl. 1950's-
1970's)
Amer. government official
O'Neill--Women's p90,340

CLAWSON, CAROL
Amer. public relations aid
Miller--Fishbait p85-86

CLAXTON, KATE (1848/1849-1924)
Amer. actress
James--Notable (1) p345-346

CLAY, ANN (fl. 1770's)
Amer. Revolutionary War
patriot
Clyne--Patriots p128,134

CLAY, MRS. CASSIUS (c1815-)
Amer. Southern farmer
Scott--Southern p108

CLAY, MRS. CLEMENT C.
See CLAY-CLOPTON, VIRGINIA
CAROLINE TUNSTALL

CLAY, LAURA (1849-1941)
Amer. suffragist, feminist,
politician
Hymowitz--Hist. p276
James--Notable (1) p346-348
Scott--Southern p108,131,173,175
Sherr--American p80-81, por.

CLAY, ODETTA LEE GRADY
Amer., mother of Mohammed
Ali
Diagram--Mothers p13-14, por.

CLAY, SHIRLEY (1902-1951)
Amer. trumpeter
Claghorn--Biog. p95

CLAYBROOK, JOAN (c1937-)
Amer. government official
O'Neill--Women's p86-87

CLAYBURGH, JILL (1944-)
Amer. actress
Anderson--People p103-104, por.
Cur. Biog. '79 p75-78, por.
Hirschhorn--Rating p84, por.
World--Who p229

CLAY-CLOPTON, VIRGINIA CARO-
LINE TUNSTALL (1825-1915)
Amer. society leader, suffra-
gist, patriot
James--Notable (1) p348-349
Wiley--Confed. p39-81, por.

CLAYDEN, MARION (fl. 1970's)
Amer. textile artist
Women's--Female p19

CLAYDON, MARGARET (fl. 1950's)
Amer. college president
Sherr--American p42

CLAYPOOL, ELIZABETH GRISCOM
See ROSS, BETSY (ELIZABETH)
GRISCOM

CLAYTON, EDITH (1897-)
Amer. hymnist
Claghorn--Biog. p95

CLAYTON, JAN (1917/1925-1983)
  Amer. actress, singer, TV
  personality
  World--Who p229

CLAYTON, LUCIE
  See GOLLIDGE, SYLVIA

CLEARY, CATHERINE B. (fl.
    1970's)
  Amer. financier, banker
  Macksey--Book p169
  O'Neill--Women's p528-529

CLEAVE, MARY
  Amer. astronaut
  Oberg--Space p19,189, por.
  O'Connor--Sally p2,21,54, por.

CLEAVELAND, AGNES MORLEY
    (fl. 1890's)
  Amer. cattle ranch manager
  Gray--Women p109-115
  Hymowitz--Hist. p178-180

CLEAVER, KATHLEEN (1945-)
  Amer. radical activist, wife
  of Eldridge Cleaver
  O'Neill--Women's p715

CLEGHORN, SARAH NORTHCLIFF
    (c1876-1959)
  Amer. poet, novelist
  Ehrlich--Oxford p18,22,343

CLEMENS, CLARA (1874-1921)
  Amer. singer, (daughter of
  Mark Twain)
  Claghorn--Biog. p96

CLEMENS, JANE LAMPTON (1802-
    1890)
  Amer., mother of Mark Twain
  Diagram--Mothers p239-241, por.

CLEMENT (daughter) (1793-c1808)
  French girl with one eye
  McFarland--Incred. p11

CLEMENT, EMMA CLARISSA
    WILLIAMS (c1874-1952)
  Amer., noted Kentucky
  mother, clubwoman
  Amer.--Mothers p213-214, por.

CLEMENTS, FIONA
  Amer. flight surgeon
  O'Neill--Women's p548

CLEMMER, MARY
  See AMES, MARY E. CLEMMER

CLEOBULINE (fl. 570's B.C.)
  Greek, daughter of Cleobulus,
  poet
  Pomeroy--Godd. p56

CLEOPATRA (1) (c69-30 B.C.)
  Graeco-Macedonian, Egyptian
  queen
  Canning--100 p120-126
  Coffin--Female p13-30, por.
  Donaldson--How p69-70
  Fraser--Heroines p88-92, por.
  Fry--1000 p40, por.
  Jones--Rutledge p182
  Kulkin--Her p70-71
  People's Almanac (2) p338-342,
  por.
  Pomeroy--Godd. p124-125,185-189,
  224-225,229
  Trease--Seven p1-29
  Who Did What p73
  Woman's Almanac p460
  World--Who p163

CLEOPATRA (2) (fl. 2nd cent.)
  Roman gynecologist
  Macksey--Book p140
  Mead--Hist., see index p534

CLEVELAND, ANN(E) NEAL (1806-
    1882)
  Amer., mother of President
  Cleveland
  Faber--Presidents' p224-226

CLEVELAND, BARBARA VILLIERS,
    DUCHESS OF
  See VILLIERS, BARBARA,
  COUNTESS OF CASTLEMAINE

CLEVELAND, EMELINE HORTON
    (1829-1878)
  Amer. surgeon, physician,
  educator, lecturer
  James--Notable (1) p349-350
  McHenry--Liberty's p74
  Sherr--American p187,204

CLEVELAND, FRANCES FOLSOM
    (1864-1947)
  Amer., noted District of
  Columbia mother, first lady
  Amer.--Mothers p102-103, por.
  James--Notable (1) p350-352
  Melick--Wives p50-51, por.

Woman's Almanac p489-
490

CLEW, HARRIET (one of three
Clew sisters) (fl. 1760's-
1770's)
Amer. hostess
Earnest--American p38-39

CLEWER, LISA (fl. 1970's)
Amer. business executive
Halcomb--Women p232-248

CLICQUOT, NICOLE-BARBE
(1777-1866)
French champagne producer
Macksey--Book p168, por.

CLIFFORD, ANNA RAWLE (1757/
1758-1828)
Amer. Revolutionary diarist
Evans--Weather. p283-302

CLIFFORD, ANNE, COUNTESS OF
DORSET (1590-1676)
English author, philanthropist
Earle--Two Cent. (1) p xvi,108,
por.

CLIFFORD, JOSEPHINE
See McCRACKIN, JOSEPHINE
WOEMPNER CLIFFORD

CLIFFORD, LINDA (fl. 1970's)
Amer. singer
Glassman--Year '79 p93

CLIFTON, LUCILLE (1936-)
Amer. poet
Chester--Rising p253-255, por.
Fisher--Third p vi,208-213

CLINE, GENEVIEVE ROSE (1878/
1879-1959)
Amer. lawyer, judge
Sicherman--Notable p153-154

CLINE, MAGGIE (1857-1934)
Amer. singer
James--Notable (1) p352-353
McHenry--Liberty's p74

CLINE, MINERVA JANE MAYO
(1847-)
Amer., noted Washington
state mother, community
worker

Amer.--Mothers p557,
por.

CLINE, PATSY (1932-1963)
Amer. singer, pianist
Claghorn--Biog. p97
O'Neill--Women's p629

CLINTON, NAOMI THOMPSON (fl.
1970's)
Amer. heroine, Carnegie
Medal winner
O'Neill--Women's p734-735

CLIVE, CAROLINE MEYSE-WIGLEY
(1801-1873/1875)
English novelist
Showalter--Lit. p321

CLIVE, CATHERINE (KITTY) R.
(1711-1785)
Irish actress, comedienne,
singer
Entertainers p91
Findlater--Player p60-70, por.

CLOCKER, MARY (fl. 1650's)
Amer. midwife
Mead--Hist. p415-416

CLODIA ("LESBIA") (c94 B.C.-)
Roman beauty
Pomeroy--Godd. p174

CLOELIA (c94 B.C.-)
Roman heroine
Zinserling--Women p64

CLOFULLIA, MADAM
See BOISDECHINES, JOSEPHINE

CLOONEY, ROSEMARY (1928-)
Amer. singer, actress
Claghorn--Biog. p97
Simon--Best p122-124, por.

CLOPTON, VIRGINIA CAROLINE
TUNSTALL CLAY
See CLAY-CLOPTON, VIRGINIA
CAROLINE TUNSTALL

CLOSE, GLENN (1947-)
Amer. actress
Cur. Biog. '84 p82-85, por.

CLOTILDA (CLOTILDE) OF BUR-
GUNDY (c475-c545)

French Saint, church builder,
nurse
Mead--Hist. p95

CLOUD, ELIZABETH ROE (fl.
1950's)
Amer., noted Oregon mother,
Indian missionary
Amer.--Mothers p448, por.

CLOUGH, ANNE JEMIMA (1820-
1892)
English educator
Macksey--Book p71

CLOUGH, PRUNELLA (1919-)
English artist
Contemp. Brit. unp.

CLOUSE, ROSE (1865-after 1900)
Amer. pianist, teacher
Claghorn--Biog. p97

CLUBB, LAURA A.
Amer. artist
Sherr--American p192

CLUSEN, RUTH C. (fl. 1970's)
Amer. political activist
O'Neill--Women's p730-731

CLYDE, JUNE (1909-)
Amer. actress
Springer--They p62,280, por.

CLYDE, MRS. (fl. 1770's)
Amer. Revolutionary War
patriot
Meyer--Petticoat p116

CLYTEMNESTRA
Grecian, sister of Helen,
wife of Agamemnon
Pomeroy--Godd. p21-22,26-27,
98-99,108,110

COALE, ANNE HOPKINSON (fl.
1770's-1800's)
Amer., sister of Francis
Cole
Earle--Two Cent. (2) p xvi, por.

COALE, MARY ABBY WILLING
(1789-)
Amer., daughter of Anne
Hopkinson Cole
Earle--Two Cent. (2) p xv, por.

COATES, ANNE V. (fl. 1960's-
1970's)
Amer. film editor
Smith--Movies p41,74-75

COATES, FLORENCE VAN LEER
EARLE NICHOLSON (1850-
1927)
Amer. poet
James--Notable (1) p353-354
McHenry--Liberty's p75

COATES, GLORIA (1938-)
Amer. singer, composer,
teacher, author
Jablonski--Ency. p506

COATES-WEST, CAROLE (1952-)
Amer. TV director
Scheuer--Tel. p92

COATSWORTH, ELIZABETH JANE
(1893-)
Amer. poet, novelist, children's
book author
Ehrlich--Oxford p49,101

COBB, GAIL A. (fl. 1970's)
Amer. policewoman
O'Neill--Women's p374

COBB, JERRIE (GERALDYN M.)
(1931-)
Amer. aviator
Gennett--Aviation p75, por.

COBB, JEWELL PLUMMER (fl. 1970's)
Amer. zoologist, professor
O'Neill--Women's p407-408

COBB, MARY ANN
Amer. Confederate patriot,
letter-writer
Wiley--Confed. p173

COBBE, FRANCES POWER (1822-
1904)
Irish antivivisectionist, writer,
philanthropist
Macksey--Book p115
Showalter--Lit. p327

COBDEN-SANDERSON, ANNIE
British bookbinder
Callen--Women p187,222

COBURN, ANN STRUTHERS (c1949-)

Amer. Episcopal priest
O'Neill--Women's p386-387

COCA, IMOGENE (1908-)
Amer. actress, comedienne
Fireman--TV p170-172
Scheuer--Tel. p92
Woman's Almanac p317-318, por.

COCHRAN(E), BARBARA ANN
(c1951-)
Amer. skier
Hollander--100 p75-76, por.
Sabin--Women p117-131, por.
Stambler--Women p107-119, por.

COCHRAN, JACQUELINE (1910-
1980)
Amer. aviatrix, cosmetologist
Boase--Sky's p122,136,189,215
Cur. Biog. '80 p452
Genett--Aviation p39-55, por.
Hazen--Interv. p372
Keil--Those, see index p322,
por.
Kulkin--Her p71-72
Longstreet--Queen p188-189
McHenry--Liberty's p75
Macksey--Book p42,250, por.
O'Neill--Women's p536,590
Reader's--Story p207
Warren--Pictorial p194
Webster's--Amer. p210
Woman's Almanac p370
World--Who p129

COCHRAN, ATHRYN
See CRAVENS, KATHRYN

COCHRAN(E), LINDA (LINDY)
(1954-)
Amer. skier
Hollander--100 p75-76, por.
Sabin--Women p117-131, por.

COCHRAN, MARGARET
See CORBIN, MARGARET
COCHRAN ("CAPTAIN
MOLLY")

COCHRAN(E), MARILYN (1950-)
Amer. skier
Hollander--100 p75-76, por.
Sabin--Women p117-131, por.

COCHRANE, ELIZABETH
See BLY, NELLIE, pseud.

COCKBURN, ALISON (or ALICIA)
(1713-1794)
Scottish poet
Avenel--Comp. (1) p108

COCKBURN, MRS.
See TROTTER, CATHERINE

COCKRELL, LILA (1922-)
Amer. mayor
Greenebaum--Politics p136
O'Neill--Women's p44,79

COCKRELL, SARAH (fl. 1850's)
Amer. pioneer settler, hotel
builder
Sherr--American p221

CODDINGTON, GRACE (fl. 1950's-
1960's)
English model, magazine
fashion editor
Keenan--Women p151,153,158-159,
por.

CODERRE, ANITA MARY (1921-)
Canadian genealogical research-
er, author
Meyer--Who's p51

CODONA, MRS. ALFREDO
See LEITZEL, LILLIAN

CODY, HARRIET (1973-)
Amer. (part of legal "marriage
contract")
O'Neill--Women's p109-110

COERR, S. DeRENNE (fl. 1970's)
Amer. printmaker, art re-
searcher
Women's--Female p118,124

COFFAL, ELIZABETH (fl. 1960's)
Amer. radio-car policewoman
O'Neill--Women's p373

COFFEY, MRS. EDWARD L.
See HAXALL, LUCY

COFFIN, ALICE VIRGINIA
Amer. P.E.O. co-founder
O'Neill--Women's p427, por.

COFFIN, ANNA (fl. 1700's)
Amer. colonial shop-owner
Sherr--American p107

COFFIN, CATHERINE (1827-1947)
Amer. abolitionist
Sherr--American p65

COFFIN (COFFYN), DIONIS
STEVENS (fl. 1640's-1660's)
Amer. colonial business woman
Sherr--American p107

COFFIN, JO (c1880-1943)
Amer. government official
Ware--Beyond p145-146, see
also index p198

COFFIN (COFFYN), MARY (1)
See STARBUCK, MARY COFFIN

COFFIN, MARY (2)
Amer. social reformer
Millstein--We p207

COFFIN, MIRIAM (1723-)
Amer. shipowner, accused
smuggler
Sherr--American p107

COFFIN, MRS. PETER (fl. 1770's)
Amer. colonial farmer, Revo-
lutionary War patriot
Millstein--We p32

COGHLAN, MRS. JOHN
See MONCRIEFFE, MARGARET

COGHLAN, ROSE (1852-1853-1932)
Irish-Amer. actress
James--Notable (1) p354-355

COGSWELL, SUE (fl. 1970's)
English squash player
McWhirter--Guinness p128

COHEN, BARBARA (1) (fl.
1960's-1970's)
Amer. editor
O'Neill--Women's p437,469

COHEN, BARBARA (2) (1945-)
Amer. TV local news
manager
Scheuer--Tel. p93

COHEN, JANE E. (1954-)
Amer. TV executive
Scheuer--Tel. p94

COHEN, JUDY
See CHICAGO, JUDY

COHEN, ZIVIA (fl. 1930's-1970's)
Israeli editor
O'Neill--Women's p481

COHN, FANNIA MARY (1885/1888-
1962)
Russian-Amer. labor leader
O'Neill--Women's p323
Sicherman--Notable p154-155

COHN, MILDRED (fl. 1960's-1970's)
Amer. chemist
O'Neill--Women's p145,164,166-167

COINCOIN, MARIE THERESE (1742-)
Amer. freed slave, plantation
owner
Sherr--American p82-83

COIT, ELEANOR G. (1894-1976)
Amer. labor educator
O'Neill--Women's p323-324

COIT, (ELIZA) LILLIE HITCHCOCK
(1843-1929)
Amer. philanthropist
Dunlap--Calif. p41, por.
Longstreet--Queen p151-153, por.
Sherr--American p20
Time--Women p161-164, por.
Woman's Almanac p211

COLBERT, CLAUDETTE (1905-)
French-Amer. actress
Engstead--Star p91-99,109-110
Hazen--Interv. p406-407
Hirschhorn--Rating p87-88, por.
Manchel--Women p55,58,67, por.
Shipman--Gold. p116-121, por.
Springer--They p62,64-65,280,
por.
Woman's Almanac p336
World--Who p229

COLBRY, VERA (fl. 1970's)
Amer. agriculturist
O'Neill--Women's p27

COLBY, ANITA (1914-)
Amer. actress, model, journal-
ist, editor
Lamparski--What. (5) p76-77, por.

COLBY, CLARA DOROTHY BEWICK
(1846-1916)
English-Amer. suffragist,
magazine founder
James--Notable (1) p355-357

Marzolf--Up p232-234
Sherr--American p138

COLCORD, JOANNA CARVER
(1882-1960)
Amer. social worker
Sicherman--Notable p155-157

COLDEN, JANE (1724-1766)
Amer. colonial botanist
Emberlin--Cont. p150-151
James--Notable (1) p357-358

COLE, ANNA VIRGINIA RUSSELL
(1846-1926)
Amer. philanthropist, social
leader
James--Notable (1) p358-359

COLE, DOLLIE
Amer. dress designer
O'Neill--Women's p260

COLE, ELIZABETH ANN
See ASHLEY, ELIZABETH

COLE, HANNAH ALLISON (fl.
1780's)
Amer., noted Missouri
mother, founder of fort, town
Amer.--Mothers p309

COLE, JANET
See HUNTER, KIM

COLE, MAX (fl. 1970's)
Amer. painter
Women's--Female p37

COLE, NATALIE (1950-)
Amer. singer, (daughter of
Nat King Cole)
Anderson--People p106, por.
Claghorn--Jazz p74
Glassman--Year '79 p93, por.
World--Who p265

COLE, OLIVIA H.H. (1942-)
Amer. artist, actress
Women's--Female p24

COLEMAN, ALICE BLANCHARD
MERRIAM (1858-1936)
Amer. missionary, church
leader
James--Notable (1) p359-360

COLEMAN, ANN (c1872-)
Amer. Alaskan librarian
Sherr--American p4

COLEMAN, GEORGIA (1912-1940)
Amer. diver
Woman's Almanac p429

COLEMAN, HELEN CORDELIA
English china painter
Callen--Women p56

COLEMAN, MARY STALLINGS (1914-)
Amer., noted Michigan mother,
Justice Michigan Supreme Court
Amer.--Mothers p282, por.
Swiger--Women p32-49

COLEMAN, REBECCA (-c1884)
British china painter
Callen--Women p56-57,222

COLEMAN, SUSAN LAWRENCE
(c1945-)
Amer. "homesteader"
O'Neill--Women's p20

COLERIDGE, MARY ELIZABETH
(1861-1907)
English poet, novelist, critic
Bernikow--World p136
Pearson--Who p45
Showalter--Lit. p341

COLERIDGE, SARA(H) HENRY
(1802-1852)
English poet, literary worker,
translator, wife of Samuel
Coleridge
Morley--Literary p195,202-203
Showalter--Lit. p322

COLET, LOUISE REVOIL (1808/
1810-1876)
French poet, salonist
Crosland--Women p29-31
Moers--Literary p283

COLETTE, ADELE-EUGENIE-SIDONIE
(-1912)
Belgian, mother of Sidonie
Gabrielle Colette
Diagram--Mothers p56-57, por.

COLETTE, SIDONIE GABRIELLE
CLAUDINE (1873-1954)

French novelist
Book--Lists (2) p114
Bree--Women p44,46-54
Cahill--Women p36-37,374
Crosland--Beyond p60-61,65,
172-175,211
Crosland--Women, see index
p251, por.
Jones--Rutledge p187
Kronenberger--Atlan. p173
Macksey--Book p191
Magill--Cycl. p225-227
Moers--Literary p283-284, see
also index p324, por.
O'Neill--Women's p672-673
Seymour-Smith--Novels p117,
por.
Seymour-Smith--Who's p83-84
Who Did What p75, por.
Woman's Almanac p249-250, por.
World--Who p33

COLIGNY, LOUISE DE (1555-1620)
French, daughter of Gaspard
de Coligny
Bainton--France p113-135, por.

COLIN, JANE (fl. 1970's)
Amer., Antarctic seal
researcher
Land--New p131-133, por.

COLINET, MARIE
See HILDEN, MARIE VON

COLLART (COLLAERT), MARIE
(1842-)
Belgian painter
Sparrow--Women p256

COLLEDGE, CECILIA (fl. 1930's)
British figure skater
Assoc. Press--Pursuit p124,146

COLLETT(E), CAMILLA WERGELAND
(1813-1895)
Norwegian novelist, feminist
Macksey--Book p81

COLLETT, GLENNA (1903-)
Amer. golfer
Hollander--100 p7,40-41, por.
People's Almanac (1) p1185

COLLEY, SARAH OPHELIA
See PEARL, MINNIE

COLLIER, CONSTANCE HARDIE
(1875/1880-1955)
English actress
Springer--They p65,280, por.

COLLIER, LUCILLE ANN
See MILLER, ANN

COLLIER, MARY ANN (1810-1866)
Amer. hymnist
Claghorn--Biog. p100

COLLINS, ANNE (fl. 1650's)
English poet
Bernikow--World p65

COLLINS, CAROLYN H. (1929-)
Amer. genealogical researcher,
writer
Meyer--Who's p53

COLLINS, CARRIE (1955-)
English-Amer. TV cable network
Scheuer--Tel. p97-98

COLLINS, CORA SUE (1927-)
Amer. child actress
Springer--They p65,280, por.

COLLINS, DOROTHY (1926-)
Canadian singer
Claghorn--Biog. p100
Lamparski--What. (3) p34-35, por.
World--Who p265

COLLINS, ELLA MAE (fl. 1950's-
1960's)
Amer. activist
O'Neill--Women's p715

COLLINS, ELLEN (1828-1913)
Amer. philanthropist, housing
reformer, Civil War patriot
James--Notable (1) p360-362

COLLINS, FANNIE B. (-1950)
Amer. teacher
Sherr--American p134

COLLINS, GAIL (fl. 1970's)
Amer. journalist, head News-
Service
O'Neill--Women's p466

COLLINS, JACKIE (1939-)
English actress, novelist
Seymour-Smith--Novels p117

COLLINS, JANET (1923-   )
Amer. ballet dancer
Toppin--Biog. p273-274

COLLINS, JENNIE C. (1828-1887)
Amer. labor reformer, wel-
fare worker, philanthropist
James--Notable (1) p362-363

COLLINS, JOAN (1933-   )
English-Amer. actress
Cur. Biog. '84 p85-88, por.
Scheuer--Tel. p98, por.

COLLINS, JOYCE (1930-   )
Amer. pianist, singer
Claghorn--Biog. p100

COLLINS, JUDY MARJORIE (1939-   )
Amer. folk-singer, guitarist,
composer, pianist
Bowman--Entertain. p20-23, por.
Claghorn--Biog. p100
Cur. Biog. '69 p102-104, por.
Glassman--Year '79 p93-94, por.
Simon--Best p130-131, por.
Smith--Movies p167-168, por.
Woman's Almanac p291, por.
World--Who p265

COLLINS, LOTTIE (1866-1910)
English music-hall singer,
dancer
Entertainers p154
People's Almanac (2) p436

COLLINS, MARJORIE (fl. 1970's)
Amer. magazine editor
Marzolf--Up p242

COLLINS, MARY CATHLEEN
See DEREK, BO (MARY
CATHLEEN)

COLLINS, PAT
Amer. TV newscaster
Gelfman--Women, see index
p185, por.
Scheuer--Tel. p98

COLLIS, SEPTIMA M. (fl.
1890's)
Amer. diarist
Sherr--American p6

COLLOT, MARIE-ANNE (1748-1821)
French sculptor
Petersen--Women p60

COLLYER, JUNE (1907-1968)
Amer. actress
Springer--They p65,280, por.

COLLYER, MARY MITCHELL (1716-
1762)
English translator, novelist
Horner--English p73 (and note)
Moers--Literary p284

COLMAN, BENITA HUME
See HUME, BENITA

COLMAN, JULIA (1828-1909)
Amer. temperance writer,
social reformer
James--Notable (1) p363-364

COLOM, AUDREY (fl. 1970's)
Amer. politician
O'Neill--Women's p707

COLONNA, VITTORIA (1490-1547)
Italian Reformation worker,
poet
Bainton--Germany p201-218, por.
Fine--Women p5-6
Macksey--Book p94
Moers--Literary p284

COLQUHOUN, MAUREEN MORFYDD
(1928-   )
British Parliament member
Vallance--Women p62,65,106-107,
110,172,174

COLSON, ELIZABETH FLORENCE
(fl. 1970's)
Amer. anthropologist
O'Neill--Women's p145,148

COLSON-MALLEVILLE, MARIE (fl.
1930's-1940's)
French film director
Smith--Movies p115

COLT, MIRIAM (fl. 1850's)
Amer. Western pioneer
Hoople--As p134-140

COLT, MIRIAM DAVIS (fl. 1850's)
Amer. author, club leader
Gray--Women p135-138

COLTER, JESSI (1947-   )
Amer. singer
Anderson--People p106-107

COLTON, ANNA
See O'DAY, ANITA

COLTON, ELIZABETH AVERY
(1872-1924)
Amer. professor, college
reformer
James--Notable (1) p364-365

COLTRANE, ALICE (1937-)
Amer. pianist
Claghorn--Biog. p291
Claghorn--Jazz p76

COLUMELLA (fl. 1st Cent. A.D.)
Roman agricultural writer
Pomeroy--Godd. p195-196

COLVIN, MRS. A.S.
Amer. journalist
Beasley--First p3

COLWELL, STELLA (1944-)
English genealogical research-
er, writer
Meyer--Who's p53

COMAN, KATHARINE (1857-1915)
Amer. economist, historian,
social reformer, educator
James--Notable (1) p365-367

COMAN, MARTHA (-1959)
Amer. journalist, club founder
Marzolf--Up p44,49

COMANECI, NADIA (1961-)
Romanian gymnast
Anderson--People p107-108
Assoc. Press--Pursuit p331-332,
por.
Cur. Biog. '77 p112-115, por.
McWhirter--Guinness p84, por.
O'Neill--Women's p562, por.
Partington--Who's p71
Woman's Almanac p54, por.
World--Who p211

COMBE, MADAME DE (-1692)
Netherlands medical woman
Mead--Hist. p418

COMBER, ELIZABETH CHOW
See HAN SUYIN

COMBS, BARBARA
See BILLINGSLEY, BARBARA

COMBS, MARY LOU (1940-)
Amer. genealogical researcher,
editor
Meyer--Who's p53

COMDEN, BETTY (1915-)
Amer. songwriter, activist,
author
Claghorn--Biog. p101
Jablonski--Ency. p350
O'Neill--Women's p637
World--Who p289

COMINI, ALESSANDRA (fl. 1970's)
Amer. college instructor
Women's--Female p114

COMISH, HANNAH (fl. 1860's)
Amer. teacher
Sherr--American p57

COMMISSIONG, JANELLE PENNY
(1953-)
Trinidad-Tobago beauty
O'Neill--Women's p743

COMNENA, ANNA (1083-1148)
Byzantine princess, physician,
medical writer, hospital admin-
istrator, historian
Macksey--Book p141
Who Did What p76

COMNENA, BERTHA
Hungarian hospital builder
Macksey--Book p141

COMPSON, BETTY (1897-1974)
Amer. actress
Lamparski--What. (2) p84-85, por.
Springer--They p67,280, por.

COMPTON, ANN WOODRUFF (1947-)
Amer. TV news correspondent
Scheuer--Tel. p99

COMPTON, HENRIA PACKER
(1827-)
Irish-Amer. Western pioneer
Fischer--Let p83-93

COMPTON, JOYCE (1907/1908-)
Amer. actress
Lamparski--What. (3) p170-171,
por.
Lamparski--What (8) p62-63, por.
Springer--They p67,280-281, por.

COMPTON, JULEEN (fl. 1970's)
Amer. actress, filmmaker
Smith--Movies p158-159,233, por.

COMPTON, LIZZIE
Amer. male impersonator,
soldier (Civil War)
Warren--Pictorial p109

COMPTON, OTELIA KATHERINE
(1859-c1944)
Amer., noted Ohio mother,
(mother of the Comptons,
educators and scientists)
Amer.--Mothers p429

COMPTON-BURNETT, IVY (1892-
1969)
English novelist
Avenel--Comp. (1) p114
Crosland--Beyond p44,53,77-88,
182,198,222
Jones--Rutledge p189
Moers--Literary p257,284-285
Seymour-Smith--Novels p118
Seymour-Smith--Who's p84
Showalter--Lit. p347
Who Did What p77

COMSTOCK, ADA LOUISE (1873-
1973)
Amer. college president
O'Neill--Women's p405
Sicherman--Notable p157-159

COMSTOCK, ANNA BOTSFORD
(1854-1930)
Amer. naturalist, illustrator
James--Notable (1) p367-369
McHenry--Liberty's p75-76

COMSTOCK, ELIZABETH LESLIE
ROUS (1815-1891)
Amer. Quaker clergyman,
reformer
James--Notable (1) p369-370
McHenry--Liberty's p76

CONANT, HANNAH O'BRIEN
CHAPLIN (1809-1865)
Amer. religious writer
James--Notable (1) p370-371

CONAT, ESTELLINA (fl. c1496)
Italian Jewish printer
Henry--Written p117-118

CONBOY, SARA AGNES McLAUGHLIN
(1870-1928)
Amer. labor leader
McHenry--Liberty's p76-77

CONCELLO, ANTOINETTE (fl.
1930's-1940's)
Amer. circus trapeze artist
Kirk--Circus p64-67, por.

CONE, CLARIBEL (1864-1929)
Amer. pathologist, art collector,
philanthropist
James--Notable (1) p371-373
Longstreet--Queen p119-122
McHenry--Liberty's p77
Rogers--Ladies p17-19, por.

CONE, CYNTHIA
Amer. anthropologist
Bowman--Social p40-43, por.

CONE, ETTA (1866-)
Amer. art patron, philanthro-
pist
Longstreet--Queen p119-123
McHenry--Liberty's p77
Rogers--Ladies p5,14,17-19,93,
por.

CONFRIN, BETSY
Amer. psychologist
Adams--Women p122

CONGDON, MARY GLASGOW PEEK
(PRINCESS REDWING) (1898-)
Amer. Indian, noted Rhode
Island mother, artist, civic
worker
Amer.--Mothers p481-482, por.

CONKLIN, PEGGY (1910/1912-)
Amer. actress
Springer--They p67,281, por.

CONKLING, HILDA (1910-)
Amer. poet, children's author
Book--Lists (2) p223

CONLEY, FLORENCE (fl. 1930's)
Amer. radio reporter
Marzolf--Up p129

CONLEY, SISTERS (fl. 1910's)
Amer. defenders of Wyandot
Indian Cemetery 1906
Sherr--American p75

CONLIN, NOREEN P. (1946-)
Amer. TV executive
Scheuer--Tel. p100

CONLON, KATHLEEN (1943-)
English novelist
Seymour-Smith--Novels p118

CONN, CANARY (1949-)
Amer. singer, journalist,
transsexual
Books--Lists (2) p327

CONNELL, THELMA (fl. 1950's-
1970's)
Amer. film editor
Smith--Movies p77,111

CONNELLY, CELIA LOGAN
KELLOGG
See LOGAN, OLIVA

CONNELLY, CORNELIA AUGUSTA
(1809-1879)
Amer. Catholic nun
James--Notable (1) p373-375
McHenry--Liberty's p77
Webster's--Amer. p218-219

CONNELLY, LAURE (fl. 1970's)
Amer. horse-racing "trainer"
O'Neill--Women's p588

CONNER, LINDA (fl. 1970's)
Amer. photographer
Women's--Female p63

CONNERS (O'CONNER), MARTHA
(fl. 1970's)
Amer. photographer
Women's--Female p63

CONNES, ELVA
See MILLER, ELVA RUBY
CONNES

CONNOLLY, MRS. HAROLD
See FIKOTOVA, OLGA

CONNOLLY, MAUREEN (CATHER-
INE) (1934-1969)
Amer. tennis player
Cur. Biog. '69 p465
Hollander--100 p107-108,116,
por.
McHenry--Liberty's p77-78
Macksey--Book p257

McWhirter--Guinness p151, por.
People's Almanac (1) p1188
Sullivan--Queens p102-104, por.
Webster's--Amer. p219
Woman's Almanac p414
World--Who p212

CONNOLLY, OLGA FIKOTOVA (fl.
1950's)
Czechoslovakian track and
field athlete
Hollander--100 p122-123, por.

CONNOLLY, SYBIL (1921-)
Welch-Irish fashion fabric
designer
Macksey--Book p268
O'Neill--Women's p243

CONNOR, CATHERINE
Amer. businesswoman
O'Neill--Women's p140

CONNOR, CHRIS (1927-)
Amer. singer
Claghorn--Biog. p102
Claghorn--Jazz p78

CONNOR, MAUREEN
Amer. sculptor
Women's--Female p87

CONNORS, BABE (1856-1918)
Amer. "madam"
People's Almanac (2) p929-930

CONOVER, CATHERINE MELLON
(c1936-)
Amer. millionaire, activist,
environmentalist
Forbes--400 ('84) p150

CONS, EMMA (1838-1912)
English philanthropist
Macksey--Book p229-230

CONSTABLE FAMILY (Ann, 1768-
1854; Mary, 1781-1865)
English, family of John
Constable
Ware--Meet p75

CONSTAT, LOUISE-FRANCOISE
(1760-1813)
French actress
Entertainers p106

CONTI, ITALIA (1873/1874-1946)
English actress, dramatic
teacher
Macksey--Book p230

CONVERSE, HARRIET MAXWELL
(-1903)
Amer. author, folklorist,
defender of Indian rights
James--Notable (1) p375-377
Sherr--American p160

CONVERSE, MARY PARKER (c1872-
1961)
Amer. navigation teacher,
Merchant Marine Captain
Sherr--American p24

CONWAY, ANN RECTOR (1770-)
Amer., noted Arkansas mother,
mother of famous sons,
patriot
Amer.--Mothers p39, por.
Sherr--American p10

CONWAY, ANNE FINCH (1631-)
English Viscountess
Mead--Hist. p405-407

CONWAY, ELAINE
Amer. TV director
Scheuer--Tel. p102-103

CONWAY, JILL KER (fl. 1970's)
Amer. college president,
historian
O'Neill--Women's p407

CONWELL, ESTHER M.
Amer. scientist
O'Neill--Women's p183,188

COOK, ALICE HANSON
Amer. educator, writer,
labor union worker
O'Neill--Women's p325,327-328

COOK, ANN TURNER (fl. 1920's)
Amer. advertising subject
Woman's Almanac p209

COOK, ANNIE (fl. 1870's-
1880's)
Amer. charitable nurse
Sherr--American p218

COOK, EDITH MAUD (-1910)
British aviatrix, parachute
jumper
Boase--Sky's p12,14
Macksey--Book p246

COOK, ELIZA (1818-1889)
English poet, editor, publisher
Jones--Rutledge p192
Showalter--Lit. p326

COOK, IVA DEAN (fl. 1970's)
Amer., noted West Virginia
mother, educator
Amer.--Mothers p578, por.

COOK, JANE BANCROFT
Amer. millionaire
Forbes--400 ('84) p86

COOK, JUDY
Amer. bowler
Hollander--100 p18-19, por.

COOK, MARTHA ANN (WOODBRIDGE)
(1807-1874)
Amer. hymnist, editor
Claghorn--Biog. p103

COOK, MAY A. (1870-)
Amer. pianist, teacher
Claghorn--Biog. p103

COOK, MRS. (-1925)
British, author of longest will
People's Almanac (1) p1331

COOK, SYLVIA (fl. 1970's)
Amer. sailor
Macksey--Book p246

COOK, TENNESSEE
See CLAFLIN, TENNESSEE

COOKE, ANNA CHARLOTTE RICE
(1853-1934)
Amer. founder of art academy
James--Notable (1) p377-378
Sherr--American p54

COOKE, ANNE
See BACON, ANNE COOKE, LADY

COOKE, FLORA JULIETTE (1864-1953)
Amer. educator
Sicherman--Notable p159-160

COOKE, HOPE
See HOPE NAMBYAL, MAHARANI
OF SIKKIM

COOKE, JEAN (1927-)
English artist
Contemp. Brit. unp., por.

COOKE, KATHERINE, LADY
KILLIGREW (fl. c1750's)
English religious worker,
(daughter of Anthony Cooke)
Bainton--Spain p101-105

COOKE, KATIE (fl. 1970's)
Canadian agricultural labor
worker
O'Neill--Women's p326

COOKE, MILDRED
See BURGHLEY, MILDRED
COOKE, LADY

COOKE, PHOEBE HEARST (c1927-)
Amer. millionaire
Forbes--400 ('84) p190

COOKE, ROSE TERRY (1827-1892)
Amer. poet, short-story
writer
Ehrlich--Oxford p55,81,88,93,95
James--Notable (1) p378-379
McHenry--Liberty's p78
Pearson--Who p208

COOKSON, CATHERINE
English novelist
Seymour-Smith--Novels p119

COOLBRITH, INA DONNA (1841-
1928)
Amer. librarian, poet
Dunlap--Calif. p43, por.
Ehrich--Oxford p417,423-424
James--Notable (1) p379-380
McHenry--Liberty's p78-79
Sherr--American p19
Time--Women p106-111, por.

COOLIDGE, ELIZABETH PENN
SPRAGUE (1864-1953)
Amer. philanthropist,
music patron, pianist
McHenry--Liberty's p79
Neuls-Bates--Women p231-238,
por.
Sicherman--Notable p160-162

COOLIDGE, GRACE ANNA GOOD-
HUE (1879-1957)

Amer., noted Vermont
mother, first lady
Amer.--Mothers p543-544, por.
Melick--Wives p66-67, por.
People's Almanac (1) p275
Sicherman--Notable p162-163
Woman's Almanac p491

COOLIDGE, MARTHA (fl. 1960's-
1970's)
Amer. filmmaker
Smith--Movies p159,233, por.

COOLIDGE, PEGGY STUART (1913-
1981)
Amer. composer, pianist
Jablonski--Ency. p508-509

COOLIDGE, RITA (1945-)
Amer. singer
Anderson--People p112, por.
Claghorn--Biog. p103-104
Glassman--Year '79 p94, por.

COOLIDGE, SUSAN
See WOOLSEY, SARAH CHAUNCEY

COOLIDGE, VICTORIA MOOR (1846-
1885)
Amer., mother of Calvin
Coolidge
Faber--Presidents' p217-219
Sherr--American p230

COONEY, JOAN GANZ (1929-)
Amer. TV executive
Adams--Women p21,79-83,87,100,
109-110,200
Cur. Biog. '70 p97-99, por.
Diamonstein--Open p70-73, por.
Firestone--Success, see index
p297
Gilbert--Part. p293-299, por.
Klever--Women p110-115, por.
McHenry--Liberty's p79
Marzolf--Up p173
100--Greatest (1) p27, por.
O'Neill--Women's p499
Scheuer--Tel. p104
Woman's Almanac p267

COONEY, MARION (fl. 1970's-1980's)
Amer. virologist, (Antarctica
researcher)
Land--New p159

COOPER, ANNA JULIA HAYWOOD
(c1859-1964)
Amer. educator, scholar
Sicherman--Notable p163-165

COOPER, CAMERON (fl. 1790's)
Amer. oil company executive
O'Neill--Women's p523

COOPER, CHARLOTTE
British tennis player
Macksey--Book p257

COOPER, DIANA, LADY (1881/
1893-1971)
British actress, beauty
Keenan--Women p51-53, por.

COOPER, EDITH EMMA
See FIELD, MICHAEL, pseud.

COOPER, GLADYS, DAME (1888-
1971)
English actress, beauty
Cur. Biog. '72 p460
Entertainers p183, por.
Johns--Dames p133-144, por.
Jones--Rutledge p193
Keenan--Women p48-50, por.
World--Who p255

COOPER, GLORIA
See VANDERBILT, GLORIA
MORGAN

COOPER, JENNIE (fl. 1860's)
Amer. Southern belle
DeLeon--Belles p110-111, por.

COOPER, JILLY (1937-)
English journalist, novelist,
humourist
Seymour-Smith--Novels p119

COOPER, JULIA DEAN
See DEAN, JULIA

COOPER, KAREN (1945-)
Amer. TV program executive
Scheuer--Tel. p105

COOPER, LOUISE FIELD (1905-)
Amer. writer
Ehrlich--Oxford p95

COOPER, MARTHA KINNEY
(1874-)

Amer., noted Ohio mother,
patriot, governor's wife, clubwoman
Amer.--Mothers p430, por.

COOPER, MILDRED ("MILLY") (fl.
1810's)
Amer. heroine
Sherr--American p129

COOPER, POLLY (fl. 1770's)
Amer. Indian Revolutionary
War patriot
Clyne--Patriots p128,134-135

COOPER, PRISCILLA
See TYLER, PRISCILLA COOPER

COOPER, SARAH BROWN INGERSOLL
(1835-1896)
Amer. kindergarten educator,
author, Bible teacher
James--Notable (1) p380-382
McHenry--Liberty's p79-80

COOPER, SARAH MARIA MASON (fl.
1860's)
Amer. Southern belle
DeLeon--Belles p109, por.

COOPER, SUSAN AUGUSTA FENI-
MORE (1813-1894)
Amer. author, philanthropist
James--Notable (1) p382-383
McHenry--Liberty's p80

COOPER, WILMA LEE (LEARY)
(1921-)
Amer. singer, guitarist,
banjoist, organist, songwriter
Claghorn--Biog. p104

COOPERPERSON, ELLEN (fl. 1970's)
Amer. feminist
Felton--Famous p258

COPE, BETTY (fl. 1970's)
Amer. TV station executive
Klever--Women p17-18,61,95-96,
108

COPELAND, ELIZABETH E. (fl.
1970's)
Amer. silversmith, enameller
Callen--Women p162,222

COPELAND, LILLIAN (fl. 1930's)

Amer. track and field athlete
Assoc. Press--Pursuit p114,129,
por.

COPENHAVER, LAURA (SCHERER)
(1868-1940)
Amer. hymnist
Claghorn--Biog. p105

COPLEY, HELEN KINNEY (c1923-)
Amer. newspaper publisher,
millionaire
Forbes--400 ('84) p124
Marzolf--Up p93
O'Neill--Women's p466
Woman's Almanac p267-268
World--Who p51

COPLEY, MARY SINGLETON
(c1710-1789)
Irish-Amer. colonial shopkeeper
James--Notable (3) p43-44

COPP, DOLLY EMERY (fl. 1830's)
Amer., noted New Hampshire
mother, pioneer
Amer.--Mothers p361-362, por.

COPPERSMITH, BARBARA CAROLE
See CARROLL, BARBARA

COPPI, HILDE (1909-1943)
German resistance fighter
Partington--Who's p73-74

COPPIN, FANNY MARION JACKSON
(1837-1913)
Amer. educator, missionary
James--Notable (1) p383-385
McHenry--Liberty's p81-82
Millstein--We p84
Reader's--Story p436
Sherr--American p199

CORBETT, ELIZABETH FRANCIS
(1887-1981)
Amer. children's book author
Ehrlich--Oxford p317

CORBIN, HANNAH LEE (1728-)
Amer. colonial feminist, suf-
fragist
DePauw--Found. p198-199
Sherr--American p238-239

Warren--Pictorial p58

CORBIN, MARGARET COCHRAN
("CAPTAIN MOLLY") (1751-
c1800)
Amer., noted Pennsylvania
mother, Revolutionary War
heroine
Amer.--Mothers p455
Booth--Women p98-99,174,300
Clyne--Patriots p19-26
DePauw--Found. p188-190
DePauw--Rem. p90
Engle--Women p26-28
Evans--Weather. p10-11
Ingraham--Album p17, por.
James--Notable (1) p385-386
McHenry--Liberty's p81
Meyer--Petticoat p61-62, 109
Millstein--We p34-35
Reifert--Women p23
Sherr--American p171,177
Somerville--Women p12-17
Webster's--Amer. p225
Whitney--Col. p158
Williams--Demeter's p243-244
Woman's Almanac p452

CORBY, ELLEN (1913-)
Amer. actress
Book--Lists (2) p370
World--Who p230

CORCORAN, NOREEN (fl. 1940's)
Amer. actress
Lamparski--What. Annual (4,5)
p292-297, por.

CORDAY, CHARLOTTE (MARIE
ANNE CHARLOTTE CORDAY
D'ARMONT) (1768-1798)
French accused criminal
Jones--Rutledge p194
Taylor--Gener. p31-32, por.
Macksey--Book p135-136, por.
World--Who p158

CORDES, GEORGENE
Amer. bowler
McWhirter--Guinness p42

CORDOVA, FRANCE (c1948-)
Amer. astrophysicist
Science Digest--100 p40, por.

CORELLI, MARIE, pseud. (1854-
1924)
English novelist
Avenel--Comp. (1) p118
Crosland--Beyond p3-4,13,44,52
Jones--Rutledge p194
Macksey--Book p188
Seymour-Smith--Novels p120
Showalter--Lit. p342-343

COREY, MARTHA (-1692)
Amer. accused witch
James--Notable (1) p386-387
Millstein--We p16-18
Sherr--American p111

COREY, MELISSA
Amer. Mormon Battalion
member
Sherr--American p18

CORI, GERTY THERESA RADNITZ
(1896-1957)
Czechoslovakian-Amer.
biochemist
Asimov--Biog. p658
McHenry--Liberty's p81
Neidle--America's p210-212, por.
O'Neill--Women's p144,164,219-
220
Opfell--Lady p183-193, por.
Sicherman--Notable p165-167
Webster's--Amer. p225-226
Woman's Almanac p361
World--Who p103

CORINNA OF TANAGRO (fl. B.C.
c1490)
Greek poet
Moers--Literary p285
Pomeroy--Godd. p52-53

CORNELIA (1) (fl. 169 B.C.--
2nd cent., B.C.)
Roman matron, mother of
the Gracchi
Pomeroy--Godd. p149-151,161,
163,170,172
Zinserling--Women p64

CORNELIA (2)
Roman, wife of L.
Aemilius Paullus
Pomeroy--Godd. p161

CORNELL, KATHARINE (1893/
1898-1974)

German-Amer. actress, pro-
ducer
Clark--Leading p134-136
Cur. Biog. '74 p457
Entertainers p205, por.
Fabian--On p162-163, por.
Gilfond--Heroines p110,112
Hazen--Interv. p83
Jones--Rutledge p194
Kulkin--Her p72-73
Lamparski--What. (2) p14-15, por.
McHenry--Liberty's p81-82
Macksey--Book p227,232
O'Neill--Women's p656
Pederson--Leaders p237, por.
Sicherman--Notable p167-169
Webster's--Amer. p226-227
Who Did What p79
World--Who p230

CORNELL, NANCY JONES (1936-)
Amer. genealogical researcher,
author, editor
Meyer--Who's p54

CORNER, BERYL DOROTHY (1910-)
British physician
Hellstedt--Women p398-403, por.

CORNER, CATERINA (c1454-1510)
Cyprus queen, Venetian
scholar
Brink--Female p24-35, por.

CORNERO, ELLENA LUCRETIA
(1646-1684)
Italian linguist, scientist
Mead--Hist. p431

CORNFORD, FRANCES CROFTS
DARWIN (1886-1960)
English poet, grandaughter
of Charles Darwin
Avenel--Comp. (1) p118-119
Morley--Literary p83,305-306

CORPRON, CARLOTTA M. (1901-)
Amer. photographer
Mitchell--Recol. p48-65,200, por.

CORREL, HELEN B. (1907-)
Amer. aquatic biologist
O'Neill--Women's p33

CORRIGAN, KATHLEEN ANN (fl.
1970's)
Amer. heroine, Carnegie

Medal winner
O'Neill--Women's p734

CORRIGAN, MAIREAD (1944-)
Irish pacifist
Cur. Biog. '78 p88-91, por.
O'Neill--Women's p711
Opfell--Lady p50-61, por.

CORRY, RUTH L. (1920-)
Amer. genealogical research-
er, writer, editor
Meyer--Who's p54

CORSE, MARY (fl. 1970's)
Amer. painter
Women's--Female p37

CORSON, JULIET (1841/1842-1897)
Amer. cookery writer, edu-
cator
Bolton--Success p9-33, por.
James--Notable (1) p387-388
McHenry--Liberty's p82

CORSON, MILLIE GADE (fl. 1920's)
Amer. swimmer
Book--Lists (2) p473-474

CORTESE, ISABELLA (-1561)
Italian scientific medical
writer
Mead--Hist. p349

COSELL, EMMY (fl. 1970's)
Amer., wife of Howard Cosell
Funt--Are p115-124, por.

COSSOTTO, FIORENZA (1935-)
Italian opera singer
Gammond--Illus. p240, por.

COST, MARCH (-1973)
English novelist
Cur. Biog. '73 p453

COSTA (COSTE), BLANCHE
MARIE DE (fl. 1566)
French teacher, author,
obstetrician
Macksey--Book p64-65
Mead--Hist. p357

COSTANZA, MARGARET ("MIDGE")
(1932-)
Amer. politician, assistant to
United States President

Cur. Biog. '78 p91-94, por.
Greenebaum--Politics p137
O'Neill--Women's p80-81

COSTELLO, DELORES (fl. 1960's-
1970's)
Amer. communications educator
Innis--Profiles p102-103, por.

COSTELLO, DOLORES (1905/1906-
1979)
Amer. actress
Lamparski--What. (2) p106-107,
por.
Springer--They p68,281, por.

COSTELLO, HELENE (1903/1905-
1957)
Amer. actress
Springer--They p68,281

COSTELLO, MARJORIE (1950-)
Amer. TV magazine editor
Scheuer--Tel. p107-108

COSTELLO, PATTY (1946-)
Amer. bowler
Hollander--100 p18, por.
O'Neill--Women's p558
Woman's Almanac p436

COSTON, CAROL, SISTER (1935-)
Amer. religious lobby organizer
O'Neill--Women's p389

COSWAY, MARIA CECELIA LOUISE
HADFIELD (1759-1838)
Irish painter
Fine--Women p77-79, por.
Kelley--Courage p220-225
Petersen--Women p46, por.

COTA-GARDENAS, MARGARITA
(1941-)
Amer. poet
Fisher--Third p viii,398

COTRUBAS, ILEANA (1939-)
Romanian opera singer
Cur. Biog. '81 p92-95, por.
Gammond--Illus. p240-241, por.

COTT, BETTY
Amer. public relations executive
Adams--Women p13,103,119-120,
177,186,204-205

COTT, NANCY F. (fl. 1780-1835)
Amer. feminist writer
Berkin--Women p187-188

COTTEN, ELIZABETH ("LIBRA")
(1893-)
Amer. singer, guitarist
Claghorn--Biog. p106

COTTEN, SALLIE SIMS SOUTHALL
(1846-1929)
Amer. woman's club leader
James--Notable (1) p388-390
Scott--Southern p157-158,162-163

COTTLE, JOSEPHINE OWAISSA
See STORM, GALE

COTTLOW, AUGUSTA (1878-1954)
Amer. pianist
Claghorn--Biog. p106

COTTMORE, MARTHA
See WINTHROP, MARTHA
COTTMORE

COTTON, ANNE
English, writer of Bacon's
Rebellion
Williams--Demeter's p162

COTTON, ELIZABETH AVERY
(1872-)
Amer. educator, reformer,
professor
Sherr--American p180

COTTON, ELIZABETH HENDERSON
Amer. suffragist
Daniels--Wash. p157,190-191,250

COUDERT, AMALIA KUSSNER
(1876-1932)
Amer. painter
Sherr--American p68

COUDRAY, ANGELIQUE MAR-
GUERITE LEBOURSIER DU,
MADAME
See LEBOURSIER, ANGELIQUE
MARGUERITE DU COUDRAY,
MADAME

COUDRAY, LOUISE LEBOURSIEUR
DU (fl. 1670's)
French medical writer
Mead--Hist. p423

COUNIHAN, ANITA KATHERINE
See COLBY, ANITA

COUPE, BETTY LOU (fl. 1900's)
Amer. child aviatrix
Boase--Sky's p14, por.

COUPERIN, CELESTE (1793-1860)
French organist
Macksey--Book p211

COUPERIN, MARGUERITE-LOUISE
(c1676-1728)
French clavecinist
Macksey--Book p211

COUPERIN FAMILY (fl. late-17th to
mid-19th cen.)
French musicians
Macksey--Book p211

COURT, MARGARET SMITH (1942-)
Australian tennis player
Cur. Biog. '73 p88-90, por.
Hollander--100 p7,107-108,112,
114,por.
Macksey--Book p257
McWhirter--Guinness p151-152,
por.
O'Neill--Women's p582
Sullivan--Queens p11-33, por.
Who Did What p80
Woman's Almanac p414-415
World--Who p212

COURTAULD, LOUISA PERINA
British goldsmith, jeweller
Callen--Women p152

COURTNEIDGE, CICELY, DAME
(c1893-1980)
English actress, comedienne
Comfort--Good p109, por.
Johns--Dames p162-178, por.
Jones--Rutledge p196
Shipman--Gold. p129-130, por.

COURTNEY, INEZ (fl. 1920's-1930's)
Amer. actress
Springer--They p68,281, por.

COURTY, MICHELINE (fl. 1970's)
French investment trust
founder
Macksey--Book p169
O'Neill--Women's p529

"COUSIN ALICE"
See HAVEN, (ALICE) EMILY
BRADLEY NEAL

COUSINS, MRS. (fl. 1910's)
British suffragist
Macksey--Book p90

COUZIN, SHARON (fl. 1970's)
Amer. filmmaker, college
instructor
Smith--Movies p159-160,233

COUZINS, PHOEBE WILSON (c1839-
1913)
Amer. lawyer, suffragist
James--Notable (1) p390-391
Sherr--American p133

COVILLAND, MARY MURPHY
Amer., member, Donner
party
Sherr--American p16

COWAN, CHARLOTTE
See RIDDELL, CHARLOTTE
ELIZA LAWSON COWAN

COWDEN-CLARKE, MARY VIC-
TORIA (1809-1898)
English novelist, journalist,
scholar, essayist
Showalter--Lit. p323

COWELL, SIDNEY FRANCES
See BATEMAN, KATE
JOSEPHINE

COWINGS, PATRICIA
Amer. physician, space
experiments
Oberg--Space p87

COWL, JANE COWLES (1883/1884-
1950)
Amer. actress, playwright,
producer
Entertainers p175
Hazen--Interv. p101-102
Holme--Journal p82-83, por.
James--Notable (1) p391-393
McHenry--Liberty's p82-83

COWLES, ANNA ROOSEVELT
(BAMIE)
Amer. sister of Franklin D.
Roosevelt

Daniels--Wash., see index p361,
por.

COWLES, BETSEY MIX (1810-1876)
Amer. educator, social reform-
er, feminist, suffragist
James--Notable (1) p393-394
Sherr--American p184,187

COWLES, FLEUR FENTON (1910-)
Amer. editor, painter, author
Lamparski--What. (4) p194-195,
por.

COWLES, FLORENCE CALL (1861-
1950)
Amer., noted Iowa mother,
author, artist
Amer.--Mothers p189-190, por.

COWLES, VIRGINIA SPENCER (1912-
1983)
Amer. journalist, newspaper
correspondent, author
Cur. Biog. '83 p463

COWLEY, ANNE P. (fl. 1960's)
Amer. spectroscopist
O'Neill--Women's p154

COWLEY, HANNAH PARKHURST
(1743-1809)
English poet, playwright
Avenel--Comp. (1) p123
Entertainers p98
Macksey--Book p227

COX, DOROTHY ISABEL
See WYNYARD, DIANA

COX, E. EVELYN (1936-)
Amer. genealogical researcher,
author
Meyer--Who's p55

COX, GERTRUDE MARY (fl. 1950's-
1970's)
Amer. professor, statistician
O'Neill--Women's p145,176

COX, IDA (1889-1968)
Amer. singer, poet
Bernikow--World p278
Claghorn--Biog. p107
Claghorn--Jazz p80

COX, LYNNE (1952/1958-)

Amer. swimmer
Hollander--100 p92-93, por.
Macksey--Book p260
O'Neill--Women's p586

COX, MARIE (fl. 1970's)
Amer. Indian organization
founder
O'Neill--Women's p718

COX, NELL
Amer. editor, filmmaker,
producer, director, writer
Scheuer--Tel. p109
Smith--Movies p160-161,234,
por.

COX, TRICIA NIXON (c1946-)
Amer., daughter of Richard
Nixon
Woman's Almanac p494

COX-McCORMACK, NANCY (1885-)
Amer. sculptor
Sherr--American p219

COYET, KARIN (fl. 1950's)
Swedish editor
Marzolf--Up p291

COYLE, GRACE LONGWELL (1892-
1962)
Amer. social worker, educator
Sicherman--Notable p169-171

COZZINI, GEORGIA (fl. 1960's)
Amer. Vice Presidential
candidate
People's Almanac (1) p127

CRABBE, SARAH ELMY (c1780's)
English, wife of George
Crabbe
Morley--Literary p74-75,406

CRABTREE, (CHARLOTTE) LOTTA
(1847-1924)
Amer. actress
Dunlap--Calif. p46-47, por.
Entertainers p136
James--Notable (1) p395-396
Kulkin--Her p73-74
McHenry--Liberty's p83
Sherr--American p13-14,18-20,
por.
Time--Women p137,139
Webster's--Amer. p232-233

CRADDOCK, CHARLES EGBERT,
pseud.
See MURFREE, MARY NOAILLES

CRAFT, ELLEN (c1826-c1897)
Amer. fugitive slave, male
impersonator, abolitionist
Book--Lists (1) p340
Chittenden--Prof. p68-87, por.
James--Notable (1) p396-398
Kulkin--Her p74-75
Reifert--Women p37-39

CRAFT, MARCELLA (1880-1959)
Amer. singer
Claghorn--Biog. p107

CRAIG, DILSEY
Amer. slave
Sherr--American p178

CRAIG, EDITH (c1870-1947)
English actress, theatrical
producer
Neuls-Bates--Women p286

CRAIG, ELIZABETH MAY ADAMS
(1888/1889-1975)
Amer. journalist, Washington
correspondent
Cur. Biog. '75 p463
O'Neill--Women's p445-446,448
Sicherman--Notable p171-173

CRAIG, ISA (1831-1903)
Scottish poet, novelist
Showalter--Lit. p331

CRAIG, LOIS (fl. 1970's)
Amer. editor
O'Neill--Women's p595

CRAIG, MAY (c1889-1975)
Amer. TV reporter, feminist,
Washington correspondent
Marzolf--Up p59,69

CRAIG, MINNIE
Amer. state legislator
Sherr--Amer. p182

CRAIGIE, PEARL MARY TERESA
(1867-1906)
Amer. novelist, essayist
Colby--Singular p175-234
Showalter--Lit. p343-344

CRAIK, DINAH MARIA MULOCK
(1826-1887)
English novelist
Jones--Rutledge p198
Magill--Cycl. p776-777
Moers--Literary p285
Morley--Literary p263-264,343
Showalter--Lit. p329

CRAIK, GEORGIANA (1831-)
English novelist
Showalter--Lit. p331

CRAIN, JEANNE (1925-)
Amer. actress
Manchel--Women p72,74, por.
Shipman--Internatl. p111-113,
por.
World--Who p230

CRAMER, BETH (fl. 1970's)
Amer. fencing coach
Jordan--Broken p86-91

CRAMER, VROW (1655-)
Netherlands obstetrician,
diarist
Mead--Hist. p441,506-507

CRAMPE, MICHIKO ITO (1947-)
Japanese-Amer. lawyer
O'Neill--Women's p361-362

CRANDALL, ELLA PHILLIPS
(1871-1938)
Amer. public health nurse
James--Notable (1) p398-399
McHenry--Liberty's p83-84

CRANDALL, PRUDENCE (1803-
1890)
Amer. educator, abolitionist,
feminist, social reformer
Chittenden--Prof. p19-34, por.
Earnest--American p98,108
Ingraham--Album p38
James--Notable (1) p399-401
Kulkin--Her p75-76
Lutz--Liberty's p84
Macksey--Book p68
Reifert--Women p73-76
Sherr--American p30,206
Stein--Lives p505-529
Taylor--Gener. p43-44, por.
Warren--Pictorial p74
Webster's--Amer. p233
Woman's Almanac p375

CRANE, CAROLINE JULIA BARTLETT
(1858-1935)
Amer. urban reformer, clergy-
man, editor, teacher
James--Notable (1) p401-402
McHenry--Liberty's p84-85

CRANE, CHERYL (1944-)
Amer., daughter of Lana
Turner and Stephen Crane
Lamparski--What. (3) p142-143,
por.

CRANE, CORA (1868-1910)
Amer. Victorian adventuress
People's Almanac (2) p144-145

CRANE, MARTHA (fl. 1920's-1960's)
Amer. radio entertainer
Marzolf--Up p123

CRANE, NATHALIA CLARA RUTH
(1913-)
Amer. poet, child author
Book--Lists (2) p223
Crosland--Women p169-170

CRANE, RUTH (fl. 1920's-1940's)
Amer. radio director, conduc-
tor
Women--Radio p10

CRANZ, CHRISTEL (1914-)
German skier
Macksey--Book p261
McWhirter--Guinness p116-117,
por.
O'Neill--Women's p565

CRAPO, JOANNA
British carsman
Macksey--Book p245

CRAPP, LORRAINE (1938-)
Australian swimmer
Beal--20th p208

CRAPSEY, ADELAIDE (1878-1914)
Amer. poet
Bernikow--World p246
Ehrlich--Oxford p168
James--Notable (1) p402-403
McHenry--Liberty's p85

CRATHORNE, ISABEL
English, daughter of John
Swinburne, wife of Thomas

Crathorne
Ware--Meet p75

CRATTY, MABEL (1868-1928)
Amer. YWCA leader, social
worker
James--Notable (1) p403-405
McHenry--Liberty's p85

CRAVENS, KATHRYN (fl. 1930's-
1940's)
Amer. radio, TV news
commentator
Marzolf--Up p129-132
O'Neill--Women's p493

CRAVENS, PENELOPE (fl. 1970's)
Amer., governor's body-
guard, airline stewardess
O'Neill--Women's p374

CRAWFORD, CHERYL (1902-)
Amer. theatrical producer
O'Neill--Women's p664

CRAWFORD, ISABELLA (1850-1887)
Canadian poet
Macksey--Book p188

CRAWFORD, JANE TODD (-1842)
Amer., first ovariotomy
patient
Sherr--American p65,78, por.

CRAWFORD, JOAN (1908-1977)
Amer. actress
Banner--Women p201-202, por.
Cur. Biog. '77 p461
Engstead--Star p54-58
Fox-Sheinwold--Gone p126-135,
158, por.
Hershey--Between p31-32,111-115
Hirschhorn--Rating p96-98, por.
Keenan--Women p78-79,81,84-85,
por.
Keylin--Hollywood p74-76, por.
Manchel--Women p40,42,70,90-
91, por.
Mordden--Movie, see index
p292, por.
100--Greatest (1) p71, por.
Shipman--Gold. p131-136, por.
Sochen--Herstory p330-332,334-
335, por.
Springer--They p68-72,281, por.
Wilson--Holly. p154-156, por.
Woman's Almanac p336-337, por.
World--Who p230

CRAWFORD, LUCY (fl. 1840's)
Amer. pioneer innkeeper,
writer
Sherr--American p146

CRAWFORD, MARIANNE
Amer. basketball player
Hollander--100 p9

CRAWFORD, PATRICIA GAIL (fl.
1960's)
Amer. heroine, Carnegie
Medal winner
O'Neill--Women's p733

CRAWFORD-SEEGER, RUTH PORTER
(1901-1953)
Amer. composer, teacher,
pianist
Claghorn--Biog. p108
Jablonski--Ency. p286
LePage--Women p43-53, por.
Neuls-Bates--Women p303-311, por.
O'Neill--Women's p636-637
Sicherman--Notable p173-174
Thomson--Amer. p135

CRAYENCOURT, MARGUERITE DE
See YOURCENAR, MARGUERITE,
MADEMOISELLE DE CRAYEN-
COURT

"CRAZY SALLY OF EPSOM"
See MAPP, MRS.

CREECH, KATHRYN H. (1951-)
Amer. TV executive
Scheuer--Tel. p110

CREED, LINDA (1949-)
Amer. singer, song writer
Pollock--In p224-231, por.

CREHAN, ADA
See REHAN, ADA

CREIGHTON, MARY LUCRETIA
(-c1875)
Amer. philanthropist
Sherr--American p141

CREQUE, BOBBIE LITTLE (fl.
1970's)
Amer. community services
intern, child care specialist
O'Neill--Women's p326

CRESPE, MARIE-MADELEINE (1760-

1796)
French ballet dancer
Migel--Ballerinas p65-70

CRESPIN, REGINE (1927-)
French opera singer
Cur. Biog. '79 p85-88, por.
Gammond--Illus. p241, por.

CREWS, LAURA HOPE (1879-1942)
Amer. actress
James--Notable (1) p405-406
Springer--They p72,281, por.

CRICKARD, MADELINE W. (1916-)
Amer. genealogical researcher,
author
Meyer--Who's p55

CRILE, SUSAN (fl. 1970's)
Amer. painter
Women's--Female p38

CRIMMINS, MARY BETY (fl.
1960's-1970's)
Amer. executive
O'Neill--Women's p524

CRIST, JUDITH KLEIN (c1922-)
Amer. film, drama critic,
journalism professor
Diamonstein--Open p74-78, por.
Marzolf--Up p170
O'Neill--Women's p458
Scheuer--Tel. p112

CRISWELL, ANNA CURRIE
Amer., mother of Wallis
Amos Criswell, clergyman
Kooiman--Silhouettes p58-63,
por.

CRITTENDEN, ALICE (fl. 1920's)
Amer. county clerk
Sherr--American p137

CRITTENDEN, MRS. HOWARD
See FISHER, LOU

CROCKER, BETTY
See HUSTED, MARJORIE
CHILD

CROCKER, HANNAH MATHER
(1752-1829)
Amer. author, feminist
James--Notable (1) p406-407

Sherr--American p98
Warren--Pictorial p69

CROCKER, LUCRETIA (1829-1886)
Amer. educator, school admin-
istrator
James--Notable (1) p407-409
McHenry--Liberty's p85-86

CROLY, JANE CUNNINGHAM (1829-
1901)
Amer. journalist, magazine
editor, woman's club leader,
feminist
James--Notable (1) p409-411
McHenry--Liberty's p86
Macksey--Book p265-266,273
Marzolf--Up p21-22
Millstein--We p75,146
O'Neill--Women's p99
Scott--Southern p151-153,156-157

CROMARTIE, HAZEL M. (fl. 1960's-
1970's)
Amer. heroine
O'Neill--Women's p734

CROMWELL, ELIZABETH (c1554-1654)
English, mother of Oliver
Cromwell
Earle--Two Cent. (1) p xvi,113,
por.

CROMWELL, EVA
See STOTESBURY, LUCRETIA
(EVA) BISHOP ROBERTS

CRONE, MARIE LUISE (1949-)
West German genealogical re-
searcher, author
Meyer--Who's p55-56

CRONIN, MARGARET
Amer. labor leader
O'Neill--Women's p328

CRONKHITE, BERNICE BROWN
Amer. educator, college dean
Hazen--Interv. p226-227

CROOK, MRS. GEORGE (fl. 1860's-
1870's)
Amer., wife of General
Time--Women p74

CROSBIE, DIANA ("FAWN"),
VISCOUNTESS (1756-1814)

English socialite
Ware--Meet p75

CROSBY, CARESSE
See JACOB, MARY PHELPS

CROSBY, FRANCES ("FANNY")
JANE (1820-1915)
Amer., blind hymnist, poet
Claghorn--Biog. p109
James--Notable (1) p411-412
McHenry--Liberty's p86-87
Macksey--Book p214
Sherr--American p30

CROSMAN, HENRIETTA FOSTER
(c1861-1944)
Amer. actress
James--Notable (1) p412-414
Springer--They p72,281, por.

CROSNIER, MADAME
French ballet, opera director,
concierge
Migel--Ballerinas p228-229

CROSS, LAURA (c1962-)
Amer., child-winner of
soap box derby
O'Neill--Women's p589

CROSS, MARY
See FISHER, MARY

CROSS, MARY ANN EVANS
See ELIOT, GEORGE, pseud.

CROSS, PATRICIA (fl. 1960's)
Amer. university dean
O'Neill--Women's p405

CROSSLEY, WINIFRED ("WINNIE")
(fl. 1930's-1940's)
English ferry pilot, aviatrix
Boase--Sky's p179

CROSSON, MARVEL (-1929)
Amer. aviatrix
Boase--Sky's p117

CROTHERS, RACHEL (1878-1958)
Amer. playwright
Chinoy--Women p129-130,137-
145, por.
Ehrlich--Oxford p317
McHenry--Liberty's p87
Macksey--Book p232

O'Neill--Women's p663
Sicherman--Notable p174-176
Webster's--Amer. p239

CROUCHER, LORENA (fl. 1970's)
Amer. "Star" farmer (Kansas)
O'Neill--Women's p21

CROUGH, MARY (1740-1818)
Amer. Revolutionary War pa-
triot, printer
Meyer--Petticoat p225
Stein--Lives no p.

CROUSE, NANCY (fl. 1860's)
Amer. Civil War patriot
Sherr--American p96

CROVO, MARIA ELENA JIMENEZ DE
(1935-)
Colombian journalist, ambassador
O'Neill--Women's p62,345

CROWE, CATHERINE STEVENS
(1800-1876)
English novelist
Showalter--Lit. p321

CROWE, SYLVIA, DAME (c1901-)
British landscape architect
Macksey--Book p166

CROWELL, GRACE NOLL (1877-1969)
Amer., noted Iowa mother,
poet
Amer.--Mothers p190-191, por.

CROWLEY, PAULINE SHOEMAKER
(1879-1960)
Amer., noted North Dakota
mother, educator
Amer.--Mothers p418, por.

CRUGER, ANNE DE LANCEY (fl.
1770's)
Amer. Revolutionary Tory
Booth--Women p257-258

CRUGER, MRS. DOUGLAS
British millionaire
Forbes--400 ('84) p47

CRUGER, LYDIA BOGGS SHEPHERD
(-1867)
Amer. patriot, hostess
Sherr--American p246

CRUIKSHANK, HELEN B. (1896-)
Scottish poet
Avenel--Comp. (1) p128

CRUMP, DIANE (fl. 1960's-
1970's)
Amer. jockey
Hollander--100 p65-66, por.
McWhirter--Guinness p92

CRUMP, IRIS (fl. 1970's)
Amer. painter
Women's--Female p38

CRUMP, MARY RUTH (1921-)
Amer. genealogical research-
er, writer
Meyer--Who's p56

CRUPE, JESSIE WANDA
See WILLIAMS, CHICKIE

CRUZ, CELIA (c1929-)
Cuban-Amer. singer
Cur. Biog. '83 p71-74, por.

CRUZ, ISABEL DE LA (fl. 1512-
1529)
Spanish religious leader
Bainton--Spain p18-27

CRUZ, SOR JUANA INES DE LA
(1651-1695)
Mexican scholar, poet,
beauty, nun
Brink--Female p119-136, por.
Hahner--Women p21-28
Henderson--Ten p73-95, por.
Macksey--Book p182

CRYER, GRETCHEN KIGER (1935-)
Amer. songwriter
Jablonski--Ency. p510-511

CUERO, DELFINA
Amer. Kumeyaay Indian
Hoople--As p166-168

CUEVAS CANCINO, ESMERELDA
ARBOLEDA DE (fl. 1960's)
Columbian transport minister,
senator, ambassador
O'Neill--Women's p61-62

CULBERTSON, JOSEPHINE MURPHY
(1899-1956)
Amer. bridge expert, wife of

Eli Culbertson
People's Almanac (1) p1167

CULBRETH, BLANCHE WALDROP
(1919-)
Amer. genealogical researcher,
author
Meyer--Who's p56

CULLAR, W. CLYTES (1920-)
Amer. genealogical researcher,
author
Meyer--Who's p56

CULLBERG, BIRGIT (1908-)
Swedish dancer, choreographer
Cur. Biog. '82 p74-78, por.
O'Neill--Women's p650

CULLETON, KATHLEEN
Amer. TV director
Scheuer--Tel. p114

CULLINAN, ELIZABETH (fl. 1950's-
1970's)
Amer. novelist, short-story
writer
McCullough--People p44-46

CULVER, MARY E.
Amer. philanthropist
Sherr--American p129

CUMBERLAND, ANNE, DUCHESS
(1743-1808)
English socialite
Ware--Meet p40,75

CUMMING, KATE (1835-1909)
Scottish-Amer. Civl War nurse,
diarist, hospital administrator
Hymowitz--Hist. p141
James--Notable (1) p414-415
Millstein--We p120
Scott--Southern p84-85
Sherr--American p2,125
Warren--Pictorial p107

CUMMINGS, CONSTANCE (1910-)
Amer. actress
Springer--They p72-73,281,283,
por.
World--Who p230

CUMMINGS, IRIS (fl. 1950's)
Amer. swimmer, army flier
Keil--Those p25,61

CUMMINGS, QUINN (1967/1968-)
Amer. child actress
Edelson--Kids p117

CUMMINS, BETTY (FOLEY)
(1923-)
Amer. singer, guitarist
Claghorn--Biog. p110

CUMMINS, MARIA SUSANNA (1827-
1866)
Amer. novelist
Earnest--American p77-78
Ehrlich--Oxford p50,58
James--Notable (1) p415-416
McHenry--Liberty's p87

CUNARD, GRACE (c1894-1967)
Amer. actress, director,
writer
Slide--Early p57, por.
Smith--Movies p12-13

CUNARD, MAUD ALICE BURKE,
LADY (1872-1948)
Amer. art patron, social
leader
Brandon--Dollar p30,128-150,
por.
Keenan--Women p34,36-37,61,
por.
Rogers--Ladies, see index
p227-228, por.

CUNARD, NANCY (1896-1965)
English eccentric reformer,
fashion leader
Keenan--Women p60-62, por.
Rogers--Ladies, see index p228

CUNEGUNDE (-1038/1040)
German nun, empress
Mead--Hist. p112

CUNEO, ANN
See CURTIS, ANN

CUNHA, MARIE DE CARNO DA
See MIRANDA, CARMEN

CUNINGGIM, MAUD MERRIMON
(1874-)
Amer. hymnist, teacher
Claghorn--Biog. p110

CUNITZ, MARIA (1610-1664)
German astronomer, writer

Macksey--Book p143
Mead--Hist. p426

CUNLIFFE-OFFLEY, MRS. FOSTER
(1780-1850)
English singer
Ware--Meet p75-76

CUNNINGHAM, ANN PAMELA (1816-
1875)
Amer. foundress, pioneer
clubwoman, patriot
James--Notable (1) p416-417
McHenry--Liberty's p87-88
Sherr--American p210,236, por.

CUNNINGHAM, CECIL (1888-1959)
Amer. actress, singer
Springer--They p73,283, por.

CUNNINGHAM, ELIZA BERTRAND
(1788-)
Scottish-Amer. patriot, noted
Arkansas mother
Amer.--Mothers p39-40, por.

CUNNINGHAM, GLADYS STORY
(1895-)
Canadian physician
Hellstedt--Women p123-137, por.

CUNNINGHAM, IMOGEN (1883-1976)
Amer. photographer
Bachtold--Gifted p35-36
Diamonstein--Open p79-84, por.
Longstreet--Queen p185-186
Munsterberg--Hist. p126,130-131
O'Neill--Women's p612
Richey--Eminent p17-43, por.
Woman's Almanac p223
Women's--Female p63
World--Who p58

CUNNINGHAM, KATE RICHARDS
O'HARE (1877-1948)
Amer. socialist, lecturer,
prison reformer
Hymowitz--Hist. p246
James--Notable (1) p417-420
McHenry--Liberty's p88-89
Sochen--Herstory p265-269
Sochen--Movers, see index p317

CUNNINGHAM, MARY ELIZABETH
(1951-)
Amer. business executive
Cur. Biog. '84 p101-105, por.

CUNNINGHAM, MINNIE FISHER
(1882-1964)
Amer. suffragist, politician,
community leader
Sicherman--Notable p176-177

CUNNISON, MARGARET (fl.
1930's-1940's)
Scottish aviatrix, instructor
Boase--Sky's p179

CUPPS, ANITA (1948-)
Amer. feminist, business
woman
Seifer--Nobody p342-384, por.

CURIE, EVE (1904-)
French author, lecturer
Jones--Rutledge p206
Macksey--Book p153

CURIE, IRENE
See JOLIOT-CURIE, IRENE

CURIE, MARIE SKLODOWSKA
(1867-1934)
Polish-French chemist,
physicist
Asimov--Biog. p536-538, por.
Bachtold--Gifted p46-50
Book--Lists (2) p8,239
Brecher--Lives p287, por.
Crovitz--Courage p153-174
Diagram--Mothers p58-59, por.
Donaldson--How p84
Fry--1000 p279, por.
Jones--Rutledge p205
Kostman--20th p78-98, por.
Kulkin--Her p76-78
Macksey--Book p152-153,157,
por.
Marks--Women p197-215, por.
Marlowe--Great p194-203, por.
O'Neill--Women's p144, por.
Opfell--Lady p147-164, por.
Palmer--Who's p92
Partington--Who's p78-79, por.
People's Almanac (2) p875-876,
1198
Prause--School p101-103
Who Did What p83
Woman's Almanac p361-362, por.
World--Who p121

CURIEL, LIDIA (c1924-)
Mexican-Amer. migrant
Lindborg--Five p41-55

CURLEE-SALISBURY, JOAN (1930-)
Amer. psychologist
Brin--Social p152

CURLEY, KATE
Amer. pioneer settler
Sherr--American p57

CURRAN, MARY KATHARINE
See BRANDEGEE, MARY KATHA-
RINE LAYNE CURRAN

CURRAN, PEARL (1883-1937)
Amer. writer
People'a Almanac (2) p1257-1258

CURRE, ZONJA (1920-1943/1944)
Albanian partisan leader
Partington--Who's p79

CURREY, LOUISE SEVIER (1903-)
Amer. humanitarian, noted
Tennessee mother
Amer.--Mothers p508-509

CURIE, MARY (1843-1905)
English novelist
Showalter--Lit. p336

CURRY, DIANE SUTHERLAND
(1939-)
Amer. labor leader, editor
O'Neill--Women's p303,309

CURTAIN, DEBORAH A.
Amer. casting, TV manager
Scheuer--Tel. p115

CURTIN, VALERIE
Amer. TV actress, writer
Scheuer--Tel. p116

CURTIS, ANN (1926/1927-)
Amer. swimmer
Hollander--100 p83-84, por.

CURTIS, CHARLOTTE MURRAY
(1930-1987)
Amer. newspaper editor,
journalist
Adams--Women p110,150,199
Diamonstein--Open p85-91, por.
Marzolf--Up p110,115
O'Neill--Women's p90,437,466-467
Woman's Almanac p268
World--Who p51

CURTIS, HARRIOT S. (fl. 1900's)
Amer. golfer
McWhirter--Guinness p75

CURTIS, JAMIE LEE (1959-)
Amer. actress
Hirschhorn--Rating p102, por.

CURTIS, LUCILE ATCHERSON
(1894-)
Amer. foreign service officer
O'Neill--Women's p90,467

CURTIS, MARGARET (fl. 1900's)
Amer. golfer
McWhirter--Guinness p75

CURTIS, MARY BARNETT (1924-)
Amer. genealogical researcher,
author
Meyer--Who's p57

CURTIS, MARY LOUISE
See ZIMBALIST, MARY LOUISE
CURTIS BOK

CURTIS, NATALIE (1875-1921)
Amer. composer, pianist,
musicologist
Claghorn--Biog. p74
James--Notable (1) p420-421
McHenry--Liberty's p58

CURWEN, ABIGAIL RUSSELL (fl.
1770's)
Amer., wife of Tory
Booth--Women p64-65

CURZON OF KEDLESTON, MARY
VICTORIA LEITER, BARON-
ESS (1868/1870-1906)
Amer. heiress, Vicereine of
India
Brandon--Dollar, see index
p210
James--Notable (1) p421-422
Longstreet--Queen p40-42, por.
McHenry--Liberty's p89
O'Neill--Women's p745-746
Peacock--Famous p264-287, por.

CUSHING, CATHERINE CHISHOLM
(1874-1952)
Amer. composer, lyricist,
playwright, librettist
Claghorn--Biog. p111

CUSHMAN, CHARLOTTE SAUNDERS
(1816-1876)
Amer. actress
Chinoy--Women p74-81, por.
Entertainers p120
Fabian--On p65-68, por.
James--Notable (1) p422-424
McHenry--Liberty's p89
People's Almanac (2) p1052-1053
Taylor--Gener. p55-56, por.
Webster's--Amer. p245

CUSHMAN, MARY NORRIS ALLERTON
See ALLERTON, MARY NORRIS

CUSHMAN, PAULINE (1833/1835-
1893/1895)
Amer. actress, Civil War spy
Ingraham--Album p29, por.
Sherr--American p7,20,219, por.

CUSHMAN, VERA CHARLOTTE
SCOTT (1876-1946)
Amer. YWCA leader, social
worker
James--Notable (1) p424-426
McHenry--Liberty's p89-90

CUST, AILEEN (fl. 1960's)
British veterinarian
Macksey--Book p155

CUSTER, ELIZABETH BACON
(1842-1933)
Amer. diarist, lecturer,
Western pioneer, wife of
General Custer
Hoople--As p75-77
Kulkin--Her p78-79
Reifert--Women p129-132
Sherr--American p74,77,182-183

CUSTIS, MARY RANDOLPH
Amer. Southern belle, wife
of Robert E. Lee
DeLeon--Belles p423, por.

CUSTIS, ELEANOR (NELLIE) PARKE
(1779-1853)
Amer., granddaughter of Mrs.
George Washington
Earle--Two Cent. (2) p xxii, por.

CUTHBERT, BETTY (1938-)
Australian track and field
athlete

Assoc. Press--Pursuit p218-219,
270, por.
McWhirter--Guinness p173
O'Neill--Women's p573,575

CUTHBERT, MARGARET ROSS
(1887-1968)
Canadian-Amer. radio
executive
O'Neill--Women's p492
Women--Radio p13-14

CUTHBERT-BROWNE, GRACE
JOHNSTON (1900-)
Australian physician
Hellstedt--Women p187-191, por.

CUTLER, HANNAH MARIA CONANT
TRACY (1815-1896)
Amer. women's rights leader,
physician, lecturer
James--Notable (1) p426-427

CUTLER, MARY SALOME
See FAIRCHILD, (MARY)
SALOME CUTLER

CUTLER, SHERRIE STEPHENS
Amer. architect
O'Neill--Women's p611-612

CUTLER, VIRGINIA (1905-)
Amer. Morman professor,
noted Utah mother
Amer.--Mothers p532, por.

"CUTPURSE, MOLL"
See FRITH, MOLLY

CUTTER, CARRIE (-1862)
Amer. Civil War nurse
Sherr--American p148,180

CUTTS, ADELE (-1899)
Amer. belle
Peacock--Famous p175-189, por.

CVIRKIENE, MARIJA (1912-)
Lithuanian painter
Women's--Female p3 supp.

D

DABERTIN, RITA (c1936-)
Amer. "Unsung Heroine of
Year" 1977
O'Neill--Women's p103

DABROWSKA, MARIA (1889-1965)
Polish writer
Partington--Who's p81, por.

DACHE, LILLY (1904-)
French-Amer. milliner, fashion
designer
O'Neill--Women's p238,247

DACIER, ANNE LEBRE, MADAME
(1651/1654-1720)
French translator, classical
scholar
Crosland--Women p56-57

DA COSTA, NOEL (1930-)
Amer. composer
Claghorn--Biog. p113

D'AGOULT, MARIE
See AGOULT, MARIE CATHERINE
SOPHIE DE FLAVIGNY

DAHL, ANNA BOE (1892-)
Amer., noted Montana mother,
rural energy program officer
Amer.--Mothers p326-327, por.

DAHL, ARLENE (1927/1928-)
Amer. actress, beauty columnist,
model
World--Who p230

DAHLGREN, ELIZABETH DREXEL
(fl. 1900's-1920's)
Amer. musician
Forma--They p83-84,209, por.

DAHL-WOLFE, LOUISE (1895-)
Amer. fashion photographer
Michell--Recol. p66-83,200-201,
por.
O'Neill--Women's p263

DAIGLER, JEREMY, SISTER
Amer. "Sister of Mercy,"
University instructor, admin-
istrator
O'Neill--Women's p392

DAILEY, IRENE (1920-)
Amer. actress
Scheuer--Tel. p117, por.
Seed--Saturday's p45-47, por.

DAILEY, THELMA (fl. 1950's-1970's)
Amer labor leader

O'Neill--Women's p324-
325

D'AILLENCOURT, SIMONE (fl.
1970's)
French model, head, model
agency
Keenan--Women p128-129,140,
144, por.

DALAGER, BETSY (1852-)
Amer. handicapped pioneer,
noted South Dakota mother
Amer.--Mothers p495-496, por.

DALAI, MARIA JOLANDA TOSONI
(1901-)
Italian physician
Hellstedt--Women p230-236, por.

D'ALBRET, JEANNE
See ALBRET, JEANNE D'

DALE, CLAMMA (1948-)
Amer. singer
Cur. Biog. '79 p95-97, por.

DALE, ELIZABETH (fl. 1830's-
1850's)
Amer. accused criminal
Sherr--American p2

DALE, ESTHER (1885-)
Amer. actress
Springer--They p77,283, por.

DALE, SANDRA
See DENNIS, SANDY

DALESSANDRO, FRANCES (fl.
1960's-1970's)
Amer. fashion editor
O'Neill--Women's p236-237

DALEY, CASS (1915-)
Amer. comedienne, actress
Lamparski--What. (4) p22-23,
por.

DALL, CAROLINE WELLS HEALEY
(1822-1912)
Amer. author, reformer
James--Notable (1) p428-429
McHenry--Liberty's p91

DAL MONTE, TOTI (1893-1975)
Italian opera singer

Tuggle--Golden p182-183,
por.

DALTON, JANE MARTIN (-1879)
Amer. novelist
Sherr--American p124

DALTON, SHIRLEY (fl. 1970's)
Amer. social reformer, moun-
tain woman
Kahn--Hill. p66-74, por.

D'ALVAREZ, MARGUERITE (1886-
1953)
English opera singer
Tuggle--Golden p57-58, por.

DALY, ELIZABETH (1879-1967)
Amer. novelist
Seymour-Smith--Novels p122

DALY, LILLIAN O'MALLEY (fl.
1940's)
Amer. Marine
O'Neill--Women's p537

DALY, MARY (fl. 1970's)
Amer. radical feminist, theo-
logian
O'Neill--Women's p398

DALY, TYNE (fl. 1980's)
Amer. actress
Scheuer--Tel. p118, por.

"DAME SHIRLEY," pseud.
See CLAPPE (CLAPP), LOUISE
AMELIA KNAPP SMITH

DAMER, ANNE SEYMOUR CONWAY
(1748/1749-1828)
English sculptor, actress,
social leader
Fine--Women p76-77
Macksey--Book p202
Munsterberg--Hist. p86,88
Petersen--Women p46-47

DAMER-DAWSON, MARGARET
British policewoman
Macksey--Book p137-138

DAMERON, EMMA (fl. 1970's)
Labor Union official
O'Neill--Women's p315

DAMIEN, ALBERTINE

See SARRAZIN, ALBERTINE
DAMIEN

DAMITA, LILI (1901/1906-)
French actress, wife of
Errol Flynn
Springer--They p77,283, por.

DAMM, SHEILA VAN
British theater manager
Macksey--Book p236

DAMON, MARY HAPPER (1858-)
Amer. missionary, noted
Hawaii mother
Amer.--Mothers p143-144, por.

DAMROW, HILDEGARD (fl. 1970's)
German legal news reporter
Marzolf--Up p281

DANA, MRS. CHARLES
See GIBSON, IRENE LANGHORNE

DANA, MARY STANLEY BUNCE
PALMER (1810-1883)
Amer. hymnist, professor,
publisher
Claghorn--Biog. p114

DANA, VIOLA (1897-)
Amer. actress
Lamparski--What. (5) p164-165,
por.

DANAHER, KAREN (1947-)
Amer. TV program director
Scheuer--Tel. p139

DANDRIDGE, DOROTHY (1923/
1924-1966)
Amer. actress
Book--Lists (2) p297
Keylin--Hollywood p77, por.
World--Who p230

DANDRIDGE, MARTHA
See WASHINGTON, MARTHA
DANDRIDGE CUSTIS

DANE, BARBARA (1927-)
Amer. singer, guitarist
Claghorn--Biog. p115

DANE, CLEMENCE, pseud. (1887-
1965)
English novelist, dramatist
Showalter--Lit. p346

DANESHVAR, JULIA PROKOFYEVNA
(1912-)
Russian painter, art instructor
Women's--Female p3 supp.

DANESI, MARISA (fl. 1960's)
West German roller-skater
McWhirter--Guinness p111-112

DANETTE, LEILA (1909-)
Amer. actress
Gold--Until p111-128, por.

DANGEVILLE, MARIE-ANN (1714-1796)
French actress
Entertainers p92
Macksey--Book p226

D'ANGOULÊME, MARGARET
See MARGUERITE D'ANGOULÊME
OF NAVARRE

DANIEL, ALICE
Amer. lawyer
O'Neill--Women's p357

DANIEL, ANN
Amer. TV executive
Scheuer--Tel. p139

DANIEL, ANNIE STURGES (1858-
1944)
Amer. physician, public health
reformer, obstetrician,
pediatrician
James--Notable (1) p429-431
O'Neill--Women's p204

DANIEL, EMILY (fl. 1880's)
British printer
Callen--Women p222

DANIEL, MARGARET TRUMAN
See TRUMAN, (MARY) MARGARET

DANIELS, BEBE (PHYLLIS) (VIR-
GINIA) (1901-1971)
Amer. actress, comedienne
Lamparski--What. (8) p74-75, por.
Shipman--Gold. p142-144, por.
Springer--They p77,79,283, por.

DANIELS, MABEL WHEELER (1878-
1971)
Amer. composer
Claghorn--Biog. p113
Jablonski--Ency. p125
Macksey--Book p216

Neuls-Bates--Women p219-222
Sicherman--Notable p177-179

DANIELS, PAMELA (1937-   )
    Amer. teacher, researcher
    Ruddick--Working p55-70,341,
    por.

DANIELS, PHILOMEN (c1838-   )
    Amer. steamboat captain
    Sherr--American p230

DANILOVA, ALEXANDRA ALICIA
    (1906-   )
    Russian-Amer. ballet dancer,
    choreographer
    Lamparski--What. (4) p116-117,
    por.
    Macksey--Book p232

DANILOVA, MARIA (1793-   )
    Russian ballet dancer
    Migel--Ballerinas p250-251

DANISI, MARISA (fl. 1960's)
    West German roller-skater
    O'Neill--Women's p565

D'ANJOU, MARGUERITE
    See ANJOU, MARGUERITE D'

DAN'KO-(ALEKSEENKO), NATALIA
    IAKOVLEVNA (1892-1942)
    Russian ceramicist
    Women's--Female p2, supp.

DANKWORTH, MRS. JOHN
    See LAINE, CLEO (CLEMETINE
    DINAH)

DANNER, BLYTHE KATHERINE
    (c1944-   )
    Amer. actress
    Cur. Biog. '81 p105-108, por.
    World--Who p230

DANSEREAU, MIREILLE (fl.
    1960's-1970's)
    Canadian filmmaker
    Smith--Movies p97

DANTAS, REGINA
    Amer. TV corporation di-
    rector
    Scheuer--Tel. p121

DANTZLER, LOUISE
    See BRIAN, MARY

D'AQUINO, IVA TOGURI
    See AQUINO, IVA IKUKO TOGURI
    ("TOKYO ROSE")

D'ARAGONA, TULLIA (c1510-1556)
    Roman courtesan, author,
    singer
    Macksey--Book p94-95

D'ARBLAY, FRANCES BURNEY
    See BURNEY, FANNY

DARBY, MARY
    Amer. Confederate government
    official
    Wiley--Confed. p146

DARCLEE, HARICLEA (1860-1939)
    Rumanian singer
    Partington--Who's p84

DARCY, CLARE
    English novelist
    Seymour-Smith--Novels p122

D'ARCY, ELLA (1851-1939)
    British short story writer,
    novelist
    Showalter--Lit. p338

DARDEN, CONSTANCE SIMONS
    DuPONT (c1904-   )
    Amer. millionaire
    Forbes--400 ('84) p149

DARDEN, MARGARET SINGLETON
    (1942-   )
    Amer. childhood educator
    Innis--Profiles p68-69, por.

DARE, ELEANOR WHITE (fl. 1600's)
    Amer. Pilgrim
    Williams--Demeter's p18-19

DARE, ETHEL (fl. 1920's)
    Amer. aviatrix, stunt pilot
    Boase--Sky's p22

DARE, VIRGINIA (1587-   )
    Amer. Pilgrim, first English
    child born in America
    James--Notable (1) p431-432
    Kulkin--Her p79-80
    McHenry--Liberty's p91
    Sherr--American p180
    Warren--Pictorial p4-5
    Webster's--Amer. p252

Woman's Almanac p51-52
World--Who p296

DARGAN, OLIVE TILFORD (1869-
1968)
Amer. poet, playwright
Ehrlich--Oxford p293,353

DARLING, FLORA ADAMS (1840-
1910)
Amer. author, organization
official, founder
James--Notable (1) p432-433
McHenry--Liberty's p91-92
Macksey--Book p273

DARLING, GRACE HORSLEY (1815-
1842)
English sea heroine
Jones--Rutledge p212
Macksey--Book p244-245

DARLING, JEAN (fl. 1929-1935)
Amer. child actress
Lamparski--What. (8) p76-77,
por.

DARLING, LUCIA
Amer. Western teacher
Sherr--American p134
Time--Women p89-90, por.

DARLINGTON, JANE EAGLESFIELD
(1928-)
Amer. genealogical researcher,
author, indexer
Meyer--Who's p61

DARLINGTON, JENNIE (fl. 1940's)
Norwegian-Amer. journalist
Land--New p9,17-18,214,221

D'ARMONT, MARIE ANNE CHAR-
LOTTE CORDAY
See CORDAY, CHARLOTTE

DARNELL, LINDA (1921-1965)
Amer. actress
Hirschhorn--Rating p104-105,
por.
Keylin--Hollywood p78, por.
Shipman--Internatl. p123-125,
por.
Springer--They p79,283, por.
World--Who p231

DARRAGH (DARRAH), LYDIA
BARRINGTON (1728-1789)
Amer. Revolutionary War spy,

patriot
Booth--Women p153-155
Clyne--Patriots p35-40
DePauw--Found. p129-130
Engle--Women p11-16, por.
Hymowitz--Hist. p34
Ingraham--Album p17
James--Notable (1) p434-435
McHenry--Liberty's p92
Mead--Hist. p488-489
Meyer--Petticoat p87-90, por.
Millstein--We p35
People's Almanac (1) p647
Sherr--American p202
Somerville--Women p56-60
Warren--Pictorial p56
Williams--Demeter's p244-245
Woman's Almanac p452

DARRIEUX, DANIELLE (1917-)
French actress, musician
Shipman--Internatl. p125-130, por.
Springer--They p79,283, por.

D'ARUSMONT, FRANCES WRIGHT
See WRIGHT, FRANCES ("FANNY")

DARWELL, JANE (1879/1880-1967)
Amer. actress
Hazen--Interv. p410
O'Neill--Women's p653
Springer--They p79,283-284, por.
World--Who p231

DARWIN, EMMA WEDGWOOD
English, wife of Darwin
Morley--Literary p115-116

DARWIN, SUSANNAH WEDGWOOD
(-1817)
English, mother of Charles
Darwin
Diagram--Mothers p62-63, por.

DARYUSH, ELIZABETH BRIDGES
(1887-1977)
English poet
Bernikow--World p166

DASHKOVA (DASHKOFF), EKATER-
INA ROMANOVA (1743/1744-
1810)
Russian Princess, author,
founder, (President), Academy
Macksey--Book p28
Mandel--Soviet p15-17

DA SILVA, MARIA HELENA

See VIERIRA DA SILVA,
MARIA HELENA

DASSEL, HERMINIA(E) BORCHARD
(-1857/1858)
German-Amer. painter
Fine--Women p103

DATER, JUDY (1941-)
Amer. photographer
Munsterberg--Hist. p143

DATINI, MARGHERITA (c1360-1423)
Italian letter-writer
Gies--Women p184-209, por.

DAT-SO-LA-LEE (c1835-1925)
Amer. Indian basket-maker
Sherr--American p144-145

D'AUBIGNE, FRANÇOISE
See MAINTENON, FRANÇOISE
D'AUBIGNE

DAUM, PAGGY (fl. 1960's-1970's)
Amer. newspaper food editor
O'Neill--Women's p468

DAUSER, SUE SOPHIA (1888-)
Amer. nurse, naval officer
McHenry--Liberty's p92

DAUSET, CARMEN
See CARMENCITA

DAVENPORT, ELIZABETH WOOLEY
(fl. 1650's)
Amer. colonial property
manager, business woman
Williams--Demeter's p86

DAVENPORT, FANNY LILY GYPSY
(1850-1898)
English-Amer. actress
James--Notable (1) p435-436
McHenry--Liberty's p92-93

DAVENPORT, JOAN M. (fl. 1970's)
Amer. government official
O'Neill--Women's p84

DAVENPORT, MARCIA (1903-)
Amer. novelist
Ehrlich--Oxford p64,143,196

DAVENPORT-ENGBERG, MARY
(fl. 1920's)

Amer. symphony conductor
Sherr--American p242

DAVEY, JEAN (fl. 1940's-1960's)
Canadian air force physician,
professor
O'Neill--Women's p551

DAVEY, MARIE AUGUSTA
See FISKE, MINNIE MADDERN

DAVEY, MARY ROGERS (1877-)
Amer. restaurant manager,
noted Montana mother
Amer.--Mothers p326

DAVID, MADELINE BLOOM (1938-)
Amer. TV network unit man-
ager
O'Neill--Women's p502

DAVID-NEAL, ALEXANDRA (1868-
1969)
French opera singer, author,
explorer
Lichtenstein--Mach. p130
Macksey--Book p242-243, por.
O'Neill--Women's p740-741
People's Almanac (2) p365-367,
por.

DAVIDOVA-MEDENE, LEA (1921-)
Latvian (Soviet) sculptor,
portraitist
Mandel--Soviet p143
Women's--Female p4 (supp.)

DAVIDS, MARIA
German artist
Sparrow--Women p287,300

DAVISON, EMILY (-1913)
British feminist
Macksey--Book p85, por.

DAVIDSON, FLORA (1924-)
English genealogical researcher,
author
Meyer--Who's p60

DAVIDSON, LADY
British Parliament member
Vallance--Women p28,51-52,54,61,
81,101

DAVIDSON, LUCRETIA MARIA
(1808-1825)

Amer. child poet
James--Notable (1) p436-438

DAVIDSON, MARGARET MILLER
(1823-1838)
Amer. child poet
James--Notable (1) p436-438

DAVIDSON, NORA FONTAINE
MAURY (fl. 1860's)
Amer. teacher
Sherr--American p237

DAVIDSON, SARA (c1943-)
Amer. writer
Diamonstein--Open p92-96, por.

DAVIDSON, SOPHIA (c1868-)
Amer. centenarian
Mitchell--Yessir p24-25, por.

DAVIE, ELSPETH
Scottish novelist
Crosland--Beyond p131

DAVIES, CLARA ULALIA MORGAN
(1835-)
Amer. church and school
worker, noted Arkansas
mother
Amer.--Mothers p40-41, por.

DAVIES, EMILY (1830-1921)
English educator, feminist,
social reformer, foundress
Macksey--Book p70-72
Marks--Women p96-98
Showalter--Lit. p331

DAVIES, MARIA THOMPSON (fl.
1920's)
Amer. photographer, sculptor, miniature painter, jeweler, suffragist
Sherr--American p218

DAVIES, MARION (1897/1900-1961)
Amer. actress
Dunlap--Calif. p49, por.
Keylin--Hollywood p79-80, por.
Manchel--Women p33,35, por.
Mordden--Movie p70,133-135,139,
por.
People's Almanac (1) p901
Shipman--Gold. p145-148, por.
Springer--They p79,284, por.
World--Who p231

DAVIES (DAVIS), MARY (c1635-
1752)
Amer. aged woman
DePauw--Rem. p40, por.

DAVIES, TREHAWKE (fl. 1900's)
English aviatrix, promoter
Boase--Sky's p15

DAVIN-MIRVAULT, MME. (1773-
1844)
French painter
Petersen--Women p63

DAVIOT, GORDON
See TEY, JOSEPHINE, pseud.

DAVIS, ADELLE (1904-1974)
Amer. nutritionist, author
Cur. Biog. '73 p93-95, por.
Cur. Biog. '74 p458
Donaldson--How p93
O'Neill--Women's p747
Sicherman--Notable p179-180
World--Who p296

DAVIS, ALICE BROWN (-1935)
Amer. Seminole Indian Chief,
leader
James--Notable (1) p438-439
Sherr--American p189-190,193

DAVIS, ALTOVISE (c1947-)
Amer. wife of Sammy Davis,
Jr.
Funt--Are p115-139, por.

DAVIS, ANGELA YVONNE (1944-)
Amer. activist, radical
Anderson--People p120-121
Cur. Biog. '72 p97-101, por.
Dunlap--Calif. p49-50
Kulkin--Her p80
O'Neill--Women's p250,470,715
People--Best p21, por.
People's Almanac (1) p613
Schoenebaum--Prof. p162-163
Woman's Almanac p510, por.
World--Who p187

DAVIS, ANNE FRANCES
See REAGAN, NANCY

DAVIS, BETTE (RUTH ELIZABETH)
(1908-)
Amer. actress
Anderson--People p121-122, por.

Banner--Women p201-202
Hazen--Interv. p403
Hirschhorn--Rating p105-107,
   por.
Jones--Rutledge p216
Lichtenstein--Mach. p259-261
McHenry--Liberty's p93
Manchel--Women, see index
   p121, por.
Marlowe--Great p338-345, por.
Mordden--Movie, see index
   p292, por.
O'Neill--Women's p652,657
Sat. Eve. Post--Movie p121,
   por.
Shipman--Gold. p149-156, por.
Sochen--Herstory p330-332,334,
   336,400, por.
Springer--They p79-84,284, por.
Webster's--Amer. p256
Woman's Almanac p329,337, por.
World--Who p231

DAVIS, BETTY JACK (1932-1953)
   Amer. singer
   Claghorn--Biog. p117

DAVIS, DOROTHY SALISBURY
   (1916-   )
   Amer. novelist
   Seymour-Smith--Novels p123

DAVIS, ELAINE
   Amer. farmer
   O'Neill--Women's p12

DAVIS, EVA WHITAKER (1892-1974)
   Amer., noted Mississippi
   mother, patriot
   Amer.--Mothers p303-304, por.

DAVIS, FRANCES (1) (fl. 1970's)
   Amer. lawyer, corporation
   executive
   O'Neill--Women's p524

DAVIS, FRANCES (2)
   See ALDA, FRANCES

DAVIS, FRANCES REED ELLIOT
   (1882-1964)
   Amer. Red Cross nurse
   Kulkin--Her p81-82
   Sicherman--Notable p180-182

DAVIS, GAIL (1925-   )
   Amer. actress, TV performer

Lamparski--What. (5) p194-195,
   por.

DAVIS, HALLIE FLANAGAN
   See FLANAGAN, HALLIE MAE
   FERGUSON

DAVIS, HANNAH (-1863)
   Amer. manufacturer (hatboxes)
   Sherr--American p147

DAVIS, HENRIETTA VINTON (fl.
   1860's-1900's)
   Amer. actress
   Chinoy--Women p92-97

DAVIS, JANE TOTAH (fl. 1940's-
   1950's)
   Amer. religious educator,
   missionary
   O'Neill--Women's p378-379

DAVIS, MRS. JEFFERSON
   See DAVIS, VARINA ANNE
   BANKS HOWELL

DAVIS, JESSIE BARTLETT (1860-
   1905)
   Amer. singer
   Claghorn--Biog. p118

DAVIS, JOAN (1907/1912-1961)
   Amer. actress, comedienne
   Springer--They p84,284, por.

DAVIS, JOSEPHINE (1902-   )
   Amer. political activist
   Gold--Until p77-94, por.

DAVIS, KATHARINE BEMENT (1860-
   1935)
   Amer. sociologist, penologist,
   social worker, philanthropist
   James--Notable (1) p439-441
   McHenry--Liberty's p93-94

DAVIS, LOU (1881-1961)
   Amer. lyricist
   Claghorn--Biog. p118

DAVIS, LOUISA J. (fl. 1890's)
   British stoneware designer,
   decorator
   Callen--Women p63,222

DAVIS, MADELYN
   Amer. producer, writer

Scheuer--Tel. p122-
123

DAVIS, MARGARET HOWELL
("LITTLE MAGGIE") (fl.
1870's)
Amer. Southern belle
DeLeon--Belles p73, por.

DAVIS, MARY FENN (1824-1886)
Amer. spiritualist, lecturer,
reformer
James--Notable (1) p441-442

DAVIS, MAXINE (1) ("MICKEY")
(fl. 1970's)
Amer. softball player
Jordan--Broken p134-137,141

DAVIS, MAXINE (2)
Amer. sociologist
Banner--Women p196-197

DAVIS, MOLLIE EVELYN MOORE
(1844-1909)
Amer. author, hostess
James--Notable (1) p442-444
McHenry--Liberty's p94

DAVIS, NANCY L. (fl. 1960's-
1970's)
Amer. lawyer, civil rights
worker, feminist
O'Neill--Women's p358

DAVIS, NELLIE VERRILL (1844-)
Amer., noted Nevada
mother, newspaper manager
Amer.--Mothers p345, por.

DAVIS, NINA SALAMAN
See SALAMAN, NINA DAVIS

DAVIS, PAULINA WRIGHT (1813-
1876)
Amer. feminist, social re-
former, suffragist, lecturer,
journalist
Gurko--Ladies p89,138-139,150,
160,171,245
Hymowitz--Hist. p99,103,105,
108,118
James--Notable (1) p444-445
McHenry--Liberty's p94
Marzolf--Up p224,227-228
Sherr--American p208
Warren--Pictorial p99

DAVIS, PAULINE MORTON
See SABIN, PAULINE MORTON

DAVIS, PHYLLIS (fl. 1970's)
Amer. advertising executive
O'Neill--Women's p519

DAVIS, REBECCA BLAINE HARDING
(1831-1910)
Amer. author
Ehrlich--Oxford p116,203,214
James--Notable (1) p445-447
McHenry--Liberty's p95
Moers--Literary p285
Seymour-Smith--Novels p123
Sherr--American p246

DAVIS, ROSALIE EDITH (1931-)
Amer. genealogical researcher,
author
Meyer--Who's p59-60

DAVIS, RUTH M.
Amer. computer scientist,
mathematician
O'Neill--Women's p89,179-180,190

DAVIS, SARAH
Amer., "perfect" wife
Sherr--American p74

DAVIS, SUSAN (fl. 1970's)
Amer. feminist, editor
Marzolf--Up p238,245

DAVIS, VARINA ANNE BANKS
HOWELL (1826-1906)
Amer., noted Mississippi
mother, Civil War diarist,
wife of Jefferson Davis
Amer.--Mothers p297, por.
DeLeon--Belles p66-68, por.
Hymowitz--Hist. p140
James--Notable (1) p447-449
Sherr--American p124,127
Wiley--Confed. p82-139, por.

DAVIS, VERA GIBRIDGE (1894-)
Amer., noted Delaware mother,
singer, politician
Amer.--Mothers p89-90, por.

DAVIS, VICKI (fl. 1970's)
Amer. fashion designer
O'Neill--Women's p248,261

DAVIS, VICKIE (1970's)

Amer. with highest tempera-
ture
Macksey--Book p13

DAVIS, "WINNIE" (VARINA ANNE)
(1864-   )
Amer. Southern belle, daugh-
ter of Jefferson Davis
DeLeon--Belles p72-73, por.
Sherr--American p206

DAVISON, ANN(E) (fl. 1950's)
British sailor, (yacht record)
Macksey--Book p245-246
McWhirter--Guinness p188

DAVYDOVA-MEDENE, LEAH
See DAVIDOVA-MEDENE, LEA

DAWIDOWICZ, LUCY S. (fl. 1970's)
Amer. historian
O'Neill--Women's p420

"DAWN" (fl. 1930's)
English model
Keenan--Women p115,117, por.

DAWN, HAZEL (1891/1894-   )
Amer. actress
Lamparski--What. (2) p100-101,
por.

DAWSON, BARBARA JOAN (fl.
1960's)
Amer., National Volunteer
Award winner, (eyeglass
reformer)
O'Neill--Women's p117-118

DAWSON, EDITH ROBINSON (fl.
1890's-1900's)
British painter, metalworker,
enameller
Callen--Women p154-156,222,
por.

DAWSON, ELIZABETH (fl. 1770's)
Amer. tavern keeper
Williams--Demeter's p199

DAWSON, MIMI WEYFORTH
(1944-   )
Amer. Commissioner, FCC
Scheuer--Tel. p124

DAY, CLARA BELLE TAYLOR (fl.
1950's-1970's)

Amer. labor union leader
O'Neill--Women's p302,314

DAY, DORIS (1924-   )
Amer. actress, singer
Anderson--People p124-125, por.
Claghorn--Biog. p119-120
Hirschhorn--Rating p107-108, por.
Manchel--Women p85, por.
Mordden--Movie p238,244,246-249,
256,284, por.
Shipman--Internatl. p130-133, por.
Simon--Best p159-161, por.
Simon--Big p264-265, por.
Sochen--Herstory p367, por.
Woman's Almanac p339, por.
World--Who p231

DAY, DOROTHY (1897-1980)
Amer. Catholic social reformer,
publisher, author, magazine
founder
Bloom--Religion p101-102, por.
Cur. Biog. '81 p461
McHenry--Liberty's p95
Marlowe--Great p295-302, por.
Nies--Seven p179-202
O'Neill--Women's p397-398
Ross--Young p25-36, por.
Signif.--Amer. p60, por.
Webster's--Amer. p262
Woman's Almanac p404
World--Who p187

DAY, EDITH (1896-1971)
Amer. singer, actress
Claghorn--Biog. p120

DAY, LARAINE (1917/1920-   )
Amer. actress
Lamparski--What. (3) p114-115,
por.
Springer--They p84-85,284, por.
World--Who p231

DAY, MARGARET
See HAUGHERY, MARGARET
GAFFNEY

DAY, WILLAMETTA KECK
Amer. millionaire
Forbes--400 ('84) p114

DAY, WORDEN (fl. 1970's)
Amer. sculptor
Women's--Female p87

DAYAN, RUTH (1917-)
Israeli craftswoman
O'Neill--Women's p100,126

DAYE, IRENE (1918-1971)
Amer. singer
Claghorn--Biog. p120
Claghorn--Jazz p88

DAYTON, ALIDA ROCKEFELLER
(c1949-)
Amer. millionaire
Forbes--400 ('84) p149-150

DEAL, BABS H. (1929-)
Amer. novelist
Ehrlich--Oxford p269

DE AMARAL, OLGA (1932-)
Columbian weaver
O'Neill--Women's p607-608

DEAN, JULIA (1830-1868)
Amer. actress
James--Notable (1) p449-450

DEAN, MAUREEN E. KANE
(c1946-)
Amer., wife of John Dean
100--Greatest (1) p93, por.

DEAN, PAT (fl. 1970's)
Amer. TV news producer
Kelver--Women p36,77,99-100,
por.

DEAN, PENNY (1955-)
Amer. swimmer
McWhirter--Cuinness p146

DEAN, VERA MICHELES (1903-
1972)
Russian-Amer. International
Affairs Specialist, writer,
teacher, editor, lecturer
Cur. Biog. '72 p461
Sicherman--Notable p182-183

DEANE, ANNA MEAD (fl. 1860's)
Amer. Southern belle
DeLeon--Belles p132, por.

DEANE, MARTHA (1)
See McBRIDE, MARY MARGARET

DEANE, MARTHA (2)
See YOUNG, MARIAN

DeANGELI, MARGUERITE (1889-)
Amer. children's book author,
illustrator
Kulkin--Her p82

DEARD(S), MARY (fl. 1700's)
Amer. goldsmith, toymaker
Callen--Women p152

DEARIE, BLOSSOM (1926-)
Amer. singer, pianist
Claghorn--Jazz p88

DEATON, LEOTI
Amer. aviatrix, (army flier)
Keil--Those, see index p325

de AYALA, JOSEFA (1630-1684)
Spanish painter
Petersen--Women p31

DE BALLI, DONA ROSA MARIA
HINOPSA (1755/1760-)
Amer., noted Texas mother,
cattle queen
Amer.--Mothers p513, por.

DE BAZUS, BARONESS
See LESLIE, MIRIAM FLORENCE
FOLLINE SQUIER

DE BEAUVOIR, SIMONE
See BEAUVOIR, SIMONE LUCIE
ERNESTINE MARIA BERTRAND
DE

DEBERNARD, DANIELE (fl. 1970's)
French skier
Assoc. Press--Pursuit p296,321

DEBI, ARUNDHATI (fl. 1960's)
East Indian actress, filmmaker
Smith--Movies p125

DE BLOIS, ELIZABETH (fl. 1770's)
Amer., friend of Benedict
Arnold
Booth--Women p161-162,227

DE BLOIS, NATHALIE (fl. 1960's-
1970's)
Amer. architectural corporate
designer
O'Neill--Women's p609-610

DEBORAH
Biblical judge, prophetess

Henry--Written p24-29
Jones--Rutledge p218
Woman's Almanac p397

DE BRETTEVILLE, SHEILA
Amer. graphic artist
Women's--Female p76

DE BRIE, CATHERINE DU ROZET
(c1620-1706)
French actress
Entertainers p63

DE BURGOS, JULIA
See BURGOS, JULIA DE

DE CARLO, YVONNE (1922/1924-)
Canadian-Amer. actress
Hirschhorn--Rating p109-110,
por.
World--Who p255

DE CISNEROS, ELEONORA
See CISNEROS, ELEANORA
BROADFOOT, DE

DECKER, MARY (1958-)
Amer. track and field athelete
Cur. Biog. '83 p95-98, por.
Hollander--100 p137-138, por.
Kulkin--Her p83-84
Stambler--Women p132-143, por.

DECKER, SARAH SOPHIA CHASE
PLATT (1852-1912)
Amer. clubwoman, social
reformer, organization
official
Hymowitz--Hist. p221
James--Notable (1) p451-452
McHenry--Liberty's p95-96

DECKERS, JEANNE (1933-)
Belgian nun, singer
Book--Lists (2) p15

DE COURT, SUZANNE (fl. c1600)
French enameller
Petersen--Women p33

DE CROW, KAREN L. (c1938-)
Amer. feminist, journalist
O'Neill--Women's p705

DECTER, MIDGE (1927-)
Amer. writer, activist
Cur. Biog. '82 p86-88, por.

DE DORLEAC, CATHERINE
See DENEUVE, CATHERINE

DEDRICK, CLAIRE (fl. 1970's)
Amer. scientist, politician,
environmentalist
O'Neill--Women's p725-726

DE DUPREY, ANA ROQUE DE
See DUPREY, ANA ROQUE DE

DEE, FRANCES JEAN (1907-)
Amer. actress
Lamparski--What. (5) p26-27, por.
Springer--They p85,284,286, por.

DEE, KIKI (1947-)
English singer
Anderson--People p125

DEE, RUBY (1924-)
Amer. actress
Cur. Biog. '70 p107-116, por.
World--Who p231

DEE, SANDRA (1942-)
Amer. actress
Hirschhorn--Rating p100, por.
Shipman--Internatl. p135-136,
por.
World--Who p231

DEER, ADA (1935-)
Amer. Indian reformer
O'Neill--Women's p718

DEERING, LADY
See WENTWORTH, FRANCES
DEERING, LADY

DE FARNESIO, ISABEL
See FARNESIO, ISABEL DE

DE FAUCIGNY, BABA DE LUCINGE
French Princess, society
fashion leader
Keenan--Women p32,56-58, por.

DE FAUVEAU, FELICIE (1802-1886)
French artist
Fine--Women p56-57

DE FEO, JAY (1929-)
Amer. painter
Women's--Female p38

DEFFAND, MARIE DE VICHY

CHAMROND, MARQUISE DU
(1697-1780)
French literary hostess,
salonist
Jones--Rutledge p219

DE FILIPPS, MARSHA L. (1947-)
Amer. genealogical researcher,
indexer, writer
Meyer--Who's p60

DE FORD, MIRIAM ALLEN
Amer. feminist, writer
Ehrlich--Oxford, see index p452
Sochen--Movers p148-149

DE FRECE, MATILDA ALICE, LADY
See TILLEY, VESTA

DE FREES, MADELINE (1919-)
Amer. poet
Chester--Rising p92-94, por.

DE GAETANI, JAN (1933-)
Amer. singer
Cur. Biog. '77 p125-128, por.

de GAULLE, JEANNE MAILLOT-
DELANNOY (-1940)
French, mother of Charles
de Gaulle
Diagram--Mothers p104-105, por.

DE GOURNAY, MARIE
See GOURNAY, MARIE LE JARS
DE

DE GRAFFENREID, CLARE
See GRAFFENREID, (MARY)
CLARE DE

DE GRASSE, IDA MAY PARK
See PARK, IDA MAY

de GREY, MABEL (fl. 1890's)
British woodcarver
Callen--Women p7,167-168

DEHARME, LISE (1902-)
French novelist, fairy-tale
writer
Crosland--Women p225-226

DE HAVEN, GLORIA (1926-)
Amer. singer, actress
Claghorn--Biog. p121

DE HAVEN, MABEL (1896-)
Amer. genealogical researcher,
author
Meyer--Who's p60

DE HAVILAND, JOAN de BEAVOIR
See FONTAINE, JOAN

DE HAVILAND, OLIVIA (1916-)
British-Amer. actress
Hirschhorn--Rating p110-111,
por.
Shipman--Gold. p156-160, por.
Springer--They p86,286, por.
Woman's Almanac p339
World--Who p231

DEH-GE-WA-NUS
See JEMISON, MARY DEHEWAMIS

DE HIRSCH, STORM (fl. 1960's-
1970's)
Amer. poet, filmmaker
Smith--Movies p161-162, por.

DEHMER, PATRICIA (c1945-)
Amer. chemical physicist
Science Digest--100 p54

DEHN, DOROTHY HARRIET (1916-)
Amer. genealogical researcher,
writer
Meyer--Who's p60

DEITCH, DONNA (fl. 1970's)
Amer. camera director
Smith--Movies p235, por.

DEIZ, MERCEDES F. (1917-)
Amer. judge, noted Oregon
mother
Amer.--Mothers p452, por.

DEJAZET, PAULINE-VIRGINIE
(1798-1875)
French actress
Entertainers p113

de JESUS, CAROLINA MARIA (fl.
1970's)
Brazilian diarist
Moffat--Revel. p288-300

DEKEN, AGATHA (AAGJI) (1741-
1804)
Netherlands poet, novelist

Who Did What (under Wolff,
Elisabeth) p332

DEKNATEL, JANE (1942-)
Amer. TV film executive
Scheuer--Tel. p126

DE KOONING, ELAINE MARIE
CATHERINE (1920-)
Amer. painter, art critic,
educator
Cur. Biog. '82 p89-92, por.
Fine--Women p212-214

DE KOVEN, JEAN (-1937)
Amer. dancer
People's Almanac (1) p583

de la FALAISE, MAXIME (fl.
1940's-1950's)
Fashion designer, writer,
actress
Keenan--Women p64,67, por,

DELAFIELD, "E.M." (EDMEE
MONICA), pseud. (1890-
1943)
British novelist, playwright
Showalter--Lit. p346

DE LAGUNA, FREDERICA ANNIS
(fl. 1940's-1970's)
Amer. anthropologist
O'Neill--Women's p145,147-148

DELAMARE, DELPHINE COUTURIER
(1822-1848)
French, inspiration, Flau-
bert's "Madame Bovary"
Book--Lists (1) p239

de la MARGE, NICOLE (fl. 1950's-
1960's)
French model
Keenan--Women p182-183,186,
190, por.

DELAND, MARGARET WADE (1857-
1945)
Amer. novelist
Ehrlich--Oxford p6,37,211
James--Notable (1) p454-456
McHenry--Liberty's p96
Sherr--American p90
Sochen--Herstory p225-227, por.
Welter--Dimity p120-129

DELANEY, SHELAGH (1939-)
English playwright, entertainer
Avenel--Comp. (1) p142
Macksey--Book p236

DELANO, JANE ARMINDA (1862-
1919)
Amer. nurse
James--Notable (1) p456-458
McHenry--Liberty's p96-97
Macksey--Book p155
Sherr--American p40,231, por.

DELANO, LAURA ("POLLY")
Amer., cousin of Franklin
Delano Roosevelt
Daniels--Wash. p56-60,200,310-314,
por.

DELANY, MARY GRANVILLE (1700-
1788)
English botanist, illustrator,
letter writer
Earle--Two Cent. (2) p470-473,
489-490,550-551, por.
Hufstader--Sisters p142-195, por.
Moers--Literary p285

DE LA PASTURE, EDMEE ELIZABETH
MONICA
See DELAFIELD, "E.M." (EDMEE
MONICA), pseud.

DE LA RAMEE, MARIE LOUISE
See "OUIDA," pseud.

DE LAROCHE, BARONNE
See LAROCHE, ELISE DE

DE LA ROCHE, MAZO (1885-1961)
Canadian novelist
Avenel--Comp. (1) p142
Jones--Rutledge p221
Magill--Cycl. p283-284
Seymour-Smith--Novels p125

DE LARROCHA, ALICIA (1923-)
Spanish pianist
O'Neill--Women's p631
World--Who p75

DELARUE-MARDRUS, LUCIE (1880-
1945)
French author
Crosland--Women, see index p250

DE LAUNAY, MME. de STAËL
See STAAL (STAHL, STAËL),
MARGUERITE JEANNE
CORDIER DELAUNAY,
BARONESS de

DELAUNAY, SONIA (c1888-1979)
Russian artist
Comfort--Good p58, por.
Cur. Biog. '77 p128-131, por.
Cur. Biog. '80 p453
Fine--Women p142,169-171
Harris--Women p60-61,63,65,97,
291-294,357
Macksey--Book p267
Munsterberg--Hist. p67-68,118
Nemser--Convers. p35-51,360,
por.
O'Neill--Women's p241,596
Petersen--Women p111-113
Woman's Almanac p106
Women's--Female p7

DeLAY, DOROTHY (c1917-)
Amer. violin teacher
O'Neill--Women's p635

DeLAY, MARIE LONG (1905-)
Amer. genealogical researcher,
columnist, writer
Meyer--Who's p60-61

DELEDDA, GRAZIA (1875-1936)
Italian novelist, short story
writer
Kulkin--Her p84-85
Macksey--Book p189
Magill--Cycl. p284-285
O'Neill--Women's p676
Opfell--Lady p80-93, por.
People's Almanac (2) p1011
Seymour-Smith--Novels p125
Seymour-Smith--Who's p94
World--Who p38

DELEHANTY, SUZANNE (fl.
1970's)
Amer. museum director
O'Neill--Women's p615

DELILAH
Biblical
Woman's Almanac p397-398

DELL, CLAUDIA (1910-)
Amer. actress
Springer--They p86,286, por.

DELLA CASA, LISA (1919/1921-)
Swiss-Amer. opera singer
Gammond--Illus. p239, por.

DELMONICO, MRS. JOHN (fl. 1980's)
Amer. millionaire
Forbes--400 ('84) p47

DEL MONDO, FE (1911-)
Filipino physician
Hellstedt--Women p413-418, por.

DE LOPEZ, ESPERANZA
Guatemalan adult educator
O'Neill--Women's p399

DELORIA, ELLA CARA (1888-1971)
Amer. Dakota Indian linguist,
anthropologist
Sicherman--Notable p183-185
Signif.--Amer. p60, por.

DELORME (or DE LORME), MARION
(1611/1613-1650)
French adventuress, courtesan
Jones--Rutledge p222

DEL RIO, DOLORES (1905-1983)
Mexican-Amer. actress
Book Lists (2) p188
Lamparski--What. (3) p62-63,
por.
Lamparski--What. (8) p80-81,
por.
Shipman--Gold. p160-162, por.
Springer--They p87,286, por.
World--Who p231

DE LUNA, BEATRICE
See NASI, (DONA) GRACIA

DE LUSSAN, ZELIE
See LUSSAN, ZELIE DE

DELUVINA (1848-)
Amer. Indian girl, friend of
Billy the Kid
Coffin--Parade p277-279

DE LYSER, FEMMY
Amer. childbirth expert
People--Best p79, por.

DE MANDIARGUES, BONA (1926-)
Italian artist, craftswoman
Women's--Female p20

DE MARCO, MARLENE (fl. 1970's)
Amer. TV director
Klever--Women p27-28,65-66,99

DeMAREST, MARY AUGUSTA LEE
(1838-1888)
Amer. lyricist
Claghorn--Biog. p122

de MARKIEVICZ, CONSTANCE
GORE-BOOTH, COUNTESS
OF
See MARKIEVICZ, CONSTANCE
GORE-BOOTH, COUNTESS
de

DE MASTER, MRS. DOUGLAS
See THOMAS, JEANETTE

de MEDICIS, CATHERINE
See CATHERINE de MEDICIS

DE MENIL, DOMINIQUE (1908-)
Amer. millionaire
Forbes--400 ('84) p128

DEMETER
Greek goddess
Fraser--Heroines p24-28, por.
Pomeroy--Godd. p44-45,76-78

DEMETRAKAS, JOHANNA (fl.
1970's)
Amer. filmmaker
Smith--Movies p162,236, por.

DeMILLE, AGNES GEORGE (1905-)
Amer. dancer, choreographer
Cur. Biog. '85 p78-83, por.
Clark--Leading p182
Entertainers p233
Gilbert--Part. p93-99, por.
Ingraham--Album p62
Jones--Rutledge p222
Kulkin--Her p86-87
Longstreet--Queen p181-184,
por.
McHenry--Liberty's p97
Macksey--Book p230
100--Greatest (1) p23, por.
O'Neill--Women's p649
People--Best p228-229, por.
Signif.--Amer. p60, por.
Stoddard--Famous p111-123, por.
Webster's--Amer. p270
Woman's Almanac p308
World--Who p70

DeMILLE, KATHERINE (1911-)
Canadian-Amer. actress
Lamparski--What. Annual (4,5)
p196-200, por.
Springer--They p87-88,286, por.

DEMONT-BRETON, VIRGINIA ELODIE,
MADAME (1859-)
French painter
Sparrow--Women p182,226,233

DE MOONING, ELAINE (fl. 1970's)
Amer. painter
Women's--Female p38

DEMOREST, CHARLOTTE (fl. 1940's)
Amer. radio director
Women--Radio p9-10

DEMOREST, ELLEN CURTIS (1824-
1898)
Amer. inventor, fashion expert
Bird--Enterprising p74-78
James--Notable (1) p459-460
Longstreet--Queen p108-109
McHenry--Liberty's p97-98
Macksey--Book p265
Warren--Pictorial p125
Woman's Almanac p133

DE MORGAN, EVELYN PICKERING
(fl. 1870's)
English painter
Sparrow--Women p71,91,117,123

DE MOSS, NANCY
Amer. musician, wife of
Arthur De Moss
Kooiman--Silhouettes p37-48, por.

DEMPSEY, MARY JOSEPH, SISTER
(1856-1939)
Amer. Catholic nun, hospital
administrator
James--Notable (1) p460-462
McHenry--Liberty's p98

DEMPSTER, CAROL (1901/1902-)
Amer. dancer, actress
Lamparski--What. (2) p192-193,
por.

DENES, AGNES (fl. 1970's)
Amer. artist
Women's--Female p102

DENEUVE, CATHERINE (1943-)

French actress
Anderson--People p126
Book--Lists (2) p256
Cur. Biog. '78 p98-101, por.
Hirschhorn--Rating p114, por.
Shipman--Internatl. p139-142,
por.
World--Who p255

DENGEL, ANNA MARIA (1892-1980)
Austrian physician
Hellstedt--Women p91-94, por.

DENISON, FLORA M. (1867-1921)
Canadian suffragist, journal-
ist, feminist
O'Neill--Women's p698

DENISON, MARY ANN ANDREWS
(c1826-1911)
Amer. novelist
James--Notable (1) p462-463

DENISON, SUSAN (1946-)
Amer. TV executive
Scheuer--Tel. p127

DENNETT, MARY COFFIN WARE
(1872-1947)
Amer. suffragist, pacifist,
social reformer
James--Notable (1) p463-465
McHenry--Liberty's p98

DENNING, ANN ELIZA WEBB
YOUNG (1844-)
Amer. writer
Sherr--American p119,221,226-
227, por.

DENNING, BERNARDINE NEWSOM
(c1930-)
Amer. government official
O'Neill--Women's p83

DENNIS, ALICE
English midwife
Mead--Hist. p398

DENNIS, JESSIE McNAB (fl. 1970's)
Amer. museum worker
Women's--Female p118

DENNIS, MARY
Amer. army officer
Macksey--Book p55

DENNIS, RUTH
See ST. DENIS, RUTH

DENNIS, SANDY (1937-)
Amer. actress
Cur. Biog. '69 p121-124, por.
Hirschhorn--Rating p115-116, por.
World--Who p231

DENNISON, JO-CARROLL (1923-)
Amer. beauty
Lamparski--What. (5) p168-169,
por.

DENNY, ANNE
Amer. correspondent
Hamblin--That p54,79-81,88-90,
182,200-202

de NOAILLES, MARIE-LAURE,
VICOMTESSE
French poet, beauty
Keenan--Women p12-14, por.

DENSEN-GERBER, JUDIANNE
(1934-)
Amer. lawyer, social activist
Cur. Biog. '83 p101-104, por.
Diamonstein--Open p97-102, por.
Gilbert--Part. p275-281, por.

DENSMORE, DANA (fl. 1970's)
Amer. feminist, editor
O'Neill--Women's p706

DENSMORE, FRANCES THERESA
(1867-1957)
Amer. Indian authority, musi-
cian, ethnomusicologist
Sherr--American p22,121-122, por.
Sicherman--Notable p185-186

DENTON, ISABEL
English inventor
Earle--Two Cent. (2) p569

DENTON, MARY FLORENCE (1857-
1947)
Amer. missionary, teacher in
Japan
James--Notable (1) p465-466

DENYS, CHARLENE (fl. 1970's)
Amer. biologist (Antarctica)
Land--New p55,69-73, por.

DE PAUW, LINDA GRANT (1960's-

1970's)
Amer. feminist, editor
O'Neill--Women's p425

DE PEYSTER, CORNELIA LUBBETSE
(fl. 1720's)
Amer. real estate owner
Williams--Demeter's p189

de PISAN, CHRISTINE
See PISAN, CHRISTINE de

DE PONTE, ROZA SOLOMON
Amer. builder of first little
theatre
Sherr--American p84

de PORCAIRAGES, AZALAIS
See PORCAIRAGES, AZALAIS de

DERAISMES, MARIA (1828-1894)
French editor, suffragist
Fine--Women p122
Macksey--Book p88

DERBY, JANE (1895-1965)
Amer. fashion expert
O'Neill--Women's p247

DERBY, MARTHA COFFIN (1783-
1832)
Amer. patriot, (wife of
Richard Derby)
Earle--Two Cent. (2) p xxiv,
790-792, por.

DEREK, BO (MARY CATHLEEN)
(1956-)
Amer. actress
Anderson--People p128-129
Mordden--Movie p269-270
People--Best p40, por.

DEREN, MAYA (c1922-1961)
Amer. film producer
O'Neill--Women's p667
Sicherman--Notable p186-188
Smith--Moives p34-35

DERIAN, PATRICIA (PAT)
(c1929-)
Amer. government official
Adams--Women p45-51

DE RIDDER, LUCILLE
See REED, LUCY

D'ERLAGER, BARONESS
See PRUE, EDWINA

DERMOT, JESSIE
See ELLIOTT, MAXINE

DEROIN, JEANNE (fl. 1840's-1850's)
French suffragist
Macksey--Book p88

de ROMERO, JOSEFINA BARCELO
See ROMERO, JOSEFINA BAR-
CELO de

de ROTHSCHILD, MRS. LEOPOLD
British woodworker
Callen--Women p168

DERRICOTTE, JULIETTE (1897-1931)
Amer. social worker, humani-
tarian
Burt--Black p13-37, por.

de SADE, MARIE ELEONORE de
MAILLE de CARMAN, COUNTESS
(1712-1777)
French, mother of Marquis de
Sade
Diagram--Mothers p224-225

DESAI, ANITA (1937-)
Amer. Indian novelist, teacher
Seymour-Smith--Novels p125

DE SASALLOW, OLGA NUÑEZ (fl.
1950's)
Nicaraguan minister of public
education, lawyer
O'Neill--Women's p61

DE SANTIS, ANNE (fl. 1970's)
Amer. journalist
O'Neill--Women's p452

DESBORDES-VALMORE, MARCELINE
(1786-1859)
French poet
Bree--Women p13
Crosland--Women p27-28, por.
Moers--Literary p285

de SELINCORT, ANNE
See SEDGWICK, ANNE DOUGLAS

DESHA, MARY (-1910)
Amer. co-founder DAR,

foundress, teacher
Sherr--American p40

DeSOTO, SARA
Spanish, daughter of explorer
Coffin--Parade p528

de SPAIN, JUNE (fl. 1970's)
Amer. "cookbook" author
Felton--Famous p74

DESSAU, INGRID (1923-)
Swedish textile designer
(rug-weaver)
O'Neill--Women's p271

DESSOFF, MARGARETHE (1874-
1944)
German choir director
Macksey--Book p219

d'ESTE, ISABELLA
See ESTE, ISABELLA d',
MARCHIONESS OF MANTUS

DESTINN, (EMMY) EMILY KITTI
(1878-1930)
Czechoslovakian opera singer
Partington--Who's p90
Tuggle--Golden p72-74, por.

de TREVINO, ELIZABETH BORTON
(1904-)
Amer. children's writer
O'Neill--Women's p691

DETTWEILER, HELEN
Amer. aviatrix, (army flier)
Keil--Those, see index p323

DEUTSCH, BABETTE (1895-)
Amer. poet, novelist,
translator, critic
Avenel--Comp. (2) p71
Bernikow--World p290
Chester--Rising p32-33, por.
Ehrlich--Oxford p156
Moers--Literary p285
Seymour-Smith--Novels p125

DEUTSCH, HELEN
Amer. feminist, writer
Hymowitz--Hist. p300

DEUTSCH, HELEN ROSENBACH
(1884-1982)

Polish-Amer. psychoanalyst
Bachtold--Gifted p73-74
Neidle--America's p207
O'Neill--Women's p413
World--Who p94

DE VALERA, SILE (fl. 1970's)
Irish politician
O'Neill--Women's p59

DEVALET, GERMAINE (1898-1945)
Belgian war heroine
Macksey--Book p59

DE VALOIS, NINETTE (1), MADAME
(fl. 13th century)
French medical woman
Mead--Hist. p218

DE VALOIS, NINETTE (2), DAME
(1898-)
Irish ballet dancer, choreog-
rapher
Jones--Rutledge p225
Macksey--Book p230,232, por.
O'Neill--Womens' p640 641
Who Did What p315
World--Who p75

DE VARONA, DONNA (1947-)
Amer. swimmer, TV sports
commentator
Scheuer--Tel. p128

DeVERE, PEARL (-1897)
Amer. "madam"
Sherr--American p26
Time--Women p144-147

DEVEREUX, MARION ("MADAME")
(-1939)
Amer. journalist, social reporter
Birmingham--Grandes p173-180,
195

DEVI, GAYATRI (MAHARANI OF
JAIPUR) (1919-)
East Indian author
O'Neill--Women's p746

DEVI, INDIRA
East Indian actress
Macksey--Book p235

DEVI, SHAKUNTALA

East Indian prodigy, mathematical wizard
O'Neill--Women's p745

de VIVONNE, CATHERINE
See VIVONNE, CATHERINE de

DEVLIN, BERNADETTE JOSEPHINE
(1947-)
Irish civil rights leader,
member of Parliament
Book--Lists (2) p257
Cur. Biog. '70 p114-117, por.
Kulkin--Her p87-88
O'Neill--Women's p714
World--Who p155

DEVLIN, JUDY (fl. 1950's-1960's)
Amer. badminton player
O'Neill--Women's p582

DEVLIN, MARGARET MARY
See ASHFORD, DAISY

DEVNEY, VERONA STUBBS (1916-)
Amer., noted Minnesota
mother, charity worker
Amer.--Mothers p294, por.

DE VOE, EMMA SMITH
Amer. suffragist, circuit
rider, lecturer
Sherr--American p135,214

DEVONSHIRE, GEORGIANA,
DUCHESS OF (1757-1806)
English social leader
Ware--Meet p23-47,49,59-61,
por.

DEVOTION, EUNICE HUNTINGTON
(1742-1827)
Amer. patriot
Flexner--Face p122, por.

DE VRIES, YUAN LIN (fl. 1970's)
Taiwan biochemist (Antarc-
tica)
Land--New p103-113,116, por.

DEWART, JANET (fl. 1970's)
Amer. radio director
O'Neill--Women's p500

DEWEY, (HATTIE) ALICE CHIP-
MAN (1858-1927)
Amer. educator

James--Notable (1) p466-
468

DEWHURST, COLLEEN (c1926-)
Canadian-Amer. actress
Cur. Biog. '74 p110-113, por.
Entertainers p266-267
World--Who p231

DE WITT, JOYCE (1949-)
Amer. TV actress
Scheuer--Tel. p128

DE WITT, LYDIA MARIA ADAMS
(1859-1928)
Amer. experimental pathologist
James--Notable (1) p468-469

DE WOLFE, ELSIE, LADY MENDL
(1856-1950)
English-Amer. actress, interior
decorator, international hostess
Forma--They p124, por.
James--Notable (1) p469-471
Keenan--Women p30-31,34, por.
Longstreet--Queen p135-139, por.
McHenry--Liberty's p98-99
O'Neill--Women's p279
Sherr--American p169

DEWSON, MARY WILLIAMS ("MOLLY")
(1874-1962)
Amer. politician, economist,
social worker, suffragist
Hymowitz--Hist. p311
McHenry--Liberty's p99
Sicherman--Notable p188-191
Sochen--Movers p151-152
Ware--Beyond p146, see also
index p198

DEY, MANJU
East Indian actress, filmmaker
Smith--Movies p124-125

DEZSO, TERRY (1931-)
Amer. feminist
Seifer--Nobody p436-477, por.

DHANVANTH, RAMA RAU, LADY
See RAMA RAU DHANVANTH,
LADY

D'HOUVILLE, GERARD, pseud.
See REGNIER, PAULE

DIA, COUNTESS OF (c1140-)

French troubadour
Bogin--Women p83,163-164
Neuls-Bates--Women p21-24

DIAMOND, FREDA (fl. 1950's-
1970's)
Amer. home furnishings consultant, designer
O'Neill--Women's p277

DIAMONSTEIN, BARBARALEE
Amer. government official
Adams--Women p24,71-73

DIANA, PRINCESS OF WALES
(1961-)
British Consort of Charles,
Prince of Wales
Cur. Biog. '83 p108-111, por.
People--Best p104-105, por.

DIANE OF POITIERS, DUCHESS
OF VALENTINOIS
See POITIERS, DIANE DE,
DUCHESS

DIAS, MARIE T. (fl. 1970's)
Amer. executive director,
(Children's World Educational
Center)
O'Neill--Women's p429

DIAZ, ABBY MORTON (1821-1904)
Amer. author, social reformer
James--Notable (1) p471-473
McHenry--Liberty's p99-100

DIAZ, ANA LAURETTA (1924-)
Guatemalan rural development
expert
O'Neill--Women's p38-39

DIBA, QUEEN FARA
See FARAH DIBA PAHLEVI,
EMPRESS

DIBBLEE, POLLY
English-Amer. Loyalist
DePauw--Found. p135-136

DICK, ELSIE (fl. 1940's)
Amer. radio director
Women--Radio p7

DICK, GLADYS ROWENA HENRY
(1881-1963)
Amer. bacteriologist,

physician, microbiologist
O'Neill--Women's p217
Sicherman--Notable p191-192

DICKASON, GLADYS MARIE (1903-
1971)
Amer. labor economist, leader
Sicherman--Notable p192-194

DICKENS, CATHERINE HOGARTH
(fl. 1830's)
English, wife of Charles
Dickens
Morley--Literary p98-100

DICKENS, ELIZABETH BARROW
(-1863)
English, mother of Charles
Dickens
Diagram--Mothers p64-67, por.
Morley--Literary p180-181

DICKENS, MONICA ENID (1915-)
English novelist
Avenel--Comp. (1) p149
Seymour-Smith--Novels p126

DICKERMAN, BEATRICE WHITNEY
See STRAIGHT, BEATRICE
WHITNEY

DICKERSON, NANCY HANSCHMAN
(c1929-)
Amer. TV Washington corres-
pondent
Marzolf--Up p165-167,196
O'Neill--Women's p498

DICKERSON, SUZANNA (fl. 1830's)
Anglo-Amer. pioneer, heroine
Sherr--American p223

DICKERSON, UNA REILLY (1881-)
Amer., noted Nevada mother,
law librarian
Amer.--Mothers p348-349, por.

DICKEY, FRANCINE (fl. 1970's)
Amer. accountant
Seed--Saturday's p125-126, por.

DICKEY, SARAH ANN (1838-1904)
Amer. educator, school foun-
dress
Chittenden--Prof. p125-141, por.
James--Notable (1) p473-475
McHenry--Liberty's p100

Sherr--American p124,
128

DICKINS, HELEN OCTAVIA (1900-   )
Amer. physician (obstetrician,
gynecologist)
O'Neill--Women's p214

DICKINSON, AMY
Amer. child baseball player
(Little League)
O'Neill--Women's p567

DICKINSON, ANGIE (1931/1932-   )
Amer. actress
Anderson--People p130-131
Cur. Biog. '81 p118-121, por.
Hirschhorn--Rating p117-118,
por.
Scheuer--Tel. p129, por.
World--Who p231

DICKINSON, ANNA (1842-1932)
Amer. social reformer, Civil
War lecturer, author,
actress
Earnest--American p127-129
Hymowitz--Hist. p150
James--Notable (1) p475-476
McHenry--Liberty's p100-101
Papachristou--Women p48, por.
Sherr--American p59,168
Smith--Daughters p373
Taylor--Gener. p25, por.

DICKINSON, ELEANOR CREEKMORE
(1931-   )
Amer. artist
Fowler--Art p148-149

DICKINSON, EMILY ELIZABETH
(1830-1886)
Amer. poet
Avenel--Comp. (2) p73-74
Benet--New p76-83, por.
Bernikow--World p205-206
Book--Lists (2) p375
Donaldson--How p95
Ehrlich--Oxford p25,61,206,225,
por.
Eills--Here p26-27
Epstein--Indiv. p23-40
Ingraham--Album p57
James--Notable (1) p477-480
Jones--Rutledge p227-228
Kaplan--Salt p145-146, por.
Kronenberger--Atlan. p224-226

Kulkin--Her p88-89
Kupferberg--First p36-38, por.
McHenry--Liberty's p101
Magill--Cycl. p293-295
Marlowe--Great p119-125, por.
Moers--Lieterary p285-286, see
also index p324, por.
Pearson--Who p85
Pederson--Leaders p122, por.
People's Almanac (3) p619
Sherr--American p97
Signif.--Amer. p17, por.
Stoddard--Famous p124-135, por.
Warren--Pictorial p130-131, por.
Webster's--Amer. p276-277
Who Did What p91
Woman's Almanac p250-251, por.
World--Who p12

DICKINSON, FRANCES (1755-1830)
Amer. convent co-founder
James--Notable (2) p509-510

DICKSON, GLORIA (1916/1917-1945)
Amer. actress
Springer--They p88,286, por.

DIDDOCK, MARGUERITE LA FLESCHE
(1862-1945)
Amer., Omaha Indian, teacher
Stein--Lives p170-172, por.

DIDION, JOAN (1934-   )
Amer. novelist, essayist,
journalist, film writer
Cur. Biog. '78 p108-111, por.
Diamonstein--Open p103-106, por.
Dunlap--Calif. p53-54
Ehrlich--Oxford p432
Moers--Literary p286
Seymour-Smith--Novels p127
Webber--Women p147-153
World--Who p12

DIDO (OR ELISSA) (9th Cent. B.C.)
Carthage Queen, foundress
Jones--Rutledge p229
Pomeroy--Godd. p161,188-189

DIDRIKSON, MILDRED ELLA ("BABE")
See ZAHARIAS, ("BABE") MILDRED
DIDRIKSON

DIEKHAUS, GRACE
Amer. TV producer
Scheuer--Tel. p129

DIEMER, EMMA LOU (1927-)
Amer. composer, artist, pro-
fessor
LePage--Women p54-70, por.

DIENERT, MILLIE
Amer. religious worker,
speaker
Kooiman--Cameos p78-85, por.

DIENES, SARI (1898-)
Hungarian-Amer. artist
Munro--Originals p97-99
Women's--Female p103

DIETERLE, DIANE (1939-)
Amer. genealogical research-
er, author
Meyer--Who's p62

DIETRICH, JUSTINA
See SIEGEMUNDIN, JUSTINE(A)
DITTRICHIN

DIETRICH, MARLENE (1901/1904-)
German-Amer. singer, enter-
tainer, actress
Claghorn--Biog. p126
Clark--Leading p141-142
Engstead--Star p70-80
Entertainers p217, por.
Hazen--Interv. p407-408
Hirschhorn--Rating p118-119,
por.
Jones--Rutledge p229
Manchel--Women p49-50, por.
Mordden--Movie, see index
p292, por.
O'Neill--Women's p658-659
Sat. Eve. Post--Movie p132,
por.
Shipman--Gold. p162-168, por.
Springer--They p88-90,286,288,
por.
Who Did What p91-92
Woman's Almanac p339-340, por.
World--Who p255-256

DIETRICH, MARTHA JANE (1916-)
Brazilian-Amer. genealogical
researcher
Meyer--Who's p62-63

DIGBY, JANE ELIZABETH
See ELLENBOROUGH, JANE
ELIZABETH DIGBY ("ANTHA"),
COUNTESS

DIGGES, ELIZABETH (-1699)
Amer. Colonial plantation owner
Williams--Demeter's p188

DIGGS, ANNIE LePORTE (1848-1916)
Canadian-Amer. politician,
social reformer, lecturer
James--Notable (1) p481-482
McHenry--Liberty's p101-102

DILHAN, JEANNE CHAUVIN,
MADEMOISELLE (1862-1926)
French lawyer
Macksey--Book p127-128

DILLARD, ANNIE (1945-)
Amer. author
Betts--Writers p58-59, por.
Cur. Biog. '83 p111-114, por.

DILLER, ANGELA (MARY ANGELICA)
(1877-1968)
Amer. music teacher, author
Sicherman--Notable p194-195

DILLER, PHYLLIS DRIVER (1917-)
Amer. actress, comedienne,
entertainer
Woman's Almanac p318, por.
World--Who p276

DILLINGHAM, MRS. (-1636)
Amer. colonist
Williams--Demeter's p40

DILLON, DIANE
Amer. writer
O'Neill--Women's p692

DILLON, FANNIE CHARLES (1881-
1947)
Amer. pianist, composer,
teacher, writer
Claghorn--Biog. p126

DILWORTH, MARY J. (fl. 1840's)
Amer. Quaker teacher
Sherr--American p227

DIMITROVA, LILYANA NIKOLOVA
(1918-1944)
Bulgarian revolutionary heroine
Partington--Who's p94, por.

DIMOCK, SUSAN (1847-1875)
Amer. physician, surgeon
James--Notable (1) p482-484

Sherr--American p89,154
Signif.--Amer. p18, por.
Sochen--Herstory p122,163, por.
Stoddard--Famous p136-148, por.
Warren--Pictorial p105
Webster's--Amer. p279-280
Woman's Almanac p376, por.
World--Who p187

DIX, DOROTHY, pseud. (1870-1951)
Amer. journalist
Ehrlich--Oxford p280
McHenry--Liberty's p157
Marzolf--Up p36-37
Sicherman--Notable p275-277
Sherr--American p19,85-86
Woman's Almanac p278, por.
World--Who p52

DIX, RUTH
Amer. medical missionary
Kooiman--Cameos p32-42, por.

DIXIE, FLORENCE CAROLINE
DOUGLAS, LADY (1857-1905)
English feminist, novelist,
explorer, traveler
Showalter--Lit. p340

DIXON, JEAN (1896/1905-1981)
Amer. actress
Springer--They p90,288, por.

DIXON, JEANE L. PINCKERT
(1918-)
Amer. psychic
Anderson--People p131-132
Cur. Biog. '73 p103-105, por.
People's Almanac (1) p4-5
People's Almanac (2) p3-4

DIXON, MARGARET (fl. c1728)
Amer. accused criminal
People's Almanac (2) p1181

DIXON, MARLENE
Amer. professor, feminist
Sochen--Movers p259-260

DIZON, SUZANNE SEARLE
(fl. 1980's)
Amer. millionaire
Forbes--400 ('84) p122

DLUGOSZEWSKI, LUCIA (1931-)

Amer. composer, poet, teacher,
pianist
Claghorn--Biog. p128
Jablonski--Ency. p513
Thomson--Amer. p139

DMITRAKOVICH, ANNA (fl. 1960's-1970's)
Russian labor union official
Mandel--Soviet p135-137

DOANE, ROSE E. (c1933-1967)
Amer. heroine
O'Neill--Women's p733

DOBBS, ELLA VICTORIA (1866-1952)
Amer. childhood educator,
suffrage worker
Snyder--Dauntless p281-320, por.

DOBSON, MARGARET
Amer. softball player
O'Neill--Women's p569

DOBSON, ROSEMARY (1920-)
Australian poet
Seymour-Smith--Who's p95

DOBSON, RUTH (fl. 1970's)
Australian ambassador to
Denmark
Macksey--Book p37
O'Neill--Women's p62

DOCK, LAVINIA LLOYD (1858-1956)
Amer. nurse, author, suffra-
gist, feminist
O'Neill--Women's p231-232
Sicherman--Notable p195-198

"DOCTORESSA"
See CORNERO, ELLENA LUCRETIA

"DOCTRESS OF EPSOM"
See MAPP, MRS.

DOD, CHARLOTTE (1871-1960)
English athlete (tennis, golf,
archery, hockey)
Macksey--Book p257
McWhirter--Guinness p9,151

DODD, CLAIRE (1908-1973)
Amer. actress
Springer--They p90,288, por.

DODD, JANE PORTER HART
(1824-1911)

Amer. craftswoman (wood-
carver, china painter)
Callen--Women p170,222

DODD, LOIS (1927-   )
Amer. artist, painter,
educator
Women's--Female p103

DODGE, ABIGAIL (1833-1896)
Amer. newspaper writer
Sherr--American p105

DODGE, GERALDINE ROCKEFELLER
(1882-1973)
Amer., wealthy woman
Woman's Almanac p211

DODGE, GRACE HOADLEY
(1856/1857-1914)
Amer. social welfare worker,
educator, philanthropist,
club founder
James--Notable (1) p489-492
Lagemann--Gen. p9-31, por.
McHenry--Liberty's p102-103
Macksey--Book p273-274
Millstein--We p151
O'Neill--Women's p112
Warren--Pictorial p143

DODGE, JOSEPHINE MARSHALL
JEWELL (1855-1928)
Amer. philanthropist, day-
nursery leader, anti-suffra-
gist
James--Notable (1) p492-493
McHenry--Liberty's p103

DODGE, MABEL
See LUHAN, MABEL GANSON
DODGE

DODGE, (MARY) ABIGAIL (1833-
1896)
Amer. journalist (Washington
correspondent), author,
humorist
Beasley--First p17-19, por.
James--Notable (1) p493-495
McHenry--Liberty's p103-104
Marzolf--Up p17-18
Sherr--American p105

DODGE, MARY ELIZABETH MAPES
(1831-1905)
Amer. children's author,

magazine editor
Ehrlich--Oxford p119,151,171,186,
por.
James--Notable (1) p495-496
Kulkin--Her p91-92
McHenry--Liberty's p104
Sherr--American p152-153
Webster's--Amer. p282
World--Who p12

DODGE, EVA F.
Amer. physician
O'Neill--Women's p211

DODGION, DOTTIE (DOROTHY)
GIAMO (1929-   )
Amer. drummer
Claghorn--Jazz p92

DODSON, BETTY (fl. 1970's)
Amer. painter
Women's--Female p39

DOE, ELIZABETH
See TABOR, ELIZABETH ("BABY
DOE") BONDUEL McCOURT

DOHAN, EDITH HAYWARD HALL
(1877-1943)
Amer. classical archaeologist
James--Notable (1) p496-497

DOHERTY, KAY (fl. 1970's)
Amer. "walker" for farm
co-ops
O'Neill--Women's p398-399

DOHRN, BERNARDINE RAE
(1942-   )
Amer. "Weathermen" leader,
radical, accused criminal
Lichtenstein--Mach. p162-164
People's Almanac (1) p613
Woman's Almanac p510
World--Who p296

DOKKEN, JULIA C. (c1947-   )
Amer. heroine
O'Neill--Women's p733

DOLE, ELIZABETH HANFORD
(1936-   )
Amer. government official,
second wife of Robert J. Dole
Cur. Biog. '83 p117-120, por.

DOLE, PHYLLIS HOLDEN

Amer., first wife of Senator
Robert J. Dole
Miller--Fishbait p118

DOLLEY, SARAH READ ADAMSON
(1829-1909)
Amer. physician
James--Notable (1) p497-499
O'Neill--Women's p201

DOLLY SISTERS (fl. 1930's-1940's)
Amer. dancers
World--Who p263

"DOLORES"
English model
Keenan--Women p109-111, por.

DOMERQUE, FAITH (1925-)
Amer. actress
Wilson--Holly. p122-125, por.

DOMINQUEZ, RITA (fl. 1970's)
Amer. art research worker
Women's--Female p124

DOMINICA, MARY, SISTER
(-1857)
Amer. nun
Sherr--American p12

DOMINIQUE, MADAME
French ballet teacher
Migel--Ballerinas p233-234,240

DOMITIEN, ELIZABETH (fl.
1970's)
African prime minister
O'Neill--Women's p47 48

DOMNA, H.
French troubadour
Bogin--Women p139,178

DONAGH, RITA (1939-)
British artist
Contemp. Brit. unp., por.

DONAHUE, HESSIE (fl. 1880's-
1890's)
Amer. boxer
Book--Lists (2) p339, por.
Felton--Famous p279-280, por.

DONALD, BARBARA KAY (1942-)
Amer. trumpeter, pianist,
saxist, trombonist,

singer
Claghorn--Jazz p93

DONALDA, PAULINE MISCHA LEON
(1884-1970)
Canadian singer
Claghorn--Biog. p130

DONALY, MARY (fl. 1730's)
Irish midwife
Mead--Hist. p479

DONEGAN, DOROTHY (1924-)
Amer. pianist
Claghorn--Biog. p130
Claghorn--Jazz p94

DONELLA
Italian nun, illuninator,
artist
Munsterberg--Hist. p12

DÖNHOFF, MARION GRÄFFIN,
COUNTESS (1909-)
German publisher, editor
Marzolf--Up p274-275,280
O'Neill--Women's p465

DONLEVY, HARRIET FARLEY
See FARLEY, HARRIET

DONLON, MARY HONOR (c1894-1977)
Amer. judge, government
official
Cur. Biog. '77 p462

DONNADIEU, MARGUERITE, pseud.
See DURAS, MARGUERITE
DONNADIEU

DONNE, MARIA DELLE (1776-1842)
Italian obstetrician, professor,
physician, surgeon
Marks--Women p119
Mead--Hist. p508,510

DONNELL-VOGT, RADKA (fl. 1950's-
1970's)
Bulgarian guiltist, painter
Miller--Lives p37-56, por.

DONNELLY, DOROTHY (1) (1880-
1928)
Amer. lyricist, actress, author
Claghorn--Biog. p130

DONNELLY, DOROTHY (2), SISTER

Amer. president, nuns'
coalition, author, professor
O'Neill--Women's p388

DONNELLY, LUCY MARTIN (1870-
1948)
Amer. college English instructor
James--Notable (1) p499-500

DONNELLY, MARY LOUISE, SISTER
(1927-)
Amer. genealogical researcher,
author
Meyer--Who's p63

DONNELLY, NELL QUINLAN
(1889-)
Amer. fashion designer,
clothing manufacturer
Bird--Enterprising p192-195

DONNELLY, RUTH (1896-)
Amer. actress, comedienne
Lamparski--What. (3) p190-192,
por.
Springer--They p90,288, por.

DONNELSON, EMILY (c1805-1854)
Amer. White House hostess
Sherr--American p217

DONNESON, SEENA (fl. 1970's)
Amer. artist
Women's--Female p103

DONOHUE, TERESA
See WALL, TESSIE

DONOVAN, FRANCES (fl. 1900's)
Amer. feminist
Hymowitz--Hist. p318-319

DOOLITTLE, HILDA (H.D.)
(1886-1961)
Amer. poet, novelist,
translator
Avenel--Comp. (2) p75
Bernikow--World p268
Chester--Rising p12-17, por.
Ehrlich--Oxford p189,196,214
Kaplan--Salt p223-226
Kronenberger--Atlan. p234
McHenry--Liberty's p104-105
Moers--Literary p287
Seymour-Smith--Novels p127-128
Seymour-Smith--Who's p154-155

Sicherman--Notable p198-201
Webster's--Amer. p284
World--Who p12

DORAN, BARBARA (fl. 1970's)
Amer. hockey player
Jordan--Broken p80-85

DORAN, MARY (1907-)
Amer. actress
Springer--They p90,288, por.

DORCAS (OR TABITHA)
Biblical
Price--God p171-174

DOREE, DORIS (1909-1971)
Amer. opera singer, teacher
Claghorn--Biog. p131

DOREMUS, SARAH PLATT HAINES
(1802-1877)
Amer. philanthropist, mis-
sionary, humanitarian
James--Notable (1) p500-501
McHenry--Liberty's p105

DOREN, ELECTRA COLLINS (1861-
1927)
Amer. pioneer librarian
Sherr--American p185

DORFMANN, ANIA (1899/1905-)
Russian pianist
Neidle--America's p243-245
O'Neill--Women's p629-630

DORION, MARIE (1786/1791-c1850)
Amer. pioneer, heroine
James--Notable (1) p502-503
Sherr--American p195

DORLHAC, HELENE
French minister
Macksey--Book p39

DORMAN, SONYA (1924-)
Amer. poet
Chester--Rising p141-144, por.

DOROSH, DARIA
Amer. painter
Women's--Female p39

DOROTHEA, QUEEN (fl. 16th cent.)
Danish religious queen, consort of Christian III, King of

DOUGLAS, ANNE (fl. 1970's)
    Amer., wife of Kirk Douglas
    Funt--Are p141-154, por.

DOUGLAS, CATHERINE (fl. 1700's)
    Amer. indentured servant
    Williams--Demeter's p60

DOUGLAS, DIANA, LADY (1943-)
    Amer. government official
    Scheuer--Tel. p133

DOUGLAS, ELLEN HOPE, pseud.
    (1921-)
    Amer. novelist
    Ehrlich--Oxford p273,284

DOUGLAS, EMILY TAFT (1899-)
    Amer. Congresswoman, Red
    Cross worker
    Chamberlin--Min. p175-180

DOUGLAS, HELEN CAHAGAN (1909-
    1980)
    Amer. actress, singer,
    Congresswoman
    Bachtold--Gifted p107
    Chamberlin--Min p180-188
    Cur. Biog. '80 p453
    Dunlap--Calif. p58
    Greenebaum--Politics p137-138
    McHenry--Liberty's p106
    Miller--Fishbait p70-71
    O'Neill--Women's p69
    People's Almanac (1) p319
    Woman's Almanac p471
    World--Who p139

DOUGLAS, JANE ("JENNIE")
    Amer. government employee
    Sherr--American p162

DOUGLAS, JUDITH HYAMS S.
    Amer. lawyer, suffrage
    leader
    Scott--Southern p181

DOUGLAS, PAMELA (fl. 1970's)
    Amer. film producer
    Smith--Movies p78-79

DOUGLAS, PAULETTE (fl. 1970's)
    Amer. TV stage, technical
    artist
    Klever--Women p52-53,67-68,101,
    106-107

DOUGLASS, MRS. DAVID (fl. 1790's)
    Amer. patriot
    DePauw--Rem. p136,138, por.

DOUGLASS, MABEL SMITH (1877-
    1933)
    Amer. educator, founder, dean
    of women's college
    James--Notable (1) p510-511
    Sherr--American p153

DOUGLASS, MARGARET (fl. 1850's)
    Amer. teacher, pioneer edu-
    cator
    Sherr--American p236

DOUGLASS, SARAH (fl. 1850's)
    Amer. Quaker teacher
    Sherr--American p199

DOUGLASS, SARAH GEORGE
    (1711-)
    Amer. frontier pioneer, noted
    Tennessee mother
    Amer.--Mothers p507

DOUGLASS, SARAH HALLAM
    (-1773/1774)
    Amer. colonial actress
    James--Notable (2) p120-122
    Williams--Demeter's p221-222

DOUGLASS, SARAH MAPPS DOUG-
    LAS (1806-1882)
    Amer. Quaker teacher, abo-
    litionist
    James--Notable (1) p511-513
    Sherr--American p199

DOURAS, MARION CECILIA
    See DAVIES, MARION

DOUSMAN, JANE (-1882)
    Amer. hostess, philanthropist
    Sherr--American p250

DOUTHIT, RUTH LONG (1909-)
    Amer. genealogical researcher,
    author
    Meyer--Who's p63

DOUVILLIER, SUZANNE THEODORE
    VAILLANDE (1778-1826)
    Amer. dancer, pantomimist
    James--Notable (1) p513-514
    McHenry--Liberty's p106

DOVE, BILLIE (1900/1903-   )
Amer. actress
Lamparski--What. (2) p168-169,
por.
Springer--They p92,288, por.

DOVI, ADI LOSALINI (fl. 1960's-
1970's)
Fijian government official
O'Neill--Women's p60

DOW, PEGGY (fl. 19th cent.)
Amer., wife of Lorenzo Dow
Earle--Two Cent. (2) p xxiii,
758,760, por.

DOWDY, BETSY
Amer. Revolutionary War
patriot
Meyer--Petticoat p206-207

DOWE, MENIE MURIEL, pseud.
See NORMAN, MRS. HENRY

DOWNER, CAROL (fl. 1970's)
Amer. director, self-
health clinic
O'Neill--Women's p706

DOWNEY, JUNE
Amer. handwriting expert
Sherr--American p256

DOWNEY, JUNE ETTA (1875-1932)
Amer. psychologist
James--Notable (1) p514-515
McHenry--Liberty's p106-107

DOWNING, LUCY WINTHROP (fl.
1630's)
Amer. colonial letter-writer
Williams--Demeter's p30

DOWNING, MARY (fl. 1630's)
Amer., niece of Governor
Winthrop
Earle--Two Cent. (2) p537-538

DOWNS, CORA (fl. 1930's-1970's)
Amer. professor, bacteriolo-
gist
O'Neill--Women's p218

DOWNS, SALLIE WARD
See WARD, SALLIE DOWNS

DOYLE, HELEN (fl. 1880's)

Amer. physician
Fischer--Let p193-204

DOYLE, SARAH ELIZABETH (1830-
1922)
Amer. educator, clubwoman
James--Notable (1) p515-517

DOZIER, BEVERLY FISHER (1933-   )
Amer. politician, community
worker, noted Florida mother
Amer.--Mothers p121, por.

DRABBLE, MARGARET (1939-   )
English novelist, critic, radio
personality
Cahill--Women p333-334,379
Crosland--Beyond p135,182,202,
227-228
Cur. Biog. '81 p125-128, por.
Moers--Literary p128,287
Seymour-Smith--Novels p129
Seymour-Smith--Who's p99
Showalter--Lit. p304-307,350
Spacks--Contemp. p18-29,178
World--Who p25

"THE DRAGON LADY"
See NGO DINH NHU, MADAME

DRAKE, FRANCES (1908-   )
Amer. actress
Springer--They p92,288, por.

DRAKE, FRANCES ANN DENNY
(1797-1875)
Amer. actress
James--Notable (1) p518-518
McHenry--Liberty's p107

DRAKE, MARGARET JOHNSON
(1914-   )
Amer. genealogical researcher,
author, indexer
Meyer--Who's p63-64

DRAKE, MARIE (1) (fl. 1930's)
Amer. musician, composer
Sherr--American p4

DRAKE, MARIE (2) (fl. 1910's)
Amer., Alaskan secretary of
education
Jones--Women (1) p155-157

DRAPER, DOROTHY (TUCKERMAN)
(1889-1969)

Amer. interior decorator
Cur. Biog. '69 p465
O'Neill--Women's p281

DRAPER, IRENE CARPENTER (fl.
1980's)
Amer. millionaire
Forbes--400 ('84) p136

DRAPER, MARGARET GREEN
(1727-c1807)
Amer. colonial, Loyalist,
publisher, printer
Booth--Women p43-46,62,109
Demeter--Primer p119-135
Marzolf--Up p8
Stein--Lives unp.
Williams--Demeter's p236

DRAPER, MARY ALDIS (c1718-
1810)
Amer. Revolutionary War
patriot, heroine
Meyer--Petticoat p38,41
Whitney--Col. p175-176

DRAPER, MARY ANNA PALMER
(1839-1914)
Amer. philanthropist,
astronomy benefactor
James--Notable (1) p518-519

DRAPER, MRS. (fl. 18th cent.)
English midwife
Mead--Hist. p475

DRAPER, RUTH (1884-1956)
Amer. monologist, actress
Chinoy--Women p114-119, por.
Entertainers p175-176
Jones--Rutledge p239
McHenry--Liberty's p107-108
Sicherman--Notable p201-202

DRAYTON, GRACE GEBBIE
Amer. advertising artist
People's Almanac (1) p356

DREIER, KATHERINE SOPHIE
(1877-1952)
Amer. art patron, artist
Sicherman--Notable p202-204

DREIER, MARY ELIZABETH
(1875-1963)
Amer. suffragist, labor
union leader

Hymowitz--Hist. p251
Neidle--America's p128,136-137,
140,146-147
O'Neill--Women's p289-290
Sicherman--Notable p204-206

DRESCHHOFF, GISELA (fl. 1970's)
German-Amer. radiation
physicist (Antarctica)
Land--New p161-175, por.

DRESSELHAUS, MILDRED S. (1930-)
Amer. electrical engineer,
professor
O'Neill--Women's p190

DRESSER, LOUISE KERLIN (1882-
1965)
Amer. actress
Springer--They p92-93,288-289,
por.

DRESSLER, MARIE (1868/1869-1934)
Canadian-Amer. actress
James--Notable (1) p519-521
Keylin--Hollywood p94-96, por.
McHenry--Liberty's p108
Mordden--Movie, see index p292,
por.
Shipman--Gold. p176-179, por.
Springer--They p93,289, por.
Webster's--Amer. p292
World--Who p256

DREW, ELIZABETH ("LIZ") (fl.
1970's)
Amer. TV interviewer
Marzolf--Up p173,197

DREW, ELIZABETH BRENNER
(1935-)
Amer. journalist, author
Cur. Biog. '79 p107-110, por.

DREW, ELLEN (1915-)
Amer. actress
Hazin--Interv. p409
Springer--They p93-94,289, por.

DREW, GEORGIANA EMMA
See BARRYMORE, GEORGIANA
EMMA DREW

DREW, LOUISA LANE (1820-1897)
English-Amer. actress, mana-
ger
Entertainers p122

James--Notable p521-523
McHenry--Liberty's p108-109
Warren--Pictorial p157

DREW, POLLY
See McVEY, LUCILLE

DREXEL, MARY KATHARINE,
MOTHER (1858-1955)
Amer. missionary, humani-
tarian, educator
McHenry--Liberty's p109
People's Almanac (1) p1304
Sicherman--Notable p206-208

DREXLER, ROSALYN (1922/1926-)
Amer. painter
Women's--Female p39

DRIESSCHE, THERESE VANDE
(fl. 1960's)
Belgian biology professor,
researcher
O'Neill--Women's p161-162

DRINKER, ELIZABETH SANDWITH
(1734-1807)
Amer. Revolutionary War
diarist, Quaker
Booth--Women p145,170,231
Evans--Weather. p22,152-184,
297-298
Hoople--As p37-40
Williams--Demeter's p259

DRINKWATER, JENNIE MARIA
(1841-1900)
Amer. author
McHenry--Liberty's p109

DRISCOLL, CLARA (1881-1945)
Amer. clubwoman, philan-
thropist, politician
James--Notable (1) p523-524
McHenry--Liberty's p109-110
Sherr--American p220,223

DRISCOLL, MARGARET CONNORS
(1915-)
Amer. judge, noted Connecticut mother
Amer.--Mothers p81, por.

DRIVERS, MRS. W. (fl. 1940's)
Australian golfer
McWhirter--Guinness p79

DROSTE-HÜLSHOFF, ANNETTE
ELISABETH, FRELIN VON
(1797-1848)
German poet
Who Did What p95

DROUET, MINOU (1947-)
French child poet
Book--Lists (2) p224
Crosland--Women p166-171, por.

DROWN, RUTH (fl. 1920's)
Amer. "radio" osteopath
Felton--Famous p228-229

DRU, JOANNE (1923-)
Amer. actress, TV performer
World--Who p232

DRUMMOND, JUNE (1923-)
South African novelist
Seymour-Smith--Novels p130

DRUMMOND, SARAH PRESCOTT
(fl. c1670's)
Amer. colonial politician,
lecturer
Williams--Demeter's p162-163

DRYDEN, RUTH TAMM (1923-)
Amer. genealogical researcher,
author
Meyer--Who's p64

DRYSDALE, BARBARA
British founder, school for
psychopathic children
Macksey--Book p77

DuBARRY, MARIE JEANNE BECU,
COMTESSE (1743/1746-1793)
French, mistress of Louis XV,
courtesan
Fry--1000 p190
Jones--Rutledge p240
Macksey--Book p99-100
Who Did What p95
World--Who p296

DUBOIS, SHIRLEY GRAHAM
See GRAHAM, SHIRLEY

DUBROW, EVELYN (fl. 1970's)
Amer. labor leader
O'Neill--Women's p285,299-300

DUBROW, MARCIA
 Amer. feminist, editor,
 journalist
 Marzolf--Up p106-107
 O'Neill--Women's p462-463

DUCE, (MURSHIDA) IVY O. (fl.
 1900's-1970's)
 Amer. director
 Chinoy--Women p12,41-44, por.

DUCHE, ESTHER
 See HILL, ESTHER DUCHE

DUCHEMIN, CATHERINE (fl. c1663)
 French artist
 Fine--Women p43

DUCHESNE, ROSE PHILIPPINE
 (1769-1852)
 Amer. missionary, nun, con-
 vent founder
 James--Notable (1) p524-526
 McHenry--Liberty's p110
 Neidle--America's p75
 People's Almanac (1) p1301

"THE DUCHESS," pseud.
 See HUNGERFORD, MARGARET
 HAMILTON

DUCKWORTH, RUTH (1919-)
 German ceramicist
 O'Neill--Women's p267

DuCOUDRAY, ANGELIQUE
 MARGUERITE, MADAME
 See LEBOURSIER, ANGELIQUE
 MARGUERITE DuCOURDRAY,
 MADAME

DUDAROVA, VERONICA (fl.
 1960's)
 Russian orchestra director,
 conductor
 Macksey--Book p221
 Mandel--Soviet p148-149

DUDEVANT, AMANDINE LUCILE
 AURORE DUPIN
 See SAND, GEORGE, pseud.

DUDLEY, DOROTHY (-1643)
 Amer. colonist
 Williams--Demeter's p42-43

DUDLEY, JANE, LADY
 See GREY, JANE, LADY

DUDLEY, HELENA STUART (1858-
 1932)
 Amer. settlement worker,
 pacifist, social reformer
 James--Notable (1) p526-527

DUDLEY, MARY WINTHROP (fl.
 1630's-1650's)
 Amer. colonist pioneer
 Williams--Demeter's p59-60,77-80

DUDZIAK, URSZULA (1943-)
 Polish singer, percussionist,
 synthesizer
 Claghorn--Jazz p96

DUDZIK, JOSEPHINE
 Polish-Amer. Civil War nurse,
 welfare worker
 Neidle--America's p75

DUERKE, ALENE BERTHA (1920-)
 Amer. Navy Admiral, nurse
 Cur. Biog. '73 p109-110, por.
 O'Neill--Women's p541

DUFAU, CLEMENTINE HELENE,
 MADEMOISELLE (1879-)
 French painter
 Sparrow--Women p182,231,240,243

DUFF, MARY ANN DYKE (1794/
 1795-1857)
 English-Amer. actress
 James--Notable (1) p527-529
 McHenry--Liberty's p110-111

DUFFEE, MARY GORDON
 Amer. Confederate poet, patriot
 Sherr--American p1

DUFFY, MARY (fl. 1900's)
 Amer. suffragist
 Millstein--We p187-188

DUFFY, MAUREEN (1933-)
 English novelist
 Seymour-Smith--Novels p130
 Seymour-Smith--Who's p101

DUGES, MARIE-JONET, MADAME
 (1730-1797)
 French midwife, writer,
 obstetrician
 Marks--Women p67
 Mead--Hist. p497-498

DUGES, MARIE LOUISE (1769-1821)

French obstetrician, medical
writer
Mead--Hist. p497-499

DUGOW, IRIS (1947-)
Amer. TV executive
Scheuer--Tel. p136

DUIGNAN-WOODS, EILEEN (fl.
1970's)
Amer. engineer
O'Neill--Women's p142

DU JARDIN, ROSAMOND NEAL
(1902-1963)
Amer. novelist, short-story
writer, poet
Ehrlich--Oxford p317,324-326

DUKE, DORIS (1912-)
Amer. heiress, journalist,
fashion editor, millionaire
Clark--Leading p158
Forbes--400 ('84) p119

DUKE, PATTY (ANNA MARIE)
(1946/1947-)
Amer. actress
Edelson--Kids p108-110, por.
Scheuer--Tel. p137
Woman's Almanac p53
World--Who p232

DUKE, ROBIN (1954-)
Canadian actress
Scheuer--Tel. p136, por.

DUKERT, BETTY (fl. 1970's)
Amer. TV producer
Klever--Women p131-134, por.

DULAC, GERMAINE (1882-1942)
French film producer
O'Neill--Women's p666-667
Smith--Movies p112-114

DULCIE OF WORMS (-1213)
Jewish scholar, martyr
Henry--Written p87

DU MAURIER, DAPHNE, LADY
BROWNING (1907-)
English novelist, playwright
Avenel--Comp. (1) p163
Baker--Women p6
Jones--Rutledge p243-244
Macksey--Book p192-192, por.
Magill--Cycl. p322-323

O'Neill--Women's p679,693
Seymour-Smith--Novels p130-131,
por.
World--Who p25

DUMESNIL, MARIE-FRANCOISE
(1711/1713-1803)
French actress
Entertainers p91-92

DUMMER, ETHEL STURGES (1866-
1954)
Amer. philanthropist
Sicherman--Notable p208-210

DUMON, MARTE
Belgian radio broadcaster
Marzolf--Up p285

DUMONT, (EMMA) ELEANORE
(-1879)
Amer. frontier saloon keeper,
gambler, pioneer
Reifert--Women p138
Sherr--American p16,144

DUMONT, LARYSE
French air force officer
O'Neill--Women's p552

DUMONT, MARGARET (1889/1890-
1965)
Amer. actress
Mordden--Movie p102, por.
Springer--They p94,289-290, por.

DUNA, STEFFI (fl. 1930's)
Hungarian actress
Springer--They p94,290, por.

DUNAWAY, (DOROTHY) FAYE
(1941-)
Amer. actress
Anderson--People p136-137, por.
Cur. Biog. '72 p114-117, por.
Hirschhorn--Rating p125, por.
Manchel--Women p14, por.
Shipman--Internatl. p154-156, por.
Woman's Almanac p340
World--Who p232

DUNBAR, BONNIE
Amer. astronaut
Oberg--Space p39,46,189,218,
231, por.
O'Connor--Sally p2,22, por.

DUNBAR, DIXIE (1918/1919-)

Amer. actress
Lamaprski--What. (8) p90-91,
por.
Springer--They p94,290, por.

DUNBAR, HELEN FLANDERS
(1902-1959)
Amer. psychiatrist, psychoanalyst
Sicherman--Notable p210-212

DUNBAR, ROXANNE (fl. 1970's)
Amer. feminist, writer
Sochen--Movers p16,257,261-262

DUNCAN, ANNE (fl. c1800)
Amer., mother of five
famous sons
Sherr--American p80

DUNCAN, DORA ANGELA
See DUNCAN, ISADORA

DUNCAN, EVELYNE WEEKS
(1906-)
Amer. community worker,
noted Missouri mother
Amer.--Mothers p315-316, por.

DUNCAN, ISADORA (1878-1927)
Amer. dancer
Brecher--Lives p343-344
Clark--Leading p34-36
Donaldson--How p102-103
Dunlap--Calif. p59, por.
Epstein--Indiv. p107-128
Fabian--On p124-126, por.
Ingraham--Album p62
James--Notable (1) p529-531
Jones--Rutledge p244
Longstreet--Queen p192
McHenry--Liberty's p111
Macksey--Book p230
Marlowe--Great p226-232, por.
May--Different p58-80, por.
Miller--Women p177-198
Millstein--We p207
People's Almanac (1) p871-872
People's Almanac (2) p1197
Richey--Eminent p209-235, por.
Rogers--Ladies p4,151-152
Sherr--American p19, por.
Signif.--Amer. p40, por.
Starr--Amer. p261,370,382-385,
por.
Stoddard--Famous p149-161, por.
Warren--Pictorial p154-155, por.

Webster's--Amer. p297
Who Did What p97-98, por.
Woman's Almanac p308-309, por.
World--Who p70

DUNCAN, MARILYN AREND (1930-)
Amer. genealogical researcher,
author, editor
Meyer--Who's p64

DUNCAN, MARY (1903-)
Amer. actress
Springer--They p94,290, por.

DUNCAN, SANDY (1946-)
Amer. actress
Cur. Biog. '80 p85-88, por.
People--Best p162, por.
World--Who p232

DUNCAN, VIVIAN (1902-)
Amer. actress, entertainer
Lamparski--What (3) p158-159,
por.

DUNCAN, SISTERS (VIVIAN AND
ROSETTA)
Amer. actresses
Hazen--Interv. p405-406
Springer--They p94,290, por.

DUNDY, ELAINE (1927-)
Amer. novelist
Seymour-Smith--Novels p131

DUNHAM, DANA
Amer. labor leader
O'Neill--Women's p302

DUNHAM, ETHEL COLLINS (1883-
1969)
Amer. pediatrician
Sicherman--Notable p212-213

DUNHAM, KATHERINE (1910-)
Amer. dancer, choreographer,
anthropologist
Adams--Great (3rd) p169, por.
Kulkin--Her p92-93
Longstreet--Queen p192
McHenry--Liberty's p111-112
O'Neill--Women's p649
Richardson--Great p72-81, por.
Signif.--Amer. p61, por.
Toppin--Biog. p289-290
Webster's--Amer. p297
Who Did What p98

Woman's Almanac p309
World--Who p70

DUNIWAY, ABIGAIL JANE SCOTT
(1834-1915)
Amer. teacher, pioneer,
feminist, suffragist
Hymowitz--Hist. p178-179
James--Notable (1) p531-533
Millstein--We p56-57,66-67
Reifert--Women p193-197
Richey--Eminent p73-96, por.
Sherr--American p57,196, por.
Time--Women p17-18,196,219,
221-225
Warren--Pictorial p121-122

DUNKLEMAN, LORETTA (fl. 1970's)
Amer. artist (drawing)
Women's--Female p25

DUNLAP, KATE (fl. 1860's)
Amer. teacher, diarist
Sherr--American p137

DUNLAP, LOUISE (fl. 1970's)
Amer. environmentalist
O'Neill--Women's p723-724

DUNLOP, MAREEN (fl. 1940's)
British ferry pilot, aviatrix
Boase--Sky's p193-195, por.

DUNN, IRENE MARIE
See DUNNE, IRENE MARIE

DUNN, JOSEPHINE (1906-)
Amer. actress
Springer--They p94,290, por.

DUNN, NATALIE (c1956-)
Amer. roller-skater
O'Neill--Women's p565

DUNN, NELL (1936-)
English novelist, journalist
Seymour-Smith--Novels p131

DUNNALLY, MARY
See DONALY, MARY

DUNNE, IRENE MARIE (1898/
1904-)
Amer. actress
Hazen--Interv. p402-403
Hirschhorn--Rating p125-126,
por.

Lamparski--What. (8) p94-95, por.
Mordden--Movie p93,100-101,150-
151,216,256, por.
Springer--They p94-96,290, por.
Shipman--Gold. p179-181, por.
Wilson--Holly. p99-101, por.
World--Who p232

DUNNE, MARY CHAVELITA (1859-
1945)
Australian story writer
Showalter--Lit. p210-215,340

DUNNETT, DOROTHY (1923-)
Scottish, portrait painter,
novelist
Seymour-Smith--Novels p131

DUNNEWALD, HELEN BISHOP
(1891-)
Amer. Dean of Women, noted
Wyoming mother
Amer.--Mothers p597-598, por.

DUNNIGAN, ALICE ALLISON (1906-)
Amer. journalist, White House
correspondent
O'Neill--Women's p450

DUNNING, EMILY
See BARRINGER, EMILY DUN-
NING

DUNNOCK, MILDRED (1900/1906-)
Amer. actress
Entertainers p215, por.
World--Who p232

DUNWOODY, GWYNETH
English Parliament member
Vallance--Women p29,61,65,68,
104

DU PARC, THERESE DE GLORIA,
MARQUISE (1633-1668)
French actress
Entertainers p66

DUPARE, FRANCOISE (1726-1778)
French artist
Harris--Women p42,171-173,180,
188,346
Petersen--Women p49-50

DUPIN, AMANDINE LUCILE AURORE
See SAND, GEORGE, pseud.

DU PLESSIS, MARIE ALICE
    BRADFORD (1824-1847)
    French, inspiration for
    Dumas' "Marguerite Gautier"
    Book--Lists (1) p239

DU PONT, EVELYN REBECCA
    (c1925-)
    Amer. millionaire
    Forbes--400 ('84) p190

DU PONT, HELENA ALLAIRE
    (c1920-)
    Amer. millionaire
    Forbes--400 ('84) p112,114

DU PONT, IRENEE JR. (fl. 1980's)
    Amer. millionaire
    Forbes--400 ('84) p149

DU PRE, JACQUELINE (1945-)
    English cellist
    Cur. Biog. '70 p121-124, por.
    O'Neill--Women's p633

DUPREE, MINNIE (1875-1947)
    Amer. actress
    Springer--They p97,200, por.

DUPREY, ANA ROQUE DE (1853-)
    Puerto Rican, feminist, suf-
    fragist, noted Puerto Rico
    mother
    Amer.--Mothers p468

DUPUY, ELIZA ANN (1814-1880)
    Amer. novelist
    James--Notable (1) p533-535
    Sherr--American p128

DURACK, FANNY (fl. 1910's)
    Australian swimmer
    Assoc. Press--Pursuit p72, por.
    Macksey--Book p259
    McWhirter--Guinness p130,132,
    por.

DURAND, MARGUERITE (fl. 1900's)
    French journalist, publisher
    Marzolf--Up p272

DURANT, ARIEL K. (1898-1981)
    Amer. author, (wife of
    Will Durant)
    Ehrlich--Oxford p54,110,177,412
    P.W.--Author p435-438,491-492

DURANT, PAULINE (fl. 1870's)
    Amer. college trustee, feminist
    Sherr--American p114

DURAS, MARGUERITE DONNADIEU
    (1914-)
    Indo-Chinese-French novelist,
    playwright, film director, film
    writer
    Bree--Women p65-68
    Crosland--Women p158-164,218,
    240, por.
    Cur. Biog. '85 p98-101, por.
    Entertainers p242
    O'Neill--Women's p668
    Seymour-Smith--Novels p131
    Seymour-Smith--Who's p102-103
    Smith--Movies p123
    Who Did What p98
    Wintle--Makers p128,139-140
    World--Who p33

DUARTE, MARIA EVA
    See PERON, (MARIA) EVA
    (EVITA) DUARTE DE

DURBIN, DEANNA (1921/1922-)
    Canadian singer, actress
    Claghorn--Biog. p135
    Edelson--Kids p17,69-71, por.
    Hazen--Interv. p418-419
    Mordden--Movie p196-198,200,
    205,218,246
    Shipman--Gold. p182-184, por.
    Springer--They p97-98,290-291,
    por.
    World--Who p232

DURGUN, DOROTHY ANN
    Amer., first Shaker "eldress"
    Sherr--American p146

DURIEUX, TILLA (1880-1971)
    Austrian actress
    Entertainers p169

DUROVA, NADEZHADA (1783-1866)
    Russian cavalry officer
    Mandel--Soviet p19-20

DURRANT, JENNIFER (1942-)
    British artist
    Contemp. Brit. unp., por.

DURST, ANI
    Amer. co-founder, carpenter
    O'Neill--Women's p318

DURYEA, VIOLA
See ALLEN, VIOLA EMILY

DUSE, ELEANORA (1858/1859-1924)
Italian actress
Entertainers p143,146
Jones--Rutledge p247
O'Neill--Women's p655
People's Almanac (2) p769-770
Who Did What p99
World--Who p256

DUSENBURY, ELINOR (fl. 1830's-
1970's)
Amer., Alaskan composer of
Alaska's flag song
Jones--Women (1) p157
Sherr--American p4

DUSIAK, MICHELE
See LEE, MICHELE

DUSSAULT, NANCY (1936-)
Amer. actress
Scheuer--Tel. p138

DUSSEK, JOSEPHA HAMBACHER
(1754-1824)
Czechoslovakian singer
Partington--Who's p105

DUSTON (DUSTIN), HANNAH
(1657-c1736)
Amer., noted New Hampshire
mother, Indian captive,
heroine
Amer.--Mothers p357, por.
James--Notable (1) p535-536
McHenry--Liberty's p112-113
Macksey--Book p53, por.
Neidle--America's p4
Reifert--Women p20-21
Sherr--American p97,106,146,
148
Warren--Pictorial p23
Williams--Demeter's p163-165

DU TERTRE, CATHERINE
GERTRUDE SCHRADERS
See CRAMER, VROW

DUTRIEUX, HELENE (c1877-1961)
French aviatrix
Boase--Sky's p12

DUTRUMBLE, GLORIA (fl. 1970's)
Amer. cook
Cohen--Meet p29-35, por.

DUTT, TORU (1856-1877)
East Indian poet, musician,
essayist, scholar
Avenel--Comp. (1) p166

DUVALL, SHELLEY (1950-)
Amer. actress
Hirschhorn--Rating p128, por.
World--Who p232

DUVERNAY, PAULINE
English ballet dancer
Migel--Ballerinas p226-228

DUX, CLAIRE (1885-1967)
Polish opera singer
Claghorn--Biog. p135

DVORAK, ANN (1912-1979)
Amer. actress
Lamparski--What. (2) p160-161,
por.
Springer--They p98,291, por.

DVORETSKAYA, MARTRYONA
Russian worker
Mandel--Soviet p43

DWIGHT, MARGARET VAN HORN
Amer. traveller
Earnest--American p54-55

DWIGHT, MARIANNE
Amer., Brook Farm subscriber
Epstein--Indiv. p97-98,102-103

DWIGHT, MINNIE RYAN (1873-1957)
Amer. feminist, noted Massa
chusetts mother
Amer.--Mothers p262-263, por.

DWYER, DORIOT ANTHONY (fl.
1940's-1970's)
Amer. orchestra "chair-
holder," flutist
O'Neill--Women's p633-634

DWYER, FLORENCE P. (1902-1976)
Amer. Congresswoman
Chamberlin--Min. p269-272
U.S.--Women (89th) p7, por.
U.S.--Women (90th) p5, por.

DWYER, KAREN (fl. 1970's)
Amer. baker
Felton--Famous p74-75

DWYER-DOBBIN, MARY ALICE

McHenry--Liberty's p115
Mead--Hist. p458-459,482-483

EARLE, SYLVIA A. (1935-)
Amer. oceanographer
Teitz--What's p100-123, por.

EARLE, VICTORIA
See MATTHEWS, VICTORIA
EARLE

EARLY, DELLOREESE PATRICIA
See REESE, DELLA

EARLY, MRS. JOHN CABELL
See CABELL, MARY WASHING-
TON

EARLY, PENNY ANN (c1943-)
Amer. jockey
Hollander--100 p65
McWhirter--Guinness p92

EASSON, MARY (fl. 1770's)
English-Amer. Tory
Booth--Women p32-33

EAST, ELIZABETH ANN THOMP-
SON (1849-1901)
Amer. teacher, noted
Mississippi mother
Amer.--Mothers p298, por.

EASTLAKE, ELIZABETH RIGBY,
LADY (1809-1893)
English art critic
Basch--Relative, see index p357
Moers--Literary p42,287

EASTMAN, ANNIS BERTHA FORD
(1852-1910)
Amer. clergyman, intellectual
James--Notable (1) p542-543
Sherr--American p160

EASTMAN, CAROLE (fl. 1970's)
Amer. film writer
Smith--Movies p73-74

EASTMAN, CRYSTAL (1881-1928)
Amer. social reformer,
feminist, pacifist
James--Notable (1) p543-545
Showalter--These p86-92, por.
Sochen--Herstory p234,266-267,
see also index p440
Sochen--Movies, see index p313

EASTMAN, HOPE (fl. 1970's)
Amer. lawyer
O'Neill--Women's p356-357

EASTMAN, LINDA ANNE (1867-1963)
Amer. librarian
Sicherman--Notable p215-216

EASTMAN, MARY BUTLER (-1837)
Amer., noted New Hampshire
mother, Revolutionary patriot
Amer.--Mothers p358

EASTMAN, MARY HENDERSON (1818-
1887)
Amer. author
Ehrlich--Oxford, see index p452
James--Notable (1) p545-546
McHenry--Liberty's p115

EASTON, FLORENCE (1884-1955)
English opera singer
Tuggle--Golden p150-151,176, por.

EASTWOOD, ALICE (1859-1953)
Canadian-Amer. botanist,
author, adventurer
Sicherman--Notable p216-217

EASTWOOD, ELIZABETH C. (1910-)
Amer. genealogical researcher,
author
Meyer--Who's p67

EATON, MRS. A.B.
Amer. founder, Ladies Pro-
tection & Relief Society
Time--Women p105

EATON, MARGARET (PEGGY)
O'NEALE (1799-1879)
Amer. socialite, hostess, wife
of Secretary Eaton
James--Notable (1) p546-548
McHenry--Liberty's p115-116
Peacock--Famous p69-79
Sherr--American p217
Webster's--Amer. p310

EAVES, ELSIE (1898-)
Amer. civil engineer
O'Neill--Women's p187

EBERHART, MIGNON GOOD (1899-)
Amer. novelist
P.W.--Author p192-194,493-494
Seymour-Smith--Novels p132
World--Who p46

EBERHART, NELLE RICHMOND
(1871-1944)
Amer. teacher, lyricist,
composer
Claghorn--Biog. p137

EBERLE, (MARY) ABASTENIA
ST. LEGER (1878-1942)
Amer. sculptor
James--Notable (1) p548-549

EBERLY, ANGELINA B. (-1860)
Amer. innkeeper, friend of
Sam Houston
Sherr--American p220

EBIGWEI, PATRICIA (fl. 1960's)
Nigerian actress
Keenan--Women p176, por.

EBNER-ESCHENBACH, MARIE VON,
BARONESS (1830-1916)
Austrian novelist
Sorell--Three p172,216

EBURNE, MAUDE (1875-1960)
Canadian actress
Springer--They p101,291, por.

ECKER, HEIDE ROSENDAHL
See ROSENDAHL, HEIDE

ECKHERT, JULIE
Amer. TV correspondent
Scheuer--Tel. p141

ECKSTEIN-DIENER, HELEN
See DINER, HELEN, pseud.

ECKSTORM, FANNIE PEARSON
HARDY (1865-1946)
Amer. writer, ornithologist,
Indian authority
James--Notable (1) p549-551
McHenry--Liberty's p116
Sherr--American p87

EDDY, BERNICE (fl. 1950's)
Amer. physician, biological
researcher
O'Neill--Women's p221

EDDY, HELEN JEROME (1897-)
Amer. actress
Springer--They p101,291,
por.

EDDY, MARY BAKER (1821-1910)
Amer., noted New Hampshire
mother, religious leader,
founder of Christian Science
Amer.--Mothers p363, por.
Bird--Enterprising p118-122
Bloom--Religion p50-75, por.
Claghorn--Biog. p138
Forma--They, see index p240,
por.
Fry--1000 p257
James--Notable (1) p551-561
Jones--Rutledge p250-251
Kostman--20th p3-20, por.
Kulkin--Her p96-97
Kupferberg--First p50
McHenry--Liberty's p116-117
Macksey--Book p115-116
Marlowe--Great p90-95, por.
O'Neill--Women's p379
People's Almanac (1) p776,1268
People's Almanac (2) p1163-1164
Sherr--American p97,99-101,107,
112-113,146-149, see index
(unpaged), por.
Signif.--Amer. p18, por.
Stoddard--Famous p173-180, por.
Warren--Pictorial p131
Webster's--Amer. p310-311
Who Did What p100
Woman's Almanac p403-404, por.
World--Who p81

EDELHEIT, MARTHA (fl. 1970's)
Amer. artist
Women's--Female p103

EDELMAN, JUDITH (fl. 1970's)
Amer. architect
O'Neill--Women's p611

EDELMAN, MARIAN WRIGHT (1939-)
Amer. lawyer, politician, co-
founder, Children's Defense
Fund
O'Neill--Women's p707,728-729
Teitz--What's p52-71, por.

EDELSHEIM-GYULA, ILONA,
COUNTESS
See HORTHY DE NAGBANYA,
MAGDALENE PURGLY DE
JOSZAHELY

EDELSON, MARY BETH (fl. 1970's)
Amer. painter

Petersen--Women p126,138-139
Women's--Female p40

EDELSTEIN, GERTRUDE
See BERG, GERTRUDE

EDELSTEIN, SUSAN (fl. 1970's)
Amer. adventurer, govern-
ment official
Lichtenstein--Mach. p337-340

EDEN, BARBARA (1924-)
Amer. actress
World--Who p232

EDER, EDITH (-1944)
Hungarian, co-founder
Zionist organization
Macksey--Book p119-120

EDERLE, GERTRUDE ("TRUDY")
CAROLINE (1906/1907-)
Amer. swimmer
Clark--Leading p111
Hazen--Interv. p398
Hollander--100 p81,90-91, por.
Ingraham--Album p50
Longstreet--Queen p192-193
McHenry--Liberty's p117
Macksey--Book p259, por.
McWhirter--Guinness p8,146,
por.
O'Neill--Women's p586
Pachter--Champ. p170, por.
People's Almanac (1) p1240-1241
Ryan--Sports p128-129
Warren--Pictorial p185
Webster's--Amer. p311
Woman's Almanac p429-430, por.
World--Who p212

EDEY, MARION (fl. 1970's)
Amer. politician
Teitz--What's p165-187, por.

EDGEWORTH, MARIA (1767-1849)
Irish novelist, educator,
feminist
Avenel--Comp. (1) p167
Jones--Rutledge p251
Kronenberger--Atlan. p251
Macksey--Book p183
Magill--Cycyl. p327-328
Moers--Literary p325, see
also index, p287
Morley--Literary, see index
p486

Seymour-Smith--Novels p132
Who Did What p100

EDINGER, TILLY (1897-1967)
German-Amer. vertibrate
paleontologist, paleoneurologist
Sicherman--Notable p218-219

EDISON, MINA MILLER (c1865-1947)
Amer., wife of Thomas Edison
People's Almanac (2) p859-860

EDISON, NANCY ELLIOTT (1810-
1871)
Canadian, mother of Thomas
A. Edison
Diagram--Mothers p68-69, por.

EDMISTON, SUSAN (fl. 1970's)
Amer. writer
Teitz--What's p247-271, por.

EDMONDS, (SARAH) EMMA E.
(1841-1898)
Amer. Union Civil War spy,
male-impersonator
Felton--Famous p40
Hoople--As p89-97
Ingraham--Album p29, por.
James--Notable (1) p561-562
Millstein--We p122,131, por.
People's Almanac (1) p648
Sherr--American p222
Warren--Pictorial p109-110
Woman's Almanac p453
World--Who p175

EDMONSTON, CATHERINE ANN (fl.
1860's)
Amer. Confederate Civil War
letter-writer
Wiley--Confed. p169-170

EDSON, KATHERINE PHILIPS (1870-
1933)
Amer. social reformer, govern-
ment official
James--Notable (1) p562-564
McHenry--Liberty's p117-118
O'Neill--Women's p341

EDWARDS, AMELIA ANN BLANFORD
(1831-1892)
English novelist, Egyptologist
Showalter--Lit. p331

EDWARDS, ELAINE SCHWARTZENBURG

(1929-   )
Amer. Senator, noted
Louisiana mother, state,
community worker, gover-
nor's wife
Amer.--Mothers p233-234, por.
Chamberlin--Min. p346-349

EDWARDS, EMILY J. (-1876)
British pottery decorator,
designer
Callen--Women p222

EDWARDS, ESTHER (-1756)
Amer. journal writer
Williams--Demeter's p110-111

EDWARDS, ESTHER G. (fl. 1970's)
Amer. executive, (record
company)
O'Neill--Women's p519

EDWARDS, JOAN (1919-1981)
Amer. composer, singer,
songwriter, author
Cur. Biog. '81 p462

EDWARDS, LOUISA E. (fl.
1870's-1890's)
British pottery designer,
decorator
Callen--Women p72,223, por.

EDWARDS, SARAH PIERPONT
(1710-1758)
Amer. Puritan mystic,
frontier housekeeper, (wife
of Jonathan Edwards)
James--Notable (1) p564-565
Warren--Pictorial p39

EGAN, JOGUES, SISTER (1918-   )
Irish-Amer. nun
Smith--Break. p59-90, por.

EGAN, NEVA (fl. 1950's-1960's)
Amer., Alaskan First Lady
Jones--Women (1) p190-197,
por.

EGBERT, ERCELL JAN (1895-   )
Amer., noted Kentucky mother,
English professor
Amer.--Mothers p222

EGERIA, ABBESS

Spanish writer
Neuls-Bates--Women p4

EGERTON, GEORGE, pseud.
See DUNNE, MARY CHAVELITA

EGGAR, SAMANTHA (1929-   )
English actress
World--Who p256

EGGERS, MARIE
German potter
Callen--Women p78

EGGLESTON, ESTELLE
See STEVENS, STELLA

EGLESFIELD, MRS. ROBERT
See GRIFFITH, MARIA THONG
PATTERSON

EGSTROM, NORMA DELORES
See LEE, PEGGY

EHINGER, ALINE N. (1891-   )
Amer., noted Delaware mother,
community worker, teacher
Amer.--Mothers p88-89, por.

EHLERS, ALICE (1890-   )
Austrian harpsichordist
Claghorn--Biog. p139

EHMANN, FREDA (-1932)
Amer. executive
Sherr--American p16-17, por.

EHRHARDT, ANNELIE (fl. 1970's)
East German track and field
athlete
McWhirter--Guinness p177, por.

EICHHOLZ, ALICE (1942-   )
Amer. genealogical researcher,
author
Meyer--Who's p68

EID, AIDA (fl. 1950's-1970's)
Lebanese agricultural economist
O'Neill--Women's p38

EIDELE
Hasidic Jew (wife of Rabbi
Isaac Rubin)
Henry--Written p209-210

EIGENMANN, ROSA SMITH (1858-1957)

Amer. ichthyologist
James--Notable (1) p565-566

EILERS, SALLY (DOROTHEA
SALLYE) (1908-)
Amer. actress
Lamparski--What. (4) p114-115,
por.
Springer--They p101-102,291,
por.

EINSTEIN, HANNAH BACHMAN
(1862-1929)
Amer. social worker
James--Notable (1) p566-568
McHenry--Liberty's p118
Neidle--America's p47

EINSTEIN, PAULINE KOCH
(1858-1920)
German, mother of Albert
Einstein
Diagram--Mothers p70-71, por.

EISEMAN, FLORENCE (1899-)
Amer. children's clothing
designer
O'Neill--Women's p261

EISEMANN-SCHIER, RUTH (fl.
1960's)
Honduran accused criminal
People's Almanac (1) p612
Woman's Almanac p508

EISENBLÄTTER, CHARLOTTE
(1903-1944)
German Nazi victim
Partington--Who's p108

EISENHOWER, IDA ELIZABETH
STOVER (1862-1946)
Amer., noted Iowa mother,
mother of Dwight Eisenhower
Amer.--Mothers p206-207, por.
Diagram--Mothers p72-73, por.
Faber--Presidents' p66-81, por.

EISENHOWER, JULIE NIXON
(1948-)
Amer. writer, (daughter of
President Nixon)
Anderson--People p141
100--Greatest (1) p8, por.
Schoenebaum--Prof. p188-189
Woman's Almanac p494

EISENHOWER, MAMIE GENEVA

DOUD (1896-1979)
Amer. First Lady, (wife of
Dwight Eisenhower)
Amer.--Mothers p ix, por.
Cur. Biog. '80 p454
Hershey--Between p53-55,155
Melick--Wives p76-78, por.
100--Greatest (1) p6, por.
People's Almanac (1) p276
Woman's Almanac p492

EISENSCHNEIDER, ELVIRA (1924-
after 1944)
German patriot, (Nazi victim)
Partington--Who's p109

EITZEN, SARAH BLOCK (1840-1917)
Amer., noted Iowa mother,
Mennonite, pioneer, midwife
Amer.--Mothers p203-204, por.

EKLUND, BRITT (1942-)
Swedish actress
People--Best p67, por.
World--Who p256

ELAM, MERRILL
Amer. architect
O'Neill--Women's p611

ELDEN, GENEVIEVE
Amer. volunteer worker
Gold--Until p335-336

ELDER, RUTH (1904-1977)
Amer. pioneer aviatrix, pilot
Hazen--Interv. p368
Macksey--Book p248

ELDRIDGE, FLORENCE (1901-)
Amer. actress
Springer--They p102,291, por.
World--Who p232

ELDRIDGE, MARIE D. (1926-)
Amer. government official
O'Neill--Women's p85

ELDRIDGE, MARY AGNES PROWSE
(1896-)
Amer., noted Nevada mother,
teacher
Amer.--Mothers p353, por.

ELDRIDGE, RONNIE (c1930-)
Amer. politician
Diamonstein--Open p107-111,
por.

Showalter--Lit. p326
Smith--Women p83-117
Woman's Almanac p251, por.
World--Who p25

ELIOT, (MAMA) CASS (c1940-1973)
Amer. singer
Simon--Best p370-372, por.

ELIOT, MARTHA MAY (1891-1978)
Amer. pediatrician, govern-
ment official
Cur. Biog. '78 p468
O'Neill--Women's p227

ELIOT-LYNN, SOPHIE
See HEATH, SOPHIE, LADY

ELISABATH (MORDECAI [MICHALS]
OF SLUTZK) (fl. 1700's)
Jewish translator
Henry--Written p118

ELISABETH OF BRANDENBURG
(1485-1545)
German Reformation worker
Bainton--Germany p111-124,
por.

ELISABETH OF BRAUNSCHWEIG
(1510-1558)
German Reformation worker
Bainton--Germany p125-144, por.

ELISSA
See DIDO

ELIZABETH (1)
Biblical, (mother of John
the Baptist)
Price--God p140-144

ELIZABETH (2), pseud.
See RUSSELL, ELIZABETH
MARY ANNETTE BEAU-
CHAMP, COUNTESS VON
ARNIM

ELIZABETH (3)
Polish-Hungarian medical
woman, (sister of Casimir
the Great)
Mead--Hist. p273-274

ELIZABETH, COUNTESS OF KENT
See KENT, ELIZABETH,
COUNTESS

ELIZABETH I (1533-1603)
British queen
Bainton--France p231-251, por.
Bernikow--World p51
Book--Lists (2) p421
Canning--100 p438-443
Davis--Women p39-59, por.
Delderfield--Kings p74-76, por.
Donaldson--How p110
Earle--Two Cent. (1) p21-23,
64 66,89,124
Earle--Two Cent. (2) p430-431,
433-434
Fry--1000 p139-140, por.
Jones--Rutledge p260-261
Kulkin--Her p98-99
Macksey--Book p24-26, por.
Marlowe--Great p17-22, por.
Mead--Hist. p339,342,381
Softly--Queens p77-80, por.
Warren--Pictorial p2-3
Who Did What p104
Williams--Demeter's p26,105-106
Woman's Almanac p461-462, por.
World--Who p156

ELIZABETH II (1926-)
British queen
Delderfield--Kings p136,145, por.
Hamblin--That p245-247
Holme--Journal p256-257, por.
Jones--Rutledge p261
Keenan--Women p21,26, por.
Kulkin--Her p100-101
Miller--Fishbait p350-353, por.
O'Neill--Women's p48
Palmer--Who's p117
Softly--Queens p124-126
Who Did What p104-105
Woman's Almanac p466-467, por.
World--Who p156

ELIZABETH BOWES-LYON (1900-)
British "Queen Mother,"
(Consort of George VI)
Cur. Biog. '81 p136-139, por.
Diagram--Mothers p76-81, por.
Jones--Rutledge p260
Keenan--Women p19-21, por.
Softly--Queens p122-124, por.

ELIZABETH, AMELIA EUGENIE
(1837-1898)
Austrian empress, (wife of

Francis Joseph)
Jones--Rutledge p259

ELIZABETH (CHARLOTTE JOSEPHINE
VICTORIA ALEXANDRA) (1894-
1956)
Rumanian princess, Grecian
queen
Partington--Who's p111

ELIZABETH OF ARAGON (1271-1336)
Portuguese queen, hospital
founder
Mead--Hist. p219

ELIZABETH OF BOHEMIA (1618-
1680)
Bohemian princess, abbess,
linguist, scholar, medical
woman
Mead--Hist. p424
People's Almanac (2) p1153

ELIZABETH OF HUNGARY, SAINT
(1207-1231)
Hungarian Saint, (daughter of
Andrew II, King of Hungary),
physician
Jones--Rutledge p261
Kulkin--Her p101-102
Mead--Hist. p221-222, por.
Partington--Who's p111

ELIZABETH OF PORTUGAL (fl.
15th cent.)
Portuguese queen
Mead--Hist. p311

ELIZABETH OF SCHÖNAU (1129-
1165)
German woman of medicine,
founder of nunnery
Marks--Women p47
Mead--Hist. p180,194

ELIZABETH OF YORK (1465/
1466-1503)
British queen
Jones--Rutledge p261
Softly--Queens p53-56, por.

ELIZABETH (PAULINE ELIZABETH
OTTILIE LOUISE) (1843-
1916)
Rumanian queen, (Consort
of Carol I)
Jones--Rutledge p145
Partington--Who's p112,404

ELIZABETH PETROVNA (1709-1762)
Russian empress, (daughter
of Peter the Great)
Jones--Rutledge p260
Macksey--Book p28

ELIZABETH STUART (1596-1662)
Bohemian queen
Jones--Rutledge p259-260

ELIZABETH WOODVILLE (1437-1492)
English queen
Softly--Queens p49-52

ELLA OF DESSAU (fl. c1690's)
Jewish child printer
Henry--Written p119-120

ELLEN, MINETTA (fl. 1930's-1940's)
Amer. radio actress
Women--Radio p5

ELLENBOROUGH, JANE ELIZABETH
DIGBY ("ANTHA"), COUNTESS
(1807-1881)
English beauty
Book--Lists (2) p438-439

ELLERBEE, LINDA (1932-   )
Amer. TV anchor/correspondent
Scheuer--Tel. p143

ELLERMAN, (ANNIE) WINIFRED
See "BRYHER" (BRYER), pseud.

ELLERS, SALLY (1908-1978)
Amer. actress
Lamparski--What. (8) p96-97,
por.

ELLET, ELIZABETH FRIES LUMMIS
(1812-1818-1877)
Amer. author, historian
James--Notable (1) p569-570
McHenry--Liberty's p119
Meyer--Petticoat, see index p247
Millstein--We p75

ELLICKSON, KATHERINE POLLAK
(fl. 1930's-1960's)
Amer. labor leader
O'Neill--Women's p298-299

ELLINGTON, KATHRYN
Amer. neurologist
Bowman--Medicine p15-19, por.

"ELLIOTT"
See ROADS, FRANC

ELLIOTT, COLLEEN MORSE (1927-)
Amer. genealogical researcher,
author, editor
Meyer--Who's p68

ELLIOTT, ELIZABETH SHIPPEN
GREEN
See GREEN, ELIZABETH SHIPPEN

ELLIOTT, ELSIE (1914-)
British founder of schools in
Hong Kong
O'Neill--Women's p737

ELLIOTT, GERTRUDE
See FORBES-ROBERTSON,
GERTRUDE ELLIOTT, LADY

ELLIOTT, HARRIET WISEMAN
(1884-1947)
Amer. educator, politician,
government official
James--Notable (1) p572-574
McHenry--Liberty's p119

ELLIOTT, MAUD (1854-1948)
Amer. biographer
Macksey--Book p189

ELLIOTT, MAUD(E) HOWE
(1854-1948)
Amer. bilinguist (Indian
languages)
Ehrlich--Oxford p12,68
O'Neill--Women's p417

ELLIOTT, MAXINE (1868/1871-
1940)
Amer. actress
Clark--Leading p17-19
Entertainers p158
Forma--They p115, por.
Hazen--Interv. p100
James--Notable (1) p576-578
McHenry--Liberty's p119-120
Macksey--Book p232

ELLIOTT, MAY GERTRUDE
(1874-1950)
Amer. actress
Entertainers p164

ELLIOTT, SARAH BARNWELL
(1848-1928)
Amer. novelist, suffragist

James--Notable (1) p578-579
McHenry--Liberty's p120
Sherr--American p219

ELLIOTT, SUSANNAH SMITH (fl.
1750-1770's)
Amer. Revolutionary War
patriot
Meyer--Petticoat p166

ELLIOTT, WENDY L. (1939-)
Amer. genealogical researcher
Meyer--Who's p68-69

ELLIS, ANITA (1920-)
Canadian-Amer. singer
Balliet--Amer. p163-178

ELLIS, CAROLINE (fl. 1940's)
Amer. radio program conduc-
tor
Women--Radio p10

ELLIS, LIZZIE RUTHERFORD (fl.
1860's)
Amer. Civil War Confederate
patriot
Sherr--American p47

ELLIS, MARY (1899-)
Amer. opera singer, actress
Springer--They p102,291, por.

ELLIS, PATRICIA (1916-1970)
Amer. actress
Springer--They p102-103,291,
por.

ELLIS, PATRICIA A. (fl. 1970's)
Amer. insurance official
O'Neill--Women's p525

ELLIS, SARAH (1810-1872)
English novelist, essayist
Showalter--Lit. p324

ELLIS, MRS. THOMAS HARDING
See TAYLOR, FANNY

ELLISON, KATHERINE WHITE (fl.
1970's)
Amer. psychologist, professor
O'Neill--Women's p423

ELLISON, LILLIAN (fl. 1970's)
Amer. wrestler
Jordan--Broken p29-55

ELLSLER, EFFIE (1854/1855-1942)
Amer. actress
James--Notable (1) p579-580

ELLSWORTH, ABIGAIL WOLCOTT
(1756-1818)
Amer., wife of Chief Justice
Oliver Ellsworth
Earle--Two Cent. (2) p xxiii,
740, por.
Flexner--Face p154, por.

ELLSWORTH, ANNIE (fl. 1840's)
Amer. secretary, pioneer
telegraph message writer
Sherr--American p66

ELLY, AMELING (1938-)
Netherlands singer
Cur. Biog. '82 p8-10, por.

ELMENDORF, MARY (fl. 1770's)
Amer. Revolutionary War
patriot
Meyer--Petticoat p97

EL SAADAWI, NAWAL
See SAADAWI, NAWAL EL

ELSIE-JEAB
See STERN, ELIZABETH

ELSNER, GISELA (1937-)
German short story writer
Herrmann--Ger. p6,115

ELSSLER, FRANJZISKA ("FANNY")
(1810-1884)
Austrian dancer
Fabian--On p62-64, por.
Jones--Rutledge p262
Migel--Ballerinas p145-167, por.

ELSTNER, ANN (1937-)
Amer. radio actress
Lamparski--What. (3) p54-55,
por.

ELSTOB, ELIZABETH (1683-1765)
English scholar, governess,
author
Brink--Female p137-160, por.
Horner--English p25 (& note)

ELZEY, HAY
See ANDREWS, ELIZA
FRANCES

EMAROT, CELESTINE (MARGUERITE
ADELAIDE)
French ballet dancer
Migel--Ballerinas p233

EMBURY, EMMA CATHERINE (1806-
1863)
Amer. author
Welter--Dimity p79

EMECHETA, BUCHI (c1941-)
African (Nigerian) writer
McCullough--People p53-54

EMELIANOVA, HELEN (fl. 1970's)
Russian scholar, writer
Mandel--Soviet p64-65

EMERALD, MAUDE
See CUNARD, MAUD ALICE
BURKE, LADY

EMERSON, ALICE FREY (fl. 1970's)
Amer. college president
O'Neill--Women's p407

EMERSON, ELLEN RUSSELL (1837-
1907)
Amer. ethnologist
McHenry--Liberty's p120-121

EMERSON, FAYE (1917-1983)
Amer. actress, TV personality
Cur. Biog. '83 p464
Lamparski--What. (2) p30-31, por.

EMERSON, GLADYS ANDERSON
(1903-)
Amer. biochemist
Emberlin--Cont. p151-152

EMERSON, GLORIA (c1929-)
Amer. journalist (foreign
correspondent)
Diamonstein--Open p112-116, por.

EMERSON, MARY MOODY (1774-
1863)
Amer. intellectual
James--Notable (1) p580-582
Sherr--American p90,103

EMERUWA, LEATRICE W. (fl. 1970's)
Amer. poet
Chester--Rising p153-155, por.

EMERY, LYDIA, DR. (c1910-)

Amer. physician
Felton--Famous p229

EMERY, MARY (c1844-1927)
Amer. socialite, philanthropist
Birmingham--Grandes, see index
p290, por.

EMERY, SARAH ELIZABETH VAN
DE VORT (1838-1895)
Amer. social reformer,
campaigner, lecturer,
politician
James--Notable (1) p582-583
Stein--Lives p167-169, por.

EMMA (1836-1885)
Hawaiian queen
James--Notable (1) p583-584
Sherr--American p54

EMMERICH, ANNA KATHERINA
(1774-1824)
German nun, visionary
Book--Lists (1) p436

EMMERICH, JOZIE
Amer. TV executive
Scheuer--Tel. p143-144

EMMET, ELLEN GERTRUDE
See RAND, ELLEN GERTRUDE
EMMET

EMMET, ROSINA
See SHERWOOD, ROSINA
EMMET

EMMONS, LUCRETIA (fl. 1770's)
Amer. Revolutionary War
patriot
Clyne--Patriots p128-129,134-135

ENCLOS, NINON (ANNE) de
See L'ENCLOS, NINON (ANNE)
de

ENDE
Italian nun, artist (illumi-
nator)
Munsterberg--Hist. p12,14

ENDER, KORNELIA (1958-)
East German swimmer
Assoc. Press--Pursuit p307,
334, por.
McWhirter--Guinness p131,135,

por.
O'Neill--Women's p586-587
Woman's Almanac p430

ENDERLEIN, OTRUM (ORTRUN)
(fl. 1960's)
East German luge athlete
O'Neill--Women's p564-565,574

ENDERS, NANNIE (fl. 1860's)
Amer. Southern belle
DeLeon--Belles p149-150, por.

ENDRESON, GURI (fl. 1860's)
Amer. Sioux Indian heroine
Sherr--American p122-123

ENDREZZE-DANIELSON, ANITA
(1952-)
Amer. Indian poet
Fisher--Third p iv, 119

ENGEL, MARIAN (fl. 1970's)
Canadian novelist, short
story writer
McCullough--People p54-55

ENGEL, SYLVETTE (fl. 1950's-
1970's)
Amer painter
Women's--Female p40

ENGELHARD, JANE
Amer. millionaire
Forbes--400 ('84) p119

ENGEL-KRÄMER, INGRID (fl.
1960's)
German diver
Assoc. Press--Pursuit p245,258

ENGLE, FLORA PEARSON
See PEARSON, FLORA ENGLE

ENNIS, ETHEL (1934-)
Amer. singer
Claghorn--Biog. p142
Claghorn--Jazz p101

ENOKI, MISWO (fl. 1970's)
Japanese feminist, pharmacist
O'Neill--Women's p708

ENTELIS, AMY R. (1951-)
Amer. TV producer
Scheuer--Tel. p145

ENTERS, ANGNA (1907-)
   Amer. dancer, painter, mime
Chinoy--Women p124-125, por.
Entertainers p230
Fabian--On p190-191, por.

EPHRON, NORA (1911-)
   Amer. author
O'Neill--Women's p478-479

EPPER, JEANNIE (fl. 1970's)
   Amer. stunt-woman
Lichtenstein--Mach. p117-119,
   121

EPSTEIN, CYNTHIA FUCHS (fl.
   1970's)
   Amer. sociologist, professor
O'Neill--Women's p423

EPSTEIN, MARIE (fl. 1930's-1950's)
   French film co-director
Smith--Movies p115-116

ERANSO, CATALINA (1592-c1650)
   Spanish (male impersonator)
   soldier
Book--Lists (1) p339
Henderson--Ten p49-72, por.

ERBE, BONNIE G.
   Amer. TV news correspondent
Scheuer--Tel. p145-146

ERDMAN, JEAN (c1917-)
   Amer. dancer, choreographer,
   teacher
Cur. Biog. '71 p115-118, por.

ERICKSON, BARBARA (fl. 1930's)
   Amer. aviatrix
Keil--Those, see index p323,
   por.

ERICKSON, LAUREL M.
   TV reporter
Scheuer--Tel. p146

ERICKSON, MELISSA (fl. 1970's)
   Amer. printmaker
Women's--Female p77

ERICSON, CAROLYN REEVES
   (1931-)
   Amer. genealogical researcher,
   author
Meyer--Who's p69-70

ERINNA (fl. 4th or 6th Cent. B.C.)
   Greek poet
Pomeroy--Godd. p137-139,199

ERLICH, MYRTLE
   See LEWIS, "TILLIE" (MYRTLE)
   ERLICH

ERNBERG, ANNA (fl. 1900's)
   Amer. craftswoman (weaver)
O'Neill--Women's p122

ERON, CAROL (fl. 1970's)
   Amer. author, editor
O'Neill--Women's p199

EROS JULIAE
   See TROTULA OF SALERNO

ERSKINE, MADGE MERCER (1882-)
   Amer., noted South Dakota
   mother, teacher
Amer.--Mothers p500, por.

ERTESZEK, OLGA
   See "OLGA" (2)

ERXLEBEN, DOROTHEA CHRISTIANA
   LEPORIN
   See LEPORIN-ERXLEBEN,
   DOROTHEA CHRISTINA

ESAU, KATHERINE (fl. 1950's)
   Russian-Amer. plant morphol-
   ogist
O'Neill--Women's p144,158

ESCALANTE, ALICIA (fl. 1960's)
   Amer. founder, Chicano Wel-
   fare Rights Group
O'Neill--Women's p716

ESCOBAR, MARISUL
   See MARISOL (ESCOBAR)

ESCODA, JOSEFA LIANES (1898-
   1945)
   Filipino, organizer of Girl
   Scouts of Philippines
O'Neill--Women's p736

ESENOVA, TO'USHAN (1915-)
   Russian poet
Mandel--Soviet p185-187

ESFANOIARI
   See SORAYA, QUEEN

ESLICK, WILLA B. (c1879-1961)
Amer. Congresswoman
Chamberlin--Min. p84-85

ESLING, CATHERINE HARBISON
(1812-1897)
Amer. hymnist
Claghorn--Biog. p143

"ESPERANZA" (fl. 1960's)
Mexican peasant
Hahner--Women p151-163

ESPERT, NURIA (1938-)
Spanish actress, director
Entertainers p288

ESPIN, VILMA (fl. 1950's)
Cuban revolutionary leader
Hahner--Women p164-171
O'Neill--Women's p714

ESPINOSA-LARSEN, ANITA
Amer. Chicano women's
worker
O'Neill--Women's p716-717

ESPINOZA, MERCEDES
Mexican-Amer. migrant
Lindborg--Five p68-83

ESPOSITO, ELAINE
Amer. medical coma record
holder
Macksey--Book p13

ESSEILY, CHARLOTTE
Lebanese textile center
manager
Macksey--Book p173

ESSEX, MARY
See BLOOM, URSULA

ESTABROOK, LIZZIE S. (TOURIEE)
(1858-1913)
Amer. composer
Claghorn--Biog. p143

ESTAUGH, ELIZABETH HADDON
(1680-1762)
Amer. colonial proprietor,
town founder
James--Notable (1) p584-585
Neidle--America's p10
O'Neill--Women's p387
Sherr--American p151-152

Warren--Pictorial p36
Williams--Demeter's p189-190

ESTE, ISABELLA D', MARCHIONESS
OF MANTUA (1474-1539)
Italian salonist, politician,
businesswoman, art collector,
archaeologist
Fine--Women p5-6
Macksey--Book p23,93-94, por.
Mead--Hist. p316-317

ESTES, ELEANOR (1906-)
Amer. children's book author
Ehrlich--Oxford, see index p453

ESTHER
Biblical
Henry--Written p23,243
Jones--Rutledge p267
Price--God p102-107
Woman's Almanac p398

ESTHER, QUEEN "CRAZY" (fl.
1770's)
Canadian-Amer. Indian accused
criminal
Booth--Women p191-192

ESTHERHAZY, CAROLINE, COUNTESS
(c1840-1917)
Amer. friend of Franz Schubert,
socialite, beauty
Daniels--Wash. p1-9,33,155

ESTY, JANET MARIE DEARHOLT
(c1944-)
Amer. medical electronics
corporation president
Rich-McCoy--Mill. p127-151, por.

ETCHERELLI, CLAIRE (fl. 1960's)
French novelist
Crosland--Women p223-224

ETHELBERGA
See BERTHAGYTA

ETHELDREDA, (AUDREY) (c630-679)
English saint, abbess, physi-
cian
Green--Saints p75-77
Macksey--Book p106
Mead--Hist. p100-101

ETHERIA (AETHERIA)
Spanish nun, traveller

Macksey--Book p237-
238

ETIENNE, GAIL (c1966-)
Amer. child of discrimination
Rivera--Special p53-76, por.

ETOLIN, MARGARET, LADY (fl.
1840's)
Russian, wife Alaskan
governor
Jones--Women (1) p27-31

ETS, MARIE HALL (1895-)
Amer. children's author,
illustrator
Smaridge--Famous p62-69
por.

ETTING, RUTH (1896-1978)
Amer. singer
Claghorn--Biog. p144
Lamparski--What. (5) p24, por.
Simon--Best p195-196, por.
World--Who p266

EUBANK, MILDRED OLEVIA
(1895-)
Amer. genealogical researcher,
teacher
Meyer--Who's p70

EUCHARIS
Roman actress
Pomeroy--Godd. p192-193,196

EUDOCIA (EUDOXIA) (ANTHENAIS)
(c401-c460)
Greek Empress, wife of
Theodosius II, hospital
founder
Macksey--Book p50
Mead--Hist. p84-85

EUGENIE (MARIE EUGENIE DE
MONTIJO DE GUZMAN)
(1826-1920)
Spanish, French empress,
wife of Napoleon III
Jones--Rutledge p268

EUMACHIA
Roman (Pompeian) business-
woman, philanthropist
Pomeroy--Godd. p200

EUNICE
Biblical

Price--God p187-
191

EUPHEMIA (fl. 1226-1257)
English abbess, hospital
builder
Mead--Hist. p223

EUROPA, MADAME
Italian-Jewish singer
Henry--Written p128

EURYCLEIA
Greek, slave of Laertes
Pomeroy--Godd. p26-27

EUSTIS, DOROTHY LEIB HARRISON
WOOD (1886-1946)
Amer. philanthropist, founder
of "Seeing Eye" dog training,
humanitarian
James--Notable (1) p585-587
McHenry--Liberty's p121
Sherr--American p152, por.

EUSTIS, EDITH
Amer. friend of Franklin
Roosevelt
Daniels--Wash., see index p361,
por.

EUSTOCHIUM (fl. c386)
Roman deaconess
Macksey--Book p105

EVALT, ELIZABETH
Australian civil servant
Macksey--Book p131

EVANICH, MANDA (fl. 1800's)
Croatian-Amer. saloon-keeper
Neidle--America's p103-105

EVANS, ABIGAIL (fl. 1950's-1970's)
Amer. circuit-rider, clergy-
man, missionary
O'Neill--Women's p380
Proctor--Women p24-26,29-30,53,
63,88,96,120-122

EVANS, ALICE CATHERINE (1881-
1975)
Amer. bacteriologist, micro-
biologist
Cur. Biog. '75 p464
O'Neill--Women's p217
Sicherman--Notable p219-221
Who Did What p107

EVANS, AUGUSTA JANE (1835-
1909)
Amer. novelist, Confederate
patriot, Southern belle
DeLeon--Belles p393, por.
Ehrlich--Oxford p256,267, por.
James--Notable (3) p625-626
McHenry--Liberty's p448-449
Scott--Southern p76-77,118
Sherr--American p2,47
Welter Dimity p105-111
Wiley--Confed. p173

EVANS, DALE
See ROGERS, DALE EVANS

EVANS, EDITH MARY BOOTH,
DAME (1888-1976)
English actress
Comfort--Good p189, por.
Cur. Biog. '77 p463
Entertainers p184, por.
Findlater--Player p193-208, por.
Johns--Dames p75-88, por.
Jones--Rutledge p269
Keylin--Hollywood p102, por.
O'Neill--Women's p658
Priestley--Part. p110-112, por.
Sherr--American p24
Shipman--Internatl. p158-160,
por.
Who Did What p107
World--Who p256

EVANS, ELIZABETH GLENDOWER
(1856-1937)
Amer. social reformer
James--Notable (1) p588-589
McHenry--Liberty's p121-122

EVANS, JANE ROSSER (fl. 1960's-
1970's)
Amer. fashion executive
O'Neill--Women's p521
Teitz--What's p145-164, por.

EVANS, JOAN (1934-)
Amer. actress
Lamparski--What. Annual
(4,5) p155-160, por.

EVANS, JONI (fl. 1970's)
Amer. editor, publisher
Adams--Women p111,148-149
O'Neill--Women's p489

EVANS, LESLIE (1946-)
British artist

Contemp. Brit. unp.,
por.

EVANS, LINDA (c1943-)
Amer. actress
Scheuer--Tel. p147

EVANS, MADGE (1909-)
Amer. actress
Hazen--Interv. p409
Lamparski--What. Annual (4,5)
p279-285, por.
Springer--They p103,291-292,
por.

EVANS, MARGARET
English novelist
Crosland--Beyond p116-120

EVANS, MARGIE (1941-)
Amer. singer
Claghorn--Jazz p103

EVANS, MARGUERITA
See EVANS, MADGE

EVANS, MARI (1923-)
Amer. poet, professor
Fisher--Third p vi,259

EVANS, MARY ANN (or MARIAN)
See ELIOT, GEORGE, pseud.

EVANS, POLLY (fl. 1750's)
Amer. Indian War patriot
Sherr--American p245

EVANS, SUE (1951)
Amer. percussionist
Claghorn--Jazz p103

EVE
Biblical
Fryer--Faces, see index p290
Gies--Women p37-38,40-41
Henry--Written p15
Woman's Almanac p398

EVERETT, BEVERLY
Amer. agriculturist ("Master
farm homemaker")
O'Neill--Women's p12

EVERETT, SERAPHINA HAYNES
(-1856)
Amer. missionary
Smith--Daughters p198-199

EVERLEIGH, ADA (AIDA) (1876-
1960)
Amer. "Madam"
McHenry--Liberty's p122

EVERLEIGH, MINNA (1878-1948)
Amer. "Madam"
James--Notable (1) p589-591
McHenry--Liberty's p122

EVERLEIGH SISTERS
Amer. "Madames"
Bird--Enterprising p150-153
People's Almanac (2) p931-932

EVERT, CHRIS (CHRISTINE MARIE)
(1954-)
Amer. tennis player
Anderson--People p145-146, por.
Cur. Biog. '73 p125-127, por.
Hollander--100 p7,112,116-117,
por.
Kulkin--Her p102-103
McHenry--Liberty's p122-123
McWhirter--Guinness p154,156,
158,163-164
100--Greatest (1) p31, por.
O'Neill--Women's p260,557,583
Sullivan--Queens p54-67, por.
Woman's Almanac p415, por.
World--Who p212-213

EWING, JULIANA HORATIA ORR
GATTY (1841-1885)
English author, children's
books
Jones--Rutledge p270
Showalter--Lit. p335

EXTER, ALEXANDRA (1882-1949)
Russian-Amer. artist
Fine--Women p165-167
Harris--Women p60-63,288-290,
357

EYCK, MARGARETHA VON (1370-
1430)
Flemish artist (miniaturist)
Fine--Women p36
Munsterberg--Hist. p18

EYMERY, MARGUERITE
See RACHILDE

EYTINGE, ROSE (1835-1911)
Amer. actress
James--Notable (1) p591-593

F

FABARES, NANETTE
See FABRAY, NANETTE

FABER, BETTY LANE
Amer. entomologist (cock-
roaches)
Felton--Famous p229-230

FABER, SANDRA (c1945-)
Amer. astronomer
Science Digest--100 p40-41, por.

FABIOLA (-399/400)
Roman physician, saint,
philanthropist, nurse
Macksey--Book p140
Mead--Hist. p78-80

FABRAY, NANETTE (1920-)
Amer. singer, actress
Claghorn--Biog. p147
Lewis--Prime p44
Scheuer--Tel. p149, por.
World--Who p267

FABBRI, TECLA
Brazilian seamstress, labor
worker, feminist
Hahner--Women p114-116

FABRICIUS, SARA
See SANDEL, CORA

"THE FABULOUS MOOLAH"
See ELLISON, LILLIAN

FAGAN, ELEANORA DE
See HOLIDAY, BILLIE (LADY
DAY)

FAHY, MARGARET CHEADLE (1902-)
Amer. genealogical researcher,
writer
Meyer--Who's p73

FAIN, BARBARA HANCOCK
Amer., wife of Colonel John
Fain, (Director, Crusade for
Christ)
Kooiman--Silhouettes p112-123,
por.

FAINLIGHT, RUTH
Amer.-English poet
Baker--Women p8

FAIRBANK, LORENA KING
(1874-)
Amer., noted South Dakota
mother, speech-drama teacher,
community worker, centenarian
Amer.--Mothers p498-499, por.

FAIRCHILD, (MARY) SALOME
CUTLER (1855-1921)
Amer. pioneer librarian
James--Notable (1) p593-594
McHenry--Liberty's p124

FAIRFAX, BEATRICE, pseud.
(1873/1878-1945)
Amer. journalist (columnist)
James--Notable (2) p491-492
Marzolf--Up p36
McHenry--Liberty's p268
Woman's Almanac p278

FAIRFAX, MARION
Amer. director, filmwriter,
playwright
Slide--Early p113, por.

FAIRFIELD, CICILY ISABEL
See WEST, REBECCA, DAME,
pseud.

FAIRFIELD, FLORA, pseud.
See ALCOTT, LOUISA MAY

FAIRLESS, MICHAEL
See BARBER, MARGARET
FAIRLESS

FAITHFULL, EMILY (1835-1895)
English novelist, publisher,
essayist, feminist, lecturer,
editor, philanthropist
Showalter--Lit. p332
Taylor--Gener. p15-16

FALANA, LOLA (1947-)
Amer. actress, singer,
dancer
Anderson--People p147, por.

FALCO, MALTHEA (1944-)
Amer. government employee
O'Neill--Women's p96

FALCONER, LANCE, pseud.
See HAWKER, MARY ELIZABETH

FALCONER, MARTHA PLATT
(1862-1941)

Amer. social worker
James--Notable (1) p594-596
McHenry--Liberty's p124

FALCONET, MRS. CAMERON
Amer., mother-in-law of
boxer Jack Johnson
Book--Lists (2) p266

FALER, JUNE H.
Amer. genealogical researcher
Meyer--Who's p73

FALK, ROSSELLA (1926-)
Italian actress
Entertainers p267, por.

FALK, SHERA DANESE (fl. 1970's)
Amer., wife of Peter Falk
Funt--Are p157-169, por.

FALKENBERG, CHARLENE (fl.
1970's)
Amer. aviatrix, pilot
Seed--Saturday's p91-92, por.

FALKENSTEIN, CLARE (fl. 1970's)
Amer. sculptor
Women's--Female p88

FALLACI, ORIANA (1930-)
Italian journalist, author
Cur. Biog. '77 p146-149, por.
Marzolf--Up p275
O'Neill--Women's p479

FALLIS, GUADALUPE VALDES
(1941-)
Amer. Chicana writer
Fisher--Third p viii,356

FAME, VIOLET, pseud.
See CURRIE, MARY

FANCHER, MOLLIE (c1848-1916)
Amer. author, clairvoyant
People's Almanac (1) p1355
People's Almanac (2) p1255-1257

FANCONI, LINDA (fl. 1970's)
Amer. agriculture 4-H
scholarship winner
O'Neill--Women's p21

FANE, THE HONORABLE MRS.
HENRY (1758-1838)
English socialite
Ware--Meet p76

FANNER, ALICE
English painter
Sparrow--Women p69,135,156

FANNIA
Roman heroine
Zinserling--Women p65

FARAH DIBA PAHLEVI, EMPRESS
(1938-)
Iranian Shahbanon, Empress
Cur. Biog. '76 p132-135, por.
Miller--Fishbait p352-354

FARBER, BEA (1940-)
Amer. harness racer
McWhirter--Guinness p90-91, por.

FARENTHOLD, FRANCES (SISSY)
(1926-)
Amer. college president,
educator, lawyer
O'Neill--Women's p408, por.

FARINA, MIMI (c1945-)
Amer. entertainer
O'Neill--Women's p711

FARJEON, ELEANOR (1881-1965)
English children's author
Kulkin--Her p103-104

FARLEY, CARRIE (c1869-)
Amer. centenarian
Mitchell--Yessir p29-34, por.

FARLEY, HARRIET (c1813-1907)
Amer. editor, social re-
former
Hymowitz--Hist. p128,132
James--Notable (1) p596-597
McHenry--Liberty's p125

FARLEY, ROSALIE LA FLESCHE
(1861-1900)
Amer. Omaha Indian
business-woman
Stein--Lives p169-170, por.

FARMER, BESS ("MISS BESS")
(1919-)
Amer. organist, accordionist,
arranger, songwriter
Claghorn--Biog. p149

FARMER, FANNIE MERRITT (1857-
1915)

Amer. dietician, head, cooking
school, teacher, author
Bird--Enterprising p159-161
James--Notable (1) p597-598
McHenry--Liberty's p125
O'Neill--Women's p131
Signif.--Amer. p28, por.
Stein--Lives p65-71
Webster's--Amer. p331
Woman's Almanac p169
World--Who p296-297

FARMER, FRANCES (1913-1970)
Amer. actress
Hazen--Interv. p410-411
Hirschhorn--Rating p131-132, por.
Shipman--Gold. p194-196, por.
Springer--They p105,292, por.
World--Who p233

FARMER, MARY (-1687)
Amer. colonial limestone mer-
chant
Williams--Demeter's p195

FARNESE, ELIZABETH (1692-1766)
Italian, wife of Philip V
Jones--Rutledge p275

FARNESE, GIULIA (fl. 1400's-
1500's)
Italian, mistress of Pope
Alexander VI
Jones--Rutledge p275

FARNESIO, ISABEL DE (1692-1766)
Italian politician
Macksey--Book p27

FARNHAM, ELIZA WOOD BURHANS
(1815-1864)
Amer. prison reformer, author,
lecturer, feminist, philanthro-
pist
James--Notable (1) p598-600
McHenry--Liberty's p125-126
Time--Women p50-51

FARNHAM, MARYNIA L. FOOT
(1899-1979)
Amer. psychiatrist, feminist,
author
Hymowitz--Hist. p300
Millstein--We p252-253
Sochen--Movers p198-200

FARNINGHAM, MARIANNE, pseud.
See HEARNE, MARY

FARQUHARSON, MARTHA, pseud.
See FINLEY, MARTHA
FARQUHARSON

FARRAND, BEATRIX JONES (1872-1959)
Amer. landscape architect
Sicherman--Notable p221-223

FARRAND, RHODA SMITH (fl. 1760's-1770's)
Amer. Revolutionary War patriot
Meyer--Petticoat p135
Sherr--American p229

FARRAR, CYNTHIA (1795-1862)
Amer. missionary
James--Notable (1) p600-601

FARRAR, ELIZA WARE ROTCH (1791-1870)
Amer. author
James--Notable (1) p601-602

FARRAR, GERALDINE (1882-1966/1967)
Amer. opera singer
Claghorn--Biog. p149
Clark--Leading p24-26
Fabian--On p144-145, por.
Holme--Journal p70-71, por.
McHenry--Liberty's p126
Mordden--Movie p16-17,32,36, 53,83
O'Neill--Women's p618-619
Sicherman--Notable p223-224
Tuggle--Golden p83-87, por.
Warren--Pictorial p153
World--Who p70

FARRAR, MARGARET FETHER-BRIDGE (1897-1967)
Amer. puzzle editor
Cur. Biog. '84 p471
McHenry--Liberty's p126-127

FARRELL, CAROL, SISTER (fl. 1980's)
Amer. nun, mayor
People's Almanac (3) p62

FARRELL, EILEEN (1920-)
Amer. singer
Claghorn--Biog. p149
McHenry--Liberty's p127
Webster's--Amer. p333
World--Who p70

FARRELL, GLENDA (1904-1971)
Amer. actress
Mordden--Movie p161-162,164, 183, por.
Springer--They p105,292, por.

FARRELL, SUZANNE (1945-)
Amer. ballet dancer
Diamonstein--Open p117-120, por.
McHenry--Liberty's p127-128
O'Neill--Women's p345
Woman's Almanac p309-310
World--Who p70

FARRINGTON, (MARY) ELIZABETH PRUETT (1898-1984)
Amer. Congresswoman
Cur. Biog. '84 p471
Miller--Fishbait p82

FARROW, MIA VILLIERS (1946-)
Amer. actress
Anderson--People p149-150, por.
Cur. Biog. '70 p132-134, por.
Hirschhorn--Rating p132, por.
People--Best p7,252-253, por.
Shipman--Internatl. p160-161, por.
World--Who p233

FARWELL, BEATRICE (fl. 1970's)
Amer. instructor
Women's--Female p114

FASSETT, CORNELIA ADELE STRONG (1831-1898)
Amer. painter
McHenry--Liberty's p128

FASTEAU, BRENDA SUE FEIGEN
Amer. feminist, lawyer, politician
O'Neill--Women's p350,356,362

FATE, MARY JANE
Amer. Athapascan Indian, president, North American Indian Women's Association
O'Neill--Women's p120, por.

FATIMA (c606-632)
Arabian, daughter of Mohammed
Jones--Rutledge p276

FATIMA, BEGUM
East Indian film director
Macksey--Book p235

FATIMAH, TAN SRI (fl. 1970's)
Indonesian Social Welfare
Minister
O'Neill--Women's p61

FAUCHALD, NORA (1803-1874)
Amer. composer
Claghorn--Biog. p149

FAUCIT, HELEN(A) SAVILLE
(1817/1820-1898)
English actress
Findlater--Player p126-127

FAUGERES, MARGARETTA VAN
WYCK
See BLEEKER, ANN(A) ELIZA

FAULKNER, ANNE SHAW (fl.
1920's)
Amer. musician (crusader
against jazz)
Felton--Famous p199

FAULKNER, KATE (-1898)
British craftswoman
(embroiderer, gesso
decorator)
Callen--Women p3,10,70-71,169,
171,223

FAULKNER, LUCY (fl. 1860's-
1970's)
British craftswoman (em-
broiderer, designer, wood
engraver, china painter),
writer
Callen--Women p70,127,172,182,
223

FAULKNER, MARY (1903-1973)
South African author
People's Almanac (3) p544

FAULKNER, MARY BELIN
DuPONT
Amer. millionaire
Forbes--400 ('84) p120

FAUNTLEROY, CONSTANCE OWEN
Amer., first woman's club
organizer
Sherr--American p67

FAURE, JEANNE (1863-1950)
Amer. singer
Claghorn--Biog. p149

FAUSET, CRYSTAL DREDA BIRD
(1893/1894-1965)
Amer. state legislator
O'Neill--Women's p78
Sicherman--Notable p224-225

FAUSET, JESSIE REDMON (1882/
1884-1961)
Amer. novelist, editor,
educator
Ehrlich--Osrord p148
Sicherman--Notable p225-227
Sochen--Herstory p296,301-302

FAUST, CAMILLE MAUCLAIR (fl.
c1900's)
Amer. art critic
Women's--Female p121

FAUSTINA, ANNIA GALERIA (1)
(THE ELDER) (c104-141 A.D.)
Roman Empress (wife of An-
tonius Pius), founder of
hospitals, medical woman
Mead--Hist. p78
Pomeroy--Godd. p204

FAUSTINA, ANNIA (2) (THE
YOUNGER) (125-175 A.D.)
Roman Empress (wife of
Marcus Aurelius)
Pomeroy--Godd. p204
Zinserling--Women p68

FAUVEAU, FELICIE DE (c1802-1886)
French-Italian sculptor
Macksey--Book p203-204
Munsterberg--Hist. p88-89

FAVILLA (fl. 2nd Cent.)
Roman medical woman
Mead--Hist. p62

FAWCETT, MILLICENT GARRETT
(1847-1929)
English bookbinder, feminist,
politician, suffragist
Callen--Women p171,190-191, por.
Jones--Rutledge p277
Macksey--Book p83-86,275-276,
por.
Palmer--Who's p121
Showalter--Lit. p337

FAWCETT, FARRAH (1947-)
Amer. actress
Anderson--People p150-151, por.

Book--Lists (2) p188
Cur. Biog. '78 p125-128, por.
People--Best p102-103,175, por.
Woman's Almanac p340
World--Who p233

FAXON, ALICIA (fl. 1970's)
Amer. art writer
Women's--Female p121

FAY, AMY (1844-1928)
Amer. pianist, letter-writer
Claghorn--Biog. p149
James--Notable (1) p602-603
Macksey--Book p214
Neuls-Bates--Women p109-121,
184-187,217-218

FAY, MARY S. (1915-)
Amer. genealogical
researcher, author
Meyer--Who's p73-74

FAYE, ALICE (1915-)
Amer. singer, actress
Claghorn--Biog. p150
Hirschhorn--Rating p132-133,
por.
Mordden--Movie p160,164,172-
175,180,183,214
Shipman--Gold. p196-198, por.
Springer--They p105,292, por.
World--Who p233

FAYE, RITA (1944-)
Amer. autoharpist
Claghorn--Biog. p150

FAYERWEATHER, SARAH HARRIS
(c1812-1878)
Amer. school administrator
Sherr--American p30,206

FAZAN, ADRIENNE (fl. 1930's-
1970's)
Amer. editor, writer
Smith--Movies p26,28,41,75

FAZENDA, LOUISE (1895-1962)
Amer. actress
Springer--They p106,292

FEALY, MAUDE (1886-)
Amer. actress
Hazen--Interv. p86-87

FEARN, ANNE WALTER (1865-1939)
Amer. physician, hospital

administrator in China
James--Notable (1) p603-604
Sherr--American p126

FEARNALL, IDA W. (1877-1947)
Amer., noted Montana
mother, educator
Amer.--Mothers p324-326, por.

FEARS, PEGGY (1906-)
Amer. entertainer, actress
Lamparski--What (3) p198-199,
por.

FEBLAND, HARRIET
Amer. painter
Women's--Female p40

FECIT, HENRIETTA JOHNSTON (fl.
1700's)
Amer. artist
Sherr--American p209

FEDCHENKO, OLGA (1845-1921)
Russian botanical explorer
Macksey--Book p239

FEDDE, ELIZABETH, SISTER (1850-
1921)
Norwegian-Amer. deaconess,
welfare worker, nurse
James--Notable (1) p605-606
Neidle--America's p76-79

FEDERKIEWICA, STEFANIE ZOFIA
See POWERS, STEFANIE

FEDERMAN, DOROTHY (fl. 1970's)
Amer. physician
O'Neill--Women's p211

FEDOROVA, NINA (1895-)
Russian novelist
Hazen--Interv. p28

FEIGE (fl. 1750's-1770's)
Jewish Hasidic, mother of
Rabbi Nahman of Bratislav
Henry--Written p209

FEINGOLD, PAULINE (fl. 1970's)
Amer. lawyer, writer
O'Neill--Women's p359-360

FEINSTEIN, DIANNE (1933-)
Amer. mayor
Cur. Biog. '79 p127-130, por.

FEINSTEIN, ELAINE (1930-)
English poet, translator,
novelist
Seymour-Smith--Novels p135

FELDER, LOIS
Amer. labor union leader
O'Neill--Women's p303

FELDMAN, PEGGY
Amer. naval midshipman,
swimmer
O'Neill--Women's p548

FELDMAN, SOPHIE
See FIELDS, TOTIE

FELDON, BARBARA (1941-)
Amer. actress
World--Who p233

FELICIE, JACOBA (fl. 1220's)
Italian physician
Marks--Women p53-55
Mead--Hist. p271

FELICITAS, CLAUDIA (1640-1705)
Hungarian wife of Emperor
Leopold I, physician,
suregon
Mead--Hist. p429

FELIX, ELISABETH (ELISA)
See RACEL (ELIZA RACHEL
FELIX)

FELL, SHEILA (1931-)
British artist
Contemp. Brit. unp., por.

FELLOWES, DAISY
Amer. socialite
Keenan--Women p9,11-12,14,24,
94,96, por.

FELLOWS, EDITH (1923-)
Amer. actress, singer
Lamparski--What. (5) p150-151,
por.
Lamparski--What. (8) p104-105,
por.
Springer--They p106,292, por.

FELTON, REBECCA ANN LATIMER
(1835-1930)
Amer., noted Georgia mother,
author, journalist, writer,

reformer, first woman Senator
Amer.--Mothers p125-126, por.
Bachtold--Gifted p89-91
Chamberlin--Min. p19-37, por.
James--Notable (1) p606-607
McHenry--Liberty's p128
Miller--Fishbait p63-64
O'Neill--Women's p65-66
Scott--Southern p68,93,148
Sherr--American p47
Warren--Pictorial p179

FENDI, ADELE
Italian business executive
O'Neill--Women's p256

FENN, MARY
See DAVIS, MARY FENN

FENNELL, DOROTHY I. (1916-1977)
Amer. mold microbiologist,
government official
O'Neill--Women's p32,90

FENNELL, HELEN
Amer. secretary, magazine
reporter
Hamblin--That p47,151,241,282

FENTON, LAVINIA, DUCHESS OF
BOLTON (1708/1709-1769)
English singer, actress
Coffin--Female p161-164
Jones--Rutledge p277

FENWICK, KATHLEEN (1902-1974)
Canadian museum director
Macksey--Book p209
O'Neill--Women's p615

FENWICK, MILLICENT VERNON
HAMMOND (1910-)
Amer. Congresswoman
Cur. Biog. '77 p153-156, por.
Lamson--In p1-36, por.
Miller--Fishbait p202
Woman's Almanac p106, por.

FERBER, EDNA (1887-1968)
Amer. novelist, short story
writer, playwright
Avenel--Comp. (2) p93
Clark--Leading p102-104
Ehrlich--Oxford, see index p453
Jones--Rutledge p277
McHenry--Liberty's p128-129
Moers--Literary p289

New York Times--Great p86-87,
por.
Ross--Young p80-90, por.
Seymour-Smith--Novels p135
Sherr--American p247,249
Sicherman--Notable p227-229
Signif.--Amer. p41, por.
Wesger's--Amer. p335-336
Woman's Almanac p251-252, por.
World--Who p13

FERCHIOU, SOFIA (fl. 1960's)
Tunisian film producer,
director
Smith--Movies p93

FEREBEE, DOROTHY (fl. 1920's-
1960's)
Amer. physician, college
instructor, obstetrician,
health director
O'Neill--Women's p227

FERGUSON, ABBIE PARK (1837-
1919)
Amer. educator
James--Notable (1) p607-610
McHenry--Liberty's p129

FERGUSON, ELIZABETH GRAEME
(1737-1801)
Amer. poet, translator, social
leader, Revolutionary War
heroine
Booth--Women p147-152,293, por.
James--Notable (1) p610-611
Kelley--Courage p12,181-183,194-
204,235
McHenry--Liberty's p129-130

FERGUSON, ELIZABETH SEXTON
(fl. 1810's)
Amer. patriot
Sherr--American p131

FERGUSON, ELVA SHARTIE
Amer. pioneer, writer,
newspaper publisher
Sherr--American p193

FERGUSON, JANE YOUNG (fl.
1770's)
Irish-Amer. Revolutionary
diarist
Evans--Weather. p28,271-282

FERGUSON, MARGARET CLAY
(1863-1951)

Amer. botanist
Sicherman--Notable p229-230

FERGUSON, MARTRESE THEK (fl.
1940's)
Amer. Marine officer
O'Neill--Women's p537

FERGUSON, MIRIAM AMANDA
WALLACE ("MA") (1875-1961)
Amer. governor
Clark--Leading p99
Sherr--American p224, por.
Sicherman--Notable p230-232
Warren--Pictorial p179
Woman's Almanac p471-472, por.
World--Who p140

FERGUSON, RENEE
Amer. feminist, writer
Millstein--We p306-307

FERGUSON, SARAH (fl. 1970's)
Amer. writer
Felton--Famous p190

FERGUSSON, ERNA (EMMA) (1888-
1964)
Amer. travel writer, dude
wrangler
Sherr--American p155

FERM, ELIZABETH (1857-1944)
Amer. leader of Utopian
"Ferrer Colony"
People's Almanac (1) p1431-1432

FERMI, LAURA CAPON (1907-)
Italian-Amer. author, refugee,
(wife of Enrico Fermi)
Cavanah--We p34-45

FERMON, NICOLE (fl. 1970's)
Amer. writer
O'Neill--Women's p403

"FERN, FANNY," pseud. (1811-1846)
Amer. author, newspaper
columnist
Earnest--American p79-80
Ehrlich--Oxford p8
James--Notable (3) p24-25
McHenry--Liberty's p317
Moers--Literary p289
Sherr--American p90
Webster's--Amer. p800

"FERNANDA FUENTES" (fl. 1960's)

Puerto Rican prostitute
Hahner--Women p122-137

FERRARIS, AMALIA (fl. 1850's)
Italian ballet dancer
Migel--Ballerinas p209,230-232,
247, por.

FERRARO, GERALDINE ANNE
(1935-   )
Amer. Representative, vice-
presidential candidate
Cur. Biog. '84 p119-122, por.

FERRARS, ELIZABETH X., pseud.
(1907-   )
British novelist
Seymour-Smith--Novels p135

FERREE, MARY WARENBUER
(-1716)
Amer. colonial landowner,
property manager
Williams--Demeter's p189

FERRETI, ZAFFIRA (fl. 1800's)
Italian anatomist
Marks--Women p119

FERRIER, KATHLEEN MARY (1912-
1953)
English opera singer
Gammond--Illus. p242, por.
Jones--Rutledge p280
Macksey--Book p221
Who Did What p110

FERRIER, SUSAN (1782-1854)
Scottish novelist
Seymour-Smith--Novels p135

FERRIN, MARY UPTON (1810-1881)
Amer. feminist
James--Notable (1) p611-612

FERRIS, HELEN (1890-1909)
Amer. children's book author
Ehrlich--Oxford p364

FERRY, SANDRA (ROCKEFELLER)
(c1935-   )
Amer. millionaire
Forbes--400 ('84) p149-150

FESSARD, MAGGIE (fl. 1960's-
1970's)
Amer., Utah homesteader
O'Neill--Women's p19

FETTI, LUCRINE (fl. c1614-c1651)
Italian artist
Fine--Women p21-22
Harris--Women p124-130,342

FEUILLERE, EDWIGE (1907-   )
French actress
Shipman--Internatl. p170-174,
por.

FFOST, GRACIE (-1965)
Amer. Congresswoman
Chamberlin--Min. p229-231

FIALKA, TAMARA
Russian worker
Mandel--Soviet p104-105

FIBINGEROVA, HELENA (fl. 1970's)
Czechoslovakian track and
field athlete
Hollander--100 p124-125
O'Neill--Women's p577

FIBISH, NANCY CONNOLLY (fl.
1970's)
Amer. labor mediator
O'Neill--Women's p338

FICHANDLER, ZELDA (c1924-   )
Amer. drama director, producer
Chinoy--Women p222-224, por.
Diamonstein--Open p121-132
O'Neill--Women's p664-665, por.

FICKLEN, NANNIE (fl. 1860's)
Amer. Southern belle
DeLeon--Belles p440, por.

"FIDDLIN' KATE"
See WARREN, MARGIE ANN

FIELD, BETTY (1918-1973)
Amer. actress
Cur. Biog. '73 p454
Springer--They p106,292-293,
por.
World--Who p233

FIELD, JESSIE
See SHAMBAUGH, JESSIE FIELD

FIELD, JOANNA, pseud. (c1905-   )
English psychologist, diarist
Moffat--Revel. p347-360

FIELD, KATE (1838-1896)
Amer. actress, journalist,

Washington correspondent,
lecturer, traveller, author
Beasley--First p20-22, por.
Hamalian--Ladies p48-56
James--Notable (1) p612-614

FIELD, MARY (1876-1968)
English educator, filmmaker
Macksey--Book p76
Smith--Movies p108

FIELD, MICHAEL, pseud. (1846-
1914)
British poet
Avenel--Comp. (1) p180

FIELD, RACHEL LYMAN (1894-
1942)
Amer. poet, children's
writer, novelist
Ehrlich--Oxford p62,134,401
James--Notable (1) p614-615
World--Who p13

FIELD, SALLY MARGARET (1946-)
Amer. actress
Anderson--People p152, por.
Cur. Biog. '79 p132-136, por.
Hirschhorn--Rating p134-135,
por.
People--Best p190, por.
Scheuer--Tel. p153, por.
World--Who p233

FIELD, SARA BARD (1882-1974)
Amer. suffragist, poet
Sicherman--Notable p232-234

FIELD, VIRGINIA (MARGARET
CYNTHIA) (1917-)
English-Amer. actress
Lamparski--What. (5) p58-59,
por.
Springer--They p106,108,293,
por.

FIELDING, SARAH (1710-1768)
English novelist, translator
Avenel--Comp. (1) p183
Horner--English p37-42,124-127
Jones--Rutledge p282
Moers--Literary p289

FIELDS, ANNIE ADAMS (1834-1915)
Amer. poet, literary hostess,
social welfare worker
Ehrlich--Oxford p31-32
James--Notable (1) p615-617

FIELDS, DOROTHY (1905-1974)
Amer. lyricist, librettist
Claghorn--Biog. p152
Cur. Biog. '74 p459
Jablonski--Ency. p227
McHenry--Liberty's p130
Sicherman--Notable p234-235
World--Who p290

FIELDS, GRACIE, DAME (1898-1978/
1979)
English singer, comedienne
Claghorn--Biog. p152
Cur. Biog. '79 p461
Entertainers p205
Hazen--Interv. p104
Jones--Rutledge p282
Shipman--Gold. p198-201, por.
Simon--Best p205-207, por.
Springer--They p108,293, por.
World--Who p267

FIELDS, MARY (c1832-1914)
Amer. mail carrier, restaurant
manager, trucker
Levenson--Women p28
Sherr--American p134
Time--Women p164-165,167

FIELDS, TOTIE (1931-1978/1979)
Amer. comedienne
Woman's Almanac p318-319
World--Who p276

FIELDS, VERNA (c1918-)
Amer. movie studio executive
Adams--Women p104-106,162

FIENNES, CELIA (1662-1741)
English traveller, diarist
Macksey--Book p181-182

FIERSON, REBA
See GLUCK, ALMA

FIESER, MARY (fl. 1970's)
Amer. chemist, author
O'Neill--Women's p165,169

FIFE, ELVIRA ELMIRA (-1894/1895)
Amer. noted twin
Sherr--American p148, por.

FIGES, EVA (1932-)
German-English novelist,
feminist
Seymour-Smith--Novels
p136

FIGNER, VERA NIKOLAYEVNA
(1852-1942)
Russian revolutionist
Macksey--Book p32
Mandel--Soviet p28

FIGUER, THERESE (fl. 1798-1812)
French dragoon
Macksey--Book p54

FIGUERO, CARMEN SANAKIA DE
(1882-)
Puerto Rican mother, music
teacher
Amer.--Mothers p469-470, por.

FIGUEROA, ANA (1907/1908-1970)
Chilean labor leader, United
Nations delegate
O'Neill--Women's p65,346-347,
por.

FIKOTOVA, OLGA (fl. 1950's-1960's)
Czechoslovakian-Amer. track
and field athlete
Assoc. Press--Pursuit p216,218,
236, por.

FILHIOL, FLORENCE MILLER
(1878-)
Amer., noted Louisiana
mother, Catholic worker,
patriot, clubworker
Amer.--Mothers p230-231, por.

FILIPOWSKA, REGINA (-1559)
Polish religious poet
Bainton--Spain p173-174

FILLEUL, ANNA ROSALIE, MME.
(-1794)
French painter
Sparrow--Women p179,186-187

FILLIPIS, MARIA TERESA DE
Italian auto racer
McWhirter--Guinness p31

FILLMORE, CAROL(E) (fl. 1930's)
Amer. aviatrix
Keil--Those p32-33,139-140,
157,235-236

FILLMORE, (MARY) ABIGAIL
POWERS (1798-1853)
Amer. First Lady, (daughter
of Millard Fillmore)

James--Notable (1) p617
Melick--Wives p37, por.
People's Almanac (1) p267
Woman's Almanac p488

FILLMORE, MYRTLE PAGE (1845-
1931)
Amer. religious leader, co-
founder of "Unity"
James--Notable (1) p617-619
McHenry--Liberty's p130-131

FILLMORE, PHOEBE MILLARD (1780-
1831)
Amer., mother of President
Fillmore
Faber--Presidents' p248-250

FILOSOFOVA, ANNA
Russian feminist, philanthro-
pist
Mandel--Soviet p24

FINCH, ANNE (-1679)
English medical woman
Mead--Hist. p405-407

FINCH, ANNE KINGSMILL, COUNTESS
OF WINCHILSEA (1661-1720)
English poet
Avenel--Comp. (1) p558
Bernikow--World p81
Kaplan--Salt p59-61
Pearson--Who p124,157

FINCH, JEAN HAYNES (1935-)
Amer. genealogical researcher
Meyer--Who's p74

FINCH, KAYE
Amer. filmmaker
Smith--Movies p162-163,238

FINDLAY, ROBERTA
Amer. filmwriter, director
Smith--Movies p82-83

FINE, DELIA
Amer. TV producer
Scheuer--Tel. p154

FINE, VIVIAN (1913-)
Amer. composer, pianist,
teacher
Claghorn--Biog. p153
Jablonski--Ency. p366
Thomson--Amer. p142-143

FISH, MARIAN (MAMIE) GRAVES
   ANTON (1853-)
   Amer. hostess, socialite
   Brandon--Dollar p17-19,194
   Felton--Famous p170-171
   Forma--They p83, por.
   James--Notable (1) p620-621

FISH, SUE ("FLYING FISH")
   O'Neill--Women's p590

FISHBACH, MARGARET (1904-
   1985)
   Amer. advertising writer,
   poet
   Cur. Biog. '85 p465

FISHELS, RIOZL (fl. 1500's)
   Polish translator, printer
   Henry--Written p118

FISHER, ANNA (c1949-)
   Amer. astronaut
   Oberg--Space p45,112-113,
   por.
   O'Connor--Sally p2,17,20,25,
   27,52-53, por.

FISHER, ANNE
   Amer. Southern belle
   DeLeon--Belles p155, por.

FISHER, CARRIE FRANCES
   (1956-)
   Amer. actress
   Anderson--People p153-154, por.
   Hirschhorn--Rating p137-138,
   por.
   World--Who p233

FISHER, CLARA (1811-1898)
   English singer, actress
   Fabian--On p60-61, por.
   James--Notable (1) p622-623
   McHenry--Liberty's p131

FISHER, DOROTHEA (1894-1974)
   British boat administrator,
   charity worker
   Macksey--Book p170

FISHER, DOROTHY CANFIELD
   (1879-1958)
   Amer., noted Vermont
   mother, novelist, essayist
   Amer.--Mothers p544, por.
   Ehrlich--Oxford p18,364

Kulkin--Her p104-105
McHenry--Liberty's p131-132
Seymour-Smith--Novels p136
Sherr--American p228
Sicherman--Notable p235-237
Webster's--Amer. p345

FISHER, FRANCES CHRISTINE
   See TIERNAN, FRANCES CHRIS-
   TINE FISHER

FISHER, KATE
   British enameller
   Callen--Women p161

FISHER, KAY (fl. 1960's-1970's)
   Amer. teacher, homesteader
   O'Neill--Women's p19

FISHER, LOU (fl. 1860's)
   Amer. Southern belle
   DeLeon--Belles p154, por.

FISHER, MARJORIE SCHUYLER
   See BARI, LYNN

FISHER, MARY (c1623-1698)
   Amer. Quaker clergyman,
   missionary
   James--Notable (1) p623-624
   Neidle--Americ's p59
   O'Neill--Women's p387
   Williams--Demeter's p124,204

FISHER, MARY FRANCES KENNEDY
   (1908-)
   Amer. cookery writer
   Cur. Biog. '83 p133-136, por.
   O'Neill--Women's p132

FISHER, WELTHY BLAKESLEY
   HONSINGER (1879/1880-1980)
   Amer. educator, organization
   official, missionary
   Cur. Biog. '69 p146-149, por.
   Cur. Biog. '81 p463
   O'Neill--Women's p430

FISHMAN, LOUISE (fl. 1970's)
   Amer. craftswoman
   Women's--Female p201

FISK, SARA ELLEN (1886-1976)
   Amer. educator
   O'Neill--Women's p428

FISKE, FIDELIA (1816-1864)

Amer. missionary, teacher
James--Notable (1) p624-625
McHenry--Liberty's p132

FISKE, HELEN MARIA
See JACKSON, HELEN MARIA
HUNT FISKE

FISKE, MINNIE MADDERN (1865-
1932)
Amer. actress, producer,
director
Chinoy--Women p57, por.
Entertainers p152
Fabian--On p104-105, por.
Gilfond--Heroines p112
Hazen--Interv. p81,98
James--Notable (1) p626-628
McHenry--Liberty's p132-133
Warren--Pictorial p157
Webster's--Amer. p347-348

FITCH, ELIZABETH
Amer., French Indian War
patriot
Sherr--American p33

FITZGERALD, ALICE (1874-1962)
Amer. nurse, teacher, public
health advisor
Kulkin--Her p105-106

FITZGERALD, CLARA SEMMES
(-1906)
Amer. Southern belle
DeLeon--Belles p118-119, por.

FITZGERALD, MRS. EDWARD
See BARTON, LUCY

FITZGERALD, ELLA (1918-)
Amer. singer
Anderson--People p154
Claghorn--Biog. p154
Claghorn--Jazz p107
Diamonstein--Open p133-138,
por.
Jablonski--Ency. p368
Jones--Rutledge p284
Longstreet--Queen p192
McHenry--Liberty's p133
O'Neill--Women's p624
Signif.--Amer. p61, por.
Simon--Best p211-214, por.
Simon--Big p12-13,325, por.
Toppin--Biog. p296-297
Webster's--Amer. p348-349

Woman's Almanac p291-292, por.
World--Who p267

FITZGERALD, EMILY McCORKLE
Amer. Alaskan pioneer, letter-
writer
Sherr--American p5

FITZGERALD, FRANCES ("FRANKIE")
(1940-)
Amer. political writer
100--Greatest (1) p38
O'Neill--Women's p481-482
P.W.--Author p441-443,496

FITZGERALD, GERALDINE (1914-)
Irish-Amer. actress
Cur. Biog. '76 p135-138, por.
Glassman--Year '79 p60,62
Springer--They p108,292, por.
World--Who p256

FITZGERALD, MABEL P. (c1872-)
English, oldest college gradu-
ate
O'Neill--Women's p745

FITZGERALD, MOLLIE McQUILLAN
(1860-)
Amer., mother of F. Scott
Fitzgerald
Diagram--Mothers p82-83, por.

FITZGERALD, RUTH CODER (1944-)
Amer. genealogical researcher,
writer
Meyer--Who's p75

FITZGERALD, SALLY RIDGEFIELD
(fl. 1970's)
Amer. editor, author, (wife
of Robert Fitzgerald)
Ehrlich--Oxford p90

FITZGERALD, ZELDA SAYRE (1900-
1948)
Amer. author, (Mrs. F. Scott
Fitzgerald
Clark--Leading p96-97
Coffin--Female p84-86, por.
Ehrlich--Oxford, see index p453,
por.
Webber--Woman p17-22

FITZGIBBON, IRENE, SISTER (1823-
1896)
English-Amer. religious worker

McHenry--Liberty's
p 133

FITZ-GIBBONS, BERNICE BOWLES
(c1895-1982)
Amer. advertising executive
Bird--Enterprising p 205-206
O'Neill--Women's p 517
Woman's Almanac p 209

FITZHERBERT, MARIA ANNE
SMYTHE (SMITH) (1756-1837)
German, friend of George IV
Jones--Rutledge p 284

FITZHUGH, ANNE (1727-1793)
Amer. Revolutionary War
patriot
Meyer--Petticoat p 168-170

FITZIV, ANNA (1888-1967)
Amer. opera singer
Tuggle--Golden p 134-135, por.

FITZPATRICK, MARGARET
See PATRICK, GAIL

FITZROY, NANCY D. (fl. 1970's)
Amer. engineer
O'Neill--Women's p 194

FITZSIMONS, MAUREEN
See O'HARA, MAUREEN

FJETTERSTRÖM, MÄRTA MÄAS
(1873-1941)
Swedish textile artist,
designer
O'Neill--Women's p 271

FLACK, AUDREY (1931-)
Amer. painter
Nemser--Convers. p 303-305,366,
por.
Women's--Female p 41

FLACK, LUISE (fl. 1910-1914)
Austrian filmmaker
Smith--Movies p 143

FLACK, ROBERTA (1940-)
Amer. pianist, singer,
composer
Anderson--People p 155, por.
Claghorn--Biog. p 154
Claghorn--Jazz p 107
Cur. Biog. '73 p 130-133, por.

Kulkin--Her p 106-107
Simon--Best p 215-216, por.
Woman's Almanac p 292
World--Who p 267

FLAGSTAD, KIRSTEN MARIE (1895-
1962)
Norwegian opera singer
Claghorn--Biog. p 155
Gammond--Illus. p 242, por.
Jones--Rutledge p 285
Macksey--Book p 218
Neidle--America's p 222
O'Neill--Women's p 619-620
People's Almanac (1) p 890-892
Who Did What p 112
World--Who p 75

FLAME, DITRA (1905-)
Amer., friend of Rudolph
Valentino
Lamparski--What. (5) p 94-95, por.

FLANAGAN, ELIZABETH (fl. 1770's)
Amer. colonial tavern keeper
DePauw--Found. p 39-40
Felton--Famous p 76

FLANAGAN, HALLIE MAE FERGUSON
(c1891-1969)
Amer. playwright, theatrical
producer, director, teacher
Chinoy--Women p 8-9,131, por.
Entertainers p 187
Sicherman--Notable p 237-239

FLANIGAN, DEBBIE (fl. 1970's)
Amer. 4-H scholarship winner
O'Neill--Women's p 21

FLANNER, HILDEGARDE
Amer. poet
Moers--Literary p 246,289

FLANNER, JANET (1892-1978)
Amer. journalist, author,
lecturer
Cur. Biog. '79 p 461
Ehrlich--Oxford p 143,312
McHenry--Liberty's p 133-134
O'Neill--Women's p 474
Warren--Pictorial p 185
World--Who p 52

FLAVIGNY, MARIE CATHERINE
SOPHIE, DE, COMTESSE
See AGOULT, MARIE CATHERINE
SOPHIE FLAVIGNY DE

FLEESON, DORIS (1901-1970)
Amer. journalist, co-founder
guild
Cur. Biog. '70 p462
Marzolf--Up p57
O'Neill--Women's p444-445
Sicherman--Notable p239-241

FLEISSER, MARIELUISE (1901-
1974)
German short-story writer,
playwright
Entertainers p217

FLEMING, AMALIA, LADY
(c1909-)
Greek physician, bacteriologist, political activist
Cur. Biog. '72 p143-145, por.

FLEMING, JANE PHILLIPS (fl.
1940's-1970's)
Amer. co-founder of WOW
(Wider Opportunities for
Women)
O'Neill--Women's p107

FLEMING, JOAN (1908-)
English novelist
Seymour-Smith--Novels p138

FLEMING, MRS. JOHN
See LASCELLES, MRS. EDWIN

FLEMING, MARJORY (MARGARET)
(1803-1811)
Scottish poet, diarist
Kupferberg--First p56-57, por.
Moffat--Revel. p21-27
People's Almanac (2) p367-368

FLEMING, PAMELA S. (1943-)
Amer. model, teacher, TV
director
Scheuer--Tel. p158

FLEMING, PEGGY GALE (1948-)
Amer. skater
Assoc. Press--Pursuit p274-275,
por.
Hollander--100 p32-33,36, por.
Kulkin--Her p108
Pachter--Champ. p186-187, por.
Ryan--Sports p88-105, por.
Woman's Almanac p434
World--Who p213

FLEMING, RHONDA (1923-)

Amer. actress
World--Who p233

FLEMING, SUSAN (1909-)
Amer. actress
Springer--They p108,293, por.

FLEMING, WILLIAMINA PATON STE-
VENS (1857-1911)
Scottish-Amer. astronomer
James--Notable (1) p628-630
McHenry--Liberty's p134
O'Neill--Women's p150

FLETCHER, ALICE CUNNINGHAM
(1838-1923)
Cuban-Amer. writer, ethnolo-
gist
Claghorn--Biog. p155
James--Notable (1) p630-633
McHenry--Liberty's p134-135
Macksey--Book p151-152
Warren--Pictorial p133

FLETCHER, ANN (fl. 1970's)
Amer. engineer, illustrator
O'Neill--Women's p194

FLETCHER, INGLIS (c1879-1969)
Amer. novelist
Ehrlich--Oxford p244

FLETCHER, JEAN (1915-1965)
Amer. architect
O'Neill--Women's p609

FLETCHER, JENNIE
British swimmer
Assoc. Press--Pursuit p72, por.

FLETCHER, LOUISE (1936-)
Amer. actress
Manchel--Women p16-17,117, por.
O'Neill--Women's p654
Shipman--Internatl. p179-180, por.
World--Who p233

FLETCHER, POLYXENA
German pianist, (pupil of
Clara Schumann)
Neuls-Bates--Women p314-315

FLEXNER, JENNIE MAAS (1882-1944)
Amer. librarian
James--Notable (1) p633-634

FLEYSHER, ELLEN (1944-)
Amer. police deputy

commissioner
O'Neill--Women's p373, por.

FLICKENSCHILDT, ELISABETH
(1905-   )
German actress
Entertainers p224

FLINT, LUCILE EVELINA DU PONT
(c1916-   )
Amer. millionaire
Forbes--400 ('84) p149

FLOOD, ANN
Amer. actress
Scheuer--Tel. p159

FLORENCE, MALVINA PRAY (1830-
1906)
Amer. dancer, comedienne,
actress
James--Notable (1) p634-635

FLORENDO, SOLEDAD ARCEGA
(1903-   )
Filipino physician
Hellstedt--Women p257-260, por.

FLORES, MARJORIE
See POWELL, YVETTE

"FLOSSIE"
See BARNEY, NATALIE
CLIFFORD

FLOWER, LUCY LOUISA COUES
(1837-1921)
Amer. social welfare worker
James--Notable (1) p635-637
McHenry--Liberty's p135

FLOWERDEN, TEMPERANCE (fl.
1600's)
English-Amer. colonist
Neidle--America's p2

FLOWERS, EMMA PAYNE (1892-   )
Amer. educator, noted
Alabama mother
Amer.--Mothers p4-5, por.

FLOWERS, RUTH
Amer. teacher, feminist,
noted Colorado mother
Amer.--Mothers p70-71, por.

FLOYD, ELIZABETH ARDERY
(1917-   )

Amer. genealogical researcher,
author
Meyer--Who's p76

FLOYD, HANNAH (-1781)
Amer. patriot
Meyer--Petticoat p69

FLOYD, PHYLLIS (fl. 1970's)
Amer. artist
Women's--Female p103

FLUCK, DIANA
See DORS, DIANA LEE

FLÜGGE-LOTZ, IRMGARD (1903-1974)
German-Amer. engineer,
mathematician
O'Neill--Women's p189
Sicherman--Notable p241-242

FLUGRATH, VIOLA
See DANA, VIOLA

FLYNN, ELIZABETH GURLEY (c1830-
1964)
Amer. communist labor leader
Archer--Famous p28-42
Banner--Women p66,108,111,125-
126, por.
Hymowitz--Hist. p246-248,256-257,
259,261
McHenry--Liberty's p136
O'Neill--Women's p712
Reader's--Story p432
Sicherman--Notable p242-246
Sochen--Herstory p232-234,239-
240,245,251,268, por.
Sochen--Movers, see index p314
Taylor--Gener. p40-41, por.
Woman's Almanac p388-389, por.
World--Who p188

FLYNT, MARGERY HOAR (-1687)
Amer. teacher
Williams--Demeter's p176

FOCH, NINA (1924-   )
Netherlands-Amer. actress
World--Who p256

FOGARTY, ANNE (1919-1980)
Amer. fashion designer
Cur. Biog. '80 p454

FOGERTY, ELSIE (1866-1945)
British school-league founder
Macksey--Book p227

FOLEY, MARGARET E. (1820-1877)
Amer. sculptor
Munsterberg--Hist. p90-91

FOLEY, MARTHA (c1897-1977)
Amer. author, editor,
magazine co-founder
Cur. Biog. '77 p463
Ehrlich--Oxford p436

FOLGER, EMILY CLARA JORDAN
(1858-1936)
Amer. Shakespearean
scholar, collector
James--Notable (1) p637-638

FOLKES, ELIZABETH
English religious martyr
Bainton--France p219

FOLLEN, ELIZA LEE CABOT
(1787-1860)
Amer. hymnist
Claghorn--Biog. p156
James--Notable (1) p638-639

FOLLETT, MARY PARKER (1868-
1933)
Amer., (personnel manage-
ment consultant), lecturer
Bird--Enterprising p177-180
James--Notable (1) p639-641
McHenry--Liberty's p136
O'Neill--Women's p99,511-512

FOLTZ, CLARA SHORTRIDGE
(1849-1934)
Amer. lawyer, feminist,
social reformer
James--Notable (1) p641-643
McHenry--Liberty's p136-137
Sherr--American p15
Time--Women p153-155

FONDA, JANE (1937-)
Amer. actress, political
activist
Anderson--People p158-159, por.
Hirschhorn--Rating p142-143,
por.
Lichtenstein--Mach., see index
p360
Manchel--Women p105,107,117,
por.
Mordden--Movie p260,275-280,
287, por.
100--Greatest (1) p12, por.
O'Neill--Women's p654,661

People--Best p78-79,124-125,245,
por.
Schoenebaum--Prof. p205
Shipman--Internatl. p180-183, por.
Smith--Movies p64-65
Woman's Almanac p330,340-341,
por.
World--Who p233

FONTAINE, JOAN (1917-)
Amer. actress
Hirschhorn--Rating p143-144, por.
O'Neill--Women's p653
Shipman--Gold. p212-215, por.
Springer--They p108-109,293, por.
World--Who p233

FONTAINE, MADEMOISELLE DE LA
(1655-1738)
French ballet dancer
Migel--Ballerinas p7-9

FONTANA, LAVINIA (1552-1614)
Italian painter
Fine--Women p10,12-13, por.
Harris--Women p21,24-31,42-43,
69,106,111-114,141,147,341
Macksey--Book p197
Munsterberg--Hist. p20-23
Petersen--Women p26-27
Sparrow--Women p28,39-41,por.
Tufts--Our p30-41, por.
Women's--Female p8

FONTANNE, LYNN (1887-1983)
English-Amer. actress
Clark--Leading p115-116
Cur. Biog. '83 p464-465
Engstead--Star p59-60,62,65
Entertainers p180
Fabian--On p154-155, por.
Hazen--Interv. p103
Jones--Rutledge p288
McHenry--Liberty's p137
Mordden--Movie p65,69-71,96-97,
142
Priestley--Part. p128-130, por.
Springer--They p109,293, por.
Talmey--Vogue p62, por.
Webster's--Amer. p354,656
Woman's Almanac p76
World--Who p256

FONTE, JEANNE DE LA
See ADOREE, RENEE

FONTES, CYNTHIA (fl. 1970's)
Amer. heroine

O'Neill--Women's
p734

FONTES, ELENA M. (fl. 1960's)
Argentinean hydrographic
research scientist (Antarctica)
Land--New p21

FONTEYN, HILDA ACHESON
(1894-)
English, mother of Margot
Fonteyn
Diagram--Mothers p84-85, por.

FONTEYN, MARGOT, DAME (1919-)
English ballet dancer
Cur. Biog. '72 p149-151, por.
Jones--Rutledge p289
Macksey--Book p236
O'Neill--Women's p40,641
Percival--Modern p7,44-47, por.
Who Did What p114
Woman's Almanac p310, por.
World--Who p75

FOOTE, ABIGAIL (fl. 1770's)
Amer. diarist
DePauw--Found. p154-155

FOOTE, ANNE (fl. 1750's)
British goldsmith, jeweller
Callen--Women p152

FOOTE, LUCINDA (fl. 1780's)
Amer., rejected Yale
applicant
Sherr--American p32

FOOTE, MARY ANNA HALLOCK
(1847-1938)
Amer. author, illustrator
Ehrlich--Oxford, see index
p453, por.
James--Notable (1) p643-645
McHenry--Liberty's p138
Time--Women p104-105,161

FORBES, AMANDA CRAWFORD
(1920-)
Amer. genealogical researcher, author
Meyer--Who's p76

FORBES, CAROL (c1913-)
Amer. agriculturalist, lawyer
O'Neill--Women's p30

FORBES, DOROTHY (DOLLY) MUR-
RAY (fl. 1740's-1770's)
Amer. Revolutionary War
"feminist"
Berkin--Women p52-53,60

FORBES, MRS. E. STANHOPE
English painter
Sparrow--Women p70,85,147,149

FORBES, ESTHER (1894-1967)
Amer. novelist
Ehrlich--Oxford p64
Magill--Cycl. p369-370
Meyer--Petticoat p160
Sicherman--Notable p246-247

FORBES, GENEVIEVE
See HERRICK, GENEVIEVE
FORBES

FORBES, KATHRYN, pseud. (1909-
1966)
Amer. short-story writer
World--Who p13

FORBES, MARY LOU WERNER
(c1927-)
Amer. newspaper woman,
editor
O'Neill--Women's p453-454

FORBES-ROBERTSON, GERTRUDE
ELLIOTT, LADY (1874-1950)
Amer. actress
James--Notable (1) p570-572

FORBES-ROBERTSON, JEAN
(-1962)
Amer.-English actress
Priestley--Part. p140-142, por.

FORCE, JULIANA RIESER (1876-
1948)
Amer. art museum director
James--Notable (1) p645-646
McHenry--Liberty's p138
O'Neill--Women's p437-438

FORCE, MADELINE
See ASTOR, MADELINE TALMADGE
FORCE

FORD, ANTONIA (fl. 1860's)
Amer. Conferderate Civil War
spy, heroine
Sherr--American p233

FORD, BETTY (ELIZABETH ANNE
BLOOMER) (1918-)
Amer. dancer, First Lady,
(Mrs. Gerald Ford)
Amer.--Mothers p273, por.
Anderson--People p160, por.
Cur. Biog. '75 p133-135, por.
Hershey--Between p59,99-100,156,
174, por.
100--Greatest (1) p4-5, por.
People--Best p28, por.
People's Almanac (1) p334
Woman's Almanac p170,494, por.
World--Who p297

FORD, CLARA BRYANT (1866-1950)
Amer., noted Michigan mother,
wife of Henry Ford, philanthropist
Amer.--Mothers p278, por.

FORD, DOROTHY GARDNER (1892-
1967)
Amer., mother of Gerald Ford
Faber--Presidents' p213-215

FORD, EILEEN OTTE (1922-)
Amer., head fashion-modelling
agency, author
Cohen--Meet p73-78, por.
Cur. Biog. '71 p136-138, por.
Firestone--Success, see index
p297

FORD, ELBUR
See PLAIDY, JEAN

FORD, ELINOR RITA, SISTER
(1931-)
Amer. nun, educator
O'Neill--Women's p391

FORD, ELIZABETH BLOOMER
See FORD, BETTY

FORD, JOSEPHINE CLAY
Amer. millionaire
Forbes--400 ('84) p108

FORD, LENA GUILBERT (-1918)
English lyricist
Claghorn--Biog. p157

FORD, LORETTA (fl. 1960's)
Amer. nurse
O'Neill--Women's p233

FORD, MARY (1924/1928-1977)
Amer. singer, (wife of Les
Paul), guitarist
Lamparski--What. (4) p102-103,
por.
Simon--Best p457-458, por.

FORD, MARY LITOGOT (1839-1876)
Amer., mother of Henry Ford
Diagram--Mothers p86-87, por.

FORD, NANCY (1935-)
Amer. songwriter
Jablonski--Ency. p510-511,518

FORD, THELMA BOOTH
See BOOTH, SHIRLEY

FORDE, FLORRIE (1876-1940)
Australian singer
Macksey--Book p229

FORDHAM, DRUECILLAR (fl. 1970's)
Amer. clergyman
Proctor--Women p23-27,34-35,53,
69,73,87-88,97-98

FOREMAN, CAROL TUCKER (1938-)
Amer. government official,
consumer activist
O'Neill--Women's p725

FOREMAN, CAROLYN THOMAS (fl.
1950's)
Amer. historian
Sherr--American p190

FOREST, SIGNEY
See STAIRS, LOUISE E.

FORLI, COUNTESS OF
See SFORZA, CATERINA

FORMAD, MARIE K. (1867-1941)
Russian-Amer. physician
Neidle--America's p204-206

FORNALSKA, MALGORZATA (1902-
1944)
Polish militarist
Partington--Who's p124-125

FORNES, MARIA (1930-)
Amer. playwright
Chinoy--Women p316-320,
por.

FORNIA-LABEY, RITA P. NEWMAN
(1878/1879-1922)
Amer. opera singer
Claghorn--Biog. p157

FORREST, CATHERINE NORTON
See SINCLAIR, CATHERINE
NORTON FORREST

FORREST, HELEN (1917-)
Amer. singer
Simon--Best p223-224, por.

FORREST, MISTRESS (fl. 1600's)
English-Amer. colonist
Warren--Pictorial p7

FORRESTER, FANNY, pseud.
See JUDSON, EMILY CHUBBUCK

FORRESTER, PATRICIA TOBACCO
(fl. 1970's)
Amer. graphic artist
Women's--Female p77

FORSMAN, EEVA-KRISTINA (fl.
1950's-1970's)
Finnish ambassador
O'Neill--Women's p62

FORSTER, MARGARET (1938-)
English biographer, novelist
Seymour-Smith--Novels p139

FORSTER-HAHN, FRANCOISE (fl.
1970's)
Amer. professor, art his-
torian
Women's--Female p114

FORSYTH, ALICE DALY (1917-)
Amer. genealogical research-
er, author
Meyer--Who's p76-77

FORT, GERTRUD VON LEE (1876-
1971)
German novelist, hymnist
Herrmann--Ger. p5,13

FORTEN, CHARLOTTE L.
See GRIMKE, CHARLOTTE L.
FORTEN

FORTESCUE-BRICKDALE, (MARY)
ELEANOR (1872-1945)
English painter, illustrator,

sained glass designer
Callen--Women p207,223
Sparrow--Women p72-73,103,114,
126,141-142

FORTISSON, BARONNE DE
See ST. LAURENT, JULIE DE

FORTNER, NANCY OWEN (fl. 1960's)
Amer. volleyball player
O'Neill--Women's p570

FORTUNA
Roman goddess
Pomeroy--Godd. p206-208

FOSSEY, DIAN (1932-)
Amer. primatologist
Cur. Biog. '85 p121-124, por.

FOSTER, ABIGAIL (ABBY) KELLEY
(1810-1887)
Amer. abolitionist, lecturer,
social reformer
Gurko--Ladies p116-117,132,135,
137-139,por.
Hymowitz--Hist. p98,100
James--Notable (1) p647-650
Kulkin--Her p110-111
Lutz--Crusade, see index p334,
por.
McHenry--Liberty's p138-139
Sherr--American p114
Warren--Pictorial p85,101-102,
por.

FOSTER, BARBARA (fl. 1970's)
Amer. printer, artist
Women's--Female p155

FOSTER, CHRISTINE
Amer. TV executive
Scheuer--Tel. p161

FOSTER, EDITH (1914-)
Amer., noted Kentucky mother,
worker for handicapped children
Amer.--Mothers p217-218, por.

FOSTER, ELEANOR (1746-)
Amer. socialite
Earle--Two Cent. (1) p xx,280,
por.

FOSTER, ELEANOR LONG (-1910)
Amer., noted Louisiana

mother, clubwoman, patriot,
community worker
Amer.--Mothers p229-230, por.

FOSTER, FAY (1886-1960)
Amer. pianist, organist,
composer, teacher
Claghorn--Biog. p157

FOSTER, GLORIA (1936-)
Amer. actress
Abdul--Famous p51-57, por.

FOSTER, HANNAH WEBSTER
(1758/1759-1840)
Amer. novelist
James--Notable (1) p650-651
McHenry--Liberty's p139
Moers--Literary p289

FOSTER, JOY (fl. 1920's)
Jamaican child tennis player
Macksey--Book p258
McWhirter--Guinness p8,146
Woman's Almanac p54

FOSTER, JODIE (1962/1963-)
Amer. actress
Anderson--People p162-163, por.
Cur. Biog. '81 p150-152, por.
Hirschhorn--Rating p146-147,
por.
Woman's Almanac p54
World--Who p234

FOSTER, JUDITH ELLEN HORTON
(1840-1910)
Amer. temperance leader,
lawyer, politician, foundress,
social reformer
James--Notable (1) p651-652
Sherr--American p70

FOSTER, MRS. LAURENCE
See FODDEN, RUMER, pseud.

FOSTER, MARGARET (1931-)
Amer. genealogical researcher
Meyer--Who's p77

FOSTER, MARJORIE (1894-1974)
British gunnery expert
Macksey--Book p256

FOSTER, SUSANNA (1924-)
Amer. singer, actress
Lamparski--What. (3) p162-163,

por.
Lamparski--What. (8) p108-109,
por.

FOTHERGILL, DOROTHY (fl. 1970's)
Amer. bowling champion
Hollander--100 p18
McWhirter--Guinness p44

FOTHERGILL, JESSIE (1851-1891)
English novelist
Showalter--Lit. p338

FOUGERET, MADAME
French food specialist
Mead--Hist. p493

FOUQUET, MARIE, VICOMTESSE DE
VAUX (fl. 17th Cent.)
French medical writer, charity
worker
Mead--Hist. p419,493

FOURMENT, HELENA (1614-)
Belgian artist's model, (wife
of Peter Rubens)
Book--Lists (1) p191

FOWLE, ELIDA BARKER RUMSEY
(1842-1919)
Amer. Civil War relief worker,
nurse, library co-founder
James--Notable (1) p652-654

FOWLER, ANN (fl. 1890's)
British lace-maker
Callen--Women p142-144

FOWLER, CLARA ANN (KATY)
See PAGE, PATTI

FOWLER, ELLEN THORNEYCROFT
(1860-1929)
British novelist, poet
Showalter--Lit. p341

FOWLER, KATE (fl. 1780's)
Amer. heroine
Sherr--American p213

FOWLER, LYDIA FOLGER (1822-1879)
Amer. pioneer physician, social
reformer, author, lecturer,
astronomer
James--Notable (1) p654-655
McHenry--Liberty's p139
Marks--Women p79-81
O'Neill--Women's p201

FOWLER, MARJORIE (fl. 1940's-
1970's)
Amer. film editor
Smith--Movies p28,74-75

FOX, ANCELLA M. (1847-1920)
Amer. singer, teacher,
writer
Claghorn--Biog. p159

FOX, ANN LEAH (c1818-1890)
Amer. spiritualist
James--Notable (1) p655-657

FOX, BERYL (fl. 1960's)
Canadian filmmaker
Smith--Movies p95-96, por.

FOX, CAROL (1926-1981)
Amer. opera producer,
manager, theater co-founder
Cur. Biog. '78 p138-141, por.
Cur. Biog. '81 p463

FOX, CATHERINE (c1839-1892)
Amer. spiritualist
McHenry--Liberty's p140

FOX, DELLA MAY (1870-1913)
Amer. singer, dancer,
actress
Claghorn--Biog. p159
James--Notable (1) p657-658
McHenry--Liberty's p139-140

FOX, EMMA AUGUSTA (1847-)
Amer., noted Michigan mother,
teacher, educator, presidential candidate
Amer.--Mothers p277, por.

FOX, KATHERINE (KATE) (c1839-
1892/1894)
Amer. spiritualist, medium
James--Notable (1) p655-657
Sherr--American p163
Webster's--Amer. p360

FOX, MARGARET (c1833-1893)
Amer. spiritualist, medium
James--Notable (1) p655-657
McHenry--Liberty's p140
Sherr--American p163
Webster's--Amer. p360

FOX, MURIEL (fl. 1960's-1970's)
Amer. public relations

executive
O'Neill--Women's p521

FOX, PAULA (fl. 1970's)
Amer. children's author
O'Neill--Women's p692

FOX, SIDNEY (1910-1942)
Amer. legal secretary, actress
Springer--They p109,293, por.

FOX SISTERS (fl. 1880's)
Amer. spiritualists
Felton--Famous p40-42
People's Almanac (1) p1393

FOX, SIV CEDERING (1939-)
Swedish-Amer. poet
Chester--Rising p307-313, por.

FOXE, FANNE (c1936-)
Amer. entertainer
Miller--Fishbait p165,180

FOY, MRS. EDWARD
See CARLETON, MRS. THOMAS

FRACCI, CARLA (1936-)
Italian ballet dancer
Cur. Biog. '75 p139-141, por.
O'Neill--Women's p644-645
World--Who p75

FRACKLETON, SUSAN STUART
GOODRICH (1848-)
Amer. potter, ceramicist
Callen--Women p87-88

FRAIBERG, SELMA (c1918-1981)
Amer. child psychoanalyst
O'Neill--Women's p229

FRAME, ALICE SEYMOUR BROWNE
(1878-1941)
Amer. missionary, educator
James--Notable (1) p658-660

FRAME, JANET (1924-)
New Zealander novelist
Avenel--Comp. (1) p193
Crosland--Beyond p136-137,227
Moers--Literary p289
Seymour-Smith--Novels p140

FRANCA, CELIA (1921-)
English ballet dancer, choreog-
rapher
World--Who p75-76

FRANCE, GEORGINA CAVE (1868-
1934)
British silversmith, jeweller,
enameller, illustrator,
children's book author, bookbinder
Callen--Women p223

FRANCES OF BRITTANY, DUCHESS
French physician
Mead--Hist. p307

FRANCESCA (1)
See ALEXANDER, FRANCESCA

FRANCESCA DA RIMINI (-c1285)
Italian, daughter of Lord of
Ravenna, (Dante's heroine)
Jones--Rutledge p294

FRANCES, ARLENE (1908-)
Amer. actress, radio, TV
personality
World--Who p234

FRANCIS, CLARE (c1946-)
English sailboat racer
O'Neill--Women's p741

FRANCIS, CONNIE (1938-)
Amer. singer
Claghorn--Biog. p159
World--Who p267

FRANCIS, GENIE ANN (1962-)
Amer. actress
Scheuer--Tel. p163, por.

FRANCIS, KAY (1903/1905-1968)
Amer. actress
Engstead--Star p115-116
Keylin--Hollywood p111, por.
Shipman--Gold. p217-221, por.
Springer--They p109-110,293,
por.
World--Who p234

FRANCIS, MILLY (c1802-1848)
Amer. Creek Indian heroine
James--Notable (1) p660-661
Sherr--American p190

FRANCIS, MIRIAM B. (1930-)
Amer. artist
Fax--Black p238-255, por.

FRANCIS, NOEL
Amer actress

Springer--They p110,293,
por.

FRANCISCO, NIA (1952-)
Amer. Navajo Indian poet
Fisher--Third p iv, 98

FRANCONERO, CONSTANCE
See FRANCIS, CONNIE

FRANK, ANNE (1929-1945)
German heroine, diarist
Jones--Rutledge p297
Kulkin--Her p111-113
Moers--Literary p289
Moffatt-Rev. p34-35
O'Neill--Women's p735
People's Almanac (2) p1307-1309,
por.
People's Almanac (3) p624
Woman's Almanac p52
World--Who p297

FRANK, MARY (1933-)
Amer. sculptor
Munro--Originals p287-308, por.
Women's--Female p88

FRANKAU, PAMELA (1908-1967)
English novelist, short story
writer, journalist
Avenel--Comp. (1) p193
Seymour-Smith--Novels p140

FRANKEL, BERNICE
See ARTHUR, BEATRICE

FRANKEL, DEXTRA (fl. 1970's)
Amer. art gallery curator
Women's--Female p118

FRANKENBURG, CAROLINE LOUISA
Amer. kindergarten founder
Sherr--American p185

FRANKENTHALER, HELEN (1928-)
Amer. painter
Fine--Women p216-219
Fowler--Art p101-123, por.
Henkes--eight p37-46,58-59
McHenry--Liberty's p140-141
Marlowe--Great p363-367, por.
Munro--Originals p207-224, por.
Munsterberg--Hist. p77-79
O'Neill--Women's p601
Parker--Old p145-146,150-151,
fig. 89,90
Woman's Almanac p226

Women's--Female p41-42
World--Who p58

FRANKFORT, ELLEN
Amer. social psychiatry
researcher, feminist, writer
100--Greatest (1) p87, por.

FRANKLAND, AGNES SURRIAGE,
LADY (1726-1783)
Amer. colonial tavern maid,
English baroness
James--Notable (1) p661-662
McHenry--Liberty's p141
Young--Revol. p28-29

FRANKLIN, ABIAH FOLGER
(1667-)
Amer., mother of Benjamin
Franklin
Diagram--Mothers p93, por.
Sherr--American p98

FRANKLIN, AGNES, LADY (fl.
1740's-1770's)
English-Amer. Tory
Booth--Women p48-49

FRANKLIN, ANN SMITH (1696-
1763)
Amer. colonial printer
Bird--Enterprising p28
Demeter--Primer p31-45
DePauw--Found. p14
James--Notable (1) p662-663
Marzolf--Up p2-3
Sherr--American p206
Taylor--Gener. p50
Warren--Pictorial p49-50
Williams--Demeter's p203-204

FRANKLIN, ARETHA (1942-)
Amer. singer
Abdul--Famous p58-65, por.
Anderson--People p165, por.
Claghorn--Biog. p159-160
Claghorn--Jazz p109
Diamonstein--Open p139-142,
por.
Kulkin--Her p113-114
O'Neill--Women's p627-628
Signif.--Amer. p62, por.
Simon--Best p227-229, por.
Woman's Almanac p292-293, por.
World--Who p267

FRANKLIN, BONNIE GAIL (1944-)
Amer. actress

Scheuer--Tel. p165, por.
World--Who p234

FRANKLIN, CHRISTINE LADD (1847-
1930)
Amer. psychologist, logician
James--Notable (2) p354-356
McHenry--Liberty's p231
Macksey--Book p151

FRANKLIN, CORA (fl. 1890's)
Amer., gold miner's wife
Sherr--American p215

FRANKLIN, DEBORAH READ (c1707-
1774)
Amer., wife of Benjamin
Franklin
James--Notable (1) p663-664
Kelley--Courage p101-138,234,
por.
Warren--Pictorial p47-49, por.

FRANKLIN, ELLEN
Amer. TV director
Scheuer--Tel. p165

FRANKLIN, ERMA (1940-)
Amer. singer
Claghorn--Biog. p160

FRANKLIN, GLADYS (fl. 1940's)
Amer. radio producer
Women--Radio p18

FRANKLIN, JANE
See MECOM, JANE FRANKLIN

FRANKLIN, MARTHA (fl. 1910's)
Amer. nurse, feminist
O'Neill--Women's p232

FRANKLIN, ROSALIND ELSIE (1920-
1958)
English biophysicist, (DNA
co-discoverer)
Fink--Great p168-176
Jones--Rutledge p297
O'Neill--Women's p161

FRANKLIN, SALLY (SARAH)
See BACHE, SALLY FRANKLIN

FRANKS, (BILHAH) ABIGAIL LEVY
(1696-1756)
Amer. pioneer, society founder
DePauw--Rem. p73-74,
por.

FRANKS, LUCINDA (fl. 1960's-
1970's)
Amer. journalist
O'Neill--Women's p452,465

FRANKS, REBECCA (1760-1823)
Amer. "Tory" belle
Booth--Women p157-158,226-227
Earle--Two Cent. (2) p669,709
Engle--Women p109-128, por.
James--Notable (1) p664-665

FRANTZ, VIRGINIA KNEELAND
(1896-1967)
Amer. surgical pathologist,
medical educator
Sicherman--Notable p247-248

FRASER, ANTONIA PAKENHAM,
LADY (1932-)
English biographer
Cur. Biog. '74 p125-127, por.
World--Who p94

FRASER, ARVONNE S. (1925-)
Amer. government official
O'Neill--Women's p23-24

FRASER, CAROLINE
Amer. philanthropist
Sherr--American p150

FRASER, DAWN (c1937-)
Australian swimmer
Assoc. Press--Pursuit p219,221,
245,257-258,261, por.
Hollander--100 p85,88
McWhirter--Guinness p17,131-
132, por.
O'Neill--Women's p586
Woman's Almanac p430-431
World--Who p213

FRASER, GRETCHEN KUNIGH
(1917/1919-)
Amer. skier
Hollander--100 p71-72, por.
McWhirter--Guinness p118-119,
por.
Woman's Almanac p432, por.

FRASER, KATHLEEN (1937-)
Amer. poet
Chester--Rising p294-300, por.

FRATELLINI, ANNIE (fl. 1970's)
French clown, school founder
O'Neill--Women's p749

FRAUSTEIN, REBAH MORGAN
(1905-)
Amer. genealogical researcher,
writer, editor
Meyer--Who's p76-77

FRAZEE, JANE (1918-1985)
Amer. Singer
Lamparski--What. (5) p40-41, por.

FRAZIER, BRENDA DIANA DUDD
(1921-)
Amer. millionaire, social leader
Keenan--Women p39,41,45-46, por.
Lamparski--What. (2) p50-51, por.

FRAZIER, MARY (fl. 1760's-1770's)
Amer. Revolutionary War patriot
Meyer--Petticoat p103

FRAZIER, MAUDE (1881-1963)
Amer. educator, state legislator
Sherr--American p144
Sicherman--Notable p248-249

FREAR, ESTHER SCHANER (1909-)
Amer., noted Delaware mother,
community worker
Amer.--Mothers p92-93, por.

FREAUFF, ANTOINETTE
See PERRY, ANTOINETTE

FREDEGUND (FREDEGONDE)
(-597 A.D.)
French consort of Chilperic I,
queen
Macksey--Book p21

FREDERICK, CHRISTINE McGAFFEY
(1883-1970)
Amer. home economist, house-
hold efficiency specialist,
business-woman
Sicherman--Notable p249-250

FREDERICK, JANE (1952-)
Amer. track and field athlete
O'Neill--Women's p579-580
Woman's Almanac p426-427

FREDERICK, NANCY GUBB (1925-)
Amer. genealogical researcher,
author
Meyer--Who's p77-78

FREDERICK, PAULINE (1) (1883-
1938)

Amer. actress
James--Notable (1) p665-668
Springer--They p110,293,295,
    por.

FREDERICK, PAULINE (2) (1908-)
    Amer. radio, TV newscaster
    Gelfman--Women, see index p185,
        por.
    Kleever--Women p122-125, por.
    Marzolf--Up, see index p302
    O'Neill--Women's p437,497-498,
        por.
    Woman's Almanac p268

FREDERIKA LOUISE, Consort of
    Paul I, King of the Hellenes
    (1917-1981)
    Greek queen, German princess
    Cur. Biog. '81 p463

FREDERIKA, SOPHIA AUGUSTA
    See CATHERINE II ("CATHERINE
    THE GREAT")

FREEDMAN, DEBORAH (1947-)
    South Amer. painter
    Miller--Lives p57-73, por.

FREEDMAN, FAIYA
    Amer. sculptor
    Woman's--Female p88

FREELAND, MRS. MARGARET
    Amer. temperance worker
    Papachristou--Women p20-21

FREEMAN, AGNES SUITER (1843-
    1931)
    Amer. "pioneer mother,"
    educator, Civil War rancher,
    physician
    Sherr--American p138
    Time--Women p16-17, por.

FREEMAN, ALICE ELVIRA
    See PALMER, ALICE ELVIRA
    FREEMAN

FREEMAN, ELIZABETH (1744-1826)
    Amer., first freed slave
    DePauw--Found. p97-98
    DePauw--Rem. p152-153, por.
    Kulkin--Her p114-115

FREEMAN, FLORENCE
    Amer. radio actress

Lamparski--What. Annual (4,5)
    p201-204, por.

FREEMAN, "INDIAN HANNAH"
    (1730-1802)
    Amer. Delaware Indian
    Sherr--American p200

FREEMAN, JO (c1946-)
    Amer. feminist, author
    O'Neill--Women's p704
    Sochen--Movers p259,271,296

FREEMAN, MARY ELEANOR WILKINS
    (1852-1930)
    Amer. novelist, short story
    writer, actress, theatre co-
    founder, feminist
    Avenel--Comp. (2) p98
    Benet--New p97-100, por.
    Chinoy--Women p293-300
    Ehrlich--Oxford p57
    McHenry--Liberty's p141
    Parker--Uneasy p51-54
    Pearson--Who p211
    Seymour-Smith--Novels p141
    Sochen--Herstory p224-225, por.
    Webster's--Amer. p367

FREEMAN, MONA (MONICA ELIZA-
    BETH) (1926-)
    Amer. actress
    Lamparski--What. (8) p110-111,
        por.

FREEMAN, PHYLLIS (fl. 1970's)
    Amer. sculptor
    Women's--Female p88

FREER, ELEANOR EVEREST (1864-
    1942)
    Amer. composer, opera singer
    Claghorn--Biog. p161

FREILICHER, JANE (1924-)
    Amer. artist
    Munro--Originals p204-205
    Women's--Female p104

FREMAULT, A.L.
    See LOUISE, ANITA

FREMONT, JESSIE ANN BENTON
    (1824-1902)
    Amer. writer, wife of John C.
    Fremont, social leader
    James--Notable (1) p668-671

Kulkin--Her p115-116
McHenry--Liberty's p142
Peacock--Famous p123-147
Starr--Amer. p98-100,104,158,
177,365-370, por.

FREMSTAD, (ANNA) OLIVE (1872-
1951)
Swedish opera singer
Claghorn--Biog. p161
Neidle--America's p223-224
Warren--Pictorial p153-154, por.
Tuggle--Golden p91-95, por.

FRENCH, ALICE
See THANET, OCTAVE, pseud.

FRENCH, ANNIE (1872-1965)
British designer, illustrator,
watercolorist
Callen--Women p205,223

FRENCH, CALLIE (fl. 1870's-1880's)
Amer. showboat entertainer
Hoople--As p156-159

FRENCH, EMMA (fl. 1880's)
Amer. legendary heroine,
pioneer
Coffin--Parade p256-257

FRENCH, MARILYN
Amer. academic, novelist
Seymour-Smith--Novels p141

FRENCH, NORA MAY
Amer. journalist, poet
Starr--Amer. p254,269,280,284

FRENDLICH, SHARON LEE (fl.
1970's)
Amer. genealogical researcher
Meyer--Who's p78

FRENI, MIRELLA (1935-)
Italian singer
Cur. Biog. '77 p169-171, por.
Gammond--Illus. p242, por.

FRENKEL-BRUNSWIK, ELSE (1908-
1958)
Polish-Amer. pathologist
Sicherman--Notable p250-252

FRERICHS, MARGARET (fl. 1970's)
Amer. clergyman
Proctor--Women p90,101-103

FREUD, AMALIE NATHANSOHN
(1835-1930)
Austrian, mother of Sigmund
Freud
Diagram--Mothers p94-97, por.

FREUD, ANNA (1895-1982)
English psychoanalyst,
(daughter of Sigmund Freud)
Cur. Biog. '79 p139-142, por.
Cur. Biog. '83 p465

FREYA FRIGG
Scandinavian midwife
Mead--Hist. p224

FRICK, HELEN CLAY (c1889-)
Amer. art expert, millionaire
Forbes--400 ('84) p148

FRICKER, SYLIVA (1940-)
Canadian singer, composer
Claghorn--Biog. p161

FRIEDAN, BETTY (1921-)
Amer. feminist, founder NOW,
social reformer, author
Adams--Women p39,151
Anderson--People p166
Banner--Women, see index p267,
por.
Clark--Leading p229-230
Cur. Biog. '70 p146-148, por.
Gilbert--Part. p327-335, por.
Hymowitz--Hist. p333,341-342,
344-345
Lichtenstein--Mach. p156
McHenry--Liberty's p142-143
Marzolf--Up p209,237-238
Millstein--We p250-252,258-261,
273, por.
100--Greatest (1) p60, por.
O'Neill--Women's p44,303-304,703
Papachristou--Women p219, por.
People--Best p203, por.
Reader's--Story p438-439
Reifert--Women p225
Schoenebaum--Prof. p217-218
Signif.--Amer. p62, por.
Sochen--Herstory p387,390-392,
398,400, por.
Sochen--Movers p189-190,238-243,
253,271
Walker--Women p14-29, por.
Warren--Pictorial p206-208, por.
Webster's--Amer. p369
Wintle--Makers p177-178, #158

Woman's Almanac p50,63,207,555-556, por.
World--Who p188

FRIEDLANDER, JUDITH
Amer. college professor,
anthropologist, activist
O'Neill--Women's p709-710

FRIEDLÄNDER, THEKLA
German singer
Neuls-Bates--Women p157,159,
161-163

FRIEDMAN, BONNIE
Amer. photographer,
editor, director
Smith--Movies p166,241, por.

FRIEDMAN, ESTHER PAULINE
See LANDERS, ANN, pseud.

FRIEDMAN, PAULINE "POPO"
ESTHER
See VAN BUREN, ABIGAIL
("ABBY"), pseud.

FRIEDMAN, SONYA
Amer. TV cable network host
Scheuer--Tel. p167

FRIEDMANN, ROSELI OCAMPO
Philippine-Amer. microbiolo-
gist, (Antarctica)
Land--New p11,189-200, por.

FRIEND, CHARLOTTE
Amer. oncologist
O'Neill--Women's p145,224

FRIES, SYLVIA
Amer. space historian
Oberg--Space p125-126

FRIESEN, LUCILLE
Amer. aviatrix, army flier
Keil--Those p56,182-183,
188-189

FRIESEN, SAMIL(L)E DIANE
See CANNON, DYAN

FRIETSCHIE, BARBARA (1766-
1862)
Amer. Civil War patriot,
heroine
Coffin--Female p5-12

Eills--Here p146-147
James--Notable (1) p673-674
McHenry--Liberty's p143-144
Meyer--Petticoat p33-34
Millstein--We p140-142
People's Almanac (1) p701
Sherr--American p95,243

FRIGANZA, TRIXIE (1870-1955)
Amer. actress, singer
Hazen--Interv. p101

FRIGG
See FREYA FRIGG

FRIGGEBO, BIRGIT (1941-)
Swedish minister
O'Neill--Women's p53

FRINK, ELISABETH (1930-)
English artist
Contemp. Brit., unp., por.

FRISSELL, TONI (1907-)
Amer. photographer
Mitchell--Recol. p102-119,201-202,
por.

FRITCHIE, BARBARA
See FRIETSCHIE, BARBARA
HAUER

FRITH, INGER (fl. 1970's)
Danish archer
Machsey--Book p256

FRITH, MOLLY (1589-1663)
English accused criminal
Macksey--Book p132-133, por.

FRITZ, BARBARA
Amer. detective
O'Neill--Women's p ff394, por.

FROMAN, JANE (1917-1980)
Amer. singer
Lamparski--What. (5) p64-65,
por.

FROMME, LYNETTE ALICE ("SQUEAKY")
(1948-)
Amer. accused criminal
Woman's Almanac p506-507, por.
World--Who p297

FROMM-REICHMANN, FRIEDA
(1890-1957)

German-Amer. psychothera-
pist, psychiatrist
Neidle--America's p207-208
Sicherman--Notable p252-255

FROST, ALICE (fl. 1940's)
Amer. radio actress
Lamparski--What. Annual (4,5)
p320-322, por.

FROST, FRANCES (1905-1959)
Amer. poet, novelist
Ehrlich--Oxford p24

FROST, HELEN
Amer. pioneer Alaskan
missionary
Jones--Women (1) p134-141, por.

FROST, JANNETT BLAKESLEE
(fl. 1870's)
Amer. author
Starr--Amer. p132-133

FROST, SARAH FRANCES
See MARLOWE, JULIA

FRY, ELIZABETH GURNEY
(1780-1845)
English Quaker, social re-
former, religious leader,
philanthropist, clergyman,
prison reformer
Brecher--Lives p304
Earle--Two Cent. (2) p xviii,
por.
Jones--Rutledge p304
Fry--1000 p215
Macksey--Book p69,107-110, por.
Marlowe--Great p33-38, por.
O'Neill--Women's p387
Taylor--Gener. p32
Who Did What p119

FRY, LAURA ANN (1857-1943)
Amer. woodcarver, cerami-
cist, designer, sculptor
Callen--Women p223, see also
index p230

FRYMAN, PATSY LOU (1934-)
Amer. labor union leader
O'Neill--Women's p312,315

FUCHS, ANKE (fl. 1970's)
German labor leader
O'Neill--Women's p345-346

FUCHS, ELAINE (c1950-)
Amer. biochemist
Science Digest--100 p48, por.

FUCHS, RUTH (fl. 1970's)
East German track and field
athlete
O'Neill--Women's p579

FUERST, SHIRLEY M. (fl. 1960's-
1970's)
Amer. painter
Women's--Female p42

FUERTES, DOLORES ADIOS
See MENKEN, ADAH ISAACS

FULGATE, CARILI ANN (1943/1944-)
Amer. accused criminal
Woman's Almanac p505

FUJIMA, MAASYA (fl. 1940's)
Japanese dancer
O'Neill--Women's p650

FULBRIGHT, ROBERTA WAUGH
(c1875-1953)
Amer. community worker,
noted Arkansas mother, social
reformer
Amer.--Mothers p45-46

FULD, CARRIE BAMBERGER FRANK
(1864-1944)
Amer. philanthropist, Institute
co-founder
James--Notable (1) p674-675

FULDHEIM, DOROTHY (c1893-)
Amer. TV anchorwoman
Klever--Women p30-32,73,103,
107, por.
Marzolf--Up p158
O'Neill--Women's p496-497
Woman's Almanac p106-107

FULFORD, MILLIE WYLIE
Amer. biochemist, space ex-
periments, payload specialist
Oberg--Space p87,113,217

FULKS, SARAH JANE
See WYMAN, JANE

FULLER, BRIDGET (-c1659)
Amer. midwife, third wife of
Samuel Fuller

FULMER, WILLA L. (1884-1968)
Amer. Congresswoman
Chamberlin--Min. p163-164

FULSTONE, MARY HILL (1892-)
Amer. physician, noted
Nebraska mother
Amer.--Mothers p352, por.

FULTON, EILEEN
Amer. actress
Scheuer--Tel. p170, por.

FULTON, MARY HANNAH (1854-
1927)
Amer. medical missionary
James--Notable (1) p685-686
McHenry--Liberty's p145
O'Neill--Women's p204-205

FULTON, SARAH BRADLEE (1740-
1835)
Amer. Revolutionary War
patriot, Mother of Boston
Tea Party
Meyer--Petticoat p29,39,42-43,
48
Williams--Demeter's p227

FULTON, SHEILA
See BROMLEY, SHEILA

FULVIA (fl. 40 B.C.)
Roman, wife of Marc Anthony
Pomeroy--Godd. p175,185-186

FUNICELLO, ANNETTE (1942-)
Amer. singer, dancer, actress
Claghorn--Biog. p163
Hirschhorn--Rating p147, por.
World--Who p234

FUNT, MARILYN (c1940-)
Amer. wife of Allen Funt
Funt--Are p327-339, por.

FUQUA, ANNA MARIE
Amer. helicopter pilot
O'Neill--Women's p543, por.

FURBER, JACKIE
Amer. agricultural labor
leader
O'Neill--Women's p9

FURBISH, (CATHARINE) KATE
(1834-1931)

Amer. botanist
James--Notable (1) p686-687
McHenry--Liberty's p145-146
O'Neill--Women's p155
Sherr--American p87

FURMAN, BESS (1894-1964)
Amer. journalist
Marzolf--Up p59-60
Sicherman--Notable p256-257

FURMAN, VIRGINIA (c1865-)
Amer. bank officer
O'Neill--Women's p526-527

FURNESS, BETTY (ELIZABETH
MARY) (1916-)
Amer. consumer advocate, TV
broadcaster
Diamonstein--Open p143-146, por.
Marzolf--Up p186
O'Neill--Women's p724-725
Scheuer--Tel. p171, por.
Springer--They p110,295, por.
World--Who p52

FURRY, ELDA
See HOPPER, HEDDA

FURSCH-MADI, EMMY (1847-1894)
Amer. opera singer
Claghorn--Biog. p163

FÜRSTENBERG, DIANE VON
See VON FÜRSTENBERG, DIANE
SIMONE MICHELLE

FURTESEVA, EKATERINA ALEX-
EYEVNA (1910-1974)
Russian politician, government
official
Cur. Biog. '74 p459
Macksey--Book p43,130-131, por.
Mandel--Soviet p287-290
O'Neill--Women's p59

FUSS, MARGARITA ("MOTHER
GRETA") (fl. c1555)
German midwife
Mead--Hist. p359

FUTTER, ELLEN VICTORIA (1949-)
Amer. college president
Cur. Biog. '85 p127-130, por.

FYODOROVA, VICTORIA (1945-)
Russian-Amer. model, actress
Woman's Almanac p76

FYODOROVA, ZOYA (c1911-)
Russian actress
Woman's Almanac p76

FYODOROVNA, MARIA, PRINCESS
DAGMAR (-1928)
Russian, mother of Nicholas II
Diagram--Mothers p184-185, por.

G

GAAL, FRANCISKA (1904-)
Hungarian singer, actress
Springer--They p114,295, por.

GAAR, PATRICIA A. (1926-)
Amer. genealogical researcher,
indexer, writer
Meyer--Who's p81

GABLIK, SUZI (fl. 1970's)
Amer. painter
Women's--Female p42

GABOR, EVA (1921/1924-)
Hungarian-Amer. actress,
singer, ice skater
Hirschhorn--Rating p149, por.
World--Who p234

GABOR, ZSA ZSA (SARI) (1919-)
Hungarian-Amer. actress
World--Who p234

GABRIEL, ANNIE (fl. 1930's)
Amer. Red Cross nurse
Sherr--American p11

GADSKI, JOHANNA (1872-1932)
German opera singer
Neidle--America's p221
Tuggle--Golden p97-99, por.

GAFFNEY, MARGARET
See HAUGHERY, MARGARET
GAFFNEY

GAFFORD, CHARLOTTE (fl.
1970's)
Amer. film writer
Smith--Movies p166-167,241

GAG, WANDA HAZEL (1893-1946)
Amer. children's book author,
illustrator
Ehrlich--Oxford p343, por.
James--Notable (2) p1-2

Kulkin--Her p117-118
McHenry--Liberty's p147
Sherr--American p121
Showalter--These p126-133
Smaridge--Famous p44-53, por.

GAGE, FRANCES DANA BARKER
(1808-1884)
Amer. social reformer, lecturer, author, Civil War humanitarian, abolitionist
James--Notable (2) p2-4
Sherr--American p115,186

GAGE, LUCY (1876-1945)
Amer. children's educator
Snyder--Dauntless p321-354, por.

GAGE, MARGARET KEMBLE, LADY
(fl. 1770's)
Amer., wife of British General
Booth--Women p21-22,24,285

GAGNE, BETTY (1923-)
Amer. health worker
Seifer--Nobody p178-216, por.

GAILLARD, MRS. EDWIN S.
See GIBSON, MARY ELIZABETH

GAINES, IRENE McCOY (c1892-1964)
Amer. civil rights reformer,
community leader, clubwoman
Sicherman--Notable p258-259

GAINES, LA DONNA ANDREA
See SUMMER, DONNA

GAINES, MYRA CLARK (1805-1885)
Amer. heiress, social leader
James--Notable (2) p6-7

GAINES, PATRICIA E. (1939-)
Amer. genealogical researcher,
editor
Meyer--Who's p81

GAINEY, CELESTE (fl. 1970's)
Amer. labor union leader
O'Neill--Women's p317

GAINOR, LAURA
See GAYNOR, JANET

GAGE, MATILDE JOSLYN (1826-
1898)
Amer. feminist, author, lecturer

James--Notable (2) p4-6
McHenry--Liberty's p147-148
Macksey--Book p86
Sherr--American p160

GALAJIKIAN, FLORENCE GRAND-
LAND (1900-)
Amer. pianist, composer
Claghorn--Biog. p165

GALE, ZONA (1874-1938)
Amer., noted Wisconsin
mother, journalist, poet,
short story writer, novelist,
playwright
Amer.--Mothers p584-585, por.
Avenel--Comp. p103
Bachtold--Gifted p8-9
Chinoy--Women p146-147,163
Ehrlich--Oxford p337-339
James--Notable (2) p7-9
Seymour-Smith--Novels p142
McHenry--Liberty's p148
Sherr--American p250
Sochen--Herstory p298,300
Sochen--Movers p123-127

GALGANI, GEMMA, SAINT (1878-
1903)
Italian Saint
Book--Lists (1) p436

GALINDO, BEATRIX (1473-1535)
Italian Professor of Latin,
philosophy, medicine,
hospital founder
Macksey--Book p64
Mead--Hist. p300,311,352

GALIZIA, FEDE (1578-c1630's)
Italian artist
Fine--Women p21-22
Harris--Women p28,31-33,41-43,
106,115-117,341
Women's--Female p8

GALLAGHER, HELEN (1926-)
Amer. actress
Scheuer--Tel. p173-174, por.

GALLAND, NANCY (fl. 1970's)
Amer. agriculturist, co-
founder Institute
O'Neill--Women's p10

GALLANT, MAVIS (1922-)
Canadian novelist

Crosland--Beyond p94,139-
140

GALLIAN, KETTI (1913-1972)
French actress
Springer--They p114,295, por.

GALLI-CURCI, AMELITA (1882-1963)
Italian opera singer
Claghorn--Biog. p165
Jones--Rutledge p308
McHenry--Liberty's p148
Macksey--Book p215
Neidle--America's p229
O'Neill--Women's p619, por.
People's Almanac (2) p775-776
Tuggle--Golden p142-144, por.

GALLIGAN, CLAIRE
Amer. swimmer
Macksey--Book p259

GALLOWAY, ANNE
Amer. labor union leader
O'Neill--Women's p303

GALLOWAY, GRACE GROWDEN (fl.
1750's-1770's)
Amer. Loyalist, diarist
DePauw--Found. p125-126,132-133
Evans--Weather. p3,154,167,171,
174,185-244,291,293,300, por.

GALLOWAY, SUSAN MOSS
Amer. painter
Women's--Female p42

GALT, EDITH BOLLING
Amer. socialite
Daniels--Wash. p30,96-100

GALTON, BLANCHE
See WHIFFEN, BLANCHE GALTON

GALVIN-LEWIS, JANE (fl. 1960's)
Amer. consultant
Innis--Profiles p18-19, por.

GALZY, JEANNE (fl. 1970's)
French writer
Crosland--Women p96-97

GAMBLE, KATHRYN
Amer. art museum director
O'Neill--Women's p616

GAMBRELL, MARY L. (c1898-1974)

Amer. college president
O'Neill--Women's p406

GAMERIN, MADAM
French balloonist
Macksey--Book p246

GAMOND, ISABELLE GATTI DE
(fl. 1860's)
Belgian educator, school
founder
Macksey--Book p72

GAMPEL, LILIT
Amer. violinist, child
celebrity
Woman's Almanac p53

GANCHEVA, ANDRIANA KUNCHEVA
See BUDEVSKA, ADRIANA
KUNCHEVA

GANDHI, INDIRA PRIYADARSHINI
NEHRU (1917-1984)
East Indian prime minister
Cur. Biog. '84 p472
Cur. Biog. '85 p485
Jones--Rutledge p309
Kulkin--Her p118-119
Kupferberg--First p66, por.
Macksey--Book p44, por.
O'Neill--Women's p39,47
Palmer--Who's p132-133
People--Best p12, por.
Whedon--Always p140-145, por.
Who Did What p121
Woman's Almanac p465-466
World--Who p164

GANDHI, PUTLIBAI (1839/1841-
1891)
East Indian, mother of
Mahatma Gandhi
Diagram--Mothers p98-99, por.

GANDY, EVELYN (fl. 1940's-
1970's)
Amer. Lieutenant Governor,
politician
O'Neill--Women's p77-78

GANNETT, DEBORAH SAMPSON
See SAMPSON, DEBORAH

GANNETT, SARAH (SALLY)
(c1923-)
Amer. millionaire
Forbes--400 ('84) p65

GANNON, ANN IDA, SISTER (fl.
1950's-1970's)
Amer. college president
O'Neill--Women's p388

GANNON, MARY
Amer. TV writer
Women--Radio p29

GANTT, ELIZABETH
Amer. research biologist
O'Neill--Women's p163

GANTT, LOVE ROSA HIRSCHMANN
(1875-1935)
Amer. physician
James--Notable (2) p10-11

GANTVOORT, MARY GRETCHEN
MORRIS (1894-1971)
Amer. concert and opera
singer
Claghorn--Biog. p166

GAPRINDASHVILI, NONA (fl. 1960's)
Russian chess player
McWhirter--Guinness p64-65, por.

GARBO, GRETA LOUISA GUSTAFSON
(1905-)
Swedish-Amer. actress
Anderson--People p169, por.
Clark--Leading p141-142
Hirschhorn--Rating p149-151, por.
Jones--Rutledge p310
Keenan--Women p79-82, por.
McHenry--Liberty's p148-149
Macksey--Book p234
Manchel--Women p38,48-49, por.
Mordden--Movie, see index p293
O'Neill--Women's p656-657,672
People's Almanac (1) p876-877
Sat Eve Post--Movie p117
Shipman--Gold. p227-235, por.
Springer--They p114-115,295,
por.
Webster's--Amer. p382
Woman's Almanac p327,341, por.
World--Who p256

GARCIA, DOMINICA (fl. 1960's-
1970's)
Thailand physician, medical
director
O'Neill--Women's p211

GARDEN, MARY (1877-1967)
Scottish opera singer

Claghorn--Biog. p166
McHenry--Liberty's p149
Neidle--America's p222
O'Neill--Women's p618
Sicherman--Notable p259-260
Signif.--Amer. p42, por.
Warren--Pictorial p153
Webster's--Amer. p383
Tuggle--Golden p49-53, por.

GARDENER, HELEN HAMILTON
(1853-1925)
Amer. author, feminist,
suffragist, social reformer,
government official
James--Notable (2) p11-13
McHenry--Liberty's p149-150
Sherr--American p163

GARDINER, ABIGAIL
Amer. Indian captive, author
Sherr--American p69

GARDINER, MRS. TUDOR
See ALBRIGHT, TENLEY EMMA

GARDNER, AVA (1922-)
Amer. actress
Hirschhorn--Rating p151-152,
por.
Mordden--Movie p194,216-218
Shipman--Internatl. p194-198,
por.
Woman's Almanac p342-343
World--Who p234

GARDNER, ELIZABETH
See BOUGUEREAU, ELIZABETH
JANE

GARDNER, HELEN (1878-1946)
Amer. art historian, educator
James--Notable (2) p13-15
McHenry--Liberty's p150

GARDNER, ISABELLA ("BELLE")
STEWART (1840-1924)
Amer. socialite, philanthropist
Birmingham--Grandes, see index
p291, por.
Chester--Rising p82-85, por.
Earnest--American p232-234
James--Notable (2) p15-17
McHenry--Liberty's p150
Sherr--American p99
Webster's--Amer. p383-384

GARDNER, JULIA ANNA (1882-1960)

Amer. geologist, stratigraphic
paleontologist
Sicherman--Notable p260-262

GARDNER, MARY SEWALL (1871-
1961)
Amer. public health nurse,
author
Sicherman--Notable p262-264

GARDNER, NANNETTE (fl. 1870's)
Amer. suffragist
Sherr--American p116-117

GARDNER, TRIXIE (fl. 1950's-1970's)
Australian-English dentist,
politician
Stobaugh--Women p93-94

GARDOS, MARIA (MARISKA) (1885-
1973)
Hungarian author, journalist
Partington--Who's p131-132, por.

GARFIELD, ELIZA BALLOU (1801-
1888)
Amer., mother of President
Garfield
Faber--Presidents' p157-167, por.

GARFIELD, LUCRETIA RUDOLPH
(1832/1833-1918)
Amer. First Lady, (wife of
President Garfield)
James--Notable (2) p17-18
Melick--Wives p48, por.
People's Almanac (1) p270
Woman's Almanac p489

GARIBALDI, ANITA (1821-1894)
Brazilian heroine
Taylor--Gener. p33

GARIBALDI, ROSA RAIMONDI
(1770-1852)
Italian, mother of Guiseppe
Garibaldi
Diagram--Mothers p102-103, por.

GARLAND, HAZEL (fl. 1950's-1970's)
Amer. editor
Marzolf--Up p91

GARLAND, JUDY (1922-1969)
Amer. singer, actress
Claghorn--Biog. p167
Clark--Leading p221-224
Cur. Biog. '69 p467

Donaldson--How p126-127
Edelson--Kids p16-20,22,32,82,
110, por.
Eills--Here p140-141
Engstead--Star p160-162,165-174
Hirschhorn--Rating p153-154, por.
Jablonski--Ency. p371-372
Jones--Rutledge p311
Keylin--Hollywood p116-119, por.
McHenry--Liberty's p150-151
Manchel--Women p57,62
Mordden--Movie, see index p293,
por.
New York Times--Great p106-107,
por.
O'Neill--Women's p453,628
Sat. Eve. Post--Movie p35-36,
por.
Shipman--Gold. p237-243, por.
Sicherman--Notable p264-267
Simon--Best p231-232, por.
Springer--They p115,117,295,
por.
Webster's--Amer. p385
Woman's Almanac p343, por.
World--Who p267

GARLAND, MARY MAGDALENE
See JACKSON, "AUNT MOLLY"

GARLAND, PHYL (fl. 1950's)
Amer. writer
Harzolf--Up p91

GARLIC, DELIA
Amer. slave
Hymowitz--Hist. p49

GARNER, NANCY R.
Amer. Navy scuba diver
O'Neill--Women's p543, por.

GARNER, PEGGY ANN (1931-1984)
Amer. child actress
Edelson--Kids p35-36,45
Lamparski--What (3) p80-81,
por.

GARNET, SARAH J. SMITH
THOMPSON (1831-1911)
Amer. teacher, community
worker
James--Notable (2) p18-19

GARNETT, ANNIE (fl. 1890's)
British weaver
Callen--Women p3

GARNETT, CONSTANCE BLACK
(1861-1946)
English translator
Avenel--Comp. (1) p202
Jones--Rutledge p311
Moers--Literary p290

GARR, TERI (1952-)
Amer. actress
Hirschhorn--Rating p155, por.

GARRARD, MARY D. (fl. 1970's)
Amer. art historian, instructor
Women's--Female p115

GARRECHT, CLAIRE
Amer. nurse, Brigadier General
O'Neill--Women's p553

GARRELS, ANNE
Amer. TV news correspondent
Scheuer--Tel. p175

GARRETT, BETTY (1919-)
Amer. actress, singer, dancer
Hirschhorn--Rating p156, por.
Shipman--Internatl. p198-199,
por.

"GARRETT, EDWARD"
See MAVO, ISABELLA FYRIE

GARRETT, ELIZABETH
See ANDERSON, ELIZABETH
GARRETT

GARRETT, EMMA (1846-1893)
Amer. educator of deaf
James--Notable (2) p19-21
McHenry--Liberty's p151-152

GARRETT, MARY ELIZABETH (1854-
1915)
Amer. philanthropist, feminist
Clark--Leading p23
James--Notable (2) p21-22
McHenry--Liberty's p151
O'Neill--Women's p198

GARRETT, MARY SMITH (1839-1925)
Amer. educator of deaf, welfare
worker
James--Notable (2) p22-23
McHenry--Liberty's p151-152

GARRETT SISTERS
British interior decorators

Callen--Women p171-172,213, por.

GARRIGUE, JEAN, pseud. (1914-1972)
Amer. poet
Avenel--Comp. (2) p104
Brinnin--Modern p116-121, por.
Ehrlich--Oxford p123,323

GARRIGUS, GERTRUDE LOUISE
See GARRIGUE, JEAN, pseud.

GARRISON, HELEN ELIZA BENSON (1811-1876)
Amer. First Lady
Lutz--Crusade p59-62

GARRISON, LUCY McKIM (1842-1877)
Amer. musician, collector
James--Notable (2) p23-24

CARRISON, MABEL (1888-1963)
Amer. opera singer
Claghorn--Biog. p167
Tuggle--Golden p153-154, por.

GARRON, ETTA R. SMALL (1887-)
Amer., noted New Jersey mother, foster mother, organist, choir director
Amer.--Mothers p371-372, por.

GARSENDA DE FORCALQUIER (c1170-)
French troubadour
Bogin--Women p109,170-173

GARSIDE, ALICE HAWES (c1909-)
Amer. educator
O'Neill--Women's p428-429

GARSOIAN, NINA G.
Amer. dean, professor
O'Neill--Women's p409

GARSON, GREER (1908-)
Irish-Amer. actress
Hirschhorn--Rating p156-157, por.
Manchel--Women p64-65, por.
Mordden--Movie p83,93,102-104, 170,207
Shipman--Gold. p243-245, por.
Springer--They p118,295-296, por.

Wilson--Hollywood p137-139, por.
World--Who p256

GARTIN, SANDY RUSSEL
Amer. TV director
Scheuer--Tel. p175

GARVEY, CYNDY (c1950-)
Amer. TV co-host
Scheuer--Tel. p176, por.

GARZONI, GIOVANNA (1600-1670)
Italian artist
Fine--Women p21-22
Harris--Women p17,27,29,32,41, 73,135-136,153,342
Parker--Old p53, fig. p53

GASCH, MARIE MANNING
See FAIRFAX, BEATRICE, pseud.

GASKELL, ELIZABETH CLEGHORN STEVENSON (1810-1865)
English novelist
Avenel--Comp. (1) p204-205
Basch--Relative, see index p352
Crosland--Beyond p70-71,109,123
Fry--1000 p227
Jones--Rutledge p312
Kronenberger--Atlan. p295
Macksey--Book p185-186
Magill--Cycl. p407-408
Moers--Literary p290, see also index p326, por.
Morley--Literary, see index p487
Seymour-Smith--Novels p143
Showalter--Lit. p324
Who Did What p121
World--Who p26

GASKIN, CATHERINE (1929-)
Irish-Australian novelist
Seymour-Smith--Novels p143

GASKIN, GEORGINA CAVE FRANCE
English silversmith, jeweler, publisher
Callen--Women p156,159,204

GASQUE, ELIZABETH (BESSIE) HAWLEY
Amer. Congresswoman
Chamberlin--Min. p115-116

GASTON, ESTHER (fl. 1770's-1780's)
Amer. Revolutionary War patriot
Meyer--Petticoat p196-197

GASTON, ROSETTA (1885-)
Amer. community leader
Innis--Profiles p78-79, por.

GATES, ELEANOR (1875-1951)
Amer. author
Ehrlich--Oxford p346

GATES, ELLEN HUNTINGTON
(1835-1920)
Amer. hymnist
Claghorn--Biog. p167

GATES, EMMA LUCY (1880-)
Amer. opera singer
Sherr--American p226

GATES, HAZEL RHOADS, SR.
(1891-1973)
Amer., noted Colorado mother,
business-woman
Amer.--Mothers p67, por.

GATES, MARGARET
Amer. lawyer, professor
O'Neill--Women's p359

GATES, SUSA YOUNG (1856-
1933)
Amer., noted Utah mother,
Morman, novelist, feminist,
genealogist
Amer.--Mothers p526-527, por.

GATES, SUSAN (fl. 1970's)
Amer. horticulturist
O'Neill--Women's p28

GATESON, MARJORIE (1891-)
Amer. actress
Springer--They p118,296, por.

GATTI, ROSA M. (1950-)
Amer. TV executive
Scheuer--Tel. p176

GATTY, MARGARET SCOTT (1807/
1809-1873)
English author, wife of
Alfred Gatty
Morley--Literary p391-392
Showalter--Lit. p323-324

GATZIMOS, BRENDA GAIL
See GAYLE, CRYSTAL

GAUCIN, DOÑA MARIA DE

Spanish nun, matador
Book--Lists (2) p15-16

GAUDARD, LUCETTE (fl. 1930's)
French film director
Smith--Movies p116

GAUDRON, MARY (1943-)
Australian lawyer
O'Neill--Women's p351

GAULT, CHARLAYNE HUNTER (fl.
1960's-1970's)
Amer. news reporter
O'Neill--Women's p462

GAUTHIER, EVA (1886-1958)
Canadian singer
Claghorn--Biog. p168
Jablonski--Ency. p230

GAUTIER, FELISA RINCON DE
(1897-)
Puerto Rican mayor
Kulkin--Her p242-243
O'Neill--Women's p78-79
Signif.--Amer. p63, por.

GAUTIER, JUDITH (1845-)
French novelist
Crosland--Women p62-67
Jones--Rutledge p314

GAUTIER, MADAME (fl. 1850's)
Amer. Western pioneer
(Yosemite Valley)
Sherr--American p23

GAY, BETTIE
Amer. "Alliance Movement"
worker
Stein--Lives p170-172, por.

GAY, DELPHINE (1804-1855)
French playwright
Bree--Women p13-14

GAY, MARIA (1879-1943)
Spanish opera singer
Claghorn--Biog. p168
Tuggle--Golden p55,57, por.

GAY, MARION (fl. 1970's)
Canadian military officer
O'Neill--Women's p552

GAY, MARY ANN HARRIS (1829-)

Amer. (Civil War) diarist)
Hymowitz--Hist. p148
Warren--Pictorial p112

GAY, PATTY (fl. 1890's)
Amer. jeweler, enameller
Callen--Women p162

GAYLE, CRYSTAL (1951-)
Amer. singer
Anderson--People p171-172, por.
Glassman--Year '79 p103-104,
por.

GAYLOR, JENNY
Amer. model
Keenan--Women p195,198-199,
por.

GAYLORD, MRS.
Amer. Revolutionary War
patriot
Meyer--Petticoat p118-119

GAYNOR, GLORIA
Amer. singer
Glassman--Year '79 p104, por.

GAYNOR, JANET (1906-1984)
Amer. actress
Engstead--Star p121-123
Hirschhorn--Rating p157, por.
Lamparski--What. (2) p178-179,
por.
Manchel--Women p58, por.
Morrden--Movie p57-65,71,195-
196,202,231
Shipman--Gold. p245-247, por.
Springer--They p118-119,296,
por.
World--Who p234

GAYNOR, JESSIE LOVEL SMITH
(1863-1921)
Amer. composer, writer
Claghorn--Biog. p168

GAYNOR, MITZI (1931-)
Amer. dancer, actress
Shipman--Internatl. p204-206,
por.
World--Who p263

GEBERTH, GERTRUDE
Austrian skier
Macksey--Book p261

GEDDES, BARBARA BEL
See BEL GEDDES, BARBARA

GEDDES, WILHELMINA MARGARET
(1887-1955)
British stained glass worker
Callen--Women p176-177

GEE, VIRGINIA (fl. 1970's)
Chinese-Amer. labor leader
O'Neill--Women's p342

GEER, VINNIE
Amer. marriage "affinities"
Book--Lists (2) p252

GEERTZ, HILDRED
Amer. social anthropologist
O'Neill--Women's p419

GEIGER, EMILY (fl. 1760's-1770's)
Amer. Revolutionary War
patriot, heroine
Meyer--Petticoat p211-213, por.
Sherr--American p212

GEIRINGER, HILDA (1893-1973)
Austrian-Amer. mathematician,
statistician, space-scientist
Sicherman--Notable p267-268

GEISLER, LISA (c1954-)
Amer. "fencer"
Jordan--Broken p86-91

GEISMAN, ELLA
See ALLYSON, JUNE

GELA (fl. 1713)
Jewish printer
Henry--Written p121-122

GELBER, SYLVIA M.
Canadian government official
O'Neill--Women's p346

GELLHORN, EDNA FISCHER (1878-
1970)
Amer., noted Missouri mother,
regional co-organizer of AAUW,
Suffragist
Amer.--Mothers p314, por.
Sicherman--Notable p268-270

GELLHORN, MARTHA (1908-)
Amer. journalist, foreign

correspondent, novelist, (3d
wife of Hemingway)
Ehrlich--Oxford p135-136,150
Marzolf--Up p55
Sochen--Herstory p316,321-322,
por.

GELMAN, POLINA
Russian aviatrix, war bomber
pilot
Macksey--Book p59

GELSTON, PHOEBE MITCHELL
(c1740-1811)
Amer. patriot, (wife of
David Gelston)
Flexner--Face p182, por.

GENAUER, EMILY (1911-)
Amer. journalist, art critic,
editor
O'Neill--Women's p452,466

GENESKO, LYNN (1955-)
Amer. swimmer
Sabin--Women p66-69,72, por.

"GENÊT," pseud.
See FLANNER, JANET

GENET, NANCY
Amer. magazine science
reporter
Hamblin--That p101-102,182,269

GENEVIEVE, SAINT (c422-512)
French saint
Jones--Rutledge p315

GENLIS, STEPHANIE FELICITE
DE CREST DE SAINT-AUBIN,
COMTESSE DE (1746-1830)
French story writer, peda-
gogical educator
Moers--Literary p291, see also
index p326, por.
Taylor--Gener. p43

GENTILESCHI, ARTEMISIA
(1593-1652/1653)
Italian painter
Fine--Women p14-17, por.
Harris--Women p118-123
Macksey--Book p197
Munsterberg--Hist. p22-26
Parker--Old p20,21-26, fig.
14, fig. 15, por.

Petersen--Women p28-30, por.
Sparrow--Women p28,31,42,45,
por.
Tufts--Our p58-69, por.
Woman's Almanac p220
Women's--Female p8

"GENTLE MARIBEL"
See ATIENZAR, MARIBEL

GENTRY, ANN HAWKINS (1791-
1870)
Amer., noted Missouri mother,
settlement founder
Amer.--Mothers p309-310, por.

GENTRY, BOBBIE LEE (1942-)
Amer. singer, guitarist,
songwriter
Claghorn--Biog. p169

GENTRY, EMMA GENE SEALE
(1939-)
Amer. genealogical researcher,
author
Meyer--Who's p82

GEORGE, GLADYS (c1904-1954)
Amer. actress
Keylin--Hollywood p120, por.
Springer--They p119,296, por.

GEORGE, MADEMOISELLE (1787-1867)
French actress
Entertainers p109

GEORGE, PHYLLIS (1949-)
Amer. TV sports broadcaster
Anderson--People p172
O'Neill--Women's p504

GEORGE, SUSAN (fl. 1970's)
Amer. world food specialist,
author
O'Neill--Women's p36

"GEORGEOUS GUSSIE"
See MORAN, GERTRUDE AUGUSTA

GEORGIEVE, RAINA (fl. 1950's)
Bulgarian plant geneticist
O'Neill--Women's p6

GERARD, MARGUERITE (1761-1847)
French artist
Fine--Women p51-53
Harris--Women p29,46,189,197-
201,348

GERBER, FRANCESCA MITZ VON
See GAYNOR, MITZI

GERE, MARGARET (1878-1965)
British painter
Callen--Women p223

GERKE, FLORENCE HOLMES
(-c1964)
Amer. landscape architect
Sherr--American p196

GERMAINE, SAINTE (c1579-1601)
French Saint
Kulkin--Her p119-120

GERMAIN, SOPHIE (1776-1841)
French mathematician
Osen--Women p83-93, por.

GEROULD, KATHERINE ELIZABETH
FULLERTON (1879-1944)
Amer. short story writer,
essayist, novelist
Ehrlich--Oxford p36
James--Notable (2) p24-27
McHenry--Liberty's p152

GEROWITZ, JUDY
See CHICAGO JUDY

GERRARD, MADY
English fashion designer
O'Neill--Women's p252-253

GERSON, BETTY LOU (fl. 1930's)
Amer. radio actress
Lamparski--What. Annual (4,5)
p265-266, por.

GERSTEN, BERTA (c1896-1972)
Polish-Amer. actress
Sicherman--Notable p270-271

GERSTUNG, MARTHA (fl. 1910's)
German swimmer
Macksey--Book p259
McWhirter--Guinness p129-130

GERTMENIAN, SUSAN (fl. 1970's)
Amer. clergyman
Proctor--Women p32-33,48-50,
60-61,82-83

"GERTRUDE," pseud.
See SIMPSON, JANE CROSS

GERVILLE-REACHE, JEANNE (1882-
1915)
French opera singer
Claghorn--Biog. p170
Tuggle--Golden p43-44, por.

GESMERAIS, MARIE MARGUERITE
See YOUVILLE, MARIE MAR-
GUERITE DUFRUS DE LA
GESMERAIS

GESTEFELD, URSULA NEWELL (1845-
1921)
Amer. religious leader
James--Notable (2) p27-28

GESTRING, MARJORIE (c1923-)
Amer. diver
McWhirter--Guinness p8
O'Neill--Women's p584

GETCHELL, MARGARET
See LA FORGE, MARGARET
GETCHELL

GEVERS, MARIE
Belgian lawyer, President law
school
Macksey--Book p126

GEYER, CELESTA (fl. 1950's-1960's)
Amer. circus "fat lady,"
record dieter
Felton--Famous p205
Macksey--Book p177

GEYER, GEORGIE ANNE (c1935-)
Amer. foreign correspondent,
author
Diamonstein--Open p147-152, por.
Marzolf--Up p85, 116
O'Neill--Women's p460

GEYSELMAN, MRS. (fl. 1880's)
British employment agency
manager
Callen--Women p115

GHELADZE, EKATERINA (c1856-
1937)
Russian, mother of Josef Stalin
Diagram--Mothers p232-233, por.

GHOSTLEY, ALICE (1926-)
Amer. actress, comedienne
World--Who p234

GHULAMALI, RAZIA
Pakistanian cement factory

manager
Macksey--Book p173

GIANNINI, DUSOLINA (1902-)
Amer. opera singer
Claghorn--Biog. p170

GIANNINI, MARGARET
Amer. physician, clinic
founder
O'Neill--Women's p208-209

GIAQUE (GIAUQUE), ELSI (1900-)
Swiss artist, weaver
O'Neill--Women's p606

GIATSINTOVA, SOFIYA
Russian actress
Macksey--Book p235

GIBBES, EMILLY
Amer. religious educator
O'Neill--Women's p397

GIBBES, SARA REEVE (1746-1825)
Amer. Revolutionary heroine,
noted South Carolina mother,
patriot
Amer.--Mothers p490

GIBBES FAMILY, MRS. AND
MARY ANN (fl. 1770's)
Amer. Revolutionary War
patriots, heroines
Meyer--Petticoat p170-171

GIBBONS, ABIGAIL HOPPER
(1801-1893)
Amer. Civil War nurse,
philanthropist, social re-
former, journalist
James--Notable (2) p28-29
McHenry--Liberty's p152-153
Macksey--Book p112

GIBBONS, IRENE
See TAYLOR, EVA

GIBBONS, JANE
Amer. patriot
Meyer--Petticoat p83,103

GIBBONS, STELLA DOROTHEA
(1902-)
English novelist, poet,
short story writer
Avenel--Comp. (1) p210

Crosland--Beyond p114,129-130
Seymour-Smith--Novels p144

GIBBS, EMMA
Amer. milliner
Time--Women p122-123

GIBBS, FLORENCE REVILLE (c1890-
1964)
Amer. Congresswoman
Chamberlin--Min. p156

GIBBS, KATHARINE (1) (1865-1934)
Amer. business educator,
founder secretarial school
Bird--Enterprising p144-145
O'Neill--Women's p511

GIBBS, KATHERINE (2)
See FRANCIS, KAY

GIBBS, MARLA (1946-)
Amer. actress
Scheuer--Tel. p180-181, por.

GIBBY, MABEL KUNCE (fl. 1960's)
Amer. government official
O'Neill--Women's p89

GIBSON, ALTHEA (1927-)
Amer. tennis player
Hollander--100 p109-110, por.
Jones--Rutledge p320
Kulkin--Her p121-122
McHenry--Liberty's p153
McWhirter--Guinness p157-158,
por.
Millstein--We p257-258
Richardson--Great p300-308, por.
Ross--Young p71-79, por.
Sullivan--Queens p102, por.
Toppin--Biog. p305-307
Webster's--Amer. p395
Woman's Almanac p415-416, por.
World--Who p213

GIBSON, CYNTHIA M.
Amer. heroine
O'Neill--Women's p735

GIBSON, ELEANOR JACK (1913-)
Amer. psychologist
Bachtold--Gifted p82-85
O'Neill--Women's p145

GIBSON, IRENE LANGHORNE (c1873-
1956)

Amer. "Gibson Girl"
Brandon--Dollar p39,153

GIBSON, JOANN (fl. 1970's)
Amer. Air Force officer
O'Neill--Women's p547

GIBSON, MARY ELIZABETH (fl.
1860's)
Amer. Southern belle
DeLeon--Belles p165-167, por.

GIBSON, WYNNE (c1907-)
Amer. actress
Lamparski--What. Annual (4,5)
p224-229, por.
Springer--They p121,296, por.

"GIBSON GIRL"
See GIBSON, IRENE LANGHORNE

GIDDENS, LINDA
Amer. water skier
McWhirter--Guinness p183

GIDEON, MIRIAM (1906-)
Amer. composer
Claghorn--Biog. p170
Jablonski--Ency. p373-374

GIEHSE, THERESE (1898-1975)
German actress
Entertainers p206

GIESLER-ANNEKE, MATHILDE
FRANZISKA
See ANNEKE, MATHILDE
FRANZISKA GIESLER

GIGANTE, PAULA M.
Amer. TV director
Scheuer--Tel. p181

GILBERT, ANNE JANE HARTLEY
(1821-1904)
English-Amer. dancer,
actress
James--Notable (2) p29-31
McHenry--Liberty's p153-154

GILBERT, CELIA (1932-)
Amer. poet, editor
Ruddick--Working p306-322,341,
por.

GILBERT, EDWINA (1931-)
Amer. airline official
Genett--Aviation p109

GILBERT, ELIZA
See MONTEZ, LOLA

GILBERT, JEAN
Amer. hospital chaplain
Proctor--Women p125-126

GILBERT, LINDA (ZELINDA)
Amer. prison welfare worker
James--Notable (2) p31-32
McHenry Liberty's p154

GILBERT, MADONNA (c1937-)
Amer. Indian school co-founder
O'Neill--Women's p718

GILBERT, MARIE DOLORES WATSON
(1844-1909)
Amer. editor
Webster's--Amer. p397-398

GILBERT, MELISSA (1964-)
Amer. actress
Scheuer--Tel. p182

GILBERT, SUSAN
Amer. writer, (M.I.T. coed)
Fenton--Famous p266-267

GILBERTO, ASTRUD (1940-)
Brazilian singer
Claghorn--Biog. p171
Claghorn--Jazz p116

GILBRETH, LILLIAN MOLLER (1878-
1972)
Amer. industrial engineer,
psychologist, management
consultant
Bachtold--Gifted p70-73
Boorstin--Americans p80-81, por.
Cur. Biog. '72 p462
Emberlin--Cont. p29-53, por.
Ingraham--Album p67,71
Marlowe--Great p218-225, por.
M.I.T.--Women p217-231,ix
O'Neill--Women's p102
Sicherman--Notable p271-273
Stoddard--Famous p193-200, por.
Woman's Almanac p94

GILDER, JEANNETTE LEONARD
(1849-1916)
Amer. editor, author, drama
critic
James--Notable (2) p32-34
McHenry--Liberty's p154

GILDER, ROSAMOND
    Amer. drama critic
    Chinoy--Women p57,226,228-230,
    por.

GILDERSLEEVE, VIRGINIA
    CROCHERON (1887-1965)
    Amer. educator, college dean
    O'Neill--Women's p404
    Sicherman--Notable p273-275

GILES, MRS. ARNETT (1901-)
    Amer. noted Mississippi
    mother, foster mother, helper
    of handicapped children
    Amer.--Mothers p304-305, por.

GILETTE (fl. 14th cent.)
    French physician, (daughter
    of Gerard of Narbonne)
    Mead--Hist. p272

GILI, KATHERINE (1948-)
    English artist
    Contemp. Brit., unp., por.

GILIANI, ALESSANDRA (1307-1326)
    Italian anatomist
    Marks--Women p51
    Mead--Hist. p225,277, por.

GILL, ARDASH
    East Indian dress designer
    O'Neill--Women's p247

GILL, JOCELYN RUTH (1916-)
    Amer. NASA cheif in-flight
    space program scientist,
    astronomer, astrophysicist
    O'Neill--Women's p88,152

GILL, LAURA DRAKE (1860-1926)
    Amer. educator
    McHenry--Liberty's p155

GILL, MARY
    Amer. patriot
    Meyer--Petticoat p195

GILL, SURJIT (fl. 1970's)
    East Indian dress designer
    O'Neill--Women's p247

GILLAIN, MARIE ANNE VICTOIRE
    See BOIVIN, (MARIE) ANNE
    VICTOIRE GILLAIN, MADAME

GILLAN, JUDY (fl. 1970's)
    Amer. co-founder, Institute
    O'Neill--Women's p10

GILLESE, EILEEN (fl. 1970's)
    Canadian Rhodes Scholar
    O'Neill--Women's p435

GILLESPIE, DOROTHY (fl. 1970's)
    Amer. painter
    Women's--Female p43

GILLESPIE, ELIZA MARIA (MOTHER
    ANGELA) (1824-1887)
    Amer. abbess, educator,
    hospital administrator, founder
    James--Notable (2) p34-35
    McHenry--Liberty's p155-156

GILLESPIE, LARRIAN (fl. 1970's)
    Amer. urologist
    O'Neill--Women's p216

GILLESPIE, MABEL EDNA (1877-
    1923)
    Amer. labor reformer, college
    founder
    James--Notable (2) p35-36
    O'Neill--Women's p291

GILLESPIE, MARCIA (c1944-)
    Amer. magazine editor
    O'Neill--Women's p479

GILLETT, EMMA MILLINDA (1852-
    1927)
    Amer. lawyer, feminist, col-
    lege founder
    James--Notable (2) p36-37
    Sherr--American p41

GILLEY, HANNAH LURVEY (fl.
    1820's-1830's)
    Amer., noted Maine mother,
    Island farmer's wife
    Amer.--Mothers p240-241

GILLIAM, BARBARA (fl. 1950's-
    1970's)
    Amer. travel consultant
    Innis--Profiles p158-159, por.

GILLIAM, DOROTHY (fl. 1950's-
    1970's)
    Amer. newspaper editor,
    author
    O'Neill--Women's p462

English actress
World--Who p256

GINOSSAR, ROSA (1890-)
Russian-Israeli lawyer
O'Neill--Women's p351

GINSBURG, ESTELLE (fl. 1970's)
Amer. artist
Women's--Female p104

GINSBURG, RUTH BADER (1933-)
Amer. judge, professor,
feminist
Gilbert--Part. p153-159, por.
O'Neill--Women's p356,362
Swiger--Women p50-66

GINTER, JOYCE (fl. 1970's)
Amer. realtor
Seed--Saturday's p108-110,
por.

GINZBURG, NATALIA (fl. 1960's-
1970's)
Italian novelist
Moers--Literary p292

GINZBERG, ROSA
See GINOSSAR, ROSA

GIOCONDA, LISA GHERARDINI
(1474/1479-)
Italian beauty, artist's
model
Book--Lists (1) p190-191

GIOSEFFI, DANIELLA (1938-)
Amer. poet
Chester--Rising p301-306, por.

GIOVANNA DI SAVOLA
See IONNA

GIOVANNI, NIKKI (1943-)
Amer. poet, children's
book author
Chester--Rising p358-361, por.
Cur. Biog. '73 p148-151, por.
Fisher--Third p vi,265
Moers--Literary p292
O'Neill--Women's p689
Webber--Woman p190-192

GIOVINCO, LUCY (fl. 1970's)
Amer. bowler
O'Neill--Women's p558

GIPPIUS, ZINAIDA (1869-1945)
Russian poet, novelist, critic
Seymour-Smith--Who's p134

GIRARD, JUDY (fl. 1970's)
Amer. TV production manager
Klever--Women p23-24,26,62-63,
99,103

GIRARDON, CATHERINE DUCHEMIN
See DUCHEMIN, CATHERINE

GIRGUS, JOAN (fl. 1970's)
Amer. college dean
O'Neill--Women's p409

"THE GIRL GERSHWIN"
See SUESSE, DANA NADINE

GIROUD, FRANÇOISE (1916-)
French novelist, poet
Crosland--Women p129,218-219,
231,240
Cur. Biog. '75 p163-165, por.
Macksey--Book p39
Marzolf--Up p279-280
O'Neill--Women's p43,53-54
Smith--Movies p123

GISELA (GIZELLA), QUEEN OF
HUNGARY (933-1095)
Hungarian Saint, (wife, St.
Stephen I)
Partington--Who's p136

GISH, DOROTHY (1898-1968)
Amer. actress
Clark--Leading p112-114
Keylin--Hollywood p124-125, por.
McHenry--Liberty's p157-158
O'Neill--Women's p655-656
Sicherman--Notable p277-278
Webster's--Amer. p401-402
Woman's Almanac p326, por.
World--Who p234

GISH, LILLIAN DIANA (1893/
1896-)
Amer. actress
Clark--Leading p112-115
Cur. Biog. '78 p159-162, por.
Engstead--Star p153-154,156
McHenry--Liberty's p157-158
Manchel--Women p30,36, por.
Mordden--Movie, see index p293,
por.
O'Neill--Women's p655-656

Shipman--Gold. p250-254, por.
Slide--Early p108,110
Smith--Movies p15
Springer--They p121,296-297, por.
Warren--Pictorial p177
Webster's--Amer. p401-402
Woman's Almanac p343-344, por.
World--Who p234-235

GIST, MALVINA BLACK (1842-)
Amer. Confederate money printer, Civil War diarist
Sherr--American p210-211

GITANA, GERTI (1887-1957)
English music-hall singer
Entertainers p180

GITELSON, FRANCES H. (1905-)
Amer. physician
Hellstedt--Women p289-291, por.

GIULIANI, VERONICA
See VERONICA, SAINT

GJØE, BIRGITTE (1511-1574)
Danish, religious school administrator
Bainton--Spain p125-127, por.

GJURICH, GILDA B. (fl. 1950's-1970's)
Amer. construction company executive
O'Neill--Women's p515

GLANVILLE-HICKS, PEGGY (1912-)
Australian music critic, composer, author
Claghorn--Biog. p174
Jablonski--Ency. p375
Thomson--Amer. p8,12,88

GLASGOW, ELLEN ANDERSON GHOLSON (1874-1945)
Amer. novelist
Avenel--Comp. p106
Clark--Leading p127-128
Earnest--American p166
Ehrlich--Oxford, see index p454
Howard--Seven p35-78
James--Notable (2) p44-49
Kronenberger--Atlan. p319
McHenry--Liberty's p158

Magill--Cycl. p422-426
Moers--Literary p292
Parker--Uneasy p131-134
Scott--Southern p4,18,214,217, 219,223-225
Seymour-Smith--Novels p145,por.
Sherr--American p238
Webster's--Amer. p403
World--Who p13

GLASPELL, SUSAN KEATING (1876/1882-1948)
Amer. playwright, novelist
Chinoy--Women p6-7,149-151,163, 247-248,251-254, por.
McHenry--Liberty's p158-159
Ehrlich--Oxford p56,347-348
James--Notable (2) p49-51
Seymour-Smith--Novels p145
Sochen--Movers p10,75-83,88,272

GLASS, META (c1881-1967)
Amer. educator, college president
Hazen--Interv. p227

GLASSE, HANNAH (fl. c1720's)
British cookbook author
Macksey--Book p14

GLEASON, KATE (1865-1933)
Amer. bank president, builder, business woman, mechanical engineer
Bird--Enterprising p171-175
James--Notable (2) p51-52
McHenry--Liberty's p159
O'Neill--Women's p187,517
Sherr--American p174

GLEED, MARY
See GRAY, MAXWELL

GLENN, ANNIE
Amer., (wife of John Glenn)
People--Best p232, por.

GLENN, CONSTANCE (fl. 1970's)
Amer. museum director
O'Neill--Women's p616

GLENN, ELINOR MARSHALL (1915-)
Amer. labor leader
O'Neill--Women's p302-303,315

GLENN, MARY (WILLCOX) BROWN (1869-1940)

Amer. social welfare leader
James--Notable (2) p52-53

GLESSNER, FRANCES M. MACBETH
(1848-1932)
Amer. silversmith
Callen--Women p162,223

GLICKMAN, GRETCHEN (fl. 1970's)
Amer. museum curator
Women's--Female p118

"GLORIA" (fl. 1930's)
English model
Keenan--Women p115,117, por.

"GLORIA JEAN" (1926/1927-   )
Amer. child actress, singer
Edelson--Kids p71-72
Lamparski--What. (4) p30-31,
por.
Lamparski--What. (8) p146-147,
por.

GLOSE, GEORGIANNA, SISTER
(fl. 1970's)
Amer. nun
Proctor--Women p147-148,152-
153,156

GLOUCESTER, ELEANOR COBHAM,
DUCHESS OF (fl. 1440's)
English accused witch, medi-
cal woman, astrologist
Leary--Golden p126n,129
Mead--Hist. p322

GLOVER, ELIZABETH (fl. 1630's)
Amer. Colonial printer
Marzolf--Up p2

GLOVER, MRS. (-1685)
Irish-Amer. accused witch
Williams--Demeter's p138

GLOVER, SARAH ANN (1785-1867)
English music teacher
Macksey--Book p212

GLUCK, ALMA (1884-1938)
Rumanian-Amer. opera
singer
Claghorn--Biog. p175
James--Notable (2) p53-55
McHenry--Liberty's p159-160
Neidle--America's p224-225
Tuggle--Golden p76-78, por.

GLUCKSMAN, MARGIE
Amer. TV director
Scheuer--Tel. p186

GLUECK, ELEANOR TOUROFF
(1898-1972)
Amer. research crimonologist,
social worker
Cur. Biog. '72 p463
McHenry--Liberty's p160
Sicherman--Notable p278-280

GLUECK, GRACE (fl. 1970's)
Amer. art critic
Women's--Female p121

GLUECKEL (GLÜKEL) OF HAMELN
(1647/1648-1724)
German diarist
Fink--Great p30-40
Henry--Written p169-177

GLYN, ELINOR SUTHERLAND (1864-
1943)
English novelist, film writer
Crosland--Beyond p5-8,11
Dunlap--Calif. p73-74, por.
Jones--Rutledge p326
Showalter--Lit. p342
Smith--Movies p16,108

GNOINSKIEJ, JADWIGE (fl. 1550's)
Polish religious, cultural
leader
Bainton--Spain p160-168

GOAD, DOLLY
See GOOD, DOLLY

GOALEN, BARBARA (c1920-   )
English model
Keenan--Women p136-138,144-146,
por.

GOCHOLASHVILI, MARIYA (fl.
1920's-1940's)
Russian plant pathologist
Macksey--Book p167

GODARE, MADAME (fl. 1770's)
Amer. flag maker of North
West territory
Sherr--American p68

GODDARD, MARY KATHERINE (1738-
1816)
Amer. Colonial printer,

People's Almanac (1) p514
People's Almanac (2) p402
Smith--Daughters, see index
p391
Sochen--Herstory p76-77,80-81,
por.
Taylor--Gener. p8-9
Woman's Almanac p541,552
World--Who p188

GODWIN, NATALIE
Amer. radio announcer
Marzolf--Up p123

GOELET, MAY WILSON, DUCHESS
OF ROXBURGH(E) (fl.
1910's)
Amer. heiress, social leader
Brandon--Dollar p31-32,71, por.

GOEPPERT-MAYER, MARIA
See MAYER, MARIA GERTRUDE
GOEPPERT

GOETHE, KATHERINA ELISABETH
TEXTOR VON (1731-1808)
German salonist, mother of
Johann Wolfgang von Goethe
Diagram--Mothers p106-107, por.

GOFF, REGINA (1917-)
Amer. educator
O'Neill--Women's p431
Signif.--Amer. p63, por.

GÖKDOGEN, NUZHET (fl. 1930's-
1950's)
Turkish astronomer
Macksey--Book p158

GOLDBERG, DORA
See BAYES, NORA

GOLDBERG, JEAN V.
Amer. TV director
Scheuer--Tel. p186

GOLDBERG, MIRIAM (fl. 1970's)
Amer. educator, professor
O'Neill--Women's p422

"GOLDBERG, MOLLIE"
See BERG, GERTRUDE

GOLDBERG, WHOOPI, pseud.
(1950-)
Amer. actress

Cur. Biog. '85 p145-147,
por.

GOLDEN, EUNICE (1970's)
Amer. painter
Women's--Female p43

GOLDEN-GOTTLIEB, PHYLLIS
Amer. TV director
Scheuer--Tel. p187

GOLDFIELD, GLADYS
See SCHMITT, GLADYS LEONORE

GOLDHABER, GERTRUDE SCHARFF
(fl. 1970's)
German-Amer. physicist
O'Neill--Women's p145,182

GOLDMAN, HETTY (1881-1972)
Amer. archaeologist, professor
O'Neill--Women's p146
Sicherman--Notable p280-282

GOLDMAN, ILENE
Amer. consumer activist, co-
founder, CAN
O'Neill--Women's p724

GOLDMARK, JOSEPHINE CLARA
(1877-1950)
Amer. social researcher, labor
reformer
McHenry--Liberty's p161
James--Notable (2) p60-61
O'Neill--Women's p291

GOLDRING, WINIFRED (1888-1971)
Amer. paleontologist
Sicherman--Notable p282-283

GOLDSCHMIDT, JOHANNA MARIA
See LIND, JENNY

GOLDSMITH, GRACE ARABELL
(1904-1975)
Amer. physician, nutritionist,
public health educator
Sicherman--Notable p283-284

GOLDSTEIN, BETTY NAOMI
See FRIEDAN, BETTY

GOLDTHWAITE, ANNE WILSON (c1875-
1944)
Amer. Southern belle, printmaker

GOOCH, ELIZA (fl. 1770's)
Amer. patriot
Young--Revol. p156-157,168-169,
211

GOOD, DOLLY (1915-1967)
Amer. singer
Claghorn--Biog. p177

GOOD, JOSEPHINE L. (fl. 1950's-
1970's)
Amer. politician, convention
director
O'Neill--Women's p75

GOOD, MARY L. (fl. 1970's)
Amer. chemist
O'Neill--Women's p165,170

GOOD, MILLIE (MILDRED)
(1913-)
Amer. singer
Claghorn--Biog. p177

GOODALL, JANE
See VAN LAWICK-GOODALL,
JANE, BARONESS

GOODAN, ALICE MAY CHANDLER
(c1893-1984)
Amer. millionaire
Forbes--400 ('84) p188

GOODELL, (RHODA) LAVINIA
(fl. 1870's)
Amer. lawyer
Sherr--American p248

GOODENOUGH, FLORENCE LAURA
(1886-1959)
Amer. developmental psychologist
Sicherman--Notable p284-286

GOODIN, JOAN M. (1934-)
Amer. labor leader
O'Neill--Women's p314

GOODIN, NATASHA
See WOOD, NATALIE

GOODING, CYNTHIA (1924-)
Amer. singer, guitarist
Claghorn--Biog. p177

GOODMAN, ELLEN (fl. 1960's-
1970's)

Amer. humorous writer,
feminist
O'Neill--Women's p467

GOODMAN, EMILY JANE (1940-)
Amer. lawyer, writer
O'Neill--Women's p359

GOODMAN, THEODOSIA
See BARA, THEDA

GOODRICH, ANN
See STORY, ANN

GOODRICH, ANNIE WARBURTON
(1866-1954)
Amer. nurse, school dean,
educator
O'Neill--Women's p232-233
Sicherman--Notable p286-288

GOODRICH, EDNA L.
Amer. teacher, consultant
O'Neill--Women's p429

GOODRICH, ELIZA (fl. 1950's-1970's)
Amer. painter, (miniaturist)
Petersen--Women p67-68

GOODRICH, FRANCES (c1891-1984)
Amer. film writer
Cur. Biog. '84 p472

GOODRICH, FRANCES LOUISA
(1856-1944)
Amer. missionary, teacher,
craftswoman (weaving)
O'Neill--Women's p122
Sherr--American p178

GOODRIDGE, SARAH (1788-1853)
Amer. portrait artist, minia-
turist, printer
Fine--Women p99-100
McHenry--Liberty's p162

GOODWILL, LINDA (fl. 1970's)
English jockey
Hollander--100 p65-66

GOODWIN, ESTELLE
See WINWOOD, ESTELLE

GOODWIN, SARAH (fl. 1745-1756)
Amer. chair-caner, Colonial
business woman
Williams--Demeter's p197

GOODY, JOAN (fl. 1970's)
Amer. architect
O'Neill--Women's p612

GOOLAGONG, EVONNE (1951-)
Australian tennis player
Cur. Biog. '71 p162-164
Hollander--100 p111-112, por.
Kulkin--Her p123-124
McWhirter--Guinness p154,164,
por.
Sullivan--Queens p68-83, por.
Who Did What p131
Woman's Almanac p416
World--Who p214

GOOLD, MARY ANN (fl. 1970's)
Amer. telephone repairwoman
Seed--Saturday's p111-112, por.

GOON, TOY LEN CHIN
Chinese-Amer. business woman,
noted Maine mother
Amer.--Mothers p244-245, por.

GOOSE, MRS. (fl. 1640's)
Amer. Colonial grocer, first
shopkeeper
Williams--Demeter's p194

GOOSENS, SIDONIE (1894/1899-)
English harpist
Jones--Rutledge p331-332

GOPOVNA, NINA (fl. 1970's)
Russian canoeist
McWhirter--Guinness p47, por.

GOQUIIOLAY-ARELLANO, REMEDIOS
(1911-)
Filipino physician
Hellstedt--Women p410-412, por.

GORDIMER, NADINE (1923-)
South African novelist,
journalist, short story writer
Avenel--Comp. (1) p218
Crosland--Beyond p141-144
Cur. Biog. '80 p131-134, por.
Moers--Literary p292
Seymour-Smith--Novels p147
Seymour-Smith--Who's p136-137

GO(U)RDIN, NATASHA
See WOOD, NATALIE

GORDON, ANNA ADAMS (1853-1931)

Amer. social reformer
James--Notable (2) p63-64
McHenry--Liberty's p162

GORDON, CAROLINE (1895-1981)
Amer. novelist, short story
writer, critic
Avenel--Comp. (2) p108
Ehrlich--Oxford, see index p454
Magill--Cycl. p440-441
Seymour-Smith--Novels p147

GORDON, DOROTHY LERNER (1889-
1970)
Amer. radio, TV personality,
children's book author
Cur. Biog. '70 p463
Marzolf--Up p122-123,134
O'Neill--Women's p495
Sicherman--Notable p288-289

GORDON, FRITZI (fl. 1970's)
British bridge player
O'Neill--Women's p592

GORDON, JANE
Amer. TV magazine editor
Scheuer--Tel. p191

GORDON, JEAN MARGARET (1865-
1931)
Amer. social welfare, suffrage
leader
James--Notable (2) p64-66
Sherr--American p85

GORDON, JULIETTE (1)
See LOW, JULIETTE MAGILL
KINZIE GORDON

GORDON, JULIETTE (2) (fl. 1970's)
Amer. artist
Women's--Female p104

GORDON, KATE M. (1861-1932)
Amer. suffragist, social re-
former
Hymowitz--Hist. p276
James--Notable (2) p66-68
Sherr--American p85

GORDON, KATHARINE
Scottish novelist
Seymour-Smith--Novels p147

GORDON, LAURA DE FORCE (1838-
1907)

Amer. lecturer, editor,
journalist, lawyer, feminist,
social reformer
James--Notable (2) p68-69
McHenry--Liberty's p162-163
Sherr--American p15

GORDON, MARY (1949-)
Amer. novelist
Cur. Biog. '81 p173-177, por.

GORDON, MARY GILMOUR (c1882-
1963)
Scottish actress
Springer--They p122,297, por.

GORDON, ODETTA HOLMES
FELIOUS
See ODETTA (ODETTE),
(HOLMES-FELIOUS) GORDON

GORDON, RUTH (1896-1985)
Amer. actress, playwright,
film writer
Cur. Biog. '72 p178-181, por.
Cur. Biog. '85 p466
Entertainers p199
Hirschhorn--Rating p161, por.
P.W.--Author p286-287,500
Woman's Almanac p107
World--Who p235

GORDON, RUTH VIDA (fl. 1970's)
Amer. structural engineer
O'Neill--Women's p193

GORDON, VIVIAN (-1931)
Amer. vice-informer
Horan--Desperate p39-40

GORDON-LAZAREFF, HELENE
(1909-)
Russian fashion leader,
magazine founder
O'Neill--Women's p475

GORE, CATHERINE GRACE
FRANCES MOODY (1799-
1861)
English novelist
Moers--Literary p292

GORE, LESLEY (1946-)
Amer. singer
Claghorn--Biog. p178
World--Who p267

GORE, MARGOT (fl. 1940's)
English aviatrix
Boase--Sky's p180,182,186,188,
193,195

GORELICK, SHIRLEY (fl. 1970's)
Amer. artist
Women's--Female p104

GORENKO, ANNA ANDREYEVNA
(1889-1966)
Russian poet
Jones--Rutledge p9
Kronenberger--Atlan. p10
Macksey--Book p192-193
Moers--Literary p272
O'Neill--Women's p683-684
Seymour-Smith--Who's p13
Who Did What p9-10
World--Who p36

GORMAN, MARGARET (fl. 1920's)
Amer. first "Miss America"
Fenton--Famous p205, por.

GORMAN, MARY (fl. 1770's)
Amer. Revolutionary War
patriot, nurse
Meyer--Petticoat p83

GORME, EYDIE (1931/1932-)
Amer. singer
Anderson--People p173
Claghorn--Biog. p179
Simon--Best p343-344, por.
World--Who p267

GORNICK, VIVIAN
Amer. feminist, writer
Adams--Women p121

GORR, RITA (1926-)
Belgian opera singer
Gammond--Illus. p243, por.

GORSUCH, ANNE (McGILL) (1942-)
Amer. government official
Cur. Biog. '82 p123-126, por.

GOSLAR, LOTTE (1917-)
German-Amer. dancer, mime
Chinoy--Women p126-127

GOTTCHALK (GOTTSCHALK),
LAURA RIDING
See RIDING, LAURA

GOTTLIEB, BARBARA (c1954-)
Amer. Food Day co-ordinator
O'Neill--Women's p731

GOTTLIEB, BESSIE (1891-1972)
Amer. humanitarian
O'Neill--Women's p721-722

GOUDAL, JETTA (c1898-)
Lamparski--What. Annual
(4,5) p95-99, por.

GOUDGE, ELIZABETH (1900-1984)
British novelist, short-story
writer, playwright
Cur. Biog. '84 p472

GOUGAR, HELEN MAR JACKSON
(1843-1907)
Amer. Indian, suffragist,
temperance reformer, feminist,
lecturer, author
James--Notable (2) p69-71
Sherr--American p67
Warren--Pictorial p141

GOUGES, OLYMPE DE (1748-1793)
French writer, feminist
Crosland--Women p20-21
Macksey--Book p79
Taylor--Gener. p7-8

GOUGH, ELEANOR FAGON
See HOLIDAY, BILLY ("LADY
DAY")

GOULD, ANNA
See TALLEYRAND PERIGORD,
ANNA GOULD, DUCHESS DE

GOULD, BEATRICE BLACKMAR
Amer. magazine co-editor
Bird--Enterprising p206-209
O'Neill--Women's p481

GOULD, CHERYL
Amer. TV news producer
Scheuer--Tel. p192

GOULD, DIANA (fl. 1960's-1970's)
Amer. filmmaker
Smith--Movies p169,243

GOULD, HANNAH FLAGG (1789/
1792-1865)
Amer. hymnist, poet
Claghorn--Biog. p179

GOULD, LOIS (c1937-)
Amer. feminist, novelist,
humorist
Sochen--Movers p283-285

GOULD, PATRICIA (fl. 1970's)
British NATO representative
O'Neill--Women's p552

GOULD, SHANE E. (1956/1957-)
Australian swimmer
Assoc. Press--Pursuit p306, por.
Hollander--100 p85-86, por.
Kulkin--Her p125-126
McWhirter--Guinness p132-133,
por.
Who Did What p132

GOURGAND, FRANÇOISE
See VESTRIS, FRANÇOISE-ROSE,
MADAME

GOURIELLI, HELENA RUBINSTEIN
See RUBINSTEIN, HELENA

GOURLEY, BERNICE
Amer. "foster" mother, noted
Washington state mother
Amer.--Mothers p562-563, por.

GOURNAY, MARIE LE JARS DE
(1565/1566-1645)
French author
Bree--Women p27-28

GOUSHA, MRS. JOSEPH R.
See POWELL, DAWN

GOUZE, MARIE-OLYMPE
See GOUGES, OLYMPE DE

GOVE, MARY
See NICHOLS, MARY SARGENT
NEAL GOVE

GOWER, PAULINE (1910-1947)
English aviatrix
Boase--Sky's p126-130,178-180,
see also index p221, por.

GOYA, GRACIA LUCIENTES
Spanish, mother of Francisco
Goya
Diagram--Mothers p108-109

GOZZADINI, BETISIA (BETTISIA)

(-1249)
Italian lawyer, lecturer
Sparrow--Women p22

GRABAU, MARY ANTIN
See ANTIN, MARY

GRABER, PHYLLIS (fl. 1970's)
Amer. tennis player
O'Neill--Women's p583

GRABLE, BETTY (1916-1973)
Amer. singer, actress
Claghorn--Biog. p180
Clark--Leading p167
Fox-Sheinwold--Gone p146-152,
por.
Hirschhorn--Rating p162-164,
por.
Keylin--Hollywood p129, por.
Manchel--Women p64,66,77, por.
Mordden--Movie, see index p293,
por.
Shipman--Gold. p257-261, por.
Sicherman--Notable p289-291
Springer--They p122,297, por.
Wilson--Holly. p145-147, por.
Woman's Almanac p344
World--Who p235

GRACE, PRINCESS OF MONACO
See KELLY, GRACE, PRINCESS
OF MONACO

GRACE, REBECCA MOTTE
See MOTTE, REBECCA BREWTON

GRAEFF, BERYL (fl. 1970's)
Amer. tax consultant
O'Neill--Women's p118

GRAEME, ELIZABETH
See FERGUSON, ELIZABETH
GRAEME

GRAF, LOUISE SPINNER (fl. 1950's)
Amer. jury foreman
Sherr--American p255

GRAFF, FRAU
See MERIAN, MARIE SIBYLLA

GRAFFENRIED, (MARY) CLARE DE
(1849-1921)
Amer. social investigator,
statistician
James--Notable (1) p452-454

Scott--Southern p121-122,127,
131,133

GRAHAM, ALICE BERRY (-1913)
Amer. hospital co-founder
Sherr--American p131, por.

GRAHAM, ANNIE ELSIE ZIMMERMAN
(1904-)
Amer. nurse, noted Alabama
mother
Amer.--Mothers p8, por.

GRAHAM, BETTE CLAIR NESMITH
(-1980)
Amer. executive
O'Neill--Women's p100,136

GRAHAM, ENNIS, pseud.
See MOLESWORTH, MARY LOUISE
STEWART

GRAHAM, FLORENCE NIGHTINGALE
See ARDEN, ELIZABETH

GRAHAM, GLORIA (1925-)
Amer. actress
Hirschhorn--Rating p164-165, por.
Shipman--Internatl. p210-212, por.

GRAHAM, ISABELLA MARSHALL
(1742-1814)
Scottish-Amer. educator,
philanthropist
James--Notable (2) p71-72
McHenry--Liberty's p163

GRAHAM, JANET
Amer. pianist
Hazen--Interv. p357

GRAHAM, KATHARINE MEYER
(1917-)
Amer. newspaper publisher
Bird--Enterprising p220-223
Cur. Biog. '71 p170-172, por.
Forbes--400 ('84) p120
Longstreet--Queen p173
McHenry--Liberty's p163-164
Macksey--Book p173-174, por.
Marzolf--Up p114-115
O'Neill--Women's p436-437,462,
514, por.
People's Almanac (1) p786
Schoenebaum--Prof. p242-243
Woman's Almanac p269, por.
World--Who p52

GRAHAM, MARGARET
British educator
Macksey--Book p77

GRAHAM, MARIA (1785-1843)
British traveler
Macksey--Book p238

GRAHAM, MARTHA (1893/1895-)
Amer. dancer, choreographer,
teacher
Bowman--Entertain. p4-15, por.
Clark--Leading p183
Fabian--On p180-181, por.
Ingraham--Album p62
Jones--Rutledge p335
Kulkin--Her p126-127
Longstreet--Queen p192
McHenry--Liberty's p164
Macksey--Book p229
100--Greatest (1) p23, por.
O'Neill--Women's p265,594,641,
646-647,650,669
Percival--Modern p12,53-60,64,
68-69,72,98, por.
Signif.--Amer. p64, por.
Stoddard--Famous p201-210,
por.
Warren--Pictorial p181-183, por.
Webster's--Amer. p420
Who Did What p133
Woman's Almanac p310-311, por.
World--Who p70

GRAHAM, MARY ANN
Amer. patriot, poet, noted
Maryland mother
Amer.--Mothers p252-253

GRAHAM, MARY BELLE GLEAMONS
(fl. 1970's)
Amer. nursing home head
O'Neill--Women's p139-140

GRAHAM, MARY J. (fl. 1840's)
Amer. pioneer
Sherr--American p132

GRAHAM, MORROW (1892-)
Amer., mother of Billy
Graham
Kooiman--Silhouettes p64-80,
por.

GRAHAM, PATRICIA ALBJERG
(fl. 1970's)
Amer. educator, college dean,

co-editor
O'Neill--Women's p425

GRAHAM, RUTH
Amer., wife of Billy Graham
Funt--Are p171-196, por.

GRAHAM, SHEILAH (1908/1910-)
English-Amer. journalist,
writer, columnist
Cur. Biog. '69 p175-177, por.
Dunlap--Calif. p75-76
O'Neill--Women's p447-448
World--Who p52

GRAHAM, SHIRLEY (1907-1977)
Amer. composer, stage
director
Cur. Biog. '77 p462

GRAHAME, MARGOT (1911-)
English actress
Springer--They p122,297, por.

GRAHN, JUDY
Amer. poet
Chester--Rising p280-288, por.

GRAHN, LUCILE (1819-1907)
Danish ballet dancer
Migel--Ballerinas p168-178, por.

GRAJALES, MARIANA (1808-1893)
Cuban patriot
Henderson--Ten p147-168, por.

GRAMATICA, IRMA (1870-1962)
Italian actress
Entertainers p161

GRAMCKO, IDA (fl. 1940's)
Venezuelan philosopher,
professor, poet, ambassador
Macksey--Book p43

GRANAHAN, KATHRYN ELIZABETH
O'HAY (1896/1900-)
Amer. Congresswoman
Chamberlin--Min. p267-269
Cur. Biog. '79 p463

GRAND, SARAH, pseud. (1855/1862-
1943)
Irish novelist
Crosland--Beyond p4-5, #14
Showalter--Lit. p204-210,342

"GRANDMA DOCTOR"
  See FRENCH, EMMA

"GRANDMA MOSES"
  See MOSES, ANNA MARY
  ROBERTSON

GRANDPIERRE-DEVERZY,
    ADRIENNE MARIE LOUISE
    (1788-)
    French artist
    Harris--Women p219-221,349

GRANGER, ETHEL (1905-)
    British holder of fashion
    record
    Macksey--Book p12

GRANN, PHYLLIS (fl. 1970's)
    Amer. publisher, editor,
    executive
    O'Neill--Women's p489

"GRANNY DOLLAR"
  See CALLAHAN, NANCY

GRANT, ANNE McVICKAR (1755-
    1838)
    Scottish-Amer. author
    Ehrlich--Oxford p98
    Kulkin--Her p127-128
    Williams--Demeter's p103-104,
    212-213

GRANT, ELLEN
  See GRANT, NELLIE

GRANT, GOGI (fl. 1950's)
    Amer. singer
    Lamparski--What. (8) p112-113,
    por.

GRANT, HANNAH SIMPSON (1798-
    1883)
    Amer., mother of Ulysses S.
    Grant
    Book--Lists (2) p266
    Diagram--Mothers p110-111, por.
    Faber--Presidents' p235-240

GRANT, JACQUELYN (fl. 1960's-
    1970's)
    Amer. theologian
    Innis--Profiles p64-65, por.

GRANT, JULIA DENT (1826-1902)
    Amer. First Lady, wife of

Ulysses S. Grant
    James--Notable (2) p72-73
    Kulkin--Her p129
    Melick--Wives p44-45, por.
    People's Almanac (1) p269
    Woman's Almanac p489

GRANT, JULIA L. (1936-)
    Amer. government official
    O'Neill--Women's p339-340

GRANT, LEE (1929/1931-)
    Amer. actress
    Anderson--People p179-180, por.
    Cur. Biog. '74 p150-153, por
    O'Neill--Women's p664
    World--Who p235

GRANT, MICKI (fl. 1970's)
    Amer. composer, lyricist, per-
    former
    Abdul--Famous p66-72, por.

GRANT, NELLIE (fl. 1870's)
    Amer., daughter of President
    Grant
    People's Almanac (1) p269

GRANT, SHELLY
    Amer. trampoline athlete
    O'Neill--Women's p562

GRANT, TIA (THU VAN) (1965/
    1966-)
    Vietnamese refugee child
    Rivera--Special p241-266, por.

GRANT, ZILPAH POLLY (1794-1874)
    Amer. educator
    Berkin--Women p183-184,189-194
    James--Notable (2) p73-75
    McHenry--Liberty's p164-165

GRANVILLE, BONITA (1923-)
    Amer. actress, TV producer
    Edelson--Kids p77-80,106, por.
    Springer--They p122-123,297, por.

GRANVILLE, CHRISTINE
  See SKARBEK, KRYSTYNA
  GIZYCKA GRANVILLE

GRASSE, PATRICIA A. (1944-)
    Amer. genealogical researcher,
    author
    Meyer--Who's p85

GRASSETT, KATIE (fl. 1890's)
British weaver, head of
school
Callen--Women p3

GRASSINI, JOSEPHINA
GIUSEPPINI (1773-1850)
Italian singer
Macksey--Book p211

GRASSO, ELLA TAMBUSSI
(1919-1981)
Amer. politician, noted
Connecticut mother
Amer.--Mothers p82, por.
Bowman--Politics p40-47, por.
Chamberlin--Min. p338-340
Cur. Biog. '75 p173-176, por.
Cur. Biog. ;81 p464
Greenebaum--Politics p99-117,
por.
McHenry--Liberty's p165
Macksey--Book p46
100--Greatest (1) p54
O'Neill--Women's p44,76, por.
Woman's Almanac p472-473
World--Who p141

GRÄSTEN, VIOLA (1910-)
Finnish textile designer
O'Neill--Women's p272

GRATTAN, SALLIE (fl. 1860's)
Amer. Southern belle
DeLeon--Belles p211, por.

GRATZ, REBECCA (1781-1869)
Amer. philanthropist, Hebrew
Sunday School founder
Baum--Jewish p30,36-38
DePauw--Rem. p74-75, por.
Earle--Two Cent. (2) p531
Ehrlich--Oxford p209
Fink--Great p49-55, por.
Henry--Written p219-227, por.
James--Notable (2) p75-76
McHenry--Liberty's p165
Macksey--Book p69
Sherr--American p203
Stein--Lives p677-682, por.

GRAU, SHIRLEY ANN (1929-)
Amer. novelist, short story
writer
Avenel--Comp. (2) p109
Ehrlich--Oxford, see index
p454

McHenry--Liberty's p165-166
Seymour-Smith--Novels p149
World--Who p14

GRAUPNER, CATHERINE HILUER
(c1777-1821)
Amer. singer
Claghorn--Biog. p182

GRAVES, MRS. A.J.
Amer. writer
Hymowitz--Hist. p67

GRAVES, DIXIE BIBB (c1882-1965)
Amer. Senator
Chamberlin--Min. p121-125

GRAVES, ELEANOR (fl. 1960's)
Amer. magazine reporter
Hamblin--That p132-135

GRAVES, NANCY STEVENSON
(1940-)
Amer. sculptor
Cur. Biog. '81 p177-180, por.
Women's--Female p26,89

GRAY, ANN MAYNARD (fl. 1970's)
Amer. TV executive
O'Neill--Women's p524
Scheuer--Tel. p196

GRAY, EILEEN (1879-1976)
Irish designer, furniture
maker
Macksey--Book p207

GRAY, ELIZABETH JANET (1902-)
Amer. children's author,
librarian, teacher
O'Neill--Women's p691

GRAY, FRANCINE DU PLESSIX
(fl. 1970's)
French-Amer. novelist
P.W.--Author p61-64,500

GRAY, GILDA (1901-1959)
Polish-Amer. actress, dancer
Hazen--Interv. p300
World--Who p263

GRAY, HANNA HOLBORN (1930-)
Amer. university president
Cur. Biog. '79 p151-154, por.
McHenry--Liberty's p156
O'Neill--Women's p411, por.
World--Who p100

GRAY, LENORA DENNIS (1873-1957)
Amer. feminist, noted Nebraska mother
Amer.--Mothers p336-337, por.

GRAY, LINDA (1940-1941-)
Amer. actress
Scheuer--Tel. p196, por.

GRAY, MARY ADELINE (fl. 1860's)
Amer. Western pioneer
Sherr--American p8

GRAY, MARY ALICE SMITH
Amer. orphan, friend James Whitcomb Riley family
Sherr--American p67

GRAY, MAXWELL (1847-1923)
British novelist, journalist
Showalter--Lit. p337

GRAYDON, RACHEL (fl. 1770's)
Amer. patriot
Meyer--Petticoat p65-66

GRAYSON, BETSY JEANNE
See DAVIS, GAIL

GRAYSON, KATHRYN (1923-)
Amer. singer, actress
Claghorn--Biog. p183
Hirschhorn--Rating p167-168, por.
Shipman--Internatl. p217-218, por.
World--Who p267

GREATOREX, ELIZA PRATT
(1819/1820-1897)
Irish-Amer. painter
James--Notable (2) p76-77

GRECCO, JULIETTE (fl. 1940's)
French singer, fashion influence
Keenan--Women p205-207, por.

GREDAL, EVA (fl. 1970's)
Danish minister
O'Neill--Women's p57

GREELEY-SMITH, NIXOLA (1880-1919)
Amer. journalist
James--Notable (2) p78-79
Marzolf--Up p37

GREEN, ADELE
Amer. organization president, feminist
Adams--Women p21,103,107,178

GREEN, ANNA KATHERINE (1846-1935)
Amer. novelist
Ehrlich--Oxford p152
James--Notable (2) p79-80
McHenry--Liberty's p166
Seymour-Smith--Novels p149
Welter--Dimity p130-144

GREEN, ANN(E) CATHERINE HOOF
(c1720-1775)
Amer. Colonial newspaper publisher, printer
Demeter--Primer p84-99
Flexner--Face p174, por.
James--Notable (2) p80-81
McHenry--Liberty's p166-167
Sherr--American p91
Stein--Lives, no p.
Warren--Pictorial p52
Williams--Demeter's p234-235

GREEN, ARDA A. (-1958)
Amer. chemist
O'Neill--Women's p164,166

GREEN, BLANCHE (fl. 1940's)
Amer. corporation executive
Hazen--Interv. p337-338

GREEN, CONSTANCE WINSOR
McLAUGHLIN (1897-1975)
Amer. historian
Sicherman--Notable p291-292

GREEN, DOROTHY
Amer. millionaire
Forbes--400 ('84) p124

GREEN, EDITH STARRETT (1910-1987)
Amer. Congresswoman
Chamberlin--Min. p251-258, por.
O'Neill--Women's p431
Sochen--Movers p232-233
U.S.--Women (89th) p9, por.
U.S.--Women (90th) p7, por.

GREEN, ELIZABETH SHIPPEN
(c1871-1954)
Amer. illustrator
Callen--Women p208, 223

GREEN, EMMA EDWARDS (1890-
1942)
Amer., noted Idaho mother,
artist, women's suffrage
worker
Amer.--Mothers p154-155, por.
Time--Women p117

GREEN, EVELYN EVERETT (1856-
1932)
British author
People's Almanac (3) p546

GREEN, FRANCES ("GREENIE")
Amer. army flier
Keil--Those p169,173-175,181,
186-188, por.

GREEN, HANNAH, pseud. (1932-)
Amer. novelist
Moers--Literary p81-82,292

GREEN, HENRIETTA HOWLAND
ROBINSON ("HETTY")
(1934-1916)
Amer. millionaire, financier
Bird--Enterprising p87
Eills--Here p88-89
Forma--They p73,75-76, por.
James--Notable (2) p81-83
Longstreet--Queen p157-163,
por.
McFarland--Incred. p123
McHenry--Liberty's p167
Macksey--Book p165
O'Neill--Women's p525-526
People's Almanac (2) p215-216
People's Almanac (3) p163-165
Sherr--American p11,152,228,
por.
Webster's--Amer. p427-428
Woman's Almanac p210, por.
World--Who p297

GREEN, JOANN (1938-)
Amer. theatrical director
Ruddick--Working p117-127,
342, por.

GREEN, JOYCE H. (fl. 1970's)
Amer. judge
O'Neill--Women's p372

GREEN, MAE
See PARKER, JEAN

GREEN, MAE RUTH (1921-)
Amer. genealogical researcher,

editor, writer
Meyer--Who's p85

GREEN, MARTY (fl. 1970's)
Amer. police officer
O'Neill--Women's p374

GREEN, MARY W.
Amer. writer
Meyer--Petticoat p19,68,92,101,
121-122,149-150,153

GREEN, MITZI (1920-1969)
Amer. child actress
Springer--They p123,297-298

GREEN, PATRICIA
Amer. clergyman
Smith--Break. p91-110, por.

GREEN, PHYLLIS (fl. 1920's)
British track and field athlete
McWhirter--Guinness p166

GREEN, RAYNA DIANE (fl. 1970's)
Amer. Cherokee Indian folk-
lore scholar, writer
O'Neill--Women's p149

GREEN, RUBY (fl. 1970's)
Amer. cotton mills worker
Kahn--Hill. p187-197, por.

GREENAWAY, KATE (CATHERINE)
(1846-1901)
English designer, children's
book author, illustrator
Callen--Women p223, see also
index p231
Jones--Rutledge p338
Macksey--Book p206-207
Munsterberg--Hist. p105,108-109
Smaridge--Famous p19-28, por.
Sparrow--Women p65-66,119,127

GREENBERG, ALICE
Amer. TV executive, director
Scheuer--Tel. p196-197

GREENBERG, BARBARA (1932-)
Amer. poet
Chester--Rising p201-205, por.

GREENBERG, IDA (fl. 1940's)
Amer., noted Colorado mother
Amer.--Mothers p69-70, por.

GREENBERG, JOANNE

See GREEN, HANNAH,
pseud.

GREENBERGER, MARCIA D.
(1946-)
Amer. feminist, government
official
O'Neill--Women's p358

GREENE, AMY
Amer. company founder,
president
Adams--Women p67-69,73,104,
160,177,194

GREENE, ANNA TERRY
See PHILLIPS, ANNA TERRY
GREENE

GREENE, ANNE (1628-)
English servant, accused
criminal
People's Almanac (2) p1181

GREENE, BELLE DA COSTA
(1883-1950)
Amer. library director,
bibliographer
James--Notable (2) p83-85
McHenry--Liberty's p167

GREENE, CATHERINE LITTLE-
field (1753-1814)
Amer., noted Rhode Island
mother, (patron of Eli
Whitney)
Amer.--Mothers p477
Booth--Women p251-253,295-296
Engle--Women p244-255
James--Notable (2) p85-86
Meyer--Petticoat p45,99,201,
224
Sherr--American p32
Woman's Almanac p371

GREENE, GAEL
Amer. novelist, radio
reporter
Lichtenstein--Mach. p5,287-291
Marzolf--Up p78-79

GREENE, GLADYS
See ARTHUR, JEAN

GREENE, MAXINE
Amer. university professor
O'Neill--Women's p416

GREENE, NANCY CATHERINE
(1943-)
Canadian skier
Cur. Biog. '69 p182-184, por.
O'Neill--Women's p566

GREENE, SARAH PRATT McLEAN
(1856-1935)
Amer. author
Ehrlich--Oxford p91
James--Notable (2) p86-87

GREENEBAUM, LOUISE G.
Amer. politician, writer
Greenebaum--Politics p144, por.

GREENEWALT, MARGARETTA
LAMMOT DU PONT (c1902-)
Amer. millionaire
Forbes--400 ('84) p149

GREENFIELD, AMY (fl. 1970's)
Amer. choreographer, film-
maker
Smith--Movies p169-170,243, por.

GREENFIELD, ELIZABETH TAYLOR
(1808/1809-1876)
Amer. singer
Claghorn--Biog. p184
Jablonski--Ency. p73
James--Notable (2) p87-89
McHenry--Liberty's p168
Signif.--Amer. p11, por.

GREENFIELD, MEG (1930-)
Amer. newspaper editor
O'Neill--Women's p437,462

GREENHOUSE, LINDA (fl. 1970's)
Amer. newspaper state bureau
chief
O'Neill--Women's p470

GREENHOW, ROSE O'NEAL (c1815-
1864)
Amer. Confederate spy
Ingraham--Album p30
James--Notable (2) p89-90
Kulkin--Her p130
McHenry--Liberty's p168
Millstein--We p130
People's Almanac (2) p425
Sherr--American p181,237-238,
por.
Warren--Pictorial p110
Webster's--Amer. p429

Woman's Almanac p454-
455

GREENSTEIN, ILISE (fl. 1970's)
Amer. artist
Women's--Female p104-105

GREENWAY, ISABELLA (-1935)
Amer. Congresswoman
Chamberlin--Min. p104-108

GREENWELL, DORA (1821-1882)
English poet
Showlater--Lit. p327

GREENWOOD, CHARLOTTE (1893-
1978)
Amer. actress
Springer--They p123,298, por.

GREENWOOD, GRACE, pseud.
(1823-1904)
Amer. Washington correspon-
dent, abolitionist, lecturer,
suffragist
Beasley--First p15-17,23, por.
James--Notable (2) p407-409
McHenry--Liberty's p248-249
Marzolf--Up p16-17
Sherr--American p25

GREENWOOD, JOAN (1921-)
English actress
Shipman--Internatl. p220-222,
por.

GREENWOOD, MARIE CHANDLER
(1901-)
Amer. postmaster, noted
Colorado mother
Amer.--Mothers p68-69, por.

GREER, GERMAINE (1939-)
Australian writer, educator,
feminist, journalist
Cur. Biog. '71 p172-175, por.
Golson--Playboy p326-351
O'Neill--Women's p705-706
Plante--Difficult p103-150,
153-173
P.W.--Author p360-362,500
Wintle--Makers p206-207, #187

GREER, JANE (1924-)
Amer. actress
Lamparski--What. Annual (4,5)
p25-30, por.

GREER, MRS. LESTER (fl. 1930's)
Amer. social reformer
Berkin--Women p385-386
O'Neill--Women's p339-340

GREGATH, ANN COCHRANE (1926-)
Amer. genealogical researcher,
author
Meyer--Who's p86

GREGG, DOROTHY
Amer. executive
O'Neill--Women's p523

GREGG, KATE L. (fl. 1910's)
Amer. scholar
Showlater--These p73-78

GREGORY, (ISABELLA) AUGUSTA
(LADY GREGORY) (1852-1932)
Irish playwright
Avenel--Comp. (1) p226-227
Entertainers p139
Jones--Rutledge p339
Kronenberger--Atlan. p338-339
Magill--Cycl. p458-459
Rogers--Ladies p10-12,139-142
Who Did What p134
World--Who p26

GREGORY, BETTINA (c1947-)
Amer. TV correspondent
Scheuer--Tel. p198

GREGORY, CYNTHIA (1946-)
Amer. ballet dancer
Bowman--Entertain. p46-47, por.
Cur. Biog. '77 p174-177, por.
Diamonstein--Open p153-157, por.
McHenry--Liberty's p168-169
O'Neill--Women's p641,644
People--Best p140-141, por.
Woman's Almanac p310
World--Who p70

GREGORY, MOLLIE (fl. 1970's)
Amer. filmmaker
Smith--Movies p170-171,243

GREGORY, PATRICIA ANN
McCONNAUGHAY (1925-)
Amer. genealogical researcher,
editor
Meyer--Who's p86

GREGORY, WELBY, LADY (fl. 1880's)
British craftswoman
Callen--Women p110

"GRENADIER SQUAW"
See "NONHELEMA"

GRENFELL, JOYCE IRENE (1910-
1979)
English actress, comedienne
Cur. Biog. '80 p455
Entertainers p235

GRENFELL, MRS. WILLIAM (1769/
1770-1851)
English, subject of portrait
Ware--Meet p76

GRENNAN, JACQUELINE
See WEXLER, JACQUELINE
GRENNAN

GRENVILLE, LILLIAN (1888-1928)
French singer
Claghorn--Biog. p184

GRES, ALIX (GRE), MADAM
(c1899-)
French fashion designer
Cur. Biog. '80 p134-137, por.

GRESE, IRMA (1923-1945)
German, accused criminal
Macksey--Book p136

GREW, MARY (1813-1896)
Amer. abolitionist, suffragist,
feminist, social reformer,
lecturer
James--Notable (2) p91-92
Lutz--Crusade, see index p335
Sherr--American p204

GREY, ELIZABETH, LADY
See ELIZABETH WOODVILLE

GREY, J.
See SNELL, HANNAH

GREY, JANE, LADY (LADY JANE
DUDLEY) (1537-1554)
English queen, martyr
Bainton--France p181
Delderfield--Kings p72-73
Donaldson--How p149-150
Jones--Rutledge p340
Kulkin--Her p131
Who Did What p135
Woman's Almanac p51
World--Who p156

GREY, NAN (1918-)
Amer. actress
Springer--They p123,298, por.

GREY, VIRGINIA (1917-)
Amer. dancer, actress
Lamparski--What (5) p52-53, por.
Springer--They p123,298, por.

GRIDLEY, MARY PUTNAM
Amer. mill president
Sherr--American p209

GRIEG, CONNIE (fl. 1970's)
Amer. executive, agriculturist
O'Neill--Women's p14-15

GRIER, PAM (1949-)
Amer. actress, founder,
corporation
100--Greatest (1) p19, por.

GRIEVE, JANET
Scottish school founder
Macksey--Book p77

GRIFFIES, ETHEL (1878-1975)
English actress
Cur. Biog. '75, p466

GRIFFIN, MRS. CHARLES
See ESTERHAZY, CAROLINE,
COUNTESS

GRIFFIN, HILDA S. (fl. 1970's)
Amer. agriculturist, sales-
woman
O'Neill--Women's p27

GRIFFIN, MARION LUCY MAHONY
(1895-c1961)
Amer. architect
O'Neill--Women's p609
Sicherman--Notable p292-294

GRIFFIN, SUSAN (1943-)
Amer. poet, playwright
Chester--Rising p362-369, por.
Chinoy--Women p187,320-323

GRIFFING, JOSEPHINE SOPHIA
WHITE (1814-1872)
Amer. social reformer
James--Notable (2) p92-94
McHenry--Liberty's p169

GRIFFITH, CORINNE (1896-)
Amer. actress, author
Lamparski--What. (2) p198-199,
por.
Springer--They p123,298, por.

GRIFFITH, DOROTHY AMBURGEY
(1924-)
Amer. genealogical researcher,
author
Meyer--Who's p86

GRIFFITH, EMILY (c1880-1947)
Amer. teacher, school founder
James--Notable (2) p94-95
Sherr--American p27

GRIFFITH, MARIA THONG PATTER-
SON (fl. 1770's)
English-Amer. Tory
Earle--Two Cent. (2) p xvi,562,
por.

GRIFFITHS, DORCAS PRINGLE
(fl. 1770's)
English-Amer. Tory
Booth--Women p47-48,60-62
Young--Revol. p27-28

GRIFFITHS, MARTHA WRIGHT
(1912-)
Amer. Congresswoman,
politician, lawyer
Chamberlin--Min. p258-264, por.
Greenebaum--Politics p79-97,
por.
Macksey--Book p129
Miller--Fishbait p374-375
O'Neill--Women's p68,70
Schoenebaum--Prof. p254-255
Sochen--Movers p250
U.S.--Women (89th) p11, por.
U.S.--Women (90th) p9, por.
Woman's Almanac p473, por.
World--Who p141

GRIFFITTS, HANNAH (1727-1817)
Amer. Quaker, poet, patriot
DePauw--Rem. p91

GRIMALDI, BENEDETTINA
Italian medical patroness
Mead--Hist. p322

GRIMES, ANNE (LAYLIN) (1912-)
Amer. singer, banjoist,

guitarist
Claghorn--Biog. p185

GRIMES, MARILLA R. (1924-)
Amer. genealogical researcher,
author
Meyer--Who's p87

GRIMES, TAMMY LEE (1934/1936-)
Amer. singer, actress, dancer
Claghorn--Biog. p185
World--Who p235

GRIMKE, ANGELINA EMILY (1880-
1958)
Amer. poet, feminist, aboli-
tionist
Bernikow--World p261
Chittenden--Prof. p50-67
Earnest--American p109,118-121
Friedman--Our p152-160
Gurko--Ladies, see index p323,
por.
Hymowitz--Hist. p80-86,103,348
Ingraham--Album p22,por.
James--Notable (2) p97-99
Kulkin--Her p132-133
Longstreet--Queen p13
Lutz--Crusade, see index p338
(under Weld)
Macksey--Book p86, 111
McHenry--Liberty's p169-170
Millstein--We p96-97
Papachristou--Women p9-10,13,
15-16, por.
Reader's--Story p433
Reifert--Women p66-70
Scott--Southern p51,55
Sherr--American p153,213
Signif.--Amer. p11, por.
Smith--Daughters p104-105,107-
109,116,124-125
Sochen--Herstory p122-124,130-
131, por.
Warren--Pictorial p83-84,119, por.
Webster's--Amer. p432
Woman's Almanac p375-376,542
World--Who p189

GRIMKE, CHARLOTTE L. FORTEN
(1838-1904)
Amer. educator, author, abo-
litionist, social reformer
Chittenden--Prof. p107-124, por.
James--Notable (2) p95-97
Kulkin--Her p109-110

Millstein--We p124,135-136
Sochen--Herstory p189

GRIMKE, SARAH MOORE (1792-
1873)
Amer. abolitionist, feminist
Chittenden--Prof. p50-67
Earnest--American p117-118,120
Friedman--Our p152-160
Gurko--Ladies, see index
p323-324, por.
Hymowitz--Hist. p20,80-86,96,
103,348
Ingraham--Album p22
James--Notable (2) p97-99
Kulkin--Her p132-133
Longstreet--Queen p13
Lutz--Crusade, see index p335
McHenry--Liberty's p169
Macksey--Book p86,111
Millstein--We p96-97,106-107
Nies--Seven p1-31
Papachristou--Women p9-10,
13-15,83,146-147, por.
Reader's--Story p433
Reifert--Women p66-70
Scott--Southern p51,61-64,71
Sherr--American p153,213
Signif.--Amer. p11, por.
Smith--Daughters p104-106,109,
124-125
Sochen--Herstory p122-124,130-
131, por.
Warren--Pictorial p83-84,119,
por.
Webster's--Amer. p432
Woman's Almanac p375-376,542
World--Who p188

GRIMM, RUTH
Amer. aviatrix, (army flier)
Keil--Those p29-30

GRINER, CAROLYN
Amer. astronautical engineer,
astronaut
O'Connor--Sally p20

GRINNELL, JOSEPHINE
Amer. Indian, accused
murderer
Sherr--American p183

GRINSTEAD, FRANCES (fl. 1920's-
1960's)

Amer. journalism professor
Marzolf--Up p251-252,255-257

GRISCOM, ELIZABETH
See ROSS, BETSY GRISCOM

GRISI, CAROLOTTA (1819-1899)
Italian ballet dancer
Migel--Ballerinas p194-207, por.

GRISI, GIULIA
Italian opera singer, wife of
Giovani Mario
Tuggle--Golden p4-5

GRISSOM, IRENE WELCH (fl. 1920's)
Amer. poet
Sherr--American p57

GRISSOT, MARIE (fl. 1700's)
Amer. midwife
Mead--Hist. p489

GRISWOLD, FLORENCE (1851-1937).
Amer. art patron
Sherr--American p34

GRISWOLD, HATTIE
Amer. poet, suffragist
Sherr--American p247

GROEBLI, RENE
Swiss free lance photographer
Hamblin--That p81-84

GROFFMA, CYNDY (fl. 1970's)
Amer. athlete (power-lifter)
Jordan--Broken p108-117

GROLLMUSS, MARIA (1896-1944)
German teacher, journalist
Parkington--Who's p144

GROOMES, FREDDIE LANG (fl.
1970's)
Amer. educator, administrator
Innis--Profiles p52-53, por.

GROSMAN, TATYANA (1904-   )
Russian-Amer. lithographer
Gilbert--Part. p11-19, por.

GROSS, MARY (1953-   )
Amer. actress
Scheuer--Tel. p201, por.

GROSS, SANDI (fl. 1970's)
Amer. artist
Women's--Female p105

GROSSFELD, MURIEL DAVIS
(c1941-)
Australian gymnast
Hollander--100 p53-54, por.

GROSSINGER, JENNIE (1892-1972)
Austrian-Amer. hotel owner,
philanthropist
Cur. Biog. '73 p455
Neidle--America's p270-272, por.
Sicherman--Notable p294-295
World--Who p198

GROSSMAN, NANCY (c1940-)
Amer. sculptor, painter
Diamonstein--Open p158-164,
por.
Nemser--Convers. p327-355,366-
367,por.
Women's--Female p89

GROSSMAN, PAULA (1919-)
Amer. teacher, transsexual
Book--Lists (2) p327

GROSSO, ELLA TAMBUSSI (1919-)
Amer. state governor
Bowman--Politics p38-45, por.
Schoenebaum--Prof. p243-244

GROSVENOR, ELSIE MAY BELL
(1878-)
English-Amer., noted District
of Columbia mother, daughter
of Alexander Graham Bell
Amer.--Mothers p99-100, por.

GROSVENOR, KALI DIANA
(1960-)
Amer. child author
Book--Lists (2) p224

GROSVENOR, VERTA MAE (1939-)
Amer. writer
P.W.--Author p292-297,501

GROTEL, MAIJA (1889-1973)
Finnish-Amer. craftswoman
O'Neill--Women's p265

GROULT, NICOLE
French couturiere
Holme--Journal p153

GROVES, GLADYS HOAGLAND
(1894-1980)
Amer. educator, marriage
counsellor
Cur. Biog. '80 p455

GRUENBERG, SIDONIE MATSNER
(1881-1974)
Amer. educator, author, lec-
turer
Cur. Biog. '74 p460
Sicherman--Notable p295-296

GRUENING, DOROTHY (fl. 1930's-
1950's)
Amer. Alaskan, wife of Ernest
Gruening
Jones--Women (1) p180-183

GRUMBACH, ARGULA VON (1492-
after 1563)
German Reformation worker
Bainton--Germany p97-109

GUALCO, SELLINA (1905-)
Italian physician
Hellstedt--Women p286-288, por.

GUBRUD, IRENE (c1946-)
Amer. singer
People--Best p228, por.

GÜDEN (GUEDEN), HILDE (1917-)
Austrian opera singer
Gammond--Illus. p243-244, por.

GUENIN, ZENA BETH
Amer. journalist
Marzolf--Up p202

GUERIN, ELSA JANE FOREST
(-1879)
Amer. male impersonator,
Western pioneer
Lichtenstein--Mach. p127-130
Time--Women p178,180,183

GUERIN, THEODORE, MOTHER
(1798-1856)
French-Amer. religious
McHenry--Liberty's p170
People's Almanac (1) p1302-1303

GUERMONPREZ, TRUDE (1910-1976)
Austrian textile artist
O'Neill--Women's p268-269

GUEST, AMY PHIPPS (fl. 1920's)
Amer. aviation patron
Keil--Those p17-19

GUEST, BARBARA (1923-   )
Amer. poet
Chester--Rising p122-125, por.

GUEST, CHARLOTTE ELIZABETH
BERTIE, LADY (1812-1875)
Welsh diarist, social reformer,
ironworks operator
Avenel--Comp. (1) p230
Macksey--Book p164

GUEST, JEAN
Amer. TV executive
Scheuer--Tel. p203

GUEVARA, ISABEL DE (fl.
1530's-1550's)
Spanish pioneer
Hahner--Women p17-20

GUEVARA, MARINA DE
Spanish nun
Bainton--Spain p40-46

GUGGENHEIM, ALICIA
See PATTERSON, ALICIA

GUGGENHEIM, DOROTHY JEAN
See HOWARD, LISA

GUGGENHEIM, "PEGGY" MAR-
GUERITE (1898-1979)
Amer. art patron, expatriate
millionaire, philanthropist
Cur. Biog. '80 p455
Fowler--Art p145
Longstreet--Queen p76
O'Neill--Women's p617
World--Who p297

GUGGENHEIMER, ELINOR
(c1913-   )
Amer. TV newscaster
Gelfman--Women p42,120,165

GUIARD, ADELAIDE LABILLE,
MADAME
See LABILLE-GUIARD,
ADELAIDE, MADAME

GUICHE, LILLIAN DE
See GISH, LILLIAN DIANA

GUILBERT, YVETTE (1867-1944)
French actress, singer
Entertainers p154

GUILFOYLE, MARGARET GEORGINA
CONSTANCE (1926-   )
Irish-Australian senator,
minister
O'Neill--Women's p60

GUILLARD, CHARLOTTE (fl. 1500's)
French pioneer printer
Marzolf--Up p270

GUILLELMA DE ROSERS (fl. 13th
Cent.)
French troubadour
Bogin--Women p135,177-178

GUILLEMOT, AGNES (fl. 1960's)
French editor
Smith--Movies p122

GUILLERM, NELLY
See VERDY, VIOLETTE

GUIMARD, MARIE-MADELEINE
(1743-1816)
French ballet dancer
Migel--Ballerinas p71-89, por.

GUINAN, MARY LOUISE CECILIA
(1884-1933)
Amer. actress, circus per-
former, hostess
Clark--Leading p105
James--Notable (2) p99-101
McHenry--Liberty's p170
World--Who p297

GUINAN, TEXAS
See GUINAN, MARY LOUISE
CECILIA

GUINEVERE
English legendary heroine
Coffin--Female p45-48, por.

GUINEY, LOUISE IMOGEN (1861-
1920)
Amer. poet, essayist, scholar
James--Notable (2) p101-102
McHenry--Liberty's p170-171

GUINNESS, GLORIA (fl. 1940's)
Mexican beauty

Keenan--Women p22-23,
por.

GUION, CONNIE MYERS (1882-
1971)
Amer. professor, clinical
medicine, physician
Kulkin--Her p133-134
O'Neill--Women's p209

GUISE, MARY (1515-1560)
Scottish, wife of James V
Jones--Rutledge p344

GULA, KASHA LINVILLE (fl.
1970's)
Amer. art critic
Women's--Female p121

GULDBERG, ESTRID (1899-)
Norwegian physician
Hellstedt--Women p179-186, por.

GULICK, ALICE WINFIELD GORDON
Amer. missionary
James--Notable (2) p102-104

GULICK, CHARLOTTE VETTER
(1910-)
Amer. founder, Camp Fire
Girls
O'Neill--Women's p112-113

GULLBERG, ELSA (1886-)
Swedish textile designer
O'Neill--Women's p272

GULLIVER, JULIA HENRIETTA
(1856-1940)
Amer. philosopher, college
president
James--Notable (2) p104-105

GUM, DELORES (fl. 1970's)
Amer. TV editor
Klever--Women p36,38-39,77-
78,96

GUMM, FRANCES
See GARLAND, JUDY

GUMP, MABEL BUSBY
See STANFORD, SALLY (MABEL
MARCIA BUSBY GOODAN,
FANSTER, BAYHAM SPAGNOLI
RAPP)

GUNDERSEN, HERDIS (1903-)
Norwegian physician
Hellstedt--Women p253-256, por.

GUNDERSON, GENEVIEVE (fl. 1970's)
Amer. Vice Presidential candi-
date
People's Almanac (1) p127

GUNNESS, BELLE (1860-c1908)
Amer. accused criminal
Woman's Almanac p503-504

GUNNING, ANN (fl. 1950's-1960's)
Amer. beauty, model
Keenan--Women p146,149, por.

GUNNING, SARAH OGAN (1910-)
Amer. poet
Bernikow--World p306

GUPTA, RUTH CHURCH (fl. 1950's-
1970's)
Amer. lawyer
O'Neill--Women's p360

GURIE, SIGRID (1911-1969)
Amer. actress
Springer--They p123,298, por.

GURNEY, ELIZA PAUL KIRKBRIDE
(1801-1881)
Amer. Quaker minister
James--Notable (2) p105-106

GURVICH, ZHENIA (fl. 1910's)
Russian member of Bund
Baum--Jewish p81-82

GUSTAFSSON, ANNA
Swedish, mother of Greta
Garbo
Diagram--Mothers p100-101, por.

GUSTAFSSON, GRETA LOUISA
See GARBO, GRETA LOUISA
GUSTAFSON

GUTA, THE NUN (fl. 12th Cent.)
French medical writer
Mead--Hist. p130-131

GUTHRIE, JANET (1937/1938-)
Amer. automobile race driver
Cur. Biog. '78 p182-185, por.
Gurtman--More p27-46, por.

Lichtenstein--Mach., see index
   p361
McHenry--Liberty's p171
McWhirter--Guinness p30-31,
   por.
O'Neill--Women's p589-590
Woman's Almanac p437-438, por.
World--Who p214

GUTMAN, SAREL (fl. 1600's)
   Jewish letter-writer
   Henry--Written p156-163

GUTTMAN, RITA (fl. 1930's-
   1970's)
   Amer. biophysicist
   O'Neill--Women's p157

GUYARD (GUIARD), ADELAIDE
   LABILLE-
   See LABILLE-GUYARD,
   ADELAIDE, MADAME

GUY-BLACHE, ALICE
   French secretary
   Macksey--Book p232-233

GUYER, CYNTHIA (fl. 1970's)
   Amer. agriculturist
   O'Neill--Women's p35

GUZIK, ANNA
   Russian-Jewish actress
   Mandel--Soviet p192

GWYN, ALTHEA (fl. 1970's)
   Amer. basketball player
   Lichtenstein--Mach. p85-89

GWYN (GWYNNE), ELEANOR
   "NELL"
   See GWYNN, NELL (ELEANOR)

GWYNETH, EVELYN VERDON
   See VERDON, GWEN

GWYNN, NELL (ELEANOR)
   (1650-1687)
   English actress, comedienne,
   mistress of Charles II
   Entertainers p75-76
   Findlater--Player p22-32, por.
   Fry--1000 p162-163, por.
   Jones--Rutledge p346
   Macksey--Book p96,224
   People's Almanac (1) p1327
   Who Did What p138
   World--Who p297

GWYNNE, ANNE (1918-)
   Amer. actress
   Lamparski--What. Annual (4,5)
   p189-193, por.
   Lamparski--What. (8) p116-117,
   por.

H

HAAS, MARY R. (fl. 1960's-1970's)
   Amer. linguist, professor
   O'Neill--Women's p416

HABEDANK, BARBARA (fl. 1970's)
   Amer. aviatrix (jet pilot)
   Lichtenstein--Mach. p177-178,
   186-187,200

HABELMAN, E. CAROLYN (1941-)
   Amer. genealogical researcher,
   author, editor
   Meyer--Who's p91

HABERSHAM, JOSEPHINE CLAY
   Amer. Southern plantation
   manager
   Scott--Southern p12,86

HACKELY, EMMA AZALIA SMITH
   (1867-1923)
   Amer. singer, humanitarian
   Claghorn--Biog. p189
   James--Notable (2) p106-108
   McHenry--Liberty's p172

HACKEMAN, VICKI (fl. 1970's)
   Amer. singer
   Glassman--Year '79 p96, por.

HACKETT, JOAN (1933-1983)
   Amer. actress
   World--Who p235

HADDAD, CLAIRE (fl. 1960's)
   Canadian fashion designer
   O'Neill--Women's p258

HADDOCK, JANET EGELSTON
   (1933-)
   Amer. genealogical researcher,
   writer
   Meyer--Who's p91

HADDON, ELIZABETH
   See ESTAUGH, ELIZABETH
   HADDON

HADEN, CHARLYNE E.

Amer. religious worker
Kooiman--Cameos p86-91, por.

HADFIELD, MARIA
See COSWAY, MARIA CECILIA
LOUISE HADFIELD

HADLEY, JANE
See BARKLEY, JANE HADLEY

HAEFKER, ANNEDORE (fl. 1970's)
West German bowler
O'Neill--Women's p558

HAENDAL, IDA
Polish violinist
Macksey--Book p221

HAENER, DOROTHY (1917-   )
Amer. labor leader
O'Neill--Women's p304

HAFEN, MARY ANN (1854-   )
Swiss-Amer. Western pioneer
Fischer--Let p101-108

HAFT, MARILYN (fl. 1970's)
Amer. deputy marshall
Adams--Women p112-114

HAGAN, HELEN EUGENIA (1893-
1964)
Amer. pianist, educator
Claghorn--Biog. p190

HAGAR
Biblical, Egyptian hand-
maiden to Sarah
Henry--Written p16,239-242
Woman's Almanac p400

HAGEDORN, JESSICA TARAHATA
(1949-   )
Filipino-Amer. writer
Fisher--Third, p x, 534

HAGEN, ALICE MARY EGAN
(1872-1972)
Canadian china painter,
potter
O'Neill--Women's p121

HAGEN, JEAN (1924-   )
Amer. actress
Lamparski--What. (5) p92,
por.

HAGEN, UTA (1919/1920-   )

German actress
Chinoy--Women p119-123, por.
Entertainers p250
World--Who p257

HAGER, ELIZABETH (BETSY)
See PRATT, ELIZABETH ("HANDY
BETSY")

HAGER, FRANCIE ("GRANNY") (fl.
1970's)
Amer. labor leader
Kahn--Hill. p39-49, por.
O'Neill--Women's p324

HAGGE, MARLENE (fl. 1970's)
Amer. golfer
McWhirter--Guinness p77

HAGIDORN, MARY (fl. 1770's)
Amer. Revolutionary War
patriot
Meyer--Petticoat p117

HAGOOD, MARGARET LLOYD
JARMAN (1907-1963)
Amer. sociologist, statistician,
demographer
Sicherman--Notable p297-298

HAGUE, PARTHENIA ANTOINETTE
(fl. 1860's)
Amer. Civil War patriot,
writer, diarist
Hymowitz--Hist. p145

HAHN, DOROTHY ANNA (1876-1950)
Amer. organic chemist
James--Notable (2) p108-109

HAHN, EMILIE (1891-1971)
Amer. music teacher
Claghorn--Biog. p190

HAHN, EMILY (1905-198)
Amer. author, geologist
Ross--Young p37-56, por.

HAIL, SUSAN O. (c1818-1857)
Amer. Western pioneer
(Oregon Trail)
Sherr--American p140

HAINES, HELEN ELIZABETH (1872-
1961)
Amer. librarian, author,
editor, educator
Sicherman--Notable p298-299

HAINES, RANDY
  Amer. TV director
  Scheuer--Tel. p209

HAINLEY, LYNDA (LYNNE) LEE
  (1951-)
  Amer. genealogical researcher
  Meyer--Who's p91

HAJOS, MARISHKA
  See "MITZIE"

HAKIMOVA, PROFESSOR (fl.
  1970's)
  Russian physician, researcher,
  author
  Mandel--Soviet p180-181

HAKKINEN, ELIZABETH SHELDON
  (1914-)
  Amer. church worker, noted
  Alaska mother
  Amer.--Mothers p23, por.

HALABY, ELIZABETH (LISA)
  (c1951-)
  Amer., consort of Hussein,
  King of Jordan
  O'Neill--Women's p751

HALASCSAK, BONNIE (1943-)
  Amer. steel worker, feminist
  Seifer--Nobody p256-294, por.

HALBERG, JULIA (c1956-)
  Amer. scientist
  O'Neill--Women's p34

HALDEMAN, SARAH ALICE (fl.
  1900's)
  Amer. banker
  Sherr--American p74

HALDORSEN, INGER ALIDA
  (1899-)
  Norwegian physician
  Hellstedt--Women p168-175,
  por.

HALE, BEATRICE FORBES-
  ROBERTSON (fl. 1910's)
  English writer
  Smith--Daughters, see index
  p376-378

HALE, CLARA (1905-)
  Amer. social activist
  Cur. Biog. '85 p164-167

HALE, LARZETTE GOLDEN (1920-)
  Amer. public accountant
  Innis--Profiles p58-59, por.

HALE, LOUISE CLOSSER (1872-1933)
  Amer. actress, author
  McHenry--Liberty's p172
  Springer--They p127,298, por.

HALE, LUCRETIA PEABODY (1820-
  1920)
  Amer. author
  Ehrlich--Oxford p29
  James--Notable (2) p109-110
  McHenry--Liberty's p172-173
  Webster's--Amer. p441-442

HALE, MARY WHITWELL (1810-1862)
  Amer. hymnist, poet
  Claghorn--Biog. p191

HALE, SARAH JOSEPHA BUELL
  (1788-1879)
  Amer., noted New Hampshire
  mother, "Mother of Thanks-
  giving," editor, novelist,
  author, hymnist
  Amer.--Mothers p365, por.
  Bird--Enterprising p14,58-66
  Claghorn--Biog. p191
  Earnest--American, see index
  p275
  Ehrlich--Oxford p205, por.
  Eills--Here p34-35
  Hymowitz--Hist. p67,127
  James--Notable (2) p110-114
  Kulkin--Her p134-135
  McHenry--Liberty's p173
  Macksey--Book p69
  Marzolf--Up p12-13
  Millstein--We p87-88
  People's Almanac (1) p160
  People's Almanac (2) p150-151
  Sherr--American p112,148
  Signif.--Amer. p11, por.
  Warren--Pictorial p124-125
  Webster's--Amer. p442

HALE, SUSAN (1833-1910)
  Amer. author, artist
  James--Notable (2) p114-115

HALE, TENNY
  Amer. psychic, astrologer
  People's Almanac (2) p4-5

HALEY, MARGARET ANGELA (1861-
  1939)

HALL, RUBY HIBLER (1912-   )
Amer. educator, community
worker, noted Oklahoma
mother
Amer.--Mothers p440, por.

HALL, SHARLOT MABRIDTH
(1870-1943)
Amer. poet, short story
writer, historian
Ehrlich--Oxford p437
Sherr--American p8

HALL, SUSAN (fl. 1970's)
Amer. painter
Women's--Female p44

HALL, SUSAN WEBB (1850-1922)
Amer. missionary to Indians,
noted North Dakota mother
Amer.--Mothers p414, por.

HALL, VERA (1905-1964)
Amer. singer
Claghorn--Biog. p192

HALL, VICKI (fl. 1970's)
Amer. artist
Women's--Female p105

HALLAM, NANCY (fl. 1750's-1775's)
English-Amer. Colonial
actress
Fabian--On p26-27, por.

HALLAM-DOUGLAS, SARAH
See DOUGLASS, SARAH
HALLAM

HALLAREN, MARY AGNES ("LIT-
TLE COLONEL") (1907-   )
Amer. army officer, director
of WAC
McHenry--Liberty's p174
O'Neill--Women's p539

HALLE, FANNINA
Russian feminist
Mandel--Soviet p9,17

HALLE, WILHELMINA (WILMA)
MARIA FRANZISKA
NORMAN-NERUDA, LADY
(1838/1839-1911)
Austrian violinist
Neuls-Bates--Women p281

HALLECK, DEEDEE (fl. 1960's-1970's)
Amer. filmmaker
Smith--Movies p171,244, por.

HALLETT, MRS. HUGHES
See SCHAUMBERJ (SCHAUMBURG),
EMILE

HALLGRIMSDOTTIR, MARIA (1905-   )
Icelander physician
Hellstedt--Women p302-305, por.

HALLINAN, HAZEL HUNKINS (c1891-
1982)
Amer. feminist
O'Neill--Women's p700, por.

HALLING, ELSE (1899-   )
Norwegian tapestry designer
O'Neill--Women's p273

HALLOCK, MARY ANNA
See FOOTE, MARY ANNA HALLOCK

HALLOWELL, ANNA (ANNE) (1831-
1905)
Amer. welfare worker, educational reformer, kindergarten
founder
James--Notable (2) p122-123
O'Neill--Women's p428

HALLWARD, ELLA F.G.
British illustrator
Callen--Women p204

HALPERT, EDITH GREGOR (1900-
1970)
Russian-Amer. art dealer,
collector
Cur. Biog. '70 p463
Sicherman--Notable p301-303

HALPIR, SALOMEE ANNE (1719-1786)
Polish oculist, physician, sur-
geon
Macksey--Book p144
Mead--Hist. p511-512

HALSBAND, FRANCES (fl. 1970's)
Amer. architect
O'Neill--Women's p612

HALSEY, MARGARET (1910-   )
Amer. novelist
Ehrlich--Oxford, see index p454

HALVERSTADT, CONSTANCE
See CUMMINGS, CONSTANCE

HAMAN, KATO (1884-1936)
Hungarian labor martyr
Partington--Who's p151

HAMBERGER, MARGOT
German insurance company
co-owner
Macksey--Book p169
O'Neill--Women's p515

HAMBLET, JULIA E. (1916-)
Amer. Marine director
O'Neill--Women's p538

HAMBLETON, KITTY
See O'NEIL, KITTY

HAMBLING, MAGGI (1945-)
English artist
Contemp. Brit. unp., por.

HAMEL, VERONICA (c1947-)
Amer. actress
Scheuer--Tel. p211-212, por.

HAMER, FANNIE LOU TOWNSEND
(1917-1977)
Amer. social reformer,
civil rights leader
Brin--Social p154-155
Diamonstein--Open p165-168,
por.
Kulkin--Her p136
O'Neill--Women's p44,701, por.
Woman's Almanac p383-384, por.
World--Who p188

HAMERSCHLAG, FREIDEL
Jewish letter writer
Henry--Written p167-168

HAMES, MARJIE PITTS (fl.
1960's-1970's)
Amer. Civil Liberties lawyer
O'Neill--Women's p360

HAMIDULLAH, ZEB-UN-NIRSA
(fl. 1950's)
Pakistani publisher, editor,
feminist
Macksey--Book p191
O'Neill--Women's p475

HAMILL, DOROTHY (1956-)

Amer. skater
Anderson--People p187-188
Assoc. Press--Pursuit p327-329,
por.
Cur. Biog. '76 p168-171, por.
Hollander--100 p36-37, por.
McWhirter--Guinness p95,100, por.
O'Neill--Women's p563, por.
Woman's Almanac p434, por.

HAMILTON, ALICE (1869-1970)
Amer. physician, bacteriologist,
researcher, toxicologist, pro-
fessor
Bachtold--Gifted p50-51
Brin--Social p155-156
Cur. Biog. '70 p463
Kulkin--Her p137-138
Marks--Women p141-147, por.
O'Neill--Women's p206,288
Sicherman--Notable p303-306
Women's Almanac p362

HAMILTON, BETSY
See MOORE, IDORA McCLELLAN
PLOWMAN

HAMILTON, CICELY VIETS DAKIN
(1837-1909)
Canadian-Amer. novelist,
children's book author,
painter
McHenry--Liberty's p210

HAMILTON, DORRANCE HILL
(c1928-)
Amer. millionaire
Forbes--400 ('84) p82

HAMILTON, EDITH (1867-1963)
German-Amer. educator,
classical scholar, author
Clark--Leading p125-127
Kulkin--Her p138-139
McHenry--Liberty's p174-175
O'Neill--Women's p414
Sicherman--Notable p306-308
Stoddard--Famous p211-217, por.
Webster's--Amer. p447

HAMILTON, ELEANOR (fl. 1970's)
Amer. writer, sex therapist
McCullough--People p75-77

HAMILTON, ELIZABETH SCHUYLER
(1757-1854)
Amer. Revolutionary War

patriot, belle, wife of
Alexander Hamilton
James--Notable (2) p123-125
Kelley--Courage p59-99,233-234

HAMILTON, EMMA LYON, LADY
(1761/1765-1815)
English mistress of Lord
Nelson
Ware--Meet p50-67,77, por.

HAMILTON, GAIL
See DODGE, (MARY) ABIGAIL

HAMILTON, (AMY) GORDON (1892-
1967)
Amer. social worker, educator
Sicherman--Notable p308-310

HAMILTON, GRACE (1907-)
Amer. noted Georgia mother,
state politician
Amer.--Mothers p135-136, por.

HAMILTON, MARGARET (1) (1902-
1985)
Amer. actress
Cur. Biog. '79 p157-161, por.
Cur. Biog. '85 p466
Springer--They p127,298, por.

HAMILTON, MARGARET (2)
(1936-)
Amer. systems analyst
Teitz--What's p226-246, por.

HAMILTON, VON GAIL (1928-)
Amer. genealogical research-
er, author
Meyer--Who's p92

HAMLIN, ANNA (1902-)
Amer. opera singer
Claghorn--Biog. p193

HAMLIN, HUYBERTIE (BERTIE)
PRUYN
Amer. socialite
Daniels--Wash., see index p362

HAMLIN, SONYA
Amer. TV producer, actress
Adams--Women p25-26,29,78

HAMM, MARGHERITA ARLINA
(1867-1907)
Canadian-Amer. journalist,

author
James--Notable (2) p125-126

HAMM-BRÜCHER, HILDEGARD
(1921-)
German minister of state
O'Neill--Women's p56

HAMMA, MARGARET
Amer. speed typist
Macksey--Book p174

HAMMAN, MARY
Amer. magazine assistant
editor
Hamblin--That p161-162

HAMMERSMITH, MARY POWELL
(1920-)
Amer. genealogical researcher,
writer
Meyer--Who's p92

HAMMETT, ELIZA GROVES (1860-
1927)
Amer. community worker,
noted Mississippi mother
Amer.--Mothers p299-300, por.

HAMMOND, CELIA (fl. 1960's)
English model
Keenan--Women p148-149,150-151,
por.

HAMMOND, HARMONY (fl. 1970's)
Amer. craftswoman
Women's--Female p20

HAMMOND, MARY DILWORTH (fl.
1860's)
Amer. Quaker-Morman teacher
Sherr--American p225

HAMOD, KAY KEESHAN (1936-)
Amer. historian
Ruddick--Working p3-24,342, por.

HAMPSHIRE, SUSAN (1941/1942-)
English actress
Cur. Biog. '74 p158-160, por.
World--Who p257

HAMPTON, ISABEL ADAMS
See ROBB, ISABEL ADAMS
HAMPTON

HANAFORD, PHEBE ANN (COFFIN)

(1829-1921)
Amer. music writer, clergy-
man, feminist
Claghorn--Biog. p194
James--Notable (2) p126-127
Sherr--American p106

HANAKAULANI-O-KAMAMALU
(1843-)
Hawaiian High Chieftess,
noted Amer. mother
Amer.--Mothers. p142-143, por.

HANANEL
See BEN JOSEPH, ROSY

HANCOCK, CORNELIA (1839/
1840-1927)
Amer. Civl War nurse,
housing reformer
James--Notable (2) p127-129
Sherr--American p152,154,200,
213,234-235

HANCOCK, DOROTHY QUINCY
(1750-1828)
Amer. Revolutionary War
patriot, (wife of John Hancock)
Earle--Two Cent. (2) p xxi,467,
714-715, por.
Flexner--Face p98
Meyer--Petticoat p55, por.

HANCOCK, JOY BRIGHT (1898-)
Amer. aviatrix, Director,
WAVES
McHenry--Liberty's p175
O'Neill--Women's p537, por.

HANCOCKS, ELIZABETH (1927-)
Canadian genealogical re-
searcher, author, indexer
Meyer--Who's p92-93

HANDLER, RUTH (c1916-)
Amer. co-founder of toy
company
Macksey--Book p172

HANEY, CAROL (1924-1964)
Amer. dancer, choreog-
rapher
World--Who p263

HANK, HELEN (c1870/1871-)
Amer. centenarian
Mitchell--Yessir p35-37, por.

HANKS, NANCY (1)
See LINCOLN, NANCY HANKS

HANKS, NANCY (2) (1927-1983)
Amer. United States govern-
ment official
Cur. Biog. '71 p180-183, por.
Cur. Biog. '83 p466
Gilbert--Part. p199-205, por.
McHenry--Liberty's p175
O'Neill--Women's p594
Schoenebaum--Prof. p268-269

HANNAH
Biblical
Henry--Written p21-23,189
Price--God p88-92

HANRAHAN, MARION
Amer. aviatrix
Keil--Those p14,198-204,206-207

HANSBERRY, LORRAINE VIVIAN
(1930-1965)
Amer. playwright
Chinoy--Women p131,257-259, por.
Entertainers p274
Ehrlich--Oxford p319
Ingraham--Album p58
McHenry--Liberty's p175-176
Moers--Literary p xv, 293
O'Neill--Women's p671
Sicherman--Notable p310-312
Toppin--Biog. p312-313
Woman's Almanac p252, por.
World--Who p14

HANSELL, ELLEN (fl. 1880's)
Amer. tennis player
Macksey--Book p257

HANSELL, LEILA DAVIDSON
(-1915)
Amer. "Sunshine Lady"
Sherr--American p179-180

HANSEN, CECILIA (1898-)
Russian-Danish violinist
Hazen--Interv. p343

HANSEN, DARLENE F.N. (1924-)
Amer. genealogical researcher,
writer
Meyer--Who's p93

HANSEN, ELLEN
See CORBY, ELLEN

HANSEN, JULIA BUTLER (1907-   )
    Amer. Congresswoman
    Chamberlin--Min. p282-286, por.
    U.S.--Women (89th) p13, por.
    U.S.--Women (90th) p11, por.
    Schoenebaum--Prof. p270-271

HANSEN, LISA (fl. 1970's)
    Amer. rower
    O'Neill--Women's p585

HANSEN, LUISA FERNANDEZ
    Chilean-Amer. nuclear physi-
    cist
    O'Neill--Women's p185

HANSEN, PEGGY ANNE (fl. 1970's)
    Amer. social reformer
    O'Neill--Women's p118-119

HANSFORD-JOHNSON, PAMELA
    (1912-   )
    English novelist, critic,
    essayist
    Avenel--Comp. (1) p235
    Seymour-Smith--Novels p153

HANSON, DORIS E. (fl. 1940's-
    1970's)
    Amer. home economist
    O'Neill--Women's p105-106

HANSON, JACKIE (1948- ,)
    Amer. field and track
    athlete, marathon star
    Woman's Almanac p426

HANSON, JANE
    Amer. TV reporter
    Scheuer--Tel. p213-214

HANSON, JEANNE
    Amer. agriculturist, dairy
    farmer
    O'Neill--Women's p13

HANSON, MARGERY DAY (1903-   )
    Amer. genealogical researcher
    Meyer--Who's p93

HANSON, NORMA (fl. 1970's)
    Amer. diver
    O'Neill--Women's p745

HANSTEEN, KIRSTEN (fl. 1940's)
    Norwegian cabinet minister
    Macksey--Book p40

HAN SUYIN (1917-   )
    Chinese novelist, physician
    Jones--Rutledge p353
    Seymour-Smith--Novels p153

HAPGOOD, ISABEL FLORENCE
    (1850-1928)
    Amer. translator, author
    James--Notable (2) p129-130
    McHenry--Liberty's p176

HARBESON, GEORGIANA BROWN
    (1894-1980)
    Amer. needlewoman, industrial
    artist, designer
    O'Neill--Women's p130

HARBOU, THEA VON (-1954)
    West German screenwriter
    Smith--Movies p141

HARDEN, ARLEEN (1945-   )
    Amer. singer, guitarist
    Claghorn--Biog. p196

HARDEN, CECIL MURRAY (c1894-   )
    Amer. Congresswoman
    Chamberlin--Min. p209-212

HARDENBERG, ANNA
    Danish, wife of Frederick
    Bainton--Spain p117-123

HARDENBROOK, MARGARET
    See PHILIPSE, MARGARET
    HARDENBROOK

HARDEY, MARY ALOYSIA, MOTHER
    (1809-1886)
    Amer. Catholic nun
    James--Notable (2) p130-132
    McHenry--Liberty's p176

HARDIE, LAURA CONSTANCE
    See COLLIER, CONSTANCE
    HARDIE

HARDIN, JACQUELINE (fl. 1960's)
    Amer. heroine, Carnegie
    Medal winner
    O'Neill--Women's p733

HARDIN, LILLIAN
    See ARMSTRONG, LIL HARDIN

HARDIN, PABLITA VELARDE (1918-   )
    Amer. Indian painter, lecturer,

writer, noted New Mexico
mother
Amer.--Mothers p384, por.

HARDING, ANN (1901/1902-1981)
Amer. actress
Mordden--Movie p68,94-95,100,
152,por.
Shipman--Gold. p265-268, por.
Springer--They p127,298, por.

HARDING, DEBORAH A. (fl. 1960's-
1970's)
Amer. Peace Corps rural
programmer
O'Neill--Women's p23

HARDING, FLORENCE KLING
(1860-1924)
Amer. First Lady, (wife of
Warren G. Harding)
James--Notable (2) p132-133
Melick--Wives p64-65, por.
People's Almanac (1) p275
Woman's Almanac p491

HARDING, FRANCES (1906-)
Amer. physician
Hellstedt--Women p321-325, por.

HARDING, PHOEBE ELIZABETH
DICKERSON (1843-1920)
Amer., mother of President
Warren G. Harding
Faber--Presidents' p219-221

HARDING, REBECCA BLAINE
See DAVIS, REBECCA BLAINE
HARDING

HARDNER, LUETTA (fl. 1970's)
Amer. farm businesswoman
O'Neill--Women's p13

HARDWICK, ELIZABETH (1916-)
Amer. critic, novelist, essay-
ist, editor
Cur. Biog. '81 p188-191, por.
Ehrlich--Oxford p140,291
Moers--Literary p293
Seymour-Smith--Novels p153
Showalter--Lit. p317-318

HARDWICK, (CATHY) KATHY
(1934-)
Korean-Amer. fashion designer
O'Neill--Women's p249,251

HARDWICK, MOLLIE
English novelist
Seymour-Smith--Novels p153

HARDY, ANNA ELIZA (1839-1934)
Amer. painter
James--Notable (2) p133-134

HARDY, ARDETH
Amer. card player
McWhirter--Guinness p63-64, por.

HARGIS, CHERYL L.
Amer. aviation machinist's mate
O'Neill--Women's p548

HARGRAFEN, MARY
See CARL, MARY, SISTER

HARGREAVES, ALICE LIDDELL
(1852-1934)
Subject of "Alice in Wonder-
land"
People's Almanac (3) p290-293,
por.

HARI, MATA (1871-1917)
Netherlands-German spy,
dancer, courtesan
Brecher--Lives p362
Coffin--Female p121-130, por.
Jones--Rutledge p525
Lichtenstein--Mach. p159-161
Macksey--Book p57
People's Almanac (1) p648,999-
1001, por.
People's Almanac (2) p1125
Who Did What p218-219, por.
Woman's Almanac p448-449, por.
World--Who p299

HARJO, JOY (1951-)
Amer. Creek Indian, poet
Fisher--Third p v, 88

HARKNESS, ANNA M. RICHARDSON
(1837-1926)
Amer. philanthropist
James--Notable (2) p134-135
McHenry--Liberty's p176-177

HARKNESS, GOERGIA EMMA (ELMA)
STILLMAN (1891-1974)
Amer. pioneer theologian,
philanthropist, clergyman,
teacher, author
Bloom--Religion p124

James--Notable (2) p135-136
Sicherman--Notable p312-314

HARKNESS, REBEKAH WEST (1915-
1982)
Amer. dance patron, composer,
philanthropist, sculptor
Cur. Biog. '74 p163-166, por.
Cur. Biog. '82 p467
Rogers--Ladies p9,13, por.
Woman's Almanac p311

HARKNESS, SARAH PILLSBURY
(fl. 1970's)
Amer. architect
O'Neill--Women's p609

HARLAN, ANN (1824-1884)
Amer., noted Iowa mother,
wife of Robert Todd Lincoln
Amer.--Mothers p186, por.

HARLAND, MARION, pseud.
See TERHUNE, MARY VIRGINIA
HAWES

HARLEY, EDITH
See TWEEDIE, MRS. ALEC

HARLOW, JEAN (1911-1937)
Amer. actress
Book--Lists (2) p215-216, por.
Hazen--Interv. p411
Hirschhorn--Rating p171, por.
James--Notable (2) p136-137
Keenan--Women p76,79, por.
Keylin--Hollywood p135-136, por.
McHenry--Liberty's p177
Manchel--Women p9,50-51, por.
Millstein--We p234, por.
Mordden--Movie, see index p293
Shipman--Gold. p271-274, por.
Springer--They p128-130,298,
por.
Webster's--Amer. p455
Woman's Alamanc p344, por.
World--Who p235

HARMAN, BELLE CARTER (fl.
1920's)
Amer. deacon, chapel builder
Sherr--American p135, por.

HARMAN, ELEANOR (fl. 1970's)
Canadian editor
O'Neill--Women's p488-489

HARMON, MARYELLEN, SISTER (fl.
1970's)
Amer. nun
O'Neill--Women's p391

HARMS, JOAN (fl. 1970's)
French TV executive
Marzolf--Up p286

HARNACK, MILDRED FISH (1902-
1943)
German Nazi victim, politician
Partington--Who's p153

HARNESS, ARMINTA J. (fl. 1970's)
Amer. air force engineer
O'Neill--Women's p541-542

HARP, HOLLY (fl. 1960's-1970's)
Amer. fashion designer, exec-
utive
O'Neill--Women's p253-254

HARPER, BEVERLY (c1942-   )
Amer. consultant, executive
O'Neill--Women's p138

HARPER, ELLA (fl. 1860's)
Amer. Confederate letter-writer
Wiley--Confed. p170

HARPER, ETHEL (1904-1979)
Amer. entertainer
World--Who p235

HARPER, FRANCES ELLEN WATKINS
(1825-1911)
Amer. poet, lecturer, social
reformer
Bernikow--World p212
Hymowitz--Hist. p152
James--Notable (2) p137-139
McHenry--Liberty's p177-178
Warren--Pictorial p88

HARPER, HEATHER (1930-   )
Irish opera singer
Gammond--Illus. p244, por.

HARPER, IDA A. HUSTED (1851-
1931)
Amer. journalist, suffragist,
feminist
James--Notable (2) p139-140
McHenry--Liberty's p178

HARPER, KATY (fl. 1970's)
Amer. air traffic controller
Innis--Profiles p194-195, por.

HARPER, MARY (c1866-)
Amer. centenarian
Mitchell--Yessir p16-18, por.

HARPER, PAT
Amer. TV news co-anchor
Scheuer--Tel. p215

HARPER, VALERIE (1940/1941-)
Amer. TV actress
Anderson--People p190, por.
Bowman--Entertain. p32-39, por.
Cur. Biog. '75 p182-185, por.
Fireman--TV p187
Kulkin--Her p139-140
World--Who p235

HARPMAN, JULIA (fl. 1920's)
Amer. journalist
Marzolf--Up p47

HARPUR, V. LORRAINE (1923-)
Canadian genealogical re-
searcher, author, editor
Meyer--Who's p93

HARRADEN, BEATRICE (1864-1936)
English novelist
Showalter--Lit. p343

HARRIMAN, FLORENCE JAFFRAY
HURST (1870-1967)
Amer. government official,
diplomat, journalist
McHenry--Liberty's p178-179
Sicherman--Notable p314-315
Ware--Beyond p147, see also
index p199

HARRIMAN, MARY (fl. 1900's)
Amer. debutante, Junior
League founder
Felton--Famous p108

HARRIMAN, MARY WILLIAMSON
AVERELL (1851-1932)
Amer. philanthropist,
businesswoman
James--Notable (2) p140-142

HARRINGTON, JANE, COUNTESS
(1755-1824)

English socialite
Ware--Meet p33,77

HARRIS, ANN SUTHERLAND (fl.
1970's)
Amer. art historian, professor
Parker--Old p46-47, 84
Women's--Female p115

HARRIS, BARBARA (1935-1937-)
Amer. singer, actress
Claghorn--Biog. p198
World--Who p235

HARRIS, CORRA MAY WHITE (1869-
1935)
Amer. novelist
James--Notable (2) p142-143

HARRIS, DILUE ROSE (c1825-1914)
Amer. historian
Sherr--American p221

HARRIS, ELIZABETH F.S. (1822-
1852)
British novelist
Showalter--Lit. p327

HARRIS, EMILY SCHWARTZ (1947-)
Amer. revolutionary, accused
criminal
Woman's Almanac p508
World--Who p297

HARRIS, EMMYLOU (1948-)
Amer. singer
Anderson--People p190-191

HARRIS, ESTHER SAY (fl. 1700's)
Amer. pioneer
Sherr--American p200

HARRIS, FRAN (fl. 1940's)
Amer. radio news reporter
Marzolf--Up 138-139,147-148

HARRIS, JEAN (1924-)
Amer. headmistress,
criminal
People--Best p76

HARRIS, JOAN SUTHERLAND (fl.
1970's)
Amer. artist
O'Neill--Women's p594

HARRIS, JULIA (1875-)
    Amer. author, journalist,
    noted Georgia mother
Amer.--Mothers p130-131, por.

HARRIS, JULIE (1925-)
    Amer. actress
Cur. Biog. '77 p190-193, por.
Entertainers p265, por.
Kufrin--Uncom. p112-131, por.
Scheuer--Tel. p216, por.
Shipman--Internatl. p227-228,
    por.
Woman's Almanac p344-345
World--Who p235

HARRIS, LA DONNA CRAWFORD
    (1931-)
    Amer. civil rights worker,
    Comanche Indian official
Diamonstein--Open p169-171, por.
O'Neill--Women's p717-718
Signif.--Amer. p64, por.

HARRIS, LUCY (1955-)
    Amer. basketball player
O'Neill--Women's p567
Woman's Almanac p438-439, por.

HARRIS, MARGARET (1943-)
    Amer. conductor, composer,
    pianist
Seed--Saturday's p16-20, por.

HARRIS, MARY (1) (fl. 1700's)
    Amer. Indian captive, wife
    of chief
Sherr--American p185

HARRIS, MARY (2)
See JONES, MARY HARRIS
    ("MOTHER JONES")

HARRIS, MARY BELLE (1874-
    1957)
    Amer. prison administrator
Sicherman--Notable p315-317

HARRIS, MAUREEN (fl. 1970's)
    Amer. bowler
McWhirter--Guinness p43

HARRIS, PATRICIA ROBERTS
    (1924-1985)
    Amer. lawyer, government
    official, law school dean
Cur. Biog. '85 p466

Diamonstein--Open p172-176, por.
McHenry--Liberty's p179
O'Neill--Women's p82,368, por.
Schoenebaum--Prof. p279-280
Signif.--Amer. p65, por.
Warren--Pictorial p197,200
Woman's Almanac p473-474
World--Who p142

HARRIS, MRS. PHIL
See FAYE, ALICE

HARRIS, RUTH BATES (fl. 1960's-
    1970's)
    Amer. space program adminis-
    trator
Innis--Profiles p88-89, por.

HARRIS, SANDRA (fl. 1970's)
    Amer. WAC
O'Neill--Women's p545

HARRIS, SARAH
See FAYERWEATHER, SARAH
    HARRIS

HARRIS, SHARON
    Amer. dress designer
Seed--Saturday's p24-26, por.

HARRISON, ANNA J. (fl. 1970's)
    Amer. chemist
O'Neill--Women's p168

HARRISON, ANNA SYMMES (1775-
    1864)
    Amer. First Lady, (wife of
    William Henry Harrison)
James--Notable (2) p143-145
Melick--Wives p30, por.
Woman's Almanac p487-488

HARRISON, BARBARA
    Amer. TV co-anchor
Scheuer--Tel. p216

HARRISON, MRS. BURTON
See HARRISON, CONSTANCE
    CARY

HARRISON, CAROLINE SCOTT
    (1832-1892)
    Amer., noted Indiana mother,
    first president general of DAR,
    artist, First Lady, (wife of
    Benjamin Harrison)
Amer.--Mothers p178, por.

British supermarket chain
director
Macksey--Book p177

HART, MRS. ERNEST (1872-)
British embroidery school
society founder, traveler,
writer
Callen--Women p116
Hamalian--Ladies p198-209

HART, JANET (fl. 1970's)
Amer. attorney
O'Neill--Women's p90,365

HART, JUDITH (fl. 1950's-
1970's)
British minister of state,
Parliament member
O'Neill--Women's p50-51
Vallance--Women, see index
p207

HART, KITTY CARLISLE (1914-)
Amer. arts administrator,
actress
Cur. Biog. '82 p140-144, por.
Springer--They p54-55,277,
por.
World--Who p228-229

HART, MARIAN RICE (c1891-)
Amer. aviatrix
Comfort--Good p145, por.
People's Almanac (3) p523

HART, MARJORY F. (fl. 1960's-
1970's)
Amer. women's program
coordinator
O'Neill--Women's p11,29

HART, MAY
British jeweller, metal-
worker, enameller
Callen--Women p157,223

HART, NANCY (fl. 1860's)
Amer. Confederate rebel
fighter
Sherr--American p48-49,245

HART, NANCY MORGAN (c1735-
1830/1840)
Amer. Revolutionary War
heroine
Booth--Women p203-207, por.

Clyne--Patriots p41-49
Hymowitz--Hist. p32
James--Notable (2) p150-151
McHenry--Liberty's p179-180
Meyer--Petticoat p128-130, por.
Reifert--Women p23
Somerville--Women p42-45
Whitney--Col. p226-228,230, por.
Williams--Demeter's p247
Woman's Almanac p452

HART, PEARL (c1872-1925)
Canadian-Amer. outlaw, West-
ern bandit
Sherr--American p7,9
Time--Women p171,174-175, por.
Williams--Legend. p41-51, por.

HARTER, LYDIA (fl. 1970's)
Amer. clergyman
Proctor--Women p56-60,64-66,92-93

HARTIGAN, GRACE (1922-)
Amer. painter
Fowler--Art p146-147
Haftmann-Paint. (1) p395
Munro--Originals p202-203
Nemser--Convers. p149-177,362-
363, por.
Women's--Female p44

HARTIN, DEBORAH (1933-)
Amer. lecturer, transsexual
Book--Lists (2) p328, por.

HARTLEY, EDNA (fl. 1970's)
Amer. sculptor
Women's--Female p90

HARTLEY, ELDA (fl. 1970's)
Amer. actress, filmmaker
Smith--Movies p177-178,245, por.

HARTLEY, VIVIEN MARY
See LEIGH, VIVIEN

HARTMAN, GRACE (fl. 1970's)
Canadian labor union leader
O'Neill--Women's p284,319

HARTMAN(N), REGINA (fl. 1750's)
German-Amer. pioneer, Indian
captive
Neidle--America's p22

HARTSHORN, EMILY (c1870/1871-)
Amer. centenarian

Mitchell--Yessir p72-73,
por.

HARTULARI, HARICLEA
See DARCLEE, HARICLEA

HARTWIG, EVA BRIGGITTA
See ZORINA, VERA

HARVEY, CLARIE COLLINS
(1903-)
Amer. churchwoman
O'Neill--Women's p398

HARVEY, CORDELIA ADELAIDE
PERRINE (1824-1895)
Amer. hospital founder,
Civil War nurse
Sherr--American p248-249

HARVEY, ETHEL BROWNE
(1885-1965)
Amer. cell biologist,
embryologist
Sicherman--Notable p319-321

HARVEY, JOANNE H. (1932-)
Amer. genealogical research-
er, editor, writer
Meyer--Who's p95-96

HARVEY, LILIAN (1906-1968)
English actress
Springer--They p130,298-299,
por.

HARVEY, MAZIE MANSON (1902-)
Amer. genealogical researcher,
writer, editor
Meyer--Who's p95

HARVEY, PAT (PATRICIA LYNN
HARVEY) (1954-)
Amer. TV newscaster
Scheuer--Tel. p218

HARWOOD, FANNY (1889-1973)
British dental surgeon
Macksey--Book p155
O'Neill--Women's p225

HARWOOD, GWEN (1920-)
Australian poet
Seymour-Smith--Who's p152

HARWOOD, ISABELLA (1840-1888)
British novelist, dramatist
Showalter--Lit. p334

HARWOOD, MARGARET (1885-)
Amer. astronomer
O'Neill--Women's p150

HASANOVITZ, ELIZABETH
Russian-Amer. factory mana-
ger, labor unionizer, writer
Baum--Jewish p132-134
Hymowitz--Hist. p207,239-242

HASBROUCK, LYDIA SAYER (1827-
1910)
Amer. dress reformer, editor
James--Notable (2) p151-152
McHenry--Liberty's p180
Sherr--American p129,165

HASCHEMEYER, AUDREY (1936-)
Amer. molecular biologist
(Antarctica)
Land--New p113-122,216-217, por.

HASEBROOCK, MARGARET ELIZA-
BETH
Amer. clubwoman, noted Ne-
braska mother
Amer.--Mothers p338-339, por.

HASHMAN, JUDY DEVLIN (1935-)
English badminton player
McWhirter--Guinness p34,36-37,
por.

HASKELL, RACHELL (fl. 1860's)
Amer. Western pioneer, diarist
Fischer--Let p58-72

HASLIP, JOAN (fl. 1970's)
English biographer
P.W.--Author p233-235,501

HASSELAER, KENAU (1526-c1588)
Netherlands shipwright
Macksey--Book p161-162, por.

HASSELTINE, ANN
See JUDSON, ANN HASSELTINE

HASSON, ESTHER VORHEES (1869-
1942)
Amer. nurse
O'Neill--Women's p534

HASTINGS, MINNETTA LITTLEWOOD
(1884-1962)
Amer. educator, noted Wisconsin mother
Amer.--Mothers p585-586, por.

HASTINGS, SELINA
    See HUNTINGDON, SELINA,
    COUNTESS OF

HASTINGS, THOMAS, LADY
    English chess player
    McWhirter--Guinness p64

HASTON, JEAN ANN (fl. 1970's)
    Amer. 4-H scholarship
    winner
    O'Neill--Women's p21

HATCHER, CORNELIA
    Amer., Alaskan clubwoman,
    Red Cross instructor
    Jones--Women (1) p184-185

HATCHER, ORIE LATHAM (1868-
    1946)
    English-Amer. scholar, voca-
    tional guidance pioneer
    James--Notable (2) p152-153
    McHenry--Liberty's p180-181

HATHAWAY, ANNE (1556/1557-
    1623)
    English, wife of William
    Shakespeare
    Jones--Rutledge p359

HATSHEPSUT (1503-1482 B.C.)
    Egyptian queen, physician
    Fry--1000 p6-7
    Macksey--Book p18-19,161, por.
    Mead--Hist. p21-22, por.

HATTIS, PHYLLIS (fl. 1970's)
    Amer. museum curator, art
    historian
    Women's--Female p118

HATTON, ANN JULIA (KEMBLE)
    CURTIS (c1757-after 1795)
    English librettist, playwright
    Claghorn--Biog. p201

HAUBRICH, KAREN (fl. 1970's)
    Amer. badminton player
    McWhirter--Guinness p37

HAUCK, MINNIE
    See HAUK, MINNIE

HAUDEBOURT-LESCOT, ANTOINETTE
    CECILE HORTENSE (1784-1845)
    French artist

Fine--Women p55-56, por.
Harris--Women p46,48,86,198,
    218-219,349

HAUGERY, MARGARET (1925-)
    Amer. aviatrix
    Genett--Aviation p108

HAUGHERY, MARGARET GAFFNEY
    (1813-1882)
    Amer. philanthropist, business
    woman, noted Louisiana mother
    Amer.--Mothers p226, por.
    Bird--Enterprising p83-85
    James--Notable (2) p153-155
    McHenry--Liberty's p181
    O'Neill--Women's p508
    Sherr--American p84, por.

HAUK, MINNIE (1851/1852-1929)
    Swiss opera singer
    Claghorn--Biog. p202
    James--Notable (2) p155-156
    McHenry--Liberty's p181-182

HAUN, CATHERINE MARGARET (fl.
    1840's)
    Amer. Western pioneer
    Time--Women p31

HAUN, WEYNETTE PARKS (1926-)
    Amer. genealogical researcher,
    author
    Meyer--Who's p95

HAUPT, ENID ANNENBERG (c1906-)
    Amer. millionaire, editor
    Forbes--400 ('84) p190

HAUPTMAN, JUDITH (fl. 1970's)
    Amer. feminist, scholar
    O'Neill--Women's p397

HAUSER, ALICE (fl. 1970's)
    Amer. teacher, art history
    Women's--Female p115

HAUSER, RITA (1934-)
    Amer. lawyer, international
    law specialist
    O'Neill--Women's p364-365

HAUTZIG, ESTHER (1930-)
    Polish-Amer. author
    Kulkin--Her p140-141

HAVA OF PRAGUE
    See BACHARACH, EVA (HAVA)

HAVEMEYER, LOUISINE WALDRON
ELDER (1855-1929)
Amer. art collector, suffra-
gist, philanthropist
James--Notable (2) p156-158
Sherr--American p171

HAVEN, (ALICE) EMILY BRADLEY
NEAL (1827-1863)
Amer. author, editor
James--Notable (2) p158-159
McHenry--Liberty's p182

HAVER, JUNE (1926-)
Amer. singer, actress
Book--Lists (2) p16
Claghorn--Biog. p202
Lamparski--What. (3) p146-147,
por.
Lamparski--What. (8) p124-125,
por.

HAVERS, ALICE (fl. 19th cent.)
English illustrator
Callen--Women p196,204

HAVILAND, JOAN DE BEAVOIR DE
See FONTAINE, JOAN

HAVILAND, LAURA SMITH
(1808-1898)
Amer. Quaker abolitionist
Hoople--As p86-89
James--Notable (2) p159-160
O'Neill--Women's p387
Sherr--American p115

HAVOC, JUNE (1916-)
Canadian actress
World--Who p257

HAWEIS, MARY
Amer. novelist, feminist
Showalter--Lit. p182-183

HAWES, BESS LOMAX (1921-)
Amer. singer, teacher
Claghorn--Biog. p202

HAWES, ELIZABETH (1903-1971)
Amer. fashion designer,
author, feminist
O'Neill--Women's p243-244
Sicherman--Notable p321-322

HAWES, HARRIET ANN BOYD
(1871-1945)

Amer. archaeologist
James--Notable (2) p160-161
McHenry--Liberty's p182-183

HAWKER, MARY ELIZABETH (1848-
1908)
Scottish novelist, short story
writer
Showalter--Lit. p337-338

HAWKES, DAPHNE
Amer. clergyman
Smith--Break. p111-135, por.

HAWKINS, LAURA
Amer. model for Twain's
"Becky Thatcher"
Sherr--American p130

HAWKINS, PAULA FICKES (1927-)
Amer. Senator
Cur. Biog. '85 p174-177

HAWKS, ANNIE SHERWOOD (1835-
1918)
Amer. hymnist
Claghorn--Biog. p203

HAWN, GOLDIE JEANNE (1945-)
Amer. actress
Anderson--People p193-194, por.
Cur. Biog. '71 p183-185, por.
Hirschhorn--Rating p174-175, por.
Mordden--Movie p229,243-244
People--Best p186-187, por.
Shipman--Internatl. p239-241, por.
World--Who p235

HAWTHORNE, SOPHIA AMELIA PEA-
BODY (1809-1871)
Amer., wife of Nathaniel Haw-
thorne, painter
Fryer--Faces, see index p291
James--Notable (2) p162-163
Sherr--American p103

HAXALL, CHARLOTTE (fl. 1860's)
Amer. Southern belle, (wife
of Robert E. Lee, Jr.)
DeLeon--Belles p128, por.

HAXALL, LUCY (fl. 1860's)
Amer. Southern belle
DeLeon--Belles p209-210, por.

HAXALL, MRS. PHIL
See TRIPLETT, MARY

HAXTON, JOSEPHINE
See DOUGLAS, ELLEN HOPE,
pseud.

HAY, ELZEY
See ANDREWS, ELIZA FRANCES

HAY, MARY GARRETT (1857-1928)
Amer. feminist, suffragist,
temperance reformer,
politician
James--Notable (2) p163-165
Sherr--American p165-166

HAYCOCK, CHRISTINE E. (fl.
1970's)
Amer. surgeon, professor
O'Neill--Women's p549

HAYD, MARIANNA (1688-1753)
German miniature painter
Macksey--Book p200

HAYDEE, MARCIA (1937/1939-)
Brazilian ballet dancer
Cur. Biog. '77 p197-200, por.
O'Neill--Women's p645

HAYDEN, MRS. CHARLES
See McGINLEY, PHYLLIS

HAYDEN, JULIE (1939-)
Amer. writer
Cahill--Women p348

HAYDEN, MARY BRIDGET,
MOTHER (1814-1890)
Irish-Amer. nun, Indian
missionary, educator
James--Notable (2) p165-166
Sherr--American p76, por.

HAYDEN, MELISSA (1923-)
Canadian-Amer. ballet
dancer
McHenry--Liberty's p183
World--Who p76

HAYDEN, SOPHIA GREGORIA
(1868/1870-1953)
Amer. architect
Callen--Women p223
O'Neill--Women's p xii,608
Sherr--American p60
Sicherman--Notable p323-324
Warren--Pictorial p159

HAYDON, JULIE (1910-)
Amer. actress
Springer--They p130-131,299, por.

HAYES, ANNA HANSEN (1886-)
Amer., noted Idaho mother,
poet, civic worker, organization official
Amer.--Mothers p153-154, por.

HAYES, DORA (fl. 1970's)
Amer. chemist
O'Neill--Women's p32, por.

HAYES, HELEN (1900-)
Amer. actress, noted New
York mother
Amer.--Mothers p396-397
Chinoy--Women p168, por.
Clark--Leading p137-138
Engstead--Star p48,50,52
Entertainers p215, por.
Fabian--On p177-179, por.
Gilfond--Heroines p112-114, por.
Hazen--Interv. p84
Hirschhorn--Rating p176-177,
por.
Ingraham--Album p62
Lewis--Prime p112
McHenry--Liberty's p183-184
100--Greatest (1) p52, por.
O'Neill--Women's p652,654,657-
658, 677
Shipman--Gold. p276-278, por.
Signif.--Amer. p65, por.
Springer--They p131,299, por.
Woman's Almanac p345-346, por.
World--Who p236

HAYES, MRS. J.A.
See DAVIS, MARGARET HOWELL
("LITTLE MAGGIE")

HAYES, JANET GRAY (1926-)
Amer. politician, mayor
O'Neill--Women's p44,79

HAYES, LUCY WARE WEBB (1831-
1889)
Amer., noted Ohio mother,
First Lady, wife of Ruther-
ford B. Hayes
Amer.--Mothers p427, por.
James--Notable (2) p166-167
Melick--Wives p46-47, por.
People's Almanac (1) p270
Woman's Almanac p489

HAYES, SOPHIA BIRCHARD (1792-
1866)
Amer., mother of President
Hayes
Faber--Presidents' p231-235

HAYES, SUSAN SEAFORTH (c1943-)
Amer. TV actress
Scheuer--Tel. p219, por.

HAYGOOD, LAURA ASKEW (1845-
1900)
Amer. educator, missionary
James--Notable (2) p167-169
McHenry--Liberty's p184
Scott--Southern p142-143

HAYLLAR, EDITH (1860-1948)
British artist
Harris--Women p54-55,93,258-
259,353

HAYMAN, HELENE
British Parliament member
Vallance--Women p53,69-70,83,
93,108,114

HAYNE, JULIA DEAN
See DEAN, JULIA

HAYNES, ELIZABETH A. ROSS
(1883-1953)
Amer. YWCA official, social
researcher, author, business
woman
Sicherman--Notable p324-325

HAYNES, PHYLLIS
Amer. TV newscaster
Gelfman--Women p45-46,68,95,
108,119-120,142,159

HAYS, ANNA MAE (fl. 1940's-
1970's)
Amer. nurse, brigadier
general
O'Neill--Women's p540

HAYS, KATHRYN
Amer. actress
Scheuer--Tel. p219

HAYS, MARY (1759/1760-1843)
English novelist, treatise
writer
Moers--Literary p293

HAYS, MOLLY LUDWIG
See PITCHER, MOLLY

HAYS, SUE PIRTLE
Amer. rodeo rider
Woman's Almanac p438

HAYWARD, BROOKE (1937-)
Amer. writer
Anderson--People p194-195

HAYWARD, SUSAN (1918/1919-1975)
Amer. actress
Cur. Biog. '75 p467
Hirschhorn--Rating p177-178, por.
Keylin--Hollywood p142, por.
Shipman--Internatl. p241-244, por.
Sicherman--Notable p325-326
Springer--They p131,299-300, por.
Woman's Almanac p346
World--Who p236

HAYWOOD, ELIZA FOWLER (c1693-
1756)
English novelist, dramatist,
journalist
Avenel--Comp. (1) p240
Horner--English p18-24,126-130
Moers--Literary p293

HAYWORTH, RITA (1918-1987)
Amer. actress, dancer
Hirschhorn--Rating p178, por.
Keenan--Women p83, por.
Manchel--Women p11,66,71,por.
Mordden--Movie p194,209-212,
215-216, por.
Shipman--Gold. p278-281, por.
Springer--They p131,300, por.
World--Who p236

HAZARD, CAROLINE (1856-1945)
Amer. college president, author,
social reformer
James--Notable (2) p169-170
Sherr--American p207

HAZELTINE, MARY EMOGENE
(1868-1949)
Amer. pioneer librarian
James--Notable (2) p170-171

HAZELTINE, NELLIE (fl. 1880's)
Amer. belle
Peacock--Famous p257-263, por.

HAZELWOOD, ADELAIDE
See WOOD, DEL

HAZEN, ELIZABETH LEE (1885-
1975)
Amer. microbiologist, my-
cologist
Sicherman--Notable p326-328

HAZEN, LITA ANNENBERG (c1910-)
Amer. millionaire
Forbes--400 ('84) p190

HAZLETON, LESLEY (fl. 1970's)
Israeli writer
Lichtenstein--Mach. p157-158

HAZZARD, SHIRLEY (1931-)
Australian novelist,
story-writer
Seymour-Smith--Novels p155

"H.D.", pseud.
See DOOLITTLE, HILDA

HEAD, EDITH (1898/1899-1981)
Amer. fashion designer
Cur. Biog. '82 p467
Dunlap--Calif. p88, por.
Engstead--Star p110-111
McHenry--Liberty's p184-185
O'Neill--Women's p255
Sat. Eve. Post--Movie p114-115
Wilson--Holly. p25-27
World--Who p297

HEAD, MARETTA (fl. 1950's)
Amer. pioneer settler
Sherr--American p122

HEAD, MARY JOHNSTON (fl.
1970's)
Amer. railroad executive
O'Neill--Women's p522

HEAGNEY, MURIEL (fl. 1920's-
1970's)
Australian author, labor
leader, feminist
O'Neill--Women's p293

HEALEY, ANNE (fl. 1970's)
Amer. sculptor
Women's--Female p90

HEALEY, CAROLINE (fl. 19th
cent.)
Amer. writer
Welter--Dimity p42-56

HEALEY, DIANE
Amer. TV executive
Scheuer--Tel. p220

HEAP, JANE
See ANDERSON, MARGARET
CAROLYN

HEARD, CUBA (fl. 1970's)
Amer. agricultural scholarship
winner
O'Neill--Women's p21

HEARD, ELIZABETH (fl. 1600's)
Amer. Colonial patriot
Williams--Demeter's p160

HEARNE, MARY (1834-1909)
English hymnist, teacher
Showalter--Lit. p332

HEARST, MILLICENT WILLSON
(c1859-1951)
Amer., wife of William Randolph
Hearst
Forma--They p106-107, por.

HEARST, PATRICIA CAMPBELL
("PATTY") (1954-)
Amer. heiress
Anderson--People p195-196, por.
Cur. Biog. '82 p151-155, por.
Dunlap--Calif. p89
Hershey--Between p193-197
People--Best p20-21, por.
People's Almanac (1) p258
Schoenebaum--Prof. p290-291
Woman's Almanac p507-508
World--Who p298

HEARST, PHOEBE APPERSON (1842-
1919)
Amer. philanthropist, noted
California mother
Amer.--Mothers p51-52
Dunlap--Calif. p88-89, por.
James--Notable (2) p171-173
McHenry--Liberty's p185
Sherr--American p12
Starr--Amer. p225,290,297,408
Warren--Pictorial p142

HEATH, LINDA M. (c1947-)
Amer. heroine
O'Neill--Women's p733

HEATH, MARY (fl. 1930's-1970's)
Amer. rancher
O'Neill--Women's p15-16

HEATH, SOPHIE, LADY (1896-
1939)
Irish aviatrix
Boase--Sky's p45-62, see also
index p221, por.
Macksey--Book p247-248,262,
por.

HEATHCOTE, MILLICENT (fl.
1960's)
British painter
Women's--Female p44

HEAZLE, JEAN (-1949)
Irish-Amer. rancher
Sherr--American p56-57

HEBARD, GRACE RAYMOND
(1861-1936)
Amer. educator, author,
suffragist
James--Notable (2) p173-174
Sherr--American p255-256

HEBDEN, KATHARINE (fl. 1640's)
Amer. Colonial physician
Williams--Demeter's p173-174

HEBERT, ANNE (1916-)
French Canadian poetess
Avenel--Comp. (1) p243

HECK, BARBARA RUCKLE (1737-
1804)
Irish-Amer. religious leader,
("Mother of Methodism")
Hymowitz--Hist. p21
James--Notable (2) p174-175
McHenry--Liberty's p185
Sherr--American p168
Williams--Demeter's p204-205
World--Who p82

HECKART, EILEEN (1919-)
Amer. actress
World--Who p236

HECKLER, MARGARET MARY
O'SHAUGHNESSY (c1932-)
Amer. Congresswoman
Chamberlin--Min. p317-321, por.
Cur. Biog. '83 p182-185, por.

Keil--Those p311,314-315
U.S.--Women (90th) p13, por.

HECTOR, ANNIE FRENCH (1825-
1902)
Irish journalist, novelist
Showalter--Lit. p328

HECUBA
Greek queen, mother of Hector
Pomeroy--Godd. p28,109
Zinserling--Women p15

HEDGEPATH, MAUREEN (fl. 1960's)
Amer. labor union leader
O'Neill--Women's p301

HEDRICK, ZELMA KATHRYN
See GRAYSON, KATHRYN

HEDWIG (HEDVIGE), QUEEN
See JADWIGA

HEER, ANNA (1862-1918)
Swiss nursing school co-founder,
physician
Marks--Women p119

HEER, MARGARETHA DE (fl. 1650's)
Netherlands artist
Harris--Women p35,144,158,343

HEGAMIN, LUCILLE NELSON (1897-
1970)
Amer. singer
Claghorn--Jazz p138

HEGAN, ALICE CALDWELL
See RICE, ALICE CALDWELL
HEGAN

HEIGHT, DOROTHY IRENE (1912-)
Amer. organization official
Cur. Biog. '72 p216-218, por.
Gilbert--Part. p111, por.
O'Neill--Women's p394-395
Warren--Pictorial p202

HEILBRON, ROSE (fl. 1940's-1950's)
English lawyer, judge
Macksey--Book p127, por.
O'Neill--Women p369

HEIM-VÖGTLIN, MARIE (1845-1916)
Swiss physician, co-founder,
nursery school

Macksey--Book p150
Marks--Women p119

HEINEL, ANNE (ANNA) (1752-
1808)
German ballet dancer
Macksey--Book p225
Migel--Ballerinas p59-64

HEINEMANN, ADA
Amer. orchestra player
Neuls-Bates--Women p204

HEINEMANN, BARBARA (1795-
1883)
Alsacian-Amer. spiritual
leader, co-founder Amana
Society
James--Notable (2) p175-177
McHenry--Liberty's p185-186
Neidel--America's p58,64-67
Sherr--American p69

HEINI, MAIJA LIISA (fl. 1970's)
Finnish editor, journalist
Marzolf--Up p269,278,293

HEISE, JAN (fl. 1970's)
Amer. marketing executive
Seed--Saturday's p140-142, por.

HEISKELL, MARIAN (fl. 1970's)
Amer. newspaper executive,
journalist
Marzolf--Up p93

HEISS, CAROL ELIZABETH (c1940-)
Amer. skater
Assoc. Press--Pursuit p208,
225-226, por.
Hollander--100 p28-29,32, por.
Kulkin--Her p141-142
Woman's Almanac p434-435

HEISS, PHYLLIS M. (1922-)
Amer. genealogical researcher,
writer
Meyer--Who's p95-96

HEKTOEN, JEANNETTE
Amer. TV director
Scheuer--Tel. p220

HELBURN, THERESA (1887-1959)
Amer. theatrical producer
Sicherman--Notable p328-330

HELD, ANNA (c1865-1918)
Polish-Amer. singer, actress
Claghorn--Biog. p206
James--Notable (2) p177-178
McHenry--Liberty's p186

HELDMAN, GLADYS (1922-)
Amer. tennis player
Woman's Almanac p416

HELEN (1) (fl. 1970's)
Amer. maid
Coles--Women p229-273

HELEN (2) (1896-)
Rumanian queen mother
Partington--Who's p157

HELEN OF TROY (fl. c1100 B.C.)
Greek beauty, physician
Coffin--Female p31-37
Marks--Women p42
Mead--Hist. p37,228
Pomeroy--Godd. p16-18,20-21

HELENA (c250-350)
Roman Saint, painter, mother
of Constantine
Green--Saints p96-98
Jones--Rutledge p362
Kulkin--Her p142
Macksey--Book p194
Munsterberg--Hist. p11
Sparrow--Women p21

HELLER, BARBARA (fl. 1970's)
Amer. environmentalist, gov-
ernment official
O'Neill--Women's p83-84

HELLER, HENELE
Jewish letter-writer
Henry--Written p163-165

HELLER, ROZ
Amer. foreign-film producer
Adams--Women p146-147,158,178,
189,204

HELLMAN, JOHANNA (1889-)
German-Swedish physician
Hellstedt--Women p33-35, por.

HELLMAN, LILLIAN (1905-1984)
Amer. playwright
Anderson--People p198

Avenel--Comp. (2) p120
Bachtold--Gifted p15-17
Chinoy--Women p129,171-178, por.
Clark--Leading p176-179
Cur. Biog. '84 p472-473
Ehrlich--Oxford, see index p454
Entertainers p224
Gilbert--Part. p91, por.
Hershey--Between p99
Ingraham--Album p58
McHenry--Liberty's p187-188
Magill--Cycl. p498-499
Moers--Literary p77-78,293
100--Greatest (1) p43, por.
O'Neill--Women's p671
Seymour-Smith--Who's p155-156
Signif.--Amer. p65, por.
Woman's Almanac p252-253
World--Who p14

HELLSTEDT, LEONE McGREGOR
(1900-1977)
Swedish physician
Hellstedt--Women p199-205, por.

HELLWIG, CHRISTINA REGINA
German poet, musician,
medical student
Mead--Hist. p426

HELM, EDITH BENHAM (c1874-
1962)
Amer. White House social
secretary
Daniels--Wash., see index p359,
363

HELMER, BESSIE BRADWELL
(1858-1927)
Amer. lawyer, editor, publisher
McHenry--Liberty's p187

HELOISE (1098/1101-1164)
French letter-writer, physi-
cian, hospital founder
Crosland--Women p41-42
Jones--Rutledge p363
Macksey--Book p141-142
Marks--Women p47
Mead--Hist. p179-180
Moers--Literary p293
Woman's Almanac p74
World--Who p298

HELSON, RAVENNA
Amer. feminist, writer
Adams--Women p5-6

HELVETIUS, ANNE-CATHERINE,
MADAME (1719-1800)
French, friend of Benjamin
Franklin
Booth--Women p115-116

HELVIN, MARIE (fl. 1970's)
Hawaiian model
Keenan--Women p128,153, por.

HEMANS, FELICIA DOROTHEA
BROWNE (1793-1835)
English poet
Avenel--Comp. (1) p243-244
Jones--Rutledge p363
Kaplan--Salt p93-95, por.
Moers--Literary p117,198,293
Morley--Literary p320-322
Who Did What p148

HEMENWAY, ABBY MARIA (1828-
1890)
Amer. Vermont historian,
anthologist
James--Notable (2) p178-179
Sherr--American p229-230

HEMENWAY, MARY PORTER TILES-
TON (1820-1894)
Amer. philanthropist
James--Notable (2) p179-181
McHenry--Liberty's p187

HEMESSEN, CATHARINA VAN (fl.
16th Cent.)
Belgian painter
Munsterberg--Hist. p22-23

HEMINGS, SALLY (1773-1835)
Amer., friend of Thomas
Jefferson
DePauw--Found. p76-79
Kelley--Courage p13,215-216,219,
226-227,230-231
People's Almanac (1) p262

HEMINGWAY, MARGAUX (MARGOT)
(1955-)
Amer., granddaughter of Ernest
Hemingway, model, actress
Anderson--People p198-199, por.
Cur. Biog. '78 p192-195, por.

Keenan--Women p142-143,153,
por.
People--Best p28,153, por.

HEMINGWAY, MARY WELSH (1908-)
Amer. wife of Ernest Heming-
way, author, journalist
Fallaci--Ego p141-158

HEMPEL, FRIEDA (1885-1955)
German opera singer
Neidle--America's p22
Tuggle--Golden p113-115, por.

HEMPERLEY, MARION R. (1923-)
Amer. genealogical researcher,
author
Meyer--Who's p96

HEMRY, SEDDA
Amer. Western pioneer
Time--Women p40-41

HENCKEN, THALASSA CRUSO
(fl. 1930's-1970's)
English TV plant specialist
O'Neill--Women's p135

HENDEE, HANNAH HUNTER (fl.
1770's-1780's)
Amer. Revolutionary War
patriot
Clyne--Patriots p66-73
Somerville--Women p52-55

HENDEE, MRS.
Amer. Colonial heroine,
Indian captive
Williams--Demeter's p168

HENDERLITE, RACHEL (fl.
1940's-1970's)
Amer. clergyman, professor
O'Neill--Women's p380

HENDERS, HARRIET (1904-1972)
Amer. opera singer
Claghorn--Biog. p206

HENDERSON, ALICE CORBIN
(1881-1949)
Amer. magazine co-founder
Ehrlich--Oxford p358
O'Neill--Women's p472

HENDERSON, ANNIE HELOISE ABEL
See ABEL, ANNIE HELOISE

HENDERSON, DOROTHY ODLE
See RICHARDSON, DOROTHY
MILLER

HENDERSON, FLORENCE (1934-)
Amer. actress, singer
Cur. Biog. '71 p187-189, por.
World--Who p268

HENDERSON, FREDDAYE
Amer. travel agency executive
Warren--Pictorial p200

HENDERSON, MARGARET (fl. 1770's)
Amer. feminist
Berkin--Women p95,98-99

HENDERSON, NATHALIE (-1934)
Amer. co-founder Junior
League
O'Neill--Women's p111

HENDERSON, ROSA DESCHAMPS
(1896-1968)
Amer. singer
Claghorn--Jazz p139

HENDRIX, HELEN HUNT (c1949-)
Amer. millionaire
Forbes--400 ('84) p107

HENDRIX, WANDA (1928-1981)
Amer. actress
Lamparski--What. (8) p128-129,
por.

HENIE, SONJA (1912-1969)
Norwegian skater
Assoc. Press--Pursuit p89,105,
108-109,111,124,146, por.
Cur. Biog. '70 p464
Hazen--Interv. p418
Hollander--100 p24-25, por.
Keylin--Hollywood p144, por.
Macksey--Book p262-263
McWhirter--Guinness p9,95
O'Neill--Women's p563
Pachter--Champ. p180-181, por.
Reader's--Story p492
Ryan--Sports p129-130
Shipman--Gold. p281-282, por.
Sicherman--Notable p330-331
Springer--They p131,133,300,
por.
Woman's Almanac p435, por.
World--Who p215

HENIN, MARIE-LOUISE (1898-
1944)
Belgian physician, dental
surgeon, war heroine
Macksey--Book p59

HENLEY, BETH (1952-)
Amer. playwright, actress
Cur. Biog. '83 p185-188, por.

HENNER, MARILU (c1952)
Amer. TV actress
Scheuer--Tel. p222, por.

HENNESSEY, ALICE E. (fl. 1970's)
Amer. executive
O'Neill--Women's p521

HENNIG, MARGARET
Amer. feminist, writer
Adams--Women p10-11,20,109

HENNING, ANNE (c1956-)
Amer. skater
Assoc. Press--Pursuit p297-298
Hollander--100 p38-39, por.
Jordan--Broken p57-66
O'Neill--Women's p564
Stambler--Women p47-59, por.

HENNING, MARGARET (fl. 1970's)
Amer. feminist, writer
Lichtenstein--Mach. p226,240-
242

HENNING-JENSEN, ASTRID (fl.
1940's-1960's)
Danish film director
Smith--Movies p101-102

HENNINGS, JOSEPHINE S. (fl.
1930's-1940's)
Amer. radio officer
Women--Radio p11

HENNIS, ANN (fl. 1750's)
Amer. heroine
Sherr--American p245

HENNISSART, MARTHA
See LATHEN, EMMA, pseud.

HENNOCK, FRIEDA BARKIN
(1904-1960)
Polish-Amer. lawyer, government official
O'Neill--Women's p365

Sicherman--Notable p332-
333

HENRICHSEN, MARGARET (fl.
1950's)
Amer. clergyman, author
O'Neill--Women's p380

HENRIETTA MARIA (1609-1669)
English queen-consort of
Charles I of England
Jones--Rutledge p364
People's Almanac (1) p530-531
Softly--Queens p84-88, por.

HENROTIN, ELLEN MARTIN (1847-
1922)
Amer. club leader, social
reformer, philanthropist
James--Notable (2) p181-183
McHenry--Liberty's p187-188
Warren--Pictorial p159

HENRY, ALICE (1857-1943)
Australian-Amer. journalist,
editor, labor leader
James--Notable (2) p183-184
Neidle--America's p125-126
O'Neill--Women's p290-291

HENRY, ANN(E) WOOD (1732/1734-
1799)
Amer. Revolutionary War
patriot
Flexner--Face p84, por.
Sherr--American p200

HENRY, CHARLOTTE (1914/1916-)
Amer. actress
Lamparski--What. Annual (4,5)
p175-179, por.
Springer--They p133,300, por.

HENRY, JEANNE HAND (1921-)
Amer. genealogical researcher,
author
Meyer--Who's p96-97

HENRY, MARGUERITE (1902-)
Amer. children's author
Ehrlich--Oxford p230

HENRY, MARY HELEN (1948-)
Australian genealogical
researcher, editor
Meyer--Who's p97

HENSCHEL, LILLIAN JUNE BAILEY
(1860-1901)
Amer. singer
Claghorn--Biog. p207-208

HENSEL, FANNY CECILE
MENDELSSOHN (1805-1847)
German composer
Neuls-Bates--Women p143-152,
por.
Woman's Almanac p52

HENSEN, JOYCE B. (1933-)
Amer. genealogical research-
er, author
Meyer--Who's p97

HENSLER, ELSIE (1836-1929)
Amer. singer
Claghorn--Biog. p208

HENSLEY, JOSEPHINE (c1844-)
Irish-Amer. dance hall owner
Sherr--American p136

HENSLEY, VIRGINIA PATTERSON
See CLINE, PATSY

HENTSCHEL-GUERNTH, DOROTHEA
(1749-)
German dietician
Macksey--Book p145
Mead--Hist. p502-503

HENTZ, CAROLINE LEE WHITING
(1800-1856)
Amer. novelist, teacher
Ehrlich--Oxford, see index p454
James--Notable (2) p184-186
McHenry--Liberty's p188

HENVILLE, SANDRA LEA
See "BABY SANDY"

HEPBURN, AUDREY (1929-)
Belgian-Amer. actress
Anderson--People p200-201, por.
Book--Lists (2) p261
Hirschhorn--Rating p179-180,
por.
Keenan--Women p11,86-87, por.
Manchel--Women p90,99, por.
Mordden--Movie p232,234-237,
266
Shipman--Internatl. p244-248,
por.
Woman's Almanac p346
World--Who p236

HEPBURN, EDITH ALICE MARY
See WICKHAM, ANNA

HEPBURN, KATHARINE (1907/
1909-)
Amer. actress
Anderson--People p201-202, por.
Clark--Leading p197-200
Cur. Biog. '69 p209-212, por.
Entertainers p233
Higham--Celeb. p11-18, por.
Hirschhorn--Rating p181-182,
por.
Horan--Desperate p33, por.
Jones--Rutledge p369
Lichenstein--Mach., see index
p361
McHenry--Liberty's p188-189
Manchel--Women, see index p121,
por.
Mordden--Movie, see index p293,
por.
O'Neill--Women's p240,652,654,
657
Priestley--Part. p120-122, por.
100--Greatest (1) p50-51, por.
Sat. Eve. Post--Movie p122-123,
por.
Shipman--Gold. p282-288, por.
Sochen--Herstory p331-333,358,
por.
Springer--They p133-134,300,
por.
Webster's--Amer. p481
Woman's Almanac p327,346-347,
por.
World--Who p236

HEPBURN-RUSTON, AUDREY
See HEPBURN, AUDREY

HEPWORTH, BARBARA, DAME
(1903-1975)
English sculptor
Cur. Biog. '75 p467
Fine--Women p180-183
Jones--Rutledge p369
Macksey--Book p208-209, por.
Munsterberg--Hist. p90-93,95
Nemser--Convers. p13-25, 359-
360, por.
O'Neill--Women's p603-604
Petersen--Women p120-121,123-124
Who Did What p150
Wintle--Makers #205 p225-226
Woman's Almanac p225
Women's--Female p90
World--Who p66

HERA
Roman goddess, queen
Pomeroy--Godd. p7-9,13

HERBERT, DOROTHEA (fl.
1770's-1780's)
Irish diarist
Mead--Hist. p457

HERBERT, MARY SIDNEY,
COUNTESS OF PEMBROKE
See PEMBROKE, MARY HER-
BERT SIDNEY, COUNTESS
OF

HERBST, JOSEPHINE FREY
(1897-1969)
Amer. novelist
Ehrlich--Oxford p351,363
Seymour-Smith--Novels p156
Sicherman--Notable p333-335

HEREDIA, pseud.
See REGNIER, PAULE

HEREFORD, LAURA (1831-1870)
English painter
Fine--Women p67

HERING, AGNES POTTS (1874-)
Irish-Amer., Alaskan pio-
neer, clubwoman, noted
Alaska mother
Amer.--Mothers p15, por.

HERLIE, EILEEN (1920-)
Scottish actress
Entertainers p250

HERMAN, ALEXIS M. (c1947-)
Amer. labor leader, government official
O'Neill--Women's p285,340-341,
por.

HERMAN, MILDRED
See HAYDEN, MELISSA

HERMAN, ROBIN (fl. 1970's)
Amer. newspaper sports-
writer
O'Neill--Women's p463

HERMANN, MILDRED R. (1891-)
Amer. Alaskan, lawyer,
government official
Jones--Women (1) p183-184

HERNANDEZ, AILEEN CLARKE
(1926-)
Amer. feminist, lawyer,
government official
Cur. Biog. '71 p189-191, por.
O'Neill--Women's p703-704
Signif.--Amer. p66, por.
Sochen--Movers p248,255

HERNANDEZ, AMALIA (fl. 1950's-
1960's)
Mexican ballet dancer, choreographer, teacher
O'Neill--Women's p650-651

HERNANDEZ, FRANCISCA
Spanish religious leader
Bainton--Spain p28-32

HERNE, CHRYSTAL KATHARINE
(1882-1950)
Amer. actress
James--Notable (2) p186-187
McHenry--Liberty's p189

HERNMARCK, HELENA B. (c1941-)
Swedish carpet designer,
tapestry artist
Macksey--Book p209
O'Neill--Women's p608

HERODIAS
Biblical
Price--God p145-147

HERON, MATILDA AGNES (1830-
1877)
Irish-Amer. actress
Entertainers p127
James--Notable (2) p187-188

HERRAD(E) OF LANDSBERG
(-1195)
German Abbess, teacher,
encyclopedic writer, poet,
physician
Macksey--Book p63
Marks--Women p47
Mead--Hist. p181,236

HERRICK, CHRISTINE TERHUNE
(1859-1944)
Amer. home economist, author
James--Notable (2) p188-189

HERRICK, ELINORE MOREHOUSE
(1895-1964)

Amer. executive, labor leader,
government official, journalist
O'Neill--Women's p333
Sicherman--Notable p335-337

HERRICK, GENEVIEVE FORBES
(1894-)
Amer. journalist
Marzolf--Up p72

HERRING, MARY STAHL (1864-
1920)
Amer., noted Louisiana
mother
Amer.--Mothers p225, por.

HERRMAN, MRS. AUGUSTINE,
LADY (fl. 1660's)
Amer. pioneer
Earle--Two Cent. (1) p xvi,
111-112, por.

HERMANN, LISELOTTE (1909-
1938)
German Nazi victim
Partington--Who's p160

HERRON, CARRIE RAND
See RAND, CAROLINE AMANDA
SHERFEY

HERSCHBERGER, RUTH (1917-)
Amer. poet, playwright
Ehrlich--Oxford p32,161,321

HERSCHEL, CAROLINE LUCRETIA
(1750-1848)
German-English astronomer,
mathematician
Asimov--Biog. p214, #297
Macksey--Book p145, por.
Marlowe--Great p28-32, por.
Osen--Women p71-81, por.
Taylor--Gener. p46

HERSENDE (fl. c1100's)
French Abbess of Fonte-
vrault
Mead--Hist. p167,178-179,217

HERSETH, CLARA NELSON (1884-
1947)
Amer. pioneer, noted North
Dakota mother
Amer.--Mothers p419-420, por.

HERSHEY, LENORE (1920-)
Amer. editor, writer,

business woman, community
leader
O'Neill--Women's p481

HERTFORD, ISABELLA, MARCHIO-
NESS OF (1760-1834)
English social leader, (friend
of George, Prince of Wales)
Ware--Meet p42-49,77, por.

HERVEY, IRENE (1910-)
Amer. actress
Springer--They p134,300, por.

HERVIN, CARRIE B. (fl. 1940's)
Amer., noted Oregon mother,
community worker
Amer.--Mothers p448-450, por.

HESS, MYRA, DAME (1890-1965)
English pianist
Jones--Rutledge p372
Macksey--Book p218
O'Neill--Women's p630
World--Who p76

HESS, THERESE M. (fl. 1970's)
Amer. homesteader
O'Neill--Women's p19

HESSE, EVA (1936-1970)
German sculptor
Nemser--Convers. p201-229,364,
por.
O'Neill--Women's p605
Parker--Old p110,152-157, fig.
92
Sicherman--Notable p337-338
Women's--Female p9

HESSELBLAD, MARIA ELIZABETH,
SISTER (-1957)
Swedish-Amer. nurse, nun
O'Neill--Women's p390

HESSELIUS, CHARLOTTE
Amer. socialite
Earle--Two Cent. (2) p xvi,425,
560-561, por.

HESTER, CAROLYN (c1937-)
Amer. singer
Claghorn--Biog. p209

HESTIA
See VESTA

HESTON, LYDIA

1840's-1860's)
Amer. abolitionist, linguist,
mathematical genius
Sherr--American p31

HICKOK, LORENA A. (1893-1908)
Amer., Roosevelt's companion,
journalist, author
Daniels--Wash. p243,248-249,
255,262-263
Sicherman--Notable p338-340

HICKS, BEATRICE ALICE (1919-)
Amer. electrical engineer,
management consultant
O'Neill--Women's p188-189,195

HICKS, ELEANOR (c1943-)
Amer. foreign service officer
Teitz--What's p211-225, por.

HICKS, LOUISE DAY (1919/1923-)
Amer. Congresswoman, lawyer,
politician
Chamberlin--Min. p341-343
Cur. Biog. '74 p174-177, por.
O'Neill--Women's p695,726
Schoenebaum--Prof. p298

HICKS, MARGARET (1858-1883)
Amer. pioneer architect,
teacher
O'Neill--Women's p608

HICKS, MARY AMALIA DANA
See PRANG, MARY AMELIA DANA
HICKS

HICKS, SHEILA (1934-)
Amer. textile artist
O'Neill--Women's p606-607
Munro--Originals p362-369, por.

HIDALGO, MARY ANN TIGHE
See TIGHE, MARY ANN

HIER, ETHEL GLENN (1889-)
Amer. composer, pianist,
teacher
Jablonski--Ency. p244

HIERONYMUS, CLARA W. (fl.
1950's)
Amer. drama critic
Chinoy--Women p228-230, por.

HIGDON, BETTINA PEARSON
(1920-)

Amer. genealogical researcher,
author
Meyer--Who's p97

HIGGINS, ALICE LOUISE
See LOTHROP, ALICE LOUISE
HIGGINS

HIGGINS, DORIA
Amer. reporter
Millstein--We p248-249

HIGGINS, MARGUERITE ("MAGGIE")
(1920-1966)
Amer. foreign correspondent,
journalist
Marzolf--Up p76-78
O'Neill--Women's p451-452
Sicherman--Notable p340-341
Woman's Almanac p269-270
World--Who p52

HIGGINS, VERA (1892-1968)
British horticulturist, writer
Macksey--Book p167

HIGGINSON, ELLA RHOADS (1862-
1940)
Amer. novelist, poet
Ehrlich--Oxford p397
Sherr--American p240

HIGHET, HELEN GILBERT
See MacINNES, HELEN CLARK

HIGHMORE, SUSANNA HIGHMORE
(1730-1812)
English wife of Duncombe,
friend of Richardson's
Horner--English p37

HIGHSMITH, PATRICIA (1921-)
Amer. novelist, short story
writer
Seymour-Smith--Novels p157-158,
por.
Seymour-Smith--Who's p161
World--Who p46

HIGHT, VROW
See CRAMER, VROW

HIGUCHI, CHAKO (fl. 1970's)
Japanese golfer
O'Neill--Women's p560-561

HIGUERA, PRUDENCIA (fl. 1840's)
Amer., daughter of California

HILL, MILDRED J. (1859-1916)
Amer. organist, concert
pianist, song-writer,
kindergarten educator
Claghorn--Biog. p211
Sherr--American p80

HILL, OCTAVIA (1836/1838-1912)
English social reformer,
author, philanthropist
Boyd, Three p95-163
Jones--Rutledge p174
Macksey--Book p117
Showalter--Lit. p334

HILL, PAMELA ("PAM") (1938-   )
Amer. TV executive pro-
ducer
Adams--Women p101,108,111,
150-152,153-154,177,184,199
Scheuer--Tel. p226

HILL, PATTY SMITH (1868-1946)
Amer. kindergarten educator,
song-writer
Burgess--Education p71-85, por.
James--Notable (2) p194-195
McHenry--Liberty's p190-191
People's Almanac (1) p851
Sherr--American p80
Snyder--Dauntless p231-280,
por.

HILL, ROBERTA (1947-   )
Amer. Oneida Indian poet
Fisher--Third p v, 122

HILL, SUSAN (1) (1942-   )
English newspaper critic,
novelist, short story writer
Baker--Women p8
Seymour-Smith--Novels p158

HILLER, SUSAN (1940-   )
Amer. artist
Contemp. Brit. unp., por.

HILLER, WENDY (1912-   )
English actress
Entertainers p240
Hirschhorn--Rating p183-184,
por.
Shipman--Gold. p288-290, por.
Springer--They p134,136,300,
por.
World--Who p257

HILLHOUSE, SARAH PORTER
(1813-1900)
Amer. educator, school
founder, publisher, editor
James--Notable (3) p88-89
McHenry--Liberty's p333
Marzolf--Up p10-11
Sherr--American p31,51
World--Who p101

HILLIS, CORA BUSSEY (1858-1924)
Amer. community worker,
noted Iowa mother
Amer.--Mothers p188-189, por.
Sherr--American p71

HILLIS, MARGARET ELEANOR
(1921-   )
Amer. choral conductor,
musician
Le Page--Women p71-84, por.
O'Neill--Women's p638

HILLMAN, BESSIE ABRAMOWITZ
(1889-1970)
Amer. labor leader
Miller--Women p149-176
Neidle--America's p138,150,161-
164, por.
O'Neill--Women's p296-297
Woman's Almanac p179
World--Who p188

HILLMAN, PONSIE BARCLAY (fl.
1960's)
Amer. labor leader
O'Neill--Women's p314-315

HILLS, CARLA ANDERSON (1934-   )
Amer. government official
Cur. Biog. '75 p194-196, por.
McHenry--Liberty's p191
100--Greatest (1) p62, por.
O'Neill--Women's p82,365-367
Schoenebaum--Prof. p298
Swiger--Women p67-82
Woman's Almanac p474

HILLS, DAPHNE ANNE (1938-   )
English genealogical researcher,
writer
Meyer--Who's p98

HILSCHER-WITTGENSTEIN, HERTA
(fl. 1970's)
Amer. photographer
Women's--Female p66

HILSZ, MARYSE (c1903-1946)
French parachutist, aviatrix
Boase--Sky's p123

HILTON, MARTHA
See WENTWORTH, MRS.
MICHAEL

HIMMELFARB, GERTRUDE (1922-)
Amer. historian, professor
Cur. Biog. '85 p184-187, por.

HIMMELSTEIN, LENA
See MALSIN, LANE BRYANT

HIND, (ELLA) CORA (1861-1942)
Canadian agricultursit, edi-
tor, journalist
Macksey--Book p166-167
O'Neill--Women's p5

HIND AL-HUNUD (fl. 5th Cent.,
A.D.)
Arabian religious leader
Woman's Almanac p445

HINES, BEA
Amer. reporter
O'Neill--Women's p464-465

HINES, MIMI (1933-)
Canadian singer
Claghorn--Biog. p213

HINESTROSA, FRANCISCA
(-1541)
Spanish-Amer. member de
Soto expedition, pioneer
Sherr--American p45
Williams--Demeter's p17-18

HINKLE, BEATRICE MOSES
(1874-1953)
Amer. pioneer psychiatrist
McHenry--Liberty's p191

HINKSON, KATHARINE JOAN
See TYNAN, KATHERINE JOAN

HINMAN, KATHERINE (fl. 1970's)
Amer. Naval Command
officer
O'Neill--Women's p543

HINSON, LOIS E. (1926-)
Amer. veterinarian
O'Neill--Women's p33

HINTON, ROSE MARIE B. (1928-)
Amer. genealogical researcher
Meyer--Who's p98

HIPP, JUTTA (1925-)
German pianist
Claghorn--Jazz p143

HIPPARCHIA
Greek philosopher, wife of
Crates
Pomeroy--Godd. p136-137

HIPPARETE
Greek, wife of Alcibiades
Pomeroy--Godd. p65,81,90,119

HIPPIUS, ZINAIDA, pseud.
See MEREZHKOVSKAVA,
ZINAIDA NIKOLA

HIPPODAMIA
Greek, wife of Pelops
Pomeroy--Godd. p19

HIPPOLET, EFFIE
See DEVI, INDIRA

HIROKO (fl. 1960's)
Japanese model
Keenan--Women p124-126, por.

HIRSCH, FIOLA (fl. c1727)
Bavarian-Jewish printer
Henry--Written p118

HIRSCH, JEANNE (c1917-)
Amer. gynecologist
O'Neill--Women's p706

HIRSCH, JENNY (1829-1902)
German feminist, newspaper
editor, gynecologist
Macksey--Book p88

HIRSCH, LOLLY (c1941-)
Amer. gynecologist
O'Neill--Women's p706

HIRSCH, GILAH (fl. 1970's)
Amer. painter
Women's--Female p45

HITCHCOCK, MRS. ALFRED
See REVILLE, ALMA

HITCHCOCK, LILLY

See COIT, (ELIZA) LILLIE
HITCHCOCK

HITE, MABEL BRADBURY (1909-)
Amer. educator, noted
Kentucky mother
Amer.--Mothers p216-217, por.

HITE, SHERE D. (1942-)
Amer. researcher, cultural
historian
O'Neill--Women's p749-750
People's Almanac (2) p928-929
World--Who p95

HITLER, KLARA PÖLZL (1800-
1907/1908)
Austrian-Hungarian, mother
of Adolf Hitler
Book--Lists (1) p285-286, por.
Diagram--Mothers p112-113, por.

HITSELBERGER, MARY ELEANOR
FITZ HUGH (1931-)
Amer. genealogical research-
er, writer
Meyer--Who's p99

HITTELMAN, MARILYN M.
Amer. heroine
O'Neill--Women's p734

HITZ, DORA (1856-)
German painter, artist
Sparrow--Women p286-287,
302-303

HITZENBERGER, ANNALIESE
(1905-)
Austrian physician
Hellstedt--Women p276-282, por.

HLASS, LAURICE
Jordanian ambassador
O'Neill--Women's p63

HOADLY, MRS. (fl. 1740's)
English, wife of Bishop
Hoadley
Ware--Meet p77

HOBART, ELLA F. (fl. 1860's)
Amer. Civil War chaplain
Warren--Pictorial p109

HOBART, ROSE (1906-)
Amer. musician, actress

Springer--They p136,300,
por.

HOBBES, JOHN OLIVER, pseud.
See CRAIGIE, PEARL MARY
THERESA

HOBBS, ABIGAIL (fl. 1700's)
Amer. accused witch
Taylor--Gener. p27

HOBBS, LUCY BEAMAN
See TAYLOR, LUCY BEAMAN
HOBBS

HOBBY, OVETA CULP (1905-)
Amer. broadcaster, lawyer,
publisher, editor, government
official, Director of WAAC
Forbes--400 ('84) p104
McHenry--Liberty's p191-192
O'Neill--Women's p82,534-535
Signif.--Amer. p66, por.
Stoddard--Famous p218-224, por.
Warren--Pictorial p194
Woman's Almanac p474
World--Who p142

HOBSON, ELIZABETH CHRISTOPHERS
KIMBALL (1841-1912)
Amer. social welfare worker,
nursing school co-founder,
nurse
James--Notable (2) p195-197
Warren--Pictorial p133-134

HOBSON, VALERIE (1917-)
Irish actress
Shipman--Gold. p290-292, por.
Springer--They p136,300,302,
por.

HOBY, ELIZABETH COOKE, LADY
(1571-)
English diarist, religious
worker
Bainton--Spain p105-110, por.
Mead--Hist. p344-345

HÖCH, HANNAH (1889-1971)
German painter
Harris--Women p58,307-309,359
Munsterberg--Hist. p132-133
O'Neill--Women's p596,599

HOCHMAN, SANDRA (1936-)
Amer. poet

Washington state mother
Amer.--Mothers p565-566, por.

HOFFMAN, JOYCE (fl. 1960's)
Amer. surfer
McWhirter--Guinness p129
O'Neill--Women's p585

HOFFMAN, MALVINA CORNELL
(1887-1966)
Amer. sculptor
Ingraham--Album p61
McHenry--Liberty's p192-193
Macksey--Book p208
O'Neill--Women's p603
Sicherman--Notable p343-345
Signif.--Amer. p42, por.
Stoddard--Famous p225-233, por.
Warren--Pictorial p182, por.

HOFFMAN, MARTHA (fl. 1960's)
Amer. bowler
McWhirter--Guinness p44

HOFFMAN, MEDORA (fl. 1880's)
Amer. pianist, linguist
Sherr--American p183, por.

HOFFMAN, VIRGINIA (fl. 1670's)
Amer. sculptor
Women's--Female p90

HOFFMAN-UDDGREW, ANNA (fl.
1910's)
Swedish filmmaker
Smith--Movies p133

HOFFMAN, BETTYE K. (1926-)
Amer. TV executive
Scheuer--Tel. p227

HOFFMAN, MATILDA
Amer., friend of
Washington Irving
Earle--Two Cent. (2) p xv,
530,531, por.

HÖFLICH, LUCIE (1883-1956)
German actress
Entertainers p174

HOFSTADTER, IRIS ADRIAN
See ADRIAN, IRIS

HOGAN, GLADYS
Amer. mother of Marilyn
Monroe

Diagram--Mothers p166-167,
por.

HOGAN, MARION G.
Amer. scientific writer,
weather specialist, executive
M.I.T.--Women p191-194, x

HOGARTH, GEORGINA (fl. 1840's)
English, sister-in-law of
Charles Dickens
Morley--Literary p100,133,407

HOGE, JANE CURRIE BLAIKIE
(1811-1890)
Amer. Civil War relief
leader, welfare worker
Bird--Enterprising p90-91,93,100
James--Notable (2) p199-201
McHenry--Liberty's p193
Sherr--American p59
Woman's Almanac p452-453

HOGG, IMA (1882-1975)
Amer. civic cultural, social
leader, philanthropist
Birmingham--Grandes, see index
p292, por.
Sicherman--Notable p345-346

HOGG, MARY EILEEN (fl. 1970's)
Canadian craftswoman
O'Neill--Women's p127

HOHENBERG, SOPHIE CHOTEK,
DUCHESS OF (1868-1914)
Austrian princess, wife of
Archduke Francis Ferdinand
of Austria
Forma--They p200-201

HOISINGTON, ELIZABETH P. (fl.
1930's-1970's)
Amer. WAAC brigadier general
O'Neill--Women's p540

HOKINSON, HELEN ELNA (1893-
1949)
Amer. cartoonist, ceramics
painter
James--Notable (2) p201-202
McHenry--Liberty's p193-194
O'Neill--Women's p749
Sherr--American p62
Webster's--Amer. ;496

HOLBROOK, CARRIE (fl. 1860's)

Amer. Southern belle
DeLeon--Belles p408-409, por.

HOLBROOK, ELIZA JANE
POITEVENT
See BICHOLSON, ELIZA JANE
POITEVENT

HOLDEN, ANN (fl. 1940's)
Amer. radio broadcaster
Marzolf--Up p144
Women--Radio p3

HOLDEN, FAY (1895-1973)
Amer. actress
Springer--They p136,302, por.

HOLDEN, JOYCE (fl. 1970's)
Canadian leader
O'Neill--Women's p316

HOLDER, MRS. (fl. 17th Cent.)
English surgeon
Mead--Hist. p444

HOLDING, ELIZABETH SANXAY
(1899-1955)
Amer. novelist
Seymour-Smith--Novels p159

HOLE, JUDITH (fl. 1970's)
Amer. TV associate archivist
Klever--Women p39-40,78-79

HOLIDAY, BILLIE ("LADY DAY")
(1915-1959)
Amer. singer
Brecher--Lives p245
Claghorn--Biog. p215
Claghorn--Jazz p144
McHenry--Liberty's p194
Macksey--Book p219
O'Neill--Women's p623-624
Sicherman--Notable p346-348
Signif.--Amer. p43, por.
Simon--Best p275-278, por.
Webster's--Amer. p497
Woman's Almanac p293, por.
World--Who p268

HOLIDAY, CATHERINE
British embroiderer
Callen--Women p107,109

HOLLAND, CECELIA (1943-)
Amer. novelist
P.W.--Author p68-69,502

HOLLAND, ELIZABETH VASSALL,
LADY (1770/1771-1845)
English salonist
Young--Revol. p184-186,213

HOLLAND, KATRIN, pseud.
See ALBRAND, MARTHA

HOLLANDER, ANNE (fl. 1970's)
Amer. art historian, writer
McCullough--People p86-87

HOLLANDER, XAVIERA (c1943-)
Netherlands-Amer. "Madam,"
author
World--Who p298

HOLLERAN, SUSAN ELLEN (1941-)
Amer. labor leader, executive
O'Neill--Women's p328

HOLLEY, JANE
Amer. aviatrix, flight engineer
O'Neill--Women's p546

HOLLEY, LESLIE (fl. 1970's)
Amer. aviatrix, Air Force
officer
O'Neill--Women's p543

HOLLEY, MARIETTA (1836-1926)
Amer. novelist, humorist,
feminist
Ehrlich--Oxford p97,169
James--Notable (2) p202-204
McHenry--Liberty's p194

HOLLEY, MARY PHELPS (1784-1846)
Amer. land speculator
Ehrlich--Oxford p84
James--Notable (2) p204-205

HOLLEY, SALLIE (1818-1893)
Amer. abolitionist, feminist
Lutz--Crusade p244-245
Sherr--American p187

HOLLIDAY, JENNIFER (1960-)
Amer. singer
Cur. Biog. '83 p192-194, por.
People--Best p162-163, por.

HOLLIDAY, JUDY (1922-1965)
Amer. actress
Entertainers p255
Hirschhorn--Rating p186-187, por.
Keylin--Hollywood p146-147, por.

Mordden--Movie p154,156,191,
229,232-234
O'Neill--Women's p637,653
Shipman--Internatl. p257-259,
por.
Sicherman--Notable p348-349
Woman's Almanac p347
World--Who p236

HOLLIDAY, POLLY DEAN (1937-)
Amer. actress
Scheuer--Tel. p228, por.

HOLLINGSWORTH, MRS. S.L.
(fl. 1930's)
Amer. social reformer
Berkin--Women p384-385

HOLLINGWORTH, LETA ANNA
(1886-1939)
Amer. educator, psychologist
Bachtold--Gifted p76-79
James--Notable (2) p206-208

HOLLINSHEAD, ARIEL (fl. 1950's-
1970's)
Amer. professor, medicine
researcher
O'Neill--Women's p222-223

HOLLISTER, GLORIA (fl. 1920's-
1930's)
Amer. zoologist, poultry
breeder
Macksey--Book p158

HOLLOWAY, DOROTHY (fl. 1940's)
Amer. radio magazine writer
Women--Radio p21

HOLM, BIRTE ROLL (c1941-)
Danish labor leader
O'Neill--Women's p320

HOLM, CELESTE (1919-)
Amer. singer, actress
Claghorn--Biog. p216
Shipman--Internatl. p259-261,
por.
World--Who p236

HOLM, ELEANOR (1914-)
Amer. swimmer
Assoc. Press--Pursuit p119,
139,160, por.
Hollander--100 p81-82, por.
Lamparski--What. (2) p58-59,
por.

HOLM, HANYA ECKERT (1893/
1898-)
German-Amer. dancer, teacher,
choreographer
Kulkin--Her p143
O'Neill--Women's p651-652

HOLM, JEANNE M. (fl. 1940's-
1970's)
Amer. aviatrix, Air Force
WAC, writer
O'Neill--Women's p533,539
Seed--Saturday's p131-134, por.

HOLM, SAXE
See JACKSON, HELEN MARIA
HUNT FISKE

HOLMAN, LIBBY (1905/1906-1971)
Amer. singer, actress
Claghorn--Biog. p216
Horan--Desperate p70-71, por.
Simon--Best p281, por.

HOLME, CONSTANCE (1881-1955)
English novelist
Crosland--Beyond p108-109,120-
123

HOLMES, ANN (fl. 1970's)
Amer. drama critic
Chinoy--Women p226-227,229-231,
por.

HOLMES, AUGUSTA MARY ANNE
(1847-1903)
French-Irish singer, composer,
song-writer
Macksey--Book p214-215

HOLMES, JEANNE M. (1922-)
Amer. technical librarian
O'Neill--Women's p29, por.

HOLMES, JULIA (fl. 1850's)
Amer. suffragist, mountain-
climber, song-writer
Sherr--American p25

HOLMES, KATE STONE (1841-1907)
Amer. civic worker, noted
Louisiana mother
Amer.--Mothers p227, por.

HOLMES, LORENDA (fl. 1770's)
English-Amer. Loyalist
DePauw--Found. p137-138

HOLMES, MARION
    Amer. fashion designer
    O'Neill--Women's p261-262

HOLMES, MARY JANE HAWES
    (1825-1907)
    Amer. novelist
    James--Notable (2) p208-209
    McHenry--Liberty's p194-195

HOLMES, MRS. OLIVER WENDELL,
    JR.
    Amer. embroiderer
    Callen--Women p130

HOLMES, VERENA (fl. 1920's-1940's)
    British mechanical engineer
    Macksey--Book p155

HOLST, AMALIA (fl. 1800's)
    German feminist, writer
    Macksey--Book p79

HOLT, BERTHA (1904-)
    Amer. sponsor of adoptions,
    noted Oregon mother
    Amer.--Mothers p451-452, por.

HOLT, EDITH (fl. 1900's-1920's)
    Amer. co-founder of blind
    organization
    O'Neill--Women's p112

HOLT, FLORENCE (fl. 1860's)
    Amer. Southern belle
    DeLeon--Belles p52, por.

HOLT, MARJORIE SEWELL
    (1920-)
    Amer. Congresswoman
    Chamberlin--Min. p352-353

HOLT, VICTORIA
    See PLAIDY, JEAN

HOLT, WINIFRED (1870-1945)
    Amer. leader in work for
    the blind, sculptor,
    philanthropist
    James--Notable (2) p209-210
    McHenry--Liberty's p195
    O'Neill--Women's p112

HOLTBY, WINIFRED (1898-1935)
    English novelist, poet
    Crosland--Beyond p22,27,108,
    123-128
    Showalter--Lit. p348-349

HOLTON, TABITHA (-1886)
    Amer. lawyer
    Sherr--American p180

HOLTZMAN, ELIZABETH (c1941-)
    Amer. Congresswoman
    Bowman--Politics p10-13, por.
    Chamberlin--Min. p353-354
    Cur. Biog. '73 p190-193, por.
    Lamson--In p69-108, por.
    100--Greatest (1) p59, por.
    O'Neill--Women's p72-73
    Schoenebaum--Prof. p307-308
    Woman's Almanac p475, por.
    World--Who p142

HOLUM, DIANNE (c1952-)
    Amer. speed skater
    Assoc. Press--Pursuit p275,278,
    297-299,327, por.
    Hollander--100 p38-39, por.

"HOLY MAID OF KENT"
    See BARTON, ELIZABETH

HOLZER, ADELA (fl. 1950's)
    Spanish-Amer. theatrical pro-
    ducer
    O'Neill--Women's p664

HOLZER, GERTRUDE
    Amer. aviatrix, army flier
    Keil--Those p71-73

HOLZER-KJEUBERB, FRIEDL (1905-)
    Austrian-Finnish ceramicist
    O'Neill--Women's p275

HOLZMAN, CATHERINE
    See HART, KITTY CARLISLE

HOMER, LOUISE DILWORTH BEATTY
    (1871-1947)
    Amer. opera singer
    Claghorn--Biog. p217
    James--Notable (2) p210-212
    McHenry--Liberty's p195-196
    Tuggle--Golden p121-122, por.

HOMSLEY, MARY E. (-1862)
    Amer. pioneer (Oregon Trail)
    Sherr--American p254-255

HONEYCUTT, PAMELA (fl. 1970's)
    Amer. labor leader, machinist's
    apprentice
    O'Neill--Women's p316

HONEYMAN, JESSIE M. (-c1948)
Amer. highway "beautifier"
Sherr--American p195

HONEYMAN, NAN WOOD (-1970)
Amer. Congresswoman
Chamberlin--Min. p112-115

HOOD, DARLA (1931/1933-1979)
Amer. child actress
Lamparski--What. (2) p136-137,
por.
Lamparski--What (8) p130-131,
por.
People's Almanac (3) p549

HOODLESS, ADELAIDE SOPHIE
HUNTER (1857-1910)
Canadian home economist,
educator, organization
founder
Macksey--Book p16,274
O'Neill--Women's p5

"HOODOO QUEEN"
See LEVEAU, MARIE

HOOF, ANN(E) CATHERINE
(-1775)
Amer., wife of Jonas Green,
printer
Sherr--American p202

HOOK, CHARLENE (1935-)
Amer. genealogical research-
er, writer, editor
Meyer--Who's p101

HOOKER, ISABELLA BEECHER
(1822-1907)
Amer. suffragist, feminist
James--Notable (2) p212-214
McHenry--Liberty's p196
Macksey--Book p15

HOOKER, JEANETTE ANNENBERG
(c1905-)
Amer. millionaire
Forbes--400 ('84) p190-191

HOOKHAM, PEGGY
See FONTEYN, MARGOT, DAME

HOOPER, ANN(E) CLARK (fl.
1760's-1770's)
Amer. Revolutionary War
patriot
Berkin--Women p52-53,60

HOOPER, ELLEN CAROLINE
STURGIS TAPPAN (1819-1888)
Amer. Transcendantalist, poet
James--Notable (2) p214-215

HOOPER, JESSIE ANNETTE JACK
(1865-1935)
Amer. suffragist, peace
advocate
James--Notable (2) p215-216

HOOVER, HULDA MINTHORN (1848-
1883)
Amer., mother of Herbert
Hoover
Faber--Presidents' p215-216

HOOVER, JULIE TARACHOW
Amer. TV executive
Scheuer--Tel. p229

HOOVER, LOU HENRY (1874/1875-
1944)
Amer., noted California
mother, First Lady, wife of
Herbert Hoover
Amer.--Mothers p53-54
James--Notable (2) p217-218
Kulkin--Her p144-145
Melick--Wives p68-69, por.
People's Almanac (1) p276
Starr--Amer. p340
Woman's Almanac p491

HOPE, LAURA LEE
See ADAMS, HARRIET

HOPE, LAWRENCE
See NICHOLSON, ADELA

HOPE NAMGYAL, MAHARANI OF
SIKKIM (1940-)
Amer.-Sikkim queen
People's Almanac (2) p729

HOPE, PATRICIA (fl. 1980's)
Amer. teacher, director
People--Best p200-201, por.

HOPEKIRK, HELEN (1856-1945)
Scottish-Amer. composer,
pianist, teacher
James--Notable (2) p218-219

HOPKINS, ELIZABETH (fl. 1600's)
Amer. Pilgrim
Williams--Demeter's p22-23

HOPKINS, EMMA CURTIS (1853-
1925)
Amer. religious leader
James--Notable (2) p219-220
McHenry--Liberty's p196-197

HOPKINS, JULIET ANN OPIE
(1818-1890)
Amer. Confederate hospital
administrator, Southern
belle
DeLeon--Belles p385, por.
James--Notable (2) p220-221
McHenry--Liberty's p197

HOPKINS, LINDA (1925-   )
Amer. singer, organist,
pianist, drummer
Claghorn--Biog. p218
Claghorn--Jazz p146

HOPKINS, MARY
Amer. millionaire
Longstreet--Queen p153-154

HOPKINS, MARY ALDEN (1876-
1960)
Amer. feminist, radical
activist
Showalter--These p40-45

HOPKINS, MIRIAM (1902-1972)
Amer. actress
Keylin--Hollywood p148, por.
Lamparski--What. (8) p132-133,
por.
Shipman--Gold. p295-298, por.
Springer--They p136,138,302,
por.
World--Who p236

HOPKINS, SARAH WINNEMUCCA
(c1844-1891)
Amer. Paiute Indian life
writer
Fischer--Let p260-270

HOPPER, GRACE MURRAY (1906-   )
Amer. engineer, mathematician,
computer specialist, naval
commander
Gilbert--Part. p59-63, por.
O'Neill--Women's p189-190,538-539,
por.
Woman's Almanac p362-363

HOPPER, HEDDA (1885/1891-1966)
Amer. columnist, actress

Brecher--Lives p210
Dunlap--Calif. p93, por.
Lewis--Prime p14,21-22,25,27
McHenry--Liberty's p197
O'Neill--Women's p447-448
Sicherman--Notable p350-351
Springer--They p138,302, por.
Webster's--Amer. p509
Woman's Almanac p276, por.
World--Who p52

HORATIA (fl. 7th Cent.)
Roman matron, sister of the
Horatii
Pomeroy--Godd. p152-153

HORBAL, KORYNE (fl. 1960's-1970's)
Amer. politician
O'Neill--Women's p75

HOREBOUT, SUSANNA(E) (1503-
1545)
Belgian painter (book illu-
minator)
Fine--Women p36
Munsterberg--Hist. p22
Sparrow--Women p253

HORENBURGIN, ANNA ELIZABETH
VON (fl. 1560's)
German midwife, writer
Mead--Hist. p359,425-426

HORENSON, BELLE
Amer. labor leader
O'Neill--Women's p313

HORGAN, SUSAN BEDSOW (1947-   )
Amer. TV producer
Scheuer--Tel. p230

HORN, CAROL (1938-   )
Amer. designer
O'Neill--Women's p248-249,252,
por.

HORN, DEBI (fl. 1970's)
Amer. inventor
Felton--Famous p83

HORN, PEGGY GRUBB (1916-   )
Amer. genealogical researcher
Meyer--Who's p101

HORN, SHIRLEY (1934-   )
Amer. singer, pianist
Claghorn--Biog. p219

HORNBECK, BERNICE M.
    Amer. research associate,
    government official
    O'Neill--Women's p25

HORNE, ALICE MERRILL (1868-
    1948)
    Amer. politician, art-writer,
    noted Utah mother
    Amer.--Mothers p527-528, por.

HORNE, ESTHER BURNETT (1955-
    1965)
    Amer. Indian, (great great
    granddaughter of Sacajawea)
    Gridley--Amer. p131-137, por.

HORNE, MARILYN B. (1934-   )
    Amer. opera singer
    Claghorn--Biog. p220
    Diamonstein--Open p177-180,
    por.
    Fabian--On p210-213, por.
    Gammond--Illus. p244, por.
    World--Who p71

HORNE, LENA (1917-   )
    Amer. singer
    Anderson--People p205-206, por.
    Claghorn--Biog. p219
    Claghorn--Jazz p147
    Cur. Biog. '85 p194-198, por.
    Entertainers p249
    Fabian--On p204-205, por.
    O'Neill--Women's p626
    People--Best p118-119, por.
    Simon--Best p283-284, por.
    Toppin--Biog. p324-326
    Warren--Pictorial p199
    Woman's Almanac p293-294
    World--Who p268

HORNER, MATINA SOURETIS
    (1939-   )
    Amer. writer, psychologist,
    educator, college president
    Adams--Women p203
    Cur. Biog. '73 p194-196, por.
    100--Greatest (1) p26, por.
    O'Neill--Women's p406-407,487
    People--Best p86, por.
    Woman's Alamanc p148,158

HORNER, VIVIAN
    Amer. TV director, cable
    executive
    Klever--Women p128-131, por.

Scheuer--Tel. p230-231,
    por.

HORNEY, KAREN DANIELS(S)EN
    (1885-1952)
    German-Amer. physician,
    psychiatrist, psychoanalyst,
    writer, teacher
    Bachtold--Gifted p74-75
    Longstreet--Queen p190-191
    McHenry--Liberty's p197-198
    Marlowe--Great p253-258, por.
    Neidle--America's p207
    O'Neill--Women's p413-414
    Pederson--Leaders p215, por.
    Sicherman--Notable p351-354
    Who Did What p158
    Woman's Almanac p36-37, por.
    World--Who p95

HORNIMAN, ANNIE ELIZABETH
    FREDERICKA (1860-1937)
    English founder theatre school,
    manager, producer, patron of
    arts
    Macksey--Book p227
    Rogers--Ladies p9-13, por.

HORNING, MARJORIE G.
    Amer. biochemist, college
    professor
    O'Neill--Women's p165,221-222

HORNSBY, LESLIE
    See "TWIGGY"

HOROWITZ, IDA (fl. 1970's)
    Amer. sculptor
    Women's--Female p90

HOROWITZ, JANICE M. (fl. 1970's)
    Amer. writer, researcher
    O'Neill--Women's p350

HORSBRUGH, FLORENCE, BARONESS
    (1889-1969)
    Scottish Parliament member,
    educator
    Cur. Biog. '70 p464
    Vallance--Women p33-34,70,91,101

HORSTMANN, DOROTHY MILLICENT
    (1911-   )
    Amer. physician, epidemiolo-
    gist, pediatrician, polio re-
    search pioneer
    O'Neill--Women's p220

HORTA, MARIA TERESA (fl. 1970's)
Portuguese author
O'Neill--Women's p727

HORTENSIA (fl. c50 B.C.)
Roman feminist, politician,
daughter of Quintus Hortensius
Macksey--Book p78
Pomeroy--Godd. p175-176,178-179

HORTHY DE NAGBANYA, MAGDA-
LENE PURGLY DE JOSZAHELY,
née COUNTESS KONA
EVELSHEIM-GYULA
(1882-1959)
Hungarian, wife of Hungarian
Regent Miklos Horthy
Partington--Who's p166

HORTON, JUANITA
See LOVE, BESSIE

HORTON, LILLIAS STERLING
See UNDERWOOD, LILLIAS
STERLING HORTON

HORTON, MILDRED HELEN McAFEE
See McAFEE, MILDRED HELEN

HORVATH, CECILE AYRES (1889-)
Amer. pianist
Claghorn--Biog. p220

HORVATH, JOAN (fl. 1960's-
1970's)
Amer. filmmaker
Smith--Movies p179

HORWICH, FRANCES RAPPAPORT
(1908-)
Amer. educator, TV personality
McHenry--Liberty's p198-199

HOSFORD, JESSIE WIEGAND
(1892-)
Amer. author, community
worker, noted New Mexico
mother
Amer.--Mothers p383, por.

HOSFORD, MARY (fl. 1830's)
Amer. early student
Sherr--American p186-187, por.

HOSKINS, JANE (1694-)
Amer. Quaker, colonial

clergyman, teacher
Berkin--Women p120-121,126

HOSMER, HARRIET GOODHUE
(1830-1908)
Amer. sculptor
Earnest--American p63-64
Fine--Women p108-111
James--Notable (2) p221-223
McHenry--Liberty's p199
Macksey--Book p206
Marlowe--Great p109-114, por.
Munsterberg--Hist. p90
Parker--Old p100-104, por.,
fig. 7,57,58
Petersen--Women p79-81, por.
Sherr--American p113,133,224,
por.
Taylor--Gener. p55-56, por.
Warren--Pictorial p154,157

HOSTETTER, HELEN (fl. 1910's-
1960's)
Amer. journalism professor
Marzolf--Up p251-252,254-255

HOTALING, DONNA REID (1932-)
Amer. genealogical researcher
Meyer--Who's p101

HOTCHKISS, HAZEL
See WIGHTMAN, HAZEL VIRGINIA

HOTHAM, AMELIA
English painter[1]
Sparrow--Women p59,88

HOUDINI, BEATRICE (BESS)
Amer. (wife of Harry Houdini)
Forma--They p62-63, por.

HOUGH, MARTI
Amer. business woman
Fenton--Famous p156-157

HOUGHTON, DEBRA (fl. 1970's)
Amer. army tank driver
O'Neill--Women's p548

HOUGHTON, DOROTHY DEEMER
(1890-1972)
Amer., community worker,
politician, organization official, noted Iowa mother
Amer.--Mothers p192-193, por.

HOULT, NORAH (1898/1901-)

Irish journalist, novelist
Seymour-Smith--Who's p166

HOUSE, TONI (fl. 1970's)
Amer. police reporter
Marzolf--Up p108

HOUSTON, JESSIE W. (c1900-)
Amer. jail missionary, writer
Diamonstein--Open p181-183,
por.

HOUSTON, MARGARET MOFFETT
LEA (c1819-1867)
Amer. Civil War diarist,
wife of General Sam Houston
Sherr--American p222

HOUSTON, MARY G. (fl. 1890's)
British bookbinder
Callen--Women p194,196

HOUTEN, BARBARA VAN,
MADEMOISELLE
Netherlands painter
Sparrow--Women p262,270,275

HOVICK, JUNE
See HAVOC, JUNE

HOVICK, (ROSE) LOUISE
See LEE, GYPSY ROSE

HOVIK, SUE (fl. 1970's)
Amer. editor
Marzolf--Up p204-205

HOVMAND, ANNELISE (fl.
1950's-1960's)
Danish film director
Smith--Movies p102

HOW, BEATRICE
English painter
Sparrow--Women p69-70,142,
148

HOWAR, BARBARA (1914-)
Amer. journalist, author
Miller--Fishbait p110

HOWARD, AGNES
Amer. Indian rancher
Rich-McCoy--Mill. p189-206,
por.

HOWARD, BESSE(E) (fl. 1940's)
Amer. radio broadcaster,

war correspondent, Red Cross
worker
Marzolf--Up p144
Women--Radio p2-3

HOWARD, BLANCHE WILLIS (fl.
1830's-1890's)
Amer. author, educator
James--Notable (2) p223-224
McHenry--Liberty's p199-200

HOWARD, CAROLINE EMILY FOX
(1829-1908)
Amer. (Mother of actress
Cordelia Howard)
James--Notable (2) p224-225

HOWARD, CATHERINE, LADY (1521-
1542)
English queen, (wife of
Henry VIII)
Earle--Two Cent. (1) p xv,88,
por.
Jones--Rutledge p153
Softley--Queens p69-71
Vance--Six p102-118
Who Did What p150, por.

HOWARD, CORDELIA (1848-1941)
Amer. actress
James--Notable (2) p224-225

HOWARD, ELIZABETH (fl. 1970's)
Amer. "craftsworker,"
carpenter
O'Neill--Women's p318

HOWARD, ELIZABETH JANE (1923-)
English novelist
Seymour-Smith--Novels p160

HOWARD, ESTELLE (c1871-)
Amer. centenarian
Mitchell--Yessir p40-41, por.

HOWARD, FANNIE (1885-)
Amer. pianist
Claghorn--Biog. p221

HOWARD, LISA (c1930-1965)
Amer. journalist, "inter-
viewer," TV reporter, actress
Marzolf--Up p167

HOWARD, LUCY
Amer. Civil Liberties Union
legal director
Ingraham--Album p76, por.

HOWARD, MABEL (1893-1972)
New Zealand official cabinet
member
Macksey--Book p40

HOWARD, MARY WOOLLEY (fl.
1910's)
Amer. mayor
Sherr--American p225

HOWARD, META (fl. 1880's)
Amer. medical missionary,
hospital founder
O'Neill--Women's p205

HOWARD, MINNIE FRANCES
(1872-)
Amer., noted Idaho mother,
physician, art patron
Amer.--Mothers p151-152, por.

HOWARD-LOCK, HELEN E.
Canadian engineer,
college professor
O'Neill--Women's p194

HOWATCH, SUSAN (1940-)
English novelist
Seymour-Smith--Novels p160

HOWE, FLORENCE (1919-)
Amer. feminist, publisher,
author
O'Neill--Women's p424-425,484

HOWE, HELEN (ALLEN) (1905-
1975)
Amer. author, satiric
monologist
Cur. Biog. '75 p467

HOWE, JULIA WARD (1819-1910)
Amer. biographer, poet,
social reformer
Avenel--Comp. (2) p126
Bernikow--World p216
Claghorn--Biog. p222
Ehrlich--Oxford, see index
p455
Gilfond--Heroines p24, por.
Hymowitz--Hist. p159,222-223
James--Notable (2) p225-229
Jones--Rutledge p385
Kulkin--Her p145-146
McHenry--Liberty's p200
Macksey--Book p189
Moers--Literary p294

Pederson--Leaders p100, por.
People's Almanac (1) p850
Sherr--American p40,98,102,207
Signif.--Amer. p18, por.
Smith--Daughters p141-143,260,
267
Warren--Pictorial p107-108,117,
por.
Webster's--Amer. p513-514
Woman's Almanac p377, por.
World--Who p14

HOWE, MARY (1882-1964)
Amer. composer, pianist
Claghorn--Biog. p222
Jablonski--Ency. p245-246

HOWE, MAUD(E)
See ELLIOTT, MAUD(E) HOWE

HOWE, PATRICIA M. (fl. 1950's-
1960's)
Amer. stock exchange executive
O'Neill--Women's p528

HOWELL, ANN
Amer. foundation director
Adams--Women p22,88,105

HOWELL, CATHERINE (fl. 1970's)
Amer. farmer
O'Neill--Women's p13

HOWELL, EMILY (1939-)
Amer. aviatrix
Genett--Aviation p95-107, por.
O'Neill--Women's p742

HOWELL, MRS. M.C. (fl. 1900's)
Amer. archer
Macksey--Book p256
McWhirter--Guinness p26-27

HOWELL, MARGARET LOUISE KEMP
(fl. 1860's)
Amer. Southern belle
DeLeon--Belles p68-69, por.

HOWELL, MARY (fl. 1770's)
Amer. Revolutionary War
patriot
Meyer--Petticoat p84

HOWES, BARBARA (1914-)
Amer. poet
Avenel--Comp. (2) p127

Brinnin--Modern p166-169, por.
Chester--Rising p76-81, por.
Ehrlich--Oxford--p19,29

HOWITT, MARY BOTHAM (1799-
1888)
English Quaker author
Basch--Relative, see index p353

HOWLAND, BETH (1947-)
Amer. actress
Scheuer--Tel. p233, por.

HOWLAND, EMILY (1827-1929)
Amer. educator, social re-
former, philanthropist
James--Notable (2) p229-231
McHenry--Liberty's p200-201
Sherr--American p175

HOWLAND, JOBYNA (1880-1936)
Amer. actress
Springer--They p139,302, por.

HOWORTH, LUCY SOMERVILLE
(1895-)
Amer. government official
Ware--Beyond p146, see also
index p200

HOXIE, VINNIE REAM (1847-1914)
Amer. sculptor, noted
District of Columbia mother
Amer.--Mothers p100-101,582,
por.
Bachtold--Gifted p27-29
Fine--Women p113
James--Notable (3) p122-123
Kulkin--Her p234
McHenry--Liberty's p341-342
Sherr--American p38-39,71,193,
231,249, por.
Woman's Almanac p222, por.

HOYO, ALICIA ERNESTINA DE LA
CARIDAD DEL COBRE
MARTINEZ
See ALONSO, ALICIA

HOYOS, ANGELA DE (fl. 1970's)
Mexican-Amer. writer
Fisher--Third p viii,393

HOYT, MRS. WILLIAM S.
Amer. embroiderer
Callen--Women p130

HRESTU, JENNIE
Amer. army flier
Keil--Those p159-160

HROTSVITHA (HROTSWITHA)
See ROSTHWITHA

HRUBA, VERA
See MILES, VERA

HSI, TZW (1835-1908)
Chinese, concubine of Chinese
emperor Hsien Feng
Book--Lists (2) p253

HSI(ANG) CHING YU (1895-1928)
Chinese Communist politician
Macksey--Book p38

HSING TZ'U-CHING (fl. c1570)
Chinese poet, calligrapher
Petersen--Women p155

HSUEH T'AO (fl. c760)
Chinese poet, artist
Petersen--Women p149-150

HSUEH, WU (HSUEN SU-SU) (c1564-
1637)
Chinese poet, painter, athlete
Petersen--Women p154

HUBBARD, GERTRUDE McCURDY
(1829-1909)
Amer., noted District of
Columbia mother, charity
worker
Amer.--Mothers p98, por.

HUBBARD, MARY GREENE (1734-
1808)
Amer., daughter of Thomas
Greene
Flexner--Face p92, por.

HUBBARD, RUTH (fl. 1950's-1970's)
Austrian-Amer. biologist,
sociologist, professor
O'Neill--Women's p159-160

HUBER, ANTJE (1924-)
German federal minister,
journalist, editor
O'Neill--Women's p56

HUBERTA, HEIDI, pseud.
See ALBRAND, MARTHA

HUBERTSE, AULKEY
Amer. colonial indentured
servant
Hoople--As p16-17
Millstein--We p27-28

HUBLEY, FAITH ELLIOTT
(1924-   )
Amer. filmmaker
Smith--Movies p59-62

HUCH, RICARDA (1864-1947)
German author, patriot,
social reformer
Herrmann--Ger. p4-5,6,8-9
Macksey--Book p188

HUCK, WINNIFRED SPRAGUE
MASON (1882-1936)
Amer. Congresswoman,
journalist
Chamberlin--Min. p44-46, por.
James--Notable (2) p231-232

HUDDLESTON, BARBARA (1939-   )
Amer. research agriculturist
O'Neill--Women's p25

HUDSON, BETTY (1949-   )
Amer. TV executive
Scheuer--Tel. p234

HUDSON, GRACE CARPENTER (fl.
1880's-1900's)
Amer. painter
Time--Women p112-113

HUDSON, MARY CLEMMER AMES
See AMES, MARY E. CLEMMER

HUDSON, ROCHELLE (1914/1915-
1972)
Amer. actress, realtor,
dancer
Lamparski--What. (3) p134-135,
por.
Springer--They p139,302-303,
por.

HUDSON, VIRGINIA CARY (1894-   )
Amer. child author, (essayist)
Book--Lists (2) p225

HUERTA, DOLORES HERNANDEZ
(1930-   )
Mexican-Amer. labor union
Leader

Bowman--Politics p14-17, por.
Newlon--Mexican p172-175
O'Neill--Women's p304-305, 315
Woman's Almanac p180
World--Who p189

HUFFMAN, BARBARA
See EDEN, BARBARA

HUFSTEDLER, SHIRLEY ANN MOUNT
(1925-   )
Amer. government official,
judge
Cur. Biog. '80 p159-161, por.
Diamonstein--Open p184-187, por.
Gilbert--Part. p191-197, por.
O'Neill--Women's p370
Woman's Almanac p523
World--Who p43

HUGHAN, JESSIE WALLACE (1875-
1955)
Amer. author, pacifist, socialist, educator, politician
Sicherman--Notable p354-355

HUGHES, ADELLA PRENTIS (1869-
1950)
Amer. concert, orchestral
manager
James--Notable (2) p232-234
O'Neill--Women's p512

HUGHES, DOROTHY PITMAN
(c1938-   )
Amer. director, day-care
center
Diamonstein--Open p188-192, por.
Walker--Women p30-46, por.

HUGHES, ELIZABETH (fl. 1870's)
Amer. writer
Starr--Amer. p395

HUGHES, ELLEN KENT (1893-   )
Australian physician
Hellstedt--Women p103-108, por.

HUGHES, IRENE
Amer. psychic
People's Almanac (1) p5
People's Almanac (2) p5-6

HUGHES, JEAN PETERS (1926-   )
Amer. actress, (wife of
Howard Hughes)
Hershey--Between p64-65
World--Who p245

HUGHES, JOAN (fl. 1940's)
British aviatrix, pilot,
instructor
Boase--Sky's p179-180,195, por.
Macksey--Book p250

HUGHES, JOSEPHINE BRAWLEY
(fl. 1870's)
Amer. teacher, feminist,
noted Arizona mother
Amer.--Mothers p27, por.

HUGHES, M. INNOCENT, SISTER
(fl. 1950's-1970's)
Amer. hospital administrator
O'Neill--Women's p390-391

HUGHES, MICHELLE
Amer. executive
Adams--Women p22-23,25,87,
104,117-118,149,159,176,
183-184,208

HUGHES, PAULA
Amer. stockbroker
Adams--Women p127-129,157,
161,188-189,194

HUGHES, SARAH TILGHMAN
(1896-1985)
Amer. lawyer, judge, organi-
zation official
Cur. Biog. '85 p468
Woman's Almanac p522-523, por.

HUGODOT, FLORENCE (fl. 1970's)
French "Sour-Prifet"
Macksey--Book p131

HULANICKI, BARBARA (fl. 1900's)
English fashion designer,
manager
Keenan--Women p100-103,106-107,
por.
O'Neill--Women's p253

HULBERT, MARY ALLEN
See PECK, MARY ALLEN

HULETT, JOSEPHINE (fl. 1970's)
Amer. labor organizer
O'Neill--Women's p304

HULL, ELIZABETH (c1862-)
Amer. centenarian
Mitchell--Yessir p12-15, por.

HULL, HANNAH HALLOWELL
CLOTHIER (1872-1958)
Amer. pacifist, suffragist
Sicherman--Notable p355-356

HULL,. HELEN ROSS (1888-1971)
Amer. novelist, educator
Cur. Biog. '71 p465

HULL, JOSEPHINE SHERWOOD
(1884/1886-1957)
Amer. actress
Springer--They p139-140,303,
por.
World--Who p237

HULL, MARGARET
See ANGLIN, MARGARET MARY

HULL, MILLIE
Amer. "Bowery queen"
Coffin--Parade p149-151

HULL, PEGGY (fl. 1910's-1940's)
Amer. foreign correspondent,
journalist
Marzolf--Up p42-43

HULTIN, JILL (fl. 1960's-1970's)
Amer. filmmaker
Smith--Movies p179-180,248

HULTIN, TEKLA (fl. 1890's)
Finnish journalist
Marzolf--Up p271

HULTON, ANN (fl. 1760's-1770's)
Amer. Revolutionary Loyalist,
letter-writer
Hoople--As p27-32
Williams--Demeter's, see index
p351-352

"HUM-ISHU-MA"
See "MOURNING DOVE"

HUME, BENITA (1906-1967)
English TV actress, wife of
Ronald Colman
Springer--They p140,303, por.

HUME, JO ANN (c1955-)
Amer. broker, executive
O'Neill--Women's p530

HUME, SOPHIA WIGINGTON (1702-
1774)

Amer. Quaker preacher
DePauw--Rem. p76-77
Hymowitz--Hist. p21
James--Notable (2) p234-235
Williams--Demeter's p204

HUMES, HELEN (1913-1981)
Amer. singer
Balliett--Amer. p42-49
Claghorn--Biog. p224
Claghorn--Jazz p148

HUMMERT, ANNE SCHUMACHER
(fl. 1930's-1940's)
Amer. radio writer, ad-
vertising executive, radio
producer
Women--Radio p21

HUMPHREY, BARBARA ANN
(BOBBI) (1950-)
Amer. flutist, alto saxist,
picolo player
Claghorn--Jazz p148

HUMPHREY, DORIS (1895-1958)
Amer. dancer, choreographer,
theatre founder
McHenry--Liberty's p201
O'Neill--Women's p647-648
Percival--Modern p12,53,66
Sicherman--Notable p356-358
World--Who p71

HUMPHREYS, MRS. DESMOND
(1860-1938)
Scottish novelist
Showalter--Lit. p341

HUMPHRY, BETTY J. (fl. 1970's)
Amer. educator
O'Neill--Women's p433

HUNGERFORD, MARGARET
HAMILTON (1850/1855-1897)
Irish novelist
Showalter--Lit. p338

HUNING, ERNESTINE FRANKE
(1845-1923)
Amer. pioneer, noted New
Mexico mother
Amer.--Mothers p377, por.

HUNNICUT, GAYLE (1943-)
Amer. actress
World--Who p237

HUNT, E. VIRGINIA (1931-)
Amer. genealogical researcher,
author, indexer, editor
Meyer--Who's p103

HUNT, ELIZABETH (fl. 1770's)
Amer. colonial midwife
DePauw--Found. p42

HUNT, EUNICE (-1862)
Amer. meetinghouse founder
Sherr--American p180

HUNT, HARRIOT KEZIA (1895-1875)
Amer. pioneer physician,
social reformer
James--Notable (2) p235-237
McHenry--Liberty's p201-202
Marks--Women p77-78
Sherr--American p102, por.
Warren--Pictorial p79

HUNT, HELEN
See JACKSON, HELEN MARIA
HUNT FISKE

HUNT, ISOBEL VIOLET (1866-1942)
English novelist
Showalter--Lit. p343

HUNT, JANE
Amer. suffragist
Sherr--American p177

HUNT, MARSHA (MARCIA VIRGINIA)
(1917/1920-)
Amer. opera singer, model,
actress
Lamparski--What. (4) p156-157,
por.
Springer--They p140,303, por.

HUNT, MARY HANNAH HANCHETT
(1830-1906)
Amer. temperance leader
James--Notable (2) p237-239
McHenry--Liberty's p202

HUNT, MOLLY
Amer. gull expert
Fenton--Famous p236

HUNT, NANCY (1927-)
Amer. journalist, transsexual
Book--Lists (2) p328

HUNT, PATRICIA

Amer. magazine nature
editor
Hamblin--That p269-270

HUNT, RUTH JUNE
Amer. millionaire
Forbes--400 ('84) p107

HUNT, RUTH RAY
Amer. millionaire
Forbes--400 ('84) p107

HUNT, VIOLET (1866-1942)
English novelist, short-
story writer
Avenel--Comp. (1) p268

HUNT (MEEKS), SWANEE
Amer. millionaire
Forbes--400 ('84) p107

HUNTER, ALBERTA (1895-1984)
Amer. singer, songwriter
Balliett--Amer. p21-31
Claghorn--Jazz p149
Cur. Biog. '79 p174-178, por.
Cur. Biog. '85 p468
Gilbert--Part. p245-253, por.
O'Neill--Women's p623

HUNTER, BARBARA (fl. 1970's)
Amer. public relations
executive
O'Neill--Women's p515-516

HUNTER, KIM (1922-)
Amer. actress
World--Who p237

HUNTER, MARIAN (fl. 1970's)
Amer. filmmaker
Smith--Movies p180,248, por.

HUNTER, MARY YOUNG
See SUTHERLAND-HUNTER,
MARY YOUNG

HUNTER, NATALIE
Amer. TV executive
Scheuer--Tel. p235

HUNTER, RITA (1933-)
English opera singer
Gammond--Illus. p244, por.

HUNTINGDON, SELINA, COUNTESS
OF (1707-1791)

English religious worker
Macksey--Book p107

HUNTINGTON, ANNA VAUGHN
HYATT (1876-1973)
Amer. sculptor, art patron
Cur. Biog. '73 p455
McHenry--Liberty's p204-205
Sherr--American p170-171
Sicherman--Notable p358-359

HUNTINGTON, ARABELLA DUVAL
YARRINGTON WORSHAM
(1849/1852-c1924)
Amer. socialite, philanthropist
Birmingham--Grandes, see index
p292, por.

HUNTINGTON, ELIZABETH T.
STODDARD (-1883)
Amer., wife of Collis P.
Huntington
Birmingham--Grandes p186-187,
192-193,196

HUNTINGTON, EMILY (1841-1909)
Amer. welfare worker
James--Notable (2) p239-240
McHenry--Liberty's p202-203

HUNTINGTON, HALLIE (c1898-)
Amer. community worker,
octogenarian
Gold--Until p333-334

HUNTLEY, BLANCHE TATHAM
(1893-)
Amer., noted Montana mother,
(mother of Chet Huntley)
Amer.--Mothers p327, por.

HUNTLEY, GERTRUDE (fl. 1930's-
1940's)
Amer. teacher, checker player
O'Neill--Women's p592

HUNTON, ADDIE D. WAITES (1875-
1943)
Amer. YWCA official
James--Notable (2) p240-241
Millstein--We p212-213

HUNTY, SHIRLEY DE LA STRICK-
LAND (1925-)
Australian track & field athlete
Assoc. Press--Pursuit p170,218-
219, por.

McWhirter--Guinness p 173,
por.

HUPPERT, ISABELLE (1955-   )
Amer. actress
Cur. Biog. '81 p 218-220, por.

HUQ, TAYYEBA (1921-   )
Bangladesh, founder
Housewives' Association
O'Neill--Women's p 119

HURD-MEAD, KATE CAMPBELL
(1867-1941)
Amer. physician, historian
of medical women
James--Notable (2) p 241-242
Macksey--Book p 150

HURDON, ELIZABETH (1868-1941)
English-Amer. gynecologist,
pathologist, physician
James--Notable (2) p 242-244
O'Neill--Women's p 212

HURNSCOT, LORAN, pseud.
English feminist, diarist
Moffat--Revel. p 335-346

HURST, FANNIE (1889-1968)
Amer. novelist
Ehrlich--Oxford p 139,303,358
Hazen--Interv. p 28-29
McHenry--Liberty's p 203
Sicherman--Notable p 359-361
Sochen--Herstory p 296-298,300,
por.
Sochen--Movers p 127-134
World--Who p 15

HURST, MARGERY
English secretarial school
founder
Macksey--Book p 174-176, por.
O'Neill--Women's p 515

HURST, SADIE DOTSON (1857-1951)
Amer. political pioneer,
prohibitionist, noted
Nebraska mother
Amer.--Mothers p 346-347

HURSTON, ZORA NEALE (c1901-
1960)
Amer. anthropologist, folklorist, novelist, teacher
Fisher--Third p vi, 159

McHenry--Liberty's p 203
Seymour-Smith--Novels p 161
Sherr--American p 43-44
Sicherman--Notable p 361-363

HURWITZ, BELLA
See CHASSEN, BELLA HURWITZ

HURWITZ, SHARI
See LEWIS, SHARI

HUSSEY, RUTH (1914/1915-   )
Amer. actress
Lamparski--What. (4) p 68-69, por.
Springer--They p 140,303, por.
World--Who p 237

HUSTED, MARJORIE CHILD (c1892-   )
Amer. home economist
Cohen--Meet p 25-27, por.
McHenry--Liberty's p 203-204

HUSTERS, PAULINE (1876-1895)
Netherlands shortest woman
Macksey--Book p 12

HUSTON, MARGO
Amer. reporter
O'Neill--Women's p 452,470-471,
por.

HUTCHINGS, FLORENCE (1864-1881)
Amer. Western pioneer
Sherr--American p 23

HUTCHINS, GRACE (1885-1969)
Amer. labor researcher,
social reformer
Sicherman--Notable p 363-365

HUTCHINSON, ABIGAIL (ABBY)
JEMIMA (1829-1892)
Amer. singer
Claghorn--Biog. p 226
James--Notable (2) p 244-245

HUTCHINSON, ANNE MARBURY
(1591-1643)
English-Amer. religious
leader, midwife
Anticaglia--12 p 1-16, por.
Bloom--Religon p 7-29
Crawford--Four, see index p 188
Fryer--Faces p 74-77
Hymowitz--Hist. p 16-17
Ingraham--Album p 9, por.
James--Notable (2) p 245-247

Kulkin--Her p146-147
McHenry--Liberty's p204
Macksey--Book p107
Mead--Hist. p411,487
Millstein--We p9,18-19
Neidle--America's p11-14,29,58
O'Neill--Women's p198
Pederson--Leaders p6, por.
Reader's--Story p92
Reifert--Women p1-9
Sherr--American p97-98,165-
166,207
Signif.--Amer. p7, por.
Smith--Daughters p39-40,145
Sochen--Herstory p45-46,49,
por.
Taylor--Gener. p28-29
Warren--Pictorial p26-29, por.
Webster's--Amer. p528
Williams--Demeter's p29-30,115-
119,125
Woman's Almanac p395,402,540
World--Who p82

HUTCHINSON, ISOBEL (1889-)
British botanical explorer
Macksey--Book p241

HUTCHINSON, JOSEPHINE (1904-)
Amer. actress
Springer--They p140,303, por.

HUTCHINSON, LUCY APSLEY
(1620-1675)
English linguist, medical
woman, author
Mead--Hist. p403-404, por.

HUTCHINSON, MARGARET H.
(fl. 1950's)
Amer. chemical engineer
O'Neill--Women's p188,191

HUTH, ANGELA (1938-)
English novelist
Seymour-Smith--Novels p161

HUTTEN, MARGARETTE
German ambassador
Macksey--Book p39

HUTTON, BARBARA (1912-1979)
Amer. heiress
Clark--Leading p158
Woman's Almanac p211-212, por.
World--Who p298

HUTTON, BETTY (1921-)
Amer. singer, comedienne,
actress
Claghorn--Biog. p226
Hirschhorn--Rating p196-197,
por.
Shipman--Gold. p304-306, por.
World--Who p237

HUTTON, INA RAY (ODESSA
COWAN) (1916-1984)
Amer. bandleader
Claghorn--Biog. p226
Claghorn--Jazz p150
Lamparski--What. (4) p122-123,
por.

HUTTON, LAUREN (1943/1944-)
Amer. model, actress
Anderson--People p208-209, por.
Keenan--Women p140-141,143,
por.
World--Who p291

HUTTON, MARION (1919-)
Amer. singer
Lamparski--What. (8) p140-141,
por.
Simon--Big p41, por.

HUTTON, MAY ARKWRIGHT (1860-
1915)
Amer. boarding house owner,
suffragist
Sherr--American p58,242

HUTTON, "MOTHER" (fl. 18th
cent.)
English botanist, pharmacist,
medical woman
Mead--Hist. p478

HUTTON, NEDENIA
See MERRILL, DINA

HUXTABLE, ADA LOUISE LAND-
MAN (c1921-)
Amer. journalist, architecture
critic, editor, author
Cur. Biog. '73 p196-199, por.
Diamonstein--Open p193-196, por.
Gilbert--Part. p207-213, por.
Marzolf--Up p84-85
O'Neill--Women's p452,464,610

HUYLER, BETTY
See GILLIES, BETTY HUYLER

HVEGER, RAGNHILD (1920-   )
Danish swimmer
Macksey--Book p259-260
McWhirter--Guinness p130
O'Neill--Women's p586

HWANG, HSIEN YUEN, JANE
(fl. 1970's)
Hong Kong Anglican priest
O'Neill--Women's p381

HYAMS, LEILA (1905-1977)
Amer. actress
Springer--They p140-141,303,
por.

HYAMS, MARJORIE (MARGIE)
(1923-   )
Amer. vibrist
Claghorn--Jazz p150

HYATT, ANNA
See HUNTINGTON, ANNA
VAUGHN HYATT

HYDE, ABBY BRADLEY (1799-
1872)
Amer. hymnist
Claghorn--Biog. p227

HYDE, ANNE (1637-1671)
English queen
Softley--Queens p91

HYDE, HELEN
Amer. painter, designer
Sparrow--Women p145,163

HYDE, IDA HENRIETTA (1857-
1945)
Amer. physiologist, zoologist,
scholar
James--Notable (2) p247-249
O'Neill--Women's p156
Stein--Fragments p225-236

HYDE, ROBIN
New Zealand poet, novelist
Seymour-Smith--Who's p171

HYERS, ANNA MADAH (1854-c1924)
Amer. singer
Claghorn--Biog. p227

HYERS, EMMA LOUISE (1853-c1916)
Amer. singer
Claghorn--Biog. p227

HYGEIA
Greek goddess of health
Marks--Women p38-39, por.

HYMAN, LIBBIE HENRIETTA (1888-
1969)
Amer. zoologist, paleontologist,
author
McHenry--Liberty's p205
Macksey--Book p154-155
O'Neill--Women's p144,156
Sicherman--Notable p365-367

HYMEN, SARALEE
Amer. TV cable executive
Scheuer--Tel. p236

HYMES, VAL (fl. 1970's)
Amer. TV-Washington cor-
respondent
Marzolf--Up p104

HYNDMAN, KATE (fl. 1930's)
Amer. labor union activist
O'Neill--Women's p328

HYPATIA (c370/380-415)
Greek philosopher, mathe-
matician, educator, beauty
Asimov--Biog. p43, (64)
Macksey--Book p62
Osen--Women p22-32, por.
Woman's Almanac p363

HYSLOP, BEATRICE FRY (1899-
1973)
Amer. historian
Sicherman--Notable p367-368

I

IAIA OF KYZIKOS
Roman painter
Munsterberg--Hist. p10-11

IAMS, LUCY VIRGINIA DORSEY
(1855-1924)
Amer. welfare worker, social
reformer
James--Notable (2) p249-251

IAN, JANIS (1950/1951-   )
Amer. singer, songwriter
Anderson--People p211
Claghorn--Biog. p229
Woman's Almanac p53
World--Who p268

IBARRURI, DOLORES (DELORES)
  (1895-   )
  Spanish Communist party
  leader
  O'Neill--Women's p695,713
  Palmer--Who's p169
  Taylor--Gener. p41-42, por.
  Who Did What p162
  Woman's Almanac p449
  World--Who p166

IBSEN, MARICHEN ALTENBURG
  (1799-1869)
  Norwegian, mother of
  Henrik Ibsen
  Diagram--Mothers p114-115, por.

ICHIKAWA, FUSAYE (1893-1981)
  Japanese feminist, activist
  O'Neill--Women's p698

ICKES, ANNA WILMARTH THOMP-
  SON
  See WILMARTH, MARY JANE
  HAWES

IGHODARO, IRENE (fl. 1950's-
  1970's)
  African (Sierra Leone/
  Nigeria) physician
  Crane--Ms. p69-81, por.

ILG, FRANCES LILLIAN (1902-
  1981)
  Amer. pediatrician, physician
  Cur. Biog. '81 p465

IL'NA, LIDIA ALEXANDROVNA
  (1915-   )
  Russian illustrator
  Women's--Female p3 (supp.)

ILOTT, PAMELA
  Amer. TV executive
  Scheuer--Tel. p237-238

ILVESSALO, KIRSTI (1920-   )
  Finnish artist, designer
  O'Neill--Women's p274-275

IMA SHALOM (fl. 70 A.D.)
  Israeli religious scholar
  Henry--Written p14,44,47-53

IMPERIA (1481-1512)
  Roman courtesan, salonnière
  Macksey--Book p94

INCHBALD, ELIZABETH SIMPSON
  (1753-1821)
  English novelist, playwright
  actress
  Avenel--Comp. (1) p271
  Horner--English p67 (and note)
  Moers--Literary p118,294

"INDIAN PEGGY" (c1800-1902)
  Amer. Shasta Indian
  Sherr--American p23, por.

INESCORT, FRIEDA (1901-   )
  Scottish-Amer. actress
  Lamparski--What. (4) p166-167,
  por.
  Springer--They p144,303, por.

INEZ, COLETTE (1931-   )
  Belgian-Amer. poet
  Chester--Rising p197-200, por.

INGALLS, LAURA (fl. 1930's)
  Amer. aviatrix, aerial acrobat
  Boase--Sky's p126

INGALLS, MADORA
  Amer., wife of prison super-
  intendent, heroine
  Sherr--American p9

INGELOW, JEAN (1820-1897)
  English novelist, poet, essayist
  Avenel--Comp. (1) p272
  Jones--Rutledge p394
  Moers--Literary p294
  Showlater--Lit. p327

INGHAM, MARY (fl. 1677)
  Amer. accused witch
  Williams--Demeter's p137-138

INGHAM, MARY HALL (1866-1937)
  Amer. social reformer, suf-
  fragist
  James--Notable (2) p252-253

INGLES, MARY DRAPER (c1718-1810)
  Amer. pioneer, Indian captive
  Sherr--American p237

INGLIS, ESTHER
  See KELLO, (H)ESTHER ENGLISH

INGLIS, FRANCES ERSKINE
  See BARCA, FANNY CALDERONE
  DE LA

INGMAN, MARY FRANCES GIL-
BERT (1923-)
Amer. genealogical re-
searcher, editor
Meyer--Who's p105

INGRAHAM, HANNAH
English-Amer. Loyalist
DePauw--Found. p144-146

INGRAM, FRANCES (1883-)
English opera singer
Claghorn--Biog. p229-230

INIQUEZ, REBECCA MATTE
DE
Chilean sculptor
Hahner--Women p79-80

INMAN, ELIZABETH MURRAY
CAMPBELL SMITH (c1726-
1785)
Scottish-Amer. Revolutionary
War patriot
Berkin--Women, see index p435,
por.

INMAN, GLORIA KAY VANDIVER
(1939-)
Amer. genealogical researcher,
author
Meyer--Who's p105

"IOLA," pseud.
See WELLS-BARNETT, IDA
BELL

IONNA (1914-)
Bulgarian queen
Partington--Who's p174

IOWA, MARIE
See DORION, MARIE

IPATESCU, ANA (1805-1875)
Romanian revolutionary
heroine
Partington--Who's p175, por.

IRAELS, BELLE LINDNER
See MOSKOWITZ, BELLE
LINDNER IRAELS

IRELAND, NORMA OLIN (1907-)
Amer. author, librarian,
indexer, genealogical
researcher

Meyer--Petticoat, p99-100,122
Meyer--Who's p106

IRENE (1) (752-803)
Greek Regent, Byzantine
empress, daughter of
Constantine V
Macksey--Book p21

"IRENE" (2)
Amer. fashion designer
Engstead--Star p34,36,116,118

IRENE, (3) SISTER
See FITZGIBBON, IRENE,
SISTER

IRENE DE BORBON DE PARMA
Netherlands princess, social
reformer, agriculturist
O'Neill--Women's p41-42

"IRIS" (fl. 1920's)
Chilean author
Hahner--Women p79

IRON, RALPH, pseud.
See SCHREINER, OLIVE

IRVINE, JESSIE S. (1836-1887)
Amer. composer
Claghorn--Biog. p230

IRVINE, LOUVA ELIZABETH (fl.
1960's-1970's)
Amer. filmmaker
Smith--Movies p180-182,248, por.

IRWIN, AGNES (1) (1841-1914)
Amer. educator, college dean
James--Notable (2) p253-255

IRWIN, AGNES (2) (1862-1938)
Canadian-Amer. actress,
singer
McHenry--Liberty's p206

IRWIN, ELISABETH ANTOINETTE
(1880-1942)
Amer. educator
James--Notable (2) p255-257

IRWIN, HARRIET (-1897)
Amer. architect
Macksey--Book p166

IRWIN, INEZ LENORE HAYNES

GILLMORE (1873-1970)
Amer. suffragist, journalist,
novelist, feminist
Showalter--These p33-40, por.
Sicherman--Notable p318-370

IRWIN, MARGARET
English novelist
Crosland--Beyond p155-158,160,
165

IRWIN, MARY KETCHUM (fl.
1860's)
Amer. Southern belle
DeLeon--Belles p190, por.

IRWIN, MAY (1862-1938)
Canadian-Amer. singer,
actress
Claghorn--Biog. p230
James--Notable (2) p257-258
McHenry--Liberty's p206-207
Macksey--Book p232
O'Neill--Women's p656

ISAACS, BARBARA (fl. 1960's-
1970's)
Amer. filmmaker
Smith--Movies p182,248

ISAACS, CAROL
Amer. TV manager
Scheuer--Tel. p238-239

ISAACS, EDITH JULIET RICH
(1878-1956)
Amer. novelist, editor,
critic
Ehrlich--Oxford p338
Sicherman--Notable p370-371

ISAACS, STELLA CHARNAUD
(BARONESS SWANS-
BOROUGH) (1894-1971)
British civil defense or-
ganizer
O'Neill--Women's p114

ISABELLA (c1180-)
French troubadour
Bogin--Women p111,173-174

ISABELLA OF ANGOULÊME
(c1187-1246)
English queen
Softly--Queens p24-26

ISABELLA I (OF CASTILE) (1451-
1504)
Spanish queen
Canning--100 p366-372
Davis--Women p25-37, por.
Fry--1000 p113
Jones--Rutledge p396
Kulkin--Her p147-148
Mead--Hist. p311, por.
Trease--Seven p71-96, por.
Warren--Pictorial p1
Who Did What p164
Woman's Almanac p460-461
World--Who p166

ISABELLA, QUEEN (1292-1358)
French queen, wife of King
Edward II, builder of hospitals
Mead--Hist. p266

ISABELLA OF FRANCE (c1292-1358)
English queen
Softly--Queens p32-35

ISABELLA OF VALOIS (1389-1409)
English queen
Softly--Queens p40-41

ISABELLA II, MARIA ISABELLA
LOUISE (1830-1904)
Spanish queen
Jones--Rutledge p396
Palmer--Who's p171

ISAKADZE, LIANA
Russian violinist
Mandel--Soviet p150

ISBELL, OLIVE MANN (-1899)
Amer. teacher
Sherr--American p21

ISELDA
French troubadour
Bogin--Women p145,178-179

ISEUT DE CAPIO (c1140-)
French troubadour
Bogin--Women p93,165-166

ISHIMINE, JOANNE
Amer. TV reporter
Scheuer--Tel. p240

ISHIMOVA, ALEXANDRA (fl. 1820's)
Russian children's author
Mandel--Soviet p18

ISHUMURE, MICHIKO (fl.
1950's-1970's)
Japanese activist,
ecologist
O'Neill--Women's p725

ISIS (c2500 B.C.)
Egyptian goddess
Pomeroy--Godd. p188,217-226

ISKIN, RUTH (fl. 1970's)
Amer. art historian
Women's--Female p115

ISLEW, BERT
See LEWIS, LILLIAN ALBERTA

ISLEY, PHYLLIS
See JONES, JENNIFER

ISNARD, MARGUERITTE
French lawyer
Macksey--Book p128

ISOM, MARY FRANCES (1865-
1920)
Amer. librarian
James--Notable (2) p258-259
McHenry--Liberty's p207

ISOM, SARAH McGEHEE (fl. 1880's)
Amer. college instructor
Sherr--American p127

ISON, JUDITH G. (1930-)
Amer. genealogical research-
er, editor
Meyer--Who's p106

ISRAEL, HANNAH ERWIN (c1743-
1821)
Amer. Revolutionary War
patriot, heroine
Meyer--Petticoat p85-86

ISRAILOVA, Z.
Russian government official
Mandel--Soviet p295

ISTOMINA, AVDOTIA (c1789-
1848)
Russian ballet dancer
Migel--Ballerinas p251-253

ITALIANO, ANNA MARIA LOUISE
See BANCROFT, ANNE

ITO, SUMAKO (fl. 1970's)
Japanese clothing designer
O'Neill--Women's p247

IUNINA, LIUBOV
Russian feminist
Mandel--Soviet p208-213,218

IVAIKINA, CLAUDIA (fl. 1970's)
Russian, hotel assistant
manager
Mandel--Soviet p108

IVANOF, VERA (fl. 1890's)
Amer., Alaskan pioneer
Jones--Women (1) p37-47

IVANOVNA, ANNA (1694-1740)
Russian ruler
Macksey--Book p28

IVERS, JULIA CRAWFORD (fl.
1910's)
Amer. film director
Slide--Early p110-111

IVES, CORA SEMMES (fl. 1860's)
Amer. Southern belle, harpist
DeLeon--Belles p118-119, por.

IVEY, JEAN EICHELBERGER (1923-)
Amer. composer, teacher
LePage--Women p85-102, por.

IVINS, MOLLY (fl. 1970's)
Amer. editor
Marzolf--Up p204
O'Neill--Women's p480

IVINS, VIRGINIA WILCOX (1827-)
Amer. Western pioneer, writer
Fischer--Let p75-82

IZARD, ANNE DE LANCY (fl. 1770's)
Amer. socialite
Earle--Two Cent. (2) p xiii,
483-484, por.

IZRAILOVNA, EVGENIA (fl. 1970's)
Russian-Jewish physician
Mandel--Soviet p192

J

JABAVU, NONTANDO ("NONI")
(c1921-)

South African writer
Avenel--Comp. (1) p273

JABLONSKI, WANDA (1920-)
Amer. reporter, editor
O'Neill--Women's p457-458

JABURKOVA, JOZKA PALECKOVA
(1896-1942)
Czechoslovakian journalist
Partington--Who's p181

JACATAQUA (fl. 1770's)
Amer. Indian, noted Maine
mother
Amer.--Mothers p237-238

JACK, MARY LETTIE MOSSMAN
(1875-)
Amer. club woman, noted
Arizona mother
Amer.--Mothers p31-32, por.

JACKSON, ABBIE CLEMENT (fl.
1940's-1970's)
Amer. churchwoman, noted
Kentucky mother
Amer.--Mothers p214-215, por.

JACKSON, ANNE (1926-)
Amer. actress
Cur. Biog. '80 p165-168, por.
McCullough--People p89-90
World--Who p237

JACKSON, "AUNT MOLLY" (1880-
1960/1961)
Amer. midwife, nurse
Coffin--Female p195-201
Coffin--Parade p413-423,591-593

JACKSON, BARBARA WARD LODS-
WORTH, LADY
See WARD, BARBARA MARY

JACKSON, ELIZABETH HUTCHIN-
SON (fl. 1770's)
Amer., mother of President
Jackson, Revolutionary War
patriot
Faber--Presidents' p260-263
Meyer--Petticoat p198-199

JACKSON, EVELYN JEAN
SEYPHERS (1927-)
Amer. genealogical researcher,
writer, editor
Meyer--Who's p109

JACKSON, FLORA (1930-1965)
Amer., heaviest woman
Macksey--Book p12

JACKSON, GLENDA (1936-)
English actress
Anderson--People p213
Cur. Biog. '71 p208-210, por.
Entertainers p286, por.
Hirschhorn--Rating p198-199, por.
Manchel--Women p105, por.
O'Neill--Women's p654,661-662
Shipman--Internatl. p269-271,
por.
Woman's Almanac p330,347
World--Who p258

JACKSON, HELEN MARIA HUNT
FISKE (1830-1885)
Amer. poet, novelist, essayist
Bernikow--World p211
Dunlap--Calif. p98, por.
Ehrlich--Oxford, see index p455
James--Notable (2) p259-261
McHenry--Liberty's p208
Moers--Literary p294
Sherr--American p14,20,25,38
Starr--Amer. p396-397
Time--Women p208
Webster's--Amer. p537-538
World--Who p15

JACKSON, JACQUELYNE J. (fl.
1970's)
Amer. professor, medical
sociologist
O'Neill--Women's p420

JACKSON, JILL (fl. 1940's)
Amer. radio sports commen-
tator, athlete
Women--Radio p11-12

JACKSON, KATE (1948-)
Amer. TV actress
Anderson--People p214-215, por.
Scheuer--Tel. p241
World--Who p237

JACKSON, LAURA RIDING
See RIDING, LAURA

JACKSON, LOTTIE WILSON (fl.
1890's)
Amer. suffragist
Hymowitz--Hist. p276

JACKSON, MAHALIA (1911-1972)

JACOBS, FRANCES (1843-1892)
Amer., noted Colorado
mother, welfare worker,
pioneer philanthropist
Amer.--Mothers p64, por.
James--Notable (2) p265-266
McHenry--Liberty's p210
Sherr--American p26

JACOBS, HAZEL
Amer., head body-guard
escort service
Lichtenstein--Mach. p232-236

JACOBS, HELEN HULL (1908-)
Amer. tennis player
Hollander--100 p100-101, por.
McWhirter--Guinness p157,163
Sullivan--Queens p100-101
Woman's Almanac p416
World--Who p215

JACOBS, JANE (1916-)
Amer. urbanologist, writer
Cur. Biog. '77 p215-218, por.

JACOBS, JESSICA (fl. 1970's)
Amer. painter
Women's--Female p46

JACOBS, MARY BELLE AUSTIN
(-c1929)
Amer. social reformer
Sherr--American p250

JACOBS, PATTIE RUFFNER
(1875-1935)
Amer., Alabama suffragist,
social reformer
James--Notable (2) p266-267
Sherr--American p1

JACOBS-BOND, CARRIE
See BOND, CARRIE JACOBS

JACOBSEN, PHEBE R. (1922-)
Amer. genealogical researcher,
writer
Meyer--Who's p109

JACOBSON, D.D. (fl. 1970's)
Amer. bowler
McWhirter--Guinness p44

JACOBSON, DOROTHY H. (fl.
1960's-1970's)
Amer. government official,

agriculturist
O'Neill--Women's p22

JACOBUS, PAULINE (1840-1930)
Amer. ceramicist
Callen--Women p89-90,223

JACOBY, MARY (fl. 1930's)
Amer. backgammon player
O'Neill--Women's p592

JACOBY, SUSAN (fl. 1970's)
Amer. writer
O'Neill--Women's p xi

JACOX, MARILYN E. (fl. 1970's)
Amer. physical chemist,
intramolecular researcher
O'Neill--Women's p90,168

JACQUETTE, YVONNE (fl. 1970's)
Amer. painter
Women's--Female p46

JÄDERSTRÖM, VIOLA
See RÖSSEL, AGDA

JADWIGA (1370/1374-1399)
Polish queen
Jones--Rutledge p400
Macksey--Book p63
Mead--Hist. p176,180-181,219-220
Partington--Who's p181
Who Did What p165

JAFFE, RONA (1932-)
Amer. novelist
Seymour-Smith--Novels p164

JAFFE, SUSAN
Amer. ballet dancer
People--Best p140, por.

JAFFEE, FLORENCE
Amer., weight-loss record
holder
Macksey--Book p177

JAGELLONICA, KATARINA
(-1583)
Swedish queen, wife of
John III
Bainton--Spain p183-204, por.

JAGGER, BIANCA (1945-)
Nicaraguan singer, fashion
leader, beauty, ex-wife
of Mick Jagger

JAMISON, JUDITH
    Amer. ballet dancer
    Bowman--Entertain. p40-45,
        por.
    Cur. Biog. '73 p202-205, por.
    O'Neill--Women's p651, por.
    Woman's Almanac p311-312

JANAUSCHEK, FRANCESCO
    ("FANNY") ROMANA
    MAGDALENA (1829/1830-
    1904)
    Bohemian actress
    James--Notable (2) p268-269

JANE SEYMOUR
    See SEYMOUR, JANE

JANEWAY, ELIZABETH HALL
    (1913-)
    Amer. novelist, essayist,
    reviewer
    Diamonstein--Open p197-202,
        por.
    Ehrlich--Oxford p152
    Moers--Literary p295

JANNEY, MARY DRAPER (fl.
    1940's-1960's)
    Amer. co-founder, WOW
    O'Neill--Women's p107

JANOWITZ, GUNDULA (1937-)
    German opera singer
    Gammond--Illus. p244, por.

JANS, ANNEKE
    See BOGARDUS, ANNETJE JANS

JANSSON, METTA (fl. 1960's-
    1970's)
    Norwegian TV anchorwoman
    Marzolf--Up p287

JANZ, KARIN (fl. 1970's)
    East German gymnast
    McWhirter--Guinness p81, por.

"JAPANESE WOMAN," unknown
    (1866-1900)
    Japanese diarist, translated
    by Lafcadio Hearn
    Moffat--Revel. p163-177

JARAMILLO, CLEOFAS MARTINEZ
    (1877-1956)
    Amer. folklorist, noted New

Mexico mother
    Amer.--Mothers p379-380, por.

JARAY, TESS (1937-)
    British artist
    Contemp. Brit. unp., por.

JARBORO, CATERINA (YARBOROUGH)
    (1903-)
    Amer. opera singer
    Claghorn--Biog. p236

JARCHO, ALICE (fl. 1960's-1970's)
    Amer. broker
    O'Neill--Women's p530

JARDIM, ANNE (fl. 1970's)
    Amer. feminist, writer, busi-
    nesswoman
    Adams--Women p10-11,20,109
    Lichtenstein--Mach. p226,240-242
    O'Neill--Women's p509

JARISH, TRINA (fl. 1970's)
    Amer. aviatrix
    O'Neill--Women's p590

JARNEVIC, DRAGOJLA (1812-1875)
    Croatian writer
    Partington--Who's p185, por.

JARRELL, HELEN IRA (1896-1973)
    Amer. superintendent of
    schools, union leader
    Sicherman--Notable p375-377

JARRELL, JOREEN
    Amer. "presbyter"
    O'Neill--Women's p394

JARRETT, MARY CROMWELL (1877-
    1961)
    Amer. social worker, social
    work educator
    Sicherman--Notable p377-379

JARVIS, ANNA M. (1864-1948)
    Amer., Mother's Day founder,
    noted West Virginia mother
    Eills--Here p48-49
    Felton--Famous p112-113
    McHenry--Liberty's p210-211
    People's Almanac (1) p939, por.
    Sherr--American p244
    Woman's Almanac p83

JARVIS, ANNA MARIE REEVES

(1836-1905)
Amer., noted West Virginia
mother, mother of Anna M.
Jarvis who was Mothers' Day
founder
Amer.--Mothers p571, por.

JARVIS, GRACE HEMRICK (1917-)
Amer. genealogical research-
er, author, editor
Meyer--Who's p110

JARVIS, LUCY HOWARD (1919/
1921-)
Amer. TV producer, editor,
corporation president
Cur. Biog. '72 p240-243, por.
Diamonstein--Open p203-210,
por.
Gelfman--Women p170
Gilbert--Part. p301-309, por.
Klever--Women p118-122, por.
Marzolf--Up p171,174,184
O'Neill--Women's p499
Scheuer--Tel. p244, por.

"JASIA"
See FORNALSKA, MAYORZATA

JASON, SYBIL (1929-)
South African child actress
Lamparski--What. (8) p144-145,
por.
Springer--They p144,303

JASPER, TERESA (TESSIE)
(1893-)
Italian-Amer. clubwoman,
community worker, noted
Massachusetts mother
Amer.--Mothers p265-266, por.

JASSIM, LINDA (fl. 1970's)
Amer. filmmaker
Smith--Movies p182,249

JAUSSI, LAUREEN RICHARDSON
(1934-)
Amer. genealogical researcher, author
Meyer--Who's p110

JAY, PENNY (1930-)
Amer. singer, songwriter
Claghorn--Biog. p237

JAY, SARAH (SALLY) LIVINGSTON

VAN BRUGH (1757-1802)
Amer., wife of John Jay,
social leader
Booth--Women p213-216,299, por.
Earle--Two Cent. (2) p xxiv,
738,767,778-779, por.

JEAN, GLORIA (1927-)
Amer. child singer, actress
Springer--They p144,303, por.

JEAN, NORMA BEASLER (1938-)
Amer. singer
Claghorn--Biog. p237

JEAN, PETIT
French, male impersonator
Sherr--American p11

JEANES, ALLENE R. (fl. 1960's)
Amer. chemist
O'Neill--Women's p31,88,164

JEANMAIRE, RENEE MARCELLE
("ZIZI") (1924/1930-)
French ballet dancer, actress
Keenan--Women p61-62, por.

JEANNE D'ARC
See JOAN OF ARC

JEANSON, BEVERLY FORREST
(1938-)
Amer. genealogical researcher,
writer
Meyer--Who's p110

JEFFERSON, JANE RANDOLPH
(1720-1776)
Amer., noted Virginia mother,
mother of Thomas Jefferson
Amer.--Mothers p548-549
Diagram--Mothers p122
Faber--Presidents' p268-271

JEFFERSON, MARTHA WAYLES
(1748-1782)
Amer., wife of Thomas Jeffer-
son
James--Notable (2) p271
Kelley--Courage p217-218
Melick--Wives p17
Meyer--Petticoat p217-218
Woman's Almanac p486

JEFFREYS, ANNE (1923-)
Amer. actress
World--Who p237

JEFFRIES, HARRIET MILDRED
See CUNARD, GRACE

JEFFRIES, MILDRED (fl. 1970's)
Amer. labor union leader,
feminist
Hymowitz--Hist. p365

JEFFRIES, ROSALIND (fl. 1970's)
Amer. artist
Fax--Black p279-293, por.

JEGER, LENA
British Parliament member
Vallance--Women, see index
p208

JEHN, JANET B. (1928-   )
Amer. genealogical re-
searcher, author, editor
Meyer--Who's p110

JEKYLL, GERTRUDE (1843-1932)
English gardening expert,
writer
Macksey--Book p17
O'Neill--Women's p134
Who Did What p166-167

JEMIMA, BARONESS VON
TAUTIPHOEUS (1807-1893)
Irish novelist
Showalter--Lit. p323

JEMISON, ALICE MAE LEE (1901-
1964)
Amer. Indian political
leader, journalist
Sicherman--Notable p379-380

JEMISON, MARY DEHEWAMIS
(1740-1831)
Irish-Amer. Tory, Indian
captive, landowner
Booth--Women p136-137,200-
201,302
DePauw--Found p121-122
James--Notable (2) p271-273
Kulkin--Her p151
McHenry--Liberty's p211
Sherr--American p159,201

JENCKES, VIRGINIA ELLIS
(1882-1975)
Amer. Congresswoman
Chamberlin--Min. p97-100

JENKIN, MARGUERITE WENDY
See BARRIE, WENDY

JENKINS, CAROL
Amer. TV newscaster
Gelfman--Women p122

JENKINS, ESSIE CYNTHIA (fl.
1960's-1970's)
Amer. librarian
Innis--Profiles p220-221, por.

JENKINS, FLORENCE FOSTER
(c1865-1944)
Amer. singer
Book--Lists (2) p162-163, por.
Felton--Famous p193-194

JENKINS, HELEN HARTLEY (1860-
1934)
Amer. philanthropist, nurse
James--Notable (2) p273-274

JENNE, CRYSTAL SNOW
Amer. (Alaskan) port mistress
Sherr--American p4

JENNER, CHRYSTIE (c1950-   )
Amer., ex-wife of Bruce
Jenner, air stewardess
People--Best p60, por.

JENNERJAHN, MARY LOU
Amer. TV executive
Scheuer--Tel. p245

JENNESS, LINDA (fl. 1970's)
Amer. presidential candidate
People's Almanac (1) p128

JENNEY, ADELINE (c1834-1968)
Amer. poet
Sherr--American p215

"JENNIE JUNE," pseud.
See CROLY, JANE CUNNINGHAM

JENNINGS, ELIZABETH (1926-   )
English poet
Avenel--Comp. (1) p278
Brinnin--Modern p180-182, por.
Seymour-Smith--Who's p181

JENNINGS, MIRIAM JOHNSON
See COLTER, JESSI

JENNINGS, SARAH, DUCHESS OF

MARLBOROUGH (1660-1744)
English social leader, builder,
wife of John Churchill
Macksey--Book p27-28

JENNISON, MRS. ROBERT F.
See BOOKER, LILLIE

JENNKY, MADAME
French motor-racer
Macksey--Book p254

JENSEN, ANN
Amer. psychic
People's Almanac (1) p6

JENSEN, ELLA (1907-)
Danish labor union official
O'Neill--Women's p320

JENSEN, ELLEN L. (fl. 1950's)
Amer. presidential candidate
People's Almanac (1) p128

JENSEN, FANNY (1890-1969)
Danish labor union pioneer
O'Neill--Women's p320

JENSEN, MARIE
German artist
Sparrow--Women p287,303

JEPSON, HELEN (1906/1907-)
Amer. opera singer
Calghorn--Biog. p238

JERGENS, ADELE (1917/1922-)
Amer. actress
Lamparski--What. (5) p84,
por.

JERITZA, MARIA, BARONESS
VON POPPER (1887/1891-)
Austrian-Amer. opera singer
Lamparski--What. (2) p114-115,
por.
Neidle--America's p221
Tuggle--Golden p208-211, por.

JEROME, JEANNETTE
See CHURCHILL, JEANNETTE
(JENNIE) JEROME, LADY
RANDOLPH

JEROME, MAUDE NUGENT (1873-
1958)
Amer. singer, actress,

popular composer, author
Claghorn--Biog. p331

JESSEN, RUTH (c1937-)
Amer. golf player
McWhirter--Guinness p76

JESSYE, EVA (1895-)
Amer. choral conductor,
author, editor
Claghorn--Biog. p238
Jablonski--Ency. p249

JESUS, CAROLINA MARIA DE (fl.
1950's)
Brazilian diarist
Hahner--Women p138-147

JETER, FELICIA
Amer. TV correspondent, co-
anchor, interviewer
Scheuer--Tel. p246

JEWELL, ISABEL (1909-1972)
Amer. actress
Springer--They p144,303-304,
por.

JEWELL, LUCINA (1874-)
Amer. composer, teacher
Claghorn--Biog. p239

JEWETT, PAULINA (fl. 1970's)
Canadian college president
O'Neill--Women's p40,407

JEWETT, SARAH ORNE (1849-1909)
Amer. novelist, story-writer
Avenel--Comp. (2) p137-138
Benét--New p92-95, por.
Ehrlich--Oxford p9-10,31-32
James--Notable (2) p274-276
Jones--Rutledge p408
Kronenberger--Atlan. p409
McHenry--Liberty's p211
Magill--Cycl. p572-574
Moers--Literary p45,177,250,295
Parker--Uneasy p11-15
Seymour-Smith--Novels p165
Sherr--American p87,90
Signif.--Amer. p19, por.
Webster's--Amer. p548
World--Who p15

JEWSBURY, GERALDINE ENDSOR
(1812-1880)
English novelist, journalist

Avenel--Comp. (1) p279
Moers--Literary p295
Showalter--Lit. p324

JEWSBURY, MARIA JANE (1800-
1833)
English poet, essayist
Moers--Literary p177,295

JEX-BLAKE, SOPHIE LOUISA
(1840-1912)
English feminist, physician,
nurse, apothecary
Callen--Women p8
Macksey--Book p150
Marks--Women p116-117, por.
Showalter--Lit. p335

JEZEBEL (c875-852 B.C.)
Biblical, Phoenician
princess, wife of Ahab of
Israel
Jones--Rutledge p408
Woman's Almanac p398-399

JHABVALA, RUTH PRAWER
(1927-)
East Indian novelist, short-
story writer
Crosland--Beyond p145-148
Cur. Biog. '77 p222-224, por.
Seymour-Smith--Novels p165

JHIRAD, JERUSHA (1891-)
East Indian physician
Hellstedt--Women p65-68, por.

JIAGGE, ANNIE (c1914-)
African (Ghana) judge
Crane--Ms. p13,20-35, por.
O'Neill--Women's p369
Macksey--Book p128

JIMULLA, VIOLA (c1878-1966)
Amer. Indian chieftess
Sherr--American p8

JOAN OF ARC (c1412-1431)
French saint, heroine,
martyr, military leader
Donaldson--How p192,194-195
Fines--Who's p139-142
Fraser--Heroines p135-140, por.
Fry--1000 p107,por.
Green--Saints p60-62
Jones--Rutledge p409
Kulkin--Her p152-153

Macksey--Book p50-52, por.
Marlowe--Great p11-16, por.
Sherr--American p39, por.
Taylor--Gener. p19-20, por.
Who Did What p168, por.
Woman's Almanac p446, por.
World--Who p88

JOANNA OF NAVARRE (c1370-1437)
English queen
Softly--Queens p41-44, por.

JOBLIN, MONIA B.
Amer. TV manager
Scheuer--Tel. p246-247

JOB'S WIFE
Biblical
Price--God p108-112

JOCHEBED
Biblical, mother of Moses
Price--God p70-73

JODWIGA, QUEEN
See JADWIGA

JOEL, EILEEN
English jockey
McWhirter--Guinness p92

JOHANN, ZITA (1904-)
Hungarian-Amer. actress
Lamparski--What. (4) p182-183,
por.
Springer--They p144,304, por.

JOHANSON, PATRICIA (1940-)
Amer. artist
Munro--Originals p462-468, por.

JOHANSSON, GRETA
Swedish diver
Macksey--Book p259

JOHANSSON-PAPE, LISA (1907-)
Finnish lamp designer
O'Neill--Women's p275

JOHN, GWEN (1876-1938)
English painter
Fine--Women p84-87, por.
Harris--Women p52,59-60,271-272,
355
Parker--Old p110-113 (fig. 62)
Petersen--Women p100, por.
Tufts--Our p198-210, por.
Women's--Female p9

JOHN, MADAME
Amer. quadroon (fictitious
heroine)
Sherr--American p83

JOHNS, ELLEN (fl. 1970's)
Amer. machinist
O'Neill--Women's p316

JOHNS, GLYNIS (1923-)
South African actress
Cur. Biog. '73 p212-215, por.
Shipman--Internatl. p271-273,
por.
World--Who p258

JOHNSEN, GRACE M. (fl. 1940's)
Amer. radio director
Women--Radio p7

JOHNSON, ADELAIDE (1847-1955)
Amer. feminist, sculptor
Sherr--American p40
Sicherman--Notable p380-381

JOHNSON, ALMA
Amer., wife of Wallace
Johnson
Kooiman--Silhouettes p87-97,
por.

JOHNSON, AMY
See MOLLISON, AMY JOHNSON

JOHNSON, AR(A)BELLA, LADY
(-1630)
Amer. Puritan, pioneer,
wife of Isaac Johnson
Williams--Demeter's p29

JOHNSON, ARTA P. (1921-)
Amer. genealogical research-
er, author, editor
Meyer--Who's p111

JOHNSON, BARBARA CRAWFORD
(fl. 1940's-1970's)
Amer. engineer
O'Neill--Women's p189,191

JOHNSON, BETS(E)Y (1942-)
Amer. fashion designer
Adams--Women p135-137,162
O'Neill--Women's p248,252, por.

JOHNSON, BUFFIE (fl. 1970's)
Amer. artist
Women's--Female p106

JOHNSON, CAROL DIAHANN
See CAROL, DIAHANN

JOHNSON, CELIA (1908-1982)
English actress
Shipman--Internatl. p273-275,
por.

JOHNSON, CLAUDIA ALTA TAYLOR
See JOHNSON, "LADY BIRD"
CLAUDIA ALTA TAYLOR

JOHNSON, DEBORAH
Amer. executive producer,
TV news
Scheuer--Tel. p247

JOHNSON, DEBORAH G. (fl. 1960's)
Amer. military officer, orbital
analyst
O'Neill--Women's p543

JOHNSON, DIANE (1934-)
Amer. novelist
Webber--Woman p154-156

JOHNSON, ELIZA McCARDLE (1810-
1876)
Amer. first lady, wife of
Andrew Johnson
James--Notable (2) p276-277
Melick--Wives p43, por.
Sherr--American p217
Woman's Almanac p489

JOHNSON, ELIZABETH JENNINGS
See HESSELIUS, CHARLOTTE

JOHNSON, ELIZABETH RUSSELL
Amer. socialite, wife of
Thomas Jennings Johnson
Earle--Two Cent. (2) p xxii,736,
por.

JOHNSON, ELLEN CHENEY (1829-
1899)
Amer. prison reformer
James--Notable (2) p277-279
McHenry--Liberty's p211-212
Macksey--Book p113

JOHNSON, EMILY PAULINE (1861/
1862-1913)
Canadian Mohawk Indian
princess, poet
Gridley--Amer. p67-73, por.

JOHNSON, FLORENCE (fl. 1890's)

British embroiderer
Callen--Women p108-109

JOHNSON, GEORGIA DOUGLAS
(1886-1967)
Amer. poet
Bernikow--World p263

JOHNSON, GLORIA T. (fl.
1950's-1960's)
Amer. labor leader,
economist
O'Neill--Women's p303,308-309,
315

JOHNSON, "GRANNY"
See JOHNSON, MRS. JACOB

JOHNSON, HELEN LOUISE
KENDRICK (1844-1917)
Amer. author, editor
McHenry--Liberty's p212

JOHNSON, MRS. JACOB (fl.
1770's)
Amer. colonial midwife
Mead--Hist. p414,487

JOHNSON, JEMIMA SUGGETT
(1753-1814)
Amer. Revolutionary War
patriot
Clyne--Patriots p129-130
Meyer--Petticoat p121-122
Sherr--American p79-80

JOHNSON, JOSEPHINE
Amer., mother of Wallace
Johnson
Kooiman--Silhouettes p81-86,
por.

JOHNSON, JOSEPHINE WINSLOW
(c1910-)
Amer. novelist
Diamonstein--Open p211-214,
por.
Ehrlich--Oxford p356-357

JOHNSON, JUDY (fl. 1940's)
English jockey
McWhirter--Guinness p92

JOHNSON, KAREN (fl. 1960's-
1970's)
Amer. filmmaker
Smith--Movies p182-183,250

JOHNSON, KATE BURR (1881-)
Amer. humanitarian, social
worker, noted North Carolina
mother
Amer.--Mothers p408, por.
Scott--Southern p207

JOHNSON, KAY (1904-)
Amer. actress
Springer--They p144-145,304,
por.

JOHNSON, KRISTEN
Amer. physicist, chemist,
cyclotron researcher
O'Neill--Women's p185,187

JOHNSON, "LADY BIRD" CLAUDIA
ALTA TAYLOR (1912-)
Amer. first lady, wife of
Lyndon B. Johnson
Hershey--Between p157,160-161,
163-165
Melick--Wives p83-85, por.
Miller--Fishbait p310,345-346,
por.
100--Greatest (1) p6, por.
O'Neill--Women's p18
Sochen--Herstory p384,409, por.
Sochen--Movers p243-247
Whedon--Always p151-152
Woman's Almanac p493
World--Who p298

JOHNSON, LARAINE
See DAY, LARAINE

JOHNSON, LORNA
Amer. air force "sailor"
O'Neill--Women's p547

JOHNSON, LUCI BAINES
See NUGENT, LUCI BAINES
JOHNSON

JOHNSON, LUCY
See GARDNER, AVA

JOHNSON, LUCY ANTEK (1945-)
Amer. TV executive
Scheuer--Tel. p248, por.

JOHNSON, MRS. LUKE (fl. 1920's)
Amer. social reformer
Scott--Southern p196

JOHNSON, LYNDA BIRD

See ROBB, LYNDA BIRD
JOHNSON

JOHNSON, MAL (fl. 1970's)
Amer. TV director
Klever--Women p134-138, por.

JOHNSON, MARGUERITE
See ANGELOU, MAYA

JOHNSON, MARIE (fl. 1970's)
Amer. sculptor
Women's--Female p90

JOHNSON, MARY McDONOUGH
(1783-1856)
Amer., mother of Andrew
Johnson
Faber--Presidents' p240-243

JOHNSON, OSA HELEN LEIGHTY
(1894-1953)
Amer. explorer, filmmaker,
author, producer
Hazen--Interv. p396
McHenry--Liberty's p212-213
Sherr--American p73, por.
Smith--Movies p24-25

JOHNSON, PAMELA HANSFORD
(1912-1981)
English novelist
Cur. Biog. '81 p466
Moers--Literary p295

JOHNSON, PHYLLIS WALKER
(1922-)
Amer. genealogical researcher, writer
Meyer--Who's p111-112

JOHNSON, REBECCA FRANKS
See FRANKS, REBECCA

JOHNSON, REBEKAH BAINES
(1881-1958)
Amer., mother of President
Lyndon Johnson
Faber--Presidents' p37-48,
por.

JOHNSON, RHODA QUICK
(1844-1939)
Amer. pioneer, noted
Oregon mother
Amer.--Mothers p447, por.

JOHNSON, RITA (1912-1965)
Amer. pianist, actress
Springer--They p145,304, por.

JOHNSON, MRS. SAMUEL
See PORTER, "TETTY"

JOHNSON, SONIA (1936-)
Amer. social activist, educator
Cur. Biog. '85 p204-208, por.

JOHNSON, SUZANNA WILLARD H.
(1730-c1810)
Amer. Indian captive, noted
New Hampshire mother
Amer.--Mothers p358-359
Sherr--American p146

JOHNSON, MRS. THOMAS JENNINGS
See HESSELIUS, CHARLOTTE

JOHNSON, THOMASINE WALKER
(1911-)
Amer. government official,
lobbyist
Earle--Two Cent. (1) p52-53

JOHNSON, VIRGINIA (1950-)
Amer. dancer
Cur. Biog. '85 p208-211, por.

JOHNSON, VIRGINIA ESHELMAN
(1925-)
Amer. psychologist
Cur. Biog. '76 p198-201, por.
Hymowitz--Hist. p359-360
Longstreet--Queen p189-190
100--Greatest (1) p26, por.
O'Neill--Women's p749
People--Best p68-69, por.
People's Almanac (2) p925-927
Sochen--Movers p252-253
Woman's Almanac p72-73,100,363

JOHNSTON, ANNIE FELLOWS (1863-
1931)
Amer. children's author
McHenry--Liberty's p213
Sherr--American p80

JOHNSTON, FRANCES BENJAMIN
(1864-1952)
Amer. periodical publisher,
feminist, photographer, lecturer
Marzolf--Up p27

Munsterberg--Hist. p126-129
Sicherman--Notable p381-383

JOHNSTON, HARRIET LANE
See LANE, HARRIET

JOHNSTON, HENRIETTA DEERING
(c1670-1728/1729)
Irish-Amer. pastel painter
DePauw--Rem. p127
Earle--Two Cent. (2) p421
Fine--Women p96-97
James--Notable (2) p281-282
McHenry--Liberty's p213
Macksey--Book p200
Petersen--Women p65
Sherr--American p209
Williams--Demeter's p210-211

JOHNSTON, JENNIFER (1930-)
Irish novelist
Seymour-Smith--Novels p165

JOHNSTON, MARY (1870-1936)
Amer. novelist
Ehrlich--Oxford, see index
p455
James--Notable (2) p282-284
McHenry--Liberty's p213-214
Magill--Cycl. p580-581

JOHNSTON, MARY HELEN
Amer. metallurgical engineer,
astronaut
Oberg--Space p84-85,90,113,
188,217,219,231, por.
O'Connor--Sally p20

JOHNSTON, MYRNA (fl. 1930's-
1970's)
Amer. cookbook editor
O'Neill--Women's p132

JOHNSTON, SUZANNE (fl. 1970's)
Amer. filmmaker
Smith--Movies p183-184

JOINER, ENFIELD (-1965)
Amer. teacher of deaf
Sherr--American p3

JOLAS, BETSY (1926-)
Amer. composer
LePage--Women p103-115, por.

JOLAS, MARIA
Amer. patron of arts

Rogers--Ladies, see index p230,
por.

JOLIOT-CURIE, IRENE (1897-1956)
French physicist, chemist
Asimov--Biog. p663 (988), por.
Jones--Rutledge p205
Kulkin--Her p155
Macksey--Book p153,157
Opfell--Lady p165-182, por.
Palmer--Who's p92,179
Who Did What p171
Woman's Almanac p363-364, por.
World--Who p122

JOLY, ANDREE (fl. 1920's)
French skater
Assoc. Press--Pursuit p89,111,
124

JONES, ADELAIDE H. (fl. 1950's)
Amer. journalist, writer
Marzolf--Up p250-251

JONES, AMANDA THEODOSIA (1835-
1914)
Amer. author, inventor,
spiritualist
James--Notable (2) p284-285
McHenry--Liberty's p214

JONES, ANNE DE LANCY (1735-
1817)
Amer. socialite
Earle--Two Cent. (2) p xxi,708,
por.

JONES, ANNIE (1865-1902)
Amer child circus star
People's Almanac (3) p548

JONES, BARBARA (1) (1937-)
Amer. track and field athlete
McWhirter--Guinness p167

JONES, BEATRIX
See FARRAND, BEATRIX JONES

JONES, CAROLYN (1933-1983)
Amer. actress
Cur. Biog. '83 p468
World--Who p237

JONES, CHARLOTTE SCHIFF
(1932-)
Amer. TV corporation president
Scheuer--Tel. p249, por.

JONES, CLARA ARAMINTA
STANTON (1913-   )
Amer. librarian, organiza-
tion official
Cur. Biog. '76 p201-204, por.
O'Neill--Women's p431

JONES, EDITH NEWBOLD
See WHARTON, EDITH
NEWBOLD JONES

JONES, ETTA (1928-   )
Amer. singer
Claghorn--Jazz p162

JONES, FRANCES (fl. 1940's)
Amer. publisher
Marzolf--Up p82-83

JONES, FRIDA (1910-1954)
Mexican painter
Women's--Female p46

JONES, GAIL (GAYL) (1949-   )
Amer. writer, professor,
actress
Fisher--Third p vi, 230

JONES, GRACE (c1951-   )
Jamaican singer
People--Best p64-65, por.

JONES, JANE ELIZABETH HITCH-
COCK (1813-1896)
Amer. lecturer, feminist
James--Notable (2) p286-286
Lutz--Crusade p222,225-227,
271

JONES, JENNIFER (1919-   )
Amer. actress
Hirschhorn--Rating p202-203,
por.
Shipman--Internatl. p279-282,
por.
World--Who p237

JONES, LEE (fl. 1940's-1960's)
Amer. journalist, editor
O'Neill--Women's p461

JONES, LILLIE MAE
See CARTER, BETTY (1)

JONES, LINDSAY (fl. 1960's-
1970's)
Amer. food fair founder

O'Neill--Women's p36-
37

JONES, LOIS MARILYN (1934-   )
Amer. geochemist (Antarctica)
Land--New p21,36,54, por.

JONES, LOIS MAILOU (1905-   )
Amer. educator, painter,
professor
O'Neill--Women's p602
Petersen--Women p124-126

JONES, MARCIA MAE (1924-   )
Amer. actress
Springer--They p145,304, por.

JONES, MARGARET (-1648)
Amer. colonial physician, mid-
wife, accused witch
Mead--Hist. p412,487
Williams--Demeter's p135

JONES, MARGO (1912-1955)
Amer. drama director, pro-
ducer
Chinoy--Women p217-221
Sherr--American p221
Sicherman--Notable p383-385

JONES, MARSHA MAE (1924-   )
Amer. actress
Lamparski--What. (4) p160-161,
por.

JONES, MARY GARDINER (c1921-   )
Amer. lawyer, government
official
Diamonstein--Open p215-219, por.
O'Neill--Women's p288,357

JONES, MARY HARRIS ("MOTHER
JONES") (1830-1930)
Irish-Amer. labor leader,
radical
Brin--Social p156
Hoople--As p176-178
Hymowitz--Hist. p245-246, por.
James--Notable (2) p286-288
Kulkin--Her p156-157
McHenry--Liberty's p214-215
Marlowe--Great p102-108, por.
Millstein--We p153,165-167
Neidle--America's p117-123, por.
Nies--Seven p95-123
O'Neill--Women's p291-292
People's Almanac (1) p97-98

Reifert--Women p166-170
Sherr--American p63,245
Signif.--Amer. p29, por.
Sochen--Herstory p183-184,256
Truman--Women p85-97,198-199,
  por.
Warren--Pictorial p145-146, por.
Webster's--Amer. p561
Woman's Almanac p177-178, por.
World--Who p189

JONES, MARY KATHARINE
  See BENNETT, MARY KATHARINE
    JONES

JONES, MATILDA SISSIERETTA
  JOYNER (1868-1933)
  Amer. singer
  Claghorn--Biog. p244
  James--Notable (2) p288-290
  McHenry--Liberty's p215
  Neuls-Bates--Women p135-142,
    por.

JONES, MAUDE HALL (1872-1954)
  Amer. business woman,
  noted Missouri mother
  Amer.--Mothers p313-314, por.

JONES, ORLO LOUISE (1929-)
  Canadian genealogical re-
  searcher
  Meyer--Who's p112-113

JONES, REBECCA (1739-1818)
  Amer. Quaker clergyman
  James--Notable (2) p290-291

JONES, RICKIE LEE (c1955-)
  Amer. singer
  Glassman--Year '79 p170, por.

JONES, RODERICK, LADY
  See BAGNOLD, ENID
    ALGERINE

JONES, RUTH
  See WASHINGTON, DINAH

JONES, RUTH GORDON
  See GORDON, RUTH

JONES, SALENA (1930-)
  Amer. singer
  Claghorn--Jazz p164

JONES, SHIRLEY (1934-)

Amer. singer, actress
Claghorn--Biog. p244
Hirschhorn--Rating p203, por.
Manchel--Women p89
World--Who p268

JONES, SISSIERETTA
  See JONES, MATILDA
    SISSIERETTA JOYNER

JONES, SYBIL (1808-1873/1877)
  Amer. Quaker minister, mis-
  sionary, speaker, noted Maine
  mother
  Amer.--Mothers p239-240
  James--Notable (2) p291-293
  McHenry--Liberty's p215

JONES, VIRGINIA
  See MAYO, VIRGINIA

JONES, WANDA
  Amer. missionary, teacher
  Kooiman--Cameos p60-65, por.

JONES, WENDY (fl. 1940's-1970's)
  Amer. (Alaskan) author
  Jones--Women (1) back cover,
    por.

JONES-FORMAN, CHRISTINE (fl.
  1970's)
  Amer. astronomer
  O'Neill--Women's p154-155, por.

JONES-GOLDSTEIN, BONNIE (fl.
  1970's)
  Amer. clergyman
  Proctor--Women p43-44,50-52,
    77-79,85,98-99

JONG, ERICA MANN (1942-)
  Amer. novelist, poet
  Anderson--People p225
  Baum--Jewish p236,257-258
  Chester--Rising p338-347, por.
  Cur. Biog. '75 p205-208, por.
  Moers--Literary p132,146,295-296
  100--Greatest (1) p40, por.
  O'Neill--Women's p689
  Seymour-Smith--Novels p82,165,
    por.
  Webber--Woman p188-189
  World--Who p15

JONKER, INGRID (1933-1965)
  Afrikaans poet, writer

Seymour-Smith--Who's
p183

JOPLIN, JANIS LYN (1943-1970)
Amer. singer
Book--Lists (2) p444
Claghorn--Biog. p245
Clark--Leading p215
Cur. Biog. '70 p209-211,464,
por.
Lichtenstein--Mach. p266
O'Neill--Women's p627
People's Almanac (2) p781-782,
1200
Sicherman--Notable p385-387
Simon--Best p307-308, por.
Talmey--Vogue p162, por.
Woman's Almanac p294-295, por.
World--Who p268

JORDAN, BARBARA (CHARLINE)
(1936-)
Amer. Congresswoman,
lawyer
Bowman--Politics p26-33, por.
Chamberlin--Min. p354
Cur. Biog. '74 p189-192, por.
Diamonstein--Open p220-225,
por.
Greenebaum--Politics p119-134,
por.
Lichtenstein--Mach. p319-322
100--Greatest (1) p58, por.
O'Neill--Women's p73
Schoenebaum--Prof. p334-335
Woman's Almanac p475-476, por.
World--Who p144

JORDAN, DOROTHY (1908-)
Amer. dancer, actress
Lamparski--What. Annual (4,5)
p64-69
Springer--They p145-146,304,
por.

JORDAN, ELIZABETH GARVER
(1865-1947)
Amer. journalist, author
James--Notable (2) p293-294
McHenry--Liberty's p215-216
Marzolf--Up p34-35

JORDAN, GRACE EDINGTON
Amer. author, community
worker, noted Idaho mother
Amer.--Mothers p156-157, por.

JORDAN, JUNE MEYER (1936-)
Amer. poet
Chester--Rising p266-273, por.
Fisher--Third p vi, 262
McCullough--People p93-94

JORDAN, MARIAN DRISCOLL
("MOLLY McGEE") (1897-1961)
Amer. entertainer
World--Who p276

JORDAN, MIRIAM (1908-)
English actress
Springer--They p146,304, por.

JORDAN, SARA CLAUDIA MURRAY
(1884-1959)
Amer. physician
Sicherman--Notable p387-388

JORDAN, SHELIA (1929-)
Amer. singer
Claghorn--Biog. p246

JORGENSEN, CHRISTINE (1926-)
Amer. actress, entertainer,
transsexual
Book--Lists (2) p329
People's Almanac (2) p727-728,
por.

"JOSEFA"
Mexican-Amer. accused
"avenger"
Sherr--American p13

JOSEPH, DAUGHTER OF
"false messiah"
Henry--Written p76

JOSEPH, GERI (fl. 1940's-1970's)
Amer. newspaper writer,
politician
O'Neill--Women's p451

JOSEPH, HELEN (1906-)
South African militant, author,
political activist
O'Neill--Women's p731

JOSEPH, MARY, MOTHER (1883-
1902)
Amer. hospital builder
Sherr--American p242
Sicherman--Notable p590-591
Time--Women p100, por.

JOSEPHINE DE BEAUCHARNAIS
(1763-1814)
French Empress, (first wife
of Napoleon)
Donaldson--How p201-202
Jones--Rutledge p61,416

JOSHEE, ANANDIBAI (1865-1887)
East Indian pioneer physician
O'Neill--Women's p204

JOSLYN, SARAH HANNAH SELLECK
(1851-1940)
Amer. art patron, philan-
thropist, noted Nebraska
mother
Amer.--Mothers p334-335, por.
Sherr--American p140-141

JOURDAIN, ELEANOR FRANCES
(c1863-1924)
English educator, psychic,
adventurer, physician,
psychologist
People's Almanac (1) p1381-1384

JOURNEYCAKE, SALLY (fl. 1830's)
Amer. Delaware Indian Chris-
tian convert
Sherr--American p190

JOY, LEATRICE (1896/1899-1985)
Amer. actress
Lamparski--What. (8) p150-151,
por.
Springer--They p146,304, por.

JOY, SALLY (fl. 1870's)
Amer. journalist
Marzolf--Up p19-20

JOYCE, ADRIAN
See EASTMAN, CAROLE

JOYCE, BRENDA (1916-)
Amer. model, actress
Springer--They p146,304,
por.

JOYCE, JOAN (1940-)
Amer. softball player
Gurtman--More p82-101, por.
Hollander--100 p79-80, por.
Jordan--Broken p127-130,139-
140,
Woman's Almanac p439, por.

JOYE, JUDY (fl. 1970's)
Amer. oceanographer
Seed--Saturday's p65-69, por.

JOYNER, MATILDA SISSIERETTA
See JONES, MATILDA SISSIERETTA
JOYNER

JOYNER, PEGGY SHOMO (1928-)
Amer. genealogical researcher,
author
Meyer--Who's p113

JUANA MARIA (fl. 1840's-1850's)
Amer. Indian, legendary
Western woman
Williams--Legend p1-13, por.

JUANITA (-1851)
Mesican accused criminal
Gray--Women p61-63

JUBIN, BRENDA (fl. 1970's)
Amer. university dean
Macksey--Book p76

JUCH, EMMA ANTONIA JOHANNA
(1865-1930)
Austrian singer
Claghorn--Biog. p246
James--Notable (2) p294-295

JUDD, DOROTHY LEONARD (1898-)
Amer. political, community
worker, noted Michigan mother
Amer.--Mothers p280

JUDD, FLORENCE
British potter
Callen--Women p54

JUDD, LAURA FISH (1804-)
Amer. writer, missionary,
noted Hawaiian mother
Amer.--Mothers p140, por.
Sherr--American p52-54

JUDD, WINNIE RUTH McKISSELL
(1905-)
Amer. accused criminal
Dunlap--Calif. p103
Horan--Desperate p77-78, por.
Woman's Almanac p505, por.
World--Who p298

JUDELS, RACHEL AND REBECCA

(fl. c1677)
German-Jewish printers
Henry--Written p118

JUDGE, ARLINE (1912-1974)
Amer. actress
Springer--They p146,304, por.

JUDITH (-977)
Queen of Falashas or Black
Jews
Taylor--Gener. p19

JUDSON, ANN HASSELTINE
(1789-1826)
Amer. missionary to Burma,
pioneer
James--Notable (2) p295-297
McHenry--Liberty's p216
Webster's--Amer. p465,565
(under Judson, Adoniram)

JUDSON, EMILY CHUBBUCK (1817-
1854)
Amer. novelist, missionary
James--Notable (2) p297-298
Webster's--Amer. p357,565
(under Judson, Adoniram)

JUDSON, SARAH HALL BOARDMAN
(1803-1845)
Amer. hymnist
Claghorn--Biog. p246
James--Notable (2) p298-300
McHenry--Liberty's p216-217
Webster's--Amer. p565

JULIA (39 B.C.-14 A.D.)
Roman empress, daughter of
Augustus
Jones--Rutledge p419
Pomeroy--Godd. p183,201-202

JULIA AGRIPPINA (fl. c50 B.C.)
Roman empress, niece of
Claudius
Zinserling--Women p67-68

JULIA ANICIA (472-)
Greek physician
Mead--Hist. p96

JULIA DOMNA (c157-217)
Roman empress, literary
salonist, medical charity
worker

Mead--Hist. p78
Pomeroy--Godd. p174
Zinserling--Women p68

JULIA MAESA (fl. c217 A.D.)
Roman empress, patriot, head of
army, (mother of Julia Mamaea)
Zinserling--Women p68

JULIA, SISTER
See McGROARTY, JULIA, SISTER

JULIANA, LOUISE EMMA MARIE
WILHELMINA (1909-)
Netherlands queen
Jones--Rutledge p419
Miller--Fishbait p347-349
O'Neill--Women's p49
Woman's Almanac p466

JULIANA OF NORWICH, DAME
(c1342-after 1416)
English mystic, religious
writer
Avenel--Comp. (1) p287
Macksey--Book p106
Moers--Literary p243,296

JULIANE MARIE, PRINCESS (1729-
1796)
Danish, stepmother of King
Christian VII of Denmark
Book--Lists (2) p253

JULIANELLI, MABEL (1919-)
Amer. shoe designer
O'Neill--Women's p247,258

JULLIARD, JACQUELINE (fl. 1970's)
Swiss chemical engineer
O'Neill--Women's p190-191

JULVES ENCARNACION LOPEZ
See ARGENTINITA

JUMEL, ELIZABETH (ELIZA) BOWEN
(1769/1775-1865)
Amer. beauty, adventuress,
second wife of Aaron Burr
James--Notable (2) p300-301
Sherr--American p172, por.

JUNE, JANE (JENNIE)
See CROLY, JANE CUNNINGHAM

JUNEAU, JOSETTE

Amer. Ottawa Indian pioneer,
city founder
Sherr--American p249

JUNG, DORA (1906-   )
Finnish textile artist
O'Neill--Women's p274

JUNGREIS, ESTHER (1938-   )
Hungarian-Amer. religious
leader
Woman's Almanac p405-406
World--Who p82

JUNKIN, MARGARET
See PRESTON, MARGARET
JUNKIN

JURADO, CONCEPCION (1864-
1931)
Mexican imposter
Book--Lists (1) p483

JURINAC, SENA (1921-   )
Yugoslavian opera singer
Gammond--Illus. p244-245, por.

JURNEY, DOROTHY (c1909-   )
Amer. editor, journalist
Diamonstein--Open p226-231,
por.
Marzolf--Up 75,79,111-113,209,
215
O'Neill--Women's p469

JURZYKOWSKI, CHRISTINE
Amer. TV corporation
president
Scheuer--Tel. p251

K

KAAHUMANU, ELIZABETH
(1772-1832)
Amer. ruler, noted Hawaii
mother
Amer.--Mothers p139, por.
James--Notable (2) p301-302
McHenry--Liberty's p218
Sherr--American p53-55

KAARRESALO-KASARI, ELLA
(fl. 1970's)
Finnish film producer,
director
Smith--Movies p112,251, por.

KACHEL, MALLEY (fl. 1970's)
German physician
Comfort--Good p87, por.

KAEL, PAULINE (1919-   )
Amer. film critic, author
Cur. Biog. '74 p192-195, por.
McHenry--Liberty's p218
O'Neill--Women's p477,669

KAGAN, HELEN(A) (1889-   )
Israeli physician
Hellstedt--Women p36-37

KAHANE, MELANIE (c1911-   )
Amer. interior designer,
corporation president
Diamonstein--Open p231-235, por.
O'Neill--Women's p282

KAHENA OF AURES
Algerian queen
McFarland--Incred. p106-107

KAHINAH DAHIYAH BINT THABITAH
IBN TIFAN
Jewish tribe leader, warrior,
prophetess
Henry--Written p65-67

KAHLERT, MARION OOLETIA
(-1904)
Amer. child, first to die in
an automobile accident
Sherr--American p42, por.

KAHLO, FRIDA (1910-1954)
Mexican painter
Harris--Women p59,61,335-337,
361-362
Petersen--Women p133-136

KAHN, FLORENCE PRAG (1866/1867-
1948)
Amer. Congresswoman
Chamberlin--Min. p48-52, por.
James--Notable (2) p302-303
McHenry--Liberty's p218-219

KAHN, MADELINE GAIL (1942-   )
Amer. actress, singer
Anderson--People p227, por.
Cur. Biog. '77 p239-243, por.
Mordden--Movie p238-239
World--Who p237

KAHN, NATALIE (fl. 1970's)

Springer--They p149,304-305,
por.

KANE, MARTHA
Amer. cosmic ray research
worker (Antarctica)
Land--New p218, por.

KANE, TOURE AISSATA (fl.
1960's-1970's)
Ismalic (Mauritania) cabinet
member
O'Neill--Women's p60

KANEKO, HELEN AOKI (1919-   )
Asian-Amer. writer
Fisher--Third p x,554

KANIZSAI, DOROTTYA
(DOROTHY) (-after 1532)
Hungarian heroine
Partington--Who's p196

KANKUS, ROBERTA A. (c1953-   )
Amer. commercial nuclear
power plant operator
O'Neill--Women's p196, por.

KANOPACKA, HALINA (fl. 1920's)
Netherlands track and field
athlete
O'Neill--Women's p573

"KANSAS CYLONE, PYTHONESS"
See LEASE, MARY ELIZABETH
CLYENS

KANTAROFF, MARYON (fl. 1970's)
Amer. sculptor
Women's--Female p91

KANTOR, ROSABETH MOSS
Amer. feminist, writer
Adams--Women p178
Lichtenstein--Mach., see index
p362

KANTOROVICH, LEAH (fl. 1970's)
Russian-Jewish nurse, heroine
Mandel--Soviet p192

KAPIOLANI (c1781-1841)
Amer. Hawaiian high
chieftess
James--Notable (2) p307-308
Sherr--American p52,55, por.

KAPLAN, MONIQUE (fl. 1970's)
French investment trust
founder
Macksey--Book p169
O'Neill--Women's p529

KAPLAN, NELLY (fl. 1950's-1970's)
French film director
Smith--Movies p120-121

KAPPEL, GERTRUDE (1884-1971)
German opera singer
Tuggle--Golden p196-197, por.

KAPPELHOFF, DORIS VON
See DAY, DORIS

KAPULE, DEBORAH (-1853)
Amer. Hawaiian queen
Sherr--American p55, por.

KARA, MANIBEN (fl. 1920's-1970's)
East Indian trade unionist,
social worker
O'Neill--Women's p254

KARAN, DONNA (c1948-1974)
Amer. fashion designer
O'Neill--Women's p254, por.

KARASZ, MARISKA (1898-1960)
Hungarian-Amer. clothes de-
signer, needlework editor
O'Neill--Women's p130

KARINSKA, BARBARA (1886-   )
Russian-Amer. costume de-
signer
Cur. Biog. '71 p210-213, por.
O'Neill--Women's p254-255

KARIYEVA, BERNARA
Russian ballet dancer
Mandel--Soviet p190, por.

KARL, ELFRIEDE (1933-   )
Austrian government official
O'Neill--Women's p56-57

KARLE, ISABELLA L. (fl. 1970's)
Amer. chemist, crystallographer
O'Neill--Women's p89,165,183,189

KARLINSEY, EDNA CATHERN
(1908-   )
Amer. teacher, noted

Washington state mother
Amer.--Mothers p561, por.

KARMEL, ROBERTA S. (1937-)
Amer. lawyer, securities
and exchange commissioner
O'Neill--Women's p367

KARPATKIN, RHODA HENDRICK
(1930-)
Amer. lawyer, head, con-
sumer's union
O'Neill--Women's p360-361

KARSAVINA, TAMARA (1885-1978)
Russian ballet dancer
Jones--Rutledge p423
Macksey--Book p230,232
Who Did What p174

KARSCH, ANNA (1722-1791)
German poet
Macksey--Book p182

KARTTUNEN, LAILA (1895-)
Finnish textile designer,
weaver
O'Neill--Women's p274

KASCHNITZ, MARIE LUISE (1901-
1974)
German poet, short-story
writer
Herrmann--Ger. p5,53

KASEBIER, GERTRUDE STANTON
(1852-1934)
Amer. photographer
James--Notable (2) p308-309
McHenry--Liberty's p220
Munsterberg--Hist. p123-126
Women's--Female p10

KASMUNAH (11th or 12th Cent.)
Spanish-Jewish poet
Henry--Written p68-70

KASSEBAUM, NANCY LANDON
(1932-)
Amer. Senator
Cur. Biog. '82 p190-194, por.

KATHERINE
See CATHERINE

KATHERINE PARR
See PARR, KATHERINE

KATHERYN HOWARD
See CATHERINE OF ARAGON

KATILIUTE, MARCEI (1913-)
Russian painter
Women's--Female p3 supp.

KATSURA YUKIKO (1913-)
Japanese painter
Munsterberg--Hist. p81-82

KATSURADA, YOSHI (fl. 1950's-
1960's)
Japanese mathematician
O'Neill--Women's p177

KATZ, GLORIA (c1943-)
Amer. film writer
Smith--Movies p73-74

KATZEN, LILA (1932-)
Amer. sculptor
Munro--Originals p225-232, por.
Nemser--Convers. p231-265,364-
365, por.
Women's--Female p91

KATZNELSON, RACHEL (fl. 1910's)
Russian journalist, feminist
Macksey--Book p190-191

KAUFFMANN, ANGELICA (1741-1807)
Swiss painter, printmaker
Fine--Women p72-75
Harris--Women p28,38,41-44,81,
174-178,190,249,346,363, por.
Jones--Rutledge p423
Macksey--Book p201
Munsterberg--Hist. p40,43-45,
105, por.
Parker--Old p9,87,90, fig. 50,
por.
Petersen--Women p43-46, por.
Sparrow--Women p58-59,67,83,
87, por.
Tufts--Our p116-121, por.
Women's--Female p10

KAUFMAN, ELAINE
Amer. restaurant owner
Adams--Women p87-88

KAUFMAN, JANE (fl. 1970's)
Amer. painter
Women's--Female p47

KAUFMAN, JOYCE

Amer. theoretical, structural
chemist, professor
O'Neill--Women's p165,169-170

KAUFMAN, SHIRLEY (1923-)
Amer. poet
Chester--Rising p126-132, por.

KAUFMAN, SUE (c1926-1977)
Amer. novelist
Macksey--Book p193
Moers--Literary p296

KAUMEYER, MARY LETA
See LAMOUR, DOROTHY

KAUR, (RAJ)KUMARI AMRIT
(1889-1964)
East Indian social reformer,
government official
Macksey--Book p120
O'Neill--Women's p61

KAVADAS, KATHRYN BANCROFT
(c1952-)
Amer. millionaire
Forbes--400 ('84) p150-151

KAVAN, ANNA (HELEN EDMONDS)
(1901-1968)
English novelist, short-
story writer
Crosland--Beyond p186-192,194-
196,212
Seymour-Smith--Novels p167

KAVANAGH, JULIA (1824-1877)
Irish novelist
Showalter--Lit. p328

KAVANAGH, MISS SPENCER
See COOK, EDITH MAUD

KAY, BEATRICE (fl. 1940's)
Amer. singer
Lamparski--What. (5) p108-
109, por.

KAY, HERMA HILL (1934-)
Amer. lawyer, professor
O'Neill--Women's p362

KAY, MARY ALMA (1930-)
Amer. genealogical research-
er, author, editor
Meyer--Who's p115

KAYE, MARY MARGARET (1908/
1909-)
English novelist
Seymour-Smith--Novels p167

KAYE, NORA (1920-1987)
Amer. ballet dancer
McHenry--Liberty's p220

KAYE-SMITH, SHEILA (1887-
1956)
English novelist
Avenel--Comp. (1) p289
Crosland--Beyond p114-115,129-
130
Magill--Cycl. p595-596
Morley--Literary p140-141
Showalter--Lit. p346

KAZAN, LAINIE (1942-)
Amer. singer
World--Who p268

KAZANKINA, TATYANA (fl.
1970's)
Russian track and field
athlete
McWhirter--Guinness p176,
por.
O'Neill--Women's p577

KAZHANOVA, DR.
Russian obstetrician, gynecologist, political leader
Mandel--Soviet p234,237-238,243-
244

KAZICKAS, JURATE (fl. 1970's)
Amer. foreign correspon-
dent
Marzolf--Up p89-90

KEAN, ELLEN TREE (1805-1880)
English actress
Findlater--Player p127-128
Jones--Rutledge p424

KEAN, JENNIE WHITLOCK (c1870-)
Amer. centenarian
Mitchell--Yessir p50-51, por.

KEAN, MRS. OTHO G.
See GRATTAN, SALLIE

KEANE, MARGARET

Amer. painter
Women's--Female p47

KEARNEY, ANNETTE GAINES
Amer. psychologist
Innis--Profiles p24, por.

KEARNEY, BELLE (1863-1939)
Amer. suffragist, temperance
worker
Hymowitz--Hist. p276
James--Notable (2) p309-310
Scott--Southern p145,149,175-
176,182
Sherr--American p125
Sochen--Herstory p217

KEARY, ANNIE (1825-1879)
English children's book
author
Showalter--Lit. p329

KEATING, ANNA-LENA
Amer. animator, filmmaker
Smith--Movies p184-185,252

KEATING, ANNE
Amer. hockey player
O'Neill--Women's p568

KEATING, S.B.
See WOOD, SALLY SAYWARD
BE(A)RRELL KEATING,
MADAM

KEATON, DIANE (1946/1949-)
Amer. actress
Anderson--People p228-229, por.
Cur. Biog. '78 p222-225, por.
Hirschhorn--Rating p207-208,
por.
Mordden--Movie p272-273
Shipman--Internatl. p290-291,
por.
World--Who p237

KECKLEY, ELIZABETH (c1818-
1907)
Amer. dressmaker, White
House modiste and confi-
dante of Mrs. Lincoln
James--Notable (2) p310-311
Millstein--We p136-137

KEE, ELIZABETH FRAZIER (1899-
1975)

Amer. Congresswoman
Chamberlin--Min. p225-226

KEEGAN, ESTHER (fl. 1860's)
Amer. labor leader
Berkin--Women p203,208,214,217,
219

KEELER, CHRISTINE (1942-)
English model
Keenan--Women p72-73, por.
Lamparski--What. (3) p28-29,
por.
People's Almanac (1) p1246-1247

KEELER, RUBY (ETHEL) (1909/
1910-)
Canadian-Amer. singer,
actress, dancer
Claghorn--Biog. p249
Cur. Biog. '71 p215-218, por.
Lamparski--What. (8) p152-153,
por.
Shipman--Gold. p321-322, por.
Springer--They p149,305, por.
Woman's Almanac p312
World--Who p263

KEEMIE, MARY KATHERINE
See FIELD, KATE

KEEN, BETTY (fl. 1950's)
Amer. journalist
Marzolf--Up p82

KEEN, DORA (1871-)
Amer. mountain climber,
traveler, author
Sherr--American p4-5

KEENE, BETTY (fl. 1940's-1970's)
Amer. organic farmer, mail-
order executive
O'Neill--Women's p17

KEENE, CAROLYN, pseud.
See ADAMS, HARRIET

KEENE, LAURA (c1820-1873)
English-Amer. actress,
theatrical manager
James--Notable (2) p311-313
McHenry--Liberty's p220-221
Macksey--Book p227
Sherr--American p40,93
Webster's--Amer. p572-573

KEEPAX, MARY
    British ceramic designer
    Macksey--Book p209

KEFFER, MARION CHRISTENA
    (1911-)
    Canadian genealogical re-
    searcher, writer, editor
    Meyer--Who's p115

KEHEW, MARY MORTON KIMBALL
    (1859-1918)
    Amer. social reformer,
    labor union leader
    James--Notable (2) p313-314
    McHenry--Liberty's p221
    O'Neill--Women's p289

KEHOE, NANCY (fl. 1970's)
    Amer. Jesuit teacher, nun
    O'Neill--Women's p398
    Proctor--Women p160-163

KEINATH, PAULINE MacMILLAN
    Amer. millionaire
    Forbes--400 ('84) p147

KEKUIAPOIWA II, HIGH CHIEFTESS
    (fl. 18th cent.)
    Amer., noted Hawaii mother
    Amer.--Mothers p139-140

KELDYSH, LYUDMILA
    VSEYOLODOVNA (1904-)
    Russian psysico-mathemati-
    cian, writer
    Macksey--Book p158

KELETI, AGNES (fl. 1950's)
    Hungarian gymnast
    Assoc. Press--Pursuit p199,223

KELLAS, ELIZA (1864-1943)
    Amer. educator
    James--Notable (2) p314-316
    McHenry--Liberty's p221-222

KELLEMS, VIVIEN (1896-1975)
    Amer. industrialist, activist,
    engineer
    Cur. Biog. '75 p468

KELLER, EVELYN FOX (1936-)
    Amer. mathematics professor,
    writer
    Ruddick--Working p77-91,342-
    343, por.

KELLER, FLORENCE (1900-)
    New Zealand nurse, physician
    O'Neill--Women's p205

KELLER, GRETA (1901-1977)
    Austrian-Amer. singer
    Claghorn--Biog. p249-250

KELLER, HELEN ADAMS (1880-1968)
    Amer., blind, deaf, humani-
    tarian, author, lecturer,
    educator
    Brecher--Lives p110,por.
    Ehrlich--Oxford p269
    Gilfond--Heroines p57-63, por.
    Holme--Journal p244-246, por.
    Jones--Rutledge p426
    Kulkin--Her p157-159
    Kupferberg--First p81, por.
    McHenry--Liberty's p222
    Macksey--Book p73
    Marlowe--Great p233-238, por.
    New York Times--Great p148-149,
    por.
    Sherr--American p3
    Pederson--Leaders p206, por.
    Sicherman--Notable p389-393
    Signif.--Amer. p43, por.
    Stoddard--Famous p234-244, por.
    Webster's--Amer. p574
    Whitman--Come p65-75
    Who Did What p175, por.
    Woman's Almanac p157-158, por.
    World--Who p189

KELLER, SUZANNE (fl. 1970's)
    Amer. sociologist, professor
    O'Neill--Women's p426-427

KELLERMAN, ANNETTE (1888-1975)
    Australian swimmer, actress
    Lamparski--What. (2) p108-109,
    por.

KELLERMAN, SALLY (1937-)
    Amer. actress
    Mordden--Movie p271-272
    World--Who p238

KELLEY, ABIGAIL (ABBY)
    See FOSTER, ABIGAIL KELLEY

KELLEY, FLORENCE (1859-1932)
    Amer. social reformer,
    feminist, humanitarian
    Banner--Women p48-49,101,117,
    136,146

Brin--Social p77-99, por.
Clark--Leading p71-72
Earnest--American p222
Friedman--Our p264-274
Hymowitz--Hist. p229-230,232
James--Notable (2) p316-319
McHenry--Liberty's p222-223
Millstein--We p143,150
O'Neill--Women's p288-289,295
Papachristou--Women p166-167,
  por.
Sochen--Herstory p229,234-
  235, por.
Warren--Pictorial p145

KELLEY, PEGGY CLARK (fl.
  1960's-1970's)
  Amer. theatrical designer
  Chinoy--Women p192,211-217,
  por.

KELLO, (H)ESTHER ENGLISH
  (1571-1624)
  French-English calligrapher,
  book and manuscript illustrator
  Petersen--Women p34

KELLOGG, CLARA LOUISE (1842-
  1916)
  Amer. opera singer, manager
  Claghorn--Biog. p250
  James--Notable (2) p319-321
  McHenry--Liberty's p223-224

KELLOGG, FANNY (fl. 1870's)
  Amer. missionary (Alaska)
  Jones--Women (1) p67-69, por.

KELLOGG, LOUISE PHELPS
  (1862-1942)
  Amer. historian
  James--Notable (2) p321-322
  McHenry--Liberty's p224
  Sherr--American p250

KELLOGG, MARION (fl. 1970's)
  Amer. business executive
  O'Neill--Women's p529-530

KELLOGG, MARY FLETCHER (fl.
  1830's-1840's)
  Amer., early college student
  Sherr--American p186-187, por.

KELLOR, FRANCES ALICE (1873-
  1952)

Amer. social reformer, economist
Sicherman--Notable p393-395

KELLOW, KATHLEEN
  See PLAIDY, JEAN

KELLY, CATHERINE
  Amer. "gangster moll"
  Macksey--Book p136

KELLY, EDNA FLANNERY (1906-)
  Amer. Congresswoman
  Chamberlin--Min. p213-218, por.
  U.S.--Women (89th) p15, por.
  U.S.--Women (90th) p15, por.

KELLY, FANNY WIGGINS (1845-
  1904)
  Canadian-Amer. Indian cap-
  tive, Amer. pioneer
  James--Notable (2) p322-323
  Sherr--American p215,254
  Time--Women p64-66

KELLY, FLORENCE FINCH (1858-
  1939)
  Amer. journalist, author
  James--Notable (2) p323-324
  Marzolf--Up p28
  Stein--Fragments no p., por.

KELLY, GRACE, PRINCESS OF
  MONACO (1929-1983)
  Amer. actress, Monacan
  princess
  Anderson--People p175-176, por.
  Cur. Biog. '77 p172-174, por.
  Cur. Biog. '82 p466
  Hershey--Between p116-117
  Hirschhorn--Rating p210-211,
  por.
  Holme--Journal p258-261, por.
  Kulkin--Her p160
  Lewis--Prime p160-161
  McHenry--Liberty's p224
  100--Greatest (1) p7, por.
  O'Neill--Women's p751
  People--Best p248-249, por.
  Sat. Eve. Post--Movie p138-139,
  por.
  Shipman--Internatl. p298-301,
  por.
  Webster's--Amer. p576
  Woman's Almanac p347-348, por.
  World--Who p238

KELLY, KATIE (c1938-   )
Amer. TV critic
Scheuer--Tel. p260

KELLY, MARY (1)
Amer., Indian captive
Time--Women p64-65

KELLY, MARY (2) (1927-   )
English novelist
Seymour-Smith--Novels p167

KELLY, MARY (3) (1941-   )
Amer. artist
Contemp. Brit. unp., por.
Parker--Old p161-168, fig.
93-97

KELLY, MARY PAT (fl. 1970's)
Amer. film writer, director
Smith--Movies p185-186,252 por.

KELLY, MYRA (1875-1910)
Amer. author, social re-
former, educator
Neidle--America's p252-253

KELLY, NANCY (1921-   )
Amer. model, actress
Springer--They p149-150,305,
por.

KELLY, PATSY (1910-1981)
Amer. comedienne, actress
Lamparski--What. (8) p154-155,
por.
Springer--They p150,305, por.
World--Who p238

KELLY, PETRA KARIN (1947-   )
West German political leader,
social activist
Cur. Biog. '84 p189-192, por.

KELLY-GADOL, JOAN (fl.
1960's-1970's)
Amer. historian, teacher
O'Neill--Women's p425-426

KELSEY, CORINNE RIDER
See RIDER-KELSEY, CORINNE

KELSEY, FRANCES OLDHAM
(1914-   )
Amer. physician, government
official
O'Neill--Women's p228

Truman--Women p178-196,198,
200-201, por.

KELTON, PERT (1906-   )
Canadian actress
Springer--They p150,305-306,
por.

KEMBLE, DOROTHY ANN (fl. 1930's-
1940's)
Amer. continuity acceptance
editor
Women--Radio p16-17

KEMBLE, FANNY (FRANCES ANNE)
(1809-1893)
English-Amer. diarist, poet,
playwright, actress
Ehrlich--Oxford p50,206-207, por.
Entertainers p118
Fabian--On p58, por.
Hymowitz--Hist. p41-45,56
James--Notable (2) p324-327
Jones--Rutledge p427
Kulkin--Her p161-162
McHenry--Liberty's p224-225
Millstein--We p103-104
Moers--Literary p188,296
Moffat--Revel. p255-269
Sherr--American p47,50
Webster's--Amer. p577-578

KEMBLE, SARAH
See SIDDONS, SARAH ("SALLY")
KEMBLE

KEMP, MAIDA SPRINGER (1910-   )
Panamanian labor union con-
sultant
O'Neill--Women's p298

KEMPE, MARGERY (1373-c1430/1440)
English mystic, evangelist,
author
Avenel--Comp. (1) p291
Jones--Rutledge p427-428

KEMPFER, HANNAH JENSEN (1830-
1943)
Amer. state legislator, social
reformer
James--Notable (2) p327-328
Sherr--American p120

KEMPRIN-SPYRI, EMILIE (1853-1901)
Swiss lawyer, teacher
Macksey--Book p129

KEMPTON, SALLY (c1943-)
Amer. writer, feminist,
journalist
Diamonstein--Open p240-243,
por.
Hymowitz--Hist. p353

KEMP-WELCH, LUCY E.
English painter
Sparrow--Women p70,115,125

KENDAL, EHRENGARDE (1667-
1743)
German, mistress of King
George I of England
Macksey--Book p97

KENDAL, MARGARET ("MADGE")
ROBERTSON, DAME (1848-
1935)
English actress
Findlater--Player p129-130
Johns--Dames p17-23, por.

KENDALL, KAY (1927-1959)
English actress
Shipman--Internatl. p301-302,
por.
World--Who p238

KENDALL, NANCY (fl. 1970's)
Amer. photographer, actress,
filmmaker
Smith--Movies p186,252

KENNEDY, ADRIENNE (1931-)
Amer. playwright
Chinoy--Women p51-56,265, por.
Webber--Woman p137-138

KENNEDY, (AIMEE) ELIZABETH
See McPHERSON, AIMEE SEMPLE

KENNEDY, CORNELIA (fl. 1970's)
Amer. judge
O'Neill--Women's p370

KENNEDY, DOLORES G. (fl.
1940's-1950's)
Amer. SPAR, WAC, WAVE
O'Neill--Women's p541

KENNEDY, ETHEL SKAKEL
(1928-)
Amer., wife of Robert Kennedy
100--Greatest (1) p108, por.
O'Neill--Women's p103

KENNEDY, FLORYNCE (1916-)
Amer. lawyer, feminist
Hymowitz--Hist. p370

KENNEDY, JACQUELINE BOUVIER
See ONASSIS, JACQUELINE
("JACKIE") BOUVIER KEN-
NEDY

KENNEDY, KATE (1827-1890)
Irish-Amer. social reformer,
feminist
James--Notable (2) p328-329
Sherr--American p19

KENNEDY, MARGARET (1896-1967)
English novelist, playwright
Avenel--Comp. (1) p291
Showalter--Lit. p348

KENNEDY, ROSE FITZGERALD
(1890-)
Amer., noted Massachusetts
mother, mother of John F.
Kennedy
Amer.--Mothers p263-264, por.
Book--Lists (2) p261
Cur. Biog. '70 p217-219, por.
Diagram--Mothers p130-133, por.
Faber--Presidents' p49-65, por.
Hershey--Between p44-47, por.
Kulkin--Her p163-164
100--Greatest (1) p109, por.
O'Neill--Women's p103
People's Almanac (1) p97
Woman's Almanac p92
World--Who p298

KENNEDY, SUZANNE
Amer. veterinarian
O'Neill--Women's p225, por.

KENNEDY, MRS. T.S.
See MALLORY, RUBY

KENNEDY-FRASER, MARJORY
(1857-1930)
British authority on Scottish
folksongs, singer
Macksey--Book p216

KENNEY, ANNIE (1879-1953)
British feminist
Macksey--Book p84-85

KENNON, MRS. (fl. 1730's)
English midwife
Mead--Hist. p475

KENNY, ELIZABETH, SISTER
(1886-1952)
Australian nurse,
physiotherapist
Jones--Rutledge p429
Marlowe--Great p259-265, por.
Sherr--American p121
Woman's Almanac p364, por.

KENT, ALLEGRA (1938-)
Amer. ballet dancer
Cur. Biog. '70 p219-221, por.

KENT, BARBARA (1906-)
Canadian actress
Springer--They p150-151,305-
306, por.

KENT, CORITA (1918-)
Amer. printmaker
Cur. Biog. '69 p236-238, por.
Women's--Female p79

KENT, DOROTHEA (1917-)
Amer. actress
Springer--They p151,306

KENT, DUCHESS OF
See MARINA, DUCHESS OF
KENT

KENT, ELIZABETH, COUNTESS
(fl. 1670's)
English medical woman,
author
Mead--Hist. p345,402

KENT, LESLIE SWIGART (fl.
1940's)
Amer. physician
O'Neill--Women's p209

KENT, LOUISE ANDREWS (1886-
1969)
Amer. novelist
Ehrlich--Oxford p36

KENT, MARJORIE
See MUTCHIE, MARJORIE
ANN

KENT, PRISCILLA (fl. 1940's)
Amer. radio free lance
writer
Women--Radio p20

KENWIX, MARGARET

English herbalist, medical
woman
Mead--Hist. p342

KENWORTHY, RUTH DEWOLFE (1889-
1971)
Amer. chorus manager
Claghorn--Biog. p251

KENYATTA, MARGARET WAMBOI
(1928-)
African (Kenyan) mayor
Crane--Ms. p82, por.

KENYON, DORIS (1897-)
Amer. actress
Lamparski--What. (4) p170-171,
por.
Springer--They p151,306, por.

KENYON, DOROTHY (1888-1972)
Amer. lawyer, activist, judge
Cur. Biog. '72 p465
Sicherman--Notable p395-397

KENYON, KATHLEEN MARY, DAME
(1906-)
British archaeologist
Jones--Rutledge p429
O'Neill--Women's p40-41
Who Did What p177-178

KENYON, NELLIE (fl. 1950's-1960's)
Amer. journalist
Marzolf--Up p62-63

KEOPUOLANI
Amer., Queen of Hawaii
Sherr--American p54-55

KEPPY, DONNA (fl. 1970's)
Amer. hog farmer
O'Neill--Women's p15

KERBIS, GERTRUDE LEMPP (fl.
1970's)
Amer. architect
Seed--Saturday's p12-15, por.
O'Neill--Women's p611

KERBY-MILLER, WILMA A. (fl.
1960's)
Amer. college dean, author
M.I.T.--Women p185-190

KERNOCHAN, SARAH (fl. 1970's)
Amer. producer, director
Smith--Movies p67

KEROUALLE, LOUISE RENEE DE,
DUCHESS OF PORTSMOUTH
AND AUBIGNY (1649-1734)
French mistress of Charles II
of England
Jones--Rutledge p430,634
Macksey--Book p96

KERR, ANITA (1927-)
Amer. pianist, singer, com-
poser
Claghorn--Biog. p252
Smith--Movies p79-80

KERR, DEBORAH JANE (1921-)
Scottish-Amer. actress
Hirschhorn--Rating p211-212,
por.
Shipman--Internatl. p302-306,
por.
Woman's Almanac p348
World--Who p258

KERR, JEAN COLLINS (1923-)
Amer. author
McHenry--Liberty's p225
World--Who p15

KERR, MARGARET
Amer. aviatrix
Keil--Those p57-59,229-230

KERR, SOPHIE (1880-1965)
Amer. author
Sherr--American p94

KERRIGAN, LOUISE EDIE
(fl. 1970's)
Amer. journalist, editor
O'Neill--Women's p100-101

KERR-TRIMMER, DEBORAH
See KERR, DEBORAH JANE

KERT, ANITA
See ELLIS, ANITA

KESSLER, GLADYS (fl. 1970's)
Amer. lawyer, judge
O'Neill--Women's p372

KETTLER, FRAU
German educator
Macksey--Book p72

KEULEN-DEELSTRA, ATJE
Netherlands skater
O'Neill--Women's p564

KEYES, EVELYN (1917-)
Amer. actress, dancer
Lamparski--What. (2) p80-81,
por.
Wilson--Holly. p39-42, por.
World--Who p238

KEYES, FRANCES PARKINSON
WHEELER (1885-1970)
Amer. novelist
Avenel--Comp. (2) p142
Banner--Women p15-16,52-53
Ehrlich--Oxford p280
Seymour-Smith--Novels p168
World--Who p15

KEYS, ANN ARMSTRONG (1845-
1910)
Irish-Amer. financier, noted
Illinois mother
Amer.--Mothers p163, por.

KEYS, MARTHA (1930-)
Amer. Congresswoman
Miller--Fishbait p117
Woman's Almanac p476

KEYSERLING, MARY DUBLIN (fl.
1930's-1940's)
Amer. economic analyst,
government official
O'Neill--Women's p288,330,337

KHAIRI, ABLA ADEL (1960-)
Egyptian swimmer
McWhirter--Guinness p146
O'Neill--Women's p586

KHALAFALLA, AIDA (fl. 1970's)
Amer. biophysicist
Seed--Saturday's p83-86, por.

KHALED, LEILA (fl. 1970's)
Palestinian hijacker
Macksey--Book p136

KHE-TAGUROVA, TAMARA
Russian economist
O'Neill--Women's p59

KHOLODNAYA, VERA
Russian actress, ballet dancer
Macksey--Book p235

KHOMYAKOVA, VALERIA L. (fl.
1940's-1970's)
Russian aviatrix, (army pilot)
O'Neill--Women's p550

KHOUREY, NADIA EL
Lebanese hotel owner,
manager, bank executive,
business woman
Macksey--Book p176

KHRISTOVA, IVANKA (fl. 1970's)
Bulgarian track and field
athlete
O'Neill--Women's p579

KIBBEE, LOIS
Amer. radio, TV actress
Scheuer--Tel. p263

KICK-IS-OM-LO SEALTH
See ANGELINE

KIDDER, MARGOT (1948-)
Canadian-Amer. actress
Hirschhorn--Rating p212, por.

KIDDER, PRISCILLA (fl. 1930's-
1970's)
Amer. fashion designer
O'Neill--Women's p260

KIEFFER, ELIZABETH CLARKE
(1899-)
Amer. genealogical re-
searcher, writer
Meyer--Who's p116

KIERA, ESTHER (1530-)
Jewish leader
Henry--Written p14,138,150-
153

KIES, MARGARET
See LINDSAY, MARGARET

KIES, MARY DIXON (c1752-)
Amer. pioneer inventor
Sherr--American p34

KIESLER, HEDWIG EVA MARIA
See LAMARR, HEDY

"KIKI DEE"
See DEE, KIKI

"KIKI OF MONTPARNASSE"
(PRIN, MARIE)
French artist's model
Book--Lists (1) p193-194

KILGALLEN, DOROTHY (1913-1965)

Amer. journalist, columnist,
TV personality
Marzolf--Up p58-59
O'Neill--Women's p445-446

KILGORE, CARRIE BURNHAM
(1836/1838-1909)
Amer., noted Vermont mother,
first balloon passenger, lawyer, feminist
Amer.--Mothers p541
James--Notable (2) p329-330

KILGORE, MARGARET (fl. 1970's)
Amer. war correspondent
Marzolf--Up p87

KILIUS, MARIKA (fl. 1960's)
German skater
Assoc. Press--Pursuit p209,227,
249

KILLGORE, NETTIE HICKS (1867-)
Amer. historian, author, noted
Arkansas mother
Amer.--Mothers p43, por.

KILLIGREW, ANNE (1660-1685)
English poet, painter
Bernikow--World p78-79
Fine--Women p69-70
Macksey--Book p198

KILLION, JANE (fl. 1970's)
Amer. track and field athlete
Lichtenstein--Mach. p37-38

KILMANNSEGGE, CHARLOTTE VON
(1675-1725)
German, mistress of British
King George I
Macksey--Book p97

KILMER, ANNIE D. (fl. 1970's)
Amer. professor, Assyriologist
O'Neill--Women's p419-420

KIM, NELLI (1957-)
Russian gymnast
Assoc. Press--Pursuit p333, por.
McWhirter--Guinness p84, por.
Woman's Almanac p423

KIMBALL, ALICE MARY (fl. 1910's)
Amer. journalist, poet
Showalter--These p52, por.

KIMBALL, ELLEN SAUNDERS
Amer. Mormon pioneer
Sherr--American p226

KIMBALL, INEZ B. (fl. 1940's)
Amer. national Girl Scouts
radio and public relations
director
Women--Radio p9

KIMBALL, ISABEL MOORE
Amer. sculptor
Sherr--American p123

KIMBRELL, MARKETA (1928-)
Czechoslovakian-Amer.
actress
Walker--Women p47-61, por.

KIMBROUGH, EMILY (1899-)
Amer. author
Ehrlich--Oxford, see index
p456

KIMMEL, CAROL KARRAKER
(1917-)
Amer. public school music
teacher, noted Illinois
mother
Amer.--Mothers p170, por.

KIMMEL, MARCIA (fl. 1970's)
Amer. artist
Women's--Female p106

KINAU, HIGH CHIEFTESS (1805-
1839)
Amer., noted Hawaii
mother, chieftess
Amer.--Mothers p141, por.

KINCAID, NANCY (fl. 1970's)
Amer. mountain woman
Kahn--Hill. p198-211, por.

KINDRED, ANNA D. DERSHEIMER
(1856-1937)
Amer. social reformer,
noted North Dakota mother
Amer.--Mothers p415, por.

KING, ALBERTA CHRISTINE
("MAMMA") WILLIAMS
(1904-1974)
Amer., mother of Martin
Luther King
Diagram--Mothers p134-135, por.

KING, ALICE (1839-1894)
English novelist
Showlater--Lit. p334

KING, ANNE
English, mother of Captain
James King
Ware--Meet p78

KING, BILLIE JEAN (1943-)
Amer. tennis player
Anderson--People p232-233
Diamonstein--Open p244-247, por.
Dunlap--Calif. p109, por.
Gilbert--Part. p169-175, por.
Hollander--100 p7,112-116, por.
Jacobs--Modern p99-119, por.
Kostman--20th p168-178, por.
Kulkin--Her p164-166
Lichtenstein--Mach., see index
p362
McHenry--Liberty's p225-226
McWhirter--Guinness p149-152,
156,158,160, por.
100--Greatest (1) p30, por.
O'Neill--Women's p260,556-557,
569,582-583, por.
Pachter--Champ. p164-165, por.
People--Best p62-63, por.
People's Almanac (1) p1188
Ryan-Sports p64-87, por.
Sabin--Women p3-23, por.
Sochen--Herstory p402, por.
Stambler--Women p34-36, por.
Sullivan--Queens p34-53, por.
Who Did What p180
Woman's Almanac p416-417, por.
World--Who p216

KING, CAMMIE
Amer. child actress
Lamparski--What. (8) p34-35,
por.

KING, CAROL WEISS (1895-1952)
Amer. lawyer
McHenry--Liberty's p226
Sicherman--Notable p397-398

KING, CAROLE KLEIN (1941-)
Amer. singer, songwriter
Anderson--People p233-234, por.
Claghorn--Biog. p253
Cur. Biog. '74 p201-203, por.
Simon--Best p318, por.
Woman's Almanac p295
World--Who p269

KING, CORETTA SCOTT (1927-)
   Amer. Civil Rights leader,
   singer, activist, writer
   Clark--Leading p206-209
   Cur. Biog. '69 p239-241, por.
   Diamonstein--Open p248-254, por.
   Gilfond--Heroines p128-133, por.
   Kulkin--Her p166-167
   100--Greatest (1) p91, por.
   O'Neill--Women's p700-701
   Woman's Almanac p384-385
   World--Who p189

KING, DEBBIE (fl. 1970's)
   Amer. agriculturist
   O'Neill--Women's p28

KING, ELIZABETH (1) (-1780)
   Amer. colonial physician
   Williams--Demeter's p173

KING, ELIZABETH (2) (c1889-
   1973)
   Amer. reporter, (Congressional Press Gallery)
   Marzolf--Up p51

KING, EVELYN "CHAMPAGNE"
   (c1960-)
   Glassman--Year '79 p120,122,
   por.

KING, GRACE ELIZABETH (1852/
   1853-1932)
   Amer. author, historian
   James--Notable (2) p331-332
   Sherr--American p86

KING, HELEN L. (1925-)
   Amer. genealogical research-
   er, author, editor
   Meyer--Who's p116-117

KING, HENRIETTA MARIA MORSE
   CHAMBERLAIN (1832-1925)
   Amer. rancher, cattlewoman
   Bird--Enterprising p132-136,138
   World--Who p200

KING, JEANETTE (c1930-)
   Amer., wife of Alan King
   Funt--Are p217-227, por.

KING, JESSIE MARION (1875-1949)
   Scottish watercolorist, illus-
   trator, bookbinder
   Callen--Women p158,196,206,223

KING, JULIE RIVE
   See RIVE-KING, JULIE

KING, LIDA SHAW (1868-1932)
   Amer. classical scholar, col-
   lege administrator
   James--Notable (2) p332-334

KING, LIZZIE (-1880)
   English-Amer. saloonkeeper
   Sherr--American p56

KING, LOUISA BOYD YEOMANS
   (1863-1948)
   Amer. writer on gardening
   James--Notable (2) p334-335
   O'Neill--Women's p134

KING, MARGARET (fl. 1970's)
   Amer. cab driver
   Seed--Saturday's p104-107, por.

KING, MARGUERITE COOPER
   Amer. government official,
   feminist
   O'Neill--Women's p92-93

KING, MARIS
   Australian diplomat
   O'Neill--Women's p62

KING, MARTHA EHEART (1923-)
   Amer. genealogical researcher,
   writer, editor
   Meyer--Who's p117

KING, MARY (fl. 1950's)
   Amer. feminist
   Berkin--Women p402-403

KING, MAXINE ("MICKI") (1943/
   1945-)
   Amer. diver
   Hollander--100 p89,96-97,142,
   por.
   Jacobs--Modern p36-51, por.
   Ryan--Sports p130-131
   Sabin--Women p132-150, por.
   Stambler--Women p120-131, por.
   Woman's Almanac p431, por.

KING, MORGANA (1930-)
   Amer. singer, actress
   Claghorn--Biog. p254
   Claghorn--Jazz p170

KING, MURIEL (c1901-1977)

Amer. fashion designer
Cur. Biog. '77 p466-467

KING, PATRICIA MILLER (fl.
1970's)
Amer. library director
O'Neill--Women's p431

KING, SUSAN
Amer. speculator, philan-
thropist
Bird--Enterprising p85-87

KING, TEDDI (-1977)
Amer. singer
Balliett--Amer. p1,5-10

KING SISTERS
Amer. singers
Simon--Big p235-236, por.

KINGSBURY, MARTHA
Amer. art professor
Women's--Female p115

KINGSBURY, SUSAN MYRA
(1870-1949)
Amer. social investigator,
educator
James--Notable (2) p335-336

KINGSFORD, ANNE BONUS
(1846-1888)
English antivivisectionist
People's Almanac (3) p647-649,
por.

KINGSFORD, FLORENCE (fl.
1890's)
British illuminator, bookbinder
Callen--Women p183,186,224

KINGSLEY, ELIZABETH SEELMAN
(c1872-1957)
Amer. puzzle expert
O'Neill--Women's p748

KINGSLEY, MARY (1852-1931)
English novelist
Showalter--Lit. p339

KINGSLEY, MARY HENRIETTA
(1862-1900)
English writer, traveller,
explorer
Hamalian--Ladies p229-249

Jones--Rutledge p433
Longford--Eminent p205-226, por.
Macksey--Book p239-240, por.
Showalter--Lit. p342

KINGSMILL, ANNE, LADY
WINCHILSEA (1661-1720)
English poet
Horner--English p25 (and note)

KINGSTON, MAXINE HONG (1940-)
Chinese-Amer. writer
Fisher--Third px, 460

KINKADE, KEBRINA
Amer. psychic
People's Almanac (2) p6

KINMONT, JILL (1937/1938-)
Amer. skier, educator
Kulkin--Her p167-168
Woman's Almanac p432

KINNEBERG, SALLY (fl. 1970's)
Amer. farm business woman
O'Neill--Women's p13-14

KINNEY, BELLE
Amer. sculptor
Sherr--American p38,126,219

KINNEY, ELIZABETH CLEMENTINE
DODGE STEDMAN (1810-1889)
Amer. hymnist
Claghorn--Biog. p254

KINNEY, ESI SYLVIA (fl. 1960's-
1970's)
Amer. ethnomusicologist
Innis--Profiles p34-35, por.

KINNEY, NARCISSA WHITE (-1901)
Amer. temperance worker,
reformer
Sherr--American p194

KINNEY, STEPHANIE SMITH (fl.
1970's)
Amer. government official
O'Neill--Women's p97

KINSEY, MARGARET B. (1920-)
Amer. genealogical researcher,
author
Meyer--Who's p177

KINSKI, NASTASSJA (1961-)

W. Ger. actress
Cur. Biog. '84 p206-210, por.
Hirschhorn--Rating p213, por.

KINSKY, COUNTESS
See SUTTNER, BERTHA,
BARONESS VON

KINTORE, HELENA
See ZIMMERMAN, HELENA,
DUCHESS OF MANCHESTER

KINZIE, JULIETTE AUGUSTA
MAGILL (1806-1870)
Amer. pioneer wife, in-
formal historian of North-
west, novelist
James--Notable (2) p336-337
McHenry--Liberty's p226
Sherr--American p250

KIRCHEVA, ELENA YANKOVA
See SNEZHINA, ELENA

KIRCHWEY, FREDA (1893-1976)
Amer. editor, publisher
Cur. Biog. '76 p470
McHenry--Liberty's p227
O'Neill--Women's p472-473
Sochen--Herstory p293,316,
319-321, por.
Sochen--Movers p134-140,213-
220

KIRK, CLARIE McKAY (1928-)
Amer. genealogical research-
er, writer
Meyer--Who's p117

KIRKLAND, CAROLINE MATILDA
STANSBURY (1801-1864)
Amer. author, editor,
journalist
James--Notable (2) p337-339
McHenry--Liberty's p227
Sherr--American p119

KIRKLAND, GELSEY (1952/1954-)
Amer. ballet dancer
Cur. Biog. '75 p221-224, por.
100--Greatest (1) p24, por.
O'Neill--Women's p641,644
People--Best p141, por.

KIRKLAND, SALLY
Amer. magazine fashion
editor
Hamblin--That p161-166

KIRKPATRICK, HELEN PAULL
(1909-)
Amer. journalist, foreign
correspondent
Marzolf--Up p70
O'Neill--Women's p443-444, por.

KIRKPATRICK, JEANE DUANE
JORDAN (1926-)
Amer. United Nations repre-
sentative
Cur. Biog. '81 p255-259, por.

KIRKSEY, LUCILE HICKS (1904-)
Amer. civic educator, religious
worker, noted Kentucky mother
Amer.--Mothers p218-219, por.

KIRKUS, VIRGINIA (1893-1980)
Amer. literary critic, author
Cur. Biog. '80 p457
McHenry--Liberty's p227-228

KIRSHNER, PEG
Amer. aviatrix, army flier
Keil--Those p293, por.

KIRSTEN, DOROTHY (1917/1919-)
Amer. opera singer
Claghorn--Biog. p255
McHenry--Liberty's p228

KIRSZENSTEIN-SZEWINSKA, IRENA
See SZEWINSKA, IRENA

KISCH, GLORIA (fl. 1970's)
Amer. sculptor
Women's--Female p91

KISKADDEN, MAUDE
See ADAMS, MAUDE

KISMARIC, CAROLINE (fl. 1970's)
Amer. photography editor
O'Neill--Women's p482

KISTIAKOWSKY, VERA
Amer. physicist, professor
O'Neill--Women's p182-183

KISTLER, RUTH (fl. 1950's)
Amer., oldest mother
Macksey--Book p11

KITCHELL, ALMA (fl. 1940's)
Amer. radio program con-
ductor
Women--Radio p10

KITT, EARTHA MAE (1928-   )
Amer. singer, dancer,
actress
Anderson--People p236-237
Claghorn--Biog. p255
People's Almanac (1) p1435-1437
World--Who p269

KITT, EDITH STRATTON (1878-   )
Amer. Western pioneer, sec-
retary, historical society
Fischer--Let p283-297
Sherr--American p9

KITTLOVA, EMMA
See DESTINN, (EMMY) EMILY
KITTI

KITTREDGE, CHARMIAN
Amer., wife of Jack London
Starr--Amer. p219,230-232,
235

KIZER, CAROLYN (1925-   )
Amer. poet
Avenel--Comp. (2) p143
Chester--Rising p145-152, por.
Webber--Woman p92-96

KLABEN, HELEN
Amer. writer
Hamblin--That p93-95,181

KLAFSKY, KATHARINA (1855-
1896)
Hungarian opera singer
Macksey--Book p215

KLAPPER, CAROL
Amer. magazine executive,
publisher
O'Neill--Women's p488

KLAUSNER, MARGOT (fl. 1930's)
Israeli filmmaker
Smith--Movies p125-126

KLAVUN, BETTY (1916-   )
Amer. artist
Munro--Originals p456-461,
por.

KLEEGMAN, SOPHIE JOSEPHINE
(1900/1901-1971)
Russian-Amer. physician,
obstetrician, gynecologist
Neidle--America's p206
Sicherman--Notable p399-400

KLEIN, ANNE (1923-1974)
Amer. fashion designer
O'Neill--Women's p245,247-249,254

KLEIN, EVELYN KAYE (fl. 1930's-
1950's)
Amer. violinist, radio performer
Lamparski--What. (4) p142-143,
por.
Women--Radio p12

KLEIN, HELENA (1885-   )
Swedish physician
Hellstedt--Women p20-22, por.

KLEIN, JO-ANN LOUISE (fl. 1970's)
Amer. heroine
O'Neill--Women's p734

KLEIN, LIESELOTTE (fl. 1960's-
1970's)
French-German civil servant
Macksey--Book p131

KLEIN, MARGARET (fl. 1960's-
1970's)
Amer. financial services editor
O'Neill--Women's p470

KLEIN, MELANIE (1882-1960)
Austrian psychoanalist
O'Neill--Women's p414
Who Did What p182
Wintle--Makers p277-278, #248

KLEIN, MIRIAM (1937-   )
Swiss singer
Claghorn--Jazz p172

KLEINOVA, MARIA V. (fl. 1950's)
Russian oceanographer
Land--New p19-20

KLIMA, M. (fl. 1900's)
Austrian tennis player
McWhirter--Guinness p152

KLINGENSMITH, FLORENCE (c1905-
1931)
Amer. aviatrix
Boase--Sky's p120-121, por.

KLINGMAN, ELOISE CLARK (1908-   )
Amer. genealogical researcher
Meyer--Who's p117

KLINK, GERTRUD SCHOTZ (1902-   )

German leader
Woman's Almanac p449

"KLONDIKE KATE" (c1881-1957)
Amer., Alaskan "gold rush
belle"
Jones--Women (1) p105-106
Sherr--American p194

KLOPSTOCK, MRS. (-1758)
German writer
Horner--English p37 (and note)

KLOTZ, MARY
See CLARKE, MAE

KLUMPKE, ANNA ELIZABETH
(1856-1942)
Amer. painter, writer
Fine--Women p118-120
Petersen--Women p76-78

KNACHE, CHRISTIANA (fl. 1970's)
East German swimmer
McWhirter--Guinness p22, por.

KNAPP, EVELYN (1908-)
Amer. actress
Springer--They p151,306, por.

KNAPP, PHOEBE PALMER (1839-
1908)
Polish composer
Claghorn--Biog. p257

KNAPPEN, BETTY COMPTON
See COMPTON, BETTY

KNAUER, VIRGINIA HARRINGTON
WRIGHT (1915-)
Amer. government official
Cur. Biog. '70 p228-231, por.
Schoenebaum--Prof. p362-363

KNECHTGES, DORIS (fl. 1950's)
Amer. bowler
McWhirter--Guinness p44

KNEF, HILDEGARD
See NEFF, HILDEGARD

KNEISEL, MARIANNE (1897-1972)
Amer. violinist, patron
Claghorn--Biog. p257

KNEPP, MARY (-1677)
English actress
Macksey--Book p224

KNEVELS, GERTRUDE (1881-1962)
Amer. novelist
Ehrlich--Oxford p100,195

KNIBBERGEN, CATHERINA VAN (fl.
1850's)
Netherlands artist
Fine--Women p36

KNICKERBOCKER, SUZY
See MEHLE, AILEEN

KNIGHT, FANNY (fl. 1850's)
Amer. diarist
Earnest--American p189-190

KNIGHT, FRANCES GLADYS (c1905-)
Amer. government official
O'Neill--Women's p91-92

KNIGHT, GLADYS MARIA (1944-)
Amer. singer
Anderson--People p239-240, por.
Claghorn--Biog. p257
Simon--Best p324-325, por.
World--Who p269

KNIGHT, JILL
British Parliament member
Vallance--Women p80,91,140,143

KNIGHT, KITTY
Amer. Revolutionary War belle,
beauty, heroine
Sherr--American p95

KNIGHT, LAURA JOHNSON, DAME
(1877-1970)
British sculptor, painter
Macksey--Book p208, por.

KNIGHT, MARGARET E. (1838-1914)
Amer. inventor
Book--Lists (2) p233-234
James--Notable (2) p339-340
McHenry--Liberty's p228
Macksey--Book p165
Marlowe--Great p126-128, por.
Sherr--American p105
Woman's Almanac p371

KNIGHT, MARY WORRELL (c1759-
1849)
Amer. patriot, Revolutionary
War heroine
Meyer--Petticoat p101

KNIGHT, SARAH KEMBLE (1666-1727)

SEMENOVNA (1905-)
Russian sculptor
Mandel--Soviet p142
Women's--Female p3, supp.

KOCH, BODIL (fl. 1950's-1960's)
Danish clergyman
O'Neill--Women's p57

KOCH, ILSE (1907-1967)
German, accused war
criminal
Macksey--Book p136

KOCHAWSKA, FRAXEDE
MARCELLINE
See SEMBRICH(K), MARCELLA

KOEDT, ANNE (fl. 1960's)
Amer. feminist, writer,
artist
Sochen--Movers p257,263-264

KOEHLER, FLORENCE (1861-1944)
Amer. artist-craftswoman,
designer, jeweller
Callen--Women p224

KOEHN, DARYL
Amer. Rhodes Scholar
O'Neill--Women's p435, por.

KOENIG, MARIE ANDRIENNE
See MURRAY, MAE

KOENIGIN, MEINE
See REDEKER, LOUISE

KOERBER, LEILA VON
See DRESSLER, MARIE

KOERT-KRONOLD, SELMA
See KRONOLD, SELMA

KOESTER, A.J. (fl. 1910's)
Amer. bowler
McWhirter--Guinness p44

KOHEN, GUTEL (c1627-)
Czechoslovakian-Jewish
printer
Henry--Written p118

KOHL, MARGUERITE C.
Amer. business executive,
publicist
O'Neill--Women's p522

KOHLER, RUTH (-1953)
Amer. journalist, editor,
noted Wisconsin mother
Amer.--Mothers p589-590, por.
Sherr--American p248

KOHLMEYER, IDA (1912-)
Amer. painter, printmaker
Women's--Female p47

KOHUT, REBEKAH BETTELHEIM
(1864-1951)
Amer. social welfare leader,
lecturer, author
Baum--Jewish p34-36,49,51-52,
178
Sicherman--Notable p403-405

KOK, AAGJE (fl. 1960's)
Netherlands swimmer
McWhirter--Guinness p135, por.

KOKES, CAROL L. (fl. 1970's)
Amer. aviatrix, naval officer
O'Neill--Women's p544

KOLB, BARBARA ANNE (1939-)
Amer. composer, conductor
Jablonski--Ency. p532
LePage--Women p116-132, por.

KOLIN, MALA
See RUBINSTEIN, MALA

KOLLONTAY, (ALEXANDRA)
ALEKSANDRA MIKHAILOVNA
(1872-1952)
Russian cabinet minister,
foreign ambassador, feminist
Macksey--Book p35
Mandel--Soviet, see index p343
Woman's Almanac p388

KOLLWITZ, KÄTHE (KAETHE)
SCHMIDT (1867-1945)
German graphic artist, painter,
sculptor
Fine--Women p150-155, por.
Harris--Women p59,65-67,242,
263-265,273,275-276,354, por.
Jones--Rutledge p438
Kronenberger--Atlan. p436
Kulkin--Her p168-169
Macksey--Book p207-208
Moffat--Revel. p237-252
Munsterberg--Hist. p109,111-115,
por.

O'Neill--Women's p596-598
Petersen--Women p116-119, por.
Sparrow--Women p286,302
Tufts--Our p178-187, por.
Woman's Almanac p222-223
Women's--Female p10

KOLTOI, ANNA (1891-1944)
Hungarian martyr, politician,
labor leader
Partington--Who's p216-217

KOMARKOVA, VERA
Amer. mountain climber,
ecologist
Lichtenstien--Mach. p17,26,
28-30

KOMAROVA, DOMNA (fl. 1970's)
Russian political leader
Mandel--Soviet p290-292

KOMAROVSKY, MIRRA (1906-)
Russian-Amer. sociologist,
feminist, educator
Banner--Women p214,218,221
O'Neill--Women's p419
Sochen--Herstory p347-348
Sochen--Movers p193-197,239

KOMER, ODESSA (1925-)
Amer. labor union leader
O'Neill--Women's p308,315

KOMISSAROVA, O. (fl. 1960's)
Russian parachutist
Macksey--Book p252

KONGAS, LEMBI (fl. 1970's)
Amer. anthropologist,
agricultural research worker
O'Neill--Women's p10

KONIE, GWENDOLINE (1938-)
African (Zambia) civil
servant, foreign service
diplomat, UN delegate
Crane--Ms. p96-111, por.

KÖNIG, BARBARA (1925-)
Bohemian short story
writer, novelist
Herrmann--Ger. p6,72

KONNER, JOAN (1931-)
Amer. TV executive
Scheuer--Tel. p269

KONOPNICKA, MARIA WASILOWSKA
(1842-1910)
Polish poet, short story writer
Partington--Who's p217-218

KOONING, ELAINE DE (1920-)
Amer. artist
Munro--Originals p248-260, por.

KOONTZ, ELIZABETH DUNCAN
(1919-)
Amer. educator, government
official
Cur. Biog. '69 p244-246, por.
Diamonstein--Open p255-259, por.
Gilbert--Part. p129-133, por.
Macksey--Book p131
O'Neill--Women's p338
Signif.--Amer. p67, por.

KOOPMAN, TOTO (fl. 1930's-1970's)
Japanese-French model
Keenan--Women p11,138,143, por.

KOPECHNE, MARY JO (c1941-1969)
Amer. secretary
Book--Lists (2) p462
People's Almanac (1) p255

KOPELAN, AMY DORN (1951-)
Amer. TV director
Scheuer--Tel. p269-270

KOPLOVITZ, KAY (1945-)
Amer. cable TV executive
Scheuer--Tel. p270, por.

KOPP, LILLIAN (c1909-1978)
Amer., first person to be
buried in a pet cemetery
Felton--Famous p172

KOPPLE, BARBARA J. (1946-)
Amer. film producer, director
O'Neill--Women's p669-670
Smith--Movies p186-187,253, por.

KOR, SEREFNUR
Turkish member NATO congress
of women officers
O'Neill--Women's p552

KORA (CALLIRHOE) (c600 B.C.)
Greek pioneer sculptor
Macksey--Book p194
Munsterberg--Hist. p12
Sparrow--Women p21

KORBUT, OLGA (1955-)
  Russian gymnast
  Assoc. Press--Pursuit p314-315,
    333, por.
  Cur. Biog. '73 p228-230, por.
  Hollander--100 p53,55-57, por.
  Kulkin--Her p169-171
  McWhirter--Guinness p82-83,
    por.
  Mandel--Soviet p154,157-158
  O'Neill--Women's p561-562, por.
  Woman's Almanac p423-424, por.
  World--Who p216

KORDA, REVA
  Amer. advertising executive
  Adams--Women p22,94-96,97-98,
    120,188
  O'Neill--Women's p521

KORDAY, HELEN M. (fl. 1940's)
  Amer. radio employment
    manager
  Women--Radio p14-15

KORĒ
  See PERSEPHONE

KOREN, ELSE ELISABETH (1832-
    1918)
  Norwegian-Amer. pioneer
  Neidle--America's p95-96

KORJUS, MILIZA (1900/1912-1980)
  Polish opera singer, actress
  Lamparski--What. (5) p152-153,
    por.
  Springer--They p152,306, por.

KORMAN, NADINE (fl. 1970's)
  Amer. bakery company
    executive
  O'Neill--Women's p139

KORNBLUH, JOYCE (fl. 1940's-
    1970's)
  Amer. labor leader
  O'Neill--Women's p327

KORNMAN, MARY
  Amer. child actress
  Edelson--Kids p55-56,58,60,
    por.

KORRIS, RISA (fl. 1970's)
  Amer. TV camerawoman,
    photographer
  O'Neill--Women's p501

KORSMO, GRETE PRYTZ (1917-)
  Norwegian designer, silver-
    smith
  O'Neill--Women's p274

KOSERSKY, RENA (fl. 1970's)
  Amer. music editor, filmmaker
  Smith--Movies p187-188,254

KOSKOW (KOSOW), SOPHIA
  See SIDNEY, SYLVIA

KOSMODEMYANSKAY(I)A, ZOYA
    ANATOLYEVNA (1923-1941)
  Russian heroine, martyr,
    partisan
  Mandel--Soviet p151

KOSMOWSKA, IRENA (IRENE)
    (1879-1945)
  Polish cabinet minister
  Macksey--Book p40-41
  O'Neill--Women's p57

KOULAKOVA, GALINA (1942-)
  Russian skier
  McWhirter--Guinness p117, por.

KOULSOUM, OUM (-1976)
  Egyptian singer, artist
  O'Neill--Women's p646

KOUPAL, JOYCE (fl. 1970's)
  Amer. environmentalist,
    activist
  O'Neill--Women's p730

KOUTIFARI, LINA (fl. 1970's)
  Greek government official
  O'Neill--Women's p555

KOVALEVSKAIA, ZINAIDA MIKHAIL-
    OVNA (1902-)
  Russian painter
  Women's--Female p3, supp.

KOVALEVSKI(Y), SONYA (SOFIE)
    (1850-1891)
  Russian mathematician, author
  Macksey--Book p152
  Mandel--Soviet p24-25, por.
  Marlowe--Great p142-146, por.
  Osen--Women p117-140, por.

KOVARSKAYA, LYDIA (1909-)
  Russian feminist, mill manager
  Mandel--Soviet p92-93

KOVNATOR, RACHEL (fl. 1910's)
Russian feminist, labor
organizer
Mandel--Soviet p56-58

KOVRIGA, MARIA DMITRIEVNA
(fl. 1930's)
Russian administrator,
physician
Macksey--Book p131

KOZLOFF, JOYCE (fl. 1970's)
Amer. painter
Women's--Female p47

KOZLOVA, OLYMPIADA (fl.
1910's-1950's)
Russian president, business
school
Mandel--Soviet p86-87

KRAL, IRENE (1932-)
Amer. singer
Claghorn--Biog. p259
Claghorn--Jazz p173

KRALOVA, HANA (fl. 1960's)
Czechoslovakian textile
designer
O'Neill--Women's p126

KRAMAR, PIRO
Amer. physician, mountain
climber
Lichtenstein--Mach. p28-29

KRAMER, ETEL THEA (fl. 1970's)
Amer. architect
O'Neill--Women's p612

KRAMER, LOUISE (fl. 1970's)
Amer. artist
Women's--Female p106-107

KRAMER, MARJORIE (fl. 1970's)
Amer. artist
Women's--Female p107

KRANDIEVSKAIA, NADEZHA
VASILEVNA (1891-)
Russian sculptor
Women's--Female p2, supp.

KRANTZ, JUDITH (1928-)
Amer. author
Cur. Biog. '82 p205-208,
por.

KRASNER, LEE (1908-1984)
Amer. painter
Cur. Biog. '74 p215-218, por.
Cur. Biog. '84 p474
Fine--Women p208-210,217
Fowler--Art p146
Harris--Women p64,332-333,361
Henkes--Eight p43-46,60
Munro--Originals p100-119, por.
Nemser--Convers. p81-111,361-
362, por.
O'Neill--Women's p596,601-602,
616
Women's--Female p47

KRAUS, LILI (1905/1908-)
Hungarian-British pianist,
professor
Cur. Biog. '75 p227-230, por.
O'Neill--Women's p631

KRAUS-BOELTE, MARIA (1836-1918)
German-Amer. kindergarten
educator
James--Notable (2) p346-348
McHenry--Liberty's p229

KRAUSE, ALVINA (c1893-1981)
Amer. acting teacher
Chinoy--Women p208-211, por.

KREAMER, MARY ELIZABETH,
SISTER (fl. 1960's)
Amer. missionary
O'Neill--Women's p391

KREBS, MARY TOMLINSON
See MAIN, MARJORIE

KREBS, NATHALIE (1895-)
Danish pioneer ceramicist
O'Neill--Women's p270

KREFETZ, BARBARA (fl. 1970's)
Amer. TV director
Kelver--Women p48-51,61,93,109,
por.

KREFT, GALINA (fl. 1970's)
Russian canoeist
McWhirter--Guinness p47

KREIN, CATHY (fl. 1970's)
Amer. TV educational director,
producer
Marzolf--Up p181-182

KREMENTZ, JILL (1940-)
Amer. photographer, author
McCullough--People p102-104

KREMER, PATI SREDNITSKY
(1867-1943)
German pioneer, revolutionary
Baum--Jewish p78-80

KREPS, JUANITA MORRIS (1921-)
Amer. government official,
economist
Cur. Biog. '77 p259-261, por.
Lamson--In p37-68, por.
McHenry--Liberty's p229-230
O'Neill--Women's p82,409-410,
por.
Woman's Almanac p476-477

KREY, LAURA (1890-)
Amer. author
Ehrlich--Oxford p374

KRISTENSEN, RUTH (fl. 1970's)
Danish labor leader
O'Neill--Women's p320

KROC, JOAN BEVERLY
Amer. corporation head,
millionaire
Forbes--400 ('84) p90

KROEGER, ALICE BERTHA
(1864-1909)
Amer. pioneer librarian,
library school director
James--Notable (2) p348-349

KROENCKE, MARY
Amer. TV anchor
Scheuer--Tel. p273

KROESEN, (MISS) J.H. (fl.
1950's)
Netherlands judge
Macksey--Book p128

KROG, KARIN (1937-)
Norwegian singer
Claghorn--Jazz p174

KRONOLD, SELMA (1861/1866-
1920)
Polish-Amer. opera singer
Claghorn--Biog. p260
James--Notable (2) p349-
350

KROSS, ANNA MOSKOWITZ (1891-
1979)
Russian-Amer. government
official, judge, feminist
Cur. Biog. '79 p466

KRÜDENER, BARBARA JULIANE
VON VIETINGHOFF, BARO-
NESS (1764-1824)
Russian-German-French
novelist, mystic
Moers--Literary p296

KRUGER, ALMA (1871-1960)
Amer. actress
Springer--They p152,306, por.

KRÜGER, AUGUSTA (fl. 1810's)
German army "secret sub-
altern"
Macksey--Book p54

KRUGER, BARBARA (fl. 1970's)
Amer. textile artist
Women's--Female p99

KRUPP VON BOHIEN UND HALBACH,
BERTHA (1886-1957)
German, wife of Friedrich
Alfred Krupp
Jones--Rutledge p441

KRUPSAK, MARY ANN(E) (1932-)
Amer. lawyer, state politician
Cur. Biog. '75 p230-232, por.
Greenebaum--Politics p138-139
100--Greatest (1) p55, por.
O'Neill--Women's p43-44,77
Schoenebaum--Prof. p366-368

KRUPSKAYA, NADEZHDA KONSTAN-
TINOVA (1869-1939)
Russian social worker, educa-
tor, revolutionary, (wife of
Lenin)
Macksey--Book p73-74, por.
Mandel--Soviet p31-33,49-50, por.
World--Who p189

KRUSELL, CYNTHIA HAGAR
(1929-)
Amer. genealogical researcher,
author
Meyer--Who's p118

KRYSINKA, MARIE
French symbolist, poet

Crosland--Women p27,86-
87

KRYSZAK, MARY OLSZEWSKI
(1875-1945)
Polish-Amer. leader, state
educator
James--Notable (2) p350-351

KSCHESSINSKA, MARHILDE
(1871-)
Russian ballet dancer
Migel--Ballerinas p270-271,
por.

KUAN TAO-SHENG (1262-1319)
Chinese painter, calligrapher
Petersen--Women p151-153

KÜBLER-ROSS, ELISABETH
(1926-)
Swiss-Amer. physician,
psychiatrist
Bowman--Medicine p42-47, por.
Cur. Biog. '80 p191-194, por.
Gilbert--Part. p265-273, por.
O'Neill--Women's p228-229
World--Who p106

KUCERA, ZDENKA (1916-)
Czechoslovakian-Amer.
librarian, genealogical
researcher, writer
Meyer--Who's p118

KUCK, LINDA (fl. 1970's)
Amer. 4-H scholarship
winner
O'Neill--Women's p20

KUDAKA, GERALDINE (1951-)
Hawaiian poet
Fisher--Third p x, 545

KUDERIKOVA, MARIE (1921-1943)
Czechoslovakian politician
Partington--Who's p233, por.

KUEHN, FRANCES (1943-)
Amer. artist
Miller--Lives p74-90

KUGLER, ANNA SARAH (1856-
1930)
Amer. medical missionary,
physician
James--Notable (2) p351-352
McHenry--Liberty's p230

KUH, KATHARINE (KATHERINE)
(c1904-)
Amer. magazine editor
Diamonstein--Open p260-264, por.

KUHAJEWSKI, GABRIELA (fl. 1970's)
Amer. TV film editor
Klever--Women p53-55,68-69,108,
por.

KUHLMAN, KATHRYN (1907/1910-
1967)
Amer. faith healer, evangelist
Cur. Biog. '74 p227-229, por.
Cur. Biog. '76 p470
O'Neill--Women's p400-401
Woman's Almanac p405, por.
World--Who p82

KUHN, IRENE CORBALLY (1900-)
Amer. journalist, columnist,
radio and TV broadcaster,
novelist
Marzolf--Up p65,141
O'Neill--Women's p494-495
Women--Radio p17

KUHN, LUCILLE R. (fl. 1950's-
1970's)
Amer. naval officer
O'Neill--Women's p547

KUHN, MARGARET E. ("MAGGIE")
(1905/1906-)
Amer. social reformer, founder,
Grey Panthers
Comfort--Good p141, por.
Cur. Biog. '78 p239-242, por.
Gilbert--Part. p103-109, por.
O'Neill--Women's p722, por.
Woman's Almanac p107
World--Who p189

KÜHN, (SUSIE) RUTH
German-Japanese spy
People's Almanac (1) p651

KULAKOVA, GALINA (fl. 1970's)
Russian skier
Assoc. Press--Pursuit p300,325
O'Neill--Women's p566

KUMIN, MAXINE WINOKUR (1925-)
Amer. poet, novelist, author
of children's books
Betts--Writers p50-53, por.
Chester--Rising p161-163, por.
World--Who p16

KUNG, SUJAN (early 12th Cent.)
Chinese painter
Petersen--Women p150-151

KUNHARDT, DOROTHY (1901-
1979)
Amer. author of children's
books, illustrator
O'Neill--Women's p692

K'UO CH'UN-CH'ING (fl. 1940's-
1950's)
Chinese soldier, male im-
personator
Book--Lists (1) p340

KUPILLAS, MARY MARTIN
(1912-)
Amer. genealogical researcher,
author
Meyer--Who's p118-119

KURISHIMA, SUMIKO (fl. 1900's)
Japanese actress
Macksey--Book p235

KURT, MELANIE (1880-1941)
Austrian opera singer,
violinist
Claghorn--Biog. p261
Tuggle, Golden p130-131, por.

KURTZ, SELMA (1874-1933)
Austrian opera singer
Tuggle--Golden p158-159, por.

KURTZ, SWOOSIE (1944-)
Amer. actress
Scheuer--Tel. p275

KUSCSIK, NINA (fl. 1970's)
Amer. track and field
athlete
Hollander--100 p7,139-140,
por.

KUSNER, KATHY (1940-)
Amer. equestrienne, jockey
Cur. Biog. '73 p232-234, por.
Hollander--100 p7,63-64, por.
McWhirter--Guinness p92
O'Neill--Women's p588
Ryan--Sports p28-45, por.

KUSSY, BELLA BLOCH (fl. 1860's)
German-Amer. milliner
Baum--Jewish p25-26

KUUSINEN, HERTTA (ELINA)
(1904-1974)
Finnish government official,
Communist leader
Cur. Biog. '74 p463

KUZNETSOVA, LARISA
Russian feminist, writer
Mandel--Soviet p205-208,212-213

KVAPILOVA, HANA KUBESOVA
(1860-1906/1907)
Czechoslovakian actress
Partington--Who's p236

KWALI, LADI (fl. 1950's)
Nigerian master potter
O'Neill--Women's p126-127

KYGER, JOANNE (1934-)
Amer. poet
Chester--Rising p223-227, por.

KYRK, HAZEL (1886-1957)
Amer. consumer economist
Sicherman--Notable p405-406

L

"L.E.L."
See LANDON, LETITIA ELIZABETH

LABANY
English midwife
Mead--Hist. p398

LaBARRE DE RAILLICOURT, MARIA
TERESA CANDELA Y SAPIEHA,
COMTESSE DE
French genealogical researcher,
author
Meyer--Who's p121

LABE, LOUISE CHARLIN PERRIN
(c1524-c1565)
French poet
Bree--Women p9,20-27,29
Crosland--Women p48-50
Moers--Literary p296
Taylor--Gener. p20-21

LABELLE, PATTI (1944-)
Amer. singer
World--Who p269

LABICHE, EMMELINE
Amer., inspiration for

"Evangeline"
Sherr--American p86, por.

LABILLE-GUIARD, ADELAIDE,
MADAME (1749-1803)
French painter
Fine--Women p45-48, por.
Harris--Women p36-37,40,42-
43,180,185-187,189,195,347
Munsterberg--Hist. p38,40-41,
por.
Parker--Old p28,32-33, fig. 20,
21, por.
Petersen--Women p55-58
Sparrow--Women p175-176,185,
188
Women's--Female p10

LABUDDE, WILHELMINE DIEFEN-
THAELER (1880-1955)
Amer. conservationist, noted
Wisconsin mother
Amer.--Mothers p585, por.

LACHAPELLE, MARIE-LOUISE
DUGES (1769-1821)
French midwife, medical
writer, physician
Marks--Women p67-68, por.
Mead--Hist. p497-501

LACHERT, HANNA (1944-)
Polish-Amer. violinist
Neidle--America's p249-250

LACKIE, ETHEL (fl. 1920's)
Amer. swimmer
Assoc. Press--Pursuit p100-
101, por.

LA COCK, JOANNE
See DRU, JOANNE

LACOMBE, ROSE (1765-c1796)
French feminist, Revolu-
tionist
Macksey--Book p79

LACY, RUBY (1922-)
Amer. genealogical re-
searcher, author
Meyer--Who's p122

LaDAME, MARY (c1885-)
Amer. government official
Ware--Beyond p148, see also
index p200

LADD, MRS. ALAN
See CAROL, SUE

LADD, CHERYL STOPPELMOOR
(1950/1951-)
Amer. TV actress, singer
Anderson--People p243, por.
People--Best p174, por.
Scheuer--Tel. p278
World--Who p238

LADD, KATE MACY (1863-1945)
Amer. philanthropist
James--Notable (2) p352-354

LADD-FRANKLIN, CHRISTINE
See FRANKLIN, CHRISTINE
LADD

LADENDORFF, MARCIA (1949-)
Amer. TV news anchor woman
Scheuer--Tel. p278-279, por.

LADEWIG, MARION
Amer. bowler
Hollander--100 p16-17, por.
People's Almanac (1) p1196

"LADY LINDY"
See EARHART, AMELIA

LADYNINA, MARINA (fl. 1930's)
Russian actress
Macksey--Book p235

LAFAYETTE, MARIE MADELEINE
PIOCHE DE LA VERGNE,
COMTESSE DE (1634-1692)
French novelist
Bree--Women p11-12,37
Crosland--Women p13,32,54-56,
235, por.
Jones--Rutledge p444
Kronenberger--Atlan. p439
Macksey--Book p181
Magill--Cycl. p614-615
Moers--Literary p296
Seymour-Smith--Novels p170, por.
Who Did What p185
World--Who p34

LAFFERTY, JANET
See BLAIR, JANET

LAFFORGUE, BRITT (fl. 1970's)
French skier
O'Neill--Women's p565

LA FLECHE, MARIE MARGUERITE
See MacKENZIE, GISELLE

LA FLESCHE, MARY GALE (1826-
1909)
Amer. Omaha Indian, noted
Nebraska mother
Amer.--Mothers p 331, por.

LA FLESCHE, SUSAN
See PICOTTE, SUSAN LA
FLESCHE

LA FLESCHE, SUSETTE
See TIBBLES, SUSETTE
"BRIGHT EYES" LA FLESCHE

LaFOLLETTE, BELLE CASE (1859-
1931)
Amer. suffragist, pacifist,
noted Wisconsin mother,
(wife of Robert M.
LaFollette)
Amer.--Mothers p 583-584, por.
James--Notable (2) p 356-358

LAFONTANT, JEWEL STRADFORD
(fl. 1970's)
Amer. lawyer, government
official
Seed--Saturday's p 135-139, por.
Swiger--Women p 83-100

LAFORET, CARMEN (fl. 1940's-
1950's)
Spanish novelist
Moers--Literary p 296

LaFORGE, MARGARET GETCHELL
(1841-1880)
Amer. department store
executive
Bird--Enterprising p 79-81
James--Notable (2) p 358
O'Neill--Women's p 509

LAGERLÖF, SELMA OTTINIANA
LOUISA (1858-1940)
Swedish novelist, poet,
short story writer
Jones--Rutledge p 444
Macksey--Book p 189, por.
O'Neill--Women's p 672
Opfell--Lady p 63-79
Seymour-Smith--Novels p 171
Seymour-Smith--Who's p 202-203
Who Did What p 186

Woman's Almanac p 253
World--Who p 40

LAGUE, LOUISE (c 1947-   )
Amer. columnist
Woman's Almanac p 277

LA GUERRE, ELISABETH-CLAUDE
JACQUET DE (1664/1665-1727)
French composer, harpsichord-
ist
Neuls-Bates--Women p xiv, 62-64

LAGUILLER, ARIETTE (c 1940-   )
French Marxist, labor leader
O'Neill--Women's p 321-322

LA HIFFE, ANN VERONICA
See CARROLL, NANCY

LAHOVARY, MARTHE
See BIBESCO, MARIE, PRINCESS

LAICH, KATHERINE (WHILHELMINA
SCHLEGEL) (1910-   )
Amer. librarian, educator,
organization official
Cur. Biog. '72 p 268-270, por.

LAIDLAW, HARRIET BURTON (1873-
1949)
Amer. suffragist, author,
teacher, lecturer, club leader
James--Notable (2) p 358-360

LAINE, CLEO (CLEMENTINE DINAH)
(1927-   )
English singer
Claghorn--Jazz p 176-177

LAING, DILYS BENNETT (1906-1960)
Welsh-Amer. poet, novelist
Bernikow--World p 323
Pearson--Who p 138

LAIRD, RUTH (fl. 1940's)
Amer. radio news reporter
Marzolf--Up p 138

LAIS (fl. c 100 A.D.)
Greek physician
Mead--Hist. p 57

LAISE, CAROL C. (fl. 1960's)
Amer. government official
O'Neill--Women's p 88, 94

LAKE, ANNA EASTON (-1899)
Amer. White House physician
O'Neill--Women's p210

LAKE, CLAUDE, pseud.
See BLIND, MATHILDE COHEN

LAKE, HARRIETTE
See SOTHERN, ANN

LAKE, LEONORA MARIE BARRY
See BARRY, LEONORA MARIE
KEARNEY

LAKE, "MOTHER"
See BARRY, LEONORA MARIE
KEARNEY

LAKE, VERONICA (1919-1973)
Amer. actress
Hirschhorn--Rating p215-216,
por.
Keenan--Women p80-81,85, por.
Keylin--Hollywood p165, por.
Lamparski--What. (8) p168-169,
por.
Shipman--Gold. p326-327, por.
World--Who p238

LAKEY, ALICE (1857-1935)
Amer. lobbyist, clubwoman
Bird--Enterprising p162-164
James--Notable (2) p360-361
O'Neill--Women's p111

LALA (fl. 1st Cent. B.C.)
Roman artist
Macksey--Book p194
Sparrow--Women p21

LALANDI, LINA
Greek harpsichordist, singer
Macksey--Book p221

LALIQUE, RENE (1860-1945)
French enameller
Callen--Women p162

LAMA, GIULIA (c1685-after 1753)
Italian painter
Harris--Women p26,29-30,165-
166,345
Petersen--Women p48, por.

LA MALINCHE
See MALINCHE

LA MARCHE, MARGUERITE DU
TERTRE DE (1638-1706)
French midwife
Marks--Women p61

LA MARCHE, MARILYN
Amer. banking official
O'Neill--Women's p529

"LA MARECHALE"
See BOOTH, CATHERINE MUM-
FORD

LAMARR, HEDY (1913/1915-)
Austrian actress
Hirschhorn--Rating p216-217,
por.
Keenan--Women p78-79, por.
Lamparski--What. (4) p14-15,
por.
People's Almanac (1) p1243
Shipman--Gold. p327-330, por.
Springer--They p155-156,307,
por.
World--Who p238

LAMARSH, JUDY (1924-1980)
Canadian government official,
lawyer
Cur. Biog. '81 p466

LAMB, ANNE CECILIA (1865-1948)
Amer., noted Maryland mother
Amer.--Mothers p251-252

LAMB, CAROLYN (CAROLINE),
LADY (1785-1828)
English novelist, (wife of
William Lamb, daughter of
Frederick Ponsonby, 3rd Earl
of Bessborough)
Jones--Rutledge p445
Moers--Literary p296

LAMB, MARTHA JOANNA READE
NASH (1826-1893)
Amer. author, historian,
editor
James--Notable (2) p361-362
McHenry--Liberty's p232

LAMB, MARY ANN (1764-1847)
English, (sister of Charles
Lamb)
Callen--Women p98
Morley--Literary p92,107,186-187,

335
Parker--Old p62-63

LAMB, MYRNA (1930-)
  Amer. feminist, playwright
  Webber--Woman p133-136

LAMBART, EVELYN (fl. 1940's-
  1970's)
  Canadian filmmaker
  Smith--Movies p95

LAMBER, JULIETTE (1836-1936)
  French socialist, feminist
  Fine--Women p123

LAMBERT, ELEANOR (c1910-)
  Amer. columnist, fashion
  expert
  Diamonstein--Open p264-267,
  por.

LAMBERT, REBECCA H.
  Amer. society founder
  Sherr--American p20

LAMBINE, JANNA (fl. 1970's)
  Amer. aviatrix, Coast
  Guard pilot
  O'Neill--Women's p549

LAMME, CORNELIE
  Netherlands painter,
  draughtsman, engraver
  Sparrow--Women p261

LAMONT, FRANCES STILES
  (1914-)
  Amer. state senator, noted
  South Dakota mother
  Amer.--Mothers p501-502, por.

LAMONT, PEGGY (1949-)
  Amer. TV director
  Scheuer--Tel. p280

"LA MORPHISE"
  See O'MURPHY, LOUISE

LAMOUR, DOROTHY (1914-)
  Amer. singer, actress
  Hirschhorn--Rating p217, por.
  Shipman--Gold. p330-332, por.
  Springer--They p156,307, por.
  World--Who p238

LAMPHERE, PHYLLIS LEE HAGMOE

Amer., League President
  O'Neill--Women's p80

LAMPKIN, DAISY ELIZABETH ADAMS
  (c1883-1965)
  Amer. social reformer, suffragist
  Sicherman--Notable p406-408

LAMPL-DE-GROOT, JEANNE (1895-)
  Netherlands physician
  Hellstedt--Women p141-145, por.

LAMY, PAULE
  Belgian lawyer
  Macksey--Book p126

LANCASTER, DUCHESS OF
  See SWYNFORD, CATHERINE,
    DUCHESS OF LANCASTER

LANCEFIELD, REBECCA CRAIGHILL
  (1895-1981)
  Amer. bacteriologist
  O'Neill--Women's p144,223

LANCHESTER, ELSA (1902-1986)
  English actress, comedienne
  Hirschhorn--Rating p219-220, por.
  Springer--They p156-157,307, por.
  World--Who p258

LANCO-STARRELS, JOSINE (fl.
  1970's)
  Amer. art museum curator
  Women's--Female p118

LANDAU, BROKSLEY ELIZABETH
  (1940-)
  Amer. lawyer, editor
  O'Neill--Women's p353

LANDAU, GENEVIEVE MILLET (fl.
  1970's)
  Amer. magazine editor, author
  O'Neill--Women's p477

LANDAU, RESEL
  Bohemian letter-writer
  Henry--Written p165-167

LANDERS, ANN, pseud. (1918-)
  Amer. columnist
  Anderson--People p244-245, por.
  Hershey--Between p233-234
  McHenry--Liberty's p143
  100--Greatest (1) p44, por.

O'Neill--Women's p452-453
Webster's--Amer. p369-370
Woman's Almanac p277-279, por.
World--Who p53

LANDES, BERTHA ETHEL KNIGHT
(1868-1943)
Amer. mayor, civic reformer
James--Notable (2) p362-363
McHenry--Liberty's p232
Sherr--American p242, por.

LANDES, SHERRI LYNN (c1955-)
Amer. riflewoman
Jordan--Broken p96-105

LANDI, ELISSA (1904-1948)
Austrian actress
Shipman--Gold. p332-334, por.
Springer--They p157,307, por.

LANDIS, JEAN
Amer. aviatrix, army flier
Keil--Those p59-61,64,230,
305-306

LANDMAN, ADA LOUISE
See HUXTABLE, ADA LOUISE
LANDMAN

LANDMAN, BARBARA
See HEINEMANN, BARBARA

LANDON, LETITIA ELIZABETH
(1802-1838)
English poet, journalist,
novelist
Avenel--Comp. (1) p301
Moers--Literary p181,296
Showalter--Lit. p321

LANDON, LYNN (c1935-)
Amer. wife of Michael
Landon
Funt--Are p229-242, por.

LANDORF, JOYCE
Amer. religious worker,
singer
Kooiman--Cameos p43-48, por.

LANDOWSKA, WANDA LOUIS
(1877-1959)
Polish pianist, harpsi-
chordist, musicologist
Jones--Rutledge p447
LePage--Women p133-144, por.

Macksey--Book p216
O'Neill--Women's p632
Who Did What p187
World--Who p77

LANDREAUX, ELIZABETH MARY
See MILES, LIZZIE

LANE, ABBE (1932/1935-)
Amer. singer, actress
World--Who p269

LANE, ANNA MARIA (fl. 1770's)
Amer. Revolutionary War nurse
Clyne--Patriots p130-131, 135

LANE, CARRIE
See CATT, CARRIE CHAPMAN
LANE

LANE, ELIZABETH, DAME (fl.
1940's-1960's)
English judge
Macksey--Book p127
O'Neill--Women's p368-369

LANE, FRANCES CORRY (1910-)
Amer. genealogical researcher,
author
Meyer--Who's p122

LANE, GERTRUDE BATTLES (1874-
1941)
Amer. magazine editor,
journalist
McHenry--Liberty's p232-233
O'Neill--Women's p472

LANE, HARRIET (1830-1903)
Amer. social leader, niece of
James Buchanan, noted
Pennsylvania mother
Amer.--Mothers p457-458, por.
James--Notable (2) p280-281
Peacock--Famous p161-174, por.
People's Almanac (1) p268
Woman's Almanac p488

LANE, HASSIE OLIVIA (1909-)
Amer. genealogical researcher,
writer
Meyer--Who's p122

LANE, LOIS
See NEILL, NOEL

LANE, LOLA MULLICAN (1909-)

Amer. actress
Lamparski--What. (4) p126-127,
por.
Springer--They p157,307, por.

LANE, PRISCILLA (1917-)
Amer. singer, actress
Springer--They p157-158,307,
por.

LANE, ROSE WILDER
See WILDER, LAURA INGALLS

LANE, ROSEMARY (1914-)
Amer. singer, actress
Springer--They p158,307, por.

LANEY, LUCY CRAFT (1854-1933)
Amer. educator
Burgess--Education p137-138
James--Notable (2) p365-367
McHenry--Liberty's p233
Sherr--American p47
Sochen--Herstory p206

LANEY, MARY (fl. 1970's)
Amer. radio, TV reporter
Seed--Saturday's p36-40, por.

LANG, JOSEPHINE (1815-1880)
German song composer
Neuls-Bates--Women p165

LANG, JUNE (1915-)
Amer. actress, dancer
Lamparski--What. (5) p90-91,
por.
Springer--They p158,307-308,
por.

LANG, MARGARET RUTHVEN
(1867-1972)
Amer. composer
Jablonski--Ency. p153

LANG, NATALIE
Amer. executive official
Adams--Women p16,38-42,102,
157,161-162,168,183,186,195

LANG, PEARL LACK (1922-)
Amer. dancer, choreographer
Cur. Biog. '70 p238-239

LANGDON, MARY
See PIKE, MARY HAYDEN
GREEN

LANGE, DOROTHEA NUTZHORN
(1895-1965)
Amer. photographer
McHenry--Liberty's p233
Marzolf--Up p66-69
Munsterberg--Hist. p133-135
O'Neill--Women's p106,612-613
Sicherman--Notable p408-410
Stoddard--Famous p245-254, por.
Webster's--Amer. p605
Women's--Female p10-11

LANGE, HELENE (1848-1930)
German educator, feminist
Macksey--Book p72

LANGE, HOPE (1933-)
Amer. actress
World--Who p238

LANGE, JESSICA (1949/1952-)
Amer. actress
Cur. Biog. '83 p224-227, por.
Hirschhorn--Rating p220-221,
por.
People--Best p107,192-193, por.

LANGE, KELLY
Amer. TV anchor woman
Scheuer--Tel. p281

LANGER, ELEANOR
Amer. telephone worker
Hymowitz--Hist. p319

LANGER, SUSANNE KATHERINA
KNAUTH (1895-1985)
Amer. philosopher, author,
educator
Avenel--Comp. (2) p145
Cur. Biog. '85 p469
McHenry--Liberty's p233-234
Stoddard--Famous p255-262, por.
Webster's--Amer. p605

LANGFORD, FRANCES (1913/1914-)
Amer. singer, actress
Claghorn--Biog. p265
Lamparski--What. (2) p88-89, por.
Springer--They p158,308, por.

LANGGASSER, ELISABETH (1899-
1950)
German poet, playwright,
novelist
Herrmann--Ger. p5,32-33

LANGHANKE, LUCILE VASCON-
CELLS
See ASTOR, MARY

LANGHORNE, NANCY WITCHER
See ASTOR, NANCY WITCHER
LANGHORNE, LADY

LANGHORNE, ORRA (fl. 1880's)
Amer. writer
Scott--Southern p122

LANGLACE, CHANTAL (fl. 1970's)
French track and field
athlete
O'Neill--Women's p576

LANGLEY, JANE PICKENS (fl.
1940's-1960's)
Amer. singer
O'Neill--Women's p117

LANGLEY, KATHERINE (c1883-
1945/1948)
Amer. congresswoman
Chamberlin--Min. p63-65
James--Notable (2) p367-368

LANGSDORFF, TONI VON (1884-)
West German physician
Hellstedt--Women p16-19, por.

LANGSTON, DICEY
See SPRINGFIELD, LAODICEA
(DICEY) LANGSTON

LANGTRY, LILLIE EMILIE CHAR-
LOTTE LE BRETON (1853-
1929)
English actress, beauty
Entertainers p140, por.
Jones--Rutledge p449
World--Who p258

LA NIÑA TORERO
See ATIENZAR, MARIBEL

LAN KUEI ("LITTLE ORCHID")
(1835-1908)
Chinese empress dowager
People's Almanac (2) p353-
357, por.

LANOETTE, EILEEN (fl. 1940's)
Amer. magazine reporter
Hamblin--That p271-272

LANSBURY, ANGELA BRIGID (1925-)
English actress
Anderson--People p245
Hirschhorn--Rating p221, por.
Shipman--Internatl. p314-318, por.
World--Who p238

LANSING, SHERRY LEE (1944-)
Amer. film executive
Cur. Biog. '81 p265-288, por.

LANSNER, FAY (fl. 1970's)
Amer. painter
Munro--Originals p205-206
Women's--Female p48

LANVIN, JEANNE, MADAME (c1867-
1946)
French couturière, fashion
designer
Holme--Journal p154, por.
World--Who p298

LANYON, ELLEN (fl. 1970's)
Amer. painter
Seed--Saturday's p27-30, por.

LANZEL, CONNIE (fl. 1970's)
Amer. lacrosse player
O'Neill--Women's p569

LAODICE
Greek, wife of Antiochus II
Pomeroy--Godd. p123

LAOURI, TAMARA (1900-)
Iranian physician
Hellstedt--Women p212-213, por.

"LA PASIONARIA"
See IBARRURI, DOLORES

LA PIERRE, CHERILYN
See "CHER"

LaPLANTE, LAURA (1904-)
Amer. actress
Lamparski--What. (2) p166-167,
por.
Lamparski--What. (8) p170-171,
por.
Springer--They p158,308, por.

LAPOINTE, RENAUDE (1912-)
Canadian senator, journalist
O'Neill--Women's p50

LAPPE, FRANCES MOORE (1944-)
    Amer. nutritionist, author
    O'Neill--Women's p35-36

LA RAMEE, MARIE LOUISE DE
    See OUIDA, pseud.

LARCOM, LUCY (1824-1893)
    Amer. poet, magazine editor,
    hymnist, mill girl, teacher
    Bagley--Mill p13-66, por.
    Bernikow--World p200
    Claghorn--Biog. p266
    Earnest--American p56-57
    Ehrlich--Oxford p27,51,55,326
    Hoople--As p173-176
    James--Notable (2) p368-369
    McHenry--Liberty's p234
    Macksey--Book p164
    Neidle--America's p116
    Sherr--American p106
    Sochen--Herstory p95-95, por.
    Taylor--Gener. p43
    Warren--Pictorial p93

LARDIE, KATHLEEN (fl. 1940's)
    Amer. educator
    Women--Radio p24-26

LARENDON, LAURE BEAUREGARD
    (fl. 1860's)
    Amer. Southern belle
    DeLeon--Belles p299-300, por.

LARIMER, SARAH (fl. 1860's)
    Amer. Indian captive
    Sherr--American p215-254
    Time--Women p64-65

LAROCHE, ELISE RAYMOND DE,
    BARONNE (1886-1919)
    French aviatrix
    Boase--Sky's p11, por.
    Macksey--Book p246

LA ROCHE, SOPHIE VON
    (1731-1807)
    German novelist, magazine
    founder, editor, social re-
    former
    Macksey--Book p182

LAROWE, NINA CHURCHMAN
    (fl. 1850's)
    Amer. Western letter-writer
    Fischer--Let p207-228

LARRIEU-LUTZ, FRANCIE (1952/
    1953-)
    Amer. track and field athlete
    Hollander--100 p131-132, por.
    Jacobs--Modern p120-132, por.
    World--Who p217

LARROCHA, ALICIA DE (1923-)
    Spanish pianist
    O'Neill--Women's p631

LARSEN, NELLA (1893-1964)
    Amer. novelist, librarian
    Sochen--Herstory p301-302

LARSON, ANNA BERTIA HUSEBOE
    (1883-)
    Amer. church worker, noted
    South Dakota mother
    Amer.--Mothers p500-501, por.

LARSON, GERALDINE ("GERI")
    (1930-)
    Amer. botanist, forestor
    O'Neill--Women's p26

LARSON, JEAN A. (1941-)
    Amer. genealogical researcher,
    author
    Meyer--Who's p123

LARSON, NICOLETTE (c1952-)
    Amer. singer
    Glassman--Year '79 p122, por.

LARSON, SUZANNE DE LEE FLAND-
    ERS
    See FOSTER, SUSANNA

LARSSON, ELIZABETH (1895-)
    Amer. physician
    Hellstedt--Women p146-149, por.

LASCELLES, MRS. EDWIN (1732-
    1813)
    British wife of Sir John
    Fleming
    Ware--Meet p78

LASKER, MARY WOODWARD (1900-)
    Amer. medical philanthropist
    Woman's Almanac p364

LASKI, MARGHANITA (1915-)
    English novelist, critic,
    broadcaster
    Jones--Rutledge p451

LASKY, ROYLE GLASER (c1930-)
Amer. business executive
O'Neill--Women's p518

LASLEY, MRS. CLINTON (fl.
1890's)
Amer. photographer, beauty
parlor operator
Time--Women p128,135,137, por.

LASOFF, ANNE (1922-)
Amer. writer
Ruddick--Working p196-212,343,
por.

LASSEN, LULU (1899-)
Danish journalist
Marzolf--Up p271-272

LASSER, LOUISE (1940/1941-)
Amer. actress
Anderson--People p245-246
Cur. Biog. '76 p221-224, por.
Manchel--Women p115-116, por.
World--Who p238

LATEAU, LOUISE (1850-1883)
French seamstress
Book--Lists (1) p436

LATHAM, EUNICE FORSYTHE (fl.
1770's)
Amer. Revolutionary War
patriot
Meyer--Petticoat p155

LATHAM, MAUDE MOORE (1871-)
Amer. musician, art
collector, writer, noted
North Carolina mother
Amer.--Mothers p405, por.

LATHBURY, MARY ARTEMISIA
(1841-1913)
Amer. hymnist
Claghorn--Biog. p266-267

LATHEN, EMMA, pseud. (1929-)
Amer. novelist, lawyer
Seymour-Smith--Novels p171
World--Who p46

LATHROP, JANE
See STANFORD, JANE ELIZA

LATHROP, JULIA CLIFFORD
(1858-1932)

Amer. social reformer, govern-
ment official
Brin--Social p157
Clark--Leading p71
Earnest--American p222
James--Notable (2) p370-372
McHenry--Liberty's p234-235
O'Neill--Women's p329
Signif.--Amer. p29, por.
World--Who p189

LATHROP, ROSE HAWTHORNE
(MOTHER MARY ALPHONSA)
(1851-1926)
Amer. nurse, author, nun,
(daughter of Nathaniel Haw-
thorne)
Book--Lists (2) p16
Ehrlich--Oxford p112
James--Notable (2) p372-374
McHenry--Liberty's p235-236

LATIMER, (MARY) ELIZABETH
WORMELEY (1822-1904)
English-Amer. author, trans-
lator
McHenry--Liberty's p236

LATIMER, LADY
See PARR, CATHERINE

LATSCH, BONNIE
Amer. Navy lieutenant
O'Neill--Women's p546

LATSIS, MARY J.
See LATHEN, EMMA, pseud.

LATYNINA, LARISSA SEMYONOVA
(1935-)
Russian gymnast
Assoc. Press--Pursuit p223,244,
260, por.
McWhirter--Guinness p83-84, por.
Macksey--Book p258, por.
O'Neill--Women's p562
Woman's Almanac p424

LAUCHIS, BETTIE E. (c1965-)
Amer. horticulturist
O'Neill--Women's p34

LAUCOTA, HERMINE
Austrian artist
Sparrow--Women p288,307

LAUDER, ESTEE (fl. 1940's-1970's)

Amer. cosmetician, millionaire
Forbes--400 ('84) p122
O'Neill--Women's p514
Woman's Almanac p133

LAUFER, BEATRICE (1922-)
Amer. composer
Jablonski--Ency. p404

LAUGHLAND, POLLY (fl. 1970's)
Amer. clergyman
Proctor--Women p42-43,82,84-
85,103,107-108

LAUGHLIN, GAIL (1868-1952)
Amer. lawyer, suffragist,
feminist, state legislator
Sicherman--Notable p410-411

LAUGHLIN, MRS. TOM
See TAYLOR, DELORES

LAUMAILLE, MADAME (fl. 1890's)
French auto racer
Macksey--Book p252
McWhirter--Guinness p29

LAUNAY, MADAME DE STAAL DE
See STAAL, (STAHL, STAËL),
MARGUERITE JEANE CORDIER
DE LAUNAY, BARONESS DE

LAUPER, CYNDI (1953-)
Amer. singer, songwriter
Cur. Biog. '85 p254-257, por.

LAUREA CONSTATIA CALENDA
(fl. 1423)
Italian physician, medical
teacher
Mead--Hist. p308

LAURENCE, MARGARET (1926-)
Canadian novelist
Crosland--Beyond p137-140
Seymour-Smith--Novels p171

LAURENCIN, MARIE (1885-1956)
French painter
Fine--Women p146,171-173
Haftmann--Paint. (1) p401
Harris--Women p58,260,295-297,
357-358
Munsterberg--Hist. p65-67
O'Neill--Women's p596-597
Petersen--Women p106-107, por.
Women's--Female p11

LAURENS, MRS. HENRY (1731-
c1768)
Amer. "founding mother"
Hymowitz--Hist. p13

LAURIE, ANNIE
See BLACK, WINIFRED SWEET

LA VALLIERE, LOUISE FRANÇOISE
DE LA BEAUME LE BLANC,
DUCHESSE (1644-1710)
French, mistress of Louis XIV
Jones--Rutledge p453
Macksey--Book p96

LAVEAU, MARIE (fl. 19th cent.)
Amer. "voodoo queen"
Sherr--American p83

LAVIN, LINDA (1937/1939-)
Amer. actress
Scheuer--Tel. p283, por.
World--Who p238

LAVIN, MARY (1912-)
Amer.-Irish short story writer
Baker--Women p4
Cahill--Women p143-144,376-377

LAW, AGNES (fl. 1920's-1940's)
Amer. radio network librarian
Women--Radio p15-16

LAW, RUTH BANCROFT (1887-)
Amer. aviatrix, stunt flier
Boase--Sky's p20-22, por.
Genett--Aviation p109

LAW, SALLIE CHAPMAN GORDON
("MOTHER OF THE CONFED-
ERACY") (1805-1894)
Amer. Confederate patriot,
nurse
McHenry--Liberty's p236

LAW, SYLVIA (fl. 1970's)
Amer. lawyer, professor
O'Neill--Women's p360

LAWATSCH, ANNA MARIE DeMUTH
(1712-1759)
Amer. hymnist
Claghorn--Biog. p267

LAWLESS, EMILY (1845-1913)
Irish poet, novelist
Showalter--Lit. p336

LAWRENCE, ANDREA MEAD
(1931/1933-)
Amer. skier
Assoc. Press--Pursuit p164,185,
187,206,225, por.
Hollander--100 p73-74, por.
O'Neill--Women's p565-566,574
Woman's Almanac p432-433

LAWRENCE, CAROL (1934/1935-)
Amer. singer, dancer,
actress
World--Who p269

LAWRENCE, ELIZABETH (fl.
1770's)
Amer. Revolutionary poet,
editor
Sherr--American p153

LAWRENCE, FLORENCE (1886-
1938)
Canadian-Amer. actress
James--Notable (2) p374-375
McHenry--Liberty's p236-237
Manchel--Women p23-24, por.
Mordden--Movie p2-5,9-10,19,
24,63,222,268

LAWRENCE, FRIEDA (1879-1956)
German, patron of arts,
(wife of D.H. Lawrence)
Rogers--Ladies, see index p231

LAWRENCE, GERTRUDE (1898-1952)
English actress
Entertainers p208, por.
Fabian--On p167-169, por.
Hazen--Interv. p104
McHenry--Liberty's p237
Macksey--Book p230,232
Priestley--Part. p124-126, por.
Springer--They p158,308, por.
World--Who p259

LAWRENCE, GUNDA JACOBSON
(1876-)
Amer., mother of Ernest
Lawrence, noted South
Dakota mother
Amer.--Mothers p499

LAWRENCE, LYDIA BEARDSALL
(1852-1910)
English, mother of David
Hubert Lawrence
Diagram--Mothers p136-137, por.

LAWRENCE, MARJORIE (1908/1909-
1979)
Austrlian-Amer. opera singer
Cur. Biog. '79 p466
O'Neill--Women's p620
World--Who p71

LAWRENCE, MARY GEORGENE BERG
WELLS (1928-)
Amer. advertising executive
Bird--Enterprising p217-220
Genett--Aviation p110
McHenry--Liberty's p434
Macksey--Book p174
100--Greatest (1) p69, por.
O'Neill--Women's p516, por.
Woman's Almanac p209-210, por.
World--Who p200-201

LAWRENCE, SUSAN
British Parliament member
Vallance--Women, see index p208

LAWRENCE, VICKI (1949-)
Amer. singer, actress
Scheuer--Tel. p284, por.

LAWRENCE, VIOLA (-1973)
Amer. film editor
Smith--Movies p17,41,74

LAWRENCE-DOW, ELIZABETH CARR
(1916-)
Amer. genealogical researcher,
author
Meyer--Who's p123

LAWRENCE-KIASEN, ALEXANDRA
DAGMAR
See LAWRENCE, GERTRUDE

LAWS, ANNIE (1855-1927)
Amer. kindergarten educator
James--Notable (2) p375-376

LAWSON, LIZZIE
British book illustrator
Callen--Women p204

LAWSON, LOUISE Q. (fl. 1950's-
1970's)
Amer. banker
O'Neill--Women's p530

LAWSON, MARJORIE
Amer. judge
Warren--Pictorial p197

LAWSON, ROBERTA CAMPBELL
(1878-1940)
Amer. Indian club leader
Gridley--Amer. p88-93, por.
James--Notable (2) p376-377
O'Neill--Women's p113-114
Sherr--American p190,192

LAWTON, ESTHER C. (fl. 1930's-
1970's)
Amer. government official
O'Neill--Women's p83

LAWTON, MARY CECILIA (fl.
1960's-1970's)
Amer. lawyer
O'Neill--Women's p365

LAXALT, THERESA ALPETCHE
(fl. 1920's-1960's)
French-Amer. hotel-
restaurant operator, noted
Nevada mother
Amer.--Mothers p350-351, por.

LAYA (fl. c100 B.C.)
Greek-Roman miniature
painter
Macksey--Book p194

LAYE, EVELYN (1900-)
English actress
Springer--They p158,160,308,
por.

LAYTON, OLIVIA CAMERON (c1898-
1975)
Amer. Girl Scout official
Cur. Biog. '76 p470

LAZAREFF, HELENE (fl. 1970's)
French magazine founder
Marzolf--Up p290

LAZARUS, EMMA (1849-1887)
Amer. poet, essayist
Baum--Jewish p38-40
Bernikow--World p218-219
Claghorn--Biog. p268
Henry--Written p247-254
James--Notable (2) p377-379
Kaplan--Salt p167-169
McHenry--Liberty's p237-238
Signif.--Amer. p19, por.
Webster's--Amer. p613
Woman's Almanac p218,253
World--Who p16

LAZARUS, HILDA MARY (1890-)
East Indian physician
Hellstedt--Women p38-41, por.

LAZARUS, IRMA (c1913-)
Amer. TV hostess
Diamonstein--Open p268-272, por.

LAZURICK, FRANCINE (1909-)
French newspaper editor,
publisher
Marzolf--Up p280
O'Neill--Women's p461

LAZURKINA, DORA
Russian labor organizer
Mandel--Soviet p35-36

LEA, BARBARA (fl. 1970's)
Amer. singer
Balliett--American p15-20

LEA, NANCY LEA
Amer., mother-in-law of Sam
Houston
Book--Lists (2) p266-267

LEA, SALLY WILDY (-1884)
Amer. civic leader, educator
Sherr--American p156

LEACH, ABBY (1855-1918)
Amer. professor, educator
James--Notable (2) p379-380
McHenry--Liberty's p238

LEACH, SUSAN (fl. 1970's)
Amer. artist
Women's--Female p155

LEACHMAN, CLORIS (1925-)
Amer. actress
Anderson--People p247, por.
Cur. Biog. '75 p232-235, por.
Hirschhorn--Rating p225, por.
Manchel--Women p113-114, por.
World--Who p238

LEAH
Biblical
Henry--Written p18-19
Price--God p52-65

LEAKEY, MARY DOUGLAS (1904/
1913-)
English archaeologist,
paleoanthropologist

Cur. Biog. '85 p257-260, por.
O'Neill--Women's p146-147
Woman's Almanac p364-365, por.
World--Who p95

LEAPMAN, EDWINA (1934-)
English artist
Contemp. Brit. unp., por.

LEAR, EVELYN SHULMAN (1929/
1931-)
Amer. opera singer
Claghorn--Biog. p268
Cur. Biog. '73 p242-245, por.
Gammond--Illus. p245, por.

LEARY, ELIZA TERRY (-1935)
Amer. hospital founder
Sherr--American p241-242

LEARY, HELEN F.M. (1935-)
Amer. genealogical research-
er, writer
Meyer--Who's p123

LEASE, MARY ELIZABETH CLYENS
(1850/1853-1933)
Irish-Amer. politician, lec-
turer, temperance worker
Bachtold--Gifted p92-95
Gray--Women p140-145, por.
James--Notable (2) p380-382
Kulkin--Her p173-174
Levenson--Women p73-74
McHenry--Liberty's p238-239
Palmer--Who's p199
Sherr--American p73
Sochen--Herstory p212-213
Stein--Lives p165-167, por.
Taylor--Gener. p35-36
Warren--Pictorial p139-141
Webster's--Amer. p614-615

LEASIA, MARY ANN (1822-1910)
Amer. Indian worker, noted
Michigan mother
Amer.--Mothers p275, por.

LEATHERBEE, MARY
Amer. magazine movie editor
Hamblin--That p161,166-169,
por.

LEATHERBEE, MARY LEE LOGAN
Amer. actress, air stunt-
woman
Keil--Those p204-206

LEAVITT, HENRIETTA SWAN (1868-
1921)
Amer. astronomer
Asimov--Biog. p544, (795)
James--Notable (2) p382-383
McHenry--Liberty's p239
O'Neill--Women's p150

LEAVITT, MARY GREENLEAF
CLEMENT (1830-1912)
Amer. teacher, missionary,
WCTU founder, social reformer
James--Notable (2) p383-385
McHenry--Liberty's p239-240
Macksey--Book p81,276

LeBEAU, LUISE (LOUISE) ADOLPHA
(1850-1927)
German composer, pianist
Neuls-Bates--Women p167-174

LEBEDEVA, SARAH DMITRIEVNA
(1881-1968)
Russian sculptor
Mandel--Soviet p141-142
Women's--Female p1-2, supp.

LEBEDINSKAIA, LIDIA IVANOVNA
(1908-)
Russian ceramic painter
Women's--Female p3, supp.

LeBLANC, NANCY E.
Amer. lawyer
O'Neill--Women's p355

LEBOURSIER, ANGELIQUE MAR-
GUERITE DuCOUDRAY,
MADAME (1712-1789)
French obstetrician, medical
writer
Macksey--Book p144
Marks--Women p66-67
Mead--Hist. p423,497,499-500

LEBOWITZ, FRANCES ANN (1950-)
Amer. humorist, writer
Cohen--Meet p189-193, por.
Cur. Biog. '82 p221-224, por.

LEBRUN, MARIE ELIZABETH LOUISE
(1755-1842)
French painter
Fine--Women p45-46,48-51,74, por.
Harris--Women p28-29,37,40-44,46,
49,83,176,180,185-194,197,200,
209,347-348

Jones--Rutledge p457
Macksey--Book p202-203
Munsterberg--Hist. p35,37-40,
47-48,52-53,145-146
Parker--Old p32-33,42,92,96-
99, fig. 53,55,56, por.
Petersen--Women p49-54, por.
Sparrow--Women p166,175-177,
191-193,198,200-201,204,
por.
Tufts--Our p126-138, por.
Woman's Almanac p220
Women's--Female p14

LECKBAND, SUSANNE M.
Amer. agricultural engineer
O'Neill--Women's p26

LECLAIR, DENISE (1952-)
Amer. anchor, cable TV
Scheuer--Tel. p286

LE CLERCQ, TANAQUIL (1929-)
Amer. dancer
McHenry--Liberty's p240
Woman's Almanac p312

LE CONTE, EMMA FLORENCE
Amer. Civil War diarist
Warren--Pictorial p112

LECOURVREUR, ADRIENNE
(1692-1730)
French actress
Entertainers p86, por.

LEDBETTER, MARIE (fl. 1970's)
Amer. parachutist
O'Neill--Women's p591

LEDERER, ESTHER PAULINE
("EPPIE")
See LANDERS, ANN, pseud.

LEDERER, EVELYN
See CAROL, SUE

LEDERMAN, JANET
Amer. therapist, educator
Adams--Women p106

LEDOUX, JEANNE PHILIBERTE
(1767-1840)
French artist
Harris--Women p188,205-206,
213,348

LEDUC, VIOLETTE (1907-1972)
French novelist
Bree--Women p69
Crosland--Women p135,201-210
Moers--Literary p297
Seymour-Smith--Novels p172

LEDYARD, FANNY
See PETERS, FANNIE LEDYARD

LEE, AGNES DICKINSON (1) (fl.
1770's)
Amer. Revolutionary War
heroine
Sherr--American p31

LEE, AGNES DICKINSON (2) (fl.
1860's)
Amer. Southern belle, (daughter of General Lee)
DeLeon--Belles p426, por.

LEE, ANN, (MOTHER) (1736-1784)
Amer. Shaker founder
Bloom--Religion p31-49, por.
Booth--Women p232-237,291
DePauw--Rem. p78
Engle--Women p165-182
Evans--Weather. p7-9
Felton--Famous p216-217
James--Notable (2) p385-387
McHenry--Liberty's p240
Neidle--America's p14,58-65,67
People's Almanac (1) p131-132
People's Almanac (2) p1336-1337
Sherr--American p80,90,146,177
Warren--Pictorial p40-41,43
Webster's--Amer. p616-617
Who Did What p190
Woman's Almanac p402-403
World--Who p89

LEE, ANNA PITTMAN (-1838)
Amer. pioneer
Sherr--American p196-197

LEE, ANNE HILL CARTER (1773-)
Amer. mother of Robert E.
Lee, noted Virginia mother
Amer.--Mothers p551
Diagram--Mothers p138-139, por.

LEE, ANNE CARTER (fl. 1860's)
Amer. daughter of General
Robert E. Lee, Southern belle
DeLeon--Belles p433, por.
Hymowitz--Hist. p140

LEE, AURA (1946-)
Romanian singer
Claghorn--Jazz p181

LEE, BARBARA (fl. 1970's)
Amer. singer
Balliett--Amer. p15-20

LEE, BRENDA (1939/1944-)
Amer. singer
Claghorn--Biog. p269

LEE, CANDY (fl. 1970's)
Amer. craftswoman
Women's--Female p20

LEE, MRS. DANIEL MURRAY
See FICKLEN, NANNIE

LEE, DORIS EMRICK (1905-1956)
Amer. painter
Henkes--Eight p31-36,57
Munsterberg--Hist. p73,76-77

LEE, DOROTHY (1911-)
Amer. actress
Springer--They p160,308, por.

LEE, FRANCES E. (fl. 1870's-
1890's)
British pottery designer,
decorator
Callen--Women p224

LEE, GWEN (1904-)
Amer. actress
Springer--They p160,308, por.

LEE, GYPSY ROSE (1914-1970)
Amer. actress, author,
burlesque queen
Brecher--Lives p137-138, por.
Cur. Biog. '70 p466
Entertainers p243, por.
McHenry--Liberty's p240-241
Sicherman--Notable p411-414
Springer--They p138-139,302,
por.
Webster's--Amer. p618
Woman's Almanac p93,312-313,
por.
World--Who p291

LEE, HARPER
See LEE, (NELLE) HARPER

LEE, HELEN (fl. 1950's-1970's)

Amer. children's clothes designer
O'Neill--Women's p247,261

LEE, JEANNE (1939-)
Amer. singer
Claghorn--Biog. p269
Claghorn--Jazz p181-182

LEE, JENNIE (1904-)
Scottish, member British
House of Commons
O'Neill--Women's p343

LEE, JOANNA
Amer. TV producer
Scheuer--Tel. p286

LEE, MRS. JOSEPH
Amer. Civil War patriot
Sherr--American p209

LEE, JULIA (1902-1958)
Amer. pianist, singer, com-
poser
Claghorn--Jazz p182

LEE, LILA (1901-1973)
Amer. actress
Springer--They p160,308, por.

LEE, LUCY
Chinese-Amer. poultry re-
search chemist
O'Neill--Women's p32-33

LEE, MARY ANN (1823/1826-1899)
Amer. pioneer ballet dancer
Fabian--On p78-79, por.
James--Notable (2) p387-388
McHenry--Liberty's p241

LEE, MARY CHUDLEIGH, LADY
(1656-1710)
English writer
Pearson--Who p158

LEE, MARY CUSTIS
Amer. granddaughter of
General Lee
DeLeon--Belles p433, por.

LEE, MICHELE (1942-)
Amer. singer, actress, dancer
Scheuer--Tel. p286, por.
World--Who p269

LEE, MILDRED (fl. 1860's)
Amer. Southern belle,
(daughter of General Lee)
DeLeon--Belles p419-420, por.

LEE, MINNIE MARY
See WOOD, JULIA AMANDA
SARGENT

LEE, MOLLIE HUSTON (1907-   )
Amer. librarian, noted
North Carolina mother
Amer.--Mothers p409-410, por.

LEE, (NELLE) HARPER (1926-   )
Amer. novelist
Seymour-Smith--Novels p172-173
World--Who p16

LEE, PEGGY (1920-   )
Amer. singer, songwriter,
actress
Claghorn--Biog. p269
Claghorn--Jazz p182
O'Neill--Women's p628
Simon--Best p349-351, por.
Simon--Big p355-356, por.
Woman's Almanac p295
World--Who p269

LEE, REBECCA (fl. 1860's)
Amer. physician
O'Neill--Women's p202

LEE, MRS. ROBERT E.
See CUSTIS, MARY RANDOLPH

LEE, MRS. ROBERT E., JR.
See HAXALL, CHARLOTTE

LEE, ROSE (1922-   )
Amer. singer, banjoist
Claghorn--Biog. p269

LEE, ROSE HUM (1904-1964)
Chinese-Amer. sociologist
Sicherman--Notable p414-415

LEE, MRS. SYDNEY SMITH
See MASON, ANNA MARIA

LEE TAI-YOUNG (fl. 1950's-
1970's)
Korean lawyer, judge
O'Neill--Women's p369

LEE, VERNON, pseud. (1856-1935)

English novelist
Colby--Singular p235-304

LEE, MRS. W.H.F.
See BOLLING, MARY TABB

LEECH, MARGARET KERNOCHAN
(1893-1974)
Amer. author, historian
Cur. Biog. '74 p464
McHenry--Liberty's p241
O'Neill--Women's p417

LEEDS, ANDREA (1914-   )
Amer. actress
Lamparski--What. Annual (4,5)
p114-119, por.
Springer--They p160-161,308,
por.

LEEDS, LILA (1928-   )
Amer. actress
Lamparski--What. Annual (4,5)
p14-18, por.

LEEN, NINA
Amer. photographer
Hamblin--That p50,58,269-270,
por.

LE FAVRE, CARRICA (fl. 1890's)
Amer. author
Felton--Famous p263

LEFFLER, DOROTHY (fl. 1940's)
Amer. director, journalist
Women--Radio p16

LEFKOWITZ, MARY L. (fl. 1970's)
Amer. classical professor,
author
O'Neill--Women's p424

LE GALLIENNE, EVA (1899-   )
English-Amer. director,
actress, author
Chinoy--Women p4-5,119-123, por.
Clark--Leading p138-139
Entertainers p212, por.
Hazen--Interv. p84-85
Longstreet--Queen p177-181, por.
McHenry--Liberty's p241-242
Webster's--Amer. p621-622
World--Who p258

LEGINSKA, ETHEL LIGGINS (1886/
1890-1970)

Keylin--Hollywood p173-176,
  por.
Manchel--Women p57,77,80, por.
O'Neill--Women's p652-653,681
People--Best p158-159
Shipman--Gold. p345-349, por.
Springer--They p161,308,310,
  por.
Woman's Almanac p348
World--Who p258

LEIGHTON, MARGARET (1922-1976)
  English actress
  Cur. Biog. '76 p471
  Entertainers p255
  World--Who p258

LEIJON, ANNA-GRETA
  Swedish labor leader,
  feminist
  O'Neill--Women's p344-345

LEININGER, BURLDENE (fl. 1930's)
  Amer. Indian labor organizer
  O'Neill--Women's p312

LEITHERSDORF, FINI (1906-)
  Hungarian-Israeli fashion
  designer, promoter
  O'Neill--Women's p246

LEITZEL, LILLIAN (1893-1931)
  German-Amer. circus aerialist
  Entertainers p193
  James--Notable (2) p388-389
  Kirk--Circus p49-52, por.
  McHenry--Liberty's p243
  McWhirter--Guinness p87-88,
    por.
  People's Almanac (2) p787-788,
    por.
  Woman's Almanac p323-324

LELONG-FERRAND, JACQUELINE
  (fl. 1930's-1950's)
  French mathematician, professor
  O'Neill--Women's p177

LEM, CAROL
  Amer. TV director
  Scheuer--Tel. p288

LEMLICH, CLARA (1970's)
  Amer. labor union organizer
  Baum--Jewish p142-143
  Hymowitz--Hist. p250
  O'Neill--Women's p291

LEMOINE, MARIE VICTOIRE (1754-
  1820)
  French artist
  Fine--Women p60
  Harris--Woman p188-189,347

"LEMONADE LUCIE"
  See HAYES, LUCY WARE WEBB

LE MONE, MARGARET
  Amer. meteorologist
  O'Neill--Women's p174-175

LENARD, KATHRYN (1934-)
  Amer. TV executive
  Scheuer--Tel. p289

L'ENCLOS, NINON (ANNE) DE
  (1620-1705/1706)
  French courtesan, writer
  Bree--Women p35-37
  Crosland--Women p53-54
  Earle--Two Cent. (1) p xv,84,
    por.
  Jones--Rutledge p461

LE NEVE, ETHEL (1883-1967)
  English accused criminal
  People's Almanac (1) p578
  People's Almanac (2) p500-501

LENGLEN, SUZANNE (1899-1938)
  French tennis player
  Hollander--100 p100-103, por.
  People's Almanac (1) p1190
  Sullivan--Queens p99
  Woman's Almanac p417
  World--Who p217

LENIN, MARIA ALEKSANDROVNA
  BLANK (c1835-1916)
  Russian, mother of Vladimir
  Ilyich Lenin
  Diagram--Mothers p140-143, por.

LENNON, MRS. JOHN
  See ONO, YOKO

LENNON SISTERS (fl. 1950's-1980's)
  Amer. singers
  Claghorn--Biog. p271
  World--Who p269

LENNOX, CHARLOTTE RAMSEY
  (1720-1804)
  Amer. novelist, translator,
  playwright
  Avenel--Comp. (1) p313

Horner--English p42-47,130-133
McHenry--Liberty's p243
Moers--Literary p297
Williams--Demeter's p212

LENNOX, SARAH, LADY
See NAPIER, SARAH LENNOX
 BUNBURY, LADY

LENROOT, KATHARINE FREDRICA
 (1891-)
 Amer. government official
Ware--Beyond p148, see also
 index p200

LENSKI, LOIS (1893-1974)
 Amer. children's book
 author, illustrator
Ehrlich--Oxford p265,307
Kulkin--Her p174-175
Smaridge--Famous p54-61, por.

LENYA, LOTTE (1898-1981)
 Austrian singer, actress
Cur. Biog. '82 p469
Fabian--On p170-172, por.
O'Neill--Women's p626
World--Who p269

LENZ, ANNE A. (fl. 1940's)
 Amer. Marine Corps officer
O'Neill--Women's p535

LEONARD, HELEN LOUISE
See RUSSELL, LILLIAN

LEONARD, JOAN (fl. 1970's)
 Amer. photographer
Women's--Female p67

LEONARD, LOUISE
See McLAREN, LOUISE
 LEONARD

LEONARD, LUCILLE PUTNAM
 (1895-)
 Amer. organization official,
 noted Rhode Island mother
Amer.--Mothers p480-481, por.

LEONARD, PRISCILLA
See BISSELL, EMILY PERKINS

LEONARD, VERA
 Amer. nurse
People--Best p88, por.

LEONOWENS, ANNA HARRIETTE
 CRAWFORD (1834-1914/1915)
 Welsh governess
Macksey--Book p72

LEONTOVICH, EUGENIE (1894/
 1900-)
 Russian-Amer. actress, dramatic coach
World--Who p239

LEOPOLD, ALICE KOLLER (1909-)
 Amer. politician, business
 executive, government official
Bachtold--Gifted p106
O'Neill--Women's p330,335

LEOPOLD, ESTELLA BERGERE
 (1927-)
 Amer. paleontologist, conservationist
O'Neill--Women's p173-174

LEOPOLDINA, D. MARIA (fl. 1797-
 1826)
 Austrian-Brazilian empress
Henderson--Ten p121-145, por.

LEPORIN-ERXLEBEN, DOROTHEA
 CHRISTINA (1713/1715-1762)
 German physician
Macksey--Book p145
Mead--Hist. p502,504
O'Neill--Women's p197

LEPPERT, ALICE JEANNE
See FAYE, ALICE

LERIS, CLAIRE JOSEPHE
See CLAIRON, CLAIRE,
 MADEMOISELLE

LERNER, GERDA (1920-)
 Austrian-Amer. professor,
 historian
Hymowitz--Hist. p82,154
O'Neill--Women's p425-426

LERNER, KAREN
 Amer. TV producer
Scheuer--Tel. p289

LE ROY, KITTY (fl. 1800's-1870's)
 Amer. Western pioneer,
 theater manager
Sherr--American p214

LERZA, CATHERINE
Amer. agricultural food
editor
O'Neill--Women's p36

LESARD, SUZANNAH
Amer. newspaper writer on
architectural, city design
O'Neill--Women's p610

"LESBIA"
See CLODIA

LESCH, MAGDALENA VON
See DIETRICH, MARLENE

LESCOT, ANTOINETTE CECILE,
MADAME HAUDEBOURT
French painter
Sparrow--Women p179-180,208

LESER, TINA (1911-)
Amer. fashion designer
O'Neill--Women's p247-248

LESKA, ANNA (fl. 1940's)
Polish (military) aviatrix
Boase--Sky's p189,193-194

LESLIE, AMY (1855-1939)
Amer. opera singer, dra-
matic critic, journalist
James--Notable (2) p389-390
O'Neill--Women's p439

LESLIE, ANNIE LOUISE BROWN
See BROWN, NANCY

LESLIE, CORINNE
Amer. dancer
People's Almanac (3) p523

LESLIE, ELIZA (ELIZABETH)
(1787-1858)
Amer. author, editor,
humorist, cookery expert
James--Notable (2) p391-393

LESLIE, MRS. FRANK
See LESLIE, MIRIAM
FLORENCE FOLLINE
SQUIER

LESLIE, JOAN (1925-)
Amer. actress
Lamparski--What. (8) p178-
179, por.
World--Who p239

LESLIE, MIRIAM FLORENCE FOLLINE
SQUIER (1836-1914)
Amer. publisher, actress,
editor, social leader, feminist,
philanthropist
Bird--Enterprising p146-150
Ehrlich--Oxford p278
Fischer--Let p313-325
James--Notable (2) p393-394
McHenry--Liberty's p243-244
Marzolf--Up p25
Sherr--American p166
Starr--Amer. p240
Warren--Pictorial p164
Webster's--Amer. p626

L'ESPERANCE, ELISE DEPEW
STRANG (1878/1879-1959)
Amer. physician, pathologist,
clinic founder
O'Neill--Women's p227
Sicherman--Notable p417-419

LESSING, DORIS MAY (1919-)
South African novelist, play-
wright, short-story writer
Avenel--Comp. (1) p313
Baker--Women p6
Cahill--Women p195-196,377
Crosland--Beyond p73,95-197,
134,141-142
Cur. Biog. '76 p230-233, por.
Jones--Rutledge p466
Moers--Literary p297
O'Neill--Women's p686
P.W.--Author p97-100,508-509
Spacks--Contemp. p30-74,178-179
Seymour-Smith--Novels p173-174,
por.
Seymour-Smith--Who's p209
Showalter--Lit. p307-313,349
Webber--Woman p79-84
Who Did What p194
Woman's Almanac p253-254
World--Who p28

LESTER, KATHERINE
See DeMILLE, KATHERINE

LESTER, MARGARET (1938-)
Australian handicapped athlete
Kulkin--Her p175

LESTOR, JOAN
British Parliament member
Vallance--Women p62,65,103,108

LE SUEUR, LUCILLE FAY
See CRAWFORD, JOAN

LESUR, ANNIE
French minister for education
Macksey--Book p39

LESZCZYNSKA, MARIA
See MARIA LESZCZYNSKA

LETCH, IDA (c1867-)
Amer. centenarian
Mitchell--Yessir p52-55, por.

LETH, MARIE GUDME (1895-)
Danish textile artist
O'Neill--Women's p270

LETOURNEAU, EVELYN PETERSON
(1900-)
Amer. college founder, noted
Texas mother
Amer.--Mothers p518-519, por.
Kooiman--Silhouettes p98-111,
por.
LEVANOVA, SVETLANA
Russian chemical engineer,
professor
Mandel--Soviet p91

LEVEAU, MARIE (1827-)
Amer. hoodoo queen
Coffin--Parade p100-103

LEVERSON, ADA (1862-1933)
English novelist
Crosland--Beyond p8-11,198
Moers--Literary p297

LE VERT, MRS. HENRY STRACHEY
Amer. Southern belle
DeLeon--Belles p183,185-186,
por.

LE VERT, OCTAVIA CELESTE
WALTON (1810/1811-1877)
Amer. author, social leader
James--Notable (2) p394-395
Peacock--Famous p102-117, por.
Sherr--American p2, por.

LEVERTOV, DENISE (1923-)
Amer. poet, war nurse,
editor, teacher, translator,
lecturer
Avenel--Comp. (2) p148
Chester--Rising p105-112, por.
Diamonstein--Open p273-277, por.

Ehrlich--Oxford p52,123,132
McHenry--Liberty's p244
O'Neill--Women's p685
Pearson--Who p139
Seymour-Smith--Who's p209
Webber--Woman p85-91
World--Who p16

LEVI, LINDA (fl. 1970's)
Amer. painter
Women's--Female p48

LEVICHEVA, VALENTINA (fl.
1940's)
Russian engineer
Mandel--Soviet p90-91

LEVI-MONTALCINI, RITA (fl.
1950's-1960's)
Italian neurobiologist
O'Neill--Women's p144,223

LEVIN, MILDRED W. (fl. 1970's)
Amer. feminist, social reformer
O'Neill--Women's p361

LEVIN, RAHEL (1771-1833)
German salonnière
Macksey--Book p101-102

LEVINA, Z.A. (fl. 1950's)
Russian musician
Mandel--Soviet p150

LEVINE, BETH (fl. 1940's-1970's)
Amer. model, shoe designer
O'Neill--Women's p239,248,258

LeVINE, DEBORAH JOY (1952-)
Amer. film producer
Scheuer--Tel. p291

LEVINE, ELLEN
Amer. TV director
Scheuer--Tel. p291-292

LEVINE, LAINIE
See KAZAN, LAINIE

LEVINE, LENA (1903-1965)
Amer. gynecologist, psychia-
trist
Sicherman--Notable p419-420

LEVINE, NAOMI (fl. 1970's)
Amer. filmmaker
Smith--Movies p256,
por.

LEVINGSTONE, MRS. (fl. 1730's)
Amer. physician
Williams--Demeter's p173

LEVINSOHN, ROANN KIM (1950-)
Amer. TV director, public
relations
Scheuer--Tel. p292-293

LEVINSON, RENA
Israeli aviatrix
O'Neill--Women's p553

LEVINSON, SARA SHERMAN
(1886-)
Romanian-Amer.-Israeli Red
Cross worker, noted Con-
necticut mother
Amer.--Mothers p79, por.

LEVI-TANAI, SARA (fl. 1940's-
1970's)
Israeli dancer, director,
composer, choreographer
O'Neill--Women's p650

LEVITT, DOROTHY (fl. 1900's)
English racer
Macksey--Book p245,252-253,
por.
McWhirter--Guinness p29, por.

LEVITT, HELEN (1913-)
Amer. photographer,
filmmaker
Munsterberg--Hist p141
O'Neill--Women's p613
Smith--Movies p188-189,256

LE VOE, SAVY (1906-1971)
Amer. pianist, singer
Claghorn--Biog. p273

LEVY, AMY (1861-1889)
English poet
Showlater--Lit. p341

LEVY, FLORENCE NIGHTINGALE
(1870-1947)
Amer. art administrator
James--Notable (2) p395-397

LEVY, MARION
See GODDARD, PAULETTE

LEVY, PHOEBE (fl. 1860's)
Amer. Southern belle
DeLeon--Belles p231, por.

LEWALD, FANNY (1811-1889)
German novelist
Moers--Literary p297

LEWIS, ALLIE MAY (1859-1930)
Amer. pianist, organist,
teacher
Claghorn--Biog. p272-273

LEWIS, AUGUSTA
See TROUP, AUGUSTA LEWIS

LEWIS, DOROTHY (fl. 1930's-1940's)
Amer. radio executive
Women--Radio p13

LEWIS, EDMONIA (1845-1890/1909)
Amer. sculptor
Adams--Great (3rd) p194, por.
Fine--Women p111-113
James--Notable (2) p397-399
McHenry--Liberty's p244-245
Petersen--Women p81-82, por.
Sherr--American p41,102
Toppin--Biog. p351-352
Tufts--Our p158-167, por.
Warren--Pictorial p154,157

LEWIS, EDNA (fl. 1970's)
Amer. cookery writer
McCullough--People p106-108

LEWIS, ELIZABETH ANNESLEY (fl.
1740's-1770's)
Amer. Revolutionary War
patriot
Meyer--Petticoat p69-70

LEWIS, ELIZABETH LANGHORNE
(c1852-1946)
Amer. suffragist
Sherr--American p236

LEWIS, ESTHER (fl. 1870's-1890's)
British pottery designer,
decorator, watercolourist
Callen--Women p75,224, por.

LEWIS, FLORA (1920-)
Amer. syndicated columnist,
foreign correspondent
Diamonstein--Open p278-283, por.
O'Neill--Women's p465-466

LEWIS, FLORENCE E. (-1917)
British pottery designer,
decorator, watercolourist
Callen Women p68,76,224, por.

LEWIS, IDA (1) (1842-1911)
Amer. lighthouse keeper
James--Notable (2) p399-400
McHenry--Liberty's p245
Macksey--Book p244-245, por.
Sherr--American p206

LEWIS, IDA (2)
See ARTHUR, JULIA

LEWIS, IDA (3) (fl. 1970's)
Canadian-Amer. magazine
founder, publisher
O'Neill--Women's p457

LEWIS, JANET (1899-)
Amer. novelist, poet
Bernikow--World p297

LEWIS, JESSICA (1890-1971)
Amer. opera singer
Claghorn--Biog. p273

LEWIS, KAY (fl. 1950's-1970's)
Amer. textile designer,
stylist
O'Neill--Women's p278-279

LEWIS, LILLIAN ALBERTA
Amer. journalist
Marzolf--Up p26

LEWIS, MARY (1900-1941)
Amer. opera singer
Claghorn--Biog. p273

LEWIS, MARY BURR
Amer. parliamentarian
Sherr--American p120

LEWIS, MARY CAULK (1880-)
Amer. community worker,
noted Delaware mother
Amer.--Mothers p85-86, por.

LEWIS, MONICA (1925-)
Amer. singer, actress
Lewis--Prime p31-32,73, por.

LEWIS, PATTI (fl. 1970's-
1980's)
Amer., wife of Jerry Lewis
Funt--Are p245-259, por.

LEWIS, ROSA OVERDEN (1867-
1952)
English hotelkeeper
World--Who p299

LEWIS, SHARI (1934-)
Amer. TV personality, (ven-
triloquist, puppeteer)
World--Who p292

LEWIS, "TILLIE" (MYRTLE) EHRLICH
(1901-1977)
Italian-Amer., head tomato
industry, agriculturist, food
executive
Bird--Enterprising p199-203
Macksey--Book p167
Marlowe--Great p316-321, por.
O'Neill--Women's p513-514

LEWISOHN, IRENE (1892-1944)
Amer. social worker, theatrical
patron, humanitarian
James--Notable (2) p400-402
McHenry--Liberty's p245-246

LEYSTER, JUDITH MOLENAER
(1609-1660)
Netherlands painter
Fine--Women p31-34, por.
Harris--Women p29,35,41-42,
137-140,342-343
Munsterberg--Hist. p26-27, por.
Petersen--Women p38-39, por.
Sparrow--Women p257,260,264
Tufts--Our p70-79, por.
Women's--Female p11

LHEVINNE, ROSINA L. (1880-1976)
Russian-Amer. pianist, edu-
cator
Cur. Biog. '77 p467
McHenry--Liberty's p246
Neidle--America's p240-241, por.
O'Neill--Women's p635

LIBBEY, LAURA JEAN (1862-1925)
Amer. novelist
James--Notable (2) p402-403
McHenry--Liberty's p246
Stein--Lives p45-52

LIBBY, LEONA M. (fl. 1940's)
Amer. nuclear physicist
O'Neill--Women's p181

LIBER, NADINE (fl. 1970's)
Amer. correspondent
Hamblin--That p163-164,248

LIBERACE, FRANCES ZUCHOWSKI
(c1891-)
Amer., mother of Liberace

LILLYBRIDGE, ANNY
Amer. army fighter
Macksey--Book p55

LILYQUIST, CHRISTINE (fl. 1970's)
Amer. museum curator
O'Neill--Women's p616

LIM, KIM (1936-)
Singapore artist
Contemp. Brit. unp., por.

LIM, SHIRLEY GEOK-LIN (fl. 1940's)
Malaysian poet
Fisher--Third p x, 531

LINCOLN, ABBEY (1930-)
Amer. singer, actress
Claghorn--Biog. p275
Claghorn--Jazz p185-186
Manchel--Women p94-95, por.

LINCOLN, ALMIRA HART
See PHELPS, ALMIRA HART LINCOLN

LINCOLN, EDITH MAAS (-1977)
Amer. pediatrician, (TB specialist)
O'Neill--Women's p206-207

LINCOLN, MARY (ANN) TODD (1818-1882)
Amer., noted Illinois mother, first lady, (wife of Abraham Lincoln)
Amer.--Mothers p162, por.
Daniels--Wash. p3-9
James--Notable (2) p404-406
Kulkin--Her p177-179
McHenry--Liberty's p247-248
Melick--Wives p39-42, por.
People's Almanac (1) p285
Sherr--American p64,79
Woman's Almanac p488-489, por.

LINCOLN, MARY JOHNSON BAILEY (1844-1921)
Amer. educator, lecturer, home economist, author
James--Notable (2) p406-407
McHenry--Liberty's p247
World--Who p100

LINCOLN, NANCY HANKS (1783/1784-1818)

Amer., noted Maryland mother, mother of Abraham Lincoln
Amer.--Mothers p174,250-251
Diagram--Mothers p147-149, por.
Faber--Presidents' p169-179
Kulkin--Her p179-180
People's Almanac (1) p289
Sherr--American p67

LINCOLN, VICTORIA ENDICOTT (1904-1981)
Amer. novelist
Ehrlich--Oxford p46

LIND, JENNY (1820-1887)
Swedish opera singer
Claghorn--Biog. p275
Coffin--Parade p338-340,579
Fabian--On p73-75, por.
Fry--1000 p240
Jones--Rutledge p472
Kirk--Circus p20-21, por.
Kulkin--Her p181
Macksey--Book p213, por.
Neidle--America's p219-220,223
People's Almanac (1) p175
Sherr--American p59,83
Smith--Women p119-171
Woman's Almanac p295-296, por.
World--Who p77

LIND, JOAN (1953-)
Amer. rower
O'Neill--Women's p584-585
Woman's Almanac p439-440

LINDBERGH, ANNE SPENCER MORROW (1906-)
Amer. aviatrix, author
Banner--Women p150-151
Boase--Sky's p137-156, see also index p221-222, por.
Clark--Leading p204-205
Cur. Biog. '76 p236-239, por.
Ehrlich--Oxford p54,181-182
Genett--Aviation p23-37, por.
McHenry--Liberty's p248
Millstein--We p258,271-272
Moers--Literary p251,297
100--Greatest (1) p111, por.
O'Neill--Women's p747-748
Woman's Almanac p107
World--Who p16

LINDBERGH, EVANGELINE LODGE LAND (1875-1954)
Amer., mother of Charles Lindbergh, Jr.

Diagram--Mothers p150-151,
por.

LIND-CAMPBELL, HJÖRDIS
(1891-)
Swedish physician
Hellstedt--Women p68-72, por.

LINDEMANN, EDNA M. (fl. 1970's)
Amer. museum curator
Women's--Female p119

LINDENFELD, LORE (fl. 1940's-
1970's)
German weaver
Miller--Lives p91-105, por.

LINDER, ANNA DORSEY (1911-)
Amer. genealogical researcher
Meyer--Who's p125

LINDFORS, ELSA VIVECA
TORSTENSDOTTER (1920-)
Swedish-Amer. actress
World--Who p258

LINDGREN, MAVIS
Canadian track and field
athlete
People's Almanac (3) p520

LINDNER, HERTHA (1920-1943)
German, Nazi victim
Partington--Who's p246-247

LINDNER, LYDIA
Amer. aviatrix
Keil--Those p64-65,98,209-210,
213-215

LINDSAY, DOROTHY STICKNEY
See STICKNEY, DOROTHY
HAYES

LINDSAY, KAY (fl. 1960's)
Amer. Antarctica geochemist
Land--New p21,37-54, por.

LINDSAY, MARGARET (1910-)
Amer. actress
Lamparski--What. Annual (4,5)
p335-340, por.
Springer--They p161,310, por.
World--Who p239

LINDSEY, CLAUDIA (fl. 1970's)
Amer. opera singer
Innis--Profiles p42-43, por.

LINDSTEN-THOMASSON, MARIANNE
(1909-)
Swedish physician
Hellstedt--Women p386-390, por.

LINDSTROM, PIA (c1939-)
Amer. TV newscaster
Gelfman--Women p14,17,90,103,
105,136-138,148-149, por.
Scheuer--Tel. p297, por.

LININGTON, ELIZABETH (1921-)
Amer. novelist
Seymour-Smith--Novels p175

LINKER, MOLLIE (fl. 1910's)
Amer. Jewish immigrant daugh-
ter
Hymowitz--Hist. p198,206,211

LINN, JO WHITE (1930-)
Amer. genealogical researcher,
author
Meyer--Who's p125

LINTHICUM, BARBARA
Amer. nurse
Talmey--Vogue p226, por.

LINTON, (ELIZABETH) "ELIZA"
LYNN (c1822-1898)
English journalist, novelist
Colby--Singular p15-45
Moers--Literary p297
Showlater--Lit. p327

LINWOOD, MARY (1755-1845)
English embroiderer, com-
poser, needlework artist
Callen--Women p113

LIPKOWSKA, LYDIA (1882-1955)
Russian opera singer
Tuggle--Golden p144-145

LIPPARD, LUCY
Amer. art critic
Parker--Old p7-8,126,130,134-135,
137,154-155
Women's--Female p122

LIPPINCOTT, SARA JANE CLARKE
See GREENWOOD, GRACE, pseud.

LIPSCOMB, DEE DEE (fl. 1970's)
Amer. painter
Women's--Female p49

LIPSTONE, JANE (1931-)
Amer. TV executive
Scheuer--Tel. p298

LIPTON, PEGGY (1947-)
Amer. singer, actress
Claghorn--Biog. p275

LISCEWSKA, ANNA DOROTHEA
(1722-1782)
German painter
Macksey--Book p200-201

"LISE"
See CHURCHILL, ODETTE
MARY CELINE BRAILLY
SANSOM

LISENHOFF, LISELOTT (fl. 1970's)
West German equestrian
McWhirter--Guinness p56

LISIEWSKA-THERBUSCH, ANNA
DOROTHEA (1721-1782)
German miniature painter
Harris--Women p36-37,42-43,79,
169-170,345-346
Macksey--Book p200
Parker--Old p92-93,96, fig. 51,
por.
Petersen--Women p48-49, por.

LISLE, ALICE, LADY (c1614-1685)
English, wife of John Lisle
Earle--Two Cent. (2) p469

LISSE, JEANNE
Guinean U.N. delegate
Macksey--Book p39

LISTON, MELBA DORETTA
(1925/1926-)
Amer. trombonist, composer
Claghorn--Biog. p276
Claghorn--Jazz p186

LISWOOD, LAURA
Amer. cable company
manager
Scheuer--Tel. p298-299

LITA (LITTE) OF REGENSBURG
(fl. c1544)
Jewish author
Henry--Written p90

LITAN, SHULAMIT (1936-)
Polish-Israeli textile

designer, craftswoman
O'Neill--Women's p126

LITTA, MARIE VON ELSNER (1856-
1883)
Amer. singer
Claghorn--Biog. p276

LITTLE, SALLY (fl. 1970's-1980's)
Amer. golfer
O'Neill--Women's p561

LITTLE, TAWNY GODIN
Amer. TV news anchor woman
Scheuer--Tel. p299

LITTLEDALE, CLARA SAVAGE
(1891-1956)
Amer. editor, author, journalist
Sicherman--Notable p421-423

"LITTLE MO"
See CONNOLLY, MAUREEN
(CATHERINE)

LITTLEWOOD, JOAN (1914-)
English theatrical director,
producer
Entertainers p246
Jones--Rutledge p475
Macksey--Book p236

LITTLEWOOD, MARGARET
Canadian aviatrix, fighter-
pilot trainer
O'Neill--Women's p551

LITTMAN, LYNNE (fl. 1970's)
Amer. filmmaker
Smith--Movies p189-190,257

LITVINENKO, LYDIA (fl. 1970's)
Russian economics researcher
Mandel--Soviet p218-222

LIVAK (LITVYAK), LYDIA (-1943)
Russian avistrix, war pilot
Macksey--Book p59
O'Neill--Women's p550

LIVELY, PENELOPE (1933-)
English children's book author
Seymour-Smith--Novels p175

LIVERMORE, HARRIET (1788-1868)
Amer. evangelist, clergyman
James--Notable (2) p409-410

LIVERMORE, MARY ASHTON RICE
(1820/1821-1905)
Amer. Civil War worker, lec-
turer, journalist, suffragist,
social reformer, noted
Massachusetts mother
Amer.--Mothers p261-262, por.
Bird--Enterprising p90-91,100
James--Notable (2) p410-413
McHenry--Liberty's p249
Sherr--American p59
Sochen--Herstory p162,164, por.
Taylor--Gener. p14
Webster's--Amer. p636-637
Who Did What p199
Woman's Almanac p452

LIVERMORE, SARAH WHITE (1789-
1874)
Amer. hymnist, poet
Claghorn--Biog. p277

LIVERS, JUDY (fl. 1970's)
Amer. firefighter
O'Neill--Women's p744

LIVIA DRUSILLA (c56-29 A.D.)
Roman empress, (third wife
of Augustus)
Fry--1000 p44
Pomeroy--Godd. p161,183-184
Zinserling--Women p66

LIVINGSTON, CORA (1806-1873)
Amer. belle
Peacock--Famous p80-89, por.

LIVINGSTON, JANE (fl. 1970's)
Amer. museum curator
Women's--Female p119

LIVINGSTON, MARGARET (1900-)
Amer. actress, (wife of Paul
Whiteman)
Springer--They p161,310

LIVINGSTON, MARGARET BEEKMAN
(fl. 1740's)
Amer. Revolutionary War
patriot
Booth--Women p91,138-139

LIVINGSTON, MILDRED RUTH
(1918-)
Canadian genealogical re-
searcher, author
Meyer--Who's p126

LIVINGSTON, MYRTLE SMITH (fl.
1920's)
Amer. playwright
Chinoy--Women p263-264

LIVINGSTON, SUSAN (fl. 1770's)
Amer. Revolutionary War
heroine
Truman--Women p15,18-26,200-201

LIVINGSTON, VIRGINIA POPE
(1907-)
Amer. genealogical researcher,
editor
Meyer--Who's p126-127

LIVINGSTONE, BEULAH (c1886-1975)
Amer. pioneer publicist
Slide--Early p10, por.

LIVINGSTONE, JANE
Amer. museum curator
O'Neill--Women's p616

LIVINGSTONE, MARY (1908/1909-
1983)
Amer. radio comedienne,
actress
Lamparski--What. (5) p10-11, por.
Woman's Almanac p320
World--Who p239

LIVRY, EMMA (-1863)
French ballet dancer
Migel--Ballerinas p232-238, por.

LLEWELLYN, DONNA M.
Amer. heroine, Carnegie
Medal winner
O'Neill--Women's p733

LLEWELLYN-SMITH, ELIZABETH
British civil servant
Macksey--Book p131

LLOYD, ALICE SPENCER GEDDES
(1876-1962)
Amer. college founder, edu-
cator
Sherr--American p80
Sicherman--Notable p423-424

LLOYD, CHRISTINE EVERT
See EVERT, CHRIS (CHRISTINE
MARIE)

LLOYD, CYNTHIA B.

Amer. economist, professor
O'Neill--Women's p420

LLOYD, DORIS (1900-1968)
English actress
Springer--They p162,310, por.

LLOYD, MARIE (1870-1922)
English actress, comedienne,
singer
Brecher--Lives p134
Entertainers p161
Jones--Rutledge p477
Macksey--Book p229
World--Who p269

LLOYD, NITA
Amer. hotel sales manager
O'Neill--Women's p525

LLOYD-GREEN, LORNA (1910-   )
Australian physician
Hellstedt--Women p391-392, por.

LOBEL, ANITA KEMPLER (1934-   )
Amer. illustrator, author of
children's books
McCullough--People p111-112

LOBELL, MIMI (fl. 1970's)
Amer. architect
O'Neill--Women's p612

LOBO, MARIA TERESA (fl. 1970's)
Portuguese clergyman
Macksey--Book p41

LO BUGLIO, RUDECINDA (CINDY)
ANN (1934-   )
Amer. genealogical researcher,
editor
Meyer--Who's p127

LOCH, JOICE NANKIVELL (1803-   )
Australian-Greek head, rug
industry
O'Neill--Women's p100,125

LOCHRIDGE, PATRICIA ("PAT")
Amer. TV news reporter
Marzolf--Up p137-138

LOCKE, ANNE
Scottish religious follower of
John Knox
Bainton--Spain p89-94

LOCKE, BESSIE (1865-1952)
Amer. educator
McHenry--Liberty's p249-250

LOCKE, EDITH RAYMOND (fl.
1940's-1970's)
Amer. magazine editor
O'Neill--Women's p474-475

LOCKE-KING, MRS. (fl. 1900's)
British motor-car racer
Macksey--Book p253-254

LOCKHART, ENID (fl. 1920's)
British tourist guide
Macksey--Book p176

LOCKHART, JUNE (1925-   )
Amer. actress
World--Who p239

LOCKPEZ, INVERNA (fl. 1970's)
Amer. painter
Women's--Female p49

LOCKRIDGE, FRANCES (c1897-1963)
Amer. novelist
Ehrlich--Oxford p358

LOCKWOOD, BELVA ANN BENNETT
McNALL (1830-1917)
Amer. lawyer, feminist, social
reformer
James--Notable (2) p413-416
Kulkin--Her p182-183
McHenry--Liberty's p250
Macksey--Book p125-126, por.
Marlowe--Great p115-118, por.
People's Almanac (1) p128
Reader's--Story p436
Reifert--Women p82-83
Sherr--American p42
Signif.--Amer. p19, por.
Stein--Fragments p213-229,727-
733, por.
Taylor--Gener. p15, por.
Warren--Pictorial p132-133, por.
Woman's Almanac p520-521, por.

LOCKWOOD, CHARLOTTE (fl. 1940's)
Amer. organist, teacher
Hazen--Interv. p359

LOCKWOOD, MARGARET (1916-   )
English actress
Shipman--Gold. p352-354, por.

Springer--They p162,164,310,
por.
World--Who p258

LOCKWOOD, MARY SMITH (1831-)
Amer. editor, club leader,
author
Sherr--American p40,151

LODEN, BARBARA (c1932-1980)
Amer. film director
Smith--Movies p54-58

LODYJENSKY, CATHERINE (fl.
1940's)
Russian physician
Neidle--America's p208-209

LOEB, CLARE SPARK (fl. 1970's)
Amer. artist
Women's--Female p107

LOEB, SOPHIE IRENE SIMON
(1876-1929)
Amer. journalist, humani-
tarian
James--Notable (2) p416-417
McHenry--Liberty's p250-251

LOEHR, DELORES
See LYNN, DIANA

LOFAS, JEANETTE (fl. 1970's)
Amer. author, foundation
co-founder
O'Neill--Women's p103

LOFTIN, TEE (c1921-)
Amer. author, publisher
O'Neill--Women's p490

LOFTS, NORAH ROBINSON (1904-
1983)
English novelist
Seymour-Smith--Novels p176

LOFTUS, BETH
Amer. psychologist,
researcher
Adams--Women p78,105,146,200

LOFTUS, MARIE CECILIA
("CISSIE") (1876-1943)
Scottish-Amer. actress,
impersonator
James--Notable (2) p417-418

LÖFVING, CONCORDIA (fl. 1870's)
Swedish-Anglo physical educa-
tor
Macksey--Book p73

LOGAN, ANNA (fl. 1860's)
Amer. Southern belle
DeLeon--Belles p240, por.

LOGAN, DEBORAH NORRIS (1761-
1839)
Amer. historical collector,
colonial social leader
James--Notable (2) p418-419

LOGAN, HANNAH
Amer. Quaker, feminist
Earnest--American p85

LOGAN, JACQUELINE (1901/1904-)
Amer. actress, journalist
Lamparski--What. (2) p156-157,
por.
Springer--They p164,310, por.

LOGAN, MRS. JOHN LEE
See TUCKER, GERTRUDE

LOGAN, KAREN (fl. 1970's)
Amer. basketball player
Hollander--100 p9-10,142, por.
O'Neill--Women's p567-568

LOGAN, MARTHA DANIEL(L) (1702/
1704-1779)
Amer. horticulturist, writer,
teacher, florist, botanist
DePauw--Rem. p48-49
James--Notable (2) p419-420
Williams--Demeter's p185-186

LOGAN, MARY SIMMERSON CUN-
NINGHAM (1838-1923)
Amer. writer, magazine editor
James--Notable (2) p421-422

LOGAN, MYRA (1908-1977)
Amer. physician, surgeon
O'Neill--Women's p214

LOGAN, OLIVE (1839-1909)
Amer. actress, playwright,
journalist, lecturer
Chinoy--Women p3,69,89, por.
James--Notable (2) p422-424

LOGUE, JOAN (fl. 1970's)

Amer. photographer
Women's--Female p67

LOHMAN, ANN TROW (1812-1878)
Amer. abortionist
Berkin--Women p250-253,264,
por.
Felton--Famous p263-264
James--Notable (2) p424-425
Macksey--Book p148

LOIR, MARIE ANNE (c1715-after
1769)
French artist
Harris--Women p42,167-168,345

LOIS
Biblical
Price--God p187-191

LOLLIA, PAULINA (-49 A.D.)
Roman empress, (wife of
Caligula)
Pomeroy--Godd. p163

LOLLOBRIGIDA, GINA (1927-)
Italian actress
Hershey--Between p131-133
Hirschhorn--Rating p230-231,
por.
Shipman--Internatl. p326-330,
por.
World--Who p258

LOMADY, MRS.
See SCHROTH, CLARA

LOMBARD, CAROLE (1908-1942)
Amer. actress, (wife of
Clark Gable)
Book--Lists (2) p189
Engstead--Star p130,132-146
Hirschhorn--Rating p231-232,
por.
James--Notable (2) p425-426
Keylin--Hollywood p182-183,
por.
McHenry--Liberty's p251
Mordden--Movie, see index
p294, por.
Shipman--Gold. p354-357, por.
Springer--They p164-166,310,
312, por.
Woman's Almanac p348-349, por.
World--Who p239

LOMBARDA (c1190-)

French troubadour
Bogin--Women p115,174-175

LOMBARDINI-SIRMEN, MADDALENA
(1745-)
Italian violinist, singer, composer
Neuls-Bates--Women p65,69,69n,
199,199n

LOMI, ARTEMISIA
See GENTILESCHI, ARTEMISIA

"LO MO"
See CAMERON, DONALDINA
MacKENZIE

LOMOND, DIANE
Amer. TV manager
Scheuer--Tel. p301

LONDA, JEWELDEAN (DEAN) JONES
(fl. 1950's-1970's)
Amer. Junior League executive
O'Neill--Women's p112

LONDON, CHARMIAN (c1870-1955)
Amer. wife of Jack London
Ehrlich--Oxford p403,440-441

LONDON, FLORA WELLMAN
Amer. (mother of Jack London)
Starr--Amer. p213,233-234

LONDON, JULIE (1926-)
Amer. singer, actress
Claghorn--Biog. p279
World--Who p239

LONG, DENISE (fl. 1960's)
Amer. basketball player
Hollander--100 p9-11, por.

LONG, JANE (c1798-1880)
Amer. early settler, "Mother
of Texas"
Sherr--American p223

LONG, JANET
Amer. TV director
Scheuer--Tel. p301

LONG, LORETTA
Amer. TV actress, educator
Scheuer--Tel. p302

LONG, MARY JANE (fl. 1850's)

Amer. Western pioneer
Time--Women p31

LONG, ROSE McCONNELL (1892-
1970)
Amer. Senator, (wife of
Henry Long)
Chamberlin--Min. p118-121
Miller--Fishbait p64-65
O'Neill--Women's p66

LONG, SHARON (c1951-)
Amer. molecular biologist
Science Digest--100 p50, por.

LONG, SHELLEY
Amer. TV actress, writer
Scheuer--Tel. p302, por.

LONG, TANIA (1913-)
Amer. foreign correspondent,
journalist
Marzolf--Up p70

LONGET, CLAUDINE GEORGETTE
(1941/1942-)
French-Amer. actress, singer,
(ex-wife of Andy Williams)
Anderson--People p255

LONGHI, BARBARA (1552-1619/
1638)
Italian painter
Fine--Women p21-22
Sparrow--Women p24,41
Women's--Female p11

LONGSHORE, HANNAH E. MYERS
(1819-1901/1902)
Amer. pioneer physician
James--Notable (2) p426-428
McHenry--Liberty's p251-252
Sherr--American p204

LONGWORTH, ALICE ROOSEVELT
(1884-1980)
Amer. socialite, (daughter
of Theodore Roosevelt)
Book--Lists (2) p261
Clark--Leading p28-30
Cur. Biog. '75 p254-258, por.
Cur. Biog. '80 p458
Daniels--Wash. p40-45,48,78,
por.
Forma--They, see index p242
(under Longworth), por.
McHenry--Liberty's p252

Miller--Fishbait p104,115
Woman's Almanac p490

LONGYEAR, MARY BEECHER (fl.
1900's)
Amer. philanthropist
Sherr--American p100

LONSDALE, KATHLEEN (1903-1971)
British physicist, crystallog-
rapher
Macksey--Book p158

LOOS, ANITA (1893-1981)
Amer. novelist, playwright,
film writer
Avenel--Comp. (2) p158
Clark--Leading p107
Cur. Biog. '74 p247-248, por.
Cur. Biog. '81 p468
Dunlap--Calif. p121, por.
Ehrlich--Oxford p416
Jones--Rutledge p481
McHenry--Liberty's p252-253
O'Neill--Women's p677
P.W.--Author p306-309,509-510
Seymour-Smith--Novels p176
Smith--Movies p15-16
World--Who p16

LOPATA, HELENA (1925-)
Amer. author
Hymowitz--Hist. p328

LOPES, MARIA (fl. 1890's)
Brazilian seamstress, labor
worker, feminist
Hahner--Women p114-116

LOPEZ, ENCARNACION
See ARGENTINITA

LOPEZ, MARIA PICASSO (1860-)
Spanish, mother of Pablo
Picasso
Diagram--Mothers p206-207, por.

LOPEZ, NANCY (1957-)
Amer. golfer
Cur. Biog. '78 p255-257, por.
Gutman--More p9-26, por.
McWhirter--Guinness p78
O'Neill--Women's p561
World--Who p217

LOPEZ, NATIVIDAD (1914-)
Filipino judge
Macksey--Book p129

LOSCH, TILLY, COUNTESS OF
CARMARVON (1907-1975)
Austrian-English dancer,
choreographer
Cur. Biog. '76 p471

LÖSER, MARGARET SIBYLLA VON
(fl. 175h cent.)
German scholar
Mead--Hist. p426

LOSH, NANCY (1867-)
Amer. centenarian
Mitchell--Yessir p26-28, por.

LOTHROP, ALICE LOUISE HIGGINS
(1870-1920)
Amer. social worker
James--Notable (2) p430-431
McHenry--Liberty's p253-254

LOTHROP, AMY
See WARNER, ANN BARTLETT

LOTHROP, HARRIETT MULFORD
STONE (1844-1924)
Amer. author
Ehrlich--Oxford p45,84
James--Notable (2) p431-432
McHenry--Liberty's p254
Warren--Pictorial p129
World--Who p16

LOT'S WIFE
Biblical
Price--God p35-39
Woman's Almanac p399

"LOTTA"
See CRABTREE, (CHARLOTTE)
LOTTA

LOTZ, IRMGARD FLÜGGE
See FLÜGGE-LOTZ, IRMGARD

LOUCHHEIM, ALINE MILTON
BERNSTEIN
See SAARINEN, ALINE MILTON
BERNSTEIN

LOUD, PATRICIA RUSSELL (1926-)
Amer. TV personality, author
Cur. Biog. '74 p249-251, por.

LOUDON, DOROTHY (1933-)
Amer. actress, singer
Cur. Biog. '84 p237-239, por.
World--Who p239

LOUGHBOROUGH, MARY ANN
WEBSTER (1863-1887)
Amer. Civil War diarist, camp
follower
Hoople--As p99-106
Hymowitz--Hist. p146-147
Sherr--American p128, por.

LOUGHLIN, MARY ANNE (1956-)
Amer. TV producer, host
Scheuer--Tel. p303

LOUIS, MARILYN
See FLEMING, RHONDA

LOUISE, ANITA (1915-1970)
Amer. actress
Springer--They p166,312, por.
World--Who p239

LOUISE, PRINCESS OF GREAT
BRITAIN, DUCHESS OF
ARGYLE (1848-1939)
English princess, daughter of
Queen Victoria
Callen--Women p5,110,166

LOUISE OF SAVOY (1476-c1531)
French regent
Macksey--Book p24

LOVE, ANN (-1858)
Amer. pioneer, innkeeper
Sherr--American p3

LOVE, BESSIE (1898-1931)
Amer. actress
Springer--They p166,168,312,
por.

LOVE, IRIS CORNELIA (1933-)
Amer. archeologist, art his-
torian
Cur. Biog. '82 p241-244, por.

LOVE, NANCY HARKNESS (1914-)
Amer. aviatrix, WAFS founder
Keil--Those, see index p327
Macksey--Book p250
Warren--Pictorial p194

LOVE, RUTH B. (c1932-)
Amer. educator
O'Neill--Women's p429

LOVEJOY, ESTHER CLAYSON POHL
(1870-1967)
Amer. physician

Kulkin--Her p183-184
O'Neill--Women's p226
Sicherman--Notable p424-426

LOVELY, PERSIS (fl. 1810's)
    Amer. friend of Indians
    Sherr--American p11

LOVEMAN, AMY (1881-1955)
    Amer. literary critic,
    magazine editor, author
    Sicherman--Notable p426-428

LOW, JULIETTE MAGILL KINZIE
    GORDON (1860-1927)
    Amer., founder of Girl
    Scouts of America
    James--Notable (2) p432-434
    Kulkin--Her p184-185
    McHenry--Liberty's p254
    Marlowe--Great p178-182, por.
    O'Neill--Women's p113
    Sherr--American p50, por.
    Signif.--Amer. p29, por.
    Webster's--Amer. p651

LOWE, ANN (1898-1981)
    Amer. fashion designer
    O'Neill--Women's p241-242

LOWE, BARBARA E.
    Amer. TV executive
    Scheuer--Tel. p304, por.

LOWE, CAROL CHANNING
    See CHANNING, CAROL

LOWE, DELLA
    Amer. Indian, labor union
    leader
    O'Neill--Women's p307

LOWELL, MAY LAWRENCE (1874-1925)
    Amer. poet, critic
    Avenel--Comp. (2) p159
    Benét--New p109-113, por.
    Bernikow--World p226-227
    Chester--Rising p4-7, por.
    Ehrlich--Oxford, see index
    p457
    James--Notable (2) p434-437
    Jones--Rutledge p487
    Kaplan--Salt p203-204, por.
    Kronenberger--Atlan. p471-472
    Kupferberg--First p93-94, por.
    Longstreet--Queen p191
    McHenry--Liberty's p254-255

Moers--Literary p297
Rogers--Ladies, see index p231
Sherr--American p102
Signif.--Amer. p30, por.
Webster's--Amer. p632
Who Did What p203
Wintle--Makers p314-315, #282
Woman's Almanac p254
World--Who p16

LOWELL, JOSEPHINE SHAW (1843-1905)
    Amer. charity worker, social
    reformer, philanthropist
    James--Notable (2) p437-439
    McHenry--Liberty's p255
    O'Neill--Women's p287
    Warren--Pictorial p143,145

LOWELL, MARIA WHITE (1821-1853)
    Amer. poet, (wife of James
    Russell Lowell)
    Bernikow--World p203
    James--Notable (2) p439-440

LOWENSTEIN-WERTHEIM, ANNE
    (-1927)
    British Princess, airplane
    pilot
    Macksey--Book p248

LOWE-PORTER, HELEN TRACY
    (1876-1963)
    Amer. translator, writer
    Sicherman--Notable p428-429

LOWER, DOROTHY M. (1914-)
    Amer. genealogical researcher,
    author
    Meyer--Who's p127

LOWERY, ELLIN PRINCE
    See SPEYER, ELLIN LESLIE
    PRINCE LOWERY

LOWERY, LIZZIE
    Amer. Indian, writer of
    Lewis & Clark expedition
    Coffin--Parade p258-259

LOWNDES, MARIE BELLOC (1868-1947)
    French novelist
    Showalter--Lit. p344

LOWNDES, MARY (fl. 1890's)
    British stained glass artist
    Callen--Women p177,224

LOWRIE, JEAN ELIZABETH
(1918-)
Amer. librarian, educator,
organization official
Cur. Biog. '73 p262-264, por.
O'Neill--Women's p430

LOWRY, EDITH ELIZABETH
(1897-1970)
Amer. religious leader,
organization executive
Sicherman--Notable p429-430

LOWRY, RHONWYN (fl. 1950's)
Amer. home demonstration
agent
O'Neill--Women's p28

LOY, MINA (1882-1966)
English-Amer. artist, poet
Bernikow--World p253-254

LOY, MYRNA (1905-)
Amer. actress
Book--Lists (2) p189
Hazen--Interv. p404
Hirschhorn--Rating p235-236,
por.
Mordden--Movie p99-100,166,
282, por.
Shipman--Gold. p357-362, por.
Springer--They p168-170,312,
por.
Woman's Almanac p349
World--Who p239

LOZIER, CLEMENCE SOPHIA
HARNED (1813-1888)
Amer. physician, reformer
James--Notable (2) p440-442
McHenry--Liberty's p255-256
Sherr--American p171

LUBCHENCO, PORTIA (1887-)
Amer. physician, noted
Colorado mother
Amer.--Mothers p66, por.

LUBETKIN, ZIVIA (c1920-)
Polish resister
Woman's Almanac p449-450

LUBICH, CHIARA (fl. 1970's)
Italian religious leader
O'Neill--Women's p399-400

LUBKIN, GLORIA B.
Amer. physicist, science

writer, editor
O'Neill--Women's p476

LUBOSHUTZ, LEA (1887-1965)
Russian violinist, music
teacher
Claghorn--Biog. p281

LUCAS, ELIZA
See PINCKNEY, ELIZA LUCAS

LUCAS, MARTHA B.
See PATE, MARTHA B. LUCAS

LUCAS, VICTORIA, pseud.
See PLATH, SYLVIA

LUCCI, SUSAN
Amer. actress
Scheuer--Tel. p305

LUCE, CLARE BOOTHE (1903-1987)
Amer. author, actress, Con-
gresswoman, Ambassador,
journalist, war correspondent,
noted New York mother
Amer.--Mothers p397
Bachtold--Gifted p107
Chamberlin--Min. p165-174, por.
Clark--Leading p168-171
Ehrlich--Oxford, see index p457
Greenebaum--Politics p53-77, por.
Jones--Rutledge p488
McHenry--Liberty's p256
Miller--Fishbait p67-71,255-256,
261
O'Neill--Women's p91, por.
People's Almanac (2) p1154
Signif.--Amer. p67, por.
Webster's--Amer. p654
Woman's Almanac p477, por.
World--Who p146

LUCE, DAW TEE TEE (fl. 1920's-
1970's)
Burmese humanitarian
O'Neill--Women's p737

LUCERO, JUDY (fl. 1970's)
Amer. Chicana poet
Fisher--Third p viii,395

LUCERO-TRUJILLO, MARCELA
CHRISTINE (fl. 1970's)
Amer. Chicana poet, instructor
Fisher--Third p ix,324,401

LUCHINS, EDITH H.

Polish-Amer. mathematician,
professor, author
O'Neill--Women's p178

LUCID, SHANNON W. (fl. 1970's-
1980's)
Amer. astronaut-trainee,
biochemist
Oberg--Space p111-112, por.
O'Connor--Sally p2,17,20-21,25,
por.
O'Neill--Women's p740, por.

LUCINGE, BABA DE FAUCIGNY
See DE FAUCIGNY, BABA LUCINGE

LUCKINBILL, LUCIE
See ARNAZ, LUCIE

"LUCKY"
French model
Keenan--Women p116,121, por.

LUCRETIA (fl. c510 B.C.)
Roman heroine
Pomeroy--Godd. p154,160-161
Zinserling--Women p63-64 ʾ

LUCY, AUTHERINE (fl. 1950's)
Amer. social reformer
O'Neill--Women's p702

LUDINGTON, SYBIL (1761-1839)
Amer. Revolutionary patriot,
heroine
Clyne--Patriots p27-34
DePauw--Found. p163-164
DePauw--Rem. p89
McHenry--Liberty's p256
Millstein--We p35
Meyer--Petticoat p209-210
Sherr--American p159, por.
Somerville--Women p24-27
Williams--Demeter's p246-247
Woman's Almanac p451

LUDLOW, INGER P. (1930-   )
Danish genealogical researcher,
translator, editor
Meyer--Who's p128

"LUDOMIR, MAID OF"
See RACHEL, HANNAH

LUDWIG, CHRISTA (1932-   )
Austrian opera singer
Cur. Biog. '71 p238-240, por.

Gammond--Illus. p246, por.
World--Who p77

LUDWIG, SARAH (fl. 1970's)
British skier
Macksey--Book p261

LUFF, ELLEN
Amer. lawyer
O'Neill--Women's p358-359

LUHAN, MABEL GANSON DODGE
(1879-1962)
Amer. art patron, author,
scholar, salon hostess
Avenel--Comp. (2) p161
Clark--Leading p83-84
Ehrlich--Oxford p106,124,389
Longstreet--Queen p111-115, por.
McHenry--Liberty's p256-257
Rogers--Ladies, see index p231,
por.
Sherr--American p157
Sicherman--Notable p430-432

LUICIME, ELEANOR
See COMPSON, BETTY

LUKENS, REBECCA WEBB PENNOCK
(1794-1854)
Amer. mill owner, ironmaster,
shipwright
Bird--Enterprising p53-56
James--Notable (2) p442-443
McHenry--Liberty's p257
Macksey--Book p163-164
Sherr--American p199, por.
Stein--Lives p1-25, por.

LULING, ELIZABETH (1930-   )
English-Amer. children's book
author
Book--Lists (2) p223

"LULU BELLE" (1913-   )
Amer. singer
Claghorn--Biog. p282

LUMAIN-DAIN, ALEXANDRA (fl.
1970's)
Amer. artist
Women's--Female p108

LUMPKIN, MARY B.T. (fl. 1890's)
Amer. garden club founder
Sherr--American p146

LUNA, BEATRICE DE
See NASI, (DONA) GRACIA

LUNA, DONYALE (c1925-1979)
Amer. model
Keenan--Women p173,175-176,
178-179, por.

LUND, ALICE (1900-   )
Swedish textile designer
O'Neill--Women's p271

LUND, CHRISTINE
Amer. TV co-anchor
Scheuer--Tel. p306

LUNDBERG, EMMA OCTAVIA
(1881-1954)
Swedish-Amer. social worker
Sicherman--Notable p432-434

LUNDEBERG, HELEN (1908-   )
Amer. artist
Munro--Originals p170-177, por.

LUNDEN, JOAN
Amer. TV personality
Scheuer--Tel. p306

LUNDGREN, INGRID (fl. 1960's-
1970's)
Swedish director
Marzolf--Up p288

LUNDIN, INGEBORG (1921-   )
Swedish glass-maker
O'Neill--Women's p273

LUNGER, MARY JANE DU PONT
(c1916-   )
Amer. millionaire
Forbes--400 ('84) p191

LUNNEY, JESSIE MAE WENCK
(1870-1961)
Amer. teacher, writer,
noted North Dakota mother
Amer.--Mothers p416-417, por.

LUPESCU, MAGDA (1896-1977)
Romanian paramour, wife of
King Carol of Romania
Cur. Biog. '77 p468
Jones--Rutledge p490
People's Almanac (1) p1243-1244

LUPINO, IDA (1918-   )
English-Amer. actress,

director
Book--Lists (2) p189
Hirschhorn--Rating p237-238, por.
O'Neill--Women's p668
Shipman--Gold. p365-366, por.
Smith--Movies p36-39, por.
Springer--They p170,312, por.
World--Who p259

LUPTON, EDITH D. (fl. 1870's-
1890's)
British pottery designer,
decorator
Callen--Women p61,224

LURIA, MIRIAM SHAPIRA (fl. 13th
Cent.)
Jewish scholar
Henry--Written p87

LURIE, ALISON (1926-   )
Amer. novelist, lecturer
Seymour-Smith--Novels p177,
por.

LUSK, GEORGIA LEE (1893/1894-
1971)
Amer. Congresswoman, edu-
cator
Chamberlin--Min. p201-203
Cur. Biog. '71 p466
Sicherman--Notable p434-435

LUSSAN, ZELIE DE (1863-1949)
Amer. singer
Claghorn--Biog. p122
James--Notable (1) p458-459

LUSSIER, YVONNE
See D'ORSAY, FIFI

LUTHER, ANGELA (c1940-   )
German terrorist
Woman's Almanac p506

LUTHER, IRENE
See RICH, IRENE

LUTHER, MARGARETHA ZIEGLER
(c1463-1534)
German, mother of Martin
Luther
Diagram--Mothers p158-159, por.

LUTHER-SCHAFER, VIVIAN (fl.
1930's)
Amer. genealogical researcher
Meyer--Who's p128

LUTYENS, ELISABETH (1908-)
English musical composer
Neuls-Bates--Women p312-322

LUTZ, BERTHA (fl. 1930's)
Brazilian member of Parlia-
ment, feminist
Macksey--Book p37

LUTZ, FRANCIE LARRIEU (1952-)
Amer. track and field athlete
Woman's Almanac p427

LUXEMBURG, ROSA (1870-1919)
Polish-German socialist
leader, activist, economist,
editor, author
Brecher--Lives p102
Fraser--Heroines p219-224, por.
Jones--Rutledge p492
Macksey--Book p35-36, por.
O'Neill--Women's p712
Palmer--Who's p210-211
Partington--Who's p251-252
Prause--School p101, por.
Taylor--Gener. p36-37, por.
Who Did What p204
Wintle--Makers p319-320, #285
Woman's Almanac p387, por.
World--Who p168

LUZ GONZALES DEL VALLE V. DE
MARINO, MARIA (c1897-1969)
Peruvian politician
Hahner--Women p85-89

LYALL, EDNA, pseud.
See BAYLEY, ADA ELLEN

LYDIA
Biblical
Price--God p175-178

LYMAN, AMY BROWN (1872-1959)
Amer. Mormon leader,
writer, social worker,
noted Utah mother
Amer.--Mothers p528-529, por.

LYMAN, DOROTHY
Amer. actress
Scheuer--Tel. p307, por.

LYMAN, MARY ELY (1887-1975)
Amer. theologian
Sicherman--Notable p435-437

LYNCH, ANNE CHARLOTTE

See BOTTA, ANNE CHARLOTTE
LYNCH

LYNCH, ELIZABETH ALLSTON
(c1728-)
Amer. patriot, (wife of
Thomas Lynch)
Flexner--Face p76, por.

LYNCH, MARY ATKINS
See ATKINS, MARY

LYNCH, PATRICIA
Amer. TV news producer
Scheuer--Tel. p307

LYND, HELEN MERRELL (1896-1982)
Amer. sociologist, author
Banner--Women p30,51,192-194,
201

LYNDON, ALICE ATKINSON
(1935-)
Amer. sculptor, photographer
Ruddick--Working p25-37,343-344,
por.

LYNDS, BEVERLY TURNER (fl.
1970's)
Amer. astronomer
O'Neill--Women's p152-153

LYNLEY, CAROL (1942/1943-)
Amer. actress
World--Who p239

LYNN, CHERYL (fl. 1970's)
Amer. singer, composer
Glassman--Year '79 p125, por.

LYNN, DIANA (1926-1971)
Amer. actress, pianist
Cur. Biog. '72 p466
Lamparski--What. (8) p186-187,
por.

LYNN, ELIZABETH COOK (1930-)
Amer. Indian (Crow Creek
Sioux) writer
Fisher--Third p iv,24,104

LYNN, JANET NOWICKI (1953-)
Amer. skater
Hollander--100 p7,34-35, por.
Jacobs--Modern p22-35, por.
Kulkin--Her p186-187
McWhirter--Guinness p9, por.
Sabin--Women p24-42, por.

LYNN, JUDY (1936-)
    Amer. singer, songwriter
    Claghorn--Biog. p283

LYNN, LORETTA WEBB (1935-)
    Amer. singer
    Anderson--People p258
    Claghorn--Biog. p283
    Cur. Biog. '73 p266-269, por.
    Dew--Women p8-33, por.
    100--Greatest (1) p83, por.
    O'Neill--Women's p629
    Simon--Best p367-369, por.
    Woman's Almanac p296, por.
    World--Who p269

LYNN, SHARON (1907-1963)
    Amer. actress
    Springer--They p170,312

LYON, JEMIMA SHEPHERD
    (fl. 1789's-1790's)
    Amer., mother of Mary Lyon
    Berkin--Women p178-179,182

LYON, LILIAN BOWES (1855-1949)
    English poet
    Bernikow--World p174

LYON, LISA
    Amer. gymnast
    People--Best p73

LYON, MARY MASON (1797-1849)
    Amer. educator, founder,
    college president
    Berkin--Women, see index p436,
        por.
    Burgess--Education p29-45, por.
    Earnest--American p56,125-126
    Fine--Women p92
    Ingraham--Album p38, por.
    James--Notable (2) p443-447
    Kulkin--Her p187-188
    McHenry--Liberty's p257-258
    Macksey--Book p68
    Neidle--America's p30
    O'Neill--Women's p264
    People's Almanac (2) p1051
    Reader's--Story p131
    Sherr--American p35,62,100,
        108,111
    Signif.--Amer. p12, por.
    Sochen--Herstory p140
    Stoddard--Famous p263-274, por.
    Warren--Pictorial p72-73, por.
    Webster's--Amer. p658

Who Did What p205
Woman's Almanac p145-146,154-
    155, por.
World--Who p100

LYONS, JOSEPHINE (fl. 1940's)
    Amer. radio advertising
    agency director
    Women--Radio p18

LYONS, RACHEL (fl. 1860's)
    Amer. Southern belle
    DeLeon--Belles p144-145, por.

LYSISTRATA
    Greek heroine
    O'Neill--Women's p554

LYTTELTON, RACHEL
    English, (wife of Sir Richard
    Lyttelton)
    Ware--Meet p78

LYTTON, ROSINA DOYLE BULWER-,
    LADY (1804-1882)
    Irish novelist
    Showalter--Lit. p322

M

MA CH'ÜAN (1768-1848)
    Chinese painter
    Petersen--Women p156

"MA PERKINS"
    See PAYNE, VICTORIA

MA SHOU-CHEN (1592-1628)
    Chinese poet, painter
    Petersen--Women p153-154

MA YA-LI (1955-)
    Chinese painter
    Petersen--Women p164

MAASS, CLARA LOUISE (1876/
    1879-1901)
    Amer. nurse
    McHenry--Liberty's p259
    O'Neill--Women's p232, por.
    Sherr--American p150,153-154,
        por.

MAASS-MOSEN, NANCY (fl. 1970's)
    Amer. painter
    Women's--Female p49

MABLEY, JACKIE ("MOMS")
(c1894-1975)
Amer. comedienne
Cur. Biog. '75 p261-264, por.
Cur. Biog. '75 p470
Woman's Almanac p319-320, por.

MABOVITZ, BLUMA (-1951)
Polish-Russian, mother of
Golda (Mabovitz) Meir
Diagram--Mothers p164-165,
por.

McAFEE, MILDRED HELEN (1900-)
Amer. educator, college
president, director, WAVES
Hazen--Interv. p231
McHenry--Liberty's p198
O'Neill--Women's p535,537
Signif.--Amer. p68, por.
Warren--Pictorial p194

McAFEE, NAOMI J.
Amer. physicist, electronics
corporation director
O'Neill--Women's p193

McALISKEY, BERNADETTE DEVLIN
See DEVLIN, BERNADETTE
JOSEPHINE

McALISTER, DOROTHY (c1900-)
Amer. government official
Ware--Beyond p148-149, see
also index p200

McALISTER, ELIZABETH (1940-)
Amer. art teacher, activist
Book--Lists (2) p17

McALLISTER, ANNABELLE COX
(1904-)
Amer. genealogical researcher,
writer
Meyer--Who's p131

McALMON, VICTORIA (fl. 1910's-
1970's)
Amer. teacher, radical
Showalter--These p109-115,
por.

McANDREW, ANNA (c1868-)
Amer. centenarian
Mitchell--Yessir p64-67, por.

McARDLE, ANDREA (1963-)

Amer. actress
World--Who p241

McARTHUR, HENRIETTA DUNCAN
(1945-)
Amer. agriculturalist, government official
O'Neill--Women's p24

MacARTHUR, JEAN
Amer., wife of Douglas
MacArthur
Miller--Fishbait p361-362

MacARTHUR, MARGARET CROWL
(1928-)
Amer. singer, autoharpist
Claghorn--Biog. p285

McAVOY, MAY (1901-1984)
Amer. actress
Lamparski--What. (3) p174-175,
por.
Lamparski--What. (8) p190-191,
por.
Springer--They p179,315

McBAIN, LAURIE (1949-)
Amer. novelist
World--Who p17

MacBETH, ANN (1875-1948)
British designer, embroiderer,
illustrator
Callen--Women p125-126,224

MacBETH, E.
Amer. track & field athlete
Macksey--Book p258

MacBETH, FLORENCE (1891-)
Amer. opera singer
Claghorn--Biog. p285

McBETH, SUSAN LAW (1830-1893)
Amer. missionary to Indians
James--Notable (2) p447-448

McBRIDE, KATHARINE ELIZABETH
(1904-1976)
Amer. educator, psychologist,
college president
Cur. Biog. '76 p471

McBRIDE, MARY MARGARET (1899-
1976)
Amer. journalist, radio per-

sonality, author
Cur. Biog. '76 p471
Lamparski--What. (3) p20-21,
  por.
McHenry--Liberty's p259
Marzolf--Up p48-49,125-126
O'Neill--Women's p437,492-493
Woman's Almanac p270
Women--Radio p1-2
World--Who p292

MacBRIDE, MAUDE GONNE
See GONNE, MAUDE

McBRIDE, PATRICIA (1942-)
  Amer. ballet dancer
World--Who p71

McBROWN, GERTRUDE P. (fl.
  1970's)
  Amer. dramatic artist
Innis--Profiles p28-29, por.

McCABE, RITA (fl. 1960's)
  Amer. business executive,
  personnel worker
M.I.T.--Women p x,24-29,34

McCAIN, MAUREEN (fl. 1970's)
  Amer. wine industrial
  executive
O'Neill--Women's p16

McCALL, DOROTHY LAWSON
  (1888-)
  Amer. author, lecturer,
  rancher, activist, noted
  Oregon mother
Amer.--Mothers p450-451, por.

McCALLA, IRISH (1929-)
  Amer. actress
Lamparski--What. Annual (4,5)
  p53-57, por.
Lamparski--What. (8) p192-193,
  por.

McCALLA, MARGARET (fl. 1860's)
  Amer. Confederate patriot,
  letter-writer
Wiley--Confed. p175

McCALLA, SARAH (fl. 1770's)
  Amer. Revolutionary War
  patriot
Meyer--Petticoat p189-193

MACALPINE, IDA (1899-1974)
  German physician (psychomatic
  medicine), medical writer
Macksey--Book p158

McCAMBRIDGE, MERCEDES (1918-)
  Amer. actress
Higham--Celeb. p138-141, por.
Hirschhorn--Rating p238-239, por.
World--Who p241

McCANNEL, LOUISE WALKER
  (c1916-)
  Amer. civic worker
Diamonstein--Open p284-288, por.

McCANNON, DINGA (fl. 1970's)
  Amer. artist
Women's--Female p108

McCARDELL, CLAIRE (1905-1958)
  Amer. fashion designer
O'Neill--Women's p239,244-245,
  247,249
Sicherman--Notable p437-439

McCARTHY, DINITIA SMITH (fl.
  1970's)
  Amer. reporter, filmmaker
Smith--Movies p191-192,261, por.

McCARTHY, JUSTINE
See KENDALL, KAY

McCARTHY, KATHRYN O'LOUGHLIN
  (1894-1952)
  Amer. Congresswoman
Chamberlin--Min. p100-103

McCARTHY, LARK (1955-)
  Amer. TV news co-anchor
Scheuer--Tel. p309

McCARTHY, MARY THERESE (1912-)
  Amer. novelist, travel writer,
  journalist, critic, editor,
  educator
Avenel--Comp. (2) p162
Cur. Biog. '69 p270-272, por.
Ehrlich--Oxford, see index p457
Howard--Seven p214-264
Jones--Rutledge p496
Kufrin--Uncom. p72-91, por.
McHenry--Liberty's p259-260
Moers--Literary p298
O'Neill--Women's p415,474,680,686

P.W.--Author p107-109,510
Seymour-Smith--Novels p66-67,
178
Seymour-Smith--Who's p237-238
Sochen--Herstory p325-326
Spacks--Contemp. p75-91,179-
180
Webber--Woman p46-50
Webster's--Amer. p662-663
Wintle Makers p323-324, #287
Woman's Almanac p254
World--Who p17

McCARTHY, SHERYL
Amer. TV news correspondent
Scheuer--Tel. p310

McCARTNEY, LOUISE SMITT (fl.
1950's-1970's)
Amer. clubwoman, noted
Alabama mother
Amer.--Mothers p10, por.

McCAUGHAN, CYNTHIA (1928-)
Amer. labor leader
O'Neill--Women's p309

MacAULAY, CATHARINE SAW-
BRIDGE (1731-1791)
English historian, Revolu-
tionary War patriot
Booth--Women, see index p326
Meyer--Petticoat p52
Moers--Literary p297

MacAULAY, ROSE (1881-1958)
English novelist, poet,
critic, travel writer,
anthropologist
Avenel--Comp. (1) p329
Crosland--Beyond, see index
p257
Jones--Rutledge p495
Morley--Literary p207
Seymour-Smith--Novels p178
Showalter--Lit. p345

McCAULEY, MARY LUDWIG HAYS
See PITCHER, MOLLY

McCHESNEY, MARTHA (1855-)
Amer. social reformer
Sherr--American p49-50

McCLELLAND, NANCY (c1877-1959)
Amer. interior decorator
O'Neill--Women's p279-280

McCLENDON, ROSE (1884-1936)
Amer. actress
James--Notable (2) p449-450

McCLENDON, SARAH (1913-)
Amer. journalist, news-
bureau owner
Miller--Fishbait p203-204
O'Neill--Women's p450-451

McCLINTOCK, BARBARA (1902-)
Amer. pathologist, biochemist,
geneticist
Cur. Biog. '84 p262-265, por.
O'Neill--Women's p144,160

McCLINTOCK, MARTHA (c1947-)
Amer. biopsychologist
Science Digest--100 p71

McCLINTOCK, MARY ANN (fl.
1840's)
Amer. feminist
Gurko--Ladies p2,96,101,105,
107, por.
Sherr--American p41

McCLOY, HELEN (1904-)
Amer. novelist
Seymour-Smith--Novels p178

McCLURE, MARY (fl. 1770's)
Amer. Revolutionary War
patriot, pioneer, heroine
Meyer--Petticoat p197-198

McCLURG, PATRICIA ANN (fl.
1970's)
Amer. church executive
O'Neill--Women's p396

McCLUSKEY, ELLEN LEHMAN (fl.
1970's)
Amer. interior decorator
O'Neill--Women's p281-282

MACCOBY, ELEANOR
Amer. psychologist, professor,
feminist
Sochen--Movers p266-268

MacCOLL, ELIZABETH (fl. 1890's)
British bookbinder
Callen--Women p194-195

McCOLLIN, FRANCES (1892-1960)
Amer. blind composer,

conductor
Claghorn--Biog. p286
Jablonski--Ency. p259-260

McCOMB, CATHERINE NAVARRE
(fl. 1780's)
Amer. social leader
Earle--Two Cent. (2) p xiv,
por.

MACOMBER, MARY LIZZIE
(1861-1916)
Amer. artist
McHenry--Liberty's p265

McCONNELL, BEATRICE (1894-)
Amer. labor leader, govern-
ment official
O'Neill--Women's p333

McCONNER, DOROTHY (fl.
1960's-1970's)
Amer. executive
O'Neill--Women's p520

McCONNEY, FLORENCE (1894-)
Canadian physician
Hellstedt--Women p120-122, por.

McCORD, LOUISA SUSANNAH
CHEVES (1810-1879)
Amer. feminist, poet, hospi-
tal organizer, Civil War
patriot, plantation manager
James--Notable (2) p450-452
Scott--Southern p83

McCORMACK, ELLEN (1926-)
Amer. Presidential candidate
Schoenebaum--Prof. p398-399
Woman's Almanac p477-478

Mc CORMACK, PATTY (1945-)
Amer. child actress
Edelson--Kids p106-107,109,
por.

Mc CORMICK, ANNE ELIZABETH
O'HARE (1881/1882-1954)
Amer. journalist, foreign
correspondent
McHenry--Liberty's p260-261
Marzolf--Up p54,56-57
O'Neill--Women's p444,452
Sicherman--Notable p439-440
Sochen--Herstory p311,313,
316-317,319

McCORMICK, EDITH ROCKEFELLER
(c1872-1932)
Amer. medical, musical and art
patron, philanthropist
Birmingham--Grande, see index
p294, por.
James--Notable (2) p452-454
Rogers--Ladies p147-148,153, por.
Woman's Almanac p210-211

McCORMICK, ELIZABETH ("FRENCHY")
(-1941)
Amer. dancer
Sherr--American p224

McCORMICK, JILL
Amer. aviatrix, army flier
Keil--Those p230,277,295-296

McCORMICK, KATHARINE DEXTER
(1875-1967)
Amer. philanthropist
Sicherman--Notable p440-442

McCORMICK, NETTIE FOWLER
(1835-1923)
Amer. businesswoman,
philanthropist
James--Notable (2) p454-455
O'Neill--Women's p510

McCORMICK, PATRICIA (PAT)
KELLER (1930-)
Amer. swimmer, diver
Assoc. Press--Pursuit p199,
220-221, por.
Hollander--100 p94-95, por.
McWhirter--Guinness p130, por.
O'Neill--Women's p584
Woman's Almanac p431

McCORMICK, RUTH HANNA
See SIMMS, RUTH HANNA
McCORMICK

McCORQUODALE, BARBARA
See CARTLAND, BARBARA
HAMILTON

McCOURT, AUGUSTA
Amer. miner's wife (of
"Silver King")
Sherr--American p28, por.

McCOURT, BABY DOE
Amer., wife of Senator
Sherr--American p28-29,40,75

McCOY, ELIZABETH (fl. 1920's-
1970's)
Amer. bacteriologist, professor
O'Neill--Women's p219

McCRACKIN, JOSEPHINE
WOEMPNER CLIFFORD
(1838-1920)
Amer. author, conservationist
James--Notable (2) p455 456

McCRARY, ELIZABETH (c1869-)
Amer. centenarian
Mitchell--Yessir p47-49, por.

McCREA, JANE (1752/1753-1777)
Amer. Indian captive,
Revolutionary War martyr
Booth--Women p131-134, por.
James--Notable (2) p456-457
McHenry--Liberty's p261
Sherr--American p161
Williams--Demeter's p250-252
Woman's Almanac p450
Young--Revol. p22-24,26-27

McCREE, JUNIE (1865-1918)
Amer. lyricist, actress
Claghorn--Biog. p287

McCREERY, MARIA MAUD
LEONARD (1883-1938)
Amer. suffragist, Socialist,
labor organizer
James--Notable (2) p457-458

McCULLAR, BERNICE BROWN
(1905-1975)
Amer. educator, journalist,
historian, author, lecturer,
noted Georgia mother
Amer.--Mothers p134 135, por.

McCULLERS, (LULA) CARSON
SMITH (1917-1967)
Amer. novelist, short story
writer, playwright
Avenel--Comp. (2) p163
Cahill--Women p180-181,377
Clark--Leading p183-184
Ehrlich--Oxford p256, por.
Howard--Seven p265-310
Jones--Rutledge p496-497
Longstreet--Queen p191
McHenry--Liberty's p261
Magill--Cycl. p680-682
Moers--Literary p108-109,247,

298-299, por.
O'Neill--Women's p681
Seymour-Smith--Novels p178, por.
Seymour-Smith--Who's p238-239
Sicherman--Notable p442-445
Webber--Woman p68-70
Webster's--Amer. p665-666
Who Did What p222
Woman's Almanac p254-255
World--Who p17

McCULLOUGH, CATHARINE GOUGER
WAUGH (1862-1945)
Amer. lawyer, suffragist
James--Notable (2) p459-460

McCULLOUGH, COLLEEN (1937-)
Australian novelist
Cur. Biog. '82 p257-260, por.
World--Who p41

McCULLOUGH, MYRTLE REED
See REED, MYRTLE

MACURDY, GRACE HARRIET (1866-
1946)
Greek scholar, teacher
James--Notable (2) p480-481

McCURDY, JEAN H. (1949-)
Amer. film executive
Scheuer--Tel. p310

McCURDY, MARY BURTON DERRICK-
SON (1908-)
Amer. genealogical researcher
Meyer--Who's p132

McCURTAIN, JANE
Amer. Choctaw Indian poli-
tician
Sherr--American p192-193

McCUTCHEON, FLORETTA DOTY
(1888-1967)
Amer. bowler
Hollander--100 p7,14-15, por.
Woman's Almanac p436, por.

McDANIEL, HATTIE (1895/1898-1952)
Amer. actress
Keylin--Hollywood p188, por.
O'Neill--Women's p681
Springer--They p179,315, por.
Sicherman--Notable p445-446
World--Who p241

McDERMOTT, ANNE (1955-   )
Amer. TV reporter, Cable
news network
Scheuer--Tel. p311

McDERMOT, JESSIE D.
See ELLIOTT, MAXINE

McDONALD, BETTY (1908-1958)
Amer. author
Ehrlich--Oxford p382

MacDONALD, CORDELIA HOWARD
See HOWARD, CORDELIA

MACDONALD, CYNTHIA
Amer. poet
Moers--Literary p97,297

MACDONALD, ELEANOR
Amer. epidemiologist
O'Neill--Women's p221

MacDONALD, FLORA (1722-1790)
Scottish heroine, loyalist
Booth--Women p69-71
DePauw--Found. p140-141
Jones--Rutledge p497
Macksey--Book p54
Sherr--American p179
Who Did What p206

MACDONALD, FRANCES (1874-
1921)
British stained-glass artist,
embroiderer, designer,
illustrator, illuminator,
enameller
Callen--Women p158-160,198,224

MacDONALD, JEANETTE (1907-
1965)
Amer. singer, actress
Claghorn--Biog. p287-288
Hazen--Interv. p403
Hirschhorn--Rating p240-241,
por.
Keylin--Hollywood p189-192, por.
Mordden--Movie, see index p294,
por.
People's Almanac (1) p905-906
Sicherman--Notable p446-447
Shipman--Gold. p367-369, por.
Simon--Best p185-186, por.
Springer--They p175-176,312,
314,por.
Woman's Almanac p349
World--Who p269

MacDONALD, JULIE (fl. 1970's)
Amer. sculptor
Women's--Female p92

MACDONALD, MARGARET R.S.W.
(1865-1933)
British designer, embroiderer,
metalworker, stained-glass
artist, illustrator, illuminator
Callen--Women p224, see also
index p231, por.

MacDONALD, MARY (fl. 1770's)
Amer. Revolutionary War
patriot
Meyer--Petticoat p101-102

McDONALD-VALESH, EVA (fl. 1890's)
Amer. Alliance movement worker
Stein--Lives p172-173, por.

MacDOUGALL, JUDITH (fl. 1970's)
Amer. filmmaker
Smith--Movies p190-191,259

MacDOUGALL, MARION
See LORNE, MARION

MacDOUGALL, PRISCILLA RUTH
Amer. activist, author
O'Neill--Women's p355-356, por.

McDOWELL, ANNE ELIZABETH
(1826-1901)
Amer. editor, journalist
James--Notable (2) p460-461

McDOWELL, KATHARINE SHERWOOD
BONNER (1849-1883)
Amer. novelist, (Longfellow's
secretary)
Ehrlich--Oxford p272
James--Notable (2) p461-462

MacDOWELL, MARIAN GRISWOLD
NEVINS (1857-1956)
Amer. patron, musician,
pianist, lecturer, (wife of
Edward MacDowell)
Sicherman--Notable p447-449

McDOWELL, MARY ELIZA (1854-1936)
Amer. settlement house direc-
tor, social reformer
James--Notable (2) p462-464
McHenry--Liberty's p261-262
O'Neill--Women's p736-737
Warren--Pictorial p150

McELHENEY, JANE
See CLARE, ADA, pseud.

MacELREE, JANE COX
Amer. millionaire
Forbes--400 ('84) p106

McELROY, COLLEEN (1935-)
Amer. poet, author
Fisher--Third p vi, 267

McENERY, RUTH
See STUART, RUTH McENERY

McEWAN, HETTY (HETTIE) M.
(fl. 1860's)
Amer. Civil War patriot
Sherr--American p219

McFADDEN, MARY JOSEPHINE
(1938-)
Amer. fashion designer
Cur. Biog. '83 p244-247, por.
O'Neill--Women's p248,250,253

McFALL, FRANCES ELIZABETH
CLARKE
See GRAND, SARAH, pseud.

McFARLAND, AMANDA (c1837-c1898)
Amer. missionary, church
founder
Jones--Women (1) p60-65, por.
Sherr--American p6

MacFARLAND, TURNER (fl. 1860's)
Amer. Southern belle
DeLeon--Belles p124, por.

McFEE, MILDRED H.
Amer. educator, college
president
Hazen--Interv. p231

McGANNON, LAURA L.
Amer. TV design manager
Scheuer--Tel. p312

McGEE, ANITA NEWCOMB (1864-
1940)
Amer. physician, government
official, Nurse Corp organizer,
noted District of Columbia
mother
Amer.--Mothers p103-104, por.
James--Notable (2) p464-466
O'Neill--Women's p534
Sherr--American p231

McGEE, MARY (fl. 1970's)
Amer. motorcyclist
O'Neill--Women's p590

McGEE, MOLLY
See JORDAN, MARIAN DRISCOLL

McGEE, PAMELA JO LEE (1947-)
Canadian Lutheran clergyman
O'Neill Women's p383

McGILL, CAROLINE (fl. 1900's-
1930's)
Amer. physician, pathologist
Sherr--American p134

MacGILL, ELSIE GREGORY
Canadian aeronautical engineer
O'Neill--Women's p188

McGILLICUDDY, FRANCES L. (fl.
1970's)
Amer. teacher
Proctor--Women p157-158

McGILVERY, HELEN
Amer. avistrix, army flier
Keil--Those p125-126

McGINLEY, PHYLLIS (1905-1978)
Amer. poet
Avenel--Comp. (2) p164
Clark--Leading p232
Cur. Biog. '78 p472
Ehrlich--Oxford p115,397,435
McHenry--Liberty's p262-263
Seymour-Smith--Who's p239
World--Who p17

McGINTY, ANNE
Amer. pioneer spinner
Sherr--American p79

McGLADE, AGNES TERESA
See O'CONNOR, UNA

MacGRAW, ALI (1939-)
Amer. model, actress
Anderson--People p260-261, por.
Hirschhorn--Rating p243, por.
Manchel--Women p104, por.
World--Who p239

McGROARTY, JULIA, SISTER
(1827-1901)
Irish-Amer. nun, educator
James--Notable (2) p466-468

McHenry--Liberty's p263
Sherr--American p41-42

McGRORY, MARY (1918-)
    Amer. journalist, columnist
    Marzolf--Up p79-80,82
    O'Neill--Women's p452-455
    Woman's Almanac p270
    World--Who p53

McGUIRE, DOROTHY (1918/1919-)
    Amer. actress
    Hirschhorn--Rating p243-244,
    por.
    Lamparski--What. (5) p176-177,
    por.
    Shipman--Internatl. p372-373,
    por.
    World--Who p241

McGUIRE SISTERS (fl. 1930's)
    Amer. singers
    .Claghorn--Biog. p289
    World--Who p270

McGUIRE, WILLA (fl. 1940's-1950's)
    Amer. water skier
    O'Neill--Women's p587

MACHA (fl. c600 B.C.)
    Irish Celtic queen, priestess,
    hospital founder
    Mead--Hist. p5

MACHAN, CATHY (fl. 1970's)
    Amer. agriculturist, editor
    O'Neill--Women's p11-12, por.

McIAN, FANNY
    English painter
    Callen--Women p27-35

McINGVALE, CYNTHIA POTTER
    (fl. 1970's)
    Amer. diver
    O'Neill--Women's p584

MacINNES, HELEN CLARK (1907-
    1985)
    Scottish-Amer. novelist
    Cur. Biog. '85 p478
    Ehrlich--Oxford p189
    McHenry--Liberty's p263
    O'Neill--Women's p681
    P.W.--Author p103-106,512-513
    Seymour-Smith--Novels p180
    World--Who p47

MacINNIS, NINA (1954-)
    Amer. swimmer
    Sabin--Women p72-75, por.

M'INTOSH, MRS. DAVID GREGG
    See PEGRAM, JENNIE

McINTOSH, MARIA JANE (1803-1878)
    Amer. author
    James--Notable (2) p468-469

MacIVER, .LOREN NEWMAN (1902/
    1909-)
    Amer. painter
    Fine--Women p144
    Henkes--Eight p14-18,52
    Harris--Women p99,334-335,361
    O'Neill--Women's p596
    Women's--Female p108

McIVER, PEARL (1893-)
    Amer. public health nurse
    O'Neill--Women's p233

MACK, HELEN (1913-)
    Amer. actress
    Springer--They p176,314, por.

MACK, MRS. (fl. 17th Century)
    Amer. pioneer, heroine, Indian
    attacker
    DePauw--Found. p176

MACK, NILA (1891-1953)
    Amer. radio director, pro-
    ducer, actress, author
    Sicherman--Notable p449-451
    Women--Radio p6

McKAIG, DIANNE (fl. 1970's)
    Amer. executive
    O'Neill--Women's p524

MACKAILL, DOROTHY (1903-)
    English actress
    Springer--They p176,314, por.

McKANE, KITTY (fl. 1920's)
    British tennis player
    McWhirter--Guinness p151

McKAY, ELEANORA FAGAN
    See HOLIDAY, BILLIE

MACKAY, ELSIE (-1928)
    British aviatrix, pilot
    Macksey--Book p248

McKAY, HEATHER PAMELA
BLUNDELL (1941-   )
Australian squash player
McWhirter--Guinness p128, por.
O'Neill--Women's p582

McKAY, (AUNT) LEPHA
Amer. pioneer educator
Sherr--American p67

MACKAY, MARY
See CORELLI, MARIE, pseud.

McKECHNIE, DONNA RUTH
(1942-   )
Amer. dancer
World--Who p263

McKETCHNIE, FLORENCE
See ELDRIDGE, FLORENCE

McKEE, EDITH (fl. 1970's)
Amer. geologist
Seed--Saturday's p57-61, por.

McKEE, FRAN (fl. 1950's-1970's)
Amer. navy line admiral
O'Neill--Women's p541,553

McKEEFE, ELLEN (1944-   )
Amer. TV bureau chief
Scheuer--Tel. p314

McKEEHAN, MARY (1751-   )
English-Amer. Revolutionary
War patriot
Woman's Almanac p451

McKENNA, MARGARET (fl. 1970's)
Amer. lawyer, government
official
Adams--Women p22,41,87,188,
109,200
O'Neill--Women's p367

McKENNA, SIOBHAN (1922/
1923-   )
Irish actress
World--Who p259

McKENNY, RUTH (1911-1972)
Amer. author
Cur. Biog. '72 p467
Ehrlich--Oxford, see index p437

MACKENZIE, JEAN KENYON (1874-
1936)

Amer. missionary, author
James--Notable (2) p469-470

MacKENZIE, GISELLE (1927-   )
Canadian-Amer. singer,
violinist, actress
Claghorn--Biog. p291
Lamparski--What. (8) p196-197,
por.
World--Who p269

MacKENZIE, LUCY (1952-   )
British artist
Contemp. Brit., unp., por.

MACKEY, MARION
Amer. aviatrix, army flier
Keil--Those p79,89,92

McKIMMON, JANE SIMPSON (1867-   )
Amer. home economist, humanitarian, noted North Carolina
mother
Amer.--Mothers p403

MACKIN, CATHERINE ("CASSIE")
(1939-1982)
Amer. TV newscaster
Gelfman--Women p24
Marzolf--Up p171,186,188-189
O'Neill--Women's p501
Woman's Almanac p270

McKINLEY, IDA SAXTON (1847-1907)
Amer. first lady, (wife of
William McKinley)
James--Notable (2) p470-471
Melick--Wives p54, por.
People's Almanac (1) p272
Sherr--American p184
Woman's Almanac p490

McKINLEY, NANCY ALLISON (1809-
1897)
Amer., mother of President
McKinley
Faber--Presidents' p222-224

McKINNEY, NINA MAE (1912-1967)
Amer. singer
Claghorn--Jazz p200
Springer--They p179,315, por.

McKINNON, JANE PRICE (fl. 1970's)
Amer. agriculturist, horti-
culturist
O'Neill--Women's p28

MACKINTOSH, ELIZABETH
See TEY, JOSEPHINE, pseud.

McKINVEN, MARY JANE
Amer. TV director
Scheuer--Tel. p314

MACKLIN, MADGE THURLOW
(1893-1962)
Amer. physician, geneticist
Sicherman--Notable p451-452

McLAIN, ELIZABETH (fl. 1970's)
Amer. city planner
Seed--Saturday's p128-130, por.

MacLAINE, SHIRLEY (1934-)
Amer. actress
Anderson--People p262, por.
Cur. Biog. '78 p267-270, por.
Hirschhorn--Rating p244-245,
  por.
Kulkin--Her p188-189
Manchel--Women p89,116, por.
100--Greatest (1) p13, por.
O'Neill--Women's p661
Ross--Young p3-14, por.
Shipman--Internatl. p339-342,
  por.
Smith--Movies p62-63, por.
Woman's Almanac p349-350, por.
World--Who p239-240

McLANE, BOBBIE JONES (1927-)
Amer. genealogical researcher,
  indexer, writer
Meyer--Who's p133

McLANE, ENID STRYKER (1896-)
Amer. teacher, noted Alaska
  mother
Amer.--Mothers p20-21, por.

McLAREN, LOUISE LEONARD
(1885-1968)
Amer. labor educator
Sicherman--Notable p452-454

McLAUGHLIN, EMILY (1928-)
Amer. actress
Scheuer--Tel. p315, por.
World--Who p241

McLAUGHLIN, MARY LOUISE M.
(1847-1939)
Amer. ceramicist, wood-
  carver, writer, artist

Callen--Women p224, see also
  index p231, por.

McLAUGHLIN, MARYA (fl. 1960's-
  1970's)
Amer. TV newscaster
Gelfman--Women p50,62,66-67,69,
  87-88
Marzolf--Up p168,186,191
O'Neill--Women's p498

McLAUGHLIN, SANDRA J. (fl.
  1950's-1970's)
Amer. banker
O'Neill--Women's p530

McLEAN, ALICE THROCKMORTON
(1886-1968)
Amer. social service organizer
McHenry--Liberty's p263-264

McLEAN, BARBARA R. (fl. 1930's-
  1950's)
Amer. film editor
Smith--Movies p26,28, por.

McLEAN, EVALYN WALSH (1886-
  1947)
Amer. mining heiress, hostess,
  socialite
James--Notable (2) p471-473
McHenry--Liberty's p264

McLEAN, KATHRYN ANDERSON
See FORBES, KATHRYN, pseud.

McLEAN, SARAH PRATT
See GREENE, SARAH PRATT
  McLEAN

McLEAN, SHEILA AVRIN
Amer. lawyer
O'Neill--Women's p361

McLEISH, ANNIE
English jeweller
Callen--Women p161

MacLEISH, MARTHA HILLARD
(1856-1947)
Amer. educator, church,
  community leader
James--Notable (2) p473-474

McLELLAN, DIANE (c1937-)
Amer. columnist
Woman's Almanac p277

McLENDON, WINZOLA (fl. 1970's)
Amer. news correspondent
O'Neill--Women's p451

McLENNON, LINDA (fl. 1970's)
Amer. letter carrier
Seed--Saturday's p88-90, por.

McLEOD, ALICE
See COLTRANE, ALICE

MacLEOD, BANDA (-1950)
Netherlands spy, World War II,
(daughter of Mata Hari)
People's Almanac (1) p649

MacLEOD, ENID (1909-)
Canadian physician
Hellstedt--Women p383-385, por.

McLEOD, MARY (1)
See BETHUNE, MARY McLEOD

MacLEOD, MARY (2) (c1615-c1706)
Scottish Gaelic poet
Avenel--Comp. (1) p339

McLOUGHLIN, MARGUERITE WADIN
(c1780-)
Canadian-Amer., noted Oregon
mother
Amer.--Mothers p443

MacLOUGHLIN, NILA
See MACK, NILA

MacMAHON, ALINE (1899-)
Amer. actress
Shipman--Gold. p369-371, por.
Springer--They p177,314, por.

McMAHON, JENNA (1937-)
Amer. TV producer, writer
Scheuer--Tel. p316

McMAIN, ELEANOR LAURA (1866-
1934)
Amer. settlement worker,
social reformer
James--Notable (2) p474-476
Sherr--American p84-85

McMANUS, JANE
See CAZNEAW, JANE MARIE
ELIZA McMANUS STORMS

McMANUS, JILL (fl. 1970's)

Amer. pianist
Claghorn--Jazz p201

McMATH, VIRGINIA KATHERINE
See ROGERS, GINGER

McMEIN, NEYSA (1888-1949)
Amer. painter, illustrator
James--Notable (2) p476-477
McHenry--Liberty's p264-265

McMILLAN, CLARA G. (c1894-1957)
Amer. Congresswoman
Chamberlin--Min. p155-156

McMILLAN, KATHY (1958-)
Amer. track & field athlete
Woman's Almanac p427

MacMILLAN, MARGARET (1860/1861-
1931)
Scottish-Amer. child educator
Brecher--Lifes p114
Jones--Rutledge p501-502
Macksey--Book p76

McMILLIN, LUCILLE FOSTER
(c1870-1949)
Amer. government official
Ware--Beyond p149, see also
index p200

McMILLION, LYNN C. (1934-)
Amer. genealogical researcher,
writer, indexer
Meyer--Who's p133-134

McMILLON, DORIS
Amer. TV news correspondent
Scheuer--Tel. p317

MacMULLAN, KATHERINE
Amer. social arbiter
Birmingham--Grandes p30-33,43

McMURRAY, LILLITA LOUISE
See CHAPLIN, LITA GREY

McNAIR, BARBARA (1939-)
Amer. singer, actress
Cur. Biog. '71 p256-259, por.

McNAMARA, MAGGIE (1931-)
Amer. actress
Lamparski--What. (8) p198-199,
por.

McNAMARA, MARGARET
    Amer. aviatrix, army flier
    Keil--Those p61-62,246
    O'Neill--Women's p116, por.

McNAY, MARION KOOGLER
    (-1950)
    Amer. art patron, philan-
        thropist
    Sherr--American p223-224

McNEELY, JUANITA (fl. 1970's)
    Amer. painter
    Women's--Female p50

McNEIL, DEE DEE (fl. 1970's)
    Amer. musical communicator
    Innis--Profiles p126-127, por.

McNEILL, LOUISE
    Amer. poet, noted West
        Virginia mother
    Amer.--Mothers p577-578, por.

McNICHOL, KRISTY (1962-)
    Amer. actress
    Anderson--People p263-264, por.
    Hirschhorn--Rating p247, por.

McNULTY, DOROTHY
    See SINGLETON, PEGGY
        ("BLONDIE")

"MACONAQUAH"
    See SLOCUM, FRANCES

McPARTLAND, MARIAN MARGARET
        TURNER PAGE (1918/1920-
        1986)
    English pianist, composer
    Claghorn--Biog. p292
    Claghorn--Jazz p202
    Cur. Biog. '76 p242-245, por.
    Simon--Best p386-387, por.
    World--Who p286

MACPHAIL, AGNES CAMPBELL
        (1800-1954)
    Canadian Parliamentary
        member, politician
    Macksey--Book p38

McPHAIL, MARION
    Amer. magazine research
        head
    Hamblin--That p180,217,284

McPHERSON, AIMEE SEMPLE
        (1890-1944)
    Amer. evangelist
    Book--Lists (2) p309
    Clark--Leading p117-119
    Dunlap--Calif. p127-128, por.
    James--Notable (2) p477-480
    Jones--Rutledge p502
    Longstreet--Queen p192
    McHenry--Liberty's p265-266
    Macksey--Book p120-121
    O'Neill--Women's p400
    People's Almanac (1) p1277-1278,
        por.
    Sherr--American p15
    Webster's--Amer. p679
    Williams--Legend. p117-137, por.
    Woman's Almanac p404, por.
    World--Who p83

McPHERSON, BERNICE M. (1901-)
    Amer. welding executive
    O'Neill--Women's p136

MACPHERSON, JAY (1932-)
    Canadian poet
    Avenel--Comp. (1) p341-342

MACPHERSON, JEANIE (-1946)
    Amer. actress, director
    Mordden--Movie p12
    Slide--Early p59-60, por.

MACPHERSON, MARY
    Scottish Gaelic poet
    Avenel--Comp. (1) p342

McPHERSON, MYRA (c1935-)
    Amer. newspaperwoman, writer
    Miller--Fishbait p108-109

McPHERSON, SANDRA (1943-)
    Amer. poet
    Chester--Rising p370-377, por.

McPHILLIPS, MARY HELEN
    Amer. TV newscaster
    Gelfman--Women p24

McQUEEN, BUTTERFLY (THELMA)
        (1911-)
    Amer. actress
    Lamparski--What. (2) p96-97,
        por.
    Springer--They p179,315-316, por.
    World--Who p241

McQUILLAN, MARION (fl. 1960's-
1970's)
British metal expert
Macksey--Book p173

McQUISTON, JOANN
Amer. magazine reporter
Hamblin--That, see index p317

MACQUOID, KATHERINE SARAH
(1824-1917)
English novelist
Showalter--Lit. p328

McRAE, CARMEN (1922-)
Amer. singer, pianist
Claghorn--Biog. p292
Claghorn--Jazz p202
Cur. Biog. '83 p247-250, por.
Simon--Best p388-389, por.

MacRAE, MEREDITH (1945-)
Amer. actress
World--Who p240

MacRAE, SHEILA STEPHENS
(1924-)
English-Amer. singer, radio
actress
World--Who p240

MACRINA
Greek physician, hospital
founder, (sister of Basil)
Mead--Hist. p79-80

MacRORIE, JANET (c1890-1950)
Amer. advertiser
O'Neill--Women's p493

McSAVENEY, EILEEN (fl. 1970's)
Amer. geologist, (Antarctica)
Land--New p21,37-54, por.

McVEY, LUCILLE (1890-1925)
Amer. actress, director
Slide--Early p105-106, por.
Smith--Movies p14

McWHINNEY, MADELINE HOUSTON
(1922-)
Amer. banker
Cur. Biog. '76 p245-248, por.
100--Greatest (1) p68, por.
O'Neill--Women's p529, por.

McWHINNIE, MARY ALICE (1922-

1980)
Amer. polar biologist (Antarc-
tica)
Land--New p20,55-73,109,137,
por.
O'Neill--Women's p163

McWHIRTER, LUELLA SMITH (1859-)
Amer. banker, suffragist,
noted Indiana mother
Amer.--Mothers p179, por.

McWILLIAMS, SARAH BREEDLOVE
See WALKER, SARAH BREED-
LOVE ("MADAM" C.J.)

MACY, ANNE SULLIVAN
See SULLIVAN, ANNE

"MADAME MOUSTACHE"
See DUMONT, (EMMA) ELEANORE

MADAR, OLGA M. (fl. 1940's-1970's)
Amer. labor leader
O'Neill--Women's p285,302
Woman's Almanac p180

"MADCAP MAGGIE"
See WHITING, MARGARET

MADDERN, MINNIE
See FISKE, MINNIE MADDERN

MADDOX, ROSE (1926-)
Amer. singer, guitarist
Claghorn--Biog. p294

MADEIRA, JEAN BROWNING
(1918/1924-1972)
Amer. opera singer
Claghorn--Biog. p294
Cur. Biog. '72 p467
O'Neill--Women's p325

MADELEVA, MARY, SISTER (1887-
1964)
Amer. educator, poet, essayist, nun, college administrator
Sicherman--Notable p741-742

MADGETT, NAOMI LONG (1923/
1925-)
Amer. poet
Fisher--Third p vii,255

MADISON, BARBARA SNYDER
(1942-)

Amer. genealogical researcher
Meyer--Who's p134

MADISON, CLEO (-1964)
Amer. actress, director
Slide--Early p52-54

MADISON, DOLLEY PAYNE TODD
(1768-1849)
Amer. first lady, wife of
President Madison
DePauw--Rem. p148-149, por.
Earle--Two Cent. (1) p315-316
Earle--Two Cent. (2) pxxiv,758,
784,787, por.
Earnest--American p49-54
Hoople--As p41-43
James--Notable (2) p483-485
Kulkin--Her p191-193
McHenry--Liberty's p266-267
Macksey--Book p102, por.
Melick--Wives p18-22, por.
People's Almanac (1) p263
Sherr--American p179,203,232,
236-237,244
Truman--Women p28-41,200, por.
Warren--Pictorial p63-65, por.
Woman's Almanac p486-487, por.
World--Who p299

MADISON, HELENE (c1913-1970)
Amer. swimmer
Hollander--100 p81-82, por.

MADISON, NELLIE (NELLY) CONWAY
(1731-1829)
Amer., noted Virginia mother,
mother of James Madison
Amer.--Mothers p549-550
Faber--Presidents' p264-267

MAEDER, CLARA FISHER
See FISHER, CLARA

MAGALASHVILI, KETEVANA
KONSTANTINOVNA (1894-
1973)
Russian portrait painter
Women's--Female p2, supp.

MAGEE, SANDRA
See "BABY SANDY"

MAGILL, ADA (-1864)
Amer. pioneer (Oregon Trail)
Sherr--American p253

MAGILL, HELEN
See WHITE, HELEN MAGILL

MAGNA MATER
Oriental mother goddess
Pomeroy--Godd. p179

MAGNANI, ANNA (1908-1973)
Italian actress
Cur. Biog. '73 p458
Fallaci--Ego. p99-111
Hirschhorn--Rating p248-249,
por.
Keylin--Hollywood p193-194, por.
O'Neill--Women's p660
Shipman--Internatl. p345-348,
por.
World--Who p259

MAGNO, JOSEPHINE (fl. 1970's)
Amer. hospice advocate,
physician
O'Neill--Women's p229

MAGNUSSEN, KAREN (1952-)
Canadian ice-skater
O'Neill--Women's p563

MAGNUSSON, LORA WILKINS (fl.
1960's-1970's)
Amer. genealogist, teacher,
noted Washington state mother
Amer.--Mothers p563-564, por.

MAGOFFIN, SUSAN SHELBY (fl.
1840's)
Amer. Western pioneer, diarist
Hoople--As p47-49
Sherr--American p156

MAGRABI, FRANCES M. (fl. 1970's)
Amer. home economist,
government official
O'Neill--Women's p27

MAGRI, LAVINIA WARREN, COUNT-
ESS
See STRATTON, MERCY LAVINIA
WARREN BUMP

MAGRUDER, JULIA (1854-1907)
Amer. novelist
James--Notable (2) p485-486

MAHLER, ALMA
See WERFEL, ALMA MAHLER
GROPIUS

MAHMEDBEKOVA, LEILA (fl. 1920's)
Turkish aviatrix
Taylor--Gener. p17

MAHMOUD, H.E. FATIMA ABDEL
(fl. 1970's)
Sudanese minister
O'Neill--Women's p42

MAHON, GIGI (fl. 1970's)
Amer. editor, financial writer
O'Neill--Women's p509

MAHONEY, MARY ELIZA (1845-
1926)
Amer. nurse, feminist
James--Notable (2) p486-487
O'Neill--Women's p231
Reader's--Story p436-437
Sherr--American p104,110
Signif.--Amer. p30, por.

MAHONEY, SHEILA
Amer. Cable TV executive
Scheuer--Tel. p319

MAHONEY, SUZANNE
See SOMERS, SUZANNE

MAHONY, MARION
See GRIFFIN, MARION LUCY
MAHONY

MAHOUT, COUNTESS OF ARTOIS
(-1329)
French linguist, hospital
builder, physician
Mead--Hist. p270-271

MAHZOLINI, ANNA MORANDI
See MORANDI, ANNA

MAILLY-NESLE, LOUISE JULIE
(1710-1751)
French, mistress of Louis XV
Macksey--Book p97

MAILLY-NESLE, MARIE-ANNE
(1717-1744)
French mistress of Louis XV
Macksey--Book p97

MAILLY-NESLE, PAULINE DE
(-1741)
French mistress of Louis XV
Macksey--Book p97

MAILMAN, CYNTHIA (1942-)
Amer. painter
Miller--Lives p106, por.

MAIMUNKOVA, ANNA KRUSTEVA
(1879-1925)
Bulgarian labor leader
Partington--Who's p254, por.

MAIN, JOHN
See PARSONS, ELSIE WORTHING-
TON CLEWS

MAIN, MARJORIE (1890-1975)
Amer. actress
Cur. Biog. '75 p470
Keylin--Hollywood p195, por.
Lamparski--What. (2) p142-143,
por.
Springer--They p177,314, por.
World--Who p240

MAINARDI, PAT (fl. 1970's)
Amer. feminist, writer,
painter
Hymowitz--Hist. p357-358
Sochen--Movers p262-263
Women's--Female p50

MAINES, RACHEL (fl. 1970's)
Amer. needlework artist,
teacher
Women's--Female p115,125

MAINOR, DOROTHY
See MAYNOR (MAINER), DOROTHY

MAINTENON, FRANÇOISE D'AUBIGNE,
MARQUISE DE (1635-1719)
French (wife of King Louis
XIV of France), foundress,
educator
Earle--Two Cent. (1) p244-245
Fine--Women p39
Macksey--Book p66,96

MAIRI NIGHEAN ALASDAIR
See MacLEOD, MARY (2)

MAI-YU, SHIH
See STONE, MARY

"THE MAJOR"
See CUSHMAN, PAULINE

MAJORS, BEVERLY (1951-)

Amer.-Afro. fashion designer
O'Neill--Women's p254

MAKAROVA, NATALIA ROMANOVNA
(1940-)
Russian-Amer. ballet dancer
Beal--20th p195
Cur. Biog. '72 p303-306, por.
O'Neill--Women's p641,643-644
People--Best p136, por.
Woman's Almanac p313
World--Who p71

MAKAROVA, NINA P.
Russian opera composer
Mandel--Soviet p151,294

MAKEBA, MIRIAM (1932-)
South African singer
Crane--Ms. p141-159, por.
Keenan--Women p175-176, por.
World--Who p269

MAKI, LUELLA
Amer. home economist
100--Greatest (1) p65, por.

MAKIN, BATHSUA (c1608-1673/
1675)
English scholar, educator,
linguist, author
Brink--Female p86-100, por.
Horner--English p2

MAKSOUTOFF, PRINCESS (fl.
1860's)
Russian, wife of Alaskan
governor
Jones--Women (1) p31-36

MALAISE, ELIZABETH (fl. 1960's)
Belgian financier, bank
director
Macksey--Book p169
O'Neill--Women's p528

MALCHI, ESPERANZA (fl. c1590's)
Turkish, Sultan's harem
lady's maid
Henry--Written p11,154-155

MALDOROR, SARAH (fl. 1970's)
French West Indies-African
feminist, filmmaker
Smith--Movies p91-92

MALET, LUCAS, pseud.
See KINGSLEY, MARY

MALHERBE, MABEL (fl. 1930's)
South African Parliament
member
Macksey--Book p41

MALIHA, LADY
Jewish letter-writer, scholar
Henry--Written p104-107

MALINA, JUDITH (1926-)
German theater founder,
actress
O'Neill--Women's p665

MALINCHE (c1504-c1528)
Indian, Mexican consort of
Cortés
Henderson--Ten p1-21, por.

MALINO, EMILY
Amer. interior decorator
O'Neill--Women's p283, por.

MALKAH
Jewish Hasidic, wife of Shalom
Rokeach
Henry--Written p209

MALLET, ELIZABETH (fl. 1700's)
English publisher, printer
Macksey--Book p162
Marzolf--Up p271

MALLET-JORIS, FRANÇOISE LILAR
(1930-)
French novelist
Crosland--Women p180-191, por.
Moers--Literary p297

MALLON, MARY ("TYPHOID MARY")
(c1870-1938)
Amer. typhoid carrier
Book--Lists (1) p426
McHenry--Liberty's p267
Macksey--Book p13
People's Almanac (1) p212
People's Almanac (2) p541-542,
por.
Webster's--Amer. p684
Woman's Almanac p503
World--Who p299

MALLORY, BOOTS (1913-)
Amer. dancer, actress
Springer--They p177,314, por.

MALLORY, MOLLA BJURSTEDT
(c1892-1959)

Norwegian-Amer. tennis player
Hollander--100 p100-101, por.
McWhirter--Guinness p163

MALLORY, RUBY (fl. 1860's)
Amer. Southern belle,
elocutionist
DeLeon--Belles p85-87, por.

MALONE, ANNIE ESTELLE
See TURNBO-MALONE, ANNIE
MINERVA ESTELLE

MALONE, DOROTHY (1925-)
Amer. actress
Hirschhorn--Rating p249-250,
por.
World--Who p240

MALONE, PATTY (1853-1896)
Amer. slave, singer
Sherr--American p1

MALONE, VIVIAN (c1942-)
Amer. student
O'Neill--Women's p701-702

MALONE, WYANNIE (fl. 1780's)
English-Amer. Loyalist
DePauw--Found. p148

MALONEY, DOROTHY ELOISE
See MALONE, DOROTHY

MALONEY, ELIZABETH (fl. 1910's-
1920's)
Amer. labor leader
O'Neill--Women's p298

MALPASS, BARBARA ANN (fl.
1950's)
Amer. male impersonator
vagrant
Felton--Famous p47

MALRAUX, CLARA (fl. 1970's)
French writer
Crosland--Women p224-225

MALSBARY, SARAH MAHON
(1868-)
Amer. centenarian
Mitchell--Yessir p56-58, por.

MALSIN, LANE BRYANT (1879-
1951)
Amer. retailer, fashion
designer

O'Neill--Women's p259
World--Who p194

MALTBY, MARGARET ELIZA (1860-
1944)
Amer. physicist
James--Notable (2) p487-488
O'Neill--Women's p180

MAMAEL
Jewish prayer-writer
Henry--Written p189-190

MAMEDOVA
Russian painter
Mandel--Soviet p142-143

"MAMMY KATE" (fl. 1770's)
Amer. Revolutionary War
patriot, heroine
Clyne--Patriots p130,135

MANCE, JEANNE (1606-1673)
French-Canadian hospital
founder, nurse, philanthropist
Mead--Hist. p417

MANCELL, ROSAMOND (1919-)
Ghanan (West African) home
economist, vocational school
founder
O'Neill--Women's p105

MANCHESTER, CONSUELO YZNAGA,
DUCHESS (c1888-1909)
Amer. socialite
Brandon--Dollar p6,65, por.

MANCHESTER, DUCHESS OF
See ZIMMERMAN, HELENA,
DUCHESS OF MANCHESTER

MANCHESTER, MELISSA (1951-)
Amer. singer, song-writer
Anderson--People p265-266, por.

MANCINI, MARIA PIA (1941-)
Italian feminist, agriculturist
O'Neill--Women's p6

MANDELA, NOMZAMO WINNIE
(fl. 1970's)
South African activist
O'Neill--Women's p731

MANDELA, WINNIE (c1934-)
South African pioneer,
activist, prisoner

Crane--Ms. p127-
128

MANDELBAUM, FREDERICKA
("MARM") (1818-1889)
Amer. accused criminal
Woman's Almanac p499
World--Who p299

MANDRELL, BARBARA (1945-)
Amer. singer, musician, TV
personality
Cur. Biog. '82 p263-267, por.
Glassman--Year '79 p125, por.

MANIGAULT, JUDITH GITON
ROYER (-1711)
(French Huguenot) Amer.
colonial agronomist, pioneer
Williams--Demeter's p52-53,178

MANKIN, HELEN DOUGLAS (1894/
1896-1956)
Amer. Congresswoman, lawyer,
state legislator
Chamberlin--Min. p191-193
Sicherman--Notable p454-456

MANKIN, "WIDOW" (fl. 1730's)
Amer. colonial druggist
Williams--Demeter's p196

MANLEY, JOAN A. DANIELS
(1932-)
Amer. publisher
O'Neill--Women's p487-488

MANLEY, MARY DE LA RIVIERE
(1663-1724)
English novelist, playwright,
story-writer
Avenel--Comp. (1) p347
Horner--English p8-18,98-102,
124
Macksey--Book p181
Moers--Literary p144,298

MANLEY, MYRA DEL (HODSON)
(1952-)
Amer. genealogical researcher,
writer, indexer
Meyer--Who's p135

MANN, ABBY (1927-)
Amer. TV producer, writer
Scheuer--Tel. p321

MANN, CAROL (1941-)
Amer. golfer
Hollander--100 p48-50, por.
McWhirter--Guinness p76-77, por.
O'Neill--Women's p561
Woman's Almanac p420

MANN, CHRIS C. (fl. 1950's-1970's)
Amer. brigadier general
O'Neill--Women's p545,553

MANN, ERIKA (1905-1969)
German-Amer. author, actress,
lecturer
Cur. Biog. '69 p470

MANN, JEAN
British Parliament member
Vallance--Women, see index p208

MANN, JESSICA (1937-)
English novelist
Seymour-Smith--Novels p182

MANN, KATINKA (fl. 1970's)
Amer. artist
Women's--Female p108

MANN, MARY TYLER PEABODY
(1806-1887)
Amer. educator
James--Notable (2) p488-490

MANN, OPAL H. (fl. 1970's)
Amer. home economist, ad-
ministrator
O'Neill--Women's p28

MANN, PAMELA (-1840)
Amer. cattle frontier woman,
hotel owner
Gray--Women p115
Sherr--American p222
Stein--Lives p359-370

MANNERS, DIANA, LADY (c1892-)
British actress
Hazen--Interv. p104

MANNES, CLARA DAMROSCH (1869-
1948)
German-Amer. pianist, music
educator
James--Notable (2) p490-491
McHenry--Liberty's p267
Neidle--America's p232-237, por.

MANNES, MARYA (1904-   )
Amer. author, literary critic,
journalist
McHenry--Liberty's p267-268

MANNEY, HENRIETTA REMSEN
MESEROLE
See WESTLEY, HELEN

MANNIN, ETHEL EDITH (1900-1978)
English novelist, short-story
writer, journalist
Avenel--Comp. (1) p347
Seymour-Smith--Novels p183

MANNING, ANNE (1807-1879)
English novelist
Showalter--Lit. p323

MANNING, JULIA (fl. 1970's)
Tanzanian judge
Macksey--Book p129

MANNING, MARIE
See FAIRFAX, BEATRICE,
pseud.

MANNING, OLIVIA (1914-   )
English novelist, journalist
Avenel--Comp. (1) p347
Baker--Women p4
Crosland--Beyond p100-101
Seymour-Smith--Novels p183

MANOCK, BETTY R. (fl. 1970's)
Amer. heroine, Carnegie
Medal winner
O'Neill--Women's p735

MANOOCHEHRIAN, MEHRAN-GUIZ
Iranian lawyer, feminist
Macksey--Book p128

MANOPPO, ANI (fl. 1940's)
Indonesian lawyer, univer-
sity dean
Macksey--Book p128

MANSFIELD, ARABELLA BABB
("BELLE") (1846-1911)
Amer. lawyer, college
teacher
James--Notable (2) p492-493
McHenry--Liberty's p268-269
Macksey--Book p124-125
O'Neill--Women's p351

Sherr--American p65-66
Signif.--Amer. p20, por.

MANSFIELD, JAYNE (1933-1967)
Amer. actress
Hirschhorn--Rating p250, por.
Keylin--Hollywood p196, por.
Lewis--Prime p142-143
Mordden--Movie p230
Shipman--Internatl. p348-350,
por.
World--Who p240

MANSFIELD, KATHERINE, pseud.
(1888-1923)
New Zealand journalist, short-
story writer, art patron,
novelist
Avenel--Comp. (1) p348
Bachtold--Gifted p11-13
Cahill--Women p59-60,375
Crosland--Beyond p11-12,33,136,
175-176
Jones--Rutledge p510
Kronenberger--Atlan. p490
Magill--Cycl. p705-707
Moers--Literary p298
Moffat--Revel. p325-334
Morley--Literary p212
Rogers--Ladies, see index p232
Seymour-Smith--Novels p183
Seymour-Smith--Who's p230
Showalter--Lit. p346
Webber--Woman p12-16
Who Did What p214
Wintle--Makers p340-341, #301
World--Who p28

MANSFIELD, MAUREEN
Amer., wife of Mike Mansfield
Miller--Fishbait p325-326

MANSI, PAULA DEI (fl. 1280's)
Italian, Jewish scribe
Henry--Written p115

MANSKI, DOROTHEE (1895-1967)
German-Amer. opera singer,
professor
Claghorn--Biog. p297

MANSUR, ABBY (-1855)
Amer. Western pioneer,
letter-writer
Fischer--Let p48-57

MANTEGNA, ANDREA (1431-1506)
Italian Renaissance painter,
engraver
World--Who p67

MANTUA, DUCHESS OF
See ELEANORA, DUCHESS OF
MANTUA

MANUEL, JANET D. (1935-   )
Amer. genealogical researcher,
author
Meyer--Who's p134

MANZOLINI, ANNE MORANDI
(1716-1774)
Italian anatomist, lecturer
Macksey--Book p144
Mead--Hist. p492,509-510

MAPLES, DORIS ELLIOTT (1918-   )
Amer. clubwoman, noted
Alabama mother
Amer.--Mothers p7-8, por.

MAPP, MRS. (fl. 18th cent.)
English medical impostor
Mead--Hist. p479-480

MAR, LAUREEN (1953-   )
Chinese-Amer. poet
Fisher--Third px,521

MARA, ADELA (c1927-   )
Amer. actress
Lamparski--What. Annual (4,5)
p124-128, por.

MARA, CLARA
Amer. fashion designer
O'Neill--Women's p249

MARA, (GERTRUDE) ELIZABETH
SCHMELING (1749-1833)
German violinist
Macksey--Book p211

MARACESCU, NATALIA (fl. 1970's)
Amer. track and field athlete
O'Neill--Women's p575

MARAIS, MIRANDO (1912-   )
Dutch singer, pianist
Claghorn--Biog. p297-298

MARAT GUTA
Jewish foresayer
Henry--Written p87-88

MARBLE, ALICE (1913-   )
Amer. tennis player
Lamparski--What. Annual (4,5)
p2-7, por.
Sullivan--Queens p101, por.
Woman's Almanac p417-418
World--Who p217

MARBURY, ELISABETH (1856-1933)
Amer. theatrical and authors'
agent
James--Notable (2) p493-495
McHenry--Liberty's p269

MARBURY, ELIZABETH (1887-1911)
Amer. salonist
Sherr--American p169

MARCELLA (325-420)
Roman saint, deaconess, nurse,
educator, hospital founder
Macksey--Book p105
Mead--Hist. p79

MARCET, JANE (1769-1858)
Swiss author, chemist,
physician
Macksey--Book p123
Moers--Literary p24,298

MARCH, MARGUERITE DU TERTRE
DE LA (fl. 1660's)
French midwife, medical writer
Mead--Hist. p423

MARCHADIE, MADAME (fl. 1720's)
Amer. midwife
Mead--Hist. p490

MARCHOCKA, ANNA TERESA (fl.
c1600's)
Polish religious writer
Bainton--Spain p177-181

MARCIA (fl. 40's-50's B.C.)
Roman, wife of Younger Cato
Pomeroy--Godd. p158,160

MARCOS, IMELDA ROMUALDEZ
(1931-   )
Philippine political leader,
wife of president
World--Who p168

MARCUS, ANN (fl. 1980's)
Amer. TV shows "co-creator"
Scheuer--Tel. p322-323

MARCUS, ANN LEE (fl. 1970's)
Amer. educator, university
dean
O'Neill--Women's p408

MARCUS, CAROL (fl. 1940's-
1950's)
Amer., wife of William
Saroyan
Book--Lists (2) p250

MARCUS, MARCIA (fl. 1970's)
Amer. artist
Women's--Female p108

MARCUS, RUTH BARCAN (fl.
1960's-1970's)
Amer. philosopher, professor
O'Neill--Women's p418-419

MARENHOLTZ-BÜLOW, BERTHA
VON (-1893)
German kindergarten pioneer
Macksey--Book p68

MARETSKAYA, VERA
Russian actress
Mandel--Soviet p148,297-298

MARGARET (1) (c1048/1050-1093)
Scottish saint, queen, wife
of King Malcolm
Green--Saints p70-72

MARGARET (2) (1353-1412)
Scandinavian queen, Regent
of Denmark and Norway
Jones--Rutledge p513
Macksey--Book p23
Who Did What p215

MARGARET (3) (1283-1290)
Scottish queen, daughter of
Eric II of Norway
Jones--Rutledge p513

MARGARET (4) (1489-1541)
Scottish queen, consort of
James IV, King of Scotland
Jones--Rutledge p513-514
Mead--Hist. p175

MARGARET, QUEEN
German physician, (wife of
Conrad IV)
Mead--Hist. p223

MARGARET OF ANGOULEME

See MARGUERITE D'ANGOULEME
OF NAVARRE

MARGARET OF ANJOU (1430-1482)
English queen, Consort of
Henry VI of England, military
heroine
Jones--Rutledge p514
Macksey--Book p23
Softly--Queens p46-49

MARGARET OF AUSTRIA (1480-1530)
Austrian regent, daughter of
Maximillian I, social reformer
Macksey--Book p24
Mead--Hist. p349

MARGARET OF FRANCE (c1282-1318)
English queen
Softly--Queens p31-32

MARGARET OF HUNGARY (1242-
1270/1271)
Hungarian saint
Partington--Who's p258

MARGARET OF NETHERLANDS
Netherlands queen, medical
woman, widow of three kings,
daughter of Emperor Maximilian
Mead--Hist. p311-312

"MARGARET" OF NEW ORLEANS
(-1882)
Amer. humanitarian
Bolton--Success p110-126, por.

MARGARET ROSE (1930-)
English princess
Jones--Rutledge p514

MARGARETA (1) (fl. 2nd Cent.)
Roman army surgeon
Mead--Hist. p62

MARGARETA (2) (fl. 1459-1470)
German nun, book illuminator,
painter
Macksey--Book p195

"MARGO" (1918-1985)
Mexican-Amer. dancer, actress
Lamparski--What. (5) p180-181,
por.
Springer--They p177,314-315,
por.
World--Who p240

MARGOLIES, MARJORIE SUE
(1943-)
Amer. TV newscaster,
broadcast journalist
Gelfman--Women p50,59,149-150,
por.

MARGOLIN, BESSIE (fl. 1930's-
1970's)
Amer. government official
O'Neill--Women's p88,336

MARGOLIN, JANET (1943-)
Amer. actress
World--Who p240

MARGOLIS, ESTHER (fl. 1970's)
Amer. printer
Macksey--Book p193
O'Neill--Women's p489, por.

MARGRETHE (OR MARGARET)
(1940-)
Danish queen
Cur. Biog. '72 p306-308, por.
O'Neill--Women's p48-49
Woman's Almanac p466

MARGUERITE OF ANGOULÊME
See MARGUERITE D'ANGOULÊME
OF NAVARRE

MARGUERITE OF BOURGOGNE (fl.
1290's)
Sicilian queen, hospital
builder
Mead--Hist. p218,230

MARGUERITE OF FLANDERS AND
OF CONSTANTINOPLE,
COUNTESS (1241-1244)
Mead--Hist. p275

MARGUERITE OF NAPLES (fl. 1414)
Italian eye specialist, poet
Marks--Women p55
Mead--Hist. p273,308

MARGUERITE D'ANGOULÊME OF
NAVARRE (1492-1549)
French poet, queen, sister
of Francis I of France,
scholar, author
Bainton--France p13-41, por.
Bree--Women p23-24
Brink--Female p36-53, por.
Crosland--Women p46-48

Fine--Women p6
Jones--Rutledge p514
Macksey--Book p24
Mead--Hist. p347
Moers--Literary p298

MARIA DE VENTADORN (c1165-)
French troubadour
Bogin--Women p99,168-169

MARIA DI NOVELLA (fl. 13th Cent.)
Italian professor of mathe-
matics
Mead--Hist. p225

MARIA FEODOROVNA (1759-1828)
Russian empress, wife of
Czar Peter I, medical school
founder
Mead--Hist. p512

MARIA HEBREA
Jewish scientist, physician
Henry--Written p90

MARIA LESZCZYNSKA (1794-1768)
French queen consort
Partington--Who's p258-259, por.

MARIA LUISA OF SAVOY (-1714)
Spanish queen, wife of
Philip V of Spain
Macksey--Book p27
People's Almanac (1) p528

MARIA OF HUNGARY AND BOHEMIA
(1505-1538)
Bohemian religious
Bainton--Spain p205-215, por.

MARIA THERESA (1717-1780)
Austrian archduchess, queen
of Hungary and Belgium,
mother of Marie Antoinette,
medical educator, hospital
philanthropist
Booth--Women p223-224
Canning--100 p503-508
Diagram--Mothers p152-157, por.
Fry--1000 p185
Jones--Rutledge p514
Macksey--Book p28, por.
Mead--Hist. p418,429,505
Trease--Seven p125-148, por.
Who Did What p215
Woman's Almanac p462-463

MARIE (1900-1961)
Yugoslovian queen, (widow of
King Alexander), (mother of
King Peter)
Partington--Who's p259

MARIE ALEXANDRIA VICTORIA
(1875-1938)
Rumanian queen, (consort of
Ferdinand I)
Partington--Who's p259-260
Sherr--American p240

MARIE ANTOINETTE (1755-1793)
French queen
Book--Lists (2) p421
Davis--Women p61-79, por.
Earle--Two Cent. (1) p386
Earle--Two Cent. (2) p558-559
Frey--1000 p190-191
Jones--Rutledge p514
Kulkin--Her p193-194
Kupferberg--First p96, por.
Macksey--Book p30-31, por.
People's Almanac (2) p403-404,
1243
Who Did What p215
World--Who p159

MARIE DE FRANCE (fl. 1175-1190)
French poet
Bree--Women p5
Crosland--Women p42-44
Mead--Hist. p162-163,228
Moers--Literary p298

MARIE DE MEDICI(S) (1573-1642)
French queen, wife of Henry IV
Jones--Rutledge p514-515

MARIE LOUISE (1791-1847)
French empress, (wife of
Napoleon)
Jones--Rutledge p515

MARIE-ELISE (1950-)
Amer. poet
Webber--Woman p202-207

MARIE-LOUISE (1933-)
Bulgarian princess
Partington--Who's p260

MARIGNY, ANNE-MARGUERITE
HENRIETTE-ROUILLE DE,
BARONESS HYDE DE
NEUVILLE (c1779-1849)

French artist
DePauw--Rem. p128,133

MARIN, LUDMILLA (fl. 1940's-1960's)
Amer. home economist, gov-
ernment official
O'Neill--Women's p38

MARINA, DUCHESS OF KENT
(1906-1968)
English princess
Keenan--Women p21, por.

MARIO, QUEEN(A) TILLOTSON
(1896-1951)
Amer. opera singer
Claghorn--Biog. p298

MARION, FRANCES (1887/1890-1973)
Amer. film writer, novelist,
director, playwright
Mordden--Movie p126
Sicherman--Notable p456-457
Slide--Early p83-91, por.
Smith--Movies p14-16,25, por.

MARISOL (ESCOBAR) (1930-)
Venezuelan-Amer. sculptor
Fine--Women p219-221
Fowler--Art p148
Nemser--Convers. p179-199,363-
364, por.
O'Neill--Women's p604
Parker--Old p151-152, fig. 91
Woman's Almanac p226, por.
Women's--Female p92

MARITZA, SARI (1910-)
British actress
Springer--They p177,315, por.

MARK, MARY ELLEN (1940-)
Amer. photographic journalist
Marzolf--Up p84

MARKEL, HAZEL KENYON (fl.
1940's)
Amer. radio director
Women--Radio p8-9

MARKHAM, BERYL (1902-1986)
British aviatrix
Boase--Sky's p113-130-133, por.

MARKHAM, ELIZABETH WINCHELL
(1852-)
Amer. poet, (mother of Edwin

Markham)
Sherr--American p196

MARKHANDEYA, KAMALA (1924-)
East Indian novelist
Avenel--Comp. (1) p348
Crosland--Beyond p145

MARKIEVICZ, CONSTANCE GORE-
BOOTH, COUNTESS DE
(1868/1876-1927)
Irish patriot, politician
Kulkin--Her p85-86
Macksey--Book p38
Marlowe--Great p204-211, por.
Taylor--Gener. p38-39, por.

MARKOVA, ALICIA, DAME (1910-)
English ballet dancer
Beal--20th p196
Fabian--On p200-201, por.
Jones--Rutledge p516
O'Neill--Women's p640-641
Who Did What p216
World--Who p77

MARKS, JANDOLIN
Amer. psychic
People's Almanac (2) p7

MARKS, JEANNETTE (AUGUSTUS)
(1875-1964)
Amer. poet, playwright,
professor
Ehrlich--Oxford p61,285

MARKS, JOSEPHINE PRESTON
PEABODY
See PEABODY, JOSEPHINE
PRESTON

MARKS, LILLIAN ALICIA
See MARKOVA, ALICIA, DAME

MARKS, LILLIAN BAYLY (1914-)
Amer. genealogical researcher,
author
Meyer--Who's p135

MARKS, SADIE
See LIVINGSTONE, MARY

MARKUS, RIKA ("RIXI") (fl.
1970's)
British bridge player
McWhirter--Guinness p63, por.
O'Neill--Women's p592

MARLAR, FANNIE MORTEU (1863-
1948)
Amer. community, religious
worker, noted Arizona mother
Amer.--Mothers p29-30, por.

MARLATT, ABBY LILLIAN (1869-
1943)
Amer. home economist, edu-
cator
James--Notable (2) p495-497
McHenry--Liberty's p269-270

MARLBOROUGH, CONSUELO VAN-
DERBILT, DUCHESS
See BALSAN, CONSUELO VAN-
DERBILT

MARLBOROUGH, DUCHESS OF
See CHURCHILL, FRANCES,
DUCHESS OF MARLBOROUGH

MARLBOROUGH, GLADYS MARIE
DEACON, DUCHESS (c1881-
1977)
Amer. socialite
Brandon--Dollar p120,122-124,
por.

MARLBOROUGH, SARAH, DUCHESS
OF
See JENNINGS, SARAH

MARLEY, MOLLY
Amer. Indian captive
Sherr--American p236

"MARLIN, MARY"
See GERSON, BETTY LOU

MARLOWE, JULIA (1866-1950)
English-Amer. actress
DePauw--Found. p146-147
Fabian--On p102-103, por.
James--Notable (2) p497-499
McHenry--Liberty's p270-271
Signif.--Amer. p31, por.
Warren--Pictorial p157

MARLOWE, MARION (1929-)
Amer. TV singer
Lamparski--What. (5) p16-17,
por.

MARMOR, HELEN (fl. 1950's-1970's)
Amer. TV newscaster
Gelfman--Women p139-140

O'Neill--Women's p498-499
Scheuer--Tel. p324-325

MARMUR, MILDRED (fl. 1970's)
Amer. publisher
O'Neill--Women's p490-491

MARNER, CAROLE SATRINA (fl.
1960's-1970's)
Amer. filmmaker
Smith--Movies p191,260

MARNO, ANNE
See BANCROFT, ANNE

MAROT, HELEN (1865-1940)
Amer. social investigator,
labor leader, social re-
former, writer, editor
James--Notable (2) p499-501
McHenry--Liberty's p271

MAROTHY-SOLTESOVA, ELENA
(1855-1938)
Czechoslovakian novelist
Partington--Who's p263

MARRINER, EDYTHE
See HAYWARD, SUSAN

MARRIOTT, ADELAIDE (c1883-   )
Canadian craftswoman
O'Neill--Women's p124

MARRIOTT, ALICE S. (fl. 1920's-
1970's)
Amer. co-founder, hotel,
restaurant chain
O'Neill--Women's p513

MARRS, STELLA (1932-   )
Amer. singer
Claghorn--Jazz p194

MARRYAT, FLORENCE (1838-1899)
English novelist, lecturer,
singer, comedienne
Showalter--Lit. p334

MARS, ANNE FRANÇOISE
HIPPOLYTE BOUTET
(1779-1847)
French comedienne, actress
Entertainers p109, por.

MARSDEN, DORIS (fl. 1910's)
Amer. magazine founder,

editor, art patron
Rogers--Ladies p143,154-157,
199-200,204-205

MARSDEN, KATE (1859-1931)
English writer, traveller
Hamalian--Ladies p185-197

MARSH, ANN (1717-1797)
Amer. patriot
DePauw--Rem. p102-103,106

MARSH, DOROTHY MARIE
See WEST, DOROTHY ("DOTTIE")
MARIE

MARSH, JEAN LYNDSEY TARREN
(1934-   )
English actress, writer
Cur. Biog. '77 p283-286, por.
Scheuer--Tel. p325
World--Who p259

MARSH, JOAN (1913-   )
Amer. actress
Springer--They p177-178,315,
por.

MARSH, MAE (1895-1968)
Amer. actress
Manchel--Women p29, por.
Sicherman--Notable p457-459
Springer--They p178,315, por.

MARSH, MARGARET
See MITCHELL, MARGARET
MUNNERLYN

MARSH, MARIAN (1913-   )
Trinidad actress
Springer--They p178,315, por.

MARSH, (EDITH) NGAIO, DAME
(1899-1982)
New Zealander theatrical
producer, novelist
Seymour-Smith--Novels p183
World--Who p47

MARSHALL, CLARA (1847-1931)
Amer. physician, dean of
medical college
James--Notable (2) p501-502
McHenry--Liberty's p271-272

MARSHALL, ELLEN CHURCH (1905-
1965)

Amer. airline stewardess, air
corp army nurse
Genett--Aviation p110

MARSHALL, EMILY
See OTIS, EMILY MARSHALL

MARSHALL, EMMA (1830-1899)
English novelist
Showalter--Lit. p330

MARSHALL, LUCY, CARLILE
(1930-)
New Zealander genealogical
researcher, writer, editor
Meyer--Who's p136

MARSHALL, MARY
Amer. (wife of Chief Justice
Marshall)
Earle--Two Cent. (2) p xv,539,
por.

MARSHALL, MARY RANDOLPH
KEITH (1737-1809)
Amer., mother of famous
sons, pioneer
Sherr--American p81

MARSHALL, MERNA (fl. 1960's-
1970's)
Amer. lawyer, judge
O'Neill--Women's p371

MARSHALL, PAULE (1929-)
Amer. novelist, lecturer,
journalist
Fisher--Third p vii,214
Washington--Black p137-138

MARSHALL, PENNY (1945-)
Amer. actress, comedienne
Anderson--People p269, por.
Cur. Biog. '80 p242-245, por.
Scheuer--Tel. p326
World--Who p240

MARSHALL, (SARAH) CATHERINE
WOOD (1914-1983)
Amer. inspirational writer,
editor, (wife of Peter
Marshall)
Cur. Biog. '83 p469
World--Who p17

MARSHALL, SUSANNAH (fl. 1770's)
Welsh loyalist, tavern keeper

Booth--Women p66-67
DePauw--Found. p133-134

MARTERTERA, AEMILIA HILARIA
See AEMILIA HILARIA MARTER-
TERA

MARTHA
Biblical, sister of Mary
Price--God p148

MARTHA, SISTER (c1751-1824)
French army surgeon
Mead--Hist. p496

MARTIN, MRS. A.E. "PADDY"
(fl. 1960's)
English golfer
McWhirter--Guinness p79

MARTIN, AGNES (1911-)
Amer. painter
Women's--Female p50

MARTIN, ALLIE BETH (1914-1976)
Amer. librarian, organization
official, educator
Cur. Biog. '75 p264-266, por.
Cur. Biog. '76 p472
O'Neill--Women's p430-431

MARTIN, ANDREA
Canadian TV writer, performer
Scheuer--Tel. p327, por.

MARTIN, ANNA (c1869-)
Amer. centenarian
Mitchell--Yessir p104-105, por.

MARTIN, ANNE HENRIETTA (1875-
1951)
Amer. social reformer,
feminist, essayist
McHenry--Liberty's p272
Sherr--American p144
Sicherman--Notable p459-461

MARTIN, BARBARA (fl. 1970's)
Amer. bishop
O'Neill--Women's p383

MARTIN, MRS. BRADLEY
Amer. philanthropist
Forma--They p46-47

MARTIN, DEBORAH BEAUMONT
(-1931)

Amer. historian
Sherr--American p247

MARTIN, EDNA (fl. 1940's-1970's)
Swedish textile designer
O'Neill--Women's p271

MARTIN, ELIZABETH MARSHALL
(fl. 1770's)
Amer. Revolutionary War
patriot, noted South Carolina mother
Amer.--Mothers p491

MARTIN, GEORGE MADDEN
(1866-1946)
Amer. author, race relations
worker
James--Notable (2) p502-504

MARTIN, HELEN REIMENSNYDER
(1868-1939)
Amer. novelist
Ehrlich--Oxford p201

MARTIN, JOAN
Amer. clergyman
O'Neill--Women's p383

MARTIN, KATHY
Amer. golfer
McWhirter--Guinness p76

MARTIN, LILLIEN JANE (1851-
1943)
Amer. psychologist
Bachtold--Gifted p64-67
James--Notable (2) p504-505
McHenry--Liberty's p272

MARTIN, LUCI
Amer. singer
Glassman--Year '79 p92, por.

MARTIN, MARIA (MARIE) (1796-
1863)
Amer. nature painter
James--Notable (2) p505-506
McHenry--Liberty's p273
Sherr--American p211

MARTIN, MARION E. (1900-)
Amer. labor leader, state
official
O'Neill--Women's p342

MARTIN, MARTHA, pseud. (fl.

1970's)
Amer., wife of a gold pros-
pector
Moffat--Revel. p301-313

MARTIN, MARY (1913-)
Amer. singer, actress, dancer
Claghorn--Biog. p300
Engstead--Star p118,120-121
McHenry--Liberty's p273
Shipman--Gold. p381-382, por.
Simon--Best p382-383, por.
World--Who p240

MARTIN, MAY (c1870-)
Amer. teacher, politician,
nonagenarian
Gold--Until p5-20, por.

MARTIN, SUSANNA (fl. 1669)
Amer. accused witch
Williams--Demeter's p140

MARTIN, VICTORIA WOODHULL
See WOODHULL, VICTORIA CLAF-
LIN

MARTIN, VIOLET FLORENCE (1862-
1915)
Irish novelist
Avenel--Comp. (1) p450
Seymour-Smith--Novels p219
Showalter--Lit. p341-342

MARTIN, VIRGINIA H. (fl. 1970's)
Amer. feminist
O'Neill--Women's p109

MARTIN FAMILY (fl. 1770's)
Amer. Revolutionary War
patriots
Meyer--Petticoat p187-189

MARTINEAU, HARRIET (1802-1876)
English moralist, political
economist, journalist, novelist,
children's book author
Avenel--Comp. (1) p351
Basch--Relative, see index p355
Earnest--American p52,55,57-58
Fine--Women p66,90
Gurko--Ladies p271-272, por.
Hamalian--Ladies p99-114
Jones--Rutledge p519
Lutz--Crusade, see index p336
Macksey--Book p123, por.
Moers--Literary p298, see also

Donaldson--How p246-247
Fry--1000 p127
Jones--Rutledge p522
Macksey--Book p24
Softly--Queens p75-77, por.
Woman's Almanac p497-498,
    por.
Who Did What p217
World--Who p157

MARY II (1662-1694)
    British queen
Delderfield--Kings p75-76, por.
Jones--Rutledge p522
Kulkin--Her p197
Softly--Queens p95-97, por.

MARY (MARY STUART, QUEEN
    OF SCOTS) (1542-1587)
    Scottish queen, mother of
    James I
Diagram--Mothers p116-117, por.
Donaldson--How p248-250
Earle--Two Cent. (1) p78-79,
    243
Earle--Two Cent. (2) p507
Fry--1000 p135
Kulkin--Her p198-199
Macksey--Book p256
People's Almanac (2) p1108
Prause--School p149-150
Who Did What p217
Woman's Almanac p462
World--Who p157

MARY (1897-1965)
    British princess, daughter
    of George V
Jones--Rutledge p522

MARY ALOYSIUS, SISTER
    (-1954)
    Amer. nun, college founder
Sherr--American p123

MARY ALPHONSA, MOTHER
    See LATHROP, ROSE
    HAWTHORNE

MARY BEATRICE ("MARY OF
    MODENA") (1658-1718)
    English, consort of James II
    of Great Britain
Jones--Rutledge p521
Softly--Queens p91-94, por.

MARY DE BOHUN (-1394)

English queen
Softly--Queens p41

"MARY GOOSE"
    See VERGOOSE, ELIZABETH
    FOSTER

MARY JOSEPH, SISTER (c1883-1955)
    Amer. nun, administrator,
    Mayo's
Sherr--American p122

MARY MAGDALENE
    Biblical
Green--Saints p91-93
Jones--Rutledge p522
Price--God p165-170
Woman's Almanac p399-400

MARY OF BETHANY
    Biblical, sister of Martha and
    Lazarus
Price--God p148-156

MARY OF BURGUNDY (MARIE DE
    BOURGOGNE) (1457-1482)
    French, duchess, (daughter
    of Charles the Bold)
Woman's Almanac p74

MARY OF CHÂTILLON (fl. c1300)
    British college founder,
    governess, educator
Macksey--Book p63

MARY OF GUELDRES
    Scottish queen, (wife of
    James II)
Leary--Golden p148,167

"MARY OF MODENA"
    See MARY BEATRICE

MARY OF TECK (1867-1953)
    British queen, consort of
    King George V
Book--Lists (2) p254
Jones--Rutledge p521-522
Softly--Queens p119-122, por.

MARY STUART
    See MARY (1542-1587)

"MARY YELLIN"
    See LEASE, MARY ELIZABETH
    CLYENS

MARZOLF, MARION
Amer. journalist, author
O'Neill--Women's p437

MASEVICH, ALLA (1957-   )
Russian astronomer, professor
Mandel--Soviet p84

MASHAM, ABIGAIL HILL, LADY
(-1734)
English, friend of Queen
Anne
Macksey--Book p28

MASINA, GIULIETTA (1921-   )
Italian actress
Shipman--Internatl. p359-361,
por.

MASKEWITZ, BETTY F. (fl.
1960's-1970's)
Amer., founder of Nuclear
Information Center
O'Neill--Women's p179

MASON, ALICE TRUMBULL (1904-
1971)
Amer. artist
Harris--Women p327-328

MASON, ANNA MARIE (fl. 1860's)
Amer. Southern belle
DeLeon--Belles p303-304, por.

MASON, MRS. BENJAMIN
See CHAMPLIN, "PEGGY"

MASON, BIDDY ("GRANDMA")
(1818-1891)
Amer. slave, social reformer,
pioneer nurse
Gray--Women p3-4,64-67
Millstein--We p53,62-63
Time--Women p213, por.

MASON, CATHY RIGBY
See RIGBY, CATHY

MASON, DEBBY (fl. 1970's)
Amer. basketball player
Hollander--100 p9

MASON, EDITH BARNES (1893-
1973)
Amer. opera singer
Claghorn--Biog. p301
Tuggle--Golden p137, por.

MASON, EMILY VIRGINIA (1815-
1909)
Amer. Southern belle, writer,
humanitarian
DeLeon--Belles p387-388, por.

MASON, LUCY RANDOLPH (1882-
1959)
Amer. YWCA worker, labor
leader, social reformer
Scott--Southern p192,194,197,
208-209
Sicherman--Notable p461-462

MASON, MARSHA (1942-   )
Amer. actress
Cur. Biog. '81 p282-285, por.
Hirschhorn--Rating p258, por.
Manchel--Women p16
World--Who p240

MASON, PRISCILLA (fl. 1790's)
Amer. feminist
Berkin--Women p83-84,89-91

MASON, SUE
Amer. aviatrix, (jet pilot)
Lichtenstein--Mach., see index
p363

MASSEE, MAY (1881-1966)
Amer. editor, children's
literature specialist
Sicherman--Notable p462-464

MASSEY, ALICE (fl. 1500's)
English midwife
Mead--Hist. p356

MASSEY, ILONA (c1912-1974)
Hungarian-Austrian opera
singer, actress
Springer--They p178,315, por.

MASSEY, LOUISA
Amer. heroine
Sherr--American p72

MASSEY, PATRICIA (1905-   )
South African physician
Hellstedt--Women p292-294, por.

MASSIE, THALIA
Amer., criminal case character
Horan--Desperate p67-68, por.

MAST, LOIS ANN (1951-   )
Amer. genealogical researcher,

author, indexer, editor
Meyer--Who's p137

MASTERS, SYBILLA (-1720)
Amer. colonial inventor
Earle--Two Cent. (2) p570
James--Notable (2) p508-509
Williams--Demeter's p178-179

MATA'AFA, MASIOFO FETAUI
(HER EXCELLENCY)
Samoan, wife of the Prime
Minister of Western Samoa
Kooiman--Silhouettes p134-142,
por.

MATARAZZO, MARIA PIA ESMER-
ELDA (fl. 1970's)
Brazilian company executive
O'Neill--Women's p525

MATHER, WINIFRED HOLT
See HOLT, WINIFRED

MATHEWS, ANN TERESA (MOTHER
BERNARDINA) (1732-1800)
Amer. convent co-founder
James--Notable (2) p509-510
McHenry--Liberty's p274

MATHEWS, JOYCE (JANE) (fl.
1940's-1950's)
Amer. actress
Lamparski--What. (8) p202-203,
por.

MATHEWS, LUCIA KLEINHAUS
(1870-1955)
Amer. painter, furniture,
woodwork decorator, wood-
carver
Callen--Women p170-171,224

MATHEWS, MARY McNAIR (fl.
1860's-1880's)
Amer. writer
Fischer--Let p177-192

MATHEWS, RITA (fl. 1970's)
Amer. biologist (Antarctica)
Land--New p119-122,217, por.

MATHIS, EDITH (1938-)
Swiss opera singer
Gammond--Illus. p246, por.

MATHIS, JUNE
Amer. film writer

Mordden--Movie
p12

MATHISON, KAROLINE (1898-)
Norwegian physician
Hellstedt--Women p156-158, por.

MATIKASHVILI, NINA
Russian veterinary surgeon
Macksey--Book p158

MATILDA (1) (MAUDE) (1102-1167)
English daughter of Henry I
of England, wife of Henry V
Jones--Rutledge p525

MATILDA (2) (fl. 12th Cent.)
French, Abbess of Fontevrault,
medical woman
Mead--Hist. p179

MATILDA (3) (fl. c983)
German, abbess of Quedlin-
burg, medical woman
Mead--Hist. p112

MATILDA ("HOLY QUEEN") (1080-
1111/1118)
English queen, hospital founder
Mead--Hist. p175
Softly--Queens p12-14

MATILDA OF BOULOGNE (1103-1152)
English queen
Softly--Queens p16-18

MATILDA OF FLANDERS (-1083)
English queen, wife of William
the Conqueror
Softly--Queen p9-12

MATILDA OF SCOTLAND (1080-1118)
English queen
Softly--Queens p12-14

MATOAKA
See POCAHONTAS

MATSUBARA, HISAKO (fl. 1970's)
Japanese short-story writer,
TV director
McCullough--People p121-123

MATTFIELD, JACQUELINE PHILLIPS
(1925-)
Amer. college president
O'Neill--Women's p408
Woman's Almanac p158

World--Who
p 100

MATTHEWS, ALVA T. (fl. 1970's)
Amer. research engineer,
consultant, mathematician
O'Neill--Women's p 189,193

MATTHEWS, ANNE (1732-1800)
Amer. convent co-founder
Williams--Demeter's p 227

MATTHEWS, GRACE ("BIG SISTER")
(fl. 1940's)
Amer. Radio, TV actress
Lamparski--What. (4) p 146-147,
por.

MATTHEWS, JESSIE (1907-)
English dancer, actress
Lamparski--What. (2) p 110-111,
por.
Shipman--Gold. p 391-393, por.
Springer--They p 178-179,315,
por.

MATTHEWS, JOYCE (fl. 1940's)
Book--Lists (2) p 251, por.

MATTHEWS, LUCIA (fl. 1970's)
Amer. painter
Women's--Female p 50

MATTHEWS, MERLE
Amer. bowler
People's Almanac (1) p 1196-1197

MATTHEWS, MRS.
See MUSGROVE, MARY

MATTHEWS, PAULINE
See DEE, KIKI

MATTHEWS, VICTORIA EARLE
(1861-)
Amer. social worker, clubwoman
James--Notable (2) p 510-511

MATTINGLY, MARIE
See MELONEY, MARIE MATTINGLY

MATTINGLY, SARAH IRWIN
See MELONEY, MARIE MATTINGLY

MATZENAUER, MARGARETE (1881-
1963)

Hungarian opera singer
Claghorn--Biog. p 303
Tuggle--Golden p 110-113, por.

MATZKIN, ROSE (fl. 1930's-1970's)
Amer. Zionist activist
O'Neill--Women's p 719-720

MATZO, EMMA
See SCOTT, LIZABETH

MAUBOURG, JEANNE (1875-)
French singer
Claghorn--Biog. p 303

"MAUD, GOOD QUEEN"
See MATILDA ("HOLY QUEEN")
(1080-1111/1118)

MAUDE
See MATILDA (1)

MAUGHAM, SYRIE (1879-1955)
English interior decorator,
wife of Somerset Maugham
O'Neill--Women's p 280

MAULIN, ANNA CATHERINE
See ZENGER, (ANNA) CATHER-
INE MAULIN

MAULSON, HANNAH (fl. 1970's)
Amer. Chippewa Indian teacher
O'Neill--Women's p 429

MAUPIN, JOYCE (1914-)
Amer. labor leader, (co-
founder of WAGE)
O'Neill--Women's p 325-326

MAURICE, MARY (fl. 1840's)
British educator
Macksey--Book p 70

MAURIER, DAPHNE DU
See DuMAURIER, DAPHNE,
LADY BROWNING

MAURY, ANTONIA CAETANA DE
PALVA PEREIRA (1866-1952)
Amer. astronomer
O'Neill--Women's p 150
Sicherman--Notable p 465-466

MAXCY, MABEL (fl. 1970's)
Amer. textile artist
Women's--Female p 99

MAXWELL, ANNA CAROLINE (1851-
1929)
Amer. nursing educator, ad-
ministrator
James--Notable (2) p511-513
Signif.--Amer. p31, por.

MAXWELL, ELSA (1883-1963)
Amer. columnist, hostess
Clark--Leading p159
Lewis--Prime p207-208
McHenry--Liberty's p274-275
Webster's--Amer. p703

MAXWELL, KATE
See WATSON, ELLA ("CATTLE
KATE")

MAXWELL, MARTHA A.
Amer. naturalist, hunter,
taxidermist, artist
Sherr--American p24, por.
Time--Women p182-183, por.

MAXWELL, MARY HAMLIN (1814-
1853)
hymnist
Claghorn--Biog. p303

MAXWELL, VERA HUPPE (1901-)
Amer. fashion designer
Cur. Biog. '77 p291-294, por.

MAY, ABIGAIL ("ABBIE") WIL-
LIAMS (ABBY W. MAY)
(1829-1888)
Amer. Civil War reformer,
humanitarian, feminist
James--Notable (2) p513-515

MAY, CATHERINE DEAN (1914-)
Amer. Congresswoman,
radio commentator
Chamberlin--Min. p274-279
U.S.--Women (89th) p17, por.
U.S.--Women (90th) p17, por.

MAY, CORDELIA SCAIFE
Amer. millionaire
Forbes--400 ('84) p101

MAY, ELAINE (1932-)
Amer. actress, director,
playwright
Entertainers p280
O'Neill--Women's p669
Smith--Movies p48-52,58, por.

Woman's Almanac p319
World--Who p241

MAY, GERALDINE PRATT (c1895-)
Amer. aviatrix, colonel,
director, WAC, WAF
McHenry--Liberty's p275
O'Neill--Women's p536-537

MAY, IRENE SOPHIE DU PONT
(c1900-)
Amer. millionaire
Forbes--400 ('84) p149

MAY, SOPHIE, pseud. (1833-1906)
Amer. children's book author
Ehrlich--Oxford p7
James--Notable (1) p344-345
McHenry--Liberty's p74
Sherr--American p90

MAYER, BESSIE BRUCE (1880-)
Amer. religious, hospital,
community worker, noted
Delaware mother
Amer.--Mothers p86-87, por.

MAYER, CONSTANCE (1778-1821)
French painter
Fine--Women p60
Harris--Women p46,205,207,213-
214,349
Munsterberg--Hist. p49

MAYER, HELENA (HELENE) (c1911-
1953)
German fencer
McWhirter--Guinness p60, por.

MAYER, JOAN
Amer. theological student
O'Neill--Women's p394, por.

MAYER, MARIA GERTRUDE GOEP-
PERT (1906-1972)
German-Amer. physicist, edu-
cator, author
Asimov--Biog. p713
Bachtold--Gifted p56-57
Cur. Biog. '72 p467
McHenry--Liberty's p275
Macksey--Book p158
Neidle--America's p212-213
O'Neill--Women's p144,182
Opfell--Lady p194-208, por.
Sicherman--Notable p466-468
Signif.--Amer. p44, por.

Warren--Pictorial p204
Webster's--Amer. p704
Woman's Almanac p365, por.
World--Who p105

MAYER, VERA
    Hungarian-Amer. TV executive
    Scheuer--Tel. p330

MAYHEW, STELLA (1875-1934)
    singer
    Claghorn--Biog. p303

MAYMI, CARMEN ROSA (1938-)
    Puerto Rican government official
    O'Neill--Women's p330,339

MAYNARD, CATHERINE (fl. 1850's)
    Amer. heroine, gardener
    Sherr--American p241

MAYNARD, JOAN
    British Parliament member
    Vallance--Women p57,62,70,196

MAYNARD, VALERIE (fl. 1970's)
    Amer. sculptor, printmaker
    Fax--Black p97-116, por.
    Women's--Female p80

MAYNOR, ASA
    Amer. TV producer
    Scheuer--Tel. p330

MAYNOR (MAINOR), DOROTHY
    (1910-)
    Amer. singer
    Claghorn--Biog. p303

MAYO, EDITH GRAHAM (fl.
    1930's-1940's)
    Amer. nurse
    Sherr--American p122

MAYO, ISABELLA FYRIE
    (1843-)
    English novelist
    Showlater--Lit. p336

MAYO, KATHERINE (1867-1940)
    Amer. journalist
    Ehrlich--Oxford p213
    James--Notable (2) p515-517

MAYO, MARY (fl. 1950's-1970's)

Amer. singer
    Balliett--Amer. p10-15

MAYO, MARY ANNE BRYANT (1845-
    1903)
    Amer. farm organizer
    McHenry--Liberty's p275-276

MAYO, SARA TEW (1869-1930)
    Amer. physician, surgeon,
    hospital founder
    James--Notable (2) p517-518
    Sherr--American p85, por.

MAYO, VIRGINIA (1920-)
    Amer. actress
    World--Who p241

MAYO, MRS. WILLIAM C.
    See WISE, MARGARETTA

MAYOR, FLORA MACDONALD
    (1872-1932)
    English novelist
    Showalter--Lit. p345

MAYSON, MARINA, pseud.
    See ROGERS, ROSEMARY

MAYWOOD, AUGUSTA (1825-1876)
    Amer. ballet dancer
    Fabian--On p80-81, por.
    James--Notable (2) p518-519
    McHenry--Liberty's p276
    Migel--Ballerinas p179-193, por.

MAZ, VERONICA (fl. 1970's)
    Amer. sociology professor,
    founder
    O'Neill--Women's p119

MAZARIN, MARIETTE (1874-1953)
    French opera singer
    Tuggle--Golden p58-59, por.

MAZE, LULA DUTY (fl. 1940's)
    Amer. banker
    O'Neill--Women's p527

MAZZETTI, LORENZA (fl. 1960's-
    1970's)
    Italian filmmaker
    Smith--Movies p129

MAZZO, KAY (1947-)
    Amer. ballet dancer
    Cur. Biog. '71 p264-266, por.

MEAD, ELIZABETH STORRS
BILLINGS (1832-1917)
Amer. college president
James--Notable (2) p519-520
McHenry--Liberty's p276

MEAD, KATE CAMPBELL HURD
See HURD-MEAD, KATE
CAMPBELL

MEAD, LUCIA TRUE AMES
(1856-1936)
Amer. pacifist, international-
ist, suffragist
James--Notable (2) p520-522

MEAD, MARGARET (1901-1978)
Amer. anthropologist,
author, noted Pennsylvania
mother
Amer.--Mothers p461, por.
Anticaglia--12 p225-243, por.
Avenel--Comp. (2) p171
Bachtold--Gifted p79-81
Berkin--Women p336-337,341
Bowman--Social p13-19, por.
Clark--Leading p220-221
Comfort--Good p97, por.
Cur. Biog. '79 p468
Emberlin--Cont. p55-79, por.
Gelfman--Woman p143
Gilbert--Part. p101, por.
Ingraham--Album p67,72, por.
Kelen--Fifty p105
Kostman--20th p117-137, por.
Kulkin--Her p199-200
Lichtenstein--Mach., see index
p363-364
Longstreet--Queen p193-194
McHenry--Liberty's p276-277
Marlowe--Great p322-327, por.
Millstein--We p244-246,256,261-
263
Moers--Literary p299
100--Greatest (1) p28, por.
O'Neill--Women's p40,145
People's Almanac (1) p25-26
Signif.--Amer. p68, por.
Sochen--Herstory p347
Sochen--Movers, see index p316
Stoddard--Famous p275-286, por.
Webster's--Amer. p706-707
Who Did What p222
Wintle--Makers p350, #310
Woman's Almanac p37,365-366,
por.
World--Who p96

MEAD, SYLVIA (ALICE) EARLE
(1935-)
Amer. marine biologist, re-
searcher
Cur. Biog. '72 p319-322, por.
O'Neill--Women's p162

MEADE, L.T. (1854-1914)
British novelist
People's Almanac (3) p546

MEADOWCRAFT, ENID LaMONTE
(1898-1966)
Amer. children's book author
Ehrlich--Oxford p82

MEADOWS, AUDREY (1922/1924-)
Amer. actress, TV personality
Scheuer--Tel. p330
World--Who p241

MEADOWS, JAYNE COTTER (1925/
1926-)
Amer. actress, (wife of Steve
Allen)
Scheuer--Tel. p331
World--Who p241

MEADOWS, MARY W. (1918-)
Amer. genealogical researcher,
writer
Meyer--Who's p137

MEADOWS-ROGERS, ARABELLA (fl.
1970's)
Amer. clergyman
Proctor--Women p41,61-62,66-67

MEAGHER, CYNDI (fl. 1970's)
Amer. newspaper reporter
O'Neill--Women's p463

MEANS, JACQUELINE (fl. 1970's)
Amer. priest
O'Neill--Women's p384

MEANS, LORELEI (fl. 1970's)
Amer. (Dakota or Sioux)
Indian co-founder, survival
school
O'Neill--Women's p718

MEANS, MARIANNE HANSEN
(1934-)
Amer. journalist
O'Neill--Women's p458

MEARA, ANNE (1924/1929-)
Amer. comedienne, TV
actress
Woman's Almanac p319
World--Who p241

MEARS, HELEN FARNSWORTH
(1872-1916)
Amer. sculptor
James--Notable (2) p522-523
McHenry--Liberty's p277-278
Sherr--American p38,249-250,
por.

MEARS, MRS. JOHN (-1765)
English, subject of portrait,
grand-daughter of Sir
Benjamin Truman
Ware--Meet p78

MEARS, MARTHA
English medical woman, writer,
obstetrician
Mead--Hist. p472-474

MECHENEN, IDA VAN (fl. 15th
Cent.)
German graphic artist
Munsterberg--Hist. p104

MECHLIN, LEILA (1874-1949)
Amer. art critic, editor,
administrator
James--Notable (2) p523-524
O'Neill--Women's p440

MECHNIKOV, ILYA ILLICH
See METCHNIKOFF, ELIE

MECHTEL, ANGELIKA (1943-)
German novelist, radio
playwright, writer
Herrmann--Germ. p6,133

MECHTHILD OF (HACKEDORN),
MAGDEBURG (1210/1212-
1282)
German nun, poet, physician
Mead--Hist. p223

MECK, NADEZHDA VON (fl.
1880's)
Russian mother of Sonia von
Meck, (patroness of Tchaikov-
sky)
Book--Lists (2) p268

MECOM, JANE FRANKLIN (1712-
1794)
Amer. Revolutionary letter
writer, sister of Benjamin
Franklin
Engle--Women p71-92
James--Notable (2) p524-525
Sherr--American p23
Warren--Pictorial p47

MEDHAVI, RAMABAI DONGRE
(1858-1922)
East Indian, religious leader,
author, humanitarian, educator
Marlowe--Great p156-160, por.

MEDICIS, CATHERINE DE
See CATHERINE DE MEDICIS

MEDICIS, MARIE DE
See MARIE DE MEDICIS

MEDILL, ELEANOR "CISSY" PAT-
TERSON (1884-1948)
Amer. newspaper publisher
Book--Lists (2) p453

MEDINA, ANN
Amer. TV newscaster
Glefman--Women p12-13,50,68,
82-83,94

MEDINA, MARIA
Austrian ballet dancer
Migel--Ballerinas p102, por.

MEDINA-SIDONIA, DUCHESS OF
(1936-)
Spanish social activist, author
Cur. Biog. '72 p322-325, por.

MEDNYANSZKY, MARIA (fl. 1920's-
1930's)
Hungarian tennis player
Macksey--Book p258
McWhirter--Guinness p147

MEEKER, JOSEPHINE (fl. 1870's)
Amer. teacher, Indian captive
Sherr--American p28-29

MEEKER, ROSE
Amer. lecturer
Time--Women p206, por.

MEFFORD, DITRA HELENA
See FLAME, DITRA

MEHLE, AILEEN
Amer. columnist, journalist
Woman's Almanac p277

MEIGS, CORNELIA (1884-1973)
Amer. historian, biographer,
short-story writer, children's
book author
Ehrlich--Oxford p329

MEINEL, MARJORIE (1917-)
Amer. astronomer
O'Neill--Women's p151

MEIR, GOLDA MABOVITCH (1898-
1978)
Israeli Prime Minister
Amer.--Mothers p587-589, por.
Comfort--Good p101, por.
Cur. Biog. '70 p284-287, por.
Cur. Biog. '79 p468
Fink--Great p177-181, por.
Fry--1000 p326
Jones--Rutledge p533
Kelen--Fifty p109
Kostman--20th p99-116, por.
Kulkin--Her p200-202
Macksey--Book p45-46, por.
Marlowe--Great p303-308, por.
O'Neill--Women's p7,46-47,284
Palmer--Who's p228
Prause--School p186-189
Whedon--Always p34-36, por.
Who Did What p223
Woman's Almanac p464-465, por.
World--Who p169

MEISLE, KATHRYN (1895-1970)
Amer. opera singer
Claghorn--Biog. p304

MEISSNER, JULIE (fl. 1970's)
Amer. ski instructor, racing
coach
O'Neill--Women's p566

MEITNER, LISE (1878-1968)
Austrian-Swedish nuclear
physicist, mathematician
Asimov--Biog. p584
Ingraham--Album p67
Jones--Rutledge p533
Kulkin--Her p202-203
Macksey--Book p153-154
O'Neill--Women's p180-181
Who Did What p223
Woman's Almanac p366, por.

MEITNER-GRAF, LOTTE (-1974)
Austrian photographer
Macksey--Book p209

MELAMUD, GRUNIE (fl. 1940's)
Russian, Jewish heroine
Mandel--Soviet p192

MELANCHTHON, KATHERINE KRAPP
German Reformation worker
Bainton--Germany p159-161

"MELANIE" (1948-)
Amer. singer, songwriter,
actress
World--Who p270

MELANTON, KAISA (1920-)
Swedish textile designer
O'Neill--Women's p271

MELBA, NELLIE, DAME (1859/1861-
1931)
Australian opera singer
Claghorn--Biog. p304-305
Fry--1000 p276-277, por.
Jones--Rutledge p533
Macksey--Book p215
Neidle--America's p222
O'Neill--Women's p618
Tuggle--Golden p6, por.
World--Who p77

MELIA, JINX (fl. 1970's)
Amer. founder of "Martha
Movement"
O'Neill--Women's p108-109,516

MELIS, CARMEN (1885-1967)
Italian opera singer
Claghorn--Biog. p305
Tuggle--Golden p54-55, por.

MELLETTE, MARGARET WYLIE
(1843-1938)
Amer., wife of first governor,
noted South Dakota mother
Amer.--Mothers p495

MELMOTH, CHARLOTTE (1749-1823)
Irish singer, actress
Claghorn--Biog. p305

MELONEY, MARIE MATTINGLY (1878-
1943)
Amer. journalist, magazine
editor

James--Notable (2) p525-526
McHenry--Liberty's p278
O'Neill--Women's p442

MELTON, NANCY LOPEZ
See LOPEZ, NANCY

MELTZER, BARBARA
Amer. TV director
Scheuer--Tel. p332, por.

MELUN, MADEMOISELLE DE
(-1679)
French nurse
Mead--Hist. p418

MELVILLE, JENNIE, pseud.
See BUTLER, GWENDOLINE

MEMMIER, RUTH LUNDEEN
(1900-)
Amer. physician
Hellstedt--Women p214-220, por.

MENCHIK-STEVENSON, VERA
(1906-1944)
British chess player
McWhirter--Guinness p64-65

MENDELSOHN, DOROTHEA
German salonist
Baum--Jewish p20-21

MENDELSON, NANCY
Amer. TV director
Scheuer--Tel. p332

MENDENHALL, DOROTHY REED
(1875-1964)
Amer. physician, noted
Wisconsin mother
Amer.--Mothers p586-587, por.
O'Neill--Women's p212
Sicherman--Notable p468-470

MENDES, GRACIA (-1569)
Portuguese businesswoman,
philanthropist
Fink--Great p18-29, por.

MENDES, MRS.
See GAUTIER, JUDITH

MENDEZ, ANA G. (1908-)
Puerto Rican-Amer. educator,
civic charitable worker, noted
Puerto Rican mother
Amer.--Mothers p473-474, por.

MENDL, ELSIE DE WOLFE, LADY
See DE WOLFE, ELSIE, LADY
MENDL

MENDOZA, LUISA DE CARVAJAL Y
(1568-1614)
Spanish Jesuit missionary,
college founder
Macksey--Book p106-107

MENDOZA-GUAZON, MARIA PAZ
Filipino physician
O'Neill--Women's p205

MENEN (MANIN), WAIZARO
(WAIZERO) (c1891-1962)
African, Empress of Gondar
(Ethiopia), wife of Emperor
Haile Selassie I
Macksey--Book p31

MENGEL, NANETTE VONNEGUT
(1913-)
Amer. university professor
Ruddick--Working p270-282,344-
345, por.

MENGES, KAY (c1912-)
Amer. aviatrix, teacher, army
flier
Keil--Those p58,137,192,196,210-
211

MENKEN, ADAH ISAACS (1835-1868)
Amer. actress
Chinoy--Women p81-87, por.
Dunlap--Calif. p136, por.
Entertainers p128, por.
James--Notable (2) p526-529
Jones--Rutledge p536
McHenry--Liberty's p278-279
People's Almanac (2) p788-790
Reifert--Women p141-143
Stein--Lives p1-36, por.

MENKEN, MARIE (c1909-1970)
Amer. filmmaker
Smith--Movies p35-36

MENNINGER, FLORA KNISELY
(1863-1945)
Amer. teacher, church worker,
noted Iowa mother
Amer.--Mothers p207-208, por.

MENON, MRS. K. RUKMINI (fl.
1970's)
East Indian ambassador

O'Neill--Women's
p62

MENTSCHIKOFF, SOIA (1915-   )
Amer. lawyer, dean law
school
O'Neill--Women's p363
Swiger--Women p101-116

MENTUAB
African, Ethiopian (Gondar)
Regent
Macksey--Book p31

MENTUHETEP (fl. c2300 B.C.)
Egyptian queen, physician
Mead--Hist. p21-22

MENUHIN, HEPHZIBAH (1922-1981)
Amer. pianist, (sister of
Yehudi Menuhin)
Jones--Rutledge p537

MENUHIN, KATHLEEN
Amer. pianist
Macksey--Book p221

MERCADER, CARIDAD
Spanish Communist
Macksey--Book p57-58

MERCER, BERYL (1882-1939)
English actress
Springer--They p179,316, por.

MERCER, LUCY PAGE
Amer. secretary (to
Eleanor Roosevelt)
Daniels--Wash., see index
p365, por.
Miller--Fishbait p104
People's Almanac (1) p296

MERCER, MABEL (1900-1984)
British-Amer. singer, com-
poser
Balliett--Amer. p149-162
Cur. Biog. '84 p476
Claghorn--Jazz p204
Cur. Biog. '73 p291-293, por.
O'Neill--Women's p625
Simon--Best p392-393, por.

MERCER, MINNIE (fl. 1910's)
Amer. socialite
Daniels--Wash., see index
p365, por.

MERCER, VIOLETTA (c1889-1947)
Amer. socialite
Daniels--Wash., see index p365

MERCHANT, MABEL STOCKTON
Amer. social reformer, feminist
Sherr--American p216

MERCHANT, MARJORIE
Argentinean golfer
McWhirter--Guinness p79

MERCOURI, MELINA (MARIA
AMALIA) (1923/1925-   )
Greek actress, politician
Anderson--People p275
O'Neill--Women's p732
Shipman--Internatl. p378-379, por.
Woman's Almanac p350
World--Who p259

MEREDITH, DOROTHY L. (1906-   )
Amer. fiber artist, educator,
weaving professor
O'Neill--Women's p266

MEREDITH, VIRGINIA (1848-1936)
Amer. agriculturist, home
economist, college dean, professor, noted Indiana mother
Amer.--Mothers p177, por.

MEREZHKOVSKAVA, ZINAIDA
NIKOLA (1869-1945)
Russian poet
Moers--Literary p xv,294

MERGLER, MARIE JOSEPHA (1851-
1901)
Amer. physician, surgeon,
educator
James--Notable (2) p529-530
Neidle--America's p202-203

MERIAN, MARIA SIBYLLA (1647-
1717)
Swiss-Flemish entomologist,
painter, engraver
Fine--Women p34-35
Harris--Women p17,27,32,35,43,
65,135,153-155,344
Macksey--Book p198-199
Mead--Hist. p426
Munsterberg--Hist. p30-31,105
Petersen--Women p38,40
Sparrow--Women p285-286,295-296
Tufts--Our p88-97, por.

MERICI, ANGELA
See ANGELA, SAINT MERICI

MERIT, PTAH (fl. c2700 B.C.)
Egyptian physician
Macksey--Book p139, por.
Mead--Hist. p16

MERIWETHER, ELIZABETH AVERY
(fl. 1870's-1880's)
Amer. suffragette
Scott--Southern p171,173-174

MERIWETHER, LEE (1935-)
Amer. actress
World--Who p241

MERIWETHER, MRS. LIDE
(1829-)
Amer. temperance worker
Scott--Southern p150

MERIWETHER, LOUISE
Amer. novelist
Washington--Black p62-66

MERIWETHER, VIRGINIA (1862-)
Amer. physician
Scott--Southern p132-133

MERKEL, UNA (1903-1986)
Amer. actress
Lamparski--What. (3) p126-127,
por.
Lamparski--What. (8) p208-209,
por.
Springer--They p179-180,316,
por.

MERMAN, ETHEL AGNES ZIMMER-
MAN (1908/1909-1984)
Amer. singer, actress
Cur. Biog. '84 p476
Claghorn--Biog. p306
Entertainers p234, por.
Fabian--On p196-199, por.
Hirschhorn--Rating p262, por.
McHenry--Liberty's p279
Mordden--Movie p171
100--Greatest (1) p46-47, por.
O'Neill--Women's p626
Simon--Best p394-396, por.
Springer--They p180,316, por.
Webster's--Amer. p716
Woman's Almanac p296-297
World--Who p241

MERMELSTEIN, PAULA (1947-)
Amer. TV executive
Scheuer--Tel. p333-334

MERMEY, FAYVELLE (1916-)
Amer. synagogue president
O'Neill--Women's p395

MERO-IRION, YOLANDA (c1877/
1887-1963)
Hungarian pianist
Claghorn--Biog. p306-307

MERRIAM, EVE (1916-)
Amer. playwright
Chinoy--Women p320,322-323

MERRIAM, FLORENCE AUGUSTA
See BAILEY, FLORENCE AUGUSTA
MERRIAM

MERRICK, CAROLINE ELIZABETH
THOMAS (1825-1908)
Amer. suffrage, temperance
leader
James--Notable (2) p530-531
Scott--Southern p144-145,174
Sherr--American p85

MERRICK, MARGE (fl. 1960's)
Amer. bowler
McWhirter--Guinness p44

MERRILL, DINA (1925-)
Amer. actress
World--Who p241

MERRILL, HELEN (1929-)
Amer. singer
Claghorn--Biog. p307
Claghorn--Jazz p204

MERRILL, LINDA
See ASHLEY, MERRILL

MERRIMAN, BRENDA (1940-)
Canadian genealogical researcher
Meyer--Who's p138

MERRITT, ANNA LEA (1844-1930)
Amer. etcher
McHenry--Liberty's p279-280

MERRIWEATHER, MARJORIE (1946-
1973)
Amer. heiress, wife of

ambassador
O'Neill--Women's p746

MERRY, ANNE BRUNTON (1769-
1808)
English-Amer. colonial
actress
Chinoy--Women p60-65, por.
James--Notable (2) p531-533
McHenry--Liberty's p280
Sherr--American p231

MESERAND, EDYTH(E) J. (fl.
1920's-1950's)
Amer. radio, TV executive
Marzolf--Up p143
O'Neill--Women's p492

MESERVE, GERTRUDE
Amer. aviatrix, army flier
Keil--Those p116-117,222

MESSALINA, VALERIA (A.D. 24-
48/49)
Roman empress, (third wife
of Emperor Claudius)
Jones--Rutledge p538
Mead--Hist. p59-60
People's Almanac (1) p993-995

MESSENGER-HARRIS, BEVERLY
(fl. 1970's)
Amer. priest
O'Neill--Women's p385

MESSER, DAISY (fl. 1970's)
Amer. miner's wife
Kahn--Hill. p50-54, por.

MESSICK, DALE (1906-)
Amer. comic-strip cartoonist
McHenry--Liberty's p280
100--Greatest (1) p76, por.
O'Neill--Women's p748-749

MESSNER, NATHALIA
See MOOREHEAD, NATALIE

MESTA, PERLE SKIRVAN (SKIRVIN)
(c1893-1975)
Amer. hostess, diplomat
Cur. Biog. '75 p470
Hershey--Between p38-49,47,53,
55,159-162
Lamparski--What. (5) p116, por.
McHenry--Liberty's p280-281

Macksey--Book p41,104
O'Neill--Women's p91
Sicherman--Notable p470-471
Woman's Almanac p478, por.
World--Who p299

MESZAROS, MARTA (fl. 1960's-
1970's)
Hungarian film director
Smith--Movies p124

METALIOUS, GRACE (1924-1964)
Amer. novelist
Seymour-Smith--Novels p186
World--Who p17

METCALF, AUGUSTA J.C. (1871-)
Amer. artist, noted Oklahoma
mother
Amer.--Mothers p439-440

METCALF, BETSEY (fl. 1790's)
Amer. manufacturer of straw
hats
Earle--Two Cent. (2) p570-571

METCHNIKOFF, ELIE (1845-1916)
Russian-French bacteriologist
World--Who p127

METHENY, LINDA JO (fl. 1960's-
1970's)
Amer. gymnast
Hollander--100 p53-54, por.

METHOT, MAYO (1904-1941)
Amer. actress
Springer--They p180-181,316,
por.

METRODORA
Greek medical writer
Mead--Hist. p63,73

METZGER, DEENA (1936-)
Amer. poet
Chester--Rising p262-265, por.

METZGER, FRANCES (fl. 1970's)
Amer. art history teacher
Women's--Female p116

METZGER, JOYCE OWEN (1934-)
Amer. genealogical researcher,
writer
Meyer--Who's p138

MEURER, DOLORES
    Amer. aviatrix, army flier
    Keil--Those p14-15,247

MEW, CHARLOTTE MARY (1869/
    1870-1928)
    English poet
    Avenel--Comp. (1) p359
    Bernikow--World p155
    Kaplan--Salt p191-192, por.
    Pearson--Who p136
    Showalter--Lit. p344

MEXIA, YNES ENRIQUETTA
    JULIETTA (1870-1938)
    Amer. botanical explorer
    James--Notable (2) p533-534

MEYER, AGNES ELIZABETH ERNST
    (1887-1970)
    Amer. journalist, philanthro-
    pist, social worker, noted
    District of Columbia mother
    Amer.--Mothers p108-109, por.
    Cur. Biog. '70 p467
    Daniels--Wash. p231,233-234
    Sicherman--Notable p471-473

MEYER, ANNIE NATHAN (1867-
    1951)
    Amer. educator, co-founder
    Barnard College
    Baum--Jewish p47, por.
    McHenry--Liberty's p281
    Macksey--Book p68
    Sicherman--Notable p473-474

MEYER, DEBBIE (c1952-)
    Amer. swimmer
    Assoc. Press--Pursuit p288,
    290-291, por.
    Cur. Biog. '69 p289-291, por.
    Hollander--100 p86-89
    McWhirter--Guinness p19, por.
    Woman's Almanac p431-432
    World--Who p218

MEYER, HELEN
    Amer. publisher
    O'Neill--Women's p485-486, por.

MEYER, LUCY JANE RIDER (1849-
    1922)
    Amer. composer, educator,
    social worker
    Claghorn--Biog. p308
    James--Notable (2) p534-536
    McHenry--Liberty's p281-282

MEYER, MARGARET (1923-)
    Amer. bacteriologist, micro-
    biologist, lecturer, educator
    Bachtold--Gifted p58-60

MEYER, MARY KEYSOR (1919-)
    Amer. genealogical researcher,
    author, editor
    Meyer--Who's p138

MEYER, MUFFIE (fl. 1960's-1970's)
    Amer. filmmaker
    Smith--Movies p192-193,261

MEYEROWITZ, HELEN (fl. 1970's)
    Amer. artist
    Women's--Female p109

MEYERS, CHRISTINE (fl. 1970's)
    Amer. advertiser
    O'Neill--Women's p525

MEYERS, ETHEL JOHNSON
    Amer. psychic
    People's Almanac (1) p8-9

MEYERS, HELEN E. (fl. 1950's)
    Amer. army dentist
    O'Neill--Women's p225

MEYERS, LINDA (fl. 1970's)
    Amer. archer
    O'Neill--Women's p558

MEYERS, MARY
    Amer. skater
    Hollander--100 p38, por.

MEYFARTH, ULRIKA (1956-)
    West German track and field
    athlete
    McWhirter--Guinness p167, por.
    O'Neill--Women's p578

MEYLAN, ELISABETH (1937-)
    Swiss short-story writer, poet
    Herrmann--Ger. p6,125

MEYLING-HYLKEMA, ELISABETH
    (1907-)
    Netherlands physician
    Hellstedt--Women p338-341, por.

MEYNELL, ALICE CHRISTI(A)NA
    GERTRUDE THOMPSON (1847-
    1922)
    English poet, essayist
    Avenel--Comp. (1) p359

Bernikow--World p140
Jones--Rutledge p539
Kaplan--Salt p181-184
Pearson--Who p133
Moers--Literary p299
Showalter--Lit. p337

MEYNELL, ALICIA (fl. 1800's)
English jockey
McWhirter--Guinness p92

MEYNELL, VIOLA (1886-1956)
English novelist
Showlater--Lit. p346

MEYOWITZ, JENNIE DELONEY
RICE (1866-)
Amer. portrait painter
Sherr--American p11

MEZEO, HELENA (fl. 1560's)
Hungarian religious sup-
porter of Stephen Szegeli
Bainton--Spain p230-235, por.

"M.F.K."
See FISHER, MARY FRANCES
KENNEDY

MIAO, LADY (fl. 1900's)
Chinese painter
Petersen--Women p162

MIBTAHIAH (fl. 5th Cent. B.C.E.)
Jewish business woman
Henry--Written p10,30-37

MIBUCHI, JOCHIKO (fl. 1970's)
Japanese judge
Macksey--Book p128

MICHAEL, GERTRUDE (1910-1965)
Amer. musician, actress
Springer--They p181,316, por.

MICHAELIS, KARIN (1872-1950)
Danish novelist, short-story
writer
Seymour-Smith--Novels p186

MICHALSKA, MARIANNA
See GRAY, GILDA

MICHAUD, BARBARA M. (fl. 1960's)
Amer. heroine, Carnegie
Medal winner
O'Neill--Women's p732

MICHEL, (CLEMENCE) LOUISE
(1830-1905)
French teacher, rebel, revolu-
tionist
Macksey--Book p55-56
Taylor--Gener. p33-34, por.

MICHELSON, GERTRUDE G. (fl.
1940's-1970's)
Amer. department store executive
O'Neill--Women's p518

MICHENER, DIANA (1940-)
Amer. photographer
Ruddick--Working p147-161,344,
por.

MIDDLETON, (PEGGY) YVONNE
See DeCARLO, YVONNE

MIDDLETON, VELMA (1917-1961)
African singer, dancer
Claghorn--Biog. p308
Claghorn--Jazz p205

MIDDLEWEEK, HELENE
See HAYMAN, HELENE

MIDLER, BETTE (1944-)
Amer. dancer, singer
Anderson--People p276-277, por.
Cur. Biog. '73 p294-296, por.
Hirschhorn--Rating p262-263, por.
100--Greatest (1) p79, por.
Simon--Best p397-398, por.
Woman's Almanac p297, por.
World--Who p270

MIEL, ALICE (fl. 1940's-1970's)
Amer. educator
O'Neill--Women's p430

MIER, ISABEL ALONSO DE (1886-)
Puerto Rican writer, civic
leader, noted Puerto Rican
mother
Amer.--Mothers p471, por.

MIGISHI, SETSUKO (1905-)
Japanese artist
Munsterberg--Hist. p81

MIGNON, CHARLOTTE
See CRABTREE, (CHARLOTTE)
LOTTA

MIHALACK, JANE (fl. 1970's)
Amer. TV studio technician
Klever--Women p55-56,69-70,
93-95,100

MIHEVIC, MIRA
Yugoslavian scholar
Mandel--Soviet p311

MIHOPOULOU, MARIA (fl. 1970's)
Greek lawyer, bank legal
advisor
O'Neill--Women's p364

MIKKELSEN, CAROLINE (fl. 1970's)
Norwegian Antarctic visitor
Land--New p16-17

MIKULSKI, BARBARA ANN (c1936-)
Amer. (Polish-Amer.) Con-
gresswoman
Cur. Biog. '85 p292-295
O'Neill--Women's p71-72

MIKUS, ELEANOR (fl. 1970's)
Amer. painter
Women's--Female p51

MILBANK, HELEN
See KIRKPATRICK, HELEN
PAULL

MILBURN, ANNA (fl. 1940's)
Amer. Presidential candidate
People's Almanac (1) p128

MILBURY, CASSANDRA MELLON
Amer. millionaire
Forbes--400 ('84) p147

MILCETIC, HELEN
See MERRILL, HELEN

MILDMAY, GRACE SHERRINGTON
(1552-1620)
English physician
Mead--Hist. p343-344

MILDNER, POLDI LEOPOLDINE
(1916-)
Austrian pianist
Hazen--Interv. p357

MILDRED (-700/725 A.D.)
English abbess, saint
Macksey--Book p106

MILDRED (664-673)
English abbess
Mead--Hist. p99

MILES, JOSEPHINE (1911-)
Amer. poet, literary scholar
Avenel--Comp. (2) p175
Bernikow--World p321
Chester--Rising p61-63, por.
O'Neill--Women's p419

MILES, LIZZIE (1895-1963)
Amer. singer
Claghorn--Biog. p309
Claghorn--Jazz p205

MILES, SARAH (1943-)
English actress
Anderson--People p277
World--Who p259

MILES, TICHI WILKERSON
Amer. newspaper head
Adams--Women p76-77

MILES, VERA (1930-)
Amer. actress
Lamparski--What. (4) p18-19,
por.
Lamparski--What. (8) p240-241,
por.
World--Who p242

MILHOLLAND, INEZ
See BOISSEVAIN, INEZ
MILHOLLAND

MILINAIRE, CATERINE (fl. 1970's)
English fashion setter, author
Keenan--Women p217-220, por.

MILLAR, FREDA I. (fl. 1970's)
Amer. banker
O'Neill--Women's p529

MILLAR, MARGARET (1915-)
Canadian-Amer. novelist
Betts--Writers p154-155, por.
Seymour-Smith--Novels p186

MILLAR, ONNIE (1919-)
Amer. sculptor
Fax--Black p202-220, por.

MILLAY, EDNA ST. VINCENT
(1892-1950)

painting and sculpture
Gilbert--Part. p21-29, por.

MILLER, ELIZABETH (1) (fl.
1850's)
British fashion designer
Macksey--Book p266

MILLER, ELIZABETH (2) (fl.
1960's)
Amer. bowler
McWhirter--Guinness p44

MILLER, ELIZABETH SMITH
(1822-1911)
Amer. feminist, social re-
former, inventor
Gurko--Ladies p67,142-145,
147,153
Hymowitz--Hist. p73,102-104
James--Notable (2) p540-541
Longstreet--Queen p58-59
McHenry--Liberty's p283
Millstein--We p73

MILLER, ELLEN
Amer. embroiderer
Callen--Women p133-134

MILLER, ELVA RUBY CONNES
(c1908-)
Amer. singer, civic worker
Book--Lists (2) p164
Lamparski--What. p76-79, por.

MILLER, EMILY CLARK HUNTING-
TON (1833-1913)
Amer. hymnist
Claghorn--Biog. p310
James--Notable (2) p541-542

MILLER, EMMA GUFFEY (1874-
1970)
Amer. government official,
suffragist, feminist
Sicherman--Notable p476-478
Ware--Beyond p149, see also
index p200

MILLER, FRIEDA SEGELKE (1890-
1973)
Amer. government official,
labor reformer
Cur. Biog. '73 p459
O'Neill--Women's p330,335
Sicherman--Notable p478-479

MILLER, HARRIET EMELINE
PHELPS (1891-1964)
Amer., noted Arizona mother,
pioneer
Amer.--Mothers p34-35, por.

MILLER, HARRIET MANN (1831-
1918)
Amer. nature writer, children's
book author
James--Notable (2) p543-545
McHenry--Liberty's p283

MILLER, IRENE BEARDSLEY
Amer. mountain climber
Lichtenstein--Mach., see index
p364

MILLER, JANICE (1938-)
Amer. animal oncologist
O'Neill--Women's p33

MILLER, JEAN (fl. 1970's)
Amer. miner, labor leader
O'Neill--Women's p316

MILLER, JEAN BAKER (fl. 1970's)
Amer. feminist, writer
Adams--Women p197-198,201,206,
212

MILLER, JODY (1941-)
Amer. singer
Claghorn--Biog. p310

MILLER, JOYCE D. (1928-)
Amer. labor leader
O'Neill--Women's p302,312-313,315

MILLER, JULIA (fl. 1970's)
Amer. filmmaker
Smith--Movies p66-67

MILLER, KATHY SWITZER (c1962-)
Amer. track and field athlete
Hollander--100 p139-140

MILLER, LEE (fl. 1920's-1930's)
Amer. model
Keenan--Women p136-138, por.

MILLER, LORINE (fl. 1970's)
Amer. labor union leader
Kahn--Hill. p147-160, por.

MILLER, MABLE (fl. 1930's)

Amer. nurse, (wife of William
"Fishbait" Miller)
Miller--Fishbait p37-38

MILLER, MARGARET HARDWICK
(1910-)
Amer. genealogical researcher,
author
Meyer--Who's p139

MILLER, MARILYN (1898-1936)
Amer. singer, dancer
Claghorn--Biog. p310
Entertainers p209
James--Notable (2) p542-543
McHenry--Liberty's p283-284
Springer--They p181-182,316,
por.
World--Who p242

MILLER, MARION (1862-)
Amer. FBI agent, club-
woman, noted California
mother
Amer.--Mothers p52-53

MILLER, MARY BRITTON (1883-
1975)
Amer. novelist
P.W.--Author p16-18,485

MILLER, MAY (fl. 1950's-1970's)
Amer. poet
Fisher--Third p vii,257

MILLER, MILLIE (fl. 1950's-1970's)
English politician, Parlia-
mentary member
Stobaugh--Women p90
Vallance--Women p29,53,57,78,
140

MILLER, MYRTIS HAWTHORNE
(1906-)
Amer. civic worker, noted
Florida mother
Amer.--Mothers p117-118, por.

MILLER, OLIVE THORNE, pseud.
See MILLER, HARRIET MANN

MILLER, PATSY RUTH (1905-)
Amer. actress
Springer--They p182,316, por.

MILLER, RUTH (fl. 1960's-1970's)

Amer. labor union leader
O'Neill--Women's p301-302

MILLER, SUSAN LINCOLN TOLMAN
(1825-1912)
Amer. missionary, educator
McHenry--Liberty's p284

MILLER, VASSAR (1924-)
Amer. poet
Chester--Rising p138-140, por.

MILLETT, KATE (1934-)
Amer. feminist, author
Banner--Women p235,240,251, por.
Clark--Leading p240
Cur. Biog. '71 p271-274, por.
Hymowitz--Hist. p361
Moers--Literary p299
Schoenebaum--Prof. p440-441
Sochen--Herstory p8,390-392,
399, por.
Sochen--Movers p263,268-269,293
Wintle--Makers p319,359-360
World--Who p190

MILLIAT, A., MADAME (fl. 1920's)
French track and field athlete
Macksey--Book p258

MILLIN, SARAH GERTRUDE LIEB-
SON (1889-1968)
South African novelist, play-
wright, short-story writer,
historian
Avenel--Comp. (1) p362-363
Jones--Rutledge p544
Macksey--Book p190
Seymour-Smith--Novels p187

MILLINER, SONYA
Amer. TV executive
Kelver--Women p42-43,81-82, por.

MILLMAN, DOROTHY K. (1922-)
Amer. genealogical researcher,
writer
Meyer--Who's p139

MILLS, ALICE FRANCIS DU PONT
Amer. millionaire
Forbes--400 ('84) p112,114

MILLS, ANN (fl. 185h cent.)
British sailor
Macksey--Book p53

MILLS, DONNA
    Amer. TV actress
    Scheuer--Tel. p339, por.

MILLS, ELIZABETH (fl. 1920's)
    English lacemaker
    Callen--Women p6, por.

MILLS, ELIZABETH SHOWN (1944-)
    Amer. genealogical researcher,
    writer
    Meyer--Who's p139-140

MILLS, ERNESTINE EVANS BELL
    (1871-1959)
    British metalworker, enameller
    Callen--Women p158,224-225

MILLS, FLORENCE (1895-1927)
    Amer. singer
    Claghorn--Biog. p311
    Claghorn--Jazz p207
    Entertainers p196,198
    James--Notable (2) p545-546
    Toppin--Biog. p369-371

MILLS, HAYLEY (1946-)
    English child actress
    Edelson--Kids p95-96, por.
    World--Who p259

MILLS, LORNA (fl. 1930's-1950's)
    Amer. bank official
    O'Neill--Women's p527

MILLS, NELLIE IRETON (1880-
    1967)
    Amer. author, civic worker,
    noted Idaho mother
    Amer.--Mothers p152, por.

MILLS, SUSAN LINCOLN TOLMAN
    (1821/1825-1912)
    Amer. missionary, teacher,
    college president, noted
    California mother
    Amer.--Mothers p51
    James--Notable (2) p546-547
    Sherr--American p16,229

MILNER, ANITA CHEEK (1936-)
    Amer. genealogical researcher,
    writer, indexer
    Meyer--Who's p140

MILNES, SHERRILL (1935-)
    Amer. opera singer

Gammond--Illus. p246-247,
    por.

MILNES-WALKER, NICOLETTE (fl.
    1970's)
    British psychologist, sailor
    Macksey--Book p246

MILSTEAD, VIOLET
    Canadian bush pilot, instruc-
    tor
    Macksey--Book p252

MIMIEUX, YVETTE CARMEN M.
    (1941/1942-)
    Amer. actress
    World--Who p242

MINER, DOROTHY EUGENIA (1904-
    1973)
    Amer. museum curator, li-
    brarian, art critic
    Sicherman--Notable p479-481

MINER, HAZEL (c1914-1920)
    Amer. child heroine
    Sherr--American p182

MINER, MYRTILLA (1815-1864)
    Amer. educator
    James--Notable (2) p547-548
    McHenry--Liberty's p284-285
    Sherr--American p41,175

MINER, SARAH LUELLA (1861-1935)
    Amer. missionary, educator
    James--Notable (2) p548-550

MINERVA
    See ATHENA (ATHENE)

MINGILAITE, BRONE (1919-)
    Lithuanian-Russian painter
    Women's--Female p4 (supp.)

MINK, PATSY TAKEMOTO (1927-)
    Amer. lawyer, Congresswoman
    Bowman--Politics p18-25, por.
    Chamberlin--Min. p309-315
    O'Neill--Women's p70
    Schoenebaum--Prof. p441-442
    Seed--Saturday's p116-120, por.
    Signif.--Amer. p69, por.
    U.S.--Women (89th) p19, por.
    U.S.--Women (90th) p19, por.

MINNAULT, D. DENISE (fl. 1970's)

Amer. museum catalog author
Women's--Female p119

MINNELLI, LIZA (1946-)
Amer. singer, actress
Anderson--People p278-279, por.
Claghorn--Biog. p312
Cur. Biog. '70 p300-302, por.
Hirschhorn--Rating p267-268,
por.
Manchel--Women p106, por.
Mordden--Movie p199,204,245,
256-257
100--Greatest (1) p17, por.
Shipman--Internatl. p394-396,
por.
Simon--Best p411-412, por.
Woman's Almanac p350-351
World--Who p270

MINNIE, MEMPHIS (1900-)
Amer. singer, poet
Bernikow--World p279

MINNIGERODE, LUCY (1871-1935)
Amer. public health nurse
McHenry--Liberty's p285

MINNIS, MARGARET KITCHENS
(1921-)
Amer. social reformer, noted
New Jersey mother
Amer.--Mothers p372, por.

MINOKA-HILL, LILLIE ROSA (1876-
1952)
Amer. Indian physician
Sicherman--Notable p481-483

MINOR, VIRGINIA LOUISA (1824-
1894)
Amer. Civil War relief
worker, suffragette
James--Notable (2) p550-551
McHenry--Liberty's p285
Papachristou--Women p104-105,
por.
Sherr--American p133
Warren--Pictorial p120

MINTER, DESIRE (fl. 1600's)
Amer. Pilgrim
Sherr--American p109

MINTER, MARY MILES (1902-1984)
Amer. actress
Higham--Celeb. p109-117, por.

MINTON, YVONNE (1938-)
Australian opera singer
Gammond--Illus. p247, por.

MINTZ, BEATRICE (1921-)
Amer. geneticist
O'Neill--Women's p145,224

MINUHIN, ESTHER (fl. 1960's)
Russian physician, sanitarium
director
Mandel--Soviet p192

MIRABEAU, SIBYLLE GABRIELE
MARIE ANTOINETTE RIQUE-
TIDE ("GYP") (-1932)
French writer
Crosland--Women p35-37

MIRABELLA, GRACE
Amer. editor
O'Neill--Women's p480-481, por.

MIRAMION, MARIE BONNEAU,
MADAME DE (1629-1696)
French philanthropist
Earle--Two Cent. (1) p xix,245,
por.

MIRANDA, CARMEN (1909-1955)
Portuguese singer, dancer
Claghorn--Biog. p312
Keylin--Hollywood p208, por.
Shipman--Gold. p403-405, por.
World--Who p259

MIRIAM (1)
Biblical prophetess
Henry--Written p19-21,249
Price--God p74-77

"MIRIAM," (2) pseud.
See AMES, MARY E. CLEMMER

MIRIKITANI, JANICE (fl. 1970's)
Japanese-Amer. writer, poet
Fisher--Third p x,540

MIRONOVA, ZOYA (fl. 1970's)
Russian United Nations
ambassador
Mandel--Soviet p295

MIRREN, HELEN (1946-)
English actress
Entertainers p291, por.

"MISS BLUE"
  See BLUE, MIRIAM

"MISS FRANCES"
  See RAPPAPORT, FRANCES

MISS, MARY (1944-   )
  Amer. artist
  Munro--Originals p393-394

MISTINGUETT (1873-1956)
  French singer, actress,
  dancer
  Entertainers p163, por.
  Jones--Rutledge p546
  Macksey--Book p229
  O'Neill--Women's p625

MISTRAL, GABRIELA (1889-1957)
  Chilean teacher, poet
  Henderson--Ten p169-191, por.
  Macksberg--Book p193
  Moers--Literary p299
  O'Neill--Women's p682,683
  Opfell--Lady p122-134, por.
  Seymour-Smith--Who's p224
  Taylor--Gener. p53-54
  Who Did What p229
  World--Who p41

"MRS. SATAN"
  See WOODHULL, VICTORIA
      CLAFIN

MITCHELL, ABBIE (1884-1960)
  Amer. singer, actress
  Claghorn--Biog. p312
  Sicherman--Notable p483-484

MITCHELL, CHARLENE (fl. 1960's)
  Amer. Presidential candidate
  People's Almanac (1) p128

MITCHELL, CHARLOTTE
  Amer. aviatrix
  Keil--Those, see index p328

MITCHELL, CHRISTINE (fl. 1970's)
  Canadian magazine editor
  O'Neill--Women's p483

MITCHELL, GILLIAN
  British-Amer. manufacturer
  Rich-McCoy--Mill. p23-48, por.

MITCHELL, GLADYS (1901-   )
  English novelist
  Seymour-Smith--Novels p187

MITCHELL, HANNAH
  English feminist, socialist
  Callen--Women p215

MITCHELL, HELEN PORTER
  See MELBA, NELLIE, DAME

MITCHELL, JACKIE (fl. 1930's)
  Amer. baseball player
  Felton--Famous p281

MITCHELL, JANE
  Amer. TV news correspondent
  Scheuer--Tel. p340

MITCHELL, JOAN (1926-   )
  Amer. painter
  Fine--Women p214-216
  Fowler--Art p147
  Haftmann--Paint. (1) p406-407
  Munro--Originals p233-247, por.
  Munsterberg--Hist. p77
  O'Neill--Women's p602
  Women's--Female p51

MITCHELL, JONI (1943-   )
  Canadian singer, songwriter
  Anderson--People p279-280, por.
  Cur. Biog. '76 p262-265, por.
  Simon--Best p413-414, por.
  Woman's Almanac p297

MITCHELL, KELLY (c1868-1915)
  Amer. gypsy queen
  Sherr--American p127

MITCHELL, LOLLY (fl. 1970's)
  Amer. public relations worker,
  wine-maker
  O'Neill--Women's p16

MITCHELL, LOUISE (fl. 1820's)
  Amer. labor union worker
  Neidle--America's p114

MITCHELL, LUCY MILLER (fl. 1900's)
  Amer. community worker,
  noted Massachusetts mother,
  educator
  Amer.--Mothers p268-269, por.

MITCHELL, LUCY MYERS WRIGHT
  (1845-1888)
  Amer. archaeologist
  McHenry--Liberty's p285-286

MITCHELL, LUCY SPRAGUE (1878-
  1967)

Amer. educator, college
administrator
Sicherman--Notable p484-487

MITCHELL, "MAGGIE" (MARGARET
JULIA) (1832-1918)
Amer. actress
James--Notable (2) p551-552
McHenry--Liberty's p286

MITCHELL, MARGARET MUNNERLYN
(1900-1949)
Amer. novelist
Avenel--Comp. (2) p179
Clark--Leading p128-129
Donaldson--How p261-262
Ehrlich--Oxford p54,249,254,257
Eills--Here p8-9
Hamblin--That p78-79
James--Notable (2) p552-554
Jones--Rutledge p547
McHenry--Liberty's p286
Macksey--Book p191
Magill--Cycl. p758-759
Moers--Literary p299
O'Neill--Women's p681
People's Almanac (3) p607-608,
por.
Seymour-Smith--Novels p187,
por.
Sherr--American p46,48-49
Webster's--Amer. p726
World--Who p18

MITCHELL, MARIA (1818-1889)
Amer. astronomer, educator
Emberlin--Cont. p152-154
Gilfond--Heroines p124-127, por.
Hoople--As p171-173, por.
Ingraham--Album p71
James--Notable (2) p554-556
Kulkin--Her p205-206
McHenry--Liberty's p287
Macksey--Book p150-151, por.
Millstein--We p75-76, por.
O'Neill--Women's p143
People's Almanac (1) p173
People's Almanac (2) p1052
Reader's--Story p437, por.
Sherr--American p107,173
Signif.--Amer. p20, por.
Stoddard--Famous p295-304,
por.
Taylor--Gener. p47, por.
Warren--Pictorial p74-75, por.
Webster's--Amer. p726
Woman's Almanac p366-367,
por.

MITCHELL, MARTHA (1918-1976)
Amer., wife of John Mitchell
Book--Lists (2) p261
People--Best p19, por.
Schoenebaum--Prof. p446-447

MITCHELL, MATTIE (DUCHESSE DE
ROCHEFOUCAULD)
Amer. belle
Peacock--Famous p272, por.

MITCHELL, PRISCILLA (1941-   )
Amer. singer
Claghorn--Biog. p313

MITCHELL, REBECCA BROWN (1834-
1908)
Amer. missionary, temperance
worker, noted Idaho mother
Amer.--Mothers p150-151, por.
Sherr--American p57

MITCHELL, SHARON
Amer. model
Felton--Famous p209

MITCHISON, NAOMI MARGARET
HALDANE (1897-1964)
Scottish novelist
Avenel--Comp. (1) p370
Crosland--Beyond p153-154,158,
160
Seymour-Smith--Novels p187
Showalter--Lit. p348

MITFORD, JESSICA LUCY (1917-   )
English-Amer. writer
Cur. Biog. '74 p279-282, por.
Dunlap--Calif. p140
P.W.--Author p380-383,516

MITFORD, MARY RUSSELL (1787-
1855)
English poet, novelist
Avenel--Comp. (1) p370-371
Magill--Cycl. p761-762
Moers--Literary p53-54,299
Morley--Literary p229-231
Seymour-Smith--Novels p187

MITFORD, NANCY FREMAN (1907-
1973)
English novelist, biographer,
editor
Avenel--Comp. (1) p371
Crosland--Beyond p57-58
Jones--Rutledge p547
Moers--Literary p300

Seymour-Smith--Novels p187-188
World--Who p28

MITTELSTAEDT-KRUBASECK,
CARLA (1912-)
German genealogical researcher
Meyer--Who's p140

MITTERMAIER, ROSI (1950-)
West German skier
Assoc. Press--Pursuit p321-322
McWhirter--Guinness p118-119,
por.
Woman's Almanac p433, por.

"MITZIE" (1891-)
Hungarian-Amer. singer,
dancer, actress
Lamparski--What. (2) p204-205,
por.

MIYAJI, KUNIE (1891-)
Japanese physician
Hellstedt--Women p62-64, por.

MIYASAKI, GAIL Y. (1949-)
Amer. wirter, TV editor
Fisher--Third p x,450

MIZRACHI, REBBETZIN (fl. 16th
Cent.)
Jewish scholar
Henry--Written p14,108-113

MOBERLY, CHARLOTTE ANNE
ELIZABETH (c1846-1937)
English educator
People's Almanac (1) p1381-1384

MOCK, JERRIE FREDRITZ (1925-)
Amer. aviatrix, noted Ohio
mother
Amer.--Mothers p433, por.
Genett--Aviation p57-73, por.

MODEJONGE, GERALDINE (fl.
1970's)
Amer. heroine
O'Neill--Women's p734

MODENA, BATHSHEBA (FIORETTA)
Jewish scholar
Henry--Written p128-129

MODENA, POMONA DE (fl. 1500's)
Jewish scholar
Henry--Written p128

MODERSOHN-BECKER, PAULA (1876-
1907)
German painter
Fine--Women p155-158, por.
Harris--Women p58-59,65-67,
273-280,355
Munsterberg--Hist. p68-70,118
O'Neill--Women's p596,598
Parker--Old p119-121, fig. 70,
72, por.
Petersen--Women p108-111, por.
Tufts--Our p188-197, por.
Women's--Female p12

MODJADJI, QUEEN
South African tribal head,
assembly head
Macksey--Book p41

MODJESKA, HELENA (1840-1909)
Polish-Amer. actress
Dunlap--Calif. p141-142, por.
Entertainers p130,132
James--Notable (2) p556-559
McHenry--Liberty's p287
Partington--Who's p282
Time--Women p139-141, por.

MÖDL, MARTHA (1912-)
German opera singer
Gammond--Illus. p247, por.

MODOTTI, TINA (1886-)
Italian actress, photographer,
political activist
Munsterberg--Hist. p137-138

MODRZEJEWSKA, HELENA OPID
See MODJESKA, HELENA

MOFFAT, AGNES K. (1905-)
Canadian physician
Hellstedt--Women p270-275, por.

MOFFAT, OLIVE (fl. 1770's)
Amer. Revolutionary War
patriot, weaver
Meyer--Petticoat p224

MOFFITT, BILLIE JEAN
See KING, BILLIE JEAN

MOFFO, ANNA (1932/1935-)
Amer. opera singer
Claghorn--Biog. p313
Gammond--Illus. p247, por.
World--Who p71

MOFTAKHARI, KHORSID
Iranian agriculturist
O'Neill--Women's p3

MOGÅRD, BRITT (1922-)
Swedish deputy minister of
education, cultural affairs
O'Neill--Women's p52-53

MOGUL, LAURA
Amer. TV advertising direc-
tor
Scheuer--Tel. p340-341

MOILLON, LOUISE (1610-1696)
French painter
Fine--Women p43-44
Harris--Women p29,32,34-35,75,
116,132,141-143,184,343
Munsterberg--Hist. p31-32
Petersen--Women p33-34

MOISANT, MATHILDE (c1879-1964)
Amer. aviatrix
Boase--Sky's p19-20

MOISE, PENINA (1797-1880)
Amer. Jewish hymn-writer,
poet
Henry--Written p228-234
James--Notable (2) p559-560
Sherr--American p209

MOKIL, SARAH (fl. 1930's)
Russian puppeteer, filmmaker
Mandel--Soviet p148

MOLBY, MARY
See MARY ALOYSIUS, SISTER

MOLESWORTH, MARY LOUISE
STEWART (1839-1921)
German children's book author
Showalter--Lit. p334

MOLL, MARY PENMAN (fl. 1880's)
Amer. teacher
Sherr--American p14

MOLLISON, AMY JOHNSON (1903-
1941)
Australian aviatrix
Boase--Sky's p90-112, see also
index p221, por.
Diagram--Mothers p123, por.
Fraser--Heroines p228-232, por.
Jones--Rutledge p413

Keil--Those p37,77,227
Kulkin--Her p154
Macksey--Book p248, por.
Palmer--Who's p177-178
Who Did What p170, por.

MOLNSKY, JOAN
See RIVERS, JOAN

MOLONY, WINIFRED D. (fl. 1940's
1970's)
Amer. agricultural attorney,
government official
O'Neill--Women's p29

MOLZA, TARQUINIA (1542-1617)
Italian singer
Neuls-BatesppWomen p50

"MONA LISA"
See GIOCONDA, LISA GHERAR-
DINI

MONS TESSA (fl. 13th Cent.)
Italian nun, nurse
Mead--Hist. p232

MONACO, GRACE POWERS (1938-)
Amer. co-founder "Candle-
lighters"
O'Neill--Women's p116-117

MONAHAN, JOHANNA (fl. 1860's)
Amer. rancher, (male imper-
sonator)
Sherr--American p58

MONCRIEFFE, MARGARET (fl.
1780's-1800's)
Amer., friend of Aaron Burr
Young--Revol., see index p221-
222

MONDALE, JOAN ADAMS (1930-)
Amer. arts consultant, his-
torian, wife of Walter Mondale
Cur. Biog. '80 p265-268, por.
Miller--Fishbait p18

MONGAN, AGNES (fl. 1930's-1970's)
Amer. museum director
O'Neill--Women's p615

MONICA (MONNICA), SAINT (c333-
387)
Roman saint, medical woman,
mother of St. Augustine
Mead--Hist. p82

MONICH, ZINAIDA
  Russian sociological writer
  Mandel--Soviet p162-163

MONK, ARLISS SHAFFER (1921-)
  Amer. genealogical research-
  er, author, indexer
  Meyer--Who's p140-141

MONK, LOES
  Amer. singer, aviatrix
  (army flier)
  Keil--Those p62-63

MONK, MARIA (1816-1849)
  Canadian-Amer. author,
  imposter
  James--Notable (2) p560-561
  McHenry--Liberty's p288

MONK, MEREDITH (1942-)
  Peruvian-Amer. dancer,
  "performer artist," composer, choreographer
  Cur. Biog. '85 p296-299, por.

MONNIER, ADRIENNE (1892-1955)
  Amer. bookstore owner,
  patron of arts
  Rogers--Ladies, see index p232

MONNIER, THYDE (MATHILDE)
  (fl. 1930's-1970's)
  French writer
  Crosland--Women p105-106

MONROE, ELIZA JONES (1747-)
  Amer., mother of James
  Monroe, noted Virginia mother
  Amer.--Mothers p550
  Faber--Presidents' p263-264

MONROE, ELIZABETH KORTRIGHT
  (1768-1830)
  Amer. first lady, wife of
  President Monroe
  Earle--Two Cent. (2) p xxiii,747,
  771, por.
  James--Notable (2) p561-562
  Melick--Wives p23-25, por.
  Woman's Almanac p487

MONROE, HARRIET (1860-1936)
  Amer. poet, editor, art
  patron, magazine publisher
  Avenel--Comp. (2) p179
  James--Notable (2) p562-564

McHenry--Liberty's p288
O'Neill--Women's p472
Rogers--Ladies, see index p232,
  por.
Signif.--Amer. p45, por.
Stoddard--Famous p305-313, por.
Warren--Pictorial p184
Webster's--Amer. p729

MONROE, MARILYN (1926-1962)
  Amer. actress
  Banner--Women p198,215, por.
  Brecher--Lives p332
  Donaldson--How p262-264
  Dunlap--Calif. p142-143, por.
  Engstead--Star p195-196
  Hirschhorn--Rating p270-271, por.
  Jones--Rutledge p552
  Keylin--Hollywood p213-216, por.
  McHenry--Liberty's p289
  Manchel--Women p12,77,84, por.
  Millstein--We p257-258, por.
  Mordden--Movie, see index p294
  New York Times--Great p200-201,
  por.
  People's Almanac (1) p1323,1333
  People's Almanac (2) p779,1205,
  por.
  People's Almanac (3) p9-12
  Priestley--Part. p130-131, por.
  Sat. Eve. Post--Movie p10-13,
  por.
  Shipman--Internatl. p401-408,
  por.
  Sicherman--Notable p487-489
  Signif.--Amer. p45, por.
  Sochen--Herstory p365-367, por.
  Webster's Amer. p730-731
  Who Did What p230, por.
  Woman's Almanac p351,329, por.
  World--Who p242

MONTAGU, ELIZABETH ROBINSON
  (1720-1800)
  English author, solonist, beauty
  Avenel--Comp. (1) p372
  Hufstader--Sisters p196-272, por.
  Macksey--Book p97,272

MONTAGU, MARY WORTLEY, LADY
  (1689-1762)
  English letter-writer, poet,
  feminist, traveler, medical
  pioneer
  Avenel--Comp. (1) p372-373
  Bernikow--World p92
  Fine--Women p63

Fry--1000 p179
Hamalian--Ladies p73-91
Hufstader--Sisters p7-141, por.
Jones--Rutledge p552
Kronenberger--Atlan. p536-537
Macksey--Book p79,182
Mead--Hist. p455-456,468-469,
   por.
Moers--Literary p300
O'Neill--Women's p197
Pearson--Who p71

MONTALEMBERT, MARCHIONESS
   DE (fl. 1780's)
   French balloon passenger
Macksey--Book p246

MONTANA, PATSY (1914-)
   Amer. singer, songwriter
Claghorn--Biog. p315

MONTANDON, PAT
   Amer. organization founder
Adams--Women p104

MONTEFIORE, JUDITH COHEN,
   LADY (fl. 1820's)
   English charity worker,
   traveler
Henry--Written p195-198,217

MONTESPAN, FRANÇOISE
   ATHENAISE ROCHECHOUART
   (1641-1707)
   French maid of honor,
   mistress of Louis XIV
Macksey--Book p96,133, por.

MONTESSORI, MARIA (1870-1952)
   Italian educator, physician
Brecher--Lives p107-108
Jones--Rutledge p553
Macksey--Book p74-76, por.
Marlowe--Great p212-217, por.
O'Neill--Women's p428
Reader's--Story p133-134, por.
Who Did What p231
Woman's Almanac p156
World--Who p100

MONTEZ, LOLA (1818-1861)
   Irish dancer
Dunlap--Calif. p143-144, por.
Eills--Here p76-77
Entertainers p121
James--Notable (2) p564-566
Jones--Rutledge p553-554

McFarland--Incred. p42-44
McHenry--Liberty's p289-290
People's Almanac (1) p954
Reifert--Women p139-141
Sherr--American p13,18
Warren--Pictorial p96
Webster's--Amer. p731
Woman's Almanac p313, por.
World--Who p263

MONTEZ, MARIA (c1920-1951)
   Spanish actress
Hirschhorn--Rating p271, por.

MONTFORT, ELEANOR DE (1215-
   1275)
   English, sister of Henry III
Gies--Women p120-142

MONTGOMERY, CATHERINE LEWIS
   (fl. 1960's-1970's)
   Amer. civic leader, educator
Innis--Profiles p188-189, por.
Sherr--American p240

MONTGOMERY, CORA
   See CAZNEAU, JANE MARIA
   ELIZA McMANUS STORMS

MONTGOMERY, ELIZABETH (1933-)
   Amer. actress
World--Who p242

MONTGOMERY, HELEN BARRETT
   (1861-1934)
   Amer. civic reformer, churchwoman, translator
James--Notable (2) p566-568

MONTGOMERY, LEILA POST (fl.
   1920's)
   Amer. philanthropist
Sherr--American p116

MONTGOMERY, MARION (1934-)
   Amer. singer
Claghorn--Biog. p315

MONTGOMERY, MELBA JOYCE
   (1938-)
   Amer. singer, songwriter
Claghorn--Biog. p315

MONTGOMERY, VAIDA (1888-1959)
   Amer. poet, editor
Ehrlich--Oxford p373

MONTOUR, CATHERINE, MADAME
(c1684-1752)
Amer. Indian interpreter,
colonial agent, linguist
James--Notable (2) p568-569
Sherr--American p201,205
Williams--Demeter's p193-194

MONTOUR, ESTHER
Amer. (Indian queen)
Sherr--American p198,205

MONTPENSIER, ANNE MARIE
LOUISE D'ORLEANS,
DUCHESSE DE (1627-1693)
French princess, author,
military heroine
Jones--Rutledge p555

MONTRESOR, FRANCES TUCKER
(fl. 1770's)
Amer. patriot, (wife of
John Montresor)
Young--Revol. p187

MONTY, GLORIA (c1921-)
Amer. TV producer
Scheuer--Tel. p342, por.

MONVOISIN, CATHERINE (-1680)
French accused criminal
Macksey--Book p133

MOODY, ANNE (1940-)
Amer. civil rights worker
Kulkin--Her p206-207

MOODY, DEBORAH, LADY
(1600-1659)
English-Amer. colony founder,
Quaker, landowner
Crawford--Four p63-83,134,143-
160,183
James--Notable (2) p569-570
Sherr--American p167
Williams--Demeter's p125-126

MOODY, HELEN WILLS
See WILLS, HELEN NEWINGTON
MOODY ROARK

MOON, APRIL (fl. 1970's)
Amer. archer
McWhirter--Guinness p27

MOON, LOTTIE DIGGES (1840-
1912)

Amer. missionary
James--Notable (2) p570-571
Kulkin--Her p207-208

MOONEY, ELIZABETH WILDE
Amer. TV director
Scheuer--Tel. p342

MOORE, ALICE RUTH
See NELSON, ALICE DUNBAR

MOORE, ANNE (fl. 1970's)
British equestrian
McWhirter--Guinness p57, por.

MOORE, ANNE CARROLL (1871-
1961)
Amer. children's librarian
pioneer, author
Kulkin--Her p209
Sicherman--Notable p489-490

MOORE, ANNIE AUBERTINE WOOD-
WARD (1841-1929)
Amer. author, musician,
translator, lecturer
James--Notable (2) p572-573

MOORE, AUGUSTA ROBERTSON
Amer. school superintendant,
Indian educator
Sherr--American p191, por.

MOORE, BARBARA (c1904-c1977)
Russian-British cross-country
walker
O'Neill--Women's p741

MOORE, CARRY
See NATION, CARRY AMELIA
MOORE

MOORE, CAROLINE RUDY (1943-)
Amer. singer, pianist, organ-
ist, teacher
Claghorn--Biog. p316

MOORE, CAROLINE T. (1907-)
Amer. genealogical researcher,
author
Meyer--Who's p141-142

MOORE, CLARA SOPHIA JESSUP
(1824-1899)
Amer. author, etiquette
writer, Civil War humanitarian
James--Notable (2) p573-574

MOORE, COLLEEN (1902-)
Amer. actress
Lamparski--What. (2) p120-121,
por.
Mordden--Movie, see index p294,
por.
Springer--They p182,317, por.

MOORE, CONSTANCE (1922-)
Amer. actress
Lamparski--What. (8) p210-211,
por.

MOORE, DENISE (-1911)
Amer. aviatrix
Boase--Sky's p12

MOORE, DOROTHY ("DOTTIE")
LOUISE SUTTON (1930-1967)
Amer. singer
Claghorn--Biog. p316

MOORE, ELIZA
Amer. Civil War patriot
Sherr--American p127

MOORE, GRACE (1) (1898/1903-
1947)
Amer. opera singer, actress
Claghorn--Biog. p316
James--Notable (2) p574-576
McHenry--Liberty's p290
Sherr--American p217
Shipman--Gold. p408-409, por.
Springer--They p182-183,317,
por.
Tuggle--Golden p211, por.

MOORE, GRACE (2) (fl. 1970's)
Amer. clergyman
O'Neill--Women's p383

MOORE, HONOR (fl. 1970's)
Amer. playwright, critic,
editor, feminist
Chinoy--Women p6,184-190

MOORE, IDORA McCLELLAN
PLOWMAN (1843-1929)
Amer. author, diarist,
reader
Sherr--American p3

MOORE, JULIA A. (1847-1920)
Amer. poet
Avenel--Comp. (2) p179
Felton--Famous p199-201, por.

MOORE, MARGARET CATHERINE
BARRY (fl. 1760's-1770's)
Amer. Revolutionary War
heroine
Sherr--American p213

MOORE, MARIANNE CRAIG (1887-
1972)
Amer. poet, critic, editor
Avenel--Comp. (2) p179-180
Bernikow--World p312-313
Betts--Writers p76-79, por.
Brinnin--Modern p237-244, por.
Chester--Rising p18-26, por.
Cur. Biog. '72 p467
Ehrlich--Oxford, see index p458,
por.
Jones--Rutledge p556
Kaplan--Salt p235-237
Kelen--Fifty p111
McHenry--Liberty's p290-291
O'Neill--Women's p675
Reader's--Story p419, por.
Seymour-Smith--Who's p248
Sicherman--Notable p490-494
Signif.--Amer. p45, por.
Talmey--Vogue p114-117
Webster's--Amer. p733
Whitman--Come p175-183
Who Did What p232
Wintle--Makers p367-369, #328
Woman's Almanac p255-256, por.
World--Who p18

MOORE, MARY TYLER (1937-)
Amer. TV actress, producer
Anderson--People p281-282, por.
Cur. Biog. '71 p279-281, por.
Hirschhorn--Rating p274-275, por.
100--Greatest (1) p98, por.
People--Best p170, por.
Woman's Almanac p264,351
World--Who p242

MOORE, MELBA (1945-)
Amer. singer, actress
Cur. Biog. '73 p305-307, por.
World--Who p270

MOORE, MOLLIE EVELYN
See DAVIS, MOLLIE EVELYN
MOORE

MOORE, MONETTE (1902-1962)
Amer. singer
Claghorn--Jazz p211

MOORE, NONNIE (fl. 1940's-1970's)
Amer. magazine fashion editor
O'Neill--Women's p475

MOORE, PATTI (fl. late 19th cent.)
Amer. police matron, welfare
worker
Sherr--American p131

MOORE, ROSALIE (1910-   )
Amer. poet
Chester--Rising p56-59, por.

MOORE, SARA JANE (1930-   )
Amer. radical, accused
criminal
Woman's Almanac p507
World--Who p299

MOORE, VANDI (1912-   )
Amer. author, church worker,
noted Wyoming mother
Amer.--Mothers p600, por.

MOORE, VIRGINIA (1903-   )
English poet
Bernikow--World p164-165

MOOREHEAD, AGNES (1906-1974)
Amer. actress
Cur. Biog. '74 p466
Hirschhorn--Rating p275-276,
por.
Keylin--Hollywood p217, por.
Shipman--Internatl. p412-415,
por.
Sicherman--Notable p494-495
World--Who p242

MOOREHEAD, NATALIE (1901-   )
Amer. actress
Lamparski--What. (8) p214-215,
por.
Springer--They p183,317, por.

MOORHEAD, ETHEL
English magazine writer,
suffragist, art patron
Rogers--Ladies p83,144,154,
190-191

MOORHOUSE, B-ANN
Amer. genealogical researcher,
editor
Meyer--Who's p142

MOORMAN, CHARLOTTE (fl. 1960's-
1970's)

Amer. cellist
Felton--Famous p201

MOOS, JEANNE (1954-   )
Amer. TV cable reporter
Scheuer--Tel. p343-344

MORALES-SCHILDT, MONA (fl.
1960's)
Swedish glass-maker
O'Neill--Women's p272

MORAN, GERTRUDE AUGUSTA
(1924-   )
Amer. tennis player
Lamparski--What. (2) p28-29,
por.
O'Neill--Women's p260
Sullivan--Queens p102

MORAN, MRS. HARRY HARRISON
(c1857-   )
Amer. oldest Civil War widow
Book--Lists (1) p411

MORAN, JULIETTE M. (fl. 1960's)
Amer. chemist, co-executive
O'Neill--Women's p518

MORAN, LOIS (1907-   )
Amer. actress
Springer--They p183,317, por.

MORAN, MARY NIMMO (1842-1899)
Scottish-Amer. painter, etcher
James--Notable (2) p576-577
McHenry--Liberty's p291

MORAN, "POLLY" (PAULINE
THERESE) (1884-1952)
Amer. vaudeville actress
Springer--They p183,317, por.

MORANDI, ANNA (1716-1774)
Italian anatomist
Marks--Women p118-119, por.

MORANI, ALMA DEA (1907-   )
Amer. physician, surgeon
Hellstedt--Women p342-348, por.
O'Neill--Women's p214

MORANTE, ELSA (1918-   )
Italian novelist
Seymour-Smith--Who's p248-249

MORARJEE, SUMATI (fl. 1970's)
East Indian shipping executive

Macksey--Book p170
O'Neill--Women's p513

MORATA, FULVIA, OF FERRARA
Italian obstetrician
Mead--Hist. p359

MORATA, OLYMPIA (1526-1555)
Italian Reformation worker
Bainton--Germany p253-267

MORELLI, RINA (1908-1976)
Italian actress
Entertainers p232

MORE, HANNAH (1745-1833)
English playwright, religious
writer, philanthropist, poet
Avenel--Comp. (1) p376
Jones--Rutledge p556
Kronenberger--Atlan. p544
Mead--Hist. p455,457
Moers--Literary p300, see also
index p330
Sherr--American p96

MOREAU, JEANNE (1928-)
French actress
Fallaci--Ego. p127-139
O'Neill--Women's p660
Shipman--Internatl. p418-422,
por.
Woman's Almanac p351-352
World--Who p259

MOREMAN, GRACE E. (fl. 1970's)
Amer. free-lance writer,
children's book author
O'Neill--Women's p286

MORENO, RITA (1931-)
Puerto Rican actress, dancer,
singer
Cur. Biog. '85 p299-302, por.
Scheuer--Tel. p344
Signif.--Amer. p69, por.
World--Who p259,263-264

MORENO, VICTORIA (1957-)
Amer. Chicana "faith
healer," poet
Fisher--Third p viii,319,397

MORES, KAREN
Australian swimmer
Hollander--100 p85

MORETON, CLARA
See MOORE, CLARA SOPHIA
JESSUP

MORFOGEN, ANN (1948-)
Amer. TV director
Scheuer--Tel. p344

MORFOVA, KHRISTINA VASILEVA
(1889-1936)
Bulgarian singer
Partington--Who's p286

MORGAN, AGNES FAY (1884-1968)
Amer. chemist, nutritionist
O'Neill--Women's p164,166
Sicherman--Notable p495-497

MORGAN, ANN HAVEN (1882-1966)
Amer. zoologist, ecologist
Sicherman--Notable p497-498

MORGAN, ANNA (1851-1936)
Amer. dramatics teacher
James--Notable (2) p577-579

MORGAN, ANNE TRACY (1873-1952)
Amer. war worker, philanthro-
pist, social worker, club
founder
Forma--They p47,209, por.
McHenry--Liberty's p291
Sicherman--Notable p498-499

MORGAN, BARBARA (1900-)
Amer. artist, photographer
Bowman--Entertain. p22-29, por.
Mitchell--Recol. p178-198,204,
por.
Women's--Female p68

MORGAN, BEVERLY C. (1929-1982)
Amer. pediatrics professor
Marks--Women p217

MORGAN, BILLIE (1922-)
Amer. singer, songwriter
Claghorn--Biog. p317

MORGAN, HANNAH (fl. 1970's)
Amer. Appalachian-market
employee
Coles--Women p71-126

MORGAN, HELEN (1900-1941)
Amer. singer, actress
Claghorn--Biog. p317-318

Clark--Leading p104-105
James--Notable (2) p579-580
McHenry--Liberty's p291-292
Simon--Best p427, por.
Springer--They p183,317-318,
   por.
World--Who p242

MORGAN, JANE (1920-   )
   Amer. singer
   Claghorn--Biog. p318
   World--Who p270

MORGAN, JAYE P. (1929-   )
   Amer. singer
   Claghorn--Biog. p318

MORGAN, JESSIE BORRER (1907-   )
   Amer. newspaperwoman,
   patriot, clubwoman, noted
   Illinois mother
   Amer.--Mothers p169, por.

MORGAN, JULIA (1872-1957)
   Amer. architect, civil
   engineer
   Bachtold--Gifted p34-35
   O'Neill--Women's p609
   People's Almanac (1) p715
   Richey--Eminent p237-263, por.
   Sherr--American p20
   Sicherman--Notable p499-501

MORGAN, LADY SYDNEY (1789-
   1859)
   Moers--Literary p300-301

MORGAN, LUCY CALISTA (1889-
   1981)
   Amer. craftswoman, weaver,
   craft school founder
   O'Neill--Women's p100,123

MORGAN, MARABEL (c1938-   )
   Amer. author, beautician
   100--Greatest p39, por.
   O'Neill--Women's p750
   People--Best p68-69
   World--Who p299

MORGAN, MARIA ("MIDDY")
   (1828-1898)
   Amer. livestock reporter
   Marzolf--Up p22

MORGAN, MARY CLARK ROCKE-
   FELLER (c1938-   )

Amer. millionaire
Forbes--400 ('84) p150

MORGAN, MARY HOPKINSON (fl.
   1770's)
   Amer. patriot
   Earle--Two Cent. (2) p xxi,587,
   589,658,724-725, por.

MORGAN, MARY KIMBALL (1861-
   1948)
   Amer. Christian Science
   educator, college founder
   James--Notable (2) p580-581
   McHenry--Liberty's p292
   Sherr--American p61,133

MORGAN, MICHELE (1920-   )
   French actress
   Shipman--Internatl. p422-426,
   por.

MORGAN, ROBIN (fl. 1970's)
   Amer. feminist, co-founder,
   women's law center, editor,
   poet, child TV actress
   Fireman--TV p177-178, por.
   Hymowitz--Hist. p349,370
   Lichtenstein--Mach. p332-333
   Moers--Literary p109,300
   O'Neill--Women's p359,704
   Sochen--Movers p258

MORGAN, SAMANTHA JANE ATKESAN
   (1843-1926)
   Amer. artist, noted West Virginia mother
   Amer.--Mothers p573, por.

MORGAN, SARAH (1841-   )
   Amer. Civil War diarist
   Sherr--American p82

MORGAN, SYDNEY OWESON, LADY
   (1780-1859)
   Irish novelist
   Smith--Women p321-375

MORGAN, WANDA (fl. 1920's)
   Amer. golfer
   McWhirter--Guinness p76

MORI, HANAE (c1925-   )
   Japanese fashion, textile
   designer

O'Neill--Women's p248

MORI, NAMIKO (fl. 1970's)
Japanese fashion designer
O'Neill--Women's p260-261

MORIARTY, MARY FARRELL
(-1887)
Amer., Irish immigrant
Sherr--American p86

MORING, JO
Amer. TV general manager
Scheuer--Tel. p345

MORINI, ERICA (ERIKA) (1906/
1911-)
Austrian violinist
O'Neill--Women's p633

MORIO, WINIFRED ("PEGGY")
(fl. 1970's)
Amer. labor leader, government official
O'Neill--Women's p333

MORISON, PATRICIA (1914/1919-)
Amer. actress
Springer--They p183,318, por.

MORISOT (MORIZOT), BERTHE
MANET (1841-1895)
French painter
Fine--Women p124-129
Haftmann--Paint. (1) p408
Harris--Women p57,66,89,231-236,
240,247,260,350-351
Kronenberger--Atlan. p545-546
Macksey--Book p205
Munsterberg--Hist. p53-56
Petersen--Women p90-94, por.
Sparrow--Women p182,211,213
Woman's Almanac p221
Women's--Female p12

MORIYAMA, MAYUMI (1927-)
Japanese labor leader,
government official
O'Neill--Women's p346

MORLACCHI, GIUSEPPINA
(1836-1886)
Italian-Amer. dancer
James--Notable (2) p581-582

MORLEY, AGNES

See CLEAVELAND, AGNES
MORLEY

MORLEY, GRACE McCANN (fl.
1930's-1960's)
Amer. art museum director
O'Neill--Women's p614

MORLEY, HELENA
See BRANT, ALICE

MORLEY, KAREN (1905-)
Amer. actress
Springer--They p184,318, por.

MORLEY, MARGARET WARNER
(1858-1923)
Amer. educator, author
McHenry--Liberty's p292

MORPURGO, RACHEL LUZZATTO
(1790-1871)
Italian, Jewish poet
Henry--Written p199-206,217

MORRA, IRENE (1913-)
Amer. film editor
Smith--Movies p18,25,28

MORRELL, OTTOLINE VIOLET
ANNE, LADY CAVENDISH
English art patron, hostess
Rogers--Ladies, see index p232-
233, por.

MORRIS, ANITA
Amer. theater performer
People--Best p164, por.

MORRIS, ANN ("QUEEN") (1878-)
Amer. forester
Sherr--American p225

MORRIS, ANNE CAREY (NANCY)
RANDOLPH (MRS. GOUVENEUR)
(fl. 1770's)
Amer. patriot
Young--Revol. p179-181,213

MORRIS, BETTY
Amer. bowler
McWhirter--Guinness p43
O'Neill--Women's p559
Woman's Almanac p436

MORRIS, CLARA (1847/1848-1925)
Canadian-Amer. actress

Chinoy--Women p67-68,73, por.
James--Notable (2) p582-583
McHenry--Liberty's p292-293

MORRIS, DELORES
    Amer. TV director
    Scheuer--Tel. p345

MORRIS, ELIZABETH (c1753-1826)
    English-Amer. actress
    McHenry--Liberty's p293

MORRIS, ELLEN THORNE (1944-)
    Amer. genealogical researcher,
    author, indexer
    Meyer--Who's p142-143

MORRIS, ESTHER HOBART
    McQUIGG SLACK (1814-1902)
    Amer., Western pioneer,
    feminist, politician, suffra-
    gist, justice-of-peace, gov-
    ernment official, noted
    Wyoming mother
    Amer.--Mothers p593, por.
    Gray--Women p75-80,85-86
    James--Notable (2) p583-585
    Levenson--Women p60,63, por.
    McHenry--Liberty's p293
    Millstein--We p65-66
    Reifert--Women p191-193
    Sherr--American p38,253-254,
    257, por.
    Signif.--Amer. p20, por.
    Time--Women p199,215-216
    Warren--Pictorial p120-121, por.
    World--Who p190

MORRIS, JAN JAMES (1927-)
    British journalist, trans-
    sexual
    Book--Lists (2) p329
    P.W.--Author p310-313,517

MORRIS, JANE BURDEN (fl.
    1970's)
    British embroiderer, wood-
    engraver
    Callen--Women p225, see also
    index p231, por.

MORRIS, JEAN SANSWENBAUGHER
    (1927-)
    Amer. genealogical researcher,
    author
    Meyer--Who's p143

MORRIS, JEANNE (c1935-)
    Amer. sportswriter
    Seed--Saturday's p21-22, por.

MORRIS, JENNY
    Amer. artist
    Callen--Women p10,15,215, por.

MORRIS, JOSIE (-1964)
    Amer. Western "cowpuncher"
    Sherr--American p225, por.

MORRIS, LEE (1916-)
    Amer. songwriter
    Claghorn--Biog. p318

MORRIS, LOUISE ELIZABETH BUR-
    TON (1905-)
    Amer. genealogical researcher,
    author, editor
    Meyer--Who's p143-144

MORRIS, LUCY SMITH (1852-1935)
    Amer. feminist, club founder,
    suffragist
    Sherr--American p247

MORRIS, MARGARET (fl. 1890's)
    British salonnière, dancer
    Macksey--Book p103-104,230, por.

MORRIS, MARGARET HILL (1737-
    1816)
    Amer. physician, Quaker,
    Revolutionary War diarist,
    noted New Jersey mother
    Amer.--Mothers p369-370, por.
    Booth--Women p111-112
    Evans--Weather. p73-109, por.
    Meyer--Petticoat p97
    Sherr--American p150

MORRIS, MARION LONGFELLOW
    (1849-1924)
    Amer. hymnist
    Claghorn--Biog. p318

MORRIS, MARY WALTON
    Amer. Revolutionary War
    patriot
    Meyer--Petticoat p68-69

MORRIS, MAY (1862-1938)
    British designer, embroider,
    textile designer, jeweller
    Callen--Women p225, see also
    index p231, por.

MORRIS, MRS. ROBERT (-1824)
Amer. Revolutionary philan-
thropist
DePauw--Found. p170-171
Earle--Two Cent. (2) p xvi,557,
por.

MORRISON, ANN (-1957)
Amer. civic worker
Sherr--American p56

MORRISON, JEANETTE HELEN
See LEIGH, JANET

MORRISON, TONI (1931-)
Amer. author
Cur. Biog. '79 p264-267, por.
Fisher--Third p vii,167-182,237
O'Neill--Women's p690
Washington--Black p35-36

MORROW, HONORE WILLSIE
(1880-1940)
Amer. novelist
Ehrlich--Oxford p351,394

MORROW, PEGLEG ANNIE (fl.
1890's)
Amer., Western dancer
Sherr--American p57-58

MORSCH, LUCILE M. (1906-1972)
Amer. librarian
Cur. Biog. '72 p468

MORSE, ANNA JUSTINA (1893-)
Amer. composer
Claghorn--Biog. p319

MORSE, ELLA MAE (1925-)
Amer. singer
Lamparski--What. (4) p118-119,
por.
Lamparski--What. (8) p218-219,
por.
Simon--Big p58-59, por.

MORSE, THEODORA ("DOLLY")
(1890-1953)
Amer. lyricist, publisher
Claghorn--Biog. p319

MORSE, (TIGER) JOAN (c1932-
1972)
Amer. fashion designer
Keenan--Women p64-65,72,
por.

MORTENSON, NORMA JEAN
See MONROE, MARILYN

MORTIMER, ALICE
English, mother of Richard,
Duke of York
Leary--Golden p131,141n

MORTIMER, ANN (fl. 1960's-1970's)
Canadian ceramist
O'Neill--Women's p127

MORTIMER, MARY (1816-1877)
Amer. educator
James--Notable (2) p585-586

MORTIMER, PENELOPE RUTH
FLETCHER (1918-)
English novelist, journalist
Avenel--Comp. (1) p380
Baker--Women p7
Crosland--Beyond p225-227
Moers--Literary p301
Seymour-Smith--Novels p189
Showalter--Lit. p349

MORTON, AZIE T.
Amer. government official
O'Neill--Women's p83, por.

MORTON, CAROLINE JOY FRENCH
(1833-1881)
Amer. pioneer ecologist,
noted Nebraska mother
Amer.--Mothers p332, por.

MORTON, MATT (fl. 1860's)
Amer. Civil War patriot
Sherr--American p125

MORTON, PATRICIA (fl. 1970's)
Amer. state government
official, mountaineer
O'Neill--Women's p93

MORTON, SARAH WENTWORTH
APTHORP (1759-1846)
Amer. poet
DePauw--Rem. p128,139, por.
James--Notable (2) p586-587
McHenry--Liberty's p294
Sherr--American p98

MOSBY, ALINE (fl. 1960's)
Amer. journalist, foreign
correspondent
Marzolf--Up p85,165
O'Neill--Women's p457

MOSEKA, AMINATA, pseud.
See LINCOLN, ABBEY

MOSELEY, LAURA WOLCOTT
(1761-1814)
Amer. Revolutionary War
patriot, (daughter of signer)
Flexner--Face p150, por.

MOSER, MARY (1) (1744-1819)
German flower and portrait
painter, craftswoman
Fine--Women p75-76
Macksey--Book p201-202
Parker--Old p87,90, fig. 36

MOSER, MARY (2)
See PROELL, ANNEMARIE
MOSER

MOSES, ANNA MARY ROBERTSON
("GRANDMA MOSES")
(1860-1961)
Amer. painter, noted New
York mother
Amer.--Mothers p393-394, por.
Comfort--Good p75, por.
Fowler--Art p31-53, por.
Haftmann--Paint. (1) p394
Jones--Rutledge p561
Kulkin--Her p210-211
McHenry--Liberty's p294
O'Neill--Women's p599-600, por.
Sherr--American p159-160,162,
229
Sicherman--Notable p501-503
Webster's--Amer. p746
Woman's Almanac p107, por.
Women's--Female p12
World--Who p59

MOSES, JUDITH (1940-)
Amer. TV reporter
Scheuer--Tel. p346

MOSHER, ELIZA MARIA (1846-
1928)
Amer. physician, educator
James--Notable (2) p587-589
McHenry--Liberty's p294-295

MOSKOWITZ, BELLE LINDNER
IRAELS (1877-1933)
Amer. social worker,
politician
Baum--Jewish p177-178
James--Notable p589-591

Neidle--America's p282
Warren--Pictorial p179

MOSKOWITZ, IDA (fl. 1900's-1910's)
Russian-Amer. realtor
Baum--Jewish p94-95,103-106

MOSS, ELIZABETH ("BETTYE")
MURPHY (fl. 1940's)
Amer. publisher, editor
Marzolf--Up p91-92

MOSS, EMMA SADLER (fl. 1950's)
Amer. physician
O'Neill--Women's p210

MOSS, LANNY (fl. 1970's)
Amer. baseball manager
O'Neill--Women's p567

MOSS, MARLOW (1890-1958)
British artist
Harris--Women p314-316,359-360
O'Neill--Women's p596

MOSS, MARTHA A. (fl. 1860's)
Amer. patriot
Sherr--American p232

MOSS, MARY
See KEENE, LAURA

MOSS, PAT (fl. 1960's)
Amer. auto racer
Macksey--Book p254
McWhirter--Guinness p32
O'Neill--Women's p589

MOSSELL, MRS. N.F. (fl. 1890's)
Amer. journalist
Marzolf--Up p25

MOSSHOLDER-HERRESHOFF, DONNA
(fl. 1970's)
Amer. painter
Women's Female p51

MOSSONG, VERNA ELAINE (1925-)
New Zealander, genealogical
researcher
Meyer--Who's p144

MOSTEL, "KATE" (KATHERINE)
CECILIA HARKIN
Amer., wife of Zero Mostel
Funt--Are p261-273,
por.

MOTEN, LUCY ELLA (1851-1933)
Amer. educator
James--Notable (2) p591-592

"MOTHER GOOSE"
See VERGOOSE, ELIZABETH
FOSTER

"MOTHER GRETA"
See FUSS, MARGARITA

"MOTHER" JONES
See JONES, MARY HARRIS

"MOTHER OF THE CONFEDERACY"
See LAW, SALLIE CHAPMAN
GORTON

MOTLEY, CONSTANCE BAKER
(1921-)
Amer. judge, state senator,
government official
Gilbert--Part. p135-141, por.
Ingraham--Album p72-73, por.
O'Neill--Women's p370
Signif.--Amer. p69, por.
Stoddard--Famous p314-324,
por.
Warren--Pictorial p209

MOTT, DEL R. (fl. 1970's)
Amer. aviation stewardess,
safety director
O'Neill--Women's p306

MOTT, ELIZA ANN MIDDAUGH (fl.
1880's)
Amer. Mormon pioneer
Sherr--American p143-144

MOTT, LUCRETIA COFFIN (1793-
1880)
Amer. Quaker, social re-
former, clergyman, abolition-
ist, noted Pennsylvania
mother
Amer.--Mothers p456-457, por.
Berkin--Women p132, por.
Earnest--American p107-110,
114-116
Gilfond--Heroines p24
Gurko--Ladies, see index
p324-325, por.
Hymowitz--Hist. p79-80,86-87,
94,96,100,110,114,121,171
Ingraham--Album p22,33, por.
James--Notable (2) p592-595

Kulkin--Her p211-213
Lutz--Crusade, see index p336,
por.
McHenry--Liberty's p295
Macksey--Book p86,110-111, por.
Millstein--We p94,98, por.
Neidle--America's p28,30
O'Neill--Women's p387
Papachristou--Women, see index
p iv, por.
Reader's--Story p433
Sherr--American p38,177,203,205
Signif.--Amer. p12, por.
Smith--Daughters p104-105,108-
109,111-113,125,146
Stoddard--Famous p325-335, por.
Taylor--Gener. p9-10, por.
Warren--Pictorial p85,88-90, por.
Webster's--Amer. p748
Woman's Almanac p374,542,544
World--Who p190

MOTTA DINIZ, FRANCISCA SEN-
HORINHA DE (fl. 1870's)
Brazilian feminist, newspaper-
woman
Hahner--Women p43-47

MOTTE, JEANNE, COMTESSE DE LA
(1756-1791)
French accused criminal
Macksey--Book p135

MOTTE, REBECCA BREWTON
(1738-1815)
Amer. Revolutionary War
heroine, patriot, noted South
Carolina mother
Amer.--Mothers p489
Booth--Women p256-257,261
Meyer--Petticoat p204
Sherr--American p209,211-212
Williams--Demeter's p247

MOULTON, ELLEN LOUISE CHAND-
LER (1835-1908)
Amer. author
McHenry--Liberty's p295-296

MOULTON, JOY WADE (1928-)
Amer. genealogical researcher,
writer
Meyer--Who's p144

MOULTON, LOUISE CHANDLER
(1835-1908)
Amer. poet, literary hostess

Ehrlich--Oxford p88
James--Notable (2) p595-596

MOULTON, MARTHA (fl. 1770's)
Amer. patriot
Booth--Women p17-18

MOULTON, SARAH BARRETT
("PINKIE") (1783-1795)
English socialite
Ware--Meet p79

"MOUNTAIN CHARLEY"
See GUERIN, ELSA JANE
FOREST

"MOUNTAIN WOLF WOMAN" (1884-
1960)
Amer. Winnebago Indian
writer
Millstein--We p171-172

MOUNTFORT, HANNAH
See ELIOT, ANN(E) MONTFORT

MOURAVIEVA, MARTHA (c1837-
1879)
Russian ballet dancer
Migel--Ballerinas p257-259, por.

"MOURNING DOVE" ("HUM-ISHU-
MA") (1888-1936)
Amer. Indian (Okanogon)
writer
Fisher--Third p v,39

MOWATT, ANNA CORA OGDEN
(1819-1870)
Amer. actress, novelist,
playwright, short-story
writer
James--Notable (2) p596-598
Kulkin--Her p213-214
McHenry--Liberty's p296
Moers--Literary p301,304
Webster's--Amer. p749

MOWATT, ANNE CORA LONGDEN,
LADY (1837-1919)
English novelist
Showalter--Lit. p333

MOWLSON, ANN RADCLIFFE,
LADY
See RADCLIFFE, ANN, LADY
MOWLSON

MOWRER, RITA SCHIVE (1927-)
Amer. genealogical researcher,
author
Meyer--Who's p144

MOYES, PATRICIA (1923-)
Anglo-Irish novelist
Seymour-Smith--Novels p190

MOYHER, GLORIA ("BIG GLO")
(c1853-)
Amer. basketball player
Jordan--Broken p91-96

MOYNIHAN, JANE (fl. 1960's-1970's)
Amer. newspaper writer,
filmmaker
Smith--Movies p193,263

MOZART, ANNA MARIA (1720-1778)
Austrian, mother of Wolfgang
Amadeus Mozart
Diagram--Mothers p168-170, por.

MOZART, MARIA ANNA (NANNERL)
(1751-1829)
Austrian musician, child
celebrity pianist, teacher,
(daughter of Mozart)
Woman's Almanac p52

MOZEE, PHOEBE ANNE OAKLEY
See OAKLEY, ANNIE

MOZLEY, ANNE (1809-1891)
English journalist
Showalter--Lit. p323

MOZLEY, HARRIETT (1803-1852)
English children's book author
Showalter--Lit. p322

M'RABET, FADELA (fl. 1970's)
Algerian feminist
Taylor--Gener. p42

MRINALINI (fl. 1910's)
East Indian actress
Macksey--Book p234-235

"MS. SOFT SOUL"
See MARRS, STELLA

MUCHMORE, DONNA (fl. 1970's)
Amer. hospital nurse,
Antarctica, wife of Harold

Muchmore
Land--New p149,151-152,154

MUDGE, GENEVRA DELPHINE
(fl. 1890's)
Amer. auto racer
Woman's Almanac p437

MUDGE, ISADOR(E) GILBERT
(1875-1957)
Amer. librarian, bibliographer
Sicherman--Notable p503-504

MUELLER, DARLENE (fl. 1970's)
Amer. farmer
O'Neill--Women's p13

MUELLER, LISEL (1924-)
Amer. poet
Chester--Rising p133-140, por.

MUELLER, MAGDALENE (fl.
1960's-1970's)
Amer. Braillist volunteer
O'Neill--Women's p118

MUELLER-HELWIG, ALEN (c1902-)
German weaver
O'Neill--Women's p267-268

MUGGE, MARY ALICE PRITCHARD
MYERS (1895-)
Amer. poet, noted Florida
mother
Amer.--Mothers p114-115, por.

MUHLERT, JAN
Amer. art museum director
O'Neill--Women's p616

MUIR, GLORIA LUDWIG (fl. 1940's-
1970's)
Amer. investment counselor
O'Neill--Women's p529

MUIR, JEAN (1) (1911-)
Amer. actress
Springer--They p184-185,318,
por.

MUIR, JEAN (2) (fl. 1960's-1970's)
Anglo-Amer. fashion designer
O'Neill--Women's p245-246

MUIRSON, GEORGEANNA (1833-
1906)

Amer. Civil War relief, hospital worker
James--Notable (3) p665-668

MUKHINA, VERA IGNA'EVNA (1889-
1953)
Russian sculptor
Mandel--Soviet p141
Women's--Female p2, supp.

MULCAHY, VIRGINIA (fl. 1960's)
Amer. heroine, Carnegie
Medal winner
O'Neill--Women's p734

MULDAUR, MARIA GRAZIA ROSA
DOMENICA D'AMATO (1942-)
Amer. singer
Claghorn--Jazz p215

MULDOWNEY, SHIRLEY "CHA CHA"
(c1940-)
Amer. drag racer
Jordan--Broken p143-154
McWhirter--Guinness p31-32, por.
O'Neill--Women's p589
Stambler--Women p95-106, por.
Woman's Almanac p440

MULHALL, LUCILLE (c1875-1940)
Amer. horsewoman, world's
original "cowgirl"
Sherr--American p189-190, por.
Time--Women p189,194-195, por.

MULLANEY, KATE (fl. 1860's)
Amer. labor leader
Berkin--Women p206,209-210,212,
214

MULLENGER, DONNA BELLE
See REED, DONNA

MULLER, AMELIA
See FAY, AMY

MULLER, ELIZA (-1876)
Amer. nurse
Sherr--American p120

MULLER, GERTRUDE AGNES (1887-
1954)
Amer. businesswoman, inventor
Sicherman--Notable p504-506

MÜLLER, MARIA (1898-1958)

Czechoslovakian opera singer
Tuggle--Golden p197, por.

MÜLLER, MARY (1820-1902)
British feminist
Macksey--Book p81

MÜLLER-PREISS, ELLEN
Austrian fencer
O'Neill--Women's p560

MULLER-SCHWARZE, CHRISTINE
(fl. 1960's)
German-Amer. psychologist
(Antarctica)
Land--New p22,23-26,50,106

MULLICAN, DOROTHY
See LANE, LOLA MULLICAN

MULLINS, PRISCILLA
See ALDEN, PRISCILLA MUL-
LINS

MULOCK, DINAH MARIA
See CRAIK, DINAH MARIA
MULOCK

MULSO, HESTER (1727-1801)
English writer
Horner--English p36-37 (& notes)

"MUMBET," pseud.
See FREEMAN, ELIZABETH

MUMFORD, MARY ENO BASSETT
(1842-1935)
Amer. civic leader, club-
woman
James--Notable (2) p598-599

MUMTAZ-MAHAL (MUMTAZA ZEMANI)
(1592-1631)
East Indian, wife of Shah
Jahan, Mogul empress (of
Taj Mahal)
World--Who p299

MUM-ZI
Nigerian grandmother at 17
McFarland--Incred. p91

MUNDAY, MISSOURI BELLE
Amer. poet, philanthropist
Sherr--American p129

MUNFORD, MARY-COOKE BRANCH

(1865-1938)
Amer. educational reformer,
civic leader
James--Notable (2) p600-601
Sherr--American p232

MUNRO, ALICE (1931-)
Canadian writer
Cahill--Women p300,378

MUNSEL, PATRICE (1925-)
Amer. opera singer
Claghorn--Biog. p321

MUNSON, JULIA (fl. 1890's)
Amer. metalworker, enameller
Callen--Women p162,225

MUNSON, MARGARET ELIZABETH
See SANGSTER, MARGARET
ELIZABETH MUNSON '

MUNSON, ONA (1906-1955)
Amer. actress
Springer--They p185,318-319,
por.

MUNSTON, CONSTANCE SYLVIA
See LILLIE, BEATRICE, LADY
PEEL

MUNTER, GABRIELE (1877-1962)
German-Amer. painter
Fine--Women p160-162
Harris--Women p58-59,95,281-282,
355-356
Munsterberg--Hist. p69-70,118
Petersen--Women p107-108
Women's--Female p12

MUONA, TOINI (1904-)
Finnish ceramist, designer
O'Neill--Women's p275

MURASAKI SHIKIBU, LADY
MURASAKI (c978-1026/1030)
Japanese novelist, diarist
Jones--Rutledge p563
Macksey--Book p62,179
Magill--Cycl. p778-779
Moers--Literary p301
Seymour-Smith--Novels p190
Who Did What p235
World--Who p42

MURAT, CATHERINE (KATRIŅA),
PRINCESS (c1824-1910)

Amer. civic worker, hotel
manager
Sherr--American p45
Time--Women p134-135, por.

MURDEN, ELIZA CRAWLY (c1790-
c1851)
Amer. composer, poet
Claghorn--Biog. p321

MURDOCK, (JEAN) IRIS (1919-)
Irish novelist, lecturer,
philosopher
Avenel--Comp. (1) p383-384
Crosland--Beyond, see index
p257
Cur. Biog. '80 p268-272, por.
Jones--Rutledge p564
Moers--Literary p301
O'Neill--Women's p40,685-686
Seymour-Smith--Novels p190,
por.
Seymour-Smith--Who's p253
Showalter--Lit. p350
Spacks--Contemp. p92-107,180
Wintle--Makers p372-373, #333
World--Who p29

MURDOCK, LOUISE CALDWELL
(1858-1915)
Amer. interior designer,
art patron
James--Notable (2) p601-602
Sherr--American p77

MURDOCK, MARGARET (1942-)
Amer. rifle shooter
McWhirter--Guinness p114
O'Neill--Women's p565
Woman's Almanac p440

MURFIN, JANE (fl. 1920's-1930's)
Amer. writer, co-director
Smith--Movies p13-14

MURFREE, MARY NOAILLES
(1850-1922)
Amer. novelist, short-story
writer
Ehrlich--Oxford p288, por.
James--Notable (2) p602-603
McHenry--Liberty's p296-297

MURGROVE, MARY (fl. 1740's)
Amer. Creek Indian colony
adviser
Williams--Demeter's p192-193

MURPHREE SISTERS (fl. 1860's)
Amer. Civil War heroines
Sherr--American p1

MURPHY, BETTY SOUTHARD
(c1929-)
Amer. attorney, labor leader,
government official
O'Neill--Women's p333,340-341,
350
Swiger--Women p117-134

MURPHY, BRIDEY
See TIGHE, VIRGINIA

MURPHY, CATHARINE
Amer. aviatrix, army flier
Keil--Those p250-251

MURPHY, CHARLOTTE P. (fl.
1950's-1970's)
Amer. lawyer, judge
Macksey--Book p129
O'Neill--Women's p371

MURPHY, (ELEANOR) PATRICIA
(1911/1912-)
Amer. restaurant owner
Neidle--America's p272-274

MURPHY, EMILY (1868-1933)
Canadian politician, judge,
author
O'Neill--Women's p352

MURPHY, JUDITH SARGENT (fl.
1790's)
Amer. feminist
Sherr--American p105

MURPHY, MARY (-1979)
Amer. dog owner
People's Almanac (3) p615

MURPHY, PAULA MULHAUSER (fl.
1970's)
Amer. auto racer
McWhirter--Guinness p32

MURPHY, SARAH BARTON (fl.
1800's)
Amer. Sunday school teacher
Sherr--American p129-130

MURPHY, VIRGINIA REED (fl.
1910's)
Amer., daughter of "Donner"

Reed (Donner party)
Hoople--As p51-60

MURRAY, ANN
See POWELL, ANN MURRAY

MURRAY, ANNE (1945-)
Canadian singer
Anderson--People p283, por.
Cur. Biog. '82 p284-287, por.
Glassman--Year '79 p130, por.
World--Who p270

MURRAY, DOLLY
See FORBES, DOROTHY
(DOLLY) MURRAY

MURRAY, ELIZABETH
See INMAN, ELIZABETH
MURRAY CAMPBELL SMITH

MURRAY, ELLEN (fl. 1860's)
Amer. abolitionist, school
founder
Sherr--American p212

MURRAY, FLORENCE KERINS
(1916-)
Amer. civic leader, lawyer,
judge, government official,
noted Rhode Island mother
Amer.--Mothers p483-484, por.
O'Neill--Women's p371

MURRAY, JEANNE
See STAPLETON, JEAN

MURRAY, JOAN (fl. 1960's)
Amer. journalist
Marzolf--Up p168-169,174

MURRAY, JUDITH SARGENT
STEVENS (1751-1820)
Amer. educational reformer,
poet, feminist, playwright,
columnist
DePauw--Found. p212-214,216
Fine--Women p93
James--Notable (2) p603-605
McHenry--Liberty's p297
Millstein--We p27,49-50
Sherr--American p105
Warren--Pictorial p69
Williams--Demeter's p309-310

MURRAY, KATHERINE
See MILLETT, KATE

MURRAY, KATHRYN (1906-)
Amer. dancing teacher,
actress
World--Who p299

MURRAY, MADALYN
See O'HAIR, MADALYN MURRAY

MURRAY, MAE (1889-1965)
Amer. actress, dancer
Mordden--Movie, see index p294
Springer--They p185,319, por.

MURRAY, MARGARET ALICE (1863-
1963)
English Egyptologist
Who Did What p235

MURRAY, MARJORIE (fl. 1960's)
Canadian missionary, artist
O'Neill--Women's p399

MURRAY, MARY LINDLEY (1720-
1782)
Amer. Revolutionary War
heroine
Booth--Women p93-94, por.
Clyne--Patriots p13-18
Meyer--Petticoat p59-60, por.
Sherr--American p169, por.

MURRAY, MICHELE (1934-1974)
Amer. poet, critic
Moers--Literary p301

MURRAY, PAULI (1910-)
Amer. author, lawyer, teach-
er, poet, professor, priest
Diamonstein--Open p289-294, por.
O'Neill--Women's p350,385, por.

MURRAY, ROBBINS ELIZABETH
(BETSY)
See ROBBINS, ELIZABETH
(BETSY) MURRAY

MURRAY, ROSEMARY (fl. 1970's)
English chemistry professor,
college vice-chancellor
O'Neill--Women's p407

MURRELL, CHRISTINE (1874-1933)
English physician
Marks--Women p118

MURRY, KATHERINE MANSFIELD
BEAUCHAMP

See MANSFIELD, KATHERINE,
pseud.

MUSCAL, RUTH (fl. 1970's)
Israeli soldier
O'Neill--Women's p553

MUSCATINE, ALLISON
Amer. Rhodes scholar
O'Neill--Women's p435, por.

MUSCHAL-REINHARDT, ROSALIE
(fl. 1970's)
Amer. priesthood student
O'Neill--Women's p378

MUSE, MARTHA TWITCHEL (fl.
1970's)
Amer. member college board
of trustees
O'Neill--Women's p407

MUSE, REYNELDA W. (1946-   )
Amer. TV news anchor re-
porter
Scheuer--Tel. p349

MUSGRAVE, THEA (1928-   )
Scottish composer, conduc-
tor, lecturer
Cur. Biog. '78 p319-322, por.
LePage--Women p145-164, por.
Macksey--Book p221, por.
O'Neill--Women's p637

MUSGROVE, MARY (c1700-c1763)
Amer. Indian leader, land-
owner
Earle--Two Cent. (1) p130-136
Friedman--Our p54-55
James--Notable (2) p605-606
Sherr--American p210

MUSHKAT, MARION (fl. 1940's-
1960's)
Polish professor, international law, United Nations
envoy
Macksey--Book p129

MUSIDORA (-1957)
French actress, feminist,
film director
Smith--Movies p114

MUSKIE, JANE FRANCES GRAY
(c1926-   )

Amer., wife of Edmund Muskie
Miller--Fishbait p112

MUSSEY, ELLEN SPENCER (1850-
1936)
Amer. lawyer, social reformer,
feminist, law school founder
James--Notable (2) p606-607
McHenry--Liberty's p297-298
Macksey--Book p68
Sherr--American p41
Signif.--Amer. p31, por.

MUSSOLINI, EDDA (1910-   )
Italian, daughter of Benito
Mussolini
People's Almanac (1) p948

MUSSOLINI, ROSA MALTONI (1858-
1905)
Italian, mother of Benito
Mussolini
Book--Lists (1) p287
Diagram--Mothers p171-173, por.

MUTCHIE, MARJORIE ANN
Amer. actress
Lamparski--What. (8) p64-65,
por.

MUTHAMMA, C.B.
East Indian government
official
O'Neill--Women's p62

MUTHE, MADAME (fl. 1940's)
German model
Keenan--Women p138-140,144, por.

MUTHEMBA, JOSINA ABIATHAR
(1945-   )
African "liberationist"
O'Neill--Women's p714

MUTHULAKSHMI
East Indian government official
Macksey--Book p90

MUUGA, LEILI ADAMOVNA (1922-   )
Russain (Estovian) painter
Women's--Female p4 (supp.)

MUZIO, CLAUDIA (1889-1936)
Italian opera singer
Tuggle--Golden p140-142, por.

MYBURGH, HELMINE

South African apartheid
fighter
O'Neill--Women's p731-732

MYELNIC, FAINA (fl. 1970's)
Russian track and field
athlete
O'Neill--Women's p577,579

MYERS, BARBARA
Amer. TV marketing director
Scheuer--Tel. p349

MYERS, CARMEL (1899-1980)
Amer. actress
Springer--They p185,319, por.

MYERS, LISA MERRYMAN
Amer. TV correspondent
Scheuer--Tel. p349

MYERS, MARGARET ELIZABETH
(1925-)
Amer. genealogical researcher
Meyer--Who's p146

MYERS, MARY ELEANOR (1905-)
Amer. genealogical researcher,
writer, editor
Meyer--Who's p146

MYERS, SARAH KERR (1940-)
Amer. geographer-sociologist
O'Neill--Women's p174

MYERSCOUGH, ANGELITA, SISTER
(fl. 1970's)
Amer. nun
O'Neill--Women's p392

MYERSON, BESS (1924-)
Amer. beauty queen, TV
personality, government
official, columnist
Bowman--Politics p4-9, por.
Macksey--Book p177
100--Greatest (1) p62, por.
Woman's Almanac p139
World--Who p54

MYRDAL, ALVA REIMER (1902-)
Swedish ambassador, United
Nations official, Ceres
Medal winner
O'Neill--Women's p40,51-52,63

MYRTIS
Greek poet, teacher of

Pindas and Corinna
Pomeroy--Godd. p52

N

NAAZ, SUSANNE
See NECKER, SUZANNE CURCHOD,
MADAME

NACHMIAS, VIVIANNE T. (fl. 1960's)
Amer. physician, anatomist,
college associate
M.I.T.--Women p x,29-34,36

NADEAU, CLAUDETTE (fl. 1970's)
Canadian federal corporation
president
O'Neill--Women's p523

NADIG, MARIE-THERESE (fl. 1970's)
Swiss skier
Assoc. Press--Pursuit p296, por.

NAGLE, FLORENCE (fl. 1960's)
British race-horse trainer
Macksey--Book p260

NAHHAS, HASHIM EL (fl. 1970's)
Egyptian filmmaker
Smith--Movies p92-93

NAIPU, SAROJINI (1879-1949)
East Indian poet, feminist,
patriot, politician, social re-
former
Avenel--Comp. (1) p387
Macksey--Book p90
Taylor--Gener. p17, por.

NAIRNE, CAROLINA(E) OLIPHANT,
BARONESS (1766-1845)
Scottish song writer, composer
Avenel--Comp. (1) p387
Macksey--Book p212

NAKATINDI, PRINCESS
Zambian government official
Macksey--Book p43

NAKAYAMA, MRS.
See TAKAGI, NORIKO

NAKIPBEKOVA SISTERS (fl. 1970's)
Russian musicians
Mandel--Soviet p149

NALECHE, BERTHOLLE LOUISETTE,
COMTESSE

See BERTHOLLE, LOUISETTE, COMTESSE DE NALECHE

NALKOWSKA, ZOFIA (1884-1954)
Polish novelist, playwright
Partington--Who's p294-295

NAMPEYO
Amer. Indian artist, (potter)
Sherr--American p8, por.

NAOMI
Biblical
Price--God p82-87

NAPIER, SARAH LENNOX BUN-
BURY, LADY (1745-1826)
English hostess, friend of
George III
Booth--Women p26-29,128,286-
287, por.

NASI, (DONA) GRACIA (1510-
c1565)
Portuguese, Jewish patroness
of letters
Henry--Written p11,119,138,
142-146,153

NASI, REYNA (fl. 1590's)
Turkish, Jewish printer
Henry--Written p119-121,142-143

NASRIDDINOVA, YADGAR (1920-)
Russian (Uzbck) engineer,
government official
Mandel--Soviet p172-176,179,181,
293, por.
O'Neill--Women's p59

NATHAN, MAUD(E) (1862-1946)
Amer. philanthropist, suf-
fragist, humanitarian, social
reformer
Banner--Women p30,159-160
James--Notable (2) p608-609
Lagemann--Gen. p33-56, por.
McHenry--Liberty's p299
O'Neill--Women's p287

NATION, CARRY AMELIA MOORE
(1846-1911)
Amer. social reformer,
temperance leader, noted
Arkansas mother
Amer.--Mothers p42-43, por.
Clark--Leading p46-49
Eills--Here p106-107

Ehrlich--Oxford p283-284
James--Notable (2) p609-611
Levenson--Women p79-81
McHenry--Liberty's p299-300
Macksey--Book p116-117, por.
Millstein--We p146,155-156, por.
O'Neill--Women's p719
People's Almanac (1) p102-103,
por.
People's Almanac (2) p1205
Sherr--American p10,75-78,129-
130,133,189,223, por.
Signif.--Amer. p21, por.
Stein--Lives p323-331
Time--Women p196,198,202-205,
por.
Webster's--Amer. p762
Woman's Almanac p381, por.
World--Who p190

NATWICK, MILDRED (1908-)
Amer. actress
Entertainers p232
World--Who p243

NAU, MARIA DOLORES BENEDICTA
JOSEFINA (1818-1891)
Amer. opera singer
Claghorn--Biog. p324

NAUSICAA
Greek princess
Pomeroy--Godd. p18-20,22,28,30
Zinserling--Women p18

NAVE, RUFINA (c1867-)
Amer. centenarian
Mitchell--Yessir p90-91, por.

NAVRATILOVA, MARTINA (1956-)
Czechoslovakian tennis player
Cur. Biog. '77 p309-312, por.
McWhirter--Guinness p164
Woman's Almanac p418
World--Who p219

NAWAZ, JAHANARA SHAH (fl. 1930's)
Pakistani feminist
Macksey--Book p90

NAZIMOVA, ALLA (1879-1945)
Russian-Amer. actress, dancer
Entertainers p168
Fabian--On p130, por.
James--Notable (2) p611-613
McHenry--Liberty's p300
Macksey--Book p233
Mordden--Movie p21-23,36,51-53,

78,210,226, por.
Slide--Early p110-113
World--Who p259

NEAGLE, ANNA, DAME (1904-   )
English actress, dancer
Johns--Dames p145-161, por.
Shipman--Gold. p415-417, por.
Springer--They p189,319, por.

NEAIRA (fl. 340 B.C.)
Corinthian slave
Pomeroy--Godd. p67-68,91-92

NEAKOK, SADIE BROWER (fl.
1880's)
Amer. (Alaskan), daughter of
King of the Arctic
Jones--Women (1) p121-122

NEAL, EMILY (ALICE)
See HAVEN, EMILY BRADLEY
NEAL

NEAL, JEAN FRANCES
Amer. pioneer
Sherr--American p23

NEAL, LOIS SMATHERS (1912-   )
Amer. genealogical researcher,
author, indexer
Meyer--Who's p149

NEAL, PATRICIA (1926-   )
Amer. actress
Book--Lists (2) p370
Hirschhorn--Rating p279-280,
por.
100--Greatest (1) p110, por.
People--Best p226-227, por.
Shipman--Internatl. p429-432,
por.
Woman's Almanac p252
World--Who p243

NEALIN, PATRICIA LORETTO
(1927-   )
Amer. TV manager
Klever--Women p21-23

NEARING, HELEN KNOTHE
(1904-   )
Amer. author, homesteader
Betts--Writers p40-43, por.
O'Neill--Women's p19-20

NECKER, ANNE LOUISE GERMAINE,
MADAME DE

See STAËL (STAËL-HOLSTEIN),
ANNE LOUISE GERMAINE
NECKER

NECKER, SUZANNE CURCHOD, MADAM
(1739/1740-1794)
Swiss-French physician, hospital founder, writer
Mead--Hist. p456,494

NEDEVA, ZLATINA (1877-1941)
Bulgarian actress, producer,
teacher
Partington--Who's p298

NEEL, ALICE HARTLEY (1900-   )
Amer. painter
Cur. Biog. '76 p281-283, por.
Fine--Women p203-205
Fowler--Art p145
Harris--Women p323-324
Kufrin--Uncom. p132-152, por.
Miller--Lives p121-129, por.
Munro--Originals p120-130, por.
Nemser--Convers. p113-147,362,
por.
O'Neill--Women's p601
Women's--Female p51-52

NEET, NAZLE BOSS (1921-   )
Amer. genealogical researcher,
editor
Meyer--Who's p149

NEETHLING, LEONORA
South African judge
Macksey--Book p129

NEFERTITI (c1390-1360 B.C.)
Egyptian queen, wife of
Akhnaton, King of Egypt
Jones--Rutledge p574

NEFF, FRANCINE IRVING (1925-   )
Amer. community worker,
United States Treasurer,
noted New Mexico mother
Amer.--Mothers p385, por.

NEFF, HILDEGARDE (1925-   )
German-Amer. actress,
singer, writer
Claghorn--Biog. p324
P.W.--Author p303-305,505
World--Who p259

NEFF, ISABELLA ELEANOR
(1830-   )

Amer. pioneer
Sherr--American p222

NEFF, MARY (fl. 1690's)
Amer., Indian captive,
nurse
Warren--Pictorial p23
Williams--Demeter's p163-165

NEGRETTE, LOLITA DOLORES
MARTINEZ ASUNSOLO LOPEZ
See DEL RIO, DOLORES

NEGRI, POLA (1894/1899-1987)
Polish-Amer. actress
Manchel--Women p37, por.
Mordden--Movie p35
Shipman--Gold. p417-421, por.
Springer--They p189,319, por.
World--Who p243

NEGRIN, SUE (fl. 1970's)
Amer. graphic artist
Women's--Female p80

NEIGHBORS, PATRICIA
Amer. corporate official
Adams--Women p22,55-57,60-61,
100,109,114-115,155-156,176,
186,208

NEIL, ROSS, pseud.
See HARWOOD, ISABELLA

NEILL, NOEL
Amer. TV actress
Lamparski--What. (8) p180-181,
por.

NEILSON, NELLIE (1873-1947)
Amer. historian
James--Notable (2) p613-614

NELL, PATRICIA A. (fl. 1960's)
Amer. Air Force captain,
medical officer
O'Neill--Women's p542

NELLI, PLAUTILLA (1523-1588)
Italian painter, abbess
Sparrow--Women p23-24

NELLIGAN, KATE (1951-)
Canadian actress
Cur. Biog. '83 p266-269, por.

NELSON, ALICE DUNBAR (1875-
1935)

Amer. poet, teacher, social
worker
Bernikow--World p260
James--Notable (2) p614-615

NELSON, ANNE H. (1925-)
Amer. labor leader
O'Neill--Women's p327

NELSON, CATHERINE SUCKLING
(1726-1768)
English, mother of Horatio,
Lord Nelson
Diagram--Mothers p180-181, por.

NELSON, CINDY (1955-)
Amer. skier
Jacobs--Modern p72-84, por.

NELSON, EDITH
Jamaican labor union official
O'Neill--Women's p322, por.

NELSON, EMILY (fl. 1970's)
Amer. sculptor
Women's--Female p93

NELSON, EVELYN
See BAKER, ("WEE") BONNIE

NELSON, GLORIA (fl. 1970's)
Amer. fashion designer
O'Neill--Women's p261

NELSON, GUNVOR (fl. 1960's-1970's)
Amer. painter, filmmaker
Smith--Movies p193-194

NELSON, HARRIET HILLIARD
(1911-)
Amer. actress, singer
Springer--They p136,300, por.
World--Who p243

NELSON, INDIANA (fl. 1970's)
Amer. novelist, painter
McCullough--People p130-131

NELSON, LINNEA J. (fl. 1920's-
1940's)
Amer. radio, advertising
agency head
Women--Radio p18

NELSON, MARJORIE (fl. 1970's)
Amer. physician
Teitz--What's p72-99, por.

NELSON, RUTH (fl. 1970's)
Amer. systems analyst
Seed--Saturday's p146-150, por.

NELSON, WANDA (fl. 1970's)
Amer. environmentalist,
activist
O'Neill--Women's p10

NEMCOVA, BOŽENA (1820-1862/
1882)
Czechoslovakian novelist,
poet, patriot
Partington--Who's p299
Who Did What p242

NEMIR, ROSA LEE (1905-   )
Amer. physician
Hellstedt--Women p295-301, por.

NEMSER, CINDY (fl. 1970's)
Amer. magazine editor
Women's--Female p122

NERENBERG, SUSAN A.
Amer. TV director
Scheuer--Tel. p353

NESBIT, EDITH (1858-1924)
English children's book
author
Avenel--Comp. (1) p389
Jones--Rutledge p576
Kronenberger--Atlan. p558
Showalter--Lit. p340

NESBIT, EVELYN (1884-1967)
Amer. actress, wife of
Harry K. Thaw
Clark--Leading p26
Forma--They, see index p242,
por.
Showalter--Lit. p340
Woman's Almanac p503
World--Who p299

NESBIT, MRS. WINIFIELD
Amer., mother of Evelyn
Nesbit
Forma--They, see index p242

NESBITT, CATHLEEN (MARY)
(1888/1889-1982)
English actress
Cur. Biog. '82 p471
World--Who p259

NESBITT, HENRIETTA (c1874-1963)
Amer., White House house-
keeper
Daniels--Wash., see index p365

NESBITT, VIRGINIA BELL (1909-   )
Amer. genealogical researcher,
writer
Meyer--Who's p150

NESKI, BARBARA (fl. 1970's)
Amer. architect
O'Neill--Women's p612

NESTOR, AGNES (1880-1948)
Amer. labor union leader
Hymowitz--Hist. p248
James--Notable (2) p615-617
McHenry--Liberty's p300-301
O'Neill--Women's p295-296,332
Sochen--Movers, see index p317

NETRASIRI, KHUNYING CHERD-
CHALONG (1909-   )
Thailand physician
Hellstedt--Women p379-382, por.

NETTLES, BEA (fl. 1970's)
Amer. photographer
Women's--Female p69

NEUBER, (FREDERIKE(A) CAROLINE
WEISSENBORN (1697-1760)
German actress, manager
Entertainers p87, por.
Macksey--Book p224, por.
Partington--Who's p302

NEUBERGER, MAURINE BROWN
(1907-   )
Amer. Senator, feminist
Bachtold--Gifted p106
Chamberlin--Min. p292-300, por.
O'Neill--Women's p66-67
Sochen--Movers p232-233
U.S.--Women (89th) p1, por.

NEUFELD, ELIZABETH FONDAL (fl.
1970's)
French-Amer. biochemist
O'Neill--Women's p145,224-225

NEUFFER, JUDITH ANN (fl. 1970's)
Amer. naval pilot, "hurricane
hunter"
O'Neill--Women's p543

NEUMANN, HANNA (-1971)
German-Anglo abstract alge-
braist
O'Neill--Women's p176

NEUMANN, THERESE (1898-1962)
German "stigmata" woman
Book--Lists (1) p437

NEUMANN, VERA
See VERA SALAFF NEUMANN

NEUVILLE, ANNE-MARGUERITE
HENRIETTE-ROUILLE,
BARONESS HYDE DE
See MARIGNY, ANNE-
MARGUERITE HENRIETTE-
ROUILLE DE, BARONESS
HYDE DE NEUVILLE

NEUVILLE, MARY DE CHAPPOTIN
DE
French religious reformer
Macksey--Book p116

NEVADA, EMMA WIXOM (1859-1940)
Amer. opera singer
Claghorn--Biog. p325-326
James--Notable (2) p617-618
McHenry--Liberty's p301
Sherr--American p143

NEVELSON, LOUISE (c1900-)
Russian-Amer. sculptor
Bowman--New p16-21, por.
Diamonstein--Open p295-297,
por.
Fine--Women p200-203
Fink--Great p154-161, por.
Fowler--Art p79-99, por.
Gilbert--Part. p73-77, por.
McHenry--Liberty's p301
Munro--Originals p131-144, por.
Munsterberg--Hist. p95-100,
118-119,145
Nemser--Convers. p53-79,360-
361, por.
100--Greatest (1) p74, por.
O'Neill--Women's p604
Petersen--Women p123-124
Woman's Almanac p224-225, por.
World--Who p59
Women's--Female p93

NEVENS, MARY McNAMARA
(1872-1965)

Irish-Amer. teacher, noted
North Dakota mother
Amer.--Mothers p417-418, por.

NEVEU, GINETTE (1919-1949)
French cellist
Macksey--Book p221

NEVIER, LEONA (fl. 1950's-1970's)
Amer. publisher, editor
O'Neill--Women's p489-490

NEVILLE, ANNE (1456-1485)
English queen, (wife of
Richard III)
Leary--Golden, see index p355-
356

NEVINS, MARTHA GRIFFITH (1860-)
Amer. teacher, suffragist,
noted Iowa mother
Amer.--Mothers p205-206, por.

NEVINS, NATALIE (1943-)
Amer. gospel singer
Claghorn--Biog. p326

NEVINS, TISH (fl. 1890's)
Amer. heroine, noted Montana
mother
Amer.--Mothers p319-320, por.

NEWBERRY, JULIA (1853/1854-1876)
Amer. heiress, diarist
Earnest--American p64,184-188

NEWBERY, JESSIE ROWAT (fl. 1880's)
British designer, embroiderer,
metalworker
Callen--Women p124-125,128,225,
por.

NEWCASTLE, MARGARET CAVEN-
DISH, DUCHESS OF (c1624-
1694)
English medical writer, play-
wright, poet, essayist,
biographer
Avenel--Comp. (1) p390
Horner, English p89-93
Macksey--Book p271
Mead--Hist. p402
Pearson--Who p26

NEWCOMB, ETHEL (1879-1959)
Amer. pianist
Claghorn--Biog. p327

Book--Lists (2) p368
Boyd--Three p167-234
Brecher--Lives p297-300
Crovitz--Courage p73-98
Donaldson--How p280-281
Fraser--Heroines p200-206, por.
Fry--1000 p256-257, por.
Jones--Rutledge p581
Kulkin--Her p215-216
Longford--Eminent p85-108,
  por.
Macksey--Book p16,110,146-148,
  por.
Marks--Women p161-174, por.
Marlowe--Great p80-84, por.
O'Neill--Women's p230-231
People's Almanac (1) p1331
People's Almanac (2) p1186
Showalter--Lit. p326
Taylor--Gener. p47-48, por.
Who Did What p245
Woman's Almanac p447, por.
World--Who p115

NIGHTINGALE, FRANCES
  ("FANNY") SMITH (c1788-
  1880)
  English, mother of Florence
  Nightingale
  Diagram--Mothers p190-191, por.

NIHELL, ELIZABETH (fl. 1740's-
  1760's)
  English midwife, writer
  Mead--Hist. p475-476

NIJINSKA, BRONISLAVA (1891-
  1972)
  Russian ballet dancer,
  choreographer
  O'Neill--Women's p639

NIKANDRE (fl. c660 B.C.)
  Greek goddess, (dedicated
  statue)
  Pomeroy--Godd. p47

NIKIFOROVA, TATIANA
  Russian clothing factory
  manager
  Macksey--Book p173

NIKOLAYEVA, CLAUDIA (1893-)
  Russian printing trade
  worker, labor leader
  Mandel--Soviet p53-54,296-297

NIKOLOVA, IORDANKA GEORGIEVA

(1911-1944)
  Bulgarian labor worker,
  politician
  Partington--Who's p204

NIKOVA, RINA
  Russian ballet dancer
  Macksey--Book p232

NILES, KATHRYN (fl. 1950's-1970's)
  Amer. cookery expert
  Felton--Famous p85-86

NILSON, ALICE
  See BABS, ALICE

NILSON, BARBRO (1899-)
  Swedish textile designer
  O'Neill--Women's p271

NILSSON, ANNA Q. (1888/1890-1974)
  Swedish photographer's model,
  actress, charity worker
  Lamparski--What. (3) p68-69,
  por.

NILSSON, (MÄRTA) BIRGIT (1918-)
  Swedish opera singer
  Claghorn--Biog. p328-329
  Gammond--Illus. p247, por.
  Neidle--America's p222
  O'Neill--Women's p620-621
  World--Who '78

NILSSON, CHRISTINE (1843-1921)
  Swedish opera singer, violinist
  Claghorn--Biog. p329
  Sherr--American p182

NIMMO, SYLVIA LEE (1937-)
  Amer. genealogical researcher,
  author, indexer
  Meyer--Who's p151

NIN, ANAÏS (1903-1977)
  French-Amer. novelist
  Avenel--Comp. (2) p192
  Betts--Writers p148-151, por.
  Cur. Biog. '75 p298-301, por.
  Cur. Biog. '77 p471
  Ehrlich--Oxford, see index p458
  Kupferberg--First p114-115, por.
  Moers--Literary p64,301
  Moffat--Revel. p86-97
  O'Neill--Women's p679-680, por.
  Seymour-Smith--Novels p192, por.
  Seymour-Smith--Who's p260-261
  Signif.--Amer. p70, por.

Webber--Woman p32-45
World--Who p35

NINON DE LENCLOS
See L'ENCLOS, NINON (ANNE)
DE

NISSEN, DOROTHY (fl. 1970's)
Amer. painter
Women's--Female p52

NISSEN, GRETA (1906-   )
Norwegian-Amer. dancer,
actress
Springer--They p189,319, por.

NITHSDALE, WINIFRED HERBERT
MAXWELL, COUNTESS OF
(-1749)
Scottish heroine
Jones--Rutledge p582

NITSCHMANN, ANNA (fl. 1740's)
Amer. Moravian leader
DePauw--Rem. p76

NIXON, AGNES (1925-   )
Amer. TV writer, producer
"All My Children"
Klever--Women p115-118, por.
Scheuer--Tel. p355

NIXON, HANNAH MILHOUS (1885-
1967)
Amer., mother of Richard
Nixon
Diagram--Mothers p192-193, por.
Faber--President's p19-35, por.
People's Almanac (1) p328-329

NIXON, JULIE
See EISENHOWER, JULIE NIXON

NIXON, MARION (1904-   )
Amer. actress
Springer--They p189,319, por.

NIXON, MARY (fl. 1770's)
Amer. Revolutionary War
patriot
Meyer--Petticoat p190,192-193

NIXON, PATRICIA ("PAT") THELMA
CATHERINE RYAN (1912-   )
Amer. teacher, first lady
Cur. Biog. '70 p315-317, por.
Hershey--Between p157-159,

169-171
Melick--Wives p86-87, por.
100--Greatest (1) p8, por.
People--Best p15, por.
People's Almanac (1) p320-321
Woman's Almanac p493-494
World--Who p299-300

NIXON, TRICIA
See COX, TRICIA NIXON

N'KANZA, LUSIBU Z.
African (Congolese) Minister
of Social Affairs
O'Neill--Women's p61

NOAILLES, ANNA BRANCOVAN,
COMTESSE DE (1876-1933)
French poet
Bree--Women p41,43-44
Crosland--Women p98-102, por.

NOBEL, ANN C. (fl. 1970's)
Amer. chemist
O'Neill--Women's p16

NOBLE, ELAINE (c1944-   )
Amer. member of Massachu-
setts House of Representatives
Lamson--In p109-143, por.
O'Neill--Women's p78

NOCHLIN, LINDA
Amer. feminist, art writer
Fine--Women p147,211, por.
O'Neill--Women's p594,596
Parker--Old p46-47,49,97,108,140
Women's--Female p116

NODDACK, IDA EVA TACKE (1896-   )
German chemist
Asimov--Biog. p656-657, (973)

NOEL, AUGUSTA, LADY (1838-
1902)
British novelist
Showalter--Lit. p334

NOEL, HATTON G., pseud.
See CAIRD, (ALICE) MONA

NOEL, SUZANNE (-1954)
French (plastic) surgeon
O'Neill--Women's p213

NOETHER, EMMY (AMALIE) (1882-
1935)

German mathematician, lec-
turer
Macksey--Book p154
O'Neill--Women's p175
Osen--Women p141-152

NOH, NORAH (fl. 1970's)
Korean fashion designer
O'Neill--Women's p254

NOLAN, DORIS (1916-)
Amer. actress
Springer--They p189-190,319-
320, por.

NOLAN, KATHY (KATHLEEN)
(1933-)
Amer. actress, labor union
leader
O'Neill--Women's p309,312,315,
por.
World--Who p243

NOLAN, MAE ELLA HUNT (1886-)
Amer. Congresswoman
Chamberlin--Min. p46-47, por.

NOLAN, MARY A.
See ROBERTSON, MARY IMO-
GENE

NOLDE, HELENE ALDEGONDE (fl.
1700-1790's)
German physician, medical
writer
Mead--Hist. p503

"NONHELEMA" ("GRENADIER
SQUAW") (fl. 1770's)
Amer. Indian Revolutionary
War patriot
Clyne--Patriots p131-132,135

NORDICA, LILLIAN, pseud. (1857-
1914)
Amer. opera singer
Claghorn--Biog. p330
James--Notable (2) p633-635
McHenry--Liberty's p304-305
Neuls-Bates--Women p122-130,
por.
Sherr--American p88
Tuggle--Golden p6, por.
Webster's--Amer. p771

NORDSTROM, FRANCES (fl. 1920's)
Amer. director
Smith--Movies p13, por.

NORELIUS, MARTHA (c1910-1955)
Amer. swimmer
Assoc. Press--Pursuit p101,119,
por.

NORENA, EIDE KAJA HANSEN
(1884-)
Norwegian opera singer
Claghorn--Biog. p330

NORMAN, MRS. HENRY (1867-)
English writer
Showalter--Lit. p344

NORMAN, JESSYE (1945/1946-)
Amer. opera singer
Claghorn--Biog. p330
Cur. Biog. '76 p292-295, por.
Gammond--Illus. p247, por.

NORMAN, JULIE BOWIE (1889-)
Amer. teacher, clubwoman,
noted Maryland mother
Amer.--Mothers p254-255

NORMAN, MARSHA WILLIAMS
(1947-)
Amer. playwright
Cur. Biog. '84 p302-305, por.

NORMAN-NERUDA, WILMA
See HALLE, WILHELMINA (WILMA)
MARIA FRANZISKA NORMAN-
NERUDA, LADY

NORMAND, MABEL ETHELREID
(1893/1898 1930)
Amer. comedienne, actress
James--Notable (2) p635-637
Keylin--Hollywood p224-225, por.
McHenry--Liberty's p305
Macksey--Book p233
Slide--Early p108

NORMANTON, HELENA (c1883-1957)
British barrister
Macksey--Book p127

NORRELL, CATHERINE DORRIS
(1901-)
Amer. Congresswoman
Chamberlin--Min. p286-289

NORRIS, DIANA STRAWBRIDGE
Amer. millionaire
Forbes--400 ('84) p82

NORRIS, KATHLEEN THOMPSON

(1880-1966)
Amer. novelist
Dunlap--Calif. p151, por.
Sicherman--Notable p509-511

NORRIS, MARY
See ALLERTON, MARY NORRIS

NORSTRAND, LUCILLE JOYCE
(fl. 1970's)
Amer. urological surgeon
O'Neill--Women's p216

NORSWORTHY, NAOMI (1877-1916)
Amer. educational psychologist
Bachtold--Gifted p67-70

NORTH, MARIANNE (1830-1890)
English botanist, traveller,
naturalist, painter
Macksey--Book p238

"NORTH, MRS."
See FROST, ALICE

NORTHCHURCH, BARONESS
See DAVIDSON, LADY

NORTHCOTT, KAYE (fl. 1970's)
Amer. journalist, editor
O'Neill--Women's p480

NORTHEN, REBECCA TYSON
(1910-)
Amer. orchid grower, noted
Wyoming mother
Amer.--Mothers p599-600, por.

NORTON, ALICE MARY
See NORTON, ANDRE, pseud.

NORTON, ALICE PELOUBET
(1860-1928)
Amer. home economics,
teacher
James--Notable (2) p637-638

NORTON, AMANDA ALLEN (fl.
1920's)
Amer. letter-writer, (sister
of Lillian Nordica)
Neuls-Bates--Women p122-123,
125-130

NORTON, ANDRE, pseud. (1912-)
Amer. novelist, librarian
Seymour-Smith--Novels p193

NORTON, CAROLINE ELIZABETH
SARAH (1808-1877)
English poet, novelist, feminist,
social worker
Avenel--Comp. (1) p393
Basch--Relative, see index p356
Macksey--Book p79-81, por.
Moers--Literary p116,301
Showalter--Lit. p323
Taylor--Gener. p12-13

NORTON, ELEANOR HOLMES
(1937-)
Amer. lawyer, civil rights
worker, government official,
feminist
Bird--Enterprising p227-230
Cur. Biog. '76 p295-298, por.
Diamonstein--Open p298-301, por.
Gilbert--Part. p143-151, por.
Halcomb--Women p174-186
Hymowitz--Hist. p337,363
Lamson--In p145-183, por.
O'Neill--Women's p366-367
Walker--Women p62-74, por.
Warren--Pictorial p200,208
Woman's Almanac p524
World--Who p148

NORTON, LILLIE
See NORDICA, LILLIAN, pseud.

NORTON, MAGGIE (fl. 1970's)
Amer. craftswoman
Women's--Female p21

NORTON, MARY TERESA HOPKINS
(1875-1959)
Amer. Congresswoman
Bachtold--Gifted p97-98
Chamberlin--Min. p52-57
Miller--Fishbait p205
Sicherman--Notable p511-512
Ware--Beyond p150, see also
index p201

NORTON-TAYLOR, JUDY (1958-)
Amer. actress
World--Who p243

NORWOOD, ELIZABETH C. (fl.
1950's-1970's)
Amer. labor leader
O'Neill--Women's p300-301

NORESTEIN, ADA
See COMSTOCK, ADA LOUISE

NOTTINGHAM, ESSEX FINCH,
COUNTESS OF (c1652-1683/
1684)
English socialite
Ware--Meet p79

NOURSE, MARY MADELINE
(1870-1959)
Amer. china painter
Callen--Women p225

NOVAES, (PINTO) GUIOMAR
(1895-1979)
Brazilian pianist
Claghorn--Biog. p331
O'Neill--Women's p630-631

NOVAK, EVA (1898-)
Amer. actress
Lamparski--What. Annual (4,5)
p143-148, por.

NOVAK, HELGA (1935-)
German-Icelandic poet
Herrmann--Ger. p6,106-107

NOVAK, JANE (1896-)
Amer. actress
Lamparski--What. Annual (4,5)
p143-148, por.

NOVAK, KIM (MARILYN PAULINE)
(1933-)
Amer. actress
Hirschhorn--Rating p284-285,
por.
Mordden--Movie p228-230
Shipman--Internatl. p446-451,
por.

NOVAK, LUCILE KAUFMANN
(1929-)
Amer. genealogical researcher,
author, editor
Meyer--Who's p152

NOVARA, SUE (fl. 1970's)
Amer. cyclist
Hollander--100 p12-13, por.
O'Neill--Women's p559-560

NOVELLA, MARIA DI (fl. 13th
Cent.)
Italian mathematics professor
Mead--Hist. p225

NOVELLO, CLARA (1818-1908)

British singer
Macksey--Book p214

NOVELLO, MARY (1818-1908)
British concert business
manager, singer
Macksey--Book p214

NOVITSKAYA, ANASTASIA (1819-)
Russian ballet dancer
Mandel--Soviet p19-20

NOWELL, ELIZABETH DAVIS (fl.
1900's)
Amer. Arctic pioneer, writer
Sherr--American p5

NOWICKI, STELLA (fl. 1970's)
Amer. labor leader
O'Neill--Women's p328

NOYES, BLANCHE WILCOX (1900-
1981)
Amer. aviatrix
Boase--Sky's p116

NOYES, CLARA DUTTON (1869-
1936)
Amer. nurse, educator,
author
McHenry--Liberty's p305-306

NUBIN, ROSETTA
See THARPE, ROSETTA, SISTER

NUGENT, LUCI BAINES JOHNSON
(1947-)
Amer., daughter of Lyndon
Johnson
Hershey--Between p167-169

NICE, MRS. (fl. 1622)
Amer. nurse
Williams--Demeter's p154

THE NUN ENSIGN
See ERANSO (ERANZO), CATA-
LINA DE

NURMI, MAILA (1921-)
Finnish-Amer. dancer, actress
Lamparski--What. Annual (4,5)
p346-350, por.
Lamparski--What. (8) p286-287,
por.

NURSE, REBECCA (1621-1692)

Amer. accused witch
James--Notable (2) p638-640
Sherr--American p103-104
Warren--Pictorial p34
Williams--Demeter's p140-141

NUSSBAUM, KAREN (1950-   )
Amer. founder, office worker's organization, labor
leader
O'Neill--Women's p305

NUSSBAUM, MRS.
See PIOUS, MINERVA

NUTHEAD, DINAH (-1695)
Amer. businesswoman, colonial
printer, noted Maryland
mother
Amer.--Mothers p250
Demeter--Primer p7-12
Marzolf--Up p1
Stein--Lives no p.
Williams--Demeter's p199-200

NUTTALL, ZELIA MARIA MAG-
DALENA (1857/1888-1933)
Amer. archaeologist
James--Notable (2) p640-642
McHenry--Liberty's p306

NUTTING, MARY ADELAIDE
(1858-1948)
Amer. nursing educator,
professor
James--Notable (2) p642-644
McHenry--Liberty's p306-307
O'Neill--Women's p232

NYAD, DIANA SNEED (1949-   )
Amer. swimmer
Cur. Biog. '79 p280-283, por.
Gurtman--More p63-81, por.
Hollander--100 p92-93, por.
Lichtenstein--Mach., see index
p365
O'Neill--Women's p586

NYMAN, GUNNEL (1909-1948)
Finnish furniture, glass
designer
O'Neill--Women's p275

NYRO, LAURA (1949-   )
Amer. singer
Claghorn--Biog. p331
World--Who p270

NYSWANDER, MARIE E. (1919-   )
Amer. physician, psychiatrist
Talmey--Vogue p230-231, por.

NZINGHA (ANN ZINGHA) (1582-
1663)
West African Amazon queen,
Mutamba
Taylor--Gener. p21-22

O

OAKEY, EMILY SULLIVAN (1829-
1883)
Amer. hymnist
Claghorn--Biog. p333

OAKLEY, ANNIE (1860-1926)
Amer. markswoman, sharp-
shooter
Coffin--Female p192-195, por.
Earnest--American p197-199
Entertainers p148
James--Notable (2) p644-646
Kirk--Circus p46-48, por.
Kulkin--Her p217-218
McHenry--Liberty's p308
Macksey--Book p229,256, por.
McWhirter--Guinness p115, por.
People's Almanac (2) p1357-1359,
por.
Sherr--American p94,153,186
Signif.--Amer. p32, por.
Webster's--Amer. p775
Woman's Almanac p324, por.
World--Who p292

OATES, JOYCE CAROL (1938-   )
Amer. novelist, poet, short
story writer, critic, professor
Cahill--Women p314-315,378-379
Cur. Biog. '70 p318-320, por.
Diamonstein--Open p302-307, por.
Ehrlich--Oxford p337
McHenry--Liberty's p308
Seymour-Smith--Novels p193
Webber--Woman p172-176
World--Who p18

OATMAN, OLIVE ANN (c 1838-1903)
Amer. Indian captive
James--Notable (2) p646-647
Sherr--American p7-8, por.
Time--Women p62,64, por.

O'BANION, NANCY (fl. 1970's)
Amer. textile artist
Women's--Female p99

OBENG, LETITIA
Ghanian aquatic biologist
Macksey--Book p159

OBER, MARGARETTE
German opera singer
Tuggle--Golden p129-130, por.

OBERG, MARGO (c1955-)
Amer. surfer
O'Neill--Women's p585

OBERON, MERLE (1911-1979)
Tasmanian-Amer. actress
Cur. Biog. '80 p461
Hirschhorn--Rating p286, por.
Shipman--Gold. p424-426, por.
Springer--They p190,320, por.
World--Who p260

OBEY, TRUDEL MIMMS (fl. 1970's)
Amer. artist
Fax--Black p131-148, por.

OBOUSSIER, HELENE (fl. 1920's)
Belgian broker
Macksey--Book p169-170

OBRAZTSOVA, ELENA (c1939-)
Russian singer
Cur. Biog. '83 p273-276, por.

O'BRIAN, JANE
See BRYAN, JANE

O'BRIEN, BAYNE PALMER (1920-)
Amer. genealogical researcher,
writer
Meyer--Who's p155

O'BRIEN, EDNA (1930-)
Irish short story writer,
novelist
Baker--Women p7
Cahill--Women p288,378
Cur. Biog. '80 p291-294, por.
P.W.--Author p114-116,518
Seymour-Smith--Novels p193,
por.
Showalter--Lit. p350
World--Who p29

O'BRIEN, ESTELLE MERLE
See OBERON, MERLE

O'BRIEN, KATE (1897-1974)
Irish novelist
Magill--Cycl. p796-797

O'BRIEN, MARGARET (ANGELA
MAXINE) (1937-)
Amer. child actress
Edleson--Kids p31-34,47-48, por.
Lamparski--What. (2) p128-129,
por.
Shipman--Gold. p427-428, por.
World--Who p244

O'BRIEN, MARY
See SPRINGFIELD, DUSTY

O'BRIEN, VIRGINIA (1921-)
Amer. singer, comedienne
Lamparski--What. (4) p46-47,
por.
Lamparski--What. (8) p224-225,
por.

O'BRIEN-MOORE, ERIN (1908-)
Amer. actress
Springer--They p190,320, por.

O'BRYAN, MOLLIE
Amer. broker, mine owner
Sherr--American p25

O'BRYANT, JOAN (1923-)
Amer. singer
Claghorn--Biog. p333

OCAMPO, ROSELI
See FRIEDMANN, ROSELI OCAMPO

O'CARROLL, MARIE MADELEINE
BERNADETTE
See CARROLL, MADELEINE

O'CASEY, EILEEN (1924-)
British biographer
P.W.--Author p245-247,518

OCCIDENTE, MARIE DEL, pseud.
See BROOKS, MARIA GOWEN

OCHOA, ELISA (fl. 1940's)
Filipino Congresswoman
Macksey--Book p40

OCHOWICZ, SHEILA YOUNG
See YOUNG, SHEILA

OCKLEMAN, CONSTANCE MARIE
See LAKE, VERONICA

OCLOO, ESTHER (fl. 1940's)
Ghanian bottling industry
executive, association founder

Macksey--Book p169
O'Neill--Women's p514

O'CONNELL, ANTHONY, SISTER
(1814-1897)
Amer. nun, Civil War nurse
James--Notable (2) p647-648
Neidle--America's p75

O'CONNELL, HELEN (1920/1921-)
Amer. singer
Lamparski--What. (3) p38-39,
por.
Simon--Best p181-182, por.
Simon--Big p290-291, por.
World--Who p270

O'CONNELL, JOAN (fl. 1970's)
Amer. agriculturist, associa-
tion co-founder
O'Neill--Women's p1

O'CONNOR, (MARY) FLANNERY
(1925-1964)
Amer. novelist, short story
writer
Avenel--Comp. (2) p194
Betts--Writers p110-115, por.
Cahill--Women p246,378
Howard--Seven p311-355
McHenry--Liberty's p308-309
Moers--Literary p301
O'Neill--Women's p682,690
Seymour-Smith--Novels p193-194
Seymour-Smith--Who's p262-263
Sicherman--Notable p512-515
Signif.--Amer. p70, por.
Webber--Woman p97-103
World--Who p18

O'CONNOR, JULIA
See PARKER, JULIA SARSFIELD
O'CONNOR

O'CONNER, MARTHA
See CONNERS, MARTHA

O'CONNOR, NANCY (c1931-)
Amer., wife of Carroll
O'Connor
Funt--Are p275-288, por.

O'CONNOR, SANDRA DAY (1930-)
Amer. Supreme Court justice
Cur. Biog. '82 p297-301, por.
People--Best p147, por.

O'CONNOR, UNA (1880-1959)
Irish actress
Springer--They p190,320, por.
World--Who p260

OCTAVIA (c69-11 B.C.)
Roman, wife of Marc
Anthony, sister of Augustus,
physician
Mead--Hist. p59-60
Pomeroy--Godd. p156,183-187

O'DAY, ANITA (1919-)
Amer. singer
Claghorn--Biog. p333
Claghorn--Jazz p224
Simon--Best p442, por.
World--Who p270

O'DAY, CAROLINE LOVE (1875-1943)
Amer. Congresswoman, artist,
social welfare worker
Chamberlin--Min. p108-112
James--Notable (2) p648-650
Ware--Beyond p150, see also
index p201

O'DAY, DAWN
See SHIRLEY, ANNE

O'DEA, ANNE CALDWELL (1867-1936)
Amer. singer, actress, lyricist
Claghorn--Biog. p333

ODETTA (ODETTE), (HOLMES-
FELIOUS) GORDON (1930-)
Amer. singer
Claghorn--Biog. p334
World--Who p270

ODILIA (OTILLA) OF HOHENBURG
(fl. 8th Cent.)
German blind abbess, physician
Mead--Hist. p102

ODLUM, DORIS (1890-)
British physician
Hellstedt--Women p49-54, por.

ODLUM, JACQUELINE
See COCHRAN, JACQUELINE

O'DONNELL, MARIE
See "MARGO"

OELMAN, RUTH (fl. 1920's)

Amer. film "location finder"
Slide--Early p10

OELRICHS, BLANCHE MARIE
See STRANGE, MICHAEL

OELSNER, MARLIES (fl. 1970's)
East German track and field
athlete
O'Neill--Women's p575-576

O'FARRELL, MARY ANN CHAPMAN
(fl. 1860's)
Irish-Amer. charitable western pioneer, gold-miner's
wife
Sherr--American p56

O'FREDERICKS, ALICE (fl. 1950's)
Danish film director
Smith--Movies p101

OGAWA, PELORHANKHE
See AI

OGLE, JANE (fl. 1970's)
Amer. fashion magazine
editor
O'Neill--Women's p480

OGLE, SANDRA K. (1943-)
Amer. genealogical researcher,
author, editor
Meyer--Who's p155

OGOT, GRACE
African (Kenyan) store
proprietor, scriptwriter,
author, broadcaster
Macksey--Book p177

O'GRADY, JANE (fl. 1960's-
1970's)
Amer. labor lobbyist
O'Neill--Women's p285,301

O'HAIR, MADALYN MURRAY
(1919-)
Amer. social activist,
lawyer, atheist, author
Cur. Biog. '77 p328-331, por.
Golson--Playboy p136-152
McHenry--Liberty's p309
People's Almanac (1) p1294
World--Who p83

O'HANLON, VIRGINIA

Amer. letter-writer, child
celebrity
People's Almanac (1) p1358-1359
Woman's Almanac p52

O'HARA, ANNE
See MARTIN, ANNE HENRIETTA

O'HARA, CATHERINE
Canadian TV writer, performer
Scheuer--Tel. p361

O'HARA, MAUREEN (1920-)
Irish actress
Hirschhorn--Rating p287-288, por.
Shipman--Internatl. p448-451, por.
Springer--They p190,320, por.
Wilson--Holly. p21-24, por.
World--Who p260

O'HARA, MARY ALSOP STURE-
VASA (1885-1980)
Amer. novelist, film writer
Cur. Biog. '81 p470
Ehrlich--Oxford p180,381
World--Who p18

O'HARE, KATE RICHARDS
See CUNNINGHAM, KATE
RICHARDS O'HARE

OHNESORGE, LENA (1898-)
West German physician
Hellstedt--Women p159-162, por.

OIKAWA-PICANTE, TERI (fl. 1970's)
Amer. museum conservator of
paintings
Women's--Female p119

O'KANE, HELEN MARGUERITE (fl.
1900's)
Amer. designer, illustrator
Callen--Women p184,225

O'KEEFFE, GEORGIA (1887-1986)
Amer. painter
Clark--Leading p184-185
Fine--Women p191-194
Fowler--Art p55-77, por.
Gilfond--Heroines p119-120, por.
Haftmann--Paint. (1) p410
Harris--Women p300-306
Henkes--Eight p8-13,50-51
Ingraham--Album p61
Longstreet--Queen p186-187
McHenry--Liberty's p309-310

Munro--Originals p75-92
Munsterberg--Hist. p71-72,74-75
100--Greatest (1) p77, por.
O'Neill--Women's p496,596,600
People--Best p130-131, por.
Petersen--Women p121-123
Talmey--Vogue p146-153, por.
Warren--Pictorial p180-181
Webster's--Amer. p777
Woman's Almanac p223-224
Women's--Female p52
World--Who p60

OKUBO, MINE (fl. 1970's)
    Amer. artist (drawing)
    Women's--Female p29

OKUMURA, KATSU (-1942)
    Amer., noted Hawaii mother
    Amer.--Mothers p144-145, por.

OLAH, SUSI (1869-1929)
    Hungarian accused criminal
    People's Almanac (2) p1118

OLANDER, JOAN LUCILLE
    See VAN DOREN, MAMIE

OLAY, RUTH (1927-)
    Amer. singer
    Claghorn--Jazz p224

OLDFIELD, ANNE ("NANCE")
    (1683-1730)
    English actress
    Entertainers p84, por.
    Findlater--Player p49-60, por.

OLDFIELD, PEARL PEDEN (1876-
    1962)
    Amer. Congresswoman
    Chamberlin--Min. p65-66

O'LEARY, CATHERINE (fl. 1870's)
    Amer. "dairy farmer,"
    (Chicago fire)
    Sherr--American p59

OLESNICKA, ZOFIA (fl. c1550)
    Polish poet
    Bainton--Spain p169-173, por.

OLFORD, BESSIE SANTMIRE
    (1893-)
    Amer. missionary, mother of
    Stephen F. Olford, evanglist
    Kooiman--Silhouettes p13-19, por.

OLFORD, HEATHER BROWN
    Irish musician, wife of Stephen
    F. Olford, evangelist
    Kooiman--Silhouettes p20-29, por.

OLGA (1) (-969/978)
    Russian regent of Kiev, (intro-
    duced Christianity to Russia),
    Saint, princess
    Macksey--Book p21

"OLGA" (2)
    Polish-Amer. fashion designer
    O'Neill--Women's p258

OLIPHANT, GRASSELLA (1929-)
    Amer. drummer
    Claghorn--Biog. p335

OLIPHANT, MARGARET WILSON
    (1828-1897)
    Scottish novelist
    Avenel--Comp. (1) p401
    Crosland--Beyond p131
    Moers--Literary p301
    Seymour-Smith--Novels p194
    Showalter--Lit. p330

OLIVAREZ, GRACIELA (fl. 1970's)
    Amer. lawyer
    O'Neill--Women's p716

OLIVER, ANNA (-1893)
    Amer. clergyman, feminist
    O'Neill--Women's p378

OLIVER, DONNA (fl. 1970's)
    Amer. research psychologist
    (Antarctica)
    Land--New p135-146, por.

OLIVER, EDITH (fl. 1960's-1970's)
    Amer. drama critic
    Chiony--Women p226,228-229,
    por.

OLIVER, EDNA MAY (1883-1942)
    Amer. actress, comedienne
    Springer--They p190,192,320,
    por.
    World--Who p244

OLIVERO, MAGDA (c1913-)
    Amer. opera singer
    Claghorn--Biog. p335
    Cur. Biog. '80 p294-297, por.

OLIVEROS, PAULINE (1932-   )
Amer. composer
Jablonski--Ency. p548
LePage--Women p165-190, por.

"OLIVIA," pseud.
See BRIGGS, EMILY POMONA
EDSON

OLMSTEAD, MARY S. (1919-   )
Amer. ambassador
O'Neill--Women's p92,95

OLMSTED, VIRGINIA L. (1916-   )
Amer. genealogical researcher,
author, indexer, editor
Meyer--Who's p155

OLOWO, BERNADETTE (fl. 1970's)
Ugandan ambassador
O'Neill--Women's p43,63

OLSEN, SANDRA (fl. 1970's)
Amer. physician
Seed--Saturday's p62-64, por.

OLSEN, TILLIE (1913-   )
Amer. short-story writer,
novelist, critic
Cahill--Women p162-163,377
Moers--Literary p301
Ruddick--Working p323-340,
344-345, por.
Seymour-Smith--Novels p194
Webber--Woman p53-67

OLSON, CAROL (fl. 1970's)
Amer. clergyman
O'Neill--Women's p382

OLSON, LYNNE (fl. 1970's)
Amer. journalist, foreign
correspondent
O'Neill--Women's p457

OLSSON, ELVY (1923-   )
Swedish prime minister
O'Neill--Women's p52

OLTMAN, FLORINE (ALMA)
(1915-   )
Amer. librarian, organization
official
Cur. Biog. '70 p327-328, por.

OLYMPIA OF ANTIOCH (fl. 390's)
Greek physician
Mead--Hist. p80

OLYMPIAS (360-408/410)
Greek Saint, (wife of Philip
II, mother of Alexander the
Great)
Pomeroy--Godd. p122
Zinserling--Women p37

OMLIE, PHOEBE JANE FAIRGRAVE
(1902/1903-1975)
Amer. aviatrix, (stunt flier),
instructor, government offi-
cial, humanitarian
Boase--Wky's p22,117-118,126
Genett--Aviation p111-112
Sicherman--Notable p515-517

O'MURPHY, LOUISE (c1737-1814)
Irish artist's model
Book--Lists (1) p191-192

ONASSIS, CHRISTINA (1950-   )
Greek heiress (daughter of
Aristotle Onassis), shipping
executive
Anderson--People p304-305, por.
Cur. Biog. '76 p298-301, por.
O'Neill--Women's p522-523
Woman's Almanac p212, por.

ONASSIS, JACQUELINE ("JACKIE")
BOUVIER KENNEDY (1929-   )
Amer. first lady (wife of John
F. Kennedy, Aristotle Onassis),
book editor
Anderson--People p306, por.
Clark--Leading p225-227
Hershey--Between p36-37,47-51,
155
Keenan--Women p22,24, por.
Kulkin--Her p218-219
Kupferberg--First p117-118, por.
Longstreet--Queen p165-168
McHenry--Liberty's p310
Macksey--Book p104
Melick--Wives p79-82, por.
Miller--Fishbait p298-300, por.
100--Greatest (1) p109, por.
O'Neill--Women's p594,751, por.
People--Best p112, por.
People's Almanac (1) p311
People's Almanac (3) p158-160
Sochen--Herstory p383-384
Woman's Almanac p492-493, por.
World--Who p300

O'NEAL, TATUM (1963-   )
Amer. actress, child celebrity
Anderson--People p307-308, por.

OPDYKE, THERESA
See HELBURN, THERESA

OPIE, AMELIA ALDERSON
(1769-1853)
English novelist
Moers--Literary p302

OPIE, IONA
British children's book author
Macksey--Book p193

OPIE, JULIET ANN
See HOPKINS, JULIET ANN
OPIE

OPPENHEIM, MERET (1913-)
German-Swiss artist
Fine--Women p177-178
Parker--Old p137,143-144,
fig. 87

OPPENHEIM, SALLY (1930-)
British Parliament member
Vallance--Women p50,57,65,79,
91,109

OPPENHEIMER, BRIDGET (fl.
1970's)
South African activist
O'Neill--Women's p731

OPPENHEIMER, LILLIAN (1898-)
Amer. origami artist,
puppeteer
Gold--Until p255-274, por.

ORCHARD, SADIE (c1863-1943)
Amer. entrepreneur
Sherr--American p155-156, por.

ORCZY, EMMUSKA (1865-1947)
Hungarian-English Baroness,
novelist, playwright
Jones--Rutledge p591-592
Seymour-Smith--Novels p195
World--Who p42

ORDWAY, ELIZABETH (fl. 1870's)
Amer. pioneer teacher
Sherr--American p241

O'REILLY, LEONORA (1870-1927)
Amer. labor leader, social
reformer
Hymowitz--Hist. p248
James--Notable (2) p651-653
Lagemann--Gen. p89-112, por.

Neidle--America's p125
O'Neill--Women's p290

OREM, DONNA M. (fl. 1970's)
Amer. journalist
O'Neill--Women's p509

ORENSTEIN, GLORIA (fl. 1970's)
Amer. art editor
Women's--Female p116

"ORINDA"
See PHILIPS, KATHERINE
FOWLER

ORKIN, RUTH (fl. 1950's)
Amer. photo-journalist, film
director
Marzolf--Up p83
Smith--Movies p39

ORLIKOVA, VALENTINA (fl. 1940's-
1970's)
Russian boat captain
Mandel--Soviet p82-83

ORMAN, SARAH
Amer. Confederate patriot
Sherr--American p43

ORMSBY-GORE, JANE (fl. 1960's)
English fashion setter
Keenan--Women p208,210-211, por.

ORNDOFF, CARLA (fl. 1960's-1970's)
Amer. Air Force lieutenant
O'Neill--Women's p544

ORNE, REBECCA TAYLOR (1727-)
Amer., wife of colonial merchant
Earle--Two Cent. (2) p xiii,502,
por.

ORON, MAIRI MHOR NAN
See MacPHERSON, MARY

ORSAY, FIFI D'
See D'ORSAY, FIFI

ORTNER, BEVERLY ("BEVA") (fl.
1960's)
Amer. bowler
McWhirter--Guinness p42, por.
O'Neill--Women's p558
People's Almanac (1) p1197

ORWELL, SONIA (1918-)

English literary hostess
Plante--Difficult. p63-101,153-173

OSBORN, EMILY MARY (1814/1834-
c1885)
British artist
Harris--Women p228

OSBORN, ETHELINDA MURRAY
(1918-)
Amer. community worker,
noted Arizona mother
Amer.--Mothers p35, por.

OSBORNE, DOROTHY (1627-1695)
English letter writer
Jones--Rutledge p593
Morley--Literary p408-409

OSBORNE, MARY (1921-)
Amer. guitarist, singer
Claghorn--Jazz p226

OSBORNE, SARAH (fl. 1680's-
1690's)
Amer. accused witch, slave
Sherr--American p103

OSBORNE, VIVIENNE (1896-1961)
Amer. actress
Springer--They p193,321, por.

OSGOOD, FRANCES SARGENT
LOCKE (1811/1812-1850)
Amer. poet
James--Notable (2) p653-655

OSGOOD, HELEN LOUISE GILSON
See GILSON, HELEN LOUISE

OSLUND, ANNA MARIE (1891-)
Swedish-Amer. teacher, li-
brarian, noted Idaho mother
Amer.--Mothers p155-156, por.

OSMER, MARGARET ("MEG")
Amer. TV reporter, pro-
ducer, newscaster
Marzolf--Up p184,187
O'Neill--Women's p505

OSMOND, (OLIVE) MARIE (1959-)
Amer. singer
Anderson--People p309-310, por.
World--Who p271

OSNATH (fl. 17th Cent.)

Jewish poet
Henry--Written p108

OSSOLI, (SARAH) MARGARET
MARCHIONESS D'
See FULLER, (SARAH) MARGARET

OST, RUTH ELIN (1886-1953)
Amer. pioneer missionary,
noted Alaska mother, midwife
Amer.--Mothers p18, por.
Jones--Women (1) p142-145

OSTENSO, MARTHA (1900-1963)
Norwegian-Amer. novelist
Ehrlich--Oxford, p341,343,392
Neidle--America's p262-264

ÖSTERBERG, MARTINA
Swedish physical educator
Macksey--Book p73

ØSTERGAARD, LISE (fl. 1970's)
Danish minister of foreign
affairs
O'Neill--Women's p57

OSTERMEYER, MICHELINE (c1923-)
French track and field athlete,
pianist
Hollander--100 p124-125

OSTINELLI, SOPHIE HENRIETTE
HEWITT (-1846)
Amer. organist, singer
Claghorn--Biog. p338

OSTROUMOVA-LEBEDEVA, ANNA
PETROVNA (1871-1955)
Russian engraver, water-
colorist
Women's--Female p1, supp.

O'SULLIVAN, MARY KENNEY (1864-
1943)
Amer. bookbinder, labor leader
Hymowitz--Hist. p230-231,248
James--Notable (2) p655-656
McHenry--Liberty's p310-311
O'Neill--Women's p289,294-295

O'SULLIVAN, MAUREEN (1911-)
Irish-Amer. actress
Edelson--Kids p44-45
Springer--They p193-194,321,
por.
World--Who p244

OSWALD, MARINA NIKOLAEVNA
(1942-)
Russian, (wife of Lee Harvey
Oswald)
People's Almanac (2) p50-52

OTIS, EMILY MARSHALL (1807-1836)
Amer. social leader, beauty
Peacock--Famous p90-101, por.

OTTENBERG, MIRIAM
Amer. journalist
Marzolf--Up p71-72,80-82
O'Neill--Women's p452-454

OTTENBERG, NETTIE PODELL
(c1887-)
Amer. association founder
O'Neill--Women's p106

OTTENDORFER, ANNA SARTORIUS
UHL (1815-1884)
Bavarian-Amer. newspaper
publisher, philanthropist
James--Notable (2) p656-657
McHenry--Liberty's p311
Neidle--America's p48-50,137

OTTIANO, RAFAELA (1894-1942)
Italian-French actress
Springer--They p194,321, por.

OTTILA (OR OTTILIA) OF HOHEN-
BURG
See ODILIA OF HOHENBURG

OTTO, ALICE (c1870-)
Amer. centenarian
Mitchell--Yessir p85-87, por.

OTTO-PETER, LUISE (1819-1895)
German feminist, newspaper
founder
Macksey--Book p87-88

OUGHTON, DIANA (1942-1970)
Amer. "weatherman"
Lichtenstein--Mach. p162-164

"OUIDA," pseud. (1839-1908)
English novelist
Avenel--Comp. (1) p406
Jones--Rutledge p595
Magill--Cycl. p813-184
Morley--Literary p82
Seymour-Smith--Novels p195
Showalter--Lit. p334

OUILMETTE, ARCHANGE (fl. 1830's)
Amer. Indian landowner
Sherr--American p64

OULD, MATTIE (fl. 1860's)
Amer. Southern belle,
socialite
DeLeon--Belles p103-104, por.
Peacock--Famous p230-238, por.

OUSLEY, MAYME H. (c1887-)
Amer. mayor
Sherr--American p132

OUSPENSKAYA, MARIA (1876-1949)
Russian-Amer. actress
Springer--They p194,321, por.
World--Who p244

OUTERBRIDGE, MARY (fl. 1870's)
Amer. tennis player
Earnest--American p229
Macksey--Book p256-257
McWhirter--Guinness p148
Sullivan--Queens p98

OVCHINNIKOVA, ALEXANDRA (fl. 1960's)
Russian technical engineer,
government official
O'Neill--Women's p59

OVERBECK, ELIZABETH GRAY
Amer. craftswoman
Callen--Women p90-92, por.

OVERTON, JULIE M. (1939-)
Amer. genealogical researcher,
author, indexer
Meyer--Who's p156

OVINGTON, MARY WHITE (1865-1951)
Amer. civil rights reformer
Sicherman--Notable p517-519

OVITZ, CAROL (fl. 1970's)
Amer. commodities broker
Seed--Saturday's p121-124, por.

OWEN, CATHERINE DALE (1925-1965)
Amer. beauty, actress
Springer--They p194,321, por.

OWEN, GRACE
British educator, (nursery

schools)
Macksey--Book p76

OWEN, JULIETTE (-1943)
Amer. ornithologist
Sherr--American p132-133, por.

OWEN, LAWRENCE (-1961)
Amer. skater
Hollander--100 p30

OWEN, LUELLA
Amer. geologist
Sherr--American p132, por.

OWEN, MARABELLE VINSON
See VINSON-OWEN, MARIBEL

OWEN, MARGARET (fl. 1910's)
Amer. typist
Macksey--Book p174

OWEN, MARIE (fl. 1890's)
Amer. detective
Macksey--Book p137

OWEN, MARIE BANKHEAD
(1869-)
Amer. historian, noted
Alabama mother
Amer.--Mothers p3, por.

OWEN, MARJORIE LEWIS
Amer. publisher, journalist,
noted Washington state
mother
Amer.--Mothers p566-567, por.

OWEN, MARY ALICIA (1858-)
Amer. authority on Indian
folklore
Sherr--American p132, por.

OWEN, NARCISSA CHISHOLM
(1831-)
Amer. teacher, noted
Oklahoma mother
Amer.--Mothers p438

OWEN, RUTH BRYAN (1885-1954)
Amer. Congresswoman,
diplomat, lecturer, author
Chamberlin--Min. p73-78, por.
Hazen--Interv. p200
McHenry--Liberty's p353

O'Neill--Women's p91
Sicherman--Notable p591-593
Ware--Beyond p151, see also
index p200

OWENS, ANGELA
Amer. TV reporter
Scheuer--Tel. p364-365

OWENS, BONNIE (1933-)
Amer. singer
Claghorn--Biog. p339

OWENS, CHARLENE B. (fl. 1950's-
1970's)
Amer. businesswoman
Innis--Profiles p96-97, por.

OWENS, ELISABETH (fl. 1940's-
1970's)
Amer. lawyer, professor,
research director
Swiger--Women p135-151

OWENS, MARGARET (1892-)
Canadian physician
Hellstedt--Women p79-84, por.

OWENS, ROCHELLE (1936-)
Amer. poet, playwright
Chester--Rising p248-252, por.
Chinoy--Women p131, por.

OWENS-ADAIR, BETHENIA
See ADAIR, BETHENIA ANGELINA
OWENS

OXENBRIDGE, MRS. (fl. 1640-
1660)
English-Amer. scholar
Williams--Demeter's p122

OZBIRN, CATHERINE FREEMAN
(c1900-1974)
Amer. organization official
Cur. Biog. '74 p467

OZICK, CYNTHIA (1928-)
Amer. author
Cur. Biog. '83 p279-283, por.
Webber--Woman p104-114

P

PAASNUORI, TYNNE (1907-)

Finnish agricultural coopera-
tive worker
O'Neill--Women's p321

PACA, ANNE HARRISON (-1780)
Amer. patriot, (wife of
William Paca)
Booth--Women p157-158

PACE, NORMA (c1923-)
Amer. economist, trade
association official
O'Neill--Women's p520

PACHAUDE, LEONARD OF AVIGNON,
DAME (fl. 15th Cent.)
French barber-surgeon
Mead--Hist. p307

PACKARD, ELEANOR (1905-1972)
Amer. journalist
Cur. Biog. '72 p468

PACKARD, ELIZABETH PARSONS
WARE (1816-1897)
Amer. social reformer,
feminist
James--Notable (2) p1-2
Sherr--American p62

PACKARD, EMMY LOU (fl. 1970's)
Amer. painter
Women's--Female p53

PACKARD, SOPHIA B. (1824-1891)
Amer. educator, college
founder
James--Notable (2) p2-4
McHenry--Liberty's p312

PADDLEFORD, CLEMENTINE
HASKIN (1900-1967)
Amer. columnist, journalist,
chef
Woman's Almanac p270-271

PADDOCK, LYDIA (fl. 1770's)
Amer. patriot
Booth--Women p35-36

PADDY, ELIZABETH (1641-)
Amer. early settler
Earle--Two Cent. (1) p xv,72,
por.

PADERSON, INGER (fl. 1970's)
Danish judge
Macksey--Book p127

PADISHAL, MADAM (fl. 17th Cent.)
Amer. early settler
Earle--Two Cent. (1) p xiii,71f,
273,275,277,315, por.

PAGE, ANITA (1910-)
Amer. actress
Lamparski--What. (5) p148, por.
Springer--They p197,321, por.

PAGE, GALE (1913-)
Amer. actress
Springer--They p197,321-322,
por.

PAGE, GERALDINE (1924-1987)
Amer. actress
Entertainers p263, por.
Shipman--Internatl. p458-460,
por.
World--Who p244

PAGE, MRS. JEREMIAH (fl. 1770's)
Amer. Revolutionary War
patriot
Sherr--American p104

PAGE, MRS. LEIGH R.
See WALLER, PAGE

PAGE, OLA MAE
Amer. servant
Gold--Until p330-331

PAGE, PATTI (1927-)
Amer. singer
Claghorn--Biog. p341
Simon--Best p450-451, por.
World--Who p271

PAGE, RUTH (1900-)
Amer. choreographer, ballet
dancer
O'Neill--Women's p642

PAGELSON, HENRIETTE (fl. 1860's-
1890's)
German dentist
Macksey--Book p149

PAGERIE, MARIE JOSEPHE ROSE
TASCHER
See JOSEPHINE DE BEAUCHAR-
NAIS

PAGE, VIOLET
See LEE, VERNON, pseud.

PAHLEVI, FARAH (1918-)
Iranian former empress,
agriculturist
O'Neill--Women's p3,40

PAIGE, SHEILA (fl. 1960's-
1970's)
Amer. filmmaker
Smith--Movies p195-197,265

PAINTER, CHARLOTTE (fl. 1970's)
Amer., Alaskan diarist
Moffat--Revel. p116-127

PAIVA, JEAN
Amer. TV cable director
of marketing
Scheuer--Tel. p367

PAKHMUTOVA, A.N. (fl. 1970's)
Russian film writer
Mandel--Soviet p148

PAKHOMOVA, LUDMIL(L)A
(1946-)
Russian ice skater
McWhirter--Guinness p97-98,
por.
O'Neill--Women's p563,574

PALEY, GRACE (1922-)
Amer. author
Cahill--Women p230,378

PALEY, JANE (1947-)
Amer. TV director
Scheuer--Tel. p367-368

PALEY, NATALIE (fl. 1920's-1930's)
French princess
Keenan--Women p12,14, por.

PALEY, MRS. WILLIAM (fl. 1930's)
Amer. fashion leader,
hostess
Keenan--Women p22-24,33-34,
por.

PALLISER, MRS. BURY (fl. 1850's)
English lacemaker
Callen--Women p140-141

PALLISER, ESTHER WALTERS
(1872-)
Amer. singer
Claghorn--Biog. p342

PALMER, ALICE ELVIRA FREEMAN
(1855-1902)
Amer. educator, college
president
Bolton--Success p223-233, por.
Burgess--Education p138
Earnest--American p213-214,218
James--Notable (3) p4-8
Kulkin--Her p219-220
McHenry--Liberty's p312-313
O'Neill--Women's p404
People's Almanac (2) p1053
Signif.--Amer. p21, por.
Webster's--Amer. p791-792

PALMER, ALISON (fl. 1970's)
Amer. priest
O'Neill--Women's p382,385

PALMER, BERTHA HONORE (1849-
1918)
Amer. socialite, art collector,
philanthropist, (wife of
Potter Palmer)
Birmingham--Grandes p126-128
Boorstin--American p149-150, por.
Earnest--American p223-228
James--Notable (3) p8-10
Longstreet--Queen p81-86, por.
McHenry--Liberty's p313
Sherr--American p45,59-60
Smith--Daughters p263-265
Webster's--Amer. p790,794

PALMER, BERTHA LOUISE SCHANTZ
(1881-)
Amer. singer, noted Arizona
mother
Amer.--Mothers p30-31, por.

PALMER, FRANCES ("FANNY")
FLORA BOND (1812-1876)
Amer. draftsman, lithographer,
folk-artist
James--Notable (3) p10-11
Petersen--Women p70

PALMER, LILLI (1914-)
German-Amer. actress, author
Shipman--Gold. p435-437, por.
World--Who p244

PALMER, LIZZIE PITTS MERRILL
(1838-1916)
Amer. philanthropist
James--Notable (3) p11-12

PALMER, MIRIAM (1946-)
Amer. poet
Chester--Rising p384-388, por.

PALMER, PHOEBE WORRALL
(1807-1874)
Amer. hymnist, evangelist,
author
Claghorn--Biog. p342
James--Notable (3) p12-14
McHenry--Liberty's p313-314

PALMER, MRS. POTTER
See PALMER, BERTHA HONORE

PALMER, SANDRA (1941-)
Amer. golfer
Hollander--100 p7,48,50
Woman's Almanac p420

PALMER, VERA JAYNE
See MANSFIELD, JAYNE

PALVANOVA, BIBI (1920-)
Russian physician
Mandel--Soviet p181-183

PAMBRUN, AUDRA (c1929-)
Amer. Indian public health
nurse
Diamonstein--Open p308-312,
por.

PAMYATNYKH, TAMARA (fl. 1940's)
Russian aviator, military air
pilot
O'Neill--Women's p550

PANACEA
Greek goddess, daughter of
Aesculapius
Marks--Women p38-39

PANATHENAEA
See ATHENA (ATHENE)

PAN CHAO (TS'AO TAKU)
(c45-c115)
Chinese scholar, historian,
poet, educator, moralist
Macksey--Book p61

PANDIT, VIJAYA LAKSHMI
(1900-)
East Indian ambassador,
diplomat, United Nations

delegate
Kulkin--Her p220-221
Macksey--Book p40
O'Neill--Women's p63-64

PANINA, COUNTESS (fl. 1910's)
Russian, cultural philanthropist
Mandel--Soviet p45,50

PANKHURST, CHRISTABEL, DAME
(1882-1958/1960)
English labor union founder,
suffragist, feminist
Macksey--Book p84
O'Neill--Women's p697
Palmer--Who's p254-255

PANKHURST, EMMELINE GOULDEN
(1858-1928)
English suffragist, feminist,
social reformer
Brecher--Lives p302
Diagram--Mothers p194-197, por.
Fry--1000 p272-273, por.
Jones--Rutledge p600
Macksey--Book p84-85
Marlowe--Great p161-165, por.
O'Neill--Women's p697
Palmer--Who's p255
People's Almanac (2) p950
Taylor--Gener. p16-17, por.
Warren--Pictorial p117-118,160,
162
Who Did What p253, por.
World--Who p190

PANKHURST, (ESTELLE) SYLVIA
(1882-1960)
English poet, feminist, social
reformer, Parliament member
Bernikow--World p150-151
Callen--Women p215, por.
Jones--Rutledge p600-601
O'Neill--Women's p697
Palmer--Who's p255-256
Vallance--Women p119-120

PANKHURST FAMILY (fl. 1880's)
English feminists
Kulkin--Her p221-222
Woman's Almanac p552

PANKLOVA, BARBARA
See NEMCOVA, BOŽENA

PANKRATOVA, ANNA (c1897-1957)

Russian sociologist, historian
of working class
Mandel--Soviet p161-162,167-168,
170

PANNELL, ANNE GARY (c1910-)
Amer. professor, educator,
association president
Diamonstein--Open p313-317,
por.

PANOVA, VERA (1905-1973)
Russian novelist, playwright
Macksey--Book p192, por.
Mandel--Soviet p153,205
O'Neill--Women's p683

"PANSY," pseud.
See ALDEN, ISABELLA
MacDONALD

PANTON, SALLY (fl. 1770's)
English-Amer. governess
Williams--Demeter's p178

PAPAS, IRENE (1926-)
Greek actress
O'Neill--Women's p660,686
World--Who p260

PAPATHANOSSIOU, ASPASIA (fl.
1940's)
Greek actress, brigade
commander
O'Neill--Women's p555

PAQUIN, MADAME (fl. 1900's)
French fashion designer
Macksey--Book p266

PARADIS (PARADIES), MARIA
THERESIA VON (1759-1834)
Austrian pianist
Neuls-Bates--Women p85-86

PARAMORE, MRS. FREDERICK W.
See HAZELTINE, NELLIE

PARDI, KATHLEEN
Amer. TV manager
Scheuer--Tel. p369-370

PARDO-BAZAN, EMILIA (1851/
1852-1921)
Spanish literary reformer
Macksey--Book p188

PARDOE, JULIA S.H. (1806-1862)
English poet, historian,
novelist
Showalter--Lit. p322

PARENT, MADELEINE (c1918-)
Canadian labor leader
O'Neill--Women's p319

PARGETER, EDITH (1913-)
English novelist, translator
Seymour-Smith--Novels p196

PARIS, DAWN EVELYN VEEN
See SHIRLEY, ANNE

PARISH, "SISTER" (fl. 1920's-
1930's)
Amer. White House decorator
O'Neill--Women's p282-283

PARK, IDA MAY (-1954)
Amer. film director
Slide--Early p60-61

PARK, MAUD MAY WOOD (-1955)
Amer. suffragist, social re-
former, feminist
Hymowitz--Hist. p279-280
McHenry--Liberty's p314
O'Neill--Women's p697
Scott--Southern p183-184
Sicherman--Notable p519-522

PARK, MERLE (1937-)
British ballet dancer
Cur. Biog. '74 p301-303, por.

PARK, PAT (fl. 1970's)
Amer. priest
O'Neill--Women's p384

PARK, ROSE (fl. 1950's)
Amer. activist
Warren--Pictorial p196

PARK, ROSEMARY (1907-)
Amer. educator, college
president, chancellor
Adams--Women p26,199
O'Neill--Women's p405-406

PARKER, BETTINA (fl. 1960's-
1970's)
Netherlands international
consultant

Lichtenstein--Mach. see index
p365

PARKER, BONNIE (1910/1911-1934)
Amer. outlaw, accused crimi-
nal
People's Almanac (1) p725-727
Woman's Almanac p504-505, por.
World--Who p300

PARKER, CECILIA (1905/1914-)
Canadian actress
Lamparski--What. (5) p140-141,
por.
Lamparski--What. (8) p228-229,
por.
Springer--They p197,322, por.

MARKER, CLAIRE (fl. 1930's)
Amer.-French film co-director
Smith--Movies p116

PARKER, CYNTHIA ANN (1827-1864)
Amer., Indian captive, pioneer
Sherr--American p221-223

PARKER, DOROTHY ROTHSCHILD
(1893-1967)
Amer. humorist, story writer,
poet
Avenel--Comp. (2) p200
Book--Lists (2) p251
Clark--Leading p100-102
Dunlap--Calif. p158, por.
Ehrlich--Oxford, see index p458,
por.
Jones--Rutledge p602
Kaplan--Salt p267-268
McHenry--Liberty's p314-315
Moers--Literary p302
Nash--Innov. p80-89, por.
New York Times--Great p226-227,
por.
O'Neill--Women's p676-677
People's Almanac (2) p707-708,
por.
Seymour-Smith--Novels p196,
por.
Sicherman--Notable p522-525
Signif.--Amer. p46, por.
Sochen--Movers p218-220
Webster's--Amer. p795
Who Did What p253
Woman's Almanac p256, por.
World--Who p18

PARKER, ELEANOR (1922-)

Amer. actress
World--Who p244

PARKER, FRANCINE (fl. 1970's)
Amer. film director
Smith--Movies p63-64,265, por.

PARKER, JEAN (1912/1915-)
Amer. actress
Lamparski--What. (5) p80-81,
por.
Springer--They p197,322, por.

PARKER, JEANNE A.
Amer. TV manager
Scheuer--Tel. p370

PARKER, JULIA SARSFIELD O'CON-
NOR (1890-1972)
Amer. labor leader
Sicherman--Notable p525-526

PARKER, MARJORIE HOLLOMAN
(fl. 1940's-1970's)
Amer. professor, educator,
author
Innis--Profiles p134-135, por.

PARKER, MARY (fl. 1940's)
Amer. aviatrix, WASP
Keil--Those, see index p329

PARKER, NANCY L. (1931-)
Amer. genealogical researcher,
editor
Meyer--Who's p160

PARKER, SUZY (1933-)
Amer. beauty, model
Keenan--Women p120-121,123,185,
por.

PARKHURST, CHARLOTTE (CHAR-
LIE) (c1812-1870)
Amer. male impersonator,
stagecoach driver
Sherr--American p21-22
Time--Women p178

PARKHURST, HELEN (1887-1973)
Amer. educator, school founder
Macksey--Book p76
Sicherman--Notable p526-527

PARKIN, MOLLY (1932-)
British journalist, novelist
Seymour-Smith--Novels p196

PARKINSON, ELIZABETH ("PAR-
KINA") (1882-1922)
Amer. singer
Claghorn--Biog. p344

PARKS, ELIZABETH RAYMOND
See ROBINS, ELIZABETH

PARKS, ROSA LEE (1913-   )
Amer. seamstress, founder
Civil Rights movement,
social reformer
Hymowitz--Hist. p339-340
Kulkin--Her p222-224
McHenry--Liberty's p315
Miller--Women p241-251
O'Neill--Women's p700
People's Almanac (2) p728-729
Sherr--American p218
Woman's Almanac p382-383, por.
World--Who p190

PARLAGHY, VILMA, PRINCESS
LWOFF (1863-   )
German painter
Sparrow--Women p287-288,316

PARLBY, IRENE (1878-1965)
Canadian feminist, politician
O'Neill--Women's p352

PARLOA, MARIA (1843-1909)
Amer. home economics
teacher, author
James--Notable (3) p16-18

PARLOW, KATHLEEN MARY (1890-
1963)
Canadian violinist
Claghorn--Biog. p344

PARNIS, MOLLIE (1905/1909-   )
Amer. fashion designer,
(couturier)
100--Greatest (1) p72, por.
World--Who p300

PARR, CATHERINE (1512-1548)
English queen
Bainton--France p161-180, por.
Jones--Rutledge p153
Softly--Queens p71-75, por.
Vance--Six p119-190
Who Did What p150, por.

PARR, HARRIET (1828-1900)
English novelist
Showalter--Lit. p330

PARRIS, ELIZABETH (BETTY) (fl.
1690's)
Amer. "beginner" of witch-
craft hysteria
Sherr--American p103

PARRISH, ANNE (1) (1760-1800)
Amer. colonial philanthropist,
educator
McHenry--Liberty's p315

PARRISH, ANNE (2) (1888-1957)
Amer. novelist
Ehrlich--Oxford p75,216,384

PARRISH, CELESTIA SUSANNAH
(1853-1918)
Amer. Southern educator
James--Notable (3) p18-20
McHenry--Liberty's p315-316
Scott--Southern p116
Sherr--American p47

PARRISH, HELEN (1922-1959)
Amer. actress, TV performer
Springer--They p197-198,322,
por.

PARRY, LILY (fl. 1970's)
Amer. golfer
McWhirter--Guinness p79

PARS, BAYAN VEDIDA (fl. 1950's)
Turkish educator
Macksey--Book p77

PARSON, LILLIAN BENDEKE (1896-   )
Amer. physician, clubwoman,
noted Minnesota mother
Amer.--Mothers p293, por.

PARSON, MARY JEAN (fl. 1960's-
1970's)
Amer. TV director
Marzolf--Up p174

PARSONS, ALICE BEAL (1886-1962)
Amer. novelist, short-story
writer
Ehrlich--Oxford p162

PARSON, BETTY PIERSON (1900-   )
Amer. museum worker
Women's--Female p119

PARSONS, ELSIE WORTHINGTON
CLEWS (1875-1941)
Amer. sociologist, anthropologist,

folklorist, author
James--Notable (3) p20-22
McHenry--Liberty's p316
Macksey--Book p240
Webster's--Amer. p798-799

PARSONS, EMILY ELIZABETH
(1824-1880)
Amer. Civil War nurse
James--Notable (3) p22-24
Sherr--American p100-101

PARSONS, ESTELLE (1927-)
Amer. actress
Cur. Biog. '75 p304-307, por.
Diamonstein--Open p318-323,
por.
Entertainers p268
World--Who p244

PARSONS, HARRIET OETTINGER
(c1906-1983)
Amer. film producer, writer
Cur. Biog. '83 p471

PARSONS, LOUELLA OETTINGER
(1881-1972)
Amer. columnist
Cur. Biog. '73 p460
Dunlap--Calif. p159, por.
Lewis--Prime p14,21-22
McHenry--Liberty's p316-317
O'Neill--Women's p447-448
Sicherman--Notable p527-529
Woman's Almanac p276
World--Who p54

PARSONS, LUCY (fl. 1840's)
Amer. teacher, (seminary
co-founder)
Sherr--American p249

PARSONS, ROSE PEABODY (1891-
1985)
Amer. organization official
Cur. Biog. '85 p472

PARTON, DOLLY REBECCA (1946-)
Amer. singer, songwriter,
actress
Anderson--People p314, por.
Claghorn--Biog. p345
Cur. Biog. '77 p338-341, por.
Dew--Women p92-121, por.
Glassman--Year '79 p133, por.
Golson--Playboy p578-607
O'Neill--Women's p629
People--Best p216, por.

Simon--Best p454-456, por.
Woman's Almanac p297-298, por.
World--Who p271

PARTON, SARA PAYSON WILLIS
See "FERN, FANNY," pseud.

PARTRIDGE, MARY
Amer. suffragist
Scott Southern p178

PARVEY, CONNIE (fl. 1970's)
Amer. clergyman, chaplain
Proctor--Women p28,122-125,130

PASKAUSKAITE, LILI (fl. 1960's-
1970's)
Lithuanian Soviet graphic
artist, book illustrator,
designer
Women's--Female p4, supp.

PASQUIER, NICOLE
French politician
O'Neill--Women's p54

PASSFIELD, LADY
See WEBB, BEATRICE POTTER

PASSOLF, PAT (fl. 1970's)
Amer. painter
Women's--Female p53

PASTA, GIUDITTA NEGRI (1798-
1865)
Italian opera singer
World--Who p78

PASTAN, LINDA (1932-)
Amer. poet
Chester--Rising p206-209, por.

PASTON, MARGARET MAUTEBY
(1423-1484)
English letter-writer, (sister
of John II)
Giles--Women p210-228

PASTORI, GIUSEPPINA (1891-)
Italian physician, biologist
Hellstedt--Women p72-75, por.
O'Neill--Women's p177

PASTORI, MARIA (fl. 1950's)
Italian mathematician
O'Neill--Women's p177

PASTRANA, JULIA (1832-1860)

Mexican Indian freak
Book--Lists (1) p451

PATAI, RAPHAEL (fl. 1960's)
Russian anthropologist,
writer
Mandel--Soviet p161-162

PATE, MARTHA B. LUCAS (1912-
1983)
Amer. educator, college
president, professor, dean
Cur. Biog. '83 p471

PATEMAN, PAT
Amer. aviatrix, writer,
army flier
Keil--Those p161-162

PATERSON, PAT (1911-)
English actress
Springer--They p198,322, por.

PATINIERE, AGNES LI, OF
DOUAI (fl. 13th Cent.)
French textile-dyer
Giles--Women p166

PATON, MARY ANNE (1802-1864)
English opera singer
Fabian--On p48-51, por.

PATRICK, LEE SALOME (c1912-
1982)
Amer. actress
Lamparski--What. (5) p136-137,
por.

PATRICK, GAIL (1911-)
Amer. actress
Engstead--Star p19-23,110
Lamparski--What (5) p78-79,
por.
Springer--They p198,322, por.

PATRICK, MARY MILLS (1850-1940)
Amer. missionary, educator,
foundress, college president
James--Notable (3) p25-26
McHenry--Liberty's p317-318

PATRICK, ROBERTA N. (fl. 1970's)
Amer. Marine colonel
O'Neill--Women's p549

PATRICK, RUTH (1907/1908-)
Amer. scientist, biologist,

limnologist, ecologist, noted
Pennsylvania mother
Amer.--Mothers p463, por.
Emberlin--Cont. p107-123, por.
O'Neill--Women's p144,158
Woman's Almanac p367

PATTERSON, ALICIA (1906-1963)
Amer. newspaper publisher,
editor
McHenry--Liberty's p318
O'Neill--Women's p448-449,478
Sicherman--Notable p529-531

PATTERSON, CONSTANCE MARIE
(fl. 1970's)
British labor union leader
O'Neill--Women's p319

PATTERSON, DELICIA
Amer. slave
Hymowitz--Hist. p57

PATTERSON, ELEANOR (CISSY)
MEDILL (1881/1884-1948)
Amer. newspaper editor, pub-
lisher
James--Notable (3) p26-28
Longstreet--Queen p173
McHenry--Liberty's p318-319
Marzolf--Up p63
O'Neill--Women's p448-449
Webster's--Amer. p802
Woman's Almanac p271

PATTERSON, ELIZABETH (1875-
1966)
Amer. actress
Springer--They p198-199,322,
por.

PATTERSON, ELIZABETH (BONA-
PARTE) (1785-1879)
Amer. belle, wife of Jerome
Bonaparte
Earle--Two Cent. (2) p786-788
James--Notable (1) p192-194
Kulkin--Her p41
McHenry--Liberty's p42
Peacock--Famous p39-60, por.
Webster's--Amer. p115-116
Young--Revol. p177,179-180,213

PATTERSON, GABBY (fl. 1940's)
English ferry pilot, aviatrix,
instructor, foundress
Boase--Sky's p179

PATTERSON, HANNAH JANE (1879-
1937)
Amer. suffragist, government
official
James--Notable (3) p28-30

PATTERSON, HELEN (-1974)
Amer. journalist, professor
Marzolf--Up p252-253

PATTERSON, MARY BAKER EDDY
See EDDY, MARY BAKER

PATTERSON, SHIRLEY (fl. 1970's)
Amer. power-lifter
Jordan--Broken p117-123

PATTI, ADELINA (ADELA JOANA
MARIA) (1843-1919)
Italian-Spanish-Amer. opera
singer
Claghorn--Biog. p346
James--Notable (3) p30-31
Jones--Rutledge p606
McHenry--Liberty's p319
Macksey--Book p215
Neidle--America's p220
Sherr--American p83
Time--Women p139
Tuggle--Golden p5, por.

PATTINSON, PENELOPE MARY
(1944-)
English genealogical researcher, writer, indexer
Meyer--Who's p161

PATTISON, LEE MARION (1890-)
Amer. pianist, composer
Claghorn--Biog. p346

PATTON, ABBY HUTCHINSON
See HUTCHINSON, ABIGAIL
("ABBY") JEMIMA

PATTON, FRANCES GRAY (1906-)
Amer. short-story writer
Ehrlich--Oxford p243,247

PATTON, JESSIE MAPLE (fl.
1970's)
Amer. film producer, editor
O'Neill--Women's p318

PATTON, MARY (fl. 1770's)
Amer. Revolutionary War
"soldier"
Sherr--American p217

PATTON, RUTH WILSON
Amer., mother of George S.
Patton
Diagram--Mothers p198-199, por.

PAU, ELENA
Italian accused criminal
Macksey--Book p136-137

PAUAHI, BERNICE (1831-)
Amer. princess, noted Hawaii
mother, school founder
Amer.--Mothers p141-142, por.

PAUKER, ANA RABINSOHN (c1894-
1960)
Rumanian Communist, feminist,
foreign minister
Fink--Great p148-153, por.
Macksey--Book p41

PAUL, ALICE (1885-1977)
English-Amer. foundress, or-
ganization official, lawyer,
suffragist, social reformer,
feminist
Banner--Women, see index p271,
por.
Clark--Leading p56-59,66-67
Cur. Biog. '77 p471
Hymowitz--Hist. p278-282, por.
Kulkin--Her p224-225
McHenry--Liberty's p319-320
Millstein--We p179,182,191-192
O'Neill--Women's p698,700
Papachristou--Women p172-174,
182, por.
People's Almanac (2) p950
Reifert--Women p197-199
Sochen--Herstory p231,234,239,
271-272,279,293,404, por.
Sochen--Movers, see index p317
Warren--Pictorial p160,162,170-
171,203-204
Woman's Almanac p551,553, por.
World--Who p190

PAUL, DOROTHY H. (1922-)
Amer. genealogical researcher,
writer
Meyer--Who's p161

PAUL, JOSEPHINE BAY
See BAY, JOSEPHINE HOLT
PERFECT

PAUL, MRS. LES
See FORD, MARY

PAUL, TILLIE (fl. 1950's)
Amer. Indian missionary,
teacher, clergyman
Jones--Women (1) p65-67

PAULA (A.D. 347-404)
Roman deaconess, saint,
scholar, hospital founder,
teacher
Macksey--Book p105
Mead--Hist. p79

PAULEKIUTE, JIEVUTE
See ROCKEFELLER, BARBARA
("BOBO") SEARS

PAULEY, GAY (fl. 1970's)
Amer. UPI's woman senior
editor
O'Neill--Women's p469

PAULEY, JANE (1950-)
Amer. TV commentator
Anderson--People p314-315
Cur. Biog. '80 p303-306, por.
O'Neill--Women's p505
Scheuer--Tel. p372-373, por.
Woman's Almanac p271

PAUR, MARIA BURGER (1862-
1899)
German pianist
Claghorn--Biog. p346

PAURUN, PHYLLIS BELLE (fl.
1970's)
Amer. graphic artist
Woman's--Female p81

PAVAN, MARISA (1932-)
Amer. actress
World--Who p244

PAVLOVA, ANNA (1881-1931)
Russian dancer
Brecher--Lives p340, por.
Fabian--On p142-143, por.
Fry--1000 p277
Holme--Journal p124-126, por.
Jones--Rutledge p608
Kulkin--Her p225-226
Macksey--Book p230, por.
Migel--Ballerinas, see index
p301, por.
O'Neill--Women's p639
People's Almanac (1) p873-874
Who Did What p255

Woman's Almanac p313-314, por.
World--Who p78

PAVLOVA, LYUBOV FEDOROVNA
(c1849-)
Russian, mother of Anna
Pavlova
Diagram--Mothers p204-205, por.

PAVLOVA, MARIA (fl. 1970's)
Russian historian
Mandel--Soviet p319

PAX, pseud.
See CHOLMONDELEY, MARY

PAXINOU, KATINA (1900-1973)
Greek actress
Cur. Biog. '73 p460
Entertainers p216, por.
World--Who p260

PAXON, MARJORIE (fl. 1940's-1960's)
Amer. editor
Marzolf--Up p104-105

PAXTON, DARLENE STEFFA WARD
(1917-)
Amer. genealogical researcher,
author
Meyer--Who's p161-162

PAYNE, DOLLEY
See MADISON, DOLLEY PAYNE
TODD

PAYNE, EDITH GERE (1875-1959)
British metalworker, gesso
worker, gilder, watercolourist
Callen--Women p225

PAYNE, ETHEL (fl. 1950's)
Amer. journalist, Washington
correspondent
Marzolf--Up p90-91

PAYNE, MARJATTA STRANDELL
Finnish-Amer. cost estimator,
English professor
O'Neill--Women's p192-193

PAYNE, MARY CALES
Amer., mother of Dolley
Madison
Sherr--American p244

PAYNE, VICTORIA (c1911-1977)

Amer. radio actress
Lamparski--What. (3) p110-111,
por.

PAYNE-GAPOSHKIN, CECELIA
HELENA (1900-1979)
English-Amer. astronomer,
professor
Gilbert--Part. p65, por.
O'Neill--Women's p151

PAYSON, JOAN WHITNEY (1903-
1975)
Amer. philanthropist,
sportswoman
Cur. Biog. '72 p338-340, por.
Cur. Biog. '75 p471
World--Who p300

PAYTON, CAROLYN R.
Amer. psychologist, Peace
Corps director
O'Neill--Women's p87, por.

PEABODY, ELIZABETH PALMER
(1804-1894)
Amer. kindergarten founder,
educator, lecturer, bookshop
owner, publisher, author,
transcendentalist
Burgess--Education p138-139
Ehrlich--Oxford p28,30,34
Epstein--Indiv. p17,79,84
Fryer--Faces p226-227
James--Notable (3) p31-34
McHenry--Liberty's p320
Macksey--Book p68
Neidle--America's p29,51
Pederson--Leaders p82, por.
Sherr--American p252
Signif.--Amer. p22, por.
Snyder--Dauntless p29-56, por.
Warren--Pictorial p73,81
Webster's--Amer. p806
World--Who p101

PEABODY, JOSEPHINE PRESTON
(1874-1922)
Amer. poet, playwright
James--Notable (3) p34-36
McHenry--Liberty's p320-321

PEABODY, KATE NICHOLS TRASK
See TRASK, KATE (KATRINA)
NICHOLS

PEABODY, LUCY WHITEHEAD

McGILL WATERBURY (1861-
1949)
Amer. missionary
James--Notable (3) p36-38
McHenry--Liberty's p321-322

"PEACHES" (fl. 1970's)
Amer. singer
Glassman--Year '79 p133, por.

PEACOCK, CYRENA
See VAN GORDON, CYRENA

PEACOCKE, ELIZABETH (fl. 1940's-
1970's)
Canadian "Savlation Army"
official
O'Neill--Women's p395

PEALE, ANNA CLAYPOOLE (1791-
1878)
Amer. painter, miniaturist
Fine--Women p96,100-103
James--Notable (3) p38-40
McHenry--Liberty's p322
Munsterberg--Hist. p60

PEALE, MARGARETTA ANGELICA
(1795-1882)
Amer. painter
James--Notable (3) p38-40
Munsterberg--Hist. p60

PEALE, SARAH MIRIAM (1800-1885)
Amer. painter
Fine--Women p96,100-103
Harris--Women p221-222,349
James--Notable (3) p38-40
McHenry--Liberty's p322
Munsterberg--Hist. p59-60
Petersen--Women p70-71,74, por.
Sherr--American p205
Tufts--Our p138-146, por.
Women's--Female p13

PEARCE, LOUISE (1885/1886-1959)
Amer. pathologist, physician
Sicherman--Notable p531-532

PEARCE, MARCELLA MORGAN
(1868-)
Amer. teacher, noted Arkansas mother
Amer.--Mothers p45, por.

PEARL, MINNIE (1912-)
Amer. singer, comedienne

Claghorn--Biog. p348
O'Neill--Women's p629
Woman's Almanac p320, por.
World--Who p271

PEARLMAN, AGNES BRANCH
(1922-)
Amer. genealogical researcher,
author, indexer
Meyer--Who's p162

PEARSALL, FRANCES (fl. 1980's)
Amer. millionaire
Forbes--400 ('84) p49

PEARSON, EDITH DU PONT (fl.
1980's)
Amer. millionaire
Forbes--400 ('84) p120

PEARSON, FLORA ENGLE (fl.
1860's)
Amer. Western pioneer
Sherr--American p243

PEARSON, JEAN (fl. 1960's-1970's)
Amer. journalist, (Antarctica)
Land--New p22,49-50,51

PEARSON, SUELA
Amer. P.E.O. co-founder
O'Neill--Women's p427, por.

PEARY, JO
Amer. writer, (wife of
Robert Peary)
Forma--They p59-60,85,119

PEAULY, MARY DE
See GOWER, PAULINE

PECK, ANNIE SMITH (1850-1935)
Amer. mountaineer, profes-
sor, explorer, feminist,
scholar, lecturer
Felton--Famous p23-24
James--Notable (3) p40-42
McHenry--Liberty's p322-323
Macksey--Book p260
Marlowe--Great p152-155, por.
Olds--Women p5-70, por.
Sherr--American p208
Signif.--Amer. p32, por.
Taylor--Gener. p59, por.
Woman's Almanac p107-108, por.

PECK, ELLEN (fl. 1970's)

Amer. activist, author, organization founder, non-parents
O'Neill--Women's p728

PECK, JULIE
See LONDON, JULIE

PECK, MARY ALLEN
Amer., friend of Woodrow
Wilson
Daniels--Wash. p93-96

PECK, ROSALINE
Amer. early settler
Sherr--American p249

PECKHAM, ISOBEL GREENE (fl.
1860's)
Amer. Southern belle
DeLeon--Belles p250-251, por.

PEDAS, MERCINA
See SIGLER, MARCY

PEDEE, LOUISE ANN (fl. 1960's)
Amer. heroine, Carnegie
Medal winner
O'Neill--Women's p733

PEDEN, IRENE CARSWELL (fl.
1970's)
Amer. professor, electrical
engineer, radio research
scientist
Land--New p74-88, por.
O'Neill--Women's p189,191-192

PEDERSEN, GINA (fl. 1890's)
Amer. pioneer, noted Wash-
ington state mother
Amer.--Mothers p558-560, por.

PEDERSEN, HELGA (fl. 1950's-
1970's)
Danish judge
O'Neill--Women's p368

PEDLAR, SYLVIA (1901-1972)
Amer. fashion designer
O'Neill--Women's p247,257

PEEL, BEATRICE LILLIE, LADY
See LILLIE, BEATRICE, LADY
PEEL

PEEL, EMMA
English TV actress
Fireman--TV p209

PEERS, JOAN (1911-   )
Amer. dancer, actress
Springer--They p199,322, por.

PEETERS, CLARA (1594-after 1657)
Belgian artist
Fine--Women p29-30
Harris--Women p28,32-35,41-43,
72,105,116,131-133,146,342
Petersen--Women p36-37, por.

PEGRAM, JENNIE (fl. 1860's)
Amer. Southern belle
DeLeon--Belles p125-126, por.

PEGRAM, MRS. JOHN
See CARY, HETTY

PEIRSE, JUANITA
English poet
Bernikow--World p182

PEIXOTTO, JESSICA BLANCHE
(1864-1941)
Amer. social economist,
professor
James--Notable (3) p42-43

PELGRIFT, KATHRYN C. (fl.
1970's)
Amer. TV executive
O'Neill--Women's p524
Scheuer--Tel. p373

PELHAM, LAURA DAINTY (fl.
1900's)
Amer. drama director
Chinoy--Women p200-203

PELHAM, MARY SINGLETON
See COPLEY, MARY SINGLETON

PELL, ANNA JOHNSON
See WHEELER, ANNA JOHNSON
PELL

PELLET, SARAH (fl. 1850's)
Amer. temperance worker
Time--Women p201

PELTIER, THERESE, MADAME
(fl. 1910's)
French, first air passenger,
sculptor, aviatrix
Boase--Sky's p10-11
Macksey--Book p246, por.

PELTZ, MARY ELLIS (OPDYCKE)

(1896-1981)
Amer. author, lecturer, opera
promoter
Cur. Biog. '82 p472

PEMBER, PHOEBE YATES LEVY
(1823-1913)
Amer. Confederate hospital
administrator, Civil War nurse,
diarist
Hymowitz--Hist. p141-142
James--Notable (3) p44-45
Millstein--We p128-129
Scott--Southern p83-84
Sherr--American p238
Wiley--Confed. p145, por.

PEMBROKE, MARY HERBERT SID-
NEY, COUNTESS OF (1561-
1621)
English poet
Bernikow--World p53

PENDLETON, ELLEN FITZ (1864-
1936)
Amer. college president,
educator
James--Notable (3) p45-47
McHenry--Liberty's p323

PENELOPE (fl. 67 A.D.)
Greek, wife of Odysseus,
mother of Telemachus
Pomeroy--Godd. p19,21,23,28
Zinserling--Women p16-18

PENFEATHER, PENELOPE, pseud.
See JOY, SALLY

PENFIELD
See PEARSON, SUELA

PENN, GULIELMA MARIA SPRINGETT
(1644-1694)
Amer., (first wife of William
Penn)
Earle--Two Cent. (1) p xvix,240,
602, por.

PENN, HANNAH CALLOWHILL (1671-
1726)
Amer., (second wife of William
Penn)
Earle--Two Cent. (1) p xix,242,
244,602, por.
James--Notable (3) p47-48
Neidle--America's p19-20
Sherr--American p201

PENNELL, ELIZABETH ROBINS
(1855-1936)
Amer. author, art critic
James--Notable (3) p48-50
McHenry--Liberty's p323

PENNELL, REBECCA (fl. 1850's)
Amer. college professor
Sherr--American p188

PENNINGTON, ANN (1893-1971)
Amer. actress, dancer
Lamparski--What. (2) p164-165,
por.

PENNINGTON, LILY MAY (1917-)
Amer. singer
Claghorn--Biog. p349

PENNINGTON, MARY ENGLE
(1897-1952)
Amer. chemist, bacteriologist,
engineer, frozen food pioneer, agricultural researcher
O'Neill--Women's p30,164
Sicherman--Notable p532-534

PENNINGTON, PATIENCE
See PRINGLE, ELIZABETH
WATIES ALLSTON

PENROSE, EVELYN
British "dowser"
People's Almanac (1) p1397

PENROSE, MARYLY BARTON
(1938-)
Amer. genealogical researcher,
author
Meyer--Who's p163

PENTZ, SARA
Amer. TV newscaster
Gelfman--Women p34-36,62,
150-151

PEPE, MARIA (fl. 1970's)
Amer. Little League baseball
player
Rivera--Special p215-239, por.

PEPPER, BARBARA (1912-1969)
Amer. actress
Springer--They p199,322, por.

PEPPER, BEVERLY (1924-)
Amer. artist

Munro--Originals p345-354,
por.

PEPPER, MRS. (fl. 1890's)
English manager, linen indus-
try, spinner
Callen--Women p3,117-118, por.

PEPPERELL, MARY SEWELL, LADY
(fl. 1760's)
Amer. baroness
Sherr--American p90

PEPPLER, MARY JO (1944-)
Amer. volleyball player,
bicyclist
Hollander--100 p141-142, por.
Jordan--Broken p155-213
O'Neill--Women's p570
Woman's Almanac p441

PEPYS, ELIZABETH ST. MICHEL
English, (wife of Samuel
Pepys)
Morley--Literary p32-33,41,187,
205

PERAGINE, FRANCES
Amer. film director
Scheuer--Tel. p374

PERATIS, KATHLEEN W. (fl. 1970's)
Amer. Civil Liberties Union
official
O'Neill--Women's p356

PERCY, EILEEN (1899-)
Irish-Amer. actress, society
editor
Lamparski--What. (4) p130-131,
por.

PERCY, FLORENCE, pseud.
See ALLEN, ELIZABETH ANNE
CHASE AKERS

PEREIRA, IRENE RICE (1907-1971)
Amer. painter
Cur. Biog. '71 p468
Fine--Women p144
Henkes--Eight p20-25,53-54
Munsterberg--Hist. p72-73
Sicherman--Notable p534-535
Tufts--Our p232-242, por.
Women's--Female p13

PERETTI, ELSA (1940-)

Italian-Amer. model, jewelry
designer
O'Neill--Women's p239,256

PEREY, MARGUERITE (1909-1975)
French scholar, researcher
Macksey--Book p158

PEREZ, IRENE (fl. 1970's)
Amer. painter
Women's--Female p53

PEREZ, SOLEDAD
Amer. Chicana writer
Fisher--Third p viii,315-316

PERICTIONE
Greek, mother of Plato
Pomeroy--Godd. p134

PERILLO, LANCELOTTI
See SPAGNUOLA, TERESA,
pseud.

PERKINS, CARMEN DE (fl. 1960's-
1970's)
Argentinean ranch-owner,
manager
Macksey--Book p167

PERKINS, CHARLOTTE
See GILMAN, CHARLOTTE
PERKINS STETSON

PERKINS, ELIZABETH PECK
(1735/1736-1807)
Amer. Revolutionary War
businesswoman, philanthropist
James--Notable (3) p50-52
Millstein--We p32-33

PERKINS, EMILY SWAN (1866-1941)
Amer. composer
Claghorn--Biog. p350

PERKINS, FRANCES (1882-1965)
Amer., noted District of
Columbia mother, government
official
Amer.--Mothers p105-106, por.
Bachtold--Gifted p98-100
Banner--Women p136,179-182,
237, por.
Clark--Leading p171-172
Ingraham--Album p47, por.
Kulkin--Her p226-227
McHenry--Liberty's p324

Macksey--Book p41, por.
Neidle--America's p140-141,144,
153,165,269
O'Neill--Women's p82,331-333
Reader's--Story p437
Sicherman--Notable p535-539
Signif.--Amer. p46, por.
Sochen--Movers p162-163
Ware--Beyond p151, see also
index p202
Warren--Pictorial p190-192, por.
Webster's--Amer. p815
Woman's Almanac p478-479, por.
World--Who p148

PERKINS, JOSEPHINE AMELIA (fl.
1830's)
Amer. accused criminal
Stein--Fragments p1-24

PERKINS, LUCY FITCH (1865-1937)
Amer. children's author
James--Notable (3) p52-53
McHenry--Liberty's p324

PERKINS, MARY FITCH WESCOTT
(-1894)
Amer. early divorcée
Berkin--Women p152-153,155-157,
168

PERKINS, MILLIE (1938-)
Amer. actress
Lamparski--What. Annual (4,5)
p324-329, por.

PERKINS, SARAH (1771-1831)
Amer. painter
DePauw--Rem. p131, por.

PERKINS, ZINA KARTCHNER (1883-)
Amer. community worker,
noted Arizona mother
Amer.--Mothers p33-34, por.

PERLMAN, ANITA (fl. 1970's)
Amer. B'nai B'rith leader
O'Neill--Women's p114-115

PERLMANN, GERTRUDE E. (1912-
1974)
Amer. chemist
O'Neill--Women's p164,168

PERNA OF FANO (fl. c1460)
Jewish - Italian physician
Henry--Written p126,128

PERON, (MARIA) EVA (EVITA)
DUARTE DE (1919-1952)
Argentinean, wife of President
Juan Perón, actress, heroine
Book--Lists (1) p453
Brecher--Lives p281-282
Fry--1000 p299, por.
Hahner--Women p90-110
Henderson--Ten p193-212, por.
Jones--Rutledge p613-614
Macksey--Book p37, por.
Palmer--Who's p261
People's Almanac (1) p363-364

PERON, ISABEL (MARIA ESTELA
MARTINEZ DE) (1931-)
Argentinean president, (third
wife of Juan Perón)
Cur. Biog. '75 p313-315, por.
Macksey--Book p37
O'Neill--Women's p48
Woman's Almanac p464

PEROVSKAYA, SOFIA (1853-1881)
Russian revolutionist, political
martyr
Macksey--Book p136
Mandel--Soviet p28-29, por.
Taylor--Gener. p34-35

PERRAULT, JESUSITA ACOSTA
(1872-1960)
Mexican-Amer. politician,
noted New Mexico mother
Amer.--Mothers p378-379, por.

PERREAU, GIGI (CHISLAINE)
(1941-)
Amer. child actress
Edelson--Kids p34-35

PERRIN, ALICE (1867-1934)
British novelist
Showalter--Lit. p344

PERRIN, ETHEL (1871-1962)
Amer. physical education
specialist
Sicherman--Notable p539-541

PERRINE, VALERIE (1943-)
Amer. actress, dancer
Book--Lists (2) p189
Cur. Biog. '75 p315-318, por.
World--Who p245

PERRY, AGNES
See BOOTH, AGNES

PERRY, ANTOINETTE (1888-1946)
Amer. actress, theatrical di-
rector
James--Notable (3) p53-54
McHenry--Liberty's p324-325

PERRY, CAROLINE SLIDELL
See BELMONT, CAROLINE
SLIDELL PERRY

PERRY, ELEANOR BAYER (c1914-
1981)
Amer. author, screenwriter
Smith--Movies p70-71,266

PERRY, FRANCES (fl. 1950's-
1970's)
British horticulturist, writer,
journalist
Macksey--Book p167
O'Neill--Women's p6

PERRY, JOANNA (-1725)
Amer. colonial bookseller
Williams--Demeter's p195

PERRY, JULIA (1927-)
Amer. composer, conductor,
teacher
Claghorn--Biog. p351
Jablonski--Ency. p549-550

PERRY, JUNE CARTER
Amer. radio performer
O'Neill--Women's p505-506

PERRY, LILLIA CABOT (c1848-1933)
Amer. artist
Harris--Women p245-246,251,352

PERRY, MARY CHASE (1868-1961)
Amer. ceramicist
Callen--Women p86-87,225

PERRY, NANCY LING ("FAHIZAH")
(1947-)
Amer. radical, revolutionary
Woman's Almanac p507
World--Who p300

PERRY, NORA (1831-1896)
Amer. author, journalist
McHenry--Liberty's p324-325

PERSEPHONE (fl. c5, 10 B.C.)
Greek goddess, daughter of
Demeter
Fraser--Heroines p24-28, por.

Pomeroy--Godd. p76-77,
216

PERSKE, BETTY
See BACALL, LAUREN

PERSSON, BIRGITTA (1303-1373)
Swedish religious order
founder
Macksey--Book p106

PERSSON-MELIN, SIGNE (fl.
1950's-1970's)
Swedish ceramicist, glass
designer
O'Neill--Women's p272-273

PERUANSKAYA, VALERIA
Russian writer
Mandel--Soviet p221-222

PESOTTA, ROSE (1896-1965)
Russian-Amer. labor leader
Sicherman--Notable p541-542

PETELSKA, EVA (fl. 1950's-1960's)
Polish film co-director
Smith--Movies p133

PETER, FRANCES
Amer. magazine editor,
author
O'Neill--Women's p438

PETER, SARAH WORTHINGTON
KING (1800-1877)
Amer. social leader, philan-
thropist, college founder,
feminist, educator
Callen--Women p225
James--Notable (3) p54-56
McHenry--Liberty's p325-326
Sherr--American p204

PETERMANN, MARY L. (-1976)
Amer. chemist, researcher
O'Neill--Women's p164,168

PETERS, BERNADETTE (1948-)
Amer. singer, actress
Anderson--People p318
Cur. Biog. '84 p320-324, por.
Mordden--Movie p257-259
World--Who p245

PETERS, ELLEN ASH (fl. 1960's-
1970's)
Amer. lawyer,

professor
O'Neill--Women's p363

PETERS, ELLIS
See PARGETER, EDITH

PETERS, FANNIE LEDYARD (c1754-
1816)
Amer. Revolutionary War
heroine
Meyer--Petticoat p154

PETERS, JANE ALICE
See LOMBARD, CAROLE

PETERS, JEAN
See HUGHES, JEAN PETERS

PETERS, MARY (1939-)
British gymnast
McWhirter--Guinness p88, por.

PETERS, KIM (fl. 1970's)
Amer. handicapped basketball
player
O'Neill--Women's p568

PETERS, ROBERTA (1930-)
Amer. opera singer
Claghorn--Biog. p351
Kufrin--Uncom. p52-71, por.
Lewis--Prime p108,161, por.
World--Who p71-72

PETERSEN, ANDREA (fl. 1950's-
1970's)
Amer. Chippewa Indian teacher
O'Neill--Women's p429-430

PETERSON, BEATRICE SOFIA
MATHILDA
See BROOKE, HILLARY

PETERSON, CYNTHIA (fl. 1970's)
Amer. architect, professor
O'Neill--Women's p612

PETERSON, DOROTHY (fl. 1930's-
1940's)
Amer. actress
Springer--They p199,322, por.

PETERSON, DOROTHY, SISTER (fl.
1970's)
Amer. nun
O'Neill--Women's p390

PETERSON, ESTHER (1906-)

Amer. consumer adviser,
feminist, government official
Diamonstein--Open p324-328, por.
O'Neill--Women's p288,299,330,
337,724, por.
Reader's--Story p438
Sochen--Movers p231-233

PETERSON, JAN (fl. 1960's)
Amer. radical, organization
founder
Lichtenstein--Mach. p314-319
O'Neill--Women's p694,729

PETERSON, JANE (1876-1965)
Amer. painter
Women's--Female p13

PETERSON, JETRET STRYKER
(1895-)
Amer. teacher, clubwoman,
noted Alaska mother
Amer.--Mothers p19-20, por.

PETERSON, KATHRYN R. (1949-)
Amer. executive, cable TV
Scheuer--Tel. p375

PETERSON, MARTHA ELIZABETH
(1916-)
Amer. college president
Cur. Biog. '69 p332-334, por.

PETERSON, SUSAN
Amer. TV executive
Scheuer--Tel. p375-376

PETIPA, MARIE SOUROVSCHIKOVA
(fl. 1860's)
Russian ballet dancer
Migel--Ballerinas p256-257

PETRACCINI, MARIA (fl. 1780's)
Italian obstetrician
Marks--Women p119

PETRE, JULIANA, LADY (1769-
1833)
English Catholic emancipator
Ware--Meet p35,79-80

PETRIDES, FREDERIQUE
Belgian violinist, conductor
Neuls-Bates--Women p247-248,
252,259-264, por.

PETRIE, KAY (fl. 1930's)

British motor-car racer
Macksey--Book p254

PETRONIA JUSTA (fl. c79 A.C.)
Roman girl, in trial
Pomeroy--Godd. p197

PETRONILLA, SAINT
French abbess
Mead--Hist. p178

PETROVIC, NADEZDA (1873-1915)
Serbian painter
Partington--Who's p326

PETRUCCINI
See PETTRACINI, MARCIA

PETRY, ANN (1912-)
Amer. novelist, journalist
Cahill--Women p132,376-377
Ehrlich--Oxford p147
Fisher--Third p vii,202
Richardson--Great p150-157, por.
Sochen--Herstory p374-375, por.
Spacks--Contemp. p108-117,181

PETTEYS, ANNA G. (-1970)
Amer. lecturer, educator,
noted Colorado mother
Amer.--Mothers p67-68, por.

PETTIT, KATHERINE (1868-1936)
Amer. settlement worker,
school founder
James--Notable (3) p56-58
McHenry--Liberty's p326
O'Neill--Women's p100,122
Sherr--American p78-79

PETTIT, LAURA MILDRED TANNER
(1895-)
Amer. musician, composer,
noted California mother
Amer.--Mothers p55-56

PETTRACINI, MARIA (fl. 1700's)
Italian physician, anatomy
teacher
Mead--Hist. p508

PETTY, LESTA JEAN (fl. 1970's)
Amer. 4-H scholarship winner
O'Neill--Women's p21

PEYTON, ANNIE COLEMAN (1852-)
Amer. educator, noted Missouri

mother
Amer.--Mothers p299, por.

PFEIFFER, EMILY JANE (1827-
1890)
British poet, essayist
Showalter--Lit. p329

PFEIFFER, IDA (1797-1806)
Austrian writer, traveller
Hamalian--Ladies p149-168

PFEIFFER, JANE CAHILL (1932-   )
Amer. nun, TV executive,
government official, engineer
Book--Lists (2) p17
Cur. Biog. '80 p313-316, por.
Lichtenstein--Mach. p10,236-239
O'Neill--Women's p519-520

PFOHL, BESSIE WHITTINGTON
(1881-   )
Amer. musician, musical
educator, noted North
Carolina mother
Amer.--Mothers p407, por.

PFOST, GRACIE BOWERS (1906-
1965)
Amer. Congresswoman
Chamberlin--Min. p229-231

PHANTOG, MRS. (fl. 1970's)
Tibetan mountaineer
McWhirter--Guinness p106

PHEBE
Biblical
Price--God p184-186

PHELPS, ALMIRA HART LINCOLN
(1793-1884)
Amer. educator, botanist,
chemist, author
James--Notable (3) p58-60
McHenry--Liberty's p326-327

PHELPS, CAROLINE (1854-1909)
Amer. philanthropist
James--Notable (3) p382-384
McHenry--Liberty's p395-396

PHELPS, ELIZABETH WOOSTER
STUART (1815-1852)
Amer. novelist, lecturer
James--Notable (3) p60-61

PHILBY, ELEANOR (fl. 1970's)
Amer. biographer
P.W.--Author p250-251,519

PHILE OF PRIENE (fl. 2nd Cent.
B.C.)
Greek magistrate
Pomeroy--Godd. p126

PHILENIA
See MORTON, SARAH WENT-
WORTH APTHORPE

PHILIPON, JEANNE MANON
See ROLAND, JEANNE MANON
PHILIPON, MADAME

PHILIPPA OF HAINAULT (1312/
1314-1369)
English queen, (wife of Ed-
ward III of England), educa-
tor, military leader
Jones--Rutledge p620
Softly--Queens p35-38, por.
Taylor--Gener. p19

PHILIPS, KATHERINE FOWLER
("ORINDA") (1631-1664)
English poet
Bernikow--World p58-59
Kaplan--Salt p41-42, por.
Moers--Literary p302

PHILIPSE, MARGARET HARDEN-
BROOK (c1650-1690)
Amer. colonial merchant,
shipowner
James--Notable (3) p61-62
Macksey--Book p162
Neidle--America's p9,269
Warren--Pictorial p16
Williams--Demeter's p175-176

PHILIPSE, MARY (1730-1825)
Amer. Revolutionary War
heroine
Earle--Two Cent. (2) p xv,540,
por.

PHILIPSON, MABEL HILTON
British Parliament member
Vallance--Women p26-28,30

PHILISTA
Greek professor of medicine,
encyclopedist, physician
Mead--Hist. p41,57

PHILLIPPS, ADELAIDE (1833-1882)
English-Amer. actress, opera
singer
James--Notable (3) p62-63

PHILLIPS, ANGELA (fl. 1970's)
Amer. photographer
Women's--Female p69

PHILLIPS, ANNA TERRY GREENE
(1813-1886)
Amer. social reformer
Lutz--Crusade, see index p337

PHILLIPS, BURRILL (1907-)
Amer. composer
Claghorn--Biog. p353

PHILLIPS, CAROLYN F.
Amer. hygienist, scholar
O'Neill--Women's p192

PHILLIPS, ELIZABETH (1685-1761)
Amer. colonial physician,
(midwife)
Mead--Hist p412,486
Williams--Demeter's p172

PHILLIPS, ESTHER MAE JONES
(1935-1984)
Amer. singer
Claghorn--Biog. p353

PHILLIPS, EUGENIA LEVY (fl.
1860's)
Amer. Southern belle, Civil
War patriot, prisoner
DeLeon--Belles p176-178, por.
Sherr--American p128

PHILLIPS, IRNA (1903-1973)
Amer. radio, TV script
writer
Cur. Biog. '74 p467
Sicherman--Notable p542-543
Women--Radio p21

PHILLIPS, LENA MADESIN
(1881-1955)
Amer. feminist, lawyer,
businesswomen's organization
founder, author, lecturer
Bird--Enterprising p165
McHenry--Liberty's p327
O'Neill--Women's p512-513
Sicherman--Notable p544-545

PHILLIPS, MARY WALKER (1923-)
Amer. craftswoman
O'Neill--Women's p131

PHILLIPS, MRS. MICHAEL
See MILLER, JULIA

PHILLIPS, MICHELE (c1944-)
Amer. singer
Simon--Best p370-372, por.

PHILLIPS, PAULINE ("POPO")
ESTHER
See VAN BUREN, ABIGAIL
("ABBY"), pseud.

PHILLIPS, MRS. PHILIP
See PHILLIPS, EUGENIA LEVY

PHILLIPS, SARAH BOWMAN (fl.
1850's)
Amer. pioneer home builder
Sherr--American p9

PHILLPOTTS, EDEN (1862-1960)
English novelist
Morley--Literary p207-208

"PHILOMENA"
See ROWE, ELIZABETH SINGER

PHIPS, MARY, LADY
Amer., wife of governor
Williams--Demeter's p142-143

PHRYNE (fl. 4th Cent. B.C.)
Greek courtesan, model,
beauty
Jones--Rutledge p620
Pomeroy--Godd. p141
Zinserling--Women p39

PHUL, ANNA MARIA VON (1786-
1823)
Amer. painter
DePauw--Rem. p132

PIAF, EDITH (1915-1963)
French singer, songwriter
Brecher--Lives p235-236
Donaldson--How p294-295
O'Neill--Women's p625-626
Simon--Best p465-466, por.
Woman's Almanac p298-299, por.
World--Who p271

PIAGGI, ANNA (fl. 1970's)

Sochen--Herstory p303-305, por.
Springer--They p199-200,322,
  por.
Warren--Pictorial p177
Webster's--Amer. p822-823
Whitman--Come p363-370
Woman's Almanac p326,352, por.
World--Who p245

PICO, MARIA ANTONIA (fl. 1810's)
  Amer. early California heroine
  Hoople--As p18-21

PICON, MOLLY (1898-)
  Amer. actress
  World--Who p245

PICOTTE, SUSAN LA FLESCHE
  (1865-1915)
  Amer. Omaha Indian physician
  Gridley--Amer. p74-80, por.
  James--Notable (3) p65-66
  Sherr--American p142, por.
  Stein--Lives p172-176, por.

PICTET, MARION MacMILLAN (fl.
  1980's)
  Amer. millionaire
  Forbes--400 ('84) p147

PIER, KATE HAMILTON (1845-1925)
  Amer. lawyer, feminist
  Sherr--American p247

PIERANGELI, MARISA
  See PAVAN, MARISA

PIERCE, ANNE KENDRICK
  (1768-1838)
  Amer., mother of President
  Pierce
  Faber--Presidents' p246-248

PIERCE, BILLIE (1905-1974)
  Amer. pianist
  Claghorn--Jazz p236

PIERCE, DIANE (1) (fl. 1970's)
  Amer. judo athlete
  O'Neill--Women's p564

PIERCE, DIANE (2) (fl. 1970's)
  Amer. clergyman
  Proctor--Women p27,52-53,
  57-58,89,164

PIERCE, JANE MEANS APPLETON

(1806-1863)
  Amer. first lady, (wife of
  Franklin Pierce), noted New
  Hampshire mother
  Amer.--Mothers p362, por.
  James--Notable (3) p66-67
  Melick--Wives p38, por.
  People's Almanac (1) p268
  Woman's Almanac p488

PIERCE, JESSIE WEBSTER (1892-)
  Amer. Indian trader, noted
  New York mother
  Amer.--Mothers p395-396, por.

PIERCE, PONCHITTA (c1942-)
  Amer. TV host, co-producer
  Scheuer--Tel. p378

PIERCE, ROXANNE
  Amer. gymnast
  O'Neill--Women's p562

PIERCE, SARAH ("SALLY") (1767-
  1852)
  Amer. educator
  James--Notable (3) p67-68
  McHenry--Liberty's p329

PIERCE, TILLIE (fl. 1860's)
  Amer. Civil War patriot,
  witness
  Millstein--We p132-134

PIERCY, MARGE (1936-)
  Amer. poet
  Chester--Rising p274-279, por.

PIERSON, GAIL (1941-)
  Amer. economist
  Teitz--What's p188-210, por.

PIFER, ALICE
  Amer. TV producer
  Scheuer--Tel. p378-379

PIGGOTT, EMELINE (fl. 1860's)
  Amer. Confederate spy
  Sherr--American p180

PIKE, MARY HAYDEN GREEN
  (1824-1908)
  Amer. author
  James--Notable (3) p68-69
  McHenry--Liberty's p329

PILBEAM, NOVA (1919-)

English actress
Springer--They p200,322, por.

PILPEL, HARRIET FLEISCHL
Amer. lawyer, feminist,
copyright authority
O'Neill--Women's p350,353, por.
Swiger--Women p152-168

PIMENOVA (fl. 1970's)
Russian scholar
Mandel--Soviet p250

PINAYEVA, LUDMILA
RHVEDOSYUK (fl. 1960's-
1970's)
Russian canoeist
McWhirter--Guinness p48

PINCHES, ROSEMARY VIVIAN
(1929-)
English genealogical researcher, author
Meyer--Who's p163-164

PINCHOT, CORNELIA ELIZABETH
BRYCE (1881-1960)
Amer. politician, suffragist
Showalter--These p120-126
Sicherman--Notable p545-547

PINCKERT, JEANE
See DIXON, JEANE L. PINCKERT

PINCKNEY, ELIZA LUCAS (1723-
1793)
English-Amer. agriculturist,
author, noted South Carolina
mother, plantation manager
Amer.--Mothers p489
Bird--Enterprising p32-36,40,106
Booth--Women p238,259-263,300
DePauw--Found. p28-29
DePauw--Rem. p61
Earle--Two Cent. (2) p480,482
Hymowitz--Hist. p32-33
Ingraham--Album p6,9
James--Notable (3) p69-71
Macksey--Book p163
Meyer--Petticoat p224
Millstein--We p23-24
Neidle--America's p9-10
Reifert--Women p21-22
Sherr--American p212
Warren--Pictorial p45-47,56
Williams--Demeter's p181-184

PINCKNEY, JOSEPHINE LYONS
SCOTT (1895-1957)
Amer. novelist
Ehrlich--Oxford p250

PINDELL, HOWARDINA (1943-)
Amer. painter
Miller--Lives p130-156
Women's--Female p54

"THE PINK LADY"
See DAWN, HAZEL

PINKHAM, LYDIA ESTES (1819-
1883)
Amer. businesswoman, patent
medicine manufacturer
Bird--Enterprising p122-127
Coffin--Female p201-215, por.
Coffin--Parade p363,583-584
Eills--Here p52-53
Felton--Famous p244-245
James--Notable (3) p71-72
Longstreet--Queen p72
McHenry--Liberty's p329
Macksey--Book p164-165, por.
O'Neill--Women's p100
Sherr--American p106-107, por.
Warren--Pictorial p126
Woman's Almanac p371-372, por.
World--Who p300

PINNEY, EUNICE GRISWOLD (1770-
1849)
Amer. primitive painter
DePauw--Rem. p128,130
Fine--Women p98-99
James--Notable (3) p72-73
Munsterberg--Hist. p61,63

PINTASSILGO, MARIA DE LOURDES
(1930-)
Portuguese minister of social
welfare
O'Neill--Women's p61

PINTONG, NILAWAN (fl. 1930's-
1970's)
Thailand magazine editor
O'Neill--Women's p475

PIOUS, MINERVA (1909-)
Russian-Amer. radio comedienne
Lamparski--What. (2) p66-67, por.

PIOZZI, HESTER LYNCH THRALE
SALUSBURY (1741-1821)

Welch author, traveller,
(friend of Dr. Johnson)
Avenel--Comp. (1) p421
Hamalian--Ladies p3-14
Jones--Rutledge p767-768
Moers--Literary p302
Morley--Literary p145,258,
316-319

PIPER, LENORE EVELINA
SIMONDS (1859-1950)
Amer. medium
James--Notable (3) p73-75

PIRAMI, EDMEA (1899-)
Italian physician
Hellstedt--Women p176-178, por.

PISAN, CHRISTINE DE (1364-
1430/1431)
French scholar, poet
Brink--Female p7-23, por.
Crosland--Women p44-46,218
Fine--Women p4
Macksey--Book p78-79,180-181,
272, por.

PISKOVA, VELA AKHMAKOVA
(1889-1925)
Bulgarian teacher, politician
Partington--Who's p331

PISSARRO, ESTHER BENSUSAN
(-1951)
British illuminator, printer,
designer, wood engraver,
radical
Callen--Women p181,183,214,225

PISTRUCCI, ELENA AND ELIZA
(fl. 1860's)
Italian-English cameo crafts-
women
Callen--Women p161-162

PITCAIRN, MRS. JOHN
Scottish, wife of chief
magistrate
Ware--Meet p80

PITCHER, MOLLY (c1754-1832)
Amer. Revolutionary War
heroine
Booth--Women p173-174, por.
Clyne--Patriots p50-57
DePauw--Found. p190-191
DePauw--Rem. p90

Evans--Weather. p10-12
Hymowitz--Hist. p30-31, por.
Ingraham--Album p14
James--Notable (2) p448-449
Kulkin--Her p227-228
McHenry--Liberty's p260
Macksey--Book p54
Meyer--Petticoat p62,107-109, por.
Millstein--We p34, por.
Reifert--Women p23-24
Sherr--American p151,198, por.
Somerville--Women p6-11
Webster's--Amer. p663
Whitney--Col. p336
Woman's Almanac p451, por.
World--Who p177

PITMAN, AGNES (1850-1946)
Amer. ceramicist, woodcarver
Callen--Women p164,169-170,225

PITOU, PENELOPE (fl. 1960's)
Amer. skier
Assoc. Press--Pursuit p229-230

PITTER, RUTH (1897-)
English poet
Avenel--Comp. (1) p421
Bernikow--World p169

PITTINGER, ALICE BUTTERWORTH
(fl. 1910's)
Amer. civic, club worker,
noted Idaho mother
Amer.--Mothers p153

PITTS, ZASU (c1900-1963)
Amer. actress, comedienne
Keylin--Hollywood p230, por.
Mordden--Movie p19-21,23
Sicherman--Notable p547-548
Springer--They p200,202,323,
por.
World--Who p245

PIX, MARY GRIFFITH (1666-c1720)
English playwright
Horner--English p8, (also note)

PIZZEY, ERIN (fl. 1970's)
English founder of Women's
Aid
O'Neill--Women's p727

PKIKHOI'KO, ANTONINA F. (fl.
1960's)
Russian physicist
O'Neill--Women's p183

PLACE, ETTA
Amer. robber
Woman's Almanac p501

PLACIDE, SUZANNE
See DOUVILLIER, SUZANNE
THEODORE VAILLANDE

PLAIDY, JEAN (1906-)
English novelist
Seymour-Smith--Novels p198,
por.
World--Who p46

PLAISTED, EMMA (fl. 1890's)
Amer. Western pioneer
Time--Women p51

PLANK, ROSINE (fl. 1970's)
Amer. agriculturist, federal
official
O'Neill--Women's p25

PLATEARIUS
See TROTULA OF SALERNO
(DAME TROTT)

PLATEN, SOPHIE VON
English, mistress of George I
Macksey--Book p97

PLATH, SYLVIA (1932-1963)
Amer. poet, novelist, feminist
Avenel--Comp. (2) p204-205
Brinnin--Modern p255-258
Chester--Rising p210-217, por.
Chinoy--Women p179-184, por.
Donaldson--How p295-296
Ehrlich--Oxford p29,54,65,144
Kaplan--Salt p289-291
Kupferberg--First p125-126, por.
McHenry--Liberty's p329-330
Moers--Literary p302, see also
index p332, por.
O'Neill--Women's p687
People's Almanac (1) p1323-1324,
por.
Seymour-Smith--Novels p199
Seymour-Smith--Who's p283-284
Sicherman--Notable p548-551
Sochen--Movers p97-98,282-285
Webber--Woman p139-146
Who Did What p263
Wintle--Makers p412-413, #374
Woman's Almanac p256-257, por.
World--Who p18

PLATT, CHRISTINA (fl. 1970's)

Amer. agriculturist, institute
co-founder
O'Neill--Women's p10

PLATT, LOUISE (1915-)
Amer. actress
Springer--They p202,323, por.

PLATT, SARAH SOPHIA CHASE
See DECKER, SARAH SOPHIA
CHASE PLATT

PLEASANT, MARY ELLEN ("MAMMY")
(c1814-1904)
Amer. boardinghouse keeper,
Western pioneer, Civil Rights
worker
James--Notable (3) p75-77
Sherr--American p16,19
Williams--Legend. p69-91, por.

PLESHETTE, SUZANNE (1937-)
Amer. actress
World--Who p245

PLESSIS, ROSE ALPHONSINE
See DU PLESSIS, MARIE ALICE
BRADFORD

PLINY, WIFE OF
Roman matron
Zinserling--Women p56

PLISETSKAYA, MAYA MIKHAILOVNA
(1925-)
Russian ballet dancer, actress
Macksey--Book p235
Mandel--Soviet p192
O'Neill--Women's p643
World--Who p78

PLOTINA (-c117 A.D.)
Roman empress, (wife of
Trajan)
Zinserling--Women p68

PLOWRIGHT, JOAN ANNE (1929-)
English actress, (wife of Sir
Laurence Olivier)
Entertainers p273
People--Best p159
World--Who p260

PLUMLEE, ELINOR (fl. 1970's)
Amer. heroine, Carnegie
Medal winner
O'Neill--Women's
p734

PLUMMER, LAURA NELSON (1879-1960)
Amer. teacher, politician,
noted North Dakota mother
Amer.--Mothers p419, por.

PLUMMER, MARY WRIGHT (1856-1916)
Amer. librarian, author
James--Notable (3) p77-78

PLUMMER, OLIVIA
Amer. religious worker
Kooiman--Cameos p13-22, por.

PLUNKET, KATHERINE (1820-1932)
English oldest person
People's Almanac (2) p941-942

PLUNKETT, MARGARET L.
Amer. labor attaché
O'Neill--Women's p337

POCAHONTAS (1595-1617)
Amer. Indian princess, noted
Virginia mother, (wife of
John Rolfe)
Amer.--Mothers p547, por.
Donaldson--How p296-297
Earle--Two Cent. (1) p xvi,
122-125, por.
Gridley--Amer. p22-32, por.
Ingraham--Album p2,5, por.
James--Notable (3) p78-81
Jones--Rutledge p628-629
Kulkin--Her p228-230
McHenry--Liberty's p330
People's Almanac (1) p105-107
Sherr--American p235,239, por.
Signif.--Amer. p7, por.
Warren--Pictorial p7-10, por.
Webster's--Amer. p830
Who Did What p264
Williams--Demeter's p10-11
Woman's Almanac p51, por.
World--Who p300

PODJAVORINSKA, LUDMILA
(-1951)
Czechoslovakian writer
Partington--Who's p332

POE, ELIZABETH (ARNOLD)
HOPKINS (1787-1811)
English-Amer. singer, actress,
(mother of Edgar Allan Poe)
Claghorn--Biog. p356

Diagram--Mothers p208-209, por.
James--Notable (3) p81-82

POILLON, CHARLOTTE AND
KATHERINE (fl. 1900's-1920's)
Amer. prizefighters, titans,
accused con-women
Felton--Famous p62-63

POILLON, CLARA LOUISE (1850-1936)
Amer. ceramicist
Callen--Women p91,225

POINTER SISTERS
Amer. singers
Claghorn--Jazz p237
Glassman--Year '79 p135, por.

POIRIER, ANNE-CLAIRE (fl. 1960's-1970's)
Canadian film director
Smith--Movies p97

POISSON, JEANNE
See POMPADOUR, JEANNE
ANTOINETTE POISSON,
MADAME DE

POITEVENT, ELIZA JANE
See NICHOLSON, ELIZA JANE
POITEVENT HOLBROOK

POITIERS, DIANE DE, DUCHESS
DE VALENTINOIS (1499-1566)
French courtesan, mistress of
Henry II of France
Jones--Rutledge p630
Macksey--Book p24,95
Mead--Hist. p347

"POKER ALICE"
See TUBBS, ALICE IVERS

POLE, ELIZABETH
See POOLE, ELIZABETH

POLIER, JUSTINE WISE (1903-)
Amer. judge
Gilbert--Part. p121-127, por.

POLIGNAT, PRINCESS OF
See SINGER, WINNARETTA
(WINNIE), PRINCESS DE
POLIGNOT

POLING, LILLIAN DIEBOLD (1880-)

Amer. humanitarian, noted
Ohio mother
Amer.--Mothers p433-434, por.

POLITE, CARLENE HATCHER
(1932-)
Amer. dancer, writer
P.W.--Author p123-126,520

POLK, ANTOINETTE
Amer. Civil War patriot
Sherr--American p217

POLK, JANE KNOX (1776-1852)
Amer., mother of President
Polk
Faber--Presidents' p252-254

POLK, MRS. (fl. 1774)
Amer. schoolmistress
Williams--Demeter's p177

POLK, SARAH CHILDRESS (1803-
1891)
Amer. first lady, wife of
James K. Polk
James--Notable (3) p82
Melick--Wives p34-35, por.
People's Almanac (1) p266
Woman's Almanac p488

POLLAK, BURGLINDE (fl. 1970's)
East German pentathlon
athlete
O'Neill--Women's p577,579-580

POLLARD, MARY (fl. 1970's)
Amer. Army camera equip-
ment repair-woman
O'Neill--Women's p545-546

POLLARD, REBECCA (c1831-1917)
Amer. educator, author
Sherr--American p71

POLLATSCHEK, ESTELLE (1876-)
Amer. aged woman
People's Almanac (2) p944

POLLITZER, ANITA LILY (1894-
1975)
Amer. suffragist, feminist
Sicherman--Notable p551-552

POLLOCK, ELSIE FRANKFURT
Amer. fashion designer,
manufacturer

Rich-McCoy--Mill. p96-126,
por.

POLLS, CAROL (fl. 1970's)
Amer. boxing judge
O'Neill--Women's p559

POLYBLANK, ELLEN ALBERTINA
(1840-1930)
English-Amer. sister, educator
James--Notable (3) p188-189

POLYDAMNA
Greek physician
Mead--Hist. p37

POLYKOFF, SHIRLEY (fl. 1930's)
Amer. advertising executive
Woman's Almanac p209

POLZUNOVA, ALLA (fl. 1970's)
Russian horsewoman
Mandel--Soviet p157

POMARES, ANITA
See PAGE, ANITA

POMEROY, SARAH B. (fl. 1970's)
Amer. classical scholar
O'Neill--Women's p423-424

POMPADOUR, JEANNE ANTOINETTE
POISSON, MADAME DE (1721-
1764)
French, mistress of Louis XV
Donaldson--How p300-301
Earle--Two Cent. (2) p461,502
Fry--1000 p180, por.
Jones--Rutledge p632
Macksey--Book p97-99, por.
Who Did What p264, por.
World--Who p159

PONCHE, (ANNA-) MARIE LA
French jockey
Macksey--Book p260
McWhirter--Guinness p93

POND, ELIZABETH (fl. 1960's-
1970's)
Amer. journalist
Marzolf--Up p87-88

PONS, LILY (ALICE JOSEPHINE)
(1904-1976)
French opera singer
Claghorn--Biog. p357

Cur. Biog. '76 p475
Lamparski--What. (2) p40-41,
 por.
McHenry--Liberty's p330
Neidle--America's p299-230
Springer--They p202-203,323,
 por.
Tuggle--Golden p220-222, por.
World--Who p72

PONSELLE, ROSE MELBA (1897-
 1981)
 Amer. opera singer
Claghorn--Biog. p357
Clark--Leading p87-89
Ingraham--Album p65
Lamparski--What. (4) p10-11,
 por.
McHenry--Liberty's p330-331
Marlowe--Great p283-287, por.
O'Neill--Women's p620
Stoddard--Famous p336-346, por.
Tuggle--Golden p159-161,164,
 179,198-199,213-214, por.
World--Who p72

PONTALBA, MICAELA ALMONESTER,
 BARONESS (1795-1874)
 Amer. building constructor,
 planner
Sherr--American p83

PONZILLO, ROSA
 See PONSELLE, ROSA MELBA

POOL, JUDITH GRAHAM (1919-1975)
 Amer. physiologist
Sicherman--Notable p553-554

POOL, MARIA LOUISE (1841-1898)
 Amer. novelist
McHenry--Liberty's p331

POOL, MARY JANE (fl. 1940's-
 1970's)
 Amer. editor
O'Neill--Women's p476

POOLE, BARBARA (fl. 1930's)
 Amer. aviatrix, army flier
Keil--Those p115,123-124

POOLE, ELIZABETH (1599-1654)
 English-Amer. Puritan, colonial
 founder
Sherr--American p113
Warren--Pictorial p36

Williams--Demeter's p30-31,
 188

POPELIN, MARIE (1846-1913)
 Belgian feminist, club founder,
 lawyer
Macksey--Book p89-90,126,274-
 275, por.

POPKES, OPAL LEE (1920-   )
 Amer. Choctaw Indian writer
Fisher--Third p v,58

POPKIN, ZELDA (1898-1983)
 Amer. author
Cur. Biog. '83 p472

POPLAVSKAYA, IRINA (fl. 1970's)
 Russian film director
Mandel--Soviet p144-145

POPOVA, KATYA ASENOVA (1924-
 1966)
 Bulgarian opera singer
Partington--Who's p334

POPOVA, LIUBOV SERBEEVNA
 (1889-1924)
 Russian painter
Fine--Women p168-199
Harris--Women p58,60-63,288,298,
 310,359
O'Neill--Women's p596

POPOVA, ZLATINA IVANOVA
 See NEDEVA, ZLATINA

POPOVICH, MARINA (fl. 1970's)
 Russian pilot, aviatrix
Mandel--Soviet p81

POPP, ADELHEID (1869-1939)
 Austrian labor leader, editor
O'Neill--Women's p293

POPP, LUCIA (1939-   )
 Czechoslovakian opera singer
Gammond--Illus. p248, por.

PORADA, EDITH
 Austrian-Amer. archaeologist,
 professor
O'Neill--Women's p147

PORCAIRAGES, AZALAIS DE
 (c1140-   )
 French troubadour

Amer. curatorial assistant
Woman's--Female p119

PORTER, SYLVIA FIELD FELDMAN
(1913-)
Amer. financial expert,
columnist, journalist,
economist
Bird--Enterprising p212-217
Bowman--Social p34-39, por.
Cur. Biog. '80 p324-327, por.
Diamonstein--Open p329-332,
por.
Gilbert--Part. p227-231, por.
Longstreet--Queen p192
McHenry--Liberty's p333-334
Marzolf--Up p58
O'Neill--Women's p449-450
Woman's Almanac p271
World--Who p54

PORTER, "TETTY" (fl. 1700's)
English, wife of Samuel
Johnson
Morley--Literary p266-267

PORTER, THEA (fl. 1960's)
English painter, fashion
designer
O'Neill--Women's p253

PORTSMOUTH, LOUISE RENEE,
DUCHESS
See KEROUALLE, LOUISE
RENEE DE, DUCHESS OF
PORTSMOUTH & AUBIGNY

POSNER, IRINA (fl. 1970's)
Amer. TV producer
Marzolf--Up p172-173

POSSONY, VALY (1905-)
Austrian potter
O'Neill--Women's p128

POST, EMILY (1873-1960)
Amer. author, etiquette
authority, columnist
Jones--Rutledge p634
McHenry--Liberty's p334
Macksey--Book p17, por.
O'Neill--Women's p747
Sicherman--Notable p554-556
Sochen--Herstory p303
Webster's--Amer. p839
World--Who p54

POST, MARION LEE
Amer. skier
O'Neill--Women's p566

POST, MARJORIE MERRIWEATHER
(1887-1973)
Amer. philanthropist, business-
woman
People's Almanac (1) p1334
Sicherman--Notable p556-557

POSTNIKOVA, VICTORIA (fl. 1970's)
Russian pianist
Mandel--Soviet p150

POTIPHAR'S WIFE
Biblical
Price--God p66-69

POTOK, ANNA MAXIMILLIAN
(c1898-)
Polish fashion designer
O'Neill--Women's p247-248,257

POTTER, (HELEN) BEATRIX (1866-
1943)
English children's book author,
illustrator
Avenel--Comp. (1) p425
Jones--Rutledge p634-635
Kulkin--Her p230-232
Macksey--Book p208, por.
Morley--Literary p91-92,326-327
O'Neill--Women's p690
Showalter--Lit. p343
Smaridge--Famous p29-36, por.
Who Did What p265
World--Who p29

POTTER, DOROTHY WILLIAMS
(1937-)
Amer. genealogical researcher,
author
Meyer--Who's p165-166

POTTER, EDITH (fl. 1930's)
Amer. physician, pathologist
O'Neill--Women's p218

POTTER, LORRAINE (fl. 1970's)
Amer. Air Force chaplain
Proctor--Women p117-119,126-130

POTTER, MARY (1900-)
English artist
Contemp. Brit. unp., por.

POTTER, SUSANNAH (c1758-1780)
Amer. "miracle" of Jemima
Wilkinson
Coffin--Parade p313

POTTKER, JANICE
Amer. feminist, author
O'Neill--Women's p403

POTTS, ELIZABETH (-1890)
Amer. accused murderer
Sherr--American p143
Time--Women p176-177, por.

POTTS, JEAN (1910-)
Amer. novelist, short-story
author
Seymour-Smith--Novels p200

POUGY, LIANE DE (fl. 19th cent.)
French writer, courtesan
Crosland--Woman p75-76

POULAIN, SIMONE A. (fl. 1950's-
1960's)
Amer. government official
O'Neill--Women's p93-94

POUND, LAURA BIDDLECOMBE
(1841-1928)
Amer. librarian, noted
Nebraska mother
Amer.--Mothers p332-333, por.

POUND, LOUISE (1872-1958)
Amer. scholar, educator,
professor, athlete
Hazen--Interv. p227
Sicherman--Notable p557-559

POUNDS, JESSIE BROWN (1861-
1921)
Amer. hymnist
Claghorn--Biog. p357-358

POUSSAINT, RENE
Amer. RV news co-anchor
Scheuer--Tel. p383-384

POUY, MRS. FREDERICK
See FYODOROVA, VICTORIA

POWDERMAKER, HORTENSE
(1900-1970)
Amer. anthropologist, author
Cur. Biog. '70 p468

Sicherman--Notable p559-
561

POWELL, ALMA WEBSTER (1874-
1930)
Amer. opera singer, teacher
Claghorn--Biog. p358

POWELL, ANN MURRAY (fl. 1770's)
Amer. pioneer milliner
Berkin--Women p54-55, 60

POWELL, DAWN (1897-1963)
Amer. novelist
Avenel--Comp. (2) p209
Seymour-Smith--Novels p200

POWELL, ELEANOR (1913-1982)
Amer. dancer, actress,
religious worker
Lamparski--What. (2) p194-195,
por.
Lamparski--What. (8) p232-233,
por.
Mordden--Movie p210
Shipman--Gold. p448-449, por.
Springer--They p203,323, por.
Woman's Almanac p314
World--Who p264

POWELL, ELIZA (fl. 1780's-1790's)
Amer. socialite
Earnest--American p37-38

POWELL, JANE (1929-)
Amer. actress, singer
Cur. Biog. '74 p321-323, por.
Shipman--Internatl. p473-474, por.
World--Who p245

POWELL, LOUISE LESSORE (fl.
1910's-1930's)
British embroiderer, dress
designer, china painter,
furniture decorator
Callen--Women p168,225

POWELL, LOUISE MATHILDE (1871-
1943)
Amer. nursing educator
James--Notable (3) p89-90

POWELL, MAUD (1868-1920)
Amer. violinist
Claghorn--Biog. p358
James--Notable (3) p90-92

McHenry--Liberty's p334
O'Neill--Women's p632-633

POWELL, PAT (fl. 1960's-1970's)
Amer. filmmaker
Smith--Movies p197,267

POWELL, SUE (fl. 1970's)
Amer. singer
Glassman--Year '79 p96, por.

POWELL, VIRGINIA (GINNY)
(-1959)
Amer. singer
Claghorn--Biog. p358

POWELL, YVETTE
Amer., (wife of Clayton
Powell)
Miller--Fishbait p190,192-193

POWER, ANNIE (fl. 1900's)
British bookbinder
Callen--Women p197,218-219,225

POWER, BILLIE JOAN (fl. 1960's)
Amer. heroine, Carnegie
Medal winner
O'Neill--Women's p733

POWER, KATHERINE ANN (c1949-)
Amer. accused criminal
People's Almanac (1) p613
Woman's Almanac p510

POWER, MRS. NICHOLAS
Amer., mother of Sarah
Helen Whitman
Book--Lists (2) p268

POWERS, MARIE (c1913-1973)
Amer. opera singer
Cur. Biog. '74 p468

POWERS, STEFANIE (1942-)
Amer. actress
People--Best p61, por.
Scheuer--Tel. p384, por.

POWLES, MATILDA
See TILLEY, VESTA,
LADY DE FRECE

POWNALL, MARY ANN (1751/
1756-1796)
English singer, songwriter
Claghorn--Biog. p358

DePauw--Rem. p138-139,
por.

POWNER, I. FLORENCE (1938-)
Amer. genealogical researcher,
writer
Meyer--Who's p166

POYNTON, DOROTHY (c1915-)
Amer. diver
Assoc. Press--Pursuit p120,139

PRALL, ELIZABETH SMITH (fl.
1830's)
Amer. early Oberlin student
Sherr--American p186, por.

PRANG, MARY AMELIA DANA HICKS
(1836-1927)
Amer. art educator, editor
James--Notable (3) p92-93

PRATT, ANNA BEACH (1867-1932)
Amer. social worker
James--Notable (3) p93-95

PRATT, ELIZABETH ("HANDY
BETSY") (1750-)
Amer. blacksmith, Revolution-
ary War patriot
Meyer--Petticoat p32-33,36-37

PRATT, JANE (c1902-)
Amer. Congresswoman
Chamberlin--Min. p193-195

PRATT, ROMANIA B.
Amer. physician, surgeon
Sherr--American p227

PRATT, RUTH SEARS BAKER
(1877-1965)
Amer. Congresswoman
Chamberlin--Min. p78-82

PRAY, ANNA MALVINA
See FLORENCE, MALVINA PRAY

PREISAND, SALLY
See PRIESAND, SALLY

PREISKEL, BARBARA SCOTT
Amer. lawyer
Innis--Profiles p48-49, por.

PRELI, SORINE A.
Amer. labor leader
O'Neill--Women's p336

PRENDERGAST, MEHITABEL WING
(1738-)
Amer. Quaker, pioneer,
patriot, noted New York
mother
Amer.--Mothers p389-390

PRENTICE, DOROTHY (fl. 1910's)
English aviatrix
Boase--Sky's p15,16-17, por.

PRENTISS, ELIZABETH PAYSON
(1818-1878)
Amer. hymnist, author
Claghorn--Biog. p359
James--Notable (3) p95-96
McHenry--Liberty's p334-335

PRENTISS, NARCISSA (1808-)
Amer. Western pioneer,
(Oregon Trail)
Sherr--American p173

PRENTISS, PAULA (1939-)
Amer. actress
World--Who p245

PREOBRAZHENSKAYA, OLGA
(fl. 1920's)
Russian film director
Mandel--Soviet p144-145
Smith--Movies p135

PRESCOTT, ELEANOR (1946-)
Amer. TV producer
Scheuer--Tel. p385

PRESCOTT, HILDA F.M. (1896-
1972)
English novelist
Morley--Literary p47-48,283

PRESLEY, CLOIE (1922-)
Amer. genealogical researcher,
indexer
Meyer--Who's p166

PRESLEY, MARY BAGGETT
(1880-1933)
Amer. post-Civil War
worker, noted Illinois mother
Amer.--Mothers p166, por.

PRESS, SUE (fl. 1970's)
Australian golfer
McWhirter--Guinness p78-79

PRESS, TAMARA (fl. 1960's)
Russian track and field athlete
Assoc. Press--Pursuit p238,270
Hollander--100 p124-125, por.

PRESS, TINA (fl. 1970's)
Amer. radio broadcaster,
executive producer
Marzolf--Up p151-154

PRESSLEY, LYNNE (fl. 1970's)
Australian Rhodes Scholar
O'Neill--Women's p435

PRESTON, ANN (1813-1872)
Amer. physician, college dean,
educator, Quaker
James--Notable (3) p96-97
McHenry--Liberty's p335
Marks--Women p108,123, por.

PRESTON, FRANCES FOLSOM
See CLEVELAND, FRANCES
FOLSOM

PRESTON, MARGARET JUNKIN (1820-
1897)
Amer. poet, Civil War letter-
writer
Ehrlich--Oxford p201
James--Notable (3) p97-98

PRESTON, MARILYN
Amer. newspaper, TV critic
Scheuer--Tel. p385-386

PRESTON, MAY WILSON (1873-1949)
Amer. illustrator
James--Notable (3) p98-100
McHenry--Liberty's p335-336

PREVIN, DORY LANGAN (1929-)
Amer. songwriter, dancer,
singer, actress
Cur. Biog. '75 p323-326, por.
Woman's Almanac p299

PREVOST, FRANÇOISE (1680-1741)
French ballet dancer
Migel--Ballerinas p11-12, por.

PREVOST, MARIE (1898-1934/1937)
Canadian-Amer. actress
Springer--They p203,323, por.

PRICE, ELLEN
See WOOD, MRS. HENRY

PRICE, FLORENCE BEATRICE
SMITH (1888-1953)
Amer. pianist, composer
Claghorn--Biog. p360
Sicherman--Notable p561-562

PRICE, JANE PALLEY
See PALEY, JANE

PRICE, JUDY (1943-)
Amer. TV executive
Scheuer--Tel. p386

PRICE, (MARY) LEONTYNE
(1927-)
Amer. opera singer
Adams--Great (3rd) p190, por.
Claghorn--Biog. p360
Cur. Biog. '78 p329-332, por.
Diamonstein--Open p333-335,
por.
Gammond--Illus. p248, por.
Ingraham--Album p65, por.
McHenry--Liberty's p336
100--Greatest (1) p84, por.
O'Neill--Women's p621-622, por.
People--Best p142, por.
Signif.--Amer. p71, por.
Toppin--Biog. p391-393
Webster's--Amer. p845
Woman's Almanac p299
World--Who p72

PRICE, MARGARET (1941-)
Welsh opera singer
Gammond--Illus. p248-249, por.

PRICE, MARY TOOZE (1915-)
Amer. "foster mother," noted
Washington state mother
Amer.--Mothers p561-562, por.

PRICE, MAYBELLE K. (1887-1973)
Amer. humanitarian, noted
Pennsylvania mother
Amer.--Mothers p458-459, por.

PRICE, RUTH (1938-)
Amer. singer, dancer
Claghorn--Biog. p360
Claghorn--Jazz p240

PRICHARD, KATHARINE SUSANNAH
(1884-1972)
Australian novelist
Avenel--Comp. (1) p428-429
Seymour-Smith--Novels p201

PRIDEAUX, SARAH T.
British bookbinder, printer
Callen--Women p194-195,226

PRIDGETT, GERTRUDE MALISSA
NIX
See RAINEY, GERTRUDE MALISSA
NIX ("MA")

PRIESAND, SALLY (1946-)
Amer. rabbi
Bloom--Religion p124-125
Ingraham--Album p68, por.
O'Neill--Women's p382
Proctor--Women p30-31,47,131-145
Woman's Almanac p396, por.
World--Who p83

PRIESKEL, BARBARA SCOTT
Amer. film executive
O'Neill--Women's p361

PRIEST, INEZ BABER (-1973)
Amer. government official,
noted California mother
Amer.--Mothers p58

PRIEST, IVY MAUDE BAKER (1905-
1975)
Amer. government official,
noted California-Utah mother
Amer.--Mothers p58,533, por.
Cur. Biog. '75 p472
Sicherman--Notable p562-563

PRIIMACHENKO, MARIIA (1908-)
Ukrainian Russian artist
Women's--Female p3, supp.

PRIMUS, PEARL (1919-)
Trinidad dancer
O'Neill--Women's p649-650

PRIN, MARIE
See "KIKI OF MONTPARNASSE"
(PRIN, MARIE)

PRINCE, MRS. FREDERICK H. (fl.
1920's-1930's)
Amer., wife of "German-
Scandinavian" millionaire
Felton--Famous p246-247

PRINCE, HELEN DODSON (fl.
1930's-1970's)
Amer. astronomer, solar
flare researcher

O'Neill--Women's p151-
152

PRINCE, LUCY TERRY
See TERRY, LUCY

PRINCE, MARY (fl. 1650's)
Amer. Quaker martyr,
colonial religious worker
Williams--Demeter's p124-125

PRINCE, MRS. SIDNEY (fl. 1930's)
Amer. philanthropist
Neuls-Bates--Women p255-256

PRINCIPAL, VICTORIA (1950-)
Amer. actress
People--Best p81, por.
Scheuer--Tel. p386, por.

PRINDLE, KAREN (fl. 1970's)
Amer. TV assistant director
Klever--Women p28-29,86-91,108-
109, por.

PRINGLE, AILEEN (1895-)
Amer. actress
Lamparski--What. (2) p174-175,
por.
Springer--They p203,323, por.

PRINGLE, ELIZABETH WATIES
ALLSTON (1845-1921)
Amer. rice planter, author
James--Notable (3) p100-101
Sherr--American p213

PRINZ, DIANNE
Amer. solar physicist
Oberg--Space p81,187,231-232,
por.

PRIOR, MARGARET BARRET
ALLEN (1773-1842)
Amer. charitable worker,
philanthropist
James--Notable (3) p101-103

PRIOR-PALMER, LUCINDA (fl.
1970's)
British horsewoman
O'Neill--Women's p588

PRISCILLA
Biblical
People's Almanac (1) p860
Price--God p179-183

PRITCHARD, MRS. FRANCIS (fl.
1660's)
Amer. colonist
Earle--Two Cent. (1) p113-114

PRITCHARD, HANNAH VAUGHAN
(1711-1768)
British actress
Findlater--Player p66-70

PROCOPE, ERNESTA G. (fl. 1970's)
Amer. insurance brokerage
executive
O'Neill--Women's p519

PROCTER, ADELAIDE ANNE (1825-
1864)
English poet
Showalter--Lit. p329

PROCTOR, ALICE (fl. 1620's)
Amer. massacre heroine
Williams--Demeter's p154

PROCTOR, BARBARA GARDNER
Amer. advertising agency
owner
Rich-McCoy--Mill. p207-227, por.

PROCTOR, ELIZABETH (fl. 1693)
Amer. accused witch
Williams--Demeter's p140

PROELL, ANNEMARIE MOSER
(1953-)
Austrian skier
Cur. Biog. '76 p327-329, por.
Kulkin--Her p232-233
McWhirter--Guinness p120, por.
O'Neill--Women's p565
Woman's Almanac p433
World--Who p220

PROLE, LOZANIA
See BLOOM, URSULA

"THE PROPHET" (fl. 1930's)
Legendary "prophet"
Coffin--Parade p80-82

PROUST, JEANNE WEIL (-1905)
French, mother of Marcel
Proust
Diagram--Mothers p212-213, por.

PROVINE, DOROTHY (1937-)
Amer. actress
World--Who p245

PROVOOST, MARY DE PEYSTER
    SCHRICK SPRATT
    See ALEXANDER, MARY
    (POLLY) SPRATT PROVOOST

PROWDA, JUDITH G. (fl. 1970's)
    Amer. writer
    O'Neill--Women's p595

PROWSE, JULIET (1936/1937-)
    British dancer
    World--Who p264

PROXMIRE, ELLEN
    Amer. hostess, (wife of
    Willis Proxmire)
    Miller--Fishbait p308

PRUE, EDWINA
    Amer. model
    Keenan--Women p111-114, por.

PRUETTE, LORINE LIVINGSTON
    (1876/1896-)
    Amer. feminist, social
    scientist, psychologist, author
    Showalter--These p68-73

PRYER, MARGARET (c1784-)
    Amer. suffragist
    Warren--Pictorial p118

PRYOR, SARA AGNES RICE (1830-
    1912)
    Amer. author, social leader,
    Civil War heroine
    James--Notable (3) p103-104

PRYOR, SUNNY
    Amer. radio disc jockey
    Marzolf--Up p146

PSAPPHO OF LESBOS
    See SAPPHO

PTAH, MERIT
    Egyptian, ancient physician
    O'Neill--Women's p197

PTASCHKINA, NELLY (1903-1920)
    Russian diarist
    Moffatt--Revel. p56-66

PUCCIARELLI, ELSA TABERNIG DE
    Argentinean professor, educa-
    tor
    Macksey--Book p77

PUCHKOVSKAYA, NADEZHDA
    Russian physician, hospital
    head
    Mandel--Soviet p85

PUDDICOMBE, ANNE (1836-1915)
    Welsh poet
    Showalter--Lit. p333

PUDEATOR, ANN (-1692)
    Amer. accused witch
    Williams--Demeter's p152-153

PUGH, SARAH (1800-1884)
    Amer. teacher, abolitionist,
    suffragist
    James--Notable (3) p104-105

PUGH, WYNETTE
    See WYNETTE, TAMMY

PUGLIESE, JULIA JONES (fl. 1930's-
    1970's)
    Amer. fencer
    O'Neill--Women's p560

PUJALS, CARMEN (fl. 1960's)
    Argentinean hydrographic
    researcher, (Antarctica)
    Land--New p21

PULITZER, LILLY (fl. 1960's)
    Amer. fashion designer
    O'Neill--Women's p249-250

PULLEN, DORIS EVELYN (1920-)
    English genealogical researcher,
    author
    Meyer--Who's p167

PULLEN, HARRIET SMITH ("MA")
    (1859-1947)
    Amer. hotel owner, Alaskan
    "gold rush belle"
    Jones--Women (1) p94-98
    Sherr--American p5

PULLINGER, DOROTHEE
    British motorcar executive
    Macksey--Book p172

PUNELLI, DIANE (fl. 1970's)
    Amer. reading-improvement
    worker
    O'Neill--Women's p117

PURCELL, POLLY JANE (1842-)

Amer. pioneer
Stein--Fragments, no p.

PURDUE, CONNIE (fl. 1950's-
1970's)
New Zealand feminist, labor
union official
O'Neill--Women's p322

PURIM, FLORA (1942-)
Brazilian singer, guitarist,
percussionist
Claghorn--Jazz p242

PURSER, SARAH (fl. 1900's)
Irish stained glass artist
Callen--Women p177,226

PUTNAM, ALICE HARVEY WHITING
(1841-1919)
Amer. pioneer kindergarten
educator
James--Notable (3) p105-106

PUTNAM, ASHLEY (1952-)
Amer. opera singer
Cur. Biog. '82 p325-328, por.

PUTNAM, BERTHA HAVEN (1872-
1960)
Amer. historian
Sicherman--Notable p563-564

PUTNAM, DEBORAH LOTHROP
(1719-1777)
Amer. Revolutionary War
patriot
Meyer--Petticoat p45

PUTNAM, EMILY JAMES SMITH
(1865-1944)
Amer. author, college dean,
educator
James--Notable (3) p106-108
McHenry--Liberty's p336-337

PUTNAM, MRS. GEORGE PALMER
See EARHART, AMELIA

PUTNAM-JACOBI, MARY C. (1842-
1906)
Amer. physician
Warren--Pictorial p127-128,143

PUTNEY, SUSANNAH (fl. 1770's)
Amer. Revolutionary War
patriot
Meyer--Petticoat p45

PUYUCAHUA, MICAELA (fl. 1760's)
Peruvian Indian heroine
Hahner--Women p29-31

PYKACEK, JUNE (fl. 1970's)
Amer. theater director
Seed--Saturday's p31-35, por.

PYLE, GLADYS (1890-)
Amer. Senator
Chamberlin--Min. p125-127

PYM, BARBARA (1913-)
Australian novelist
Crosland--Beyond p54,181-185
Seymour-Smith--Novels p203

PYTHIA (fl. 9th Cent. B.C.)
Greek prophetess
Book--Lists (2) p306
Pomeroy--Godd. p33

PYTHIAS (fl. c380's-320's B.C.)
Greek histologist, embryologist, botanist, biologist, (wife
of Aristotle)
Mead--Hist. p39-40

Q

QUANT, MARY (1934-)
English fashion designer
Keenan--Women p90-91,96-101,
127, por.
Macksey--Book p268-270, por.
O'Neill--Women's p236,249
World--Who p204

QUARLES, NORMA
Amer. TV newscaster
Gelfman--Women p9,26,77-78,93-
94,97,112-113,128,154-155, por.
Marzolf--Up p192-193
Scheuer--Tel. p389

QUATRO, SUZI (c1951-)
British singer
Glassman--Year '79 p137

QUEDENS, EUNICE
See ARDEN, EVE

"QUEEN ANN"
See MORRIS, ANN

QUEEN, NORMA YERGER (fl. 1940's)
Amer. war worker
Berkin--Women p357-359

QUEENSBERRY, CATHERINE
("KITTY") HYDE, DUCHESS
(-1777)
British hostess
Earle--Two Cent. (2) p472-473

QUEIROZ, CARLOTTA PEREIRA
DE (1892-)
Brazilian physician
Hellstedt--Women p85-90, por.

QUELER, EVE (ROBIN) (c1936-)
Amer. conductor, pianist,
foundress
Cur. Biog. '72 p354-357, por.
LePage--Women p191-207, por.
McHenry--Liberty's p338
O'Neill--Women's p638
Walker--Women p75-89, por.

QUIGG-LENNOX, NAOMI M.
(1921-)
Amer. genealogical researcher,
author
Meyer--Who's p169

QUIGLEY, JANE
See ALEXANDER, JANE

QUIGLEY, JUANITA (1931-)
Amer. child actress
Springer--They p206,323, por.

QUIGLEY, MAUD (1900-)
Amer. genealogical researcher,
indexer
Meyr--Who's p169

QUIMBY, EDITH HINKLEY (1891-
1982)
Amer. physicist
Cur. Biog. '83 p472

QUIMBY, HARRIET (1884-1912)
Amer. aviatrix
Boase--Sky's p18-19, por.
Genett--Aviation p112
Keil--Those p10-11
McHenry--Liberty's p338
Macksey--Book p246-247

QUIMBY, HELEN SHERWOOD (1870-)
Amer. violinist, pianist,
teacher
Claghorn--Biog. p363

QUIN, ANN

English novelist
Crosland--Beyond p192-196

QUINCY, DOROTHY
See HANCOCK, DOROTHY
QUINCY

QUINN, JANE BRYANT (1939-)
Amer. magazine, newspaper
columnist
Scheuer--Tel. p389

QUINN, MARIE GEOGHEGAN (fl.
1970's)
Irish Parliamentary secretary
O'Neill--Women's p59

QUINN, MARTHA
Amer. TV video jockey
Scheuer--Tel. p389-390

QUINN, SALLY (1941-)
Amer. TV co-anchor, journalist
Gelfman--Women p9,20-31,67,75,
96, por.
Miller--Fishbait p111
O'Neill--Women's p502

QUINTON, AMELIA STONE (1833-
1926)
Amer. Indian reformer, hu-
manitarian, club leader
James--Notable (3) p108-110
Warren--Pictorial p133

QUINTON, CORNELIA BENTLEY
SAGE (fl. 1910's-1960's)
Amer. art museum director
O'Neill--Women's p614

QUITSLAND, SONIA (fl. 1970's)
Amer. religions professor,
feminist
O'Neill--Women's p397

QUOIREZ, FRANÇOISE
See SAGAN, FRANÇOISE, pseud.

R

RAABEOVA, HEDVIKA (fl. 1910's-
1930's)
Czechoslovakian filmmaker
Smith--Movies p100

RABB, HARRIET (fl. 1960's-1970's)
Amer. Laywer, assistant

dean
O'Neill--Women's p363

RABB, KATE MILNER (1866-1937)
Amer. teacher, author,
noted Indiana mother
Amer.--Mothers p181, por.

RABENO, GEORGETTE (fl. 1960's)
Madagascar judge
O'Neill--Women's p369

RABIN, MRS. YITZHAK
Israeli, (wife of Israeli
prime minister)
Whedon--Always p158-159

RABINOFF, SOPHIE (1888-1957)
Russian-Amer. physician
Neidle--America's p205

RABINOVITZ, FRANCINE FISHER
(fl. 1970's)
Amer. professor, scholar
O'Neill--Women's p422

RABINOWITCH-KEMPNER, LYDIA
(1871-1935)
Lithuanian-Amer. bacteriologist, biologist
Neidle--America's p210

RABOFF, FRAN (fl. 1970's)
Amer. sculptor
Women's--Female p94

RACEY, LINDA (1869-)
Amer. centenarian
Mitchell--Yessir p101-103, por.

RACHEL
Biblical
Henry--Written p18-19,21
Price--God p52-65

RACHEL (ELIZA RACHEL FELIX)
(1821-1858)
French-Swiss actress
Entertainers p122
Fink--Great p72-78, por.
Jones--Rutledge p647
Macksey--Book p227
Marlowe--Great p85-89, por.
Smith--Women p377-420
Who Did What p269

RACHEL, HANNAH (c1815-1892)

Polish rabbi
Fink--Great p67-71
Henry--Written p213-214

RACHILDE (MARGUERITE EYMERY)
(1860-1953)
French writer
Crosland--Women p68-71

RACHLIN, MARJORIE B. (fl. 1950's-
1970's)
Amer. labor leader, ERA,
feminist
O'Neill--Women's p325

RADCLIFFE, ANN, LADY MOWLSON
(-c1661)
English educator
Macksey--Book p65-66

RADCLIFFE, ANN WARD (1764-1821/
1823)
English novelist, journalist,
antiquary
Avenel--Comp. (1) p435
Horner--English p68-72,74-76
Jones--Rutledge p648
Magill--Cycl. p879-880
Moers--Literary p302-303, see
also index p332
Morley--Literary p239,298-300
Seymour-Smith--Novels p204
Woman's Almanac p257
World--Who p47

RADCLIFFE, MARY
British writer, feminist
Macksey--Book p79

RADEGONDE (518-587)
German saint, physician,
nurse, wife of Clothaire
Mead--Hist. p95-96

RADEMACHER, CAROL SIMS (1928-)
Amer. genealogical researcher,
author, editor
Meyer--Who's p171

RADEWALD, BETTE MILLER (1931-)
Amer. genealogical researcher,
author, indexer
Meyer--Who's p171

RADFORD, GAIL (1941-)
Australian government official,
lobbyist
O'Neill--Women's p708

RADNER, GILDA (1946-)
    Amer. comedienne, dancer,
    actress
    Anderson--People p323, por.
    Cur. Biog. '80 p327-329, por.
    People--Best p178-179, por.

RADNITZ, GERTY (-1957)
    Amer. pathologist
    Webster's--Amer. p225,854

RADZIWILL, LEE BOUVIER,
    PRINCESS (1933-)
    Amer. interior decorator,
    socialite, sister of Jackie
    Onassis
    Anderson--People p324
    Cur. Biog. '77 p353-356, por.

RAE, CHARLOTTE (1926-)
    Amer. actress
    Scheuer--Tel. p391, por.

RAEBURN, AGNES, R.S.W. (1872-
    1955)
    British watercolourist,
    designer, illustrator
    Callen--Women p208,226

RAFATDJAH, SAFIEH (1903-)
    Iranian physician
    Hellstedt--Women p249-252, por.

RAGGIO, LOUISE BALLERSTEDT
    (fl. 1970's)
    Amer. lawyer, reformer
    Swiger--Women p169-186

RAGGIO, OLGA (1926-)
    Amer. museum curator
    O'Neill--Women's p616

RAGNONI, BARBARA, SISTER
    (fl. c1500)
    Italian artist
    Sparrow--Women p23,35

RAGUSA, PAULA
    See PRENTISS, PAULA

RAHAB
    Biblical
    Price--God p78-81

RAHIMOVA, IBODAT
    Russian political leader
    Mandel--Soviet p179-181

RAIMOND, C.E.
    See ROBINS, ELIZABETH

RAINE, ALLEN, pseud.
    See PUDDICOMBE, ANNE

RAINE, KATHLEEN (JESSIE)
    (1908-)
    English poet, translator,
    critic
    Avenel--Comp. (1) p435-436
    Bernikow--World p177-178
    Seymour-Smith--Who's p300

RAINER, LUISE (1910/1912-)
    Austrian actress
    Shipman--Gold. p459-460, por.
    Springer--They p206,323, por.
    World--Who p246

RAINEY, BARBARA ALLEN
    See ALLEN, BARBARA

RAINEY, GERTRUDE MALISSA NIX
    PRIDGETT ("MA") (1886-1939)
    Amer. singer, poet
    Bernikow--World p272-273
    Claghorn--Biog. p366
    Claghorn--Jazz p245-246
    James--Notable (3) p110-111
    McHenry--Liberty's p339
    Macksey--Book p219
    O'Neill--Women's p623
    Sherr--American p48
    Simon--Best p477, por.
    World--Who p271

RAINEY, RACHEL (fl. 1970's)
    Amer. naval quartermaster
    O'Neill--Women's p544

RAINIER, PRIAULX
    French composer
    Macksey--Book p221

RAINS, LILIORE GREEN (fl. 1980's)
    Amer. millionaire
    Forbes--400 ('84) p124

RAISA, ROSA (1893-1963)
    Polish opera singer
    Claghorn--Biog. p366
    Tuggle--Golden p145-147, por.

RAITT, BONNIE (1949-)
    Amer. singer
    Anderson--People p324-325

Lichtenstein--Mach. p268-
271

RALPH, JESSIE (1864-1944)
Amer. actress
Springer--They p206,323-324,
por.

RALSTON, ESTHER (1902-)
Amer. actress
Lamparski--What. (2) p206-207,
por.
Lamparski--What. (8) p239-239,
por.
Springer--They p206,324, por.

RALSTON, VERA HRUBA
See MILES, VERA

RAMA RAU, DHANVANTHI, LADY
East Indian educator
O'Neill--Women's p746

RAMA RAU, SHANTHA (1923-)
East Indian novelist
Avenel--Comp. (1) p438
O'Neill--Women's p746

RAMABAI, SARASVATI PANDITA
(1858-1922)
East Indian kindergarten
pioneer, missionary
Macksey--Book p68

RAMATI, RAQUEL (fl. 1970's)
Amer. architect, (city
planner)
O'Neill--Women's p610

RAMBAUT, MARY LUCINDA (1816-
1900)
Amer. educator, Indian
rights advocate
James--Notable (1) p197-198
McHenry--Liberty's p42-43
Sherr--American p165
Warren--Pictorial p133

RAMBEAU, MARJORIE (1889-1970)
Amer. actress
Hazen--Interv. p102
Springer--They p206-207,324,
por.
World--Who p246

RAMBERT, MARIE, DAME (1888-
1982)

Polish-British ballet company
director
Cur. Biog. '81 p324-328, por.
Cur. Biog. '82 p472
Fry--1000 p331
Jones--Rutledge p651
Macksey--Book p232
O'Neill--Women's p639
Who Did What p270

RAMBOUILLET, CATHERINE DE
VIVONNE SAVELLI, MARQUISE
DE (1588-1665)
French salonist, literary
hostess
Fine--Women p40
Jones--Rutledge p651

RAMBOVA, NATASHA (NATACHA)
(c1897-1966)
Amer. costume designer,
(2nd wife of Valentino)
O'Neill--Women's p254

RAMEE, MARIE LOUISE DE LA
See OUIDA, pseud.

RAMEY, ESTELLE
Amer. physician, physiologist,
endrocrinologist, feminist,
professor
Bowman--Medicine p24-31, por.
100--Greatest (1) p88, por.

RAMIREZ, ROSITA RIVERA (1906-)
Filipino physician
Hellstedt--Women p313-315, por.

RAMOS, ELAINE ABRAHAM (fl.
1970's)
Amer. Tlingit Indian, college
vice-president
Gridley--Amer. p162-168, por.

RAMOS, MARY (fl. 1970's)
Mexican-Amer. migrant
Lindborg--Five p55-63

RAMSAY, ALICE HUYLER (fl. 1900's)
Amer. car driver
O'Neill--Women's p741

RAMSAY, MARTHA LAURENS (1759-
1811)
Amer. South Carolina "blue-
stocking"
James--Notable (3) p111-113

RAMSAY, REGINA
    Amer. religious speaker
    Kooiman--Cameos p23-31, por.

RAMSEY, CAROLINE
    Amer. model
    Adams--Women p47,50

RAMSEY, LORENE (fl. 1970's)
    Amer. softball player
    Jordan--Broken p137

RANCKEN, SAIMA TAWAST
    (1900-)
    Finnish physician
    Hellstedt--Women p221-222, por.

RAND, AYN (1905-1982)
    Russian-Amer. philosopher,
    novelist
    Avenel--Comp. (2) p213
    Clark--Leading p203-204
    Cur. Biog. '82 p331-335
    McHenry--Liberty's p339
    Seymour-Smith--Novels p204
    Seymour-Smith--Who's p301
    Webster's--Amer. p854-855
    World--Who p19

RAND, CAROLINE AMANDA
    SHERFEY (1826-1905)
    Amer. philanthropist
    James--Notable (3) p113-115
    Starr--Amer. p269,276-277,
        280-281,284

RAND, ELLEN GERTRUDE EMMET
    (1875-1941)
    Amer. portrait painter
    James--Notable (3) p115-116

RAND, MARIE GERTRUDE (1886-
    1970)
    Amer. experimental psycholo-
    gist, researcher, opthamologist
    Sicherman--Notable p565

RAND, SALLY (1904-1979)
    Amer. dancer, entertainer
    McHenry--Liberty's p339-340
    Webster's--Amer. p855
    Woman's Almanac p314
    World--Who p264

RANDAL, JUDITH (fl. 1970's)
    Amer. newspaper science
    correspondent
    O'Neill--Women's p461

RANDALL, CLAIRE (c1921-)
    Amer. religious worker
    O'Neill--Women's p393-394

RANDALL, ELIZABETH
    Amer. TV executive
    Scheuer--Tel. p392

RANDALL, HARRIET BULPITT
    (1904-1975)
    Amer. public health worker,
    noted California mother
    Amer.--Mothers p56-57

RANDALL, RUTH PAINTER (1892-
    1908)
    Amer. biographer
    Ehrlich--Oxford p330

RANDOLPH, ANNE CAREY
    See MORRIS, ANNE CAREY
    (NANCY) RANDOLPH (MRS.
    GOUVERNEUR MORRIS)

RANDOLPH, GEORGINA ANN
    See RICE, CRAIG, pseud.

RANDOLPH, IDELL BINGMAN (1876-
    1933)
    Amer. mother of Senator
    Jennings Randolph, noted
    West Virginia mother
    Amer.--Mothers p574, por.

RANDOLPH, JOYCE (1925-)
    Amer. TV actress
    Lamparski--What. (8) p242-243,
    por.

RANDOLPH, MARTHA JEFFERSON
    (1772-1836)
    Amer., daughter of Thomas
    Jefferson
    James--Notable (3) p116-117
    Kulkin--Her p233

RANDOLPH, MARY RANDOLPH (1762-
    1828)
    Amer. cookbook author
    James--Notable (3) p117-118

RANKIN, ANABELLE, DAME (fl.
    1970's)
    Australian cabinet member,
    ambassador
    Macksey--Book p37
    O'Neill--Women's p59-60,
    62

RANKIN, JEANNETTE PICKERING
(1880-1973)
Amer. pioneer congress-
woman, feminist, pacifist
Bachtold--Gifted p95-97
Chamberlin--Min. p5-18, por.
Greenebaum--Politics p9-27, por.
Hazen--Interv. p199
Hymowitz--Hist. p283
Ingraham--Album p37
Lamparski--What. (2) p60-61,
por.
Longstreet--Queen p193
McHenry--Liberty's p340
Macksey--Book p41
Miller--Fishbait p60-63
O'Neill--Women's p67
People's Almanac (2) p572
Rader's--Story p437
Reifert--Women p215-216
Richey--Eminent p181-207, por.
Sherr--American p51,137
Sicherman--Notable p566-568
Signif.--Amer. p47, por.
Warren--Pictorial p166-167, por.
Webster's--Amer. p857
Woman's Almanac p479-480, por.
World--Who p149

RANKIN, JUDY TORLUERMKE
(1945-)
Amer. golfer
O'Neill--Women's p557,561
Woman's Almanac p420-421, por.
World--Who p220

RANKIN, OLIVE PICKERING
(1854-)
Amer., noted Montana mother
of 6 famous children, of
Jeannette Rankin
Amer.--Mothers p320-321

RAPOPORT, LYDIA (1923-1971)
Austrian-Amer. social worker,
educator
Sicherman--Notable p568-569

RAPOPORT, SEREL SEGAL (fl.
1850's)
Jewish prayer writer
Henry--Written p187-188

RAPPAPORT, FRANCES (1908-)
Amer. TV "teacher"
Lamparski--What. (4) p190-191,
por.

RAPPOLD, MARIE (BERGER)
WINTEROTH (1880-1957)
Amer. opera singer
Claghorn--Biog. p367

RASHED, SAMIA SADEEK (fl. 1970's)
Egyptian lawyer, professor,
feminist, activist
O'Neill--Women's p350,355

RASKIN, BARBARA (fl. 1970's)
Amer. novelist, journalist
O'Neill--Women's p4

RASKIN, JUDITH (1928-1984)
Amer. opera singer
Cur. Biog. '85 p472-473

RASMUSSEN, FRANKA (1909-)
Danish weaver, teacher
O'Neill--Women's p270

RASPUTIN, MARIA (1898-)
Russian, duaghter of Rasputin,
animal trainer
Higham--Celeb. p290-296, por.
Lamparski--What. (4) p38-39,
por.

RATCLIFF, BERNICE (fl. 1970's)
Amer. labor union worker,
mountain woman
Kahn--Hill. p147-160, por.

RATCLIFFE, MARY-CURTIS (fl.
1970's)
Amer. sculptor
Women's--Female p155

RATEB, AISHA (fl. 1970's)
Egyptian lawyer, professor
O'Neill--Women's p363

RATHBONE, ELEANOR FLORENCE
(1892-1946)
English Parliamentary member
Stobaugh--Women p33-48
Vallance--Women, see index p210

RATHBONE, JOSEPHINE ADAMS
(1856/1864-1941)
Amer. librarian, editor,
educator
James--Notable (3) p118-119

RATHBUN, MARY JANE (1860-1943)
Amer. marine zoologist,

carcinologist
James--Notable (3) p119-121

RATIA, ARMI (fl. 1940's-1970's)
Finnish textile designer
O'Neill--Women's p236,275-276

RATNAYAKE, MAY (1892-)
Sri Lankan physician
Hellstedt--Women p95-99, por.

RATNER, SARAH (fl. 1960's)
Amer. biochemist
O'Neill--Women's p145,164,224

RATTLEY, JESSIE MENIFIELD (fl.
1950's-1970's)
Amer. business school
operator
Innis--Profiles p172-173, por.

RATTRAY, GILLIAN (fl. 1970's)
English-Amer. hockey coach
Jordan--Broken p78-80

RAU, SANTHA RAMA
See RAMA RAU, SANTHA

RAUBAL, ANGELA MARIA "GELI"
(1908-1931)
German, niece of Adolph
Hitler
Book--Lists (2) p453

RAVAN, GENYA (1941-)
Polish-Amer. singer
Claghorn--Biog. p368

RAVEN, ARLENE (fl. 1970's)
Amer. art writer
Women's--Female p116

RAVEN, CLARA (fl. 1920's-1940's)
Amer. Army physician
O'Neill--Women's p210

RAVERST, GWEN DARWIN (1885-
1957)
English author, (grand-
daughter, Charles Darwin)
Morley--Literary p115-117

RAVITZ, MYRNA (fl. 1970's)
Amer. filmmaker
Smith--Movies p197-198,267

RAVKIND, EDNA FRANKFURT

(c1908-)
Amer. fashion designer, manu-
facturer
Rich-McCoy--Mill. p96-126, por.

RAWLINGS, MARJORIE KINNAN
(1898-1953)
Amer. novelist, noted Florida
mother
Amer.--Mothers p115-116, por.
Avenel--Comp. (2) p214
Ehrlich--Oxford, see index p459
McHenry--Liberty's p340
Magill--Cycl. p884-885
Seymour-Smith--Novels p205
Sherr--American p43
Sicherman--Notable p569-571
Signif.--Amer. p48, por.
World--Who p19

RAWLINSON, MABEL
Amer. librarian, aviatrix,
singer, army flier
Keil--Those p203-207

RAWLS, BETSY
Amer. golfer
Hollander--100 p48-49
McWhirter--Guinness p73-74, por.

RAWLS, KATHERINE (fl. 1930's)
Amer. swimmer
Hollander--100 p81

RAWNSLEY, MRS. WILLINGTON (fl.
1890's)
Amer. furniture wood decorator, designer
Callen--Women p169

RAWSON, ELEANOR S. (fl. 1970's)
Amer. editor, publisher, co-
founder of publishing company
O'Neill--Women's p489

RAWSON, REBECCA (1656-1692)
Amer., daughter of Edward
Rawson, Secretary of State
Earle--Two Cent. (1) p xv,526,
por.

RAY, CHARLOTTE E. (1850-1911)
Amer. lawyer, teacher
James--Notable (3) p121-122
McHenry--Liberty's p340-341
Macksey--Book p125

RAY, DIXY LEE (1914-   )
Amer. government official,
governor, marine biologist,
zoologist
Cur. Biog. '73 p345-348, por.
Emberlin--Cont. p154-155
Greenebaum--Politics p139-140
McHenry--Liberty's p341
O'Neill--Women's p76-77
Schoenebaum--Prof. p509-510
Woman's--Almanac p480
World--Who p149

RAYBURN, METZE JONES
Amer., wife of Sam Rayburn
Miller--Fishbait p228-229

RAYE, MARTHA (1916-   )
Amer. singer, comedienne,
dancer, TV performer
Claghorn--Biog. p368
Mordden--Movie p138
Scheuer--Tel. p394
Springer--They p208,324, por.
Woman's Almanac p320-321
World--Who p246

RAYL, HANNAH JO (fl. 1970's)
Amer. labor leader
O'Neill--Women's p309,315

RAYMOND, C.E., pseud.
See ROBINS, ELIZABETH

RAYMOND, CARRIE B. (fl. 1880's)
Amer. musician, organist,
choir conductor
Sherr--American p140

RAYMOND, ELEANOR (1887-   )
Amer. architect, (solar
pioneer)
O'Neill--Women's p609

RAYMOND, MARILYN A. (fl. 1970's)
Amer. executive, food service
company, dietition
O'Neill--Women's p524

RAYMOND, SARAH
Amer. teacher
Time--Women p91

RAYNAL, JACKIE (fl. 1960's-
1970's)
French editor, director
Smith--Movies p122

RAYNER, CLAIRE (1931-   )
English writer, broadcaster
Seymour-Smith--Novels p205

RAZETO, STELLA
Amer. film director
Slide--Early p113

READ, CATHERINE (-1786)
English pastel portrait painter
Fine--Women p71
Petersen--Women p47
Sparrow--Women p58,61,84

READ, DEBORAH
See FRANKLIN, DEBORAH READ

READ, LADY (fl. 1710's)
English eye surgeon, (wife of
Sir William Read)
Mead--Hist. p477-478

READ, MARY (1680-1720/1721)
English pirate, male impersona-
tor, soldier, sailor
Macksey--Book p133-134, por.
Woman's Almanac p498-499

"READ, MISS," pseud. (1913-   )
English teacher, novelist
Seymour-Smith--Novels p205

READING, STELLA CHARNAUD
ISAACS, MARCHIONESS OF
(1894-1971)
British politician, social worker,
organization official, social
welfare leader
Cur. Biog. '71 p469

READY, MARTHA A.
See SILKS, MATTIE (MARTHA)

REAGAN, BARBARA B. (fl. 1970's)
Amer. economist, professor,
writer
O'Neill--Women's p421

REAGAN, NANCY (1921/1923-   )
Amer., wife of President
Ronald Reagan, actress
Anderson--People p329-330
Cur. Biog. '82 p338-342, por.
People--Best p9, por.

REAGE, PAULINE, pseud.
French novelist

Seymour-Smith--Novels
p205

REAM, VINNIE
See HOXIE, VINNIE REAM

REBAY, HILLA (1890-1967)
Alsatian-Amer. museum
director, painter
Sicherman--Notable p571-572

REBECCA (REBEKAH)
Biblical, (wife of Isaac)
Henry--Written p17-18
Price--God p40-51

REBOURS, MADAME
French medical woman
Mead--Hist. p493

RECAMIER, FRANÇOISE JULIE
ADELAÏDE JEANNE BERNARD
(1777/1779-1849/1850)
French beauty, salonist,
politician, social leader
Jones--Rutledge p656
Macksey--Book p102,271

RECTOR, ELLEN (fl. 1970's)
Amer. mountain woman
Kahn--Hill. p137-146, por.

RECTOR, FLORENCE KENYON
HAYDEN (fl. 1820's)
Amer. architect
Sherr--American p185

"RED BIRD"
See BONNIN, GERTRUDE
SIMMONS

REDD, ELVIRA "VI" (1930-)
Amer. saxist, singer
Calghorn--Jazz p247

REDDI, MUTHULAKSHIMI
(1930's-1960's)
East Indian member of state
legislative assembly, social
reformer
Macksey--Book p39-40,120

REDDY, HELEN (1941-)
Australian-Amer. singer,
songwriter
Anderson--People p330-331,
por.

Cur. Biog. '75 p340-343, por.
Simon--Best p483-484, por.
Woman's Almanac p299-300
World--Who p271

REDEKER, LOUISE
German singer
Neuls-Bates--Women p164-165

REDFORD, LOLA VAN WAGENEN
(1938-)
Amer. consumer activist, (wife
of Robert Redford)
O'Neill--Women's p724
Walker--Women p90-104, por.

REDGRAVE, LYNN (1943-)
English actress
Cur. Biog. '69 p358-360, por.
O'Neill--Women's p659
Scheuer--Tel. p396
Shipman--Internatl. p495-496,
por.
World--Who p260

REDGRAVE, VANESSA (1937-)
English actress, political
activist
Anderson--People p332-333, por.
Entertainers p287
Hirschhorn--Rating p317-318,
por.
O'Neill--Women's p654,659
Shipman--Internatl. p496-500,
por.
World--Who p260

REDMAN, MARY (fl. 1770's)
Amer. Revolutionary War
"teenage" patriot
Meyer--Petticoat p86

REDMON, ANNE (1943-)
Amer. novelist
Seymour-Smith--Novels p205

REDMUND, DONNA (fl. 1970's)
Amer. mountain woman
Kahn--Hill. p174-186, por.

REDPATH, JEAN (1937-)
Scottish folksinger
Cur. Biog. '84 p344-347, por.

REECE, FLORENCE (fl. 1970's)
Amer. songwriter, mountain
woman

Kahn--Hill. p27-38,
por.

REECE, LOUISE GOFF (c1899-1970)
Amer. Congresswoman
Chamberlin--Min. p289-290

REED, BETTY LOU (1927-)
Amer. politician
Greenebaum Politics p140 141

REED, CAROLYN COULTER (1939-)
Amer. labor leader
O'Neill--Women's p307
Woman's Almanac p176

REED, DONNA (1921-1986)
Amer. actress, TV performer
Hirschhorn--Rating p318, por.
Lamparski--What. (5) p170-171,
por.
World--Who p246

REED, DOROTHY
See MENDENHALL, DOROTHY
REED

REED, ELIZABETH ARMSTRONG
See REED, MYRTLE

REED, ESTHER DeBERDT (1746-
1780)
English-Amer. Revolutionary
War patriot, letter-writer,
philanthropist
DePauw--Found. p169,171-172
Engle--Women p31-44, por.
Ingraham--Album p10,12-13, por.
James--Notable (3) p123-124
Meyer--Petticoat p133-135
Somerville--Women p46-47
Williams--Demeter's p258 259
Woman's Almanac p450

REED, LUCY (1921-)
Amer. singer
Claghorn--Biog. p370
Claghorn--Jazz p248

REED, MARGARET
Amer., Donner Lake woman
Sherr--American p22

REED, MARY (1854-1943)
Amer. missionary
James--Notable (3) p124-126
McHenry--Liberty's p342

REED, MYRTLE (1874-1911)
Amer. novelist
James--Notable (3) p126-127
McHenry--Liberty's p342-343

REED, NELL QUINLAN DONNELLY
(1889-)
Amer. fashion designer
O'Neill--Women's p259-260

REED, PHYLLIS (fl. 1970's)
Amer. advertising agent
Innis--Profiles p122-123, por.

REED, SUSAN KAREN (1927-)
Amer. harpist, singer
Claghorn--Biog. p370

REEL, ESTELLE (fl. 1890's)
Amer. educator
Sherr--American p255
Time--Women p199

REEL, MRS. VINCENT
See CHI CHENG

REES, ELLA DWENDOLEN
See RHYS, JEAN

REES, MINA S. (1902-)
Amer. mathematician, educator,
scientist, government official,
college dean
M.I.T.--Women p x,34-40
O'Neill--Women's p175-176

REES, ROSEMARY (fl. 1940's)
English ferry pilot, aviatrix
Boase--Sky's p179,192-193,195

REESE, DELLA (1932-)
Amer. singer
Claghorn--Biog. p370
Claghorn--Jazz p248
Cur. Biog. '71 p338-340, por.
World--Who p271

REESE, LIZETTE WOODWORTH
(1856-1935)
Amer. poet, lyricist
Bernikow--World p222
Claghorn--Biog. p370
Ehrlich--Oxford p224
James--Notable (3) p127-128
McHenry--Liberty's p343
Sherr--American p93-94

REESE, SARAH T. BOLTON
  Amer. poet
  Sherr--American p129

REESER, MARY HARDY (-1951)
  Amer., unusual death
  (internal flame)
  Felton--Famous p210-211

REEVE, CLARA (1729-1807)
  English novelist, critic
  Avenel--Comp. (1) p439
  Horner--English p70 (and note)
  Moers--Literary p303

REEVE, VERA (1910-)
  Amer. genealogical researcher,
  author
  Meyer--Who's p172

REEVE, VIRGINIA WATSON (1885-)
  Amer. patriot, noted New
  Jersey mother
  Amer.--Mothers p371

REEVES, ELIZABETH (fl. 1920's-
  1940's)
  Amer., radio director of
  public relations
  Women--Radio p19

REEVES, EMMA BARRETT (1901-)
  Amer. genealogical researcher,
  author
  Meyer--Who's p172

REEVES, HELEN MATHERS (1853-
  1920)
  English novelist
  Showlater--Lit. p339

REEVES, MAUD CELESTE COLMER
  (1886-)
  Amer. conservationist, noted
  Mississippi mother
  Amer.--Mothers p303, por.

REFSHAUGE, JOAN (1906-)
  Australian physician
  Hellstedt--Women p333-337, por.

REGAN, AGNES GERTRUDE (1869-
  1943)
  Amer. social welfare leader,
  educator
  James--Notable (3) p128-130

REGINE (1929-)
  French night club entrepreneur
  Cur. Biog. '80 p329-332, por.

REGNIER, MADAME (-1872)
  French "silent" woman
  McFarland--Incred. p155

REGNIER, PAULE (1875-)
  French novelist
  Crosland--Women p67-68

REHAN, ADA (1857/1860-1916)
  Irish-Amer. actress
  Entertainers p148
  James--Notable (3) p130-131
  McHenry--Liberty's p343
  Webster's--Amer. p863-864

REHOR, GRETE (1910-)
  Austrian government minister
  O'Neill--Women's p56

REICHARD, GLADYS AMANDA
  (1893-1955)
  Amer. anthropologist
  Sicherman--Notable p572-574

REICHERT, JULIA (fl. 1970's)
  Amer. filmmaker
  Smith--Movies p198-199,267, por.

REICHERT, OSSI (fl. 1950's)
  German skier
  Assoc. Press--Pursuit p185,187,
  206, por.

REID, CHARLOTTE THOMPSON
  (c1913-)
  Amer. Congresswoman
  Chamberlin--Min. p302-307
  Cur. Biog. '75 p343-346, por.
  U.S.--Women (89th) p21, por.
  U.S.--Women (90th) p21, por.

REID, CHRISTIAN
  See TIERNAN, FRANCES
  CHRISTINE FISHER

REID, DOROTHY DAVENPORT
  (1895-)
  Amer. film director, (Mrs.
  Wallace Reid)
  Slide--Early p73-82, por.
  Smith--Movies p40

REID, EDITH C. (fl. 1970's)

Amer. cardiologist
Innis--Profiles p202-203, por.

REID, ELIZABETH ANN (fl. 1970's)
Australian feminist, govern-
ment official
Macksey--Book p131
O'Neill--Women's p708

REID, ELIZABETH MILLS (1858-
1931)
Amer. philanthropist
James--Notable (3) p132-133

REID, HELEN ROGERS (1882-1970)
Amer. newspaper publisher
Cur. Biog. '70 p469
Marzolf--Up p63-64,92
O'Neill--Women's p441-442
Sicherman--Notable p574-575
Signif.--Amer. p48, por.

REID, JUDITH P. (1945-)
Amer. genealogical researcher,
writer
Meyer--Who's p172-173

REID, KATE (1930-)
Canadian-Amer. actress
Cur. Biog. '85 p337-341, por.

REID, PATRICIA KIMBERLY
See STANLEY, KIM

REID, MRS. WHITELAW
See REID, ELIZABETH MILLS

REIDMILLER, CARRIE (fl. 1890's)
Amer. restaurant manager
Sherr--American p25

REIGNOLDS, CATHERINE ("KATE")
MARY (1836-1911)
English-Amer. actress,
dramatic reader, teacher
James--Notable (3) p133-134

REILLY, JEANNE LENNOX (1942-)
Amer. labor leader, engineer
O'Neill--Women's p313-314

REILLY, TRISH
Amer. TV newscaster
Glefman--Women p18-19,42-43,
76,107-108, por.

REIMACKER-LEGOT, MARGUERITE

DE (fl. 1960's)
Belgian cabinet minister
Macksey--Book p37

REINDEER, MARY
Eskimo, head of reindeer
industry
Sherr--American p5

REINER, MAX
See CALDWELL, TAYLOR

REINERT, M. ANN (1936-)
Amer. genealogical researcher,
writer
Meyer--Who's p173

REINHARDT, AURELIA ISABEL
HENRY (1877-1948)
Amer. college president,
educator, religious worker
James--Notable (3) p134-136
McHenry--Liberty's p343-344

REINIG, CHRISTA (1926-)
German poet
Herrmann--Ger. p7,87

REINIGER, LOTTE (fl. 1910's-1950's)
West German filmmaker
Smith--Movies p142,268

REINKING, ANN (c1941-)
Amer. dancer
People--Best p160, por.

REISENBERG, NADIA, MADAME
(1904-)
Russian-Amer. pianist, teacher
Neidle--America's p238-240, por.

REISINGER, JOY A. (1934)
Amer. genealogical researcher,
editor
Meyer--Who's p173

REISS, JOHANA DE LEEUW (1932-)
Dutch-Amer. teacher, author,
editor
Kulkin--Her p235-236

REITSCH, HANNA (1912-)
German aviatrix, test pilot,
glider pilot
Boase--Sky's p9,113,197-213, see
also index p222-223, por.
Macksey--Book p250-251, por.

REITZ, MRS. DENEYS
South African government
official
Macksey--Book p41

REJANE, GABRIELLE CHARLOTTE
(1856-1920)
French actress, comedienne
Entertainers p141-142
Jones--Rutledge p658

REJTO-SAGINE, ILDIKO
Hungarian fencer
O'Neill--Women's p560

REJU, GABRIELLE CHARLOTTE
See REJANE, GABRIELLE
CHARLOTTE

REMICK, LEE (1935-)
Amer. actress
Anderson--People p334, por.
Manchel--Women p93,113, por.
Shipman--Internatl. p502-504,
por.
World--Who p246

REMINGTON, DEBORAH (1930-)
Amer. painter
Women's--Female p54

REMOND, SARAH PARKER (1826-
1887)
Amer. antislavery lecturer,
physician
James--Notable p136-137

REMY, NAHIDA (fl. 1890's)
Jewish feminist, author
Henry--Written p237

RENAUD, MADELEINE (1900/
1905-)
French actress, theatre
co-founder
Entertainers p221-222
O'Neill--Women's p659

RENAULT, MARY, pseud. (1905-
1983)
English novelist
Crosland--Beyond p165-170
Cur. Biog. '84 p478
O'Neill--Women's p684
Seymour-Smith--Novels p206,
por.
World--Who p29

RENDEL, LEILA (1910's)
Swedish educator, boarding
school founder
Macksey--Book p76

RENDELL, RUTH (1930-)
English novelist
Seymour-Smith--Novels p206

RENDLESHAM, CLARE, LADY (fl.
1960's)
English fashion leader
Keenan--Women p24,26-27, por.

RENEE OF FERRARA
Italian Reformation worker
Bainton--Germany p235-251, por.

RENEE OF FRANCE
French, Christian, scholar,
(daughter of Anne of Brittany
and Louis XII)
Mead--Hist. p347

RENGER, ANNEMARIE (1919-)
German government official
Macksey--Book p39
O'Neill--Women's p43,49

RENICK, JEANE
Amer. TV executive
Scheuer--Tel. p397

RENNSELAER, CATHERINE VAN
SCHUYLER
See SCHUYLER, CATHERINE
VAN RENSSELAER

RENO, TERRY (fl. 1970's)
Amer. model
Kulkin--Her p236

RENOIR, MARGUERITE (fl. 1930's)
French film editor
Smith--Movies p117-118

RENSE, PAIGE (c1933-)
Amer. interior decorator,
designer
O'Neill--Women's p262-263

RENSON, MARCELLE (fl. 1920's)
Belgian lawyer
Macksey--Book p126

RENSSELAER, MARIA VAN (fl.
1670's)

Amer. colonist, letter-writer
Hoople--As p7-9

RENTMEISTER, JEAN R. (1935-   )
Amer. genealogical researcher,
author, indexer
Meyer--Who's p173

RENZULLO, VITTORIA (fl. 1970's)
Amer., city police captain
O'Neill--Women's p373

REPPLIER, AGNES (1855-1950)
Amer. essayist
James--Notable (3) p137-139
McHenry--Liberty's p344

RESNICK, NOEL
Amer. association director
Scheuer--Tel. p398

RESNIK, JUDITH A. (1948-1986)
Amer. astronaut, electrical
engineer
Oberg--Space p47,111-112, por.
O'Connor--Sally p2,14, por.
O'Neill--Women's p740, por.

RESNIK, REGINA (1923-   )
Amer. opera singer
Claghorn--Biog. p371
Fabian--On p208-209, por.
Gammond--Illus. p249, por.

RESOR, HELEN LANSDOWNE
Amer. advertising executive
Woman's Almanac p209

RESTELL, MADAME
See LOHMAN, ANN TROW

RESTIVO, SALLY JO (fl. 1970's)
Amer. editor
Marzolf--Up p110-111

RETHBERG, ELISABETH (1894-
1976)
German opera singer
Tuggle--Golden p216-218, por.

REUTHER, ROSEMARY RADFORD
(fl. 1960's-1970's)
Amer. scholar, feminist
O'Neill--Women's p398

REVELLE, CARRIE CAROLINE
MILLIGAN (1880-1965)

Amer. cooking expert, noted
Maryland mother
Amer.--Mothers p254

REVERE, DEBORAH HITCHBOURN
(1704-1777)
Amer., mother of Paul Revere
Diagram--Mothers p216-217

REVIER, DOROTHY (1904-   )
Amer. actress
Springer--They p208,324, por.

REVILLE, ALMA (1879-1982)
English film writer, (Mrs.
Alfred Hitchcock)
Smith--Movies p107-108

REYNAL, JEANNE (1902-   )
Amer. artist, craftswoman
Munro--Originals p178-188, por.
Women's--Female p22

REYNOLDS, BERTHA E. (fl. 1900's)
Amer. physician
Sherr--American p247-248

REYNOLDS, DEBBIE (MARIE
FRANCES) (1932-   )
Amer. actress, comedienne,
singer
Anderson--People p336
Engstead--Star p148,161,164
Hirschhorn--Rating p321-322, por.
Mordden--Movie p206-207
People's Almanac (2) p1150, por.
Shipman--Internatl. p508-510, por.
Woman's Almanac p352-353
World--Who p246

REYNOLDS, FRANCES (1729-1807)
English portrait painter,
(sister of Joshua Reynolds)
Fine--Women p71-72

REYNOLDS, MALVINA (1900/1901-
1978)
Amer. singer, song-writer
Bowman--Entertain. p44-47, por.
Claghorn--Biog. p372
Dunlap--Calif. p167
Woman's Almanac p108

REYNOLDS, MARY ELLEN
See MILLER, MARILYN

REYNOLDS, MYRA (1853-1936)

Amer. teacher, English
scholar
James--Notable (3) p139-140

REYNOLDS, PHEBE (fl. 1770's-
1780's)
Amer. Revolutionary War
patriot
Clyne--Patriots p96-103

REZNIKOFF, SARAH YETTA
Amer. seamstress, milliner
Baum--Jewish p61,69-70,205

RHOADS, GERALDINE (1914-)
Amer. magazine editor
O'Neill--Women's p476-477

RHODE, RUTH BRYAN OWEN
See OWEN, RUTH BRYAN

RHODES, LEAH
Amer. fashion (costume)
designer
Wilson--Holly. p104-107, por.

RHODES, MARY (c1782-1853)
Amer. nun, school foundress
James--Notable (3) p140-141

RHODES, ZANDRA (fl. 1960's)
English fashion designer
Keenan--Women p72,216-217,
por.
O'Neill--Women's p252

RHYS, JEAN (1894-1979)
Welsh-Dominican novelist,
short-story writer
Avenel--Comp. (1) p441
Crosland--Beyond p148,172-176,
185
Cur. Biog. '72 p364-367, por.
Moers--Literary p303
Plante--Difficult p7-61,153-173
Seymour-Smith--Novels p207
Seymour-Smith--Who's p307-308
Showalter--Lit. p348
Spacks--Contemp. p118-136,181
World--Who p29

RICE, ALICE CALDWELL HEGAN
(1870-1942)
Amer. novelist, children's
book author
Ehrlich--Oxford p292-293
James--Notable (3) p141-142

McHenry--Liberty's p344
Sherr--American p80

RICE, CRAIG, pseud. (1908-1957)
Amer. novelist
Seymour-Smith--Novels p207

RICE, FLORENCE M. (1907-1974)
Amer. activist, actress,
(daughter of Grantland Rice)
Hazen--Interv. p404
O'Neill--Women's p723
Springer--They p208,324, por.

RICE, FRANCES (fl. 1970's)
Amer. art research worker
Women's--Female p125

RICE, JOAN MOORE (1954-)
Amer. gymnast
Kulkin--Her p237

RICE-DAVIES, MANDY (1944-)
English "party-girl"
Lamparski--What. (3) p30-31,
por.

RICE PEREIRA, IRENE
See PEREIRA, IRENE RICE

RICH, ADRIENNE CECILE (1929-)
Amer. poet, feminist, critic,
teacher, socialist
Avenel--Comp. (2) p217
Chester--Rising p189-196, por.
Cur. Biog. '76 p342-345, por.
Moers--Literary p303
O'Neill--Women's p687-688, por.
Ruddick--Working p xiii-xxiv,345
Webber--Woman p123-132

RICH, IRENE (1891/1897-)
Amer. actress
Hazen--Interv. p404-405
Springer--They p209,324, por.
World--Who p246

RICH, JEAN, pseud. (1923-1975)
Amer. cargo-airline owner
Rich-McCoy--Mill. p152-168, por.

RICHARDS, ANN (1935-)
Amer. singer
Claghorn--Biog. p374
Claghorn--Jazz p249-250

RICHARDS, CORNELIA WELLS WALTER

See WALTER, CORNELIA
WELLS

RICHARDS, ELLEN HENRIETTA
SWALLOW (1842-1911)
Amer. chemist, home econo-
mist, nutritionist
Bachtold--Gifted p44-46
Bird--Enterprising p155-159
James--Notable (3) p143-146
Kulkin--Her p238-239
McHenry--Liberty's p345
Macksey--Book p15-16,151
Marlowe--Great p129-133, por.
O'Neill--Women's p103-104
Reader's--Story p437
Sherr--American p88-89,101
Signif.--Amer. p33, por.
Warren--Pictorial p126
Woman's Almanac p168-169

RICHARDS, MRS. GEORGE F.
(fl. 1910's)
Amer. journalist
Marzolf--Up p51

RICHARDS, LAURA ELIZABETH
HOWE WARD (1850-1943)
Amer. novelist, short-story
writer, children's book author,
noted Maine mother
Amer.--Mothers p241-242, por.
James--Notable (3) p146-148
McHenry--Liberty's p345-346
Macksey--Book p189
Sherr--American p89
Webster's--Amer. p514,871
World--Who p19

RICHARDS, LINDA (1841-1930)
Amer. pioneer nursing
educator
James--Notable (3) p148-150
Kulkin--Her p239-240
McHenry--Liberty's p346
Neidle--America's p191
O'Neill--Women's p231
Sherr--American p41,110
Warren--Pictorial p135

RICHARDS, LYDIA (c1863-1935)
Amer. civil engineer, land
developer
Sherr--American p182

RICHARDS, MARY ATHERTON

(1869-)
Amer. educator, noted Hawaii
mother
Amer.--Mothers p145, por.

RICHARDS, MARY FALLON (1920-)
Amer. genealogical researcher,
writer
Meyer--Who's p174

RICHARDS, RENEE (1935-)
Amer. tennis player, transexual
Book--Lists (2) p329-330

RICHARDS, SUZANNE (fl. 1970's)
Amer. labor lawyer
O'Neill--Women's p314

RICHARDSON, CHARLOTTE SMITH
(1775-after 1806)
Amer. hymnist
Claghorn--Biog. p374

RICHARDSON, DORCAS NELSON
(1740/1741-1834)
Amer. Revolutionary War
patriot, noted South Carolina
mother
Amer.--Mothers p490
Meyer--Petticoat p181-183

RICHARDSON, DOROTHY MILLER
(1872/1873-1957)
English novelist
Avenel--Comp. (1) p442
Crosland--Beyond p15,17-18,33-
41,197
Magill--Cycl. p895-896
Moers--Literary p304
Papachristou--Women p139-141
Seymour-Smith--Novels p207
Showalter--Lit. p248-262,345
Who Did What p274

RICHARDSON, ETHEL FLORENCE
See RICHARDSON, HENRY HAN-
DEL, pseud.

RICHARDSON, HENRY HANDEL,
speud. (1870-1946)
Australian novelist
Avenel--Comp. (1) p442-443
Magill--Cycl. p896-897
Moers--Literary p304
Showalter--Lit. p345

RICHARDSON, JOSEPHINE
British Parliament member
Vallance--Women p50,53,65,70,
77,142

RICHARDSON, KATHARINE BERRY
(-1933)
Amer. physician, surgeon
Sherr--American p131, por.

RICHARDSON, LINDA
Amer. TV executive, director
Scheuer--Tel. p400

RICHERT, SHIRLEY (fl. 1970's)
Amer. printmaker, painter
Women's--Female p81

RICHEY, ANNIE
Amer., accused cattle rustler
Sherr--American p255-256

RICHEY, HELEN (fl. 1940's)
Amer. aviatrix
Boase--Sky's p126,189
Keil--Those p4,98

RICHIER, GERMAINE (1904-1959)
French sculptor
Fine--Women p174-176
Munsterberg--Hist. p94-95
Tufts--Our p222-231, por.

RICH-McCOY, LOIS (1941-)
Amer. author
Rich-McCoy--Mill. p237

RICHMAN, JOAN (fl. 1970's)
Amer. TV correspondent,
executive, producer
Marzolf--Up p171,184
O'Neill--Women's p503-504
Scheuer--Tel. p403

RICHMAN, JULIA (1855-1912)
Amer. educator
James--Notable (3) p150-152
Stein--Lives p13-30, por.

RICHMOND, JUNE (1915-1962)
Amer. singer
Claghorn--Jazz p250

RICHMOND, MARY (1861-1928)
Amer. social worker
Bird--Enterprising p185-188
Earnest--American p222

James--Notable (3) p152-154
McHenry--Liberty's p346-347

RICHTER, ELISE (1864-1943)
Austrian professor
O'Neill--Women's p412

RICHTER, GISELA MARIE AUGUSTA
(1882-1972)
English-Amer. classical archaeologist, museum curator
Sicherman--Notable p575-577

RICHTER, MARGA (c1926-)
Amer. composer, pianist
LePage--Women p208-225, por.

RICHTER, ULRIKE (fl. 1970's)
East German swimmer
McWhirter--Guinness p139, por.
O'Neill--Women's p587

RICKER, MARILLA MARKS YOUNG
(1840-1920)
Amer. lawyer, suffragist
James--Notable (3) p154-156
Sherr--American p146-147

RICKERT, EDITH (1871-1938)
Amer. author, medievalist,
English professor, educator
James--Notable (3) p156-157
McHenry--Liberty's p347

RICKET, MRS. TOWNSEND
Amer. silver miner
Sherr--American p12

RICKETTS, SARAH LIVINGSTONE
Amer., wife of William Ricketts
Earle--Two Cent. (2) p ix, por.

RICKOFF, REBECCA DAVIS (fl.
1870's)
Amer. educator, noted Ohio
mother
Amer.--Mothers p428-429

RIDDELL, CHARLOTTE ELIZA LAW-
SON COWAN (1832-1906)
Irish novelist
Showalter--Lit. p332

RIDDICK, KATHLEEN (-1973)
British conductor
Macksey--Book p221

RIDE, SALLY KRISTEN (1951-)
Amer. astronaut, astro-
physicist
Cur. Biog. '83 p318-321, por.
O'Neill--Women's p740, por.

RIDER-KELSEY, CORINNE (1880-
1947)
Amer. singer
Claghorn--Biog. p375
James--Notable (3) p157-158

RIDGE, LOLA (1873-1941)
Irish-Amer. poet
Kernikow--World p251-252
James--Notable (3) p158-160

RIDGELY, MABEL LLOYD (1872-
after 1957)
Amer. patriot, suffragist,
community worker, noted
Delaware mother
Amer.--Mothers p85, por.

RIDGEWAY, ROZANNE L. (fl.
1960's-1970's)
Amer. ambassador
O'Neill--Women's p96

RIDING, LAURA (1901-)
Amer. poet, novelist, critic,
editor
Avenel--Comp. (2) p218
Seymour-Smith--Who's p309-310

RIDKER, CAROL
Amer. sociologist, potter
O'Neill--Women's p128, por.

RIDLEN, COLLEEN ALICE
(1926-)
Amer. genealogical researcher,
author
Meyer--Who's p174

RIDLER, ANNE (1912-)
English poet
Bernikow--World p181
Brinnin--Modern p285-291

RIDOUT, HESTER ANN CHASE
(-1886)
Amer. philanthropist
Sherr--American p91

RIE, LUCY (1902-)
Austrian-English potter
O'Neill--Women's p267

RIEDESEL, FREDERICA LOUISA
CHARLOTTE MASSOW,
BARONESS VON (1746-1808)
Amer. Revolutionar War
"camp-follower"
DePauw--Found. p187
Earle--Two Cent. (2) p712
Engle--Women p129-152, por.
Young--Revol. p14,31,35-39,52,
55,62,201

RIEFENSTAHL, LENI (BERTA HELENE
AMALIA) (1902-)
German film director, producer,
photographer, actress, dancer
Cur. Biog. '75 p354-358, por.
Jones--Rutledge p666
Macksey--Book p234
O'Neill--Women's p667
Smith--Movies p137-140, por.
Who Did What p275
Wintle--Makers p442-443, #403

RIEPP, BENEDICTA, MOTHER
(1825-1862)
Amer. nun, school founder
James--Notable (3) p160-161
McHenry--Liberty's p347-348

RIESEL, YETTA (fl. 1970's)
Amer. labor leader, feminist
O'Neill--Women's p303,308

RIGBY, CATHY (1952-)
Amer. gymnast
Hollander--100 p53-55
Kulkin--Her p240-241
O'Neill--Women's p562
Ryan--Sports p132
Sabin--Women p98-116, por.
Stambler--Women p21-33, por.
Woman's Almanac p424, por.

RIGBY, ELIZABETH
See EASTLAKE, ELIZABETH
RIGBY, LADY

RIGER, ELEANOR
Amer. sports producer
O'Neill--Women's p502,557

RIGG, DIANA (1938-)
British actress
Cur. Biog. '74 p336-339, por.
World--Who p260

RIGGIN, AILEEN
Amer. diver

Assoc. Press--Pursuit p82-83,
101, por.

RIISNA, ENE (1942-   )
Estonian producer, TV news
director
Scheuer--Tel. p401

RIKER, JANETTE
Amer. western pioneer,
frontier woman, farmer,
(Oregon Trail)
Millstein--We p60-61
Reifert--Women p105-106

RIKKI (RIKKI KILSDONK)
Netherlands designer
O'Neill--Women's p258

RILEY, BRIDGET LOUISE (1931-   )
English painter
Contempt.--Brit., unp., por.
Cur. Biog. '81 p340-344, por.
Fine--Women p183-184
Macksey--Book p209
O'Neill--Women's p602
Women's--Female p54

RILEY, CORINNE BOYD (1894-   )
Amer. Congresswoman
Chamberlin--Min. p290-291

RILEY, MARIE
Amer., restored blind woman
People's Almanac (3) p676-677

RILEY, RANNY
Amer. executive, company
founder
Adams--Women p110,117,144-145,
183-184

RINCON DE GAUTIER FELISA
See GAUTIER, FELISA RINCON
DE

RIND, CLEMENTINA (c1740-1774)
Amer. colonial newspaper
publisher, editor, printer
Demeter--Primer p100-118
James--Notable (3) p161-162
Marzolf--Up p6-8
Sherr--American p239
Stein--Lives, no p.
Williams--Demeter's p235-236

RINDGE, MAY KNIGHT (1865-1941)

Amer. rancher, (wife of
Frederick Hastings Rindge)
Dunlap--Calif. p169
Sherr--American p16

RINEHART, MARY ROBERTS (1876-
1958)
Amer. novelist, playwright
Avenel--Comp. (2) p219
Clark--Leading p106
Ehrlich--Oxford p137,213,382
McHenry--Liberty's p348
O'Neill--Women's p672
Seymour-Smith--Novels p207
Sicherman--Notable p577-579
Webster's--Amer. p875-876
World--Who p47

RING, BLANCHE (1872-1961)
Amer. singer, actress
Claghorn--Biog. p376

RINGGOLD, FAITH (1930/1934-   )
Amer. painter, sculptor,
teacher, lecturer
Fine--Women p147-148
Innis--Profiles p206-207, por.
Miller--Lives p157-175, por.
Munro--Originals p409-416, por.
Women's--Female p55

RINGO, MARILYN (1949-   )
Amer. TV director, producer
Scheuer--Tel. p402

RINKER, "OLD MOM"
Amer. patriot, (Revolutionary
War spy)
Meyer--Petticoat p86-87

RINKOFF, BARBARA
See RICH, JEAN, pseud.

RINSER, LUISE (1911-   )
German teacher, literary
critic, author
Herrmann--Ger. p6,58-59

RIO, ANITA (1873-1971)
Amer. singer
Claghorn--Biog. p376

RIPERTON, MINNIE (1947-1979)
Amer. singer
World--Who p271

RIPLEY, MARTHA GEORGE ROGERS

(1843-1912)
Amer. physician, humanitarian
James--Notable (3) p162-163
Sherr--American p121-122

RIPLEY, SARAH ALDEN BRADFORD
(1793-1867)
Amer. scholar
James--Notable (3) p163-164
Sherr--American p103

RIPLEY, SOPHIA WILLARD DANA
(1803-1861)
Amer. transcendentalist,
(Brook Farm)
Epstein--Indiv., see index p174
James--Notable (3) p164-166
Sherr--American p114

RIPPIN, JANE PARKER DEETER
(1882-1953)
Amer. social worker, Girl
Scout executive
Sicherman--Notable p579-580

RIPPIN, SARAH (fl. 1950's-1970's)
Israeli magazine editor
O'Neill--Women's p482

RISDON, ELIZABETH (1887-1958)
English actress
Springer--They p209,324-325,
por.

RISHER, SARAH W. (fl. 1970's)
Amer. "affirmative action"
director
O'Neill--Women's p139

RISTORI, ADELAIDE (1822-1906)
Italian actress
Entertainers p122-123

"RITA," pseud.
See HUMPHREYS, MRS. DESMOND

RITA OF CASCIA, SAINT (1381-
1487)
Italian foundress
Book--Lists (1) p436

RITCHIE, MRS. ALBERT
See CABELL, LIZZIE

RITCHIE, ANNA CORA MOWATT
See MOWATT, ANNA CORA
OGDEN

RITCHIE, JEAN (1) (1913-)
English agriculturist
O'Neill--Women's p38

RITCHIE, JEAN (2) (1922-)
Amer. singer, (folklorist),
author
Claghorn--Biog. p376
McHenry--Liberty's p348

RITCHIE, ROXANNE
Amer. M.I.T. coed
Felton--Famous p266-267

RITNER, SUSAN (fl. 1970's)
Amer. university administrator
O'Neill--Women's p406

RITTENHOUSE, JESSIE B. (1869-
1948)
Amer. poet, editor, critic
Ehrlich--Oxford p116,134
James--Notable (3) p166-168
McHenry--Liberty's p348-349

RITTER, FANNY RAYMOND (fl.
1870's)
Amer. musical patron, historian
Neuls-Bates--Women p188-190

RITTER, NELLIE MILLER (1882-)
Amer. community worker,
noted Arizona mother
Amer.--Mothers p32-33, por.

RITTER, THELMA (1905-1969)
Amer. actress
Cur. Biog. '74 p468
Keylin--Hollywood p240, por.
Shipman--Internatl. p510-512,
por.
Hirschhorn--Rating p323-324,
por.
World--Who p246

RITTLE, EDINA (fl. 12th Cent.)
English physician, hospital
head
Macksey--Book p141
Mead--Hist. p167-168,224

RIVE-KING, JULIE (1854/1857-1937)
Amer. pianist
Claghorn--Biog. p376
James--Notable (3) p168-169
McHenry--Liberty's p349

RIVERA, CHITA (1933-)
Puerto Rican-Amer. dancer,
actress, singer, comedienne
Cur. Biog. '84 p351-355, por.
World--Who p264

RIVERA, MARINA (1942-)
Amer. Chicana writer, poet
Fisher--Third p viii, 407

RIVERS, JOAN (1935/1937-)
Amer. actress, comedienne
Anderson--People p338
Cur. Biog. '70 p352-354, por.
Scheuer--Tel. p404
Woman's Almanac p321
World--Who p278

RIVERS, MARY M. (fl. 1960's)
Amer. heroine
O'Neill--Women's p733

RIVERS, PEARL
See NICHOLSON, ELIZA JANE
POITEVENT HOLBROOK

RIVES, AMELIE LOUISE, PRINCESS
TROUBETZKOY (1863-1945)
Amer. novelist
Ehrlich--Oxford p230,233
James--Notable (3) p169-171

RIVET, JACKIE (fl. 1970's)
Amer. filmmaker
Seed--Saturday's p41-44, por.

RIVIERE, ISABELLE, MADAME
(fl. 1900's)
French novelist
Crosland--Women p103-104

RIVLIN, ALICE MITCHELL (1931-)
Amer. government official,
scholar, economist
Bowman--Social p45-47, por.
Cur. Biog. '82 p355-358, por.
O'Neill--Women's p421

RIZENROVA, L'UDMILA
See PODJAVORINSKA, LUDMILA

RIZPAH
Biblical
Price--God p98-101

ROACH, EILEEN
Amer. aviatrix, army flier

Keil--Those p137-138,208,
277

ROADS, FRANC
Amer. P.E.O. co-founder
O'Neill--Women's p427, por.

ROARK, HELEN MILLS
See WILLS, HELEN NEWINGTON
MOODY ROARK

ROBALINO, ISABEL
Ecuadorian senator
Macksey--Book p39

ROBB, INEZ CALLAWAY (c1901-1979)
Amer. journalist, columnist
Cur. Biog. '79 p472

ROBB, ISABEL ADAMS HAMPTON
(1860-1910)
Amer. nurse, labor leader,
educator
James--Notable (3) p171-172
O'Neill--Women's p295

ROBB, LYNDA BIRD JOHNSON
Amer., daughter of President
Lyndon B. Johnson
Hershey--Between p162-167,169

ROBBINS, CARIA (1794-)
Amer. colonial traveller
Earle--Two Cent. (2) p797-799

ROBBINS, ELIZABETH LE BARON
(1745-1829)
Amer. colonial patriot
Flexner--Face p160, por.

ROBBINS, ELIZABETH (BETSY)
MURRAY (-1853)
Amer. social reformer, aboli-
tionist, prison reformer, text-
book writer
Berkin--Women p52-54,57-60

ROBBINS, JANE ELIZABETH (1860-
1946)
Amer. social worker, physician
James--Notable (3) p172-174

ROBBINS, MARGARET DREIR (fl.
1900's-1910's)
Amer. labor leader, sociologist
Hymowitz--Hist. p233,252,
256

ROBBINS, MARY LOUISE
Amer. physician, microbiologist
Bowman--Medicine p21-23, por.

ROBBINS, REGINA
Amer. state trooper
O'Neill--Women's p374

ROBERTI, LYDA (1906-1938)
Polish actress
Springer--They p209,325, por.

ROBERTS, ANN CLARK ROCKE-
FELLER (c1934-)
Amer. millionaire
Forbes--400 ('84) p150

ROBERTS, BEVERLY (1914-)
Amer. actress
Springer--They p209,325, por.

ROBERTS, EIRLYS (fl. 1950's-
1970's)
British consumer activist,
magazine editor
Macksey--Book p177
O'Neill--Women's p723

ROBERTS, ELIZABETH MADOX
(1886-1941)
Amer. novelist, poet
Avenel--Comp. (2) p219
Ehrlich--Oxford p293
James--Notable (3) p174-175
McHenry--Liberty's p349
Magill--Cycl. p907-909
Seymour-Smith--Novels p208
Sherr--American p81
Webster's--Amer. p879

ROBERTS, JUNE E. (fl. 1960's)
Amer. heroine
O'Neill--Women's p733

ROBERTS, KATE (1891-)
Welsh short story writer,
novelist
Avenel--Comp. (1) p445

ROBERTS, LIL(L)IAN (c1929-)
Amer. hospital worker,
labor leader
Berkin--Women, see index
p439, por.

ROBERTS, LYDIA JANE (1879-
1965)

Amer. nutritionist, home
economist, educator
Sicherman--Notable p580-581

ROBERTS, MARY (-1761)
Amer. portrait painter
Williams--Demeter's p211

ROBERTS, MARY MAY (1877-1959)
Amer. nurse, editor
Sicherman--Notable p581-583

ROBERTS, SYLVIA (fl. 1950's-
1970's)
Amer. lawyer, feminist
O'Neill--Women's p353-354

ROBERTSON, AGNES KELLY
See BOUCICAULT, AGNES
ROBERTSON

ROBERTSON, ALICE MARY (1854-
1931)
Amer. Congresswoman, pioneer
postmistress, Indian educator
Book--Lists (2) p473
Chamberlin--Min. p38-43, por.
James--Notable (3) p177-178
McHenry--Liberty's p350
Miller--Fishbait p205
Sherr--American p190-192

ROBERTSON, ANNA MARY
See MOSES, ANNA MARY ROBERT-
SON ("GRANDMA MOSES")

ROBERTSON, ANNE ELIZA WORCHES-
TER (1820/1826-1905)
Amer. missionary, teacher,
Indian linguist, noted Oklahoma
mother
Amer.--Mothers p437
James--Notable (3) p178-179

ROBERTSON, ETHEL FLORENCE
RICHARDSON
See RICHARDSON, HENRY
HANDEL, pseud.

ROBERTSON, ISOBEL RUSSELL
(1908-)
South African physician
Hellstedt--Women p364-368, por.

ROBERTSON, JEANNIE SMILLIE
(1877/1878-1981)
Canadian physician

Hellstedt--Women p1-4,
por.

ROBERTSON, MARION G. ("PAT")
(c1930-)
Amer. flight attendant,
associate officer
O'Neill--Women's p305-306,315

ROBERTSON, MARY IMOGENE
(c1906-1948)
Amer. author, feminist,
actress
Papachristou--Women p181-182,
por.

ROBERTSON, MURIEL (1883-1973)
British medical researcher,
physician
Macksey--Book p157

ROBERTSON, NAN
Amer., handicapped journalist
People--Best p234-236, por.

ROBERTSON, PAT MARION GORDON
(1930-)
Amer. TV network president
Scheuer--Tel. p404-405

ROBESON, ESLANDA CARDOZA
GOODE (1896-1965)
Amer. civil rights reformer,
anthropologist, author
Sicherman--Notable p583-584

ROBESON, LILA P. (1880-1960)
Amer. opera singer, teacher
Claghorn--Biog. p378

ROBICHAUD, BERYL (fl. 1940's-
1970's)
Amer. publishing executive
O'Neill--Women's p519

ROBIE, MARIE (fl. 1940's)
Amer. golfer
McWhirter--Guinness p78

ROBINEAU, ADELAIDE ALSOP
(1865-1929)
Amer. ceramicist
Callen--Women p85-86,226

ROBINS, DEBBIE (1956-)
Amer. executive, theatrical
producer
Scheuer--Tel. p405

ROBINS, DENISE (1897-)
English novelist
Seymour-Smith--Novels p208

ROBINS, ELIZABETH (1862-1936/
1952)
Amer. novelist, actress,
suffragette
Ehrlich--Oxford p292,308
Showalter--Lit. p218-222,342

ROBINS, EVA (fl. 1970's)
Amer. labor arbitrator,
government official
O'Neill--Women's p327

ROBINS, MARGARET DREIER
(1868-1945)
Amer. philanthropist, labor
reformer
Banner--Women p71-72
Clark--Leading p71
James--Notable (3) p179-181
McHenry--Liberty's p350
Millstein--We p152-153
Neidle--America's p126-132,146,
149-150,154
O'Neill--Women's p284,289-290

ROBINSON, ANN (fl. 1790's)
Amer. colonial actress
Chinoy--Women p193-197

ROBINSON, DOLLIE LOWTHER (fl.
1950's-1970's)
Amer. labor leader, government official
O'Neill--Women's p337

ROBINSON, EMMA (1814-1890)
English novelist
Showalter--Lit. p325

ROBINSON, GRACE (fl. 1930's-
1940's)
Amer. journalist
Marzolf--Up p47-48

ROBINSON, HARRIET JANE HANSON
(1825-1911)
Amer. suffrage leader, femin-
ist, merchant, author
Bagley--Mill p69-113, por.
Hymowitz--Hist. p125-126
James--Notable (3) p181-182

ROBINSON, JANE MARIE BANCROFT
(1847-1932)

Amer. educator, historian,
philanthropist, foundress
James--Notable (3) p183-184

ROBINSON, JEAN (1934-)
Amer. bicycler
Hollander--100 p12-13

ROBINSON, MARY DARBY
("PERDITA") (1758-1800)
English actress, author
Jones--Rutledge p670

ROBINSON, MONA DEAN (1928-)
Amer. genealogical researcher,
indexer, writer
Meyer--Who's p174

ROBINSON, RUBY DORIS SMITH
(1942-1967)
Amer. civil rights reformer
Berkin--Women p401-402
Sicherman--Notable p585-587

ROBINSON, THERESE ALBERTINE
LOUISE VON JAKOB (1797-
1869/1870)
German-Amer. author, trans-
lator
McHenry--Liberty's p350-351

ROBINSON, MARY
See ROBSON, MAY MARY
JEANNETTE

ROBISON, PAULA (1941-)
Amer. flutist
Cur. Biog. '82 p358-361, por.

ROBSART, AMY (1532-1560)
English socialite, (wife of
Robert Dudley, Earl of
Leicester, daughter of
Sir John Robsart)
Jones--Rutledge p670

ROBSON, ELEANOR
See BELMONT, ELEANOR
ELISE ROBSON

ROBSON, FLORA, DAME (1902-
1984)
English actress
Cur. Biog. '84 p478
Entertainers p219
Johns--Dames p104-116, por.
Jones--Rutledge p670-671
Shipman--Gold. p479-481, por.

Springer--They p209,325,
por.

ROBSON, MAY MARY JEANNETTE
(1858-1942)
Australian-Amer. actress
Hazen--Interv. p402
James--Notable (3) p184-185
McHenry--Liberty's p351
Springer--They p209,325, por.
World--Who p247

ROBU, GALINA (fl. 1970's)
Russian puppeteer
Mandel--Soviet p148

ROBUSTI, MARIETTA (1560-1590)
Italian portrait painter
Macksey--Book p195
Munsterberg--Hist. p20
Women's--Female p13

ROCHE, JOSEPHINE ASPINWALL
(1886-1976)
Amer. industrialist, social
reformer, labor leader, gov-
ernment official, lecturer
Bird--Enterprising p181-183
Cur. Biog. '76 p475
O'Neill--Women's p288,298
Ware--Beyond p151-152, see also
index p202

ROCHE, MARY ELIZABETH (1920-)
Amer. singer
Claghorn--Biog. p379
Claghorn--Jazz p253

ROCHE, SOPHIE VON
See LA ROCHE, SOPHIE VON

ROCHEFORT, CHRISTINE (1917-)
French novelist
Crosland--Women p219-221

ROCHEFOUCAULD, DUCHESS DE
See MITCHELL, MATTIE,
DUCHESS OF ROCHEFOUCAULD

ROCHESTER, ANNA
See HUTCHINS, GRACE

ROCHOW, DAWN
Amer. aviatrix
Keil--Those p169,173

ROCKBURNE, DOROTHEA (fl.
1970's)

Amer. sculptor
Women's--Female p94

ROCKEFELLER, ABBY GREENE
ALDRICH (1874-1948)
Amer. philanthropist, art
patron, (wife of John D.
Rockefeller, Jr.)
James--Notable (3) p185-187
McHenry--Liberty's p351-352
Sherr--American p170

ROCKEFELLER, BARBARA ("BOBO")
SEARS (1917-)
Amer. socialite, craftswoman,
(wife of Winthrop Rockefeller)
Birmingham--Grande p125,141-
142
O'Neill--Women's p127-128

ROCKEFELLER, EDITH
See McCORMICK, EDITH
ROCKEFELLER

ROCKEFELLER, ELIZABETH DAVI-
SON (c1813-1889)
Amer., mother of John D.
Rockefeller
Diagram--Mothers p218-219, por.

ROCKEFELLER, GERALDINE (fl.
1980's)
Amer. socialite
Birmingham--Grandes p133-134

ROCKEFELLER, "HAPPY" (MAR-
GARETTA) FITLER (1926-)
Amer. socialite, (wife of
Nelson Rockefeller)
Book--Lists (2) p261
100--Greatest (1) p90, por.

ROCKEFELLER, HOPE ALDRICH
(fl. 1980's)
Amer. millionaire
Forbes--400 ('84) p149-150

ROCKEFELLER, MARTHA BAIRD
(1895-1971)
Amer. pianist
Claghorn--Biog. p379

ROCKINGHAM, MARY, LADY
(fl. 1770's)
English-Amer. patriot
Young--Revol. p96-99,114 and
n.,129,138-139,193,207

ROCKWELL, KATHLEEN
See "KLONDIKE KATE"

ROCKWELL, MARTHA (fl. 1960's)
Amer. cross-country skier
O'Neill--Women's p566

RODDE, DOROTHEA VON (1770-
1824)
German philosopher, linguist,
scholar, medical woman
Macksey--Book p145
Mead--Hist. p502

RODGERS, DOROTHY (c1909-)
Amer. columnist, inventor
Diamonstein--Open p336-338, por.

RODGERS, ELIZABETH FLYNN
(1847-1939)
Amer. labor leader, insurance
society executive
James--Notable (3) p187-188

RODIANA, HONORATA (ONORATA)
(-1472)
Italian painter
Macksey--Book p195

RODIONOVA, ALEXANDRA (fl.
1910's)
Russian physician, labor
leader
Mandel--Soviet p42,44,49

RODMAN, ELLEN
Amer. TV director
Scheuer--Tel. p405-406

RODMAN, HENRIETTA
Amer. feminist
Banner--Women p107,139
Sochen--Herstory p245,292-293
Sochen--Movers, see index p318

RODNINA, IRINA (1949-)
Russian ice skater, skier
Assoc. Press--Pursuit p299,327,
329
McWhirter--Guinness p96,98-99,
por.
O'Neill--Women's p563

RODRIGUEZ, GLORIA (fl. 1960's)
Amer. heroine
O'Neill--Women's p733

RODRIGUEZ, ROSALINDA (1948-   )
Amer. Chicano activist, feminist, city councilwoman
Seifer--Nobody p296-341, por.

ROE, FRANCES
Amer., army wife
Tine--Women p72,74

ROEBLING, MARY GRINDHART
(1905/1906-   )
Amer. governor of American
Stock Exchange, banker
O'Neill--Women's p527-528

ROEDERSTEIN, OTTILIE,
MADEMOISELLE
Swiss painter
Sparrow--Women p289,305,311

ROELOFSE, SARAH (fl. 1600's)
Netherlands-Amer. linguist
Neidle--America's p9

ROEMER, ELIZABETH (fl. 1950's-
1970's)
Amer. astronomer, professor,
researcher
O'Neill--Women's p152

ROGERS, CLARA KATHLEEN
BARNETT (1844-1931)
English-Amer. singer, teacher
Claghorn--Biog. p380

ROGERS, DALE EVANS (1912-   )
Amer. singer, songwriter,
actress, (wife of Roy Rogers)
Claghorn--Biog. p144
Kooiman--Cameos p49-59, por.
World--Who p232-233

ROGERS, EDITH NOURSE (1881-
1960)
Amer. Congresswoman
Chamberlin--Min. p57-61
McHenry--Liberty's p352
Miller--Fishbait p72-73
O'Neill--Women's p67-68
Sicherman--Notable p587-589
Signif.--Amer. p48, por.
Warren--Pictorial p179

ROGERS, ELIZABETH ANN (1829-
1921)
Anglican sister, educator
James--Notable (3) p188-189

ROGERS, GINGER (1911-   )
Amer. singer, actress, dancer
Claghorn--Biog. p381
Engstead--Star p44,48-49
Hazen--Interv. p407
Hirschhorn--Rating p327-328,
por.
Manchel--Women p67
Mordden--Movie, see index p295
O'Neill--Women's p648,653
Shipman--Gold. p481-485, por.
Springer--They p210-211,325-
326, por.
Woman's Almanac p314-315
World--Who p264

ROGERS, GRACE RAINEY (1867-
1943)
Amer. art collector, philanthropist
James--Notable (3) p189-190

ROGERS, HARRIET BURBANK (1834-
1919)
Amer. educator of deaf mutes
James--Notable (3) p190-191
McHenry--Liberty's p352
Macksey--Book p73
Sherr--American p107

ROGERS, JEAN (1916-   )
Amer. actress
Lamparski--What. (8) p252-253,
por.

ROGERS, JENNIE (fl. 1870's-1880's)
Amer. "Madam"
Time--Women p142-143

ROGERS, LOU (fl. 1920's-1930's)
Amer. political cartoonist,
illustrator
Showalter--These p97-103

ROGERS, MARY CECILIA (1820-1841)
Amer. inspiration for Edgar
Allen Poe's "Mystery of Marie
Roget"
Book--Lists (1) p239

ROGERS, MARY JOSEPH, MOTHER
(1882-1955)
Amer. founder, religious
order
McHenry--Liberty's p352-353
Sicherman--Notable p590-591

ROGERS, MRS. MAXWELL (fl.
1960's)
Amer. weightlifter
McWhirter--Guinness p186

ROGERS, MELODY
Amer. TV host
Scheuer--Tel. p406

ROGERS, MILLICENT A. (c1900-
1953)
Amer. beauty, heiress
Keenan--Women p14-16, por.

ROGERS, MRS. ROBERT (fl.
1770's)
Amer. patriot
Young--Revol. p39-43,49-52,
193,202

ROGERS, ROSEMARY (1932/1933-)
East Indian-Amer. novelist
Seymour-Smith--Novels p208
World--Who p19

ROHE, VERA-ELLEN
See VERA-ELLEN

ROHLES, ANNA KATHARINE
GREEN
See GREEN, ANNA KATHARINE

ROIPHE, ANNE (1935-)
Amer. novelist
Moers--Literary p239,304

ROJAS, GLORIA
Amer. TV newscaster
Gelfman--Women, see index
p186, por.
Scheuer--Tel. p407

ROLAND, JEANNE MANON
PHILIPON, MADAME (1754-
1793)
French patriot, editor, poli-
tician, social leader, child
psychologist
Crosland--Women p21-22
Macksey--Book p31, por.
Mead--Hist. p492-493

ROLAND, RITA (fl. 1960's-1970's)
Amer. film editor
Smith--Movies p76

ROLDAN, LOUISE (LUISA) (1656-

1704)
Spanish wood-carver, sculptor
Macksey--Book p197
Munsterberg--Hist. p86
Petersen--Women p31-32

ROLFE, BARI (1916-)
Amer. dancer, mime
Chinoy--Women p127-128

ROLFE, REBECCA
See POCAHONTAS

ROLLE, ESTHER
Amer. TV actress
World--Who p247

ROLLEN, BERIT (fl. 1970's)
Swedish journalist
Marzolf--Up p276

ROLLIN, BETTY (1936-)
Amer. TV newscaster
Gelfman--Women p65-66,98-99
Scheuer--Tel. p407

ROMAN, NANCY GRACE (1925-)
Amer. astronomer, astrophysi-
cist, space scientist
O'Neill--Women's p88,153

ROMANELLI, ELAINE (fl. 1970's)
Amer. editor, writer
O'Neill--Women's p557

ROMANESCU, ARISTIZZA (1854-1918)
Rumanian actress
Partington--Who's p354

ROMANOVA, MARIA
Russian ballet dancer
Macksey--Book p235
O'Neill--Women's p640

ROMBAUER, IRMA VON STARKLOFF
(1877-1962)
Amer. author, cookery expert
McHenry--Liberty's p353
O'Neill--Women's p132
Sicherman--Notable p593-595
World--Who p300

ROMERO, JOSEFINA BARCELO DE
(1901-)
Puerto Rican-Amer. politician,
noted Puerto Rico mother
Amer.--Mothers p472-473, por.

ROMEU, MARTA ROBERT DE
(1890-   )
Puerto Rican-Amer. physician,
civic worker, politician,
noted Puerto Rico mother
Amer.--Mothers p472, por.

ROMIEU, MARIE (fl. c1581)
French physiologist, author
Mead--Hist. p357-358

ROMNEY, LENORE LAFOUNT
Amer. humanitarian, commun-
ity, political worker, noted
Michigan mother
Amer.--Mothers p281, por.

ROMUALD, MARY (c1895-   )
Amer., Alaskan nursing nun
Jones--Women (1) p132-134

RONCHEZ, LYDIA (fl. 1970's)
Amer. labor official
O'Neill--Women's p315

RONCHI, VITTORIA NUTI (fl.
1950's-1970's)
Italian plant researcher,
professor of genetics,
feminist
O'Neill--Women's p40-41

RONELL, ANN (c1910-   )
Amer. composer, lyricist,
conductor
Jablonski--Ency. p440

RONGE, BERTHA
English kindergarten pioneer
Macksey--Book p68

RONGE, JOHAN (fl. 1890's)
German kindergarten pioneer
Macksey--Book p68

RONNE, EDITH (fl. 1940's)
Norwegian-Amer. early inhabi-
tant, Antarctica
Land--New p17,22

RONNEL, ANN (fl. 1940's-1950's)
Amer. film composer
Smith--Movies p80

RONNER, HENRIETTE, MADAME
(1821-   )
Netherlands painter

Sparrow--Women p261,279,
281

RONSTADT, LINDA (1946-   )
Amer. singer
Anderson--People p343, por.
Claghorn--Biog. p382
Cur. Biog. '78 p352-356, por.
Glassman--Year '79 p140, por.
People--Best p210, por.
Simon--Best p504-505, por.
Woman's Almanac p300, por.
World--Who p272

RONZONE, BERTHA BISHOP (1885-   )
Amer. shopkeeper, noted
Nevada mother
Amer.--Mothers p349-350, por.

ROOKE, SARAH ("SALLY") J.
(1908-   )
Amer. telephone operator,
flood heroine
Sherr--American p155

ROOKES, MARIAN AGNES
See BOOTH, AGNES

ROOS, BARBARA (fl. 1970's)
Amer. producer-writer, film-
maker
Smith--Movies p199-200,269

ROOSEVELT, ALICE
See LONGWORTH, ALICE ROOSE-
VELT

ROOSEVELT, ALICE HATHAWAY
LEE (1861-1884)
Amer. first lady, (1st wife of
Theodore Roosevelt)
James--Notable (3) p191-192
Melick--Wives p55, por.

ROOSEVELT, ANNA ELEANOR
See ROOSEVELT, (ANNA)
ELEANOR

ROOSEVELT, ANNA HALL (1863-
1892)
Amer. socialite, mother of
Eleanor Roosevelt
Daniels--Wash., see index p366
Diagram--Mothers p220-221, por.
O'Neill--Women's p738

ROOSEVELT, BETSY CUSHING

Amer. daughter-in-law of
Franklin Delano Roosevelt
Daniels--Wash. p267-271,276

ROOSEVELT, BLANCHE TUCKER
(1853-1898)
Amer. singer, writer,
journalist
Claghorn--Biog. p382

ROOSEVELT, EDITH KERMIT
CAROW (1861-1948)
Amer. first lady, (wife of
Theodore Roosevelt), noted
Connecticut mother
Amer.--Mothers p78-79
Daniels--Wash. p41-42,71
James--Notable (3) p192-193
Melick--Wives p56-57, por.
Woman's Almanac p490

ROOSEVELT, (ANNA) ELEANOR
(1884-1962)
Amer. social reformer, first
lady, (wife of Franklin D.
Roosevelt)
Adams--Women p44
Amer.--Mothers p394-395, por.
Anticaglia--12 p184-207, por.
Banner--Women p174-184,231-232,
por.
Brin--Social p125-150, por.
Clark--Leading p131-134
Daniels--Wash., see index p367,
por.
Donaldson--How p318-319
Gilfond--Heroines p70-77, por.
Hazen--Interv. p153-154
Hymowitz--Hist. p310-311
Ingraham--Album p54, por.
Jones--Rutledge p675
Keil--Those p26,44,47-48
Kelen--Fifty p132
Kulkin--Her p243-245
Kupferberg--First p134-135, por.
McHenry--Liberty's p354
Macksey--Book p42-43, por.
Marlowe--Great p245-252, por.
Melick--Wives p70-73, por.
Miller--Fishbait, see index p387,
por.
Millstein--We p232-233,242-243,
273, por.
Neidle--America's p129,131-133,
141,144-145,153-154, por.
New York Times--Great p248-249,
por.

O'Neill--Women's, see index p788
Palmer--Who's p277
Pederson--Leaders p212, por.
People's Almanac (1) p296
Reifert--Women p203-212,216-217
Sherr--American p162-163,170
Sicherman--Notable p595-601
Signif.--Amer. p49, por.
Sochen--Herstory p317,326-330,
345-346,383, por.
Sochen--Movers p151-161
Stoddard--Famous p347-360, por.
Ware--Beyond p152, see also
index p202
Warren--Pictorial p190-192,195,
por.
Webster's--Amer. p890-891
Whedon--Always p155-158, por.
Woman's Almanac p491-492, por.
World--Who p300

ROOSEVELT, MRS. JAMES (fl.
1860's)
Amer. social worker
Warren--Pictorial p113

ROOSEVELT, MARTHA ("MITTIE")
BULLOCH (1835-1884)
Amer., (mother of Theodore
Roosevelt)
Faber--Presidents' p141-153, por.

ROOSEVELT, RUTH (fl. 1970's)
Amer. writer, co-founder SFF
O'Neill--Women's p103

ROOSEVELT, SARA DELANO (1854-
1941)
Amer., mother of Franklin D.
Roosevelt
Book--Lists (2) p253, por.
Daniels--Wash., see index p367,
por.
Diagram--Mothers p222-223, por.
Faber--Presidents' p97-113, por.
Sherr--American p163,170

ROOSTEIN, ADEL (fl. 1970's)
Amer. mannequin-maker
Cohen--Meet p81-86, por.

ROOT, HELEN (fl. 1890's)
Amer. theater manager
Sherr--American p256

ROOT, KARA SMART
Amer. poultry business

ROSENBERG, ETHEL GREENGLASS
(1915-1953)
Amer. accused spy
Brecher--Lives p63
McHenry--Liberty's p355-356
Sicherman--Notable p601-604
Webster's--Amer. p896
World--Who p300

ROSENBERG, META
Amer. executive producer,
writer
Adams--Women p99-100,102,107-
108,160,164,184
Scheuer--Tel. p409

ROSENBERG, RUTH BLAUSTEIN
(fl. 1980's)
Amer. millionaire
Forbes--400 ('84) p114

ROSENBERG, SHELI
Amer. lawyer, feminist
O'Neill--Women's p358

ROSENBALTT, JOAN RAUP (fl.
1970's)
Amer. statistician
O'Neill--Women's p89,178

ROSENBALTT, WIBRANDIS (1504-
1564)
German Reformation worker
Bainton--Germany p79-96, por.

ROSENDAHL, HEIDE (c1948-)
West German field and track
athlete
Hollander--100 p135-136, por.

ROSENKOWITZ, SUE
South African mother
Macksey--Book p11

ROSENSTEIN, NETTIE (1897-)
Amer. fashion designer,
philanthropist
O'Neill--Women's p241,243,247

ROSENTHAL, ANNA HELLER (1872-
1941)
Russian feminist, Bund member
Baum--Jewish p82-83

ROSENTHAL, BEATRICE (fl. 1930's-
1940's)
Amer. company manager
O'Neill--Women's p257

ROSENTHAL, IDA COHEN (1889-
1973)
Russian-Amer. manufacturer,
dressmaker, company founder
Bird--Enterprising p190-192
O'Neill--Women's p257
Sicherman--Notable p604-605

ROSENTHAL, JANE
Amer. TV film director
Scheuer--Tel. p410

ROSENTHAL, JEAN (1912-1969)
Amer. lighting designer
Sicherman--Notable p605-607

ROSENTHAL, LYOVA HASKELL
See GRANT, LEE

ROSENTHAL, RACHEL (fl. 1970's)
Amer. sculptor
Women's--Female p94

ROSENWALD, AUGUSTA ("GUSSIE")
NUSBAUM (fl. 1890's)
Amer. socialite
Birmingham--Grandes p97-98,100,
102

ROSENWALD, EDITH
See STERN, EDITH ROSENWALD

ROSER, C.E. (fl. 1970's)
Amer. painter
Women's--Female p55

ROSHONE, EDNA (fl. 1960's)
Amer. heroine
O'Neill--Women's p732

"ROSIE, THE RIVETER"
See BONAVITA, ROSE (ROSINA)

ROSS, AMANDA McKITTRICK (1861-
1939)
Irish novelist
Avenel--Comp. (1) p449

ROSS, ANNIE (1930-)
English singer, songwriter
Claghorn--Jazz p256
Simon--Best p336-337, por.

ROSS, BETSY (ELIZABETH) GRIS-
COM (1752-1836)
Amer. patriot, flag-maker,
noted Pennsylvania mother
Amer.--Mothers p455-456, por.

Booth--Women p278-279
DePauw--Found. p161-163,166
DePauw--Rem. p95
James--Notable (3) p198-199
Kulkin--Her p246-247
McHenry--Liberty's p356
Meyer--Petticoat p81-82, por.
Millstein--We p35
People's Almanac (2) p1242
Sherr--American p202
Webster's--Amer. p897
Whitney--Col. p352-353, por.
World--Who p300

ROSS, BEVERLY ("BUDDY")
MORGAN (1914-)
Amer. singer
Claghorn--Biog. p384

ROSS, DIANA (1944-)
Amer. singer, actress
Abdul--Famous p109-117, por.
Anderson--People p344, por.
Bowman--Entertain. p40-43, por.
Cur. Biog. '73 p363-366, por.
Glassman--Year '79 p24,140,142,
por.
Manchel--Women p108,110, por.
100--Greatest (1) p17, por.
People--Best p114, por.
People's Almanac (2) p1147, por.
Simon--Best p506-507, por.
Woman's Almanac p304-305, por.
World--Who p272

ROSS, ELIZABETH GRISCOM
See ROSS, BETSY (ELIZABETH)
GRISCOM

ROSS, ISHBEL (ISABEL) (1897-1975)
Scottish-Amer. biographer,
novelist, journalist
Marzolf--Up, see index p307
P.W.--Author p252-255,523

ROSS, KATHARINE (1942/1943-)
Amer. actress
Hirschhorn--Rating p330, por.
Manchel--Women p98,101, por.
World--Who p247

ROSS, LILLIAN (1926/1927-)
Amer. journalist, novelist,
biographer, short-story writer
Avenel--Comp. (2) p222
Ehrlich--Oxford p379
Seymour-Smith--Novels p209

ROSS, MARGARET (1922-)
Amer. genealogical researcher,
author, editor
Meyer--Who's p175-176

ROSS, MARION (1928-)
Amer. actress
Scheuer--Tel. p411

ROSS, MARTIN
See MARTIN, VIOLET FLORENCE

ROSS, NELLIE TAYLOE (1876-1977)
Amer. governor, noted Wyoming
mother
Amer.--Mothers p595-596, por.
Cur. Biog. '78 p475
Levenson--Women p66
McHenry--Liberty's p356
O'Neill--Women's p76
Sherr--American p254, por.
Signif.--Amer. p50, por.
Ware--Beyond p152-153, see also
index p202
Warren--Pictorial p179
Webster's--Amer. p898
Woman's Almanac p480
World--Who p150

ROSS, PAT
Amer. author, editor
Ross--Young p109, por.

ROSS, SHIRLEY (1914-)
Amer. actress
Springer--They p211,326, por.

ROSS, SUSAN DELLER (c1652-1700)
Amer. Civil Liberties worker,
feminist
O'Neill--Women's p357

ROSSE, SUSAN PENELOPE (c1652-
1700)
British artist
Harris--Women p156-157,344, por.

RÖSSEL, AGDA (1910-)
Swedish diplomat, UN delegate
O'Neill--Women's p63-64

ROSSEN, ELLEN (1946-)
Amer. TV news producer
Scheuer--Tel. p411

ROSSETTI, CHRISTINA GEORGINA
(1830-1894)

English poet
Avenel--Comp. (1) p450-451
Bernikow--World p123-124
Fry--1000 p245
Jones--Rutledge p678
Kaplan--Salt p125-126, por.
Kronenberger--Atlan. p653-654
Magill--Cycl. p918-920
Moers--Literary p304, see also
  index p333, por.
Pearson--Who p129
Showalter--Lit. p331
Who Did What p279

ROSSETTI, LUCY MADDOX BROWN
  (fl. 1870's)
  English artist
  Fine--Women p81-83

ROSSI, ALICE S.
  Amer. feminist, sociologist,
  writer, college professor
  M.I.T.--Women px,51-127,106n,
  136
  Sochen--Movers p255-257

ROSSI, PROPERZIA DI (c1490-1530)
  Italian painter, sculptor
  Fine--Women p8-9
  Macksey--Book p195
  Parker--Old p3,9,17-18, fig. 3
  Petersen--Women p26-27

ROSSITER, MARGARET (fl. 1970's)
  Amer. professor of science,
  history
  O'Neill--Women's p142

ROSSNER, JUDITH (1935-)
  Amer. novelist, feminist
  Seymour-Smith--Novels p209
  World--Who p19

ROSTWITHA (HROSVITHA) (935-
  1000)
  German nun, poet, playwright
  Macksey--Book p180
  Mead--Hist. p112-113
  Who Did What p159

ROTH, ENID (fl. 1970's)
  Amer. TV news director
  O'Neill--Women's p503

ROTH, LAURA M. (fl. 1970's)
  Amer. professor, solid state
  theorist
  O'Neill--Women's p183

ROTH, LILLIAN (1910-)
  Amer. actress, singer, writer
  Lamparski--What. (3) p24-25,
  por.
  Springer--They p211-212,326,
  por.
  World--Who p272

ROTHENBERG, SHERIBEL (fl.
  1970's)
  Amer. lawyer, feminist
  O'Neill--Women's p358

ROTHENBERG, SUSAN (1945-)
  Amer. painter
  Cur. Biog. '85 p344-347

ROTHENBERGER, ANNELIESE
  (1924-)
  German opera singer
  Gammond--Illus. p249, por.

ROTHMAN, STEPHANIE (c1925-)
  Amer. comedienne, director,
  filmmaker
  O'Neill--Women's p669
  Smith--Movies p58-59,269, por.

ROTHMANN, LORRAINE
  Amer. co-founder, gynecologi-
  cal self-help clinic
  O'Neill--Women's p706

ROTHSCHILD, AMALIE (fl. 1970's)
  Amer. photographer, filmmaker
  Smith--Movies p200-201, por.

ROTHSCHILD, DOROTHY
  See PARKER, DOROTHY ROTHS-
  CHILD

ROTHSCHILD, EMMA (1948-)
  English professor
  O'Neill--Women's p35

ROTHSCHILD, MIRIAM LOUISA
  (1908-)
  British zoologist, marine
  biologist, entomologist,
  parasitologist
  O'Neill--Women's p158-159

ROTSCHILD, KLARA (1903-1976)
  Hungarian fashion designer
  O'Neill--Women's p242

ROUGET, MARIE
  See MARIE-NOËL

ROUNTREE, MARTHA (1916-   )
Amer. journalist, radio, TV
personality
Marzolf--Up p158

ROURKE, CONSTANCE MAYFIELD
(1885-1941)
Amer. cultural historian,
critic, educator
Avenel--Comp. (2) p223
James--Notable (3) p199-200
McHenry--Liberty's p356-357
Sherr--American p118

ROUSSEAU, LILLIAN McKIM
See PULITZER, LILLY

ROUSSEL, SIMONE
See MORGAN, MICHELE

ROUSSIETSKI, SALOMEE ANNE
See HALPIR, SALOMEE ANNE

ROUSSILON, ALICE
Amer. patriot, heroine
Sherr--American p68

ROUTH, MARTHA (fl. 1790's)
English-Amer. Quaker
clergyman
Earle--Two Cent. (2) p603-604

ROWAND, MARY LOUISE MORRIS
(1918-   )
Amer. clergyman, noted
Texas mother
Amer.--Mothers p519-520, por.
O'Neill--Women's p380-381,394

ROWBOTHAM, SHEILA (fl. 1970's)
English feminist, author
O'Neill--Women's p418
Showalter--Lit. p314

ROWE, ELIZABETH SINGER (1674-
1737)
English poet
Horner--English p25 (and note)
Mead--Hist. p477

ROWLAND, BETTY JANE (fl. 1930's)
Amer. burlesque queen
Lamparski--What. (5) p100, por.
Lamparski--What. (8) p256-257,
por.

ROWLAND, SARAH (fl. 1770's)

Amer. patriot
Sherr--American p37

ROWLANDS, ALICE MARION
See HART, MRS. ERNEST

ROWLANDS, GENA (VIRGINIA
CATHRYN) (c1936-   )
Amer. actress
Cur. Biog. '75 p363-366, por.
Higham--Celeb. p104-108, por.
Hirschhorn--Rating p331, por.
World--Who p247

ROWLANDSON, ESTHER (fl. 1670's)
Amer. Indian captive
Earle--Two Cent. (1) p144-145

ROWLANDSON, MARY WHITE (c1635-
c1678)
Amer. Indian captive, writer
Avenel--Comp. (2) p223
Hoople--As p9-16
James--Notable (3) p200-202
McHenry--Liberty's p357
Neidle--America's p4
Sherr--American p111-112
Sochen--Herstory p39-40
Warren--Pictorial p20-23
Williams--Demeter's p154-159

ROWSON, SUSANNA HASWELL (c1762-
1824)
English-Amer. novelist, poet,
playwright, lyricist, librettist,
teacher, educator, actress
Avenel--Comp. (2) p223-224
Claghorn--Biog. p385
DePauw--Rem. p128, por.
Earle--Two Cent. (2) p xiv, por.
Earnest--American p30-31,43
James--Notable (3) p202-204
McHenry--Liberty's p357
Moers--Literary p304
Neidle--America's p31-33
Seymour-Smith--Novels p209
Signif.--Amer. p8, por.
Sochen--Herstory p142
Webster's--Amer. p900
Williams--Demeter's p312-313

ROXBOROUGH, MILDRED BOND (fl.
1970's)
Amer. activist leader
O'Neill--Women's p702

ROXBURGH(E), DUCHESS OF
See GOELET, MAY WILSON

ROY, MRS. CLARINDA (c1863-)
Amer. centenarian
Mitchell--Yessir p42-43, por.

ROY, GABRIELLE (1909-)
Canadian novelist
Avenel--Comp. (1) p453
Crosland--Beyond p140-141
Crosland--Women p227-228
Seymour-Smith--Novels p209

ROYAL, DORIS (fl. 1970's)
Amer. agricultural leader
O'Neill--Women's p15

ROYALL, ANNE NEWPORT (1769-
1854)
Amer. journalist, Washington
correspondent, traveler, pub-
lisher, editor
Beasley--First p3-5
Ingraham--Album p71
James--Notable (3) p204-205
McHenry--Liberty's p357-358
Marzolf--Up p11-12
Sherr--American p42,245-246
Webster's--Amer. p900
Woman's Almanac p271-272

ROYCE, MRS. JOSIAH
See HEAD, KATHARINE

ROYCE, SARAH (1819-1891)
English-Amer., mother of
Josiah Royce
Starr--Amer. p143-144,359

ROYCE, SARAH ELEANOR BAY-
LISS (1819-1891)
Amer. Western pioneer,
teacher, diarist
Hoople--As p60-62
James--Notable (3) p205-206
Time--Women p34-37,52-53,
118

ROYDE-SMITH, NAOMI GWADYS
(-1964)
Welsh novelist, playwright
Avenel--Comp. (1) p453

ROYE, ELEANORE DE (1535-1564)
French, wife of Louis de
Boudon, Prince de Condé
Bainton--France p83-86, por.

ROZANOVA, OLGA VLADIMIROVNA

(1886-1918)
Russian artist
Fine--Women p167-168
Harris--Women p61-63,299-358

ROZEANU, ANGELICA (fl. 1950's)
Rumanian table tennis player
Macksey--Book p258
McWhirter--Guinness p147, por.

RUAROWNA, MARGARETA (fl.
c1620's)
Polish religious poet
Bainton--Spain p174-176

RUBENS, BERNICE (1927-)
Welsh novelist
Seymour-Smith--Novels p209

RUBIN, BARBARA JO (1949-)
Amer. jockey
Cur. Biog. '69 p380-382, por.
Hollander--100 p65-66
McWhirter--Guinness p92

RUBIN, RUTH ROSENBLATT (1898-
1953)
Amer. pianist, composer
Claghorn--Biog. p385

RUBIN, VERA C. (1928-)
Amer. astronomer
O'Neill--Women's p151

RUBINSTEIN, HELENA (1870/1872-
1965)
Polish-Amer. cosmetician,
fashion designer, philanthro-
pist
Banner--Women p156-157,165, por.
Brecher--Lives p49, por.
Comfort--Good p182, por.
Fink--Great p121-125, por.
Kulkin--Her p248-249
Longstreet--Queen p104-108, por.
McHenry--Liberty's p358
Macksey--Book p171-172,271, por.
Neidle--America's p269-270,277-281
O'Neill--Women's p257,518
People's Almanac (3) p507-508,
por.
Sicherman--Notable p607-608
Signif.--Amer. p50, por.
Sochen--Herstory p291-292
Woman's Almanac p134, por.
World--Who p205

RUBINSTEIN, MALA (c1907-)
Polish cosmetician
Macksey--Book p172
O'Neill--Women's p518, por.

RUSS, MARY CAROLINA (fl.
1770's)
English accused criminal
Earle--Two Cent. (2) p xx,482,
675-679, por.

RUDDICK, SARA (1935-)
Amer. teacher
Ruddick--Working p128-146,
345-346, por.

RUDE, SOPHIE FREMIET, MADAM
(1797-1867)
French painter
Sparrow--Women p179, por.

RUDERSDORFF, HERMINE (1822-
1882)
Ukrainian singer, teacher
Claghorn--Biog. p386

RUDIE, EVELYN (fl. 1950's)
Amer. child actress
Lamparski--What. (8) p258-259,
por.

RUDIE, YVONNE (1892-)
French-Amer. actress
Gold--Until p334

RUDKIN, MARGARET FOGARTY
(1897-1967)
Amer. bakery founder,
executive
O'Neill--Women's p135
Sicherman--Notable p609-610

RUDOLPH, WILMA GLODEAN
(1940-)
Amer. track and field athlete
Assoc. Press--Pursuit p218,237-
238,242, por.
Hollander--100 p126-128, por.
Kulkin--Her p249-250
McHenry--Liberty's p358-359
McWhirter--Guinness p175, por.
O'Neill--Women's p575
Pachter--Champ. p206-207, por.
People's Almanac (3) p551
Ryan--Sports p46-63, por.
Woman's Almanac p427-428, por.
World--Who p221

RUDRUD, JUDY L.
Amer. executive, publishing
company
Scheuer--Tel. p414, por.

RUECK, KELLY
Amer. flight attendant
O'Neill--Women's p303,305-306,
por.

RUEGGER, ELSA (1881-1924)
Swiss-Amer. cellist
Claghorn--Biog. p386

RUETHER, ROSEMARY (1936-)
Amer. historian, theologian
Gilbert--Part. p113-119, por.

RUFFIN, JOSEPHINE ST. PIERRE
(1843-1924)
Amer. politician, clubwoman,
Civil War patriot, feminist
Hymowitz--Hist. p223
James--Notable (3) p206-208
Macksey--Book p273
Papachristou--Women p120-121

RUFFNER, PATTIE RUFFNER (1875-
1935)
Amer. suffrage leader
Sherr--American p1

"RUHAMAH," pseud.
See SCIDMORE, ELIZA RUHAMAH

RUKEYSER, MURIEL (1913-1980)
Amer. poet
Avenel--Comp. (2) p224
Bernikow--World p330
Brinnin--Modern p299-302, por.
Chester--Rising p68-75, por.
Cur. Biog. '80 p463
McHenry--Liberty's p359
Moers--Literary p304
O'Neill--Women's p680-681
Pearson--Who p95
Webber--Woman p51-52
World--Who p19

RULE, JANICE (1931-)
Amer. actress
World--Who p247

RUMSEY, ELIDA BARKER
See FOWLE, ELIDA BARKER
RUMSEY

RUMSEY, MARY ANN (fl. 1820's)
Amer., namer of city
Sherr--American p115

RUMSEY, MARY HARRIMAN (1881-
1934)
Amer. social welfare leader,
co-founder Junior League
James--Notable (3) p208-209
McHenry--Liberty's p359-360
O'Neill--Women's p111
Ware--Beyond p153, see also
index p202

RUNCIE, CONSTANCE FAUNT LE
ROY (1836-1911)
Amer. composer, pianist,
club leader
Claghorn--Biog. p386
McHenry--Liberty's p360

RUNGE, BLANCHE
Amer. TV director
Scheuer--Tel. p415

RUNYON, BRENDA (fl. 1910's-
1920's)
Amer. banker
Sherr--American p216, por.

RUPERT, ELINORE PRUITT
Amer. Western pioneer
Time--Women p53,56-57

RUSAD, LAILI (fl. 1950's-1960's)
Indonesian ambassador
O'Neill--Women's p62

RUSAKOVA, NINA
Russian aviatrix, test pilot
Mandel--Soviet p80,83

RUSH, BARBARA (1930-)
Amer. actress
World--Who p247

RUSH, JULIA STOCKTON (1759-
1848)
Amer. Revolutionary War
patriot
Booth--Women p266,299

RUSH, OLIVE (fl. 1930's)
Amer. fresco painter
Sherr--American p157

RUSHEN, PATRICE LOUISE (1954-)

Amer. pianist
Claghorn--Jazz p257

RUSIECKI, SALOMEE ANNE
See HALPIR, SALOMEE ANNE

RUSS, GIANNINA (1878-1951)
Italian opera singer
Tuggle--Golden p40-41, por.

RUSS, JOANNA (1937-)
Amer. novelist
Webber--Woman p157-163

RUSSELL, ANNIE (1864-1936)
English-Amer. actress
James--Notable (3) p209-211
McHenry--Liberty's p360

RUSSELL, BARBARA (fl. 1940's)
Amer. aviatrix, army flier
Keil--Those p231-233

RUSSELL, DIANA E.H.
Amer. activist, sociology
professor, co-editor
O'Neill--Women's p709-710

RUSSELL, ELIZABETH MARY
ANNETTE BEAUCHAMP,
COUNTESS VON ARNIM
(1866-1941)
Australian novelist, letter
writer, essayist, social re-
former
Jones--Rutledge p30
Macksey--Book p184
Moers--Literary p272

RUSSELL, ELIZABETH SHULL
(1913-)
Amer. zoologist, geneticist
O'Neill--Women's p145,157-158,
223-224

RUSSELL, ELLA (1864-1935)
Amer. singer
Claghorn--Biog. p387

RUSSELL, GAIL (1924-1861)
Amer. actress
Shipman--Internatl. p516-517,
por.

RUSSELL, JANE (ERNESTINE JANE
GERALDINE) (1921-)
Amer. actress, model

Hirschhorn--Rating p331-332,
por.
Shipman--Internatl. p517-519,
por.
World--Who p247

RUSSELL, JANE ANNE (1911-1967)
Amer. biochemist, endocrin-
ologist
Sicherman--Notable p610-611

RUSSELL, LADY
See HOBY, ELIZABETH COOKE,
LADY

RUSSELL, LETTY MANDEVILLE
(fl. 1970's)
Amer. clergyman
O'Neill--Women's p381

RUSSELL, LILLA (c1885-1977)
New Zealander agriculturist
O'Neill--Women's p5-6

RUSSELL, LILLIAN (1861-1922)
Amer. opera singer, actress
Banner--Women p6-7,163, por.
Claghorn--Biog. p387
Hazen--Interv. p85-86
James--Notable (3) p211-213
McHenry--Liberty's p360-361
Sherr--American p70
Warren--Pictorial p157, por.
Webster's--Amer. p905
World--Who p272

RUSSELL, LISE ANN (fl. 1970's)
Amer. golfer
O'Neill--Women's p561

RUSSELL, MARY BAPTIST, MOTHER
(1829-1898)
Irish-Amer. nun, superior
James--Notable (3) p213-214
McHenry--Liberty's p361

RUSSELL, OLIVE RUTH (fl. 1970's)
Canadian psychology professor, author, euthanasia
activist
O'Neill--Women's p728

RUSSELL, RACHEL WRIOTHESLEY,
LADY (1636/1641-1723/1728)
English socialite
Earle--Two Cent. (2) p xix, por.

RUSSELL, ROSALIND (1907/1912-
1976)
Amer. actress
Cur. Biog. '77 p472
Fox-Sheinwold--Gone p136-145,
por.
Hirschhorn--Rating p332-333, por.
Keylin--Hollywood p249-250, por.
Mordden--Movie, see index p295
Shipman--Gold. p492-494, por.
Springer--They p212,214,326,
por.
Woman's Almanac p353, por.
World--Who p247

RUSSIER, GABRIELLE (-1969)
French teacher
Book--Lists (2) p61-62

RUSSO, NANCY FELIPE (fl. 1970's)
Amer. psychologist, scientist,
administrator
O'Neill--Women's p433

RUST, ELEANOR FRANCIS DU PONT
(c1907-)
Amer. millionaire
Forbes--400 ('84) p149

RUST, NORMA (fl. 1970's)
Amer. clergyman
Proctor--Women p85-87,91-92,106

RUSTAD, GURO (fl. 1960's)
Norwegian political reporter
Marzolf--Up p286-287

RUSTAMOVA, ZEBINISO (fl. 1970's)
Russian archer
McWhirter--Guinness p24, por.

RUTH
Biblical
Price--God p82-87
Woman's Almanac p400

RUTHERFORD, ANN (1920-)
Canadian-Amer. actress
Lamparski--What. (4) p34-35,
por.
Lamparski--What. (8) p260-261,
por.
Springer--They p214,326, por.
World--Who p247

RUTHERFORD, LUCY
See MERCER, LUCY PAGE

RUTHERFORD, MARGARET, DAME
(1892-1972)
English actress, comedienne
Cur. Biog. '72 p470
Entertainers p191, por.
Johns--Dames p123-132, por.
Jones--Rutledge p687
Keylin--Hollywood p251, por.
Shipman--Internatl. p519-522,
por.
World--Who p260-261

RUTHERFORD, MILDRED LEWIS
(1851-1928)
Amer. educator
James--Notable (3) p214-215

RUTHERFORD, MINNIE URSULA
OLIVER
See FULLER, MINNIE URSULA
OLIVER SCOTT RUTHERFORD

RUTHERFURD, ALICE MORTON
(-1917)
Amer. socialite
Daniels--Wash. p168,171-172

RUTKIEWICZ, WANDA (fl. 1970's)
Polish mountaineer
McWhirter--Guinness p105-106

RUTLEDGE ANN MAY(E)S (1813/
1816-1835)
Amer., legendary friend of
Abraham Lincoln
James--Notable (3) p216-217
Sherr--American p64

RUTLEDGE, ELIZABETH (-1792)
Amer. Revolutionary War
patriot
Meyer--Petticoat p165

RUTSTEIN, LILLIAN
See ROTH, LILLIAN

RUYS, A. CHARLOTTE (1898-)
Netherlands physician
Hellstedt--Women p163-167, por.

RUYSCH, RACHEL (1664-1750)
Netherlands painter, museum
director
Fine--Women p35-38
Harris--Women p29,32,34-35,41-44,
65,78,141,152,154,158-160,
344-345

Macksey--Book p198
Mead--Hist. p430
Munsterberg--Hist. p26,28
Parker--Old p57, por.
Petersen--Women p41-42
Sparrow--Women p260-261,265
Tufts--Our p98, por.
Women's--Female p13

RYAN, ANNE (1889-1954)
Amer. painter, college artist
Munsterberg--Hist. p72-73
O'Neill--Women's p602
Sicherman--Notable p611-613

RYAN, ELIZABETH ("BUNNY")
(c1891-1979)
Amer. lawn tennis player
Brecher--Lives p318
McWhirter--Guinness p151,155-
156, por.

RYAN, IRENE (1903-1973)
Amer. actress
World--Who p247

RYAN, JOAN
Amer. sports writer, columnist
O'Neill--Women's p463

RYAN, LUANN
Amer. archer
McWhirter--Guinness p24
O'Neill--Women's p558

RYAN, PATRICIA
Amer. managing editor
People--Best p6, por.

RYAN, PATTY
Amer. aviatrix, (Air Force
cadet)
Lichtenstein--Mach. p182-183,
187-188

RYAN, PEGGY (1924-)
Amer. comedienne, actress
World--Who p247

RYDELIUS, EDIT V. (1903-)
Swedish kindergarten teacher
O'Neill--Women's p321

RYDEN, HOPE
Amer. airline stewardess,
photographer, writer, filmmaker

Smith--Movies p201-202,
270

RYE, MARIA (1829-1903)
British social reformer
Macksey--Book p114-115

RYKIEL, SONIA (SONYA)
(c1931-)
French fashion designer
O'Neill--Women's p251

RYSANEK, LEONIE (1926/1928-)
Austrian opera singer
Gammond--Illus. p249, por.

RYSKAL, INNA (1944-)
Russian volleyball player
McWhirter--Guinness p181
O'Neill--Women's p570

RYSSDAL, SIGNE
Norwegian lawyer
Macksey--Book p129

RYSTE, RUTH (1932-)
Norwegian minister of social
affairs
O'Neill--Women's p58

S

SAADAWI, NAWAL EL (1930-)
Egyptian feminist, physician,
psychiatrist, novelist
O'Neill--Women's p709

SAAL, ROLLENE (fl. 1970's)
Amer. editorial director
O'Neill--Women's p436,438,488

SAAR, BETYE (1926-)
Amer. construction artist
Miller--Lives p176-184, por.
Munro--Originals p355-361, por.
Women's--Female p95

SAARINEN, ALINE MILTON BERN-
STEIN LOUCHHEIM (1914-
1972)
Amer. art critic, TV corres-
pondent, editor
Cur. Biog. '72 p470
Diamonstein--Open p340-343, por.
Marzolf--Up p169-170,174
Sicherman--Notable p613-614

SAARINEN, LOJA (fl. 1920's)
Finish architectonic fabric
designer
O'Neill--Women's p264-265

SABBE
See SAMBATHE

SABIA, LAURA (fl. 1970's)
Canadian labor leader
O'Neill--Women's p319

SABIN, ELLEN CLARA (1850-1949)
Amer. school administrator,
college president
James--Notable (3) p217-218
Sherr--American p249

SABIN, FLORENCE RENA (1871-
1953)
Amer. anatomist, researcher,
educator, physician
Bachtold--Gifted p51-56
Burgess--Education p87-109, por.
Ingraham--Album p65,67
Kulkin--Her p250-251
McHenry--Liberty's p362
O'Neill--Women's p144,223
Richey--Eminent p45-71, por.
Sherr--American p27,38,93
Sicherman--Notable p614-617
Stoddard--Famous p361-371, por.
Woman's Almanac p367, por.

SABIN, PAULINE MORTON (1887-
1955)
Amer. prohibition repeal
leader, party official, interior
decorator, social reformer
Sicherman--Notable p617-618

SABIROVA, MALKIA (1943-)
Russian ballet dancer
Mandel--Soviet p183-184

SABUCO, OLIVA BARRERA (1562-)
Spanish author
Mead--Hist. p352-353

SACAJAWEA (1786/1787-c1812)
Amer. Shoshone Indian guide,
interpreter, noted Idaho,
Montana mother
Amer.--Mothers p149-150,319,
por.
Gray--Women p5-20, por.

Gridley--Amer. p47-53, por.
Ingraham--Album p21, por.
James--Notable (3) p218-219
Kulkin--Her p252-253
McHenry--Liberty's p362-363
Miller--Women p29-46
Millstein--We p54,59-60
Sherr--American p58,134,136-
137,182-183,186,194-197,
215,232-233,255, por.
Signif.--Amer. p12, por.
Taylor--Gener. p58-59, por.
Time--Women p17-21,24, por.
Warren--Pictorial p65-67, por.
Webster's--Amer. p910
Woman's Almanac p51
World--Who p130

SACHS, NELLY LEONE (1891-1970)
German-Amer. poet, play-
wright
Cur. Biog. '70 p470
Fink--Great p142-148, por.
Macksey--Book p193
Opfell--Lady p135-146, por.
World--Who p43

SACKVILLE-WEST, VICTORIA
MARY (1892-1962)
English poet, novelist,
horticulturist, biographer
Avenel--Comp. (1) p457-458
Jones--Rutledge p689
Kaplan--Salt p257-258
Moers--Literary p304-305
Morley--Literary p114,130
Seymour-Smith--Novels p210
Showalter--Lit. p347
Who Did What p282

SADAT, JIHAN (c1933-)
Egyptian first lady, (wife of
President Anwar Sadat),
feminist, social activist
O'Neill--Women's p695,708
Whedon--Always p159-161

SADLIER, MARY ANNE MADDEN
(1820-1903)
Irish-Amer. novelist
James--Notable (3) p219-220
McHenry--Liberty's p363

SAFFORD, MARY JANE (JOANNA)
(1834-1891)
Amer. Civil War nurse,
physician, humanitarian

James--Notable (3) p220-222
McHenry--Liberty's p363

SAFKA, MELANIE (fl. 1960's-1970's)
Amer. song writer
Pollock--In p202-209, por.

SAGAN, FRANÇOISE, pseud.
(1935-)
French novelist, playwright
Crosland--Women p192-200, see
also index p254
Seymour-Smith--Novels p210, por.
Seymour-Smith--Who's p324
World--Who p35

SAGAN, LEONTINE
West German filmmaker
Smith--Movies p140-141

SAGE, KAY LINN (1898-1963)
Amer. painter, poet
Fine--Women p197-198
Harris--Women p319-320,338,360
Sicherman--Notable p618-619

SAGE, LETITIA ANN (fl. 1780's-
1810's)
British pioneer balloon
passenger
Macksey--Book p246

SAGE, MARGARET OLIVIA SLOCUM
(1828-1918)
Amer. philanthropist, (Mrs.
Russell Sage)
James--Notable (3) p222-223
McHenry--Liberty's p363-364
Sherr--American p177
Warren--Pictorial p142
Webster's--Amer. p911
Woman's Almanac p211
World--Who p205

SAGER, RUTH (1918-)
Amer. geneticist, biology
professor
McHenry--Liberty's p364
O'Neill--Women's p145,161

SAID, AMINA EL (fl. 1970's)
Egyptian journalist, writer
O'Neill--Women's p480

SAIDAMINOVA, DILORAM (UZBEK)
(1944-)
Russian composer

Mandel--Soviet p150-
151

SAIKOWSKI, CHARLOTTE (fl.
1970's)
Amer. newspaper editor
O'Neill--Women's p457

SAIN, DOROTHY M. (fl. 1970's)
Amer. journalist, labor
leader
O'Neill--Women's p306-307,315

SAINT, EVA MARIE (1924-   )
Amer. actress
Hirschhorn--Rating p334, por.
Shipman--Internatl. p525-526,
por.
World--Who p247

ST. CLAIR, SALLY (fl. 1770's)
Amer. soldier, (male imper-
sonator)
Ingraham--Album p17

ST. CYR, LILI (LILY) (1917-   )
Amer. burlesque player
Lamparski--What. (5) p70-71,
por.

ST. DENIS, RUTH (1877-1968)
Amer. dancer, choreographer
Anticaglia--12 p137-155, por.
Dunlap--Calif. p174, por.
Fabian--On p120-121, por.
McHenry--Liberty's p364-365
Macksey--Book p229
O'Neill--Women's p647
Sicherman--Notable p620-621
Signif.--Amer. p51, por.
Webster's--Amer. p912

ST. GEORGE, KATHARINE (1896-
1983)
Amer. Congresswoman,
business executive
Chamberlin--Min. p203-207
Cur. Biog. '83 p474
Miller--Fishbait p77

ST. JAMES, SUSAN (1946-   )
Amer. actress
World--Who p247

ST. JOHN, JILL (1940-   )
Amer. actress
World--Who p247

ST. JOHN FIELD, VIRGINIA
See FIELD, VIRGINIA (MARGARET
CYNTHIA)

ST. JOHNS, ADELA ROGERS
(1894-   )
Amer. film writer, lecturer,
TV personality, journalist,
novelist, noted California
mother
Amer.--Mothers p54-55
Cur. Biog. '76 p355-358, por.
Dunlap--Calif. p174-175
McHenry--Liberty's p365
Marzolf--Up p34,39
Mordden--Movie p63
O'Neill--Women's p441
Slide--Early p10, por.
Woman's Almanac p272, por.
World--Who p55

ST. JOHNS, KATHLEEN (1954-   )
Amer. TV executive
Scheuer--Tel. p420

ST. LAURENT, JULIE DE (fl.
1770's)
Amer. patriot
Young--Revol. p104-107,110,121,
208

ST. PHALLE, NIKI DE (1930-   )
French-Amer. sculptor
Munsterberg--Hist. p97,101,103

SAINTE-MARIE, BUFFY (BEVERLY)
(1940/1942-   )
Canadian-Amer. Cree Indian
singer, guitarist, songwriter
Bowman--Entertain. p12-19, por.
Claghorn--Biog. p389
Cur. Biog. '69 p387-389, por.
O'Neill--Women's p717
Pollock--In p57-65, por.
Woman's Almanac p300, por.
World--Who p272

SAKAJAWEA
See SACAJAWEA

SAKIN, GENIA (fl. 1930's-1940's)
Lithuanian plastic surgeon,
Army major
O'Neill--Women's p213-214

SALAMAN, NINA DAVIS (1877-1925)
Jewish poet, translator

Henry--Written p205,217,
255

SALAMAN, PEGGY (fl. 1930's)
British debutante, aviatrix
Boase--Sky's p122

SALE-BARKER, WENDY (fl. 1940's)
English aviatrix, ferry pilot
Boase--Sky's p180,182

SALISBURY, MARY (fl. c1754)
Amer. boarding school
director
Williams--Demeter's p177

SALLE, MARIE (1707-1756)
French ballet dancer
Macksey--Book p225
Migel--Ballerinas p15-30, por.

SALMELA-JARVINEN, MARTTA
(1892-   )
Finnish politician
O'Neill--Women's p321

SALMENHAARA, KYLLIKKI
(1915-   )
Finnish designer
O'Neill--Women's p275

SALMINEN, LEENA (fl. 1970's)
Finnish editor
Marzolf--Up p278

SALMON, LUCY MAYNARD (1853-
1927)
Amer. historian
James--Notable (3) p223-225
McHenry--Liberty's p365-366

SALMON, MARY (fl. 1750's)
Amer. colonial blacksmith
DePauw--Found. p32-33

SALM-SALM, AGNES ELISABETH
WINONA LECLERQ JOY,
PRINCESS (1840-1912)
Amer. war relief worker
McHenry--Liberty's p366

SALOME (1)
Biblical, mother of James
and John
Price--God p157-160
Woman's Almanac p400-401

SALOME (2) (fl. 1st cent. A.D.)
Biblical, Roman dancer
People's Almanac (1) p900-901

SALOME, ALEXANDRA (fl. 78-68
B.C.)
Judea queen, wife of Alexan-
der
Henry--Written p2

SALOMON, ALICE (1872-1948)
German school founder,
feminist
Macksey--Book p73,88

SALPE (fl. 1st Cent. B.C.)
Greek physician, poet
Mead--Hist. p41,57

SALT, BARBARA (fl. 1950's-1960's)
British ambassador
Macksey--Book p38

SALTER, MARY TURNER (1856-
1938)
Amer. singer, composer,
teacher
Claghorn--Biog. p389
Jablonski--Ency. p174

SALTER, SUSANNA MEDORA
(c1860-   )
Amer. mayor, temperance
worker
Felton--Famous p143, por.
Sherr--American p73
Time--Women p199,222, por.

SALUZZIO, MARGUERITE (fl.
c1460's)
Italian physician
Mead--Hist. p308

SALVINA (fl. 4th Cent.)
Roman physician
Mead--Hist. p81

SAMAROFF, OLGA HICKENLOOPER
(1882-1948)
Amer. pianist, music teacher,
educator
Claghorn--Biog. p390
James--Notable (3) p225-227
McHenry--Liberty's p366-367

SAMBATHE (SABBE) (fl. 1st Cent.,

B.C.E.)
Greek-Jewish, Alexandrian
sibyl
Henry--Written p38-43

SAMISH, ZDENKA
Israeli food technologist
Macksey--Book p159

SAMOILOVA, NATASHA
(CONCURDIA) (1876-)
Russian editor, feminist,
writer, labor leader
Mandel--Soviet p35,40-41,47,54

SAMPE, ASTRID (1909-)
Swedish textile designer
O'Neill--Women's p272

SAMPER, GABRIELA (c1918-1974)
Colombian filmmaker
Smith--Movies p130-131

SAMPSON, DEBORAH (1760-1827)
Amer. Revolutionary soldier,
male impersonator
Book--Lists (1) p339
Booth--Women p266-270
Clyne--Patriots p89-95
DePauw--Found. p192-193
DePauw--Rem. p90,95, por.
Evans--Weather. p10,303-334,
por.
Hymowitz--Hist. p31-32
Ingraham--Album p17, por.
James--Notable (3) p227-228
Kulkin--Her p253-254
McHenry--Liberty's p367
Meyer--Petticoat p156-163, por.
Millstein--We p35,44-45
People's Almanac (1) p139-140
People's Almanac (2) p564-565
Reifert--Women p24
Sherr--American p111
Somerville--Women p28-35
Whitney--Col. p359-361, por.
Williams--Demeter's p241-243
Woman's Almanac p451

SAMPSON, EDITH SPURLOCK
(1901-1979)
Amer. jurist, lawyer, UN
delegate
Cur. Biog. '80 p463
Signif.--Amer. p72, por.

SAMPSON, SYLVIA CHURCH

(1768-1836)
Amer. socialite
DePauw--Rem. p116, por.

SAMPTER, JESSIE ETHEL (1883-1938)
Amer. poet, Zionist
James--Notable (3) p228-229

SAMSON, JULIE ANN (fl. 1980's)
Amer. physics student
(Antarctica)
Land--New p217-219, por.

SAMSON, PRUNELLA J. (fl. 1970's)
English WRAC officer
O'Neill--Women's p551

SANCHEZ, SONIA (1935-)
Amer. poet
Chester--Rising p238-241, por.

SAND, GEORGE, pseud. (1804-1876)
French novelist
Bree--Women p40-41
Crosland--Women, see index p255,
por.
Donaldson--How p324-326
Kronenberger--Atlan. p671-672
Macksey--Book p185, por.
Magill--Cycl. p936-938
Moers--Literary p305-310, see
also index p333, por.
Moffat--Revel. p79-85
People's Almanac (2) p855-856
Seymour-Smith--Novels p211, por.
Smith--Women p221-269
Taylor--Gener. p50-51, por.
Who Did What p283
Woman's Almanac p257-258, por.

SAND, LAUREN JOY
Amer. TV director
Scheuer--Tel. p422

SANDA, DOMINIQUE (1951-)
French actress
World--Who p261

SANDEL, CORA (1880-1974)
Norwegian novelist
Seymour-Smith--Novels p211
Seymour-Smith--Who's p326

SANDERS, ALTINA (fl. 1940's)
Amer. eyeglass designer
O'Neill--Women's p255-256

SANDERS, BEULAH (1935-)
    Amer. welfare rights activist
    O'Neill--Women's p726-727

SANDERS, CLAUDIA (1902-)
    Amer. restauranteur, (wife
    of Colonel Sanders), noted
    Kentucky mother
    Amer.--Mothers p221, por.

SANDERS, ELIZABETH ELKINS
    (1762-1851)   ˡ
    Amer. social critic, pamphle-
    teer
    James--Notable (3) p229-230

SANDERS, ESTELLE SCHULZE
    (1905-)
    Amer., church, civic worker,
    noted Louisiana mother
    Amer.--Mothers p232-233, por.

SANDERS, MARION K. (c1905-)
    Amer. magazine editor,
    government official, journalist
    O'Neill--Women's p475

SANDERS, MARLENE (1931-)
    Amer. TV executive, producer,
    correspondent, anchorwoman
    Adams--Women p24-25,104,108-
    111,154,157,176,188,199
    Cur. Biog. '81 p351-354, por.
    Gelfman--Women, see index p186,
    por.
    Marzolf--Up p169,174-176,184-186
    O'Neill--Women's p504
    Scheuer--Tel. p423
    Smith--Movies p80-82,270, por.
    Walker--Women p105-121, por.
    Woman's Almanac p272

SANDERSON, SIBYL SWIFT (1865-
    1903)
    French-Amer. opera singer
    Claghorn--Biog. p390
    James--Notable (3) p230-232
    McHenry--Liberty's p367
    Starr--Amer. p348-383

SANDES, FLORA (fl. 1910's)
    English nurse, heroine,
    soldier
    Macksey--Book p57

SANDFORD, CHRISTINE (1893-
    1975)

British school founder,
    (Addes Ababa)
    Macksey--Book p77

SANDFORD-MORGAN, ELMA LINTON
    (1890-)
    Australian physician
    Hellstedt--Women p42-48, por.

SANDLER, BERNICE (1928-)
    Amer. Congresswoman,
    feminist
    O'Neill--Women's p402-403,432
    Woman's Almanac p158

SANDLER, MARION O. (fl. 1970's)
    Amer. banker
    O'Neill--Women's p528
    Woman's Almanac p181

SANDOZ, HENRIETTA (fl. 1880's)
    Swiss-Amer. writer
    Neidle--America's p97

SANDOZ, MARI (1896/1900-1966)
    Amer. biographer, historian,
    novelist, teacher
    Ehrlich--Oxford p394, por.
    Sherr--American p138-139
    Sicherman--Notable p621-623

SANDOZ, ROBERTA ("BOBBY")
    Amer. aviatrix
    Keil--Those, see index p330

SANDRART, ESTHER BARBARA
    VON (1651-1729)
    German naturalist, writer,
    illustrator
    Mead--Hist. p426

SANDS, DIANA PATRICIA (1934-1973)
    Amer. actress
    World--Who p248

SANDWINA, KATIE BRUMBACH
    (1884-1952)
    German weight lifter
    Macksey--Book p258
    McWhirter--Guinness p186, por.

SANFORD, ISABEL GWENDOLYN
    (1917/1933-)
    Amer. TV actress
    People--Best p176, por.
    Scheuer--Tel. p423, por.
    World--Who p248

SANFORD, MARIA LOUISE (1836-
1920)
Amer. college professor,
feminist, humanitarian
Burgess--Education p139-140
James--Notable (3) p232-234
McHenry--Liberty's p367-368
Sherr--American p38,120, por.

SANGER, ELEANOR N. (fl. 1930's-
1940's)
Amer. radio station program
director
Women--Radio p6-7

SANGER, MARGARET HIGGINS
(1883-1966)
Amer. social reformer, birth
control pioneer
Anticaglia--12 p156-183, por.
Archer--Famous p70-84
Banner--Women p53,102,109,116,
por.
Brin--Social p101-123, por.
Clark--Leading p73-77
Gilfond--Heroines p64-69, por.
Hymowitz--Hist. p199,294-298
Ingraham--Album p54, por.
Kostman--20th p34-55, por.
Kulkin--Her p254-255
Longstreet--Queen p97-102
McHenry--Liberty's p368
Macksey--Book p120,156, por.
Marlowe--Great p239-244, por.
Miller--Women p199-240
Millstein--We p205-207,223-226,
por.
O'Neill--Women's p720
Palmer--Who's p286
Papachristou--Women p191-193,
196, por.
Peoples' Almanac (2) p446
Reader's--Story p435
Reifert--Women p187-190
Ross--Young p57-70, por.
Sherr--American p160,167,169
Sicherman--Notable p623-627
Signif.--Amer. p51, por.
Smith--Daughters, see index
p386
Sochen--Herstory p274,295,336-
337, por.
Sochen--Movers p104-106
Stoddard--Famous p372-386, por.
Taylor--Gener. p39-40, por.
Warren--Pictorial p150-152, por.
Webster's--Amer. p916

Woman's Almanac p26, por.
World--Who p190-191

SANGSTER, MARGARET ELIZABETH
MUNSON (1838-1912)
Amer. poet, editor
Ehrlich--Oxford p117-118
James--Notable (3) p234-235
McHenry--Liberty's p369
Signif.--Amer. p33, por.

SAN JUAN, OLGA (1927-)
Amer. dancer
Lamparski--What. (5) p146-147,
por.

SANSAN (fl. 1960's)
Chinese writer
Cavanah--We p176-185

SANSOM, EMMA (-1900)
Amer. Civil War heroine,
diarist
Sherr--American p1, por.

SANSOM, ODETTE MARIE CELINE
BRAILLY
See CHURCHILL, ODETTE MARY
CELINE BRAILEY SANSOM

SANSONE, MARY (1916-)
Amer. activist, organization
director
Seifer--Nobody p40-87, por.

SANTAELLA, IRMA (fl. 1960's-
1970's)
Puerto Rican-Amer. lawyer,
humanitarian
O'Neill--Women's p364

SANTAMARIA, FRANCES KARLEN
(fl. 1970's)
Amer. diarist
Moffat--Revel. p109-115

SANTI, TINA
Amer. corporate official
Adams--Women p57-61,87,101,104

SANTMYER, HELEN HOOVEN
(1895-)
Amer. novelist
Cur. Biog. '85 p357-360, por.

SANTORO, SUZANNE (1946-)
Amer. artist

618 / Santos

Parker--Old p127, fig.
79-80

SANTOS, JOCELINA (c1956-)
Amer. food specialist
O'Neill--Women's p21

SANTY, PATRICIA
Amer. physician (science
psychology)
Oberg--Space p32

SAPHO
See SCUDERY, MADELEINE
(MAGDALEINE) DE

SAPPHO (600/610 B.C.-c580 B.C.)
Greek poet
Jones--Rutledge p695
Kronenberger--Atlan. p674
Macksey--Book p178
Magill--Cycl. p944-945
Moers--Literary p310
Pomeroy--Godd. p53-56
Who Did What p284
Woman's Almanac p258-259, por.
World--Who p43
Zinserling--Women p20-21

SARABHAI, ANUSUYA(BEN)
(1885-)
East Indian labor leader
O'Neill--Women's p293-294

SARAGOSSA (SARAGOZA),
AUGUSTINA (1786-1857)
Spanish soldier, patriot,
heroine
Woman's Almanac p447

SARAH (1)
Biblical
Henry--Written p2,15-16
Price--God p17-34
Woman's Almanac p400

SARAH (2) (570-632 C.E.)
Arabic Yeminite Jewish poet
Henry--Written p62-64

SARAH (3) OF ST. GILES (fl.
1320's)
French, head of medical
school
Mead--Hist. p214,269

SARAH (DONNA) (fl. 13th Cent.)

Jewish letter-writer
Henry--Written p102-104

SARANDON, SUSAN (1946-)
Amer. actress
Hirschhorn--Rating p336, por.

SARGENT, PEGGY
Amer. magazine, film editor
Hamblin--That p68-71,243-244,
por.

SARNOFF, DOROTHY
Amer. actress, opera singer,
TV "teacher"
Fireman--TV p261, por.

SAROSA, JULIE SULLANTI (fl.
1970's)
Indonesian UN official
Macksey--Book p40

SARRAUTE, NATHALIE (1900/
1903-)
Russian-French novelist,
critic, lawyer, playwright
Bree--Women p60-65
Crosland--Women p153-158,163-
164, por.
Moers--Literary p310
O'Neill--Women's p680
Seymour-Smith--Novels p212,
por.
Seymour-Smith--Who's p328-329
Wintle--Makers p462-463, #422

SARRAZIN, ALBERTINE DAMIEN
(1937-1967)
French novelist
Bree--Women p69
Crosland--Women p171-179, por.

SARSON, EVELYN K. (fl. 1960's)
Amer. children's TV writer
O'Neill--Women's p729

SARTAIN, EMILY (1841-1927)
English-Amer. painter, mez-
zotint engraver, art educator,
etcher, illustrator
James--Notable (3) p235-236
McHenry--Liberty's p369

SARTIKA, IBU DEWI (1884-1942)
Indonesian girl's school
pioneer
Macksey--Book p73

SARTON, MAY (1912-)
Amer. novelist, poet
Avenel--Comp. (2) p229
Betts--Writers p46-49, por.
Chester--Rising p64-67, por.
Cur. Biog. '82 p381-385, por.
Ehrlich--Oxford, see index p460
McCullough--People p148-149
Seymour-Smith--Novels p212

SARTRE, MARQUISE DE
French physician, mathematician, naturalist, (wife of D'Estoublon)
Mead--Hist. p419

SARU-HASHI, KATSUKO
Japanese geochemist
O'Neill--Women's p174

SASALLOW, OLGA NUÑEZ DE
See DE SASALLOW, OLGA NUÑEZ

SASS, SYLVIA
Hungarian opera singer
Gammond--Illus. p249-250, por.

SASSO, SANDY (1947-)
Amer. rabbi
Proctor--Women p62-63,131-134, 136-145
Smith--Break. p38-58, por.

SATUR, DOROTHY MAY (1902-)
East Indian physician
Hellstedt--Women p237-239, por.

SATZ, NATALIA
Russian director, children's theatre
Mandel--Soviet p191

SAUER, MARIE ELIZABETH (fl. 18th Cent.)
German gypsy queen, midwife
Mead--Hist. p503

SAUNDERS, CICELY
English hospice founder
O'Neill--Women's p229

SAUNDERS, DORIS EVANS (1928-)
Amer. publishing director, editor
O'Neill--Women's p486-487

SAUNDERS, NELL
Amer. boxer
Felton--Famous p284

SAUNIER-SEITE, ALICE (1925-)
French government official
O'Neill--Women's p54-55

SAUVAGEOT, MARCELLE (-1934)
French writer
Crosland--Women p109-110

SAUVE, JEANNE (1922-)
Amer. state governor-general
Cur. Biog. '84 p361-365, por.
O'Neill--Women's p51

SAVAGE, AUGUSTA CHRISTINE (1892-1962)
Amer. sculptor
Sicherman--Notable p627-629

SAVAGE, ETHEL DELL (1881-1939)
English novelist
Showalter--Lit. p345

SAVCHENKO, MELANIE (fl. 1910's)
Russian physician
Mandel--Soviet p42-43

SAVINOVA, IRINA (fl. 1970's)
Russian poet
Mandel--Soviet p152-153

SAVITCH, JESSICA (1947-1984)
Amer. journalist, TV anchorwoman
Cur. Biog. '83 p341-344, por.
Cur. Biog. '84 p479
Klever--Women p29-30,79-81,96, 106, por.
O'Neill--Women's p506-507

SAVITSKAYA, SVETLANA ("SVETA") (c1948-)
Russian engineer, (aerobatics), astronaut
Macksey--Book p251
Oberg--Space p32
O'Connor--Sally p21-22
O'Neill--Women's p590

SAVOLAINEN, ANN W. (fl. 1940's-1970's)
Amer. nuclear director
O'Neill--Women's p184-185

SAWAMATSU, KAZUKO (fl. 1970's)
   Japanese tennis player
   O'Neill--Women's p583

SAWYER, ADA LEWIS (-1911)
   Amer. lawyer
   O'Neill--Women's p351-352

SAWYER, CAROLINE MEHITABLE
   FISHER (1812-1894)
   Amer. poet, editor
   James--Notable (3) p236-237

SAWYER, DIANE (c1945-)
   Amer. TV news co-anchor
   Scheuer--Tel. p426

SAWYER, JANET (fl. 1970's)
   Amer. painter
   Women's--Female p56

SAWYER, MARY
   Amer., subject of "Mary had
   a little lamb"
   Sherr--American p112

SAWYER, RUTH (1880-1970)
   Amer. children's book author
   Kulkin--Her p256
   Sicherman--Notable p629-631

SAWYER, RUTH BURR (1912-)
   Amer. educator, noted
   Florida mother
   Amer.--Mothers p120-121, por.

SAXE, SUSAN EDITH (c1950-)
   Amer. accused criminal
   People's Almanac (1) p613
   Woman's Almanac p510

SAXON, CELIA (-1935)
   Amer. educator
   Sherr--American p210

SAXON, ISABELLE (fl. 1860's)
   English western writer
   Fischer--Let p237-244

SAXTORPH, MATTHIAS (1740-
   1800)
   Danish professor of obstet-
   rics
   Mead--Hist. p506

SAYER, DOROTHY LEIGH (1893-
   1957)

   English novelist, translator,
   playwright, amateur theologian
   Jones--Rutledge p697
   Macksey--Book p191
   Morley--Literary p42-43
   O'Neill--Women's p677
   Seymour-Smith--Novels p212, por.
   Showalter--Lit. p348
   Sochen--Movers p183-185
   World--Who p47

SAYRE, RUTH BUXTON (1896-)
   Amer. agriculturist, noted
   Iowa mother
   Amer.--Mothers p193-194, por.
   O'Neill--Women's p8

SCALAMANDRE, FLORA ADRIANA
   (1907-)
   Amer. textile, wallpaper
   designer
   O'Neill--Women's p276-277, por.

SCAMARDELLA, ROSE ANN
   Amer. TV news anchorwoman
   Gelfman--Women p23,25-26,100-
   101,125, por.
   Scheuer--Tel. p426

SCANLAN, ELENORE (fl. 1930's-
   1940's)
   Amer. radio advertising agency
   buyer
   Women--Radio p18

SCANNELL, NANCY (fl. 1970's)
   Amer. newspaper sportswriter
   O'Neill--Women's p463

SCARAVAGLIONE, CONCETTA
   (1900-1975)
   Amer. sculptor
   Fine--Women p144

SCHACHENMANN, GERTRUD DINA
   (1910-)
   Swiss physician
   Hellstedt--Women p404-406, por.

SCHACHER-ELEK, ILONA (fl.
   1930's-1950's)
   Hungarian fencer
   O'Neill--Women's p560

SCHACTER, FRANCES
   Amer. psychology professor
   O'Neill--Women's p422

SCHAEFER, HELEN
Amer. aviatrix, army flier
Keil--Those p230-231

SCHAEFER, MARY CHERUBIN
(1886-)
Amer. teacher, writer
Claghorn--Biog. p392

SCHAEFFER, MARGARET G. (fl.
1970's)
Amer. judge
O'Neill--Women's p370

SCHAKOWSKY, EUGENIE, COUNT-
ESS (fl. 1910's)
German aviatrix, instructor
Boase--Sky's p21

SCHALHEIMER, MARIE SOPHIE
CONRING (fl. 1690's)
German linguist, scientist,
theologian, writer, food
chemist, dietician
Mead--Hist. p426-427

SCHAPIRO, ANGELA P. (fl. 1940's)
English TV association presi-
dent
Scheuer--Tel. p428

SCHAPIRO, MIRIAM (1923-)
Canadian-Amer. painter,
feminist
Bachtold--Gifted p37-38
Munro--Originals p272-281
Ruddick--Working p283-305,346,
por.
Women's--Female p56

SCHARFF, MARY (fl. 1970's)
Amer. basketball player
Hollander--100 p9, por.

SCHARRER, BERTA VOGEL (fl.
1960's)
Amer. anatomist
O'Neill--Women's p144,223

SCHARY, HOPE SKILLMAN
(c1920-)
Amer. fashion leader, textile
executive
Diamonstein--Open p344-348, por.

SCHAUMBERJ (SCHAUMBURG),
EMILIE (fl. 1860's)

Amer. social leader, belle
Peacock--Famous p190-205, por.

SCHAW, JANET (fl. 1770's)
Scottish-Amer. patriot
Booth--Women p30-32

SCHECHTER, MATHILDE ROTH
(1859-1924)
German-Amer. president,
theological seminary, noted
New York mother
Amer.--Mothers p392-393

SCHECHTER, RUTH LISA (1928-)
Amer. poet
Chester--Rising p184-188, por.

SCHEERER, JEANNETTE (fl. 1900's-
1950's)
Amer. clarinetist
Neuls-Bates--Women p253-254,
265-272

SCHEFF, FRITZI (1879/1882-1954)
Austrian actress, singer
Hazen--Interv. p86
Neidle--America's p230-231

SCHEIBLICH, CHRISTINA (fl.
1970's)
East German rower
McWhirter--Guinness p113
O'Neill--Women's p572,584

SCHEIN, VIRGINIA
Amer. feminist, writer
Adams--Women p100

SCHEINBERG, MRS. BERNARD
(c1854-1911)
Austrian mother (of 69
children)
McFarland--Incred. p14

SCHELL, MARIA MARGARETHE
ANNA (1926-)
Austrian actress
World--Who p261

SCHELLHAMMER, MARIE SOPHIE
CONRING
See SCHALHEIMER, MARIE
SOPHIE CONRING

SCHENIRER, SARAH (1873-1925)
Polish-Austrian founder girls'

schools
Fink--Great p126-131, por.

SCHENK, LYNN A. (fl. 1970's)
Amer. feminist, founder
Equal Rights Advisors
O'Neill--Women's p359

SCHEUER, LAURA
Amer. TV lawyer
Scheuer--Tel. p430

SCHIAPARELLI, ELSA (1890/
1891-1973)
Italian-French fashion
designer
Cur. Biog. '74 p469
Keenan--Women p69-71, por.
Macksey--Book p268, por.
O'Neill--Women's p241
World--Who p301

SCHIFF, DOROTHY (1903-)
Amer. newspaper editor,
publisher
Fink--Great p162-168, por.
Longstreet--Queen p174-175
McHenry--Liberty's p369-370
O'Neill--Women's p449
Woman's Almanac p272-273
World--Who p55

SCHIFFKORN, GERHILDE (fl.
1960's)
Austrian skier
Macksey--Book p261

SCHIFFMAN, CAROL MEHR (1928-)
Amer. genealogical researcher
Meyer--Who's p180

SCHIMMEL, GERTRUDE D.T.
(1918-)
Amer. policewoman, writer
O'Neill--Women's p373
Walker--Women p122-136, por.

SCHJERFBECK, HELENE (fl. 1860's)
Finnish artist
Sparrow--Women p291,310,313

SCHLAFLY, PHYLLIS STEWART
(1924-)
Amer. author, social, politi-
cal activist
Cur. Biog. '78 p360-363, por.
Lichtenstein--Mach. see index

p366
Schoenebaum--Prof. p572-573
Woman's Almanac p559-560, por.
World--Who p191

SCHLATTER, RACHEL (fl. 1770's)
Amer. Revolutionary War
patriot
Meyer--Petticoat p103

SCHLEE, NICHOLAEVNA SANINA
See VALENTINA

SCHLEI, MARIE (fl. 1970's)
German minister for economic
cooperation
O'Neill--Women's p55-56

SCHLETZ, ELKE
See SOMMER, ELKE

SCHLOSS, CLARA F. (fl. 1950's-
1970's)
Amer. labor official
O'Neill--Women's p336

SCHLÖZER, DOROTHEA VON RODDE
See RODDE, DOROTHEA VON

SCHMIDT, KATE (KATHY) (fl.
1970's)
Amer. track and field athlete
McWhirter--Guinness p171, por.
O'Neill--Women's p577,579

SCHMIDT, KÄTHE
See KOLLWITZ, KÄTHE (KAETHE)
SCHMIDT

SCHMIDT-FISCHER, HILDEGARD
(1906-)
West German physician
Hellstedt--Women p316-320, por.

SCHMIDT-NIELSEN, BODIL (fl.
1970's)
Amer. physiologist
O'Neill--Women's p221

SCHMITT, GLADYS LEONORE
(1909-1972)
Amer. author, teacher, editor
Cur. Biog. '72 p470

SCHNEIDER, DEBORAH (fl. 1950's)
Amer. contest winner
Felton--Famous p202

SCHORR, LIA
Amer. cosmetologist
People--Best p75, por.

SCHRADERS, CATHERINE
GERTRUDE DE TERTDE
See CRAMER, VROW

SCHREIBER-FAVRE, NELLY (fl.
1900's)
Swiss lawyer
Macksey--Book p129

SCHREINER, JAN (fl. 1970's)
Amer. Army commandant
O'Neill--Women's p546

SCHREINER, OLIVE (1855-1920)
South African novelist,
feminist
Avenel--Comp. (1) p462
Colby--Singular p47-110
Jones--Rutledge p701
Macksey--Book p81,188
Magill--Cycl. p954-955
Moers--Literary p310
Seymour-Smith--Novels p213
Showalter--Lit. p195-204,339
Who Did What p286

SCHREINER-YANTIS, NERTI
(1930-)
Amer. genealogical researcher,
author
Meyer--Who's p180

SCHRIECK, LOUISE VAN DER,
SISTER (1813-1886)
Dutch-Amer. religious
McHenry--Liberty's p370-371

SCHRIFT, SHIRLEY
See WINTERS, SHELLEY

SCHRÖDER-DEVRIENT, WILHEL-
MINE (1804-1860)
German opera singer
Partington--Who's p370

SCHROEDER, BECKY (fl. 1970's)
Amer. inventor
O'Neill--Women's p744-745

SCHROEDER, PATRICIA (1940-)
Amer. Congresswoman
Chamberlin--Min. p354-355
Cur. Biog. '78 p367-370, por.

Greenebaum--Politics p141
O'Neill--Women's p45,72, por.
Swiger--Women p187-200
Woman's Almanac p480-481, por.

SCHRÖTER, CORONA VON (1751-
1802)
German singer, composer
Neuls-Bates--Women p87

SCHROTH, CLARA (fl. 1940's-1950's)
Amer. gymnast
McWhirter--Guinness p87

SCHUCHAT, MOLLY G. (fl. 1970's)
Amer. anthropologist
O'Neill--Women's p234,236

SCHUCKMAN, KAREN (fl. 1970's)
Amer. gymnast
Jordan--Broken p69-76

SCHULMAN, NINA (fl. 1970's)
Amer. filmmaker
Smith--Movies p202,271

SCHULMAN, PAT
Amer. teacher
Gold--Until p334-335

SCHULTZ, SIGRID LILLIAN (1893-)
Amer. foreign correspondent
Marzolf--Up p55,69-70
O'Neill--Women's p442

SCHUMACHER-PERCY, ULLA (1918-)
Swedish textile designer
O'Neill--Women's p271-272

SCHUMANN, CLARA JOSEPHINE
WIECK (1819-1896)
German pianist, composer,
music teacher, (wife of Robert
Schumann)
Kulkin--Her p257
Macksey--Book p212-213, por.
Neuls-Bates--Women, see index
p348, por.
Woman's Almanac p300-301

SCHUMANN, ELIZABETH (1885/
1891-1952)
German opera singer
Claghorn--Biog. p395
Jones--Rutledge p702
Macksey--Book p217, por.
Tuggle--Golden p131-132, por.

SCHUMANN, MARGIT (fl. 1970's)
East German luge athlete
O'Neill--Women's p564-565

SCHUMANN-HEINK, ERNESTINE
ROSSLER (1861-1936)
Czechoslovakian-Amer. opera
singer
Claghorn--Biog. p395
Hazen--Interv. p285-287
James--Notable (3) p240-242
McHenry--Liberty's p371
May--Different p105-118, por.
Neidle--America's p226-228
O'Neill--Women's p617
Tuggle--Golden p126-128, por.
Webster's--Amer. p924

SCHUPAK, LENORE H. (fl. 1970's)
Amer. environmental engineer
O'Neill--Women's p196

SCHURMAN, ANNA MARIA VON
(1607-1678)
Netherlands scholar, poet,
sculptor, feminist, linguist,
glass engraver, ivory and
wood carver, engraver
Brink--Female p68-85, por.
Fine--Women p30-31, por.
Macksey--Book p65,197-198,
por.
Marlowe--Great p23-27, por.
Mead--Hist. p430, por.
Munsterberg--Hist. p28-30, por.

SCHURR, CATHLEEN (fl. 1970's)
Amer. co-founder, feminist
theater
Chinoy--Women p293-300

SCHURZ, MARGARETHE MEYER
(1832-1876)
German-Amer. educator,
kindergarten founder, noted
Wisconsin mother
Amer.--Mothers p581, por.
James--Notable (3) p242-243
Sherr--American p252
Snyder--Dauntless p17-28, por.

SCHUST, FLORENCE
See KNOLL-BASSETT, FLORENCE
SCHUST

SCHUYLER, CATHERINE VAN
RENSSELAER (1733/1734-1803)

Amer. colonial hostess, Revolu-
tionary War patriot
James--Notable (3) p243-244
Meyer--Petticoat p92-95

SCHUYLER, LOUISE LEE (1837-1926)
Amer. welfare work leader,
Civil War philanthropist, hu-
manitarian
James--Notable (3) p244-246
McHenry--Liberty's p371-372
Woman's Almanac p452

SCHWAGER, VIRGINIA, SISTER (fl.
1940's-1970's)
Amer. nun, hospital president
O'Neill--Women's p390

SCHWALB, SUSAN (1944-   )
Amer. graphic artist
Miller--Lives p185-201, por.
Women's--Female p82

SCHWARTZ, CONSTANCE
See SHAPIRO, DEE

SCHWARTZ, DOROTHY
Amer. TV executive
Scheuer--Tel. p434-435

SCHWARTZ, FELICE N. (fl. 1960's-
1970's)
Amer. executive, founder
O'Neill--Women's p106-107

SCHWARTZ, HELENE (fl. 1970's)
Amer. lawyer, writer
O'Neill--Women's p350

SCHWARTZ, MARY E. (1940-   )
Amer. genealogical researcher,
author, editor
Meyer--Who's p181

SCHWARTZ, MELAINIE (-1897)
German air-ship builder
Macksey--Book p170

SCHWARTZ, PEPPER
Amer. sociologist, researcher
Adams--Women p117

SCHWARTZ, SYDNEE M. (1941-   )
Amer. labor leader, lobbyist
O'Neill--Women's p308

SCHWARTZE, THERESE (TERESA),

MADEMOISELLE (1852-1918)
Netherlands painter pastellist
Sparrow--Women p262,270-271,273,
275, por.
Women's--Female p57

SCHWARZER, THERESA F. (fl.
1970's)
Amer. genoscientist
O'Neill--Women's p174

SCHWARZHAUPT, ELISABETH
(1901-)
West German health minister
O'Neill--Women's p55

SCHWARZKOPF, ELISABETH
(1951-)
Polish-German opera singer
Gammond--Illus. p250, por.
O'Neill--Women's p621
World--Who p79

SCHWEBER, MIRIAM (fl. 1970's)
Amer. biochemist, DNA
researcher
O'Neill--Women's p161

SCHWIMMER, ROSIKA (1877-1948)
Hungarian-Amer. feminist,
pacifist, author
Forma--They p231-232, por.
James--Notable (3) p246-249
McHenry--Liberty's p372-373
Neidle--America's p51-53
O'Neill--Women's p699
Warren--Pictorial p167-168

SCHWINDEL, ROSA ELIZABETH
German gem cutter, wax-
modeller
Macksey--Book p200

SCHWOMEYER, JUDY (fl. 1960's-
1970's)
Amer. ice skater
McWhirter--Guinness p100

SCHYGULLA, HANNA (1943-)
Silesian actress
Cur. Biog. '84 p372-376, por.

SCICOLONE, SOFIA VILLANI
See LOREN, SOPHIA

SCIDMORE, ELIZA RUHAMAH
(1856-1928)

Amer. traveler, author
McHenry--Liberty's p373

SCOTT, ANN (LONDON) (1929-1975)
Amer. feminist, poet
Sicherman--Notable p633-634

SCOTT, BARBARA ANN (1928-)
Canadian skater
Assoc. Press--Pursuit p163,167,
por.
Lamparski--What. (2) p122-123,
por.

SCOTT, BLANCHE STUART ("BET-
TY") (1892-1970)
Amer. pioneer aviatrix, pilot
Boase--Sky's p18
People's Almanac (2) p673-674,
por.
Woman's Almanac p369

SCOTT, CHARLOTTE ANGAS (1858-
1931)
English-Amer. mathematician,
professor
James--Notable (3) p249-250
O'Neill--Women's p176

SCOTT, DOROTHY
See HANCOCK, DOROTHY QUINCY

SCOTT, DRU
Amer. executive
Adams--Women p23,69-71,73,103,
116,167-168

SCOTT, E. NAN (fl. 1970's)
Amer. physician, (Antarctica)
Land--New p11,147-160, por.

SCOTT, EVELYN D. (1893-1963)
Amer. poet, novelist, diarist
Ehrlich--Oxford p285
Moffat--Revel. p98-108

SCOTT, GLORIA DEAN (1938-)
Amer. president, Girl Scouts
of America
O'Neill--Women's p119, por.

SCOTT, HAZEL DOROTHY (1920-
1981)
Trinidad-Amer. pianist, singer
Claghorn--Biog. p396
Claghorn--Jazz p263
Cur. Biog. '81 p472
Miller--Fishbait p187-190

SCOTT, IRENE FEAGIN (fl.
1960's-1970's)
Amer. lawyer, tax-court
judge
O'Neill--Women's p369-370
Swiger--Women p201-219

SCOTT, LEADER, pseud.
See BAXTER, LUCY E. BARNES

SCOTT, LIZABETH (1922/1923-   )
Amer. actress
Lamparski--What. (3) p106-107
World--Who p248

SCOTT, MARGARET, LADY (fl.
1890's)
English golfer
Macksey--Book p256
McWhirter--Guinness p67

SCOTT, MARTHA (1914-   )
Amer. actress
World--Who p248

SCOTT, MASHA (fl. 1940's)
Russian-Amer. teacher,
feminist
Mandel--Soviet p9-10,67-68

SCOTT, ROSALIE VIRGINIA
See McCLENDON, ROSE

SCOTT, SHEILA (1927-   )
English aviatrix, pilot
Boase--Sky's p215
Cur. Biog. '74 p353-356, por.
O'Neill--Women's p590
Woman's Almanac p370

SCOTT, SHIRLEY (1924-   )
Amer. pianist
Claghorn--Jazz p264

SCOTT-MAXWELL, FLORIDA
(1883-   )
Amer. actress, psychologist,
feminist, diarist, short-story
writer
Moffat--Revel. p361-373

SCOTTO, RENATA (1933/1936-   )
Italian-Amer. opera singer
Cur. Biog. '78 p370-373, por.
Gammond--Illus. p250, por.
Glassman--Year '79 p142-143,
por.

People--Best p143, por.
World--Who p79

SCOVEL, BETTIE J. (fl. 1880's)
Amer. potter
Callen--Women p88

SCRIPPS, ELLEN BROWNING (1836-
1932)
English-Amer. journalist, pub-
lisher, philanthropist, college
and museum founder
James--Notable (3) p250-252
McHenry--Liberty's p373
Marzolf--Up p18
Sherr--American p12,14, por.
Webster's--Amer. p928
Woman's Almanac p273
World--Who p55

SCRIVENER, CHRISTINE (1925-   )
French secretary of state
O'Neill--Women's p55

SCUDDER, ELIZA (1821-1896)
Amer. hymnist
Claghorn--Biog. p397

SCUDDER, IDA SOPHIA (1870-1960)
Amer. physician, missionary
Sicherman--Notable p634-636

SCUDDER, JANET (1869-1940)
Amer. sculptor
James--Notable (3) p252-253
McHenry--Liberty's p373-374

SCUDDER, VIDA DUTTON (1861-
1954)
Amer. author, educator,
social reformer, scholar
McHenry--Liberty's p374
O'Neill--Women's p111
Sicherman--Notable p636-638

SCUDERY, MADELEINE (MAGDA-
LEINE) DE (1607-1701)
French novelist, poet
Bree--Women p37-38
Crosland--Women p51-52,58, por.
Jones--Rutledge p705
Macksey--Book p181
Magill--Cycl. p958-959
Who Did What p287

SCULLY, JANE, SISTER (fl. 1970's)
Amer. college president,

corporation director
O'Neill--Women's p392

SCULLY, JULIA (fl. 1960's-1970's)
Amer. magazine editor,
photographer
O'Neill--Women's p476

SCULLY, VIOLET SIMPSON
(1902-)
English-Amer. community
worker, noted Illinois mother
Amer.--Mothers p168, por.

SEAMAN, AUGUSTA HUIELL (1879-
1950)
Amer. novelist
Ehrlich--Oxford p194

SEAMAN, BARBARA
Amer. feminist, author
100--Great (1) p86, por.

SEAMAN, ELIZABETH COCHRANE
See BLY, NELLIE, pseud.

SEAMAN, MOTHER
English religious martyr
Bainton--France p219

SEARGEANT, MARY ELIZABETH
(1855-1921)
Amer. collector of Indian
relics, noted Arizona mother
Amer.--Mothers p28, por.

SEARIGHT, PATTI (c1925-)
Amer. radio program director
Marzolf--Up p146

SEARS, CYNTHIA LOVELACE
(1937-)
Amer. author
Ruddick--Working p251-269,346,
por.

SEARS, ELEONORA RANDOLPH
(1881-1968)
Amer. horseman, tennis
player, socialite
Hollander--100 p7,58-60,100,
por.
Ryan--Sports p132-133
Sicherman--Notable p638-639
Woman's Almanac p411

SEAVEY, HELEN (fl. 1770's)

Amer. Revolutionary War
patriot
Meyer--Petticoat p82

SEBASTIAN, DOROTHY (1903-1957)
Amer. model, actress
Springer--They p218,326, por.

SEBERG, JEAN (1938-1979)
Amer. actress
Cur. Biog. '79 p473
Hirschhorn--Rating p339-340,
por.

SEBIRI, CELIA (fl. 1970's)
Amer. jeweler-designer
O'Neill--Women's p248,256

SECHLER, SUSAN (fl. 1970's)
Amer. agriculturist, govern-
ment official
O'Neill--Women's p37

SEDDON, MARGARET RHEA (c1948-)
Amer. astronaut
Oberg--Space p24,110-111,113,
por.
O'Connor--Sally p2,25,53, por.
O'Neill--Women's p740, por.

SEDGWICK, ANNE DOUGLAS (1873-
1935)
Amer. novelist
Ehrlich--Oxford p181
James--Notable (3) p255-258
McHenry--Liberty's p375

SEDGWICK, CATHARINE MARIA
(1789-1867)
Amer. novelist, educator
Beach--Daughters p1-39
Ehrlich--Oxford p50,62-63
McHenry--Liberty's p375
Moers--Literary p310

SEDLACKOVA, MARIE
Moravian, Nazi victim
Partington--Who's p373

SEDLAK, BONNIE (fl. 1970's)
Amer. developmental biologist
Seed--Saturday's p79-82, por.

SEDLAK, VALERIA (fl. 1970's)
Amer. Army meteorologist
O'Neill--Women's p546

SEDODE, JULIA BARBARA DE
LAMA "BABLA" (1858-)
African teacher
Crane--Ms. p14-15

SEE, CAROLYN (fl. 1970's)
Amer. novelist
Halcomb--Women p249-264

SEED, SUZANNE (fl. 1970's)
Amer. author, photographer
Seed--Saturday's p157-158, por.

SEEDAT, ZUBEDA KASSIM (fl.
1970's)
South African lawyer
O'Neill--Women's p361

SEEGER, MARGARET (PEGGY)
(1935-)
Amer. singer
Claghorn--Biog. p398

SEEGER, RUTH CRAWFORD
See CRAWFORD-SEEGER, RUTH
PORTER

SEELEY, BLOSSOM (1891-1974)
Amer. vaudeville star, singer
Lamparski--What. (4) p202-203,
por.

SEELY, MARILYN JEANNE (1940-)
Amer. singer, songwriter
Claghorn--Biog. p398-399

SEELYE, SARA EMMA EDWARDS
(1841-1901)
Amer. Civil War nurse, spy,
noted Michigan mother
Amer.--Mothers p276, por.

SEGAL, LORE
Austrian-Amer. translator,
children's book author
McCullough--People p150-151

SEGAL, VIVIENNE (1897-)
Amer. singer, actress
Claghorn--Biog. p399
Lamparski--What. (3) p150-151,
por.
Lamparski--What. (8) p264-265,
por.
Springer--They p218,326-327,
por.

SEGALE, BLANDINA, SISTER
(c1850-)
Amer. nun, teacher
Time--Women p95,98-99,101

SEGHERS, ANNA, pseud. (1900-
1983)
East German novelist, short-
story writer
Cur. Biog. '83 p473
Herrmann--Ger. p5,37-38
Seymour-Smith--Novels p214

SEGERMAN, NAN (1949-)
Amer. TV sound technician
O'Neill--Women's p504

SEGUR, SOPHIE ROSTOPCHINE,
COMTESSE DE (1799-1874)
French-Russian children's
book author
Crosland--Women p33-34
Moers--Literary p310

SEGURA, DEBI
Amer. TV cable news anchor
Scheuer--Tel. p437

SEIBEL, RUTH ROBINSON
(1907-)
Amer. genealogical researcher,
editor, writer
Meyer--Who's p182

SEIBERLING, DOROTHY
Amer. art editor
Hamblin--Life p217,279-280

SEID, RUTH
See SINCLAIR, JO, pseud.

SEIDEL, DEBORAH
Amer. lawyer
O'Neill--Women's p354

SEIDEL, DIANA E. (fl. 1970's)
Amer. filmmaker
Smith--Movies p202-203,272

SEIDENBERG, FAITH
Amer. civil rights and civil
liberties lawyer
O'Neill--Women's p355,705, por.

SEIDLER, MAREN (c1953-)
Amer. track and field athlete

Hollander--100 p124-125, por.
O'Neill--Women's p579

SEIFER, NANCY
Amer. social reformer, writer
Hymowitz--Hist. p362

SEIFERT, ELIZABETH (1897/1898-
1983)
Amer. novelist
Cur. Biog. '83 p473

SEI SHOHNAGON (fl. 11th Cent.)
Japanese lady-in-waiting
Who Did What p288

SEITZ, BEATRICE WEST (1912-)
Amer. genealogical researcher,
author
Meyer--Who's p182

SEKAQUAPTEWA, HELEN (1898-)
Amer. Hopi Indian writer
Fisher--Third p v,31-37

SELBY, CECILY CANNON (fl. 1970's)
Amer. corporation official
O'Neill--Women's p519

SELINCOURT, ANNE DE
See SEDGWICK, ANNE DOUGLAS

SELL, HILDEGARDE LORETTA
See "HILDEGARDE"

SELLER, PHYLLIS
See BROOKS, PHYLLIS

SELLINS, FANNIE MOONEY (1872-
1919)
Amer. labor organizer
O'Neill--Women's p297

SELMER, RAGNIHILD (fl. 1970's)
Norwegian Supreme Court
judge
Macksey--Book p129

SELZNICK, JOYCE (c1928-1981)
Amer. filmmaker
Smith--Movies p65,69-70

SEMBRICH(K), MARCELLA (1858-
1935)
Polish-Russian-Amer. opera
singer
Claghorn--Biog. p399

James--Notable (3) p258-260
McHenry--Liberty's p375-376
Neidle--America's p224-226
Sherr--American p158
Tuggle--Golden p6, por.

SEMENOVA, ULIANA (fl. 1970's)
Russian basketball player
O'Neill--Women's p567

SEMMEL, JEAN (fl. 1970's)
Amer. painter
Women's--Female p57

SEMMES, MYRA EULALIE KNOX (fl.
1860's)
Amer. Southern belle, society
hostess, actress, musician,
philanthropist
DeLeon--Belles p113-114, por.

SEMPLE, ELLEN CHURCHILL (1863-
1932)
Amer. anthrop-geographer,
professor
James--Notable (3) p260-262
McHenry--Liberty's p376
O'Neill--Women's p412
Who Did What p288

SEMPRONIA
Roman matron, co-conspirator
of Catiline
Pomeroy--Godd. p171-172,185
Zinserling--Women p56-57

SENCEVICKY, LORRAINE COWLES
(1926-)
Amer. genealogical researcher,
writer, editor
Meyer--Who's p182

SENDEROWITZ, JUDITH (1942-)
Amer. activist
O'Neill--Women's p728

SENESH, HANNAH (1921-1944)
Hungarian-Israeli, World War
II heroine
Kulkin--Her p258-259
Moffat--Revel. p67-74

SENGSTACKEN, AGNES
Amer. Western pioneer
Reifert--Women p105,108

SENKRAH, ARMA LEORETTE HOFFMAN

woman's club pioneer
James--Notable (3) p265-268
McHenry--Liberty's p377
Time--Women p106

SEVERINE (1855-1929)
French journalist
Moers--Literary p310

SEVERSON, ANNE (fl. 1970's)
Amer. teacher, film co-
director
Smith--Movies p272, por.

SEVIER, CATHERINE SHERRILL
("BONNY KATE") (1754/
1756-1836)
Amer. Revolutionary War
patriot, Western pioneer
Meyer--Petticoat p123-124
Sherr--American p3,218

SEVIER, CLARA DRISCOLL
See DRISCOLL, CLARA

SEVIGNE, MARIE DE RABUTIN-
CHANTAL, MARQUISE DE
(1626-1696)
French letter-writer, scholar,
salonist
Bree--Women p11,37
Brink--Female p101-118, por.
Crosland--Women p52-53, por.
Earle--Two Cent. (2) p xiv,506-
508, por.
Jones--Rutledge p709
Kronenberger--Atlan. p696-697
Mead--Hist. p419
Moers--Literary p310
Who Did What p288-289
World--Who p36

SEWALL, LUCY ELLEN (1837-1890)
Amer. physician
James--Notable (3) p268-269
Sherr--American p110

SEWALL, MAY ELIZA WRIGHT
(1844-1920)
Amer. educator, feminist,
suffragist, club woman,
social reformer, pacifist
James--Notable (3) p269-271
McHenry--Liberty's p377-378
Sherr--American p66

SEWARD, ANNA (1747-1809)

English poet, letter-writer
Avenel--Comp. (1) p467
Jones--Rutledge p709
Moers--Literary p310
Showalter--Lit. p327

SEWELL, EDNA BELLE SCOTT
(1881-1967)
Amer. farm woman's leader
Sicherman--Notable p641-642

SEWELL, ELIZABETH MISSING
(1815-1906)
English novelist, educator
Showalter--Lit. p325

SEXTON, ANNE GRAY HARVEY
(1928-1974)
Amer. poet
Avenel--Comp (2) p231
Brinnin--Modern p316-320, por.
Chester--Rising p170-183, por.
Diamonstein--Open p349-352, por.
McHenry--Liberty's p378
Moers--Literary p133,310
Seymour-Smith--Who's p335
Sicherman--Notable p642-644
Webber--Woman p115-117
Wintle--Makers p473-474, #430
Woman's Almanac p259, por.
World--Who p20

SEYMOUR, ANNE ECKERT (1909-)
Amer. radio director, actress
Lamparski--What. Annual (4,5)
p263-267, por.
Women--Radio p4-5

SEYMOUR, JANE (c1509-1537)
English queen, wife of
Henry VIII
Jones--Rutledge p404
Softly--Queens p63-66, por.
Vance--Six p76-88

SEYMOUR, LYNN (1939-)
Canadian ballet dancer
Cur. Biog. '79 p344-348, por.

SEYMOUR, MARY FOOT (1846-1893)
Amer. stenographer, business
college founder, magazine
editor, journalist
Bird--Enterprising p141-144
James--Notable (3) p271-272
O'Neill--Women's p511

SEYRIG, DELPHINE (1932-)
French actress
Entertainers p280-281, por.

SFORZA, BONA
Polish religious, wife of
Sigismund I
Bainton--Spain p135-155, por.

SFORZA, CATERINA (1463-1509)
Italian author, soldier,
stateswoman
Fine--Women p5

SHADD, MARY ANN
See CARY, MARY ANN SHADD

SHADIYEVA, TAIJIKHAN (fl.
1920's)
Russian-Turkish editor,
feminist
Taylor--Gener. p54

SHAFER, HELEN ALMIRA (1839-
1894)
Amer. educator
McHenry--Liberty's p378-379

SHAFFER, CATHARINE (fl. 1970's)
Amer. TV executive
Kelver--Women p43-44,82,84,
100-101,108

SHAFFER, DEBORAH (fl. 1970's)
Amer. filmmaker, feminist
Smith--Movies p273, por.

SHAFFER, ELAINE (1926-1973)
Amer. flutist
Macksey--Book p221

SHAFFER, GENE
Amer. aviatrix, army flier
Keil--Those p28,249-250,262-263

SHAFFER, MARGARET T.
Amer. corporate executive,
business consultant
O'Neill--Women's p138

SHAHENIAN, MARGARET (fl.
1960's-1970's)
Amer. Wine Institute director
O'Neill--Women's p16

SHAIN, EVA (fl. 1970's)
Amer. heavy-weight fighter
O'Neill--Women's p744

SHAINESS, NATALIE
Amer. psychiatrist
People's Almanac (1) p33-35

SHAKESPEARE, MARY ARDEN
(c1538-1608)
English, mother of William
Shakespeare
Diagram--Mothers p226-227

SHAKHOVSKAYA, EUGENIE, PRIN-
CESS
Russian aviatrix, pilot, execu-
tioner, member of Secret Police
Macksey--Book p57

SHALALA, DONNA EDNA (1941-)
Amer. government official,
professor, educator
O'Neill--Women's p422

SHALOM, IMA
See IMA SHALOM

SHALVI, ALICE (1926-)
German-Israeli professor
O'Neill--Women's p416

SHAM'AH SHABAZI
Jewish poet
Henry--Written p60-61

SHAMBAUGH, JESSIE FIELD (1881-
1971)
Amer. rural educator, founder
of 4-H, noted Iowa mother
Amer.--Mothers p191-192, por.
Sherr--American p70
Sicherman--Notable p644-645

SHANAHAN, EILEEN (fl. 1970's)
Amer. reporter, government
official
Marzolf--Up p107-109
O'Neill--Women's p85-86,456-457

SHANGE, NTOZAKE (1948-)
Amer. playwright, poet
Chinoy--Women p187,320,323-324,
por.
Cur. Biog. '78 p380-383, por.
Fisher--Third p vii,281

SHANK, THERESA (c1951-)
Amer. basketball player
Stambler--Women p144-155,
por.

SHANNON, DEL, pseud.
See LININGTON, ELIZABETH

SHANNON, JULIA
Amer. photographer, midwife
Time--Women p130

SHANNON, KATHLEEN (fl. 1950's-
1970's)
Canadian filmmaker
Smith--Movies p95

SHANNON, PEGGY (c1907-1941)
Amer. dancer, actress
Springer--They p218,327, por.

SHAPIRO, DEE (fl. 1970's)
Amer. artist
Women's--Female p111

SHAPSNIKOFF, ANTESIA
Amer. religious leader
Sherr--American p5

SHARAWI, MRS. HUDA (fl. 1920's)
Egyptian pioneer feminist
Taylor--Gener. p42

SHARP, ABIGAIL
See GARDNER, ABIGAIL

SHARP, ELLA WING
Amer. philanthropist
Sherr--American p118

SHARP, EVELYN (-1944)
Amer. aviatrix, army flier
Keil--Those p232-235

SHARP, JANE (fl. 1670's)
English midwife, publisher,
medical writer
Marks--Women p63
Mead--Hist. p395-396,476

SHARP, KATHARINE LUCINDA
(1865-1914)
Amer. librarian, school
founder
James--Notable (3) p272-273
Sherr--American p64

SHARP, RETA R. (fl. 1970's)
Amer. heroine
O'Neill--Women's p734

SHARP, SUSIE MARSHALL (1907-)

Amer. judge
O'Neill--Women's p371, por.
Woman's Almanac p523

SHARPLES (SHARPLALES), ELLEN
WALLACE (1769-1849)
English painter
DePauw--Rem. p131, por.
Petersen--Women p65-66, por.

SHARPLES, ROLINDA (1794-1838)
English painter
Petersen--Women p65-66, por.

SHARRER, ETHEL V. (fl. 1800's)
Amer. postmaster
Sherr--American p96

SHARROCK, LINDA CHAMBERS
(1949-)
Amer. singer
Claghorn--Jazz p365

SHATNER, MARCY (c1947-)
Amer. ballet dancer, (wife of
William Shatner)
Funt--Are p291-310, por.

SHATTUCK, LYDIA WHITE (1822-
1889)
Amer. naturalist, botanist,
teacher
James--Notable (3) p273-274

SHATTUCK, SARAH HARTWELL
(fl. 1770's)
Amer. Revolutionary War
heroine
Sherr--American p105

SHAVER, DOROTHY (1897-1959)
Amer. retail business executive
O'Neill--Women's p517
Sicherman--Notable p645-646

SHAW, ANNA HOWARD (1847-1919)
English-Amer. physician,
lecturer, suffragist, clergyman
Banner--Women p39-41,91-92,
125,131, por.
Clark--Leading p50-52
Earnest--American p213,249
Gray--Women p121-127,134, por.
Hoople--As p151-157
Hymowitz--Hist. p177,250-251,
273-274
James--Notable (3) p274-277

McHenry--Liberty's p379
Macksey--Book p87
Millstein--We p177
Neidle--America's p43-46
Sherr--American p99-100,115-116,
125-126
Signif.--Amer. p34, por.
Warren--Pictorial p159,166, por.

SHAW, AURORA C. (1913-)
Amer. genealogical researcher,
author
Meyer--Who's p183

SHAW, BESSIE GURLEY
Irish, mother of George
Bernard Shaw
Diagram--Mothers p228-229, por.

SHAW, CHARLOTTE PAYNE-
TOWNSHEND (-1943)
Irish, wife of George Bernard
Shaw
People's Almanac (2) p1198

SHAW, HESTER
English midwife
Mead--Hist. p395

SHAW, MARLENA (1944-)
Amer. singer
Claghorn--Jazz p266

SHAW, MARY G. (1860-1929)
Amer. actress, feminist
Chinoy--Women p98-107, por.
Hazen--Interv. p87
James--Notable (3) p277-278

SHAW, PAULINE AGASSIZ (1841-
1917)
Swiss-Amer. educational
philanthropist
James--Notable (3) p278-280
Neidle--America's p48,50-51

SHAW, SUSAN
English broker
Macksey--Book p170

SHAW, WINI (1910-)
Amer. singer, actress
Springer--They p218,327, por.

SHAY, DOROTHY (c1921-1978)
Amer. singer, actress
Lamparski--What. Annual (4,5)
p315-319, por.

SHAZAR-KATZNELSON, RACHEL
(1888-)
Russian-Israeli co-founder,
Workers' Council
O'Neill--Women's p293

SHCHETININA, ANNA (fl. 1920's-
1940's)
Russian sea captain
Macksey--Book p245
Mandel--Soviet p82

SHEARER, MOIRA (1926-)
Scottish ballet dancer, actress
World--Who p79

SHEARER, (EDITH) NORMA (1900/
1904-1983)
Canadian actress
Hirschhorn--Rating p343, por.
Mordden--Movies, see index p295
Shipman--Gold. p497-502, por.
Springer--They p218-220,327,
por.
Woman's Almanac p353
World--Who p248

SHEDD, MARGARET (1900-)
Amer. novelist
P.W.--Author p139-141,524

SHEEDY, ALEXANDRA (c1962-)
Amer. child celebrity
Woman's Almanac p52

SHEEHAN, JEAN ELLEN DuPONT
(c1923-)
Amer. millionaire
Forbes--400 ('84) p191

SHEEHY, GAIL HENION (1937-)
Amer. author, journalist,
editor
Adams--Women p10,83-87,162
O'Neill--Women's p478
World--Who p55

"SHEENA, QUEEN OF THE JUNGLE"
See McCALLA, IRISH

SHEERER, MARY G.
Amer. potter
Callen--Women p88-89

SHEFFIELD, MARY E. (fl. 1860's)
Amer. Civil War teacher,
charity worker
Millstein--We p132

SHEIL, LILY
  See GRAHAM, SHEILAH

SHELDON, KARIN (fl. 1960's)
  Amer. environmental lawyer
  O'Neill--Women's p357-358

SHELDON, MARY DOWNING
  See BARNES, MARY DOWNING
  SHELDON

SHELIKOF, NATALYA (fl. 1780's-
  1790's)
  Russian, wife of first Russian
  Alaskan manager
  Jones--Women (1) p9-13

SHELL, ELIZABETH PETRIE (fl.
  1770's-1780's)
  Amer. patriot, Revolutionary
  War heroine
  Meyer--Petticoat p114-115

"SHELL FLOWER"
  See WINNEMUCCA, SARAH

SHELLEY, GLADYS (1918-)
  Amer. dancer, actress,
  lyricist
  Claghorn--Biog. p402

SHELLEY, HARRIET WESTBROOK
  English, first wife of Percy
  Bysshe Shelley
  Morley--Literary p183,204,335

SHELLEY, KATE (c1866-1912)
  Amer. heroine
  Sherr--American p72

SHELLEY, MARY WOLLSTONECRAFT
  GODWIN (1797-1851)
  English novelist, short-story
  writer
  Avenel--Comp. (1) p472-473
  Jones--Rutledge p713
  Kronenberger--Atlan. p702
  Kulkin--Her p259-260
  Magill--Cycl. p969-970
  Moers--Literary p310-311, see
    also index p334, por.
  Pearson--Who p271
  People's Almanac (2) p409
  Seymour-Smith--Novels p215,
    por.
  Warren--Pictorial p68-70
  Who Did What p290
  World--Who p48

SHELLY, MARY JOSEPHINE (1902-
  1976)
  Amer. Air Force colonel, educator, organization official
  Cur. Biog. '76 p475-476

SHEN, LINDA
  Amer. TV newscaster
  Gelfman--Women p43,96,109,125-
  126

SHEPARD, ELIZA
  Amer., sister of Jack London
  Starr--Amer. p231-232,234,236,
  261

SHEPHERD, CYBILL (1950-)
  Amer. actress, model
  World--Who p248

SHEPITKO, LARISA (1940-)
  Russian filmmaker
  Mandel--Soviet p144,146

SHEPPARD, ELIZABETH SARA
  (1830-1862)
  English novelist
  Showalter--Lit. p330

SHEPPARD, EUGENIA BENBOW
  (1910-)
  Amer. editor, fashion columnist
  Diamonstein--Open p353-356, por.
  O'Neill--Women's p263

SHEPPARD, KATHARINE (1848-1934)
  New Zealander WCTU leader,
  feminist, suffragist
  Macksey--Book p81-83,276, por.

SHEPPARD, PEGGY (fl. 1950's)
  Amer. industrial worker
  Hymowitz--Hist. p320

SHER-GILL, AMRITA (1913-1941)
  East Indian painter
  Munsterberg--Hist. p82-83

SHERIDAN, ANN (CLARA LOU)
  (1915/1916-1967)
  Amer. actress
  Book--Lists (2) p189
  Engstead--Star p112-114
  Hirschhorn--Rating p344-345,
    por.
  Keylin--Hollywood p261-262, por.
  Shipman--Gold. p502-505,
    por.

SHIELDS, LORA MANGUM
Amer. Indian botanist,
college instructor
O'Neill--Women's p160

SHIGENOBU, FUSAKO ("AUNTIE")
(c1946-)
Japanese terrorist
Woman's Almanac p506

SHIH, HSIO-YEN (1934-)
Canadian gallery director
O'Neill--Women's p614

SHIH, NELLIE Y.Y. (1903-)
Chinese-Amer. church worker,
social worker, noted
Massachusetts mother
Amer.--Mothers p267-268, por.

SHIH MAI-YU
See STONE, MARY (SHIH
MAI-YU)

SHIH MEI
Chinese film editor, director
Smith--Movies p99

SHILEY, JEAN
Amer. track and field athlete
Assoc. Press--Pursuit p129,131-
132

SHILLARD-SMITH, CHRISTINE
See LESER, TINA

SHIMSHI, SIONA (1939-)
Lithuanian-Israeli textile
designer, ceramist, painter,
sculptor
O'Neill--Women's p126

SHINN, MILICENT WASHBURN
(1858-1940)
Amer. author, editor,
child psychologist
James--Notable (3) p285-286

SHINODA, TOKO (fl. 1970's)
Japanese artist, calligrapher
O'Neill--Women's p600-601

SHIPLEY, ELIZABETH (fl. 1730's)
Amer. Quaker clergyman
Sherr--American p37

SHIPMAN, NELL (c1892-)

Canadian film writer, actress,
director, producer, photographer
Slide--Early p106-107, por.
Smith--Movies p14-15

SHIPP, ELLIS REYNOLDS (1847-
1933)
Amer. Mormon, physician,
school founder, noted Utah
mother
Amer.--Mothers p525-526, por.
Sherr--American p227

SHIPPEN, MARGARET ("PEGGY")
See ARNOLD, MARGARET
("PEGGY") SHIPPEN

SHIPTON, "MOTHER" (c1486-1561)
English prophetess
Jones--Rutledge p715
People's Almanac (1) p12-13

SHIRE, TALIA (1946-)
Amer. actress
World--Who p248

SHIRLEY, ANNE (1918-)
Amer. actress, columnist
Hazen--Interv. p410
Lamparski--What. (5) p202-203,
por.
Springer--They p221-222,327,
por.

"SHIRLEY," DAME, pseud.
See CLAPPE (CLAPP), LOUISE
AMELIA KNAPP SMITH

SHIRLEY, MYRA BELLE
See STARR, BELLE SHIRLEY

SHIRLEY, PENN
See GREENWOOD, GRACE, pseud.

SHIRREFF, EMILY ANN ELIZA
(1814-1897)
English college founder,
pioneer educator
Macksey--Book p72

SHIRTLIFFE, ROBERT, pseud.
See SAMPSON, DEBORAH

SHLONSKY, VERDINA
Israeli composer
Macksey--Book p221

SHOEMAKER, ANN (1891-)
Amer. actress
Springer--They p222,327-328,
por.

SHOEN, UEMURA (1875-1949)
Japanese artist
Munsterberg--Hist. p81

SHONAGON, SEI (963/967-)
Japanese diarist, poet
Moffat--Revel. p75-78

"SHOPP, BE BE" (1950-)
Amer. beauty
Lamparski--What. (4) p72-73,
por.

SHORE, DINAH (FRANCES
"FANNIE" ROSE) (1917-)
Amer. singer, TV performer
Anderson--People p358-359, por.
Claghorn--Biog. p403
Higham--Celeb. p33-39, por.
Lewis--Prime p249-256, por.
100--Greatest (1) p100-101, por.
O'Neill--Women's p627
Simon--Best p529-530, por.
Woman's Almanac p301
World--Who p272

SHORE, JANE (c1445-c1527)
English, mistress of Edward
IV
Jones--Rutledge p716
Leary--Golden p219,256,270-271

SHORE, LOUISE (1824-1895)
English poet
Showlater--Lit. p328

SHORT, ANNABELLE
See ROSS, ANNIE

SHORT, ESTHER (fl. 1840's-1860's)
Amer. city founder, philan-
thropist
Sherr--American p243

SHORT, MERCY (fl. 1690's)
Amer., Indian captive,
witch accuser
Williams--Demeter's p150-151,160

SHORT, RENEE
British Parliament member
Vallance--Women p20-21,65,68-69,
96,141

SHOTWELL, ODETTE (fl. 1960's-
1970's)
Amer. research chemist,
government official
O'Neill--Women's p32

SHOUMATOFF, ELIZABETH AVINOFF
(c1888-1980)
Russian-Amer. painter
Daniels--Wash. p290,294-295,
308-310,317-318

SHOWALTER, ELAINE
Amer. author
Showalter--These (appendix)

SHRIDHARANI, SHRIMATI
East Indian, dance-music
school director
O'Neill--Women's p651

SHRIDHARANI, SUNDARI
East Indian dancer
O'Neill--Women's p651

SHRIMPTON, JEAN ROSEMARY
(1942-)
English model, writer
Keenano--Women p128,133-135,
148-153,190-193, por.

SHRIVER, EUNICE KENNEDY
(1921-)
Amer., wife of Sargent
Shriver
Talmey--Vogue p196-200, por.

SHU SHUEN
Hong Kong filmmaker
Smith--Movies p99

SHUB, ESTHER (fl. 1920's-1940's)
Russian filmmaker
O'Neill--Women's p667
Smith--Movies p135-136

SHULER, BEVERLY SLOAN (1927-)
Amer. genealogical researcher,
editor
Meyer--Who's p184

SHURA, KASHINA
See HARDWICK, (CATHY) KATHY

SHURTLEFF, ROBERT
See SAMPSON, DEBORAH

SHUTTA, ETHEL (1896-1976)

Amer. singer, actress
Claghorn--Biog. p404

SHYLER, NETTIE ROGERS (1862-
1939)
Amer. suffragist, clubwoman
James--Notable (3) p287

SIBELIUS, HELENA (1905-)
Finnish physician
Hellstedt--Women p283-285, por.

SIBLEY, ANTOINETTE (1939-)
British ballet dancer
Cur. Biog. '70 p392-394, por.

SIBLEY, MARY EASTON (1800-1878)
Amer. educator, college co-
founder
James--Notable (3) p288
Sherr--American p132

SIDAMON-ERISTOFF, ANNE PHIPPS
(c1934-)
Amer. millionaire
Forbes--400 ('84) p148

SIDBURY, CHARLOTTE M.
(-1904)
Amer. businesswoman
Sherr--American p221

SIDDALL, ELIZABETH ELEANOR
(1814-1862)
English milliner's assistant,
model of Dante Gabriel
Rossetti
Harris--Women p229-230,350

SIDDONS, SARAH ("SALLY")
KEMBLE (1755-1831)
English actress
Entertainers p103
Findlator--Player p91-123, por.
Fry--1000 p208-209, por.
Jones--Rutledge p717
Kulkin--Her p260-261
Macksey--Book p226, por.
People's Almanac (1) p1329
Ware--Meet p37-38,80
Who Did What p291
World--Who p261

SIDHWA, BAPSI
English novelist
Crosland--Beyond p145

SIDNEY, MARGARET
See LOTHROP, HARRIETT
MULFORD STONE

SIDNEY, MARY, COUNTESS OF
PEMBROKE
See PEMBROKE, MARY HERBERT
SIDNEY, COUNTESS OF

SIDNEY, SYLVIA (1910-)
Amer. actress
Cur. Biog. '81 p380-383, por.
Lamparski--What. (3) p84-85,
por.
Shipman--Gold. p505-507, por.
Springer--They p222,328, por.
World--Who p248

SIDORISHINA, Z.P. (fl. 1950's)
Russian aviatrix, Arctic pilot
Mandel--Soviet p80-81

SIEBELS, MRS. EMMET
See GOLDTHWAITE, ANNE
WILSON

SIEBERT, FLORENCE (1897-)
Amer. chemist, researcher
O'Neill--Women's p217-218

SIEBERT, MURIEL (1932-)
Amer. banker, investment
counselor
Gilbert--Part. p233-237, por.
100--Greatest (1) p69, por.
O'Neill--Women's p528
Warren--Pictorial p204

SIEBOLD, CHARLOTTE VON (1761-
1859)
German obstetrician, physician
Marks--Women p69-70
Mead--Hist. p475,503-504, por.

SIEBOLD, REGINA JOSEPH
HENNING VON (1761-)
German obstetrician
Marks--Women p69
Mead--Hist. p503

SIEFF, REBECCA (-1966)
British co-founder, Zionist
organization
Macksey--Book p119

SIEGEMUNDIN, JUSTINE(A)

DITTRICHIN (1645/1650-
1705)
German medical writer,
obstetrician
Marks--Women p65-66
Mead--Hist. p427-429,501, por.

SIEGL, SIGRUN (fl. 1970's)
East German track and field
athlete
O'Neill--Women's p577-578

SIGEA, ALOYSIA (fl. 165h Cent.)
Spanish teacher, physician,
theologian
Macksey--Book p64
Mead--Hist. p352

SIGEA, LUISA (1522-1560)
Portuguese linguist, tutor
Bainton--Spain p65-68

SIGEAN, STELLA
South African minister of
education
Macksey--Book p41

SIGLER, MARCY (fl. 1960's)
Amer. "eclipse-chaser"
Lichtenstein--Mach. p228-231

SIGNORET, SIMONE (1921-1985)
French actress
Cur. Biog. '85 p474
Shipman--Internatl. p545-549,
por.
World--Who p261

SIGOURNEY, LYDIA HOWARD
HUNTLEY (1791-1865)
Amer. poet, hymnist
Claghorn--Biog. p404
Earnest--American p67,97,241
Ehrlich--Oxford p81,88
James--Notable (3) p288-290
McHenry--Liberty's p379-380
Sherr--American p34,72
Webster's--Amer. p948

SIGURDSEN, GERTRUDE (1923-)
Swedish cabinet officer
O'Neill--Women's p345

SIIMES, AUNE (1909-)
Finnish designer, ceramist
O'Neill--Women's p275

SIKHARANE, JOYCE (fl. 1970's)
South African prisoner
Crane--Ms. p123-126

SILCOTT, JANE ("JANE") (1842-
1895)
Amer. Indian heroine, scout
Sherr--American p57

SILKO, LESLIE MARMON (1948-)
Amer. Pueblo Indian novelist,
poet
Fisher--Third p v,18-23,49,70,92
McCullough--People p157-159

SILKS, MATTIE (MARTHA) (1847-
1929)
Amer. Western pioneer
People's Almanac (2) p929
Sherr--American p27-28

SILKWOOD, KAREN GAY (1946-1974)
Amer. nuclear technician,
safety researcher
O'Neill--Women's p729
People's Almanac (3) p15-18

SILL, ANNA PECK (1816-1889)
Amer. educator, school
founder
Hymowitz--Hist. p225
James--Notable (3) p290-291
McHenry--Liberty's p380

SILLANPÄÄ, MIINA (1866-1952)
Finnish cabinet minister
Macksey--Book p39
O'Neill--Women's p59,344

SILLIMAN, MARIANNA DU PONT
(c1911-)
Amer. millionaire
Forbes--400 ('84) p149

SILLIMAN, MARY FISH (1736-1804)
Amer. Revolutionary War
heroine, noted Connecticut
mother
Amer.--Mothers p76-77
Meyer--Petticoat p150-151

SILLS, BEVERLY (1929-)
Amer. opera singer
Claghorn--Biog. p404
Cur. Biog. '69 p397-400, por.
Cur. Biog. '82 p392-396, por.

Diamonstein--Open p357-361, por.
Gammond--Illus. p250, por.
Glassman--Year '79 p143, por.
McHenry--Liberty's p380
100--Greatest (1) p112, por.
O'Neill--Women's p622
Signif.--Amer. p72, por.
Woman's Almanac p301-302, por.
World--Who p72

SILVA, MARIA HELENA DA
See VIERIRA DA SILVA, MARIA
    HELENA

SILVER, FRANCES ("FRANKIE")
STUART (-1833)
Amer. accused criminal
Woman's Almanac p499

SILVERMAN, BELLE
See SILLS, BEVERLY

SILVERMAN, IDA (1882-c1973)
Amer. leader in Israel
founding, noted Rhode Island
mother
Amer.--Mothers p479-480, por.

SIMBERG-EHRSTRÖM, UHRA
BEATA (1914-)
Finnish textile designer
O'Neill--Women's p274

SIMBURG, WYOMIA TYUS
See TYUS, WYOMIA

SIMCHAK, MORAG McLEOD (1914-)
English-Amer. labor leader
O'Neill--Women's p336

SIMIONATO, GIULIETTA (1910-)
Italian opera singer
Gammond--Illus. p250-251, por.

SIMKHOVITCH, MARY MELINDA
KINGSBURY (1867-1951)
Amer. settlement worker,
housing reformer
McHenry--Liberty's p381
Sicherman--Notable p648-651

SIMMANCE, ELIZA (1873-1928)
British pottery designer,
decorator
Callen--Women p63,65-66,226

SIMMES, SARAH (fl. 1600's)

Amer. colonial pioneer
Williams--Demeter's p75

SIMMONS, ADELE (fl. 1970's)
Amer. college president
O'Neill--Women's p410-411

SIMMONS, ELEANOR BOOTH (c1869-
1950)
Amer. reporter, journalist
Marzolf--Up p44

SIMMONS, FRIEDA BARKIN
See HENNOCK, FRIEDA BARKIN

SIMMONS, JEAN (1929-)
English actress
Edelson--Kids p80,83-84
Hirschhorn--Rating p345-346, por.
Shipman--Internatl. p551-554, por.
World--Who p261

SIMMONS, SUE
Amer. TV anchorwoman
Scheuer--Tel. p448

SIMMS, DAISY FLORENCE (1873-
1923)
Amer. YWCA leader
James--Notable (3) p291-293

SIMMS, RUTH HANNA McCORMICK
(1880-1944)
Amer. Congresswoman
Chamberlin--Min. p66-73, por.
James--Notable (3) p293-295
McHenry--Liberty's p381-382

SIMON, ANNE
Amer. TV sports reporter
Scheuer--Tel. p448

SIMON, CARLY (1945-)
Amer. singer, songwriter
Anderson--People p359-360, por.
Claghorn--Biog. p405
Cur. Biog. '76 p372-374, por.
Glassman--Year '79 p143, por.
Kulkin--Her p261-262
Simon--Best p531-532, por.
Woman's Almanac p302
World--Who p272

SIMON, DOROTHY M. (fl. 1960's-
1970's)
Amer. research physical
chemist, corporation official

M.I.T.--Women p x, 41-44
O'Neill--Women's p189,519

SIMON, ESTHER ANNENBERG
(c1902-)
Amer. millionaire
Forbes--400 ('84) p191

SIMON, GLORIA
Amer. bowler
McWhirter--Guinness p44

SIMON, KATE (fl. 1960's)
Amer. travel writer
People's Almanac (2) p659

SIMON, MARGARET MILLER
(1922-)
Amer. genealogical researcher
Meyer--Who's p185

SIMON, MARY (fl. 1970's)
Amer. 4-H scholarship winner
O'Neill--Women's p20-21

SIMON, SIMONE (1914-1985)
French actress
Lamparski--What. (2) p70-71,
por
People's Almanac (1) p1242-1243
Springer--They p222-223,329,
por.

SIMONE, BENDA, MADAME
(1877-c1967)
French author
Crosland--Women p102-104

SIMONE, NINA (1933-)
Amer. singer, pianist,
songwriter
Claghorn--Biog. p405
Claghorn--Jazz p270
Simon--Best p536-537, por.
World--Who p272

SIMONS, MARY SULLIVAN (fl.
1970's)
Amer. newspaper, magazine
editor
O'Neill--Women's p482

SIMONS, SUSAN
Amer. TV manager
Scheuer--Tel. p449

SIMPSON, ABBY ROCKEFELLER

(c1957-)
Amer. millionaire
Forbes--400 ('84) p150

SIMPSON, ADELE SMITHLINE
(1903-)
British-Amer. fashion designer
Cur. Biog. '70 p397-399, por.
O'Neill--Women's p242-243,247
World--Who p301

SIMPSON, BELLE GOLDSTEIN
(fl. 1900's-1930's)
Amer., Alaskan realtor, store
owner
Jones--Women (1) p159,161

SIMPSON, CAROLE
Amer. TV correspondent
Scheuer--Tel. p449

SIMPSON, EDNA OAKES (1891-)
Amer. Congresswoman
Chamberlin--Min. p279

SIMPSON, ELIZABETH (1)
See INCHBALD, ELIZABETH
SIMPSON

SIMPSON, ELIZABETH (2) (1923-)
English genealogical research-
er, editor
Meyer--Who's p185-186

SIMPSON, ELIZABETH SLOAN
See SIMPSON, SLOAN

SIMPSON, JANE CROSS (1811-1886)
Scottish poet, religious writer
Showalter--Lit. p324

SIMPSON, JOANNE (fl. 1960's-
1970's)
Amer. meteorologist, government official
O'Neill--Women's p172

SIMPSON, MARGARET BURNETT
(1874-1974)
Amer. church, community
worker, noted Wyoming mother
Amer.--Mothers p594-595, por.

SIMPSON, MARY MICHAEL, CANON
(1926-)
Amer. priest
O'Neill--Women's p386

SIMPSON, MYRTLE LILLIAS
  (1931-)
  Scottish explorer, (Arctic)
  Macksey--Book p243

SIMPSON, SLOAN (1917-)
  Amer. actress, model
  Lamparski--What. (4) p138-139,
  por.

SIMPSON, VALERIA (c1946-)
  Amer. singer
  Glassman--Year '79 p84, por.

SIMPSON, VIVIAN (c1904-)
  Amer. lawyer
  O'Neill--Women's p352

SIMPSON, WALLIS WARFIELD
  See WINDSOR, (BESSIE)
  WALLIS WARFIELD SIMPSON,
  DUCHESS OF

SIMRIL, HARRIET (fl. 1870's)
  Amer., post-Civil War worker
  Millstein--We p137-138

SIMS, GINNY (VIRGINIA) (1916-)
  Amer. singer
  Lamparski--What. (3) p94-95,
  por.

SIMS, NAOMI (1949-)
  Amer. wig-maker
  Keenan--Women p172-173,178,
  por.
  O'Neill--Women's p238-239

SINATRA, NANCY (1941-)
  Amer. singer (daughter of
  Frank Sinatra)
  Claghorn--Biog. p405-406

SINCLAIR, ADELAIDE HELEN
  GRANT MacDONALD
  (1900-1982)
  Canadian government official,
  lecturer
  Cur. Biog. '83 p473
  O'Neill--Women's p550-551

SINCLAIR, CATHERINE (1800-1864)
  Scottish novelist
  Showalter--Lit. p32

SINCLAIR, CATHERINE NORTON
  FORREST (1817-1891)

English-Amer. actress, manager
  James--Notable (1) p646-647
  Macksey--Book p227

SINCLAIR, D.B.
  See SINCLAIR, ADELAIDE HELEN
  GRANT MacDONALD

SINCLAIR, JO, pseud. (1913-)
  Amer. short-story author,
  playwright
  Seymour-Smith--Novels p217

SINCLAIR, MAY (1863/1865-1946)
  English novelist
  Crosland--Beyond p13-15,125,169
  Magill--Cycl. p990-991
  Showalter--Lit. p342

SINCOTTA, GAIL (fl. 1970's)
  Amer. banker, activist
  O'Neill--Women's p694,730

SINGER, CARLA
  Amer. TV executive
  Scheuer--Tel. p450, por.

SINGER, DULCY
  Amer. TV executive, producer
  Scheuer--Tel. p450

SINGER, ELIZABETH
  See ROWE, ELIZABETH SINGER

SINGER, JUNE
  Amer. psychoanalyst
  Lichtenstein--Mach. p295-296,346-
  347

SINGER, MAXINE F. (fl. 1970's)
  Amer. scientist, DNA
  researcher
  O'Neill--Women's p159

SINGER, WINNARETTA (WINNIE),
  PRINCESSE DE POLIGNOT
  (c1865-1943)
  Amer. socialite
  Brandon--Dollar p180-189, por.

SINGLETON, MARGARET ("MARGIE")
  LOUISE (1935-)
  Amer. singer, songwriter
  Claghorn--Biog. p406

SINGLETON, PENNY ("BLONDIE")
  (1908-1952)

Amer. radio star, actress,
singer, dancer
Lamparski--What. (2) p98-99,
por.
Springer--They p225,329, por.

SINGMASTER, ELSIE (1879-1958)
Amer. novelist, children's
book author, short-story
writer
Ehrlich--Oxford p213
Magill--Cycl. p994-996

SINKFORD, JEANNE CRAIG (fl.
1960's-1970's)
Amer. dentistry dean,
professor
Innis--Profiles p154-155, por.

SINKO, PEGGY TUCK (1949-)
Amer. genealogical researcher,
writer
Meyer--Who's p186

SIOUSSAT, HELEN J. (fl. 1930's-
1950's)
Amer. radio, TV network
executive
Marzolf--Up p134-136
O'Neill--Women's p437,493-494,
por.
Women--Radio p7

SIPILA, HELVI L. (1915-)
Finnish UN official
O'Neill--Women's p65,286

SIRANI, ELISABETTA (1638-1665)
Italian painter, etcher,
printmaker
Fine--Women p17-20
Harris--Women p25,29,41-43,77,
147-150,152,343-344
Macksey--Book p197
Munsterberg--Hist. p105,107
Parker--Old p26-27, fig. 16,17
Petersen--Women p27-29
Sparrow--Women p28-30,43,46
Tufts--Our p80-87, por.
Women's--Female p13

SIROLA, JOYCE
See RANDOLPH, JOYCE

SISK, MILDRED GILLARS (fl.
1930's-1940's)
Amer., accused of treason,

World War II
Lamparski--What. (2) p10-11, por.

SISON, HONORIE (fl. 1900's)
Filipino physician
Macksey--Book p150

SISSON, SARAH MARTHA (1942-)
Amer. genealogical researcher,
writer
Meyer--Who's p186

SISTER A. OF SANTA MARTA (fl.
c1500)
Sienese nun, painter
Sparrow--Women p23,34-35

SISTER B. OF SANTA MARTA (fl.
c1500)
Sienese nun, painter
Sparrow--Women p23,34

SISTLER, BARBARA J. (1942-)
Amer. genealogical researcher
Meyer--Who's p186

SITES, SHARON (fl. 1960's)
Amer. yacht sailor
McWhirter--Guinness p188

SITWELL, EDITH, DAME (1887-1964)
English poet, critic, biographer,
anthologist
Avenel--Comp. (1) p479
Bernikow--World p158-159
Book--Lists (2) p422
Brinnin--Modern p333-337, por.
Jones--Rutledge p720-721
Keenan--Women p64,68
Kronenberger--Atlan. p716-717
Macksey--Book p192
Moers--Literary p312
Morley--Literary p61,252,394
O'Neill--Women's p676
Seymour-Smith--Who's p342-343
Who Did What p292
Wintle--Makers p484-485, #440
World--Who p30

SJOO, MONICA (fl. 1970's)
English painter
Women's--Female p57

SKARBEK, KRYSTYNA GIZYCKA
GRANVILE (1915-1952)
Polish-British spy
Macksey--Book p59-60, por.

SKATES, SUZI
    Amer. "roller-skater,"
    business woman
    Felton--Famous p161

SKELSEY, ALICE F. (fl. 1970's)
    Amer. author
    O'Neill--Women's p4

SKILES, JACQUELINE (fl. 1970's)
    Amer. graphic artist
    Women's--Female p82-83

SKILLERN, DAPHNE (c1928-   )
    British policewoman,
    department chief
    O'Neill--Women's p375

SKINNER, CONSTANCE LINDSAY
    (1877-1939)
    Canadian-Amer. historian
    James--Notable (3) p295-296
    McHenry--Liberty's p382

SKINNER, CORNELIA OTIS (1901-
    1979)
    Amer. actress, humorist,
    author, monologist
    Avenel--Comp. (2) p234
    Cur. Biog. '79 p473
    Ehrlich--Oxford, see index p460
    Hazen--Interv. p81-82
    Jones--Rutledge p721
    World--Who p248

SKINNER, DOROTHY WENDELL
    (1733-1822)
    Amer., colonial merchant's
    daughter
    Flexner--Face p96, por.

SKIPWORTH, ALISON (1863-1952)
    English actress
    Springer--They p225-226,329,
    por.

SKLOVER, THEODORA K. (c1938-   )
    Amer. TV consultant, pro-
    ducer
    Scheuer--Tel. p451

SKLODOWSKA, MANYA
    See CURIE, MARIE SKLODOWSKA

SKOBLIKOVA, LIDIA (LYDIA)
    (c1940-   )
    Russian ice skater

Assoc. Press--Pursuit p228,247,
    por.
McWhirter--Guinness p102, por.

SLADE, MARY BRIDGES CANEDY
    (1826-1882)
    Amer. hymnist, teacher
    Claghorn--Biog. p407

SLAGLE, ELEANOR CLARKE (1872-
    1942)
    Amer. leader, occupational
    therapy
    James--Notable (3) p296-298

SLATER, COURTENAY (c1934-   )
    Amer. economist, government
    official
    O'Neill--Women's p85

SLATER, HANNAH (fl. 1820's)
    Amer. inventor, (textile
    industry)
    Sherr--American p207

SLAUGHTER, CONSTANCE ("CON-
    NIE") TONA (fl. 1960's-1970's)
    Amer. judge
    O'Neill--Women's p372,702

SLAUGHTER, LINDA W. (1843-   )
    Amer. author, educator, post-
    mistress, politician, noted
    North Dakota mother
    Amer.--Mothers p413-414, por.
    Sherr--American p182

SLAYDEN, ELLEN M. (fl. 1910's)
    Amer. political diarist, re-
    porter
    Daniels--Wash. p52-53,61,74,93-
    94,105,174-175

SLEDGE SISTERS (fl. 1970's)
    Amer. singers
    Glassman--Year '79 p143,145, por.

SLEIGH, SYLVIA (fl. 1970's)
    Amer. painter
    Parker--Old p124-126, fig. 77
    Women's--Female p58

SLENCZYNSKI, RUTH (1925-   )
    Amer. pianist
    Claghorn--Biog. p407
    People's Almanac (3) p548

SLESIN, AVIVA (fl. 1970's)
Amer. graphic artist,
film editor, filmmaker
Smith--Movies p203,274

SLESINGER, TESS (1905-1945)
Amer. novelist, short-story
writer, feminist
Baum--Jewish p230-232
Moers--Literary p312
Sochen--Herstory p323-326

SLESSOR, MARY (1848-1915)
Scottish missionary (to
Nigeria)
Kulkin--Her p262-263

SLEZAK, EVA (1946-)
Czechoslovakian-Amer.
genealogical, researcher,
writer, editor
Meyer--Who's p186

SLICK, GRACE WING (1939/1940-)
Amer. singer, model
Anderson--People p364-365
Claghorn--Biog. p407
Cur. Biog. '82 p399-402, por.
Lichtenstein--Mach. p251,266-
267
Woman's Almanac p302
World--Who p273

SLICK, JONATHAN
See STEPHENS, ANN(A)
SOPHIA WINTERBOTHAM

SLIPPEY, ALICE ELIZABETH (fl.
1970's)
Amer. 4-H scholarship winner
O'Neill--Women's p21

SLIVKA, ROSE (fl. 1950's-1970's)
Amer. crafts writer, maga-
zine editor
O'Neill--Women's p263-264

SLOAN, EMILY (fl. 1910's-1920's)
Amer. poet, politician, lawyer
Sherr--American p134

SLOAN, MARGARET
Amer. feminist, editor
Millstein--We p285

SLOANE, PATRICIA (fl. 1970's)
Amer. painter, filmmaker
Women's--Female p58

SLOCUM, FRANCES ("MACONA-
QUAH") (1773-1847)
Amer. Indian captive, noted
Indiana mother
Amer.--Mothers p173, por.
Booth--Women p194-195
James--Notable (3) p298-299
Sherr--American p67,205

SLOCUM, MARIANNA
Amer. Bible translator
Kooiman--Cameos p66-77, por.

SLOCUMB, MARY HOOKS (POLLY)
(1760-1836)
Amer. Revolutionary War
patriot, heroine
Engle--Women p17-25
Meyer--Petticoat p184-187
Sherr--American p178-179, por.

SLONIMSKAYA, VERA (fl. 1910's)
Russian food collector, pro-
fessor
Mandel--Soviet p55

SLOOP, MARY T. MARTIN (1873-
1962)
Amer. educator, social worker,
physician, noted North Carolina mother, school founder
Amer.--Mothers p406, por.

SLOWE, LUCY DIGGS (1885-1937)
Amer. teacher, school admin-
istrator, college dean
James--Notable (3) p299-300

SLYE, MAUD CAROLINE (1869/
1879-1954)
Amer. pathologist, professor,
researcher
O'Neill--Women's p217
Sicherman--Notable p651-652
Woman's Almanac p367-368

SMALL, TESS (fl. 1940's)
Amer. bowler
McWhirter--Guinness p44

SMALLWOOD, LaVIECE MOORE
(1935-)
Amer. genealogical researcher,
writer
Meyer--Who's p187

SMEAL, ELEANOR MARIE CUTRI
(1939-)

Amer. social activist, organi-
zation official
Cur. Biog. '80 p366-369, por.
O'Neill--Women's p99,120-121,
705, por.
World--Who p191

SMEDLEY, AGNES (1892/1894-1950)
Amer. foreign correspondent,
journalist, lecturer, novelist
James--Notable (3) p300-302
McHenry--Liberty's p382-383
O'Neill--Women's p713

SMEDLEY, MENELLA BUTE (1820-
1877)
British novelist, poet
Showlater--Lit. p327

SMILEY, JULIE (fl. 1960's-1970's)
Amer. "Future Farmers"
president
O'Neill--Women's p21

SMIRNOVA, M.N.
Russian film scenarist
Mandel--Soviet p148

SMIRNOVA, TATIANA
Russian ballet dancer
Migel--Ballerinas p253

SMITH, ABBY HADASSAH (1797-
1878)
Amer. feminist, suffragist
Felton--Famous p143-146
James--Notable (3) p302-304
McHenry--Liberty's p383
Sherr--American p31

SMITH, ABIGAIL ADAMS (fl.
1780's)
Amer., daughter of President
John Adams
Earle--Two Cent. (2) p xvi,xxii,
575-576,737, por.

SMITH, ALEXIS (1921-)
Amer. actress
World--Who p248-249

SMITH, ALICE GULLEN (fl. 1930's)
Amer. librarian, professor,
noted Florida mother
Amer.--Mothers p118-119, por.

SMITH, ALICE MARY (1839-1884)

English composer
Macksey--Book p214
Neuls-Bates--Women p214-215

SMITH, ALICE MAUD (fl. 1920's)
Amer. nurse, physician, poet
Sherr--American p243

SMITH, ALLISON (fl. 1970's)
Amer. Air Force captain,
optometrist
O'Neill--Women's p544

SMITH, ALYS PEARSALL
English, wife of Bertrand
Russell
People's Almanac (2) p860-862,
por.

SMITH, AMANDA BERRY (1837-1915)
Amer. evangelist, missionary,
orphanage founder
Bloom--Religion p125-126
James--Notable (3) p304-305
McHenry--Liberty's p383-384
O'Neill--Women's p400
Sherr--American p62

SMITH, ANNE (fl. 1970's)
Amer. magazine managing
editor
Adams--Women p26,101

SMITH, APRIL
Amer. TV producer, writer
Scheuer--Tel. p453

SMITH, ATHALIE IRVINE (c1931-)
Amer. millionaire
Forbes--400 ('84) p140

SMITH, BARBARA LEIGH-
See BODICHON, BARBARA
LEIGH-SMITH

SMITH, BARBARA T. (fl. 1970's)
Amer. sculptor
Women's--Female p95

SMITH, BESSIE (ELIZABETH)
(1894/1898-1937)
Amer. singer, poet, song-
writer
Bernikow--World p276
Claghorn--Biog. p408
Claghorn--Jazz p271-272
Donaldson--How p342-343

Eills--Here p134-135
Jablonski--Ency. p290-291
Kulkin--Her p263-264
Lichtenstein--Mach. p263-265
McHenry--Liberty's p384
Macksey--Book p219, por.
O'Neill--Women's p623
People's Almanac (1) p897-898
People's Almanac (2) p1206
Sherr--American p216
Signif.--Amer. p53, por.
Simon--Best p545-546, por.
Warren--Pictorial p199
Webster's--Amer. p959
Woman's Almanac p302-303, por.
World--Who p273

SMITH, BETTY MESSER (fl. 1970's)
    Amer. miner's wife, mountain
    woman
    Kahn--Hill. p50-54, por.

SMITH, BETTY WEHNER (1904-1972)
    Amer. novelist
    Avenel--Comp. (2) p235
    Cur. Biog. '72 p471
    Ehrlich--Oxford p86,90-91,152,
        331
    Magill--Cycl. p998
    Seymour-Smith--Novels p217
    World--Who p20

SMITH, BEULAH MORGAN (fl.
    1930's)
    Amer. clubwoman, community
    worker, noted Kentucky
    mother
    Amer.--Mothers p220-221, por.

SMITH, CABELL
    Amer. TV technician
    Gelfman--Women p109-110
    O'Neill--Women's p317, por.

SMITH, CAROLINE LOUISA
    SPRAGUE (1827-1886)
    Amer. hymnist
    Claghorn--Biog. p408

SMITH, CHARLOTTE TURNER
    (1749-1806)
    English poet, novelist
    Avenel--Comp. (1) p483-484
    Horner--English p67, (and note)
    Kaplan--Salt p73-75
    Moers--Literary p312
    Seymour-Smith--Novels p218

SMITH, CHLOETHIEL W. (c1910-)
    Amer. architect, city planner
    Diamonstein--Open p362-366, por.
    O'Neill--Women's p610

SMITH, CLARA (1894-1935)
    Amer. singer
    Claghorn--Jazz p272

SMITH, CONNIE (1941-)
    Amer. singer
    Claghorn--Biog. p409

SMITH, CORNELIA (-1755)
    Amer. newspaper publisher,
    printer
    Williams--Demeter's p202-203

SMITH, DEBORAH (fl. 1970's)
    Amer. 4-H scholarship winner
    O'Neill--Women's p21

SMITH, DELLA MAE (fl. 1970's)
    Amer. labor union worker,
    mountain woman
    Kahn--Hill. p75-82, por.

SMITH, DODIE
    See ANTHONY, C.L., pseud.

SMITH, DODY WILSON (fl. 1940's-
    1970's)
    Amer. Waves officer, writer
    O'Neill--Women's p533

SMITH, DOROTHY JACQUELINE
    KEELY
    See SMITH, KEELY

SMITH, ELINOR (1911-)
    Amer. child aviatrix
    Boase--Sky's p22,126

SMITH, ELIZA ROXEY SNOW
    See SNOW, ELIZA ROXEY

SMITH, ELIZABETH GERRIT (fl.
    1850's)
    Amer., first "bloomer" wearer
    Sherr--American p175

SMITH, ELIZABETH LEE ALLEN
    (1817-1877)
    Amer. hymnist
    Claghorn--Biog. p409

SMITH, ELIZABETH MURRAY

See INMAN, ELIZABETH MURRAY
CAMPBELL SMITH

SMITH, ELIZABETH OAKES PRINCE
(1806-1893)
Amer. lecturer, poet, social
reformer, novelist
Ehrlich--Oxford p7
James--Notable (3) p309-310

SMITH, ELSKE V.P.
Monacan solar physicist
O'Neill--Women's p153

SMITH, EMILY JAMES
See PUTNAM, EMILY JAMES
SMITH

SMITH, EMMA HALE (1804-1879)
Amer. Mormon, religious
worker, wife of Joseph Smith
James--Notable (3) p311-312
Sherr--American p63

SMITH, ERMINNIE ADELE PLATT
(1836-1886)
Amer. ethnologist, geologist
James--Notable (3) p312-313

SMITH, ETHEL (1) (1910-   )
Amer. organist, actress
Lamparski--What. (3) p118-119,
por.

SMITH, ETHEL (2) (1921-   )
Amer. singer
Claghorn--Biog. p409

SMITH, FANNY MORRIS (fl. 1900's)
Amer. club woman
Neuls-Bates--Women p190-191

SMITH, FLORENCE MARGARET
See SMITH, STEVIE
(FLORENCE MARGARET)

SMITH, FRANCIS
See ROGERS, DALE EVANS

SMITH, GARLAND
Amer. artist
Showalter--These p115-120

SMITH, GLADYS MARY
See PICKFORD, MARY

SMITH, HANNAH WHITALL (1832-

1911)
Amer. religious leader, author,
evangelist, feminist, temperance
reformer
James--Notable (3) p313-316
McHenry--Liberty's p385

SMITH, HAZEL BRANNON (1914-   )
Amer. newspaper publisher,
editor, journalist
Cur. Biog. '73 p384-386, por.
Marzolf--Up p83
O'Neill--Women's p452,458-459
Woman's Almanac p274

SMITH, HELEN CELLIAST (fl.
1870's-1890's)
Amer. Indian teacher,
mediator
Sherr--American p194

SMITH, HELEN MARTIN (c1910-1969)
Amer. bridge player
O'Neill--Women's p592

SMITH, HILDA WORTHINGTON
(1888-   )
Amer. government official
O'Neill--Women's p323
Ware--Beyond p154, see also
index p203

SMITH, IDA VAN (fl. 1960's-1970's)
Amer. aviatrix, flight instruc-
tor
Innis--Profiles p138-139, por.

SMITH, JACLYN (1947/1948-   )
Amer. TV actress, model
Anderson--People p365, por.
People--Best p128,175, por.
Scheuer--Tel. p454-455
World--Who p249

SMITH, JACQUELINE (1) (1933-   )
Amer. TV executive
Scheuer--Tel. p455

SMITH, JACQUELINE (2) (fl. 1970's)
British parachute jumper
McWhirter--Guinness p108, por.

SMITH, JEAN WHEELER (1942-   )
Amer. chemist, professor,
food specialist, writer
Washington--Black p18-20

SMITH, JESSIE WILCOX (1863-1935)
Amer. cover designer, illus-
trator, painter
Callen--Women p208-209,226
James--Notable (3) p316-317
McHenry--Liberty's p385-386

SMITH, JOAN BARTON (1942-)
Amer. cheese-maker
Sherr--American p207

SMITH, JOANNA (1614-1687)
Amer. colonial physician
Mead--Hist. p414-415

SMITH, MRS. JOSEPH (fl. c1780's)
English socialite
Ware--Meet p80

SMITH, JULIA (1911-)
Amer. composer, pianist,
teacher, author
Claghorn--Biog. p410
Jablonski--Ency. p450

SMITH, JULIA EVELINA (1792-
1886)
Amer. feminist, suffragist
Felton--Famous p143-146
James--Notable (3) p302-304
McHenry--Liberty's p383
Sherr--American p31

SMITH, KAREN
Amer. agriculturist
O'Neill--Women's p2

SMITH, KATE (1909-1986)
Amer. singer
Claghorn--Biog. p410
McHenry--Liberty's p386
100--Greatest (1) p81, por.
O'Neill--Women's p626-627
People's Almanac (1) p907
People's Almanac (2) p1154-1155
Simon--Best p547-548, por.
Springer--They p226,329, por.
Webster's--Amer. p962
Woman's Almanac p303-304
World--Who p273

SMITH, KATE DOUGLAS
See WIGGIN, KATE DOUGLAS
SMITH

SMITH, KEELY (1932-)
Amer. singer, comedienne

Claghorn--Biog. p410
Claghorn--Jazz p274
World--Who p273

SMITH, LELA (fl. 1970's)
Amer. photographer, filmmaker
Smith--Movies p203-204,274

SMITH, LILLIAN EUGENIA (1897-
1966)
Amer. feminist, author, editor,
social reformer
Berkin--Women p372-373,381
Ehrlich--Oxford p262
Sicherman--Notable p652-654

SMITH, LIZ (MARY ELIZABETH)
(1923-)
Amer. columnist, journalist
Woman's Almanac p277

SMITH, LUCILLE BISHOP (1892-)
Amer. cookery expert, noted
Texas mother
Amer.--Mothers p521, por.

SMITH, LULA CARSON
See McCULLERS (LULA) CARSON
SMITH

SMITH, MADELEINE-HAMILTON
(1835/1836-1928)
Scottish accused criminal
People's Almanac (1) p571-572
People's Almanac (2) p498-499

SMITH, MAGGIE (1934-)
English actress
Cur. Biog. '70 p405-407, por.
Entertainers p283
Shipman--Internatl. p559-561,
por.
World--Who p261

SMITH, MAMIE ROBINSON (1883-
1946)
Amer. singer
Claghorn--Jazz p274-275

SMITH, MARGARET BAYARD
HARRISON (1778-1844)
Amer. letter-writer, author,
social leader, hostess
Earnest--America p49-53,86,89,
241-242
James--Notable (3) p317-318

SMITH, MARGARET CHASE
(1897-   )
Amer. Senator
Bachtold--Gifted p100-103
Chamberlin--Min. p138-150, por.
Clark--Leading p195-197
Gilfond--Heroines p91-95, por.
Greenebaum--Politics p29-51,
   por.
Ingraham--Album p72-73, por.
Kulkin--Her p264-265
McHenry--Liberty's p386-387
Macksey--Book p41
Miller--Fishbait p74-76,205
O'Neill--Women's p66-67
Schoenebaum--Prof. p610-611
Signif.--Amer. p73, por.
Stoddard--Famous p387-398,
   por.
Truman--Women p162-164,167-
   178,200, por.
U.S.--Women (89th) p3, por.
U.S.--Women (90th) p1, por.
Warren--Pictorial p204
Woman's Almanac p481, por.
World--Who p151

SMITH, MARTHA KERGAN (1824-
1918)
Amer. pioneer, noted Iowa
mother
Amer.--Mothers p200-201, por.

SMITH, MARY ALICE (fl. 1800's)
Amer., friend of James
Whitcomb Riley, actress
Sherr--American p67

SMITH, MARY ELLEN (1)
See PLEASANT, MARY ELLEN
("MAMMY")

SMITH, MARY ELLEN (2) (1862-
1933)
British cabinet member
O'Neill--Women's p50

SMITH, MARY HEATHMAN
("GRANNY")
English-Amer. physician,
surgeon, midwife, nurse
Sherr--American p225

SMITH, MARY LOUISE (1914-   )
Amer. politician, noted
Iowa mother
Amer.--Mothers p194-195, por.

Cur. Biog. '76 p380-383, por.
O'Neill--Women's p44,74

SMITH, MARY LOUISE RILEY (1843-
1927)
Amer. hymnist
Claghorn--Biog. p410

SMITH, MARY MATTIE (fl. 1970's)
Amer. labor leader
O'Neill--Women's p305

SMITH, MAUDE E.
Amer. mother of "Chuck"
Smith
Kooiman--Silhouettes p150-160,
por.

SMITH, MAYBELLE (1924-1972)
Amer. singer
Claghorn--Biog. p410
Claghorn--Jazz p274

SMITH, MIRANDA (fl. 1960's)
Amer. urban agriculturist
O'Neill--Women's p36

SMITH, NIXOLA GREELEY
See GREELEY-SMITH, NIXOLA

SMITH, NORA ARCHIBALD
See WIGGIN, KATE DOUGLAS
SMITH

SMITH, PAMELA COLEMAN (c1877-   )
Amer. painter, illustrator
Callen--Women p226

SMITH, PATRICIA FALKEN
Amer. TV executive writer,
story consultant
Scheuer--Tel. p455-456

SMITH, PATTI (c1946-   )
Amer. singer, poet, song-
writer
Lichtenstein--Mach., see index
p367
World--Who p273

SMITH, ROBIN B. (fl. 1960's-
1970's)
Amer., publisher's president,
general manager
O'Neill--Women's p488

SMITH, ROBYN CAROLINE (1944-   )

Amer. jockey, (wife of Fred
Astaire)
Cur. Biog. '76 p383-385, por.
McWhirter--Guinness p92-93,
por.
100--Greatest (1) p33, por.
O'Neill--Women's p588
People--Best p70-71, por.
Stambler--Women p60-70, por.
Woman's Almanac p441-442

SMITH, RUBY DORIS
See ROBINSON, RUBY DORIS
SMITH

SMITH, SARA MAHALA REDWAY
See BENSON, SALLY (SARA)
SMITH

SMITH, SARAH (1)
See STRETTON, HESBA, pseud.

SMITH, SARAH (2) (fl. 1770's)
Amer. Revolutionary War
patriot
Meyer--Petticoat p64-65

SMITH, SARAH (3) (1804-1877)
Amer. wife of Asa Smith,
clergyman
Time--Women p24-25,27,30

SMITH, SOPHIA M. (1796-1870)
Amer. educator, college
founder, philanthropist
Callen--Women p193, por.
James--Notable (3) p318-320
McHenry--Liberty's p387
Macksey--Book p69
Sherr--American p105,107

SMITH, STEVIE (FLORENCE
MARGARET) (1902-1971)
English poet, novelist
Jones--Rutledge p724
Kaplan--Salt p281-282

SMITH, SUKI (SUE LANIADO)
(1950-)
Amer. TV promotion manager
Scheuer--Tel. p456

SMITH, THELMA J. (fl. 1970's)
Amer. executive
O'Neill--Women's p530

SMITH, VIRGINIA BEATRICE

(1924-)
Amer. college president
Cur. Biog. '78 p387-390, por.

SMITH, VIRGINIA THRALL (1836-
1903)
Amer. charitable worker,
pioneer in child care
James--Notable (3) p320-321

SMITH, VIVIAN LEATHERBERRY
(c1908-)
Amer. millionaire
Forbes--400 ('84) p117

SMITH, ZEPHANIA HOLLISTER (fl.
1840's-1870's)
Amer. feminist
Sherr--American p31

SMITH, ZILPHA DREW (c1852-1926)
Amer. social worker
James--Notable (3) p321-323
McHenry--Liberty's p387

SMITH BROWNSTEIN, ELIZABETH
(fl. 1930's)
Amer. TV editorial/research
director
Scheuer--Tel. p456

SMOKE, MARCIA JONES (fl. 1960's)
Amer. canoeist
McWhirter--Guinness p49

SMOLEN, VIVIAN (fl. 1940's)
Amer. radio actress
Lamparski--What. (4) p92-93,
por.

SMOYER, ANNA MYRTLE
See WALKER, NANCY

SMYTH, ETHEL MARY, DAME
(1858-1944)
British composer, suffragist,
feminist, author, journalist,
pianist
Jones--Rutledge p725-726
Macksey--Book p216-217, por.
Neusl-Bates--Women, see index
p349, por.
O'Neill--Women's p636

SMYTHE, MABEL MURPHY (fl.
1970's)
Amer. ambassador to Cameroon
O'Neill--Women's p96

SMYTHE, PAT (fl. 1940's)
British horsewoman
Macksey--Book p260, por.

SNAPP, HELEN
Amer. army flier
Keil--Those p210-211

SNEDDEN, BARBARA A. (1926-)
Amer. genealogical researcher,
author
Meyer--Who's p189

SNELL, HANNAH (1723-1792)
British marine, (male
impersonator)
Macksey--Book p52-53

SNELL, NANCY
Amer. shop manager,
adventurer
Lichtenstein--Mach. p46-48,285

SNELSON, DEBRA G. (fl. 1970's)
Amer. Coast Guard officer
O'Neill--Women's p549

SNEVE, VIRGINIA DRWING HAWK
(1933-)
Amer. author, Indian his-
torian, noted South Dakota
mother
Amer.--Mothers p502-503, por.

SNEZHINA, ELENA (1881-1944)
Bulgarian actress
Partington--Who's p387-388, por.

SNODGRESS, CARRIE (1946-)
Amer. actress
Hirschhorn--Rating p348, por.
World--Who p249

SNOOK, NETA (fl. 1920's-1930's)
Amer. aviatrix
Boarse--Sky's p68
Macksey--Book p248,250

SNOW, ANNA RABLEN (1861-)
Amer. Alaskan pioneer,
singer, dancer
Sherr--American p4

SNOW, BARBARA
See JOHNSON, PAMELA
HANSFORD

SNOW, ELIZA ROXEY (1804-1887)
Amer. hymnist, Mormon leader,
poet
Claghorn--Biog. p411
James--Notable (3) p307-309
McHenry--Liberty's p384-385
Sherr--American p226-227, por.

SNOW, PHOEBE LAUB (1952-)
Amer. singer, guitarist, com-
poser
Claghorn--Jazz p276

SNOW, VALAIDA (1900-1956)
Amer. trumpeter, singer
Claghorn--Jazz p276

SNOWDEN, MARY (fl. 1970's)
Amer. painter
Women's--Female p58

SNYDER, ALICE DOROTHEA (1887-
1943)
Amer. professor, author,
educator
James--Notable (3) p323-324

SNYDER, JOAN (1940-)
Amer. painter
100--Greatest (1) p75, por.
Women's--Female p58

SNYDER, LILLIAN (fl. 1870's)
Amer. pioneer, flag-maker
Sherr--American p226

SNYDER, LINDA (fl. 1970's)
Amer. blind lawyer
O'Neill--Women's p352-353

SNYDER, LUCIA (fl. 1940's)
Amer. radio writer
Women--Radio p20

SNYDER, RHODA (fl. 1870's)
Amer. pioneer, town co-
founder
Sherr--American p225-226

SNYDER, RUTH BROWN (1895-1928)
Amer. accused criminal
People's Almanac (1) p580-581
Woman's Almanac p504, por.

SOBEL, REBECCA
Amer. TV news correspondent
Scheuer--Tel. p458

SOBIROUS, MARIE BERNADETTE
See BERNADETTE OF LOURDES,
SAINT

SOCHEN, JUNE (fl. 1970's)
Amer. author, feminist
Sochen--Herstory, cover
(jacket), por.

SÖDER, KARIN (fl. 1970's)
Swedish foreign minister
O'Neill--Women's p43,52

SODERQUIST, BERTHA (c1898-)
Amer. Peace Corps worker
Comfort--Good p212, por.

SODERSTRÖM (SOEDERSTROEM),
ELISABETH (1926/1927-)
Swedish opera singer
Cur. Biog. '85 p393-397, por.
Gammond--Illus. p251, por.

SOEMARIO, ROESIAL (fl. 1950's)
Indonesian feminist
Macksey--Book p90-91

SOEWONDO, NANI (fl. 1940's)
Indonesian lawyer
Macksey--Book p90,128

SOFKA, MELANIE
See "MELANIE"

SOKOLOW, ANNA (1915-)
Amer. choreographer,
director, teacher, ballet
dancer
Cur. Biog. '69 p407-410, por.
Percival--Modern p64,66

SOLASCO, BELLA (fl. 1950's-
1970's)
Russian "retired" woman
Mandel--Soviet p281-282

SOLDAN-BROFELDT, VENNY
(1860-)
Finnish artist
Sparrow--Women p291

SOLIMAN, PATRICIA (fl.
1960's-1970's)
Amer. editor, publisher
O'Neill--Women's p489

SOLNTSEVA, JULIA (YULIA) (fl.

1960's)
Russian actress, filmmaker
Mandel--Soviet p146
Smith--Movies p136

SOLOMAN, SUSAN (fl. 1970's)
Amer. museum curator
Women's--Female p119

SOLOMON, HANNAH GREENEBAUM
(1858-1942)
Amer. charity worker, organi-
zation founder
Fink--Great p79-85, por.
James--Notable (3) p324-325
McHenry--Liberty's p387-388

SOLOMON, JOAN (fl. 1970's)
Amer. model agent
O'Neill--Women's p137-138

SOLOMON, MARGARET GREY
("MOTHER SOLOMON")
(1815-1890)
Amer. Indian, noted Ohio
mother
Amer.--Mothers p425-426

SOLOMON, VICKI
Amer. TV traffic manager
Kelver--Women p44-45,85-86

SOLTYSIK, PATRICIA (c1949-1974)
Amer. accused criminal
Woman's Almanac p507

SOLWOSKA, MARIA, pseud.
See FRENCH, MARILYN

SOMERS, SUZANNE (1945-)
Amer. actress
Anderson--People p366-367, por.
Scheuer--Tel. p459
World--Who p249

SOMERVILLE, EDITH ANNA OENONE
(1858/1861-1949)
Irish novelist
Avenel--Comp. (1) p487-488
Showalter--Lit. p341

SOMERVILLE, MARY FAIRFAX
(1780-1872)
Scottish mathematician,
physicist, author
Jones--Rutledge p728
Osen--Women p95-116, por.

Smith--Women p173-219
Taylor--Gener. p46, por.

SOMERVILLE, NELLIE NUGGENT
(1863-1952)
Amer. reformer, state
legislator, lawyer, noted
Mississippi mother, feminist
Amer.--Mothers p301-302, por.
Scott--Southern p203-205
Sherr--American p124
Sicherman--Notable p654-656

SOMERVILLE, EDITH (1858-1949)
Irish novelist
Seymour-Smith--Novels p219

SOMMER, ELKE (1941-   )
Amer. actress
World--Who p249

SOMMERS, TISH
Amer. organization official
O'Neill--Women's p108, por.

SOMOGI, JUDITH (1941/1943-   )
Amer. opera conductor
O'Neill--Women's p638-639

SONDERGAARD, GALE (1899-1985)
Amer. actress
Springer--They p226,329, por.

SONE, MONICA (1919-   )
Japanese-Amer. author
Kulkin--Her p265-266

SONNENDAY, MARGARET L.
Amer. church organization
president
O'Neill--Women's p394

SONNINO, EVE
Italian-Amer. shoe designer
O'Neill--Women's p258-259

SONTAG, SUSAN (1933-   )
Amer. novelist, critic,
filmmaker, philosopher,
essayist
Avenel--Comp. (2) p236
Cur. Biog. '69 p413-415, por.
McCullough--People p163-165
McHenry--Liberty's p388
O'Neill--Women's p688-689
Seymour-Smith--Novels p219
Seymour-Smith--Who's p346

Smith--Movies p52-54, por.
World--Who p97

SONTHIEL, URSULA
See SHIPTON, "MOTHER"

SOONG, MAYLING
See CHIANG KAI-SHEK, MAYLING
SOONG, MADAME

SOPHIA (1) (1630-1714)
German electress of Hanover
Jones--Rutledge p728

SOPHIA (2) (1657-1704)
Russian regent, sister of
Peter the Great
Book--Lists (2) p17
Macksey--Book p28

SOPHIA DOROTHEA OF CELLE (1666-
1726)
English queen
Softly--Queens p100

SOPHIA OF MECHLENBURG
German queen, mother of
Christian IV of Norway and
Denmark, social reformer in
midwifery
Mead--Hist. p348-349

"SOPHIE MAY," pseud.
See MAY, SOPHIA, pseud.

SORABJI, CORNELIA (c1868-1954)
East Indian lawyer, author
Macksey--Book p128

SORAY, TÜRKAN (fl. 1970's)
Turkish actress, filmmaker
Smith--Movies p144

SORAYA, QUEEN
Persian ex-queen
Hamblin--Life p110-111

SOREFF, HELEN (1960's-1970's)
Danish painter
Women's--Female p58

SORETH (fl. 1700's)
Jewish Hasidic woman
Henry--Written p210

SOREL, AGNES (1409/1422-1450)
French mistress of Charles VII

Leary--Golden p80,87n,
147

SORMA, AGNES (1865-1927)
Austrian actress
Entertainers p152

SOROUR, JACKIE (fl. 1940's)
Amer. aviatrix
Boase--Sky's p186, por.

SORRELLS, CONNIE M. (fl. 1960's)
Amer. heroine
O'Neill--Women's p733

SORYA, FRANÇOISE
See AIMEE, ANOUK

SOTHERN, ANN (1909/1912-)
Amer. actress
Shipman--Gold. p507-510, por.
Springer--They p226-228,329,
por.
World--Who p249

SOTHERN, GEORGIA (c1917-)
Amer. burlesque queen
Lamparski--What. (4) p84-85,
por.

SOTKA, KATHY
Amer. psychic
People's Almanac (2) p8

SOTOMAYER, MARTA (fl. 1970's)
Amer. Chicano social work
administrator
O'Neill--Women's p409

SOTOMAYOR, MARIA DE ZAYAS
Y SIBYL OF MADRID
(c1590-c1661)
Spanish scholar
Brink--Female p54-67

SOUCHE, HALLIE (fl. 1930's-
1970's)
Amer. banker
O'Neill--Women's p526-527

SOULE, CAROLINE AUGUSTA
WHITE (1824-1903)
Amer. author, church
worker, social reformer,
lecturer, clergyman
James--Notable (3) p325-327

SOUTAR, JUDY COOK (1944-)
Amer. bowler
Jacbos--Modern p11-21, por.
McWhirter--Guinness p44
O'Neill--Women's p558-559
Woman's Almanac p436-437, por.

SOUTHARD, LYDA (fl. 1900's)
Amer. accused murderer
Sherr--American p58

SOUTHCOTT, JOANNA (1750-1814)
English prophetess
Jones--Rutledge p730
People's Almanac p1101

SOUTHGATE, ELIZA
See BOWNE, ELIZA SOUTHGATE

SOUTHWORTH, EMMA DOROTHY
ELIZA NEVITTE (1819-1899)
Amer. novelist
Ehrlich--Oxford p177,224
James--Notable (3) p327-328
McHenry--Liberty's p388
Webster's--Amer. p966-967

SOWELL, ANNE WINDFOHR (c1939-)
Amer. millionaire
Forbes--400 ('84) p138

SPACEK, "SISSY" (MARY ELIZA-
BETH) (1949-)
Amer. actress
Anderson--People p368-369
Cur. Biog. '78 p397-400, por.
Hirschhorn--Rating p348-349, por.
World--Who p249

SPAFFORD, BELLE SMITH (c1895-
1982)
Amer. Mormon, author, noted
Utah mother
Amer.--Mothers p530-531, por.

SPAGNUOLA, TERESA (fl. 1670's)
Spanish medicinal botanist,
writer
Mead--Hist. p431-432

SPAIN, JAYNE (c1941-)
Amer. director, company
president, government
official
Diamonstein--Open p367-371, por.

SPAIN, JAYNE BAKER (1927-)

Amer. company manager
Bird--Enterprising p224-227
O'Neill--Women's p523

SPALDING, CATHERINE, MOTHER
(1793-1858)
Amer. foundress, nun
James--Notable (3) p328-330
McHenry--Liberty's p388-389

SPALDING, ELIZA HART (1807-
1851)
Amer. Western pioneer, mis-
sionary (to Oregon)
James--Notable (3) p330-331
Millstein--We p52
Sherr--American p58,197,254,
257
Time--Women p24,48
Welter--Dimity p92

SPARK, MURIEL SARAH CAMBERG
(1918-)
Scottish novelist, critic, poet
Avenel--Comp. (1) p490
Baker--Women p7-8
Crosland--Beyond p54-57
Cur. Biog. '75 p393-395, por.
Jones--Rutledge p731
Seymour-Smith--Novels p220,
por.
Seymour-Smith--Who's p347
Spacks--Contemp. p137-149,
181-182
World--Who p31

SPARKES, CATHERINE (fl. 1870's)
British china painter
Callen--Women p53,67-68,226

SPARKS, MILDRED HOTCH (1901-)
Amer. clubwoman, politician,
noted Alaska mother
Amer.--Mothers p21-22, por.

SPARROWK, CORA (1950's-1970's)
Amer. religious leader
O'Neill--Women's p396

SPEAKMAN, MARJORIE WILLOUGHBY
(1890-)
Amer. businesswoman, noted
Delaware mother
Amer.--Mothers p88, por.

SPEAKMAN, MARY N. (1920-)
Amer. genealogical researcher,
writer, editor
Meyer--Who's p189-190

SPEAKS, OLEY (1874-1948)
Amer. singer, composer
Claghorn--Biog. p413-414

SPEER, LENA BROCK ("MOM")
(-1967)
Amer. singer
Claghorn--Biog. p414

SPENCER, ANNA CARPENTER
GARLIN (1851-1931)
Amer. clergyman, social
reformer
James--Notable (3) p331-333

SPENCER, ANNE (1882-)
Amer. poet
Bernikow--World p265

SPENCER, CAROLINE ELIZABETH,
LADY (1763/1764-1812)
English actress
Ware--Meet p26-27,80

SPENCER, CHARLOTTE, LADY
(1769-1802)
English socialite
Ware--Meet p26,80

SPENCER, CORNELIA PHILLIPS
(1825-1908)
Amer. author, feminist, col-
lege founder, educator, noted
North Carolina mother
Amer.--Mothers p401-402, por.
James--Notable (3) p333-334
Scott--Southern p72-73,94,125-
126,156,172
Sherr--American p178-179,181

SPENCER, DANIELLE (1965-)
Amer. actress
World--Who p249

SPENCER, DOROTHY (fl. 1930's-
1960's)
Amer. film editor
Smith--Movies p26,28,41,74

SPENCER, ELEANOR (1890-1973)
Amer. pianist
Claghorn--Biog. p414

SPENCER, ELIZABETH (1921-)

Amer. novelist, short-story
writer
Avenel--Comp. (2) p237
Ehrlich--Oxford p270
Seymour-Smith--Novels p220

SPENCER, JEAN
English artist
Contemp. Brit., unp., por.

SPENCER, LAVINIA, COUNTESS
(1762-1831)
English socialite
Ware--Meet p24,26-27,81, por.

SPENCER, LILY MARTIN (1822-1902)
Amer. painter
Fine--Women p105-108
Fowler--Art p144
Harris--Women p226-227,350
James--Notable (3) p334-336
McHenry--Liberty's p389
Munsterberg--Hist. p60-62
Petersen--Women p84-87, por.
Women's--Female p14

SPENCER, SUSAN
Amer. TV news correspondent
Scheuer--Tel. p460

SPENCER (SPENSER), VIOLET
See COOK, EDITH MAUD

SPERBER, PAULA (1951-)
Amer. bowler
Hollander--100 p18-19, por.
Sabin--Women p81-97, por.

SPERLING, KAREN (fl. 1970's)
Amer. filmmaker
Smith--Movies p83-86,275, por.

SPERO, NANCY (1926-)
Amer. painter
Miller--Lives p202-212, por.

SPEWACK, BELLA COHEN (1899-)
Hungarian librettist, play-
wright, journalist
Claghorn--Biog. p414
Neidle--America's p259-260

SPEYER, ELLIN LESLIE PRINCE
LOWERY (1849-1921)
Amer. philanthropist, society
hostess
James--Notable (3) p336-337

SPEYER, LEONORA VON STOSCH
(1872-1956)
Amer. violinist, poet
Bernikow--World p249
Ehrlich--Oxford p137,224

SPHEERIS, PENNY (fl. 1970's)
Amer. filmmaker
Smith--Movies p204-205,275

SPICER, DOROTHY (fl. 1930's)
British aviatrix
Boase--Sky's p92,126-129, por.

SPILIMBERG, IRENE DI
See DI SPILIMBERG, IRENE

SPINDLER, PEARL G. (fl. 1940's-
1970's)
Amer. labor leader, lawyer,
government official
O'Neill--Women's p286

SPINELLY, ANDREE ("SPI") (fl.
1920's-1930's)
French, eccentric actress,
beauty
Keenan--Women p62-64, por.

SPIVEY, VICTORIA (1908-1976)
Amer. singer, pianist
Claghorn--Jazz p278

SPOCK, MILDRED STOUGHTON
(1876-1968)
Amer., mother of Dr.
Benjamin Spock
Diagram--Mothers p230-231, por.

SPOFFORD, GRACE HARRIET (1887-
1974)
Amer. music educator, ad-
ministrator
Sicherman--Notable p656-657

SPOFFORD, HARRIET ELIZABETH
PRESCOTT (1835-1921)
Amer. novelist
Ehrlich--Oxford p54,227
James--Notable (3) p337-339
McHenry--Liberty's p389-390

SPOONER, WINIFRED (-1933)
English aviatrix
Boase--Sky's p118,122,126

SPORER, ANDREA D.

Amer. executive, satellite
communications
Scheuer--Tel. p461

SPOTTED-WOLF, MINNIE (fl.
1940's)
Amer. Indian marine
O'Neill--Women's p541

SPRAGUE, KATE CHASE
See CHASE, KATE

SPRINGETT, GULIELMA
See PENN, GULIELMA MARIA
SPRINGETT

SPRINGFIELD, DUSTY (1939-)
English singer
World--Who p273

SPRINGFIELD, LAODICEA (DICEY)
LANGSTON (1760-)
Amer. Revolutionary War
patriot, heroine
Engle--Women p3-10, por.
Meyer--Petticoat p126-128

SPRY, CONSTANCE (1886-1960)
English lecturer, florist,
author, horticulturist
Macksey--Book p17
O'Neill--Women's p134

SPURLOCK, EDITH
See SAMPSON, EDITH SPUR-
LOCK

SPURLOCK, JEANNE (fl. 1960's-
1970's)
Amer. psychiatrist
O'Neill--Women's p229

SPYCHAJOWA-KURKOWSKA,
JANINA (fl. 1930's-1940's)
Polish archer
McWhirter--Guinness p25
O'Neill--Women's p558

SPYRI, JOHANNA HEUSSER (1827-
1901)
Swiss children's book author
Macksey--Book p186

"SQUAW SACHEM" (-1667)
Amer. Indian leader
Sherr--Amer. p107

SQUIRES, DELPHINE ANDERSON
(1868-)
Amer. publisher, editor,
noted Nevada mother
Amer.--Mothers p347-348, por.

SREDNITSKY, PATI
See KREMER, PATI SREDNITSKY

STAAL (STAHL, STAEL), MAR-
GUERITE JEANNE CORDIER
DELAUNAY, BARONESS DE
(1693-1750)
French anatomist
Macksey--Book p143
Mead--Hist. p491

STABLER, PHOEBE (fl. 1900's)
British sculptor, ceramicist,
metalworker, enameller
Callen--Women p71,226

STACK, CAROL (fl. 1970's)
Amer. sociologist, writer
Hymowitz--Hist. p338

STACY, HOLLIS (fl. 1970's)
Amer. golfer
McWhirter--Guinness p75

STACY, JESS ALEXANDRIA (1904-)
Amer. singer
Claghorn--Jazz p278

STADE, FREDERICA VON (1945/
1946-)
Amer. opera singer
Gammond--Illus. p251, por.
World--Who p72

STAEHR-NIELSEN, EVA (1895-)
Danish ceramist
O'Neill--Women's p270

STAËL (STAËL-HOLSTEIN), ANNE
LOUISE GERMAINE NECKER,
MADAME DE (1766-1817)
French historian, critic,
novelist
Bree--Women p12,40-41
Crosland--Women p59-60,235, por.
Jones--Rutledge p734
Kronenberger--Atlan. p730-731
Macksey--Book p100-101, por.
Magill--Cycl. p1014
Mead--Hist. p456, por.

Moers--Literary p312-313, see
also index p334, por.
Who Did What p296
Woman's Almanac p250
Women's--Female p7
World--Who p36

STAFFORD, JEAN (1915-1979)
Amer. novelist, short-story
writer
Avenel--Comp. (2) p237-238
Cur. Biog. '79 p473
Ehrlich--Oxford, see index p461
Moers--Literary p313
Seymour-Smith--Novels p220
Seymour-Smith--Who's p350
World--Who p20

STAFFORD, JO (1918-   )
Amer. singer
Claghorn--Biog. p415
Simon--Best p553-554, por.
World--Who p273

STAGEBERG, SUSIE W. (1877-1961)
Amer. politician, religious,
social reformer, noted
Minnesota mother
Amer.--Mothers p290-291, por.

STAGG, BESSIE (fl. 1950's-1970's)
Amer. newspaper editor
O'Neill--Women's p455

STAGG, CAMILLE
Amer. newspaper food-editor
O'Neill--Women's p468

STAGG, MARY (fl. 1710's-1730's)
English-Amer. colonial actress,
dancer, theatre owner
Macksey--Book p224

STAHL, LESLEY (1941-   )
Amer. TV newscaster,
anchorwoman
Gelfman--Women p32-34,50-51,
62-63,84,95, por.
Marzolf--Up p189
O'Neill--Women's p502-503

STAHL, MADAME DE
See STAËL (STAËL-HOLSTEIN),
ANNE LOUISE GERMAINE
NECKER, MADAME DE

STAIR, LOIS HARKRIDER (1923-

1981)
Amer. religious leader, moder-
ator
O'Neill--Women's p394

STAIR, PATTY (1869-1926)
Amer. organist, composer,
conductor, teacher
Claghorn--Biog. p416

STAIRS, LOUISE E. (1892-   )
Amer. organist, composer,
teacher
Claghorn--Biog. p416

STALLKNECHT, KIRSTEN (1937-   )
Danish labor leader, govern-
ment official
O'Neill--Women's p284,320

STAMBERG, SUSAN (c1939-   )
Amer. radio producer, TV
anchorwoman
Marzolf--Up p151
O'Neill--Women's p499-500

STAMM, LAURA (fl. 1970's)
Amer. hockey coach
O'Neill--Women's p569

STANARD, JANE STITH RICHMOND
(-1824)
Amer., inspiration of Edgar
Allen poe
Ehrlich--Oxford p236

STANFIELD, AGNES
See CLARE, ADA, pseud.

STANFORD, JANE ELIZA LATHROP
(1825/1828-1905)
Amer. philanthropist,
university co-founder
James--Notable (3) p340-342
Longstreet--Queen p154-156, por.
Macksey--Book p69
Sherr--American p21, por.
Starr--Amer. p325-334
Warren--Pictorial p143

STANFORD, SALLY (MABEL MARCIA
BUSBY GOODAN FANSTER
BAYHAM SPAGNOLI RAPP
GUMP) (1903-1982)
Amer. mayor, businesswoman,
millionaire
Dunlap--Calif. p191-192, por.

Felton--Famous p146
O'Neill--Women's p79-80

STANHOPE, HESTER LUCY, LADY
(1776-1839)
English explorer, author,
traveller, prophetess
Hamalian--Ladies p92-98
Jones--Rutledge p735
Morley--Literary p194,200-201
Smith--Women p421-470
Taylor--Gener. p57-58, por.

STANLEY, AILEEN (1893-)
Amer. actress
Chinoy--Women p107-113, por.

STANLEY, CHARLOTTE (fl. 1770's)
Amer. patriot
Young--Revol. p21,23-25n,26n,
29,187,200

STANLEY, KIM (1921/1928-)
Amer. actress, singer
Entertainers p253
World--Who p249

STANLEY, LOUISE (1883-1954)
Amer. agriculturist, govern-
ment official, home economist
O'Neill--Women's p22
Sicherman--Notable p657-659

STANLEY, WINIFRED C. (1909-)
Amer. Congresswoman,
lawyer
Chamberlin--Min. p159-163

STANNUS, EDRIS
See DE VALOIS, NINETTE,
DAME

STANSFIELD, GRACE
See FIELDS, GRACIE, DAME

STANTON, ELIZABETH CADY
(1815-1902)
Amer. suffragist, social
reformer, editor, feminist,
noted New York mother
Amer.--Mothers p392, por.
Archer--Famous p156-171
Banner--Women p15-16,23-24,
88,91-92, por.
Earnest--American, see index
p279
Fine--Women p92,94-95,105, por.

Gilfond--Heroines p22, por.
Gurko--Ladies, see index p326-
327, por.
Hoople--As p181-183, por.
Hymowitz--Hist. p73,86,88-121,
136,149,159,184,274,278,348,
see also index p398, por.
Ingraham--Album p26,33-34,37,
por.
James--Notable (3) p342-347
Kulkin--Her p266-268
Lutz--Crusade, see index p337
McHenry--Liberty's p390
Macksey--Book p86
Marlowe--Great p74-79, por.
Marzolf--Up p224-227
Millstein--We p96,98-99,108-112,
172-173, por.
Neidle--America's p28,30,39-45
Nies--Seven p61-93
O'Neill--Women's p387,483
Papachristou--Women, see index
p vi, por.
Pederson--Leaders p99, por.
Reader's--Story p432
Reifert--Women p84-101
Sherr--American p38,75,160,
164,166,174-177, por.
Signif.--Amer. p23, por.
Smith--Daughters, see index p388
Sochen--Herstory p124-125, see
index p446, por.
Warren--Pictorial p89-90,98-100,
114-115,117,137,159, por.
Woman's Almanac p542-544,546-
547,549, por.
World--Who p191

STANVILLE, MARTHA PELL
Amer. TV executive
Scheuer--Tel. p463

STANWOOD, CORDELIA (1865-1958)
Amer. pioneer ornithologist,
nature-writer, photographer
Sherr--American p88

STANWYCK, BARBARA (1907-)
Amer. actress
Engstead--Star p39-42
Hazen--Interv. p405
Hirschhorn--Rating p351-352,
por.
Lichtenstein--Mach. p259-261
Manchel--Women p68,72, por.
Mordden--Movie, see index p295
Shipman--Gold. p510-515, por.

Springer--They p228-229,330, por.
Woman's Almanac p353-354
World--Who p249

STAPLETON, BESSIE LACKEY
(1861-)
Amer. PTA state organizer,
noted Mississippi mother
Amer.--Mothers p300, por.

STAPLETON, JEAN (1923-)
Amer. actress
Anderson--People p372
Cur. Biog. '72 p407-410, por.
100--Greatest (1) p102, por.
Scheuer--Tel. p463, por.
World--Who p249

STAPLETON, MAUREEN (1925-)
Amer. actress
Entertainers p266
World--Who p249

STAPLETON, RUTH CARTER
(1929-1983)
Amer. evangelist, (sister of
Jimmy Carter)
O'Neill--Women's p401
World--Who p84

STARBUCK, DOROTHY L. (fl.
1940's-1970's)
Amer. government official
O'Neill--Women's p87

STARBUCK, MARY COFFIN
(COFFYN) (1644/1645-1717)
Amer. Quaker clergyman
James--Notable (3) p347-349
Sherr--American p107
Williams--Demeter's p129-130

STARIN, MARY ELIZABETH (fl.
1950's)
Amer. genealogical researcher,
writer
Meyer--Who's p190

STARK, ELIZABETH PAGE
("MOLLY") (1736/1737-1814)
Amer. Revolutionary War
patriot, noted New
Hampshire mother
Amer.--Mothers p360, por.
Meyer--Petticoat p45,92-93
Sherr--American p147,229

STARK, FREYA MADELINE (1893-)
British travel writer, explor-
er, (daughter of Robert
Stark, sculptor)
Avenel--Comp. (1) p497
Macksey--Book p243

STARK, MABEL (1892-)
Canadian-Amer. animal trainer
Woman's Almanac p324

STARK, MOLLY
See STARK, ELIZABETH PAGE
("MOLLY")

STARK, SHIRLEY (fl. 1970's)
Amer. sculptor
Fax--Black p19-38, por.

STARKE, PAULINE (1901-1977)
Amer. actress
Lamparski--What. Annual (4,5)
p42-47, por.

STARKLOFF, IRMA LOUISE VON
See ROMBAUER, IRMA LOUISE
VON STARKLOFF

STARR, BELLE SHIRLEY (1848/
1849-1889)
Amer. Western heroine, out-
law, legendary "bandit queen"
of the Southwest
Coffin--Female p131-139, por.
James--Notable (3) p349-350
Levenson--Women p69-70, por.
McHenry--Liberty's p390-391
Macksey--Book p136
Millstein--We p66
People's Almanac (1) p108-109
Reifert--Women p143-144
Sherr--American p10,129,193,
por.
Time--Women p171, por.
Woman's Almanac p500, por.
World--Who p301

STARR, ELIZA ALLEN (1824-1901)
Amer. writer, poet, lecturer
James--Notable (3) p350-351

STARR, ELLEN GATES (1859-1935/
1940)
Amer. socialist, social reformer, co-founder Hull House,
bookbinder
Callen--Women p198-199,226

Clark--Leading p31-32
Hymowitz--Hist. p227
James--Notable (3) p351-353
Macksey--Book p117-118
Sherr--American p60
Signif.--Amer. p34, por.

STARR, FRANCES (1886-1973)
Amer. actress
Springer--They p229,330, por.

STARR, KAY (1922/1923-)
Amer. singer
Claghorn--Biog. p417
Simon--Best p557-558, por.

STARRETT, MARION H. (1930-)
Amer. genealogical researcher
Meyer--Who's p191

STARTZ, JANE (fl. 1970's)
Amer. artist, (educational
media)
Women's--Female p155

STASOVA, HELENA (1873-1966)
Russian political leader,
feminist, cabinet member,
writer
Mandel--Soviet p32-33,49-50

STASOVA, NADEZHDA (1850-)
Russian mathematician
Mandel--Soviet p24

STATON, DAKOTA (1932-)
Amer. singer
Claghorn--Jazz p279

STEAD, CHRISTINA ELLEN (1902-
1983)
Australian novelist
Crosland--Beyond p136,148,
177-181,185
Moers--Literary p313
Seymour-Smith--Novels p221
Seymour-Smith--Who's p350-351
World--Who p31

STEAD, KAREN
Amer. athlete, child celebrity
Woman's Almanac p54

STEARNS, AGNES JUNE (1939-)
Amer. singer
Claghorn--Biog. p417

STEARNS, LUTIE EUGENIA (1866-
1943)
Amer. pioneer librarian, lecturer, social reformer
James--Notable (3) p353-354

STEARNS, MARY BETH (-1973)
Amer. scientist, executive
(automobile industry), inventor
O'Neill--Women's p184,520

STEBBINS, EMMA (1815-1852)
Amer. painter, sculptor
James--Notable (3) p354-355
Sherr--American p98,170

STEBER, ELEANOR (1916-)
Amer. opera singer
Claghorn--Biog. p418

STECHER, RENATE (fl. 1970's)
East German track and field
athlete
Assoc. Press--Pursuit p313,315,
339
McWhirter--Guinness p12, por.

STECKEL, ANITA (fl. 1970's)
Amer. painter
Women's--Female p58-59,111

STECKLING, ADRI
See ADRI

STEDING, PEGGY (fl. 1970's)
Amer. racquetball player
O'Neill--Women's p582

STEDMAN, MRS. (fl. 1770's)
Amer. Revolutionary War
patriot
Meyer--Petticoat p35

STEEL, DOROTHY DYNE (1884-1965)
English croquet player
Macksey--Book p256, por.
McWhirter--Guinness p50-51, por.

STEEL, FLORA ANNIE WEBSTER
(1847-1929)
English novelist, suffragist
Showalter--Lit. p337

STEEL, KATHERINE ("KATE")
FISHER (c1724-1785)
Amer. Revolutionary War

patriot, pioneer, heroine
Meyer--Petticoat p125-126

STEELE, ELIZABETH MAXWELL
(fl. 1770's)
Amer. Revolutionary War
patriot
Meyer--Petticoat p202
Sherr--American p181

STEEN, MARGUERITE (1894-1975)
English author
Cur. Biog. '75 p474

STEENBERG, RISË
See STEVENS, RISË

STEEVENS, MADAME (fl. 1720's)
Irish hospital builder
Mead--Hist. p479

STEFFENS, SHARON (fl. 1970's)
Amer. agriculturist
O'Neill--Women's p1,8

STEGHAGEN, EMMA (fl. 1920's)
Amer. labor union worker
Hymowitz--Hist. p248

STEHLING, WENDY
Amer. author
People--Best p75, por.

STEIN, EDITH (1891-1942)
German nun
Book--Lists (2) p17-18

STEIN, GERTRUDE (1874-1946)
Amer. novelist, poet
Avenel--Comp. (2) p239-240
Bernikow--World p232-233
Book--Lists (2) p222
Brandon--Dollar p191-192
Cahill--Women p42-43,374
Chester--Rising p1-3, por.
Donaldson--How p349
Dunlap--Calif. p193, por.
Ehrlich--Oxford, see index p461
Fink--Great p132-141, por.
Howard--Seven p30-34
Ingraham--Album p61, por.
James--Notable (3) p355-359
Jones--Rutledge p738
Kelen--Fifty p160
Kronenberger--Atlan. p732-733
Kulkin--Her p268-270

Longstreet--Queen p141-149, por.
McHenry--Liberty's p391-392
Moers--Literary p313-314, see
also index p334, por.
O'Neill--Women's p678-679
People's Almanac (2) p1198-1199
Richey--Eminent p153-179, por.
Rogers--Ladies, see index p235,
por.
Seymour-Smith--Novels p221
Seymour-Smith--Who's p351-351
Signif.--Amer. p53, por.
Sorell--Three p71-128, por.
Stoddard--Famous p399-409, por.
Warren--Pictorial p184
Webster's--Amer. p979
Who Did What p297
Wintle--Makers p495-496, #452
Woman's Almanac p259-260
World--Who p21

STEIN, NANETTE (MARIA ANNA)
(1769-1833)
Austrian pianist
Macksey--Book p212

STEIN, PAT (fl. 1970's)
Amer. painter
Woman's--Female p59

STEINBACH, SABINA VON (fl.
c1220's-c1300)
German sculptor, artist
Macksey--Book p194-195
Munsterberg--Hist. p84-85
Women's--Female p15

STEINBECK, ELAINE SCOTT (fl.
1950's-1960's)
Amer., third wife of John
Steinbeck
Ehrlich--Oxford p144, por.

STEINEM, GLORIA (1934-)
Amer. feminist, magazine
editor, journalist, NOW
founder
Anderson--People p374-375
Clark--Leading p241,244
Cur. Biog. '72 p412-414, por.
Diamonstein--Open p372-378, por.
Gilbert--Part. p161-167, por.
Ingraham--Album p76, por.
Kostman--20th p155-167, por.
Lichtenstein--Mach., see index
p367

Macksey--Book p221
Marzolf--Up p243-244
100--Greatest (1) p61, por.
O'Neill--Women's p40,44,479-480,
484
Schoenebaum--Prof. p620-621
Sochen--Herstory p398,401, por.
Walker--Women p137-152, por.
Warren--Pictorial p206-208, por.
Woman's Almanac p558-559, por.
World--Who p191

"STELLA DALLAS"
See ELSTNER, ANN

STELLA FAMILY
French painters
Petersen--Women p33

STELLMAN, JEANNE M. (fl.
1970's)
Amer. labor leader, chemist,
author
O'Neill--Women's p326

STELOFF, (IDA) FRANCES
(1887-)
Amer. bookseller, book mart
owner, founder
Gilbert--Part. p1-9, por.
Warren--Pictorial p183, por.

STEN, ANNA (1908/1910-)
Russian actress
Shipman--Gold. p515-517, por.
Springer--Tehy p229-230,330,
por.

STENHOLM, KATHERINE (fl.
1950's-1970's)
Amer. speech, drama instructor, filmmaker
Smith--Movies p205,276

STENHOUSE, CAROLINE (1900-)
New Zealander physician
Hellstedt--Women p192-198, por.

STENHOUSE, FANNY
Amer. writer on Mormonism
Hymowitz--Hist. p185-186
Sherr--American p226

STEPHANE, NICOLE (fl. 1940's-
1970's)
French actress, producer
Smith--Movies p54,119-120

STEPHEN, MARGARET (fl. 1790's)
English obstetrician, medical
writer
Mead--Hist. p477

STEPHENS, ALICE BARBER (1858-
1932)
Amer. illustrator
Callen--Women p208
James--Notable (3) p359-360
McHenry--Liberty's p392

STEPHENS, ANN(A) SOPHIA WIN-
TERBOTHAM (1810-1886)
Amer. editor, novelist, poet,
journalist
Ehrlich--Oxford p7,74-75
James--Notable (3) p360-362
McHenry--Liberty's p392
Macksey--Book p186

STEPHENS, ANNIE
Amer. Western pioneer
Sherr--American p241

STEPHENS, KATE (1853-1938)
Amer. professor, author,
editor
James--Notable (3) p362-363

STEPHENS, SUE (fl. 1970's)
Amer. Naval Academy lieutenant
O'Neill--Women's p548

STEPHENSON, FRANCES (-1973)
British, wife of David Lloyd
George
Macksey--Book p103

STEPHENSON, MARION (fl. 1960's-
1970's)
Amer. radio executive
Marzolf--Up p148-149
O'Neill--Women's p496,518

STEPOVICH, MATILDA (fl. 1950's)
Amer., wife of Alaskan Gov-
ernor Michael Stepovich
Jones--Women (1) p185

STERLING, ANTOINETTE (1850-
1904)
Anglo-Amer. singer
Claghorn--Biog. p419

STERLING, CLAIRE (fl. 1940's-
1950's)

Amer. foreign correspondent
Marzolf--Up p85

STERLING, JAN (1923-)
Amer. actress
World--Who p249

STERN, CATHERINE BRIEGER
(1894-1973)
German-Amer. educator
Sicherman--Notable p659-660

STERN, DANIEL, pseud.
See AGOULT, MARIE CATHERINE
SOPHIE DE FLAVIGNY

STERN, EDITH ROSENWALD
(c1895-1980)
Amer. socialite, philan-
thropist
Birmingham--Grandes, see
index p297

STERN, ELIZABETH (1890-1954)
Amer. writer, social worker
Baum--Jewish p125-126,206,
214-215
Hymowitz--Hist. p198,201-202,
211,214,324-325

STERN, FRANCES (1873-1947)
Amer. social worker, dietician
James--Notable (3) p363-364

STERN, GLADYS BRONWYN (1890-
1973)
English novelist
Avenel--Comp. (1) p499
Seymour-Smith--Novels p222
Showalter--Lit. p347

STERN, LINA SOLOMONOVNA (fl.
1930's-1940's)
Russian physiologist
Mandel--Soviet p192

STERN, MARJORIE HEFTER (fl.
1970's)
Amer. labor leader, feminist
O'Neill--Women's p303,307-308

STERN, SUSAN (1943-1976)
Amer. weatherwoman, radical
Lichtenstein--Mach. p163-165,
294-295

STERNBURG, JANET (fl. 1970's)

Amer. filmmaker, writer,
feminist
Smith--Movies p205,277

STERNE, AGNES (-1759)
British, mother of Laurence
Sterne
Book--Lists (2) p253

STERNE, ELIZABETH LUMLEY
English, wife of Laurence
Sterne
Morley--Literary p63-65

STERNE, HEDDA (1916-)
Rumanian-Amer. artist
Munro--Originals p95-97

STETSON, AUGUSTA EMMA SIM-
MONS (1842-1928)
Amer. Christian Science
leader
James--Notable (3) p364-366
McHenry--Liberty's p392-393

STETSON, CHARLOTTE PERKINS
See GILMAN, CHARLOTTE
PERKINS STETSON

STETTHEIMER, FLORINE (1871-
1944)
Amer. painter
Harris--Women p58,64,94,266-
267,354
James--Notable (3) p366-368
Petersen--Women p101-103

STEVENS, ALICE HARDIE (1900-)
Amer. community worker,
teacher, noted Wyoming mother
Amer.--Mothers p598-599, por.

STEVENS, ALZINA PARSONS (1844/
1849-1900)
Amer. labor leader, journalist,
settlement worker, feminist,
author, social reformer
James--Notable (3) p368-369

STEVENS, CONNIE (1938-)
Amer. singer, actress, TV
personality
Claghorn--Biog. p420
World--Who p249

STEVENS, GEORGIA LYDIA,
MOTHER (1870-1946)

Amer. musician, nun, school
co-founder, teacher
James--Notable (3) p369-370

STEVENS, JANE (fl. 18th cent.)
English medical "imposter"
Mead--Hist. p479,481

STEVENS, JULIE
Amer. radio actress
Lamparski--What. (3) p98-99,
por.
Lamparski--What. (3) p254-255,
por.

STEVENS, LILLIAN MARION NOR-
TON AMES (1844-1914)
Amer. social reformer
James--Notable (3) p370-372
Sherr--American p88,90

STEVENS, MARIETA (fl. 1850's)
Amer. hotel-keeper
Brandon--Dollar p63-64,67,79-80

STEVENS, MAY (1924-   )
Amer. painter
Miller--Lives p213-227, por.
Ruddick--Working p103-116,
346-347, por.
Women's--Female p112

STEVENS, MINNIE (-1919)
Amer. heiress
Brandon--Dollar p63-67,79-80,
127-131, por.

STEVENS, NETTIE MARIA (1861-
1912)
Amer. biologist, geneticist
James--Notable (3) p372-373
McHenry--Liberty's p393

STEVENS, RISË (1913-   )
Amer. opera singer
Claghorn--Biog. p420
Lamparski--What. (4) p50-51,
por.
World--Who p72

STEVENS, RUBY
See STANWYCK, BARBARA

STEVENS, STELLA (1936-   )
Amer. actress
World--Who p249

STEVENSON, ALICE (1861-1973)
British, oldest woman
Macksey--Book p12

STEVENSON, BIRGIT
See NILSSON, (MÄRTA) BIRGIT

STEVENSON, ELIZABETH CLEGHORN
See GASKELL, MRS. ELIZABETH
CLEGHORN STEVENSON

STEVENSON, MATILDA COXE EVANS
(1849-1915)
Amer. ethnologist, anthro-
pologist
James--Notable (3) p373-374
McHenry--Liberty's p393-394

STEVENSON, RACHEL (fl. 1940's)
Amer. radio performer
Marzolf--Up p134

STEVENSON, SARAH ANN HACKETT
(1841-1909)
Amer. physician, teacher,
author
James--Notable (3) p374-376
McHenry--Liberty's p394
O'Neill--Women's p202-203

STEVENSON, VANDERGRIFT
OSBOURNE
Amer., wife of Robert Lewis
Stevenson
Brecher--Lives p184, por.

STEWARD, SUSAN SMITH McKINNEY
(1848-1918)
Amer. physician
O'Neill--Women's p202,207

STEWART, AMII (fl. 1970's)
Amer. singer
Glassman--Year '79 p37,146, por.

STEWART, DEBORAH M. CLENAHAN
Amer. socialite
Earle--Two Cent. (2) p xvii,589,
740, por.

STEWART, DIANA (fl. 1970's)
Amer. bishop
O'Neill--Women's p383

STEWART, DIANE J. (fl. 1970's)
Amer. heroine, Carnegie

medal winner
O'Neill--Women's p735

STEWART, ELINORE PRUITT
RUPERT (1878-)
Amer. Western pioneer,
homesteader
Hoople--As p140-143
Hymowitz--Hist. p180,183

STEWART, ELIZA DANIEL (1816-
1908)
Amer. temperance reformer,
suffragist
James--Notable (3) p376-377
McHenry--Liberty's p394-395
Sherr--American p187

STEWART, ELLA
See WINTER, ELLA

STEWART, ELLEN (c1928-)
Amer. theatrical producer
Cur. Biog. '73 p392-395, por.
Gilbert--Part. p33-41, por.
O'Neill--Women's p665

STEWART, GWENDA (fl. 1900's-
1920's)
English ambulance driver,
motor-car racer
Macksey--Book p253, por.
McWhirter--Guinness p30, por.

STEWART, HELEN JANE WISER
(1854-c1926)
Amer. ranch owner, noted
Nevada mother
Amer.--Mothers p346, por.
Sherr--American p144

STEWART, ISABEL MAITLAND
(1878-1963)
Canadian-Amer. nursing
educator
Sicherman--Notable p660-662

STEWART, MARGOT (fl. 1970's)
Amer. artist
Women's--Female p112

STEWART, MARIA W. MILLER
(1803-1879)
Amer. teacher, lecturer,
social reformer
James--Notable (3) p377-378
Warren--Pictorial p85

STEWART, MARY (1916-)
English educator
Macksey--Book p77

STEWART, MARY FLORENCE ELINOR
RAINBOW (1916-)
English novelist
O'Neill--Women's p686-687
Seymour-Smith--Novels p223, por.
World--Who p48

STEWART, MAYDELLE
Amer. agricultural literature
indexer
O'Neill--Women's p29

STEWART, PAMELA ANNE
Amer. heroine, Carnegie
Medal winner
O'Neill--Women's p735

STEWART, RAMONA (1922-)
Amer. novelist
P.W.--Author p144-147,526

STEWART, SARAH E. (-1976)
Mexican-Amer. microbiologist
O'Neill--Women's p88,220-221

STICKEL, LUCILLE FARRIER (fl.
1950's-1970's)
Amer. biologist
O'Neill--Women's p33,89

STICKNEY, DOROTHY HAYES
(1900/1903-)
Amer. actress
Fabian--On p148-149, por.
World--Who p249

STIEHM, JUDITH (fl. 1970's)
Amer. educator, professor
Halcomb--Women p200-215

STILL, NANCY (1926-)
Finnish designer, (glass and
wood)
O'Neill--Women's p275

STILLMAN, MILDRED (WHITNEY)
(1890-1950)
Amer. hymnist
Claghorn--Biog. p421

STIMPSON, CATHARINE R. (1936-)
Amer. magazine editor,
professor

O'Neill--Women's p424, por.
Ruddick--Working p71-76,347,
por.

STIMSON, JULIA CATHERINE
(1881-1948)
Amer. nurse, educator
James--Notable (3) p378-380
McHenry--Liberty's p395

STINSON, KATHARINE (1896-)
Amer. aviatrix
Boase--Sky's p20-21
Genett--Aviation p113

STIRLING, ELIZABETH (1819-1895)
English organist, composer
Macksey--Book p214

STIRLING, KITTY
Amer. Revolutionary War
patriot
Meyer--Petticoat p75,78,80,106

STIRLING, LINDA (1921-)
Amer. actress
Lamparski--What. (5) p124-125,
por.

STIRLING, MARION (fl. 1940's-
1970's)
Amer. archaeologist, geographer
O'Neill--Women's p147, por.

STITT, SUSAN (fl. 1970's)
Amer. museum director
O'Neill--Women's p615

STIX, MARGUERITE (1907-1975)
Austrian-Amer. sculptor,
designer, craftswoman
Diamonstein--Open p379-384,
por.
O'Neill--Women's p255

STOCKARD, VIRGINIA ALICE
COTTEY
Amer. college founder
O'Neill--Women's p427

STOCKHAM, ALICE BUNKER
(fl. 1880's)
Amer. writer
Felton--Famous p268-269

STOCKTON, ANNIS BOUDINOT

(1736-1801)
Amer. colonial poet, Revolu-
tionary War patriot
Booth--Women p100-102,113,299,
por.
Kelley--Courage p12,175-194,198,
234-235
Meyer--Petticoat p73-74
Sherr--American p153-154

STOCKTON, KATE BRADFORD
(fl. 1880's-1930's)
Amer. politician, Socialist
Sherr--American p216

STOCKTON, MARTHA MATILDA
BRUSTAR (1821-1885)
Amer. hymnist
Claghorn--Biog. p421

STODDARD, CORA FRANCES (1872-
1936)
Amer. temperance educator
James--Notable (3) p380-381

STODDARD, MRS. SIMEON
Amer. social leader
Earle--Two Cent. (1) p75-76,
por.

STOECKEL, ELLEN BATTELL (1851-
1939)
Amer. philanthropist, music
patron
James--Notable (3) p381-382

STOEDTER, HELGA (fl. 1970's)
German-Amer. lawyer
O'Neill--Women's p354

STOERMER, GRACE R. (fl. 1920's)
Amer. banker
O'Neill--Women's p526

STOESS, MRS. M. DE W.
See HOWELL, MARGARET
LOUISE KEMP

STOFFELS, HENDRICKJE (-1667)
Netherlands artist's model
Book--Lists (1) p191

STOKES, MARIANNE(A) (fl.
1880's-1890's)
German-English painter
Sparrow--Women p72,79,129

Papachristou--Women, see index
p vi, por.
Sherr--American p59,104-106,
114,153,186,252, por.
Signif.--Amer. p24, por.
Smith--Daughters, see index
p388-389
Sochen--Herstory p175,177,
por.
Warren--Pictorial p75-77,83,101-
102,117,120,159, por.
Webster's--Amer. p996-997
Woman's Almanac p146-147,547-
548
World--Who p191

STONE, MARY (SHIH MAI-YU)
(1873-1954)
Chinese physician
O'Neill--Women's p203

STONE, MARY KATHERINE (fl.
1960's)
Amer. educator, noted
Alabama mother
Amer.--Mothers p9, por.

STONE, MAY (fl. 1890's-1930's)
Amer. settlement school
co-founder
O'Neill--Women's p122
Sherr--American p79

STONE, PAULENE (fl. 1950's-
1970's)
English model
Keenan--Women p147-150-151,
158,160, por.

STONE, SARAH (fl. c1730's)
English medical writer
Mead--Hist. p476-477

STONE, SYLVIA (1928-)
Canadian-Amer. artist
Munro--Originals p334-344, por.

STONE, VIRGINIA (fl. 1950's-
1970's)
Amer. actress, singer,
swimmer
Smith--Movies p40,77

STONEHOUSE, RUTH (1894-1941)
Amer. actress, director
Slide--Early p54, por.

STONEMAN, ABIGAIL (fl. 1760-
1777)
Amer. publican of colonial
Rhode Island, Massachusetts,
& New York, tavern-owner
James--Notable (3) p390-391
Sherr--American p206

STONEMAN, BERTHA
See FERGUSON, ABBIE PARK

STONGER, KAROL (fl. 1970's)
Amer. syndicated sportswriter
O'Neill--Women's p463

STOPES, MARIE CHARLOTTE
CARMICHAEL (c1880-1959)
English feminist, paleontologist,
birth control clinic founder
Brecher--Lives p300
Comfort--Good p121, por.
Jones--Rutledge p743
Macksey--Book p120,156-157, por.
O'Neill--Women's p720
Palmer--Who's p300
People's Almanac (2) p921-923
Wintle--Makers p502-503, #458

STORCH, MARCIA (1933-)
Amer. obstetrician, gynecolo-
gist
Walker--Women p153-165, por.

STORER, MARIA (c1750-1795)
Amer. singer, actress
Claghorn--Biog. p422

STORER, MARIA LONGWORTH
NICHOLS (1849-1932)
Amer. ceramicist, metalworker,
music patron
Callen--Women p226, see also
index p232, por.
James--Notable (3) p391-393
McHenry--Liberty's p397

STORM, GALE (1921/1924-)
Amer. singer, actress
Claghorn--Biog. p422
Lamparski--What. (5) p104-105,
por.
Lamparski--What. (8) p272-273,
por.
World--Who p249

STORMS, JANE MARIA ELIZA

McMANUS
See CAZNEAU, JANE MARIA
ELIZA McMANUS STORMS

STORNI, ALFONSINA (1892-1938)
Argentinian poet
Hahner--Women p172-174

STORY, ADELINE (fl. 1970's)
Amer. banker
Seed--Saturday's p151-152, por.

STORY, ANN (1742-1817)
Amer. pioneer, Revolutionary
War heroine, noted Vermont
mother
Amer.--Mothers p537, por.
Sherr--American p230

STOTESBURY, LUCRETIA (EVA)
BISHOP ROBERTS (1865-1946)
Amer. socialite, philanthropist
Birmingham--Grandes, see index
p298, por.
Daniels--Wash. p123-125

STOUDER, SHARON (fl. 1960's)
Amer. swimmer
Assoc. Press--Pursuit p257-258
Hollander--100 p87-88

STOUGHTON, LOUISE (fl. c1870's)
Amer. writer
Earnest--American p190-193

STOUT, PENELOPE THOMSON
(1622-1732)
Netherlands diarist
Crawford--Four, see index p190

STOVALL, THELMA L. (1919-)
Amer. clubwoman, government
official, politician, noted
Kentucky mother
Amer.--Mothers p215-216, por.
O'Neill--Women's p77

STOVE, BETTY (fl. 1970's)
Amer. tennis player
McWhirter--Guinness p156,160,
por.

STOVENOUR, JUNE
See HAVER, JUNE

STOVER, CLARA MAE LEWIS

(1882-1975)
Amer. business woman, noted
Missouri mother
Amer.--Mothers p315, por.

STOW, FREELOVE BALDWIN (1728-)
Amer. Revolutionary War pa-
triot, noted Connecticut mother
Amer.--Mothers p75-76

STOW, MARIETTA (fl. 1880's)
Amer. pioneer fashion design-
er, politician
Time--Women p223, por.

STOWE, EMILY (1831-1903)
Canadian physician, feminist,
suffragist
Macksey--Book p89
O'Neill--Women's p203-204

STOWE, HARRIET ELIZABETH
BEECHER (1811-1896)
Amer. novelist, librettist,
noted Connecticut mother
Amer.--Mothers p77-78, por.
Avenel--Comp. (2) p242-243
Beech--Daughters p209-247, por.
Benét--New p48-55, por.
Betts--Writers p22-27, por.
Boorstin--Americans p62-63, por.
Claghorn--Biog. p423
Earnest--American, see index
p279
Ehrlich--Oxford, see index p461,
por.
Fine--Women p92-93
Fry--1000 p246
Gilfond--Heroines p102-104, por.
Hymowitz--Hist. p68
Ingraham--Album p25-26,58, por.
James--Notable (3) p393-402
Jones--Rutledge p743
Kronenberger--Atlan. p745-747
Kulkin--Her p272-273
Longford--Eminent p178-204, por.
Lutz--Crusade p247-254
McHenry--Liberty's p397-398
Macksey--Book p33,111-112,184-
185, por.
Magill--Cycl. p1034-1035
Millstein--We p104-106
Moers--Literary p314-315, see
also index p334, por.
Papachristou--Women p69-70
Pederson--Leaders p95, por.

People's Almanac (1) p175
People's Almanac (2) p1186
Seymour-Smith--Novels p223
Sherr--American p31-32,41,44,
   81,87,90,184,187,229
Signif.--Amer. p13, por.
Smith--Daughters, see index
   p389
Sochen--Herstory p42,146, por.
Stoddard--Famous p410-420, por.
Warren--Pictorial p103-104, por.
Webster's--Amer. p997-998
Who Did What p300
Woman's Almanac p145,168,260
World--Who p21

STOWE, MARY F. (fl. 1970's)
   Amer. police officer
   O'Neill--Women's p373-374

STOWE, MARY L. (fl. 1890's)
   Amer. Vice Presidential
   candidate
   People's Almanac (1) p127

STOWE, SALLY A. (fl. 1960's-
   1970's)
   Amer. banker
   O'Neill--Women's p528

STOWE-GULLEN, AUGUSTA
   (-1943)
   Canadian physician
   O'Neill--Women's p204

STRADA, NANNI (fl. 1960's-
   1970's)
   Italian fashion designer
   Keenan--Women p91,103-104,
   por.

STRAIGHT, BEATRICE WHITNEY
   (1918-)
   Amer. actress
   World--Who p250

STRAIGHT, DOROTHY (1958-)
   Amer. child author
   Book--Lists (2) p224

STRAIGHT, DOROTHY WHITNEY
   (1887-1968)
   Amer. organization officer
   O'Neill--Women's p111

STRAND, CHICK (fl. 1960's-
   1970's)

Amer. college film instructor,
   filmmaker
Smith--Movies p206-207,277

STRANEY, SHIRLEY GARTON
   Amer. genealogical researcher,
   writer
   Meyer--Who's p192-193

STRANG, RUTH MAY (1895-1971)
   Amer. educator, author
   Cur. Biog. '71 p470
   Sicherman--Notable p662-663

STRANGE, MICHAEL (1890-1950)
   Amer. poet, actress
   James--Notable (3) p490-491
   McHenry--Liberty's p419-420

STRASBERG, SUSAN ELIZABETH
   (1938-)
   Amer. actress, author
   World--Who p250

STRASSER, ROBIN (1945-)
   Amer. TV actress
   Scheuer--Tel. p469, por.

STRATAS, TERESA (1938-)
   Canadian opera singer
   Cur. Biog. '80 p381-384, por.

STRATTON, DOROTHY CONSTANCE
   (1899-)
   Amer. educator, naval officer,
   government official
   McHenry--Liberty's p398
   Signif.--Amer. p73, por.
   Warren--Pictorial p194

STRATTON, (MERCY) LAVINIA
   WARREN BUMPUS, COUNTESS
   MAGRI (1841-1919)
   Amer. midget, (wife of Tom
   Thumb)
   Kirk--Circus p27, por.
   People's Almanac (1) p110
   Sherr--American p30
   Woman's Almanac p323, por.

STRATTON, MARY CHASE PERRY
   (1867-1961)
   Amer. ceramicist
   Sherr--American p117

STRATTON-PORTER, GENE
   See PORTER, GENE STRATTON

STRAUS, ELLEN SULZBERGER
(fl. 1920's)
  Amer. radio station executive
Adams--Women p74-77,107
O'Neill--Women's p115

STRAUSS, ANNA LORD (1899-1979)
  Amer. civic leader, editor
Cur. Biog. '79 p474

STRAYER, SARA BARKER
  See WILSON, MARGERY

STREEP, MERYL (MARY LOUISE)
(1949/1950-)
  Amer. actress
Cur. Biog. '80 p388-391, por.
Entertainers p291
Hirschhorn--Rating p355, por.
Mordden--Movie p281-282
People--Best p187, por.

STREETER, RUTH CHENEY (1895-)
  Amer. marine director
McHenry--Liberty's p398-399
O'Neill--Women's p535,546-547
Signif.--Amer. p74, por.

STREETER, VIRGINIA
  Amer. nutritionist, army flier
Keil--Those p149-150,162-164,
  261-262

STREISAND, BARBRA JOAN
(1942-)
  Amer. singer, actress
Anderson--People p377-378, por.
Claghorn--Biog. p424
Glassman--Year '79 p146, por.
Hirschhorn--Rating p355-356,
  por.
McHenry--Liberty's p399
Manchel--Women p94,105,107,
  112, por.
Mordden--Movie p62,245,250-
  256,288
100--Greatest (1) p18, por.
O'Neill--Women's p627,654
People--Best p116-117, por.
Shipman--Internatl. p567-569,
  por.
Simon--Best p559-561, por.
Talmey--Vogue p44, por.
Webster's--Amer. p1001
Woman's Almanac p354, por.
World--Who p250

STRENGEL, MARIANNE (fl. 1930's)
  Amer. director, textile art
  studio
O'Neill--Women's p265

STRETTON, HESBA, pseud. (1832-
  1911)
  English children's book author
Showalter--Lit. p332

STRETTON, JULIA CECILIA COLLIN-
  SON DEWINTON (1812-1878)
  English novelist
Showalter--Lit. p324-325

STRICKLAND, AGNES (1796-1874)
  English historian
Avenel--Comp. (1) p504

STRICKLAND, LILY TERESA (1887-
  1958)
  Amer. song-writer, author
Claghorn--Biog. p424
Sherr--American p213

STRICKLAND, SHIRLEY DE LA
  HUNTY
  See HUNTY, SHIRLEY DE LA
  STRICKLAND

STRIDER, MARJORIE (fl. 1970's)
  Amer. painter, sculptor
Women's--Female p59,96

STRIDER, NANCY (fl. 1970's)
  Amer. sculptor
Women's--Female p96

STRINASACCHI, REGINA
  Italian violinist
Nuels-Bates--Women p65,199,199n

STRITCH, ELAINE (1925/1928-)
  Amer. actress, singer
World--Who p250

STROMSTEN, AMY (fl. 1960's-
  1970's)
  Amer. photographer
Miller--Lives p228-244, por.
Women's--Female p71

STROND, CAROL J.
  Amer. TV director of research
Scheuer--Tel. p470

STRONG, ANNA LOUISE (1885-1970)

Amer. radical, journalist,
poet
Cur. Biog. '70 p471
Ehrlich--Oxford p391
McHenry--Liberty's p399-400
Nies--Seven p147-178
Sicherman--Notable p664-666

STRONG, HARRIET WILLIAMS
RUSSELL (1844-1929)
Amer. agriculturist, environ-
mentalist
James--Notable (3) p405-406
Sherr--American p22-23

STRONG, SUSAN (1875-)
Amer. opera singer
Claghorn--Biog. p425

STRONGIN, LYNN (1939-)
Amer. poet
Chester--Rising p314-321, por.

STROUD, F. AGNES N. (fl.
1970's)
Amer. Indian radiobiologist
O'Neill--Women's p162

STROYEVA, VERA (fl. 1970's)
Russian filmmaker
Mandel--Soviet p144,146
Smith--Movies p136

STROZZI, BARBARA
Italian singer, composer
Macksey--Book p211

STRUTHERS, SALLY ANN(E)
(1948-)
Amer. actress
Anderson--People p378-379
Cur. Biog. '74 p402-404, por.
Scheuer--Tel. p470, por.
World--Who p250

STRYKER-RODDA, HARRIET
(1905-)
Amer. genealogical researcher,
author, editor
Meyer--Who's p193

STUART, DONNA VALLEY (1927-)
Amer. genealogical researcher,
editor, indexer
Meyer--Who's p194

STUART, GLORIA (1910-)

Amer. actress
Lamparski--What. (5) p36-37, por.
Springer--They p230,330, por.

STUART, JANE (1) (1812-1888)
Amer. artist, daughter of
Gilbert Stuart
Fine--Women p99-100,103-105
Munsterberg--Hist. p59
Petersen--Women p66-68

STUART, JANE (2) (1830-1891)
Amer. Civil War relief and
hospital worker
James--Notable (3) p665-668

STUART, JESSIE BONSTELLE
See BONSTELLE, JESSIE

STUART, MARY
Amer. actress
Scheuer--Tel. p470-471

STUART, MICHELLE
Amer. artist
Munro--Originals p438-446, por.

STUART, MIRANDA
See BARRY, JAMES (MIRANDA)
("DR.")

STUART, RUTH McENERY (1849-
1917)
Amer. author
Ehrlich--Oxford p277,285
James--Notable (3) p407-408
McHenry--Liberty's p400

STUART-WORTLEY, EMMELINE
CHARLOTTE ELIZABETH
MANNERS, LADY (1806-1855)
English poet, travel writer
Showalter--Lit. p322

STUBBES, KATHERINE (fl. 1600's)
English religious worker
Bainton--Spain p95-99

STUBBS, JEAN (1926-)
English novelist
Cahill--Women p268,378
Seymour-Smith--Novels p224

STUBER, RUTH
Amer. timpanist, marimba
player
Neuls-Bates--Women p261

STÜCKELBERGER, CHRISTINE (fl.
1970's)
Swiss equestrian
McWhirter--Guinness p56
O'Neill--Women's p588

STUECKGOLD, GRETE (1895-)
English-Amer. opera singer
Claghorn--Biog. p425

STURE-VASA, MARY
See O'HARA, MARY ALSOP
STURE-VASA

STURGIS, CAROLINE
See HOOPER, ELLEN CAROLINE
STURGIS TAPPAN

STURGIS, ELLA (c1859-)
Amer. Western pioneer
Time--Women p73, por.

STURGIS, ELLEN
See HOOPER, ELLEN CAROLINE
STURGIS TAPPAN

STURGIS, KATHERINE BOUCET
(1903-)
Amer. physician, noted
Pennsylvania mother
Amer.--Mothers p462, por.
Diamonstein--Open p385-390,
por.

STURGIS, MARGARET CASTEL (fl.
1910's-1930's)
Amer. physician, surgeon,
hospital officer
O'Neill--Women's p213

STURTEVANT, BRERETON (1921-)
Amer. lawyer, government
official
O'Neill--Women's p85

STUTMAN, JUDITH C. (fl. 1970's)
Amer. government official
O'Neill--Women's p118

STUTSMAN, GRACE MAY (fl.
1920's-1930's)
Amer. hymnist
Claghorn--Biog. p425

STUTZ, GERALDINE (GERI)
VERONICA (1924-)
Amer. department store

official, fashion editor
Adams--Women p24-25,97-98,
109,176
Cur. Biog. '83 p376-379, por.
100--Greatest (1) p70, por.
O'Neill--Women's p518

STUYVESANT, ELIZABETH (fl.
1910's-1970's)
Amer. dancer, settlement
worker, birth-control advocate
Showalter--These p92-97

STYERS, ALETA (fl. 1960's-1970's)
Amer. corporate planner,
government official
O'Neill--Women's p525

SUAREZ, INES DE (1507-1572)
Spanish-Chilean philanthropist,
social arbitrator
Henderson--Ten p23-48, por.

SUBLIGNY, MARIE-THERESE
PERDOU DE (1666-1736)
French ballet dancer
Migel--Ballerinas p9-10, por.

SUCKLEY, MARGARET (DAISY)
Amer. cousin of Franklin D.
Roosevelt
Daniels--Wash. p300-301,309-310,
por.

SUCKOW, RUTH (1892-1960)
Amer. novelist
Ehrlich--Oxford, see index p461
Sicherman--Notable p666-667

SUESSE, DANA NADINE (1911-)
Amer. pianist, author, com-
poser
Jablonski--Ency. p457
World--Who p293

SUFFOLK, ALICE, DUCHESS OF
(-1475)
English hospital builder
Mead--Hist. p321-322

SUGGS, LOUISE (1923-)
Amer. golfer
McWhirter--Guinness p73-74, por.
Signif.--Amer. p74, por.

SUIKO
Japanese ruler
Macksey--Book p21-22

SUKENICK, LYNN (1927-)
    Amer. poet
    Chester--Rising p289-293, por.

SULEIMANOVA, KHADYCHA (fl.
    1960's-1970's)
    Russian feminist
    Mandel--Soviet p176

SULLAM, SARA COPPIA (1590-
    1641)
    Italian, Jewish scholar, poet,
    singer, musician
    Henry--Written p132-134

SULLAVAN, MARGARET BROOKE
    (1909/1911-1960)
    Amer. actress
    Hirschhorn--Rating p356-357,
    por.
    Keylin--Hollywood p262-263, por.
    Shipman--Gold. p520-522, por.
    Springer--They p230-231,330,
    por.
    World--Who p250

SULLIVAN, MRS. ALGERNON S.
    (fl. 1860's)
    Amer. Southern relief or-
    ganizer
    Warren--Pictorial p113

SULLIVAN, ANNE (1866-1936)
    Amer., teacher of Helen
    Keller
    James--Notable (2) p481-483
    Kulkin--Her p189-191
    McHenry--Liberty's p266
    Macksey--Book p73
    Marlowe--Great p233-238
    Sherr--American p3
    Signif.--Amer. p34, por.
    Stoddard--Famous p234-244,
    por.
    Webster's--Amer. p574
    Woman's Almanac p157-158,
    por.
    World--Who p100

SULLIVAN, ELINOR SMITH
    See SMITH, ELINOR

SULLIVAN, ELIZABETH (1) (fl.
    1970's)
    Amer. Creek Indian writer
    Fisher--Third p v,26

SULLIVAN, ELIZABETH (2) (BETTY)
    (fl. 1940's-1950's)
    Amer. chemist
    O'Neill--Women's p30-31,164

SULLIVAN, KATHLEEN
    Amer. TV news co-anchorwoman
    Schuer--Tel. p471

SULLIVAN, (KATHY) KATHRYN
    (fl. 1980's)
    Amer. astronaut, marine
    geophysicist
    Oberg--Space p111, por.
    O'Connor--Sally p2,20,23, por.
    O'Neill--Women's p740, por.

SULLIVAN, LEONOR ALICE KRETZER
    (1903/1904-)
    Amer. Congresswoman, con-
    sumer advocate
    Chamberlin--Min. p232-239
    Greenebaum--Politics p142
    O'Neill--Women's p68-70
    Schoenebaum--Prof. p629-630
    U.S.--Women (89th) p23, por.
    U.S.--Women (90th) p23, por.
    Woman's Almanac p124,481

SULLIVAN, MARY JOSEPHINE QUINN
    (1877-1939)
    Amer. art teacher, collector,
    patron
    James--Notable (3) p408-410
    Sherr--American p170

SULLIVAN, MAXINE (1911-1987)
    Amer. singer
    Claghorn--Biog. p426
    Claghorn--Jazz p282

SULLIVAN, SUSAN
    Amer. actress
    Scheuer--Tel. p471, por.

SULPICIA (fl. 63 B.C.-14 A.D.)
    Roman poet
    Pomeroy--Godd. p173-174

SUMAC, YMA (1927-)
    Peruvian singer
    Lamparski--What. (4) p54-55,
    por.

SUMMER, DONNA (1948/1949-)
    Amer. singer

Anderson--People p379-380
Cur. Biog. '69 p383-386, por.
Glassman--Year '79 p44,47,49,
157, por.
People--Best p221, por.
World--Who p273

SUMMERHAYES, MARTHA (fl.
1870's)
Amer. Western pioneer,
author
Fischer--Let p137-148
Reifert--Women p129
Sherr--American p7

SUMMEROUR, SHIRLEY (fl. 1970's)
Amer. carpet mill worker,
mountain woman
Kahn--Hill. p161-173, por.

SUMMERS, COLLEEN
See FORD, MARY

SUMMERS, ELAINE (fl. 1970's)
Amer. filmmaker
Smith--Movies p207-208,277, por.

SUMMERSBY, KATHLEEN (KAY)
(c1908-1975)
Amer., friend of Dwight
Eisenhower
Hershey--Between p53-54

SUMMERSKILL, EDITH CLARA,
BARONESS (1901-1980)
English physician, politician,
feminist, Parliamentary mem-
ber
Cur. Biog. '80 p466
Jones--Rutledge p749
Vallance--Women, see index p210

SUMMERSKILL, SHIRLEY
British Parliament member
Vallance--Women p60,103,115,143

SUMNER, HELEN LAURA
See WOODBURY, HELEN LAURA
SUMNER

SUMNER, JESSIE (c1909-)
Amer. Congresswoman, judge
Chamberlin--Min. p152-155
Miller--Fishbait p71-72

SUMTER, MARY CANTEY (CANTY)

JEIMESSON (1723-1818)
Amer. plantation owner,
pioneer
Booth--Women p254-255,300

"SUMURUN" (fl. 1920's)
English model
Keenan--Women p111-113,118-119,
por.

SUN, CHINGLING SOONG
See SUN YAT-SEN, CHINGLING
SOONG, MADAME

"SUNDAY LADY"
See McCHESNEY, MARTHA

SUNDE, GERNER
See BLODGETT, FERN

SUNDELIUS, MARIE LOUISE
SUNDBORG (1884-1958)
Swedish opera singer
Neidle--America's p223

SUNDSTROM, EBBA (fl. 1920's-
1930's)
Amer. orchestra conductor,
violinist
Neuls-Bates--Women p248-249

SUNG, BETTY LEE (fl. 1940's-
1970's)
Chinese-Amer. professor,
author
O'Neill--Women's p327,420-421

SUNTZEFF, VALENTINA (1891-)
Russian-Amer. physician
Neidle--America's p213-215, por.

SUN YAT SEN, CHINGLING SOONG,
MADAME (1890-1981)
Chinese Deputy Chairman of
People's Republic of China,
patriot, feminist, (wife of
Sun Yat-Sen)
Cur. Biog. '81 p472
Marlowe--Great p271-276, por.

SUPRUN, KSENIYA
Russian painter
Macksey--Book p208

SURNACHEVSKAYA, RAYA (fl.
1940's)

Russian aviatrix, combat pilot
O'Neill--Women's p550

SURRATT, MARY EUGENIA JEN-
KINS (1817/1820-1865)
Amer., accused co-
conspirator in Lincoln
assassination
James--Notable (3) p410-411
McHenry--Liberty's p400-401
Millstein--We p138-140
Sherr--American p94
Warren--Pictorial p110-111
Webster's--Amer. p1010
World--Who p301

SURRIAGE, AGNES
See FRANKLAND, AGNES
SURRIAGE, LADY

SUSANN, JACQUELINE ("JACKIE")
(1921-1974)
Amer. novelist, actress
Cur. Biog. '72 p420-423, por.
Cur. Biog. '74 p470
Hershey--Between p28-29,66-68,
por.
McHenry--Liberty's p401
Macksey--Book p192
P.W.--Author p148-151,527
Seymour-Smith--Novels p224,
por.
World--Who p21

SUSLOVA (SUSLOWA), NADEZHDA
(NADEYA) (fl. 1860's)
Russian physician
Macksey--Book p150
Marks--Women p119

SUSONG, EDITH O'KEEFE (fl.
1910's)
Amer. publisher, journalist
Marzolf--Up p61

SUSSKIND, JOYCE (c1935-)
Amer., wife of David Susskind
Funt--Art p313-325, por.

SUSSMAN, JUDY
See BLUME, JUDY SUSSMAN

SUTCLIFF, ROSEMARY (1920-)
Amer. children's book author
Kulkin--Her p273

SUTHERLAND, EFUA (1924-)

African (Ghana) poet, film
director
Crane--Ms. p36-56, por.
Smith--Movies p93

SUTHERLAND, ELIZABETH
See CARPENTER, LIZ

SUTHERLAND, JOAN, DAME
(1926-)
Australian opera singer
Claghorn--Biog. p427
Gammond--Illus. p251, por.
Jones--Rutledge p750
O'Neill--Women's p621
World--Who p80

SUTHERLAND, HARRIS, ANN
See HARRIS, ANN SUTHERLAND

SUTHERLAND-HUNTER, MARY
YOUNG
New Zealander painter
Sparrow--Women p71-72,126,130

SUTRO, ROSE LAURA (1870-1957)
Amer. pianist
Claghorn--Biog. p427

SUTTNER, BERTHA, BARONESS
VON (1843-1914)
Austrian pacifist, journalist,
editor
Kulkin--Her p274-275
Macksey--Book p33
Opfell--Lady p1-17, por.

SUTTON, CAROL (c1933-)
Amer. editor
Marzolf--Up p216
O'Neill--Women's p437,468-469

SUTTON, MARY JANE ODELL (1860-
1962)
Amer. pioneer, noted Washington state mother
Amer.--Mothers p558, por.

SUTTON, MAY (1887-1975)
English-Amer. tennis player
Dunlap--Calif. p27-28, por.
Lamparski--What. (5) p112-113,
por.
McWhirter--Guinness p148
Woman's Almanac p418

SUZMAN, JANET (1939-)

South African actress
Cur. Biog. '76 p392-395, por.
Entertainers p289, por.

"SUZY"
See MEHLE, AILEEN

SVARTZ, NANNA (1890-   )
Swedish physician
Hellstedt--Women p55-61, por.

SVENDSEN, GRO (1841-1878)
Norwegian-Amer. pioneer,
teacher
Neidle--America's p94-95

SVETLANOVA, E.
Russian writer, feminist
Mandel--Soviet p213-218

SWADOS, ELIZABETH (1951-   )
Amer. composer, director,
author
Cur. Biog. '79 p386-389, por.
Jablonski--Ency. p567

SWAIN, CLARA A. (1834-1910)
Amer. pioneer physician
James--Notable (3) p411-413
McHenry--Liberty's p401

SWAIN, LOUISA ANN (c1800-   )
Amer., first woman voter
Sherr--American p256

SWAIN, SUSAN (1954-   )
Amer. TV producer
Scheuer--Tel. p473

SWALLOW, ELLEN HENRIETTA
See RICHARDS, ELLEN
HENRIETTA SWALLOW

SWAN, ANNA (1846-1888)
Canadian-Amer. giantess
Entertainers p135

SWAN, DOTTIE (1916-   )
Amer. singer, songwriter
Claghorn--Biog. p427

SWANSON, DARLENE
Amer. religious worker
Kooiman--Cameos p126-136, por.

SWANSON, GLORIA MAY JOSEPHINE
(1898/1899-1983)

Amer. actress
Cur. Biog. '83 p474
Holme--Journal p223, por.
Manchel--Women p35,45, por.
Mordden--Movies, see index
p296, por.
Sat. Eve. Post--Movie p127, por.
Shipman--Gold p522-527, por.
Springer--They p231,233,330,
332, por.
Woman's Almanac p354
World--Who p250

SWANSON, KATRINA
Amer. deacon
O'Neill--Women's p382,385

SWANWICK, ANNA (1813-1897)
English translator, traveler,
feminist
Showalter--Lit. p325

SWARTHOUT, GLADYS (1904-1969)
Amer. opera singer
Claghorn--Biog. p428
Cur. Biog. '69 p474
Lamparski--What. (2) p20-21,
por.
Springer--They p233,332, por.

SWARTZ, MAUD(E) O'FARRELL
(1879-1937)
Irish-Amer. labor leader,
government official
James--Notable (3) p413-415
Neidle--America's p31,144,146,
153
O'Neill--Women's p284,290

SWEDBERG, JEAN C.
Amer. heroine, Carnegie
Medal winner
O'Neill--Women's p735

"SWEDISH NIGHTINGALE"
See LIND, JENNY

SWEEN, JANE C. (1931-   )
Amer. genealogical researcher,
writer
Meyer--Who's p195

SWEET, BLANCHE (1895/1896-   )
Amer. actress
Lamparski--What. (8) p276-277,
por.
World--Who p250

SWEET, WINIFRED
See BLACK, WINIFRED SWEET

SWENSON, INGA (1932/1934-)
Amer. actress
Scheuer--Tel. p473

SWENSON, MAY (1919-)
Amer. poet
Avenel--Comp. (2) p245
Brinnin--Modern p364-367, por.
Chester--Rising p86-91, por.

SWENSSON, ALMA CHRISTINE
LIND (1859-1939)
Amer. musician, college co-
founder, noted Iowa mother
Amer.--Mothers p204-205, por.

SWIDLER, ARLENE ANDERSON
Amer. author, translator,
editor, magazine co-founder
O'Neill--Women's p398

SWIFT, BETTY (J.) (1922-)
Amer. genealogical researcher,
author
Meyer--Who's p196

SWIFT, GINA (fl. 1970's)
Amer. pentathlete
O'Neill--Women's p580

SWIFT, KAY (1897-)
Amer. composer, lyricist,
pianist
Jablonski--Ency. p458-459

SWIFT, LELA (fl. 1940's)
Amer. TV director
Marzolf--Up p158,162,177

SWIGER, ELINOR PORTER (fl.
1970's)
Amer. lawyer, author,
lecturer
Swiger--Women p224

SWINDLER, MARY HAMILTON
(1884-1967)
Amer. archaeologist,
classicist
Sicherman--Notable p667-669

SWISSHELM, JANE GREY CANNON
(1815-1884)
Amer. social reformer,

feminist, abolitionist, journal-
ist, teacher, publisher, author
Beasley--First p3,6-9,23,por.
James--Notable (3) p415-417
Marzolf--Up p14-16
Sherr--American p122,205
Stein--Lives p205-227
Taylor--Gener. p32-33

SWIT, LORETTA (1937-)
Amer. actress
Scheuer--Tel. p474, por.
World--Who p250

SWITZER, KATHERINE V. (c1946-)
Amer. cosmetics executive,
marathon runner
Lichtenstein--Mach. p341-342
O'Neill--Women's p576, por.

SWITZER, MARY ELIZABETH (1900-
1971)
Amer. government official
Cur. Biog. '71 p471
O'Neill--Women's p227
Sicherman--Notable p669-670

SWOBODA, HARRIET N. (fl. 1960's)
Amer. heroine, Carnegie
Medal winner
O'Neill--Women's p732-733

SWOYER, ANN MYRTLE
See WALKER, NANCY

SWYNFORD, CATHERINE, DUCHESS
OF LANCASTER (c1350-1403)
English, wife of John of Gaunt
Jones--Rutledge p753
Macksey--Book p92

SYDENSTRICKER, CAROLINE
STULTING (1892-)
Amer. mother of Pearl Buck,
noted West Virginia mother
Amer.--Mothers p576

SYDENSTRICKER, PEARL
See BUCK, PEARL SYDEN-
STRICKER

SYERS, MADGE (fl. 1900's)
British ice skater
Macksey--Book p261

SYFERS, JUDY
Amer. feminist, writer

Hymowitz--Hist.
p357

SYKES, ELIZABETH
Amer. TV director
Scheuer--Tel. p474

SYKES, GLORIA (fl. 1970's)
Amer. defendant in
unusual law case
Felton--Famous p147

SYLVA, CARMEN, pseud.
See ELIZABETH (PAULINE
ELIZABETH OTTILIE
LOUISE)

SYLVESTER, C.
See WOOD, EMMA CAROLINE,
LADY

SYMONDS, REBEKAH (fl. 1660's-
1680's)
English-Amer., mother of
merchant John Hall
Earle--Two Cent. (1) p140,144
Earle--Two Cent. (2) p495

SYMS, SYLVIA (fl. 1940's-1970's)
Amer. singer
Balliett--Amer. p91-103

SYNDER, NANCY (fl. 1970's)
Amer. government official
O'Neill--Women's p23

SYSE, GLENNA (fl. 1950's-1970's)
Amer. drama critic
Chinoy--Women p226-228,230-
231, por.

SZEKELY, DEBORAH (c1921-)
Amer. manager, health spa
founder
Diamonstein--Open p391-401,
por.

SZEKELY, EVA (fl. 1940's-1950's)
Hungarian swimmer
Assoc. Press--Pursuit p180,
193,198,212

SZEMES, MARIANNE (fl. 1960's-
1970's)
Hungarian film writer, film
director
Smith--Movies p124

SZEWINSKA, IRENA (1946-)
Polish track and field athlete
Assoc. Press--Pursuit p270,313,
339
McWhirter--Guinness p174, por.
O'Neill--Women's p575,577

SZOLD, HENRIETTA (1860-1945)
Amer.-Israeli editor, Zionist
leader, founder of Hadassah
Baum--Jewish p32-33,39,42-46,
184
Bloom--Religion p77-99, por.
Fink--Great p86-104, por.
James--Notable (3) p417-420
Kulkin--Her p275-276
McHenry--Liberty's p401-402
Macksey--Book p119
Marlowe--Great p183-189, por.
O'Neill--Women's p719
Sherr--American p94
Signif.--Amer. p35, por.
Woman's Almanac p382
World--Who p191

SZUMOWSKA, ANTOINETTE (1868-
1938)
Polish-Amer. pianist
Claghorn--Biog. p429

T

TABA, HILDA (1902-1967)
Estonian-Amer. educator,
professor, author
Sicherman--Notable p670-672

TABAKOVA, TSVETANA BORISOVA
(1905-1936)
Bulgarian opera singer
Partington--Who's p407, por.

TABANKIN, MARGERY ANN (fl.
1970's)
Amer. humanitarian, government official
O'Neill--Women's p726

TABEI, JUNKO (1940-)
Japanese mountain climber
Macksey--Book p263, por.
McWhirter--Guinness p105
O'Neill--Women's p740
Woman's Almanac p368

TABER, GLADYS LEONAE BAGG
(1899-1980)

Amer. novelist
Cur. Biog. '80 p466
Ehrlich--Oxford p91

TABICK, JACQUELINE (c1949-)
English rabbi
O'Neill--Women's p382

TABITHA
See DORCAS

TABOR, AUGUSTA PIERCE
(1833-1895)
Amer., wife of millionaire
miner, Western pioneer
Sherr--American p28-29, por.

TABOR, ELIZABETH ("BABY
DOE") BONDUEL McCOURT
(1854-1935)
Amer. silver mine owner,
pioneer recluse
Williams--Legend. p93-115, por.
Woman's Almanac p75-76

TACHA, ATHENA (1936-)
Greek-Amer. sculptor
Munro--Originals p392-393

TADYSHEVA, OLGA (fl. 1960's)
Russian shepherd, member
of Congress
Mandel--Soviet p295-296

TAEUBER, IRENE BARNES
(1906-1974)
Amer. demographer, popula-
tion authority
Sicherman--Notable p672-673

TAEUBER-ARP, SOPHIE (1889-1943)
Swiss artist
Fine--Women p173-174
Harris--Women p60-61,291,311-
313,321,359

TAFOLLA, CARMEN (1951-)
Amer. Chicana writer, poet,
bilingual educator
Fisher--Third p ix,410

TAFT, HELEN HERRON (1861-1943)
Amer. first lady, musician,
teacher, wife of William
Howard Taft
James--Notable (3) p420-421
Melick--Wives p58-59, por.
Woman's Almanac p490

TAFT, JESSIE (1882-1960)
Amer. psychologist, social
work educator
Sicherman--Notable p674-675

TAFT, LOUISA MARIA TORREY
(c1828-1907)
Amer. mother of President
Taft
Faber--Presidents' p125-139, por.

TAGGARD, GENEVIEVE (1894-1948)
Amer. poet, educator
Bernikow--World p288
Ehrlich--Oxford, see index p461
James--Notable (3) p421-423
McHenry--Liberty's p403
Sherr--American p52
Showalter--These p62-68

TAGLIONI, AMALIA (1801-1881)
Swedish ballet dancer
Fabian--On p46-47, por.

TAGLIONI, MARIE (1804-1884)
Italian ballet dancer
Jones--Rutledge p755
Macksey--Book p225
Migel--Ballerinas p115-144, see
also index p303, por.
Who Did What p303
World--Who p80

TAIT, AGNES (c1897-)
Amer. artist
Harris--Women p64,317-318,360

TAI-YOUNG, LEE (fl. 1950's-1960's)
Korean lawyer, judge
O'Neill--Women's p369

TAKA, TOYOKO (1925-)
Japanese labor leader
O'Neill--Women's p322

TAKAGI, NORIKO (fl. 1960's)
Japanese badminton player
McWhirter--Guinness p37

TAKAHASHI, HISAKO (1927-)
Japanese labor leader
O'Neill--Women's p346

TAKAHASHI, NOBUKO
Japanese labor organization
official
O'Neill--Women's p347,
por.

TAKASHIMA, SHIZUYE (1928-)
Japanese-Amer. artist, author
Kulkin--Her p276-277

TAKAYAMA, SHIGERI (c1899-1977)
Japanese activist, civil rights
leader
O'Neill--Women's p723

TAKEDA, MARGUERITE HU (fl.
1970's)
Amer. government official
O'Neill--Women's p27

TAKEUCHI, SHIGEYO (1881-)
Japanese physician
Hellstedt--Women p5-7, por.

TALBOT, CATHERINE (1720/1721-
1770)
English essayist, letter-writer
Horner--English p37 (and note)
Moers--Literary p315

TALBOT, MARION (1858-1948)
Amer. university dean,
professor
Berkin--Women p325-328,332,
por.
James--Notable (3) p423-424

TALBOT, MARY ANNE (1778-1808)
British seaman
Macksey--Book p54

TALBOT, NITA (1930-)
Amer. actress, comedienne
World--Who p250

TALCOTT, ELIZA (1836-1911)
Amer. missionary, teacher,
nurse
James--Notable (3) p424-425

TALIAFERRA, DELLAREESE
See REESE, DELLA

TALIAFERRO, MABEL
Amer. actress
Hazen--Interv. p410

TALLCHIEF, MARIA (1925-)
Amer. Indian ballet dancer
Gridley--Amer. p138-153, por.
Ingraham--Album p62, por.
Kufrin--Uncom. p2-16, por.
Kulkin--Her p277-278
McHenry--Liberty's p403-404

O'Neill--Women's p641-642
Signif.--Amer. p75, por.
Webster's--Amer. p1017
Woman's Almanac p315

TALLCHIEF, MARJORIE (1927-)
Amer. Indian ballet dancer
Gridley--Amer. p138-153, por.
O'Neill--Women's p642

TALLENT, ANNIE (fl. 1890's)
Amer. pioneer, educator,
writer
Sherr--American p214-215

TALLEY, FAY STAINBROOK
(1916-)
Amer. genealogical researcher
Meyer--Who's p199

TALLEY, MARION NEVADA (1907-)
Amer. opera singer
Claghorn--Biog. p431

TALLEYRAND-PERIGORD, ANNA
GOULD, DUCHESSE DE (1876-
1961)
Amer. heiress
Brandon--Dollar p33,77-98,102,
por.

TALLIEN, JEANNE
See CHIMAY, JEANNE MARIE
IGNACE THERESE DE CARAR-
RUS, PRINCESS OF (TALLIEN,
MADAME)

TALLY-FROST, E. STEPHENIE
(1917-)
Amer. genealogical researcher,
author, editor
Meyer--Who's p198

TALMA, LOUISE J. (1906-)
French-Amer. composer,
professor
Claghorn--Biog. p431
Jablonski--Ency. p460-461
LePage--Women p226-240, por.
Thomson--Amer. p175-176

TALMADGE, BETTY SHINGLER (fl.
1970's)
Amer. head, meat packaging
corporation
O'Neill--Women's p14

TALMADGE, CONSTANCE (c1900-

1973)
Amer. actress, comedienne
Keylin--Hollywood p264, por.

TALMADGE, NORMA (1893/1897-
1957)
Amer. actress
Hazen--Interv. p408
Keylin--Hollywood p265, por.
Mordden--Movie p52-53
Springer--They p237,332, por.
World--Who p250

TALMEY, ALLENE (1902/1903-)
Amer. editor, journalist
Diamonstein--Open p402-407,
por.

TALVJ, pseud.
See ROBINSON, THERESE
ALBERTINE LOUISE VON
JAKOB

TAMIRIS, HELEN (1902/1905-1966)
Amer. ballet dancer, cheoreog-
rapher
McHenry--Liberty's p404
O'Neill--Women's p648
Sicherman--Notable p675-677

TANAKA, ATSUKO (1932-)
Chinese painter
Munsterberg--Hist. p81

TANAKA, KINUYO
Japanese actress, film
director
Macksey--Book p235
Smith--Movies p130

TANAQUIL
Roman heroine
Zinserling--Women p64

TANDY, JESSICA (1909-)
English actress
Cur. Biog. '84 p389-393, por.
World--Who p261

T'ANG SOU-YÜ
Chinese art critic
Petersen--Women p160

TANGUAY, EVA (1878-1947)
Canadian-Amer. actress,
singer
Entertainers p167

James--Notable (3) p425-427
McHenry--Liberty's p404

"TANIA"
See BUNKE BIDER, HAYDEE
TAMARA

TANNER, BEATRICE STELLA
See CAMPBELL, BEATRICE
STELLA TANNER

TANNER, LUCRETIA DEWEY (fl.
1960's-1970's)
Amer. labor economist
O'Neill--Women's p339

TANNING, DOROTHEA (1910-)
Amer. painter
Fine--Women p210-212
Harris--Women p100,338,362
Petersen--Women p133
Women's--Female p59

TAN SRI, FATIMAH (fl. 1970's)
Malaysian clergyman
Macksey--Book p40

TAPPAN, CAROLINE STURGIS
See HOOPER, ELLEN CAROLINE
STURGIS TAPPAN

TAPPAN, EVA MARCH (1854-1950)
Amer. children's book author,
teacher, biographer, historian
Ehrlich--Oxford p65
James--Notable (3) p427-428

TAPPAN, JULIA
Amer. antislavery worker
Hymowitz--Hist. p79

TAPPAN, SUSAN
Amer. antislavery worker
Hymowitz--Hist. p79

TAPPER, BERTHA FEIRING (1859-
1915)
Norwegian-Amer. pianist,
teacher
Claghorn--Biog. p431

TAPPER, JOAN (1947-)
Amer. book publisher's head
O'Neill--Women's p490

TARBELL, IDA MINERVA (1857-
1944)

Amer. editor, author,
journalist, feminist
Boorstin--Americans p51, por.
Ehrlich--Oxford, see index p461
Hazen--Interv. p304-306
James--Notable (3) p428-431
Kulkin--Her p278-279
McHenry--Liberty's p404-405
Marzolf--Up p41-42
O'Neill--Women's p471-472
Reifert--Women p183 184
Sherr--American p205
Signif.--Amer. p53, por.
Smith--Daughters p142,169-170,
181,184-185,295-298
Sochen--Movers p17-18
Webster's--Amer. p1019
Woman's Almanac p274
World--Who p56

TARDY, KAREN
Canadian-Amer. TV sales
director
Scheuer--Tel. p475-476

TARRANT, SARAH
See FRIETSCHIE, BARBARA
HAUER

TASHJIAN, ELIZABETH (fl.
1930's-1970's)
Amer. nut museum curator
Felton--Famous p10, por.

TASHMAN, LILYAN (1899-1934)
Amer. model, actress
Springer--They p237,332, por.
World--Who p250

TASTU, AMABLE, MADAME (1798-
1885)
French poet, children's book
author
Moers--Literary p315

TATE, CAROLINE
See GORDON, CAROLINE

TATE, ELLALICE TATE
See PLAIDY, JEAN

"TATOO LADY"
See HULL, MILLIE

TAUB, NADINE (fl. 1970's)
Amer. law professor, feminist
O'Neill--Women's p360

TAÜBER-ARP, SOPHIE (1889-1943)
Swiss painter
Munsterberg--Hist. p70-71

TAUSSIG, HELEN BROOKE (c1898-
1986)
Amer. physician, heart
surgeon, professor
Diamonstein--Open p408-412, por.
Gilbert--Part. p51-57, por.
Ingraham--Album p67
McHenry--Liberty's p404-405
O'Neill--Women's p145,207-208
Signif.--Amer. p75, por.
Woman's Almanac p368

TAVINS, PAULA (fl. 1970's)
Amer. craftswoman
Women's--Female p22

TAWNEY, LENORE (1925-)
Amer. weaver
Munro--Originals p325-333, por.
O'Neill--Women's p606

TAX, MEREDITH (fl. 1970's)
Amer. feminist, writer
Hymowitz, Hist. p350

TAYLOR, ALICE BEMIS (-1942)
Amer. philanthropist
Sherr--American p25

TAYLOR, ALMA (1895-1974)
British actress
Macksey--Book p233

TAYLOR, ANN (1782-1866)
British Parliamentary member
Morley--Literary p81-82
Vallance--Women p58,62,73,104

TAYLOR, ANNIE EDSON (1858-
c1924)
Amer. daredevil, stunt
woman
Book--Lists (2) p140
Felton--Famous p28-29, por.
Sherr--American p172, por.

TAYLOR, BETTY
Amer. aviatrix
Keil--Those p210-212

TAYLOR, BUNNY (fl. 1970's)
Amer. baseball "little leaguer"
O'Neill--Women's p567

TAYLOR, CHARLOTTE (fl. 1970's)
Amer. government official
O'Neill--Women's p517

TAYLOR, CHARLOTTE ANN (fl. 1840's)
Amer. philanthropist
Sherr--American p117

TAYLOR, DELORES (fl. 1970's)
Amer. filmmaker
Smith--Movies p67-68

TAYLOR, DYANNA
Amer. photographer,
mountain climber
Lichtenstein--Mach. p23-25

TAYLOR, ELIZABETH (1) (1932-)
English actress
Anderson--People p383-384, por.
Book--Lists (2) p250
Cur. Biog. '85 p407-411, por.
Edelson--Kids p87-89, por.
Hershey--Between p59,66,71,
100,123-124,127,129-130
Hirschhorn--Rating p358-359,
por.
McHenry--Liberty's p405-406
Manchel--Women p83,87,89,91,
94,98,100, por.
Mordden--Movie, see index p296
100--Greatest p14-15, por.
O'Neill--Women's p654,751-782
People--Best p110-111, por.
People's Almanac (2) p1155-1156
Shipman--Internatl. p569-573,
por.
Sochen--Herstory p364-367, por.
Webster's--Amer. p1022-1023
Woman's Almanac p354-355, por.
World--Who p250

TAYLOR, ELIZABETH (2)
Amer. rancher
Gray--Women p117
Sherr--American p142

TAYLOR, ELIZABETH COLES (1912-
1975)
English novelist, short-story
writer
Baker--Women p5
Seymour-Smith--Novels p225

TAYLOR, ELLA (c1868-)
Amer. centenarian

Mitchell--Yessir p109-112,
por.

TAYLOR, (IDA) ESTELLE (1899-
1958)
Amer. model, actress
Springer--They p237,332-333,
por.
World--Who p250

TAYLOR, EVA (1896-)
Amer. singer
Claghorn--Jazz p287

TAYLOR, FANNY (-1897)
Amer. belle
Peacock--Famous p118-122, por.

TAYLOR, GAY SMART
See HURNSCOT, LORAN, pseud.

TAYLOR, JANE (1783-1824)
English poet
Morley--Literary p81-82

TAYLOR, JEAN S. (fl. 1970's)
Amer. editor
Marzolf--Up p111,211-212

TAYLOR, JOAN (fl. 1970's)
Amer. bowler
McWhirter--Guinness p42

TAYLOR, JOANNE (fl. 1930's-
1940's)
Amer. radio retail advertiser
Women--Radio p12

TAYLOR, JULIET (c1945-)
Amer. casting director
Chinoy--Women p232-235, por.

TAYLOR, KATE (1949-)
Amer. singer, pianist
Claghorn--Biog. p432

TAYLOR, KOKO (1938-)
Amer. singer
Claghorn--Jazz p287

TAYLOR, LAURETTE COONEY
(1884-1946)
Amer. actress
James--Notable (3) p431-433
McHenry--Liberty's p406

TAYLOR, LILY ROSS (1886-1969)

Amer. classicist
Sicherman--Notable p677-678

TAYLOR, LISA (fl. 1970's)
Amer. TV producer
Klever--Women p27,64-65

TAYLOR, LUCY BEAMAN HOBBS
(1833-1910)
Amer. dentist
Bird--Enterprising p110-112
James--Notable (3) p433-435
McHenry--Liberty's p406-409
Macksey--Book p148-149
O'Neill--Women's p225
Reader's--Story p437
Sherr--American p184-185, por.
Warren--Pictorial p79
Woman's Almanac p32, por.

TAYLOR, MARGARET MACKAIL
SMITH (1788-1852)
Amer. first lady, wife of
Zachary Taylor
Melick--Wives p36
People's Almanac (1) p267
Woman's Almanac p487

TAYLOR, MARY (1817-1893)
New Zealander feminist,
writer
Moers--Literary p315

TAYLOR, PHOEBE ATTWOOD
(1909/1910-1976)
Amer. novelist
Seymour-Smith--Novels p225

TAYLOR, RACHEL ANNAND
(1876-)
Amer. poet
Bernikow--World p145

TAYLOR, ROSEMARY DRACHMAN
(1899-)
Amer. author
Ehrlich--Oxford p437

TAYLOR, RUTH ASHTON
Amer. TV news reporter
Scheuer--Tel. p478

TAYLOR, SALLY (fl. 1970's)
Amer. rancher, (llama
raiser)
O'Neill--Women's p17

TAYLOR, SARAH STROTHER (1760-
1822)
Amer., mother of Zachary
Taylor, noted Virginia mother
Amer.--Mothers p550
Faber--Presidents' p250-251

TAYLOR, STELLA (1929-)
Amer. swimmer
McWhirter--Guinness p146

TAYLOR, SUSIE KING (1848-1912)
Amer. Civil War nurse, camp
follower, slave, teacher
Hoople--As p97-99, por.
Kulkin--Her p280
Millstein--We p129

TAYLOR, WENDY (1945-)
English artist
Contemp. Brit., unp., por.

TAYLOR, WINIFRED
British detective
Macksey--Book p138

TCHERKASOVA, MARINA (1962-)
Russian ice skater
McWhirter--Guinness p99, por.

TCHERKASSKY, MARIANNA (1952-)
Amer. dancer
Cur. Biog. '85 p411-414, por.

TEASDALE, SARA (1884-1933)
Amer. poet
Bernikow--World p280-281
Claghorn--Biog. p433
Ehrlich--Oxford, see index p461
James--Notable (3) p435-436
McHenry--Liberty's p407
O'Neill--Women's p673-674
Sherr--American p133
Webster's--Amer. p1025
World--Who p21

TEASDALE, VERREE (1906-)
Amer. actress
Springer--They p237,333, por.

TEASLEY, MARIE WRIGHT (fl.
1940's-1970's)
Amer. newspaper editor
Innis--Profiles p176-177, por.

TEBALDI, RENATA (1922-)

Italian opera singer
Gammond--Illus. p251-252, por.
World--Who p80

TEEBAY, SUSAN (fl. 1970's)
Amer., defendant in
unusual law case
Felton--Famous p147

TEEPLES, MRS. C.A. (fl. 1870's-
1880's)
Amer. Western pioneer
Fischer--Let p94-100

TEERLINC, LEVINA (c1520-1576)
Flemish painter
Fine--Women p27-28
Harris--Women p19,25-26,42,
102-104,340
Petersen--Women p34
Tufts--Our p42-49, por.

TEJADO, RAQUEL
See WELCH, RAQUEL

TEKAKWITHA, KATERI (CATHER-
INE) (1656-1680)
Amer. Mohawk Indian, con-
vert to Catholicism
James--Notable (3) p436-437
McHenry--Liberty's p407
People's Almanac (1) p1300
Sherr--American p160
Signif.--Amer. p8, por.
Webster's--Amer. p1025-1026

TE KANAWA, KIRI (c1946-)
New Zealander opera singer
Cur. Biog. '78 p411-414, por.
People--Best p142, por.

TELKES, MARI(A) DE (1900-)
Hungarian engineer,
physical chemist
O'Neill--Women's p188-189,750

TELLES, LUCY TOM PARKER (fl.
1920's-1930's)
Amer. Indian basket-maker
Sherr--American p23

TELVA, MARION (1897-1962/1965)
Amer. opera singer
Claghorn--Biog. p433

TEMPEL, GUDRUN
German writer
Macksey--Book p193

TEMPEST, MARIE (MARY) SUSAN
ETHERINGTON, DAME (1864-
1942)
English actress
Entertainers p151-152, por.
Johns--Dames p41-56, por.
Jones--Rutledge p760
World--Who p261

TEMPLE, ALICE (1871-1946)
Amer. kindergarten educator
Snyder--Dauntless p187-229, por.

TEMPLE, LADY
See BOWDOIN, AUGUSTA, LADY
TEMPLE

TEMPLE, SHIRLEY
See BLACK, SHIRLEY TEMPLE

TEMPLETON, FAY (1865-1939)
Amer. actress, singer
Hazen--Interv. p98
James--Notable (3) p437-439
McHenry--Liberty's p408

TEMPLETON, LUCY CURTIS (fl.
1910's)
Amer. telegraph editor
Marzolf--Up p61-62

TEMPSKI, ARMINE VON
See VON TEMPSKI, ARMINE

TENELLA
See CLARKE, MARY BAYARD
DEVEREUX

TENNANT, EMMA (1937-)
English novelist
Seymour-Smith--Who's p361

TENNEY, TABITHA GILMAN (1762-
1837)
Amer. novelist
Ehrlich--Oxford p13
James--Notable (3) p439
Sherr--American p147

TENNILLE, TONY (1943-)
Amer. singer
Anderson--People p76-77, por.
World--Who p273

TENNYSON, EMILY SELLWOOD (1813-
1896)
English, wife of Alfred, Lord
Tennyson

Morley--Literary p112,114,
152

"TENTH MUSE"
See MUSIDORA

TEODORINI, ELENA (THEODORINI)
(1857-1926)
Rumanian singer
Partington--Who's p410, por.

TEPPERMAN, JEAN (1945-)
Amer. poet
Hymowitz--Hist. p309-310,319,
368
Pearson--Who p296

TERENTIA (fl. 1st Cent. B.C.)
Roman, wife of Cicero
Pomeroy--Godd. p205
Zinserling--Women p56

TERESA
See also THERESA

TERESA, FRANCES (1907-)
Amer. hospital worker
Gold--Until p61-75, por.

TERESA, MOTHER (1) (1910-)
Yugoslavian nun, missionary
Book--Lists (2) p18
Cur. Biog. '73 p403-406, por.
Jones--Rutledge p762
Macksey--Book p121, por.
O'Neill--Women's p40,389-390,
por.
Palmer--Who's p304
People--Best p84, por.
Woman's Almanac p405

TERESA, MOTHER (2) (c1766-1846)
Amer. religious
McHenry--Liberty's p408

TERESA DE CEPEDA Y AHUMADA
See THERESA OF AVILA

TERESA OF LISIEUX
See THERESE OF LISIEUX,
SAINT

TERESA SPAGNUOLA, pseud.
Spanish medical botanist,
writer
Mead--Hist. p431-432

TERESHKOVA-NIKOLAYEVA,

VALENTINA (VLADIMIROVNA)
(1937-)
Russian cosmonaut, aviatrix
Boase--Sky's p215
Kulkin--Her p281-282
Macksey--Book p243,251-252, por.
Mandel--Soviet p94-99,290,293,
por.
Oberg--Space p108-109
O'Conner--Sally p21
O'Neill--Women's p739-740, por.
Woman's Almanac p370-371, por.
World--Who p133

TERHUNE, MARY VIRGINIA HAWES
(1830-1922)
Amer. novelist, cook-book
author
Bolton--Success p90-109, por.
Ehrlich--Oxford, see index p461-
462
James--Notable (3) p439-441
McHenry--Liberty's p409

TERNAN, ELLEN
English, friend of Charles
Dickens
Morley--Literary p100,133-134,
221

TERRELL, GAIL
Amer. TV sales manager
Klever--Women p40-42,81,100,
109, por.

TERRELL, MARY ELIZA CHURCH
(1863-1954)
Amer. feminist, social reform-
er, civil rights leader, com-
poser, educator, author
Adams--Great (3rd) p119, por.
Claghorn--Biog. p434
Millstein--We p161-163,213-215
Papachristou--Women p121,123,
142-143, por.
Sicherman--Notable p678-680
Signif.--Amer. p55, por.
Sochen--Herstory p187-188,206-
207,229, por.
Toppin--Biog. p422-425
Woman's Almanac p390-391
World--Who p191

TERRELL, RHA
Amer. singer
Simon--Big p329-330, por.

TERRY, ADOLPHINA FLETCHER

(1881-)
Amer. politician, writer,
humanitarian, noted Arkansas
mother
Amer.--Mothers p46-47, por.

TERRY, ALICE (fl. 1920's-1930's)
Amer. actress, director
Slide--Early p114-115

TERRY, ELLEN ALICIA, DAME
(1847/1848-1928/1929)
English actress
Brecher--Lives p333-334, por.
Entertainers p136-137, por.
Findlater--Player p131-160, por.
Frey--1000 p272
Johns--Dames p7-16, por.
Jones--Rutledge p762
Kulkin--Her p282-283
Longford--Eminent p151-177,
por.
Morley--Literary p169-170,356
Who Did What p306, por.
World--Who p261

TERRY, LUCY (fl. 1740's)
Amer. slave, poet
DePauw--Found. p90-91
Williams--Demeter's p166-168

TERRY, MEGAN (1932-)
Amer. feminist, playwright
Chinoy--Women p131,285-292,
294, por.

TERRY, ROSE
See COOKE, ROSE TERRY

TESORO, GIULIANA (fl. 1970's)
Italian chemist, (polymer
expert)
O'Neill--Women's p168-169

TETRAULT, JEANNE (fl. 1970's)
Amer. homesteader, author
O'Neill--Women's p19

TETRAZZINI, LUISA, (MADAM
BAZELLI) (1871-1940)
Italian opera singer
Claghorn--Biog. p434
Dunlap--Calif. p202, por.
Jones--Rutledge p762
Macksey--Book p215
Neidle--America's p221
O'Neill--Women's p618

Tuggle--Golden p10-11, por.
World--Who p80

TETSUO, TAMAYO (1888-)
Japanese physician
Hellstedt--Women p30-32, por.

TEWKESBURY, JOAN (c1936-)
Amer. playwright, screen-
writer
O'Neill--Women's p670

TEWS, CHRISTY
Amer. mountain climber
Lichtenstein--Mach. p23-26

TEY, JOSEPHINE, pseud. (1897-
1952)
Scottish novelist, playwright
Avenel--Conp. (1) p338
Morley--Literary p461,463
Seymour-Smith--Novels p225-226
World--Who p48

TEYTE, MAGGIE, DAME (1888/1889-
1976)
English opera singer
Cur. Biog. '76 p477
Tuggle--Golden p149-150, por.

THADEN, LOUISE McPHETRIDGE
(1905/1906-)
Amer. aviatrix
Boase--Sky's p117
Genett--Aviation p115

THANE, ELSWYTH (1900-)
Amer. novelist, playwright
Ehrlich--Oxford p237,346

THANET, OCTAVE, pseud. (1850-
1934)
Amer. novelist
Ehrlich--Oxford, see index p462
James--Notable (1) p671-673
McHenry--Liberty's p142
Sherr--American p10

THARP, TWYLA (1941/1942-)
Amer. ballet dancer,
choreographer
Cur. Biog. '75 p401-404, por.
McHenry--Liberty's p409-410
100--Greatest (1) p25, por.
O'Neill--Women's p652
People--Best p139, por.
Percival--Modern p94-95,117, por.

Woman's Almanac p316
World--Who p72

THARPE, ROSETTA, SISTER
(1921-1973)
Amer. singer, guitarist
Claghorn--Biog. p435
Claghorn--Jazz p289-290
Simon--Best p570-571, por.

THATCHER, MARGARET HILDA
ROBERTS (1925-   )
English prime minister
Cur. Biog. '75 p404-407, por.
Jones--Rutledge p763
Macksey--Book p46
O'Neill--Women's p43,49-50
Palmer--Who's p305
People--Best p12, por.
Vallance--Women, see index p211

THAW, EVELYN NESBIT
See NESBIT, EVELYN

THAW, MRS. WILLIAM
Amer., mother of Harry
Thaw
Forma--They, see index p244,
por.

THAXTER, CELIA LAIGHTON (1835-
1894)
Amer. poet, noted New
Hampshire mother
Amer.--Mothers p364, por.
Ehrlich--Oxford p15,17, por.
James--Notable (3) p441-443
McHenry--Liberty's p410
Sherr--American p87,149

THEBOM, BLANCHE (1919-   )
Amer. opera singer
Claghorn--Biog. p435

THEODORA (508-548)
Byzantine (Roman) empress,
social reformer, hospital
founder, actress
Fry--1000 p58
Jones--Rutledge p764
Macksey--Book p93,105-106,
por.
Mead--Hist. p92

THEODORE, ATHENA
Amer. magazine editor,
sociologist, writer

Adams--Women p11-12,122,152-
153,172

THEODORIDES, ELENA
See TEODORINI, ELENA
(THEODORINI)

THEODOSIA, SAINT
Roman physician
Mead--Hist. p77-78

THERBUSCH, ANNA DOROTHEA
LISIEWSKA-
See LISIEWSKA-THERBUSCH,
ANNA DOROTHEA

THERESA
See TERESA

THERESA OF AVILA (1515-1582)
Spanish saint, social reformer,
poet, mystic
Bainton--Spain p47-64
Book--Lists (2) p447
Crovitz--Courage p25-45
Fry--1000 p133
Jones--Rutledge p762
Kulkin--Her p280-281
Mead--Hist. p355
Moers--Literary p123-124,128,
246,315-316
Who Did What p306
Woman's Almanac p402
World--Who p91

THERESA OF JESUS, SAINT
See THERESA OF AVILA

THERESA OF LISIEUX, SAINT
(1873-1897)
French nun
Green--Saints p104-105
Jones--Rutledge p765
Moers--Literary p246,316
Palmer--Who's p305

THESLEFF, ELLEN
Finnish painter
Sparrow--Women p292,314

THIBLE, MADAME (fl. 1780's)
French pioneer aeronaut,
balloon passenger
Macksey--Book p246

THIBODEAU, ANITA M. (fl. 1960's)
Amer. heroine, Carnegie

Medal winner
O'Neill--Women's p734

THIRKELL, ANGELA MARGARET
MACKAIL (1890-1961)
English novelist
Crosland--Beyond p88-94,129
Jones--Rutledge p765

THOBEN, PATRICIA JOAN (1933-
1977)
Amer. handicapped,
government official
O'Neill--Women's p119-120

THOBURN, HELEN (1885-1932)
Amer. hymnist
Claghorn--Biog. p435

THOBURN, ISABELLA (1840-1901)
Amer. missionary
James--Notable (3) p443-444
McHenry--Liberty's p410-411

THOMAS, ALMA W. (1891/1892-
1978)
Amer. painter, teacher
Munro--Originals p95,189-197,
por.
O'Neill--Women's p602-603

THOMAS, BETTY
Amer. actress
Scheuer--Tel. p478-479

THOMAS, CARLA (1942-)
Amer. singer
Claghorn--Biog. p435

THOMAS, CAROLYN GOLD HILL,
pseud. (fl. 1940's)
Amer. novelist
Ehrlich--Oxford p386

THOMAS, MRS. E. (fl. 1920's)
British motor-car racer
Macksey--Book p254

THOMAS, EDITH MATILDA (1854-
1925)
Amer. poet
Ehrlich--Oxford p158,296
James--Notable (3) p444-446
McHenry--Liberty's p411

THOMAS, EVELYN WARD
See ANTHONY, EVELYN, pseud.

THOMAS, HELEN (1920-)
Amer. journalist, (White
House correspondent)
Marzolf--Up p109-110
100--Greatest (1) p36-37, por.
O'Neill--Women's p450, por.
Woman's Almanac p264,274, por.

THOMAS, JANE BLACK (1720-)
Amer. patriot, Revolutionary
War heroine, noted South
Carolina mother
Amer.--Mothers p489
Meyer--Petticoat p210-211
Millstein--We p35

THOMAS, JEAN (1881-)
Amer. novelist
Ehrlich--Oxford p289

THOMAS, JEANETTE (fl. 1970's)
Amer. seal research worker,
(Antarctica), (wife of Douglas
De Master)
Land--New p11,123-134, por.

THOMAS, JUDY
Amer. TV newscaster
Gelfman--Women p58,119,146

THOMAS, LERA M. (1893-)
Amer. Congresswoman
Chamberlin--Min. p315-316

THOMAS, MARTHA CAREY (1857-
1935)
Amer. college president,
Quaker feminist, suffragist
Banner--Women p38-41,92-93
Burgess--Education p140-141
Clark--Leading p21-24
Coffin--Female p215-223, por.
Earnest--American p218-220
James--Notable (3) p446-450
McHenry--Liberty's p411
O'Neill--Women's p323,404
Sherr--American p198
Signif.--Amer. p35, por.
Webster's--Amer. p1031-1032
Woman's Almanac p156
World--Who p101

THOMAS, MARY FRAME MYERS
(1816-1888)
Amer. physician, suffragist,
editor
James--Notable (3) p450-451

THOMAS, MAUDE O. (fl. 1880's)
Amer. newspaperwoman,
pioneer
Sherr--American p189

THOMAS, MRS.
Amer. midwife
Mead--Hist p411

THOMAS, SHERRY
Amer. homesteader, author
O'Neill--Women's p19

THOMAS, TASHA (fl. 1970's)
Amer. musical record
producer
Innis--Profiles p38-39, por.

THOMAS, VIVIA (-1870)
Amer. male impersonator,
soldier
Sherr--American p189

THOMAS, WALTRAUD
German representative,
NATO conference
O'Neill--Women's p552

THOMPKINS, PAULINE
Amer. college president
O'Neill--Women's p409, por.

THOMPSON, ANNA WILMARTH
ICKES
See WILMARTH, MARY JANE
HAWES

THOMPSON, ANNE
Amer. lawyer, prosecutor
O'Neill--Women's p364

THOMPSON, BETTY A. (fl.
1950's-1970's)
Amer. lawyer
O'Neill--Women's p355

THOMPSON, CHRISTINA GERTRUDE
See MEYNELL, ALICE
CHRISTI(A)NA GERTRUDE
THOMPSON

THOMPSON, CLARA (MABEL)
(1893-1958)
Amer. psychiatrist, psychoanalyst
Sicherman--Notable p680-
683

THOMPSON, DOROTHY (1893-1961)
Amer. journalist, columnist,
foreign correspondent, news
bureau head
Clark--Leading p143-146
Ehrlich--Oxford, see index p462
McHenry--Liberty's p411-412
Macksey--Book p190
Marlowe--Great p277-282, por.
Marzolf--Up p54-56
O'Neill--Women's p443
Sherr--American p228
Sicherman--Notable p683-686
Sochen--Herstory p316-317,319,
344-345,347,353,357-358,360,
por.
Sochen--Movers p185-189,197
Warren--Pictorial p190
Webster's--Amer. p1034
Woman's Almanac p274-275, por.
World--Who p56

THOMPSON, ELIZA JANE TRIMBLE
("MOTHER") (1816-1905)
Amer. temperance worker,
social reformer
James--Notable (3) p451-452
Sherr--American p186

THOMPSON, ELIZABETH
See BUTLER, ELIZABETH
SOUTHERDEN THOMPSON,
LADY

THOMPSON, ELIZABETH ROWELL
(1821-1899)
Amer. philanthropist, social
reformer
James--Notable (3) p452-454

THOMPSON, ELSA KNIGHT (fl.
1950's-1970's)
Amer. radio broadcaster
O'Neill--Women's p710

THOMPSON, FLORA (1877-1947)
English novelist
Seymour-Smith--Novels p226

THOMPSON, FRANKLIN, pseud.
See EDMONDS, (SARAH) EMMA E.

THOMPSON, HANNAH
Amer.-Canadian, mother of
Robert N. Thompson
Kooiman--Silhouettes p124-133,
por.

THOMPSON, HELEN
Amer. author
Berkin--Women p328-333,340-341

THOMPSON, HELEN MULFORD
(1908-1974)
Amer. orchestra manager,
organization executive
Sicherman--Notable p686-688

THOMPSON, KATHERINE W.
(1910-)
Amer. genealogical researcher,
author
Meyer--Who's p201

THOMPSON, KAY (1911/1913-)
Amer. singer, entertainer,
author
McHenry--Liberty's p412
World--Who p21

THOMPSON, LEA (1945-)
Amer. TV news anchorwoman
Scheuer--Tel. p480

THOMPSON, LYDIA (1836-1908)
English actress, dancer,
manager
Chinoy--Women p88-92, por.
Entertainers p129

THOMPSON, MALVINA
Amer. secretary (to
Eleanor Roosevelt)
Daniels--Wash. p249,278-279

THOMPSON, MARGARET
British painter, (mural tile
panels)
Callen--Women p77

THOMPSON, MARTHA LUNN
Amer. heroine, Carnegie
Medal winner
O'Neill--Women's p734

THOMPSON, MARY (fl. 1960's)
Amer. child patent-holder
O'Neill--Women's p744

THOMPSON, MARY HARRIS
(1829-1895)
Amer. physician, surgeon,
lecturer
James--Notable (3) p454-455
O'Neill--Women's p204

THOMPSON, RUTH (1) (1887/1888-
1970)
Amer. attorney, Congress-
woman
Chamberlin--Min. p222-225

THOMPSON, RUTH (2) (fl. 1970's)
Amer. clergyman
Proctor--Women p35-37,69-73,80,
90-91,107

THOMPSON, SADA CAROLYN
(1929-)
Amer. actress
Cur. Biog. '73 p412-414, por.
Diamonstein--Open p413-416, por.
World--Who p251

THOMPSON, SARAH (fl. 1860's)
Amer. patriot
Ingraham--Album p30

THOMPSON, SUE (1926-)
Amer. singer, guitarist
Claghorn--Biog. p437

THOMPSON, SUSAN (fl. 1970's)
Amer. golfer
McWhirter--Guinness p79

THOMPSON, TERESA (c1952-)
Amer. child patent-holder
O'Neill--Women's p744

THOMPSON-CLEWRY, PAMELA (fl.
1960's-1970's)
African Sierre Leone University professor, scientist, home
economist
O'Neill--Women's p105

THOMS, ADAH B. SAMUELS (c1863-
1943)
Amer. pioneer nurse
James--Notable (3) p455-457
O'Neill--Women's p232, por.

THOMSON, MARY ANN (1834-1923)
English-Amer. hymnist
Claghorn--Biog. p437

THOMSON, MARY MOORE DABNEY
(1887-)
Amer., college president,
noted Ohio mother
Amer.--Mothers p430-431

THOMSON, PAT (fl. 1970's)
Amer. film editor
Smith--Movies p208-209,278

THOMSON, THYRA GODFREY
(1916-)
Amer. state government official, noted Wyoming mother
Amer.--Mothers p602, por.

THORBORG, KERSTIN (c1897-1970)
Swedish opera singer
Cur. Biog. '70 p471

THORN, LAURA SIMPSON (c1950-)
Amer. millionaire
Forbes--400 ('84) p150

THORNBURG, BETTY
See HUTTON, BETTY

THORNDIKE, ANNELIE (fl. 1950's-
1960's)
East German filmmaker
Smith--Movies p103

THORNDIKE, SYBIL, DAME
(1882-1976)
English actress
Entertainers p173-174
Findlater--Player p174-192, por.
Johns--Dames p24-40, por.
Jones--Rutledge p767
Priestley--Part. p147-149, por.
Who Did What p308
World--Who p261

THORNE, FLORENCE CALVERT
(1877-1973)
Amer. labor researcher,
editor
Sicherman Notable p688-689

THORNE, OLIVE
See MILLER, HARRIET MANN

THORNTON, LEE (fl. 1970's)
Amer. TV Washington
correspondent
Marzolf--Up p193-195

THORNTON, NAOMI (1935-)
Amer. actress, producer
Ruddick--Working p228-240,
347, por.

THORPE, ROSE ALMORA

HARTWICK (1850-1939)
Amer. poet, children's book
author
Ehrlich--Oxford p314,333,422
James--Notable (3) p457-458
McHenry--Liberty's p412-413
Sherr--American p119

THORSELL, ELISABETH (1945-)
Swedish genealogical researcher,
writer
Meyer--Who's p201

THORSSON, INGA (1915-)
Swedish foreign affairs
minister
O'Neill--Women's p53

THRALE, HESTER LYNCH SALUS-
BURY
See PIOZZI, HESTER LYNCH
THRALE SALUSBURY

THULIEZ, LOUISE
Belgian heroine
Macksey--Book p57

THULIN, INGRID (1929-)
Swedish actress
World--Who p261-262

THUMB, MRS. TOM
See STRATTON, (MERCY)
LAVINIA WARREN BUMPUS

THURBER, JEANETTE MEYERS
(1850-1946)
Amer. music patron
James--Notable (3) p458-459
McHenry--Liberty's p413

THURSBY, EMMA CECILIA (1857-
1931)
Amer. singer, teacher
Claghorn--Biog. p438
James--Notable (3) p459-461

THURSTON, JEAN MERRILL (1936-)
Amer. genealogical researcher,
writer
Meyer--Who's p201

THURSTON, MATILDA SMYRELL
CALDER (1875-1958)
Amer. missionary, educator
Sicherman--Notable p689-691

TIARKS, HENRIETTA (fl. 1950's)
English debutante
Keenan--Women p42-43,47, por.

TIBBETS, ELIZA (fl. 1870's)
Amer. orange tree donor
Sherr--American p17-18

TIBBETTS, IRENE LYONS (1883-
1973)
Amer. educator, poet, dancer,
noted Minnesota mother
Amer.--Mothers p291-292, por.

TIBBLES, SUSETTE ("BRIGHT
EYES") LA FLESCHE (1854-
1903)
Amer. Omaha Indian leader,
reformer, politician, author,
lecturer, painter, book
illustrator
Gray--Women p97-108
James--Notable (3) p461-462
Kulkin--Her p171-172
McHenry--Liberty's p231-232
Sherr--American p138, por.
Stein--Lives p167-169, por.
Time--Women p206-209, por.

TIBORS (c1130-)
French troubadour
Bogin--Women p81,162-163

TIBURTIUS, FRANZISKA (1843-
1927)
German educator
Macksey--Book p72

TICKEY, BERTHA (BLAZIN)
REAGAN (c1914-)
Amer. softball player
Hollander--100 p79-80, por.
O'Neill--Women's p569

TICKHILL, TERRY LEE (fl.
1960's-1970's)
Amer. student chemist
(Antarctica)
Land--New p21-22,47-48, por.

TIDBLAD, INGA (1901-1975)
Swedish actress
Entertainers p218, por.

TIDMARSH, CHRISTINE
English model
Keenan--Women p109,111, por.

TIEGS, CHERYL (1947-)
Amer. model, TV personality
Anderson--People p386
Cur. Biog. '82 p411-413, por.
People--Best p100, por.

TIERNAN, FRANCES CHRISTINE
FISHER (1846-1920)
Amer. novelist
James--Notable (3) p462-463
McHenry--Liberty's p414
Sherr--American p178,181

TIERNEY, GENE (1920-)
Amer. actress
Hirschhorn--Rating p361-362, por.
Lamparski--What. (5) p8-9, por.
Lamparski--What. (8) p280-281,
por.
Shipman--Internatl. p578-580,
por.
World--Who p251

TIETJENS, EUNICE (1884-1944)
Amer. poet
James--Notable (3) p463-465

TIGHE, MARY ANN (1948-)
Amer. TV executive
Scheuer--Tel. p481, por.

TIGHE, VIRGINIA
Amer. actress
People's Almanac (2) p1217-1219,
por.

TIKTINER, REBECCA (-c1550)
Polish book printer
Henry--Written p88-89,92-101

TILLER, KATHERINE (fl. 1970's)
Amer. political worker,
mountain woman
Kahn--Hill. p55-65, por.

TILLEY, MONIKA (fl. 1970's)
Austrian-Amer. fashion
designer (swimsuits)
O'Neill--Women's p248,260

TILLEY, VESTA, LADY DE FRECE
(1864-1952)
English actress
Entertainers p152
Jones--Rutledge p769

TILLSON, CHRISTIANA HOLMES

TOLSTOY, ALEXANDRA LVOVNA
(1884-1979)
Russian-Amer. social reformer,
lecturer, (daughter of Leo
Tolstoy)
Cur. Biog. '79 p474
Lamparski--What. (3) p88-89,
por.

TOLSTOY, MARYA NIKOLAYEVNA
VOLKONSKAYA (-1830)
Russian, mother of Leo Tol-
stoy
Diagram--Mothers p234-235, por.

TOLSTOY, SOPHIE BEHRS (1844-
1919)
Russian, wife of Leo Tolstoy
Moffat--Revel. p138-147

TOMALING, SUSAN
See SARANDON, SUSAN

TOMARA, SONIA (1897-)
Russian journalist
Marzolf--Up p70

TOMASIA, DE MATTEO DE
CASTRO ISIAE (fl. 14th
Cent.)
Italian surgeon
Mead--Hist. p278

TOMASZEWICZOWNA, ANNA (fl.
1870's-1890's)
Polish physician
Macksey--Book p150

TOMLIN, LILY (MARY JEAN)
(1937/1939-)
Amer. actress, comedienne
Anderson--People p388, por.
Bowman--Entertain. p4-11, por.
Cur. Biog. '73 p415-417, por.
Mordden--Movie p232,240-244,
280, por.
100--Greatest (1) p96, por.
O'Neill--Women's p662
Woman's Almanac p321-322, por.
World--Who p251

TOMPKINS, SALLY LOUISA (1833-
1916)
Amer. Civil War patriot,
Confederate Army nurse,
hospital founder
Bird--Enterprising p96
Hymowitz--Hist. p141

James--Notable (3) p471-472
McHenry--Liberty's p415
Macksey--Book p55,149
O'Neill--Women's p226
Scott--Southern p85
Sherr--American p236-237
Webster's--Amer. p1045
Wiley--Confed. p144-145, por.

TOMSUDEN, RUTH (fl. 1970's)
Amer. Navy captain
O'Neill--Women's p451

TONG, KAITY
Chinese-Amer. TV corres-
pondent, co-anchor
Scheuer--Tel. p483-484

TONKIN, MURIEL (1918-)
English genealogical research-
er, writer
Meyer--Who's p202

TONNA, CHARLOTTE ELIZABETH
BROWNE (1790-1846)
English novelist, memoir writer
Moers--Literary p24-26,38,316

TOOMBS, MRS. ROBERT (fl. 1860's)
Amer. Confederate, Civil War
heroine
Sherr--American p51

TOOMER, JEAN (1894-1967)
Amer. author
Ehrlich--Oxford p148

TOROREK, LILY (fl. 1970's)
Israeli fashion designer
O'Neill--Women's p257

TORERA, LA NIÑA (fl. 1970's)
Spanish bullfighter
O'Neill--Women's p744

TORRE, MARIE (1924-)
Amer. journalist, TV news-
caster, radio personality
Gelfman--Women p60
Klever--Women p32-34,72-73,
96-97, por.
Marzolf--Up p177
O'Neill--Women's p453

TORRE, SUSANA
Amer. architect
O'Neill--Women's p608

TORREY, MARY IDE (1817-1869)
Amer. hymnist
Claghorn--Biog. p441

TORSTENDOTTER, ELSA VIVECA
See LINDFORS, ELSA VIVECA
TORSTENSDOTTER

TORTULA
See TROTULA OF SALERNO
(DAME TROTT)

TOSCANO, CARMEN
Mexican-Amer. filmmaker,
Chicana writer
Fisher--Third p ix,317-318
Smith--Movies p131

TOSHCHAKOVA, DR. (fl. 1950's)
Russian anthropologist
Mandel--Soviet p189-191

TOSHIKO
See AKIYOSHI, TOSHIKO

TOTINO, ROSE (fl. 1950's-1970's)
Amer. executive
O'Neill--Women's p523

TOUISSANT, JEANNE
French jewelry designer
O'Neill--Women's p255

TOUPIN, MARIE
See DORION, MARIE

TOUREL, JENNIE (1910-1973)
Canadian opera singer
Claghorn--Biog. p441
Cur. Biog. '74 p471
Sicherman--Notable p694-695

TOURISCHEVA, LUDMILLA
(1952-)
Russian golfer, gymnast
McWhirter--Guinness p85-86,
por.
O'Neill--Women's p562
Woman's Almanac p424-425

TOUROFF, ELEANOR (1898-1972)
Amer. research criminologist
Webster's--Amer. p406 (under
Glueck, Sheldon),1047

TOUSSAINT, CHERYL (c1954-)
Amer. track and field athlete

Sabin--Women p43-60,
por.

TOVAR, INES HERNANDEZ (1947-)
Amer. Chicana writer, profes-
sor, editor, poet
Fisher--Third p ix,413

TOVELL, "BILLIE"
Amer. international marketing
specialist
O'Neill--Women's p25

TOVIM, SARAH BAT (fl. 1700's)
Jewish prayer-writer
Henry--Written p180-187,258

TOWLE, CHARLOTTE HELEN (1896-
1966)
Amer. social worker, educator
Sicherman--Notable p695-697

TOWLE, KATHERINE AMELIA
(1898-)
Amer. educator, university
dean, Marine officer
McHenry--Liberty's p415
O'Neill--Women's p536,538

TOWNE, LAURA MATILDA (1825-
1901)
Amer. educator
James--Notable (3) p472-474
McHenry--Liberty's p415-416
Sherr--American p212

TOWNSEND, CLAIRE (c1952-)
Amer. movie studio official
Adams--Women p41-42

TOWNSEND, CLAUDIA
Amer. White House press
secretary
O'Neill--Women's p81, por.

TOWNSEND, EDNA WAUGH (1908-)
Amer. genealogical researcher,
writer, editor
Meyer--Who's p203

TOWNSEND, MARION
See MARLOWE, MARION

TOWNSEND, MARJORIE RHODES
(c1930-)
Amer. electrical engineer,
government official

O'Neill--Women's p90,
190

TOWNSEND, MARY ASHLEY VAN
VOORHIS (c1832-1901)
Amer. poet, novelist
Ehrlich--Oxford p116,281

TOWNSEND, SALLY (1760-1842)
Amer. Revolutionary War
heroine, "teen-age" patriot
Clyne--Patriots p58-65
Meyer--Petticoat p142-144,146

TOYOTA, TRITIA
Amer. TV co-anchorwoman
Scheuer--Tel. p484

TRACY, CARRIE BROWN (-1942)
Amer., mother of Spencer
Tracy
Diagram--Mothers p236

TRACY, MARTHA (1876-1942)
Amer. physician, medical
college dean
James--Notable (3) p474-475

TRADER, ELLA KING NEWSOM
(1838-1919)
Amer. Confederate, Civil
War nurse, hospital ad-
ministrator
James--Notable (3) p475-476
Scott--Southern p86
Woman's--Almanac p455

TRADER, GEORGIA (AND
FLORENCE) (fl. 1910's)
Amer. philanthropists,
humanitarians
Sherr--American p184

"TRAFFORD, F.G."
See RIDDELL, CHARLOTTE
ELIZA LAWSON COWAN

TRAHEY, JANE
Amer. advertising executive
Lichtenstein--Mach. p242

TRAMBLEY, ESTELA PORTILLO
(1936-)
Amer. Chicana writer
Fisher--Third p ix,349

TRAPP, MARIA AUGUSTA VON

(1905-)
Austrian-Amer. singer
Cavanah--We p48-56
Neidle--America's p231
Woman's Almanac p305, por.
World--Who p273

TRAQUAIR, PHOEBE ANNA MOSS
(1852-1936)
British illuminator, calligrapher, bookbinder, mural
painter, embroiderer, metalworker, enameller
Callen--Women p122-123,185-186,
192,226, por.

TRASK, KATE ("KATRINA")
NICHOLS (1853-1922)
Amer. author, philanthropist
James--Notable (3) p476-478
McHenry--Liberty's p416

TRAUBEL, HELEN FRANCESCA
(1903-1972)
Amer. opera singer
Claghorn--Biog. p442
Cur. Biog. '72 p472
McHenry--Liberty's p416
Sicherman--Notable p697-699
Signif.--Amer. p54, por.
World--Who p73

TRAUTMANN, CLAUDINE (fl.
1970's)
French car driver
Macksey--Book p254
O'Neill--Women's p589

TRAVELL, JANET GAEME (1901-)
Amer. physician
O'Neill--Women's p210

TRAVERS, MARY ELLIN (1936/
1937-)
Amer. singer
Claghorn--Biog. p442
Simon--Best p460-462, por.

TREADWELL, SOPHIE (1890-1970)
Amer. playwright, journalist
Chinoy--Women p7,157-162, por.

TREADWIN, MRS. E.
British lacemaker
Callen--Women p140,142

TREGILLIS, HELEN COX (1944-)

Amer. genealogical researcher,
author
Meyer--Who's p203

TREMOILLE, MARY (MARIE) ANNE
URSINS DE LA
See URSINS, MARY (MARIE)
ANNE DE LA TREMOILLE

TREMULIA, JEAN (fl. 1970's)
Amer. florist
Seed--Saturday's p101-102, por.

"TRENT, HELEN"
See STEVENS, JULIE

TRETIAKOVA, OKTIABRINA
Russian hydraulic engineer
Mandel--Soviet p89,91

TREVILLE, ABIGAIL
See STONEMAN, ABIGAIL

TREVILLE, YVONNE DE (LE
GIERCE) (1881-1954)
Amer. singer
Claghorn--Biog. p442

TREVOR, CLAIRE (1909/1912-)
Amer. actress
Hirschhorn--Rating p366-367,
por.
Shipman--Gold. p542-544, por.
Springer--They p241,334, por.
World--Who p251

TRIAS, JENNIE
Amer. TV director
Scheuer--Tel. p485-486

TRICE, MARGUERITE GWYNNE
See GWYNNE, ANNE

TRICO, CATALINA (c1581-)
Netherlands-Amer. immigrant
Williams--Demeter's p51-52

TRIGERE, PAULINE (1912-)
French-Amer. fashion designer
McHenry--Liberty's p416-417
Neidle--America's p275-277, por.
O'Neill--Women's p242,247
Woman's Almanac p134-135

TRILLING, DIANA RUBIN (1905-)
Amer. author, literary critic
Cur. Biog. '79 p396-398, por.

TRIMIAR, MARIAN ("TYGER")
(1953-)
Amer. boxer
Woman's Almanac p442

TRINTIGNANT, NADINE MARQUAND
(fl. 1960's-1970's)
French editor, director
Smith--Movies p122

TRIOLET, ELSA (1896/1903-1970)
Russian-French novelist,
short-story writer
Crosland--Women p195,226-227

TRIPLETT, MARY (fl. 1860's)
Amer. Southern belle
DeLeon--Belles p147-148, por.
Peacock--Famous p230,235, por.

TRISTAN, FLORA (1803/1804-1844)
French writer, feminist,
socialist
Crosland--Women p28-29
Fine--Women p42
Moers--Literary p316-317, see
also index p335

TROCK, PAULA (1889-)
Danish weaver
O'Neill--Women's p270

TROCTA
See TROTULA OF SALERNO
(DAME TROTT)

TROEDSSON, INGEGERD (1929-)
Swedish deputy minister of
health, social affairs
O'Neill--Women's p53

TROISGROS, SIMONE (1904-)
French labor leader
O'Neill--Women's p321

TROLLOPE, FRANCES MILTON
(1780-1863)
English novelist
Avenel--Comp. (1) p528
Earnest--American p47,57-58,
67-68,71
Ehrlich--Oxford, see index p462
Longstreet--Queen p1-9,16-17,
26-27,103, por.
Moers--Literary p24,317
Morley--Literary p73,242
Neidle--America's p26,30,35
Warren--Pictorial p153

TROTMAN, LILA
Amer. religious worker
Kooiman--Cameos p111-125, por.

TROTMAN, MARY
Amer. aviatrix, army flier
Keil--Those p128-129

TROTT, DAME (TROTTA)
See TROTULA OF SALERNO
(DAME TROTT)

TROTT, EDNA RUBY LOUISE
(1920-)
Amer. teacher of exceptional
children, noted Maryland
mother
Amer.--Mothers p255-256

TROTTA, LIZ (ELIZABETH)
(1937-)
Amer. TV reporter, war
correspondent
Marzolf--Up p168,171,173,175,
193
O'Neill--Women's p501-502
Scheuer--Tel p486

TROTTER, CATHERINE (1679-
1749)
English playwright, author
Horner--English p7-8, also note

TROTULA OF SALERNO (DAME
TROTT) (fl. 11th cent.)
Italian physician, (gynecolo-
gist, obstetrician)
Macksey--Book p63,141
Marks--Women p44-47, por.
Mead--Hist. p119,127-152

TROUBETZKOY, AMELIE FRANCES
RIVES, PRINCESS
See RIVES, AMELIE LOUISE,
PRINCESS TROUBETZKOY

TROUP, AUGUSTA LEWIS (c1848-
1920)
Amer. labor leader, journalist
Hymowitz--Hist. p136
James--Notable (3) p478-479
O'Neill--Women's p294
Sherr--American p32-33
Warren--Pictorial p143
Woman's Almanac p177

TROUTMAN, JOANNA (-1880)

Amer. designer of Texas flag
Sherr--American p49,220, por.

TROY, ANN
Amer. historian, museum
director
Sherr--American p153

TROY, DOROTHY & HELEN (fl.
1930's)
Amer., Alaskan daughters of
governor
Jones--Women (1) p176-178

TROYANOS, TATIANA (1938-)
Amer. opera singer
Cur. Biog. '79 p398-402, por.
Gammond--Illus. p252, por.

TRUDEAU, MARGARET JOAN
SINCLAIR (1948-)
Canadian, wife of Prime
Minister Pierre Trudeau
Anderson--People p390
People--Best p28-29, por.

TRUITT, ANNE (1921-)
Amer. sculptor
Munro--Originals p314-324, por.

TRUMAN, BESS (ELIZABETH) WAL-
LACE (1885-1982)
Amer. first lady, wife of
Harry S. Truman
Cur. Biog. '83 p475
Melick--Wives p74-75, por.
Miller--Fishbait p188,337
100--Greatest (1) p92, por.
People's Almanac (1) p302-303
Woman's Almanac p492

TRUMAN, (MARY) MARGARET
(1924-)
Amer. singer, author, daughter of President Truman
Claghorn--Biog. p443
100--Greatest (1) p92, por.
People's Almanac (1) p303

TRUMAN, MARTHA ELLEN YOUNG
(1852-1947)
Amer., mother of President
Truman, noted Missouri
mother
Amer.--Mothers p311, por.
Faber--President's p82,
por.

TRUMBULL, FAITH ROBINSON
(1718-1780)
Amer. Revolutionary War
patriot, noted Connecticut
mother
Amer.--Mothers p75
Clyne--Patriots p132,136
Earle--Two Cent. (1) p262-263
Meyer--Petticoat p141, por.
Sherr--American p32
Somerville--Women p40-41

TRUMP, ROSEMARY (1944-)
Amer. labor union leader
O'Neill--Women's p306,315

TRUTH, SOJOURNER (1797-1883)
Amer. abolitionist, feminist,
clergyman, noted Michigan
mother
Adams--Great (3rd) p33, por.
Amer.--Mothers p274, por.
Bloom--Religion p126
Gilfond--Heroines p49-52, por.
Gurko--Ladies p139,207,214-215
Ingraham--Album p24-25, por.
James--Notable (3) p479-481
Kulkin--Her p284-286
Levenson--Women p10-12,15,
por.
McHenry--Liberty's p417
Macksey--Book p112
Millstein--We p101-102,116-117,
por.
Papachristou--Women p35-36,
por.
People's Almanac (2) p158-159
Reader's--Story p432
Reifert--Women p70-72
Sherr--American p115-116, por.
Signif.--Amer. p14, por.
Taylor--Gener. p11-12, por.
Toppin--Biog. p425-427
Warren--Pictorial p87-88, por.
Webster's--Amer. p1054
Woman's Almanac p547, por.
World--Who p191

TRUXTON, BETTY
Amer. army nurse, religious
worker
Kooiman--Cameos p137-148, por.

TRYFOROS, LYNNE (c1943-)
Amer., friend of Dr. Herman
Tarnower (Scarsdale Diet
physician)
People--Best p76, por.

TS' AO MIAO-CH'ING (fl. 14th
Cent.)
Chinese poet, calligrapher,
painter
Petersen--Women p155

TS'AO TAKU
See PAN CHAO

TSENG, YU-HO (1923-)
Chinese painter
Munsterberg--Hist. p81-83

TSE-TUNG, MADAME MAO
See CHIANG CHING

TSIN, KING (-1907)
Chinese feminist
Taylor--Gener. p16

TUAL, DENISE PIAZZA (fl. 1920's-
1930's)
French film editor, director
Smith--Movies p119

TUBBS, ALICE IVERS (c1851-1930)
English-Amer. gambler
Sherr--American p215, por.

TUBMAN, HARRIET ROSS (1820/
1826-1913)
Amer. abolitionist, liberator
Adams--Great (3rd) p32, por.
Brin--Social p7-29, por.
Gilfond--Heroines p41-48, por.
Hymowitz--Hist. p58-60,142-143,
por.
Ingraham--Album p24-25, por.
James--Notable (3) p481-483
Kulkin--Her p286-288
McHenry--Liberty's p417-418
Macksey--Book p54-55,112, por.
Marlowe--Great p69-73, por.
Miller--Women p83-114
Millstein--We p100-101,122-123,
por.
Nies--Seven p33-59
Pederson--Leaders p116, por.
Reader's--Story p432
Reifert--Women p40-49
Sherr--American p158
Signif.--Amer. p24, por.
Sochen--Herstory p165-166,189,
249, por.
Stoddard--Famous p421-430, por.
Toppin--Biog. p427-431
Warren--Pictorial p86-87, por.
Webster's--Amer. p1055

Woman's Almanac p454, por.
World--Who p192

TUCHMAN, BARBARA MAYER
WERTHEIM (1912-)
Amer. historian, journalist
Bowman--Social p20-23, por.
McHenry--Liberty's p418
O'Neill--Women's p81,327-328,418
Signif.--Amer. p76, por.
World--Who p98

TUCHMAN, JESSICA
Amer. government official,
presidential advisor
O'Neill--Women's p81-82

TUCHOK, WANDA
Amer. film writer
Smith--Movies p15, por.

TUCHOLLA, KÄTHE SCHEFFLER
(1910-1943)
German, Fascist victim,
hockey player
Partington--Who's p421-422

TUCKAMONY, PEG (fl. 1700's)
Amer. Indian basket-maker
Sherr--American p201

TUCKER, ANNE (fl. 1970's)
Amer. photographer
Women's--Female p72

TUCKER, CHARLOTTE MARIA
(1825-1893)
English religious book writer
Showalter--Lit. p328

TUCKER, GERTRUDE (fl. 1860's)
Amer. Southern belle
DeLeon--Belles p239, por.

TUCKER, JENNIFER M. (fl.
1970's)
Amer. Army officer
O'Neill--Women's p546

TUCKER, JULIA (c1939-)
Amer. policewoman
O'Neill--Women's p374-375

TUCKER, MARCIA (fl. 1970's)
Amer. museum association
curator
Women's--Female p120

TUCKER, SOPHIE KALISH (1884-
1966)
Russian-Amer. singer, enter-
tainer
Claghorn--Biog. p444
McHenry--Liberty's p418-419
O'Neill--Women's p625
Sicherman--Notable p699-700
Simon--Best p576-577, por.
Springer--They p241-242,334,
por.
Webster's--Amer. p1055-1056
Woman's Almanac p305-306, por.
World--Who p273

TUCKER, TANYA (1938-)
Amer. singer
Dew--Women p122-149, por.
Glassman--Year '79 p162, por.

TUFNELL, MERIEL (fl. 1970's)
English jockey
Macksey--Book p260
McWhirter--Guinness p93

TUFTY, BARBARA (fl. 1940's-
1970's)
Amer. author
O'Neill--Women's p143

TUFTY, ESTHER VAN WAGONER
Amer. journalist
O'Neill--Women's p446-447

TULA, DONA
See BARCELO, GERTRUDIS

TULES, DONA (-1852)
Amer. gambling house opera-
tor, patriot
Sherr--American p156

TULEY, CATHY (1950-)
Amer. feminist, labor union
worker
Seifer--Nobody p218-255, por.

TULLIA (79-45 B.C.)
Roman, daughter of Cicero
Pomeroy--Godd. p157-158

TULLY, ALICE (1902-)
Amer. music patron
Cur. Biog. '84 p403-406, por.

TULLY, GRACE (1900-)
Amer., employee of FDR

Daniels--Wash., see index
p369, por.

TULLY, MARY JEAN (fl. 1970's)
Amer. feminist, president
NOW
O'Neill--Women's p707

TURBEVILLE, SARAH (fl. 1700's)
English oculist
Mead--Hist. p400

TRUECK, ROSALYN (1914-   )
Amer. pianist, harpsichord-
ist, conductor, teacher,
author
LePage--Women p241-255, por.
O'Neill--Women's p632

TURELL (TURRELL), JANE COL-
MAN (1708-1735)
Amer. poet
James--Notable (3) p483-484
Williams--Demeter's p213-214

TURFREY, MARY (fl. 1700's)
Amer. teacher
Williams--Demeter's p176

"TURIA" (THURIA) (fl. 1st Cent.
B.C.)
Roman matron
Pomeroy--Godd. p158-159,161

TURISCHEVA, LUDMIL(L)A
(1952-   )
Russian gymnast
Assoc. Press--Pursuit p316,333
World--Who p223

TURK, MARION G. (1914-   )
Amer. genealogical researcher,
writer
Meyer--Who's p203

TURNBO-MALONE, ANNIE MINERVA
ESTELLE (1869-1957)
Amer. social service director,
philanthropist
Innis--Profiles p166-167, por.
Sicherman--Notable p700-702

TURNBULL, AGNES SLIGH (1888-
1982)
Amer. novelist
Ehrlich--Oxford p199, por.

TURNBULL, EDITH
British bagpipe player, major
Macksey--Book p220-221

TURNBULL, JULIA ANNA (1822-
1887)
Canadian-Amer. ballet dancer
James--Notable (3) p484-485

TURNER, CHARLOTTE
See SMITH, CHARLOTTE TURNER

TURNER, DORIS
Amer. labor leader
O'Neill--Women's p301,315

TURNER, ELIZA L. SPROAT RAN-
DOLPH (1826-1903)
Amer. author, suffragist,
woman's club leader
James--Notable (3) p485-486

TURNER, FLORENCE E. (1888/
1900-1946)
Amer. actress, producer,
director
James--Notable (3) p486-487
McHenry--Liberty's p419
Macksey--Book p233
Slide--Early p103

TURNER, HELEN NEWTON
Australian physician, geneti-
cist
O'Neill--Women's p42

TURNER, JULIA JEAN
See TURNER, LANA (JULIA
JEAN)

TURNER, KERENHAPPUCH (fl.
1780's)
Amer. war heroine, nurse
Sherr--American p179

TURNER, L. PATTON (1912-   )
Amer. genealogical researcher,
writer
Meyer--Who's p204

TURNER, LANA (JULIA JEAN)
(c1920-   )
Amer. actress
Book--Lists (2) p190, por.
Dunlap--Calif. p207, por.
Hirschhorn--Rating p367-368, por.

Mordden--Movies p195
Shipman--Gold. p544-547, por.
Springer--They p242,334, por.
Woman's Almanac p355
World--Who p251

TURNER, SHIRLEY J. (fl. 1950's)
Amer. genealogical researcher,
writer
Meyer--Who's p204

TURNER, TINA (ANNIE MAE)
BULLOCK (1938-)
Amer. singer
Claghorn--Biog. p445
Cur. Biog. '84 p410-413, por.
Simon--Best p578-579, por.
World--Who p273-274

TURPEINEN, KAISA (1911-)
Finnish physician
Hellstedt--Women p407-409, por.

TURPIN, ELLA WHEELER (1876-)
Amer. community worker,
painter, educator, noted
Montana mother
Amer.--Mothers p324, por.

TURRALL, JENNY
Australian swimmer
Hollander--100 p85-86, por.

TUSHINGHAM, RITA (1942-)
English actress
World--Who p262

TUSSAUD, MARIE GROSHOLTZ,
MADAME (1760-1850)
Swiss waxworks founder
Brecher--Lives p140
Jones--Rutledge p782
Macksey--Book p202

TUTHILL, LOUISA CAROLINE
HUGGINS (1798/1799-1879)
Amer. author
James--Notable (3) p487-488

TUTIN, DOROTHY (1930-)
English actress
Entertainers p278

TUTTIET, MARY GLEED
See GRAY, MAXWELL

TUTTLE, JULIA DE FOREST

STURTEVANT (fl. 1870's)
Amer. landowner, town pro-
moter
Sherr--American p44

TUTWILER, JULIA STRUDWICK
(1841-1916)
Amer. educator, prison re-
former, poet, college founder
James--Notable (3) p488-490
McIlenry--Liberty's p419
Scott--Southern p113,116-117,148
Sherr--American p2-3

TUUMI, RAIJA (1923-)
Finnish designer
O'Neill--Women's p275

TUVE, IDA MARIE LASEN (1872-)
Amer. educator, noted South
Dakota mother
Amer.--Mothers p496-497

TUVE, ROSEMOND (1903-1964)
Amer. literary scholar, teacher
Sicherman--Notable p702-703

TUVIM, JUDITH
See HOLLIDAY, JUDY

TVERDYANSKAYA, LIKIYA
Russian artist
Macksey--Book p208

TWEED, BLANCHE OELRICHS
THOMAS BARRYMORE
See STRANGE, MICHAEL

TWEEDIE, MRS. ALEC (1866-1940)
English writer, traveller
Hamalian--Ladies p57-69

TWELVETREES, HELEN JURGENS
(1907-1958)
Amer. actress
Springer--They p242,334, por.

"TWIGGY" (1949-)
English model
Keenan--Women p149-151,153-
155,202, por.
Woman's Almanac p135
World--Who p301

TWINNING, LOUISA(E) (1820-1911)
British social reformer,
archaeologist
Macksey--Book p114

TYLER, ADELINE BLANCHARD,
SISTER (1805-1875)
Amer. nurse, deaconess,
Civil War hospital adminis-
trator
James--Notable (3) p491-493

TYLER, ALICE SARAH (1859-1944)
Amer. librarian, educator
James--Notable (3) p493-494

TYLER, ANNE (1941-)
Amer. author
Cur. Biog. '81 p430-434, por.

TYLER, ARMIRA WILSON (1780-1856)
Amer. patriot
Earle--Two Cent. (2) p xvi, por.

TYLER, JULIA GARDINER (1820-
1889)
Amer. first lady, (second
wife of John Tyler)
James--Notable (3) p494-496
Melick--Wives p32-33, por.
People's Almanac (1) p266
Sherr--American p172
Woman's Almanac p488

TYLER, LETITIA CHRISTIAN
(1790-1842)
Amer. first lady, (first wife
of President Tyler)
James--Notable (3) p496-497
Melick--Wives p31, por.
People's Almanac (1) 266
Woman's Almanac p488

TYLER, MARY ARMISTEAD (1761-1797)
Amer., mother of John Tyler,
noted Virginia mother
Amer.--Mothers p550
Faber--Presidents' p254-255

TYLER, PRISCILLA COOPER
(1816-1889)
Amer. actress, White House
hostess
James--Notable (3) p497-498

TYLER-ODAM, DOROTHY (fl. 1930's)
British track and field
athlete
Assoc. Press--Pursuit p155,172

TYNAN, KATHERINE JOAN (1861-
1931)
Irish poet, novelist

Showalter--Lit. p341

TYNELL, HELIN HELENA (1918-)
Finnish potter, designer
O'Neill--Women's p275

TYNES, MARY "MOLLY" ELIZABETH
(fl. 1860's)
Amer. Civil War heroine
Sherr--American p235,239

TYÖLÄJÄRVI, PIRKKO ANNIKKI
(1938-)
Finnish minister of social
affairs and health
O'Neill--Women's p58-59

"TYPHOID MARY"
See MALLON, MARY

TYSHKYEVICH, TAMARA (fl. 1950's)
Russian track and field athlete
McWhirter--Guinness p178, por.

TYSON, CICELY (c1939-)
Amer. actress, model
Abdul--Famous p118-124, por.
Bowman--Entertain. p24-31, por.
Cur. Biog. '75 p422-425, por.
Keenan--Women p175-176,178, por.
Manchel--Women p108-109,112-114,
por.
O'Neill--Women's p662
Woman's Almanac p355
World--Who p251

TYUS, WYOMIA (1945-)
Amer. track and field athlete
Hollander--100 p129-130, por.
McWhirter--Guinness p165, por.
Ryan--Sports p132
Stambler--Women p71-83, por.
Woman's Almanac p428
World--Who p223

TZ'U-HSI (TZE-HSI, YEHONALA)
(1834-1908)
Chinese dowager empress,
painter
Jones--Rutledge p784
Macksey--Book p33-34, por.
Palmer--Who's p313
Petersen--Women p160,162-163

U

UBALDINA OF PISA, SISTER (fl.
12th Cent.)

Italian nurse
Mead--Hist. p169

UCCELLO, ANN
Amer. mayor, politician
Ingraham--Album p68,
por.

UDALTSOVA, NADEZHDA
ANDREEVNA (1885-1961)
Russian artist
Harris--Women p297-298

UDEL (ODELL)
Polish, Jewish Hasidic
woman, duaghter of Baal
Shem
Henry--Written p209

UELAND, CLARA HAMPSON
(1860-1927)
Amer. suffragist, civic
reformer, kindergarten
founder
James--Notable (3) p498-499
Sherr--American p122

UEMURA, TAMAKI (fl. 1940's)
Japanese clergyman
O'Neill--Women's p380

UGGAMS, LESLIE (1943-)
Amer. singer
Claghorn--Biog. p447
World--Who p274

UHL, ALICE (fl. 1890's)
Amer. music club founder,
builder
Sherr--American p118, por.

UHNAK, DOROTHY (1930/1933-)
Amer. policewoman, novelist
Seymour-Smith--Novels p229
World--Who p48

UJLAKI-REJITO, ILDIKO (1937-)
Hungarian fencer
McWhirter--Guinness p59

ULANOVA, GALINA SERGEYEVNA
(1908/1912-)
Russian ballet dancer
Jones--Rutledge p785
Macksey--Book p235
O'Neill--Women's p639-640,643
Who Did What p313
World--Who p80

ULANOVA, LYUBOV
Russian aviatrix, jet airline
pilot
Macksey--Book p251

ULLMANN, LIV JOHANNE (1939-)
Norwegian actress
Cur. Biog. '73 p420-423, por.
O'Neill--Women's p661
Shipman--Internatl. p588-591,
por.
Woman's Almanac p355
World--Who p262

ULLYOT, JOAN
Amer. physician, researcher,
marathon runner
Adams--Women p160,163-164,177
Lichtenstein--Mach. p36-37,196

ULRIC, LENORE (1892/1894-1970)
Amer. actress
Springer--They p246,334-335,
por.

ULRICHA DE FOSCHUA
German oculist
Mead--Hist. p272

UMEKI, MIYOSHI (1929/1930-)
Japanese-Amer. actress,
singer
World--Who p251

UNDERHILL, RUTH MURRAY (1884-
1984)
Amer. anthropologist, educator,
Indian authority, author
Cur. Biog. '84 p480

UNDERWOOD, AGNESS ("AGGIE")
MAY WILSON (1902-)
Amer. newspaper editor
Marzolf--Up p53
O'Neill--Women's p451

UNDERWOOD, LILLIES STIRLING
HORTON (1851-1921)
Amer. physician
James--Notable (3) p499-501

UNDSET, SIGRID (1882-1949)
Norwegian novelist
Cavanah--We p81-87
Jones--Rutledge p786
Kronenberger--Atlan. p817
Macksey--Book p189-190
Magill--Cycl. p1100-1102

Moers--Literary p92,231,317
O'Neill--Women's p673
Opfell--Lady p94-106, por.
People's Almanac (2) p1012
Seymour-Smith--Novels p229
Woman's Almanac p260-261
World--Who p44

UNGERELEIDER, JOY
Amer. museum director
O'Neill--Women's p615

UNTERMEYER, JEAN STARR (1886-
1970)
Amer. poet
Ehrlich--Oxford p308

UNWIN, MARY (1724-1796)
English nurse
Morley--Literary p71,148-149,
295-298

UNZER, JOHANNA CHARLOTTE
OF ALTONA (1724-1782)
German scientific writer
Mead--Hist. p502

UPTON, HARRIET TAYLOR (1853-
1945)
Amer. politician, author,
feminist
James--Notable (3) p501-502

URBACH, LILY (fl. 1970's)
Amer. printmaker, graphic
artist
Women's--Female p155

URRACA OF PORTUGAL (fl. 13th
Cent.)
Portuguese hospital
philanthropist
Mead--Hist. p176,219

URRY, MICHELLE
Amer. magazine executive
Adams--Women p24,87,101-103,
107,129-132,158,176

URSINS, MARY (MARIE) ANNE DE
LA TREMOILLE (1642-1722)
French painter
Macksey--Book p27

URSO, CAMILLA (1842-1902)
French-Amer. violinist
Claghorn--Biog. p447

James--Notable (3) p502-503
McHenry--Liberty's p421
Neuls-Bates--Women p198-201

URSULA OF MÜNSTERBERG (1491/
1495-after 1534)
German nun
Bainton--Germany p45-53

URZICEANU, AURA
See LEE, AURA

USHAKOVA, YELIZVETA (fl. 1940's)
Russian rural economist
Macksey--Book p167

USTOVOLSĶAYA, GALINA
Russian composer
Macksey--Book p221, por.

UTLEY, FREDA (1898-1978)
English-Amer. journalist,
author, lecturer
Cur. Biog. '78 p477

V

VACANI, MADAME (fl. 1910's-
1940's)
English dancing teacher
Keenan--Women p38,42, por.

VĂCĂRESCU, HELENE (1866-1947)
Rumanian poet, novelist
Macksey--Book p189

VACCARO, BRENDA (1939-)
Amer. actress
World--Who p251

"VAGUE, VERA"
See ALLEN, BARBARA JO

VAIL, MARGE (fl. 1920's-1930's)
Amer. radio actress
Lamparski--What. (3) p130-131,
por.

VAIL, MYRTLE (1888-)
Amer. radio actress
Lamparski--What. (3) p130-131,
por.

VALADON, SUZANNE (1865-1940)
French model, painter
Bachtold--Gifted p31-34
Book--Lists (1) p192-193
Fine--Women p136-140

Haftmann--Paint. (1) p423
Harris--Women p259-261,354
Munsterberg--Hist. p65-66,115-116
O'Neill--Women's p596,598
Parker--Old p121-123, (fig. 73),
   por.
Petersen--Women p95-97, por.
Tufts--Our p169-177, por.
Women's--Female p14

VALDA, GUILIA (1855-1925)
   Amer. singer
   Claghorn--Biog. p449

VALDEZ, ADELIA RIVERA DE
   (1874-)
   Amer. agricultural worker,
   noted Colorado mother
   Amer.--Mothers p65, por.

VALENTE, CATERINA (1932-)
   French-German singer
   World--Who p274

VALENTE, RENEE
   Amer. TV film producer
   Scheuer--Tel. p491

VALENTINA (1904-)
   Russian-Amer. fashion
   designer
   O'Neill--Women's p242-243

VALENTINE, ANNA MARIE
   BOOKPRINTER (1863-1947)
   Amer. ceramicist
   Callen--Women p226

VALENTINE, CARLA
   Amer. film editor, art
   director
   Smith--Movies p209-210

VALENTINE, HELEN
   Amer. magazine founder,
   editor
   O'Neill--Women's p475

VALENTINE, LILA HARDAWAY
   MEADE (1865-1921)
   Amer. educational reformer,
   suffragist
   James--Notable (3) p504-505
   Sherr--American p238

VALERIA (fl. 138-78 B.C.)
   Roman, wife of Sulla

Pomeroty--Godd. p157

VALIAN, VIRGINIA (1942-)
   Amer. psychology professor
   Ruddick--Working p162-178,347,
   por.

VALITON, MARY RAE (1863-1946)
   Amer. pioneer, dormitory
   matron, noted Montana mother
   Amer. Mothers p322, por.

VALLAYER-COSTER, ANNE (1744-1818)
   French painter
   Fine--Women p45
   Harris--Women p32,35,41-43,82,
   152,179-184,197,346-347
   Petersen--Women p58-60, por.
   Women's--Female p14

VALLE, INGER LOUISE ANDVIG
   (fl. 1970's)
   Norwegian minister of
   consumer affairs, justice
   O'Neill--Women's p58

VALLEJO, ISABEL ARR (fl. 1940's)
   Paraguayan diplomat
   O'Neill--Women's p63

VALLERIA, ALWINA (1848-1925)
   Amer. singer
   Claghorn--Biog. p449

VALLI, ALIDA (1921-)
   Italian actress
   Shipman--Internatl. p593-597, por.

VALOIS, ISABELLA OF
   See ISABELLA OF VALOIS

VALOIS, NINETTE DE
   See DE VALOIS, NINETTE (2),
   DAME

"VAMPIRA"
   See NURMI, MAILA

VAN AKEN, CAROL G. (fl. 1960's)
   Amer. science & engineering
   specialist
   M.I.T.--Women p v-vii,x

VAN ALSTYNE, FRANCES
   See CROSBY, FRANCES ("FAN-
   NY") JANE

VAN ALSTYNE, NANCY (1733/

1738-)
Amer. colonial Indian fighter,
patriot, "Patriot Mother" of
Mohawk Valley, Revolutionary
War heroine
DePauw--Found. p194
Meyer--Petticoat p112-114

VAN BEUREN, HOPE HILL (c1934-)
Amer. millionaire
Forbes--400 ('84) p82

VAN BLARCOM, CAROLYN
CONANT (1879-1960)
Amer. nurse, midwife
Sicherman--Notable p703-704

VAN BOSSE, MARIE PHILIPPINE,
MADAME
See BILDERS, MARIE PHILIPPINE
VAN BOSSE, MADAME

VAN BRUGH, IRENE, DAME (1872-
1949)
English actress
Johns--Dames p57-65, por.

VAN BUREN, ABIGAIL ("ABBY"),
pseud. (1918-)
Amer. columnist
Anderson--People p396
100--Greatest (1) p44, por.
O'Neill--Women's p452-453
Woman's Almanac p278-279, por.
World--Who p56

VAN BUREN, HANNAH HOES
(1783-1819)
Amer. first lady, wife of
Martin Van Buren
James--Notable (3) p505-506
Melick--Wives p29, por.
Woman's Almanac p487

VAN BUREN, MARIA (MARY)
HOES VAN ALEN (1747-1818)
Amer., mother of President
Van Buren
Faber--Presidents' p257-259

VANCE, CLARA
See DENISON, MARY ANN
ANDREWS

VANCE, ELEANOR P. (fl. 1900's)
Amer. weaver
O'Neill--Women's p123-124

VANCE, NINA (c1914-1980)
Amer. director, producer
Chinoy--Women p220-221

VANCE, VIVIAN (1912-1979)
Amer. actress
World--Who p251

VAN CLEVE, CHARLOTTE CLARK
(1819-1907)
Amer. pioneer, humanitarian,
noted Minnesota mother
Amer.--Mothers p287-288, por.

VAN CLEVE, RUTH G. (fl. 1970's)
Amer. lawyer, government
official
O'Neill--Women's p84,88

VAN CORTLANDT, MARI
See VAN RENNSELAER, MARI
VAN CORTLANDT

VAN COTT, MARGARET ("MAGGIE")
ANN NEWTON (1830-1914)
Amer. clergyman, evangelist
James--Notable (3) p506-507
Welter--Dimity p93

VANDEGRIFT, MARY HUDSON (fl.
1930's)
Amer. founder, gasoline
marketing company
O'Neill--Women's p514

VAN DEMAN, ESTHER BOISE
(1862-1937)
Amer. archaeologist
McHenry--Liberty's p422

VAN DE MEER, ANNE (fl. 1970's)
Netherlands track and field
athlete
McWhirter--Guinness p182

VANDERBILT, ALVA ERTSKIN
SMITH BELMONT HAZARD
(1853-1933)
Amer. socialite, suffragist,
politician, feminist, philan-
thropist
Brandon--Dollar p52-55,58,60-
62,158
Clark--Leading p59-60
Forma--They p50-52,132,152,209,
por.
Hymowitz--Hist. p251,281

VAN HOOSEN, BERTHA (1863-1952)
Amer. feminist, obstetrician,
physician, surgeon
O'Neill--Women's p213
Sicherman--Notable p706-707

VAN HORN, EDITH (1923-   )
Amer. feminist
O'Neill--Women's p316

VAN HORN, JUNE
Amer. Air Force cadet
Licthenstein--Mach. p181-183,
185,188

VAN HORNE, BETSEY (fl. 1770's)
Amer. patriot
Young--Revol. p30-32

VAN HORNE, HANNAH
See CARLETON, MRS. THOMAS

VAN HORNE, HARRIET (1920-   )
Amer. journalist, columnist
100--Greatest (1) p38, por.
Women--Radio p22
Scheuer--Tel. p493

VAN HOUTEN, BARBARA
See HOUTEN, BARBARA VAN,
MADEMOISELLE

VAN KLEECK, MARY ABBY (1883-
1972)
Amer. social reformer, labor
leader
Hymowitz--Hist. p207,262
O'Neill--Women's p285,329
Sicherman--Notable p707-709

VAN LAWICK-GOODALL, JANE,
BARONESS (1934-   )
English researcher, anthro-
pologist, ethnologist, writer
Bowman--Social p24-33, por.
O'Neill--Women's p149
P.W.--Author p396-398,528
World--Who p98

VAN LEW, ELIZABETH L. (1818-
1900)
Amer. Civil War abolitionist,
Union spy
Bird--Enterprising p167
Ingraham--Album p30
James--Notable (3) p508-510
Kulkin--Her p289

McHenry--Liberty's p422
Sherr--American p237
Warren--Pictorial p110
Woman's Almanac p455

VAN MÖRL, MARIA (1812-1868)
German, stigmata witness
Book--Lists (1) p436

VAN NESS, MARCIA BURNS (1782-
1832)
Amer. social leader, feminist,
patriot, philanthropist
Earle--Two Cent. (2) p xxii, por.
Peacock--Famous p11-17, por.

VAN OOSTERWITJK (OOSTERWYCK),
MARIA (1630-1693)
Netherlands painter
Parker--Old p51-54, (fig. 30)
Petersen--Women p41

VAN RENNSELAER, CATHERINE
See SCHUYLER, CATHERINE
VAN RENNSELAER

VAN RENNSELAER, MARI VAN
CORTLANDT (1645-1688/1689)
Amer. colonial administrator
James--Notable (3) p510-511

VAN RENNSSELAER, MARIANA ALLEY
GRISWOLD (1851-1934)
Amer. art critic, historian
James--Notable (3) p511-513
McHenry--Liberty's p423

VAN RENNSELAER, MARTHA (1864-
1932)
Amer. home economist, pro-
fessor
James--Notable (3) p513-514
O'Neill--Women's p104-105
Sherr--American p163

van RIJN, NEELTJEN WILLEMDOCH-
TER van SUYDTBROUCK
(1750-1640)
Netherlands, mother of Rem-
brandt van Rijn
Diagram--Mothers p214-215, por.

van SCHAAK, MARIE
See ST. CYR, LILI (LILY)

VAN SCHURMAN, ANNA
See SCHURMAN, ANNA MARIE VON

VAN SLYKE, HELEN LENORE VOGT
(1919-1979)
Amer. novelist, journalist
Seymour-Smith--Novels p230

VAN STRA(A)TEN, FLORENCE
WILHELMINA (1913-)
Amer. physical chemist,
meteorologist, professor
Emberlin--Cont. p155-156

VAN SUYDTBROUCK, NEELTJEN
See van RIJN, NEELTJEN
WILLEMSDOCHTER van
SUYDTBROUCK

VAN UPP, VIRGINIA (fl. 1940's)
Amer. film producer
Smith--Movies p26-27, por.

VAN VORST, MARIE LOUISE
(1867-1936)
Amer. social reformer,
author, singer
Hymowitz--Hist. p238-239
James--Notable (3) p514-515

van VRIES, MARGARET HARDEN-
BROEK (fl. 1660's)
Netherlands-Amer. business-
woman
Neidle--America's p269

VAN WAGENER, ISABELLA
See TRUTH, SOJOURNER

VAN WATERS, MIRIAM (1887-1974)
Amer. penologist, prison
reformer, social worker
Cur. Biog. '74 p471
Sicherman--Notable p709-711

VAN ZANT, MARIE (1861-1919/
1920)
French-Amer. opera singer
Claghorn--Biog. p451
James--Notable (3) p515-517
McHenry--Liberty's p423

VARAIGNE, DOMINIQUE
See SANDA, DOMINIQUE

VARDA, AGNES (1928-)
French film director,
photographer
Cur. Biog. '70 p424-426, por.
O'Neill--Women's p668
Smith--Movies p120-122

VARE, GLENNA COLLETT (1903-)
Amer. golfer
People's Almanac (1) p1185
Woman's Almanac p420
World--Who p223

VARGA, JULIA KOTEL (1889-)
Hungarian-Amer. community,
church worker, noted Con-
necticut mother
Amer.--Mothers p80, por.

VARNAY, ASTRID (1918-)
Swedish-Amer. opera singer
Claghorn--Biog. p451

VARNHAGEN, RAHEL LEVIN (1771-
1833)
German salonist, diarist
Fink--Great p41-48, por.
Moers--Literary p317

VARNOD, WIDOW (fl. 1730's)
French teacher
Williams--Demeter's p177

VARSI, DIANE (1937/1938-)
Amer. actress
World--Who p252

VAS, JUDIT (fl. 1960's)
Hungarian director
Smith--Movies p124

VASSALL, ELIZABETH (fl. 1790's)
Amer.-English loyalist, social-
ite
Earnest--American p202

VASSEUR, MARIE LE (1674-1767)
French mother-in-law of Jean
Jaques Rousseau
Book--Lists (2) p253

VASSILET, MRS. FYODOR (MADAME)
(1816-1872)
Russian mother
Macksey--Book p11
McFarland--Incred. p14

VATA, SHKURTE PAL (1952-1967)
Albanian heroine
Partington--Who's p430

VAUBRUN, MARGUERITE THERESE,
MARQUISE DE (fl. c1670's)
French socialite
McFarland--Incred. p59

VAUGHAN, SARAH LOIS (1924-)
    Amer. singer, pianist
    Claghorn--Biog. p451
    Claghorn--Jazz p298
    Cur. Biog. '80 p407-411, por.
    O'Neill--Women's p628
    Simon--Best p585-586, por.
    Women's Almanac p306
    World--Who p274

VAUGHN, THERESA (c1898-)
    English bigamist
    McFarland--Incred. p25

VAUTRIN, MINNIE (1886-1941)
    Amer. missionary, educator
    James--Notable (3) p517-518

VEDRES, NICOLE (fl. 1940's-1950's)
    French journalist, filmmaker
    Smith--Movies p117

VEGA, MARYLOIS P. (fl. 1960's-
    1970's)
    Amer. magazine researcher
    Marzolf--Up p98-99

VEIJJABU, PIERRA HOON (1909-)
    Thailand physician
    O'Neill--Women's p210

VEIL, SIMONE ANNIE JACOB
    (1927-)
    French administrator, feminist
    Cur. Biog. '80 p411-414, por.
    Jones--Rutledge p793
    O'Neill--Women's p54

VELARDE, PABLITA (1918-)
    Amer. Pueblo Indian artist
    Gridley--Amer. p94-104, por.
    Kulkin--Her p290

VELASQUEZ, LORETA JANETA
    (1838/1842-1897)
    Amer. male impersonator,
    Confederate soldier, Civil
    War spy
    Felton--Famous p48
    Macksey--Book p55
    Millstein--We p122-123

VELEY, MARGARET (1843-1887)
    English novelist, poet
    Showalter--Lit. p336

VELEZ, LUPE (1908/1910-1944)

Mexican actress
    Springer--They p246,335, por.

VELHO DA COSTA, MARIA (fl.
    1970's)
    Portuguese author
    O'Neill--Women's p727

VELIMESIS, MARGERY L. (fl.
    1940's-1970's)
    Amer. psychologist
    O'Neill--Women's p375

VELUT, ALMA
    Amer. aviatrix, army flier
    Keil--Those p55-56,238

VENABLE, EVELYN (1913-)
    Amer. actress, college
    instructor
    Lamparski--What. (3) p166-167,
    por.
    Springer--They p246,335, por.

VENGEROVA, ISABELLE (1877-1956)
    Russian-Amer. pianist, profes-
    sor
    Claghorn--Biog. p452
    O'Neill--Women's p635

VENIER, MARIE (fl. 1590-1619)
    French actress
    Macksey--Book p223

VENKER, MARY (fl. 1970's)
    Amer. golfer
    McWhirter--Guinness p79

VENNESLAND, BIRGIT (fl. 1960's)
    Norwegian-Amer. biochemist
    O'Neill--Women's p164,167-168

VENTURI, DENISE
    See BROWN, DENISE SCOTT

VERA-ELLEN (1926-1981)
    Amer. dancer, actress
    Cur. Biog. '81 p474
    Lamparski--What. Annual (4,5)
    p250-256, por.
    Shipman--Internatl. p601-602,
    por.

VERA SALAFF NEUMANN (1910-)
    Amer. fashion designer
    Macksey--Book p268
    O'Neill--Women's p277-278

Rich-McCoy--Mill. p1-22,
por.

VERDESI, ELIZABETH HOWELL
(fl. 1970's)
Amer. historian
O'Neill--Women's p396-397

VERDON, GWEN (1925-)
Amer. dancer, actress
World--Who p264

VERDY, VIOLETTE (1933-)
French-Amer. ballet dancer,
opera ballet director
Cur. Biog. '69 p437-439, por.
Cur. Biog. '80 p414-417, por.
O'Neill--Women's p642

VERE, CLEMENTINE DE (1864-1954)
Amer. opera singer
Claghorn--Biog. p452

VERELST, MARIA (MARIAN) (1680-
1744)
Netherlands painter
Fine--Women p36

VERGINIA (1) (fl. 449 B.C.)
Roman maiden
Pomeroy--Godd. p153

VERGINIA (2) (fl. 300's B.C.)
Roman slave of Appius
Claudius
Zinserling--Women p63

VERGNE, MARIE MADELEINE
See LAFAYETTE, MARIE
MADELEINE PIOCHE DE LA
VERGNE, COMTESSE DE

VERGOOSE, ELIZABETH FOSTER
(c1648/1665-1690/1752)
Amer. nursery-rhyme singer
Coffin--Female p143-147
Fenton--Famous p191-192
People's Almanac (1) p940
Williams--Demeter's p208

VERHULST, MAYKEN
Netherlands painter
Petersen--Women p36

VERNON, MABEL (1883-1975)
Amer. suffragist, feminist,
pacifist

Sicherman--Notable p711-
712

VERONE, MARIA
French suffragist
Macksey--Book p89

VERONICA, SAINT
Biblical
Green--Saints p87-89
Jones--Rutledge p795

VERONICA GIULIANI, SAINT (1660-
1697)
Italian nun
Book--Lists (1) p436

VERRETT, SHIRELY (1933-)
Amer. singer
Claghorn--Biog. p453
Gammond--Illus. p252, por.

VERSAILLES, ELIZABETH STARR
(1909-)
Amer. genealogical researcher,
author
Meyer--Who's p207

VERUSHKA (c1943-)
German countess, model
Keenan--Women p132-133,153,
por.

VESLEY, JANE DE (fl. 1920's)
French weightlifter
Macksey--Book p258
McWhirter--Guinness p187

VESPUCCI, ELENA "AMERICA"
(1804-)
Italian-Amer. adventuress
People's Almanac (2) p159-161

VESTA
Greek goddess
Pomeroy--Godd. p184,210-211

VESTRIS, FRANÇOISE-ROSE,
MADAME (1743-1804)
French actress
Entertainers p99
Who Did What p318

VESTRIS, LUCIA (LUCY) ELIZA-
BETTA, MADAME (1797-1856)
English actress-manager,
singer

Entertainers p113
Findlater--Player p128

VESTRIS, THERESE (1726-1808)
Italian ballet dancer
Migel--Ballerinas p46-49

VIANELLO, A.
Italian roller-skater
Macksey--Book p261

VICKERS, JULIA (fl. 1970's)
New Zealander librarian,
mountain climber, research
assistant (Antarctica)
Land--New p81-88, por.

VICKREY, FANNY RANDOLPH (fl.
1890's)
Amer. social reformer
Stein--Lives p169-170, por.

VICTOIRE (fl. 1950's)
French model, boutique
head
Keenan--Women p118,121, por.

VICTOIRE, DUCHESS OF KENT
(1786-)
German-English, mother of
Queen Victoria
Diagram--Mothers p244-247, por.

VICTOR, FRANCES AURETTA FUL-
LER (1826-1902)
Amer. poet, historian
Ehrlich--Oxford p398
James--Notable (3) p518-519
McHenry--Liberty's p423-424

VICTOR, METTA VICTORIA FUL-
LER (1831-1885)
Amer. author
James--Notable (3) p519-520
McHenry--Liberty's p424-425

VICTOR, SALLY JOSEPH(S)
(JOSEPHA) (1894/1905-1977)
Amer. millinery designer
Cur. Biog. '77 p473
O'Neill--Women's p238,247

VICTOR, WILMA L. (fl. 1970's)
Amer. Choctaw Indian
educator
Gridley--Amer. p154-161,
por.

VICTORIA (1819-1901)
English queen
Basch--Relative, see index p359
Brecher--Lives p311-314, por.
Canning--100 p543-548
Delderfield--Kings p121-126, por.
Donaldson--How p375-376
Fry--1000 p250-251, por.
Holme--Journal p22-23, por.
Jones--Rutledge p797-798
Kulkin--Her p291-292
Kupferberg--First p170-171, por.
Longford--Eminent, see index
p255, por.
Macksey--Book p255
Moers--Literary p317
Plamer--Who's p317
People's Almanac (2) p413,1196
People's Almanac (3) p271-276,
por.
Softly--Queens p113-116
Who Did What p318-319
Woman's Almanac p463, por.
World--Who p158

VICTORIA, ADELAIDE MARY (1840-
1901)
German empress
Jones--Rutledge p798

VIERA DA SILVA, MARIA HELENA
(1908-)
Brazilian-Portuguese painter
Fine--Women p176-177
Haftmann--Paint. (1) p423
Munsterberg--Hist. p78,80-81
O'Neill--Women's p600
Woman's Almanac p225
Women's--Female p14

VIGEE-LE BRUN, ELIZABETH
See LE BRUN, MARIE ELISABETH
LOUISE

VIGRI, CATERINA DA (CATHERINE
OF BOLOGNA) (1413-1463)
Italian painter, saint, abbess,
medical teacher, nurse
Fine--Women p6-7
Macksey--Book p195
Marks--Women p52
Mead--Hist. p310
Sparrow--Women p23,33

VILAR, ESTHER (1935-)
German writer
P.W.--Author p399-401,529

Vilar / 721

VILAR, LOLA (1900-   )
Spanish physician
Hellstedt--Women p206-211, por.

VILLA, AMELIA CHOPITEA (-1942)
Mexican-Amer. migrant
Lindborg--Five p63-68

VILLALOBOS, MARIA PATRICIA
KRCZYN
Mexican law professor,
activist, lawyer
O'Neill--Women's p364

VILLARD, FANNY GARRISON (1844-
1928)
Amer. philanthropist, suffragist, pacifist
James--Notable (3) p520-522

VILLARIÑO, LUZ M. (fl. 1970's)
Amer. labor official
O'Neill--Women's p338-339

VILLERE, LAURE (1823-1850)
Amer. Southern belle
DeLeon--Belles p293, por.

VILLERS, MADAME (fl. 18th-19th
cent.)
French artist
Harris--Women p47,217,349

VILLIERS, BARBARA, COUNTESS
OF CASTLEMAINE (1640/
1641-1709)
English courtesan, mistress
of Charles II
Earle--Two Cent. (2) p xix,
por.
Jones--Rutledge p182
Macksey--Book p96

VILMORIN, LOUISE DE (fl. 1930's)
French writer
Crosland--Women p107-108

VILSONS, VELTA (fl. 1940's-
1960's)
Latvian-Canadian weaver
O'Neill--Women's p125

VINCENT, MARY ANN FARLOW
(1818-1887)
Amer. actress
James--Notable (3) p522-523

VINCENTI, JULIA RIVERA DE (fl.
1960's-1970's)
Puerto Rican cabinet officer
O'Neill--Women's p345

VINOGRASKAYA, KATERINA (fl.
1920's)
Russian film writer
Mandel--Soviet p147-148

VINSON, ADDIE (1852-   )
Amer. slave
Hoople--As p83-86

VINSON, HELEN (1907-   )
Amer. actress
Springer--They p246,335, por.

VINSON, PHYLLIS TUCKER
Amer. TV executive
Scheuer--Tel. p495-496

VINSON-OWEN, MARIBEL (-1961)
Amer. skater, coach, sports
columnist
Assoc. Press--Pursuit p111,124,
146
Hollander--100 p27,30-31, por.
O'Neill--Women's p563

VIONNET, MADELEINE (1877-1975)
French couturier
Macksey--Book p266
O'Neill--Women's p240

VIORST, JUDITH
Amer. poet, columnist, chil-
dren's books author, editor
Diamonstein--Open p417-420, por.
O'Neill--Women's p478

VISCOPOLEANU, VIORICA (fl.
1970's)
Rumanian track and field
athlete
O'Neill--Women's p578

VISHNEVSKAYA, GALINA
PAVLOVA (1926-   )
Russian opera singer
Gammond--Illus. p252, por.

VISSCHER, ANNA (1583/1584-1651)
Netherlands glass-engraver
Macksey--Book p197-198

VISSCHER, MARIA (1595-1649)

Netherlands glass-engraver
Macksey--Book p197-198

"VITAGRAPH GIRL"
See TURNER, FLORENCE E.

VITO, MARY DE (fl. 1970's)
Amer. gunnery expert
Macksey--Book p256

VITTI, MONICA (1931-)
Italian actress
Shipman--Internatl. p603-606,
por.

VIVIEN, RENEE (PAULINE TARN)
(1877-1909)
French poet
Bree--Women p44
Crosland--Women p77-81

VIVONNE, CATHERINE DE (1588-
1665)
Italian salonnier
Macksey--Book p95-96,181, por.

VLACHOS, ELENI (HELEN) (1911-)
Greek publisher, editor,
refugee
Cavanah--We p188-197
O'Neill--Women's p460,555

VLASEK, JUNE
See LANG, JUNE

VOGDES, ADA A. (fl. 1860's-1870's)
Amer. Western pioneer
Time--Women p67-68

VOGE, VICTORIA (fl. 1970's)
Amer. naval flight surgeon
O'Neill--Women's p543-544
Oberg--Space p112

VOGELSANG, JUDITH (fl. 1960's-
1970's)
Amer. filmmaker
Smith--Movies p210-211,279

VOIPIO, ANNI (fl. 1940's-1970's)
Finnish reporter, corres-
pondent
Marzolf--Up 277

VOLBORTH, JUDITH IVALOO
(1950-)
Amer. Apache/Comanche

Indian poet
Fisher--Third p v,96

VOLKENSTEIN, LIUDMILLA
Russian revolutionary prisoner,
feminist
Mandel--Soviet p27-28

VOLKERSZ, VERONICA (fl. 1940's)
Amer. aviatrix
Boase--Sky's p182-183,186,188,
192-195

VOLLMER, LULA (LOUISE SMITH)
(1898-1955)
Amer. playwright
Chinoy--Women p151-152

VOLNER, JILL WINE (1943-)
Amer. lawyer
Woman's Almanac p524, por.

VOLODINA, MARIA (fl. 1960's)
Russian head, electrical power
Mandel--Soviet p90

von ARNIM, ELIZABETH
See RUSSELL, ELIZABETH MARY
ANNETTE BEAUCHAMP,
COUNTESS von ARNIM

VONDERMUHLL, VALERIE
Amer. magazine reporter
Hamblin--That, see index p320,
por.

VON EBNER-ESCHENBACH, MARIE,
BARONESS
See EBNER-ESCHENBACH, MARIE
VON, BARONESS

VON FURSTENBERG, BETSY (1932-)
German actress
World--Who p252

VON FURSTENBERG, DIANE SIMONE
MICHELLE (c1946-)
Belgian-Amer. fashion designer
Anderson--People p398
Cur. Biog. '76 p409-411, por.
People--Best p99, por.
Woman's Almanac p120,135-136
World--Who p297

VON JANUSCHOWSKY, GEORGINE
(1859-1914)
Austrian-Amer. singer
Claghorn--Biog. p454

von KAPPELHOFF, DORIS
See DAY, DORIS

von LANGSDORFF, TONI
See LANGSDORFF, TONI von

VON LEHNDORFF, VERA,
COUNTESS
See VERUSHKA

VON LESCH, MARIE MAGDALENA
See DIETRICH, MARLENE

von LORINGHOVEN, ELSA von
FREITAG, BARONESS
German eccentric party-goer
Felton--Famous p178-179

von MARTINEZ, MARIANNE
See MARTINEZ, MARIANNE von

VON MISES, HILDA
See GEIRINGER, HILDA

VON PARADIS, MARIA THERESIA
See PARADIS, MARIA THERESIA

von PLATEN, RUTH CHANDLER
(1897-)
Amer. millionaire
Forbes--400 ('84) p146

VON POPPER, MARIE JERITZA,
BARONESS
See JERITZA, MARIA

VON REUTER, FLORIZEL (1890-)
Amer. violinist
Claghorn--Biog. p454

von RIEDESEL, FREDERIKA,
BARONESS (fl. 1770's-1780's)
Amer. writer, wife of general
Booth--Women, see index p328,
por.
Williams--Demeter's p228,270-272

von ROCHE, SOPHIE
See LA ROCHE, SOPHIE von

von RODDE, DOROTHEA
See RODDE, DOROTHEA von

von RORQUE, MADAME
See HOLBROOK, CARRIE

VON SALTZA, CHRIS

Amer. swimmer
Hollander--100 p87-88, por.

von SCHRÖTER, CORONA
See SCHRÖTER, CORONA von

VON STADE, FREDERICA (1945-)
Amer. opera singer
Cur. Biog. '77 p414-417, por.

von STARKLOFF, IRMA LOUISE
See ROMBAUER, IRMA von
STARKLOFF

VON STEINBACH, SABINA
See STEINBACH, SABINA von

VON TAUTIPHOEUS, JEMIMA,
BARONESS
See JEMIMA, BARONESS von
TAUTIPHOEUS

VON TEMPSKI, ARMINE (1899-1943)
Amer. author
Ehrlich--Oxford p406,440-441

VON VIETINGHOFF, BARBARA
JULIANE
See KRÜDENER, BARBARA
JULIANE von VIETINGHOFF,
BARONESS

von WEREFKIN, MARIANNE (1870-
1938)
Russian artist
Fine--Women p159-160, por.

VON WRANGELL, BARONESS (fl.
1830's)
Russian, wife of Alaskan
governor
Jones--Women (1) p26

VORHEES-HASSON, ESTHER
See HASSON, ESTHER VORHEES

VORONINA, INGA (fl. 1970's)
Russian skater
O'Neill--Women's p564

VORSE, MARY HEATON MARVIN
(1874-1966)
Amer. journalist, social re-
former, journalist
Hymowitz--Hist. p258
Sicherman--Notable p712-714
Sochen--Movers, see index p319

VORST, MARIE VAN
See VAN VORST, MARIE
LOUISE

VOYNICH, ETHEL LILIAN (c1864-
1960)
Irish novelist, political
radical
Showlater--Lit. p343

VRANA, ETHEL
Amer. clergyman
Proctor--Women p37-38

VREELAND, DIANA DALZIEL
(c1903-)
Scottish-Amer. fashion edi-
tor, journalist, museum
consultant
Cur. Biog. '78 p445-448, por.
Gilbert--Part. p215-217, por.
Keenan--Women p68-69, por.
McHenry--Liberty's p424-425
100--Greatest (1) p72, por.
O'Neill--Women's p244,262,480
Woman's Almanac p136, por.

VYTILINGAM, KAMALA ISREAL
(1901-)
East Indian physician
Hellstedt--Women p226-229, por.

W

WADE, BETSY (1929-)
Amer. editor, labor leader
Marzolf--Up p79, 108
O'Neill--Women's p315,465

WADE, ERNESTINE (1939-)
Amer. radio actress
Lamparski--What. (3) p14-15,
por.

WADE, JENNIE (fl. 1860's)
Amer. Civil War patriot
Sherr--American p200

WADE, (SARAH) VIRGINIA
(1945-)
English tennis player
Cur. Biog. '76 p412-414, por.
O'Neill--Women's p583, por.
Sullivan--Queens p92-97, por.
World--Who p223

WADLEY, ELLEN (fl. 1940's-1960's)

Amer. radio producer
Marzolf--Up p144-145

WAGAR, MARGARET (fl. 1970's)
Amer. bridge player
O'Neill--Women's p592

WAGLE, ASHA (1944-)
English investment firm
executive
O'Neill--Women's p746

WAGLE, PREMILA (1920-)
East Indian clothing exporter
O'Neill--Women's p746

WAGLUM, JINNIE (fl. 1790's)
Amer. Revolutionary War
patriot
Clyne--Patriots p132-133,136

WAGNER, COSIMA (1837/1840-1930)
Hungarian music patron, wife
of Richard Wagner
Neuls-Bates--Women p175-178

WAGNER, JANE TIFFANY (fl. 1940's)
Amer. radio broadcaster
Marzolf--Up p141-142

WAGNER, LINDSAY (1949-)
Amer. actress
Manchel--Women p114-115, por.

WAGSTAFF, ANN T. (1939-)
Amer. genealogical researcher,
indexer
Meyer--Who's p211

WAHLMAN, MARY (fl. 1970's)
Amer. pharmacist
Seed--Saturday's p70-73, por.

WAHLÖÖ, PER (1926-1975)
Swedish novelist (with hus-
band, Maj Sjöwall)
Seymour-Smith--Novels p217

WAIGHT, LAVINIA (fl. 1820's)
Amer. union worker
Neidle--America's p114

WAIN, BEA (fl. 1940's)
Amer. singer, radio personality
Simon--Big p71-72,
por.

WAISBROOKER, LOIS
Amer. radical writer
Sherr--American p240

WAITE, CATHERINE VAN VALKEN-
BURG (1829-1913)
Canadian-Amer. suffragist,
lawyer, legal journalist
James--Notable (3) p523-525

WAITE, MARY GEORGE JORDON
(1918-)
Amer. clubwoman, noted
Alabama mother
Amer.--Mothers p6-7, por.

WAITZ, GRETE (1953-)
Nor. track and field athlete
Cur. Biog. '81 p434-436, por.

WAKELY, SHELAGH (1932-)
English artist
Contemp. Brit., unp., por.

WAKOSKI, DIANE (1937-)
Amer. poet
Avenel--Comp. (2) p259
Webber--Woman p164-171

WALASIEWICZ, STANISLAWA
See WALSH, STELLA

WALCOTT, MARY MORRIS VAUX
(1860-1940)
Amer. artist, naturalist
James--Notable (3) p525-526
McHenry--Liberty's p426

WALD, LILLIAN D. (1867-1940)
Amer. nurse, social reformer,
humanitarian
Banner--Women p69,99,101-102
Brin--Social p158
Earnest--American p222
Fink--Great p105-111, por.
Gilfond--Heroines p17-21, por.
James--Notable (3) p526-529
Kulkin--Her p292-293
Lagemann--Gen. p59-86, por.
McHenry--Liberty's p426-427
O'Neill--Women's p736
People's Almanac (2) p1055
Sherr--American p35,168
Signif.--Amer. p36, por.
Sochen--Herstory p215,217,239,
por.
Warren--Pictorial p148-149

Webster's--Amer. p1083
Woman's Almanac p380-381, por.
World--Who p192

WALD, PATRICIA M. (1928-)
Amer. lawyer, government
official
O'Neill--Women's p367

WALDMAN, ANNE (1945-)
Amer. poet
Chester--Rising p378-383, por.
Lichtenstein--Mach. p6,251,273-
277,334,342

WALDMAN, DIANE (fl. 1970's)
Amer. museum curator
O'Neill--Women's p616

WALDO, FAITH SAVAGE (1683-1760)
Amer., wife of Cornelius Waldo
Earle--Two Cent. (2) p xvi, por.

WALDO, JANET
Amer. TV actress
Lamparski--What. (5) p166-167,
por.

WALDO, REBECCA SALISBURY
(1731-1811)
Amer., wife of Daniel Waldo
Earle--Two Cent. (2) p xvi,
554-555, por.

WALDO, RUTH FANSHAW (1885-1975)
Amer. advertising executive
Sicherman--Notable p715-716

WALES, LUCY (fl. 1830's)
Amer. teacher
Sherr--American p129

WALEWSKA, MARIE, COUNTESS
(1787/1789-1817)
Polish duchess, Napoleon's
mistress
Partington--Who's p440-441, por.

WALFORD, LUCY BETHIA COLQU-
HOUN (1845-1915)
Scottish novelist
Showalter--Lit. p336

WALKER, ALICE (1944-)
Amer. poet, essayist, colum-
nist, novelist
Cahill--Women p363,379

Cur. Biog. '84 p430-433, por.
Fisher--Third p vii,151,184,294
O'Neill--Women's p689-690
P.W.--Author p167-168,530
Ruddick--Working p92-102,347-
    348, por.
Washington--Black p89-90
Webber--Women p193-201

WALKER, ANN(E)
    See WELCH, ANN

WALKER, BRENDA (fl. 1970's)
    Amer. physical therapist
    Innis--Profiles p92-93, por.

WALKER, CINDY
    Amer. dancer, composer
    Claghorn--Biog. p458

WALKER, EDYTH (1867/1870-1950)
    Amer. opera singer, teacher
    Claghorn--Biog. p458
    James--Notable (3) p529-530

WALKER, ELIZABETH (fl. 1800's)
    Amer., legendary inn-
    keeper's daughter
    Coffin--Parade p291-293

WALKER, ELMEDA McHARGUE (fl.
    1900's)
    Amer. weaver
    O'Neill--Women's p122

WALKER, MRS. JOHN (fl. 1770's)
    Amer. Revolutionary War
    patriot
    Meyer--Petticoat p217

WALKER, "MADAME" C.J.
    See WALKER, SARAH BREED-
    LOVE ("MADAME" C.J.)

WALKER, MAGGIE LENA (1867-
    1934)
    Amer. banker, noted
    Virginia mother, philan-
    thropist
    Adams--Great (3rd) p85, por.
    Amer.--Mothers p552-553, por.
    Bird--Enterprising p167-170
    Burt--Black p38-53, por.
    James--Notable (3) p530-531
    McHenry--Liberty's p427
    Marlowe--Great p190-193, por.
    O'Neill--Women's p526

Sherr--American p238
Signif.--Amer. p36, por.
Woman's Almanac p181

WALKER, MARGARET ABIGAIL
    (1915-   )
    Amer. poet
    Bernikow--World p325-326
    Fisher--Third p vii,249
    Pearson--Who p294

WALKER, MARTHA I'ANS (fl. 1770's)
    English-Amer. Revolutionary
    War diarist, wife of rebel
    Evans--Weather. p52-72

WALKER, MARY (1) (fl. 1770's)
    Amer. landowner, voter
    Williams--Demeter's p190

WALKER, MARY (2) (fl. 1830's-
    1840's)
    Amer. pioneer, missionary
    Time--Women p24-27,30,48,51

WALKER, MARY EDWARDS (1832-
    1919)
    Amer. male impersonator,
    Civil War nurse, spy, sur-
    geon, physician, dress re-
    former
    Felton--Famous p270-272
    Ingraham--Album p71
    James--Notable (3) p532-533
    Kulkin--Her p294-295
    Longstreet--Queen p45-47
    McHenry--Liberty's p427-428
    O'Neill--Women's p199,534, por.
    Reifert--Women p81
    Sherr--American p126,173
    Signif.--Amer. p25, por.
    Taylor--Gener. p48, por.
    Warren--Pictorial p109
    Woman's Almanac p499
    World--Who p110

WALKER, MARY RICHARDSON
    (1811-1897)
    Amer. Western pioneer, mis-
    sionary's wife, geologist,
    botanist, scholar
    Bird--Enterprising p47-48
    Millstein--We p54,56,121
    Reifert--Women p119-120
    Sherr--American p240

WALKER, NANCY (1921/1922-   )

Amer. actress
Kulkin--Her p295-296
World--Who p252

WALKER, NELLA (fl. 1920's-1950's)
Amer. actress
Springer--They p249,335, por.

WALKER, NELLE VERNE (1874-1973)
Amer. sculptor
Sherr--American p72

WALKER, SARAH BREEDLOVE
("MADAME" C.J.) (1869-1919)
Amer. cosmetics manufacturer,
millionaire, noted Missouri
mother
Adams--Great (3rd) p84, por.
Amer.--Mothers p312, por.
Bird--Enterprising p130-131
James--Notable (3) p533-535
McHenry--Liberty's p428
Macksey--Book p170-171
O'Neill--Women's p100,512
Sherr--American p66,82,133,
163,166-167,171, por.
Sochen--Herstory p291
Toppin--Biog. p435-437
Warren--Pictorial p200
Webster's--Amer. p1086
Woman's Almanac p136,138

WALL, LUCILLE (fl. 1940's)
Amer. radio actress
Lamparski--What. (4) p82-83, por.

WALL, SUSANNAH (fl. 1790's)
Amer. colonial actress
Chinoy--Women p193-197

WALL, TESSIE (1869-1932)
Amer. "Madame"
People's Almanac (2) p930-931

WALLACE, CAROLYN L. (fl. 1970's)
Amer. heroine, Carnegie
Medal winner
O'Neill--Women's p735

WALLACE, ELLEN
See SHARPLES (SHARPLALES),
ELLEN WALLACE

WALLACE, FLORENCE RICHARDSON
(1875-)
Amer. farmer, noted Vermont
mother
Amer.--Mothers p542-543, por.

WALLACE, JOAN S. (fl. 1970's)
Amer. government official,
agriculturist
O'Neill--Women's p22-23

WALLACE, LILA BELL ACHESON
(1889/1890-1984)
Amer. millionaire, journalist,
editor, magazine co-founder
Cur. Biog. '84 p481
Forbes--400 ('84) p188
O'Neill--Women's p473
Webster's--Amer. p10,1087
(under Wallace, De Witt)
World--Who p56

WALLACE, LURLEEN BURNS (1926-
1968)
Amer. humanitarian, governor,
noted Alabama mother
Amer.--Mothers p10-11, por.
Woman's Almanac p481-482

WALLACE, MADGE GATES (1862-
1952)
Amer., mother-in-law of Harry
Truman
Book--Lists (2) p254

WALLACE, MIRIAM AMANDA
See FERGUSON, MIRIAM AMANDA
WALLACE ("MA")

WALLACE, MOLLY (fl. 1790's)
Amer. orator
Berkin--Women p77,83,87-89

WALLACE, NELLIE (1870-1948)
English comedienne
Entertainers p161

WALLACE, RUBY ANN
See DEE, RUBY

WALLACE, SIPPIE (1898-1926)
Amer. pianist, organist,
singer
Claghorn--Jazz p302

WALLACE, ZERALDA GRAY
SANDERS (1817/1818-1901)
Amer. temperance worker,
feminist, lecturer, noted
Indiana mother
Amer.--Mothers p176-177, por.
James--Notable (3) p535-536

WALLENDA, HELEN
(fl. 1920's-1950's)
German circus performer
Kirk--Circus p78-79

WALLER, ANNE (fl. 1740's)
Amer. shopkeeper
Williams--Demeter's p198

WALLER, JUDITH CARY (1889-1973)
Amer. radio station manager
Marzolf--Up p120-122
O'Neill--Women's p491-492
Sicherman--Notable p716-717
Women--Radio p8

WALLER, PAGE (fl. 1860's)
Amer. southern belle
DeLeon--Belles p222, por.

WALLERSTEIN, JUDITH (fl. 1970's)
Amer. children's counsellor
O'Neill--Women's p422

WALPURGA, SAINT (754-778/780)
English-German abbess,
monastery founder, woman
of medicine
Jones--Rutledge p809
Macksey--Book p106
Marks--Women p43
Mead--Hist. p102

WALSH, ALIDA (fl. 1970's)
Amer. artist
Women's--Female p112

WALSH, EFTHALIA
Amer. religious writer
O'Neill--Women's p378

WALSH, JULIA M. (fl. 1940's-
1970's)
Amer. investment broker
O'Neill--Women's p530

WALSH, LOUISE FORSYTH (1886-
1971)
Amer. community worker,.
noted Alaska mother
Amer.--Mothers p17, por.

WALSH, MARNIE (fl. 1970's)
Amer. Sioux Indian poet
Fisher--Third p v-vi,113

WALSH, MOLLIE (-1902)

Amer., Alaskan "gold rush
belle"
Jones--Women (1) p98-101

WALSH, STELLA (1911-)
Polish track and field athlete
Hollander--100 p118-119, por.
People's Almanac (1) p1193
Woman's Almanac p428
World--Who p223

WALTER, ALICE GRANBERY (1908-)
Amer. genealogical researcher,
author
Meyer--Who's p212

WALTER, CORNELIA WELLS (c1813-
1898)
Amer. journalist
James--Notable (3) p536-537

WALTER, FLORENCE G. (1884-1972)
Amer. bookbinding designer
Women's--Female p155

WALTER, LUCY (MRS. BARLOW)
(c1630-1658)
English, mistress of Charles II
Macksey--Book p96

WALTERS, ANNA LEE (1946-)
Amer. Pawnee/Oloe Indian poet
fisher--Third p vi,109

WALTERS, BARBARA (1931-)
Amer. TV newscaster, jour-
nalist, anchorwoman, inter-
viewer
Anderson--People p401-402, por.
Clark--Leading p236-237
Cur. Biog. '71 p432-434, por.
Diamonstein--Open p422-425, por.
Gelfman--Women, see index p186,
por.
Gilbert--Part. p325, por.
McHenry--Liberty's p428
Marzolf--Up, see index p309
100--Greatest (1) p104-105, por.
O'Neill--Women's p504-505
People--Best p180-181, por.
Scheuer--Tel. p499-500, por.
Sochen--Herstory p400, por.
Woman's Almanac p264-265,275,
por.
World--Who p56

WALTERS, LYDIA MILNER (fl. 1850's)

Amer. Western pioneer
Millstein--We p51

WALTON, DOROTHY CAMBER (fl.
1770's)
Amer. Revolutionary War
patriot
Sherr--American p45

WALTON, OCTAVIA
See LeVERT, OCTAVIA CELESTE
WALTON

WALWORTH, ELLEN HARDIN (1832-
1915)
Amer. clubwoman, author,
DAR co-founder
James--Notable (3) p537-538
Sherr--American p40,62

WAMBAUGH, SARAH (1882-1955)
Amer. author, political
scientist, lecturer, consultant
McHenry--Liberty's p428-429

WANG, JULIANA (fl. 1970's)
Amer. cinematographer
O'Neill--Women's p317
Smith--Movies p211-212,280, por.

WANGCHUCK, DECHHEN WANG-MO
Bhutan government official
O'Neill--Women's p40,41-42

WANG PING (fl. 1950's-1960's)
Chinese film director
Smith--Movies p99

WANNGÅARD, HANNA (1892-)
Swedish labor worker,
teacher
O'Neill--Women's p321

WARBURTON, A.M. (fl. 1970's)
British ambassador
O'Neill--Women's p62

WARD, ANITA (1957-)
Amer. singer
Glassman--Year '79 p164, por.

WARD, BARBARA MARY (1914-
1981)
English economist, writer,
educator, editor, author,
journalist
Cur. Biog. '77 p424-427, por.

Cur. Biog. '81 p474-475
World--Who p98

WARD, CLARA (1924-1973)
Amer. singer
Claghorn--Biog. p460
Claghorn--Jazz p303

WARD, MRS. DUDLEY (fl. 1920's)
English socialite
Keenan--Women p19, por.

WARD, ELIZABETH STUART PHELPS
(1844-1911)
Amer. novelist, philanthropist
Ehrlich--Oxford p26,47
James--Notable (3) p538-540
McHenry--Liberty's p429
Welter--Dimity p111-120

WARD, GENEVIEVE, DAME (1837/
1838-1922)
English actress
Johns--Dames p4-6, por.

WARD, MRS. H.O.
See MOORE, CLARA SOPHIA
JESSUP

WARD, HELEN (fl. 1930's)
Amer. singer
Simon--Big p98-99

WARD, HORTENSE SPARKS MALSCH
(1872-1944)
Amer. lawyer, social reformer
James--Notable (3) p540-541
McHenry--Liberty's p429-430
Sherr--American p222

WARD, MRS. HUMPHREY (1851-1920)
Tasmanian novelist, philanthro-
pist, religious reformer
Avenel--Comp. (1) p542
Colby--Singular p111-174
Crosland--Beyond p2,52-53
Jones--Rutledge p811
Macksey--Book p116
Moers--Literary p317
Seymour-Smith--Novels p233
Showalter--Lit. p227-232,338
Who Did What p324

WARD, IRENE (fl. 1940's-1970's)
British Parliament member
Macksey--Book p38

WARD, JUSTINE BAYARD (1879-
1975)
Amer. teacher, school
co-founder
Claghorn--Biog. p460

WARD, MAISIE (1889-1975)
English-Amer. publisher,
author, lecturer, activist,
publishing house co-founder
Cur. Biog. '75 p475

WARD, MARIANNE I. (fl. 1960's)
Amer. heroine, Carnegie
Medal winner
O'Neill--Women's p734

WARD, MARY AUGUSTA ARNOLD
See WARD, MRS. HUMPHREY

WARD, MARY JANE (1905-)
Amer. novelist
Ehrlich--Oxford p311,324

WARD, NANCY (c1738-1822)
Amer. Cherokee Indian
soldier, Revolutionary War
heroine
Booth--Women p79-81,302
DePauw--Found. p123
Gridley--Amer. p39-46
James--Notable (3) p541-543
McHenry--Liberty's p430
Macksey--Book p53-54
Millstein--We p36
Sherr--American p216-217
Signif.--Amer. p9, por.

WARD, SALLIE DOWNS
Amer. social leader
Peacock--Famous p148-160, por.

WARD, WINIFRED LOUISE (1884-
1975)
Amer. children's theater
specialist
Sicherman--Notable p717-718

WARD-THOMAS, EVELYN BRIDGET
PATRICIA STEPHENS
See ANTHONY, EVELYN, pseud.

WARDEL, LYDIA (fl. 1600's)
Amer. Quaker activist
Williams--Demeter's p129

WARDLAW, ELIZABETH, LADY

(1677-1727)
Scottish poet, balladist
Avenel--Comp. (1) p542

WARDLE, ELIZABETH WARDLE
(1834-1902)
British embroiderer
Callen--Women p8,226

WARE, HARRIET (1877-1962)
Amer. composer, pianist
Claghorn--Biog. p460
Jablonski--Ency. p187

WARE, HELEN (1877-)
Amer. violinist, composer
Claghorn--Biog. p460

WARE, MARY LOVELL PICKARD
(1798-1849)
Amer. religious worker
Beach--Daughters p43-75, por.

WARFF, ANN (fl. 1960's)
Swedish glass-maker
O'Neill--Women's p272

WARFIELD, WALLIS
See WINDSOR, (BESSIE) WALLIS
WARFIELD SIMPSON, DUCHESS
OF

WARING, LON (fl. 1950's)
Amer. ice-skater
McWhirter--Guinness p97

WARNE, MARGARET ("PEGGY")
VLIET ("AUNT PEGGY")
(1751-1840)
Amer. Revolutionary War
nurse, midwife, medical
asisstant, obstetrician
Clyne--Patriots p133,136
Meyer--Petticoat p97
Sherr--American p154

WARNE, MARY
See MARCH, MAE

WARNER, AMALES PUSEY (fl.
1900's)
Amer. college founder
Sherr--American p37

WARNER, ANNA
See BAILEY, ANNA WARNER
("MOTHER BAILEY")

WARWICK, MRS. ABRAM
See CHEVALIER, SALLY

WARWICK, (MARIE) DIONNE
(1941-)
Amer. singer
Claghorn--Biog. p462
Cur. Biog. '69 p442-444, por.
Simon--Best p593-594, por.
World--Who p274

WASER, ANNA (c1679-1713)
Swiss painter
Munsterberg--Hist. p31,33, por.

WASHBURN, FLORINDA (fl. 1850's)
Amer. Western pioneer,
milliner
Millstein--We p52

WASHBURN, MARGARET FLOY
(1871-1939)
Amer. psychologist, profes-
sor, editor, author
Emberlin--Cont. p156-157
James--Notable (3) p546-548
McHenry--Liberty's p431
O'Neill--Women's p144,412

WASHBURN, PATTY BENJAMIN
(1792-)
Amer., noted Maine mother
Amer.--Mothers p239, por.

WASHINGTON, BERNADINE C. (fl.
1970's)
Amer. radio station executive
O'Neill--Women's p520

WASHINGTON, DINAH (1924-1963)
Amer. singer
Claghorn--Biog. p462
Claghorn--Jazz p304
Simon--Best p595-596, por.
World--Who p274

WASHINGTON, ELIZABETH FOOTE
(-1812)
Amer. Revolutionary War
diarist
Evans--Weather. p335-360

WASHINGTON, EUGENIA (-1900)
Amer. co-founder, DAR
Sherr--American p40-41

WASHINGTON, FREDI (1903-)

Amer. dancer, actress
Springer--They p249,335, por.

WASHINGTON, MARTHA DANDRIDGE
CUSTIS (1732-1802)
Amer. first lady, wife of
George Washington
Booth--Women, see index p228,
por.
DePauw--Found. p51,169-170,186
DePauw--Rem. p142-146, por.
Earle--Two Cent. (2) p xxii,466,
511,554,740, por.
Earnest--American, see index
p280
Engle--Women p209-235, por.
Evans--Weather. p168,335,338,
357
Flexner--Face p230, por.
Ingraham--Album p13, por.
James--Notable (3) p548-550
Kulkin--Her p296-297
Melick--Wives p8-11, por.
Meyer--Petticoat, see index p252,
por.
People's Almanac (1) p279
Sherr--American p154,165
Signif.--Amer. p9, por.
Warren--Pictorial p59-63, por.
Williams--Demeter's p269-270
Woman's Almanac p486

WASHINGTON, MARY BALL (1707/
1708-1789)
Amer. mother of George
Washington, noted Virginia
mother
Amer.--Mothers p548-549, por.
Diagram--Mothers p250-253, por.
Faber--Presidents' p196-209, por.
Sherr--American p233-234

WASHINGTON, ORA (fl. 1920's-
1970's)
Amer. tennis player
O'Neill--Women's p583

WASON, BETTY (1912-)
Amer. journalist, foreign
correspondent
Marzolf--Up p140-141
O'Neill--Women's p494

WASSER, ANNA (1676/1679-1710/
1713)
Swiss painter
Macksey--Book p199-200

WASSERSTEIN, WENDY (c1950-)
Amer. playwright
Chinoy--Women p188, por.

WASTE, JOAN
English martyr
Bainton--France p219-220

WATERBURY, LUCY McGILL
See PEABODY, LUCY WHITE-
HEAD McGILL WATERBURY

WATERFORD, LOUISA, LADY
(1818-1891)
English painter
Sparrow--Women p60,63,66,99,
101

WATERMAN, NAN (c1922-)
Amer. organization official
O'Neill--Women's p731

WATERS, CLARA ERSKINE CLEMENT
(1834-1916)
Amer. art historian, world
traveler
James--Notable (3) p550-551

WATERS, ETHEL (1900-1977)
Amer. singer, actress
Adams--Great (3rd) p168, por.
Claghorn--Biog. p462
Claghorn--Jazz p305
Cur. Biog. '77 p473
Entertainers p216
Ingraham--Album p62
Lamparski--What. (2) p36-37,
por.
McHenry--Liberty's p431-432
Macksey--Book p236
O'Neill--Women's p624
Signif.--Amer. p77, por.
Simon--Best p597-598, por.
Toppin--Biog. p441-444
Warren--Pictorial p199
Webster's--Amer. p1100
World--Who p274

WATERS, LYDIA (fl. 1850's-1870's)
Amer. Western pioneer,
diarist
Hoople--As p63-65

WATIE, SARAH CAROLINE BELL
(1820-)
Amer. Cherokee Indian,
Civil War Confederate patriot,

noted Oklahoma mother
Amer.--Mothers p437

WATKINS, ALTHERIA (fl. 1970's)
Amer. WAF policewoman
O'Neill--Women's p547

WATKINS, ELAINE
Amer. agriculturist, police-
woman
O'Neill--Women's p13

WATKINS, FRANCES ELLEN
See HARPER, FRANCES ELLEN
WATKINS

WATSON, ANNA (c1871-)
German-Amer. centenarian
Mitchell--Yessir p116-118, por.

WATSON, BARBARA L. (1944-)
Amer. TV executive
Scheuer--Tel. p502

WATSON, BARBARA M. (1918-)
Amer. government official
O'Neill--Women's p92
Warren--Pictorial p200

WATSON, CAROLINE (c1760-1814)
English engraver
Sparrow--Women p59,89

WATSON, ELLA ("CATTLE KATE")
(c1862-1888/1889)
Amer. cattle rancher
Gray--Women p116-117
Sherr--American p253, por.
Williams--Legend. p53-67, por.

WATSON, FRANCES NASH (1890-
1971)
Amer. pianist
Claghorn--Biog. p463

WATSON, LILIAN D. (1932-)
Australian genealogical re-
searcher
Meyer--Who's p214

WATSON, LILLIAN SMITH (-1967)
Amer., Alaskan telephone
operator
Jones--Women (1) p127-131

WATSON, LUCILE (1879-1962)
Canadian-Amer. actress

Springer--They p250,335, por.
World--Who p252

WATSON, MARIAN ETOILE
Amer. TV arts editor
Scheuer--Tel. p503

WATSON, MAUD (fl. 1880's)
British tennis player
Macksey--Book p257

WATSON, MYRA (fl. 1970's)
Amer. mountain woman
Kahn--Hill. p114-125, por.

WATSON, PATRICIA ("TRICIA")
(c1949-)
Amer. chemist
Science Digest--100 p56-57, por.

WATSON, SARAH
Amer., wife of John Cotton
Dana
Starr--Amer. p44,46

WATSON, VERA (-1978)
Amer. mountain climber,
computer programmer
Lichtenstein--Mach. p16-18,30-31

WATT, LINNIE (1875-1890)
British pottery designer,
decorator, faience artist
Callen--Women p77,227, por.

WATTEVILLE, HENRIETTA
BENIGNA JUSTINE ZINZEN-
DORF VON (1725-1789)
Amer. colonial educator,
college founder, religious
leader
James--Notable (3) p551-552
Neidle--America's p21-22
Sherr--American p198

WATTS, DOROTHY CHAMBERS
(1911-)
Amer. genealogical researcher,
writer, indexer
Meyer--Who's p214

WATTS, HEATHER (1953-)
Amer. ballet dancer
Cur. Biog. '83 p430-433, por.

WATTS, HELEN (1927-)
English opera singer

Gammond--Illus. p252,
por.

WATTS, MARY
British painter, designer,
architect, architectural
ceramicist
Callen--Women p7,166,227

WAUNEKA, ANNIE DODGE (1910-)
Amer. Navajo Indian, social
reformer
Brin--Social p157-158
Gridley--Amer. p119-130, por.
Kulkin--Her p297-298

WAY, AMANDA M. (1828-1914)
Amer. temperance-suffrage
reformer, clergyman, nurse,
feminist, social reformer
James--Notable (3) p552-553

WAY, KATHERINE (1903-)
Amer. nuclear physicist,
professor
O'Neill--Women's p181

WAYMAN, EUNICE
See SIMONE, NINA

WAYNE, FRANCES (1924-)
Amer. singer
Claghorn--Jazz p306

WAYNE, JUNE (1918-)
Amer. lithographer, graphic
artist
Diamonstein--Open p426-431, por.
Munro--Originals p282-288, por.
Women's--Female p83

WAYNE, MABEL (1904-)
Amer. composer, pianist,
singer
Claghorn--Biog. p463
Jablonski--Ency. p308-309

WAYNE, SUSAN
Amer. singer, filmmaker
Smith--Movies p212-214,281

WEATHERFORD, DOROTHY (fl.
1970's)
Amer. artist, craftswoman
O'Neill--Women's p248,251

WEAVER, EULA (c1889-)

Amer. athlete (walker)
People's Almanac (3) p525

WEAVER, HARRIET SHAW (1876-
1961)
English patron of arts
Rogers--Ladies, see index
p236, por.

WEAVER, MARJORIE (1913-)
Amer. singer, model,
actress
Springer--They p250,335÷336,
por.

WEBB, AILEEN OSBORN (1892-
1979)
Amer. organization official,
craftswoman, watercolorist,
woodcarver, enamelist,
ceramicist
Cur. Biog. '79 p475
Gilbert--Part. p31, por.
O'Neill--Women's p100,124

WEBB, BEATRICE POTTER (1858-
1943)
English Socialist, social
reformer, economist, his-
torian
Brecher--Lives p305, por.
Fry--1000 p287
Jones--Rutledge p815
Macksey--Book p118-119
Moers--Literary p317
O'Neill--Women's p292-293
Showalter--Lit. p340
Who Did What p325
Wintle--Makers p555-565, #509
World--Who p192

WEBB, JUNE ELLEN (1934-)
Amer. singer, songwriter
Claghorn--Biog. p464

WEBB, MARY GLADYS MEREDITH
(1881-1927)
English novelist
Avenel--Comp. (1) p547
Crosland--Beyond p54,108-117,
121-122,130,133,170
Jones--Rutledge p815
Magill--Cycl. p1133-1134
Morley--Literary p140
Seymour-Smith--Novels p234
Showalter--Lit. p345

WEBBER, ANNA (fl. 1880's)
Amer. Western teacher
Time--Women p92,95

WEBER, ALICIA (c1945-)
Amer. TV photographer
O'Neill--Women's p501

WEBER, CHARLOTTE COLKET
(c1943-)
Amer. millionaire
Frobes--400 ('84) p82

WEBER, ENID W. (fl. 1970's)
Amer. labor leader, govern-
ment official
O'Neill--Women's p333

WEBER, LOIS (1881-1939)
Amer. film director, writer,
actress, producer
James--Notable (3) p553-555
McHenry--Liberty's p432
O'Neill--Women's p666
Slide--Early p34-51, por.
Smith--Movies p11-12, por.

WEBSTER, MRS. DANIEL
Amer., wife of Daniel Webster
Earle--Two Cent. (2) p xxv,804,
por.

WEBSTER, ELEANOR (fl. 1960's)
Amer. chemist, professor
M.I.T.--Women p x,201-205

WEBSTER, JEAN (1876-1916)
Amer. author
James--Notable (3) p555-556
McHenry--Liberty's p432-433

WEBSTER, MARGARET (1905-1972)
Amer. theatrical director,
producer, actress
Chinoy--Women p192, por.
Cur. Biog. '73 p464
Sicherman--Notable p718-721

WEBSTER, MARY REEVE (fl. 1680's)
Amer., accused witch
Williams--Demeter's p138

WEBSTER, MAY
See WHITTY, MAY, ("DAME")

WEDDINGTON, SARAH RAGLE

(1945-   )
Amer. lawyer, activist,
government official
Adams--Women p100,123-125,177
O'Neill--Women's p354

WEDEL, CYNTHIA CLARK (c1908-   )
Amer. church official, be-
haviorial scientist
Bloom--Religion p126
Cur. Biog. '70 p437-438, por.
Diamonstein--Open p432-436,
por.
Macksey--Book p121
O'Neill--Women's p393-394

WEED, ELLA (1853-1894)
Amer. educator
James--Notable (3) p556-557

WEED, ETHEL BERENICE (1906-
1975)
Amer. military officer (WAC)
Sicherman--Notable p721-723

WEEDEN, ELIZABETH (fl. 1670's-
1680's)
Amer. midwife
Mead--Hist. p410

WEEKS, HELEN C.
See CAMPBELL, HELEN STUART

WEEKS, JENNIE N. (1902-   )
Amer. genealogical researcher,
author
Meyer--Who's p215

WEGNER, SANDRA DeFORE (1938-   )
Amer. genealogical researcher
Meyer--Who's p215

WEHNER, BETTY
See SMITH, BETTY WEHNER

WEICKER, CAMILLE
Amer., wife of Senator
Lowell Weicker
People--Best p230-231, por.

WEIDENFELD, SHEILA (fl. 1970's)
Amer. TV producer
Klever--Women p26,63-64,95,
107-108,por.

WEIDLER, VIRGINIA (1927-1968)
Amer. child actress

Edelson--Kids p28-30, por.
Springer--They p250,336, por.

WEIGEL, HELENE (1900-1971)
Amer. actress
Entertainers p216

WEIGEL, KATHERINE (-1539)
Polish religious martyr
Bainton--Spain p156-159

WEIKEL, SALLY ANN (1930-   )
Amer. genealogical researcher,
author
Meyer--Who's p215

WEIL, MINA ROSENTHAL (1859-   )
Amer. educator, social
worker, noted North Carolina
mother
Amer.--Mothers p402-403, por.

WEIL, SIMONE (1909-1943)
French author, philosopher,
humanitarian
Crosland--Women, see index p255,
por.
Donaldson--How p382-383
Marlowe--Great p346-350, por.
Seymour-Smith--Who's p387
Wintle--Makers p560-561, #512

WEIL, SUZANNE (1933-   )
Amer. TV program executive
Scheuer--Tel. p504-505, por.

WEILL, CLAUDIA (1947-   )
Amer. film producer, director
O'Neill--Women's p663
Smith--Movies p214,282, por.

WEINER, RUTH (fl. 1960's-1970's)
Austrian-Amer. chemist, en-
vironmentalist, professor
Neidle--America's p215-217
O'Neill--Women's p170

WEINSHIENK, ZITA (c1933-   )
Amer. judge
Diamonstein--Open p437-441, por.

WEINSTEIN, HANNAH (fl. 1950's-
1970's)
Amer. film producer
Smith--Movies p65-66,282

WEINSTEIN, MIRIAM (c1948-   )

Amer. filmmaker
Smith--Movies p215,282

WEINSTEIN, PAULA
Amer. film studio executive
Adams--Women p101

WEINSTOCK, ANNA
Amer. labor mediator,
government official
O'Neill--Women's p285,330-331

WEINTRAUBEN, BARBARA AUGS-
BURG (fl. 1600's)
German medical writer
Mead--Hist. p360,426

WEIR, IRENE (1862-1944)
Amer. painter, teacher,
writer
James--Notable (3) p557-559

WEIR, MARY BRINKLEY (1783-
1840)
Amer. composer
Claghorn--Biog. p466

WEIS, JESSICA McCULLOUGH
(1901-1963)
Amer. Congresswoman
Chamberlin--Min. p280-282

WEISBERG, SUZANNE (fl. 1970's)
Amer. artist
Women's--Female p113

WEI SHUO
Chinese artist (calligrapher)
Petersen--Women p148-149

WEISS, MYRA TANNER (fl. 1950's-
1960's)
Amer. Vice Presidential
candidate
People's Almanac (1) p127

WEISS, SUSAN ARCHER TALLEY
(fl. 1890's-1900's)
Amer. poet, literary patron
Ehrlich--Oxford p235

WEISSTEIN, NAOMI (1939-)
Amer. psychology professor
Ruddick--Working p241-250, por.

WEIZMANN, VERA CHATZMAN
(1881-1966)

Russian co-founder, Zionist
organization
Macksey--Book p119-120

WELBORN, NANCY (fl. 1970's)
Amer. softball player
Jordan--Broken p137,139-141

WELBY, AMELIA BALL COPPUCK
(1819/1821-1966)
Amer. poet
Sherr--American p96

WELCH, OLA-FLORENCE
Amer., early school friend of
Richard Nixon
People's Almanac (1) p320

WELCH, RAQUEL (1940-)
Amer. actress
Anderson--People p403-404, por.
Cur. Biog. '71 p436-438, por.
Hirschhorn--Rating p374, por.
Mordden--Movies p267-268,275
Shipman--Internatl. p611-613,
por.
World--Who p253

WELD, ANGELINA GRIMKE
See GRIMKE, ANGELINA EMILY

WELD, THERESA (1893-)
Amer. skater
Hollander--100 p22-23, por.
McWhirter--Guinness p99-100

WELD, TUESDAY (SUSAN KER)
(1943-)
Amer. actress
Cur. Biog. '74 p428-431, por.
Hirschhorn--Rating p374-375,
por.
Shipman--Internatl. p613-614,
por.
World--Who p253

WELDON, FAY (fl. 1970's)
English novelist, playwright
Baker--Women p5
Crosland--Beyond p58,195-196,
199,204-210,213-214,228
Seymour-Smith--Novels p234

WELITCH, LJUBA (1912/1913-)
Bulgarian-Amer. opera singer
Claghorn--Biog. p467

WELKER, CHRISTY
    Amer. TV executive
    Scheuer--Tel. p507

WELL, SIMONE (1903-1943)
    French philosopher
    Moers--Literary p xix,88,212,
    282,318, por.

WELLAUER, MARALYN ANN (1949-)
    Amer. genealogical researcher,
    author
    Meyer--Who's p216

WELLES, CLARA BARCK (1868-)
    Amer. silversmith, designer
    Callen--Women p162,227

WELLES, SOPHIA WOODHOUSE (fl.
    1820's)
    Amer. inventor
    Sherr--American p35

WELLESLEY, ANNE HILL, LADY
    MORNINGTON (c1743-)
    Irish, mother of Arthur
    Wellesley, Duke of
    Wellington
    Diagram--Mothers p254-255, por.

WELLESLEY, DOROTHY (1891-1956)
    English poet
    Bernikow--World p162

WELLHOUSE, (MARY) ANN WALCHER
    (1928-)
    Amer. genealogical researcher
    Meyer--Who's p216

WELLS, ALICE STEBBINS
    Amer. social worker, police-
    woman
    Felton--Famous p148-150, por.
    Macksey--Book p137

WELLS, ARDIS ARLEE (1917-)
    Amer. singer, songwriter
    Claghorn--Biog. p467

WELLS, CAROLYN (1862-1942)
    Amer. anthologist, poet,
    novelist, children's book
    author
    Ehrlich--Oxford p193
    James--Notable (3) p559-560
    McHenry--Liberty's p433

WELLS, CHARLOTTE FOWLER
    (1814-1901)
    Amer. teacher, phrenologist,
    publisher, lecturer, journalist,
    businesswoman
    James--Notable (3) p560-561

WELLS, DELILAH AND SARAH
    (fl. 1630's)
    Amer. sisters, town namesake
    Sherr--American p245

WELLS, EMMELINE BLANCHE WOOD-
    WARD (1828-1921)
    Amer. religious leader,
    feminist, suffragist, noted
    Utah mother
    Amer.--Mothers p525, por.
    James--Notable (3) p561-563
    McHenry--Liberty's p433-434
    Sherr--American p227
    Time--Women p218

WELLS, FAITH McCAIN (-1961)
    Amer., mother-in-law of
    Sherwood Eliot Wirt
    Kooiman--Silhouettes p143-149,
    por.

WELLS, IDA BELL
    See WELLS-BARNETT, IDA BELL

WELLS, JULIA
    See ANDREWS, JULIE

WELLS, KATE GARNETT (1838-1911)
    English-Amer. social reformer,
    art writer
    Callen--Women p46
    James--Notable (3) p563-565

WELLS, KITTY (1919-)
    Amer. singer, guitarist
    Claghorn--Biog. p467

WELLS, LOUISA M. (-1886)
    Amer. company operator
    Sherr--American p106

WELLS, LOUISA SUSANNAH (fl.
    1770's)
    English "Tory"
    Williams--Demeter's p257-258

WELLS, MARGUERITE MILTON
    (1872-1959)

Amer. suffragist, civic
leader
Sicherman--Notable p723-725

WELLS, MARY GEORGENE BERG
See LAWRENCE, MARY
GEORGENE BERG WELLS

WELLS, REBECCA (fl. 1750's)
Amer. real estate agent,
colonial realtor
Williams--Demeter's p189

WELLS-BARNETT, IDA BELL
(1862-1931)
Amer. journalist, lecturer,
editor, feminist, social
reformer
Adams--Great (3rd) p109, por.
Brin--Social p151
Burt--Black p54-70, por.
Hoople--As p178-181
James--Notable (3) p565-567
Kulkin--Her p298-299
McHenry--Liberty's p434-435
Marzolf--Up p25
Millstein--We p150
O'Neill--Women's p440
Papachristou--Women p123-124,
145
Sherr--American p60-61,218
Signif.--Amer. p37, por.
Toppin--Biog. p446-448
Truman--Women p70-85,108,199,
por.
Webster's--Amer. p1115

WELSH, KIT (1667-1739)
British soldier
Woman's Almanac p446-447

WELSH, LILIAN (1858-1938)
Amer. physician, educator
James--Notable (3) p567-568

WELTER, BLANCA ROSA
See CHRISTIAN, LINDA

WELTON, CAROLINE J. (c1842-
1884)
Amer. sportswoman,
mountain climber
Sherr--American p35

WELTY, EUDORA (1909-)
Amer. short-story writer,

novelist
Avenel--Comp. (2) p262
Cahill--Women p7,96-97,376
Clark--Leading p183
Cur. Biog. '75 p431-433, por.
Diamonstein--Open p442-445, por.
Ehrlich--Oxford, see index p463
Howard--Seven p166-213
McHenry--Liberty's p435
Magill--Cycl. p1139-1141
Moers--Literary p261,318
O'Neill--Women's p681-682
Pearson--Who p288
Seymour-Smith--Novels p235
Seymour-Smith--Who's p387-388
Signif.--Amer. p77, por.
Spacks--Contemp. p150-172,182-
183
Webber--Woman p23-31
Webster's--Amer. p1115-1116
Who Did What p327
World--Who p22

WEMLINGER, CLAIRE
See TREVOR, CLAIRE

WENDELL, ELLA VON ECHTEL
(-1931)
Amer. real estate profiteer,
recluse
Horan--Desperate p74-75, por.

WENNER, KATE (1947-)
Amer. TV news producer
Scheuer--Tel. p508

WENONAH (fl. 1800's)
Amer. Sioux Indian, legendary
heroine
Coffin--Parade p529,608
Sherr--American p123, por.

WEN SHU (1595-1634)
Chinese painter
Petersen--Women p156

WENTWORTH, CECILE DE (c1853-
1933)
Amer. painter
McHenry--Liberty's p435

WENTWORTH, FRANCES DEERING,
LADY (-1813)
Amer. belle
Young--Revol., see index p224-
225, por.

WENTWORTH, MRS. MICHAEL (fl.
1770's)
Amer. patriot
Young--Revol. p91-93,111 & n,
132,140

WENTWORTH, SARAH (fl. 1780's)
Amer. (first) novelist
Ingraham--Album p58

WERBERMACHER, HANNAH RACHEL
(1805-)
Polish, Jewish Hasidic rabbi
Henry--Written p11,212-214

WEREFKIN, MARIANNE VON
See VON WEREFKIN, MARIANNE

WERFEL, ALMA MAHLER GROPIUS
(1879-1964)
Austrian composer, feminist
Dunlap--Calif. p216-217
Sorell--Three p1-69, por.

WERLEIN, ELIZEBETH THOMAS
(1883-1946)
Amer. leader, preserving
New Orleans French quarter
James--Notable (3) p568-569

WERLEY, MERYL (fl. 1970's)
Amer. la crosse player
O'Neill--Women's p569

WERNER, JOYCE
Amer. TV cable manager
Scheuer--Tel. p508

WERNER, MARY LOU
See FORBES, MARY LOU
WERNER

WERSHBA, SHIRLEY
Amer. TV news producer
Scheuer--Tel. p509

WERTHEIM, BARBARA
See TUCHMAN, BARBARA
MAYER WERTHEIM

WERTMÜLLER, LINA (1930/1931-)
Italian film director, writer
Cur. Biog. '76 p430-433, por.
O'Neill--Women's p669
Smith--Movies p126-128, por.
World--Who p283

WERTZ, JEANNE
Amer. business consultant
Woman's Almanac p180

WESCOTT, MARY FITCH
See PERKINS, MARY FITCH
WESCOTT

WESLEY, SUSANNA ANNESLEY
(1669-1742)
English, "Mother of Methodism," mother of John Wesley
(religious leader)
Diagram--Mothers p256-258, por.
Taylor--Gener. p30, por.

WEST, DOROTHY (1910-)
Amer. magazine editor, short-
story writer, novelist
Pearson--Who p189

WEST, DOROTHY ("DOTTIE")
MARIE (1932-)
Amer. singer, songwriter
Claghorn--Biog. p468
Glassman--Year '79 p165,167, por.

WEST, JESSAMYN (1902-1984)
Amer. novelist
Bachtold--Gifted p19-22
Betts--Writers p152-153, por.
Cur. Biog. '77 p433-436, por.
Cur. Biog. '84 p489
Diamonstein--Open p446-449, por.
Dunlap--Calif. p217, por.
Ehrlich--Oxford, see index p463
McHenry--Liberty's p435-436
P.W.--Author p178-180,532

WEST, JOELLA
Amer. TV director
Scheuer--Tel. p509

WEST, LILLIE
See LESLIE, AMY

WEST, MAE (1892/1893-1980)
Amer. actress, singer, play-
wright, director, author
Banner--Women p199-200, por.
Claghorn--Biog. p469
Clark--Leading p142
Coffin--Female p167-177, por.
Comfort--Good p199, por.
Cur. Biog. '81 p475
Engstead--Star p98-102

WESTON, HANNAH WATTS (1758-
1855)
Amer. Revolutionary War
heroine, patriot
Sherr--American p90

WESTON, NANCY
Amer. slave
Hymowitz--Hist. p52

WESTPHAL, JEANNE (fl. 1970's)
Amer. government official
O'Neill--Women's p84-85

WESTPHALEN, JENNY VON
See MARX, JENNY VON
WESTPHALEN

WESTWOOD, JEAN MILES (1923-)
Amer. political leader
O'Neill--Women's p74

WETAMOO ("SQUAW SACHEM OF
POCASSET") (fl. 1670's)
Amer. Indian warrior
Gridley--Amer. p13-21
Sherr--American p208

WETHERED, JOYCE (1901-)
English golfer
People's Almanac (1) p1186
Woman's Almanac p421

WETHERELL, ELIZABETH
See WARNER, SUSAN BOGERT

WETHERELL, EMMA ABBOTT
See ABBOTT, EMMA

WETHERS, DORIS LOUISE (fl.
1950's-1970's)
Amer. pediatrician
Innis--Profiles p148-149, por.

WEXLER, ANNE (c1930-)
Amer. political worker,
government official
Diamonstein--Open p450-455,
por.
O'Neill--Women's p81

WEXLER, JACQUELINE GRENNAN
(1926-)
Amer. college president, nun
Adams--Women p50
Cur. Biog. '70 p441-443, por.
O'Neill--Women's p406

WEYAND, RUTH (fl. 1930's-1960's)
Amer. labor lawyer
O'Neill--Women's p285,334,349-350

WHALEY, (AUNT) LYDIA (c1840-
1926)
Amer. weaver, craftswoman,
basket-maker
O'Neill--Women's p123

WHALL, VERONICA (1887-)
British stained glass artist
Callen--Women p175,227

WHARTON, EDITH NEWBOLD JONES
(1862-1937)
Amer. novelist, short-story
writer
Avenel--Comp. (2) p264-265
Betts--Writers p38-39, por.
Brandon--Dollar, see index p214
Cahill--Women p6,373
Clark--Leading p79-83
Crosland--Beyond p1,13,44-45,
179
Daniels--Wash. p164-165,168-170
Earnest--American p231-232
Ehrlich--Oxford, see index p463,
por.
Gilfond--Heroines p104
Holme--Journal p175-177, por.
Howard--Seven p28-30
Ingraham--Album p58
James--Notable (3) p570-573
Jones--Rutledge p822
Kronenberger--Atlan. p865-866
Kulkin--Her p299-300
Longstreet--Queen p125-133, por.
McHenry--Liberty's p436-437
Magill--Cycl. p1148-1150
Moers--Literary p318
O'Neill--Women's p673
Parker--Uneasy p179-183
Seymour-Smith--Novels p235, por.
Seymour-Smith--Who's p391-392
Sherr--American p106
Signif.--Amer. p55, por.
Webster's--Amer. p1119
Who Did What p328
Wintle--Makers p566-567, #517
Woman's Almanac p261
World--Who p221

WHATELEY, ANNE, SISTER (c1561-
c1600)
English nun, friend of William
Shakespeare

British needlework designer
Callen--Women p100, por.

WHIFFEN, BLANCHE GALTON
(1854-1936)
English-Amer. actress
James--Notable (3) p579-580

WHIGHAM, MARGARET (fl. 1930's)
British debutante
Keenan--Women p44-45, por.

WHIPPLE, CORNELIA WRIGHT
(1816-1890)
Amer., girl's school founder,
noted Minnesota mother
Amer.--Mothers p286, por.

WHISTLER, ANNA MATILDA
McNEILL (1804-1881)
Amer., mother of James
McNeill Whistler
Diagram--Mothers p259-261, por.
People's Almanac (1) p941

WHISTLER, PEGGY
See EVANS, MARGARET

WHITAKER, ANN (fl. 1970's)
Amer. surface physics
specialist
O'Connor--Sally p20

WHITAKER, ELIZABETH FOULKS
(fl. 1800's)
Amer. pioneer, Indian captive, fur trader
Sherr--American p186

WHITALL, ANN (fl. 1770's)
Amer. Quaker, heroine
Earle--Two Cent. (2) p606-607
Sherr--American p152

WHITCHER, FRANCES MIRIAM
BERRY (1811/1814-1852)
Amer. humorist, caricaturist
Ehrlich--Oxford p177
James--Notable (3) p580-581
McHenry--Liberty's p438

WHITCHURCH, ANNA K. (fl.
1970's)
Amer. industrial psychologist
Seed--Saturday's p143-144, por.

WHITCOMB, JOANNE (fl. 1970's)

Amer. clergyman
Proctor--Women p30-46,57,75-77,
81,89,107

WHITE, ALICE (1907-)
Amer. actress
Springer--They p253,337, por.

WHITE, ALMA BRIDWELL (1862-1946)
Amer. church founder, bishop
James--Notable (3) p581-583
McHenry--Liberty's p438-439

WHITE, ANNA (1831-1910)
Amer. Shaker eldress, social
reformer
James--Notable (3) p583-584

WHITE, ANTONIA (1899-)
English novelist, translator,
journalist
Showalter--Lit. p349

WHITE, BARBARA EHRLICH (fl.
1970's)
Amer. author
Women's--Female p117

WHITE, BETTY (1917-)
Amer. actress
World--Who p253

WHITE, CAROLINA (1886-1935)
Amer. opera singer
Claghorn--Biog. p470

WHITE, CHERYL (fl. 1970's)
Amer. jockey
Hollander--100 p65-66

WHITE, DIANA (fl. 1900's)
British book illustrator
Callen--Women p182

WHITE, EARTHA MARY MAGDALENE
(1876-1974)
Amer. social welfare, community leader, businesswoman
Sicherman--Notable p726-728

WHITE, EDITH (1855-)
Amer. Western pioneer
Fischer--Let p271-282

WHITE, EDNA NOBLE (1879-1954)
Amer. educator, home economist, child development pioneer

Sicherman--Notable p728-
729

WHITE, ELEANOR
See DARE, ELEANOR WHITE

WHITE, ELIZA ORNE (1856-1947)
Amer. children's book author
James--Notable (3) p584-585

WHITE, ELIZABETH (fl. 1900's)
Amer. pioneer fruit-grower
Sherr--American p154

WHITE, ELIZABETH PEARSON
(1914-)
Amer. genealogical researcher,
editor
Meyer--Who's p217

WHITE, ELLEN GOULD HARMON
(1827-1915)
Amer. co-founder, Seventh
Day Adventist Church
James--Notable (3) p585-588
McHenry--Liberty's p439
O'Neill--Women's p379-380
Sherr--American p116
Warren--Pictorial p131
Woman's Almanac p404-405
World--Who p84

WHITE, GRACE MILLER (1868-
1965)
Amer. novelist
Ehrlich--Oxford p114

WHITE, HELEN MAGILL (1853-1944)
Amer. educator, novelist
James--Notable (3) p588-589
McHenry--Liberty's p439-440
Sicherman--Notable p729-730

WHITE, JOSEPHINE (1873-1956)
Amer., Alaskan gold-rush
pioneer
Sherr--American p5

WHITE, KATHARINE ELKUS (1906-
1985)
Amer. Ambassador (to Den-
mark), mayor
Cur. Biog. '85 p476

WHITE, KATHARINE S. (c1893-1977)
Amer. magazine fiction editor
O'Neill--Women's p473-474

WHITE, KATHERINE ELIZABETH
See WILSON, MARIE KATHERINE
ELIZABETH

WHITE, LYNNE
Amer. TV weathercaster
Scheuer--Tel. p512

WHITE, MARGARET
See BOURKE-WHITE, MARGARET

WHITE, MARGARET DAVIS FISHER
(1874-)
Amer., noted New Jersey
mother
Amer.--Mothers p371

WHITE, MARGITA EKLUND (1937-)
Amer. government official
O'Neill--Women's p80

WHITE, MARTHA (fl. 1970's)
Amer. marathon runner
O'Neill--Women's p576

WHITE, MARY (-1921)
Amer., daughter of William
Allen White
Sherr--American p74

WHITE, MARY ANN HATTEN (1830-
1924)
Amer., mother of William
Allen White, noted Iowa mother
Amer.--Mothers p201-202, por.

WHITE, MARY JARRETT (fl. 1920's)
Amer., Georgia voter
Sherr--American p51

WHITE, MARY LUELLA NESMITH
Amer. Western pioneer, teacher
Time--Women p90-91

WHITE, PEARL (1889-1938)
Amer. actress
Banner--Women p166, por.
James--Notable (3) p589-590
Keylin--Hollywood p281, por.
McHenry--Liberty's p440
Manchel--Women p26-27, por.
Mordden--Movie p24-25
World--Who p253

WHITE, RUTH (1914-1969)
Amer. producer, composer,
actress, electronics expert

Smith--Movies p215-216,
283

WHITE, SUE SHELTON (1887-1943)
Amer. suffragist, lawyer,
government official,
feminist, politician
James--Notable (3) p590-592
Scott--Southern p205-206
Showalter--These p45-52
Ware--Beyond p154-155, see
also index p203

WHITE, SUSANNA
See WINSLOW, SUSANNA FULLER
WHITE

WHITE, WILLYE (c1940-)
Amer. track & field athlete
Jordan--Broken p1-27
Woman's Almanac p428-429

"WHITE ROSE OF THE MIAMIS"
See SLOCUM, FRANCES
("MACONAQUAH")

WHITEHEAD, LENORE R. (1917-)
Amer. genealogical researcher,
editor, indexer
Meyer--Who's p217

WHITEHOUSE, MARY (1910-)
English moral reformer,
teacher, journalist, broadcaster
Jones--Rutledge p824

WHITELY, OPEL (fl. 1920's)
Amer. "counterfeit" diarist
Sherr--American p197

WHITING, (EMILY) LILIAN
(1847-1942)
Amer. journalist, author
James--Notable (3) p592-593

WHITING, MARGARET (1924-)
Amer. singer
Simon--Best p608-609, por.
World--Who p274

WHITING, MARGARET C. (fl.
1890's)
Amer. embroiderer
Callen--Women p133-134

WHITING, SARAH FRANCES (1847-

1942)
Amer. physicist, astronomer,
professor
James--Notable (3) p593-595
O'Neill--Women's p149
Sherr--American p114

WHITLEY, EDYTHE JOHNS RUCKER
(1900-)
Amer. genealogical researcher,
author
Meyer--Who's p218

WHITMAN, MRS. MARCUS (fl.
1800's)
Amer. missionary's wife
Stein--Fragments p39-68

WHITMAN, MARINA VON NEUMANN
(1935-)
Cur. Biog. '73 p432-434, por.
O'Neill--Women's p421

WHITMAN, NARCISSA (1808-1847)
Amer. missionary, Western
pioneer
Gray--Women p21-35, por.
Hoople--As p110-116,125-127
James--Notable (3) p595-597
Kulkin--Her p302-303
Millstein--We p53,58, por.
Reifert--Women p126-128
Sherr--American p243,254,257
Time--Women p47-48,51-52

WHITMAN, RUTH (1922-)
Amer. poet
Chester--Rising p102-104, por.

WHITMAN, SARAH HELEN POWER
(1803-1878)
Amer. poet, essayist, spiri-
tualist, (fiancée of Edgar
Allan Poe)
Ehrlich--Oxford p69-70
James--Notable (3) p597-599
McHenry--Liberty's p440
Sherr--American p208, por.

WHITMORE, JOAN
South African hydrological
researcher
Macksey--Book p159

WHITMORE, MRS. THOMAS (fl.
1760's)
Amer. pioneer settler, nurse,

McWhirter--Guinness p77-78, por.
Sabin--Women p151-166, por.
Woman's Almanac p421-422, por.
World--Who p224

WIAT, MRS. (fl. 1700's)
    Amer. midwife
    Mead--Hist. p411

WICHMAN, SHARON (fl. 1960's)
    Amer. swimmer
    McWhirter--Guinness p134, por.

WICK, TEMPE (fl. 1770's-1780's)
    Amer. Revolutionary War
    patriot
    Clyne--Patriots p74-81

WICKER, IREENE (1905-)
    Amer. radio singer, actress,
    film writer
    Lamparski--What. (2) p158-159,
    por.

WICKERSHAM, ELIZABETH ("LIZ")
    Amer. TV news co-host
    Scheuer--Tel. p513

WICKHAM, ANNA (1884-1947)
    Australian poet
    Bernikow--World p152-153
    Showalter--Lit. p346

WICKSELL, ANNA (fl. 1920's)
    Swedish Parliamentary member
    Macksey--Book p41

WIDDEMER, MARGARET (1890-1978)
    Amer. poet, novelist
    Ehrlich--Oxford p109,139,174,
    197

WIDEN, SOFIA (1900-c1960)
    Swedish textile artist
    O'Neill--Women's p271

WIDNALL, SHEILA E. (fl. 1970's)
    Amer. engineer, professor,
    government official
    O'Neill--Women's p189,192

WIECK, CLARA
    See SCHUMANN, CLARA
    JOSEPHINE WIECK

WIECK, DOROTHEA (1907/1908-)
    Swiss actress

Springer--They p254,338,
por.

WIELAND, JOYCE (c1930-)
    Canadian filmmaker
    Smith--Movies p97

WIESEL, ELIE (1928-)
    Rumanian-Amer. novelist
    World--Who p22

WIESLANDER, ROSE
    See STOKES, ROSE HARRIET
    PASTOR

WIESNER, ELIZABETH (fl. 1970's)
    Amer. priest
    O'Neill--Women's p386

WIEWIORSKA, HELENA (1888-1967)
    Polish lawyer
    Macksey--Book p129

WIGGIN, KATE DOUGLAS SMITH
    (1856-1923)
    Amer. author, kindergarten
    educator
    Earnest--American p103-104
    Ehrlich--Oxford, see index p463
    James--Notable (3) p605-607
    Jones--Rutledge p826
    Kulkin--Her p305-306
    McHenry--Liberty's p444
    Sherr--American p87,89-90
    Signif.--Amer. p37, por.
    Snyder--Dauntless p87-123, por.
    Webster's--Amer. p1133
    World--Who p101

WIGGINS, ELLA MAY (1889-1929)
    Amer. poet
    Bernikow--World p309-310

WIGGINS, LILLIAN (fl. 1960's)
    Amer. newspaper editor,
    foreign correspondent,
    politician
    O'Neill--Women's p459

WIGHTMAN, FRIEDA
    See INESCORT, FRIEDA

WIGHTMAN, HAZEL VIRGINIA
    HOTCHKISS (1886/1887-1974)
    Amer. tennis player
    Hollander--100 p98-100, por.
    McHenry--Liberty's p444

Macksey--Book p257, por.
McWhirter--Guinness p161, por.
Sherr--American p14
Sicherman--Notable p731-732
Sullivan--Queens p98-99
Who Did What p329

WIGMAN, MARY (1886-1973)
German dance educator,
choreographer, dancer
Cur. Biog. '69 p448-451, por.
Cur. Biog. '73 p464
O'Neill--Women's p646-647

WIGNELL, ANN BRUNTON
See MERRY, ANN BRUNTON

WIIK, MARIA (1853-)
Finnish artist
Sparrow--Women p290,309,313

WILBERFORCE, MARION (fl.
1940's)
British aviatrix
Boase--Sky's p179,186

WILCOX, ELLA WHEELER (1850-
1919)
Amer. poet, journalist
Avenel--Comp. (2) p268
Bernikow--World p220-221
Ehrlich--Oxford p336
James--Notable (3) p607-609
Jones--Rutledge p826
McHenry--Liberty's p444-445
Moers--Literary p318
People's Almanac (2) p605, por.
Sherr--American p34,248
Stein--Lives p433-439
Webster's--Amer. p1134

WILCOX, SHIRLEY LANGDON
(1942-)
Amer. genealogical researcher,
author, editor
Meyer--Who's p218

WILDE, JANE FRANCESCA ELGEE,
LADY (1824/1826-1896)
Irish patriot, author,
(mother of Oscar Wilde)
Diagram--Mothers p262-265, por.

WILDE, KIRSTIE (fl. 1970's-1980's)
Amer. TV news field anchor
Scheuer--Tel. p513

WILDENHAIN, MARGUERITE (1896-)
Amer. potter
O'Neill--Women's p268

WILDER, FRANCES FARMER (1897-)
Amer. radio executive
Women--Radio p14

WILDER, LAURA INGALLS (1867-
1957)
Amer. novelist, teacher, edi-
tor, children's book author,
noted Missouri mother
Amer.--Mothers p312-313, por.
Ehrlich--Oxford, see index p463,
por.
McHenry--Liberty's p445
Kulkin--Her p306-307
O'Neill--Women's p692-693
Sherr--American p74,118,122,131,
158,214,250, por.
Sicherman--Notable p732-734
World--Who p22

WILDESEN, LESLIE (c1944-)
Amer. archeologist
O'Neill--Women's p26

WILDING, FAITH (fl. 1970's)
Amer. painter
Women's--Female p61

WILES, MARIE DAVIS (1912-)
Amer. genealogical researcher,
author
Meyer--Who's p218-219

WILEY, DOROTHY (fl. 1960's-1970's)
Amer. teacher, filmmaker
Smith--Movies p193-194

WILEY, JENNY SELLARDS
Amer. Indian captive
Sherr--American p80

WILEY, LEE (1915-1975)
Amer. singer, composer
Claghorn--Jazz p312
Simon--Best p613, por.

WILEY, OLIVE FUCIER THOMAS
(1902-)
Amer. communist worker,
noted Rhode Island mother
Amer.--Mothers p482-483, por.

WILHELMI, JANE RUSSELL

Hymowitz--Hist. p189-190
Ingraham--Album p41
James--Notable (3) p613-619
Jones--Rutledge p828
Kulkin--Her p307-308
Levenson--Women p78-79
McHenry--Liberty's p446-447
Macksey--Book p32,276, por.
Papachristou--Women, see index
p vii, por.
People's Almanac (2) p1052
Scott--Southern p144-145,150,155
Sherr--American p38,59,61,72,125,
248,250
Signif.--Amer. p25, por.
Warren--Pictorial, see index
p136-141, por.
Webster's--Amer. p1137-1138
Woman's Almanac p377-378, por.
World--Who p192

WILLARD, NANCY (1936-)
Amer. poet
Chester--Rising p256-261, por.

WILLE, LOIS (1931-)
Amer. journalist
O'Neill--Women's p458

WILLEBRANDT, MABEL WALKER
(1889-1963)
Amer. lawyer, government
official
Sicherman--Notable p734-737

WILLETS, MARY
Amer. physician
Marks--Women p112

WILLETT, MRS. RALPH (1746-1815)
English, wife of Ralph Willett
Ware--Meet p81

WILLIAMS, ABIGAIL (fl. 1710's-
1740's)
Amer. pioneer, witch accuser
Sherr--American p103

WILLIAMS, ANNA WESSELS
(1863-1954)
Amer. physician, bacteri-
ologist
Sicherman--Notable p737-739

WILLIAMS, ANNIE L. (-1977)
Amer. literary agent
O'Neill--Women's p527

WILLIAMS, AUGUSTA
See MAYWOOD, AUGUSTA

WILLIAMS, BARBARA (1942-)
Amer. ice hockey coach
Woman's Almanac p442

WILLIAMS, BETTY (SMYTH)
(1943-)
North Ireland peace activist
Cur. Biog. '79 p434-437, por.
O'Neill--Women's p711
Opfell--Lady p50-61, por.
People's Almanac (2) p1048-1049
Woman's Almanac p386-387

WILLIAMS, CHEE CHEE
Amer. TV news reporter
Scheuer--Tel. p514-515

WILLIAMS, CHICKIE (1919-)
Amer. singer, songwriter
Claghorn--Biog. p474

WILLIAMS, CICELY D. (1893-)
Jamaican physician, professor,
public health worker
O'Neill--Women's p207

WILLIAMS, CINDY (1948-)
Amer. actress
Anderson--People p407, por.
World--Who p253

WILLIAMS, ELIZABETH SPRAGUE
(1869-1922)
Amer. social worker
James--Notable (3) p619-620

WILLIAMS, ELIZABETH WHITNEY
(fl. 1900's)
Amer. lighthouse-keeper,
writer
Sherr--American p116

WILLIAMS, ELLA GWENDOLYN REES
See RHYS, JEAN

WILLIAMS, ESTHER (1923-)
Amer. swimmer, actress,
business woman
Dunlap--Calif. p221, por.
Lamparski--What. (2) p44-45,
por.
People's Almanac (2) p726-727
Shipman--Internatl. p619-621, por.
World--Who p253

WILLIAMS, EUNICE (1696-1786)
Amer. pioneer, Indian captive
Neidle--America's p4

WILLIAMS, FANNIE BARRIER
(1855-1944)
Amer. lecturer, clubwoman,
feminist, hospital co-founder
James--Notable (3) p620-622
McHenry--Liberty's p447-448
Millstein--We p156-157
O'Neill--Women's p696
Sherr--American p61
Sochen--Herstory p187-188
Stein--Fragments p91-96

WILLIAMS, FLORENCE (1865-)
Amer. newspaper editor,
writer
Scott--Southern p120

WILLIAMS, HANNAH ENGLISH
(1692-1722)
Amer. scientist, colonial
biologist
Williams--Demeter's p178-179

WILLIAMS, HELEN MARIE (1762-
1827)
English political letter-writer,
novelist, poet, musician,
politician
Moers--Literary p44,125,318

WILLIAMS, INDIANA FLETCHER
Amer. college founder
Sherr--American p239

WILLIAMS, IVY (fl. 1920's)
English lawyer
Macksey--Book p126-127

WILLIAMS, JEAN L. (fl. 1950's-
1970's)
Amer. science and industrial
animator, filmmaker
Smith--Movies p216,283

WILLIAMS, JESSICA (1948-)
Amer. pianist, composer
Claghorn--Jazz p314

WILLIAMS, KATHLYN (fl. 1910's-
1940's)
Amer. film director, actress
Slide--Early p102-103, por.

WILLIAMS, LORRAINE ANDERSON
(1923-)
Amer. educator, historian,
author, professor
O'Neill--Women's p411

WILLIAMS, MARIETTA
See SULLIVAN, MAXINE

WILLIAMS, MARION (1927-)
Amer. gospel singer
Claghorn--Jazz p315

WILLIAMS, MARY
See FRIETSCHE, BARBARA

WILLIAMS, MARY ALICE (1949-)
Amer. executive, TV cable
anchor
Scheuer--Tel. p515

WILLIAMS, MARY LOU (1910-1981)
Amer. pianist, guitarist, com-
poser
Claghorn--Biog. p475-476
Claghorn--Jazz p315
Cur. Biog. '81 p476
Gilbert--Part. p79-89, por.
Kufrin--Uncom. p154-173, por.
O'Neill--Women's p631-632
Simon--Best p621, por.

WILLIAMS, MARY LYDE HICKS (fl.
1900's)
Amer. painter
Sherr--American p179

WILLIAMS, MARY WILHELMINE
(1878-1944)
Amer. historian
James--Notable (3) p622-623

WILLIAMS, MYRNA
See LOY, MYRNA

WILLIAMS, PEGGY LENORE
("PELENORE") (1948-)
Amer. clown
O'Neill--Women's p749
Woman's Almanac p324

WILLIAMS, MRS. ROBERT
See CUTTS, ADELE

WILLIAMS, SARAH (fl. 1870's)
Amer. suffragist
Sherr--American p187

WILLIAMS, SHERLEY (fl. 1970's)
Amer. author
Fisher--Third p vii,289

WILLIAMS, SHIRLEY VIVIEN
TERESA BRITTAIN (1930-)
British Parliamentary member,
politician
Cur. Biog. '76 p441-444, por.
Jones--Rutledge p831
Vallance--Women, see index p211

WILLIAMS, SUSAN (fl. 1970's)
Amer. sculptor
Women's--Female p97

WILLIAMS, VANESSA (1963-)
Amer. former beauty contest
winner, musician
Cur. Biog. '84 p454-456

WILLIAMS, VICKI (fl. 1970's)
Amer. wrestler
Jordan--Broken p45-48

WILLIAMSON, MIRIAM PIERCE
(1822-1890)
Amer. physician
Amer.--Mothers p426

WILLIM, STEPHANIE (fl. 1970's)
Amer. child gymnast
O'Neill--Women's p562

WILLING, ANNE
See BINGHAM, ANN(E) WILLING

WILLING, AVA
See ASTOR, AVA WILLING

WILLING, JENNIE FOWLER (1834-
1916)
Canadian-Amer. clergyman,
temperance reformer
James--Notable (3) p623-625

WILLIS, BEVERLY
Amer. architect
Rich-McCoy--Mill. p169-188,
por.

WILLIS, FRANCES ELIZABETH
(1899-)
Amer. career ambassador
O'Neill--Women's p90-91

WILLIS, LOVE MARIE (WHITCOMB)

(1824-1908)
Amer. hymnist
Claghorn--Biog. p477

WILLIS, MARY (fl. 1880's)
Amer. library founder
Sherr--American p51

WILLIS, OLYMPIA BROWN
See BROWN, OLYMPIA

WILLIS, SARA PAYSON
See FERN, FANNY, pseud.

WILLMOTT, ELLEN (-1932)
English gardening expert
O'Neill--Women's p134

WILLOUGHBY, CATHERINE, DUCHESS
OF SUFFOLK (1519/1520-1580)
English socialite
Bainton--France p253-279, por.

WILLOUGHBY, FRANCES LOIS (fl.
1940's)
Amer. Navy physician
O'Neill--Women's p209

WILLOUGHBY, LADY
English medical woman
Mead--Hist. p401

WILLS, HELEN NEWINGTON MOODY
ROARK (1905/1906-)
Amer. tennis player
Dunlap--Calif. p170, por.
Hazen--Interv. p382
Hollander--100 p7,104-107, por.
Jones--Rutledge p832
McHenry--Liberty's p448
O'Neill--Women's p583
Pachter--Champ. p154-155, por.
People's Almanac (1) p1190-1191
Reader's--Story p493
Ryan--Sports p131
Sullivan--Queens p99-100, por.
Warren--Pictorial p185-186, por.
Webster's--Amer. p1141-1142
Woman's Almanac p418
World--Who p224

WILLS, JUDY (fl. 1960's)
Amer. trampoline athlete
McWhirter--Guinness p180, por.

WILLSON, MARY ANN (1810-1825)
Amer. painter

DePauw--Rem. p128,134-135
Petersen--Women p68-69

WILMARTH, MARY JANE HOWES
(1873-1935)
Amer. social reformer, state
legislator
James--Notable (2) p251-252
(under Ickes)

WILMS, EVA (fl. 1970's)
West German pentathlete
O'Neill--Women's p580

WILSON, ALICE (c1881-1964)
Canadian geologist
O'Neill--Women's p171

WILSON, ANN (c1950-   )
Amer. singer, flutist
Glassman--Year '79 p106

WILSON, ANNA (-1911)
Amer. Omaha Indian pro-
prietor, philanthropist
Sherr--American p140

WILSON, AUGUSTA JANE EVANS
See EVANS, AUGUSTA JANE

WILSON, CAIRINE (fl. 1930's)
Canadian Senator
Macksey--Book p38

WILSON, DAGMAR (c1916-   )
Amer. illustrator, peace
activist
Diamonstein--Open p461-466,
por.
O'Neill--Women's p710

WILSON, DEBORAH (fl. 1660's)
Amer. Quaker activist
Williams--Demeter's p129

WILSON, DOROTHY (1909-   )
Amer. stenographer,
actress
Springer--They p254-255,338,
por.

WILSON, EDITH BOLLING GALT
(1872-1961)
Amer. first lady, (second
wife of Woodrow Wilson)
Daniels--Wash., see index
p370, por.

Melick--Wives p61-63, por.
Sicherman--Notable p739-741
Woman's Almanac p490, por.

WILSON, ELIZABETH MILLER (fl.
1870's)
Amer. postmaster
Sherr--American p197

WILSON, ELLEN LOUISE AXSON
(1860-1914)
Amer. first lady, (first wife
of Woodrow Wilson)
Daniels--Wash. p62-63,75-76,83
James--Notable (3) p626-628
Melick--Wives p60
Woman's Almanac p490

WILSON, ELSIE JANE (-1965)
New Zealander-Amer. director
Slide--Early p57-58

WILSON, ERICA
English needlewoman
O'Neill--Women's p130-131, por.

WILSON, ETHEL DAVIS (1888/
1890-1980)
South African-Canadian novel-
ist, short-story writer
Avenel--Comp. (1) p557
Seymour-Smith--Novels p237
Seymour-Smith--Who's p399

WILSON, FLORENCE (fl. 1840's)
Amer. principal, Cherokee
Indian school
Sherr--American p192

WILSON, GRACE (1890-1962)
Amer. singer
Claghorn--Biog. p478

WILSON, HARRIETTE (1789-1846)
English author, courtesan
Macksey--Book p102

WILSON, HELEN HOPEKIRK
See HOPEKIRK, HELEN

WILSON, JANE (fl. 1970's)
Amer. painter, film writer
O'Neill--Women's p663-664
Women's--Female p61

WILSON, JESSIE WOODROW (1826/
1830-1888)

English-Amer., (mother of
Woodrow Wilson), noted Vir-
ginia mother
Amer.--Mothers p551-552, por.
Faber--Presidents' p115-123, por.

WILSON, LOIS (1894/1896-)
Amer. actress
Lamparski--What. (5) p138-139,
por.
Lamparski--What. (8) p294-295,
por.
Springer--They p255,338, por.

WILSON, LUZENA STANLEY (fl.
1840's-1850's)
Amer. Western pioneer, hotel
owner
Fischer--Let p151-165
Time--Women p131,134

WILSON, MARGARET (1882-1973)
Amer. novelist
Ehrlich--Oxford p352

WILSON, MARGARET BERENICE
BUSH (1919-)
Amer. organization official,
lawyer
Cur. Biog. '75 p443-446, por.
O'Neill--Women's p361

WILSON, MARGARET D. (fl. 1960's-
1970's)
Amer. philosopher, professor
O'Neill--Women's p427

WILSON, MARGERY (1898-)
Amer. film director
Slide--Early p62-72, por.

WILSON, MARIE KATHERINE
ELIZABETH (1916/1917-1972)
Amer. actress, radio, TV
personality
Lamparski--What. (3) p72-73,
por.
Springer--They p255,338, por.
World--Who p253

WILSON, MARY (1) (fl. 1870's)
Amer. suffragist
Sherr--American p116-117

WILSON, MARY (2) (1943-)
Amer. singer
Woman's Almanac p304-305, por.

WILSON, MARY K. ("KITTY")
(1927-)
Amer. singer, bassist, songwriter
Claghorn--Biog. p478

WILSON, MATILDA RAUSCH (1883-
1966)
Amer. philanthropist, community worker, noted Michigan
mother
Amer.--Mothers p279, por.

WILSON, MAY (fl. 1970's)
Amer. sculptor
Women's--Female p97

WILSON, NANCY (1937-)
Amer. singer
Claghorn--Biog. p479
Claghorn--Jazz p317
Glassman--Year '79 p106

WILSON, RAMONA C. (1945-)
Amer. Colville Indian poet
Fisher--Third p vi,102

WILSON, ROSEMARY (fl. 1970's)
Amer. photographer
Women's--Female p72

WILSON, SARAH (1) (1750-)
English-Amer. adventuress,
accused criminal
Book--Lists (1) p482
James--Notable (3) p628
Macksey--Book p134-135

WILSON, SARAH (2) (fl. 1870's)
Amer. philanthropist
Sherr--American p199

WILSON, SHIRLEY B. (1937-)
Amer. genealogical research-
er, writer
Meyer--Who's p219-220

WILSON, WILMA (fl. 1980's)
Amer., wife in famous court
case
People--Best p206-207, por.

WILSON, WYOMING (fl. 1970's)
Amer. mountain woman
Kahn--Hill. p85-105,110-112, por.

WILTON, MARIE

See BANCROFT, MARIE EFFIE
WILTON, LADY

WIMMER, ELIZABETH JANE (fl.
1840's)
Amer. gold discoverer
Sherr--American p12

WINANS, ANN (1928-)
Amer. engineering secretary,
feminist
Seifer--Nobody p388-435, por.

WINANT, ETHEL
Amer. TV executive
Scheuer--Tel. p516

WINBORNE, REBECCA M. (-1918)
Amer. Civil War (Confederate)
flag-maker
Sherr--American p181

WINCHELL, CONSTANCE MABEL
(1896-1983)
Amer. librarian
Cur. Biog. '84 p481

WINCHESTER, LYDIA ELIZABETH
(fl. 1880's)
Amer. well-water "donor"
Sherr--American p96

WINCHESTER, SARAH PARDEE
(c1837-1922)
Amer. eccentric millionaire,
"mystery house" builder
Dunlap--Calif. p222, por.
McFarland--Incred. p153-154
Sherr--American p20

WINCHILSEA, ANNE FINCH
See FINCH, ANNE KINGSMILL,
COUNTESS OF WINCHILSEA

WINDHAM, MARGARET LEONARD
(1924-)
Amer. genealogical researcher,
writer, editor
Meyer--Who's p220

WINDSOR, CLAIRE (1897-1972)
Amer. actress
Lamparski--What. (2) p186-187,
por.

WINDSOR, (BESSIE) WALLIS WAR-
FIELD SIMPSON, DUCHESS OF

(1896-1986)
Amer. socialite, wife of Ed-
ward VIII
Brandon--Dollar p145-147
Clark--Leading p149-151
Horan--Desperate p206, por.
Keenan--Women p16-19, por.
McHenry--Liberty's p449
Miller--Fishbait p253
100--Greatest (1) p93, por.
O'Neill--Women's p751
People's Almanac (2) p863-864
Webster's--Amer. p1148
World--Who p301

WINEMA (c1836-1920)
Amer. Modoc Indian peace-
maker
Gridley--Amer. p61-66, por.
Sherr--American p194

WINER, LINDA (fl. 1970's-1980's)
Amer. theater critic
Chinoy--Women p226-227,230-231

WINER, LUCY (fl. 1970's)
Amer. theatrical director,
playwright, feminist
Chinoy--Women p300-307

WINE-VOLNER, JILL
Amer. lawyer, prosecutor
O'Neill--Women's p366, por.

SINFIELD, MARGARET (fl. 1960's-
1970's)
English politician
Stobaugh--Women p94-95

WINFREY, LEE (1932-)
Amer. TV newspaper critic
Scheuer--Tel. p516

WING, TOBY (1913-)
Amer. actress
Springer--They p255,338, por.

WINGER, DEBRA (1955-)
Amer. actress
Cur. Biog. '84 p460-463, por.

WINGO, ELIZABETH B. (1907-)
Amer. genealogical researcher,
author
Meyer--Who's p220

WINGRO, EFFIEGENE L. (1883-1962)

Amer. Congresswoman
Chamberlin--Min. p82-84

WINN, KAY (fl. 1930's-1940's)
Amer. radio advertiser
Women--Radio p18

WINNEMUCCA, SARAH (c1844-1891)
Amer. Paiute Indian leader,
author, army scout
Gridley--Amer. p54-60, por.
James--Notable (3) p628-630
McHenry--Liberty's p449-450
Richey--Eminent p125-151, por.
Sherr--American p144
Signif.--Amer. p26, por.
Time--Women p196,209,212,214-
215, por.
Truman--Women p42-53, por.
Woman's Almanac p378-379, por.
World--Who p131

WINOKUROW, ELSA (1883-   )
West German physicist
Hellstedt--Women p10-15, por.

WINONA
See WENONAH

WINSER, BEATRICE (1869-1947)
Amer. librarian, museum
director
James--Notable (3) p630-632

WINSLOW, ANNA GREEN (fl. 1770's-
1780's)
Amer. colonial diarist
Earle--Two Cent. (1) p297-299,
415-416
Earle--Two Cent. (2) p552-554,
641
Williams--Demeter's p229,299

WINSLOW, CATHERINE MARY
REIGNOLDS
See REIGNOLDS, CATHERINE
("KATE") MARY

WINSLOW, MARY CHILTON (c1608-
1679)
Amer. Mayflower Pilgrim
Sherr--American p109
Williams--Demeter's p23

WINSLOW, OLA ELIZABETH (c1885-
1977)
Amer. teacher, author
Ehrlich--Oxford p9

WINSLOW, PENELOPE (fl. 1650's)
Amer. colonial wife
Earle--Two Cent. (1) p xvi, por.
Earle--Two Cent. (2) p505

WINSLOW, SUSANNA FULLER WHITE
(-before 1675)
Amer. Pilgrim
Williams--Demeter's p23

WINSLOW, THYRA SAMTER (1893-
1961)
Amer. journalist, author
Baum--Jewish, see index p290

WINSOR, JACQUELINE (JACKIE)
(1941-   )
Canadian-Amer. artist
Munro--Originals p431-437, por.
Women's--Female p113

WINSOR, KATHLEEN (1916/1919-   )
Amer. novelist
Ehrlich--Oxford p344
Seymour-Smith--Novels p237

WINSTON, CAROLINE (1948-   )
Amer. TV executive
Scheuer--Tel. p517

WINSTON, SUSAN
Amer. TV executive producer
Scheuer--Tel. p517

WINSTONE, NORMA (1941-   )
English singer
Claghorn--Jazz p318

WINTER, ALICE VIVIAN AMES (1865-
1944)
Amer. woman's club leader,
author
James--Notable (3) p632-633

WINTER, ELLA (1898-1980)
Australian journalist, social
activist, author
Cur. Biog. '80 p468
O'Neill--Women's p397,427, por.

WINTERS, JANET LEWIS
See LEWIS, JANET

WINTERS, SHELLEY (1922/1924-   )
Amer. Actress
Anderson--People p413-414, por.
Hirschhorn--Rating p378-379,
por.

Shipman--Internatl. p621-626,
   por.
Woman's Almanac p356
World--Who p253

WINTHROP, HANNAH (c1726-1790)
   Amer. letter, writer, Revol-
   lutionary War patriot
   Booth--Women p19-20,144,177-
   178
   Williams--Demeter's p272-273

WINTHROP, MARGARET (c1591-
   1647)
   Amer., wife of John Winthrop,
   colonial patriot, printer
   James--Notable (3) p633-634
   Neidle--America's p1,4-7
   Williams--Demeter's p26,28,39,
   116

WINTHROP, MARTHA (fl. 1640's)
   Amer., fourth wife of John
   Winthrop
   Williams--Demeter's p89-90

WINTHROP, MARY
   See DUDLEY, MARY WINTHROP

WINTRINGHAM, MARGARET
   British Parliamentary member
   Vallance--Women p26-28,30,121

WINWAR, FRANCES (1900-)
   Amer. biographer, literary
   critic
   Ehrlich--Oxford p375

WINWOOD, ESTELLE (1883-)
   English actress, comedienne
   World--Who p262

WIRTH, MAY
   Australian-Amer. circus
   horseback rider
   Kirk--Circus p57-59, por.

WISCHNEWETZKY, FLORENCE
   KELLEY
   See KELLEY, FLORENCE FINCH

WISDOM, ANN (fl. 1960's)
   British motor-car driver
   Macksey--Book p254

WISE, AUDREY
   British Parliamentary member

Vallance--Women p62,68,80,
   94

WISE, LOUISE WATERMAN (1874-
   1947)
   Amer. charity worker, Zionist
   James--Notable (3) p634-636
   O'Neill--Women's p720

WISE, MARGARETTA (fl. 1860's)
   Amer. Southern belle
   DeLeon--Belles p307, por.

WISER, VIVIAN (fl. 1950's-1970's)
   Amer. archivist, historian,
   agriculturist, writer
   O'Neill--Women's p29

WISINGER-FLORIAN, OLGA (1844-
   1926)
   Austrian painter
   Sparrow--Women p288

WISTER, SARAH ("SALLY")
   (1761-1804)
   Amer. Revolutionary War
   patriot, diarist
   Booth--Women p145-147,186,294
   Evans--Weather. p15,110-151,291
   Sherr--American p201-203

"WITCH OF WALL STREET"
   See GREEN, HENRIETTA HOW-
   LAND ROBINSON ("HETTY")

WITHERINGTON, PEARL (fl. 1940's)
   French spy
   Macksey--Book p59

WITHERS, JANE (1926/1927-)
   Amer. child actress
   Edelson--Kids p25-27, por.
   Springer--They p256,338, por.
   World--Who p253

WITHERSPOON, CORA (1890-1957)
   Amer. actress
   Springer--They p256,338, por.

WITKE, ROXANE (fl. 1970's)
   Amer. historian, professor,
   writer, editor
   O'Neill--Women's p421

WITT, CARRIBELLE (fl. 1960's)
   Amer. food industry founder
   O'Neill--Women's p137

WITTENMYER, ANNIE TURNER
(1827-1900)
Amer. Civil War dietician,
social reformer, lecturer,
author, humanitarian
Bird--Enterprising p93-95
James--Notable (3) p636-638
McHenry--Liberty's p450
Sherr--American p70-71,128
World--Who p192

WITTIG, MONIQUE (c1936-)
French novelist
Crosland--Women p211-216, por.
Moers--Literary p247,298,318

WITTPENN, CAROLINE BAYARD
STEVENS (1859-1932)
Amer. welfare worker
James--Notable (3) p638-639
Woman's Almanac p390

WIXOM, EMMA
See NEVADA, EMMA

WOERISHOFFER, ANNA
Amer., post-Civil War era
humanitarian
Neidle--America's p48

WOERISHOFFER, (EMMA) CAROLA
(1885-1911)
Amer. social reformer,
philanthropist
James--Notable (3) p639-641
Neidle--America's p48,137-138

WOFF, MARY EVALINE
See MADELEVA, MARY, SISTER

WOFFINGTON, MARGARET ("PEG")
(1714/1717-1760)
Irish actress
Entertainers p92
Findlater--Player p76-90, por.
Macksey--Book p226
Who Did What p332

WOHLERS, JEANNE
Amer. industrial executive
Adams--Women p34-38,42,177,
194

WOHMANN, GABIRELLE (1932-)
German short-story writer,
novelist
Herrmann--Ger. p6,101

WOJCIECHOWSKA, MAIA TERESA
(1927-)
Polish-Amer. publisher, chil-
dren's book author
Cur. Biog. '76 p447-450, por.
Kulkin--Her p309

WOLCOTT, LAURA R. (fl. 1850's)
Amer. physician
Sherr--American p249

WOLD, ANITA (fl. 1970's)
Norwegian track and field
athlete
O'Neill--Women's p566

WOLD, EMMA (1871-1950)
Amer. lawyer, social reformer,
feminist, activist
World--Who p192

WOLF, CHRISTA (1929-)
German author
Herrmann--Ger. p6,92-93

WOLF, FRUMENT (FANI) (late
1700's-1849)
Jewish-German community,
charity worker
Henry--Written p191-194

WOLFE, CAROLYN (1890-)
Amer. government official
Ware--Beyond p155,see also
index p203

WOLFE, CATHARINE LORILLARD
(1828-1887)
Amer. philanthropist
James--Notable (3) p641-642

WOLFE, DONNA (1951-)
Amer. executive, associate
director, cable TV
Scheuer--Tel. p519

WOLFE, ELSIE DE
See DeWOLF, ELSIE, LADY
MENDL

WOLFE, MILDRED NUNGESTER
(1912-)
Amer. artist, teacher, noted
Mississippi mother
Amer.--Mothers p305-306, por.

WOLFENSTEIN, MARTHA (c1911-

1976)
Amer. psychologist
Baum--Jewish p242-243

WOLFERT, HELEN (fl. 1940's-
1960's)
Amer. poet
Chester--Rising p51-55, por.

WOLFF, ELENA
See LUPESCU, MAGNA

WOLFF, ELISABETH (1738-1804)
Netherlands novelist
Who Did What p332

WOLFF, MABEL OLSON (1895-   )
Amer. Red Cross worker,
noted Minnesota mother
Amer.--Mothers p292, por.

WOLFGANG, MYRA KOMAROFF
(c1914-1976)
Amer. labor leader
Diamonstein--Open p467-470,
por.
O'Neill--Women's p299

WOLFSON, THERESA (1897-1972)
Amer. labor economist,
educator
Sicherman--Notable p742-744

WOLLMAN, BETTY KOHN (1836-   )
Amer. abolitionist, philan-
thropist, noted Iowa mother
Amer.--Mothers p202-203, por.

WOLLSTEIN, MARTHA (1868-1939)
Amer. pathologist, medical
researcher
James--Notable (3) p642-644

WOLSTENHOLME-ELMY, ELIZABETH
C. (1834-1918)
English military suffragette,
writer
Showalter--Lit. p332

WOLLSTONECRAFT, MARY
See SHELLEY, MARY WOLL-
STONECRAFT GODWIN

WOLYNSKI, MARA
Amer. TV reporter
Scheuer--Tel. p521

WONG, ANNA MAY (LU TSONG)
(c1907-1961)
Chinese-Amer. actress
Keylin--Hollywood p282, por.
Sicherman--Notable p744-745
Springer--They p256,338-339,
por.
World--Who p253

WOOD, ANN (fl. 1850's)
Amer. slave
Chittenden--Prof. p35-49

WOOD, ANNE HIGGINS (1917-   )
Amer. genealogical researcher,
author
Meyer--Who's p221

WOOD, CHRISTINE KNOX (1923-   )
Amer. genealogical researcher,
author, editor
Meyer--Who's p221

WOOD, CLARA MAY (c1884-   )
Amer. pioneer, banker
Sherr--American p195

WOOD, DEL
Amer. singer, pianist
Claghorn--Biog. p482

WOOD, EDITH ELMER (1871-1945)
Amer. housing economist,
humanitarian, author
James--Notable (3) p644-645
O'Neill--Women's p721

WOOD, ELLEN PRICE (MRS. HENRY)
(1814-1887)
English novelist
Avenel--Comp. (1) p559
Jones--Rutledge p838
Morley--Literary p263
Seymour-Smith--Novels p238
Showalter--Lit. p325

WOOD, EMMA CAROLINE, LADY
(1802-1879)
English novelist
Showalter--Lit. p322

WOOD, FRIEDA (fl. 1970's)
Amer. bowler
McWhirter--Guinness p43

WOOD, JULIA AMANDA SARGENT

(1825-1903)
Amer. author, pioneer
Minnesota newspaper editor
James--Notable (3) p646-647

WOOD, MARY ANNE PATON
See PATON, MARY ANNE

WOOD, MARY ELIZABETH (1861-
1931)
Amer. missionary, librarian
James--Notable (3) p647-648
McHenry--Liberty's p450-451

WOOD, MATILDA ALICE VICTORIA
See LLOYD, MARIE

WOOD, MATILDA CHARLOTTE
VINING (1831-1915)
Amer. actress, theatre
manager
James--Notable (3) p648-649

WOOD, NAN (fl. 1960's-1970's)
Amer. company founder,
executive, feminist
O'Neill--Women's p514

WOOD, NATALIE (1938-1981)
Amer. actress
Andersen--People p416-417
Book--Lists (2) p251
Cur. Biog. '82 p476
Edelson--Kids p89-91, por.
Hirschhorn--Rating p379-380,
por.
Manchel--Women p82-83,91, por.
People--Best p250, por.
People's Almanac (2) p135
Shipman--Internatl. p627-629,
por.
Woman's Almanac p356
World--Who p253

WOOD, PEGGY (1892-1978)
Amer. actress, author
Cur. Biog. '78 p478
Lamparski--What. (4) p88-89,
por.
World--Who p253

WOOD, SALLY SAYWARD
BE(A)RRELL KEATING,
MADAM (1759-1854)
Amer. novelist, noted
Maine mother

Amer.--Mothers p238
James--Notable (3) p649-650
Warren--Pictorial p70

WOOD, SARA BARD FIELD
See FIELD, SARA BARD

WOOD, VIRGINIA (1882-1941)
English novelist, critic
Avenel--Comp. (1) p560-562

WOOD, VIRGINIA STEELE (fl. 1950's)
Amer. genealogical researcher,
author
Meyer--Who's p221-222

WOODWARD, NEIL SACHSE (1920-)
Amer. genealogical researcher,
writer, editor
Meyer--Who's p222

WOODBERRY, MARY DODGE (fl.
1600's)
Amer. Puritan voter
Williams--Demeter's p122

WOODBURY, HELEN LAURA SUMNER
(1876-1933)
Amer. labor historian, govern-
ment official
James--Notable (3) p650-652
McHenry--Liberty's p451

WOODHAM-SMITH, CECIL BLANCHE
FITZGERALD (1896/1897-1977)
British historian, biographer
O'Neill--Women's p418

WOOD-HILL, MABEL
See HILL, MABEL WOOD

WOODHOUSE, BARBARA (1910-)
Irish animal trainer
Cur. Biog. '85 p456-460

WOODHOUSE, ELEANOR (fl. 1610's)
English surgeon
Mead--Hist. p522

WOODHOUSE, MARGARET CHASE
GOING (1890-1984)
Amer. Congresswoman, econo-
mist, educator, author
Chamberlin--Min. p188-191
Cur. Biog. '85 p477

WOODHOUSE, SOPHIA (fl. 1810's)

Amer. inventor
Earle--Two Cent. (2) p570

WOODHULL, VICTORIA CLAFLIN
(1838-1927)
Amer. social reformer, Presidential candidate, feminist, journalist, stockbrocker
Earnest--American p130-132, 249-250
Gurko--Ladies p230,243-249,287
Hymowitz--Hist. p164-174, por.
James--Notable (3) p652-655
Longstreet--Queen p61-70, por.
McHenry--Liberty's p451-452
Macksey--Book p165-166,169, por.
May--Different p7-33, por.
Millstein--We p154
Papachristou--Women p74-82, por.
People's Almanac (1) p128, por.
Signif.--Amer. p26, por.
Smith--Daughters, see index p391-392
Sochen--Herstory p177-178
Taylor--Gener. p52-53, por.
Warren--Pictorial p131-132
Webster's--Amer. p1156-1157
Woman's Almanac p547-548, por.
World--Who p192

WOODIE, EFFIE (fl. 1970's)
Amer. mountain woman
Kahn--Hill. p126-136, por.

WOODROW, NANCY MANN WADDEL
(c1866-1935)
Amer. author
James--Notable (3) p655-656

WOODRUFF, JUDY
Amer. TV network correspondent
Scheuer--Tel. p522

WOODS, KATHARINE PEARSON
(1853-1923)
Amer. author, teacher, social service worker
James--Notable (3) p656-657

WOODS, MARGARET LOUISA
BRADLEY (1856-1945)
English novelist, poet, playwright
Showalter--Lit. p339

WOODS, MEHITABLE ELLIS ("AUNTIE")
Amer. Civil War patriot
Sherr--American p71

WOODS, PATRICIA RUDY (1946-)
Amer. singer
Claghorn--Biog. p484

WOODS, ROSE MARY (1917-)
Amer. secretary (Presidential)
Schoenebaum--Prof. p676-677

WOODS, SYLVIA (fl. 1930's-1970's)
Amer. labor union activist
O'Neill--Women's p328

WOODSMALL, RUTH FRANCES
(1883-1963)
Amer. YWCA leader, government official, organization official, author
Sicherman--Notable p746-747

WOODVILLE, ELIZABETH
See ELIZABETH WOODVILLE

WOODWARD, AGNES (fl. 1900's)
Amer. whistler
Sherr--American p15

WOODWARD, ALICE BOLINGBROKE
(1862-)
English book illustrator, stained-glass artist
Callen--Women p196,204

WOODWARD, ELLEN SULLIVAN
(1887-1971)
Amer. government official, state legislator
Sicherman--Notable p747-749
Ware--Beyond p155, see also index p204

WOODWARD, JOANNE GIGNILLIAT
(1930/1931-)
Amer. actress
Anderson--People p417-418
Hirschhorn--Rating p380-381, por.
Manchel--Women p15,83,98-100, por.
People--Best p116, por.
Shipman--Internatl. p629-632, por.
Woman's Almanac p356-357, por.
World--Who p253